CIVIL PROCEDURE

CIVIL PROCEDURE

Doctrine, Practice, and Context

STEPHEN N. SUBRIN
Professor of Law
Northeastern University School of Law

MARTHA L. MINOW
Professor of Law
Harvard University Law School

MARK S. BRODIN
Professor of Law
Boston College School of Law

THOMAS O. MAIN, Esq.
Boston, Massachusetts

ASPEN LAW & BUSINESS
A Division of Aspen Publishers, Inc.
Gaithersburg   New York

Permissions
Aspen Law & Business
1185 Avenue of the Americas
New York, NY 10036

Printed in the United States of America

Library of Congress Cataloging-in-Publication Data

Civil procedure: doctrine, practice, and context /
 Stephen Subrin . . . [et al.].
  p. cm.
 Includes index.
 ISBN 0-7355-1200-0 (casebound)
  1. Civil procedure—United States. 2. Law students—United
States—Handbooks, manuals, etc. I. Subrin, Stephen, 1958–
KF8841.C554 2000
347.73′5—dc21   99-059291

About Aspen Law & Business, Law Education Division

With a dedication to preserving and strengthening the long-standing tradition of publishing excellence in legal education, Aspen Law & Business continues to provide the highest quality teaching and learning resources for today's law school community. Careful development, meticulous editing, and an unmatched responsiveness to the evolving needs of today's discerning educators combine in the creation of our outstanding casebooks, coursebooks, textbooks, and study aids.

ASPEN LAW & BUSINESS
A Division of Aspen Publishers, Inc.
A Wolters Kluwer Company
www.aspenpublishers.com

Dedication

I dedicate this book to over three decades of
Northeastern Law students who have insisted that intelligence,
compassion, and justice must go hand in hand, and to Joan,
who has done the same—and then some.
—Stephen N. Subrin

I dedicate this book to Harvard Law students who have, since 1981,
helped me to make procedure more civil, and to Joe Singer, who
inspires accessible casebooks and other improvements of daily life.
—Martha Minow

I dedicate this book to my late father, Herman Brodin,
who instilled in me a keen sense of justice and equity.
—Mark S. Brodin

I dedicate this book to my parents, who always seem to
know the way, and to Paula, with whom I read maps.
—Thomas O. Main

Summary of Contents

Contents

Preface

The impetus for this book grew out of our own experience as law students and professors. We find that students learn most effectively when legal doctrine, its context, and how doctrine actually works in practice are integrated. Empirical and theoretical research support the notion that we learn and remember at our best as a result of intense, sustained experiences in which we must perform concrete tasks that call upon a number of our faculties. Many of our deepest learning experiences have come from teaching a new course, helping a client solve a problem, or writing an article or a book—experiences that call upon a combination of knowledge, insight, values, clarity, advocacy, judgment, and endurance. These are the lessons that stick.

We wanted a civil procedure course that created a more unified learning experience. Civil procedure doctrine can seem remote from the reality of torts, crimes, contracts, and land. And yet perhaps no other legal subject so calls into question the major issues of law and practicing law in the United States: separation of powers, federalism, the adversarial relationship, efficiency, fairness, power and powerlessness, justice, and fees. In a civil procedure course one finds, for example, the conceptual challenges of *Erie,* the ethical dimensions of discovery, and the practical necessities of hard and fast rules. Moreover, this is a field in flux, and studying the underlying values and historical context of procedure helps one make some sense of the inherent uncertainty and change.

Often students say that they know the doctrine, yet (frustratingly) they cannot meaningfully apply it. We wanted to develop a course in which students applied the doctrine they were learning. Seven years ago, Steve Subrin and several of his students at Northeastern University School of

Law confronted the challenge of creating a more unified civil procedure course. They put two real cases, with practice-oriented exercises, at the center of a contextual, philosophic, and multidisciplinary study of civil procedure. They reprinted fewer opinions, but retained more of the procedure and factual context by not severely editing them. They also reprinted longer excerpts of pertinent articles to demonstrate the flow of an extended argument. The students were given challenging questions to contemplate or answer, but they were not given questions that required additional reading or expert knowledge. Finally, they employed *orientation essays* to illuminate certain doctrines and to elucidate the contextual and practical environments that influenced, and were influenced by, those doctrines.

We have remained true to the vision of Steve Subrin and his students—the vision of creating a civil procedure course that not only taught the doctrine but also applied it and illuminated the integral role of civil procedure in every substantive area of the law. Many features of this book promote that vision:

- Orientation essays that are introduced by the symbols **D**, **P**, or **C**, which indicate whether the essay focuses on doctrine, or practice, or context, or a combination of these.
- Pleadings and files of two real cases are threaded throughout the book.
- To maintain a manageable size yet cover all of the essentials, the authors have carefully edited the book's cases.
- There is complete integration of contextual materials and practice exercises.
- Thomas Main helped design the founding materials as a law student, and became a co-author of this text as he entered practice and added a law-practice perspective to this course.
- Martha Minow and Mark Brodin brought original materials and different perspectives that contributed to this effort to reinvent a course in civil procedure.

We are grateful to those who aided and abetted this project. In particular, Jeff Stern, a distinguished trial lawyer at Sugarman, Rogers, Barshak & Cohen in Boston, Massachusetts, helped us develop the materials for the wrongful death action involving the roll-over of a Jeep. Jane Picker, Ken Kowalski, and the Fair Employment Law Clinic at Cleveland-Marshall College of Law, Cleveland State University, helped us develop the materials for the Title VII class action against the Cleveland Ohio Fire Department. In both cases, we have changed the names and, in a few instances for pedagogical purposes, certain facts.

Many Northeastern University School of Law students and graduates inspired Steve's vision for this book, and participated in its initial preparation and later iterations. He gives special thanks to Mary Azzarito, John Becker, David Brenner, Kent Brintnall, Kevin Brown, Shawn Bush, Stephanie Cucurullo, Rachel Dimitruk, Genna Carver, Liz Goldstein, Amy Hubert, Vik Kanwar, Dovie King, Amber Klinge, Aileen Lachs, Mark McGrath, Laura Matlow, David Plotkin, Judy Prosper, Joel Rosen, Sasha Rosebush, Nicole Voigt, Jason Walta, Angela Wessels, and Debra Williams.

Martha thanks Laurie Corzett, Katie Cook, Naomi Ronen, and many generations of civil procedure students.

Mark thanks the hundreds of civil procedure students over the years who, he insists, have taught him far more than he has taught them.

Thomas thanks Grace Petrola, Sandy Heffley, and countless others who contributed time and expertise to this project. He also thanks Hill & Barlow, Boston, Massachusetts, and Platinum Equity Holdings, Los Angeles, California, who wittingly shared (and in important respects shouldered) his commitment to this text.

All of the authors sincerely thank Greg Pingree for helping to clarify the collective voice of this book. The authors also thank Bernard Johnston, Melody Davies, and Jay Boggis of Aspen Publishers for their assistance and patience. And finally, the authors thank Carol McGeehan, our Acquisitions Editor, for her support, guidance, and belief in this project. The final product is truly a collaborative effort.

> Stephen N. Subrin
> Martha L. Minow
> Mark S. Brodin
> Thomas O. Main

February 2000

Acknowledgments

The authors gratefully acknowledge the permissions granted to reproduce the following materials.

American Bar Association, "Discovery," Litigation (Winter 1997).

Aspen, Marvin E., "The Search for Renewed Civility in Litigation." 28 Val. U. L. Rev. 513 (1994).

Ball, Milner, *The Promise of American Law: A Theological, Humanistic View of Legal Process* 48-62, 136-138 (University of Georgia Press 1981).

Bernstein, Lisa, "Understanding the Limits of Court-Connected ADR: A Critique of Federal Court-Annexed Arbitration Programs," 141 U. Pa. L. Rev. 2169 (1993). Copyright © 1993 University of Pennsylvania Law Review.

Brazil, Wayne, "The Adversary Character of Civil Discovery: A Critique and Proposals for Change," 31 Vand. L. Rev. 1295 (1978). Copyright © 1978 Vanderbilt Law Review.

Burbank, Stephen, "The Rules Enabling Act of 1934," 130 U. Pa. L. Rev. 1015 (1982). Copyright © 1982 University of Pennsylvania Law Review.

Chayes, Abram, "The Role of the Judge in Public Law Litigation," 89 Harv. L. Rev. 1281 (1976). Copyright © 1976 by the Harvard Law Review Association.

Clark, Charles E., "Comments," Proceedings of the Institute at Washington, D.C., on the Federal Rules of Civil Procedure (American Bar Association October 6, 1938). Copyright © 1938 American Bar Association. Reprinted by permission.

Coombe, George W., Jr., "The Resolution of Transnational Commercial Disputes: A Perspective from North America," 5 Ann. Surv. Int'l & Comp. L. (Golden Gate University School of Law) 13 (1999).

Delgado, Richard, "Fairness and Formality: Minimizing the Risk of Prejudice in Alternative Dispute Resolution," 1985 Wisc. L. Rev. 1359 (1985). Used by permission of the author and the Wisconsin Law Review.

Devitt, Edward J., "Should Jury Trial Be Required in Civil Cases? A Challenge to the Seventh Amendment," 47 J. Air L. & Comm. 495 (1982).

Eastman, Herbert, "Speaking Truth to Power: The Language of Civil Rights Litigators." Reprinted by permission of The Yale Law Journal Company and Fred B. Rothman & Company from The Yale Law Journal, Vol. 104, pages 763-879.

Editorial, "Requirement That Attorneys Perform Pro Bono Work." This article originally appeared in the February 25, 1991 issue (Vol. 17, No. 8, p. 18) of The Connecticut Law Tribune. Copyright © 1991, The Connecticut Law Tribune.

Edwards, Harry T., "Alternative Dispute Resolution: Panacea or Anathema?" Harv. L. Rev. 668 (1986). Copyright © by the Harvard Law Review Association.

Fiss, Owen M., "Against Settlement." Reprinted by permission of The Yale Law Journal Company and Fred B. Rothman & Company from The Yale Law Journal, Vol. 93, pages 1073-1090.

Fuller, Lon, "The Forms and Limits of Adjudication," 92 Harv. L. Rev. 353 (1978). Reprinted by permission of the Lon L. Fuller Trust.

Galanter, Marc, "Jury Shadows: Reflections on the Civil Jury and the Litigation Explosion," *The American Civil Jury* 16-18 (1987).

Gunning, Isabelle R., "Diversity Issues in Mediation: Controlling Negative Cultural Myths," J. Disp. Resol. 55 (1995).

Hans, Valerie P., and Neil Vidmar, *Judging the Jury* (1986).

James, Fleming, Jr., Geoffrey Hazard, & John Leubsdorf, *Civil Procedure* (4th ed. 1992).

Kalven, Harry, "The Dignity of the Civil Jury," 50 U. Va. L. Rev. 1055, 1059-67 (1964).

Kamp, Allen, "The History Behind *Hansberry v. Lee*." This work was originally published in 20 U.C. Davis L. Rev. 481 (1987). Copyright © 1987 by The Regents of the University of California. Reprinted with permission.

Kieve, Loren, "Discovery Reform," 77 A.B.A. J. 79 (1991).

King, Martin Luther, Jr., "Letter from a Birmingham City Jail."

Landsman, Stephen, "Defense of the Adversarial Process," *Readings on Adversarial Justice: The American Approach to Adjudication* 33-39 (West 1988).

Lieberman, Jethro K., and James F. Henry, "Lessons from the Alternative Dispute Resolution Movement," 53 U. Chi. L. Rev. 424 (1986).

Luban, David, *Lawyers and Justice: An Ethical Study* (Princeton University Press 1988).

Luban, David, *Legal Modernism* (University of Michigan Press 1994).

Marcus, Richard L., "Discovery Containment Redux," 39 B.C. L. Rev. 747 (1998).

Mashaw, Jerry L., "The Supreme Court's Due Process Calculus—Three Factors in Search of a Theory of Value," 44 U. Chi. L. Rev. 28, 28-30, 46-59 (1976).

Menkel-Meadow, Carrie, "Pursuing Settlement in an Adversary Culture: A Tale of Innovation Co-opted or 'The Law of ADR,'" 19 Fla. St. U. L. Rev. 1 (1991).

Michelman, Frank, 'The Supreme Court and Litigation Access Fees," 1973 Duke L.J. 1153, 1172-77.

Minow, Martha, "Judge for the Situation: Judge Jack Weinstein, Creator of Temporary Administrative Agencies." This article originally appeared at 97 Colum. L. Rev. 2010 (1997). Reprinted by permission.

Minow, Martha, *Not Only for Myself: Identity, Politics & the Law* 99-100 (1997). Copyright © 1997. Reprinted by permission of The New Press.

Olson, Walter K., "Dentists, Bartenders, and Lawyer Unpopularity." Manhattan Institute for Civil Justice Memo No. 37 (April 1999). http://manhattan.institute.org/htm/cjm_37.htm. Reprinted with permission of the Manhattan Institute for Policy Research and Walter K. Olson.

Pierce, Richard J., "The Due Process Counterrevolution of the 1990s?" This article originally appeared at 96 Colum. L. Rev. 1973 (1996). Reprinted by permission of The Columbia Law Review and Richard J. Pierce.

Posner, Richard A., "An Economic Approach to Legal Procedure and Judicial Administration, 2 J. Legal Stud. 399 (1973). Copyright © 1973 by the University of Chicago. Reprinted by permission of the University of Chicago and Richard A. Posner.

Ramirez, Deborah A., "The Mixed Jury and the Ancient Custom of Trial by Jury de Medietate Linguae: A History and a Proposal for Change. Volume 74:5, Boston University Law Review (1994) 777–818. Reprinted with permission. © 1994 Trustees of Boston University. Forum of original publication.

Resnik, Judith, "Managerial Judges and Court Delay: The Unproven Assumptions." 8 Judge's Journal (1994). Reprinted with permission of Judith Resnik, Arthur Liman Professor of Law, Yale Law School.

Ross, William G., "The Ethics of Hourly Billing by Attorneys," 44 Rutgers L. Rev. 1 (1991).

Sander, Frank E.A., "Varieties of Dispute Processing." The Pound Conference: Perspectives on Justice in the Future (American Bar Association, 1979).

Schrag, Philip G., "Bleak House 1968: A Report on Consumer Test Litigation." 44 N.Y.U. L. Rev. 115 (1969).

Schwarzer, William, "Managing Civil Litigation: The Trial Judge's Role," 61 Judicature 400 (1978).

Shapiro, David L., "Class Actions: The Class as Party and Client." Volume 73, Number 4, the Notre Dame Law Review (May 1998) 913-961. Reprinted with permission. © by Notre Dame Law Review, University of Notre Dame.

Simon, William, "The Ideology of Advocacy." 1978 Wisc. L. Rev. 29.

Stryker, Lloyd Paul, *The Art of Advocacy* (1954).

Subrin, Stephen N., "David Dudley Field and the Field Code: An Historical Analysis of an Earlier Procedural Vision." From 6 Law and History Review. Copyright 1988 by Board of Trustees of the University of Illinois. Used with permission of the University of Illinois Press.

Thornburg, Elizabeth G., "Giving the 'Haves' a Little More: Considering the 1998 Discovery Proposals." Originally appearing in Vol. 52, No. 1 of the SMU Law Review. Reprinted with permission from the SMU Law Review and the Southern Methodist University School of Law.

Trangsrud, Roger H., "Mass Trials in Mass Tort Cases: A Dissent." 1989 U. Ill. L. Rev. 69. © Board of Trustees of the University of Illinois.

Tyler, Tom R., and E. Allan Lind, "A Relational Model of Authority in Groups," 25 Adv. in Exper. Soc. Psych. 115 (1992).

VanBuskirk, Walter, "Lifting a Truck."

CIVIL PROCEDURE

1

![black square]

An Introduction to Civil Procedure

Recognizing that different students approach a subject in different ways, this introductory section includes discussions of the importance and contents of civil procedure, along with a brief explanation of sources for key rules and doctrines, suggestions for studying, and comments on the unique features of this casebook. The introduction also suggests that law can be understood as a kind of theater with rules and practices for translating social harms into a drama recognized by the legal world.

Finally, this opening section introduces a central theme of the course through discussion of one notable case, *United States v. Hall,* 472 F.2d 261 (5th Cir. 1972). The theme is that the law imposes limitations on the power of courts. The doctrinal issue is contempt power—the question of whether a court has power to hold a nonparty in contempt. Arising in the larger context of a school desegregation suit, *Hall* presents judicial analysis of both common law precedents and a rule about judicial power to punish nonparties for violating a court order.

The second section of this chapter addresses the constitutional foundations for due process, or the right to be heard, a right that guides the structure of procedure in the United States. Because landmark Supreme Court opinions have addressed the scope of due process in reviewing decisions by administrative agencies, these opinions provide the centerpiece, but the frameworks and values that emerge pervade procedural rules and practices in the courts as well. Indeed, the values behind due process are critical to the doctrines governing access to court, jurisdiction, and preclusion, as developed in later parts of the book.

1

The final section of this chapter considers access to lawyers and to the legal system. Affected by due process and also by legislative and judicial and bar initiatives, the access issues are, of course, prior to every other topic in the field of procedure.

A. WHAT STUDENTS SHOULD KNOW FROM THE START

1. Why Procedure Matters

Most starting law students have some sense of the subjects to be addressed in criminal law, property, contracts, and torts. The media and personal encounters make these fields familiar to nonlawyers. Many students have signed leases for apartments and entered into oral or written employment contracts. Some have been involved in automobile accidents or injured by defective products. Others have had close encounters with the criminal law through following highly visible murder trials, serving on juries, or watching the experiences of friends and family members. However, few students, if any, have thought about why some cases are in federal court and some in state court, or whether an accident victim may file successive suits for each separate injury suffered in an incident, or what steps initiate and terminate a lawsuit.

Yet from the moment a lawyer meets a prospective client and begins to learn the details of the problem for which assistance is sought, the lawyer must think about such procedural dimensions. How could the client's story be translated into a "complaint," which is the document that commences litigation? What elements would comprise a viable "claim for relief" and thus survive the defendant's available procedural challenges, which may charge lack of jurisdiction, improper venue, failure to join a necessary party, or failure to plead with sufficient specificity? How can the "discovery" (pretrial fact investigation) process be used to develop evidence sufficient to support the "allegations" in the complaint? Is the amount of money likely to be recovered on a prevailing claim adequate to make the litigation worth the costs, including attorneys' fees? Or should the lawyer encourage the client to drop the claim, settle the claim, or pursue mediation or another alternative to litigation?

Even lawyers who never plan to go to court (the majority of the profession) must concern themselves with procedural matters. The business lawyer who drafts a contract must consider what could happen if either party fails to perform and litigation arises. Will my client have to chase the breaching party to its distant home state to file a suit to enforce the contract, or will we have to defend a suit charging breach in that distant forum? Should we negotiate for a "forum selection clause" and a "choice of law clause" to specify where any litigation over the contract would take place, and under what normative rules?

The skills used in mastering the world of procedure are highly useful in other legal endeavors. Drafting complaints and answers helps lawyers refine the skill of sorting out points of agreement and disagreement in other contexts. Studying the Federal Rules of Civil Procedure and procedural statutes highlights the delicate art of statutory construction and interpretation. Mastering the line of Supreme Court opinions governing personal jurisdiction involves close reading of evolving case law and learning to see how legal concepts and factual distinctions matter over time in judge-made law. Fact gathering and managing information to prepare for litigation are skills crucial even to lawyers who never pursue court actions.

Although at times procedure may seem to involve petty details (do weekends count in assessing when a ten-day deadline kicks in?), it also engages the largest questions law can engage: What should a society value? How should it resolve disputes? What role should citizens have in governance? What are the roles and limits of democratic institutions like legislatures? What power should be held and used by the nonmajoritarian institution of the court? Can words restrict the actions of people entrusted with power? What can remedy a wrong? What is a lie? How should economic disparities affect access to justice? These large questions underlie and shape the subject. Now let's consider what that subject is.

2. What Is "Civil Procedure"?

The "Civil" in "Civil Procedure" means noncriminal. Although a criminal case may result in imprisonment or a fine and the moving party is always the government, in a civil case, the remedies include monetary compensation or an order directing the defendant to do or stop doing something. Often, both plaintiff and defendant are private parties, although in some instances the government may be either plaintiff or defendant.

"Procedure" is meant to contrast with "substance." The rights and duties governing daily activities of people and institutions constitute substantive law. For instance, a torts course teaches about the various forms of conduct about which a plaintiff can complain and obtain redress under such doctrines as negligence, assault, and defamation; the doctrines themselves are composed of elements that must be proven before a court can order a remedy.

In contrast, a procedure course concentrates on the *methods* by which the substantive law can be enforced, typically, although not exclusively, by courts. Thus, procedure determines how disputes are channeled into a legal form; civil procedure addresses the channeling of disputes into courts and the methods for resolving them there. The topics range from the mundane, such as what documents must be filed and what information must be set forth in each, to those basic to defining governmental power in the United States, such as what power to resolve disputes is retained by the states and what by the federal government (subject matter jurisdiction); which source of law—state or federal—applies to a dispute when it is litigated (the federalism issue epitomized by the case of *Erie Railroad v. Tomkins*, 304 U.S. 64 (1938)); and when a person's liberty may be affected by government power (due process, personal jurisdiction). Some issues involve high degrees of technical precision, such as the standard for granting summary judgment. Every issue, even the most technical, also involves important social policies and values. Summary judgment, for example, raises the fundamental question of whether disputes should be resolved by the professional judge or by lay citizens summoned to serve on juries. In sum, the civil procedure course concerns the premises and operations of the adversarial system of justice, the scope of due process, the ethical issues posed for a lawyer entrusted with representing the interests of another, and the proper balance between efficiency and fairness.

The basic line between procedure and substance, so central to the very definition of civil procedure, will not always be clear or obvious. Indeed, in this respect, the debates over the line between procedure and substance mirror debates over most other lines drawn by the law. Procedure and substance, in particular, are often closely wedded as well as mutually defining.

3. Meeting the Players and the Institutions

If substantive law announces norms and the consequences for their breach, procedural law converts a conflict over norms and breach into a case amenable to trial. Procedures translate conflicts into cases for trial, even when the dispute never goes to trial and instead ends in settlement or moves through alternative processes such as mediation or arbitration. Procedural law translates disputants into parties. As parties, people appear in court; party or potential party status affects even out -of-court conversations. This section will briefly introduce terms used in the federal courts, terms that you need to know in order to work with the materials in this chapter. A more comprehensive survey of terms appears in Chapter 3 and describes both the elements and stages of a lawsuit, and the issues that procedural rules address. You will soon see why civil procedure is often described as "lawyers' law," because the basic vocabulary is foreign to nonlawyers and the vocabulary actually reflects institutions and professional practices that compose the world of lawyers.

a. Parties

The complaining party, who may be an individual, a corporation, or a collection of individuals, becomes the *plaintiff* or plaintiffs; those named in terms of fault or responsibility for the plaintiffs' claims become the *defendant* or defendants. Thus identified, the plaintiffs and defendants are adversaries on opposite sides of the lawsuit. Historically in the American system, progress in pursuing a civil case depends on the parties' initiatives rather than on the decision of a judge or prosecutor. Even with court changes enlarging the roles of judges and administrators as managers of the docket, the tradition of party control in practice puts the burden on the parties' lawyers, who in turn will be influenced by their own assessment of the merits of their client's position, by their predictions about proceeding, and by the method they will use for assessing attorneys' fees. The general rule is that each party pays its own attorneys' fees, so estimates of the party's ability to pay influence the attorney. Many lawyers in the tort field offer clients contingency fee arrangements, meaning a promise by the client to give the lawyer a percentage (typically one-third) of any recovered damages, with no obligation to pay if there is no recovery. Some statutes require that a losing defendant pay the attorneys' fees incurred by a prevailing plaintiff. Variations in these payment methods affect the attorney's calculus of the costs and risks of filing the suit, undertaking extensive investigation, hiring expert witnesses, and settling before trial or before judgment.

Sometimes, disputes involve more than two sides, such that simple opposition cannot capture the varied interests and obligations at issue. The Federal Rules of Civil Procedure thus permit plaintiffs and defendants to construct lawsuits that vary the bipolar two-party lawsuit structure through devices such as joinder, intervention, class action, and interpleader, each of which will be explored later in the course.

b. Jurisdiction

This general term refers to the power of a tribunal over a case. It actually has two dimensions: *jurisdiction over the subject matter* and *jurisdiction over the person*. To have subject matter jurisdiction, a court must be authorized by the Constitution and statutes to decide cases dealing with this kind of subject. The federal district (trial) courts have power to hear only the kinds of lawsuits specified by Congress under two categories: the suit raises a federal question, under federal statutes or the U.S. Constitution, or the suit involves parties satisfying diversity of citizenship (the plaintiff and defendant are citizens of different states or one of them is a citizen of a foreign country) *and* more than a statutory minimum amount is in controversy (currently set by Congress at $75,000). Specialized courts (dealing, for example, with patents or tax matters) have even more restricted spheres of subject matter jurisdiction. State trial courts include some with *general jurisdiction*—able to decide most cases—and those with specialized jurisdiction, such as the housing court (for landlord/tenant matters) or juvenile court (for offenses by minors).

Trial courts hear the initial dispute and presentation of evidence; appellate courts review the record developed in the course of the trial in light of claims of error in legal interpretation or application. The federal system has thirteen United States Courts of Appeals, and the Supreme Court of the United States, which has discretionary appellate jurisdiction over cases coming from the federal courts of appeals as well as from state supreme courts if, and only if, those cases depend on an issue of federal law. State systems have varying names for their trial, appellate, and highest courts.

Jurisdiction over the person, or personal jurisdiction, must also be satisfied before a court can proceed with a case. This means that the court selected by the plaintiff must have authority to direct the defendant to appear and to bind the defendant with a judgment. Thus, the defendant must be subject to suit in the state in which the court is located, which in turn means that the defendant resides there or has engaged in conduct with sufficient connection to the state to make it fair to impose personal jurisdiction there.

c. Remedies

There are various kinds of relief a court may order after being persuaded that the plaintiff's claims are meritorious. Remedies may include money damages to compensate the plaintiff; money damages to punish the defendant; a declaration of the rights and duties of the parties; and orders, called injunctions, that direct the defendant to stop the harmful conduct or to start new conduct as required by law.

4. Sources for the Rules and Doctrines

The rules governing civil procedure come from several sources. Most law school civil procedure courses focus heavily on the federal courts and thus rely substantially on the Federal Rules of Civil Procedure. Congress has authorized the Supreme Court to prescribe rules to govern the conduct of federal district courts and courts of appeals (as well as rules of evidence), so long as those rules do not "abridge, enlarge or modify any substantive right," 28 U.S.C. §2072(b).* Congress specified the mechanism for developing these rules: the Judicial Conference, composed

---

*Congressional enactments are codified and organized by numbered titles. Title 28 collects the laws governing the federal judiciary and judicial procedure.

of the chief judge of each of the district courts and courts of appeals and members of the Supreme Court, authorizes the appointment of a standing committee which screens proposed rules. 28 U.S.C. §2072. The Judicial Conference also authorizes the appointment of advisory committees to focus on particular topics, such as civil rules or evidence rules. The advisory committees, comprised of judges, practitioners, and scholars, consider proposed amendments and new rules, gather comments from judges and lawyers, and send revised proposals to the standing Committee on Practice and Procedure. That committee reports to the Judicial Conference, which then recommends rule changes to the Supreme Court. The Supreme Court then decides whether to transmit such proposed rules to Congress, which in turn has the chance to reject the proposal or else, through inaction, let the proposal become part of the rules. 28 U.S.C. §2074. In addition, Congress has on its own initiative adopted legislation to alter one or more rules or promote alternative processes for reforming rules. *See* Civil Justice Reform Act of 1990, Pub. L. No. 101-650, 104 Stat. 5089 (codified as amended at 28 U.S.C. §§471-482). Federal district courts also have large numbers of local rules. Approximately half of the states have adopted the Federal Rules of Civil Procedure for their own state procedural rules.

No less important, however, are court-made doctrines. Some predate the codified rules of procedure; some interpret those rules; and some interpret constitutional or legislative norms to provide for procedural rules. Thus, for example, the doctrines governing a right to a hearing and what a hearing must include interpret the Due Process Clause of the Fourteenth Amendment to the U.S. Constitution. The doctrines governing the remedial powers of the courts grow from common law practices and statutory interpretation. The doctrine of personal jurisdiction stems from the Due Process Clauses of the Fifth and Fourteenth Amendments as well as interpretations of state statutes. (In this and other areas, experts' judgments about the trends in case law and about admirable decisions are collected in a Restatement of Law, under the auspices of the American Law Institute.) Subject matter jurisdiction involves judicial interpretations of statutes governing the courts. Allocation of power between the trial judge and jury depends on common law and constitutional doctrines about burden of proof as well as judicial interpretation of rules governing juries and the conduct of trials. Doctrines addressing the effects of a prior judgment on a subsequent lawsuit—the preclusion, or res judicata rules—grow from common law decisions as well as from interpretations of the Full Faith and Credit Clause of the Constitution (Art. IV Sec. 1), the Due Process clauses, and judicial interpretations of statutes; again, a Restatement of the law of judgments reflects the views of experts. Finally, special rules governing complex litigation have grown not only from the Federal Rules of Civil Procedure, but also from congressional action, precedents, and the work of a multidistrict panel of judges addressing the subject.

5. How to Approach Studying

Learning procedure, like learning most of the law, requires that you actively engage the materials. Develop a habit of pursuing questions and imagining the events surrounding the materials you read. Rather than memorizing the materials, you will get more out of the course if you focus your time in some or all of these ways:

First, carefully read all assignments before class, and read them critically. You should argue with the material. Ask: why was the case decided this way? Does the doctrine announced by the court make sense? Does its application to this circumstance make sense? What alternatives are there, and would they be better? Generate hypothetical situations, or "what ifs." What if the facts were slightly different? Would that produce a different result in the eyes of the court that produced the opinion? Should it produce a different result? What if the motion were a different motion? What if the case were in state rather than federal court? What if the judge sat without a jury? Learning in law requires playing with the facts and doctrine, not memorizing and repeating rules.

Second, always ask where a given case is in the life cycle of procedure. Has there already been a trial, and is the case now on appeal—and if so, in what court? Or is the case at an earlier stage, such as a challenge to the complaint through a motion to dismiss? Is a trial court's grant or rejection of such a motion now on appeal? These questions will arise in all your courses; become aware of the procedural posture of every case you study. Also ask what will happen next, procedurally?

Third, look up what you do not know. If a rule or statute is mentioned and seems relevant, look it up. It will often be in your rule and statute supplement.

Fourth, when analyzing a rule or statute, always start with the exact language of the relevant rule or statute, just as courts do. Consider if there are any ambiguous words; in what ways can the ambiguity be resolved?

Fifth, think hard about facts. What "facts" are described in the judicial opinion? What is the source for those facts—an adversarial trial, the statements in the plaintiff's complaint, an empirical study, one witness's sworn statement? What is contested or contestable about the facts? What could resolve the contest? Which facts seem crucial to the judgment by a court or by you? Legal doctrine, abstracted from facts, is slippery if not worthless. It is the facts of any case that shape its ultimate result, putting the matter on one side or another of a legal rule or convincing a decision-maker to change the rule. A wise lawyer once said, "I could find the law easier than the facts. When I was stumped or made a mistake, it was usually because of elusive facts."

Sixth, try to make sense of what you read by learning about its historical and political context. This book offers sources toward that end. Statutes and cases are made by people who reflect the times in which they live and respond to the world they have known. Many procedural issues are explicable only in relationship to prior debates and reforms. Being mindful of such context will help you remember and understand the law, and will also help you explain it and persuade others about your views.

Seventh, develop your own study materials as the course proceeds. An outline that you construct from your notes on the readings and class discussion will help you get your hands around the material and to manage the large amount of information and analysis you will need to know by the end of the course. Include not only cases and their results but also underlying issues of values and statements of rules and exceptions.

Eighth, form a study group to discuss and debate the materials with your classmates. Propose hypotheticals and try to work them out together. By the middle of the course, take a look at old exams and tackle them together. This will help you do law rather than simply study it; you want to get in the habit of applying doctrine, forming arguments, predicting court action, and evaluating unsatisfactory decisions. All of this is easier and more fun to do when learning with and from other students.

Ninth, remember that law is about real people and groups. Ask what effect the law has on them and what happened after the cases were over.

Tenth, do not worry if many aspects of this and other courses do not make immediate sense or hang entirely together. Much understanding of law depends on understanding each part's relationship to the others; many aspects of each course will make more sense as you learn other aspects. Be patient and determined.

6. About This Book

Casebooks collect leading and illustrative judicial opinions, relevant statutes, and rules and present them in an order that helps make sense of doctrine and rules. This book also includes exercises that place you in the role of lawyer and judge to help develop the critical skills of analysis, research, fact investigation, strategy formulation, document drafting, written and oral advocacy, and ability to make informed judgments in the face of necessarily limited information. The book further includes historical, empirical, and jurisprudential materials to help you see the litigation system in its broader contexts and to expose the value choices behind both the existing system and proposals for reform.

Explanatory orientations are placed throughout the text and are identified by icons that indicate orientations in the nature of doctrine, practice, or context—to wit, **D** , **P** , **C** , respectively.

For focus and coherence, this book continually uses the files of two actual cases. The first, brought by a surviving spouse, is a wrongful death action arising out of a motor vehicle accident. The second is an employment discrimination class action. By offering materials that reveal how these two cases move through the litigation process, the book provides chronological set pieces around which you can organize and remember what you have learned. The two cases also permit a realistic and sophisticated exploration of procedural doctrine and procedural decision making. They allow you to see the relationship between decisions made early on and the later stages of the litigation. They also vividly demonstrate the importance of facts and how one arranges them into different stories for different audiences or purposes. Because practicing lawyers follow through with individual cases, rather than jump each day to new problems, these materials simulate real features of practice, in which procedural topics remain interconnected in the life history of particular cases. Finally, the two cases provide a good deal of substantive law, to create a realistic sense of the interplay between substance and process.

This book was written to afford a window into actual law practice, to provide historical and empirical contexts for procedural rules and choices, and to create active roles for students to engage with problem solving, legal analysis, counseling, factual investigation, and recognizing and resolving ethical issues. The aspiring lawyer who uses this book should become a problem solver. From the initial meeting with the potential client, through the early thought process (Is there a claim for relief? What remedies are available, and do they make litigation worthwhile? Who will pay attorneys' fees?) to the choice of an appropriate court, designation of the parties, and development of legal theories and strategies, the lawyer, and here, you, move through the stages of litigation framed by procedural rules. Deciding what type of complaint to bring, conducting discovery of factual material, posturing for settlement, planning and defending motions, and developing a strategy regarding the jury—each process compels you to make choices—choices that are affected by procedural and substantive rules and by ethical and philosophic considerations.

7. One More Prelude

That great observer of American democracy, Alexis de Tocqueville, recognized in the 1830s that "scarcely any political question arises in the United States that is not resolved, sooner or later, into a judicial question." I Tocqueville, *Democracy in America*, 280 (1953). Lawyers are pivotal players in American society. They serve as legislators, administrators, judges, public and corporate officials, and as advocates and advisors. This course begins your preparation to assume these roles in the practice of law, and in the society you will influence.

8. Law as Theater

Most fundamentally, legal procedures enable the process of translating harms in the world into terms that are recognized by lawyers and judges.

Crucial to that process of translation are the facts and the substantive law (rules of contract, tort, and so forth). Yet also vital are elements of presentation: style, tone, rhetoric, and drama. At the heart of the trial process are efforts by the parties (usually through their lawyers) to persuade the decision makers—whether judges or juries—to believe their version of the facts and law. Thus, for lawyers it is crucial to tell a story that compels and that helps to make sense of the materials that surround the dispute.

Professor Milner Ball has proposed a way of understanding these elements by exploring the significance of metaphor and the function of courts as theater.

■MILNER S. BALL, THE PROMISE OF AMERICAN LAW: A THEOLOGICAL, HUMANISTIC VIEW OF LEGAL PROCESS
48-62, 136-138 (1981)

THE ELEMENT OF METAPHOR

The case which an attorney presents for judgment in court is an admixture of fact and law. The facts are called facts because they are not, we hope, fiction. The interaction of the facts and the law is guided by a logic that may be described, following John Dewey, as an "experimental and flexible logic," or a logic "relative to consequences rather than to antecedents."

The selection of facts and law is guided by their interaction with one another and with a third element, their potential for presentation in court. The elements of presentation—rules of evidence, the case of the opposing side, the dynamics of the proceeding (including surprise and improvisation), the quality of evidence and witnesses, and the compellingness of the law—are considered just as carefully by an attorney as are the facts and the law. The dominant element in the presentation with which he will be concerned is the need to persuade the appropriate decision-makers, first to a judgment that the claim is judicially cognizable, and then to a judgment favorable to the party represented.

The consequential logic, which to a degree governs the selection of facts and law, coupled with the attorney's need for a persuasive presentation, distinguishes the legal case from a scientific investigation. Dewey, for example, hastened to add to his description of the workings of experimental logic the demurrer that "I do not for a moment set up this procedure as a model of scientific investigation; it is too precommitted to the establishment of a particular and partisan conclusion to serve as such a model." What distinguishes the case from scientific investigation helps to establish it as a form of dramaturgy. . . . The methods are better understood as those of playwrights, actors, and directors, and may be described as the making of metaphor.

What is meant by metaphor? In reference to the play *The Cherry Orchard*, Francis Fergusson [in *The Idea of a Theater* (1949), at 166] explained that "the larger elements of the composition—the scenes or episodes, the setting and the developing story—are composed in such a way as to make a poetry of the theater; but the 'text' as we read it literally, is not." The poetry, the metaphor, is not necessarily to be found in the words of the text. Rather, it is to be found in the histrionic elements which "can only be seen in performance or by imagining a performance." . . .

The passage from fact to metaphor is what the advocate seeks. It is the passage from the materials of fact and law (the text) by means of courtroom presentation (the performance) to a persuasive statement of what is to be done in a given situation (the metaphor).

The advocate's presentation of a case, the creation of courtroom metaphor, is marked by the coincidence of the opposites of fact and illusion. Illusion here is not falsehood but facts selected and established through artful, sometimes fortuitous, sequence. This convergence is the paradox of theater. . . . At its best the presentation of a case is a coincidence of reality and illusion, not in the sense of perjury, but in the sense of theatrical metaphor—the reenactment of relevant and material elements for reflection and judgment. Although elusive, this paradoxical interplay of reality and illusion does seem to correspond with the deeper truth of the way we experience life, which is to say that it is a strength, and not a weakness or fault in both the playhouse and the courtroom.

DEFENDING THE ANALOGY: IS COURTROOM ACTION REALLY METAPHOR?

Several objections may legitimately be raised to viewing the courtroom as a theater. One is that it asks too much and the wrong things of the word metaphor. A brief defense of its use here may prove useful.

"Metaphor," Lon Fuller has observed, "is the traditional device of persuasion. Eliminate metaphor from the law and you have reduced its power to convince and convert." Certainly the law does employ metaphors. Fuller illustrated his point with a consideration of the metaphor "constructive notice." An additional point is attempted here: attorneys not only use linguistic metaphors but also produce histrionic metaphors. Constructive notice is a metaphor. A presentation which makes out a case of constructive notice is also a metaphor. Like the performance of a play, the presentation of the advocate's case seeks to persuade, and it does so openly. It is a metaphor and not a lie. . . .

. . . The court case is a tacit comparison in which presentation of selected fact and law is substituted for the events themselves and the prior law.

There are several reasons for the substitution. The plainest is that the past cannot be reproduced exactly, so that in the nature of things some substitution cannot be avoided. Another is constitutional policy which may require deliberate exclusion of certain evidence in criminal cases. A third reason arises from the task of judgment, which requires interpretation rather than a formless flow of information. Finally, and most basically, the very theory of our justice system, as Justice Holmes put it, "is that the conclusions to be reached in a case will be induced only by evidence and argument in open court, and not by any outside influence." This process is to be preserved even against *truthful* outside influences. . . .

TRIALS PERSUADE. DOES THEATER?

Besides maintaining that it overloads "metaphor," another possible objection to the position adumbrated here is that, if, as has been maintained, it is the precommitment of a case to a partisan conclusion that distinguishes it from scientific investigation, then this same precommitment distinguishes it as well from theater. In other words, judicial proceedings are not theater because theater is its own end (art for art's sake) or has some end other than that of persuading to a judgment (entertainment or cathartic excitation to pity or fear, for example).

Yet, art in general and theater in particular do persuade to some conclusion. If the objective is parochial or political, then the artist's product may be perhaps, corruptly, propagandistic. If the objective is broad (for instance, a view or experience of human life), then it is contemplative. Either way, there is an objective of persuasion. . . .

Of course, a play does not guide its audience, as a case guides the jury, to either an immediate decision or to a decision with immediate consequences for the life, freedom, or property of another. Judgments made in response to a play, other than critical ones about the play's quality, are longer range and have to do more with perceptions of life and one's own identity. The question is whether this difference destroys the proposition that the case is theater or only distinguishes the theater of the courtroom from that of the playhouse. The latter alternative has been chosen here. . . .

THE FUNCTIONS OF JUDICIAL THEATER

. . . It is the theatrical character of courts that makes them spaces of freedom, human places where the story of beginning is augmented as it comes alive.

COMMUNICATING NONVERBAL INFORMATION

It may be that live performance communicates nonverbally some of the information that the decision-maker must take into account. Demeanor evidence is an example. While it is undeniable that documents lack the capacity to convey nonverbal information, it has been contested that videotape may do so as well as live presentation. Opinion on the issue will likely continue to be divided, since the communication of nonverbal information is not easily tested or analyzed. It would seem, however, that what is true of plays is true as well of cases: "The little ritual of performance, given just a modicum of competence, can lend to the events represented another dimension, a more urgent reality."

REDIRECTING AGGRESSION

Further, the theatrical character of lawsuits also allows them to redirect aggression. Aggression, the need to fight and have revenge, is acted out and is thereby ritually expressed and controlled. It is in this sense that "[t]he right to sue and defend in the courts is the alternative of force."

The continued capacity of lawsuits to rechannel aggression depends upon several factors, one of which is their gravity, that is, their convictive and absorptive power. . . .

Besides their gravity, another, more decisive factor that maintains legal proceedings as an alternative to other forms of aggression is their fairness. The procedures and conventions of the courtroom set judicial proceedings apart from the world of common, daily affairs. . . . Acceptance of judicial proceedings must be voluntary and is consequently dependent upon the perceived fairness of the courts.

If acceptance of the rules of play ultimately depends upon their fairness, acceptance of the play world they mark off depends upon that world's making good on its express and implied promises. Playgoers bring with them to the theater a "willing suspension of disbelief," a willingness not to see an actor and a bare stage when presented with Macbeth and Birnam Wood come to Dunsinane. . . .

Participants in judicial proceedings also bring with them a willing suspension of disbelief. It is manifested in their willingness to observe the rules and forms of the proceedings, their willingness to abide by the outcome of the proceedings, and their willingness not to dismiss the legitimacy of the legal system, characterized though it may be by curious formulae, arcane rites, and untoward results. Like the license granted theater, this willingness will answer for any sustained length of time only to the system's reasonable degree of success in doing what it promises, in this case, justice.

ENCOURAGING IMPARTIALITY

Courts may not always or even frequently do justice, but their theatrical quality does contribute to their potential for doing justice by encouraging disinterestedness in the decision-makers. As actors, the judge and jury are asked to play parts in a government of laws and not of people. Fulfillment of the roles enables judgments that rise above prejudice and that, therefore, will more likely be just. Not the least hoped-for result of the theatrical trappings and conventions of judicial proceedings is to educe such performances.

Judge and jury are audience as well as actors and in this capacity also may be encouraged to make unprejudiced judgments. . . .

When courtroom theater is effectively and really that — *i.e.*, when it is theater, when it is dramatic — then decision-makers are put in position to judge not so much with blindfolded as with equal eyes.

INDUCING CREATIVITY IN JUDGMENT

To the suggestions that live presentation may communicate nonverbal information, redirect aggression, and encourage impartiality, there may be added another: it is perhaps an inducement to creativity in judgment. Of the cases that come to court, one estimate placed at 30 to 40 percent of the total those that can be decided but one way because they clearly fall within the ambit of a clearly and authoritatively stated rule. Even in these "clear" cases, live presentation may promote the search for imaginative alternatives if it makes disposition less mechanical by giving force and appeal to the position of the party against whom the rule is to be applied. . . .

It should not be concluded from the foregoing discussion that live presentation seduces courts into making undisciplined judgments. Judges may yield to bias and prejudice but not in consequence of live presentation. A legal judgment may be creative without being undisciplined. In this regard it is like fine art. Although original, as Kant observed, "there is still no fine art in which something mechanical, capable of being at once comprehended and followed in obedience to rules, and consequently something *academic* does not constitute the essential condition of the art." The formal requirement that judges, unlike artists, state reasons for what they have done offers added assurance that discipline will be exercised.

THE PERFORMANCE AS A WHOLE

If the advocate's presentation of his client's case is a form of theater which is played to the judge or jury and which contributes to judgment, there is also the theater of the courtroom itself — embracing all that goes on within — played to the public at large. It is the function of this drama to provide an image of legitimate society. In this sense, it is importantly an end in itself. As is true of theater generally, so of judicial theater: the performance is the "good" consumed. The courts are not so much in the business of producing decisions — finding facts, fixing liability, convicting the guilty, protecting the innocent, etc. — as they are of giving a performance. . . .

In fulfilling what John Marshall saw as its duty to say what the law is, the judicial branch does not merely utter decisions, disembodied words. It is the exemplar of law. In its ceremony, its costuming, its performance, and its treatment of participants, it embodies the legitimate exercise of power within a given sphere. Judicial theater is itself a continuous way of saying, in things and acts within appointed spaces, "what the law is." . . .

LAW AS METAPHOR

As I noted in the preface, lawyers speak a reductive language. They do so necessarily, for the disposition of cases requires it. Tort litigation, for example, is possible only if the human body is analyzed into parts keyed to cases. Paradoxically, this alchemy that reduces life to the immediate needs of courtroom judgment is meant ultimately to augment and humanize life. As Archibald MacLeish has said, the "business of the law is to make sense of the confusion of what we call human life—to reduce it to order *but at the same time* to give it possibility, scope, even dignity." The law is marked by a pull in opposite directions, a simultaneity of reduction and augmentation. This is the very stuff of metaphor.

If law is a metaphor, what is it a metaphor of? What is the other thing meant when we talk in terms of law? [Professor James Boyd] White notes how "one has the feeling about a legal argument that it involves everything." When we speak the language of law, we may mean *everything*: law may be a metaphor of life and death.

Law is a metaphor of death when the practice of it is dull, restrictive, a routine drudgery, despairing. In this event, it is a metaphor of the attorney's death. Law is a metaphor of death, too, when it crushes the troubled and the troubling or oppresses the powerless. In this circumstance, it is a metaphor of the society's death. . . .

Law may mean death but does not have to. It can be a metaphor of life. It becomes a metaphor of life for the lawyer when it is an enterprise of the imagination, a language which, controlled, is a vehicle of deliberate commitment. This is to claim that the lawyer, with law as the given term of the metaphor, can define the meaning of the other term, without having to accept such meaning as may be assigned by the law itself, by any institution, or by default. In White's vision, the lawyer works out an identity. "You define a mind and character, very much as the historian or poet or novelist might be said to do. At the end of thirty years you will be able to look at shelves of briefs, think back on negotiations and arguments . . . and say, 'Here is what I have found it possible to say.'"

. . . The lawyer must be able to use legal language, the medium of translation, competently and creatively. But another capacity is of equal, even more critical, importance. The lawyer must not only conjure legal arguments; he must also be able to hear the poor and blacks and others whose grievances cry out to be translated. These faculties, insofar as they require more than imagination, may be said to depend upon conscience, or heart. White has taught us to animate the imagination. How to inspirit the heart is another question.

Its answer will come from legal education that ventures the risk of a pilgrimage undertaken with as well as for others. The pilgrimage will be rare even though it follows a circular course, seeking to achieve that which gives it origin. Such education, like life, will be filled with amazement, always starting from and always on the way to the New Beginning.

B. AN OPENING CASE: THE POWER AND LIMITS OF COURTS

In *United States v. Hall*, 472 F.2d 261 (5th Cir. 1972), the Court of Appeals for the Fifth Circuit asks whether the district court judge may punish—or indeed do anything to—someone who was not a party to the relevant lawsuit. What are the limits of judicial power as announced in this opinion? Have those limits changed because of this decision, or does this decision simply confirm pre-existing limits? When the court looks to a rule to answer the question before it, where does that rule come from? When there is more than one relevant rule, what should a court do? When applying established rules to new facts, does the court change the rules, and if so, how?

1. *Background of* United States v. Hall [*]

Eric Hall was arrested on March 9, 1972, for violating an emergency *ex parte* injunction issued pursuant to one of a series of decisions involving the Duval County, Florida, public schools, then the thirteenth largest school district in the country. Duval County maintained a dual school system divided along racial lines despite the United States Supreme Court's decision in *Brown v. Board of Education*, 347 U.S. 482 (1954), forbidding such deliberate segregation. In 1960, a group of black parents sued the school board on behalf of their school-aged children. The court found that the school board had maintained a racially divided school system "as a matter of policy, custom and usage" and had "not adopted any plan whatever for eliminating racial discrimination in the public system." *Braxton v. Board of Public Instruction for Duval County*, 326 F.2d 616, 620 (5th Cir. 1964).

By 1971, the Duval County School Board remained either incapable of or unwilling to comply with the court's order. Only 60 of the 30,000 black students in the school system participated in desegregated schooling; most black students attended all-black schools, even if that required

---

[*] Thanks to Vik Kanwar and Dovie Yoana King, students at the Northeastern University School of Law, for research.

commuting to distant schools. *Mims v. Duval County School Board,* 329 F. Supp. 123, 125 (D. Fla. 1971). The district court therefore ordered remedial action, including a plan to pair Ribault and Raines High Schools, which would yield two integrated schools. This decision was in line with the Supreme Court's 1971 opinion in *Swann v. Charlotte-Mecklenburg Board of Education,* 402 U.S. 1 (1971), which detailed the duties of school districts and the powers of district courts to ensure plans to work realistically and effectively to end racial segregation in public schools.

Soon after the court's desegregation order was put into effect, racial violence erupted at Ribault High School—the formerly predominantly white school. In response to the violence, administrators shut down the school on at least two occasions. These and subsequent events were reported in Otis Perkins, *End to Disruptions at Schools Ordered Here,* Florida Times-Union, March 6, 1972. On February 18, 1972, black students at Ribault organized a walkout; white students and black students then engaged in fights that damaged school property. Despite the participation of both groups of students, school officials blamed the black students and charged and suspended 12 of them. The administrators then recruited 30 extra teachers to be present on campus. The administration also alerted sheriffs in the vicinity, rearranged lunch schedules, and eliminated one class period to avoid confrontations between the racial groups. Then, a white faculty member removed from the cafeteria bulletin board several posters relating to Black History week, including one with a picture of philosopher and prisoner advocate Angela Davis and the caption, "THIS IS WAR."* Black students replaced the posters, and then white students took them down. This incident produced a 20-minute delay in classes, and 50 white students and 125 black students then gathered on the school patio in a "free for all" fight. Black students then tried to organize another boycott.

School authorities held black students largely responsible for the unrest that day. The authorities also believed that black adults from outside the school were encouraging students to defy police and school authorities. The school administrators petitioned the district court for injunctive relief to bar such outsiders from school premises. In response, the court issued an *ex parte* injunction on Sunday, March 5, 1972. Among those intended to be covered by the injunction were members of the Florida Black Front, an organization that modeled itself on the Black Panthers. The injunction was served directly on some members of that group, but not to Eric Hall, who was associated with the group. Eric Hall's lawyer, William Sheppard, recalled that Eric intended to go to the school to support the black students following the incident over the posters. Whether

---

*Angela Davis became a fugitive after August 7, 1970, when she was accused of involvement in Jonathan Jackson's attempted hostage trade for the Soledad Brothers—an effort that ended in a deadly shootout. She later became a philosopher and university professor.

Hall supported or opposed integration was not entirely clear; he did seek to inspire active strategies for asserting rights.[*]

Hall learned of the injunction from another member of the Black Front. He asked his lawyer what would happen if he went to the high school. Sheppard recalled his response: "I told him honestly that I thought he'd get picked up in three minutes." Sheppard also recalls that Hall next telephoned the famous leftist lawyer, William Kunstler, for a second opinion.[†] Kunstler reportedly told Hall that as a nonparty to the suit, he could do what he wanted to do. Hall entered the campus, was immediately arrested, and was then charged with contempt. The case that bears his name has been cited with approval by the United States Supreme Court. *See Washington v. Washington State Commercial Passenger Fishing Vessel Assn.*, 443 U.S. 658, 692 n.32 (1979); *Golden State Bottling Co. v. NLRB*, 414 U.S. 168, 180 (1973).

Duval County never fully integrated its school system, and controversy still surrounds its schools. Despite a court-approved agreement with the National Association for the Advancement of Colored People (NAACP) in 1996, Duval County administrators prefer voluntary integration through specialized magnet programs. The NAACP, by contrast, favors a school choice plan limiting students' options in order to ensure racial balance in the schools and is concerned that the school system plans to build new schools solely in predominantly white suburbs. The school board filed a motion to end the federal court involvement in the system.

A final word on two of the principals involved in the case: the senior judge on the appellate panel assigned to the case, Judge John Minor Wisdom, was one of the champions of the civil rights movement who enforced Supreme Court school desegregation rulings despite personal attacks and threats of physical violence.

Less than a week after completing his jail term for contempt, Eric Hall was shot by a security guard in a Jacksonville, Florida, nightclub. After his photograph appeared in a newspaper story about the incident, a former parole officer from South Florida recognized him as someone known as Kenneth Hall, wanted for robbery in South Florida. Hall was removed from his hospital bed and tried and convicted in South Florida. Reportedly, by the early 1980s, he had become a prisoners' rights activist.

---

[*]Interviews by Vik Kanwar with William Sheppard, Jan. 10, 1998 and March 17, 1998.

[†]Kunstler, a cofounder of the Center for Constitutional Rights, represented the Chicago 7 defendants and many Black Panthers.

2. The Opinion

■ **UNITED STATES v. HALL***
472 F.2d 261 (5th Cir. 1972)

WISDOM, Circuit Judge.

This case presents the question whether a district court has power to punish for criminal contempt a person who, though neither a party nor bearing any legal relationship to a party, violates a court order designed to protect the court's judgment in a school desegregation case. We uphold the district court's conclusion that in the circumstances of this case it had this power, and affirm the defendant's conviction for contempt.

On June 23, 1971, the district court entered a "Memorandum Opinion and Final Judgment" in the case of *Mims v. Duval County School Board.* The court required the Duval County Florida school board to complete its desegregation of Duval County schools, in accordance with the Supreme Court's decision in *Swann v. Charlotte-Mecklenburg Board of Education,* 402 U.S. 1 (1971), by pairing and clustering a number of schools which had theretofore been predominantly one-race schools. This order culminated litigation begun eleven years before, *Braxton v. Board of Public Instruction.* This Court affirmed the district court's order in *Mims v. Duval County School Board,* 447 F.2d 1330 (5th Cir. 1971). The district court retained jurisdiction to enter such orders as might be necessary in the future to effectuate its judgment.

Among the schools marked for desegregation under the plan approved by the district court was Ribault Senior High School, a predominantly white school. The plan directed pairing of Ribault with William E. Raines Senior High School, a predominantly black school, so that the black enrollment would be 59 percent at Raines and 57 percent at Ribault. After the desegregation order was put into effect racial unrest and violence developed at Ribault, necessitating on one occasion the temporary closing of the school. On March 5, 1972, the superintendent of schools and the sheriff of Jacksonville filed a petition for injunctive relief in the case with the district court. This petition alleged that certain black adult "outsiders" had caused or abetted the unrest and violence by their activities both on and off the Ribault campus. The petition identified the appellant Eric Hall, allegedly a member of a militant organization known as the "Black Front," as one of several such outsiders who, in combination with black students and parents, were attempting to prevent the normal operation of Ribault through student boycotts and other activities. As relief the petitioners requested an order "restraining all Ribault Senior High School students and any person acting independently or in concert with them from interfering with the orderly operation of the school and the Duval

---

*Eds. Note: In this case and throughout this book we have omitted textual citations; textual omissions are indicated with ellipses. We have retained the original footnote numbering.

County School system, and for such other relief as the court may deem just and proper."

At an *ex parte* session on March 5, 1972, the district court entered an order providing in part:

1. All students of Ribault Senior High School, whether in good standing or under suspension, and other persons acting independently or in concert with them and having notice of this order are hereby enjoined and restrained from

(a) Obstructing or preventing the attendance in classes of students and faculty members;

(b) Harassing, threatening or intimidating any faculty, staff member or employee of Ribault Senior High School or the Duval County School Board;

(c) Harassing, threatening or intimidating any student en route to and from school;

(d) Destroying or attempting to destroy, defacing or attempting to deface any structure, buildings, materials or equipment of Ribault Senior High School or the Duval County School Board;

(e) Committing any other act to disrupt the orderly operation of Ribault Senior High School or any other school of the Duval County School System;

2. Until further order of this Court, no person shall enter any building of the Ribault Senior High School or go upon the school's grounds except the following:

(a) Students of Ribault Senior High School while attending classes or official school functions;

(b) The faculty, staff, and administration of Ribault Senior High School and other employees of the Duval County School Board having assigned duties at the school;

(c) Persons having business obligations which require their presence on the school's premises;

(d) Parents of Ribault Senior High School students or any other person who has the prior permission of the principal or his designee to be present on the school's premises;

(e) Law enforcement officials of the City of Jacksonville, the State of Florida or the United States Government.

The order went on to provide that "anyone having notice of this order who violates any of the terms thereof shall be subject to arrest, prosecution and punishment by imprisonment or fine, or both, for criminal contempt under the laws of the United States of America. . . ." The court ordered the sheriff to serve copies of the order on seven named persons, *including Eric Hall.* Hall was neither a party plaintiff nor a party defendant in the *Mims* litigation, and in issuing this order the court did not join Hall or any of the other persons named in the order as parties.

On March 9, 1972, four days after the court issued its order, Hall violated that portion of the order restricting access to Ribault High School by appearing on the Ribault campus. When questioned by a deputy United States marshal as to the reasons for his presence, Hall replied that he was on the grounds of Ribault for the purpose of violating the March 5 order. The marshal then arrested Hall and took him into custody. After a nonjury trial, the district court found Hall guilty of the charge of criminal contempt and sentenced him to sixty days' imprisonment.

On this appeal Hall raises two related contentions. Both contentions depend on the fact that Hall was not a party to the *Mims* litigation and the fact that, in violating the court's order, he was apparently acting independently of the *Mims* parties. He first points to the common law rule that a nonparty who violates an injunction solely in pursuit of his own interests cannot be held in contempt. Not having been before the court as a party or as the surrogate of a party, he argues that in accordance with this common law rule he was not bound by the court's order. Second, he contends that Rule 65(d) of the Federal Rules of Civil Procedure prevents the court's order from binding him, since Rule 65(d) limits the binding effect of injunctive orders to "parties to the action, their officers, agents, servants, employees, and attorneys, and . . . those persons in active concert or participation with them who receive actual notice of the order by personal service or otherwise." We reject both contentions.

For his first contention, that a court of equity has no power to punish for contempt a nonparty acting solely in pursuit of his own interests, the appellant relies heavily on the two leading cases of *Alemite Manufacturing Corp. v. Staff*, 42 F.2d 832 (2d Cir. 1930), and *Chase National Bank v. City of Norwalk*, 291 U.S. 431 (1934). In *Alemite* the district court had issued an injunction restraining the defendant and his agents, employees, associates, and confederates from infringing the plaintiff's patent. Subsequently a third person, not a party to the original suit and acting entirely on his own initiative, began infringing the plaintiff's patent and was held in contempt by the district court. The Second Circuit reversed in an opinion by Judge Learned Hand, stating that "it is not the act described which the decree may forbid, but only that act when the defendant does it." 42 F.2d at 833. In *Chase National Bank* the plaintiff brought suit against the City of Norwalk to obtain an injunction forbidding the removal of poles, wires, and other electrical equipment belonging to the plaintiff. The district court issued a decree enjoining the City, its officers, agents, and employees, "and all persons whomsoever to whom notice of this order shall come" from removing the equipment or otherwise interfering with the operation of the plaintiff's power plant. The Supreme Court held that the district court had violated "established principles of equity jurisdiction and procedure" insofar as its order applied to persons who were not parties, associates, or confederates of parties, but who merely had notice of the order. *See also Regal Knitwear Co. v. NLRB*, 324 U.S. 9, 13 (1945); *Scott v. Donald*, 165 U.S. 107 (1896).

This case is different. In *Alemite* and *Chase National Bank* the activities of third parties, however harmful they might have been to the plaintiffs' interests, would not have disturbed in any way the adjudication of rights and obligations as between the original plaintiffs and defendants. Infringement of the *Alemite* plaintiff's patent by a third party would not have upset the defendant's duty to refrain from infringing or rendered it more difficult for the defendant to perform that duty. Similarly, the defendant's duty in *Chase National Bank* to refrain from removing the plaintiff's equipment would remain undisturbed regardless of the activities of third parties, as would the plaintiff's right not to have its equipment removed by the defendant. The activities of Hall, however, threatened both the plaintiffs' right and the defendant's duty as adjudicated in the *Mims* litigation. In *Mims* the plaintiffs were found to have a constitutional right to attend an integrated school. . . . In short, the activities of persons contributing to racial disorder at Ribault imperiled the court's fundamental power to make a binding adjudication between the parties properly before it.

Courts of equity have inherent jurisdiction to preserve their ability to render judgment in a case such as this. This was the import of the holding in *United States v. United Mine Workers of America*, 330 U.S. 258 (1947). There the district court had issued a temporary restraining order forbidding a union from striking, though there was a substantial question of whether the Norris-LaGuardia Act had deprived the district court of jurisdiction to issue such an order. The Supreme Court upheld the defendants' contempt conviction for violation of this order. As an alternative holding the Court stated that the contempt conviction would have been upheld even if the district court had ultimately been found to be without jurisdiction. This holding affirmed the power of a court of equity to issue an order to preserve the status quo in order to protect its ability to render judgment in a case over which it might have jurisdiction. . . .

The integrity of a court's power to render a binding judgment in a case over which it has jurisdiction is at stake in the present case. . . .

The principle that courts have jurisdiction to punish for contempt in order to protect their ability to render judgment is also found in the use of *in rem* injunctions. Federal courts have issued injunctions binding on all persons, regardless of notice, who come into contact with property which is the subject of a judicial decree. . . . A court entering a decree binding on a particular piece of property is necessarily faced with the danger that its judgment may be disrupted in the future by members of an undefinable class—those who may come into contact with the property. The *in rem* injunction protects the court's judgment. The district court here faced an analogous problem. The judgment in a school case, as in other civil rights actions, inures to the benefit of a large class of persons, regardless of whether the original action is cast in the form of a class action. . . . At the same time court orders in school cases, affecting as they do large numbers of people, necessarily depend on the cooperation of the entire community for their implementation.

As this Court is well aware, school desegregation orders often strongly excite community passions. School orders are, like *in rem* orders, particularly vulnerable to disruption by an undefinable class of persons who are neither parties nor acting at the instigation of parties. In such cases, as in voting rights cases, courts must have the power to issue orders similar to that issued in this case, tailored to the exigencies of the situation and directed to protecting the court's judgment. . . .

The appellant also asserts that Rule 65(d) of the Federal Rules of Civil Procedure prevents the court's order from binding him.[3] He points out that he was not a party to the original action, nor an officer, agent, servant, employee, or attorney of a party, and denies that he was acting in "active concert or participation" with any party to the original action.

In examining this contention we start with the proposition that Rule 65 was intended to embody "the common-law doctrine that a decree of injunction not only binds the parties defendant but also those identified with them in interest, in 'privity' with them, represented by them or subject to their control." . . . Literally read, Rule 65(d) would forbid the issuance of *in rem* injunctions. Note, *Binding Nonparties to Injunction Decrees*, 49 Minn. L. Rev. 719, 736 (1965). But courts have continued to issue *in rem* injunctions notwithstanding Rule 65(d), since they possessed the power to do so at common law and since Rule 65(d) was intended to embody rather than to limit their common law powers.

Similarly, we conclude that Rule 65(d), as a codification rather than a limitation of courts' common-law powers, cannot be read to restrict the inherent power of a court to protect its ability to render a binding judgment. We hold that Hall's relationship to the *Mims* case fell within that contemplated by Rule 65(d). By deciding *Mims* and retaining jurisdiction the district court had, in effect, adjudicated the rights of the entire community with respect to the racial controversy surrounding the school system. Moreover, as we have noted, in the circumstances of this case third parties such as Hall were in a position to upset the court's adjudication. This was not a situation which could have been anticipated by the draftsmen of procedural rules. In meeting the situation as it did, the district court did not overstep its powers.

We do not hold that courts are free to issue permanent injunctions against all the world in school cases. Hall had notice of the court's order. Rather than challenge it by the orderly processes of law, he resorted

---

3. Rule 65(d) provides:

Form and Scope of Injunction or Restraining Order. Every order granting an injunction and every restraining order shall set forth the reasons for its issuance; shall be specific in terms; shall describe in reasonable detail, and not by reference to the complaint or other document, the act or acts sought to be restrained; and is binding only upon the parties to the action, their officers, agents, servants, employees, and attorneys, and upon those persons in active concert or participation with them who receive actual notice of the order by personal service or otherwise.

to conscious, willful defiance. *See Walker v. Birmingham,* 388 U.S. 307 (1967).

It is true that this order was issued without a hearing, and that ordinarily injunctive relief cannot be granted without a hearing. *See* 7 J. Moore, *Moore's Federal Practice* ¶ 65.04[3] & n.8a (1972). But we need not hold that this order has the effect of a preliminary or permanent injunction. Rather, the portion of the court's order here complained of may be characterized as a temporary restraining order, which under Rule 65(b) may be issued *ex parte.* . . .

We hold, then, that the district court had the inherent power to protect its ability to render a binding judgment between the original parties to the *Mims* litigation by issuing an interim *ex parte* order against an undefinable class of persons. We further hold that willful violation of that order by one having notice of it constitutes criminal contempt. The judgment of the district court is affirmed.

C. THE RIGHT TO BE HEARD: ELEMENTS AND HISTORY OF DUE PROCESS

> "nor shall any State deprive any person of life, liberty, or property, without due process of law"
>
> Amendment 14, section 1, U.S. Constitution*

This basic phrase, "due process of law," is the Constitution's most basic notion of procedure. But what does it mean? The phrase most simply refers to a right to be heard, but as interpreted by theorists and by courts the meaning of that right has evolved and changed shape over time. A heated debate over these issues in the context of a highly charged political period produced six separate opinions in the Supreme Court case of *Joint Anti-Fascist Refugee Committee v. McGrath,* 341 U.S. 123 (1951). In that case, three organizations challenged the decision of the Attorney General of the United States both to list them as "totalitarian, fascist, communist, or subversive," and to furnish that information to the Loyalty Review Board of the United States Civil Service Commission. The three organizations claimed that this governmental action was taken without notice to them or an opportunity for them to present a defense, and injured them in a national climate that was decidedly anti-Communist. The majority view of

---

* *Eds. Note:* The Fourteenth Amendment specifically sets limits on what state governments may do. For limitations on the federal government, *see* Amendment 5: "nor [shall any person] be deprived of life, liberty, or property, without due process of law."

the Supreme Court Justices interpreted "due process" to require the organizations the opportunity to be heard and to present their own evidence before being labeled pejoratively by the Attorney General.

In his concurring opinion in the case, Justice Felix Frankfurter suggested two reasons for notice and hearing: "No better instrument has been devised for *arriving at truth* than to give a person in jeopardy of a serious loss notice of the case against him and opportunity to meet it. Nor has a better way been found for *generating the feeling,* so important to a popular government, *that justice has been done.*" 341 U.S. 149, 171-172 (emphasis added). He continued: "The heart of the matter is that democracy implies respect for the elementary rights of men, however suspect or unworthy; a democratic government must therefore practice fairness; and fairness can rarely be obtained by secret, one-sided determination of facts decisive of rights."

At the same time, Justice Frankfurter acknowledged that "'due process,' unlike some legal rules, is not a technical conception with a fixed content unrelated to time, place and circumstances. Expressing as it does in its ultimate analysis respect enforced by law for that feeling of just treatment which has evolved through centuries of Anglo-American constitutional history and civilization, 'due process' cannot be imprisoned within the treacherous limits of any formula. . . . It is a delicate process of adjustment inescapably involving the exercise of judgment by those whom the Constitution entrusted with the unfolding of the process." 341 U.S. at 162-163.

Nearly twenty years later, a group of attorneys for poor people gave the Justices a further opportunity to interpret due process. *Goldberg v. Kelly* posed the question: does due process require notice and a hearing before the government terminates public assistance (or welfare) benefits? As you read the background to the case and the Supreme Court opinions, consider the values behind the idea of due process and the specific contours that idea took in this setting.

1. *Background of* Goldberg v. Kelly

Presidents John F. Kennedy and Lyndon B. Johnson promoted programs to address poverty; these became the "War on Poverty" declared by President Johnson in 1964. These federal programs included public assistance, health care, housing assistance, job training, public education, and legal services for poor people. Activists and lawyers working on behalf of poor people found a model in the civil rights movement. "Activists, perhaps naively and certainly optimistically, viewed the federal courts as the ultimate protectors of individual rights and, under the appropriate circumstances, arbiters of social change." Martha F. Davis, *Brutal Need: Lawyers and the Welfare Rights Movement, 1960-1973* (1993), at 1.

Activists and lawyers hoped to use law to make public assistance more certain and reliable, even though the state had long treated welfare as a gift rather than a right. Even progressive lawyers in the 1960s stopped short of arguing that the Constitution mandated welfare as a right. Instead, the lawyers argued that once an individual established eligibility, under a statute, for public assistance, the state had to comply with constitutional principles, such as equal protection and the right to travel in the implementation of the benefit. Before *Goldberg v. Kelly*, federal and state welfare laws had allowed benefits to be terminated as soon as a caseworker determined that the recipient was ineligible. Sometimes, caseworkers used the threat of termination to shake up recipients and make them pliant.

For due process to apply, however, public assistance had to somehow fit the predicates of "life, liberty, or property." Here, a landmark article written by Charles Reich helped. The Yale Law School professor argued that government benefits including licenses and jobs, as well as welfare payments, effectively operate like property and deserve legal protections like property, if the state is not to require extraordinary abilities to coerce those who depend on these resources.*

Recent legislative changes have altered the underlying federal benefits program established in the 1970s, as described in the next excerpt.

■ RICHARD J. PIERCE, JR., THE DUE PROCESS COUNTERREVOLUTION OF THE 1990s?
96 Colum. L. Rev. 1973, 1989-1992 (1996)

. . . The Second Circuit's 1994 opinion in *Colson v. Sillman* [35 F.3d 106 (2d Cir. 1994)] illustrates the ways in which changes in the language of the statutes that govern the availability of benefits can convert a protected "property" right into an unprotected "privilege." A New York statute authorized state provision of medical services to disabled children. When the State withdrew the services it was previously providing to the plaintiff, his parents filed an action pursuant to the Civil Rights Act of 1871. They argued that the procedures the State used to terminate the plaintiff's benefits did not meet the minimum standards required by due process. The court held that due process protections did not apply to the termination decision because the statute did not confer on beneficiaries any "property" right protected by due process.

The second circuit wrote a well-reasoned opinion in which it held that due process did not apply to a decision to withdraw a benefit previously

---

*For a thorough discussion of the influences on Reich's thought, see Martha Davis, *Brutal Need: Lawyers and the Welfare Rights Movement 1960-1973*, at 82-86 (1993). Lawyers for poor people, notably those working at the federally funded Mobilization for Youth Legal Unit in New York City, and others at the Center on Social Welfare Policy in New York City, took up these ideas in a test case challenging terminations of public benefits.

made available under the statute. The Second Circuit distinguished cases such as *Goldberg* and *Eldridge*, where the applicable statutes entitled any individual with specified characteristics to receipt of the benefits at issue. The New York statute qualified the availability of health benefits to otherwise eligible individuals in two ways. First, the statute authorized provision of "such medical service . . . as in the judgment of the commissioner is needed." Second, the statute qualified the availability of benefits with reference to potential fiscal constraints: "The department shall . . . provide, within the limits of the appropriations made therefor, such medical service. . . ." The statute conferred no protected "property" right on an otherwise eligible beneficiary because the statutory provisions that conferred discretion on the agency and that limited the availability of benefits with reference to potential fiscal constraints had the effect of negating any inference that the statutory benefits were an "entitlement."

In 1996, Congress enacted major amendments to the statutes that now govern the availability of all forms of welfare [Personal Responsibility and Work Opportunity Act of 1996, Pub. L. No. 104-193, 110 Stat. 2105]. The amendments have two dominant characteristics. They confer more discretion on (state) agencies, and they authorize these agencies to limit the benefits made available based on potential fiscal constraints. When the inevitable constitutional challenge reaches a Supreme Court already looking for an opportunity to reduce the scope of the interests protected by due process, the results will be predictable. The Court will adopt the Second Circuit's reasoning in *Colson* to hold that neither welfare benefits nor Medicare benefits are property interests protected by due process. That series of opinions will signal the end of the largest single battle in the due process counterrevolution. . . .

The statute abolishes the AFDC program that provided the vehicle for the Court's revolutionary decision in *Goldberg v. Kelly*. It substitutes for AFDC a system of "block grants to states for temporary assistance for needy families." The first provision of the block grant part of the statute begins: "The purpose of this part is to increase the flexibility of states. . . ." That provision concludes with the following statement: "NO INDIVIDUAL ENTITLEMENT.—This part shall not be interpreted to entitle any individual . . . to assistance under any State program funded under this part." In short, the statute provides the Court abundant evidence to support a holding that welfare is no longer a form of "property" within the meaning of the Due Process Clause. Indeed, it is hard to imagine how the Court could support a reaffirmation of its holding in *Goldberg*, given the many provisions of the welfare reform act that negate any implication that it confers a property right on welfare beneficiaries.

Social Security benefits are likely to survive the counterrevolution for a few years, but their exclusion from the scope of the property interests protected by due process is inevitable. All of the major political actors in the budget debate have taken Social Security "off the table" for the moment. Anyone who can read, however, knows that Social Security is not actuarially viable in its present form. Within a few years, Congress will have to amend the Social Security statute in ways that are broadly analogous to the amendments to the welfare statutes. Once those amendments become law, the then-existing precedents with respect to welfare will support the conclusion that Social Security benefits also fail to qualify as "property" protected by due process.

At this point in the counterrevolution, only one major category of "new property" will remain subject to due process—the jobs of government employees who can be discharged only for cause. Classifying a government job as a constitutionally-protected "property" right of the incumbent has long been viewed as a bizarre anachronism even by many scholars who support most of the results of the due process revolution. It will seem even more anachronistic in a legal environment in which legislatures, rather than courts, determine the procedures appropriate for decisions to place prisoners in solitary confinement, for decisions to deprive welfare beneficiaries of "the very means by which to live," and for decisions to withdraw medical benefits from handicapped children. The Court will find a way to hold that government employees no longer have a constitutionally-protected right to their jobs in this environment. The only interesting question is how the Court will support such a holding.

2. The Complaint

Civil litigation starts with a complaint, filed by the plaintiff. As you read the complaint that launched the decision now known as *Goldberg v. Kelly,* consider why the initial filing is captioned *Kelly v. Wyman.* (Answer: the plaintiff class was led by Kelly; the plaintiffs won at the district court level, and the caption for the appeal listed the appellant (defendant) first. But by that time, the head of the state agency had changed, so the name had changed.) Consider how the plaintiffs' lawyers framed the lawsuit. Why did they frame the suit to include more than one plaintiff? The Federal Rule governing complaints requires only that the document give the defendants notice of the claims against them, a "short and plain statement of the claim showing that the pleader is entitled to relief" along with a demand for that relief. Fed. R. Civ. P. 8. Why did the plaintiffs' lawyers provide more detail than was required?

JOHN KELLY, et al., Plaintiffs, v. GEORGE K. WYMAN, et al., Defendants.	Civil Action No. 394-1968 COMPLAINT FOR DECLARATORY JUDGMENT INJUNCTIVE RELIEF

I

This is an action for injunctive and declaratory relief authorized by Title 42 U.S.C. 1983 to secure rights, privileges and immunities established by the Fourteenth Amendment to the Constitution of the United States and the Social Security Act, Title 42 U.S.C. 301 et seq., and the regulations promulgated thereunder. Jurisdiction is conferred on this Court by Title 28 U.S.C. 1343(3) and (4) providing for original jurisdiction of this Court in suits authorized by Title 42 U.S.C. 1983; and jurisdiction is further conferred on this Court by 28 U.S.C. 2201 and 2202 relating to declaratory judgments.

II

This is a proper case for determination by a three-judge court pursuant to Title 28 U.S.C. 2281 and 2284, in that it seeks an injunction to restrain the defendants from applying, enforcing, executing and implementing Sections 213(2), 214, 304, 325, 350(2) (6), and 353(2) of the New York Social Services Law, Section 351.22 and 356.4 of Volume 18, Official Compilation of Code Rules and Regulations of the State of New York (hereafter referred to as 18 N.Y.C.R.R.), Sections 84.2-84.23 of 18 N.Y.C.R.R., promulgated by the New York State Board of Social Welfare to supersede Section 351.22 and 356.4 on March 1, 1968, and related statutes, rules and regulations, insofar as these statutes and regulations require termination or suspension of financial aid in the form of public assistance [Aid to Families with Dependent Children (AFDC), Aid to the Aged, Blind and Disabled (AABD) and Home Relief (HR)] prior to the granting of adequate notice and opportunity to be heard on the grounds of the invalidity of said statutes and regulations under the Constitution and laws of the United States.

III

This action seeks an injunction and declaratory judgment restraining the enforcement of, and declaring unconstitutional the aforesaid state statutes and statewide rules and regulations, on their face and as applied and interpreted by defendants, on the grounds that said statutes, rules and regulations, and actions taken pursuant thereto deprive plaintiffs of the due process of law guaranteed by the Fourteenth Amendment to the United States Constitution and, so far as the AFDC and AABD programs are concerned, deprive plaintiffs of the "fair hearing" guaranteed by the Social Security Act, in that said statutes, rules and regulations deny to plaintiffs an opportunity for a hearing prior to termination or suspension of financial aid under the public assistance program.

IV

Plaintiffs John Kelly, Randolph Young, and Juan DeJesus are adult citizens of the United States and residents of the City and State of New York who received public assistance until aid was terminated without notice and without a hearing.

Plaintiffs Pearl McKinney and Pearl Frye are adult citizens of the United States and residents of the City and State of New York who received public assistance until aid was terminated without a hearing.

Plaintiff Altagracia Guzman is an adult citizen of the United States who faces imminent termination of her public assistance benefits if she does not accede to a demand of the New York City Department of Social Service, for which demand the Department has no basis in law.

V

Plaintiffs bring this action pursuant to Rule 23 of the Federal Rules of Civil Procedure on behalf of themselves and all other recipients of public assistance who are similarly situated. All public assistance recipients are similarly affected by the statutes, rules and regulations challenged herein in that all are by statute, rule and regulation made subject to peremptory *ex parte* termination of their aid. The persons in the class are so numerous as to make joinder impractical; there are common questions of law and fact; plaintiffs' claims are typical of the claims of the class; and the representative plaintiffs will fairly and adequately protect the interests of the class. The parties opposing the class have acted or refused to act on grounds generally applicable to the class.

VI

Defendant George K. Wyman is the Commissioner of the Department of Social Services of the State of New York and is charged with statewide administration of the public assistance program and with establishing regulations to carry out the statutory provisions of said program.

Defendant Maurice C. Hunt is Acting Commissioner of the Department of Social Services of the City of New York and is responsible for administering the public assistance program in the City of New York.

Defendants Hugh R. Jones, as Chairman of the State Board of Social Welfare, and Mrs. Omar Adams, Dorothy I. Height, Richard G. Kimmerer, John M. Galbraith, Edward J. Johannes, Jr., Arthur G. Hopkins, Mrs. Monica M. McConville, John P. Hale, Mrs. Alexander E. Holstein, Jr., Frederick A. Klingenstein, George F. Berlinger, Theodore C. Jackson, Jose Lopez, and David Bernstein, as members of the State Board of Social Welfare, are responsible for the promulgation of rules governing the policies and conduct of the Department of Social Services of the State of New York.

VII

The aforesaid public assistance programs created by the New York Social Services law provide financial aid to certain needy persons. Persons who meet the statutory criteria receive financial aid as a matter of statutory entitlement.

VIII

At all times relevant hereto the State of New York and defendants, in order to receive federal funds for the Aid to Families with Dependent Children and Aid to the Aged, Blind, and Disabled programs have been required by the Social Security Act, Title 42 U.S.C. §301 et seq., to have formulated a "state plan" for said programs in conformity with the provisions of the Act and the United States Constitution. The Social Security Act, as interpreted by regulations of the United States Department of Health, Education and Welfare requires that a "state plan" provide for granting an opportunity for a fair hearing before the State agency to any individual aggrieved by an action of a local Department of Social Services.

IX

1. Plaintiff John Kelly is twenty-nine years old and was a recipient of Home Relief in the amount of $80.05 semi-monthly from August 1967, until January 1, 1968.

2. Plaintiff Kelly was the victim of a hit and run accident in June, 1966, which resulted in serious injury, repeated hospitalization and inability to work.

3. On December 16, 1967, plaintiff Kelly was ordered by his caseworker to move out of the Broadway Central Hotel in which he was then residing and in which he desired to reside and into the Barbara Hotel which charged equal rates but which Mr. Kelly knew to be inhabited by drug addicts and drunkards.

4. Plaintiff Kelly moved into the Barbara Hotel as a result of his caseworker's order, but moved out of this hotel within a short time since he considered it a serious threat to his health and safety. Mr. Kelly moved into the apartment of a friend.

5. On January 8, 1968, plaintiff Kelly was informed by the hotel desk clerk at the Barbara Hotel where he received his mail that Mr. Kelly's caseworker had terminated his case and had instructed the clerk to return a check which was mailed to Mr. Kelly for a winter coat which the Department had previously decided Mr. Kelly required.

6. Plaintiff Kelly did not receive his assistance check due January 16, 1968.

7. Plaintiff Kelly attempted to visit his caseworker at the Gramercy Welfare Center, 110 East 28th Street, New York, N.Y. on January 8 and January 16, 1968, and on both occasions was refused an interview.

8. Plaintiff Kelly was informed on both occasions that his case had been terminated because he had violated his caseworker's instructions to move into the Barbara Hotel and remain there or suffer immediate termination of his case.

9. On January 23, 1968, a social worker at Mobilization for Youth, Inc. telephoned the Gramercy Welfare Center and was informed that Mr. Kelly's case had been terminated. Her efforts to re-open Mr. Kelly's case were ineffective.

10. Plaintiff Kelly has no assets, no means of support and remains unable to work pending further surgery which was occasioned by his 1966 automobile accident. Since his termination Mr. Kelly has been living on the charity of his friends.

[The complaint provides details of the background and situation of additional plaintiffs including financial status and the manner in which public assistance was terminated.] . . .

XV

Sections 213(2), 304, 325 and 353(2) of the New York Social Services Law, and 18 N.Y.C.R.R. Section 356.4 as in effect and as amended by 18 N.Y.C.R.R. Section 84.2-84.23. effective March 1, 1968, prescribing the hearing procedure in the public assistance program, and Sections 214, 304(6), 325 and 350(2)(b) and 18 N.Y.C.R.R. 351.22 prescribing the manner of termination or suspension of aid in the public assistance program, on their face, and as interpreted and applied to plaintiffs and members of their class, deprive the plaintiffs of the right of due process of law guaranteed by the Fourteenth Amendment to the United States Constitution and, to the extent applicable, of the "Fair Hearing" guaranteed by the Social Security Act in that said statutes and the regulations adopted in enforcement thereof authorize and require effective action terminating and suspending financial aid prior to the granting of reasonable notice and opportunity for a hearing which meets due process standards. The termination and withdrawal of financial aid may, under the present regulations, extend for a period of several months before a hearing is held and a decision is rendered, even though plaintiffs had been receiving such aid and are in vital need of such aid for food, shelter and medical care and even though plaintiffs are prepared to prove that they are and have been eligible. Such deprivation is contrary to the purpose of the Social Security Act.

XVI

Plaintiffs have no adequate remedy at law and defendants will continue to cause and threaten to cause irreparable injury to plaintiffs unless enjoined by this Court. Plaintiffs Kelly, Young and DeJesus will not be afforded any administrative hearing since they received aid through the Home Relief program. Plaintiff Frye is awaiting the hearing she has requested. Plaintiff McKinney only received her notice of termination on Friday, January 26.

XVII

Plaintiffs have no adequate resources with which to support themselves and their families in the absence of their public assistance grants.

WHEREFORE, plaintiffs respectfully pray on behalf of themselves and all others similarly situated that this Court:

1. Assume jurisdiction of this cause and convene a three-judge Court pursuant to Title 28 U.S.C. §2281.

2. Enter a temporary restraining order and a preliminary injunction ordering the defendants to refrain from

  1. refusing to pay the named plaintiffs herein their regular public assistance grants and

  2. terminating aid to any recipient of public assistance without giving advance written notice stating the reasons for such action and without affording such recipients an opportunity for a hearing prior to withdrawal of aid.

3. Enter a declaratory judgment pursuant to Title 28 U.S.C. Sections 2201 and 2202 and Rule 57 of the Federal Rules of Civil Procedure declaring that Sections 213(2), 214, 304, 325, 350(2)(b) and 353(2) of the New York Social Service Law and related provisions, and the regulations and rules issued pursuant thereto, violate the Fourteenth Amendment to the United States Constitution and the Social Security Act on their face and as applied, insofar as they authorize and require termination or suspension of public assistance prior to granting reasonable notice and opportunity for a hearing meeting due process standards.

4. Enter a preliminary and permanent injunction restraining the defendants, their successors in office, agents and employees from terminating or suspending the aid of any public assistance recipient prior to the granting of reasonable and adequate notice and opportunity for a hearing which satisfies the standards of due process of law.

5. Allow plaintiffs their costs herein, grant them and all others similarly situated such additional or alternative relief including payment of all monies wrongfully withheld, as the Court may deem to be just and appropriate.

Respectfully submitted,
[Attorneys' names]

(Sworn to January 26, 1968.)

3. Reading the Case

As you read the opinions in this and other cases that follow, please consider the following different ways you can analyze opinions in procedural cases and be prepared to discuss them in class, based on the model of *Goldberg v. Kelly*. These methods will serve you well for the entire course and beyond.

The underlying story. First, it is often helpful to try to figure out what led to the dispute prior to the lawsuit. Who were the parties, what did they do prior to the litigation that led to the dispute, and what do they want to achieve in the lawsuit?

The procedural posture. Second, you can read a case in order to follow and understand the procedure. This approach has three aspects: (1) You must consider the precise procedural question before each court. (2) You should also analyze what procedural steps took place previously. This will help you preview procedural concepts before you get to them in greater detail, and it will help you review what you already know. (3) Finally, you should also consider the outcome at each level of court, that is, what the circuit court did with the district court decision, and what the Supreme Court did with the circuit court decision. Also ask what will happen next in the case now that the Supreme Court has spoken.

Lawyer and judge strategies. Third, you can consider the strategies of each of the participants. Why did the lawyers act as they did? This includes analyzing why they made their procedural choices and why plaintiffs seek particular types of relief. What are the Justices' strategies in writing their opinions? The judges are trying to gain votes from other judges, and are trying to influence future behavior and subsequent decisions.

Holdings and procedural doctrine. Fourth (some students and teachers like to start with this), you will want to consider what the case holds. What doctrine will lawyers and legislators take from the case? Is there reasoning that will be valuable to later cases? How closely do the Justices try to link their decision to the facts of the particular case?

Other viewpoints of your choice. Fifth, you might consider judicial opinions from the points of view of other disciplines that interest you. For example, history: what does this case tell you about the procedural, intellectual, and factual history of the times? If you like novels, consider the plot and characters involved. If you like film, imagine the courtroom scenes and others that precede and follow them.

4. The Supreme Court's Response

■ GOLDBERG v. KELLY
397 U.S. 254 (1970)

Justice BRENNAN delivered the opinion of the Court:

The question for decision is whether a State that terminates public assistance payments to a particular recipient without affording him the opportunity for an evidentiary hearing prior to termination denies the recipient procedural due process in violation of the Due Process Clause of the Fourteenth Amendment.

This action was brought in the District Court for the Southern District of New York by residents of New York City receiving financial aid under the federally assisted program of Aid to Families with Dependent Children (AFDC) or under New York State's general Home Relief program.* Their complaint alleged that the New York State and New York City officials administering these programs terminated, or were about to terminate, such aid without prior notice and hearing, thereby denying them due process of law. At the time the suits were filed there was no requirement of prior notice or hearing of any kind before termination of financial aid. However, the State and city adopted procedures for notice and hearing after the suits were brought, and the plaintiffs, appellees here, then challenged the constitutional adequacy of those procedures.

The State Commissioner of Social Services amended the State Department of Social Services' Official Regulations to require that local social services officials proposing to discontinue or suspend a recipient's financial aid do so . . . [by] giving notice to the recipient of the reasons for a proposed discontinuance or suspension at least seven days prior to its effective date, with notice also that upon request the recipient may have the proposal reviewed by a local welfare official holding a position superior to that of the supervisor who approved the proposed discontinuance or suspension, and, further, the recipient may submit, for purposes of the review, a written statement to demonstrate why his grant should not be discontinued or suspended. The decision by the reviewing official whether to discontinue or suspend aid must be made expeditiously, with written notice of the decision to the recipient. . . .

[Under an additional city procedure, a] caseworker who has doubts about the recipient's continued eligibility must first discuss them with the recipient. If the caseworker concludes that the recipient is no longer eligible, he recommends termination of aid to a unit supervisor. If the latter

*Eds. Note: AFDC was established by the Social Security Act of 1935, 49 Stat. 627, as amended, 42 U.S.C. §601-610 (1964 ed. and Supp. IV). It is a categorical assistance program supported by federal grants-in-aid but administered by the state according to regulations of the Secretary of Health, Education and Welfare . . . "Home Relief is a general assistance program financed and administered solely by New York state and local governments . . . "

concurs, he sends the recipient a letter stating the reasons for proposing to terminate aid and notifying him that within seven days he may request that a higher official review the record, and may support the request with a written statement prepared personally or with the aid of an attorney or other person. If the reviewing official affirms the determination of ineligibility, aid is stopped immediately and the recipient is informed by letter of the reasons for the action. Appellees' challenge to this procedure emphasizes the absence of any provisions for the personal appearance of the recipient before the reviewing official, for oral presentation of evidence, and for confrontation and cross-examination of adverse witnesses. However, the letter does inform the recipient that he may request a post-termination "fair hearing." This is a proceeding before an independent state hearing officer at which the recipient may appear personally, offer oral evidence, confront and cross-examine the witnesses against him, and have a record made of the hearing. If the recipient prevails at the "fair hearing" he is paid all funds erroneously withheld. . . . A recipient whose aid is not restored by a "fair hearing" decision may have judicial review. . . .

The constitutional issue to be decided, therefore, is the narrow one whether the Due Process Clause requires that the recipient be afforded an evidentiary hearing *before* the termination of benefits. The District Court held that only a pre-termination evidentiary hearing would satisfy the constitutional command, and rejected the argument of the state and city officials that the combination of the post-termination "fair hearing" with the informal pre-termination review disposed of all due process claims. . . . Although state officials were party defendants in the action, only the Commissioner of Social Services of the City of New York appealed. We noted probable jurisdiction. . . . We affirm.

Appellant does not contend that procedural due process is not applicable to the termination of welfare benefits. Such benefits are a matter of statutory entitlement for persons qualified to receive them. Their termination involves state action that adjudicates important rights. The constitutional challenge cannot be answered by an argument that public assistance benefits are "a 'privilege' and not a 'right.'" *Shapiro v. Thompson*, 394 U.S. 618, 627 n.6 (1969). Relevant constitutional restraints apply as much to the withdrawal of public assistance benefits as to disqualification for unemployment compensation, *Sherbert v. Verner*, 374 U.S. 398 (1963); or to denial of a tax exemption, *Speiser v. Randall*, 357 U.S. 513 (1958); or to discharge from public employment, *Slochower v. Board of Higher Education*, 350 U.S. 551 (1956). The extent to which procedural due process must be afforded the recipient is influenced by the extent to which he may be "condemned to suffer grievous loss," *Joint Anti-Fascist Refugee Committee v. McGrath*, 341 U.S. 123, 168 (1951) (Frankfurter, J., concurring), and depends upon whether the recipient's interest in avoiding that loss outweighs the governmental interest in summary adjudication. Accordingly, as we said in *Cafeteria & Restaurant Workers Union v. McElroy*, 367 U.S. 886,

895 (1961), "consideration of what procedures due process may require under any given set of circumstances must begin with a determination of the precise nature of the government function involved as well as of the private interest that has been affected by governmental action." *See also Hannah v. Larche,* 363 U.S. 420, 440, 442 (1960).

It is true, of course, that some governmental benefits may be administratively terminated without affording the recipient a pre-termination evidentiary hearing. But we agree with the District Court that when welfare is discontinued, only a pre-termination evidentiary hearing provides the recipient with procedural due process. *Cf. Sniadach v. Family Finance Corp.,* 395 U.S. 337 (1969). For qualified recipients, welfare provides the means to obtain essential food, clothing, housing, and medical care. Thus the crucial factor in this context—a factor not present in the case of the blacklisted government contractor, the discharged government employee, the taxpayer denied a tax exemption, or virtually anyone else whose governmental entitlements are ended—is that termination of aid pending resolution of a controversy over eligibility may deprive an eligible recipient of the very means by which to live while he waits. Since he lacks independent resources, his situation becomes immediately desperate. His need to concentrate upon finding the means for daily subsistence, in turn, adversely affects his ability to seek redress from the welfare bureaucracy.

Moreover, important governmental interests are promoted by affording recipients a pre-termination evidentiary hearing. From its founding the Nation's basic commitment has been to foster the dignity and well-being of all persons within its borders. We have come to recognize that forces not within the control of the poor contribute to their poverty. This perception, against the background of our traditions, has significantly influenced the development of the contemporary public assistance system. Welfare, by meeting the basic demands of subsistence, can help bring within the reach of the poor the same opportunities that are available to others to participate meaningfully in the life of the community. At the same time, welfare guards against the societal malaise that may flow from a widespread sense of unjustified frustration and insecurity. Public assistance, then, is not mere charity, but a means to "promote the general Welfare, and secure the Blessings of Liberty to ourselves and our Posterity." The same governmental interests that counsel the provision of welfare, counsel as well its uninterrupted provision to those eligible to receive it; pre-termination evidentiary hearings are indispensable to that end.

Appellant does not challenge the force of these considerations but argues that they are outweighed by countervailing governmental interests in conserving fiscal and administrative resources. These interests, the argument goes, justify the delay of any evidentiary hearing until after discontinuance of the grants. Summary adjudication protects the public fisc by stopping payments promptly upon discovery of reason to believe that a recipient is no longer eligible. Since most terminations are accepted without challenge, summary adjudication also conserves both the fisc and administrative time and energy by reducing the number of evidentiary hearings actually held.

We agree with the District Court, however, that these governmental interests are not overriding in the welfare context. The requirement of a prior hearing doubtless involves some greater expense, and the benefits paid to ineligible recipients pending decision at the hearing probably cannot be recouped, since these recipients are likely to be judgment-proof. But the State is not without weapons to minimize these increased costs. Much of the drain on fiscal and administrative resources can be reduced by developing procedures for prompt pre-termination hearings and by skillful use of personnel and facilities. Indeed, the very provision for a post-termination evidentiary hearing in New York's Home Relief program is itself cogent evidence that the State recognizes the primacy of the public interest in correct eligibility determinations and therefore in the provision of procedural safeguards. Thus, the interest of the eligible recipient in uninterrupted receipt of public assistance, coupled with the State's interest that his payments not be erroneously terminated, clearly outweighs the State's competing concern to prevent any increase in its fiscal and administrative burdens. . . .

II

We also agree with the District Court, however, that the pre-termination hearing need not take the form of a judicial or quasi-judicial trial. We bear in mind that the statutory "fair hearing" will provide the recipient with a full administrative review.[14] Accordingly, the pre-termination hearing has one function only: to produce an initial determination of the validity of the welfare department's grounds for discontinuance of payments in order to protect a recipient against an erroneous termination of his benefits. . . . Thus, a complete record and a comprehensive opinion, which would serve primarily to facilitate judicial review and to guide future decisions, need not be provided at the pre-termination stage. We recognize, too, that both welfare authorities and recipients have an interest in relatively speedy resolution of questions of eligibility, that they are used to dealing with one another informally, and that some welfare departments have very burdensome caseloads. These considerations justify the limitation of the pre-termination hearing to minimum procedural safeguards, adapted to the particular characteristics of welfare recipients, and to the limited nature of the controversies to be resolved. We wish to

14. Due process does not, of course, require two hearings. If, for example, a State simply wishes to continue benefits until after a "fair" hearing there will be no need for a preliminary hearing.

add that we, no less than the dissenters, recognize the importance of not imposing upon the States or the Federal Government in this developing field of law any procedural requirements beyond those demanded by rudimentary due process. . . .

In the present context these principles require that a recipient have timely and adequate notice detailing the reasons for a proposed termination, and an effective opportunity to defend by confronting any adverse witnesses and by presenting his own arguments and evidence orally. These rights are important in cases such as those before us, where recipients have challenged proposed terminations as resting on incorrect or misleading factual premises or on misapplication of rules or policies to the facts of particular cases.

We are not prepared to say that the seven-day notice currently provided by New York City is constitutionally insufficient per se, although there may be cases where fairness would require that a longer time be given. Nor do we see any constitutional deficiency in the content or form of the notice. New York employs both a letter and a personal conference with a caseworker to inform a recipient of the precise questions raised about his continued eligibility. Evidently the recipient is told the legal and factual bases for the Department's doubts. This combination is probably the most effective method of communicating with recipients.

The city's procedures presently do not permit recipients to appear personally with or without counsel before the official who finally determines continued eligibility. Thus a recipient is not permitted to present evidence to that official orally, or to confront or cross-examine adverse witnesses. These omissions are fatal to the constitutional adequacy of the procedures.

The opportunity to be heard must be tailored to the capacities and circumstances of those who are to be heard. It is not enough that a welfare recipient may present his position to the decision maker in writing or secondhand through his caseworker. Written submissions are an unrealistic option for most recipients, who lack the educational attainment necessary to write effectively and who cannot obtain professional assistance. Moreover, written submissions do not afford the flexibility of oral presentations; they do not permit the recipient to mold his argument to the issues the decision maker appears to regard as important. Particularly where credibility and veracity are at issue, as they must be in many termination proceedings, written submissions are a wholly unsatisfactory basis for decision. The secondhand presentation to the decision maker by the caseworker has its own deficiencies; since the caseworker usually gathers the facts upon which the charge of ineligibility rests, the presentation of the recipient's side of the controversy cannot safely be left to him. Therefore a recipient must be allowed to state his position orally. Informal procedures will suffice; in this context due process does not require a particular order of proof or mode of offering evidence. . . .

In almost every setting where important decisions turn on questions of fact, due process requires an opportunity to confront and cross-examine adverse witnesses. . . . Welfare recipients must therefore be given an opportunity to confront and cross-examine the witnesses relied on by the department.

"The right to be heard would be, in many cases, of little avail if it did not comprehend the right to be heard by counsel." *Powell v. Alabama*, 287 U.S. 45, 68-69 (1932). We do not say that counsel must be provided at the pre-termination hearing, but only that the recipient must be allowed to retain an attorney if he so desires. . . .

Finally, the decision maker's conclusion as to a recipient's eligibility must rest solely on the legal rules and evidence adduced at the hearing. To demonstrate compliance with this elementary requirement, the decision maker should state the reasons for his determination and indicate the evidence he relied on, though his statement need not amount to a full opinion or even formal findings of fact and conclusions of law. And, of course, an impartial decision maker is essential. We agree with the District Court that prior involvement in some aspects of a case will not necessarily bar a welfare official from acting as a decision maker. He should not, however, have participated in making the determination under review. Affirmed.

Justice BLACK, dissenting:

In the last half century the United States, along with many, perhaps most, other nations of the world, has moved far toward becoming a welfare state, that is, a nation that for one reason or another taxes its most affluent people to help support, feed, clothe, and shelter its less fortunate citizens. The result is that today more than nine million men, women, and children in the United States receive some kind of state or federally financed public assistance in the form of allowances or gratuities, generally paid them periodically, usually by the week, month, or quarter. Since these gratuities are paid on the basis of need, the list of recipients is not static, and some people go off the lists and others are added from time to time. These ever-changing lists put a constant administrative burden on government and it certainly could not have reasonably anticipated that this burden would include the additional procedural expense imposed by the Court today.

. . . [W]hen federal judges use this judicial power for legislative purposes, I think they wander out of their field of vested powers and transgress into the area constitutionally assigned to the Congress and the people. That is precisely what I believe the Court is doing in this case. Hence my dissent.

The more than a million names on the relief rolls in New York, and the more than nine million names on the rolls of all the 50 States were not put there at random. The names are there because state welfare officials believed that those people were eligible for assistance. Probably in the officials' haste to make out the lists many names were put there erroneously in order to alleviate immediate suffering, and undoubtedly some people are drawing relief who are not entitled under the law to do so. Doubtless some draw relief checks from time to time who know they are not eligible, either because they are not actually in need or for some other reason. Many of those who thus draw undeserved gratuities are without sufficient property to enable the government to collect back from them any money they wrongfully receive. But the Court today holds that it would violate the Due Process Clause of the Fourteenth Amendment to stop paying those people weekly or monthly allowances unless the government first affords them a full "evidentiary hearing" even though welfare officials are persuaded that the recipients are not rightfully entitled to receive a penny under the law. In other words, although some recipients might be on the lists for payment wholly because of deliberate fraud on their part, the Court holds that the government is helpless and must continue, until after an evidentiary hearing, to pay money that it does not owe, never has owed, and never could owe. I do not believe there is any provision in our Constitution that should thus paralyze the government's efforts to protect itself against making payments to people who are not entitled to them.

Particularly do I not think that the Fourteenth Amendment should be given such an unnecessarily broad construction. That Amendment came into being primarily to protect Negroes from discrimination, and while some of its language can and does protect others, all know that the chief purpose behind it was to protect ex-slaves. . . .

I would have little, if any, objection to the majority's decision in this case if it were written as the report of the House Committee on Education and Labor, but as an opinion ostensibly resting on the language of the Constitution I find it woefully deficient. . . .

The procedure required today as a matter of constitutional law finds no precedent in our legal system. Reduced to its simplest terms, the problem in this case is similar to that frequently encountered when two parties have an ongoing legal relationship that requires one party to make periodic payments to the other. Often the situation arises where the party "owing" the money stops paying it and justifies his conduct by arguing that the recipient is not legally entitled to payment. The recipient can, of course, disagree and go to court to compel payment. But I know of no situation in our legal system in which the person alleged to owe money to another is required by law to continue making payments to a judgment-proof claimant without the benefit of any security or bond to insure that these payments can be recovered if he wins his legal argument. . . .

The Court apparently feels that this decision will benefit the poor and needy. In my judgment the eventual result will be just the opposite. . . . Thus the end result of today's decision may well be that the government, once it decides to give welfare benefits, cannot reverse that decision until the recipient has had the benefits of full administrative and judicial review, including, of course, the opportunity to present his case to this Court. Since this process will usually entail a delay of several years, the inevitable result of such a constitutionally imposed burden will be that the government will not put a claimant on the rolls initially until it has made an exhaustive investigation to determine his eligibility. . . .

For the foregoing reasons I dissent from the Court's holding. The operation of a welfare state is a new experiment for our Nation. For this reason, among others, I feel that new experiments in carrying out a welfare program should not be frozen into our constitutional structure. They should be left, as are other legislative determinations, to the Congress and the legislatures that the people elect to make our laws.

[Chief Justice BURGER and Justice STEWART also dissented.]

Comments and Questions

1. In what court did this case start—and where did it end?

2. Which due process clause is invoked in this case—from the Fifth or Fourteenth Amendment—and why?

3. Describe the underlying story: who are the plaintiffs and defendants, and how do they disagree? What happened that led to the disagreement, and what do the parties want to achieve through the lawsuit?

4. Does the Supreme Court rule that welfare is property for purposes of triggering the due process protections? How does the majority on the Court deal with this question? Does the Court respond to Justice Black's argument in dissent? What are the strongest elements of Justice Black's view?

5. What would be the "full service," maximum elements of procedure that could ever be "due"? Use the formal court trial as a model for comparing expansive elements of process with the narrower elements at issue in *Goldberg v. Kelly*. How important are the following: advance notice, access to counsel, the opportunity to testify, the opportunity to cross-examine witnesses, the requirement of a written record of testimony, and the requirement of a statement of reasons accompanying the decision? Which elements of process does the *Goldberg* Court find necessary in the termination of welfare benefits, and which ones not necessary? What principles or factors affect this set of distinctions?

6. Who will pay for the additional process required by the Court? Will the monies available for benefits need to be reduced by the administrative costs in conducting pretermination hearings? How will the Court's opinion influence termination decisions by the state agency? How will the Court's opinion influence the agency's initial decisions about who is eligible for benefits?

7. What values are served by the particular elements of process discussed by the majority? Remember Justice Frankfurter's emphasis on arriving at the truth and on generating the feeling that justice has been done, *Joint Anti-Fascist Committee v. McGrath, supra.* Many scholars have written about how perceptions of fairness affect the purposes of litigation.

In the following excerpt, Frank Michelman identifies values behind process in his discussion of access fees, such as filing fees, that make it difficult if not impossible for impoverished individuals to file lawsuits. Which of the values he identifies persist, even for potential parties who have little or no chance of prevailing on the merits?

Following Professor Michelman, Tom Tyler and Allan Lind consider procedural values in light of social psychology and political stability. Again, consider what aspects of their argument stand independent from any claims by parties that should prevail on the merits. Can and should the legitimacy of the legal system be secured by procedural rights, even if outcomes are systematically biased against certain groups?

■ FRANK L. MICHELMAN, THE SUPREME COURT AND LITIGATION ACCESS FEES: THE RIGHT TO PROTECT ONE'S RIGHTS
1973 Duke L.J. 1153, 1172-1177 (1973)

. . . [T]here are generally accepted reasons for making litigation possible. I think we take little risk of serious distortion if we try to frame those reasons in terms of the values (ends, interests, purposes) that are supposed to be furthered by allowing persons to litigate.

I have been able to identify four discrete, though interrelated, types of such values, which may be called dignity values, participation values, deterrence values, and (to choose a clumsily neutral term) effectuation values. *Dignity values* reflect concern for the humiliation or loss of self-respect which a person might suffer if denied an opportunity to litigate. *Participation values* reflect an appreciation of litigation as one of the modes in which persons exert influence, or have their wills "counted" in societal decisions they care about. *Deterrence values* recognize the instrumentality of litigation as a mechanism for influencing or constraining individual behavior in ways thought socially desirable.[73] *Effectuation values* see litigation as an important

---

73. A possibly more accurate (but less distinct) label would have been "social welfare values." The category is intended to stand for all interpretations of litigation as a means for maximizing value across society, as distinguished from securing to the victorious party his due. In a given case, value maximization might be effectuated through an act of redistribution of wealth (the immediate impact of the judgment or decree itself), rather than through an act of (negative or affirmative) deterrence strictly speaking (the impact on future behavior of knowledge of the decision and its grounds). . . .

means through which persons are enabled to get, or are given assurance of having, whatever we are pleased to regard as rightfully theirs. . . .

Dignity values. These seem most clearly offended when a person confronts a formal, state-sponsored, public proceeding charging wrongdoing, failure, or defect, and the person is either prevented from responding or forced to respond without the assistance and resources that a self-respecting response necessitates.

The damage to self-respect from the inability to defend oneself properly seems likely to be most severe in the case of criminal prosecution, where representatives of civil society attempt in a public forum to brand one a violator of important societal norms. . . .

Of course, one immediately sees that there are some nominally "civil" contexts where the would-be litigant is trying to fend off accusatory action by the government threatening rather dire and stigmatizing results (for example, a proceeding to divest a parent of custody of a child on grounds of unfitness), which are exceedingly difficult to distinguish from standard criminal contexts in dignity value terms. Still these cases do not by themselves show that the dignity notion is uncontainable. Challenging though it may be in a few cases to draw the line between the quasi-criminal and the noncriminal context, the determination usually will not be insuperably difficult.

But this is hardly to say that dignity considerations are entirely absent from civil contexts. Perhaps there is something generally demeaning, humiliating, and infuriating about finding oneself in a dispute over legal rights and wrongs and being unable to uphold one's own side of the case. How serious these effects are seems to depend on various factors including, possibly, the identity of the adversary (is it the government?), the origin of the argument (did the person willingly start it himself?), the possible outcomes (will the person, or others, feel that he has been determined to be a wrongdoer?), and how public the struggle has become (has it reached the courts yet?). . . .

Participation values. The illumination that may sometimes flow from viewing litigation as a mode of politics has escaped neither courts nor legal theorists. But I can see no way of trenchantly deploying that insight so as to rank litigation contexts for purposes of a selective access-fee relief rule. (Certainly the Supreme Court's emergent rule cannot be construed to reflect any such ranking.)

But if participation values cannot help us differentiate among litigation contexts, they can contribute significantly to the argument for a broad constitutional right of court access. Participation values are at the root of the claim that such a right can be derived from the first amendment, a claim that I shall not pursue. And they also help inspire the analogy between general litigation rights and general voting rights. . . .

Deterrence values. Litigation is often, and enlighteningly, viewed as a process, or part of a process, for constraining all agents in society to the performance of duties and obligations imposed with a view to social welfare. A possible link between deterrence values and access fees is, of course, supplied by the obvious frustration of those values which results if the person in the best position, or most naturally motivated, to pursue judicial enforcement of such constraints is prevented by access fees from doing so. . . .

Effectuation values. In the effectuation perspective we view the world from the standpoint of the prospective litigant as distinguished from that of society as a whole or as a collectivity. Value is ascribed to the actual protection and realization of those interests of the litigant which the law purports to protect and effectuate (in this perspective one would shamelessly refer to those interests as the litigant's "rights") and more generally to a prevailing assurance that those interests will be protected; and litigation is regarded as a process, or as a part of a process, for providing such protection and assurance. . . .

■ TOM R. TYLER AND E. ALLAN LIND, A RELATIONAL MODEL OF AUTHORITY IN GROUPS
25 Advances in Experimental Social Psychology 115, 133-140 (1992)

The research . . . shows that a key factor affecting legitimacy across a variety of settings is the person's evaluation of the fairness of the procedures used by the authority in question. The studies that have included behavioral measures show much the same pattern of results with respect to measures of obedience and other behaviors linked to authority. Evaluations of both the favorability of the authority's decision and its fairness, in distributive justice terms, have occasionally been found to exert an effect on legitimacy independent of that exerted by procedural fairness. Nevertheless, it is clear that in terms of both the strength of effects and the ubiquity of effects, neither outcome factor is nearly as important as procedural justice in determining whether an authority is viewed as legitimate.[12]

Why is procedural justice so central to legitimacy? One explanation can be found in some of the original theorizing on procedural justice issues. In their discussion of the problems of dispute resolution in groups Thibaut and Walker (1975) noted the potential harm that the process of

---

[12]As noted above, it is important to distinguish personal satisfaction from attitudes such as legitimacy. We are not saying that people are happy if they receive unfavorable outcomes through a fair procedure. We are saying, however, that they 1) are more likely to accept the decision and 2) are less likely to blame the authorities and/or institutions they have dealt with. As a consequence, they are more likely to follow the authority's directives in the future.

resolving disputes could do to social relationships within a group or society: poorly resolved disputes can threaten enduring relationships. They suggested that the use of procedures regarded by all parties as fair facilitates the maintenance of positive relations among group members—preserving the "fabric of society"—even in the face of the conflict of interest that exists in any group whose members have different preference structures and different beliefs with respect to what the group should strive for and how it should manage its affairs (Thibaut & Walker, 1975, p. 67).

A second reason for the pre-eminence of procedural justice concerns in judgments of the legitimacy of authority is found in another analysis by Thibaut and Walker (1978). In many social situations it is not at all clear what decision or action is correct in an objective sense. Indeed, it could be argued that most group decisions concern questions for which, at least at the time the decision is made, there is no way of knowing what course of action will work out best. In these circumstances, Thibaut and Walker argue, what is critical to good decision making is the appearance of fairness, and fairness is most obviously achieved when procedures that are accepted as just are used to generate the decision. In other words, absent objective indicators of the correctness of a decision, the best guarantee of decision quality is the use of good—which is to say fair—procedures. . . .

A third and final reason for the importance accorded procedural justice concerns in judgments of legitimacy has to do with links between perceptions of procedures and other cognitions about groups. In an earlier analysis (Lind & Taylor, 1988) we have argued that procedures are widely viewed as essential elements of groups, that perceptions of procedures are key features of cognitions about groups. It is no accident, for example, that the drafting of a constitution is generally one of the first enterprises of any group that intends to function on a continuing basis. Through the design of procedures a group gives itself form and makes specific its values and goals. Because procedures are widely viewed as manifestations of group values, we argue, they take on enormous symbolic significance in cognitions about groups. According to this line of thought, perceptions of procedures have greater impact on evaluations of groups than do perceptions of outcomes, because outcomes are generally viewed as one-time responses to particular situations while procedures have an enduring quality that makes an unfair procedure much more threatening than a single unfair outcome. In much the same way, the procedures used by an authority to reach a decision might be seen as an expression of the authority's values, and the judgment that an authority uses unfair procedures might be viewed with greater concern than the judgment that a particular decision is unfair.

Whatever the explanation, the results reviewed above suggest that the use of fair procedures is an important element, perhaps the key element, for the effective exercise of legitimate authority. . . .

Effectively exercising authority is a core issue within any organized group. Hence, the questions which we have been examining are always important. But they become especially important in situations of resource scarcity, where social conflict is more likely and where allocation is especially problematic. As we noted above, the empowerment of authorities seems to be a response of groups to problems such as social conflict and the allocation of scarce or diminishing resources, and yet it is precisely in such situations that the actions of authorities are most likely to be controversial. . . .

The possibility of heightened social conflict was viewed as especially problematic for American government authorities during the 1970's because the United States was in an historic period during which it seemed particularly vulnerable to social unrest. Alienation from and distrust of legal, political, and industrial authorities was quite high. Since the legitimacy of authorities is often viewed as a "cushion of support" that helps societies to survive difficult periods in history, the weakness of the support underlying the American legal, political, and economic systems seemed to point to a potentially dangerous vulnerability to destructive social unrest. . . .

We believe that the social issues that are likely to emerge as central concerns of the 1990's may also emphasize the importance of legitimacy and authority processes. . . .

5. Costs of Process

Process has costs. What role should costs play in determining how much process is due in a given circumstance? The Supreme Court addressed this issue in *Mathews v. Eldridge*, which followed shortly after *Goldberg v. Kelly*. As you read *Eldridge*, consider whether the Court simply applies *Goldberg*'s standard for interpreting how much process is due, or instead changes the standard. In either instance, why did this decision come out differently?

■ MATHEWS, SECRETARY OF HEALTH, EDUCATION AND WELFARE v. ELDRIDGE
424 U.S. 319 (1976)

Justice POWELL delivered the opinion of the Court:

The issue in this case is whether the Due Process Clause of the Fifth Amendment requires that prior to the termination of Social Security disability benefit payments the recipient be afforded an opportunity for an evidentiary hearing.

Cash benefits are provided to workers during periods in which they are completely disabled under the disability insurance benefits program created by the 1956 amendments to Title II of the Social Security Act. 70 Stat. 815, 42 U.S.C. § 423. Respondent Eldridge was first awarded benefits in June 1968. In March 1972, he received a questionnaire from the state agency charged with monitoring his medical condition. Eldridge completed the questionnaire, indicating that his condition had not improved and identifying the medical sources, including physicians, from whom he had received treatment recently. The state agency then obtained reports from his physician and a psychiatric consultant. After considering these reports and other information in his file the agency informed Eldridge by letter that it had made a tentative determination that his disability had ceased in May 1972. The letter included a statement of reasons for the proposed termination of benefits, and advised Eldridge that he might request reasonable time in which to obtain and submit additional information pertaining to his condition.

In his written response, Eldridge disputed one characterization of his medical condition and indicated that the agency already had enough evidence to establish his disability. The state agency then made its final determination that he had ceased to be disabled in May 1972. This determination was accepted by the Social Security Administration (SSA), which notified Eldridge in July that his benefits would terminate after that month. The notification also advised him of his right to seek reconsideration by the state agency of this initial determination within six months.

Instead of requesting reconsideration Eldridge commenced this action challenging the constitutional validity of the administrative procedures established by the Secretary of Health, Education and Welfare for assessing whether there exists a continuing disability. He sought an immediate reinstatement of benefits pending a hearing on the issue of his disability. 361 F. Supp. 520 (W.D. Va. 1973). The Secretary moved to dismiss on the grounds that Eldridge's benefits had been terminated in accordance with valid administrative regulations and procedures and that he had failed to exhaust available remedies. In support of his contention that due process requires a pre-termination hearing, Eldridge relied exclusively upon this Court's decision in *Goldberg v. Kelly*, 397 U.S. 254 (1970), which established a right to an "evidentiary hearing" prior to termination of welfare benefits. The Secretary contended that *Goldberg* was not controlling since eligibility for disability benefits, unlike eligibility for welfare benefits, is not based on financial need and since issues of credibility and veracity do not play a significant role in the disability entitlement decision, which turns primarily on medical evidence. . . .

Procedural due process imposes constraints on governmental decisions which deprive individuals of "liberty" or "property" interests within the meaning of the Due Process Clause of the Fifth or Fourteenth Amendment. The Secretary does not contend that procedural due process is inapplicable to terminations of Social Security disability benefits. . . . Rather, the Secretary contends that the existing administrative procedures, detailed below, provide all the process that is constitutionally due before a recipient can be deprived of that interest.

This Court consistently has held that some form of hearing is required before an individual is finally deprived of a property interest. *Wolff v. McDonnell,* 418 U.S. 539, 557-558 (1974). *See, e.g., Phillips v. Commissioner,* 283 U.S. 589, 596-597 (1931). The "right to be heard before being condemned to suffer grievous loss of any kind, even though it may not involve the stigma and hardships of a criminal conviction, is a principle basic to our society." *Joint Anti-Fascist Comm. v. McGrath,* 341 U.S. 123, 168 (1951) (Frankfurter, J., concurring). The fundamental requirement of due process is the opportunity to be heard "at a meaningful time and in a meaningful manner." *Eldridge* agrees that the review procedures available to a claimant before the initial determination of ineligibility becomes final would be adequate if disability benefits were not terminated until after the evidentiary hearing stage of the administrative process. The dispute centers upon what process is due prior to the initial termination of benefits, pending review.

In recent years this Court increasingly has had occasion to consider the extent to which due process requires an evidentiary hearing prior to the deprivation of some type of property interest even if such a hearing is provided thereafter. In only one case, *Goldberg v. Kelly,* 397 U.S. at 266-271, has the Court held that a hearing closely approximating a judicial trial is necessary. In other cases requiring some type of pre-termination hearing as a matter of constitutional right the Court has spoken sparingly about the requisite procedures. *Sniadach v. Family Finance Corp.,* 395 U.S. 337 (1969), involving garnishment of wages, was entirely silent on the matter. In *Fuentes v. Shevin,* 407 U.S. 67, 96–97 (1972), the Court said only that in a replevin suit between two private parties the initial determination required something more than an *ex parte* proceeding before a court clerk. Similarly, *Bell v. Burson,* 402 U.S. 535, 540 (1971), held, in the context of the revocation of a state-granted driver's license, that due process required only that the pre-revocation hearing involve a probable-cause determination as to the fault of the licensee, noting that the hearing "need not take the form of a full adjudication of the question of liability." *See also North Georgia Finishing, Inc. v. Di-Chem, Inc.,* 419 U.S. 601, 607 (1975). More recently, in *Arnett v. Kennedy, supra,* we sustained the validity of procedures by which a federal employee could be dismissed for cause. They included notice of the action sought, a copy of the charge, reasonable time for filing a written response, and an opportunity for an oral appearance. Following dismissal, an evidentiary hearing was provided.

These decisions underscore the truism that "'[d]ue process,' unlike some legal rules, is not a technical conception with a fixed content unrelated to time, place and circumstances." *Cafeteria Workers v. McElroy,* 367

U.S. 886, 895 (1961). "[D]ue process is flexible and calls for such procedural protections as the particular situation demands." *Morrissey v. Brewer*, 408 U.S. 471, 481 (1972). Accordingly, resolution of the issue whether the administrative procedures provided here are constitutionally sufficient requires analysis of the governmental and private interests that are affected. More precisely, our prior decisions indicate that identification of the specific dictates of due process generally requires consideration of three distinct factors: First, the private interest that will be affected by the official action; second, the risk of an erroneous deprivation of such interest through the procedures used, and the probable value, if any, of additional or substitute procedural safeguards; and finally, the Government's interest, including the function involved and the fiscal and administrative burdens that the additional or substitute procedural requirement would entail. *See, e.g., Goldberg v. Kelly.*

The principal reasons for benefits terminations are that the worker is no longer disabled or has returned to work. As Eldridge's benefits were terminated because he was determined to be no longer disabled, we consider only the sufficiency of the procedures involved in such cases.

The continuing-eligibility investigation is made by a state agency acting through a "team" consisting of a physician and a nonmedical person trained in disability evaluation. The agency periodically communicates with the disabled worker, usually by mail—in which case he is sent a detailed questionnaire—or by telephone, and requests information concerning his present condition, including current medical restrictions and sources of treatment, and any additional information that he considers relevant to his continued entitlement to benefits.

Information regarding the recipient's current condition is also obtained from his sources of medical treatment. If there is a conflict between the information provided by the beneficiary and that obtained from medical sources such as his physician, or between two sources of treatment, the agency may arrange for an examination by an independent consulting physician. Whenever the agency's tentative assessment of the beneficiary's condition differs from his own assessment, the beneficiary is informed that benefits may be terminated, provided a summary of the evidence upon which the proposed determination to terminate is based, and afforded an opportunity to review the medical reports and other evidence in his case file. He also may respond in writing and submit additional evidence.

The state agency then makes its final determination, which is reviewed by an examiner in the SSA Bureau of Disability Insurance. If, as is usually the case, the SSA accepts the agency determination it notifies the recipient in writing, informing him of the reasons for the decision, and of his right to seek de novo reconsideration by the state agency. Upon acceptance by the SSA, benefits are terminated effective two months after the month in which medical recovery is found to have occurred.

If the recipient seeks reconsideration by the state agency and the determination is adverse, the SSA reviews the reconsideration determination and notifies the recipient of the decision. He then has a right to an evidentiary hearing before an SSA administrative law judge. The hearing is nonadversary, and the SSA is not represented by counsel. As at all prior and subsequent stages of the administrative process, however, the claimant may be represented by counsel or other spokesmen. . . .

Despite the elaborate character of the administrative procedures provided by the Secretary, the courts below held them to be constitutionally inadequate, concluding that due process requires an evidentiary hearing prior to termination. In light of the private and governmental interests at stake here and the nature of the existing procedures, we think this was error.

Since a recipient whose benefits are terminated is awarded full retroactive relief if he ultimately prevails, his sole interest is in the uninterrupted receipt of this source of income pending final administrative decision on his claim. His potential injury is thus similar in nature to that of the welfare recipient in *Goldberg*, the nonprobationary federal employee in *Arnett*, and the wage earner in *Sniadach*.

Only in *Goldberg* has the Court held that due process requires an evidentiary hearing prior to a temporary deprivation. It was emphasized there that welfare assistance is given to persons on the very margin of subsistence. . . . Eligibility for disability benefits, in contrast, is not based upon financial need. Indeed, it is wholly unrelated to the worker's income or support from many other sources, such as earnings of other family members, workmen's compensation awards, tort claims awards, savings, private insurance, public or private pensions, veterans' benefits, food stamps, public assistance, or the "many other important programs, both public and private, which contain provisions for disability payments affecting a substantial portion of the work force. . . ." *Richardson v. Belcher*, 404 U.S. 84, 85-87 (Douglas, J., dissenting).

As *Goldberg* illustrates, the degree of potential deprivation that may be created by a particular decision is a factor to be considered in assessing the validity of any administrative decisionmaking process. The potential deprivation here is generally likely to be less than in *Goldberg*, although the degree of difference can be overstated. . . . Thus, in contrast to the discharged federal employee in *Arnett*, there is little possibility that the terminated recipient will be able to find even temporary employment to ameliorate the interim loss.

As we recognized last Term in *Fusari v. Steinberg*, 419 U.S. 379, 389 (1975), "the possible length of wrongful deprivation of . . . benefits [also] is an important factor in assessing the impact of official action on the private interests." The Secretary concedes that the delay between a request for a hearing before an administrative law judge and a decision on the claim is currently between 10 and 11 months. Since a terminated recipient must first obtain a reconsideration decision as a prerequisite to invoking his right to an evidentiary hearing, the delay between the actual cutoff of benefits and final decision after a hearing exceeds one year.

In view of the torpidity of this administrative review process, and the typically modest resources of the family unit of the physically disabled worker, the hardship imposed upon the erroneously terminated disability recipient may be significant. Still, the disabled worker's need is likely to be less than that of a welfare recipient. In addition to the possibility of access to private resources, other forms of government assistance will become available where the termination of disability benefits places a worker or his family below the subsistence level. In view of these potential sources of temporary income, there is less reason here than in *Goldberg* to depart from the ordinary principle, established by our decisions, that something less than an evidentiary hearing is sufficient prior to adverse administrative action.

An additional factor to be considered here is the fairness and reliability of the existing pre-termination procedures, and the probable value, if any, of additional procedural safeguards. Central to the evaluation of any administrative process is the nature of the relevant inquiry. *See Mitchell v. W. T. Grant Co.*, 416 U.S. 600, 617 (1974); Friendly, *Some Kind of Hearing*, 123 U. Pa. L. Rev. 1267, 1281 (1975). In order to remain eligible for benefits the disabled worker must demonstrate by means of "medically acceptable clinical and laboratory diagnostic techniques," 42 U.S.C. §423(d)(3), that he is unable "to engage in any substantial gainful activity by reason of any medically determinable physical or mental impairment. . . ." In short, a medical assessment of the worker's physical or mental condition is required. This is a more sharply focused and easily documented decision than the typical determination of welfare entitlement. In the latter case, a wide variety of information may be deemed relevant, and issues of witness credibility and veracity often are critical to the decisionmaking process. *Goldberg* noted that in such circumstances "written submissions are a wholly unsatisfactory basis for decision."

By contrast, the decision whether to discontinue disability benefits will turn, in most cases, upon "routine, standard, and unbiased medical reports by physician specialists," *Richardson v. Perales*, 402 U.S. 389, 404 (1971), concerning a subject whom they have personally examined. . . . To be sure, credibility and veracity may be a factor in the ultimate disability assessment in some cases. But procedural due process rules are shaped by the risk of error inherent in the truthfinding process as applied to the generality of cases, not the rare exceptions. The potential value of an evidentiary hearing, or even oral presentation to the decisionmaker, is substantially less in this context than in *Goldberg*.

The decision in *Goldberg* also was based on the Court's conclusion that written submissions were an inadequate substitute for oral presentation because they did not provide an effective means for the recipient to communicate his case to the decisionmaker. Written submissions were viewed as an unrealistic option, for most recipients lacked the "educational attainment necessary to write effectively" and could not afford professional assistance. In addition, such submissions would not provide the "flexibility of oral presentations" or "permit the recipient to mold his argument to the issues the decision maker appears to regard as important." 397 U.S. at 269. In the context of the disability-benefits-entitlement assessment the administrative procedures under review here fully answer these objections. . . .

A further safeguard against mistake is the policy of allowing the disability recipient's representative full access to all information relied upon by the state agency. In addition, prior to the cutoff of benefits the agency informs the recipient of its tentative assessment, the reasons therefor, and provides a summary of the evidence that it considers most relevant. Opportunity is then afforded the recipient to submit additional evidence or arguments, enabling him to challenge directly the accuracy of information in his file as well as the correctness of the agency's tentative conclusions. These procedures, again as contrasted with those before the Court in *Goldberg*, enable the recipient to "mold" his argument to respond to the precise issues which the decisionmaker regards as crucial. . . .

In striking the appropriate due process balance the final factor to be assessed is the public interest. This includes the administrative burden and other societal costs that would be associated with requiring, as a matter of constitutional right, an evidentiary hearing upon demand in all cases prior to the termination of disability benefits. The most visible burden would be the incremental cost resulting from the increased number of hearings and the expense of providing benefits to ineligible recipients pending decision. No one can predict the extent of the increase, but the fact that full benefits would continue until after such hearings would assure the exhaustion in most cases of this attractive option. Nor would the theoretical right of the Secretary to recover undeserved benefits result, as a practical matter, in any substantial offset to the added outlay of public funds. The parties submit widely varying estimates of the probable additional financial cost. We only need say that experience with the constitutionalizing of government procedures suggests that the ultimate additional cost in terms of money and administrative burden would not be insubstantial.

Financial cost alone is not a controlling weight in determining whether due process requires a particular procedural safeguard prior to some administrative decision. But the Government's interest, and hence that of the public, in conserving scarce fiscal and administrative resources is a factor that must be weighed. At some point the benefit of an additional safeguard to the individual affected by the administrative action and to society in terms of increased assurance that the action is just, may be outweighed by the cost. Significantly, the cost of protecting those whom the preliminary administrative process has identified as likely to be found undeserving may in the end come out of the pockets of the deserving since resources available for any particular program of social welfare are not unlimited.

But more is implicated in cases of this type than ad hoc weighing of fiscal and administrative burdens against the interests of a particular category of claimants. The ultimate balance involves a determination as to when, under our constitutional system, judicial-type procedures must be imposed upon administrative action to assure fairness. We reiterate the wise admonishment of Mr. Justice Frankfurter that differences in the origin and function of administrative agencies "preclude wholesale transplantation of the rules of procedure, trial, and review which have evolved from the history and experience of courts." *FCC v. Pottsville Broadcasting Co.*, 309 U.S. 134, 143 (1940). The judicial model of an evidentiary hearing is neither a required, nor even the most effective, method of decision-making in all circumstances. The essence of due process is the requirement that "a person in jeopardy of serious loss [be given] notice of the case against him and opportunity to meet it." *Joint Anti-Fascist Comm. v. McGrath*, 341 U.S., at 171-172 (Frankfurter, J., concurring). All that is necessary is that the procedures be tailored, in light of the decision to be made, to "the capacities and circumstances of those who are to be heard," *Goldberg v. Kelly*, 397 U.S., at 268-269 (footnote omitted), to insure that they are given a meaningful opportunity to present their case. In assessing what process is due in this case, substantial weight must be given to the good-faith judgments of the individuals charged by Congress with the administration of social welfare programs that the procedures they have provided assure fair consideration of the entitlement claims of individuals. *See Arnett v. Kennedy*, 416 U.S. 171, 202 (White, J., concurring in part and dissenting in part). This is especially so where, as here, the prescribed procedures not only provide the claimant with an effective process for asserting his claim prior to any administrative action, but also assure a right to an evidentiary hearing, as well as to subsequent judicial review, before the denial of his claim becomes final. *Cf. Boddie v. Connecticut*, 401 U.S. 371, 378 (1971).

We conclude that an evidentiary hearing is not required prior to the termination of disability benefits and that the present administrative procedures fully comport with due process. The judgment of the Court of Appeals is Reversed.

Justice STEVENS took no part in the consideration or decision of this case.

Justice BRENNAN, with whom Justice MARSHALL concurs, dissented:
. . . [T]he Court's consideration that a discontinuance of disability benefits may cause the recipient to suffer only a limited deprivation is no argument. It is speculative. Moreover, the very legislative determination

to provide disability benefits, without any prerequisite determination of need in fact, presumes a need by the recipient which is not this Court's function to denigrate. Indeed, in the present case, it is indicated that because disability benefits were terminated there was a foreclosure upon the Eldridge home and the family's furniture was repossessed, forcing Eldridge, his wife, and their children to sleep in one bed. Finally, it is also no argument that a worker, who has been placed in the untenable position of having been denied disability benefits, may still seek other forms of public assistance.

Comments and Questions

Relevant —

1. Note that the membership of the Court changed between the time of the decisions in *Goldberg* and *Mathews*. Sitting in 1970 were justices Hugo Black, Harry A. Blackmun, William J. Brennan, Warren E. Burger, William O. Douglas, John M. Harlan, Thurgood Marshall, Potter Stewart, and Byron R. White. By 1976, President Nixon's nominees, Lewis F. Powell and William H. Rehnquist, had replaced Hugo Black and John Harlan, and President Ford's nominee, John Paul Stevens, replaced William O. Douglas (although Justice Stevens did not participate in the *Mathews* decision). How relevant is this to explaining the results?

2. The Court in *Mathews v. Eldridge* articulates a three-factor test, calling for a comparison of (1) the private interest affected by proposed governmental deprivation, (2) the risk of error created by the procedures under challenge, and (3) the burden imposed on the government by more expansive procedural requirements. Does this balancing test better guide judicial interpretations of due process than the pre-existing calls for flexible, evolving judgments? Does the balancing test make any difference to the actual results in cases like *Goldberg* and *Mathews*?

How does the balancing test build upon or move away from the basic values of due process? Materials from two leading commentators help address this question.

■ JERRY L. MASHAW, THE SUPREME COURT'S DUE PROCESS CALCULUS—THREE FACTORS IN SEARCH OF A THEORY OF VALUE
44 U. Chi. L. Rev. 28, 28-30, 46-59 (1976)

During the 1970s the Supreme Court has undertaken an intensive review of administrative hearing procedures for conformity with constitutional requirements of due process of law. The landmark case of *Goldberg v. Kelly* in 1970 confirmed the Court's unwillingness to limit its review by traditional notions of property interests and also suggested, in its specification of the constitutionally requisite elements of adjudicatory procedure, that the Court was prepared to assume a highly interventionist posture. What followed was a "due process revolution"—a flood of cases seeking to extend, or simply to apply, *Goldberg's* precepts.

The basic task that this burgeoning due process case load has presented to the courts has been to give content to the requirements of due process while maintaining an appropriate judicial role in the design of administrative procedures. Although *Goldberg* may have indicated the Court's willingness to impose a detailed model of requisite adjudicatory procedure upon a particular administrative function, no recent Supreme Court has believed that a single model is readily and consistently applicable to all administrative functions. What is required, therefore, are general criteria for review that will lend consistency and principle to the Court's decisions while permitting different administrative functions to be reviewed on their own terms. At the same time, those general criteria should be sufficiently concrete to structure administrative behavior without resort to a judicial test of every procedure that lacks some element of the paradigm process advanced by *Goldberg*.

In the Court's latest attempt to formulate this due process calculus, *Mathews v. Eldridge*, Justice Powell's majority opinion articulates a set of criteria with a comprehensiveness that suggests a preliminary integration of the Court's recent efforts. In the majority's words, from which there is no dissent, the Court must consider:

> first, the private interest that will be affected by the official action; second, the risk of an erroneous deprivation of such interest through the procedures used, and the probable value, if any, of additional or substitute procedural safeguards; and finally, the Government's interest, including the function involved and the fiscal and administrative burdens that the additional or substitute procedural requisites would entail.

Although this functional formulation impliedly invites an intrusive, particularistic review and specification of procedures, it is tempered by judicial restraint. "In assessing what process is due in this case, substantial weight must be given to the good-faith judgment of the individuals charged by Congress with the administration of the social welfare system that the procedures they have provided assure fair consideration of the entitlement claims of individuals."

The thesis of this article is that the *Eldridge* approach is unsatisfactory both as employed in that case and as a general formulation of due process review of administrative procedures. The failing of *Eldridge* is its focus on questions of technique rather than on questions of value. That focus, it is argued, generates an inquiry that is incomplete because unresponsive to the full range of concerns embodied in the due process clause. . . .

The Supreme Court's analysis in *Eldridge* is not informed by systematic attention to any theory of the values underlying due process review. The approach is implicitly utilitarian but incomplete, and the Court overlooks alternative theories that might have yielded fruitful inquiry. My purpose is, first, to articulate the limits of the Court's utilitarian approach, both in *Eldridge* and as a general schema for evaluating administrative procedures, and second, to indicate the strengths and weaknesses of three alternative theories—individual dignity, equality, and tradition. These theories, at the level of abstraction here presented, require little critical justification: they are widely held, respond to strong currents in the philosophic literature concerning law, politics, and ethics, and are supported either implicitly or explicitly by the Supreme Court's due process jurisprudence.[61]

61. In early due process cases the Supreme Court concentrated on tradition. The oft-cited statement in *Davidson v. New Orleans*, 96 U.S. 97, 104 (1877), that the Court's approach to due process problems should be "by the gradual process of judicial inclusion and exclusion," epitomizes the conservative, precedent-oriented, historical approach. As governmental functions increased, however, the Court was faced with due process problems that had no compelling historical analogies. If the Court was not to be a continual stumbling block to "progress," a more flexible approach was needed. Indeed, the history of due process in the Supreme Court might be characterized as a continuous search for a theory of due process review that combines the legitimacy of the evolutionary theory with a flexibility that permits adaptation to contemporary circumstances. Dignitary or natural right, utilitarian, and egalitarian theories have all been incorporated to this end.

Dignitary ideas, although used occasionally in a supportive role both before 1900 and in some contemporary cases, were employed most frequently as the primary mode of analysis from about 1933 through the early 1950s. The proliferation of new government functions associated with the New Deal legislation and, later, with emergency war measures, stimulated a judicial reaction that was captured in the Court's emphasis on individual rights and dignitary values. The reactive natural rights style, predicated upon the Justices' perception of the "fair" solution in each case, had an ad hoc quality that soon became disturbing. The apparent inconsistency of the Supreme Court's due process jurisprudence led Sanford Kadish in a seminal article to describe the Supreme Court's decisions as in "chaotic array." Kadish, *Methodology and Criteria in Due Process Adjudication—A Survey and Criticism*, 66 Yale L.J. 319 (1957).

In the late 1950s and early 1960s various utilitarian formulations began to supply a structure for analysis. In *Cafeteria & Restaurant Workers Local 473 v. McElroy*, 367 U.S. 886, 895 (1961), for example, the Court, per Mr. Justice Stewart, stated that two factors must be considered in due process cases: "the precise nature of the government function involved . . . [and] of the private interest that has been affected by government action." The statement of the utilitarian approach culminates in the *Eldridge* opinion's three-factor calculus.

Equality as a due process value has received considerable attention in criminal (or quasi-criminal) cases, but little outside that area. Perhaps the best example of the explicit use of equality concerns with respect to an administrative function is found in *Ashbacker Radio Corp. v. FCC*, 326 U.S. 327, 330 (1945). There the Court, per Mr. Justice Douglas, stated that the right to a hearing "becomes an empty thing" unless all parties affected by the process have an equal opportunity to be heard.

A. UTILITARIANISM

Utility theory suggests that the purpose of decisional procedures—like that of social action generally—is to maximize social welfare. Indeed, the three-factor analysis enunciated in *Eldridge* appears to be a type of utilitarian, social welfare function. That function first takes into account the social value at stake in a legitimate private claim; it discounts that value by the probability that it will be preserved through the available administrative procedures, and it then subtracts from that discounted value the social cost of introducing additional procedures. When combined with the institutional posture of judicial self-restraint, utility theory can be said to yield the following plausible decision-rule: "Void procedures for lack of due process only when alternative procedures would so substantially increase social welfare that their rejection seems irrational."

The utilitarian calculus is not, however, without difficulties. The *Eldridge* Court conceives of the values of procedure too narrowly; it views the sole purpose of procedural protections as enhancing accuracy, and thus limits its calculus to the benefits or costs that flow from correct or incorrect decisions. No attention is paid to "process values" that might inhere in oral proceedings or to the demoralization costs that may result from the grant-withdrawal-grant-withdrawal sequence to which claimants like *Eldridge* are subjected. Perhaps more important, as the Court seeks to make sense of a calculus in which accuracy is the sole goal of procedure, it tends erroneously to characterize disability hearings as concerned almost exclusively with medical impairment and thus concludes that such hearings involve only medical evidence, whose reliability would be little enhanced by oral procedure. As applied by the *Eldridge* Court the utilitarian calculus tends, as cost-benefit analyses typically do, to "dwarf soft variables" and to ignore complexities and ambiguities.

The problem with a utilitarian calculus is not merely that the Court may define the relevant costs and benefits too narrowly. However broadly conceived, the calculus asks unanswerable questions. For example, what is the social value, and the social cost, of continuing disability payments until after an oral hearing for persons initially determined to be ineligible? Answers to those questions require a technique for measuring the social value and social cost of government income transfers, but no such technique exists. Even if such formidable tasks of social accounting could be accomplished, the effectiveness of oral hearings in forestalling the losses that result from erroneous terminations would remain uncertain. In the face of these pervasive indeterminacies the *Eldridge* Court was forced to retreat to a presumption of constitutionality.

Finally, it is not clear that the utilitarian balancing analysis asks the constitutionally relevant questions. The due process clause is one of those Bill of Rights protections meant to insure individual liberty in the face of contrary collective action. Therefore, a collective legislative or administrative decision about procedure, one arguably reflecting the intensity of the contending social values and representing an optimum position from the contemporary social perspective, cannot answer the constitutional question of whether due process has been accorded. A balancing analysis that would have the Court merely redetermine the question of social utility is similarly inadequate. There is no reason to believe that the Court has superior competence or legitimacy as a utilitarian balancer except as it performs its peculiar institutional role of insuring that libertarian values are considered in the calculus of decision. . . .

B. INDIVIDUAL DIGNITY

The increasingly secular, scientific, and collectivist character of the modern American state reinforces our propensity to define fairness in the formal, and apparently neutral language of social utility. Assertions of natural or "inalienable" rights seem, by contrast, somewhat embarrassing. Their ancestry, and therefore their moral force, are increasingly uncertain. Moreover, their role in the history of the due process clause makes us apprehensive about their eventual reach. It takes no peculiar acuity to see that the tension in procedural due process cases is the same as that in the now discredited substantive due process jurisprudence—a tension between the efficacy of the state and the individual's right to freedom from coercion or socially imposed disadvantage.

Yet the popular moral presupposition of individual dignity, and its political counterpart, self-determination, persist. State coercion must be legitimized, not only by acceptable substantive policies, but also by political processes that respond to a democratic morality's demand for participation in decisions affecting individual and group interests. At the level of individual administrative decisions this demand appears in both the layman's and the lawyer's language as the right to a "hearing" or "to be heard," normally meaning orally and in person. To accord an individual less when his property or status is at stake requires justification, not only because he might contribute to accurate determinations, but also because a lack of personal participation causes alienation and a loss of that dignity and self-respect that society properly deems independently valuable.

. . . Notwithstanding its difficulties, the dignitary theory of due process might have contributed significantly to the *Eldridge* analysis. The questions of procedural "acceptability" which the theory poses may initially seem vacuous or at best intuitive, but they suggest a broader sensitivity than the utilitarian factor analysis to the nature of governmental decisions. Whereas the utilitarian approach seems to require an estimate of the quantitative value of the claim, the dignitary approach suggests that the Court develop a qualitative appraisal of the type of administrative decision involved. While the disability decision in *Eldridge* may be narrowly characterized as a decision about the receipt of money payments, it may also be considered from various qualitative perspectives which seem pertinent in view of the general structure of the American income-support system.

That system suggests that a disability decision is a judgment of considerable social significance, and one that the claimant should rightly perceive as having a substantial moral content. The major cash income-support programs determine eligibility, not only on the basis of simple insufficiency of income, but also, or exclusively, on the basis of a series of excuses for partial or total nonparticipation in the work force: agedness, childhood, family responsibility, injury, disability. A grant under any of these programs is an official, if sometimes grudging, stamp of approval of the claimant's status as a partially disabled worker or nonworker. It proclaims, in effect, that those who obtain it have encountered one of the politically legitimate hazards to self-sufficiency in a market economy. The recipients, therefore, are entitled to society's support. Conversely, the denial of an income maintenance claim implies that the claim is socially illegitimate, and the claimant, however impecunious, is not excused from normal work force status.

These moral and status dimensions of the disability decision indicate that there is more at stake in disability claims than temporary loss of income. They also tend to put the disability decision in a framework that leads away from the superficial conclusion that disability decisions are a routine matter of evaluating medical evidence. Decisions with substantial "moral worth" connotations are generally expected to be highly individualized and attentive to subjective evidence. The adjudication of such issues on the basis of documents submitted largely by third parties and by adjudicators who have never confronted the claimant seems inappropriate. Instead, a court approaching an analysis of the disability claims process from the dignitary perspective might emphasize those aspects of disability decisions that focus on a particular claimant's vocational characteristics, his unique response to his medical condition, and the ultimate predictive judgment of whether the claimant should be able to work.

C. EQUALITY

Notions of equality can . . . significantly inform the evaluation of any administrative process. One question we might ask is whether an investigative procedure is designed in a fashion that systematically excludes or undervalues evidence that would tend to support the position of a particular class of parties. If so, those parties might have a plausible claim that the procedure treated them unequally. Similarly, in a large-scale inquisitorial process involving many adjudicators, the question that should be posed is whether like cases receive like attention and like evidentiary development so that the influence of such arbitrary factors as location are minimized. In order to take such equality issues into account, we need only to broaden our due process horizons to include elements of procedural fairness beyond those traditionally associated with adversary proceedings. These two inquiries might have been pursued fruitfully in *Eldridge*. First, is the state agency system of decision making, which is based on documents, particularly disadvantageous for certain classes of claimants? There is some tentative evidence that it is. Cases such as *Eldridge* involving muscular or skeletal disorders, neurological problems, and multiple impairments, including psychological overlays, are widely believed to be both particularly difficult, due to the subjectivity of the evidence, and particularly prone to be reversed after oral hearing.

Second, does the inquisitorial process at the state agency level tend to treat like cases alike? If the GAO's* study is indicative, the answer is decidedly no. According to that study, many, perhaps half, of the decisions are made on the basis of records that other adjudicators consider so inadequate that a decision could not be rendered. The relevance of such state agency variance to *Eldridge*'s claim is twofold: first, it suggests that state agency determinations are unreliable and that further development at the hearing stage might substantially enhance their reliability; alternatively, it may suggest that the hierarchical or bureaucratic mode of decision making, with overhead control for consistency, does not accurately describe the Social Security disability system. And if consistency is not feasible under this system, perhaps the more compelling standard for evaluating the system is the dignitary value of individualized judgment, which . . . implies claimant participation.

D. TRADITION OR EVOLUTION

Judicial reasoning, including reasoning about procedural due process, is frequently and self-consciously based on custom or precedent. In part, reliance on tradition or "authority" is a court's institutional defense against illegitimacy in a political democracy. But tradition serves other values, not the least of which are predictability and economy of effort. More importantly, the inherently conservative technique of analogy to custom and precedent seems essential to the evolutionary development and the preservation of the legal system. Traditional procedures are legitimate not only because they represent a set of continuous expectations, but because the body politic has survived their use.

The use of tradition as a guide to fundamental fairness is vulnerable, of course, to objection. Since social and economic forces are dynamic, the processes and structures that proved functional in one period will not

---

* *Eds. Note*: The Federal General Accounting Office surveyed state disability determinations to assess consistency. The study found definite inconsistencies both among state agencies and between state agencies and the federal adjudicators.

necessarily serve effectively in the next. Indeed, evolutionary development may as often end in the extinction of a species as in adaptation and survival. For this reason alone tradition can serve only as a partial guide to judgment.

Furthermore, it may be argued that reasoning by analogy from traditional procedures does not actually provide a perspective on the values served by due process. Rather, it is a decisional technique that requires a specification of the purposes of procedural rules merely in order that the decision maker may choose from among a range of authorities or customs the particular authority or custom most analogous to the procedures being evaluated.

This objection to tradition as a theory of justification is weighty, but not devastating. What is asserted by an organic or evolutionary theory is that *the purposes of legal rules cannot be fully known.* Put more cogently, while procedural rules, like other legal rules, should presumably contribute to the maintenance of an effective social order, we cannot expect to know precisely how they do so and what the long-term effects of changes or revisions might be. Our constitutional stance should therefore be preservative and incremental, building carefully, by analogy, upon traditional modes of operation. So viewed, the justification "we have always done it that way" is not so much a retreat from reasoned and purposive decision making as a profound acknowledgment of the limits of instrumental rationality.

Viewed from a traditionalist's perspective, the Supreme Court's opinion in *Eldridge* may be said to rely on the traditional proposition that property interests may be divested temporarily without hearing, provided a subsequent opportunity for contest is afforded. *Goldberg v. Kelly* is deemed an exceptional case, from which *Eldridge* is distinguished.

CONCLUSION

The preceding discussion has emphasized the way that explicit attention to a range of values underlying due process of law might have led the *Eldridge* Court down analytic paths different from those that appear in Justice Powell's opinion. The discussion has largely ignored, however, arguments that would justify the result that the Court reached in terms of the alternative value theories here advanced. Those arguments are now set forth.

First, focus on the dignitary aspects of the disability decision can hardly compel the conclusion that an oral hearing is a constitutional necessity prior to the termination of benefits when a full hearing is available later. Knowledge that an oral hearing will be available at some point should certainly lessen disaffection and alienation. Indeed, Eldridge seemed secure in the knowledge that a just procedure was available. His desire to avoid taking a corrective appeal should not blind us to the support of dignitary values that the de novo appeal provides.

Second, arguments premised on equality do not necessarily carry the day for the proponent of prior hearings. The Social Security Administration's attempt to routinize and make consistent hundreds of thousands of decisions in a nationwide income-maintenance program can be criticized both for its failures in its own terms and for its tendency to ignore the way that disability decisions impinge upon perceptions of individual moral worth. On balance, however, the program that Congress enacted contains criteria that suggest a desire for both consistency and individualization. No adjudicatory process can avoid tradeoffs between the pursuit of one or the other of these goals. Thus a procedural structure incorporating (1) decisions by a single state agency based on a documentary record and subject to hierarchical quality review, followed by (2) appeal to de novo oral proceedings before independent administrative law judges, is hardly an irrational approach to the necessary compromise between consistency and individualization.

Explicit and systematic attention to the values served by a demand for due process nevertheless remains highly informative in *Eldridge* and in general. The use of analogy to traditional procedures might have helped rationalize and systematize a concern for the "desperation" of claimants that seems as impoverished in *Eldridge* as it seems profligate in *Goldberg*; and the absence in *Eldridge* of traditionalist, dignitary, or egalitarian considerations regarding the disability adjudication process permitted the Court to overlook questions of both fact and value—questions that, on reflection, seem important. The structure provided by the Court's three factors is an inadequate guide for analysis because its neutrality leaves it empty of suggestive value perspectives.

Furthermore, an attempt by the Court to articulate a set of values that informs due process decision making might provide it with an acceptable judicial posture from which to review administrative procedures. The *Goldberg* decision's approach to prescribing due process—specification of the attributes of adjudicatory hearings by analogy to judicial trial—makes the Court resemble an administrative engineer with an outdated professional education. It is at once intrusive and ineffectual. Retreating from this stance, the *Eldridge* Court relies on the administrator's good faith—an equally troublesome posture in a political system that depends heavily on judicial review for the protection of countermajoritarian values. . . .

■ RICHARD A. POSNER,* AN ECONOMIC APPROACH TO LEGAL PROCEDURE AND JUDICIAL ADMINISTRATION
2 J. Legal Stud. 399, 400-408, 417-420, 441-448 (1973)

I. A FRAMEWORK OF ANALYSIS

An important purpose of substantive legal rules (such as the rules of tort and criminal law) is to increase economic efficiency. It follows (as demonstrated in Parts II and III) that mistaken imposition of legal liability, or mistaken failure to impose liability, will reduce efficiency. Judicial error is therefore a source of social costs and the reduction of error is a goal of the procedural system. The reader may challenge the last proposition by citing, for example, the rule excluding from criminal trials evidence obtained by an illegal search. Such evidence is highly probative; its exclusion reduces the accuracy of the fact-finding process in criminal trials. But this type of exclusionary rule is exceptional, and is recognized—and often bitterly criticized—as such.

Even when the legal process works flawlessly, it involves costs—the time of lawyers, litigants, witnesses, jurors, judges, and other people, plus paper and ink, law office and court house maintenance, telephone service, etc. These costs are just as real as the costs resulting from error: in general we would not want to increase the direct costs of the legal process by one dollar in order to reduce error costs by 50 (or 99) cents. The economic goal is thus to minimize the sum of error and direct costs.

Despite its generality, this formulation provides a useful framework in which to analyze the problems and objectives of legal procedure. It is usable even when the purpose of the substantive law is to transfer wealth or to bring about some other noneconomic goal, rather than to improve efficiency. All that is necessary is that it be possible, in principle, to place a price tag on the consequences of failing to apply the substantive law in all cases in which it was intended to apply, so that our two variables, error cost and direct cost, remain commensurable.

To illustrate the utility of the economic approach, consider the question whether the defendant in an administrative action (such as deportation, license revocation, or the withdrawal of a security clearance) should be entitled to a trial-type hearing. The tendency in the legal discussion of this question has been to invoke either a purely visceral sense of fairness or a purely formal distinction between penal and nonpenal sanctions. The economic approach enables the question to be framed in rational and

---

* *Eds. Note:* Judge Richard A. Posner now serves on the Court of Appeals for the Seventh Circuit. Previously, as a professor at the University of Chicago Law School, he helped launch the use of economic analysis in the study of law. He has since written extensively on jurisprudence and explored the uses of literature, pragmatism, feminism, and other approaches in legal studies and decision making.

functional terms. We ask first whether error costs would be substantially increased by denial of a trial-type hearing. Error costs (discussed in detail in the next part) may here be regarded as the product of two factors, the probability of error and the cost if an error occurs. If the facts on which the outcome of the administrative proceeding turns are the kind most accurately determined in a trial-type hearing, the probability of error if such a hearing is denied is apt to be great. If, in addition, the cost of an error if one occurs would be substantial because the sanction applied by the agency, whether in formal legal terms penal or not, imposes heavy costs on a defendant, total error costs are likely to be significantly increased by the denial of a trial-type hearing. The increment in error costs must be compared with the direct costs of a hearing; but these will often be low. The cost inquiries required by the economic approach are not simple and will rarely yield better than crude approximations, but at the very least they serve to place questions of legal policy in a framework of rational inquiry.

II. The Costs of Error in Civil Actions

AN ANALYSIS OF ERROR COSTS IN ACCIDENT CASES

Suppose a company inflicts occasional injuries on people with whom it cannot contract due to very high transaction costs. Victims of these injuries could prevent them only at prohibitive cost (we will initially assume), but the company can purchase various relatively inexpensive safety devices that would reduce the accident rate significantly. In the absence of legal sanctions it has no incentive to purchase such devices since, due to the costs of transacting, it cannot sell anyone the benefits of the devices in increasing safety. If the tort law makes it liable for the costs of these accidents, and is enforced flawlessly, the company will purchase the optimum quantity of safety devices. If the law is not enforced flawlessly, a suboptimum quantity of safety equipment will be procured.

The goal of a system of accident liability is to minimize the total costs of accidents and of accident avoidance. If we assume that the only feasible method of accident avoidance is the purchase of a particular type of safety equipment, then those total costs are minimized by purchasing the quantity of that equipment at which the marginal product of safety equipment in reducing accident costs is equal to the marginal cost of the equipment. This marginal product is the rate at which the number of accidents inflicted by the company declines as the quantity of safety equipment purchased increases, multiplied by the cost per accident. The marginal cost of safety equipment is simply the unit price of such equipment if, as we shall assume, that price does not vary with the amount of equipment that the company purchases.

The company, however, is not interested in minimizing the social costs of accidents and accident avoidance; it is interested only in minimizing its private accident and accident-avoidance costs. The former are the social costs of the firm's accidents multiplied by the probability that the firm will actually be held liable—forced to pay—for those costs. Since legal error presumably causes erroneous impositions as well as erroneous denials of liability, we must add a third term to the firm's cost function: the amount of money that it is forced to pay out in groundless claims. That amount is a function of the legal error rate and disappears when that rate is zero. We ignore it for the moment.

The company minimizes its private accident and accident-avoidance costs by equating the marginal product of safety equipment in reducing its accident liability to the marginal private cost of that equipment (which we assume is the same as the marginal social cost). This marginal private product is simply the marginal social product weighted by the probability of the firm's being held liable. If that probability is one, the marginal social and private products are the same. But when the probability is less than one—that is, when the legal-error rate is positive—they diverge, leading to a social loss. . . . The higher the error rate, the greater the reduction in the purchase of safety equipment and the greater the social loss.

The analysis is incomplete because we have ignored the possible effect of a positive error rate, operating through the third term in the company's cost function (liability resulting from groundless claims), on the firm's purchase of safety equipment. Suppose that the errors against the company took the form exclusively of accident victims' exaggerating the extent of their injuries. By increasing the company's private accident costs, these errors would increase the marginal private product of safety equipment. Thus, while errors in favor of the company would lower the company's marginal private product curve . . . errors against the company would shift it back upward. In fact, however, although all errors in favor of the company operate to lower its marginal-product curve, only some errors against the company operate to raise it. The purchase of additional safety equipment will not prevent the erroneous imposition of liability in a case in which no accident would have occurred in any event—the victim fabricated it—or in which the accident was inflicted by someone else and could not have been prevented by the defendant. Such errors do not increase the value of safety equipment to the firm and hence the marginal private product of that equipment. But even here a qualification is necessary. Additional safety equipment might strengthen the company's defense against a suit arising out of an accident actually caused by someone else. The company might be able to argue that, in view of all of the safety precautions it had taken, it could not have caused the accident. Still, it seems a reasonable conclusion that a positive error rate will result in a net reduction in the company's marginal private product of safety, and hence in a net social loss.

[According to this model, the] social loss will be greater, the more serious the accident. . . .

To be sure, the stakes have another effect. . . . [A]n increase in the stakes in a case will usually induce the parties to spend more money on the litigation. This in turn will reduce the probability of an erroneous result, and so, by our previous analysis, the social loss from error. Aggregate error costs might actually be smaller in a class of big cases than in a class of small ones. . . .

Thus far we have assumed that legal error will have no effect on the behavior of accident victims. In fact, by increasing expected accident costs net of compensation, error encourages prospective victims to engage in self-protection. If adequate compensation were paid in every accident case, the net cost of accidents to the victims would be zero and their incentive to take precautions also zero. But if by reason of error the expected compensation is only (say) 80 per cent of the expected accident cost, the net cost of accidents to victims becomes positive and they have an incentive to adopt precautions that cost less than the uncompensated accident costs that they prevent.

The effect of error is thus to shift safety incentives from injurers to victims. If the victims can prevent the same accidents at lower cost than the injurers, such a shift will produce a net social gain rather than a social loss, but where this is possible the injurers should not be liable in the first place. If, as we assume, the substantive law places liability where it will encourage the most efficient methods of loss avoidance, the shift in safety incentives brought about by error in the legal process will produce a net social loss. But the loss may be slight. . . .

The analysis of legal-error costs would be very different if the purpose of the underlying substantive law were not to improve the allocation of resources but were instead to compensate victims of certain accidents. The amount of undercompensation due to legal error would be equal to the product of the error rate, the cost per accident, and the number of accidents that occur for which the injurer should be held liable. That number will be greater the higher the error rate, for we know from the previous discussion that the number of accidents rises with the error rate, and therefore undercompensation must rise with the error rate. Besides the error rate, the principal factors determining the total amount of undercompensation are the effectiveness of the law (albeit imperfectly enforced) in deterring accidents, and the scope of the law. For identical error rates, the number of accidents occurring for which the injurer should be held liable will be greater if the legal standard is strict liability than if it is negligence. The costs of error are therefore likely to be higher under a strict-liability than under a negligence standard if failure to compensate where compensation is due is reckoned as a cost, and not merely as a transfer of wealth. Finally, to make undercompensation commensurable with the social loss . . . we need to know the rate at which a dollar in undercompensation is equated to a dollar in scarce resources consumed; it need not be one to one. In short the cost of legal error may differ dramatically depending on whether the purpose of the underlying substantive law is viewed as allocative or distributive.

BIASED AND UNBIASED ERROR

It is useful to distinguish between "biased" and "unbiased" error. Unbiased error in our usage is any error that is as likely to operate against one party to the dispute as it is to operate against the other. Such an error gives judgment to undeserving plaintiffs in about half of the erroneously decided cases and to undeserving defendants in the other half; accepting perjured testimony is an example. A biased error is one more likely to defeat plaintiffs than defendants or vice versa. The previous analysis assumed unbiased error.

Two types of biased error may, in turn, be distinguished. The first arises from a deliberate decision to bias a source of error (as in the rule that the guilt of a criminal defendant must be proved beyond a reasonable doubt). Consider a social-loss function that consists of two terms: the social loss . . . due to failure to impose liability on injurers in all cases in which they should be held liable, and the social loss that results when the judicial system awards compensation to a victim who could have averted an accident by appropriate safety precautions at lower cost than the injurer.

Assume that if the parties have the same burden of proof, the probability of an accurate determination of liability in both situations will be 90 percent, meaning that in 10 percent of the cases in which injurers should be held liable they are not held liable, while in 10 percent of the cases in which victims should be held liable (denied compensation) for failure to take cost justified safety precautions they receive compensation. Now let the standard of proof be changed to require that the defendant prove nonliability to a certainty. Victims will win every case. The probability of injurers' being held liable when they should be held liable will rise to one, causing the social loss from legal errors favoring injurers to fall to zero. But the probability of victims' being held liable when they fail to take proper safety precautions will fall to zero, which will cause the social loss from such failures to rise. We cannot be certain whether our total loss function will be higher or lower without knowing the specific values of the relevant parameters, but probably it will be higher. What we have done, in effect, is to impose a standard either of strict injurer liability (with no contributory negligence) or strict victim liability, depending on which probability has gone to zero. Both standards are less efficient than the alternatives. The effects of moderate bias, however, cannot be appraised a priori.

A second type of biased error occurs when a source of error affects the parties' chances unequally. Consider the rule—still followed in some states—that the victim of an accident must prove his freedom from contributory negligence. In a fatal accident to which there were no witnesses, the effect of the rule, if followed to the letter, would often be to prevent recovery even though the victim was in fact free from contributory negligence; the rule would never operate in favor of victims. But courts do not apply the rule in such cases. Instead they presume in the absence of contrary evidence that the victim was exercising due care. The effect is to increase the injurer's incentive to take precautions and reduce the victim's. This is an improvement if we assume that the injurer is more likely to be negligent than the victim; the modified rule is better if the reverse is more likely. . . .

SETTLEMENT OUT OF COURT

The . . . preceding parts considered the costs of erroneous judicial determinations. Now we turn to the direct costs of legal dispute resolution. These include the costs of trials . . . and the costs of settling cases without, or before completion of, litigation.

Since settlement costs are normally much lower than litigation costs, the fraction of cases settled is an important determinant of the total direct cost of legal dispute resolution. The necessary condition for settlement is that the plaintiff's minimum offer—the least amount he will take in settlement of his claim—be smaller than the defendant's maximum offer. This is not a sufficient condition: the parties may find it impossible to agree upon a mutually satisfactory settlement price. But we shall assume that settlement negotiations are rarely unsuccessful for this reason and therefore that litigation occurs only when the plaintiff's minimum offer is greater than the defendant's maximum offer. The plaintiff's minimum offer is the expected value of the litigation to him plus his settlement costs, the expected value of the litigation being the present value of the judgment if he wins, multiplied by the probability (as he estimates it) of his winning, minus the present value of his litigation expenses. The defendant's maximum offer is the expected cost of the litigation to him and consists of his litigation expenses, plus the cost of an adverse judgment multiplied by the probability as he estimates it of the plaintiff's winning (which is equal to one minus the probability of his winning), minus his settlement costs. Anything that reduces the plaintiff's minimum offer or increases the defendant's maximum offer, such as an increase in the parties' litigation expenditures relative to their settlement costs, will reduce the likelihood of litigation. Hence measures to reduce litigation costs might actually increase the total costs of legal dispute resolution, by making trials, which are usually costlier than settlements, more attractive than before the measures were introduced.

Anything that increases the plaintiff's minimum settlement offer or reduces the defendant's maximum offer will increase the likelihood of litigation. An increase in the plaintiff's subjective probability of prevailing or in his stakes will do this, but so will an increase in the defendant's subjective probability of prevailing since it will induce him to reduce his maximum settlement offer. An increase in the defendant's stakes in the case will reduce the likelihood of litigation by leading him to increase his maximum settlement offer. In the important special case where the stakes to the parties are the same, it can be shown that an increase in those stakes will increase the likelihood of litigation. In that case, litigation cannot possibly occur unless the plaintiff's subjective probability of prevailing is greater than one minus the defendant's subjective probability, for otherwise the plaintiff's minimum settlement offer will be equal to or smaller than the defendant's maximum offer. Assuming that this minimum condition for litigation is satisfied, any increase in the stakes must increase the likelihood of litigation by making the plaintiff's minimum settlement offer grow faster than the defendant's maximum settlement offer.

The approach suggested here assumes that the subjective probabilities, the stakes, and the costs of litigation and of settlement are mutually independent, but they are not. A change in the stakes will affect the amount of money that the parties spend on litigation and this in turn will alter the probabilities of a particular outcome. Settlement costs are probably a function of both litigation costs and stakes. A change in one party's expenditures on litigation, triggered by a change in the stakes or subjective probability of winning of that party may lead the other party to alter his expenditures on the case, which may induce a further change in the first party's expenditures. . . . The interdependence of the parties' expenditures makes it impossible to predict the level of those expenditures unless special, and somewhat arbitrary, assumptions about the parties' reaction patterns are adopted. This indeterminacy makes the conditions for settlement indeterminate, since not only the plaintiff's and defendant's litigation costs but also their subjective probabilities of prevailing if the case is litigated are functions of their expenditure decisions. . . .

THE INTERACTION BETWEEN ERROR COSTS AND DIRECT COSTS

The relationship between error costs and direct costs can be summarized in a loss function having three terms. The first term is error cost. This is a function of the probability of error, which in turn is a function of the fraction of cases litigated, the amount of private expenditures on litigation, and the amount of public expenditures. The second term is the sum of the private and public expenditures in cases that are litigated, and is equal to the total of those expenditures in all cases multiplied by the fraction of cases litigated. The third term is the total expenditures (all private) on cases that are settled, and is equal to the total private expenditures in all cases multiplied by the fraction of cases settled multiplied by the fractional cost of settling rather than litigating. An increase in the fraction of cases litigated, or in the public or private expenditures on litigation, will reduce the probability and hence cost of an erroneous judicial determination. An increase in public expenditures on litigation will reduce the relative cost advantage of settling rather than litigating (the government's subsidy of litigation has increased), and an increase in the relative cost advantages of settling will reduce the fraction of cases tried.

These relationships make clear why it is difficult to predict a priori the effect on overall efficiency of changes in the relevant variables. For example, an increase in the fraction of cases litigated will increase the social costs of legal dispute resolution only if the difference between the total costs of litigating cases and the total costs of settling them is greater than the reduction in error costs brought about by increasing the fraction of litigated cases. Otherwise it will reduce the total costs of legal dispute resolution. An increase in public expenditures will reduce error costs both directly and by inducing a larger fraction of cases to be tried, but it will increase the total direct costs of legal dispute resolution both directly and by making litigation relatively more attractive than settlement. Thus there can be no presumption that increasing the public expenditures on the court system will increase social welfare. An expenditure of another $1 million on the court system might cost society several millions — or benefit society by several millions. Finally, an increase in the fractional cost of settlement versus litigation, by lowering the cost of settlement relative to that of litigation, will reduce the direct costs of legal dispute resolution but indirectly increase the error costs. Thus, as argued earlier, measures that increase the attractiveness of settlement in comparison to litigation cannot be regarded as unequivocally desirable.

[Professor Posner then examines several examples of the "complex interplay between error and direct costs," including discovery, substantive law reform, the jury, and res judicata. Also examined is delay in court.]

To most experts in judicial administration, delay between the filing and final disposition of a legal claim is an unmitigated evil and the proper focus of judicial reform. This is an odd way to look at the matter. Delay is an omnipresent feature of social and economic life. It is only excessive delay that is undesirable, and what is excessive can be determined only by comparing the costs and benefits of different amounts of delay. . . .

The effect of the usual procedural reforms that are suggested (greater use of summary judgment, admissions, judicial notice, and the like) is to increase the productivity of litigation expenditures. The relationship to delay is obscure. An increase in the productivity of evidence will, as we have seen, induce litigants to purchase more of it. Thus, while it is repeatedly suggested that delay in Interstate Commerce Commission proceedings (for example) could be reduced if only the ICC would permit evidence without the cumbersome procedures, such as the best-evidence rule and the right of cross-examination, of common law proceedings, such simplification would induce the parties to increase the quantity of their litigation inputs—expert witnesses and the like—and this might result in even more protracted proceedings, albeit ones of higher quality.

The proposal to reduce delay by adding judges—usually considered the sovereign remedy—ignores several realistic possibilities that might undermine the effectiveness of the measure. The reduction in delay brought about by the addition of judges might be offset by the lower settlement rate in the personal-injury area, and perhaps in other areas, that can be foreseen if delay is reduced; the additional litigation would create a new source of delay. Moreover, with litigation a speedier method of dispute resolution, disputants who under existing conditions of delay substitute other methods of dispute resolution (such as arbitration) because they value prompt resolution would be attracted back to the courts, and again a new source of delay would be created. An analogy may be drawn to building a new freeway: by improving road transportation the freeway induces some people who previously used other modes of transportation to switch to driving, and this leads to new congestion.

The essential point is that minimization of delay is not an appropriate formulation of the goal of judicial reform. The goal, it has been argued in this article, is to minimize the sum of the error costs and of the direct costs of legal dispute resolution. The problem of delay must be placed within that larger framework of inquiry. Indeed, unless that is done, delay cannot even be defined in a meaningful fashion.

There is now a substantial literature of economic analysis of procedure and administration of justice. *See,* for example, Gary S. Becker and William M. Landes, *Essays in the Economics of Crime and Punishment* (1974). Judge Richard A. Posner's general work, *Economic Analysis of Law* (2d ed. 1977), provides an overview of the general analysis framework within which the above-excerpted essay fits. For a criticism of that framework, see Arthur A. Leff, *Economic Analysis of Law: Some Realism about Nominalism,* 60 Va. L. Rev. 45 (1974).

Practice Exercise No. 1: Designing a Sound Dispute Resolution Process

What are the minimal elements of a fair process for resolving a dispute, and what additional elements are worth the additional cost? For the moment, imagine that you are free to design the resolution process under each of the following circumstances:

1. You rented an apartment before moving to start law school; you gave the landlord a security deposit of one month's rent before obtaining

the apartment, and now expect it back after finishing your lease, but the landlord has retained the security deposit and claims that you left marks on the walls and floors that justify this retention. How would you want to resolve your dispute with the landlord? Identify setting, participants, purposes, and the directions for the proceeding.

2. You own 2000 residential apartment rental units and face regular disputes with tenants over matters such as repairs, noise, unpaid rent, and security deposits. What procedures would you want established for managing these disputes—keeping in mind that they are numerous and frequent?

3. Which procedural elements identified in (1) and (2) above would be in common? Which would differ? If you now were legislating for all tenants and landlords a procedural system for disputes between them, what elements would you specify?

D. ACCESS TO LAWYERS AND TO THE LEGAL SYSTEM

When should the due process right to be heard ensure a right to a lawyer? When should that right encompass rights of access to the formal setting of the courtroom? One due process case decided by the Supreme Court before *Goldberg* and one decided after *Mathews* address these questions. Complicating the question of access to a lawyer is the issue of communication between clients and lawyers who may come from different social, economic, and cultural worlds. Questions of access could be resolved outside the constitutional framework through legislation, voluntary contributions by the bar, or the creation of cheaper, quicker processes inside and outside the formal judicial setting. When would such approaches be desirable?

1. Access to Court

■ BODDIE v. CONNECTICUT
401 U.S. 371 (1971)

Justice HARLAN delivered the opinion of the Court:

Appellants, welfare recipients residing in the State of Connecticut, brought this action in the Federal District Court for the District of Connecticut on behalf of themselves and others similarly situated, challenging, as applied to them, certain state procedures for the commencement of litigation, including requirements for payment of court fees and costs for service of process, that restrict their access to the courts in their effort to bring an action for divorce.

It appears from the briefs and oral argument that the average cost to a litigant for bringing an action for divorce is $60. Section 52-259 of the Connecticut General Statutes provides: "There shall be paid to the clerks of the supreme court or the superior court, for entering each civil cause, forty-five dollars. . . ." An additional $15 is usually required for the service of process by the sheriff, although as much as $40 or $50 may be necessary where notice must be accomplished by publication.

There is no dispute as to the inability of the named appellants in the present case to pay either the court fees required by statute or the cost incurred for the service of process. The affidavits in the record establish that appellants' welfare income in each instance barely suffices to meet the costs of the daily essentials of life and includes no allotment that could be budgeted for the expense to gain access to the courts in order to obtain a divorce. Also undisputed is appellants' "good faith" in seeking a divorce.

Assuming, as we must on this motion to dismiss the complaint, the truth of the undisputed allegations made by the appellants, it appears that they were unsuccessful in their attempt to bring their divorce actions in the Connecticut courts, simply by reason of their indigency. The clerk of the Superior Court returned their papers "on the ground that he could not accept them until an entry fee had been paid." Subsequent efforts to obtain a judicial waiver of the fee requirement and to have the court effect service of process were to no avail.

Appellants thereafter commenced this action in the Federal District Court seeking a judgment declaring that Connecticut's statute and service of process provisions, "requiring payment of court fees and expenses as a condition precedent to obtaining court relief [are] unconstitutional [as] applied to these indigent [appellants] and all other members of the class which they represent." As further relief, appellants requested the entry of an injunction ordering the appropriate officials to permit them "to proceed with their divorce actions without payment of fees and costs." Our conclusion is that, given the basic position of the marriage relationship in this society's hierarchy of values and the concomitant state monopolization of the means for legally dissolving this relationship, due process does prohibit a State from denying, solely because of inability to pay, access to its courts to individuals who seek judicial dissolution of their marriages.

At its core, the right to due process reflects a fundamental value in our American constitutional system. Our understanding of that value is the basis upon which we have resolved this case.

Perhaps no characteristic of an organized and cohesive society is more fundamental than its erection and enforcement of a system of rules defining the various rights and duties of its members, enabling them to govern their affairs and definitively settle their differences in an orderly, predictable manner. Without such a "legal system," social organization and cohesion are virtually impossible; with the ability to seek regularized resolution of conflicts individuals are capable of interdependent action that enables them to strive for achievements without the anxieties that would beset them in a disorganized society. Put more succinctly, it is this injection of the rule of law that allows society to reap the benefits of rejecting what political theorists call the "state of nature."

American society, of course, bottoms its systematic definition of individual rights and duties, as well as its machinery for dispute settlement, not on custom or the will of strategically placed individuals, but on the common-law model. It is to courts, or other quasi-judicial official bodies, that we ultimately look for the implementation of a regularized, orderly process of dispute settlement. Within this framework, those who wrote our original Constitution, in the Fifth Amendment, and later those who drafted the Fourteenth Amendment, recognized the centrality of the concept of due process in the operation of this system. Without this guarantee that one may not be deprived of his rights, neither liberty nor property, without due process of law, the State's monopoly over techniques for binding conflict resolution could hardly be said to be acceptable under our scheme of things. Only by providing that the social enforcement mechanism must function strictly within these bounds can we hope to maintain an ordered society that is also just. It is upon this premise that this Court has through years of adjudication put flesh upon the due process principle. . . .

Recognition of this theoretical framework illuminates the precise issue presented in this case. As this Court on more than one occasion has recognized, marriage involves interests of basic importance in our society. *See, e.g., Loving v. Virginia,* 388 U.S. 1 (1967); *Skinner v. Oklahoma,* 316 U.S. 535 (1942); *Meyer v. Nebraska,* 262 U.S. 390 (1923). It is not surprising, then, that the States have seen fit to oversee many aspects of that institution. . . .

[A]lthough they assert here due process rights as would-be plaintiffs, we think appellants' plight, because resort to the state courts is the only avenue to dissolution of their marriages, is akin to that of defendants faced with exclusion from the only forum effectively empowered to settle their disputes. Resort to the judicial process by these plaintiffs is no more voluntary in a realistic sense than that of the defendant called upon to defend his interests in court. For both groups this process is not only the paramount dispute-settlement technique, but, in fact, the only available one. In this posture we think that this appeal is properly to be resolved in light of the principles enunciated in our due process decisions that delimit rights of defendants compelled to litigate their differences in the judicial forum.

These due process decisions, representing over a hundred years of effort by this Court to give concrete embodiment to this concept, provide, we think, complete vindication for appellants' contentions. In particular, precedent has firmly embedded in our due process jurisprudence two important principles upon whose application we rest our decision in the case before us.

Prior cases establish, first, that due process requires, at a minimum, that absent a countervailing state interest of overriding significance, persons forced to settle their claims of right and duty through the judicial process must be given a meaningful opportunity to be heard. . . .

Due process does not, of course, require that the defendant in every civil case actually have a hearing on the merits. . . . What the Constitution does require is "an opportunity . . . granted at a meaningful time and in a meaningful manner," *Armstrong v. Manzo,* 380 U.S. 545, 552 (1965) (emphasis added), "for [a] hearing appropriate to the nature of the case," *Mullane v. Central Hanover Tr. Co., supra,* at 313. . . .

Our cases further establish that a statute or a rule may be held constitutionally invalid as applied when it operates to deprive an individual of a protected right although its general validity as a measure enacted in the legitimate exercise of state power is beyond question. Thus, in cases involving religious freedom, free speech or assembly, this Court has often held that a valid statute was unconstitutionally applied in particular circumstances because it interfered with an individual's exercise of those rights.

No less than these rights, the right to a meaningful opportunity to be heard within the limits of practicality, must be protected against denial by particular laws that operate to jeopardize it for particular individuals. . . .

The State's obligations under the Fourteenth Amendment are not simply generalized ones; rather, the State owes to each individual that process which, in light of the values of a free society, can be characterized as due.

Drawing upon the principles established by the cases just canvassed, we conclude that the State's refusal to admit these appellants to its courts, the sole means in Connecticut for obtaining a divorce, must be regarded as the equivalent of denying them an opportunity to be heard upon their claimed right to a dissolution of their marriages, and, in the absence of a sufficient countervailing justification for the State's action, a denial of due process.

The arguments for this kind of fee and cost requirement are that the State's interest in the prevention of frivolous litigation is substantial, its use of court fees and process costs to allocate scarce resources is rational, and its balance between the defendant's right to notice and the plaintiff's right to access is reasonable.

In our opinion, none of these considerations is sufficient to override the interest of these plaintiff-appellants in having access to the only avenue open for dissolving their allegedly untenable marriages. . . .

We are thus left to evaluate the State's asserted interest in its fee and cost requirements as a mechanism of resource allocation or cost recoupment. Such a justification was offered and rejected in *Griffin v. Illinois,* 351 U.S. 12 (1956). In *Griffin* it was the requirement of a transcript beyond the means of the indigent that blocked access to the judicial process. While in

Griffin the transcript could be waived as a convenient but not necessary predicate to court access, here the State invariably imposes the costs as a measure of allocating its judicial resources. Surely, then, the rationale of *Griffin* covers this case.

In concluding that the Due Process Clause of the Fourteenth Amendment requires that these appellants be afforded an opportunity to go into court to obtain a divorce, we wish to re-emphasize that we go no further than necessary to dispose of the case before us, a case where the bona fides of both appellants' indigency and desire for divorce are here beyond dispute. We do not decide that access for all individuals to the courts is a right that is, in all circumstances, guaranteed by the Due Process Clause of the Fourteenth Amendment so that its exercise may not be placed beyond the reach of any individual, for, as we have already noted, in the case before us this right is the exclusive precondition to the adjustment of a fundamental human relationship. . . . Reversed.

[Justice DOUGLAS' and Justice BRENNAN's concurring opinions are omitted.]

Justice BLACK, dissenting:

This is a strange case and a strange holding. Absent some specific federal constitutional or statutory provision, marriage in this country is completely under state control, and so is divorce. When the first settlers arrived here the power to grant divorces in Great Britain was not vested in that country's courts but in its Parliament. And as recently as 1888 this Court in *Maynard v. Hill*, 125 U.S. 190, upheld a divorce granted by the Legislature of the Territory of Oregon. Since that time the power of state legislatures to grant divorces or vest that power in their courts seems not to have been questioned. It is not by accident that marriage and divorce have always been considered to be under state control. The institution of marriage is of peculiar importance to the people of the States. . . .

The Court here holds, however, that the State of Connecticut has so little control over marriages and divorces of its own citizens that it is without power to charge them practically nominal initial court costs when they are without ready money to put up those costs. The Court holds that the state law requiring payment of costs is barred by the Due Process Clause of the Fourteenth Amendment of the Federal Constitution. Two members of the majority believe that the Equal Protection Clause also applies. I think the Connecticut court costs law is barred by neither of those clauses.

It is true, as the majority points out, that the Court did hold in *Griffin v. Illinois*, 351 U.S. 12 (1956), that indigent defendants in criminal cases must be afforded the same right to appeal their convictions as is afforded to a defendant who has ample funds to pay his own costs. . . . [T]here are strong reasons for distinguishing between the two types of cases.

Criminal defendants are brought into court by the State or Federal Government to defend themselves against charges of crime. They go into court knowing that they may be convicted, and condemned to lose their lives, their liberty, or their property, as a penalty for their crimes. Because of this great governmental power the United States Constitution has provided special protections for people charged with crime. . . .

Civil lawsuits, however, are not like government prosecutions for crime. Civil courts are set up by government to give people who have quarrels with their neighbors the chance to use a neutral governmental agency to adjust their differences. In such cases the government is not usually involved as a party, and there is no deprivation of life, liberty, or property as punishment for crime. Our Federal Constitution, therefore, does not place such private disputes on the same high level as it places criminal trials and punishment. There is consequently no necessity, no reason, why government should in civil trials be hampered or handi-capped by the strict and rigid due process rules the Constitution has provided to protect people charged with crime. . . . The rules set out in the Constitution itself provide what is governmentally fair and what is not. Neither due process nor equal protection permits state laws to be invalidated on any such nonconstitutional standard as a judge's personal view of fairness. The people and their elected representa-tives, not judges, are constitutionally vested with the power to amend the Constitution. . . .

Comments and Questions

1. Which of these values are crucial to the majority opinion, and why? What is their role in the Court's analysis?
   a. the interests of individuals involved in marriage and divorce are so fundamental that the state must act very carefully in govern-ing them;
   b. the state monopoly over the techniques of binding conflict resolution in the area of divorce cannot be conducted in a mode that deprives an individual of liberty or property;
   c. the state monopoly over the techniques of binding conflict resolution cannot be conducted in a mode that deprives an individual of liberty or property;
   d. the individual plaintiffs have untenable marriages;
   e. the state here offers no mechanisms for waiving access fees for divorce upon demonstration of the parties' indigency.

2. Which of the rationales offered by Justice Black in dissent do you find most persuasive?
   a. accommodation of indigents in criminal litigation is not a com-pelling analogy for the treatment of indigents in civil litigation, where the state itself does not threaten to deprive a person of life, liberty, or property;

  b. nothing in the language of the Constitution empowers a judge
     to invalidate state laws on the basis of personal views of fairness;
  c. dissatisfaction with the system should lead to action by the peo-
     ple and their elected representatives, not by judges.

3. What rejoinders does the majority offer to the arguments in the
dissent? Which do you find most persuasive?

4. How can the *Boddie* decision support an indigent mother's claim to
waive the costs of a transcript necessary to appeal a civil court judgment
terminating her parental rights for abuse or neglect? How can the decision in *Boddie* be distinguished to avoid supporting that mother's claim?
For the Supreme Court's decision on the subject, *see M.L.B. v. S.L.J.,* 519
U.S. 102 (1996).

2. Access to a Lawyer

■ LASSITER v. DEPARTMENT OF SOCIAL
SERVICES OF DURHAM COUNTY,
NORTH CAROLINA
452 U.S. 18 (1981)

Justice STEWART delivered the opinion of the Court:

In the late spring of 1975, after hearing evidence that the petitioner,
Abby Gail Lassiter, had not provided her infant son William with proper
medical care, the District Court of Durham County, N.C., adjudicated him
a neglected child and transferred him to the custody of the Durham
County Department of Social Services, the respondent here. A year later,
Ms. Lassiter was charged with first-degree murder, was convicted of second-
degree murder, and began a sentence of 25 to 40 years of imprisonment.[1]

In 1978 the Department petitioned the court to terminate Ms.
Lassiter's parental rights because, the Department alleged, she "has not

---

1. The North Carolina Court of Appeals, in reviewing the petitioner's conviction, indicated that the murder occurred during an altercation between Ms. Lassiter, her mother, and
the deceased:

"Defendant's mother told [the deceased] to 'come on.' They began to struggle and deceased fell or was knocked to the floor. Defendant's mother was beating deceased with a
broom. While deceased was still on the floor and being beaten with the broom, defendant
entered the apartment. She went into the kitchen and got a butcher knife. She took the
knife and began stabbing the deceased who was still prostrate. The body of deceased had
seven stab wounds. . . ." *State v. Lassiter,* No. 7614SC1054 (June 1, 1977). After her conviction was affirmed on appeal, Ms. Lassiter sought to attack it collaterally. Among her arguments was that the assistance of her trial counsel had been ineffective because he had failed
to "seek to elicit or introduce before the jury the statement made by [Ms. Lassiter's mother,]
'And I did it, I hope she dies.'" Ms. Lassiter's mother had, like Ms. Lassiter, been indicted on
a first-degree murder charge; however, the trial court granted the elder Ms. Lassiter's motion
for a nonsuit. The North Carolina General Court of Justice, Superior Court Division, denied
Ms. Lassiter's motion for collateral relief. File No. 76-CR-3102 (Mar. 20, 1979).

had any contact with the child since December of 1975" and "has willfully left the child in foster care for more than two consecutive years without showing that substantial progress has been made in correcting the conditions which led to the removal of the child, or without showing a positive response to the diligent efforts of the Department of Social Services to strengthen her relationship to the child, or to make and follow through with constructive planning for the future of the child."

Ms. Lassiter was served with the petition and with notice that a hearing on it would be held. Although her mother had retained counsel for her in connection with an effort to invalidate the murder conviction, Ms. Lassiter never mentioned the forthcoming hearing to him (or, for that matter, to any other person except, she said, to "someone" in the prison). At the behest of the Department of Social Services' attorney, she was brought from prison to the hearing, which was held August 31, 1978. The hearing opened, apparently at the judge's instance, with a discussion of whether Ms. Lassiter should have more time in which to find legal assistance. Since the court concluded that she "has had ample opportunity to seek and obtain counsel prior to the hearing of this matter, and [that] her failure to do so is without just cause," the court did not postpone the proceedings. Ms. Lassiter did not aver that she was indigent, and the court did not appoint counsel for her.

A social worker from the respondent Department was the first witness. She testified that in 1975 the Department "received a complaint from Duke Pediatrics that William had not been followed in the pediatric clinic for medical problems and that they were having difficulty in locating Ms. Lassiter. . . ." She said that in May 1975 a social worker had taken William to the hospital, where doctors asked that he stay "because of breathing difficulties [and] malnutrition and [because] there was a great deal of scarring that indicated that he had a severe infection that had gone untreated." The witness further testified that, except for one "prearranged" visit and a chance meeting on the street, Ms. Lassiter had not seen William after he had come into the State's custody, and that neither Ms. Lassiter nor her mother had "made any contact with the Department of Social Services regarding that child." When asked whether William should be placed in his grandmother's custody, the social worker said he should not, since the grandmother "has indicated to me on a number of occasions that she was not able to take responsibility for the child" and since "I have checked with people in the community and from Ms. Lassiter's church who also feel that this additional responsibility would be more than she can handle." The social worker added that William "has not seen his grandmother since the chance meeting in July of '76 and that was the only time."

After the direct examination of the social worker, the judge said:

> I notice we made extensive findings in June of '75 that you were served with papers and called the social services and told them you weren't coming; and

the serious lack of medical treatment. And, as I have said in my findings of the 16th day of June '75, the Court finds that the grandmother, Ms. Lucille Lassiter, mother of Abby Gail Lassiter, filed a complaint on the 8th day of May, 1975, alleging that the daughter often left the children, Candina, Felicia and William L. with her for days without providing money or food while she was gone.

Ms. Lassiter conducted a cross-examination of the social worker, who firmly reiterated her earlier testimony. The judge explained several times, with varying degrees of clarity, that Ms. Lassiter should only ask questions at this stage; many of her questions were disallowed because they were not really questions, but arguments.

Ms. Lassiter herself then testified, under the judge's questioning, that she had properly cared for William. Under cross-examination, she said that she had seen William more than five or six times after he had been taken from her custody and that, if William could not be with her, she wanted him to be with her mother since, "He knows us. Children know they family. . . . They know they people, they know they family and that child knows us anywhere. . . . I got four more other children. Three girls and a boy and they know they little brother when they see him." Ms. Lassiter's mother was then called as a witness. She denied, under the questioning of the judge, that she had filed the complaint against Ms. Lassiter, and on cross-examination she denied both having failed to visit William when he was in the State's custody and having said that she could not care for him.

The court found that Ms. Lassiter "has not contacted the Department of Social Services about her child since December, 1975, has not expressed any concern for his care and welfare, and has made no efforts to plan for his future." Because Ms. Lassiter thus had "wilfully failed to maintain concern or responsibility for the welfare of the minor," and because it was "in the best interests of the minor," the court terminated Ms. Lassiter's status as William's parent.

On appeal, Ms. Lassiter argued only that, because she was indigent, the Due Process Clause of the Fourteenth Amendment entitled her to the assistance of counsel, and that the trial court had therefore erred in not requiring the State to provide counsel for her. The North Carolina Court of Appeals decided that "[while] this State action does invade a protected area of individual privacy, the invasion is not so serious or unreasonable as to compel us to hold that appointment of counsel for indigent parents is constitutionally mandated." *In re Lassiter*, 43 N.C. App. 525. The Supreme Court of North Carolina summarily denied Ms. Lassiter's application for discretionary review, and we granted certiorari to consider the petitioner's claim under the Due Process Clause of the Fourteenth Amendment.

For all its consequence, "due process" has never been, and perhaps can never be, precisely defined. "[Unlike] some legal rules," this Court has said, due process "is not a technical conception with a fixed content unrelated to time, place and circumstances." *Cafeteria Workers v. McElroy,* 367 U.S. 886, 895. Rather, the phrase expresses the requirement of "fundamental fairness," a requirement whose meaning can be as opaque as its importance is lofty. Applying the Due Process Clause is therefore an uncertain enterprise which must discover what "fundamental fairness" consists of in a particular situation by first considering any relevant precedents and then by assessing the several interests that are at stake.

The pre-eminent generalization that emerges from this Court's precedents on an indigent's right to appointed counsel is that such a right has been recognized to exist only where the litigant may lose his physical liberty if he loses the litigation. Thus, when the Court overruled the principle of *Betts v. Brady,* 316 U.S. 455, that counsel in criminal trials need be appointed only where the circumstances in a given case demand it, the Court did so in the case of a man sentenced to prison for five years. *Gideon v. Wainwright,* 372 U.S. 335. And thus *Argersinger v. Hamlin,* 407 U.S. 25, established that counsel must be provided before any indigent may be sentenced to prison, even where the crime is petty and the prison term brief.

That it is the defendant's interest in personal freedom, and not simply the special Sixth and Fourteenth Amendments right to counsel in criminal cases, which triggers the right to appointed counsel is demonstrated by the Court's announcement in *In re Gault,* 387 U.S. 1, that "the Due Process Clause of the Fourteenth Amendment requires that in respect of proceedings to determine delinquency which may result in commitment to an institution in which the juvenile's freedom is curtailed," the juvenile has a right to appointed counsel even though those proceedings may be styled "civil" and not "criminal." *Id.* at 41 (emphasis added). Similarly, four of the five Justices who reached the merits in *Vitek v. Jones,* 445 U.S. 480, concluded that an indigent prisoner is entitled to appointed counsel before being involuntarily transferred for treatment to a state mental hospital. The fifth Justice differed from the other four only in declining to exclude the "possibility that the required assistance may be rendered by competent laymen in some cases." *Id.* at 500 (separate opinion of Powell, J.).

Significantly, as a litigant's interest in personal liberty diminishes, so does his right to appointed counsel. In *Gagnon v. Scarpelli,* 411 U.S. 778, the Court gauged the due process rights of a previously sentenced probationer at a probation-revocation hearing. In *Morrissey v. Brewer,* 408 U.S. 471, 480, which involved an analogous hearing to revoke parole, the Court had said: "Revocation deprives an individual, not of the absolute liberty to which every citizen is entitled, but only of the conditional liberty properly dependent on observance of special parole restrictions." Relying on that discussion, the Court in *Scarpelli* declined to hold that indigent probationers have, per se, a right to counsel at revocation hearings, and instead left the decision whether counsel should be appointed to be made on a case-by-case basis.

Finally, the Court has refused to extend the right to appointed counsel to include prosecutions which, though criminal, do not result in the defendant's loss of personal liberty. The Court in *Scott v. Illinois*, 440 U.S. 367, for instance, interpreted the "central premise of *Argersinger*" to be "that actual imprisonment is a penalty different in kind from fines or the mere threat of imprisonment," and the Court endorsed that premise as "eminently sound and [warranting] adoption of actual imprisonment as the line defining the constitutional right to appointment of counsel." *Id.*, at 373. The Court thus held "that the Sixth and Fourteenth Amendments to the United States Constitution require only that no indigent criminal defendant be sentenced to a term of imprisonment unless the State has afforded him the right to assistance of appointed counsel in his defense." *Id.*, at 373-374.

In sum, the Court's precedents speak with one voice about what "fundamental fairness" has meant when the Court has considered the right to appointed counsel, and we thus draw from them the presumption that an indigent litigant has a right to appointed counsel only when, if he loses, he may be deprived of his physical liberty. It is against this presumption that all the other elements in the due process decision must be measured.

The case of *Mathews v. Eldridge*, 424 U.S. 319, 335, propounds three elements to be evaluated in deciding what due process requires, viz., the private interests at stake, the government's interest, and the risk that the procedures used will lead to erroneous decisions. We must balance these elements against each other, and then set their net weight in the scales against the presumption that there is a right to appointed counsel only where the indigent, if he is unsuccessful, may lose his personal freedom.

This Court's decisions have by now made plain beyond the need for multiple citation that a parent's desire for and right to "the companionship, care, custody, and management of his or her children" is an important interest that "undeniably warrants deference and, absent a powerful countervailing interest, protection." *Stanley v. Illinois*, 405 U.S. 645, 651. Here the State has sought not simply to infringe upon that interest, but to end it. If the State prevails, it will have worked a unique kind of deprivation. A parent's interest in the accuracy and justice of the decision to terminate his or her parental status is, therefore, a commanding one.

Since the State has an urgent interest in the welfare of the child, it shares the parent's interest in an accurate and just decision. For this reason, the State may share the indigent parent's interest in the availability of appointed counsel. If, as our adversary system presupposes, accurate and just results are most likely to be obtained through the equal contest of opposed interests, the State's interest in the child's welfare may perhaps best be served by a hearing in which both the parent and the State acting for the child are represented by counsel, without whom the contest of interests may become unwholesomely unequal. North Carolina itself acknowledges as much by providing that where a parent files a written answer to a termination petition, the State must supply a lawyer to represent the child. N.C. Gen. Stat. §7A-289.29 (Supp. 1979).

The State's interests, however, clearly diverge from the parent's insofar as the State wishes the termination decision to be made as economically as possible and thus wants to avoid both the expense of appointed counsel and the cost of the lengthened proceedings his presence may cause. But though the State's pecuniary interest is legitimate, it is hardly significant enough to overcome private interests as important as those here, particularly in light of the concession in the respondent's brief that the "potential costs of appointed counsel in termination proceedings . . . is [sic] admittedly de minimis compared to the costs in all criminal actions."

Finally, consideration must be given to the risk that a parent will be erroneously deprived of his or her child because the parent is not represented by counsel. North Carolina law now seeks to assure accurate decisions by establishing the following procedures: A petition to terminate parental rights may be filed only by a parent seeking the termination of the other parent's rights, by a county department of social services or licensed child-placing agency with custody of the child, or by a person with whom the child has lived continuously for the two years preceding the petition. §7A289.24. A petition must describe facts sufficient to warrant a finding that one of the grounds for termination exists, §7A289.25 (6), and the parent must be notified of the petition and given 30 days in which to file a written answer to it, §7A289.27. If that answer denies a material allegation, the court must, as has been noted, appoint a lawyer as the child's guardian ad litem and must conduct a special hearing to resolve the issues raised by the petition and the answer. §7A-289.29. If the parent files no answer, "the court shall issue an order terminating all parental and custodial rights . . . ; provided the court shall order a hearing on the petition and may examine the petitioner or others on the facts alleged in the petition." §7A289.28. Findings of fact are made by a court sitting without a jury and must "be based on clear, cogent, and convincing evidence." §7A289.30. Any party may appeal who gives notice of appeal within 10 days after the hearing. §7A289.34.

The respondent argues that the subject of a termination hearing— the parent's relationship with her child—far from being abstruse, technical, or unfamiliar, is one as to which the parent must be uniquely well informed and to which the parent must have given prolonged thought. The respondent also contends that a termination hearing is not likely to produce difficult points of evidentiary law, or even of substantive law, since the evidentiary problems peculiar to criminal trials are not present and since the standards for termination are not complicated. In fact, the respondent reports, the North Carolina Departments of Social Services are themselves sometimes represented at termination hearings by social workers instead of by lawyers.

Yet the ultimate issues with which a termination hearing deals are not always simple, however commonplace they may be. Expert medical and psychiatric testimony, which few parents are equipped to understand and fewer still to confute, is sometimes presented. The parents are likely to be people with little education, who have had uncommon difficulty in dealing with life, and who are, at the hearing, thrust into a distressing and disorienting situation. That these factors may combine to overwhelm an uncounseled parent is evident from the findings some courts have made. . . . The respondent is able to point to no presently authoritative case, except for the North Carolina judgment now before us, holding that an indigent parent has no due process right to appointed counsel in termination proceedings.

The dispositive question, which must now be addressed, is whether the three *Eldridge* factors, when weighed against the presumption that there is no right to appointed counsel in the absence of at least a potential deprivation of physical liberty, suffice to rebut that presumption and thus to lead to the conclusion that the Due Process Clause requires the appointment of counsel when a State seeks to terminate an indigent's parental status. . . .

If, in a given case, the parent's interests were at their strongest, the State's interests were at their weakest, and the risks of error were at their peak, it could not be said that the *Eldridge* factors did not overcome the presumption against the right to appointed counsel, and that due process did not therefore require the appointment of counsel. But since the *Eldridge* factors will not always be so distributed, and since "due process is not so rigid as to require that the significant interests in informality, flexibility and economy must always be sacrificed," *Gagnon v. Scarpelli*, 411 U.S. at 788, neither can we say that the Constitution requires that appointment of counsel in every parental termination proceeding. We therefore adopt the standard found appropriate in *Gagnon v. Scarpelli*, and leave the decision whether due process calls for the appointment of counsel for indigent parents in termination proceedings to be answered in the first instance by the trial court, subject, of course, to appellate review. . . .

The Department of Social Services was represented at the hearing by counsel, but no expert witnesses testified, and the case presented no specially troublesome points of law, either procedural or substantive. While hearsay evidence was no doubt admitted, and while Ms. Lassiter no doubt left incomplete her defense that the Department had not adequately assisted her in rekindling her interest in her son, the weight of the evidence that she had few sparks of such an interest was sufficiently great that the presence of counsel for Ms. Lassiter could not have made a determinative difference. True, a lawyer might have done more with the argument that William should live with Ms. Lassiter's mother—but that argument was quite explicitly made by both Lassiters, and the evidence that the elder Ms. Lassiter had said she could not handle another child, that the social worker's investigation had led to a similar conclusion, and that the grandmother had displayed scant interest in the child once he had been removed from her daughter's custody was, though controverted, sufficiently substantial that the absence of counsel's guidance on this point did not render the proceedings fundamentally unfair.

Finally, a court deciding whether due process requires the appointment of counsel need not ignore a parent's plain demonstration that she is not interested in attending a hearing. Here, the trial court had previously found that Ms. Lassiter had expressly declined to appear at the 1975 child custody hearing, Ms. Lassiter had not even bothered to speak to her retained lawyer after being notified of the termination hearing, and the court specifically found that Ms. Lassiter's failure to make an effort to contest the termination proceeding was without cause. In view of all these circumstances, we hold that the trial court did not err in failing to appoint counsel for Ms. Lassiter. . . .

For the reasons stated in this opinion, the judgment is affirmed.

Chief Justice BURGER, concurring:

I join the Court's opinion and add only a few words to emphasize a factor I believe is misconceived by the dissenters. The purpose of the termination proceeding at issue here was not "punitive." On the contrary, its purpose was protective of the child's best interests. Given the record in this case, which involves the parental rights of a mother under lengthy sentence for murder who showed little interest in her son, the writ might well have been a "candidate" for dismissal as improvidently granted. However, I am content to join the narrow holding of the Court, leaving the appointment of counsel in termination proceedings to be determined by the state courts on a case-by-case basis.

Justice BLACKMUN, with whom Justice BRENNAN and Justice MARSHALL join, dissenting:

The Court today denies an indigent mother the representation of counsel in a judicial proceeding initiated by the State of North Carolina to terminate her parental rights with respect to her youngest child. The Court most appropriately recognizes that the mother's interest is a "commanding one," and it finds no countervailing state interest of even remotely comparable significance, see ante, at 27-28, 31. Nonetheless, the Court avoids what seems to me the obvious conclusion that due process requires the presence of counsel for a parent threatened with judicial termination of parental rights, and, instead, revives an ad hoc approach thoroughly discredited nearly 20 years ago in *Gideon v. Wainwright*, 372 U.S. 335 (1963). Because I believe that the unique importance of a parent's interest in the care and custody of his or her child cannot constitutionally be extinguished through formal judicial proceedings without the benefit of counsel, I dissent.

This Court is not unfamiliar with the problem of determining under what circumstances legal representation is mandated by the Constitution. In *Betts v. Brady*, 316 U.S. 455 (1942), it reviewed at length both the tradition behind the Sixth Amendment right to counsel in criminal trials and the historical practices of the States in that area. The decision in *Betts*—that the Sixth Amendment right to counsel did not apply to the States and that the due process guarantee of the Fourteenth Amendment permitted a flexible, case-by-case determination of the defendant's need for counsel in state criminal trials—was overruled in *Gideon v. Wainwright*, 372 U.S., at 345. . . .

Outside the criminal context, however, the Court has relied on the flexible nature of the due process guarantee whenever it has decided that counsel is not constitutionally required. The special purposes of probation revocation determinations, and the informal nature of those administrative proceedings, including the absence of counsel for the State, led the Court to conclude that due process does not require counsel for probationers. *Gagnon v. Scarpelli*, 411 U.S. 778, 785-789 (1973). In the case of school disciplinary proceedings, which are brief, informal, and intended in part to be educative, the Court also found no requirement for legal counsel. *Goss v. Lopez*, 419 U.S. 565, 583 (1975). Most recently, the Court declined to intrude the presence of counsel for a minor facing voluntary civil commitment by his parent, because of the parent's substantial role in that decision and because of the decision's essentially medical and informal nature. *Parham v. J.R.*, 442 U.S. 584, 604-609 (1979).

In each of these instances, the Court has recognized that what process is due varies in relation to the interests at stake and the nature of the governmental proceedings. Where the individual's liberty interest is of diminished or less than fundamental stature, or where the prescribed procedure involves informal decisionmaking without the trappings of an adversarial trial-type proceeding, counsel has not been a requisite of due process. Implicit in this analysis is the fact that the contrary conclusion sometimes may be warranted. Where an individual's liberty interest assumes sufficiently weighty constitutional significance, and the State by a formal and adversarial proceeding seeks to curtail that interest, the right to counsel may be necessary to ensure fundamental fairness. To say this is simply to acknowledge that due process allows for the adoption of different rules to address different situations or contexts.

It is not disputed that state intervention to terminate the relationship between petitioner and her child must be accomplished by procedures meeting the requisites of the Due Process Clause. Nor is there any doubt here about the kind of procedure North Carolina has prescribed. North Carolina law requires notice and a trial-type hearing before the State on its own initiative may sever the bonds of parenthood. The decisionmaker is a judge, the rules of evidence are in force, and the State is represented by counsel. The question, then, is whether proceedings in this mold, that relate to a subject so vital, can comport with fundamental fairness when the defendant parent remains unrepresented by counsel. As the Court today properly acknowledges, our consideration of the process due in this context, as in others, must rely on a balancing of the competing private and public interests, an approach succinctly described in *Mathews v. Eldridge.* As does the majority, I evaluate the "three distinct factors" specified in *Eldridge.* . . .

At stake here is "the interest of a parent in the companionship, care, custody, and management of his or her children." *Stanley v. Illinois,* 405 U.S. 645, 651 (1972). This interest occupies a unique place in our legal culture, given the centrality of family life as the focus for personal meaning and responsibility. "[Far] more precious . . . than property rights," *May v. Anderson,* 345 U.S. 528, 533 (1953), parental rights have been deemed to be among those "essential to the orderly pursuit of happiness by free men," *Meyer v. Nebraska,* 262 U.S. 390, 399 (1923), and to be more significant and priceless than "'liberties which derive merely from shifting economic arrangements.'" *Stanley v. Illinois,* 405 U.S., at 651, quoting *Kovacs v. Cooper,* 336 U.S. 77, 95 (1949) (Frankfurter, J., concurring). Accordingly, although the Constitution is verbally silent on the specific subject of families, freedom of personal choice in matters of family life long has been viewed as a fundamental liberty interest worthy of protection under the Fourteenth Amendment. Within the general ambit of family integrity, the Court has accorded a high degree of constitutional respect to a natural parent's interest both in controlling the details of the child's upbringing, and in retaining the custody and companionship of the child.

In this case, the State's aim is not simply to influence the parent-child relationship but to extinguish it. A termination of parental rights is both total and irrevocable. Unlike other custody proceedings, it leaves the parent with no right to visit or communicate with the child, to participate in, or even to know about, any important decision affecting the child's religious, educational, emotional, or physical development. . . .

The magnitude of this deprivation is of critical significance in the due process calculus, for the process to which an individual is entitled is in part determined "by the extent to which he may be 'condemned to suffer grievous loss.'" *Goldberg v. Kelly,* 397 U.S. 254, 263 (1970), *quoting Joint Anti-Fascist Refugee Committee v. McGrath,* 341 U.S. 123, 168 (1951) (Frankfurter, J., concurring). Surely there can be few losses more grievous than the abrogation of parental rights. Yet the Court today asserts that this deprivation somehow is less serious than threatened losses deemed to require appointed counsel, because in this instance the parent's own "personal liberty" is not at stake.

I do not believe that our cases support the "presumption" asserted, that physical confinement is the only loss of liberty grievous enough to trigger a right to appointed counsel under the Due Process Clause. Indeed, incarceration has been found to be neither a necessary nor a sufficient condition for requiring counsel on behalf of an indigent defendant. The prospect of canceled parole or probation, with its consequent deprivation of personal liberty, has not led the Court to require counsel for a prisoner facing a revocation proceeding. On the other hand, the fact that no new incarceration was threatened by a transfer from prison to a mental hospital did not preclude the Court's recognition of adverse changes in the conditions of confinement and of the stigma that presumably is associated with being labeled mentally ill. *Vitek v. Jones*, 445 U.S. 480, 492, 494 (1980). For four Members of the Court, these "other deprivations of liberty," coupled with the possibly diminished mental capacity of the prisoner, compelled the provision of counsel for any indigent prisoner facing a transfer hearing.

Moreover, the Court's recourse to a "pre-eminent generalization," misrepresents the importance of our flexible approach to due process. . . .

Rather than opting for the insensitive presumption that incarceration is the only loss of liberty sufficiently onerous to justify a right to appointed counsel, I would abide by the Court's enduring commitment to examine the relationships among the interests on both sides, and the appropriateness of counsel in the specific type of proceeding. The fundamental significance of the liberty interests at stake in a parental termination proceeding is undeniable, and I would find this first portion of the due process balance weighing heavily in favor of refined procedural protections. The second *Eldridge* factor, namely, the risk of error in the procedure provided by the State, must then be reviewed with some care.

The method chosen by North Carolina to extinguish parental rights resembles in many respects a criminal prosecution. Unlike the probation revocation procedure reviewed in *Gagnon v. Scarpelli*, on which the Court so heavily relies, the termination procedure is distinctly formal and adversarial. The State initiates the proceeding by filing a petition in district court.*

In addition, the proceeding has an obvious accusatory and punitive focus. In moving to terminate a parent's rights, the State has concluded that it no longer will try to preserve the family unit, but instead will marshal an array of public resources to establish that the parent-child separation must be made permanent. . . .

[T]he State here has prescribed virtually all the attributes of a formal trial as befits the severity of the loss at stake in the termination decision — every attribute, that is, except counsel for the defendant parent. The provision of counsel for the parent would not alter the character of the proceeding, which is already adversarial, formal, and quintessentially legal.

---

* *Eds. Note:* Section 2281 was repealed in 1976. Section 2284 sets forth the current law concerning three-judge courts.

It, however, would diminish the prospect of an erroneous termination, a prospect that is inherently substantial, given the gross disparity in power and resources between the State and the uncounseled indigent parent.

The prospect of error is enhanced in light of the legal standard against which the defendant parent is judged. As demonstrated here, that standard commonly adds another dimension to the complexity of the termination proceeding. Rather than focusing on the facts of isolated acts or omissions, the State's charges typically address the nature and quality of complicated ongoing relationships among parent, child, other relatives, and even unrelated parties. . . .

The legal issues posed by the State's petition are neither simple nor easily defined. The standard is imprecise and open to the subjective values of the judge. A parent seeking to prevail against the State must be prepared to adduce evidence about his or her personal abilities and lack of fault, as well as proof of progress and foresight as a parent that the State would deem adequate and improved over the situation underlying a previous adverse judgment of child neglect. The parent cannot possibly succeed without being able to identify material issues, develop defenses, gather and present sufficient supporting nonhearsay evidence, and conduct cross-examination of adverse witnesses.

The Court, of course, acknowledges, that these tasks "may combine to overwhelm an uncounseled parent." I submit that that is a profound understatement. . . .

The risk of error . . . is several-fold. The parent who actually has achieved the improvement or quality of parenting the State would require may be unable to establish this fact. The parent who has failed in these regards may be unable to demonstrate cause, absence of willfulness, or lack of agency diligence as justification. And errors of fact or law in the State's case may go unchallenged and uncorrected. Given the weight of the interests at stake, this risk of error assumes extraordinary proportions. By intimidation, inarticulateness, or confusion, a parent can lose forever all contact and involvement with his or her offspring.

The final factor to be considered, the interests claimed for the State, do not tip the scale against providing appointed counsel in this context. The State hardly is in a position to assert here that it seeks the informality of a rehabilitative or educative proceeding into which counsel for the parent would inject an unwelcome adversarial edge. As the Assistant Attorney General of North Carolina declared before this Court, once the State moves for termination, it "has made a decision that the child cannot go home and should not go home. It no longer has an obligation to try and restore that family."

The State may, and does, properly assert a legitimate interest in promoting the physical and emotional well-being of its minor children. But this interest is not served by terminating the rights of any concerned, responsible parent. . . .

The State also has an interest in avoiding the cost and administrative inconvenience that might accompany a right to appointed counsel. But, as the Court acknowledges, the State's fiscal interest "is hardly significant enough to overcome private interests as important as those here." . . .

The Court's analysis is markedly similar to mine; it, too, analyzes the three factors listed in *Mathews v. Eldridge*, and it, too, finds the private interest weighty, the procedure devised by the State fraught with risks of error, and the countervailing governmental interest insubstantial. Yet, rather than follow this balancing process to its logical conclusion, the Court abruptly pulls back and announces that a defendant parent must await a case-by-case determination of his or her need for counsel. . . .

The Court's own precedents make this clear. In *Goldberg v. Kelly*, the Court found that the desperate economic conditions experienced by welfare recipients as a class distinguished them from other recipients of governmental benefits. In *Mathews v. Eldridge*, the Court concluded that the needs of Social Security disability recipients were not of comparable urgency, and, moreover, that existing pre-termination procedures, based largely on written medical assessments, were likely to be more objective and evenhanded than typical welfare entitlement decisions. . . .

Moreover, the case-by-case approach advanced by the Court itself entails serious dangers for the interests at stake and the general administration of justice. . . .

The problem of inadequate representation is painfully apparent in the present case. . . .

It is perhaps understandable that the District Court Judge experienced difficulty and exasperation in conducting this hearing. But both the difficulty and the exasperation are attributable in large measure, if not entirely, to the lack of counsel. An experienced attorney might have translated petitioner's reaction and emotion into several substantive legal arguments. The State charged petitioner with failing to arrange a "constructive plan" for her child's future or to demonstrate a "positive response" to the Department's intervention. A defense would have been that petitioner had arranged for the child to be cared for properly by his grandmother, and evidence might have been adduced to demonstrate the adequacy of the grandmother's care of the other children. The Department's own "diligence" in promoting the family's integrity was never put in issue during the hearing, yet it is surely significant in light of petitioner's incarceration and lack of access to her child. Finally, the asserted willfulness of petitioner's lack of concern could obviously have been attacked since she was physically unable to regain custody or perhaps even to receive meaningful visits during 21 of the 24 months preceding the action.

Petitioner plainly has not led the life of the exemplary citizen or model parent. It may well be that if she were accorded competent legal representation, the ultimate result in this particular case would be the same. But the issue before the Court is not petitioner's character; it is whether she was given a meaningful opportunity to be heard when the State moved to terminate absolutely her parental rights. In light of the unpursued avenues of defense, and of the experience petitioner underwent at the hearing, I find virtually incredible the Court's conclusion today that her termination proceeding was fundamentally fair. . . .

Finally, I deem it not a little ironic that the Court on this very day grants, on due process grounds, an indigent putative father's claim for state-paid blood grouping tests in the interest of according him a meaningful opportunity to disprove his paternity, *Little v. Streater*, but in the present case rejects, on due process grounds, an indigent mother's claim for state-paid legal assistance when the State seeks to take her own child away from her in a termination proceeding. In *Little v. Streater*, the Court stresses and relies upon the need for "procedural fairness," the "compelling interest in the accuracy of [the] determination," the "not inconsiderable" risk of error, the indigent's "fac[ing] the State as an adversary," and "fundamental fairness."

. . . If the Court in *Boddie v. Connecticut*, 401 U.S. 371 (1971), was able to perceive as constitutionally necessary the access to judicial resources required to dissolve a marriage at the behest of private parties, surely it should perceive as similarly necessary the requested access to legal resources when the State itself seeks to dissolve the intimate and personal family bonds between parent and child. It will not open the "floodgates" that, I suspect, the Court fears. On the contrary, we cannot constitutionally afford the closure that the result in this sad case imposes upon us all. I respectfully dissent.

[Justice STEVENS' dissenting opinion is omitted.]

Comments and Questions

1. What are the benefits and problems of the *Lassiter* Court's case-by-case decision making about the right to publicly funded counsel?

2. Note that in the termination of parental rights at issue in *Lassiter*, the state assumes the role of moving party, or plaintiff, and the parent is the defendant. The child is not a party to the lawsuit. Even if the parent has no attorney, the state agency will have counsel, and in many circumstances, the child will also have an attorney, a guardian *ad litem* (pending the litigation), appointed by the court to protect his or her interests.

3. Many states now provide counsel for parents risking termination of parental rights.

4. Publicly funded legal services programs either hire salaried attorneys or provide contracts with private attorneys to represent low-income individuals in certain cases. Given the limited resources available for this purpose, how should those attorneys' services be allocated? Do the due process considerations regarding the private interest at stake help

determine the relative importance of claims on divorce, termination of parental rights, housing, income support, and health care access? What other considerations should influence the allocation decisions made by states and agencies providing services for poor people?

5. What dynamics influence the relationships between poor clients and their lawyers? Do poor clients, and should poor clients, direct the lines of their representation in court actions? Consider Lucie White, *Subordination, Rhetorical Survival Skills and Sunday Shoes: Notes on the Hearing of Mrs. G,* 38 Buffalo L. Rev. 1(1990). This article is based upon the author's work as a legal aid lawyer in North Carolina from 1982 to 1986. Professor White eloquently describes her own difficulty in understanding the client's perspective, and the irony that it was when Mrs. G. told her own story in her own voice that she became empowered and persuasive.

3. Pro Bono Work

People who cannot afford to pay lawyers may find access to legal representation through the donated legal services of individual lawyers or law firms. A long tradition of such *pro bono publico** service among lawyers today takes many forms. Some large law firms and law departments of corporations include pro bono work as an important part of their own practice, and expect individual lawyers to participate. Other firms offer individual lawyers opportunities to spend time working in legal aid clinics or public defender services. Many law schools house clinics that serve low-income clients and support student work at legal aid clinics and governmental agencies. Some bar associations promote and organize pro bono efforts. The American Bar Association, in its Model Rules of Professional Responsibility, exhorts its members to undertake pro bono service.

For decades, lawyers have debated whether pro bono service should be required for all lawyers. To date, no state bar has made pro bono service mandatory. By 1997, at least fourteen law schools accredited by the American Bar Association had adopted mandatory pro bono programs requiring from 20 to 60 hours of work prior to graduation. *See* Neta Ziv, *Law Schools Fostering a Commitment to Public Service—What More Can Be Done?,* 15 (May 1997), cited in Nitza Milagros Escalera, *A Christian Lawyer's Mandate to Provide Pro Bono Publico Service,* 66 Fordham L. Rev. 1393, 1396 (1998). Although the American Bar Association has consistently rejected proposals for a mandatory pro bono service duty, in January, 1995, the Bar of the City of New York's Committee on Legal Assistance urged all of the

* *Pro bono publico* means for the public good or general welfare; pro bono legal work is usually understood as offering services to indigents without charge. *Black's Legal Dictionary* 1203 (6th ed. 1990).

law schools in the state to institute mandatory pro bono programs. What arguments in addition to those offered below would help evaluate such a proposal?

■ EDITORIAL, DON'T FORCE ATTORNEYS TO DO PRO BONO WORK
17 Conn. Law Trib. (No. 8), Feb. 25, 1991, at 18

Mandatory pro bono is a bad idea. Although the proposal keeps surfacing in Connecticut and other states, we believe it should be firmly rejected.

The usual pro bono proposal is that every lawyer legally be required, without compensation, to spend at least a set minimum number of hours each year representing poor people. One variant of the proposal is that law firms may satisfy the requirement by one or a few lawyers assuming the pro bono obligation for all lawyers in the firm by taking added pro bono duties. Another proposal variant is that lawyers may buy their way out of the obligation by paying a bounty to be used in employing legal aid or other lawyers to assume the obligation—similar to the much maligned means of avoiding the military draft during the Civil War by paying to have someone else take one's place.

We fully recognize that a serious shortfall exists in providing legal services to the poor, a shortfall that is a disgrace in a society that boasts of its democratic ideals, including equality of access by all citizens to the system of justice. We strongly support the equal access ideal but take issue with mandatory pro bono as a means of achieving that ideal. The end is laudable; the means are objectionable, and objectionable for several obvious reasons.

First of all, mandatory pro bono is inequitable. The proposal is that lawyers be required to donate substantial time and effort to providing needed legal services to the poverty segment of the society when no other occupational group servicing the poor is required to donate its services to the poor—not physicians, not nurses, not social workers, not school teachers, not the police, not any other occupation. Only lawyers are to be coerced. This is patently inequitable.

In addition, coerced representation by a blanket requirement imposed on lawyers too often will result in less than the zealous and enthusiastic representation that all clients are entitled to. Furthermore, effective legal representation of the poor requires expertise in one or more fields of law that commonly involve the poor, such as divorce, child custody and support, welfare and other governmental entitlements, tenant eviction, consumer fraud and immigration. Many lawyers have no expertise in any of these fields of law, nor in criminal defense, another broad field of needed representation of poor persons. And a high percentage of legal work for poverty clients involves in court representation, a phase of the practice as to which many lawyers lack skill or experience.

Are lawyers capable of learning to represent clients in these various areas of the law? Most lawyers, yes. However, if coerced into the representation, will they learn to do so, through training programs or otherwise? Frequently, no. For many lawyers, learning to provide effective representation to the poor in needed problem areas is a substantial undertaking. If the representation is coerced, this learning often will be haphazard or worse, to the clients' acute disadvantage. Finally, making a mandatory pro bono scheme work fairly and honestly could be very difficult and expensive to administer and enforce.

We strongly support efforts being made by the Connecticut Bar Association and other bar associations to promote and expand voluntary pro bono. These are useful endeavors that can help materially in easing the shortfall in appropriate legal representation of the poor. However, we recognize that the principal responsibility for providing legal services to the poor and funding those services is in the larger community, including all levels of government. The top priority should be funding that will enable existing legal aid and public defender offices to hire enough lawyers to fill the need. These offices have proven that they can provide the poor with effective representation, but the legal aid agencies in particular are so seriously understaffed that they can accommodate only a minority of those who qualify and need their services.

Until the larger community is willing to finance adequately access to the legal system by those who cannot afford to pay for that access, serious inequities in the American justice system will remain. Trying to force lawyers to assume the responsibilities of the larger community is not an acceptable or workable solution.

■ EDITORIAL, DISSENT: LAWYERS HAVE SPECIAL DUTY TO SOCIETY
17 Conn. Law Trib. (No. 8), Feb. 25, 1991, at 18

As a member of the Editorial Board, I dissent from its opinion that lawyers should not be required to do pro bono work.

Our legal system exists to insure a just and orderly society. Lawyers exist so that our legal system can work. But our system will work only if those who need lawyers can get them. If lawyers turn their backs on those who need them, our legal system no longer insures a just and orderly society. If that happens, the justification for lawyers disappears.

In short, lawyers have a duty to see that those who really need lawyers get them. Voluntary pro bono programs are all well and good, but they are inadequate. One need only turn to the Interest on Lawyers Trust Accounts program to prove that. When IOLTA was voluntary, various bar efforts to increase participation had some modest success, but when IOLTA was made mandatory, participation quadrupled.

The majority of the Editorial Board gives two main reasons for opposing mandatory pro bono programs. (1) Other professions have no such requirement, and (2) lawyers will do a poorer job if the representation is mandatory.

As for the first point, I would have thought lawyers might want to be proud to set a good example for other professions to follow. On the second point, either the majority is factually wrong, in which case its argument disappears, or the majority is factually right, in which case we disgrace our profession. Until mandatory pro bono is tried and has failed, I am not willing to assume that we will disgrace our profession.

2

Remedies and Stakes

A. INTRODUCTION

Voltaire wrote: "I was never ruined but twice: once when I lost a lawsuit, and once when I won one." *An Editor's Treasury: A Continuing Anthology of Prose, Verse, and Literary Curiosities* 1032 (Herbert Meyer ed. 1968). The costs—economic and emotional—of litigation should never be underestimated; what, then, are the benefits? The ability of courts to order remedies stands as the most concrete benefit, and these remedies can include money damages, orders to direct a defendant to cease the offending behavior or to undertake new behavior, and declarations of rights and duties. Although most remedies must await the plaintiffs' success in demonstrating entitlement to relief, courts are also authorized under special circumstances to order provisional, temporary relief even before the litigation is completed.

This chapter explores the range of remedial options as well as the practices limiting their availability. Attorneys' fees are included for two practical reasons. First, under limited circumstances, one party may be ordered to pay another party's attorneys' fees; second, this benefits the parties and encourages deterrence and settlement comparable to money damages or other remedies.

The chapter closes with a section on judicial power to enforce court-ordered remedies through use of the contempt power—and peaceful protest, an alternative to court often pursued by social movements.

Broadly speaking, judicial power over remedies can be understood as part of the larger topic of what is at stake in litigation.

B. PROVISIONAL RELIEF

Should a plaintiff ever be able to use the law to obtain relief before proving the elements of the claim? Exceptional, but still frequently used, are devices for *securing the judgment* and for *maintaining the status quo.* Both stem from the equity powers of courts. The Federal Rules of Civil Procedure joined law and equity in the federal court system in 1938. Originally, these two judicial systems on this continent were largely separate and reflected the English judicial system, which had separate courts of law and equity until the passage of the Judicature Acts of the 1870s. The law and equity courts in England evolved as complementary systems, with the King's equity courts affording relief where the common law courts, the only courts with juries, did not.* Equitable relief therefore traditionally was a last resort, available when the formalities and limitations of the common law system precluded a just result. Nevertheless, equitable relief is now common in the merged system and is actually provided for by some statutes.

Before the merger, law and equity involved different sets of procedures. For example, no jury existed at equity; the jury served only the law courts. Pleadings at law faced strict categories; joinder was a rarity. Fact-finding mechanisms now known as discovery originated with equity. Yet common law courts in the United States permitted some discovery by the mid-nineteenth century. This example indicates the kind of interdependency that grew between the two systems, which made merger all the more welcome. Finally, the remedies in equity primarily were injunctive relief, while at law the remedies ordinarily were limited to money damages. Currently, the Federal Rules cover the entire system of merged law and equity and tend to reflect the flexibility of equity rather than the rigidity of law. Vestiges of the old division remain, however, in the tensions between justice and efficiency, and in many standards and rules.

1. Securing the Judgment: Attachments, Garnishments and Sequestration

Plaintiffs often bring a civil lawsuit in order to obtain or recover real or personal property or to receive money. Their lawyers would very much

---

*The Seventh Amendment to the United States Constitution directs that in suits at common law, "the right of trial by jury shall be preserved." As interpreted by Amercian courts, the amendment directs courts to use tests informed by the historical line between equity and common law jurisdictions in determining which cases will have a jury, if the parties so request. *See* Chapter 5, *infra.*

like to "tie up" defendants' property, pending the outcome of litigation. Sometimes, this is called "securing the judgment." For instance, plaintiffs' lawyers would like to put an attachment or a lien on real estate belonging to the defendant. The real estate could be the subject of the lawsuit or could be unrelated, but would represent the defendants' assets and thus their ability to pay the judgment. Alternatively, plaintiffs' attorneys could seek a preliminary injunction to enjoin the defendant from transferring the real estate. In many jurisdictions, lawyers, after obtaining a lien, a restraining order, or a preliminary injunction, will then file a notice of *lis pendens* in the registry of deeds, warning anyone who may want to acquire an interest in the realty of the pending litigation that the attachment could prevent them from obtaining unburdened title to the property.

More frequently, plaintiffs' lawyers prefer to trigger a process that would direct a public official, such as a sheriff, to take defendants' personal property to a neutral location or order the defendants' banks or employers to cut off the defendants' access to funds or wages. This process, often called sequestration, attaches property or funds pending the outcome of litigation; often this procedure removes property from the person in possession, pending some further action or proceedings affecting the property. This helps plaintiffs in two major ways. First, plaintiffs are assured that the defendants' resources will be available to collect if the plaintiffs win their lawsuits. If the property that has been secured is the very item at issue in the lawsuit (for instance, an installment vendor as plaintiff has sought to *replevy* the merchandise sold to the defendant), then the winning plaintiff will have less trouble turning a paper victory in court into actual recovery of the asset in question. Second, tying up a defendant's asset—such as a bank account or wages—puts intense pressure on the defendant to settle, regardless of the merits of the case. Plaintiffs generally like to secure such attachments prior to notifying defendants. Otherwise, defendants could harm or transfer the asset or dissipate the money before the end of the lawsuit.

Prior to the late 1960s, methods of securing the judgment before trial faced minimal or no restrictions. Indeed, in many jurisdictions as late as the mid-1960s, a lawyer would often commence a lawsuit by attaching the defendant's property prior to notifying the defendant of either the attachment or the suit. A plaintiff's lawyer would at that time *trustee* any of the defendants' bank accounts that could be located; under this procedure, the banks would be directed to pay no funds to the defendants, even before the defendants received notice. Lawyers had commenced suits in this fashion for centuries (or at least this was the common belief), and they took the legality of these practices for granted.

In the 1960s, however, reflecting the due process revolution in the courts, some lawyers challenged these deprivations of property as violations of the Fourteenth Amendment's guarantee of due process and similar state constitutional provisions. Landmark cases, many brought by legal services lawyers defending poor clients when creditors sought to seize their limited assets or installment sales purchases, successfully established that (1) due process guarantees applied to prejudgment contexts and (2) insufficient procedural protections had been in place.

Thus, in June 1969, the Supreme Court struck down Wisconsin's prejudgment wage garnishment statute in *Sniadach v. Family Finance Corp.*, 395 U.S. 337 (1969). The Court ruled that an employee was entitled under the constitution to notice and a hearing before the attachment of wages. In *Goldberg v. Kelly*, 397 U.S. 254 (1970), the Court held that due process required notice and a hearing prior to the termination of public welfare benefits. Other cases extended the requirement of notice and a right to be heard prior to even a temporary deprivation of property or liberty. *See Bell v. Burson*, 402 U.S. 535 (1971) (suspension of a driver's license); *Stanley v. Illinois*, 405 U.S. 645 (1971) (removal of custody of children from unwed father after death of mother). The next reading, *Fuentes v. Shevin*, 407 U.S. 67 (1972), followed these cases; it was argued on November 8, 1971, when the Court lacked two members. By the time the opinion was issued, Justices Powell and Rehnquist were seated on the Court, but they played no role in the decision.

■ FUENTES v. SHEVIN
407 U.S. 67 (1972)

Justice STEWART delivered the opinion of the Court:

We here review the decisions of two three-judge federal District Courts that upheld the constitutionality of Florida and Pennsylvania laws authorizing the summary seizure of goods or chattels in a person's possession under a writ of replevin. Both statutes provide for the issuance of writs ordering state agents to seize a person's possessions, simply upon the ex parte application of any other person who claims a right to them and posts a security bond. Neither statute provides for notice to be given to the possessor of the property, and neither statute gives the possessor an opportunity to challenge the seizure at any kind of prior hearing. The question is whether these statutory procedures violate the Fourteenth Amendment's guarantee that no State shall deprive any person of property without due process of law.

I

The appellant in No. 5039, Margarita Fuentes, is a resident of Florida. She purchased a gas stove and service policy from the Firestone Tire and Rubber Co. (Firestone) under a conditional sales contract calling for monthly payments over a period of time. A few months later, she purchased a stereophonic phonograph from the same company under the same sort of contract. The total cost of the stove and stereo was about $500, plus an additional financing charge of over $100. Under the contracts, Firestone retained title to the merchandise, but Mrs. Fuentes was entitled to possession unless and until she should default on her installment payments. For more than a year, Mrs. Fuentes made her installment payments. But then, with only about $200 remaining to be paid, a dispute developed between her and Firestone over the servicing of the stove. Firestone instituted an action in a small-claims court for repossession of both the stove and the stereo, claiming that Mrs. Fuentes had refused to make her remaining payments. Simultaneously with the filing of that action and before Mrs. Fuentes had even received a summons to answer its complaint, Firestone obtained a writ of replevin ordering a sheriff to seize the disputed goods at once.

In conformance with Florida procedure, Firestone had only to fill in the blanks on the appropriate form documents and submit them to the clerk of the small-claims court. The clerk signed and stamped the documents and issued a writ of replevin. Later the same day, a local deputy sheriff and an agent of Firestone went to Mrs. Fuentes' home and seized the stove and stereo.

Shortly thereafter, Mrs. Fuentes instituted the present action in a federal district court, challenging the constitutionality of the Florida prejudgment replevin procedures under the Due Process Clause of the Fourteenth Amendment. She sought declaratory and injunctive relief against continued enforcement of the procedural provisions of the state statutes that authorize prejudgment replevin.

II

Under the Florida statute challenged here, "[a]ny person whose goods or chattels are wrongfully detained by any other person . . . may have a writ of replevin to recover them. . . . " Fla. Stat. Ann. §78.01 (Supp. 1972-1973). There is no requirement that the applicant make a convincing showing before the seizure that the goods are, in fact, "wrongfully detained." Rather, Florida law automatically relies on the bare assertion of the party seeking the writ that he is entitled to one and allows a court clerk to issue the writ summarily. It requires only that the applicant file a complaint, initiating a court action for repossession and reciting in conclusory fashion that he is "lawfully entitled to the possession" of the property, and that he file a security bond in at least double the value of the property to be replevied conditioned that plaintiff will prosecute his action to effect and without delay and that if defendant recovers judgment against him in the action, he will return the property, if return thereof is adjudged, and will pay defendant all sums of money recovered against plaintiff by defendant in the action. Fla. Stat. Ann. §78.07 (Supp. 1972-1973). On the sole basis of the complaint and bond, a writ is issued "command[ing] the officer to whom it may be directed to replevy the goods and chattels in possession of defendant . . . and to summon the defendant to answer the complaint." Fla. Stat. Ann. §78.08 (Supp. 1972-1973). If the goods are "in any dwelling house or other building or enclosure," the officer is required to demand their delivery; but if they are not delivered, "he shall cause such house, building or enclosure to be broken open and shall make replevin according to the writ. . . ." Fla. Stat. Ann. §78.10 (Supp. 1972-1973).

Thus, at the same moment that the defendant receives the complaint seeking repossession of property through court action, the property is seized from him. He is provided no prior notice and allowed no opportunity whatever to challenge the issuance of the writ. After the property has been seized, he will eventually have an opportunity for a hearing, as the defendant in the trial of the court action for repossession, which the plaintiff is required to pursue. And he is also not wholly without recourse in the meantime. For under the Florida statute, the officer who seizes the property must keep it for three days, and during that period the defendant may reclaim possession of the property by posting his own security bond in double its value. But if he does not post such a bond, the property is transferred to the party who sought the writ, pending a final judgment in the underlying action for repossession.

The Pennsylvania law differs, though not in its essential nature, from that of Florida. As in Florida, a private party may obtain a prejudgment writ of replevin through a summary process of ex parte application to a prothonotary. As in Florida, the party seeking the writ may simply post with his application a bond in double the value of the property to be seized. Pa. Rule Civ. Proc. 1073(a). There is no opportunity for a prior hearing and no prior notice to the other party. On this basis, a sheriff is required to execute the writ by seizing the specified property. Unlike the Florida statute, however, the Pennsylvania law does not require that there ever be opportunity for a hearing on the merits of the conflicting claims to possession of the replevied property. The party seeking the writ is not obliged to initiate a court action for repossession. Indeed, he need not even formally allege that he is lawfully entitled to the property. The most that is required is that he file an "affidavit of the value of the property to be replevied." Pa. Rule Civ. Proc. 1073(a). If the party who loses property through replevin seizure is to get even a post-seizure hearing, he must initiate a lawsuit himself. He may also, as under Florida law, post his own counterbond within three days after the seizure to regain possession. Pa. Rule Civ. Proc. 1076. . . .

IV

For more than a century the central meaning of procedural due process has been clear: "Parties whose rights are to be affected are entitled to be heard; and in order that they may enjoy that right they must first be notified." . . . It is equally fundamental that the right to notice and an opportunity to be heard "must be granted at a meaningful time and in a meaningful manner." *Armstrong v. Manzo*, 380 U.S. 545, 552.

The primary question in the present cases is whether these state statutes are constitutionally defective in failing to provide for hearings "at a meaningful time." The Florida replevin process guarantees an opportunity for a hearing after the seizure of goods, and the Pennsylvania process allows a post-seizure hearing if the aggrieved party shoulders the burden of initiating one. But neither the Florida nor the Pennsylvania statute provides for notice or an opportunity to be heard before the seizure. The issue is whether procedural due process in the context of these cases requires an opportunity for a hearing before the State authorizes its agents to seize property in the possession of a person upon the application of another.

The constitutional right to be heard is a basic aspect of the duty of government to follow a fair process of decision making when it acts to deprive a person of his possessions. The purpose of this requirement is not only to ensure abstract fair play to the individual. Its purpose, more particularly, is to protect his use and possession of property from arbitrary encroachment—to minimize substantively unfair or mistaken deprivations of property, a danger that is especially great when the State seizes goods simply upon the application of and for the benefit of a private party. So viewed, the prohibition against the deprivation of property without due process of law reflects the high value, embedded in our constitutional and political history, that we place on a person's right to enjoy what is his, free of governmental interference.

. . . It has long been recognized that "fairness can rarely be obtained by secret, one-sided determination of facts decisive of rights. . . . [And] no better instrument has been devised for arriving at truth than to give a person in jeopardy of serious loss notice of the case against him and opportunity to meet it." *Joint Anti-Fascist Refugee Committee v. McGrath*, 341 U.S. 123, 170-172.

If the right to notice and a hearing is to serve its full purpose, then, it is clear that it must be granted at a time when the deprivation can still be prevented. . . .

The Florida and Pennsylvania prejudgment replevin statutes fly in the face of this principle. To be sure, the requirements that a party seeking a writ must first post a bond, allege conclusorily that he is entitled to specific goods, and open himself to possible liability in damages if he is wrong, serve to deter wholly unfounded applications for a writ. But those requirements are hardly a substitute for a prior hearing, for they test no more than the strength of the applicant's own belief in his rights. . . .

The minimal deterrent effect of a bond requirement is, in a practical sense, no substitute for an informed evaluation by a neutral official. More specifically, as a matter of constitutional principle, it is no replacement for the right to a prior hearing that is the only truly effective safeguard against arbitrary deprivation of property. . . .

V

The right to a prior hearing, of course, attaches only to the deprivation of an interest encompassed within the Fourteenth Amendment's protection. In the present cases, the Florida and Pennsylvania statutes were applied to replevy chattels in the appellants' possession. The replevin was not cast as a final judgment; most, if not all, of the appellants lacked full title to the chattels; and their claim even to continued possession was a matter in dispute. Moreover, the chattels at stake were nothing more than an assortment of household goods. Nonetheless, it is clear that the appellants were deprived of possessory interests in those chattels that were within the protection of the Fourteenth Amendment.

A

A deprivation of a person's possessions under a prejudgment writ of replevin, at least in theory, may be only temporary. The Florida and Pennsylvania statutes do not require a person to wait until a post-seizure hearing and final judgment to recover what has been replevied. Within three days after the seizure, the statutes allowing him to recover the goods if he, in return, surrenders other property—a payment necessary to secure a bond in double the value of the goods seized from him. But it is now well settled that a temporary, nonfinal deprivation of property is nonetheless a "deprivation" in the terms of the Fourteenth Amendment. *Sniadach v. Family Finance Corp.*, 395 U.S. 337; *Bell v. Burson*, 402 U.S. 535. Both *Sniadach* and *Bell* involved takings of property pending a final judgment in an underlying dispute. In both cases, the challenged statutes included recovery provisions, allowing the defendants to post security to quickly regain the property taken from them. Yet the Court firmly held that these were deprivations of property that had to be preceded by a fair hearing.

B

The appellants who signed conditional sales contracts lacked full legal title to the replevied goods. The Fourteenth Amendment's protection of "property," however, has never been interpreted to safeguard only the rights of undisputed ownership. Rather, it has been read broadly to extend protection to "any significant property interest," including statutory entitlements.

. . . Clearly, the [appellant's] possessory interest in the goods, dearly bought and protected by contract, was sufficient to invoke the protection of the Due Process Clause. . . .

It is enough to invoke the procedural safeguards of the Fourteenth

Amendment that a significant property interest is at stake, whatever the ultimate outcome of a hearing on the contractual right to continued possession and use of the goods.

C

Nevertheless, the District Courts rejected the appellants' constitutional claim on the ground that the goods seized from them—a stove, a stereo, a table, a bed, and so forth—were not deserving of due process protection, since they were not absolute necessities of life. The courts based this holding on a very narrow reading of *Sniadach v. Family Finance Corp., supra,* and *Goldberg v. Kelly, supra,* in which this Court held that the Constitution requires a hearing before prejudgment wage garnishment and before the termination of certain welfare benefits. They reasoned that *Sniadach* and *Goldberg,* as a matter of constitutional principle, established no more than that a prior hearing is required with respect to the deprivation of such basically "necessary" items as wages and welfare benefits.

This reading of *Sniadach* and *Goldberg* reflects the premise that those cases marked a radical departure from established principles of procedural due process. They did not. Both decisions were in the mainstream of past cases, having little or nothing to do with the absolute "necessities" of life but establishing that due process requires an opportunity for a hearing before a deprivation of property takes effect. . . .

The household goods, for which the appellants contracted and paid substantial sums, are deserving of similar protection. While a driver's license, for example, "may become (indirectly) essential in the pursuit of a livelihood," *ibid.,* a stove or a bed may be equally essential to provide a minimally decent environment for human beings in their day-to-day lives. It is, after all, such consumer goods that people work and earn a livelihood in order to acquire.

No doubt, there may be many gradations in the "importance" or "necessity" of various consumer goods. Stoves could be compared to television sets, or beds could be compared to tables. But if the root principle of procedural due process is to be applied with objectivity, it cannot rest on such distinctions. The Fourteenth Amendment speaks of "property" generally. . . .

VI

There are "extraordinary situations" that justify postponing notice and opportunity for a hearing. *Boddie v. Connecticut,* 401 U.S. at 379. These situations, however, must be truly unusual. Only in a few limited situations has this Court allowed outright seizure without opportunity for a prior hearing. First, in each case, the seizure has been directly necessary to secure an important governmental or general public interest. Second, there has been a special need for very prompt action. Third, the State has kept strict control over its monopoly of legitimate force; the person initiating the seizure has been a government official responsible for determining, under the standards of a narrowly drawn statute, that it was necessary and justified in the particular instance. Thus, the Court has allowed summary seizure of property to collect the internal revenue of the United States, to meet the needs of a national war effort, to protect against the economic disaster of a bank failure, and to protect the public from misbranded drugs and contaminated food.

The Florida and Pennsylvania prejudgment replevin statutes serve no such important governmental or general public interest. . . .

Nor do the broadly drawn Florida and Pennsylvania statutes limit the summary seizure of goods to special situations demanding prompt action. . . .

The statutes, moreover, abdicate effective state control over state power. Private parties, serving their own private advantage, may unilaterally invoke state power to replevy goods from another. No state official participates in the decision to seek a writ; no state official reviews the basis for the claim to repossession; and no state official evaluates the need for immediate seizure. There is not even a requirement that the plaintiff provide any information to the court on these matters. The State acts largely in the dark. . . .

VIII

We hold that the Florida and Pennsylvania prejudgment replevin provisions work a deprivation of property without due process of law insofar as they deny the right to a prior opportunity to be heard before chattels are taken from their possessor. . . .

For the foregoing reasons, the judgments of the District Courts are vacated and these cases are remanded for further proceedings consistent with this opinion. It is so ordered.

[Justice WHITE's dissenting opinion is omitted.]

Comments and Questions

1. Even in federal court actions, state rules govern most plaintiffs' efforts to seize property for purposes of securing the action. *See* Fed. R. Civ. P. 64.

2. Notice that the primary question in *Fuentes v. Shevin* is not whether the defendant is entitled to a hearing on the underlying merits of the plaintiff's claim, but whether due process entitles the defendant to notice and an opportunity to be heard before any action tying up the defendant's assets pending the final adjudication on the merits.

3. As often happens in law, the innovations marked by *Fuentes v. Shevin* produced strong reactions. While some scholars wrote articles celebrating the decision, others criticized it for potentially making life worse for consumers in various ways. Additional procedures could drive up the costs for sellers or the costs of borrowing by consumers. Stores might close in poor neighborhoods if vendors were no longer able to secure their installment sales. Creditor-sellers could force installment sales purchasers to sign contractual terms permitting the creditor or its agent simply to take any goods over which there was a dispute. Creditors might simply engage in self-help remedies of repossession, permitted under the Uniform Commercial Code, with no involvement from the state.

In *Flagg Brothers, Inc. v. Brooks*, 436 U.S. 149 (1978), the Supreme Court made clear that due process is not part of self-help remedies; the Supreme Court clarified this because no overt official involvement occurs where a creditor threatens to sell repossessed goods to satisfy a debt. Remember, then, that the Fourteenth Amendment is implicated only when a *state* has taken an action depriving a person of life, liberty, or property. What precisely was the state action involved in *Fuentes* that was sufficient to trigger the protections of the Fourteenth Amendment?

4. The Court itself reacted to *Fuentes v. Shevin* in two subsequent cases. In *Mitchell v. W. T. Grant Co.*, 416 U.S. 600 (1974), the Court upheld a sequestration procedure despite its failure to ensure notice prior to the plaintiff's seizure of the defendant's property. The Court found the Louisiana procedure at issue adequate because (1) the seller-creditor, as well as the buyer, had current, real interests in the property; (2) Louisiana required a verified petition or affidavit giving "specific facts" about "the nature of the claim and the amount thereof, if any, and the grounds relied upon for the issuance of the writ," whereas the Florida and Pennsylvania procedures at issue in *Fuentes* had permitted the plaintiff to proceed with "bare conclusory claims of ownership or lien"; and (3) the Louisiana procedure required judicial involvement and control. Justices Powell and Rehnquist, absent from the decision in *Fuentes*, joined the majority in *Mitchell*. Justice Stewart dissented from *Mitchell* and accused the majority of overruling *Fuentes* without admitting it. Then, in *North Georgia Finishing, Inc. v. Di-Chem, Inc.*, 419 U.S. 601 (1975), the Court rejected as constitutionally deficient the Georgia proceeding for garnishment. A bank account had been impounded with no bond pending litigation on an alleged debt. The Court found due process violated by (1) the absence of notice or an opportunity for the defendant to have an early hearing; (2) the lack of participation by a judicial officer; (3) no requirement for an affidavit by someone with personal knowledge of the facts; (4) no requirement that the creditor demonstrate at least a probable cause for the garnishment; and (5) the burden placed on the defendant to file a bond in order to challenge the garnishment. Justice Stewart's concurrence,

echoing a famous statement by Mark Twain, expressed his gratification that "my report of the demise of *Fuentes v. Shevin* . . . seems to have been greatly exaggerated." Justice Powell concurred, stressing the failure of the Georgia procedure to provide a prompt and adequate postgarnishment hearing; Justices Blackmun and Rehnquist dissented, emphasizing that *Fuentes* should have little force because it was decided only by four votes on a court with two vacant seats.

5. In *Connecticut v. Doehr*, 501 U.S. 1 (1991), Justice White wrote for a unanimous Court that a state statute authorizing the prejudgment attachment of real estate without prior notice or hearing, without a showing of extraordinary circumstance, and without a requirement that the person seeking the attachment post a bond, is a violation of the Due Process Clause of the Fourteenth Amendment. In this case, the plaintiff in an assault and battery case had obtained an attachment, with court approval, on the basis of an affidavit with five one-sentence paragraphs asserting probable cause that he would win his case. In his opinion, Justice White wrote: "It is self-evident that the judge could make no realistic assessment concerning the likelihood of an action's success based upon these one-sided, self-serving and conclusory submissions." White further wrote that "although the majority of the Court does not reach the issue," Justices Marshall, Stevens, O'Connor and he would hold that due process also requires the plaintiff to post a bond or other security in addition to the requirement that she make a showing of exigent circumstances.

6. In 1993, the Supreme Court ruled that, absent exigent circumstances, the Fifth Amendment's Due Process Clause requires the government to afford notice and a meaningful opportunity to be heard before seizing, under a federal forfeiture statute, property used or intended to be used in a drug-related offense. *United States v. James Daniel Good Real Property*, 510 U.S. 493 (1993). As a postconviction measure and an extra deterrent to crime, the federal government and many states have authorized prosecutors to seize goods used in the commission of the crime or purchased with the proceeds of the crime. The Court made clear, however, that neither the law enforcement purpose nor compliance with Fourth Amendment rules about criminal searches and seizures exempts the government from the requirements of due process.

The Court distinguished its prior decision permitting seizure of movable property, such as a yacht, without prior notice or hearing, *Calero-Toldeo v. Pearson Yacht Leasing Co.*, 416 U.S. 663 (1974), precisely because real property cannot be moved or concealed and owners are less able to frustrate governmental interests in forfeitable real property. In finding notice and hearing necessary prior to the forfeiture of real property, the Court relied in part on the three-part test announced in *Mathews v. Eldridge*, 424 U.S. 319 (1976), which recognized the strong private interest in the property, the unacceptable risk of error in an *ex parte* seizure, and the special need for neutral procedures, given the government's pecuniary interest in the forfeiture proceeding as well as the government's lack of a burden to present evidence on the statutory defense of innocence of ownership. The Court also reasoned that less extreme measures could adequately preserve the property and the court's jurisdiction, so there was "no pressing need" for prejudgment seizure in the case, unlike other contexts such as collection of delinquent income taxes. In a separate opinion joined by Justice Scalia and in part by Justice O'Connor, Chief Justice Rehnquist disagreed with the application of *Mathews v. Eldridge* to civil forfeiture and disputed the requirement of notice and hearing prior to forfeiture of any real property. 510 U.S. at 72-73. Justice O'Connor's separate opinion approved the application of *Mathews v. Eldridge* to civil forfeitures but disagreed with the majority's application of its test.

How would you justify the use of the *Mathews v. Eldridge* test in the postjudgment forfeiture context, and how would you argue against it? Would the case come out differently in the prejudgment relief contexts of *Mitchell* and *Di-Chem*, with an assessment of individual components of due process, such as posting a bond, judicial involvement, and a proffer of facts rather than a conclusory affidavit? And how would the case come out under *Doehr* and *James Daniel Good Real Property*?

7. What explains the Court's resurgent concern for due process in *Doehr* and *James Daniel Good Real Property*?

8. What, if any, due process requirements should apply to a rule providing for automatic eviction from public or publicly subsidized housing of any tenant who is suspected of engaging in illicit drug activities? What about a tenant who has a relative (e.g., a minor child) so suspected?

9. What kinds of governmental interests should outweigh private interests in property threatened by forfeiture? Would a governmental "War on Drugs" provide the "exigent circumstances" required in *Fuentes* or the "pressing need" specified in *James Daniel Good Real Property*?

Practice Exercise No. 2: Drafting a Constitutional
Attachment Statute

The Arkansas Supreme Court struck down the state's prejudgment attachment code as inadequate under *Fuentes, Di-Chem,* and *Mitchell. Barbara McCrory and Thomas McCrory v. Thomas J. Johnson and Jacquetta Alexander,* 296 Ark. 231, 755 S.W.2d 566 (1988). In that case, the defendant had failed to pay the monthly rent for a house; the rental agent gave notice that she should pay rent or else vacate the premises; he then placed a termination notice requesting her to vacate the premises within ten days, and shortly after that period expired, the rental agent removed all personal property (furniture, appliances, and household items) from the residence and deposited them at a local storage facility. The realtor then filed a complaint for the missing rent along with an affidavit for attachment, requiring the support of a bond, which is money or other security proffered to the court in an amount set by the judge to cover potential incidental and consequential costs incurred by the restrained party, pending judgment or final relief. A clerk issued the writ of attachment.

Imagine that an Arkansas state representative has asked you to draft a new statute governing attachment. It should respond to the defects highlighted in the *McCrory* case and also should reflect the Supreme Court's line of cases. Be sure to address these questions: (1) What kind of showing should be made before property can be attached? To whom? (2) When should notice and an opportunity to be heard be assured to the property owner, and should the timing here be affected by the plaintiff's concerns about sufficient assets to satisfy any judgment? (3) Should any exceptions be anticipated to permit postponement of notice and opportunity to be heard, for instance, to meet the needs of a national war effort, or to protect against the economic failure of a bank? (4) How would you deal with the dangers that increased procedural protections in this area will prompt more self-help actions by lenders, will increase the costs of borrowing or renting, or otherwise will make life worse for consumers and poor people? (5) What definitions and provisions should be in the proposed statute?

2. Maintaining the Status Quo

Sometimes a plaintiff wants above all to ensure that the defendant will stop engaging in a harmful activity or refrain from undertaking one. Yet during the time entailed in litigation, the defendant could act in harmful ways that would make a final remedy inadequate or unable to protect the plaintiff. In that situation, the plaintiff may again rely on the equitable powers of the courts to seek provisional relief known as temporary restraining orders and preliminary injunctions. The crucial question is under what circumstances these extraordinary orders should be granted prior to the litigation on the merits? (For the federal practice, *see* Fed. R. Civ. P. 65.) The case that follows provides some guidelines.

■ AMERICAN HOSPITAL SUPPLY CORP. v. HOSPITAL PRODUCTS LTD.

780 F.2d 589 (7th Cir. 1986)

POSNER, Circuit Judge.

A supplier terminated a distributor, who sued for breach of contract and got a preliminary injunction. . . . The supplier, Hospital Products (as we shall call the affiliated corporations that are the defendants), a small firm now undergoing reorganization in bankruptcy, is one of the world's two principal manufacturers of "reusable surgical stapling systems for internal surgical procedures" ("surgical stapling systems," for short). The terminated distributor, American Hospital Supply Corporation, the world's largest distributor of medical and surgical supplies, in 1982 became the exclusive distributor in the United States of Hospital Products' surgical stapling systems. The contract of distribution was for three years initially, but provided that it would be renewed automatically for successive one-year periods (to a limit of ten years) unless American Hospital Supply notified Hospital Products at least 90 days before the three years were up (or any successive one-year period for which the contract had been renewed) that it wanted to terminate the contract; and this meant, by June 3, 1985.

On that day Hospital Products hand-delivered a letter to American Hospital Supply demanding to know whether it intended to renew the contract and reminding it that if it failed to respond by the end of the day this would mean that the contract had been renewed. American Hospital Supply responded the same day in a letter which pointed out that since it wasn't terminating, the contract was, indeed, renewed. But on the next day Hospital Products announced that it was going to treat the contract as having been terminated, and on June 7 it sent a telegram to American Hospital Supply's dealers informing them that effective June 3 American Hospital Supply was "no longer the authorized distributor of [Hospital Products'] stapling products."

American Hospital Supply forthwith brought this diversity breach of contract suit against Hospital Products and moved for a preliminary injunction, which was granted on July 8 after an evidentiary hearing. The injunction forbids Hospital Products to take any action in derogation of American Hospital Supply's contract rights so long as the injunction is in force (i.e., pending the outcome of the trial). It also requires Hospital Products to notify American Hospital Supply's dealers that American Hospital Supply is still Hospital Products' authorized distributor, and this has been done. Hospital Products counterclaimed, alleging breach of contract, fraud, and unfair competition. . . .

A district judge asked to decide whether to grant or deny a preliminary injunction must choose the course of action that will minimize the costs of being mistaken. Because he is forced to act on an incomplete record, the danger of a mistake is substantial. And a mistake can be costly. If the judge grants the preliminary injunction to a plaintiff who it later turns out is not entitled to any judicial relief—whose legal rights have not been violated—the judge commits a mistake whose gravity is measured by the irreparable harm, if any, that the injunction causes to the defendant while it is in effect. If the judge denies the preliminary injunction to a plaintiff who it later turns out is entitled to judicial relief, the judge commits a mistake whose gravity is measured by the irreparable harm, if any, that the denial of the preliminary injunction does to the plaintiff.

These mistakes can be compared, and the one likely to be less costly can be selected, with the help of a simple formula: grant the preliminary injunction if but only if $P \times H_p > (1 - P) \times H_d$, or, in words, only if the harm to the plaintiff if the injunction is denied, multiplied by the probability that the denial would be an error (that the plaintiff, in other words, will win at trial), exceeds the harm to the defendant if the injunction is granted, multiplied by the probability that granting the injunction would be an error. That probability is simply one minus the probability that the plaintiff will win at trial; for if the plaintiff has, say, a 40 percent chance of winning, the defendant must have a 60 percent chance of winning $(1.00 - .40 = .60)$. The left-hand side of the formula is simply the probability of an erroneous denial weighted by the cost of denial to the plaintiff, and the right-hand side simply the probability of an erroneous grant weighted by the cost of grant to the defendant.

This formula, a procedural counterpart to Judge Learned Hand's famous negligence formula, *see United States v. Carroll Towing Co.*, 159 F.2d 169, 173 (2d Cir. 1947), is not offered as a new legal standard; it is intended not to force analysis into a quantitative straitjacket but to assist analysis by presenting succinctly the factors that the court must consider in making its decision and by articulating the relationship among the factors. It is actually just a distillation of the familiar four (sometimes five) factor test that courts use in deciding whether to grant a preliminary injunction. The court asks whether the plaintiff will be irreparably harmed if the preliminary injunction is denied (sometimes also whether the plaintiff has an adequate remedy at law), whether the harm to the plaintiff if the preliminary injunction is denied will exceed the harm to the defendant if it is granted, whether the plaintiff is reasonably likely to prevail at trial, and whether the public interest will be affected by granting or denying the injunction (i.e., whether third parties will be harmed—and these harms can then be added to Hp or Hd as the case may be). The court undertakes these inquiries to help it figure out whether granting the injunction would be the error-minimizing course of action, which depends on the probability that the plaintiff is in the right and on the costs to the plaintiff, the defendant, or others of granting or denying the injunction. . . . The formula is new; the analysis it capsulizes is standard. . . .

We have now to apply these precepts, and we begin with the balance of harms. Hospital Products points out, irrelevantly as it seems to us, that American Hospital Supply did not prove more than a handful of lost sales as a result of the mailgram of June 7 which announced the termination of American Hospital Supply's distributorship to its dealers. The reason is simply that American Hospital Supply promptly asked for and promptly received a preliminary injunction to head off any losses by restoring its distributorship. The question is not whether there was an actual loss but whether there was an impending loss that the preliminary injunction prevented, how great it was, and whether it could have been made up by a judgment for damages after trial.

Although American Hospital Supply was able to replace Hospital Products' line of surgical stapling systems in the interval between the mailgram of June 7 and the entry of the preliminary injunction a month later, the mailgram, unless retracted as ordered by the injunction, might have impaired American Hospital Supply's goodwill, a factor emphasized in other cases where terminated dealers sought preliminary injunctions. The suddenness of the termination and the urgent mode of announcement might have made the dealers think that American Hospital Supply must have engaged in unethical or unreasonable conduct. We do not put much weight on this point, however. It is speculative, and any harm may have been cured by the retraction, in which event the harm could not support the rest of the injunction.

But in addition, on June 7 American Hospital Supply was holding a large unsold inventory of Hospital Products' surgical stapling systems. To help Hospital Products overcome serious financial problems, American Hospital Supply had advanced it millions of dollars—part in loans, part by buying more of the product than it needed and keeping the excess in inventory. The mailgram jeopardized its investment because dealers might be reluctant to buy Hospital Products' goods from American Hospital Supply, not wanting to become enmeshed in a legal dispute between it and its supplier or perhaps even fearing that there might be some defect in the particular items being sold by American Hospital Supply. True, its investment would probably not be totally wiped out. . . .

What made the loss (whatever exactly it was in dollar terms) irreparable was not only or mainly the difficulty that American Hospital Supply might encounter down the road in quantifying its loss, although this difficulty has been stressed in other cases where a distributor sought a preliminary injunction in part to protect goodwill; it was Hospital Products' insolvency, which was apparent when the district judge granted the preliminary injunction, even though the firm had not yet declared bankruptcy. . . .

We conclude that there was a threat of irreparable harm to the plaintiff; and although the dollar amount of that harm is not known with any precision and we hesitate to call it great, it seems substantial. We must next consider the irreparable harm to the defendant from the injunction. The district judge found there would be none, because American Hospital Supply—which has billions of dollars in sales and earns substantial profits—will be good for any money judgment that Hospital Products may obtain on its counterclaim. This ground is not entirely satisfactory. There is a difference between the damages caused Hospital Products by the breach of contract or other (alleged) misconduct committed by American Hospital Supply before this suit began, damages which we may assume American Hospital Supply is good for, and damages caused Hospital Products by the preliminary injunction—that is, by an order fastening Hospital Products to American Hospital Supply for another year. Those are not the damages that Hospital Products seeks to recover on its counterclaim, and while there may be considerable overlap between the injunction damages and the counterclaim damages, we cannot say that the overlap is complete.

But we may not overlook the bond that a plaintiff who obtains a preliminary injunction is required to post [see Fed. R. Civ. P. 65(c)] and that this plaintiff did post, in an amount, $5 million, whose adequacy Hospital Products does not challenge. . . .

But what of the fact that an award of damages on the injunction bond, even if it made Hospital Products' creditors whole (and it might not), might not come in time to save the company itself? Many reorganizations in bankruptcy end in liquidation, and Hospital Products' reorganization may end there too, before the case is tried on the merits and therefore before the injunction bond can be enforced; and even if the company is successfully reorganized, the shareholders may be wiped out, and all the stock come into the hands of creditors. But the full financial losses to Hospital Products' shareholders from the bankruptcy are not the correct measure of the harm from granting the injunction. Bankruptcy is not, not intentionally anyway, a device for reducing wealth, but a device for distributing the impact of a business failure over various claimants to the bankrupt's assets. The costs that bankruptcy imposes, as distinct from the costs that the underlying failure imposes, are therefore merely the costs of administering the bankruptcy proceeding. Nevertheless these costs are not negligible. . . . A preliminary injunction that will or may precipitate a firm into bankruptcy is therefore a source of costs which ought to be considered in deciding whether to grant such an injunction.

A related and often more significant type of cost, but one whose implications for legal policy are more ambiguous, is the cost of the business failure itself. If the firm's assets would be worth less on the auction block than as part of a going concern, this might seem a powerful argument against granting a preliminary injunction that increased the risk of failure. . . .

We need penetrate no further into this maze; it is enough that the effect of a preliminary injunction in precipitating insolvency is a factor arguing against the grant of the injunction (how strongly we shall not have to decide). Reflection on this overlooked point might conceivably persuade the district judge to grant a motion to dissolve the preliminary injunction, should such a motion be made, as it can be at any time. *See, e.g., Winterland Concessions Co. v. Trela,* 735 F.2d 257, 259-60 (7th Cir. 1984). But it does not persuade us that the preliminary injunction was in error. . . .

The district judge was persuaded that Hospital Products, not American Hospital Supply, had broken the contract, implying a very high P. He undoubtedly was correct if the contract was renewed on June 3 and in force the next day when Hospital Products announced that the contract was terminated. But we must consider as did he whether American Hospital Supply repudiated the contract before this announcement. That would make this a case of anticipatory breach of contract—American Hospital Supply indicates that it will not perform its obligations under the renewed contract, Hospital Products therefore treats the contract as terminated. Hospital Products points to a letter from American Hospital Supply which threatens to end financial assistance to Hospital Products and call its loans unless Hospital Products agrees to modify the contract in American Hospital Supply's favor. American Hospital Supply responds with much show of reason that it had advanced millions of dollars to Hospital Products beyond anything that it was contractually obligated to do, and therefore had every right to condition the making of new loans or the extension of existing ones on contract concessions. Hospital Products says that no loans were due and what the letter referred to as financial assistance was a euphemism for money due on goods sold and delivered—to which another round of replies asserts that if no loans were due, Hospital Products had nothing to worry about and that American Hospital Supply actually had bought far more surgical stapling products from Hospital Products than it needed or was contractually obligated to buy, so that what looked like payment on the contract really was financial assistance.

This legal badminton is inconclusive; but as nearly as we can determine, the able and experienced district judge who resolved the uncertainty in American Hospital Supply's favor was on solid ground in doing so. . . .

Last, Hospital Products argues that the injunction is against the public interest. All such an argument means, as we said earlier, is that the injunction has effects on nonparties, in this case the members of the consuming public, which is to say the hospitals that are the ultimate purchasers of surgical stapling systems. Of course these effects must be taken into account in deciding whether to issue the injunction; when as here they are urged as reasons against the grant of the injunction, they are part of H_d in our formula, that is, they are part of the harm (to the defendant—but also to anyone else adversely affected) if the injunction is granted. If the injunction had been denied, Hospital Products would have sold its products directly to dealers in the United States, and American Hospital

Supply presumably would have sold its newly developed line to dealers, too, thus increasing the number of competing producers from two to three. From this it can be argued that renewal of the contract was anti-competitive because it has postponed American Hospital Supply's entry into the market as a competitor of Hospital Products. If "reusable surgical stapling systems for internal surgical procedures" constitute an economically meaningful market—meaning that if the producers colluded expressly or tacitly, they could raise the price of the product significantly without experiencing such a drastic loss of sales (as customers switched to substitutes, or producers of other products switched to making this product) as to make the price increase unprofitable—Hospital Products might have a winning argument; it is easier for two firms to collude without being detected than for three to do so. But Hospital Products has not tried to show that its product constitutes a genuine market and hence that there is a real danger of collusion; perhaps it has not tried to do so because it would be pointing to itself as one of the two colluders. . . .

SWYGERT, Senior Circuit Judge, dissenting:

. . . Parties seeking a preliminary injunction must meet four requirements. They must show that: (1) they have no adequate remedy at law and will suffer irreparable harm if the relief is not granted; (2) the irreparable harm they would suffer outweighs the irreparable harm defendants would suffer from an injunction; (3) they have some likelihood of success on the merits; and (4) the injunction would not disserve the public interest. [Judge Swygert then applied the four-part test to these facts.]

I would have preferred to avoid commenting on the majority's attempt to reduce the well-developed and complex law of preliminary injunctions to a "simple" mathematical formula. But because of the potentially far-reaching and baneful consequences of today's decision, I must regretfully voice my concerns. . . .

My quarrel . . . is not with *Carroll Towing* but rather with the majority's attempt today to create its equitable analogue. A quantitative approach may be an appropriate and useful heuristic device in determining negligence in tort cases, but it has limited value in determining whether a preliminary injunction should issue. Proceedings in equity and cases sounding in tort demand entirely different responses of a district judge. The judgment of the district judge in a tort case must be definite; the judgment of the district judge in an injunction proceeding cannot, by its very nature, be as definite. The judgment of a district judge in an injunction proceeding must be flexible and discretionary—within the bounds of the now settled four-prong test. . . .

Ironically, the majority never attempts to assign a numerical value to the variables of its own formula. We are never told how to measure P or

H_p or H_d. I believe, and the majority appears to concede, that a numerical value could never be assigned to these variables. Who can say, for instance, what exactly the probability is that the granting of the injunction was an error? How then will the majority's formula ease in a meaningful way the responsibilities of the district courts? Judges asked to issue a preliminary injunction must, in large part, rely on their own judgment, not on mathematical quanta. . . .

The majority disavows any effort to force the district courts into a "quantitative straitjacket," but I suspect that today's decision may lead to just that. District judges operate under enormous pressure to be decisive and precise. Much rides on their smallest decisions. Like a Homeric Siren the majority's formula offers a seductive but deceptive security. Moreover, the majority's formula invites members of the Bar to dust off their calculators and dress their arguments in quantitative clothing. The resulting spectacle will perhaps be entertaining, but I do not envy the district courts of this circuit and I am not proud of the task we have given them. . . .

Comments and Questions

1. What are the differences between a temporary restraining order and a preliminary injunction? You may want to review the treatment of the issue in *United States v. Hall, supra.*

2. Does it make sense that *Fuentes* and the cases that followed it insisted on the requirement of notice and the right to be heard prior to deprivation, but that temporary restraining orders can be granted *ex parte*? Why or why not? How are the situations different?

3. According to the majority and dissent in *American Hospital Supply Corporation*, what are the prerequisites for a preliminary injunction? Are they the same for a temporary restraining order in federal court?

4. How would you make Judge Posner's formula understandable to a mathphobic judge?

5. What faults does the dissent find with Judge Posner's use of the formula? Do you agree?

C. FINAL RELIEF

1. Equitable and Declaratory Relief

Equity law and procedure historically developed in England as the King's effort to provide more flexible and discretionary justice—and to give more power to the King for offering such justice. (The King may also have used the law courts in London to consolidate royal power.) The law courts generally used procedures and techniques thought to be more predictable than their equitable counterparts. The usual remedy available in the law courts was money damages; the equity courts, in contrast, offered injunctions (orders to stop the offending conduct or to comply with a legal duty); an accounting (reviewing of financial books, with reallocation of any monies wrongly placed in one account rather than another); rescission and reformation of contracts; and other tailor-made remedies. In the contemporary American federal system, which has merged law and equity, courts can consider requests for both kinds of relief. However, equitable relief is supposed to be available only when money damages would not be adequate. Consider the following case on this matter.

■ WALGREEN CO. v. SARA CREEK PROPERTY CO.
966 F.2d 273 (7th Cir. 1992)

Posner, Circuit Judge.

This appeal from the grant of a permanent injunction raises fundamental issues concerning the propriety of injunctive relief. The essential facts are simple. Walgreen has operated a pharmacy in the Southgate Mall in Milwaukee since its opening in 1951. Its current lease, signed in 1971 and carrying a 30-year, 6-month term, contains, as had the only previous lease, a clause in which the landlord, Sara Creek, promises not to lease space in the mall to anyone else who wants to operate a pharmacy or a store containing a pharmacy. Such an exclusivity clause, common in shopping-center leases, is occasionally challenged on antitrust grounds— implausibly enough, given the competition among malls; but that is an issue for another day, since in this appeal Sara Creek does not press the objection it made below to the clause on antitrust grounds.

In 1990, fearful that its largest tenant—what in real estate parlance is called the "anchor tenant"—having gone broke was about to close its store, Sara Creek informed Walgreen that it intended to buy out the anchor tenant and install in its place a discount store operated by Phar-Mor Corporation, a "deep discount" chain, rather than, like Walgreen, just a "discount" chain. Phar-Mor's store would occupy 100,000 square feet, of which 12,000 would be occupied by a pharmacy the same size as Walgreen's. The entrances to the two stores would be within a couple of hundred feet of each other.

Walgreen filed this diversity suit for breach of contract against Sara Creek and Phar-Mor and asked for an injunction against Sara Creek's letting the anchor premises to Phar-Mor. After an evidentiary hearing, the judge found a breach of Walgreen's lease and entered a permanent injunction against Sara Creek's letting the anchor tenant premises to Phar-Mor until the expiration of Walgreen's lease. He did this over the defendants' objection that Walgreen had failed to show that its remedy at law—damages—for the breach of the exclusivity clause was inadequate. Sara Creek had put on an expert witness who testified that Walgreen's damages could be readily estimated, and Walgreen had countered with evidence from its employees that its damages would be very difficult to compute, among other reasons because they included intangibles such as loss of goodwill.

Sara Creek reminds us that damages are the norm in breach of contract as in other cases. Many breaches, it points out, are "efficient" in the sense that they allow resources to be moved into a more valuable use. Perhaps this is one—the value of Phar-Mor's occupancy of the anchor premises may exceed the cost to Walgreen of facing increased competition. If so, society will be better off if Walgreen is paid its damages, equal to that cost, and Phar-Mor is allowed to move in rather than being kept out by an injunction. That is why injunctions are not granted as a matter of course, but only when the plaintiff's damages remedy is inadequate. Walgreen's is not, Sara Creek argues; the projection of business losses due to increased competition is a routine exercise in calculation. Damages representing either the present value of lost future profits or (what should be the equivalent, *Carusos v. Briarcliff, Inc.*, 76 Ga. App. 346, 351-52, 45 S.E.2d 802, 806-07 (1947)) the diminution in the value of the leasehold have either been awarded or deemed the proper remedy in a number of reported cases for breach of an exclusivity clause in a shopping-center lease. . . . Why, Sara Creek asks, should they not be adequate here?

Sara Creek makes a beguiling argument that contains much truth, but we do not think it should carry the day. For if, as just noted, damages have been awarded in some cases of breach of an exclusivity clause in a shopping-center lease, injunctions have been issued in others. . . . The choice between remedies requires a balancing of the costs and benefits of the alternatives. *Hecht Co. v. Bowles*, 321 U.S. 321, 329 (1944); *Yakus v. United States*, 321 U.S. 414, 440 (1944). The task of striking the balance is for the trial judge, subject to deferential appellate review in recognition of its particularistic, judgmental, fact-bound character. . . . As we said in an appeal from a grant of a preliminary injunction—but the point is applicable to review of a permanent injunction as well—"The question for us [appellate judges] is whether the [district] judge exceeded the bounds of permissible choice in the circumstances, not what we would have done if we had been in his shoes. . . ."

The plaintiff who seeks an injunction has the burden of persuasion — damages are the norm, so the plaintiff must show why his case is abnormal. But when, as in this case, the issue is whether to grant a permanent injunction, not whether to grant a temporary one, the burden is to show that damages are inadequate, not that the denial of the injunction will work irreparable harm. "Irreparable" in the injunction context means not rectifiable by the entry of a final judgment. . . . It has nothing to do with whether to grant a permanent injunction, which, in the usual case anyway, is the final judgment. The use of "irreparable harm" or "irreparable injury" as synonyms for inadequate remedy at law is a confusing usage. It should be avoided.

The benefits of substituting an injunction for damages are twofold. First, it shifts the burden of determining the cost of the defendant's conduct from the court to the parties. If it is true that Walgreen's damages are smaller than the gain to Sara Creek from allowing a second pharmacy into the shopping mall, then there must be a price for dissolving the injunction that will make both parties better off. Thus, the effect of upholding the injunction would be to substitute for the costly processes of forensic fact determination the less costly processes of private negotiation. Second, a premise of our free-market system, and the lesson of experience here and abroad as well, is that prices and costs are more accurately determined by the market than by government. . . .

The costs and benefits of the damages remedy are the mirror of those of the injunctive remedy. The damages remedy avoids the cost of continuing supervision and third-party effects, and the cost of bilateral monopoly as well. It imposes costs of its own, however, in the form of diminished accuracy in the determination of value, on the one hand, and of the parties' expenditures on preparing and presenting evidence of damages, and the time of the court in evaluating the evidence, on the other.

The weighing up of all these costs and benefits is the analytical procedure that is or at least should be employed by a judge asked to enter a permanent injunction, with the understanding that if the balance is even the injunction should be withheld. The judge is not required to explicate every detail of the analysis and he did not do so here, but as long we are satisfied that his approach is broadly consistent with a proper analysis we shall affirm; and we are satisfied here. The determination of Walgreen's damages would have been costly in forensic resources and inescapably inaccurate. . . . The lease had ten years to run. So Walgreen would have had to project its sales revenues and costs over the next ten years, and then project the impact on those figures of Phar-Mor's competition, and then discount that impact to present value. All but the last step would have been fraught with uncertainty. . . .

Damages are not always costly to compute, or difficult to compute accurately. . . . But this is not such a case and here damages would be a costly and inaccurate remedy; and on the other side of the balance some of the costs of an injunction are absent and the cost that is present seems low. The injunction here, like one enforcing a covenant not to compete (standardly enforced by injunction), is a simple negative injunction — Sara Creek is not to lease space in the Southgate Mall to Phar-Mor during the term of Walgreen's lease — and the costs of judicial supervision and enforcement should be negligible. There is no contention that the injunction will harm an unrepresented third party. It may harm Phar-Mor but that harm will be reflected in Sara Creek's offer to Walgreen to dissolve the injunction. (Anyway Phar-Mor is a party.) . . .

The only substantial cost of the injunction in this case is that it may set off a round of negotiations between the parties. In some cases, illustrated by *Boomer v. Atlantic Cement Co.*, 26 N.Y.2d 219 (1970), this consideration alone would be enough to warrant the denial of injunctive relief. The defendant's factory was emitting cement dust that caused the plaintiffs harm monetized at less than $200,000, and the only way to abate the harm would have been to close down the factory, which had cost $45 million to build. An injunction against the nuisance could therefore have created a huge bargaining range (could, not would, because it is unclear what the current value of the factory was), and the costs of negotiating to a point within it might have been immense. If the market value of the factory was actually $45 million, the plaintiffs would be tempted to hold out for a price to dissolve the injunction in the tens of millions and the factory would be tempted to refuse to pay anything more than a few hundred thousand dollars. Negotiations would be unlikely to break down completely, given such a bargaining range, but they might well be protracted and costly. There is nothing so dramatic here. Sara Creek does not argue that it will have to close the mall if enjoined from leasing to Phar-Mor. Phar-Mor is not the only potential anchor tenant. *Liza Danielle, Inc. v. Jamko, Inc.*, 408 So. 2d 735, 740 (Fla. App. 1982), on which Sara Creek relies, presented the converse case where the grant of the injunction would have forced an existing tenant to close its store. The size of the bargaining range was also a factor in the denial of injunctive relief in *Gitlitz v. Plankinton Building Properties, Inc.*, 228 Wis. 334, 339-40 (1938).

To summarize, the judge did not exceed the bounds of reasonable judgment in concluding that the costs (including forgone benefits) of the damages remedy would exceed the costs (including forgone benefits) of an injunction. . . .

Comments and Questions

1. How can nonmonetary costs and benefits be included in the comparison of equitable relief and damages? Consider a case in which the plaintiffs demonstrated that unconstitutional race discrimination by public officials explains the pattern of student enrollment in the public schools. Would it be possible or desirable to imagine money damages as an alternative to an injunctive order directing the officials to change the method of student assignment to the schools?

2. Sometimes, the relief a party wants most is a clarification of the law as applied to particular facts. For example, an investor may be reluctant to

finance an entrepreneur without a clear announcement that the proposed enterprise will breach no patents owned by someone else; or the administrator of a new governmental task force may want a declaratory judgment that the meetings will be held in private before proceeding with the risk of litigation over this issue. Congress has empowered courts to issue clarifications, or declaratory judgments, under the Declaratory Judgment Act, 28 U.S.C. §§2201 and 2202, and most states have similar legislation authorizing suits that permit parties to obtain a declaration of rights. Also, a request for a declaratory judgment may be coupled with a request for other relief, including damages or an injunction. The difficulty posed by declaratory relief on its own arises from the constitutional requirement that courts refrain from acting in the absence of a concrete, live controversy; Article III of the Constitution limits federal courts to considering only actual cases or controversies, rather than hypothetical issues. Can you frame a specific request for a declaratory judgment in *Connecticut v. Doehr* that ensures an actual case or controversy?

3. A court may issue a negative injunction, directing the defendant to cease the offending conduct. Such relief may be available even without a showing of irreparable harm. (Remember that irreparable harm is the standard for obtaining preliminary but not permanent injunctive relief.) *See Continental Airlines Inc. v. Intra Brokers, Inc.*, 24 F.3d 1099 (9th Cir. 1994) (affirming injunction against the selling of airline discount coupons).

4. Equitable relief has been granted in the form of long-term injunctions directing the desegregation of racially segregated schools, the improvement of prison conditions found to violate the Eighth Amendment ban on cruel and unusual punishment, the alteration of institutions for persons with mental disabilities in light of demonstrated statutory violations, and the redirection of public housing management found to violate statutory and constitutional guarantees. *See, e.g., Finney v. Hutto*, 410 F. Supp. 251 (E.D. Ark. 1976) (prison conditions); *Halderman v. Pennhurst State School and Hospital*, 673 F.2d 647 (3d Cir. 1982) (en banc) (mental hospital); *Perez v. Boston Housing Authority*, 379 U.S. 703 (1980) (public housing); *Swann v. Charlotte-Mecklenburg Board of Education*, 402 U.S. 1 (1971) (school desegregation). These injunctive orders often are very specific, indicating, for example, how the defendants should assign and transport students and teachers to schools; how patients should be evaluated and treated; how health and safety standards in housing should be devised and administered; and what resources should be available to individual prisoners. Courts also have ordered and directed the clean-up of polluted waters; *see* Charles Haar, *Boston Harbor: A Case Study*, 19 B.C. Envtl. Aff. L. Rev. 641 (1992); courts have also redirected public funds to promote racial and class integration in suburbs, not just in urban areas; *see* David Kirp, John Dwyer, and Larry Rosenthal, *Our Town: Race, Housing, and the Soul of Suburbia* (1996). To assist a court in monitoring the implementation of such orders, judges have exercised their authority to appoint judicial officers, such as masters or monitors. *See* Fed. R. Civ. P. 53.

5. Settlement of lawsuits that seek injunctive relief can produce *consent decrees*, which are settlements negotiated by parties but approved and enforced by the court which retains jurisdiction over the dispute. *See* Larry Kramer, *Consent Decrees and the Rights of Third Parties,* 87 Mich. L. Rev. 321 (1988). This form of dispute resolution resembles both a private contract and a court judgment. It is often used to terminate public law and institutional reform litigation where the goal is to ensure enforcement of a statute or government regulation, such as antitrust and employment discrimination regulations. Although the terms of the consent decree must be approved by the court, the parties contribute language, ideas, and voluntary compliance to the process. Violations of either kind of consent decree can trigger judicial enforcement through contempt hearings and sanctions. A court may approve a consent decree after finding liability or violation by the defendant; alternatively, the parties may propose and the judge may approve a consent decree prior to such a finding. This flexibility promotes settlement, but also may prompt questions about the use of judicial resources to enforce a privately constructed settlement. *See* Jeremy A. Ralkin and Neal E. Devins, *Averting Government by Consent Decree: Constitutional Limits on the Enforcement of Settlements with the Federal Government,* 40 Stan. L. Rev. 203 (1987).

What difference would it make — to the parties and to the public — for a court to enforce a consent decree right after the suit is filed, compared with one produced after the introduction of massive evidence at trial? *See United States v. American Telephone and Telegraph Co.,* 522 F Supp. 131 (D.D.C. 1982). The Supreme Court has addressed further questions about consent decrees, such as the binding of third parties and the circumstances permitting modification. *See Martin v. Wilks,* 490 U.S. 755 (1989) (effect on third parties); *Rufo v. Inmates of the Suffolk County Jail,* 502 U.S. 367 (1992) (modification permitted in light of significant change in facts or law warranting suitably tailored revision).

6. What role does a judge play in crafting the elements of equitable relief — and does this task draw the judge beyond the conventional role assigned in the adversary system? Debates over judicial action in cases yielding complex injunctions appear in both scholarship and the popular media. *See, e.g.,* Derrick Bell, *The Dialectics of School Desegregation,* 32 Ala. L. Rev. 281 (1981); Colin Diver, *The Judge as Political Powerbroker: Superintending Structural Change in Public Institutions,* 65 Va. L. Rev. 43 (1979); Owen Fiss, *The Forms of Justice,* 93 Harv. L. Rev. 1 (1979).

Practice Exercise No. 3: Equitable Relief in
Carpenter and *City of Cleveland*

Equitable remedies, including injunctions and declaratory relief, combine with money damages to create the range of possible remedies available in a lawsuit. How does a plaintiff come to know what relief to seek? It helps to consult a lawyer to learn about what relief might be available and in what scope. The lawyer, in turn, will investigate relevant case law, assess probabilities of success in the litigation, and estimate the costs of litigation. But even before this kind of investigation, the lawyer's counsel about the contrasts among equitable and damage remedies can help a client clarify goals and choices. It is this kind of advice that you should try to develop in this exercise in the context of two situations, both of which became real cases. These two cases will recur throughout this book to show unfolding stages of litigation and decision points for lawyers and clients. As you read the following descriptions, keep in mind the difference between the types of final relief that may be sought in each case. Imagine that the plaintiff(s) in each case have asked you what kind of relief they could obtain if they prevail in their lawsuits. What would you tell them?

1. The *Carpenter* Case: Nancy Carpenter wants to file a suit in Massachusetts following the death of her husband, Charles Carpenter, who was a passenger in a Jeep CJ-7. Randall Dee was driving the jeep at the time of the fatal accident. Dee allegedly lost control of the jeep, and it rolled over, pinning Charles Carpenter under the vehicle and killing him. Dee could have been acting recklessly in at least the following acts and omissions: speeding, failing to stop at an intersection, and modifying the jeep with the use of a suspension lift kit and hugely oversized tires. At the time of the incident, the jeep was owned by Twyla Burell, the ex-girlfirend of Randall Dee. Burell maintained a minimum liability insurance policy on the jeep, worth a total of $10,000. You have not yet had the jeep inspected.

Apparently, Randall Dee is not a wealthy man. He is unmarried and lives with his brother in a house they bought from the estate of their deceased father. Randall Dee's interest in the home may be his only substantial asset.

2. The *City of Cleveland* Case: A group of women believe they have faced sex discrimination in recruitment, training, testing, hiring, and employment practices affecting firefighters at the Cleveland, Ohio, Fire Department. They may have claims under federal civil rights statutes: Title VII (deprivation of employment opportunities on the basis of sex) and under the United States Constitution (equal protection). The defendants are likely to be the City of Cleveland, the officers and members of the Civil Service Commission of Cleveland, and the Fire Chief.

Given their claims, what would you tell each client about potential equitable relief? Assume that the Federal Rules of Civil Procedure or identical state rules apply; you may want to re-read Fed. R. Civ. P. 65. What kinds of injunctions could be available—and how would they redress the plaintiffs' injuries? Is there any way to indicate that monetary damages would be inadequate, and that therefore equitable relief would be in order?

2. Enforcement of Equitable Relief

Sometimes described as "the least dangerous branch," courts lack police or other direct resources to ensure enforcement of their rulings. Thus, even when a plaintiff wins and a court renders a final judgment, the dispute may not be over. First, the claimant needs a document, which is entitled a judgment, Fed. R. Civ. P. 58. *See also* Fed. R. Civ. P. 54(a) ("judgment" in federal court applies to decrees including equitable decrees). Executing or enforcing that judgment, where the defendant does not comply voluntarily, can lead to further proceedings. Under Fed. R. Civ. P. 70, the court can enforce some equitable decrees by appointing a person to engage in the required behavior (such as conveying title to property) at the cost of the disobedient party.

If the recalcitrant defendant fails to comply with an equitable order (Fed. R. Civ. P. 70), the court—at its own motion or at the request of the plaintiff—may hold contempt proceedings. Civil contempt proceedings are brought by the dissatisfied party trying to enforce the court order and are conducted according to the rules of civil procedure, but in a more summary fashion. They can entail either an order to pay the plaintiff for damage done by failure to comply with the original order or a penalty for failure to comply, including fines and imprisonment. (Of course, imposing fines is somewhat strange as a response for failure to comply with an equitable order, since equitable relief itself is available only if money damages would be inadequate.)

In criminal contempt proceedings, based on government prosecutions of the original defendant under a reasonable doubt standard, the court may punish disobedience through fines or imprisonment; the focus is less enforcement of the original order or redressing the plaintiff's wrong than ensuring respect for the court. To be frank, the distinction between criminal and civil contempt remains unclear; the Supreme Court has called this area of law a "hodge-podge," and for good reason. *United States v. United Mine Workers*, 330 U.S. 258, 364 (1971). More about the law of contempt follows later in this chapter.

3. Damages

Stemming from law rather than equity, the remedy of money damages poses often difficult questions of valuation. How much money does a specific legal violation warrant? Consider the following case.

■ CAREY v. PIPHUS
435 U.S. 247 (1978)

Justice POWELL delivered the opinion of the Court:

In this case, brought under 42 U.S.C. §1983, we consider the elements and prerequisites for recovery of damages by students who were suspended from public elementary and secondary schools without procedural due process. The Court of Appeals for the Seventh Circuit held that the students are entitled to recover substantial nonpunitive damages even if their suspensions were justified, and even if they do not prove that any other actual injury was caused by the denial of procedural due process. We disagree, and hold that in the absence of proof of actual injury, the students are entitled to recover only nominal damages.

I

Respondent Jarius Piphus was a freshman at Chicago Vocational High School during the 1973-1974 school year. On January 23, 1974, during school hours, the school principal saw Piphus and another student standing outdoors on school property passing back and forth what the principal described as an irregularly shaped cigarette. The principal approached the students unnoticed and smelled what he believed was the strong odor of burning marihuana. He also saw Piphus try to pass a packet of cigarette papers to the other student. When the students became aware of the principal's presence, they threw the cigarette into a nearby hedge.

The principal took the students to the school's disciplinary office and directed the assistant principal to impose the "usual" 20-day suspension for violation of the school rule against the use of drugs. The students protested that they had not been smoking marihuana, but to no avail. Piphus was allowed to remain at school, although not in class, for the remainder of the school day while the assistant principal tried, without success, to reach his mother. . . .

A suspension notice was sent to Piphus' mother, and a few days later two meetings were arranged among Piphus, his mother, his sister, school officials, and representatives from a legal aid clinic. The purpose of the meetings was not to determine whether Piphus had been smoking marihuana, but rather to explain the reasons for the suspension. Following an unfruitful exchange of views, Piphus and his mother, as guardian ad litem, filed suit against petitioners in Federal District Court under 42 U.S.C. §1983 and its jurisdictional counterpart, 28 U.S.C. §1343, charging that Piphus had been suspended without due process of law in violation of the Fourteenth Amendment. The complaint sought declaratory and injunctive relief, together with actual and punitive damages in the amount of $3,000. Piphus was readmitted to school under a temporary restraining order after eight days of his suspension.

Respondent Silas Brisco was in the sixth grade at Clara Barton Elementary School in Chicago during the 1973-1974 school year. On September 11, 1973, Brisco came to school wearing one small earring. The previous school year the school principal had issued a rule against the wearing of earrings by male students because he believed that this practice denoted membership in certain street gangs and increased the likelihood that gang members would terrorize other students. Brisco was reminded of this rule, but he refused to remove the earring, asserting that it was a symbol of black pride, not of gang membership.

The assistant principal talked to Brisco's mother, advising her that her son would be suspended for 20 days if he did not remove the earring. Brisco's mother supported her son's position, and a 20-day suspension was imposed. Brisco and his mother, as guardian ad litem, filed suit in Federal District Court under 42 U.S.C. §1983 and 28 U.S.C. §1343, charging that Brisco had been suspended without due process of law in violation of the Fourteenth Amendment. The complaint sought declaratory and injunctive relief, together with actual and punitive damages in the amount of $5,000. Brisco was readmitted to school during the pendency of proceedings for a preliminary injunction after 17 days of his suspension.

Piphus' and Brisco's cases were consolidated for trial and submitted on stipulated records. The District Court held that both students had been suspended without procedural due process. It also held that petitioners were not entitled to qualified immunity from damages under the second branch of *Wood v. Strickland*, 420 U.S. 308 (1975), because they "should have known that a lengthy suspension without any adjudicative hearing of any type" would violate procedural due process. . . . Despite these holdings, the District Court declined to award damages because: "Plaintiffs put no evidence in the record to qualify their damages, and the record is completely devoid of any evidence which could even form the basis of a speculative inference measuring the extent of their injuries. Plaintiffs' claims for damages therefore fail for complete lack of proof."

The court also stated that the students were entitled to declaratory relief and to deletion of the suspensions from their school records, but for reasons that are not apparent the court failed to enter an order to that effect. Instead, it simply dismissed the complaints. No finding was made as to whether respondents would have been suspended if they had received procedural due process.

On respondents' appeal, the Court of Appeals reversed and remanded. It first held that the District Court erred in not granting declaratory and injunctive relief. It also held that the District Court should have considered evidence submitted by respondents after judgment that tended to prove the pecuniary value of each day of school that they missed while suspended. The court said, however, that respondents would not be entitled to recover damages representing the value of missed school time if petitioners showed on remand "that there was just cause for the suspension[s] and that therefore [respondents] would have been suspended even if a proper hearing had been held."

Finally, the Court of Appeals held that even if the District Court found on remand that respondents' suspensions were justified, they would be entitled to recover substantial "nonpunitive" damages simply because they had been denied procedural due process. *Id.*, at 31. Relying on its earlier decision in *Hostrop v. Board of Junior College Dist. No. 515*, 523 F.2d 569 (7th Cir. 1975), *cert. denied*, 425 U.S. 963 (1976), the court stated that such damages should be awarded "even if, as in the case at bar, there is no proof of individualized injury to the plaintiff, such as mental distress. . . ." 545 F.2d, at 31. We granted certiorari to consider whether, in an action under §1983 for the deprivation of procedural due process, a plaintiff must prove that he actually was injured by the deprivation before he may recover substantial "nonpunitive" damages. 430 U.S. 964 (1977).

II

Title 42 U.S.C. §1983, Rev. Stat. §1979, derived from §1 of the Civil Rights Act of 1871, 17 Stat. 13, provides:

> Every person who, under color of any statute, ordinance, regulation, custom, or usage, of any State or Territory, subjects, or causes to be subjected, any citizen of the United States or other person within the jurisdiction thereof to the deprivation of any rights, privileges, or immunities secured by the Constitution and laws, shall be liable to the party injured in an action at law, suit in equity, or other proper proceeding for redress.

The legislative history of §1983, elsewhere detailed, *e.g.*, *Monroe v. Pape*, 365 U.S. 167, 172-183 (1961); *id.*, at 225-234 (Frankfurter, J., dissenting in part), demonstrates that it was intended to "[create] a species of tort liability" in favor of persons who are deprived of "rights, privileges, or immunities secured" to them by the Constitution.

Petitioners contend that the elements and prerequisites for recovery of damages under this "species of tort liability" should parallel those for recovery of damages under the common law of torts. In particular, they urge that the purpose of an award of damages under §1983 should be to compensate persons for injuries that are caused by the deprivation of constitutional rights; and, further, that plaintiffs should be required to prove not only that their rights were violated, but also that injury was caused by the violation, in order to recover substantial damages. Unless respondents prove that they actually were injured by the deprivation of procedural due process, petitioners argue, they are entitled at most to nominal damages.

Respondents seem to make two different arguments in support of the holding below. First, they contend that substantial damages should be awarded under §1983 for the deprivation of a constitutional right whether or not any injury was caused by the deprivation. This, they say, is appropriate both because constitutional rights are valuable in and of themselves, and because of the need to deter violations of constitutional rights. Respondents believe that this view reflects accurately that of the Congress that enacted §1983. Second, respondents argue that even if the purpose of a §1983 damages award is, as petitioners contend, primarily to compensate persons for injuries that are caused by the deprivation of constitutional rights, every deprivation of procedural due process may be presumed to cause some injury. This presumption, they say, should relieve them from the necessity of proving that injury actually was caused.

A

Insofar as petitioners contend that the basic purpose of a §1983 damages award should be to compensate persons for injuries caused by the deprivation of constitutional rights, they have the better of the argument. Rights, constitutional and otherwise, do not exist in a vacuum. Their purpose is to protect persons from injuries to particular interests, and their contours are shaped by the interests they protect. . . .

The Members of the Congress that enacted §1983 did not address directly the question of damages, but the principle that damages are designed to compensate persons for injuries caused by the deprivation of rights hardly could have been foreign to the many lawyers in Congress in 1871. Two other sections of the Civil Rights Act of 1871 appear to incorporate this principle, and no reason suggests itself for reading §1983 differently. To the extent that Congress intended that awards under §1983 should deter the deprivation of constitutional rights, there is no evidence that it meant to establish a deterrent more formidable than that inherent in the award of compensatory damages.[10]

B

It is less difficult to conclude that damages awards under §1983 should be governed by the principle of compensation than it is to apply this principle to concrete cases. But over the centuries the common law of torts has developed a set of rules to implement the principle that a person

---

10. This is not to say that exemplary or punitive damages might not be awarded in a proper case under §1983 with the specific purpose of deterring or punishing violations of constitutional rights. [The Court cited several lower court decisions upholding punitive awards in §1983 cases.] Although we imply no approval or disapproval of any of these cases, we note that there is no basis for such an award in this case. The District Court specifically found that petitioners did not act with malicious intention to deprive respondents of their rights or to do them other injury, and the Court of Appeals approved only the award of "nonpunitive" damages.

We also note that the potential for liability of §1983 defendants for attorney's fees, *see* Civil Rights Attorney's Fees Awards Act of 1976, 42 U.S.C. §1988, provides additional—and by no means inconsequential—assurance that agents of the State will not deliberately ignore due process rights.

should be compensated fairly for injuries caused by the violation of his legal rights. These rules, defining the elements of damages and the prerequisites for their recovery, provide the appropriate starting point for the inquiry under § 1983 as well.

It is not clear, however, that common-law tort rules of damages will provide a complete solution to the damages issue in every § 1983 case. In some cases, the interests protected by a particular branch of the common law of torts may parallel closely the interests protected by a particular constitutional right. In such cases, it may be appropriate to apply the tort rules of damages directly to the § 1983 action. In other cases, the interests protected by a particular constitutional right may not also be protected by an analogous branch of the common law torts. In those cases, the task will be the more difficult one of adapting common-law rules of damages to provide fair compensation for injuries caused by the deprivation of a constitutional right.

Although this task of adaptation will be one of some delicacy—as this case demonstrates—it must be undertaken. The purpose of § 1983 would be defeated if injuries caused by the deprivation of constitutional rights went uncompensated simply because the common law does not recognize an analogous cause of action. . . .

C

The Due Process Clause of the Fourteenth Amendment provides: "[N]or shall any State deprive any person of life, liberty, or property, without due process of law. . . ." This Clause "raises no impenetrable barrier to the taking of a person's possessions," or liberty, or life. *Fuentes v. Shevin*, 407 U.S. 67, 81 (1972). Procedural due process rules are meant to protect persons not from the deprivation, but from the mistaken or unjustified deprivation of life, liberty, or property. Thus, in deciding what process constitutionally is due in various contexts, the Court repeatedly has emphasized that "procedural due process rules are shaped by the risk of error inherent in the truth-finding process. . . ."

In this case, the Court of Appeals held that if petitioners can prove on remand that "[respondents] would have been suspended even if a proper hearing had been held," 545 F.2d, at 32, then respondents will not be entitled to recover damages to compensate them for injuries caused by the suspensions. The court thought that in such a case, the failure to accord procedural due process could not properly be viewed as the cause of the suspensions. The court suggested that in such circumstances, an award of damages for injuries caused by the suspensions would constitute a windfall, rather than compensation, to respondents. 545 F.2d at 32. We do not understand the parties to disagree with this conclusion. Nor do we.

The parties do disagree as to the further holding of the Court of Appeals that respondents are entitled to recover substantial—although unspecified—damages to compensate them for "the injury which is 'inherent in the nature of the wrong,'" 545 F.2d, at 31, even if their suspensions were justified and even if they fail to prove that the denial of procedural due process actually caused them some real, if intangible, injury. Respondents, elaborating on this theme, submit that the holding is correct because injury fairly may be "presumed" to flow from every denial of procedural due process. Their argument is that in addition to protecting against unjustified deprivations, the Due Process Clause also guarantees the "feeling of just treatment" by the government. *Anti-Fascist Committee v. McGrath*, 341 U.S. 123, 162 (1951) (Frankfurter, J., concurring). They contend that the deprivation of protected interests without procedural due process, even where the premise for the deprivation is not erroneous, inevitably arouses strong feelings of mental and emotional distress in the individual who is denied this "feeling of just treatment." They analogize their case to that of defamation per se, in which "the plaintiff is relieved from the necessity of producing any proof whatsoever that he has been injured" in order to recover substantial compensatory damages. C. McCormick, *Law of Damages* §116 at 423 (1935).

. . . Petitioners' argument is . . . that such injury cannot be presumed to occur, and that plaintiffs at least should be put to their proof on the issue, as plaintiffs are in most tort actions.

We agree with petitioners in this respect. As we have observed in another context, the doctrine of presumed damages in the common law of defamation per se "is an oddity of tort law, for it allows recovery of purportedly compensatory damages without evidence of actual loss." The doctrine has been defended on the grounds that those forms of defamation that are actionable per se are virtually certain to cause serious injury to reputation, and that this kind of injury is extremely difficult to prove. Moreover, statements that are defamatory per se by their very nature are likely to cause mental and emotional distress, as well as injury to reputation, so there arguably is little reason to require proof of this kind of injury either. But these considerations do not support respondents' contention that damages should be presumed to flow from every deprivation of procedural due process. . . .

First, it is not reasonable to assume that every departure from procedural due process, no matter what the circumstances or how minor, inherently is as likely to cause distress as the publication of defamation per se is to cause injury to reputation and distress. . . .

Moreover, where a deprivation is justified but procedures are deficient, whatever distress a person feels may be attributable to the justified deprivation rather than to deficiencies in procedure. But as the Court of Appeals held, the injury caused by a justified deprivation, including distress, is not properly compensable under §1983. This ambiguity in causation, which is absent in the case of defamation per se, provides additional need for requiring the plaintiff to convince the trier of fact that he actually suffered distress because of the denial of procedural due process itself.

Finally, we foresee no particular difficulty in producing evidence that mental and emotional distress actually was caused by the denial of procedural due process itself. . . . In sum, then, although mental and emotional distress caused by the denial of procedural due process itself is compensable under §1983, we hold that neither the likelihood of such injury nor the difficulty of proving it is so great as to justify awarding compensatory damages without proof that such injury actually was caused. . . .

Because the right to procedural due process is "absolute" in the sense that it does not depend upon the merits of a claimant's substantive assertions, and because of the importance to organized society that procedural due process be observed, *see Boddie v. Connecticut*, 401 U.S. 371, 375 (1971); *Anti-Fascist Committee v. McGrath*, 341 U.S. at 171-172 (Frankfurter, J., concurring), we believe that the denial of procedural due process should be actionable for nominal damages without proof of actual injury. We therefore hold that if, upon remand, the District Court determines that respondents' suspensions were justified, respondents nevertheless will be entitled to recover nominal damages not to exceed one dollar from petitioners.

The judgment of the Court of Appeals is reversed, and the case is remanded for further proceedings consistent with this opinion.

Comments and Questions

1. How do you read the opinion's decision to approve only nominal damages? Does this suggest that due process is not worth very much in financial terms, or that deterrence of due process violations should be secured through means other than the threat of money damages? How does footnote 10 bear on this issue? Under what circumstances could the plaintiffs have obtained more than nominal damages for a due process violation?

2. If you served as counsel to a school board after this decision, what guidelines would you advise for designing procedures for school suspensions?

3. Valuations problems arise even where damages are sought for harm to a building or piece of land. Thus, in *Trinity Church in the City of Boston v. John Hancock Mutual Life Ins. Co.*, 399 Mass. 43 (Mass. 1987), the Church claimed that the life insurance company and other defendants caused structural damage to the church building while constructing the John Hancock Tower Building; the construction caused physical settlement, which in turn undermined the structural integrity of the church building. For relief, the plaintiff sought to recover the cost of repairing the interior and exterior of the church, as well as compensation for the

structural damage. Fair market value, the usual measure of damages, proved unavailing. The court therefore considered using the cost of reproduction less depreciation, and ruled in favor of replacement or restoration costs. *Id.* at 51. *See also Peevyhouse v. Garland Coal Mining Co.*, 382 P.2d 109 (Okla. 1962), *cert. denied,* 375 U.S. 906 (1963) (measure of damages to land from stripmining normally would be cost of restoration unless economic waste would result; here, recovery is to be measured by diminution of market value).

4. Punitive Damages

Under the traditional common law approach, compensatory damages seek to return the plaintiff to the position he or she enjoyed prior to the harm. Sometimes, further monetary relief seems appropriate to deter future wrongful conduct and to express public disapproval of the injuring behavior. The common law thus developed *punitive damages,* typically left to the jury to assess, based on "the gravity of the wrong and the need to deter similar wrongful conduct." *Pacific Mutual Life Insurance Co. v. Haslip,* 499 U.S. 1(1991). That jury determination would in turn be reviewed by the trial and appellate courts under a standard of reasonableness. In recent years, reformers have argued that punitive damage awards are increasing in frequency, amounts, and unpredictability. *See generally* Cass R. Sunstein, Daniel Kahneman, and David Schkade, *Assessing Punitive Damages,* 107 Yale L.J. 2071 (1998). Others respond that the problems have been much overstated and reflect faulty generalizations from a few outlying cases. *See, e.g.,* Geoffrey T. Miller, *Behind the Battle Lines: A Comparative Analysis of the Necessity to Enact Comprehensive Federal Products Liability Reforms,* 45 Buffalo L. Rev. 241 (1997); Product Liability Fairness Act, 1995: Hearings on S. 565 Before the Subcomm. On Consumer Affairs, Foreign Commerce, and Tourism, 104th Cong. 505 (1995) (testimony of Dr. Stephen Daniels, Senior Research Fellow, American Bar Foundation). Similar debates surround the use of punitive damages in the context of arbitration. *See* Stuart C. Goldberg, 1991 Report of the Public Investors Arbitration Bar Association As to the Authority of Arbitrators to Award Punitive Damages in Securities Arbitration, 1991 Pub. Investors Arb. B. Assn. 1. Besides generating legislative proposals, the debate over punitive damages has inspired a search by litigants for federal constitutional authority to limit the scope of punitive damages. The Court has rejected claims that the Excessive Fines Clause of the Eighth Amendment sets a limit on punitive damages, *Browning-Ferris Industries of Vermont v. Kelco Disposal, Inc.,* 492 U.S. 257 (1989), but has concluded that the Due Process Clause of the Fourteenth Amendment could, in certain cases, limit jury and judicial discretion in this area. *Pacific Mutual Life Insurance Co. v. Haslip, supra.*

In *Honda Motor Co. v. Oberg*, 512 U.S. 415 (1994), the Supreme Court found a procedural defect in an Oregon rule prohibiting judicial review of the jury's award of punitive damages unless the court could affirmatively say there is no evidence for the verdict. After reviewing eighteenth and nineteenth century English and American cases addressing excessive damages, the Court reasoned that judicial review has long been an important part of the process of awarding punitive damages. Oregon's constitutional provision to the contrary departs from tradition and thus presumptively violates due process without adequate substitutes to guard against arbitrary awards. Justice Ginsburg, joined by Chief Justice Rehnquist, dissented, not from the idea that due process should restrict punitive damage procedures, but from the application of due process to the Oregon context. *Id.*

However, in *BMW v. Gore*, 517 U.S. 559 (1996), the Court rejected a punitive damages award in Alabama despite the state court's adherence to the procedural safeguard of judicial review. The Court found the award of punitive damages "grossly excessive," and, therefore, a violation of Fourteenth Amendment due process. Dr. Ira Gore sued the auto distributor, BMW of North America, for fraud after discovering that the $40,000 new auto he had purchased from an authorized dealer had been repainted; BMW admitted a nationwide nondisclosure policy on its routine practice of repairing and repainting damaged new cars where the damage amounted to less than 3 percent of the car's total value. An Alabama jury found BMW liable for $4,000 diminution in value to Gore's car, then imposed $4 million in punitive damages, calculated by multiplying Gore's $4,000 in damages by the approximate number of undisclosed repaintings nationwide. The Alabama Supreme Court reduced the award to $2 million after concluding that the jury had erred in including in its calculations BMW's acts outside the jurisdiction.

Writing for the majority, Justice Stevens, who also had written the majority opinion in *Honda*, found the $2 million punitive damages grossly excessive in light of the state's legitimate interests in punishing and deterring illegal conduct within the state. The Court identified three "guideposts" to clarify what constitutes unconstitutional excessiveness in punitive damage awards. Most important is (1) How reprehensible is the defendant's conduct? Less important, but also relevant are (2) the ratio of the award to the actual or potential harm inflicted and (3) a comparison of the award to civil or criminal penalties that could be imposed for comparable misconduct. The Court found BMW's conduct not reprehensible because it only involved monetary loss, it reflected a reasonable effort to comport with uninterpreted state statutes, and it ceased upon a finding of unlawfulness. Noting that no "mathematical bright line" could demarcate constitutionality, the Court found the 500 to 1 ratio of award to damages excessive in light of precedents and reason and when compared with comparable legislatively created sanctions. A concurring opinion by Justice Breyer cited procedural defects in the Alabama judicial review of punitive awards. Dissenting opinions by Justices Scalia and Ginsburg expressed concern about this federal intrusion into state law.

Not long thereafter, in *Gasperini v. Center for Humanities, Inc.*, 518 U.S. 415 (1996), the Supreme Court, by a vote of five to four, approved a federal court's application of a New York State procedure empowering appellate courts to review jury verdicts under a reasonableness standard. Because the federal district court was sitting in diversity, it properly could apply a state legal standard of this nature with no injury to the federally guaranteed right to a jury trial.

Comments and Questions

1. States rights arguments are invoked both by justices who support due process review of punitive damages and by those who oppose it. How can this be?

2. How do you assess Justice Scalia's dissenting view, in *BMW*, that the Fourteenth Amendment affords "an opportunity to contest the reasonableness of a damages judgment in state court; but [not a] federal guarantee [that] a damages award actually be reasonable"? *BMW, supra,* at 68.

3. Assess the Court's three guideposts for constitutional review of punitive damages awards. How do you think lower courts will interpret it? Would a bright-line rule be better, and can you articulate such a rule?

4. What kind of proof and what legal standard are needed for punitive damages? In typical common law cases, the moving party must show that the defendant acted egregiously, and usually this involves acting with malice or with reckless or callous indifference. The interaction between this standard and an underlying claim that itself requires demonstration of defendant's intention or state of mind can be very complex. Recently ruling in *Kolstad v. American Dental Assn.*, 119 S. Ct. 2118 (1999), the Supreme Court held that although a plaintiff may seek punitive damages in a Title VII employment discrimination case, success in proving intentional discrimination does not itself guarantee evidence to support punitive damages. The Court rejected a standard of egregiousness and approved the standard of malice or reckless or callous indifference for demonstrating a basis for punitive damages. The Court also ruled that common law agency principles would limit liability on supervisors or the entire entity for conduct by individuals that might itself justify punitive damages.

Practice Exercise No. 4: Damages in *Carpenter* and *City of Cleveland*

Imagine that the *Carpenter* and *City of Cleveland* plaintiffs have asked you to predict the scope of damages they could receive if they prevailed in their claims.

1. What damages would be available for Nancy Carpenter, the plaintiff in the jeep case? If she was pregnant at the time her husband, Charles, was killed, could this affect her damages? If Charles did not die instantly, but instead remained conscious for minutes or hours after the accident, should this affect the level of damages awarded? Why or why not? Substantive tort law doctrine will govern these questions; even in the absence of full knowledge of torts, though, try to reason your way to the kinds of damages Nancy Carpenter could claim. What further information would you need to assess the value of her claims? What witnesses, including experts, would you need to establish such value(s) at trial?

2. What damages would be available to women plaintiffs who claim they were denied recruitment, training, testing, hiring, and employment opportunities at the Cleveland Fire Department?

5. *Enforcement of Damages*   **D P**

If the defendant refuses to pay money damages, the plaintiff must first be sure to obtain a judgment, which in federal court is described in Federal Rule 58. That judgment must be entered in the docket. Fed. R. Civ. P. 79(a); *see also* Forms 31 and 32 (at the end of the Federal Rules). The original judgment merely identifies the defendant's obligation to the plaintiff; it does not order payment (compared with an injunction, which directly orders conduct). Federal Rule 69 provides the process for enforcing a judgment for the payment of money. This involves a writ of execution, absent an alternative specified by the court or a relevant federal statute. Federal law does not provide many details of the enforcement process; therefore, the law of the state in which enforcement is sought will govern. State laws permit the use of proceedings to supplement or aid the enforcement of a judgment; these may include actions for garnishment of wages, contempt, and appointment of a receiver. Charles Alan Wright, Arthur R. Miller, and Richard Marcus, 12 *Federal Practice and Procedure* §3012 (West 1997).

To collect from a defendant who does not pay on his own initiative, the plaintiff (now called the judgment creditor because she is owed a sum by the defendant/judgment debtor) must initiate another legal proceeding. Some state statutes permit judgment creditors to obtain a lien on property by recording the judgment in a registry of deeds or in the location for filings under the Uniform Commercial Code. The judgment-creditor also can obtain a writ of execution for a piece of defendant's property, which authorizes the sheriff to seize the property, sell it—generally at public auction—and turn over the proceeds to the plaintiff. Through a discovery process, the plaintiff may even compel the defendant to disclose the location of assets to satisfy the judgment. Another option for the plaintiff is to execute the judgment against the income of the defendant, resulting in garnishment of wages if the defendant does not pay the installment as ordered. Even if assets exist or income exists, however, the plaintiff may have difficulty taking control of them. Many state statutes exempt certain property from liens so that the defendant can remain able to house, clothe, and feed his or her family; many statutes also limit wage garnishment. (It is worth asking, to what extent should due process "notice and right to be heard" principles apply to procedures to execute a final judgment?)

Other hurdles for the plaintiff include the sheltering effects of bankruptcy, under which the defendant's total assets may be outweighed by total debts, and the prioritization of creditors, which assures secured creditors, first dibs on the defendant's assets.

It may also be difficult or impossible to collect on a judgment because of a lack of assets owned by the judgment debtor, because assets are exempt, or because prior liens exist. Consequently, plaintiffs and their lawyers often try to locate defendants who have insurance or sufficient assets to pay a judgment without causing the plaintiff to spend additional money and time to collect.

D. ATTORNEYS' FEES AND THE ECONOMICS OF RELIEF

Technically, attorneys' fees are not a remedy but simply the professional's charge for services. The "American Rule" about attorneys' fees directs that each party pay his or her own attorney. Yet alterations of that rule—by statute, regulation, or judicial decision—have significant effects on lawyers' decisions to take a given case and whether to pursue or to settle it. Accordingly, courts can and do award attorneys' fees under relevant authorities, and this practice becomes inextricably tied to the availability and scope of remedies for plaintiffs. The connection between fees and remedies is also manifest in practices such as "contingency fee" arrangements, where an attorney agrees to represent a plaintiff in a tort suit for no fee other than a specified share (often one-third) of any victory in court or settlement. Judicial rules, ethical rules, and statutes governing fee arrangements and awards thus become crucial to an understanding of what litigation can bring to parties, and indeed, of how the American legal system operates.

1. Attorneys' Fees: The "American Rule"

Under the "American Rule," the losing party does not pay the prevailing party's attorneys' fees. As the name might imply, this is not the rule everywhere else. In England and much of Europe, for example, losers typically are required to pay the opposing lawyer's fees as well as their own lawyer's fees; costs follow victory. What differences emerge in practice under these rules?

Defenders of the American Rule maintain that it permits the poor, as well as the rich, to litigate. Poor folks would not otherwise be able to sue, the argument goes, because of the fear that if they lose they would have to pay the opponent's legal fees. Moreover, the American Rule encourages innovative claims, while the English rule directs plaintiffs, and their lawyers, to be more risk averse.

Advocates of the English Rule emphasize that it deters frivolous or marginal litigation and that it more fully compensates the prevailing party for the troubles of litigation. It is worth noting that in practice, the English Rule exempts cases where the losing party's lawyer is financed through legal aid, which, in turn, is available to low-income people. Also, in the English practice a taxing officer determines fees (for both solicitors and barristers) with reference to a fee schedule, which tends to run 60-70 percent of actual fees. Further, applications for taxation of costs may be made at points before the end of the litigation, such as the award of preliminary relief, and therefore fees may be awarded to a party that does not prevail in the end. In Germany, the losing party pays fees to the degree that the winning party was successful, or what may be known as "less-than-full" fee compensation. Thus, "if the remedy sought was payment of DM300,000, and if the plaintiff is successful only in relation to the amount of DM100,000, the plaintiff has to bear two-thirds of the costs." Peter F. Schlosser, *Lectures on Civil-Law Litigation Systems and American Cooperation With Those Systems,* 45 Kan. L. Rev. 9, 18 (1996). This rule deters plaintiffs from seeking enormous damages.

Fee rules also reflect other differences between the English and United States legal systems and cultures. England virtually abolished juries in civil cases (except for libel and malicious prosecution) over fifty years ago. Cases are tried before judges, whose decisions on damages as well as liability are narrowly bound by precedent. England does not have distinct sovereign states which apply their own common law rules. For all these reasons, outcomes tend to be more predictable in England than in the United States.

In contrast, the jury remains a vital part of the United States civil justice system, and a case that might seem marginal when filed may nonetheless persuade a jury. Moreover, substantive and procedural rules evolve rapidly and in varied directions across the 50 states, producing a more volatile and less precedent-bound legal world than in England. Propositions that might at one time have been thought highly speculative have become accepted law.

For a comparison of the two attorneys' fees models and an assessment of their probable impact on attorney conduct and results in particular cases, using economics to model the risk preferences of lawyers and their clients, *see* Steven Shavell, Suit, Settlement and Trial: A Theoretical Analysis Under Alternative Methods for the Allocation of Legal Costs, 11 J. Legal Stud. 55 (1982).

2. Fee-Shifting Statutes

Even at common law, the American Rule governing attorneys' fees had exceptions. The Supreme Court has concluded that when a party acts in "bad faith," courts have inherent authority to assess fees to reimburse the opposing party. Some courts have ruled that when a lawyer or litigant acts in a way that creates a "common fund" for the benefit of others, the resulting fund can be "taxed" for the fair value of the lawyer's work, to prevent a windfall to the beneficiaries. In the 1960s and 1970s, some lower federal courts adopted the theory that losing defendants could be ordered to pay plaintiffs' attorneys' fees where those plaintiffs acted as "private attorneys general." The Supreme Court rejected this theory in *Alyeska Pipeline Service Co. v. Wilderness Society*, 421 U.S. 240 (1975), and concluded that Congress, rather than the courts, should determine the kinds of cases warranting a fee shift. The Court recognized that a fee shift fundamentally provides an incentive to plaintiffs to file suit, an incentive to lawyers to represent those plaintiffs, and a deterrent to defendants at risk of such suits.

Congress responded to *Alyeska* by adopting the Civil Rights Attorney's Fees Act of 1976, 42 U.S.C. §1988. By 1995, Congress had included fee-shifting provisions in over 180 pieces of legislation that addressed topics ranging from environmental protection and civil rights to intellectual property and banking. *See, e.g.,* Clean Air Act Amendments of 1977, 42 U.S.C. §7622(e)(2); Equal Access to Justice Act, 28 U.S.C. §2412(b); Handicapped Children's Protection Act of 1988, 20 U.S.C. §1415(e)(4)(B); Violence Against Women Act of 1994, 108 Stat. 1796 §40303; Patent Infringement Act, 35 U.S.C. §285; Electronic Fund Transfer Act, 15 U.S.C. §§1693m(a) and (f). By creating monetary incentives for attorneys to pursue these and other claims, Congress intended to promote enforcement of selected federal statutory rights.

Yet unlike the English Rule, which directs that the loser pay the attorneys' fees of the opponent, many of these American statutes, as interpreted by the courts, provide only for shifting *prevailing* plaintiffs' fees to the defendants; a losing plaintiff is not obliged to pay the defendants' attorneys' fees. This pro-plaintiff, one-way shift structure encourages enforcement efforts without penalizing the unsuccessful plaintiff. Yet even under a statute with this structure, a court may order the plaintiff who brings a totally frivolous or groundless suit to pay the defendant's attorneys' fees. *See, e.g., Chirstianburg Garment Co. v. EEOC*, 434 U.S. 412 (1978) (interpreting Title VII). A similar result can occur under Fed. R. Civ. P. 11:

a court may order "payment of some or all of the reasonable attorneys' fees and other expenses" as a sanction for filing a pleading or motion without adequate inquiry, unwarranted by existing law or fact, or based on a frivolous argument for new law.

3. Attorneys' Fees and Settlement

As a monetary incentive and deterrent, attorneys' fees become part of the package of possibilities that influence settlement of lawsuits. If Congress authorizes attorneys' fees for a prevailing plaintiff, then the defendant must include the possible liability for plaintiff's attorneys' fees in the calculus of the costs and benefits of proceeding to trial, compared with the costs and benefits of settlement. Similarly, the plaintiff must consider the risk of losing not only on the merits, but also of foregoing attorneys' fees, in deciding whether to file initially, as well as whether to proceed or to settle. How should a statutory policy promoting certain kinds of lawsuits be reconciled with a judicial policy promoting settlement? When should the value of attorneys' fees themselves be on the bargaining table for settlement of a lawsuit? The following cases address these complex issues.

■ MAREK v. CHESNY
473 U.S. 1 (1985)

Chief Justice BURGER delivered the opinion of the Court:
We granted certiorari to decide whether attorney's fees incurred by a plaintiff subsequent to an offer of settlement under Federal Rule of Civil Procedure 68 must be paid by the defendant under 42 U.S.C. §1988, when the plaintiff recovers a judgment less than the offer.

I

Petitioners, three police officers, in answering a call on a domestic disturbance, shot and killed respondent's adult son. Respondent, in his own behalf and as administrator of his son's estate, filed suit against the officers in the United States District Court under 42 U.S.C. §1983 and state tort law.

Prior to trial, petitioners made a timely offer of settlement "for a sum, including costs now accrued and attorney's fees, of ONE HUNDRED THOUSAND ($100,000) DOLLARS." Respondent did not accept the offer. The case went to trial and respondent was awarded $5,000 on the state-law "wrongful death" claim, $52,000 for the §1983 violation, and $3,000 in punitive damages.

Respondent filed a request for $171,692.47 in costs, including attorney's fees. This amount included costs incurred after the settlement offer. Petitioners opposed the claim for postoffer costs, relying on Federal Rule of Civil Procedure 68, which shifts to the plaintiff all "costs" incurred subsequent to an offer of judgment not exceeded by the ultimate recovery at trial. Petitioners argued that attorney's fees are part of the "costs" covered by Rule 68. The District Court agreed with petitioners and declined to award respondent "costs, including attorney's fees, incurred after the offer of judgment." 547 F. Supp. 542, 547 (N.D. Ill. 1982). The parties subsequently agreed that $32,000 fairly represented the allowable costs, including attorney's fees, accrued prior to petitioners' offer of settlement. Respondent appealed the denial of postoffer costs.

The Court of Appeals reversed. The court rejected what it termed the "rather mechanical linking up of Rule 68 and section 1988." It stated that the District Court's reading of Rule 68 and § 1988, while "in a sense logical," would put civil rights plaintiffs and counsel in a "predicament" that "cuts against the grain of section 1988." Plaintiffs' attorneys, the court reasoned, would be forced to "think very hard" before rejecting even an inadequate offer, and would be deterred from bringing good-faith actions because of the prospect of losing the right to attorney's fees if a settlement offer more favorable than the ultimate recovery were rejected. The court concluded that "[t]he legislators who enacted section 1988 would not have wanted its effectiveness blunted because of a little known rule of court." We granted certiorari. We reverse.

II

Rule 68 provides that if a timely pretrial offer of settlement is not accepted and "the judgment finally obtained by the offeree is not more favorable than the offer, the offeree must pay the costs incurred after the making of the offer." The plain purpose of Rule 68 is to encourage settlement and avoid litigation. The Rule prompts both parties to a suit to evaluate the risks and costs of litigation, and to balance them against the likelihood of success upon trial on the merits. This case requires us to decide whether the offer in this case was a proper one under Rule 68, and whether the term "costs" as used in Rule 68 includes attorney's fees awardable under 42 U.S.C. §1988.

. . . [Does] the term "costs" in Rule 68 include[] attorney's fees awardable under 42 U.S.C. §1988[?] By the time the Federal Rules of Civil Procedure were adopted in 1938, federal statutes had authorized and defined awards of costs to prevailing parties for more than 85 years. *See* Act of Feb. 26, 1853, 10 Stat. 161; *see generally Alyeska Pipeline Service Co. v. Wilderness Society*, 421 U.S. 240 (1975). Unlike in England, such "costs" generally had not included attorney's fees; under the "American Rule," each party had been required to bear its own attorney's fees. The

"American Rule" as applied in federal courts, however, had become subject to certain exceptions by the late 1930's. Some of these exceptions had evolved as a product of the "inherent power in the courts to allow attorney's fees in particular situations." *Alyeska, supra*, at 259. . . .

The authors of Federal Rule of Civil Procedure 68 were fully aware of these exceptions to the American Rule. The Advisory Committee's Note to Rule 54(d), 28 U.S.C. App., p. 621, contains an extensive list of the federal statutes which allowed for costs in particular cases; of the 35 "statutes as to costs" set forth in the final paragraph of the Note, no fewer than 11 allowed for attorney's fees as part of costs. Against this background of varying definitions of "costs," the drafters of Rule 68 did not define the term; nor is there any explanation whatever as to its intended meaning in the history of the Rule.

In this setting, given the importance of "costs" to the Rule, it is very unlikely that this omission was mere oversight; on the contrary, the most reasonable inference is that the term "costs" in Rule 68 was intended to refer to all costs properly awardable under the relevant substantive statute or other authority. In other words, all costs properly awardable in an action are to be considered within the scope of Rule 68 "costs." Thus, absent congressional expressions to the contrary, where the underlying statute defines "costs" to include attorney's fees, we are satisfied such fees are to be included as costs for purposes of Rule 68. . . .

Here, respondent sued under 42 U.S.C. §1983. Pursuant to the Civil Rights Attorney's Fees Awards Act of 1976, 90 Stat. 2641, as amended, 42 U.S.C. §1988, a prevailing party in a §1983 action may be awarded attorney's fees "as part of the costs." Since Congress expressly included attorney's fees as "costs" available to a plaintiff in a §1983 suit, such fees are subject to the cost-shifting provision of Rule 68. This "plain meaning" interpretation of the interplay between Rule 68 and §1988 is the only construction that gives meaning to each word in both Rule 68 and §1988.

Unlike the Court of Appeals, we do not believe that this "plain meaning" construction of the statute and the Rule will frustrate Congress' objective in §1988 of ensuring that civil rights plaintiffs obtain "'effective access to the judicial process.'" *Hensley v. Eckerhart*, 461 U.S. 424, 429 (1983), *quoting* H.R. Rep. No. 94-1558, p. 1 (1976). Merely subjecting civil rights plaintiffs to the settlement provision of Rule 68 does not curtail their access to the courts, or significantly deter them from bringing suit. Application of Rule 68 will serve as a disincentive for the plaintiff's attorney to continue litigation after the defendant makes a settlement offer. There is no evidence, however, that Congress, in considering §1988, had any thought that civil rights claims were to be on any different footing from other civil claims insofar as settlement is concerned. Indeed, Congress made clear its concern that civil rights plaintiffs not be penalized for "helping to lessen docket congestion" by settling their cases out of court. . . .

Moreover, Rule 68's policy of encouraging settlements is neutral, favoring neither plaintiffs nor defendants; it expresses a clear policy of favoring settlement of all lawsuits. Civil rights plaintiffs—along with other plaintiffs—who reject an offer more favorable than what is thereafter recovered at trial will not recover attorney's fees for services performed after the offer is rejected. But, since the Rule is neutral, many civil rights plaintiffs will benefit from the offers of settlement encouraged by Rule 68. . . .

To be sure, application of Rule 68 will require plaintiffs to "think very hard" about whether continued litigation is worthwhile; that is precisely what Rule 68 contemplates. This effect of Rule 68, however, is in no sense inconsistent with the congressional policies underlying §1983 and §1988. Section 1988 authorizes courts to award only "reasonable" attorney's fees to prevailing parties. In *Hensley v. Eckerhart, supra,* we held that "the most critical factor" in determining a reasonable fee "is the degree of success obtained." *Id.,* at 436. We specifically noted that prevailing at trial "may say little about whether the expenditure of counsel's time was reasonable in relation to the success achieved." *Ibid.* In a case where a rejected settlement offer exceeds the ultimate recovery, the plaintiff—although technically the prevailing party—has not received any monetary benefits from the postoffer services of his attorney. This case presents a good example: the $139,692 in postoffer legal services resulted in a recovery $8,000 less than petitioners' settlement offer. Given Congress' focus on the success achieved, we are not persuaded that shifting the postoffer costs to respondent in these circumstances would in any sense thwart its intent under §1988.

Rather than "cutting against the grain" of §1988, as the Court of Appeals held, we are convinced that applying Rule 68 in the context of a §1983 action is consistent with the policies and objectives of §1988. Section 1988 encourages plaintiffs to bring meritorious civil rights suits; Rule 68 simply encourages settlements. There is nothing incompatible in these two objectives.

III

Congress, of course, was well aware of Rule 68 when it enacted §1988, and included attorney's fees as part of recoverable costs. The plain language of Rule 68 and §1988 subjects such fees to the cost-shifting provision of Rule 68. Nothing revealed in our review of the policies underlying §1988 constitutes "the necessary clear expression of congressional intent" required "to exempt . . . [the] statute from the operation of" Rule 68. *Califano v. Yamasaki,* 442 U.S. 682, 700 (1979). We hold that petitioners are not liable for costs of $139,692 incurred by respondent after petitioners' offer of settlement. The judgment of the Court of Appeals is Reversed.

[Concurring opinions of Justices POWELL and REHNQUIST are omitted.]

Justice BRENNAN, with whom Justice MARSHALL and Justice BLACKMUN join, dissenting:

The question presented by this case is whether the term "costs" as it is used in Rule 68 of the Federal Rules of Civil Procedure and elsewhere throughout the Rules refers simply to those taxable costs defined in 28 U.S.C. §1920 and traditionally understood as "costs"—court fees, printing expenses, and the like—or instead includes attorney's fees when an underlying fees-award statute happens to refer to fees "as part of" the awardable costs. Relying on what it recurrently emphasizes is the "plain language" of one such statute, 42 U.S.C. §1988, the Court today holds that a prevailing civil rights litigant entitled to fees under that statute is per se barred by Rule 68 from recovering any fees for work performed after rejecting a settlement offer where he ultimately recovers less than the proffered amount in settlement.

I dissent. The Court's reasoning is wholly inconsistent with the history and structure of the Federal Rules, and its application to the over 100 attorney's fees statutes enacted by Congress will produce absurd variations in Rule 68's operation based on nothing more than picayune differences in statutory phraseology. Neither Congress nor the drafters of the Rules could possibly have intended such inexplicable variations in settlement incentives. Moreover, the Court's interpretation will "seriously undermine the purposes behind the attorney's fees provisions" of the civil rights laws, *Delta Air Lines, Inc. v. August,* 450 U.S. 346, 378 (1981) (Rehnquist, J., dissenting)—provisions imposed by Congress pursuant to §5 of the Fourteenth Amendment. Today's decision therefore violates the most basic limitations on our rulemaking authority as set forth in the Rules Enabling Act, 28 U.S.C. §2072, and as summarized in *Alyeska Pipeline Co. v. Wilderness Society,* 421 U.S. 240 (1975). Finally, both Congress and the Judicial Conference of the United States have been engaged for years in considering possible amendments to Rule 68 that would bring attorney's fees within the operation of the Rule. That process strongly suggests that Rule 68 has not previously been viewed as governing fee awards, and it illustrates the wisdom of deferring to other avenues of amending Rule 68 rather than ourselves engaging in "standardless judicial lawmaking." *Delta Air Lines, Inc. v. August, supra* 450 U.S. at 378 (Rehnquist, J., dissenting).

I

The Court's "plain language" analysis, goes as follows: Section 1988 provides that a "prevailing party" may recover "a reasonable attorney's fee as part of the costs." Rule 68 in turn provides that, where an offeree obtains a judgment for less than the amount of a previous settlement offer, "the offeree must pay the costs incurred after the making of the offer." Because "attorney's fees" are "costs," the Court concludes, the "plain meaning" of Rule 68 per se prohibits a prevailing civil rights plaintiff from recovering fees incurred after he rejected the proposed out-of-court settlement.

The Court's "plain language" approach is, as Judge Posner's opinion for the court below noted, "in a sense logical." 720 F.2d 474, 478 (CA7 1983). However, while the starting point in interpreting statutes and rules is always the plain words themselves, "[t]he particular inquiry is not what is the abstract force of the words or what they may comprehend, but in what sense were they intended to be understood or what understanding they convey when used in the particular act." We previously have been confronted with "superficially appealing argument[s]" strikingly similar to those adopted by the Court today, and we have found that they "cannot survive careful consideration." *Roadway Express, Inc. v. Piper*, 447 U.S. 752, 758 (1980). So it is here. . . .

For a number of reasons, "costs" as that term is used in the Federal Rules should be interpreted uniformly in accordance with the definition of costs set forth in §1920:

First. The limited history of the costs provisions in the Federal Rules suggests that the drafters intended "costs" to mean only taxable costs traditionally allowed under the common law or pursuant to the statutory predecessor of §1920. Nowhere was it suggested that the meaning of taxable "costs" might vary from case to case depending on the language of the substantive statute involved—a practice that would have cut against the drafters' intent to create uniform procedures applicable to "every action " in federal court. Fed. Rule Civ. Proc. 1.

Second. The Rules provide that "costs" may automatically be taxed by the clerk of the court on one day's notice, Fed. Rule Civ. Proc. 54(d) — strongly suggesting that "costs" were intended to refer only to those routine, readily determinable charges that could appropriately be left to a clerk, and as to which a single day's notice of settlement would be appropriate. Attorney's fees, which are awardable only by the court and which frequently entail lengthy disputes and hearings, obviously do not fall within that category.

Third. When particular provisions of the Federal Rules are intended to encompass attorney's fees, they do so explicitly. Eleven different provisions of the Rules authorize a court to award attorney's fees as "expenses" in particular circumstances, demonstrating that the drafters knew the difference, and intended a difference, between "costs," "expenses," and "attorney's fees."

Fourth. With the exception of one recent Court of Appeals opinion and two recent District Court opinions, the Court can point to no authority suggesting that courts or attorneys have ever viewed the cost-shifting provisions of Rule 68 as including attorney's fees. . . .

Fifth. We previously have held that words and phrases in the Federal Rules must be given a consistent usage and be read in *pari materia*, reasoning that to do otherwise would "attribute a schizophrenic intent to the drafters." *Id.*, at 353. Applying the Court's "plain language" approach consistently throughout the Rules, however, would produce absurd results that would turn statutes like §1988 on their heads and plainly violate the restraints imposed on judicial rulemaking by the Rules Enabling Act. For example, Rule 54(d) provides that "costs shall be allowed as of course to the prevailing party unless the court otherwise directs." Similarly, the plain language of Rule 68 provides that a plaintiff covered by the Rule "must pay the costs incurred after the making of the offer"—language requiring the plaintiff to bear both his postoffer costs and the defendant's postoffer costs. If "costs" as used in these provisions were interpreted to include attorney's fees by virtue of the wording of §1988, losing civil rights plaintiffs would be required by the "plain language" of Rule 54(d) to pay the defendant's attorney's fees, and prevailing plaintiffs falling within Rule 68 would be required to bear the defendant's postoffer attorney's fees.

Had it addressed this troubling consequence of its "plain language" approach, perhaps the Court would have acknowledged that such a reading would conflict directly with §1988, which allows an award of attorney's fees to a prevailing defendant only where "the suit was vexatious, frivolous, or brought to harass or embarrass the defendant," [citation] and that the substantive standard set forth in §1988 therefore overrides the otherwise "plain meaning" of Rules 54(d) and 68. But that is precisely the point, and the Court cannot have it both ways. . . .

Sixth. As with all of the Federal Rules, the drafters intended Rule 68 to have a uniform, consistent application in all proceedings in federal court. In accordance with this intent, Rule 68 should be interpreted to provide uniform, consistent incentives "to encourage the settlement of litigation." *Delta Air Lines, Inc. v. August, supra,* 450 U.S. at 352. Yet today's decision will lead to dramatically different settlement incentives depending on minor variations in the phraseology of the underlying fees-award statutes—distinctions that would appear to be nothing short of irrational and for which the Court has no plausible explanation.

Congress has enacted well over 100 attorney's fees statutes, many of which would appear to be affected by today's decision. . . . Under the "plain language" approach of today's decision, Rule 68 will operate to include the potential loss of otherwise recoverable attorney's fees as an incentive to settlement in litigation under these statutes. . . .

The result is to sanction a senseless patchwork of fee shifting that flies in the face of the fundamental purpose of the Federal Rules—the provision of uniform and consistent procedure in federal courts. Such a construction will "introduce into [Rule 68] distinctions unrelated to its goal . . . and [will] result in virtually random application of the Rule." . . .

In sum, there is nothing in the history and structure of the Rules or in the history of any of the underlying attorney's fee statutes to justify

such incomprehensible distinctions based simply on fine linguistic variations among the underlying fees-award statutes—particularly where, as in
Roadway Express, the cost provision can be read as embodying a uniform
definition derived from §1920. As partners with Congress, we have a responsibility not to carry "plain language" constructions to the point of
producing "untenable distinctions and unreasonable results." *American
Tobacco Co. v. Patterson,* 456 U.S. 63, 71 (1982). . . .

II

A

Although the Court's opinion fails to discuss any of the problems
reviewed above, it does devote some space to arguing that its interpretation
of Rule 68 "is in no sense inconsistent with the congressional policies
underlying §1983 and §1988." The Court goes so far as to assert that its
interpretation fits in smoothly with §1988 as interpreted by *Hensley v.
Eckerhart,* 461 U.S. 424 (1983).

The Court is wrong. Congress has instructed that attorney's fee entitlement under §1988 be governed by a reasonableness standard. Until
today the Court always has recognized that this standard precludes
reliance on any mechanical "bright-line" rules automatically denying a
portion of fees, acknowledging that such "mathematical approach[es]"
provide "little aid in determining what is a reasonable fee in light of all
the relevant factors." 461 U.S. at 435-436, n.11. Although the starting
point is always "the number of hours reasonably expended on the litigation," this "does not end the inquiry": a number of considerations set
forth in the legislative history of §1988 "may lead the district court to adjust
the fee upward or downward." *Id.,* at 433-434. We also have emphasized
that the district court "necessarily has discretion in making this equitable
judgment" because of its "superior understanding of the litigation." *Id.,* at
437. Section 1988's reasonableness standard is, in sum, "acutely sensitive
to the merits of an action and to antidiscrimination policy." *Roadway
Express, Inc. v. Piper,* 447 U.S. at 762.

Rule 68, on the other hand, is not "sensitive" at all to the merits of an
action and to antidiscrimination policy. It is a mechanical per se provision
automatically shifting "costs" incurred after an offer is rejected, and it
deprives a district court of all discretion with respect to the matter by
using "the strongest verb of its type known to the English language—
'must.'" *Delta Air Lines, Inc. v. August, supra,* 450 U.S. at 369. The potential
for conflict between §1988 and Rule 68 could not be more apparent.

Of course, a civil rights plaintiff who unreasonably fails to accept a settlement offer, and who thereafter recovers less than the proffered amount
in settlement, is barred under §1988 itself from recovering fees for unpro-
ductive work performed in the wake of the rejection. This is because "the

extent of a plaintiff's success is a crucial factor in determining the proper amount of an award of attorney's fees," 461 U.S. at 440 (emphasis added); hours that are "excessive, redundant, or otherwise unnecessary" must be excluded from that calculus, *id.*, at 434. To this extent, the results might sometimes be the same under either §1988's reasonableness inquiry or the Court's wooden application of Rule 68. Had the Court allowed the Seventh Circuit's remand in the instant case to stand, for example, the District Court after conducting the appropriate inquiry might well have determined that much or even all of the respondent's postoffer fees were unreasonably incurred and therefore not properly awardable.

But the results under §1988 and Rule 68 will not always be congruent, because §1988 mandates the careful consideration of a broad range of other factors and accords appropriate leeway to the district court's informed discretion. Contrary to the Court's protestations, it is not at all clear that "[t]his case presents a good example" of the smooth interplay of §1988 and Rule 68, ante, at 9, because there has never been an evidentiary consideration of the reasonableness or unreasonableness of the respondent's fee request. It is clear, however, that under the Court's interpretation of Rule 68 a plaintiff who ultimately recovers only slightly less than the proffered amount in settlement will per se be barred from recovering trial fees even if he otherwise "has obtained excellent results" in litigation that will have far-reaching benefit to the public interest. . . .

To discuss but one example, Rule 68 allows an offer to be made any time after the complaint is filed and gives the plaintiff only 10 days to accept or reject. The Court's decision inevitably will encourage defendants who know they have violated the law to make "low-ball" offers immediately after suit is filed and before plaintiffs have been able to obtain the information they are entitled to by way of discovery to assess the strength of their claims and the reasonableness of the offers. The result will put severe pressure on plaintiffs to settle on the basis of inadequate information in order to avoid the risk of bearing all of their fees even if reasonable discovery might reveal that the defendants were subject to far greater liability. Indeed, because Rule 68 offers may be made recurrently without limitation, defendants will be well advised to make ever-slightly larger offers throughout the discovery process and before plaintiffs have conducted all reasonably necessary discovery.

This sort of so-called "incentive" is fundamentally incompatible with Congress' goals. Congress intended for "private citizens . . . to be able to assert their civil rights" and for "those who violate the Nation's fundamental laws" not to be able "to proceed with impunity." . . .

Other difficulties will follow from the Court's decision. For example, if a plaintiff recovers less money than was offered before trial but obtains potentially far-reaching injunctive or declaratory relief, it is altogether unclear how the Court intends judges to go about quantifying the "value" of the plaintiff's success. . . .

B

Indeed, the judgment of the Court of Appeals below turned on its determination that an interpretation of Rule 68 to include attorney's fees is beyond the pale of the judiciary's rulemaking authority. *Ibid.* Congress has delegated its authority to this Court "to prescribe by general rules . . . the practice and procedure of the district courts and courts of appeals of the United States in civil actions." 28 U.S.C. §2072. This grant is limited, however, by the condition that "[s]uch rules shall not abridge, enlarge or modify any substantive right." *Ibid.* The right to attorney's fees is "substantive" under any reasonable definition of that term.

Comments and Questions

1. First, let's walk through *Marek v. Chesney*, the landmark case that interpreted Fed. R. Civ. P. 68. That ruling encourages parties to make realistic offers to their opponent by penalizing the party who refuses an offer of judgment and later receives a less favorable judgment at trial. But before *Marek* the penalty was minor: it provided for a shift only of "costs" as a penalty, and costs (such as filing fees) are generally quite small. *Marek* adds teeth to the penalty by construing "costs" to include attorneys' fees. This means that where a fee-shifting statute allows a prevailing party to recover attorneys' fees as part of costs, Rule 68 can curtail any fees otherwise due if the prevailing party rejected a settlement offer more favorable than the ultimate judgment. Fee-shifting statutes that do not include attorneys' fees as part of costs apparently avoid this operation of Rule 68.

2. Importantly, *Marek* was decided at a time when §1988 (the Civil Rights Attorneys Fees Act) was the most commonly used of the federal fee-shifting statutes and the most common exception to the American Rule. Previous to *Marek* (*see Christiansburg Garment Co. v. EEOC*, 434 U.S. 412 (1978)), the Supreme Court had interpreted §1988 as authorizing courts to order defendants to pay the attorneys' fees of prevailing plaintiffs, but generally *not* to authorize courts to order plaintiffs to pay the attorneys' fees of prevailing defendants (the exception is where the plaintiff's suit is "frivolous, unreasonable, or without foundation"—much like a Rule 11 violation). *Marek* is therefore a "one-way" fee-shift rule, permitting shifts of attorneys' fees only from plaintiff to defendant; it is a "pro-plaintiff" rule, given the Court's view of the importance of encouraging enforcement of the civil rights laws.

3. Consider the plaintiff who wins under §1983; normally that plaintiff would then be entitled also to win attorneys' fees under §1988. But *Marek* ruled that Fed. R. Civ. P. 68 includes attorneys' fees within the scope of "costs" that can be shifted to the plaintiff who rejects a settlement offer that turns out to be greater than ultimate recovery. By rejecting a

settlement offer that exceeded ultimate judgment, under Fed. R. Civ. P. 68, the plaintiff now cannot shift to the defendant its attorneys' fees *incurred after rejecting the settlement offer and will have to pay those fees unless the plaintiff's prior arrangement with the attorney* imposed no such obligation on the plaintiff. Under what circumstances might an attorney sign such a contract?

4. The basic idea in *Marek's* majority view—besides a "plain language" interpretation of Fed. R. Civ. P. 68—is that the value of the attorneys' work up until the settlement offer deserves acknowledgment, but that the attorneys' work subsequent to a rejected settlement offer is not worthwhile when the ultimate recovery is less than the offer.

5. Meantime, can the plaintiff who rejected the settlement offer now be liable for the defendant's attorneys' fees? The language of Fed. R. Civ. P. 68 suggests as much, once "costs" is construed to include "fees": "If the judgment finally obtained by the offeree is not more favorable than the offer, the offeree must pay the costs incurred after the making of the offer." Yet the Court in *Marek* does not direct the plaintiff to pay the attorneys' fees of the defendant that were incurred subsequent to the rejection of the settlement offer. The opinion's only comment on this issue appears in its footnote 1, where the Court notes that the District Court refused to shift the petitioner-defendant's attorneys' fees to the respondent-plaintiff, and the petitioner-defendant did not contest this issue before the Supreme Court.

This makes sense in light of the interpretation of §1988. Because §1988 has been construed as a one-way shift (absent extreme circumstances), the courts will not direct plaintiffs in §1983 cases to pay the attorneys' fees of defendants even if Fed. R. Civ. P. 68 is triggered. Moreover, a defendant who makes a successful Rule 68 offer still is not a "prevailing party" if the plaintiff did have some recovery. Several courts thus have concluded that a defendant cannot recover its fees after making a successful Rule 68 offer. *See, e.g., EEOC v. Bailey Ford, Inc.,* 26 F.3d 570, 571 (5th Cir. 1994); *O'Brien v. City of Greer's Ferry,* 873 F.2d 1115, 1120 (8th Cir. 1989).

6. Is an accepted settlement offer adequate as "substantially prevailing" for purposes of triggering attorneys' fees under §1988 (or other fee-shifting statutes that permit a shift of fees to benefit the prevailing party)? The answer is: maybe. The settlement *can* be treated as evidence of substantially prevailing, *see Nadeau v. Helgmoe,* 581 F.2d 275 (1st Cir. 1978), but the settlement offer can include a waiver of attorneys' fees, and/or a specification that the plaintiff "is not the substantially prevailing party." A court also may review the terms of the settlement to determine whether it should count as "*substantially* prevailing" or instead as only partially prevailing. This is especially likely if the plaintiff has rejected a settlement offer that ended up being larger than the ultimate judgment.

7. Although "costs" covered by federal awards of costs to prevailing parties are usually quite limited, they can include the costs of a plaintiff's

experts following a judgment for the plaintiff. *See* Peter L. Murray, A Comparative Law Experiment, 8 Inc. Intl. & Comp. L. Rev. 2115, 2138 (1998). In addition, Fed. R. Civ. P. 26(a)(4)(C) authorizes the judge to require a party seeking discovery to pay the reasonable fee of an expert responding to the discovery, or a fair portion of the fees and expenses incurred by the opposing party in obtaining facts and opinions from the expert.

8. If you were on an Advisory Committee considering proposed changes to Fed. R. Civ. P. 68, what would you recommend? Keep in mind the *Marek* dissent's concern that the Rules Enabling Act boundaries may be breached by a procedural rule with substantive effects. Try to work out the specific language for a new rule, and explain what you are pursuing and how the rule would handle different cases. Try applying your rule to *Marek*, and to the *Carpenter* case. Assume that Ultimate Auto, the retailer who sold the kits allowing the defendant to modify the suspension of the jeep is the only defendant. The plaintiff's lawyer thinks the case is worth $500,000; Ultimate Auto thinks it is worth $300,000. What would each be tempted to offer under the rule, and why? What happens if the jury comes in with $0? $200,000? $400,000? $600,000?

4. Offer of Settlement

What if the defendant offers a settlement whose terms include waiver of the attorneys' fees, notwithstanding a statutory provision calling for the defendant to pay the fee of a prevailing plaintiff? In *Evans v. Jeff D.*, 475 U.S. 717 (1986), the lawyers for a class-action plaintiff group of children with disabilities faced precisely this question when the defendant offered to settle and provide "virtually all of the injunctive relief" to improve the children's health care treatment as sought in the complaint—provided that the plaintiffs would waive statutory attorneys' fees. The plaintiff's attorney claimed that this offer violated the statute and would undermine its purpose of promoting precisely this kind of successful lawsuit. The lawyer claimed that he faced an ethical conflict between the interests of his current client and the interests of potential future clients with similar claims whose cases he would not be able to take because of the risk of foregoing attorneys' fees even in a successful case. The Supreme Court rejected this argument:

> Although respondents contend that Johnson, as counsel for the class, was faced with an "ethical dilemma" when petitioners offered him relief greater than that which he could reasonably have expected to obtain for his clients at trial (if only he would stipulate to a waiver of the statutory fee award), . . . we do not believe that the "dilemma" was an "ethical" one in the sense that Johnson had to choose between conflicting duties under the prevailing norms of professional conduct. Plainly Johnson had no *ethical*

obligation to seek a statutory fee award. His ethical duty was to serve his clients loyally and competently. Since the proposal to settle the merits was more favorable than the probable outcome of the trial, Johnson's decision to recommend acceptance was consistent with the highest standards of our profession. 475 U.S. at 727–28.

Comments and Questions

1. Special problems in *Evans v. Jeff D.* arose because the client was (a) a class action and (b) composed of children with disabilities. Therefore, the option of a full discussion between attorney and client about whether to accept a settlement that waives attorneys' fees was unavailable. Could an individual, competent adult client make a sensible choice about whether or not to waive attorneys' fees as part of a settlement offer?

2. Perhaps the most widespread response to the issue presented in *Evans v. Jeff D.* is the use of contractual provisions between lawyers and their clients that forbid the client from waiving court-awarded fees. Are there any problems with this kind of agreement? Should rules of professional ethics forbid it?

3. Taking *Evans v. Jeff D.* and *Marek v. Chesny* together, what policies seem the basis for the federal tendency toward settlement and toward litigation encouraged by pro-plaintiff fee shifts? Would you strike the balance differently? What factors are most relevant to this judgment? Note how the balance affects (a) when lawsuits should be filed; (b) when already filed lawsuits should be settled; and (c) when lawsuits should be followed through to judgments and precedential effects.

5. Assessing the Value of Legal Services

When a court awards attorneys' fees, how should those fees be calculated? Billing practices by attorneys vary widely. Traditionally, lawyers in this country have billed for each hour of service, but lawyers charge different hourly rates based on their years of experience, demonstrated expertise, access to colleagues with other expertise, or other reputational features. Percentage contingent fees are a long-standing alternative, especially in the field of personal injuries; the attorney and client agree by contract that the attorney will share a specified percentage of any award or settlement. Increasingly, lawyers explore other billing practices, including set fees for certain services, yearly salary (for in-house counsel, pre-paid legal services plans, or legal aid lawyers), or a mixture of methods. Should the attorneys' fees awarded under a fee-shifting statute be subjected to a judicial inquiry as to their reasonableness—and if so, measured how? Should the court inquire about the relationship between the fees and the amount recovered? The following case illuminates these questions.

■ CITY OF RIVERSIDE v. RIVERA
477 U.S. 561 (1986)

Justice BRENNAN announced the judgment of the Court and delivered an opinion in which Justice MARSHALL, Justice BLACKMUN and Justice STEVENS join:

The issue presented in this case is whether an award of attorney's fees under 42 U.S.C. §1988 is per se "unreasonable" within the meaning of the statute if it exceeds the amount of damages recovered by the plaintiff in the underlying civil rights action.

I

Respondents, eight Chicano individuals, attended a party on the evening of August 1, 1975, at the Riverside, California, home of respondents Santos and Jennie Rivera. A large number of unidentified police officers, acting without a warrant, broke up the party using tear gas and, as found by the District Court, "unnecessary physical force." Many of the guests, including four of the respondents, were arrested. The District Court later found that "[t]he party was not creating a disturbance in the community at the time of the break-in." . . . Criminal charges against the arrestees were ultimately dismissed for lack of probable cause.

On June 4, 1976, respondents sued the city of Riverside, its Chief of Police, and 30 individual police officers under 42 U.S.C. §§1981, 1983, 1985(3), and 1986 for allegedly violating their First, Fourth, and Fourteenth Amendment rights. The complaint, which also alleged numerous state-law claims, sought damages and declaratory and injunctive relief. On August 5, 1977, 23 of the individual police officers moved for summary judgment; the District Court granted summary judgment in favor of 17 of these officers. The case against the remaining defendants proceeded to trial in September 1980. The jury returned a total of 37 individual verdicts in favor of the respondents and against the city and five individual officers, finding 11 violations of §1983, 4 instances of false arrest and imprisonment, and 22 instances of negligence. Respondents were awarded $33,350 in compensatory and punitive damages: $13,300 for their federal claims, and $20,050 for their state-law claims.

Respondents also sought attorney's fees and costs under §1988. They requested compensation for 1,946.75 hours expended by their two attorneys at a rate of $125 per hour, and for 84.5 hours expended by law clerks at a rate of $25 per hour, a total of $245,456.25. The District Court found both the hours and rates reasonable, and awarded respondents $245,456.25 in attorney's fees. The court rejected respondents' request for certain additional expenses, and for a multiplier sought by respondents to reflect the contingent nature of their success and the high quality of their attorneys' efforts.

Petitioners appealed only the attorney's fees award, which the Court of Appeals for the Ninth Circuit affirmed. *Rivera v. City of Riverside*, 679 F.2d 795 (1982). Petitioners sought a writ of certiorari from this Court. We granted the writ, vacated the Court of Appeals' judgment, and remanded the case for reconsideration in light of *Hensley v. Eckerhart*, 461 U.S. 424 (1983). On remand, the District Court held two additional hearings, reviewed additional briefing, and reexamined the record as a whole. The court made extensive findings of fact and conclusions of law, and again concluded that respondents were entitled to an award of $245,456.25 in attorney's fees, based on the same total number of hours expended on the case and the same hourly rates. The court again denied respondents' request for certain expenses and for a multiplier.

Petitioners again appealed the fee award. And again, the Court of Appeals affirmed, finding that "the district court correctly reconsidered the case in light of *Hensley*. . . ." 763 F.2d 1580, 1582 (1985). The Court of Appeals rejected three arguments raised by petitioners. First, the court rejected petitioners' contention that respondents' counsel should not have been compensated for time spent litigating claims other than those upon which respondents ultimately prevailed. Emphasizing that the District Court had determined that respondents' attorneys had "spent no time on claims unrelated to the successful claims," *ibid.*, the Court of Appeals concluded that "[t]he record supports the district court's findings that all of the plaintiffs' claims involve a 'common core of facts' and that the claims involve related legal theories." *Ibid.* The court also observed that, consistent with *Hensley*, the District Court had "considered the degree of success [achieved by respondents' attorneys] and found a reasonable relationship between the extent of that success and the amount of the fee award." 763 F.2d, at 1582. Second, the Court of Appeals rejected the argument that the fee award was excessive because it exceeded the amount of damages awarded by the jury. Examining the legislative history of §1988, the court found no support for the proposition that an award of attorney's fees may not exceed the amount of damages recovered by a prevailing plaintiff. Finally, the court found that the District Court's "extensive findings of fact and conclusions of law" belied petitioners' claim that the District Court had not reviewed the record to determine whether the fee award was justified. . . .

II

A

. . . Congress enacted the Civil Rights Attorney's Fees Awards Act of 1976, 42 U.S.C. §1988, which authorized the district courts to award reasonable attorney's fees to prevailing parties in specified civil rights litigation. [T]he statute itself does not explain what constitutes a reasonable fee. . . .

Hensley v. Eckerhart, 461 U.S. 424 (1983), announced certain guidelines for calculating a reasonable attorney's fee under §1988. Hensley stated that "[t]he most useful starting point for determining the amount of a reasonable fee is the number of hours reasonably expended on the litigation multiplied by a reasonable hourly rate." Id., at 433. This figure, commonly referred to as the "lodestar," is presumed to be the reasonable fee contemplated by §1988. The opinion cautioned that "[t]he district court . . . should exclude from this initial fee calculation hours that were not 'reasonably expended'" on the litigation. Id., at 434 (quoting Senate Report, at 6). . . .

B

Petitioners argue that the District Court failed properly to follow Hensley in calculating respondents' fee award. We disagree. The District Court carefully considered the results obtained by respondents pursuant to the instructions set forth in Hensley, and concluded that respondents were entitled to recover attorney's fees for all hours expended on the litigation. First, the court found that "[t]he amount of time expended by counsel in conducting this litigation was reasonable and reflected sound legal judgment under the circumstances." The court also determined that counsel's excellent performances in this case entitled them to be compensated at prevailing market rates, even though they were relatively young when this litigation began. See Johnson, 488 F.2d, at 718-719 ("If a young attorney demonstrates the skill and ability, he should not be penalized for only recently being admitted to the bar").

The District Court then concluded that it was inappropriate to adjust respondents' fee award downward to account for the fact that respondents had prevailed only on some of their claims, and against only some of the defendants. The court first determined that "it was never actually clear what officer did what until we had gotten through with the whole trial," so that "[u]nder the circumstances of this case, it was reasonable for plaintiffs initially to name thirty-one individual defendants . . . as well as the City of Riverside as defendants in this action." . . .

The District Court also considered the amount of damages recovered, and determined that the size of the damages award did not imply that respondents' success was limited:

> [T]he size of the jury award resulted from (a) the general reluctance of jurors to make large awards against police officers, and (b) the dignified restraint which the plaintiffs exercised in describing their injuries to the jury. For example, although some of the actions of the police would clearly have been insulting and humiliating to even the most insensitive person and

were, in the opinion of the Court, intentionally so, plaintiffs did not attempt to play up this aspect of the case.

Id., at 188-189. The court paid particular attention to the fact that the case "presented complex and interrelated issues of fact and law," *id.*, at 187, and that "[a] fee award in this civil rights action will . . . advance the public interest." . . .

Based on our review of the record, we agree with the Court of Appeals that the District Court's findings were not clearly erroneous. We conclude that the District Court correctly applied the factors announced in *Hensley* in calculating respondents' fee award, and that the court did not abuse its discretion in awarding attorney's fees for all time reasonably spent litigating the case.

III

Petitioners, joined by the United States as amicus curiae, maintain that *Hensley*'s lodestar approach is inappropriate in civil rights cases where a plaintiff recovers only monetary damages. In these cases, so the argument goes, use of the lodestar may result in fees that exceed the amount of damages recovered and that are therefore unreasonable. Likening such cases to private tort actions, petitioners and the United States submit that attorney's fees in such cases should be proportionate to the amount of damages a plaintiff recovers. Specifically, they suggest that fee awards in damages cases should be modeled upon the contingent-fee arrangements commonly used in personal injury litigation. In this case, assuming a 33% contingency rate, this would entitle respondents to recover approximately $11,000 in attorney's fees.

The amount of damages a plaintiff recovers is certainly relevant to the amount of attorney's fees to be awarded under §1988. *See Johnson*, 488 F.2d, at 718. It is, however, only one of many factors that a court should consider in calculating an award of attorney's fees. We reject the proposition that fee awards under §1988 should necessarily be proportionate to the amount of damages a civil rights plaintiff actually recovers.

A

As an initial matter, we reject the notion that a civil rights action for damages constitutes nothing more than a private tort suit benefiting only the individual plaintiffs whose rights were violated. Unlike most private tort litigants, a civil rights plaintiff seeks to vindicate important civil and constitutional rights that cannot be valued solely in monetary terms. . . .

B

A rule that limits attorney's fees in civil rights cases to a proportion of the damages awarded would seriously undermine Congress' purpose in enacting §1988. Congress enacted §1988 specifically because it found that the private market for legal services failed to provide many victims of civil rights violations with effective access to the judicial process. These victims ordinarily cannot afford to purchase legal services at the rates set by the private market. . . . Moreover, the contingent fee arrangements that make legal services available to many victims of personal injuries would often not encourage lawyers to accept civil rights cases, which frequently involve substantial expenditures of time and effort but produce only small monetary recoveries. . . .

Justice POWELL, concurring in the judgment:

I join only the Court's judgment. The plurality opinion reads our decision in _Hensley v. Eckerhart,_ 461 U.S. 424 (1983), more expansively than I would, and more expansively than is necessary to decide this case. For me affirmance—quite simply—is required by the District Court's detailed findings of fact, which were approved by the Court of Appeals. On its face, the fee award seems unreasonable. But I find no basis for this Court to reject the findings made and approved by the courts below. . . .

Federal Rule of Civil Procedure 52(a) provides that "[f]indings of fact [by a district court] shall not be set aside unless clearly erroneous. . . ." The Court of Appeals did not disagree with any of the foregoing findings by the District Court. I see no basis on which this Court now could hold that these findings are clearly erroneous. To be sure, some of the findings fairly can be viewed as conclusions or matters of opinion, but the findings that are critical to the judgments of the courts below are objective facts. . . .

Petitioners argue for a rule of proportionality between the fee awarded and the damages recovered in a civil rights case. Neither the decisions of this Court nor the legislative history of §1988 support such a "rule." The facts and circumstances of litigation are infinitely variable. . . .

Berger → I join Justice Rehnquist's dissenting opinion. I write only to add that it would be difficult to find a better example of legal nonsense than the fixing of attorney's fees by a judge at $245,456.25 for the recovery of $33,350 damages.

The two attorneys receiving this nearly quarter-million-dollar fee graduated from law school in 1973 and 1974; they brought this action in 1975, which resulted in the $33,350 jury award in 1980. Their total professional experience when this litigation began consisted of Gerald Lopez' 1-year service as a law clerk to a judge and Roy Cazares' two years' experience as a trial attorney in the Defenders' Program of San Diego County. For their services the District Court found that an hourly rate of $125 per hour was reasonable.

Can anyone doubt that no private party would ever have dreamed of paying these two novice attorneys $125 per hour in 1975, which, considering inflation, would represent perhaps something more nearly a $250 per hour rate today? . . .

This fee award plainly constitutes a grave abuse of discretion which should be rejected by this Court—particularly when we have already vacated and remanded this identical fee award previously—rather than simply affirming the District Court's findings as not being either "clearly erroneous" or an "abuse of discretion." The Court's result will unfortunately only add fuel to the fires of public indignation over the costs of litigation.

Justice REHNQUIST, with whom the CHIEF JUSTICE, Justice WHITE, and Justice O'CONNOR join, dissenting:

I see no escape from the conclusion that the District Court's finding that respondents' attorneys "reasonably" spent 1,946.75 hours to recover a money judgment of $33,350 is clearly erroneous, and that therefore the District Court's award of $245,456.25 in attorney's fees to respondents should be reversed. The Court's affirmance of the fee award emasculates the principles laid down in *Hensley,* and turns §1988 into a relief Act for lawyers.

A brief look at the history of this case reveals just how "unreasonable" it was for respondents' lawyers to spend so much time on it. Respondents filed their initial complaint in 1976, seeking injunctive and declaratory relief and compensatory and punitive damages from the city of Riverside, its Chief of Police, and 30 police officers, based on 256 separate claims allegedly arising out of the police breakup of a single party. Prior to trial, 17 of the police officers were dismissed from the case on motions for summary judgment, and respondents dropped their requests for injunctive and declaratory relief. More significantly, respondents also dropped their original allegation that the police had acted with discriminatory intent. The action proceeded to trial, and the jury completely exonerated nine additional police officers. Respondents ultimately prevailed against only the city and five police officers on various §1983, false arrest and imprisonment, and common negligence claims. No restraining orders or injunctions were ever issued against petitioners, nor was the city ever compelled to change a single practice or policy as a result of respondents' suit. The jury awarded respondents a total of $33,350 in compensatory and punitive damages. Only about one-third of this total, or $13,300, was awarded to respondents based on violations of their federal constitutional rights. . . .

The analysis of whether the extraordinary number of hours put in by respondents' attorneys in this case was "reasonable" must be made in light of both the traditional billing practices in the profession, and the fundamental principle that the award of a "reasonable" attorney's fee under §1988 means a fee that would have been deemed reasonable if billed to affluent plaintiffs by their own attorneys. . . .

Comments and Questions

1. What response did the plurality give to the dissent's claim that it was wasteful to spend $245,456.25 in attorneys' fees to win $33,350 in compensation? What response would you have given?

2. Should attorneys' fees be calculated any differently when the relief is injunctive, versus when the relief is money damages?

3. Does the central difficulty in *City of Riverside* stem from hourly billing? What other ways of assessing the value of lawyers' work could provide compensation and incentive to lawyers to undertake appropriate cases? Consider the following excerpt on the ethics of hourly billing by attorneys as you consider these questions.

■ WILLIAM G. ROSS, THE ETHICS OF HOURLY BILLING BY ATTORNEYS
44 Rutgers L. Rev. 1 (1991)

For the past two decades, most attorneys in private civil practice have based their fees almost entirely upon the number of hours that they have expended on services for their clients. Originally hailed for its objectivity and efficiency, hourly billing increasingly has been assailed for encouraging inefficiency, excessive litigation, and fraud. . . .

During the past decade, economic changes in the legal profession have stimulated substantial increases in billable hours, making annual billings in excess of 2,000 hours per lawyer commonplace in many firms. It therefore is not surprising that the methods by which attorneys calculate their time are being scrutinized more closely by individuals within and outside the legal profession. Clients may have acquiesced to questionable billing practices in the past; however, these practices are likely to encounter more resistance as attorneys record ever-increasing totals of hours. Although a number of firms are experimenting with alternatives to hourly billing and some critics of hourly billing have predicted its demise, time remains the principal basis for billing, and it seems likely to remain the primary means of billing for the foreseeable future. Moreover, even alternative methods of billing are based at least in part upon expenditures of time. Therefore, it is useful to examine the ethical considerations faced by attorneys who base their billings in whole or in part upon time. . . .

HOW WIDESPREAD IS UNETHICAL BILLING?

Because there is no practical manner of verifying the accuracy of most time records, every attorney who has billed time knows that time billing creates rich opportunities for fraud. If she misrepresents her hours, an attorney is vulnerable only to her conscience and questions from senior attorneys or clients. For honest attorneys, conscience ordinarily will check any base instincts. For less scrupulous attorneys, the fear of questions or complaints from senior attorneys or clients may not provide much restraint. . . .

With the number of billable hours steadily climbing at major firms, many attorneys may suspect that fraud accounts for some of the inflation. Pressured by their firms to bill substantial numbers of hours, many lawyers—especially associates at large firms—may be exaggerating the time that they spend on client business or doing unnecessary work. However, until recently, the subject of fraudulent billing among otherwise respectable firms has remained largely taboo in polite circles. Only recently has this subject begun to attract attention in the courts and among scholars. Chief Justice Rehnquist ruefully has observed that "if one is expected to bill more than two thousand hours per year, there are bound to be temptations to exaggerate the hours actually put in." . . .

In short, [my survey] tends to support [the thesis] that fraudulent billing occurs but remains the exception rather than the rule. Only 12.3% of the private practitioners and 15.2% of the corporate counsel who responded to the survey's question about padding of hours stated that they believe that lawyers "frequently" pad their hours to deliberately bill clients for work which they never performed. But some 38% of the private practitioners and 40.7% of the corporate counsel stated that they believe that lawyers "occasionally" pad their hours. Only 42.4% of the private practitioners and 35.6% of the corporate counsel stated that the perceived that such padding "rarely" occurs, and only 7.3% of the former and 8.5% of the latter contended that it virtually "never" occurs. While 35.5% of the private practitioner[s] and 39.7% of the corporate counsel stated that they lacked any specific knowledge of such padding, 58.9% of the private practitioners and 54% of the corporate counsel averred that they personally knew of at least "some" instances of padding. Some 5.6% of the private practitioners and 6.3% of the corporate counsel stated that they knew of "many" such instances. . . .

In narrative comments to the survey, many attorneys denied that fraudulent billing or unnecessary work is widespread. A number of respondents explained that they were so busy with necessary work that they would have no reason to pad their hours or to perform make-work assignments even if they lacked moral scruples. . . .

On the other hand, a number of attorneys in the survey castigated hourly billing. A partner in a Portland, Oregon firm, for example, stated that "'padding hours' is an increasing problem. I have heard stories of lawyers billing 400 to 600 hours per month. These stories are generally not told with outrage, but often with admiration." Similarly, a corporate counsel, who previously had practiced with a Wall Street firm and a small regional firm, stated that "padding . . . is encouraged. The philosophy in many firms is 'do whatever you can get away with.'" . . .

As noted above, associates experience intense pressure to bill substantial numbers of hours because many firms evaluate the work of associates and even some partners heavily or even primarily in terms of the number of hours billed. . . . Moreover, many associates may spend excessive time on assignments because they feel intense pressure to make certain that their work is thorough and accurate. . . . Although partners routinely tell associates to record all of the time spent on a particular project and that the time will be discounted if it appears disproportionate to the results accomplished, partners obviously must feel a temptation to bill as much recorded time as possible without arousing the client's suspicions. The pressure to bill a large number of hours is especially intense for associates in large firms, since associates in those firms often lack opportunities to impress senior attorneys with the quality of their work. . . .

SPECIAL PROBLEMS INVOLVING LITIGATION

The danger of make-work is particularly acute in pretrial discovery. There is agreement that hourly billing encourages excess discovery. Judge Reavley recently observed that "an attorney may resort to sharp tactics to increase billable hours as the resulting delays and additional activity—repeated requests, motions, protracted depositions and trials—mean more hours of attorney time." Similarly, Professor Brazil has noted that "sophisticated obstructionist maneuvering during discovery . . . can be very lucrative for lawyers. Since discovery constitutes such a significant percentage of most litigation activity, lawyers understand that they must make money during discovery." An attorney who bills by the hour therefore may encounter "a great economic temptation to protract and complicate discovery."

[The article then discusses how the liberal discovery provisions of the Federal Rules of Civil Procedure seem to encourage the sort of protracted litigation that encourages attorneys to adopt tactics that inflate client bills.]

6. The Contingency Fee

An American innovation, the contingency fee is the leading alternative to hourly billing by attorneys. Typically, the client signs an agreement drafted by the attorney that promises to pay the attorney a specified percentage, usually one-third, of any recovery achieved through the litigation, and simultaneously makes it clear that the client will owe no fee if there is no recovery. State judicial and ethics rules make clear that such arrangements do not violate traditional norms against champerty, in which a person not a party to a suit agrees to invest in it in return for a share in the profits, while also providing for judicial review to ensure reasonable terms in contingency agreements.

What effect does this billing practice have on attorneys? The contingency fee in a real sense makes the lawyer an investor or joint venturer with the client. To proceed with the lawsuit, the lawyer has to invest time and potentially further resources for experts, court costs, and investigative work. The lawyer therefore must make judgments about which cases are worth taking "on speculation"; some must pay off if the lawyer is to stay in business over time.

The contingency fee also affects how much time a lawyer puts into a case, what the lawyer does with that time, and how the lawyer views settlements (and clients). One economic analysis suggests that the lawyer "should continue to devote hours to [a given contingency fee case] only as long as each additional hour increased his fee by at least as much as his opportunity cost," meaning the cost of foregoing work on another matter. Kevin M. Clermont and John D. Currivan, *Improving on the Contingent Fee*, 63 Cornell L. Rev. 529 (1978). Perhaps lawyers paid on a contingent fee basis will spend fewer hours on a case than would be optimal for the client (if the case appears to be a losing one), and lawyers paid on an hourly basis will put in more than the optimal number of hours. One study, based on court records and interviews with 371 hourly fee lawyers and 267 contingent fee lawyers from twelve state and federal courts concluded that:

> the contingent fee lawyer appears sensitive to the potential return to be achieved from a case, which is closely related to the stakes. The hourly fee lawyer's return from a case is not as tied to stakes, and other types of considerations (*e.g.*, the client's goals, the nature of the forum, etc.) have a greater influence.

Herbert M. Kritzer, William L. F. Felstiner, Austin Sarat, and David M. Trubek, *The Impact of Fee Arrangement on Lawyer Effort*, 19 L. & Socy. Rev. 251 (1985).

In *Venegas v. Mitchell,* 495 U.S. 82 (1990), the Supreme Court considered whether a federal fee-shifting statute invalidates contingent-fee contracts that would require a prevailing plaintiff to pay his attorney more than the statutory award against the defendant. Mitchell was hired three months before the trial of Venegas' civil rights suit against city police officers (alleging false arrest and perjured trial), after the bulk of preparation had been completed. Mitchell obtained a $10,000 nonrefundable retainer and a right to share in 40 percent of the gross amount of any recovery. After trial, the defendants unsuccessfully moved to set aside the judgment and then appealed. Mitchell pursued and obtained statutory attorneys' fees under 42 U.S.C. §1988, which the court calculated by multiplying the hours of attorney time by a market-based hourly rate. Mitchell then sought 40 percent of the judgment proceeds. The court agreed to enforce the contingency fee arrangement. On review, the Supreme Court concluded that private fee arrangements may exist alongside statutory fee-shifts, and therefore permitted enforcement of the contingency fee arrangement at issue. Again, perhaps the problem in the case arose from the method for assessing the value of the lawyer's time.

Practice Exercise No. 5: Fee Arrangements in
Carpenter and *City of Cleveland*

Return to the *Carpenter* and *City of Cleveland* cases. Assume that you have been approached by the plaintiff(s) in each case to represent them. Estimate the relief available and the statutory attorneys' fees (if any). Should you take these cases, and, if so, under what contractual terms for attorneys' fees?

E. CONTEMPT

A party or lawyer who disobeys a court order or court rule risks being found in contempt of court. On occasion, individuals deliberately disobey court orders just as they may disobey a statute in order to protest or challenge a rule or norm they consider to be unjust. In recent years, protestors have violated rules governing access to abortion clinics and military settings. *See, e.g., Jayne Bray v. Alexandria Women's Health Clinic,* 506 U.S. 263 (1993) (pro-life protest); *United States and Connecticut v. Carmen E. F. Vasquez,* 145 F.3d 74 (2nd Cir. 1998) (same); *United States v. Albertini,* 472 U.S. 676 (1985) (anti-nuclear protest); *United States v. Springer,* 51 F.3d 861 (9th Cir. 1995) (same).

When someone disobeys a statute and faces criminal or civil consequences, there usually is a chance to offer a defense and a challenge to the law at issue in the course of a judicial hearing.

After a court finds a party in contempt for violating its order, should that party be able to defend the noncompliance? Would failing to give such an opportunity undermine due process or substantive justice? Or would giving such an opportunity invite further violations of court orders and disrespect for judicial power? The leading case on the subject grew out of the civil rights effort, led by the Reverend Martin Luther King, Jr., to challenge racial segregation in Birmingham, Alabama. David Luban described the historical context for the case in the following excerpt.

■ DAVID LUBAN, LEGAL MODERNISM
218-220 (1994)

In January 1963, the Southern Christian Leadership Conference (SCLC) held a retreat in Georgia to discuss strategy for a concerted attack

on segregation in Birmingham, Alabama. Project C for "confrontation"—
would consist of demonstrations and boycotts of Birmingham's downtown
businesses during the normally busy Easter shopping season.

Birmingham itself had recently begun to display some sentiment for
change in its segregationist ways. A group of whites headed by the Chamber of Commerce president campaigned to alter Birmingham's municipal
government by abolishing the offices of the three segregationist commissioners (including the notoriously racist commissioner of public safety,
Theophilus Eugene "Bull" Connor) who then ran the city. The voters
agreed to move to a mayoral system, and in a special election, Connor was
defeated by a more moderate segregationist named Albert Boutwell.
Connor went to court to demand that he be allowed to finish his term of
office as commissioner of public safety and while this matter was pending,
Birmingham was governed by what were in effect two city governments,
each passing its own laws and conducting city business after its own
fashion; municipal checks were signed by both Connor and Boutwell.
Some Birmingham whites hoped that the SCLC would cancel the Easter
demonstrations to give the new government a chance to show what it
could do, but the SCLC leadership—which had previously canceled
demonstrations to allow the run-off election between Connor and
Boutwell to proceed without the pressure of demonstrations—went ahead
with Project C.

A Birmingham city ordinance required the demonstrators to obtain a
parade permit from the city commission. On April 3, Mrs. Lola Hendricks,
representing the demonstrators, approached Connor to request a permit;
Connor replied, "No, you will not get a permit in Birmingham, Alabama
to picket. I will picket you over to the City Jail." On April 5—one week
before Good Friday—Connor replied to a second, telegraphic, request
for a parade permit with another refusal. The demonstrators proceeded
with their protests.

Project C included plans for the Reverend Martin Luther King, Jr., to
place himself in a position to be arrested on Good Friday, April 12.

Late Wednesday evening, April 10, Connor obtained an ex parte
injunction from Alabama Circuit Court Judge W. A. Jenkins, Jr., forbidding civil rights leaders, including all the leaders of Project C, from
taking part in or encouraging demonstrations. The injunction was served
at 1:00 A.M. on Thursday, and the SCLC leadership debated how to
respond to it. King feared that complying with the injunction would
deflate the protest, as had happened the previous summer in Albany,
Georgia. He went ahead with the planned demonstration the following
day and was arrested; a second demonstration took place on Easter Sunday, April 14. Subsequently, Judge Jenkins found several of the demonstrators guilty of criminal contempt and sentenced each of them (including
King) to five days in jail and a $50 fine. It is this conviction that the *Walker*
Court upheld.

This ends the sequence of events recounted in *Walker* and King's Letter. But the largest chronicle of the Birmingham campaign did not end with King's arrest. The demonstrators subsequently embarked on a strategy of marches by schoolchildren, leading to literally thousands of arrests. As the demonstrations continued, Bull Connor upped the level of official response, ordering the fire hoses and police dogs be turned on the demonstrators. Television news horrified its audiences with the spectacle of children bowled over by hoses that hit with enough force to rip the bark off trees. White moderates and the SCLC leadership undertook negotiations that led to a settlement announced on May 10. On May 11, the Ku Klux Klan staged a rally; after the meeting, the motel where King had been staying and the home of his brother were bombed. Crowds of angry blacks rioted, and President Kennedy eventually sent in federal troops. A month later, Alabama Governor George Wallace personally blocked the entrance of a University of Alabama building to prevent the entrance of two black students whose admission had been ordered by a federal court. Evidently this action was the last straw. The same day, President Kennedy spoke on national television to announce that he was seeking comprehensive civil rights legislation that eventually became the Civil Rights Act. This announcement and the march were the culminating events of Project C.

But let us return to King's original April arrest. While King was in jail, eight white clergymen—significantly, they were liberals who had publicly opposed Governor George Wallace's "Segregation Forever!" speech—took out a full-page advertisement in the Birmingham News denouncing the demonstrations. King responded from his cell, writing in the newspaper's margins until he was able to obtain paper; after he was permitted visitors, King's manuscript was typed by his friends and returned to him in jail for revisions. His Letter from Birmingham Jail attracted little attention at first. It was eventually printed by the American Friends Service Committee and reprinted in numerous periodicals; its fame and influence grew, and by now it is perhaps the most famous document to emerge from the civil rights movement. . . .

Point and counterpoint: King's Letter has become one of the great classics in the literature of civil disobedience, both for its philosophy and for the soul-stirring magnificence of its language. No one has called Potter Stewart's *Walker* opinion a classic (in what might be called the literature of civil obedience), but its status as a Supreme Court precedent makes it the functional equivalent of a classic. Both *Walker* and the *Letter* address an ancient question, a question that more than any other defines the very subject of legal philosophy: that, of course, is the question whether we lie under an obligation to obey unjust legal directives, including directives ordering our punishment for disobeying other unjust directives. All political philosophy, from Plato's *Apology* and *Crito* on, is driven by this question; all our political hopes and aspirations are contained in the descriptive and argumentative materials we use to answer it.

■ WALKER v. CITY OF BIRMINGHAM
388 U.S. 307 (1967)

Justice STEWART delivered the opinion of the Court:

On Wednesday, April 10, 1963, officials of Birmingham, Alabama, filed a bill of complaint in a state circuit court asking for injunctive relief against 139 individuals and two organizations. The bill and accompanying affidavits stated that during the preceding seven days:

[R]espondents (had) sponsored and/or participated in and/or conspired to commit and/or to encourage and/or to participate in certain move- ments, plans or projects commonly called "sit-in" demonstrations, "kneel-in" demonstrations, mass street parades, trespasses on private property after being warned to leave the premises by the owners of said property, congre- gating in mobs upon the public streets and other public places, unlawfully picketing private places of business in the City of Birmingham, Alabama; violation of numerous ordinances and statutes of the City of Birmingham and State of Alabama. . . .

It was alleged that this conduct was "calculated to provoke breaches of the peace," threaten[ed] the safety, peace and tranquility of the City, and placed an undue burden and strain upon the manpower of the Police Department.

The bill stated that these infractions of the law were expected to continue and would "lead to further imminent danger to the lives, safety, peace, tranquility and general welfare of the people of the City of Birm- ingham," and that the "remedy by law [was] inadequate." The circuit judge granted a temporary injunction as prayed in the bill, enjoining the petitioners from, among other things, participating in or encouraging mass street parades or mass processions without a permit as required by a Birmingham ordinance.

Five of the eight petitioners were served with copies of the writ early the next morning. Several hours later four of them held a press confer- ence. There a statement was distributed, declaring their intention to disobey the injunction because it was "raw tyranny under the guise of maintaining law and order." At this press conference one of the petition- ers stated: "That they had respect for the Federal Courts, or Federal Injunctions, but in the past the State Courts had favored local law enforce- ment, and if the police couldn't handle it, the mob would."

That night a meeting took place at which one of the petitioners announced that "[i]njunction or no injunction we are going to march tomorrow." The next afternoon, Good Friday, a large crowd gathered in the vicinity of Sixteenth Street and Sixth Avenue North in Birmingham. A group of about 50 or 60 proceeded to parade along the sidewalk while a crowd of 1,000 to 1,500 onlookers stood by, "clapping, and hollering, and [w]hooping." Some of the crowd followed the marchers and spilled out into the street. At least three of the petitioners participated in this march.

Meetings sponsored by some of the petitioners were held that night and the following night, where calls for volunteers to "walk" and go to jail were made. On Easter Sunday, April 14, a crowd of between 1,500 and 2,000 people congregated in the midafternoon in the vicinity of Seventh Avenue and Eleventh Street North in Birmingham. One of the petitioners was seen organizing members of the crowd in formation. A group of about 50, headed by three other petitioners, started down the sidewalk two abreast. At least one other petitioner was among the marchers. Some 300 or 400 people from among the onlookers followed in a crowd that occupied the entire width of the street and overflowed onto the sidewalks. Violence occurred. Members of the crowd threw rocks that injured a newspaperman and damaged a police motorcycle.

The next day the city officials who had requested the injunction applied to the state circuit court for an order to show cause why the petitioners should not be held in contempt for violating it. At the ensuing hearing the petitioners sought to attack the constitutionality of the injunction on the ground that it was vague and overbroad, and restrained free speech. They also sought to attack the Birmingham parade ordinance upon similar grounds, and upon the further ground that the ordinance had previously been administered in an arbitrary and discriminatory manner.

The circuit judge refused to consider any of these contentions, pointing out that there had been neither a motion to dissolve the injunction, nor an effort to comply with it by applying for a permit from the city commission before engaging in the Good Friday and Easter Sunday parades. Consequently, the court held that the only issues before it were whether it had jurisdiction to issue the temporary injunction, and whether thereafter the petitioners had knowingly violated it. Upon these issues the court found against the petitioners, and imposed upon each of them a sentence of five days in jail and a $50 fine, in accord with an Alabama statute.

The Supreme Court of Alabama affirmed. That court, too, declined to consider the petitioners' constitutional attacks upon the injunction and the underlying Birmingham parade ordinance. . . .

Without question the state court that issued the injunction had, as a court of equity, jurisdiction over the petitioners and over the subject matter of the controversy. And this is not a case where the injunction was transparently invalid or had only a frivolous pretense to validity. We have consistently recognized the strong interest of state and local governments in regulating the use of their streets and other public places. . . . When protest takes the form of mass demonstrations, parades, or picketing on public streets and sidewalks, the free passage of traffic and the prevention of public disorder and violence become important objects of legitimate state concern. As the Court stated, in *Cox v. State of Louisiana*, "We emphatically reject the notion . . . that the First and Fourteenth Amendments afford the same kind of freedom to those who would communicate ideas by conduct such as patrolling, marching, and picketing on streets and highways, as these amendments afford to those who communicate ideas by pure speech." 379 U.S. 536, 555. . . .

The generality of the language contained in the Birmingham parade ordinance upon which the injunction was based would unquestionably raise substantial constitutional issues concerning some of its provisions. *Schneider v. State of New Jersey*, 308 U.S. 147; *Saia v. People of State of New York*, 334 U.S. 558; *Kunz v. People of State of New York*, 340 U.S. 290. The petitioners, however, did not even attempt to apply to the Alabama courts for an authoritative construction of the ordinance. Had they done so, those courts might have given the licensing authority granted in the ordinance a narrow and precise scope. . . . [Here] it could not be assumed that this ordinance was void on its face.

The breadth and vagueness of the injunction itself would also unquestionably be subject to substantial constitutional question. But the way to raise that question was to apply to the Alabama courts to have the injunction modified or dissolved. The injunction in all events clearly prohibited mass parading without a permit, and the evidence shows that the petitioners fully understood that prohibition when they violated it.

The petitioners also claim that they were free to disobey the injunction because the parade ordinance on which it was based had been administered in the past in an arbitrary and discriminatory fashion. In support of this claim they sought to introduce evidence that, a few days before the injunction issued, requests for permits to picket had been made to a member of the city commission. One request had been rudely rebuffed, and this same official had later made clear that he was without power to grant the permit alone, since the issuance of such permits was the responsibility of the entire city commission. Assuming the truth of this proffered evidence, it does not follow that the parade ordinance was void on its face. The petitioners, moreover, did not apply for a permit either to the commission itself or to any commissioner after the injunction issued. Had they done so, and had the permit been refused, it is clear that their claim of arbitrary or discriminatory administration of the ordinance would have been considered by the state circuit court upon a motion to dissolve the injunction.

This case would arise in quite a different constitutional posture if the petitioners, before disobeying the injunction, had challenged it in the Alabama courts, and had been met with delay or frustration of their constitutional claims. . . .

The rule of law that Alabama followed in this case reflects a belief that in the fair administration of justice no man can be judge in his own case, however exalted his station, however righteous his motives, and irrespective of his race, color, politics, or religion. This Court cannot hold that the petitioners were constitutionally free to ignore all the procedures of the law and carry their battle to the streets. . . .

Affirmed.

APPENDIX TO OPINION OF COURT
[THE FULL TEXT OF DR. KING'S SPEECH]

In our struggle for freedom we have anchored our faith and hope in the rightness of the Constitution and the moral laws of the universe.

Again and again the Federal judiciary has made it clear that the privileges guaranteed under the First and the Fourteenth Amendments are too sacred to be trampled upon by the machinery of state government and police power. In the past we have abided by Federal injunctions out of respect for the forthright and consistent leadership that the Federal judiciary has given in establishing the principle of integration as the law of the land.

However we are now confronted with recalcitrant forces in the Deep South that will use the courts to perpetuate the unjust and illegal system of racial separation.

Alabama has made clear its determination to defy the law of the land. Most of its public officials, its legislative body and many of its law enforcement agents have openly defied the desegregation decision of the Supreme Court. We would feel morally and legally responsible to obey the injunction if the courts of Alabama applied equal justice to all of its citizens. This would be sameness made legal. However the issuance of this injunction is a blatant [example] of difference made legal.

Southern law enforcement agencies have demonstrated now and again that they will utilize the force of law to misuse the judicial process.

This is raw tyranny under the guise of maintaining law and order. We cannot in all good conscience obey such an injunction, which is an unjust, undemocratic and unconstitutional misuse of the legal process.

We do this not out of any disrespect for the law but out of the highest respect for the law. This is not an attempt to evade or defy the law or engage in chaotic anarchy. Just as in all good conscience we cannot obey unjust laws, neither can we respect the unjust use of the courts.

We believe in a system of law based on justice and morality. Out of our great love for the Constitution of the U.S. and our desire to purify the judicial system of the state of Alabama, we risk this critical move with an awareness of the possible consequences involved.

Chief Justice WARREN, with whom Mr. Justice BRENNAN and Mr. Justice FORTAS join, dissenting.

Petitioners in this case contend that they were convicted under an ordinance that is unconstitutional on its face because it submits their First and Fourteenth Amendment rights to free speech and peaceful assembly to the unfettered discretion of local officials. They further contend that the ordinance was unconstitutionally applied to them because the local officials used their discretion to prohibit peaceful demonstrations by a group whose political viewpoint the officials opposed. The Court does not dispute these contentions, but holds that petitioners may nonetheless be convicted and sent to jail because the patently unconstitutional ordinance was copied into an injunction—issued ex parte without prior notice or hearing on the request of the Commissioner of Public Safety—forbidding all persons having notice of the injunction to violate the ordinance without any limitation of time. I dissent because I do not believe that the fundamental protections of the Constitution were meant to be so easily evaded, or that "the civilizing hand of law" would be hampered in the slightest by enforcing the First Amendment in this case.

The salient facts can be stated very briefly. Petitioners are Negro ministers who sought to express their concern about racial discrimination in Birmingham, Alabama, by holding peaceful protest demonstrations in that city on Good Friday and Easter Sunday 1963. For obvious reasons, it was important for the significance of the demonstrations that they be held on those particular dates. A representative of petitioners' organization went to the City Hall and asked to see the person or persons in charge to issue permits, permits for parading, picketing, and demonstrating. She was directed to Public Safety Commissioner Connor, who denied her request for a permit in terms that left no doubt that petitioners were not going to be issued a permit under any circumstances. He said, "No you will not get a permit in Birmingham, Alabama to picket. I will picket you over to the City Jail," and he repeated that twice. A second, telegraphic request was also summarily denied, in a telegram signed by Eugene "Bull" Connor, with the added information that permits could be issued only by the full City Commission, a three-man body consisting of Commissioner Connor and two others. According to petitioners' offer of proof, the truth of which is assumed for purposes of this case, parade permits had uniformly been issued for all other groups by the city clerk on the request of the traffic bureau of the police department, which was under Commissioner Connor's direction. The requirement that the approval of the full Commission be obtained was applied only to this one group.

Understandably convinced that the City of Birmingham was not going to authorize their demonstrations under any circumstances, petitioners proceeded with their plans despite Commissioner Connor's orders. On Wednesday, April 10, at 9 in the evening, the city filed in a state circuit court a bill of complaint seeking an ex parte injunction. The complaint recited that petitioners were engaging in a series of demonstrations as "part of a massive effort . . . to forcibly integrate all business establishments, churches, and other institutions" in the city, with the result that the police department was strained in its resources and the safety, peace, and tranquillity were threatened. It was alleged as particularly menacing that petitioners were planning to conduct "kneel-in" demonstrations at churches where their presence was not wanted. The city's police dogs were said to be in danger of their lives. Faced with these recitals, the Circuit Court issued the injunction in the form requested, and in effect ordered petitioners and all other persons having notice of the order to refrain for an unlimited time from carrying on any demonstrations without a permit. A permit, of course, was clearly unobtainable; the city would not have sought this injunction if it had any intention of issuing one.

Petitioners were served with copies of the injunction at various times on Thursday and on Good Friday. Unable to believe that such a blatant and broadly drawn prior restraint on their First Amendment rights could be valid, they announced their intention to defy it and went ahead with the planned peaceful demonstrations on Easter weekend. On the following Monday, when they promptly filed a motion to dissolve the injunction, the court found them in contempt, holding that they had waived all their First Amendment rights by disobeying the court order.

These facts lend no support to the court's charges that petitioners were presuming to act as judges in their own case, or that they had a disregard for the judicial process. They did not flee the jurisdiction or refuse to appear in the Alabama courts. Having violated the injunction, they promptly submitted themselves to the courts to test the constitutionality of the injunction and the ordinance it parroted. They were in essentially the same position as persons who challenge the constitutionality of a statute by violating it, and then defend the ensuing criminal prosecution on constitutional grounds. It has never been thought that violation of a statute indicated such a disrespect for the legislature that the violator always must be punished even if the statute was unconstitutional. On the contrary, some cases have required that persons seeking to challenge the constitutionality of a statute first violate it to establish their standing to sue. Indeed, it shows no disrespect for law to violate a statute on the ground that it is unconstitutional and then to submit one's case to the courts with the willingness to accept the penalty if the statute is held to be valid.

The Court concedes that "[t]he generality of the language contained in the Birmingham parade ordinance upon which the injunction was based would unquestionably raise substantial constitutional issues concerning some of its provisions." That concession is well-founded but minimal. I believe it is patently unconstitutional on its face. . . . When local officials are given totally unfettered discretion to decide whether a proposed demonstration is consistent with "public welfare, peace, safety, health, decency, good order, morals or convenience," as they were in this case, they are invited to act as censors over the views that may be presented to the public. The unconstitutionality of the ordinance is compounded, of course, when there is convincing evidence that the officials have in fact used their power to deny permits to organizations whose views they dislike. . . .

I do not believe that giving this Court's seal of approval to such a gross misuse of the judicial process is likely to lead to greater respect for the law any more than it is likely to lead to greater protection for First Amendment freedoms. The ex parte temporary injunction has a long and odious history in this country, and its susceptibility to misuse is all too apparent from the facts of the case. . . . Respect for the courts and for judicial process was not increased by the history of the labor injunction.

Justice DOUGLAS, Justice, with whom the CHIEF JUSTICE, Justice BRENNAN, and Justice FORTAS concur, dissenting:

The record shows that petitioners did not deliberately attempt to circumvent the permit requirement. Rather they diligently attempted to obtain a permit and were rudely rebuffed and then reasonably concluded that any further attempts would be fruitless.

The right to defy an unconstitutional statute is basic in our scheme. Even when an ordinance requires a permit to make a speech, to deliver a sermon, to picket, to parade, or to assemble, it need not be honored when it is invalid on its face. . . .

Yet by some inscrutable legerdemain these constitutionally secured rights to challenge prior restraints invalid on their face are lost if the State takes the precaution to have some judge append his signature to an ex parte order which recites the words of the invalid statute. The State neatly insulates its legislation from challenge by mere incorporation of the identical stifling, overbroad, and vague restraints on exercise of the First Amendment freedoms into an even more vague and pervasive injunction obtained invisibly and upon a stage darkened lest it be open to scrutiny by those affected. . . .

The Court today lets loose a devastatingly destructive weapon for infringement of freedoms jealously safeguarded not so much for the benefit of any given group of any given persuasion as for the benefit of all of us. We cannot permit fears of "riots" and "civil disobedience" generated by slogans like "Black Power" to divert our attention from what is here at stake—not violence or the right of the State to control its streets and sidewalks, but the insulation from attack of ex parte orders and legislation upon which they are based even when patently impermissible prior restraints on the exercise of First Amendment rights, thus arming the state courts with the power to punish as a "contempt" what they otherwise could not punish at all. Constitutional restrictions against abridgments of First Amendment freedoms limit judicial equally with legislative and executive power. Convictions for contempt of court orders which invalidly abridge First Amendment freedoms must be condemned equally with convictions for violation of statutes which do the same thing. I respectfully dissent.

Comments and Questions

1. Note that after its decision in *Walker*, the Supreme Court held that the Birmingham parade-permit ordinance violated the First Amendment because it gave unfettered discretion to city officials to restrict speech.

Shuttlesworth v. City of Birmingham, 394 U.S. 147 (1967). Also, the Court ruled there that Reverend Shuttlesworth could overturn his conviction for parading without a permit. Why do you think the Supreme Court treated Reverend Shuttlesworth's action in violation of the law differently from Reverend King's violation of a court order predicated on the same law? Do you think there is a distinction here worth maintaining? For one effort to address these issues, *see* Alexander Bickel, *Civil Disobedience and the Duty to Obey,* 8 Gonz. L. Rev. 199 (1973).

2. In *Walker,* the court announced exceptions to Alabama's collateral bar rule. What are those exceptions, and how would you apply them to the facts of the *Shuttlesworth* case?

3. What kind of rule is the collateral bar rule, and how can it be changed? Note that in *Walker,* the state's collateral bar rule was found to apply even in the face of federal constitutional claims. Some state courts have rejected the collateral bar rule. *See In re Berry,* 68 Cal. 2d 137 (1968). What are the arguments for retaining and rejecting it?

4. Further historical context can be found in Alan Westin and Barry Mahoney, *The Trial of Martin Luther King* (1974), and Taylor Branch, *Parting the Waters* (1988), and the award-winning Public Broadcasting Service series, Eyes on the Prize.

5. Long before the Supreme Court's decision in *Walker,* back at the time of his arrest for violating the Alabama court order, Reverend Martin Luther King, Jr. wrote a response to a statement by eight Alabama clergymen urging him and others in the black community to stop their program of "direct action," including sit-ins, boycotts, and marches against racial segregation. King's direct-action approach pursued tenets of civil disobedience in response to the Southern resistance to integration, which had been mandated by the Supreme Court since its decision in *Brown v. Board of Education,* 374 U.S. 483 (1954). King was awarded the Nobel Peace Prize for his struggle for civil rights. He was murdered in Memphis in April 1968. Following his assassination, major urban areas in the United States erupted in violence. As you read portions of Reverend King's letter, consider what you find persuasive, and why, and whether any of his arguments join issue with the majority opinion in *Walker.* You can also find the full text of King's letter in *Civil Disobedience: Theory and Practice* 72-89 (ed. Hugo Bedav 1969).

■ MARTIN LUTHER KING, JR., LETTER FROM BIRMINGHAM CITY JAIL
A Testament of Hope: The Essential Writings and Speeches of Martin Luther King, Jr., 289 (*James M. Washington, ed. 1986*)

The following is the public statement directed to Martin Luther King, Jr., by eight Alabama clergymen:

We the undersigned clergymen are among those who, in January, issued "An Appeal for Law and Order and Common Sense," in dealing with racial problems in Alabama. We expressed understanding that honest convictions in racial matters could properly be pursued in the courts, but urged that decisions of those courts should in the meantime be peacefully obeyed.

Since that time there had been some evidence of increased forbearance and a willingness to face facts. Responsible citizens have undertaken to work on various problems which cause racial friction and unrest. In Birmingham, recent public events have given indication that we all have opportunity for a new constructive and realistic approach to racial problems.

However, we are now confronted by a series of demonstrations by some of our Negro citizens, directed and led in part by outsiders. We recognize the natural impatience of people who feel that their hopes are slow in being realized. But we are convinced that these demonstrations are unwise and untimely.

We agree rather with certain local Negro leadership which has called for honest and open negotiation of racial issues in our area. And we believe this kind of facing of issues can best be accomplished by citizens of our own metropolitan area, white and Negro, meeting with their knowledge and experience of the local situation. All of us need to face that responsibility and find proper channels for its accomplishment.

Just as we formerly pointed out that "hatred and violence have no sanction in our religious and political traditions," we also point out that such actions as incite to hatred and violence, however technically peaceful those actions may be, have not contributed to the resolution of our local problems. We do not believe that these days of new hope are days when extreme measures are justified in Birmingham.

We commend the community as a whole, and the local news media and law enforcement officials in particular, on the calm manner in which these demonstrations have been handled. We urge the public to continue to show restraint should the demonstrations continue, and the law enforcement officials to remain calm and continue to protect our city from violence.

We further strongly urge our own Negro community to withdraw support from these demonstrations, and to unite locally in working peacefully for a better Birmingham. When rights are consistently denied, a cause should be pressed in the courts and in negotiations among local leaders, and not in the streets. We appeal to both our white and Negro citizenry to observe the principles of law and order and common sense.

Bishop C. C. J. Carpenter, Bishop Joseph A. Durick, Rabbi Milton L. Grafman, Bishop Paul Hardin, Bishop Nolan B. Harmon, Rev. George M. Murray, Rev. Edward V. Ramage, Rev. Earl Stallings

April 12, 1963

My dear Fellow Clergymen,

While confined here in the Birmingham City Jail, I came across your recent statement calling our present activities "unwise and untimely." Seldom, if ever, do I pause to answer criticism of my work and ideas. If I sought to answer all of the criticisms that cross my desk, my secretaries would be engaged in little else in the course of the day, and I would have no time for constructive work. But since I feel that you are men of genuine goodwill and your criticisms are sincerely set forth, I would like to answer your statement in what I hope will be patient and reasonable terms. . . .

Several months ago our local affiliate here in Birmingham invited us to be on call to engage in a nonviolent direct action program if such were deemed necessary. We readily consented and when the hour came we lived up to our promises. So I am here, along with several members of my staff, because we were invited here. I am here because I have basic organizational ties here.

Beyond this, I am in Birmingham because injustice is here. Just as the eighth century prophets left their little villages and carried their "thus saith the Lord" far beyond the boundaries of their home towns; and just as the Apostle Paul left his little village of Tarsus and carried the gospel of Jesus Christ to practically every hamlet and city of the Graeco-Roman world, I too am compelled to carry the gospel of freedom beyond my particular home town. Like Paul, I must constantly respond to the Macedonian call for aid.

Moreover, I am cognizant of the interrelatedness of all communities and states. I cannot sit idly by in Atlanta and not be concerned about what happens in Birmingham. Injustice anywhere is a threat to justice everywhere. We are caught in an inescapable network of mutuality, tied in a single garment of destiny. Whatever affects one directly affects all indirectly. Never again can we afford to live with the narrow, provincial "outside agitator" idea. Anyone who lives inside the United States can never be considered an outsider anywhere in this country.

You deplore the demonstrations that are presently taking place in Birmingham. But I am sorry that your statement did not express a similar concern for the conditions that brought the demonstrations into being. I am sure that each of you would want to go beyond the superficial social analyst who looks merely at effects, and does not grapple with underlying causes. I would not hesitate to say that it is unfortunate that so-called demonstrations are taking place in Birmingham at this time, but I would say in even more emphatic terms that it is even more unfortunate that the white power structure of this city left the Negro community with no other alternative.

In any nonviolent campaign there are four basic steps: 1) Collection of the facts to determine whether injustices are alive. 2) Negotiation. 3) Self-purification and 4) Direct Action. We have gone through all of these steps in Birmingham. There can be no gainsaying of the fact that racial injustice engulfs this community.

Birmingham is probably the most thoroughly segregated city in the United States. Its ugly record of police brutality is known in every section of this country. Its unjust treatment of Negroes in the courts is a notorious reality. There have been more unsolved bombings of Negro homes and churches in Birmingham than any city in this nation. These are the hard, brutal and unbelievable facts. On the basis of these conditions Negro leaders sought to negotiate with the city fathers. But the political leaders consistently refused to engage in good faith negotiation. . . .

When we discovered that Mr. Connor was in [a run-off election], we decided again to postpone action so that the demonstrations could not be used to cloud the issues. At this time we agreed to begin our nonviolent witness the day after the run-off.

This reveals that we did not move irresponsibly into direct action. We too wanted to see Mr. Connor defeated; so we went through postponement after postponement to aid in this community need. After this we felt that direct action could be delayed no longer.

CREATIVE TENSION

You may well ask, "Why direct action? Why sit-ins, marches, etc.? Isn't negotiation a better path?" You are exactly right in your call for negotiation. Indeed, this is the purpose of direct action. Nonviolent direct action seeks to create such a crisis and establish such creative tension that a community that has constantly refused to negotiate is forced to confront the issue. It seeks so to dramatize the issue that it can no longer be ignored. I just referred to the creation of tension as a part of the work of the nonviolent resister. This may sound rather shocking. But I must confess that I am not afraid of the word tension. I have earnestly worked and preached against violent tension, but there is a type of constructive nonviolent tension that is necessary for growth. Just as Socrates felt that it was necessary to create a tension in the mind so that individuals could rise from the bondage of myths and half-truths to the unfettered realm of creative analysis and objective appraisal, we must see the need of having nonviolent gadflies to create the kind of tension in society that will help men to rise from the dark depths of prejudice and racism to the majestic heights of understanding and brotherhood. So the purpose of the direct action is to create a situation so crisis-packed that it will inevitably open the door to negotiation. We, therefore, concur with you in your call for negotiation. Too long has our beloved Southland been bogged down in the tragic attempt to live in monologue rather than dialogue.

One of the basic points in your statement is that our acts are untimely. Some have asked. "Why didn't you give the new administration time to act?" The only answer that I can give to this inquiry is that the new administration must be prodded about as much as the outgoing one before it acts. We will be sadly mistaken if we feel that the election of Mr. Boutwell will bring the millennium to Birmingham. While Mr. Boutwell is much more articulate and gentle than Mr. Connor, they are both segregationists, dedicated to the task of maintaining the status quo. The hope I see in Mr. Boutwell is that he will be reasonable enough to see the futility of massive resistance to desegregation. But he will not see this without pressure from the devotees of civil rights. My friends, I must say to you that we have not made a single gain in civil rights without determined legal and nonviolent pressure. History is the long and tragic story of the fact that privileged groups seldom give up their privileges voluntarily. Individuals may see the moral light and voluntarily give up their unjust posture; but as Reinhold Niebuhr has reminded us, groups are more immoral than individuals.

We know through painful experience that freedom is never voluntarily given by the oppressor; it must be demanded by the oppressed. Frankly, I have never yet engaged in a direct action movement that was "well timed," according to the timetable of those who have not suffered unduly from the disease of segregation. For years now I have heard the words "Wait!" It rings in the ear of every Negro with a piercing familiarity. This "Wait" has almost always meant "Never." It has been a tranquilizing thalidomide, relieving the emotional stress for a moment, only to give birth to an ill-formed infant of frustration. We must come to see with the distinguished jurist of yesterday that "justice too long delayed is justice denied." We have waited for more than three hundred and forty years for our constitutional and God-given rights. The nations of Asia and Africa are moving with jet-like speed toward the goal of political independence, and we still creep at horse and buggy pace toward the gaining of a cup of coffee at a lunch counter. I guess it is easy for those who have never felt the stinging darts of segregation to say, "Wait." But when you have seen vicious mobs lynch your mothers and fathers at will and drown your sisters and brothers at whim; when you have seen hate-filled policemen curse, kick, brutalize and even kill your black brothers and sisters with impunity; when you see the vast majority of your twenty million Negro brothers smothering in an airtight cage of poverty in the midst of an affluent society; when you suddenly find your tongue twisted and your speech stammering as you seek to explain to your six-year-old daughter why she can't go to the public amusement park that has just been advertised on television, and see tears welling up in her little eyes when she is told that Funtown is closed to colored children, and see the depressing clouds of inferiority begin to form in her little mental sky, and see her begin to distort her little personality to unconsciously developing a bitterness toward white people; when you have to concoct an answer for a five-year-old son asking in agonizing pathos: "Daddy, why do white people treat colored people so mean?"; when you take a cross country drive and find it necessary to sleep night after night in the uncomfortable corners of your automobile because no motel will accept you; when you are humiliated day in and day out by nagging signs reading "white" and "colored"; when your first name becomes "nigger" and your middle name becomes "boy" (however old you are) and your last name becomes "John," and when your wife and mother are never given the respected title "Mrs."; when you are harried by day and haunted at night by the fact that you are a Negro, living constantly at tip-toe stance never quite knowing what to expect next, and plagued with inner fears and outer resentments; when you are forever fighting a degenerating sense of "nobodiness"; then you will understand why we find it difficult to wait. There comes a time when the cup of endurance runs over, and men are no longer willing to be plunged into an abyss of injustice where they experience the blackness of corroding despair. I hope, sirs, you can understand our legitimate and unavoidable impatience.

BREAKING THE LAW

You express a great deal of anxiety over our willingness to break laws. This is certainly a legitimate concern. Since we so diligently urge people to obey the Supreme Court's decision of 1954 outlawing segregation in the public schools, it is rather strange and paradoxical to find us consciously breaking laws. One may well ask, "how can you advocate breaking some laws and obeying others?" The answer is found in the fact that there are two types of laws: There are *just* and there are *unjust* laws. I would agree with Saint Augustine that "An unjust law is no law at all."

Now what is the difference between the two? How does one determine when a law is just or unjust? A just law is a man-made code that squares with the moral law or the law of God. An unjust law is a code that is out of harmony with the moral law. To put it in the terms of Saint Thomas Aquinas, an unjust law is a human law that its not rooted in eternal and natural law. Any law that uplifts human personality is just. Any law that degrades human personality is unjust. All segregation statutes are unjust because segregation distorts the soul and damages the personality. It gives the segregator a false sense of superiority, and the segregated a false sense of inferiority. To use the words of Martin Buber, the great Jewish philosopher, segregation substitutes an "I-it" relationship for the "I-thou" relationship, and ends up relegating persons to the status of things. So segregation is not only politically, economically and sociologically unsound, but it is morally wrong and sinful. Paul Tillich has said that sin is separation. Isn't segregation an existential expression of man's tragic separation, an expression of his awful estrangement, his terrible sinfulness? So I can urge men to disobey segregation ordinances because they are morally wrong.

Let us turn to a more concrete example of just and unjust laws. An unjust law is a code that a majority inflicts on a minority that is not binding on itself. This is difference made legal. On the other hand a just law is a code that a majority compels a minority to follow that it is willing to follow itself. This is sameness made legal.

Let me give another explanation. An unjust law is a code inflicted upon a minority which that minority had no part in enacting or creating because they did not have the unhampered right to vote. Who can say that the legislature of Alabama which set up the segregation laws was democratically elected? Throughout the state of Alabama all types of conniving methods are used to prevent Negroes from becoming registered voters and there are some counties without a single Negro registered to vote despite the fact that the Negro constitutes a majority of the population. Can any law set up in such a state be considered democratically structured?

These are just a few examples of unjust and just laws. There are some instances when a law is just on its face and unjust in its application. For instance, I was arrested Friday on a charge of parading without a permit. Now there is nothing wrong with an ordinance which requires a permit for a parade, but when the ordinance is used to preserve segregation and to deny citizens the First Amendment privilege of peaceful assembly and peaceful protest, then it becomes unjust. . . .

THE WHITE MODERATE

We can never forget that everything Hitler did in Germany was "legal" and everything the Hungarian freedom fighters did in Hungary was "illegal." It was "illegal" to aid and comfort a Jew in Hitler's Germany. But I am sure that if I had lived in Germany during that time I would have aided and comforted my Jewish brothers even though it was illegal. If I lived in a Communist country today where certain principles dear to the Christian faith are suppressed, I believe I would openly advocate disobeying these anti-religious laws. I must make two honest confessions to you, my Christian and Jewish brothers. First, I must confess that over the last few years I have been gravely disappointed with the white moderate. I have almost reached the regrettable conclusion that the Negro's great stumbling block in the stride toward freedom is not the White Citizen's Councilor or the Ku Klux Klanner, but the white moderate who is more devoted to "order" than to justice; who prefers a negative peace which is the absence of tension to a positive peace which is the presence of justice; who constantly says "I agree with you in the goal you seek, but I can't agree with your methods of direct action"; who paternalistically feels that he can set the timetable for another man's freedom; who lives by the myth of time and who constantly advises the Negro to wait until a "more convenient season." Shallow understanding from people of good will is more frustrating than absolute misunderstanding from people of ill will. Lukewarm acceptance is much more bewildering than outright rejection.

I had hoped that the white moderate would understand that law and order exist for the purpose of establishing justice, and that when they fail to do this they become dangerously structured dams that block the flow of social progress. . . .

You spoke of our activity in Birmingham as extreme. At first, I was rather disappointed that fellow clergymen would see my nonviolent efforts as those of the extremist. I started thinking about the fact that I stand in the middle of two opposing forces in the Negro community. One is a force of complacency made up of Negroes who, as a result of long years of oppression, have been so completely drained of self-respect and a sense of "somebodiness" that they have adjusted to segregation, and of a few Negroes in the middle class who, because of a degree of academic and economic security, and because at points they profit by segregation, have unconsciously become insensitive to the problems of the masses. The other force is one of bitterness and hatred and comes perilously close to advocating violence. It is expressed in the various black nationalist groups that are springing up over the nation, the largest and best known being Elijah Muhammad's Muslim movement. This movement is nourished by the contemporary frustration over the continued existence of racial discrimination. It is made up of people who have lost faith in America, who have absolutely repudiated Christianity, and who have concluded that the white man is an incurable "devil." I have tried to stand between these two forces saying that we need not follow the "do-nothingism" of the complacent or the hatred and despair of the black nationalist. There is the more excellent way of love and nonviolent protest. I'm grateful to God that, through the Negro church, the dimension of nonviolence entered our struggle. If this philosophy had not emerged, I am convinced that by now many streets of the South would be flowing with floods of blood. And I am further convinced that if our white brothers dismiss as "rabble rousers" and "outside agitators" those of us who are working through the channels of nonviolent direct action and refuse to support our nonviolent efforts, millions of Negroes, out of frustration and despair, will seek solace and security in black nationalist ideologies, a development that will lead inevitably to a frightening racial nightmare. . . .

EXTREMISTS FOR LOVE

. . . [A]s I continued to think about the matter, I gradually gain[ed] a bit of satisfaction from being considered an extremist. Was not Jesus an extremist in love—"Love your enemies, bless them that curse you, pray for them that despitefully use you." Was not Amos an extremist for justice—"Let justice roll down like waters and righteousness like a mighty stream." Was not Paul an extremist for the gospel of Jesus Christ—"I bear in my body the marks of the Lord Jesus." Was not Martin Luther an extremist—"Here I stand; I can do none other so help me God." Was not John Bunyan an extremist—"I will stay in jail to the end of my days before I make a butchery of my conscience." Was not Abraham Lincoln an extremist—"This nation cannot survive half slave and half free." Was not Thomas Jefferson an extremist—"We hold these truths to be self-evident, that all men are created equal." So the question is not whether we will be extremist but what kind of extremist will we be. Will we be extremists for

hate or will we be extremists for love? Will we be extremists for the preservation of injustice—or will we be extremists for the cause of justice? In
that dramatic scene on Calvary's hill, three men were crucified. We must
not forget that all three were crucified for the same crime—the crime of
extremism. Two were extremists for immorality, and thusly fell below their
environment. The other, Jesus Christ, was an extremist for love, truth, and
goodness, and thereby rose above his environment. So, after all, maybe
the South, the nation and the world are in dire need of creative
extremists. . . .

[In this portion of his letter, Doctor King criticizes white churches
that "stand on the sideline and merely mouth pious irrelevancies and
sanctimonious trivialities, and speak about obeying law, but neither about
'right' nor 'injustice.'" He also criticizes most moderate whites: "I guess
I should have realized that few members of a race that has oppressed race
can understand or appreciate the deep groans and passionate yearnings
of those that have been oppressed and still fewer have the vision to see
that injustice must be rooted out by strong, persistent and determined
action."]

BULL CONNOR'S POLICE

I must close now. But before closing, I am impelled to mention one
other point in your statement that troubled me profoundly. You warmly
commended the Birmingham police force for keeping "order" and
"preventing violence." I don't believe you would have so warmly
commended the police force if you had seen its angry violent dogs literally
biting six unarmed, nonviolent Negroes. I don't believe you would so
quickly commend the policemen if you would observe their ugly and inhuman treatment of Negroes here in the city jail; if you would watch them
push and curse old Negro women and young Negro girls; if you would see
them slap and kick old Negro men and young boys; if you will observe
them, as they did on two occasions, refuse to give us food because we
wanted to sing our grace together. I'm sorry that I can't join you in your
praise for the police department.

It is true that they have been rather disciplined in their public
handling of the demonstrators. In this sense they have been rather
publicly "nonviolent." But for what purpose? To preserve the evil system of
segregation. Over the last few years I have consistently preached that
nonviolence demands that the means we use must be as pure as the ends
we seek. So, I have tried to make it clear that it is wrong to use immoral
means to attain moral ends. But now I must affirm that it is just as wrong,
or even more so, to use moral means to preserve immoral ends. Maybe
Mr. Connor and his policemen have been rather publicly nonviolent, as
Chief Pritchett was in Albany, Georgia, but they have used the moral
means of nonviolence to maintain the immoral end of flagrant racial

injustice. T. S. Eliot has said that there is no greater treason than to do the right deed for the wrong reason.

I wish you had commended the Negro sit-inners and demonstrators of Birmingham for their sublime courage, their willingness to suffer and their amazing discipline in the midst of the most inhuman provocation. One day the South will recognize its real heroes. They will be the James Merediths, courageously and with a majestic sense of purpose facing jeering and hostile mobs and the agonizing loneliness that characterizes the life of the pioneer. They will be old oppressed, battered Negro women, symbolized in a seventy-two year old woman of Montgomery, Alabama, who rose up with a sense of dignity and with her people decided not to ride the segregated buses, and responded to one who inquired about her tiredness with ungrammatical profundity: "My feet is tired, but my soul is rested." They will be the young high school and college students, young ministers of the gospel and a host of their elders courageously and non-violently sitting-in at lunch counters and willingly going to jail for conscience's sake. One day the South will know that when these disinherited children of God sat down at lunch counters they were in reality standing up for the best in the American dream and the most sacred values in our Judeo-Christian heritage, and thusly, carrying our whole nation back to those great wells of democracy which were dug deep by the founding fathers in the formulation of the Constitution and the Declaration of Independence.

Never before have I written a letter this long (or should I say a book?). I'm afraid that it is much too long to take your precious time. I can assure you that it would have been much shorter if I had been writing from a comfortable desk, but what else is there to do when you are alone for days in the dull monotony of a narrow jail cell other than write long letters, think strange thoughts, and pray long prayers?

If I have said anything in this letter that is an overstatement of the truth and is indicative of an unreasonable impatience, I beg you to forgive me. If I have said anything in this letter that is an understatement of the truth and is indicative of my having a patience that makes me patient with anything less than brotherhood, I beg God to forgive me.

I hope this letter finds you strong in the faith. I also hope that circumstances will soon make it possible for me to meet each of you, not as an integrationist or a civil rights leader, but as a fellow clergyman and a Christian brother. Let us all hope that the dark clouds of racial prejudice will soon pass away and the deep fog of misunderstanding will be lifted from our fear-drenched communities and in some not too distant tomorrow the radiant stars of love and brotherhood will shine over our great nation with all of their scintillating beauty.

Yours for the cause of Peace and Brotherhood
Martin Luther King, Jr.

Comments and Questions

One possible rejoinder to King's Letter From Birmingham City Jail follows the logic of civil disobedience: if a person or group wants to dramatize the injustice of a law by disobeying it, they should be willing to take the consequences of that disobedience. This would strengthen their impact—either by producing martyrs or by dramatizing the perceived injustice. It would also express ultimate respect for the rule of law and the law's rules for bringing about change. According to this view, we see the outer limit of judicial remedies for potential injustices when protestors take their claims to the streets rather than to the courts. How should defenders of Reverend King respond? How does this debate affect your view of the collateral bar rule? These issues are discussed in Abe Fortas, *Concerning Dissent and Civil Disobedience* (1968). Justice Fortas joined the dissenting opinion in *Walker.*

3

Thinking Like a Trial Lawyer, Pleadings, and Simple Joinder

A. INTRODUCTION

In Chapters 3, 4 and 5, we turn to the major steps in civil litigation. Chapter 3 covers the requirements for a complaint and also considers how many plaintiffs and defendants can and should be joined, and what responses the defendant can and should make. Chapter 4 addresses the discovery process, which is central to civil litigation. Chapter 5 discusses the right of trial by jury and the many methods that have evolved to instruct and constrain juries.

It is important that you begin to internalize your own sense of the chronological flow of a civil lawsuit from the filing of the initial pleadings; through discovery and motions; through trial, verdict, and judgment; and then to the concept of finality. To this end, we have provided various ways in which you can gain perspective on the entire process. After this introduction, we provide a brief description of the major aspects of a case in the chronological order in which they typically take place. You will find it helpful to refer back to this section whenever you are learning a new topic, so that you can continually see where what you are studying fits into the larger picture. Also, throughout the remainder of the book most of the practice exercises will focus on one or both of the real lawsuits that run throughout the course.

B. THE STAGES AND ESSENTIAL CONCEPTS OF A CIVIL LITIGATION   D P

Most civil cases are introduced to plaintiffs' lawyers when a client comes to the office and expresses dissatisfaction with the behavior of others. As the client describes what is wrong, the lawyer considers whether this is a situation for which the law gives any relief. Assume, for instance, the potential client, Joe, says, "I was in an elevator yesterday, and a passenger, Sally, didn't say hello to me." If this is the whole story, the lawyer would probably think that the law does not recognize snubbing as a wrong. In other words, the action of Sally the passenger was not legally "cognizable." Thus, whether the law will give relief is sometimes called a question of *cognizability*.

The underlying concept (or "unit of measurement" if you like scientific analogies) the lawyer would use in reaching this result is called the *cause of action* or *claim showing that the pleader is entitled to relief*. Causes of action are a shorthand for what events or circumstances must have taken place (or, in some instances, will take place) before a court will grant relief.

Each cause of action or claim has components, called *elements*. Suppose Joe said instead: "I was walking down the street and I think Sally tripped me, or perhaps she was just careless in sticking out her leg." The attorney might now think about both negligence and battery. The lawyer might say to herself: "Sally, as another pedestrian, had a 'duty' to Joe to refrain from unreasonable conduct, and perhaps she breached that duty by acting 'unreasonably' in tripping Joe, and that caused him harm ('cause in fact') which was foreseeable or within the risk Sally took ('proximate cause'), and since he broke his leg as a result of her action, he has suffered 'harm' or sustained 'damages.' So if the facts are true, there may be a cause of action for negligence because all five elements (of the negligence cause of action) are present: duty, unreasonable conduct (breach of duty), cause in fact, proximate cause, and harm or damages."

Perhaps Sally acted intentionally; if so, there is a cause of action for battery with these elements: an (1) intentional and (2) unwanted touching. (The touching itself is considered enough harm to make a cognizable case, but in this instance there is the additional damage of a broken leg.)

The same cause of action may permit multiple *theories*. For instance, in an automobile personal injury case, the cause of action may be negligence. Behind that cause of action may be theories (what some trial lawyers call "factual theories of the case") that include the defendant's not wearing her prescription glasses, speeding, driving with knowledge of defective brakes, driving with a dirty windshield that obscured vision, and/or driving under the influence of alcohol.

Throughout this course, we will deal with many causes of action from many different fields. This will require us to consider what are the elements of those causes of action. Please remember that different jurisdictions, lawyers, and law professors choose to treat or express the elements somewhat differently. So, do not be alarmed if in your torts class "negligence" and "battery" are explained a bit differently than in this rendition.

If, after talking to the potential client and possibly performing further investigation, a lawyer is satisfied that there is at least one provable cause of action, she will discuss fees and perhaps take the case. Then, the lawyer will have to decide in which states the defendant can be sued; this is a question of *personal jurisdiction*. Let's say you are an Oregon lawyer, and Sally, who lives in California, allegedly caused Joe to trip on a street in Oregon. He has come to discuss the case with you in Oregon. You would probably conclude quickly, since Oregon has typical personal jurisdiction statutes, that Sally could be sued on the facts of this case either in Oregon or in California. If you decide California is a better *forum* state—a state in which a court sits, and where a suit has been or will be brought—you would help Joe find a lawyer in California, since you have probably not been admitted to practice law there.

It probably makes sense to sue in Oregon, where your client lives and where the accident occurred; this would also mean that you could handle the case and earn a fee. Next, you would have to decide in which Oregon court to commence suit. Oregon, like all other states, has a state court system and at least one federal district court (remember, federal district courts are trial courts). The issue of "what court is empowered to hear this type of case" is called a question of *subject matter jurisdiction*. A combination of constitutional provisions and statutes grant different courts the right to hear different types of cases. For instance, in any given state, either the state constitution or statutes will give at least one trial court the authority to hear most types of cases. This broad grant of power to a trial court is called a grant of *general subject matter jurisdiction*.

Article III of the United States Constitution describes what cases Congress is permitted to authorize the federal district courts to hear. This grant of power is considerably narrower than the authorization provided in state constitutions and statutes. Thus, subject matter jurisdiction in the federal courts is commonly called *limited subject matter jurisdiction*. The limited subject matter jurisdiction for federal district courts can be found primarily in Title 28, in the "1330" sections of the United States Code. (After Congress passes a bill, it becomes an Act. Acts are assigned to a Title, by subject matter. Peruse these sections either in your rules supplement or in the United States Code volumes in the library.) The two major grants of limited subject matter jurisdiction to the federal district courts are called *federal question* and *diversity of citizenship*. See if you can find where these grants appear in your supplement. Sometimes, grants of limited subject matter jurisdiction to the federal district courts appear in various substantive statutes granting specific rights (scattered throughout the Code), so that Title 28 is not the only title in which one can find such grants of federal subject matter jurisdiction.

Even after the lawyer decides in what court system and in what state to commence a suit (and please keep in mind that litigation is not the only rational alternative to resolve disputes), she must determine where within the state or within the federal system the case can be brought. This question is geographic, but it is different from personal jurisdiction or subject matter jurisdiction. This additional issue is called *venue*. For instance, if the suit of Joe against Sally is brought in an Oregon Circuit Court, a trial court of the Oregon state judicial system, one still must decide in which geographic section of the state to bring the case. Typical state venue statutes look to the county in which the cause of action arose (in this instance, it would be where Sally allegedly tripped Joe) or where the defendant resides. (*See, e.g.*, Or. Rev. Stat. §14.080.) Congress has placed venue restrictions on where plaintiffs can commence cases in federal court. Try to find the relevant section(s) in your supplement.

The plaintiff must have not only personal jurisdiction over the defendant or defendants, subject matter jurisdiction in the appropriate court, and proper venue, but the defendants must also be appropriately notified of the commencement of suit. The "due process" requirements of notice and the right to be heard were explored at length in Chapter 1 and again in several cases concerning provisional relief in Chapter 2. These issues of personal jurisdiction, subject matter jurisdiction, venue, and *notice* raise fascinating and complex issues of federalism, separation of powers, and elemental fairness, and they occupy much of the second half of the materials in this book.

In the case of *Joe v. Sally*, as Joe's lawyer, you may have the opportunity to choose either a state court in Oregon or California, or a federal court in either state, if the potential damages were in excess of $75,000. Assuming Joe is a citizen of Oregon and Sally is a citizen of California, and the potential damages were sufficient, there would be diversity of citizenship within the meaning of Title 28, Sec. 1332. Note that this would then be a case where there is *concurrent subject matter jurisdiction* among state courts and federal courts. Unless Congress makes a grant of *exclusive subject matter jurisdiction*, then a case that would have federal subject matter jurisdiction will also have state subject matter jurisdiction. On the other hand, if, for instance, Congress says that only federal courts can hear a certain type of case, such as actions alleging certain types of anti-competitive behavior specifically prescribed in the Sherman Anti-Trust Act (15 U.S.C. §4), then the plaintiff's lawyer would be unable to bring that exact violation into a state trial court. Many first-year law students assume that if there is a federal question, such as a violation of a federal civil rights act, then the case can only be brought in federal court. This is *not* true. Again, unless Congress grants exclusivity to the federal court system, there is concurrent subject matter jurisdiction and the plaintiff has its choice of state or federal courts.

Returning to the case of *Joe v. Sally*, let us assume as Joe's lawyer that you have decided to bring the case in the Circuit Court of Oregon (a state court with general subject matter jurisdiction) sitting in the County of Yamhill. You will have checked what is called the *long-arm statute* of Oregon to make sure that Sally, a California citizen, can be sued in Oregon for a tort she allegedly committed there (Rule 4(c) of the Oregon Rules of Civil Procedure would indeed permit this exercise of personal jurisdiction). Also, you will have checked the applicable Oregon venue statute and complied with it in choosing the location of the court in Oregon in which to sue. You will then draft a *complaint* in accordance with Oregon's procedural rules. If the case were in a federal court, such pleading rules would appear in the Federal Rules of Civil Procedure. The pleading rules and cases interpreting them (as well as local culture, and in some instances, local rules) will tell you how precise you must be in your complaint about the facts and the specific relevant causes of action and their elements. You will have to check the applicable *statute of limitations* to make certain that the complaint has been filed within a statutorily prescribed time or, depending on the state law, that each defendant (in this case "Sally") is "served" the complaint (*service of process*) or (again depending on statutes and their constitutionality) otherwise notified about the case. You will also have to decide whether you can and desire to file a *jury claim.* This is usually a question of both constitutional right and trial strategy.

A plaintiff's lawyer also must consider *joinder* issues at the beginning of a case. If you choose to raise both negligence and battery causes of action against Sally, that would be called joinder of causes of action or, in the language of the Federal Rules, *joinder of claims.* If Joe tells you that the doctor who treated him for his broken leg after Sally tripped him did a bad job in setting the splint, then you will consider whether Joe has a negligence action against the doctor (often called a *malpractice* cause of action). Whether one can and should join Sally and the doctor as defendants in the same lawsuit is called a *joinder of parties* issue.

One reason that plaintiffs' lawyers begin their analysis of potential cases by considering causes of action is that the defendant, in answering the plaintiff, can promptly bring a *motion to dismiss* the case because of the plaintiff's failure to state a cause of action, or, in the words of Fed. R. Civ. P. 12(b)(6), "failure to state a claim upon which relief can be granted." This is, again, the concept of cognizability. Even if what the complaint says is true, is it the type of circumstance of which the courts take cognizance?

As you will find out, the defendant, either by motion or in its answer, has many options and many responsibilities. The defendant can challenge personal jurisdiction, subject matter jurisdiction, venue, and notice (service of process). The defendant, if filing an *answer,* must admit or deny the allegations. The defendant must state, or waive by not stating, *affirmative defenses.* Affirmative defenses are defenses that the defendant has to the plaintiff's causes of action, even if the case is in an appropriate court and the plaintiff otherwise has a good cause of action. In the case of Joe against Sally, Sally might claim, for example, that Joe's own negligence contributed to the fall, or that he consented to contact, or that the applicable statute of limitations has already run. The defendant can also *counterclaim* against the plaintiff for damages or relief that the defendant seeks from the plaintiff. In some instances, such counterclaims are compulsory. In federal court, for example, Fed. R. Civ. P. 13(a) mandates *compulsory counterclaims* if the defendant has a claim that "arises out of the transaction or occurrence that is the subject matter of the opposing party's claim" (although the rule is more complicated than this abbreviated statement of it). Perhaps Joe slandered Sally immediately after the incident. Lawyers might then debate whether this is a compulsory or *permissive counterclaim.*

Sally may have good reason to believe that if she is responsible to Joe, someone else is responsible to her for what she owes Joe. Let's say that Sally was acting as a messenger for a delivery company when the accident happened, and that the company had agreed to indemnify her for any harm caused while she made deliveries. Sally could bring a complaint for indemnification against the company, called an *impleader* or *third-party practice*. In federal court, impleader is covered by Fed. R. Civ. P. 14. If there are co-defendants, they may have claims against each other, which are called *cross-claims* in some states and in Fed. R. Civ. P. 13(g).

In some instances a plaintiff must join certain parties, or the case cannot go forward. These are called issues of *necessary and indispensable parties*, and are covered by Fed. R. Civ. P. 19. There are also more complex joinder issues, such as *intervention* (Fed. R. Civ. P. 24), *interpleader* (Fed. R. Civ. P. 22), and *class actions* (Fed. R. Civ. P. 23), which, along with necessary and indispensable parties, are covered in the final chapter of this book.

Assuming that the case survives preliminary motions, the parties may then engage in *discovery*. Most states, as well as the federal courts, have a group of procedures whereby one party may gain information from the other parties, and, in some instances, even from nonparty witnesses. Fed. R. Civ. P. 26 through 37 cover the discovery provisions, and are drafted to permit quite liberal discovery. In many federal courts and some state courts, selected information is subject to *mandatory disclosure* in the earliest stages of the litigation. Additional discovery is obtained by other methods, including written questions to opposing parties called *interrogatories*, written and oral *depositions*, requests to inspect documents, and motions to inspect real or personal property. In oral depositions, one party normally forces another and/or other witnesses to appear in person before a stenographer (or another method of recording) to answer a series of oral questions under oath, which may be admissible at trial as permitted by Fed. R. Civ. P. 32. Court orders may limit the amount and scope of discovery; there are sanctions for interfering with legitimate discovery and for abuse of the discovery rules; and many district courts also have local rules that limit discovery. All ninety-four federal district courts, and many state trial courts, have *local rules* and *standing orders* of judges that supplement the rules found throughout the country or in a given state. Consequently, a lawyer in federal court, for example, must know not only the Federal Rules of Civil Procedure, but also the applicable local rules and standing orders of the individual judges.

To understand the procedure that logically likely comes next, you must understand the concepts of the *burden of production* and the *burden of persuasion*. At the trial of a case, the party with the burden of proof, usually the plaintiff, must have a sufficiency of evidence as to each element of at least one cause of action to permit a reasonable fact finder to find that each element is true. This is called the *burden of production*. Let's say that Joe in fact sued Sally for negligence, the case reached a jury trial, and Joe's lawyer examined the witnesses in court and offered whatever evidence she had in favor of Joe. Assume that she was done with her part of the case, which is called *resting*. If the defendant's lawyer does not think there was a sufficiency of evidence to permit reasonable juries to find that all of the elements are true, that lawyer can move for a *directed verdict* (now called *judgment as a matter of law* in Fed. R. Civ. P. 50). For instance, in the case of Joe against Sally, if Joe's lawyer offered no evidence from which reasonable people could infer that Sally acted intentionally or unreasonably, then the trial judge, upon the defendant's motion, would grant a directed verdict, meaning that the jury would have to find for the defendant. This is because Joe would not have met his "production" burden.

But it is logical that even if Joe survives a motion for directed verdict, he may not ultimately win. Let's say that Joe describes in open court how Sally carelessly tripped him, and also presents other potentially believable evidence of each element of his negligence case. This would mean that he would survive a directed verdict motion because he has met his production burden, that is, produced a sufficiency of evidence to permit reasonable jurors to find that each element is true. But the jury may not actually believe all or part of Joe's testimony, or it may find that what he said to Sally did not in their minds add up to negligence or unreasonable conduct. Thus the jury might find for the defendant, because Joe did not persuade them that each element is true. In that instance, Joe did not meet the persuasion burden. In civil cases, the plaintiff must ordinarily persuade the fact finder by a *preponderance of the evidence* that each element is more likely than not to be true (or, as it is sometimes said, that the scale of justice tips at least a little bit in favor of the plaintiff as to each element of the plaintiff's cause of action). You can now see that in the normal case, the plaintiff has three burdens with respect to the merits of his or her case: he or she must plead correctly in the complaint, then meet the production burden, and then, in order to ultimately win, meet the persuasion burden.

If, after discovery, it appears that there is no way a plaintiff can win his or her case because it is predictable that at the trial the plaintiff will not have a sufficiency of evidence to meet the production burden, the defendant can then bring a motion for *summary judgment*. This will dispose of the case after (or during) discovery but before trial. This motion is described in Fed. R. Civ. P. 56.

Occasionally, a plaintiff can win a case at summary judgment or directed verdict. Let's say that the cause of action is nonpayment of a promissory note, and that it is clear through discovery that the plaintiff lent the defendant money, got a valid promissory note in return, and that the defendant, without any affirmative defense, has not paid. If the elements of a plaintiff's cause of action are self-evident, why have a trial? The plaintiff should win on a summary judgment motion. And if the plaintiff has not filed a summary judgment motion, she could still win this case, after defendant has rested, at the directed verdict stage.

There are other important motions, such as the motion for *judgment notwithstanding the verdict* (*judgment n.o.v.*), new trial motions, and motions to vacate judgment, but for the most part we will leave those until later in the course. You will see in *Wilkins v. Eaton Corporation*, 790 F.2d 515 (6th Cir. 1986), your next case in this course, that the motion for judgment n.o.v. raises precisely the same question as a directed verdict motion, and requires the judge to apply exactly the same test, but that judgment n.o.v. is brought *after* the jury has rendered its verdict. (The Federal Rules refer to both directed verdict and judgment n.o.v. motions as motions for judgment as a matter of law.) You will discuss later in the course why a judge might deny a motion for directed verdict, and then, after the jury has found for one party (usually the plaintiff), grant a judgment n.o.v. on behalf of the opposing party (usually the defendant).

Trials usually begin with each side giving *opening statements*. The plaintiff's lawyer then introduces her case first, with *direct examination* of each witness. Then the defendant's lawyer will ordinarily *cross-examine* those witnesses. At the trial, as the parties introduce evidence, the attorneys may raise *objections* to some of the questions asked or exhibits offered. The judge will apply rules of *evidence* in assessing the validity of the counsel's objections. If the question is a proper one, the judge will *overrule* the objection, and the witness must answer the question. If the judge finds that the question is improperly framed by counsel or that counsel seeks *inadmissible* testimony, she will *sustain* the objection, which means that the lawyer will have to reframe the question or move on to another matter.

Assume this is a jury case. Once both sides rest, assuming neither side wins on a motion for directed verdict, each side will give *closing arguments*. These will be preceded or followed by the judge's *instructing* the jury. The jury will render its *verdict*. The verdict will later become a *judgment*. If the plaintiff wins, he, she, or it can use formal methods to *execute on the judgment*—that is, force the defendant to pay it. Bear in mind, though, that in some cases the plaintiff will be seeking injunctive relief. She may seek a *temporary restraining order* at the beginning of the case to stop the defendant from doing irreparable harm, and then seek to have that judgment become a *preliminary* injunction, stopping the defendant from doing something prior to trial. If the plaintiff wins, the injunction may become a *permanent injunction.*

In most instances, in both state and federal courts, the losing party can appeal only from a *final judgment.* In the federal court system, the party that loses at the district court level has a right to appeal to the United States Court of Appeals. If the appeal is lost at this level, the losing party can apply to the United States Supreme Court for review. This is called a petition for a *writ of certiorari.* (Supreme Court review is governed by 28 U.S.C. §§1253-1258.)

If a party loses in the state trial court of general jurisdiction, then the party usually has the right to appeal to an intermediate appellate court. If the appeal is lost at this level, the losing party can appeal to the state's highest court, but that court usually has discretion over which cases it will hear. Some of the appellate decisions at the highest state court level can be reviewed by the United States Supreme Court, but only if that decision involved federal law. 28 U.S.C. §1257.

Generally, appellate courts insist that the party seeking review have objected to the decision or ruling it is appealing at the time the decision was originally made. Additionally, appellate courts usually require that the trial court's decision be based on the same point. Consequently, a good trial lawyer is always keeping a close eye on the proceedings, looking to object to questionable decisions so that she has a viable, appealable point in the event of a later unfavorable final judgment.

Can you imagine why appellate courts are reluctant to let a party who only loses on a preliminary matter appeal that point at that time to an appellate court? What if, for instance, Sally files a motion to dismiss for improper venue and loses. Why shouldn't she be permitted to appeal then on this matter? This would be called an *interlocutory appeal.* Still, appeals of interlocutory orders sometimes are allowed under 28 U.S.C. §1292(b) if (i) the question involved is one of law; (ii) the question is controlling; (iii) there are substantial grounds for a difference of opinion; and (iv) immediate appeal materially advances the ultimate termination of litigation. For example, appeals from interlocutory orders of the district courts regarding injunctions are sometimes allowed because of the final and irreparable effect on the rights of the parties, and because the evaluation is completely separate from the merits of the case and is unreviewable on appeal. 28 U.S.C. §1292(a).

Once a case reaches final judgment, the concept of *res judicata* (literally "a matter adjudged") applies. Let's say that a jury renders a defendant's verdict in the case of *Joe v. Sally,* which then becomes a judgment. A year later, Joe decides to go to another lawyer to try again. Intuitively, this would be both unfair to Sally and expensive for the court system. The defense to the second case would be *res judicata,* because plaintiffs are not permitted to bring the same case twice. Even if Joe decided to sue in case

one alleging only battery, and now tries to bring a case for negligence arising from the same incident, res judicata would apply. In modern parlance,
one would say that Joe is not permitted to split his claim, a concept also
called *claim preclusion.*

Sometimes, an issue is decided in one case, and is relevant to a new
claim between the same parties in a subsequent case. Assume that A sues B
on a promissory note and wins a case for installments not paid up until
the time of the verdict. (Assume further that the note does not have an
"acceleration clause" making all of the installments due upon any single
failure to pay.) Subsequently, B continues not to pay, and A sues for the
subsequent installments owed. A will probably not have to reprove the validity of the promissory note, because that issue has already been litigated
between the same parties. The second court would say that A can *collaterally estop* B from denying that the note was valid. In other words, the
second fact finder, whether judge or jury, would summarily have to find
that the note was a valid one. This concept is usually called *issue preclusion.*

Unfortunately some courts use the term *res judicata* to cover both
claim preclusion and issue preclusion. In any event, the issues of res judicata and collateral estoppel are covered near the end of this book—
appropriate, given their finality.

It is now time to explore more deeply the concepts of cause of action,
element, production burden, and persuasion burden, as a prelude to
lessons on pleading and the history of pleading.

C. PLEADING AND AMENDMENTS

At the heart of a trial lawyer's thinking and strategy about civil litigation are the fundamental concepts of claims, elements, burden of production, and burden of persuasion. A lawsuit usually begins when there has
been a dispute and a party or parties to that dispute, and their lawyers, believe that they are entitled to relief because the law recognizes the injury
they have suffered, and permits the court to intervene and provide injunctive, monetary or declaratory relief. A *cause of action* is one shorthand term
for what the plaintiff must prove in order to win a litigation. The corresponding term used by the Federal Rules of Civil Procedure, however, is a
claim showing that the pleader is entitled to relief. Why the Federal Rules use
the phrase "claim showing the pleader is entitled to relief" rather than the
previously used term, "cause of action," is something you should consider
throughout this chapter. Each cause of action or claim connotes a group
of circumstances for which a court will grant relief. These circumstances,
in turn, are divided into parts called elements. In this section, we will provide several examples of causes of action and their elements. In civil litigation, a judge often asks the plaintiff's lawyer what her *prima facie case* is.

This can mean that the judge is asking either for an enumeration of the elements of the plaintiff's claim (or cause of action) or for a short description of the evidence as to each of those elements.

Putting aside for now jurisdictional and notice issues, we have seen that plaintiffs have three obligations in order to win in civil litigation. First, if they are in federal court, they must state a claim for which they are entitled to relief. In some state courts, the procedural rules also require a statement of the facts underlying the cause of action. Second, after satisfying their initial pleading obligation, plaintiffs must meet a production burden. This is shorthand for the idea that a plaintiff must present sufficient evidence to permit a reasonable person to find that each element of the claim (or cause of action) is true. Finally, in order to prevail, a plaintiff must meet a burden of persuasion by persuading the fact finder that each element is true.

Federal Rules of Civil Procedure 7, 8, and 9 lay out the requirements for a federal complaint, and 12(b)(6) describes the motion that a defendant may bring to challenge whether the plaintiff's complaint correctly describes a claim for which relief can be granted. The cases that follow will demonstrate the continuing debate in procedure about how specifically the plaintiff must allege the elements of a claim (or cause of action). *Conley v. Gibson,* 355 U.S. 41 (1957), suggests a more liberal pleading standard (often called *notice pleading*) and rejects the need for specificity. "Simplicity," including ease of pleading, was one of the themes behind the enactment of the Federal Rules of Civil Procedure. However, some federal courts began to require stricter pleading, particularly in civil rights cases brought against public officials, as you will see in the Court of Appeals' opinion in *Leatherman*—an opinion that later was reversed by the Supreme Court. In the face of what some perceive as unwarranted litigiousness in our society, a heightened pleading requirement (sometimes called *fact pleading*) is thought to help prevent the filing of frivolous claims. Both fact and notice pleading have their advantages and disadvantages, as you will see. In either case, a plaintiff's lawyer must consider not only what the rules require him to put in a pleading; even where notice pleading is permitted, a lawyer may wish to plead with greater specificity for strategic reasons. For instance, a fuller story in a pleading may help educate the judge to see the case in a more favorable light, or it may lead to an earlier and more advantageous settlement.

In this section, you also will study the responses that a defendant must make, and may make, to a complaint. For instance, the defendant will have the choice, if appropriate, of either challenging through a motion or in an answer whether the complaint sufficiently states a claim for which relief can be granted. This section will also expose you to the rules for amending pleadings. Indeed, a fundamental tenet of the simplicity theme of the drafters of the Federal Rules was ease of amendment.

By the end of the section, you should know the fundamental rules of pleading complaints and answers, as well as the rules governing amendments. You should also be thinking about pleadings from the points of view of the parties, lawyers, judges and the court system, and society.

1. Claims, Elements, and Burdens of Proof

■ WILKINS v. EATON CORPORATION
790 F.2d 515 (6th Cir. 1986)

Contie, Circuit Judge.

The defendant-appellant, Eaton Corporation (Eaton), appeals from the district court's denial of its motion for judgment notwithstanding the verdict as well as the court's ruling on evidentiary matters. The jury had returned a verdict for plaintiff-appellee, Ned Wilkins, finding that Eaton had discriminated against Wilkins on the basis of age in violation of the Age Discrimination in Employment Act (ADEA), 29 U.S.C. §§621 et seq., and in willful violation of the ADEA.

On February 27, 1981, Ned Wilkins was fired by Eaton Corporation. Wilkins had been employed since July 16, 1968 as a pilot in Eaton's Flight Operations. At the time of his termination, Wilkins was 51 years of age.

Wilkins began flying at the age of sixteen. When he was hired by Eaton in 1968, he was moved to Kalamazoo, Michigan where he flew a Cessna 411. When Eaton began using a Lear Jet aircraft, Wilkins was relocated to Cleveland, Ohio. Wilkins was trained and qualified to fly the new aircraft. He was an Assistant Chief Pilot from 1972 to 1980 and trained other Eaton pilots in the operation of Lear Jets. Throughout his flying career, he had an exemplary safety record and received very high performance ratings from his superiors. In addition to his piloting abilities, Wilkins developed a temperature control system for the Lear Jet, wrote a computer program for scheduling aircraft trips and crew assignments, and helped service and maintain the automatic pilots.

During the 1970s, Eaton's Flight Operations expanded and in 1979 there were some management changes. In September 1979, Eaton retained a consulting firm, Aviation Consultants, Inc., to evaluate and make recommendations concerning the Flight Operations. Aviation Consultants issued a report in January 1980 which recommended several changes, most important of which was the development of a standardized flight checklist. A checklist is a list of operations to be performed in an aircraft and is supposedly designed for safety purposes.

Pursuant to another recommendation of Aviation Consultants, the Flight Operations was reorganized. A new management position was created, Flight Manager, which was filled by Mr. Doug Collier. Mr. Greg Kuta became the new Chief Pilot, a position directly under the Flight Manager, after the previous Chief Pilot retired. The plaintiff was not considered for the position of Flight Manager, being told he was a "very negative person," and he was not offered the position of Chief Pilot despite his interest in that position. Wilkins was also "demoted" during the same time period from Assistant Chief Pilot to Captain Pilot when Eaton decided to send all pilots to safety school. By sending pilots to safety school, the need for an Assistant Chief Pilot to perform various duties was eliminated.

Shortly after Kuta's appointment, Eaton implemented a policy whereby the management would designate a "Trip Captain" for each flight, who would then designate a pilot-in-command for that flight. During one of Wilkins' scheduled flights, a younger, less experienced pilot was designated as Trip Captain. As a result, Wilkins refused to fly and he was temporarily suspended from piloting duties by Kuta. After discussions with management, Wilkins was permitted to present his grievances in writing, and thereafter Eaton announced that the senior pilot would be pilot-in-command on all future flights.

In August 1980, Kuta began developing a flight checklist by soliciting advice from several sources. In October 1980, Kuta asked Wilkins to use the new checklist in a simulator and to report his impression to Kuta. Wilkins informed Kuta that the checklist was too lengthy. Kuta responded that use of the checklist would be mandatory for all pilots. This fact was later announced to all pilots at a pilot meeting which Wilkins attended.

On February 9, 1981, Wilkins flew to Middletown, Delaware. Wilkins noticed that his co-pilot was occupied with the checklist rather than helping him sight other airplanes. Upon his return to Cleveland, Wilkins told Kuta that the checklist compromised safety and that he did not intend to use it. Kuta stated that all pilots were required to use the checklist in order to fly for Eaton, and Wilkins responded that he might have to work elsewhere.

On February 26, 1981, Wilkins went on a round trip flight to New York City and when he returned he was confronted by Kuta regarding the checklist. Wilkins stated he had not used the checklist, and intended to never use the checklist because he believed safety would be compromised. Kuta told him that he would lose his job and proceeded to remove Wilkins from a scheduled flight on the following day. Wilkins testified at trial that he "could not accept the conditions that [Kuta] attached to continued flying," and when Kuta called him on February 27 to discuss his intentions, Wilkins stated he would not fly if required to use the checklist. Wilkins also stated that he would like to draft a memo as he had been allowed to do in regards to his disagreement with the Trip Captain policy. However, he was called on the following Monday, March 2, 1981, and again was informed that his refusal to use the checklist would result in termination. Wilkins again refused to fly under those conditions, and proceeded to finish his memo for consideration by management. His termination was effective February 27, 1981. Subsequent to his termination Mr. Terry Ross was promoted to Captain Pilot. Ross was 27 years old.

Wilkins filed a complaint on February 26, 1982, alleging that Eaton had fired him because of his age in violation of the Age Discrimination in Employment Act (ADEA), 29 U.S.C. §§621 et seq. He requested damages and reinstatement. The case was tried before a jury.

In support of his claim of age discrimination, Wilkins testified that he believed the flight checklist was discriminatory because it was biased to the younger, inexperienced pilot by virtue of its completeness and requirement for rigorous execution. And it was biased against the older, more experienced pilots by requiring them to divert their attention to a simple housekeeping chore and take their attention from more important items which would be observing for other traffic, other airplanes in the sky, unusual conditions, wherein true flight safety would lie.

On cross-examination, Wilkins agreed that Eaton had probably believed the checklist would increase safety. Wilkins also testified that he was not aware of anyone else who had told Kuta that they would not use the checklist. He also wrote a computer program which generated two graphs, which were then admitted into evidence. One graph showed the number of pilots, while the other depicted the average age of active pilots over a several year period. The data used to generate the graphs consisted of each pilot's date of birth, date of hire and date that the individual became an inactive pilot by virtue of termination, transfer, retirement or otherwise. Wilkins testified that this graph showed that the average age of active pilots had been decreasing around the time he was terminated.

Mr. Terry Saylor also testified on behalf of Wilkins. Saylor was a pilot for Eaton at the time Wilkins was fired. At that time he was 33 years of age. Saylor testified that he, too, did not use the checklist despite knowing it was mandatory, believing it to be unsafe and inefficient. He stated that he believed the checklist was biased against older and more experienced pilots although he did not state his reasons for that conclusion. He also gave the following testimony: I had been out on a trip [on February 26, 1981], and when I returned I was talking with Greg Kuta who was chief pilot at that time. And we got into a discussion about the checklist that we were using at that point. At that time there was a discussion about me not using it. I didn't agree with the checklist, and we had a long discussion about it. When asked if Mr. Kuta knew that Saylor was not using the checklist, Saylor stated, "Somebody had been talking to him about it. . . ." When asked a second time whether Kuta knew on February 26, 1981 that he did not use the checklist, Saylor responded, "If somebody else had told him." Saylor was not disciplined by Kuta, but was told to "kind of bear with him at that point, that there was going to be some revisions made to the checklist." Wilkins argued that Saylor's testimony showed that he had been treated differently than Saylor on the basis of age. Eaton attempted to introduce into evidence a letter written by Saylor to management which stated, inter alia, that Saylor disagreed with the checklist, but nonetheless followed company policy. The district court did not permit this into evidence, reasoning that it was a prior inconsistent statement and Eaton had failed to lay the proper foundation.

Eaton presented the following evidence. Mr. Sadler, who had overall responsibility for Flight Operations, testified that Wilkins was fired because he "elected not to comply with one of our regulations concerning the operations of our Flight Department" and that age was never considered. Mr. Campbell, Manager of Employee Relations for Eaton, testified that Eaton usually did not terminate employees immediately, giving them three months to turn their behavior around. He stated that this procedure was not used with Wilkins, however, for the following reasons: [H]e refused to follow the checklist, which was a procedure in place, and he said he would not, and was not, and was not working hand in hand with the manager at that time, and he said he would not follow the checklist and would not fly the airplane as long as the checklist was in place, and he walked off the job, and he was asked again if he would come back, and he refused. He testified that age played no factor in Wilkins' dismissal.

Kuta testified that Wilkins refused to use the checklist and was informed that termination could result from such refusal. He also testified that Saylor had never outright refused to use the checklist.

The case was submitted to the jury over Eaton's motion for directed verdict. The jury returned a verdict for Wilkins awarding $228,116, representing $114,083 in back pay, and the same amount for a willful violation of the ADEA. The district court also ordered reinstatement and pension fund contribution. The judgment was later amended in order to subtract prejudgment interest, thereby totaling $194,330.

Eaton filed a motion for judgment notwithstanding the verdict or, in the alternative, a new trial. The district court denied both of these motions. In denying Eaton's motion for judgment notwithstanding the verdict, the court reasoned that Wilkins had established a prima facie case of age discrimination, and that he had presented adequate evidence to rebut Eaton's articulated reason for dismissing him. Specifically, the court held that the jury could reasonably conclude, based on a permitted inference that the checklist was not enforced uniformly, that Eaton's articulated reason for firing Wilkins was merely a pretext for age discrimination. The court next concluded that the graph was properly admitted into evidence and that Eaton's arguments merely went to the weight to be given that evidence. Further, since Eaton failed to introduce Saylor's letter during Saylor's testimony, the letter was properly not admitted because the opposing party would not have had an opportunity to question Saylor regarding his prior inconsistent statement. Eaton's motion for a new trial was therefore denied.

Eaton argues on appeal that the district court erred in denying its motion for judgment notwithstanding the verdict, and again challenges certain evidentiary rulings. For the reasons set forth below, we reverse the judgment of the district court and remand this case for entry of judgment notwithstanding the verdict in favor of the appellant.

In an age discrimination case under the ADEA, the plaintiff carries the ultimate burden of persuasion to establish by a preponderance of the evidence that, as an individual protected by the statute, he was dismissed, demoted, or not hired because of his age. Although there may be more than one reason for an employee's discharge, a plaintiff can prevail if he establishes that "but for" his employer's motive to discriminate against him because of his age, he would not have been discharged.

To make out a prima facie case of age discrimination, thereby avoiding a directed verdict at the close of plaintiff's evidence, a plaintiff must demonstrate that: (1) he was a member of a protected class; (2) he was discharged; (3) he was qualified for the position; and (4) he was replaced by a younger person. We agree with the district court that Wilkins carried his burden of establishing a prima facie case. It is clear that Wilkins, being 51 years old, was a member of a protected class at the time of discharge. He therefore satisfied the first two criteria.

Eaton argues that by virtue of his insubordination, Wilkins was not "qualified" for his position as a pilot. We find this argument unpersuasive. To be qualified for a position means that the individual was doing his job well enough to rule out the possibility that he was fired for inadequate job performance, absolute or relative. There is no indication in the record that Wilkins was anything but a superb pilot. Although Wilkins' refusal to fly may serve as a legitimate reason for dismissal, we do not believe that speaks to his ability to fly an airplane.

Eaton also argues that Wilkins was not replaced by a younger individual. Shortly after Wilkins was discharged, a 27 year old co-pilot, Terry Ross, was promoted to Captain Pilot. Wilkins identified Ross as the individual who took over his former duties. Although it is natural, to an extent, for older employees to be replaced by younger employees who are moving up the employment ladder, we do not believe that fact precludes the establishment of a prima facie case in this situation. Ross was next in line for being promoted to Captain Pilot, but Wilkins also provided some evidence that the average age of active pilots was decreasing. We believe that the combination of these factors adequately satisfies the last element. . . . Therefore, the district court did not err by denying Eaton's motion for directed verdict at the close of plaintiff's case.

Eaton clearly satisfied its production burden by coming forth with a legitimate nondiscriminatory reason for Wilkins' discharge. The evidence is uncontradicted that Wilkins was not using the checklist when told to do so, and, more importantly, he informed his superior, Greg Kuta, that he would not fly if he were required to use the checklist. Wilkins' account of the events leading to his discharge agrees with the accounts of Eaton's witnesses. Further, all of Eaton's witnesses testified that Wilkins' outright refusal to use the checklist was the basis for his dismissal and that his age was never considered.

Once an employer has articulated a legitimate reason for its action, the plaintiff has the burden of showing, by a preponderance of the evidence, that the stated reason is a mere pretext or "cover-up" for what was in truth a discriminatory purpose. The fact finder may not focus on the soundness of the employer's business judgment, since the ADEA was only intended to protect the older worker from arbitrary classifications on the basis of age. The ADEA did not change the fact that an employer may make a subjective judgment to discharge an employee for any reason that is not discriminatory. In other words, when an employer meets its burden of articulating a legitimate nondiscriminatory reason for discharge, the presumption of discrimination created by establishing a prima facie case is destroyed. The factual inquiry encompassing the ultimate question in the case then proceeds to a new level of specificity.

The dispositive motivational issue requires a consideration of the two opposing reasons for discharge to determine whether Wilkins' discharge would not have occurred but for defendant's motive to discriminate against him because of his age. The burden of producing evidence of "pretext" essentially merges with the burden of persuasion, which always lies with the plaintiff. If the plaintiff has failed to carry this ultimate burden of production, the court is compelled to grant judgment for the defendant upon a proper motion for directed verdict or judgment notwithstanding the verdict. The question before the court is whether the plaintiff produced sufficient evidence for this case to be submitted to a jury and for the jury verdict to be upheld.

For a case to be properly submitted to the jury, there must be more than a scintilla of evidence supporting the claim. When the evidence is such that without weighing the credibility of the witnesses there can be but one reasonable conclusion as to the verdict the court should determine the proceeding by non-suit, directed verdict or by judgment notwithstanding the verdict. By such direction of the trial the result is saved from the mischance of speculation over legally unfounded claims. In determining whether the evidence is sufficient to be sent to the jury or to support a jury verdict, the evidence, and reasonable inferences therefrom, is to be viewed in the light most favorable to the non-moving party and the court must not consider the credibility of witnesses nor weigh the evidence. To do otherwise is to substitute the court's opinion for that of the jury.

In the case at bar, we believe that the evidence simply cannot support a conclusion that the Eaton Corporation fired Wilkins on the basis of his age. Wilkins principally relied on the fact that Saylor, who was younger than Wilkins, was not fired when he did not use the checklist. We are totally unpersuaded, however, that Saylor and Wilkins acted in the same manner. Saylor never informed the Eaton management that he refused to use the checklist and would not fly if required to use the checklist. Wilkins even testified that, to the best of his knowledge, he was the only pilot who informed management that he simply would not fly if required to adhere to the company policy. This is significantly different conduct than Saylor's.

In fact, this was the second time Wilkins refused to work unless management abandoned a particular policy and agreed with his point of view. There was no evidence at all that Eaton adopted this checklist as a pretext for discriminating against Wilkins; even Wilkins testified that Eaton management probably thought the checklist would increase the safety of flights.

Nor are we persuaded by the argument that the checklist itself was discriminatory. The testimony indicates that Wilkins and Saylor believed the checklist discriminated against older and more experienced pilots because the checklist required them to spend time on housekeeping chores which should not be occupying their time. Since all pilots were required to use the checklist, there was no classification based on age or experience. The fact that pilots were essentially required to "waste time" is not evidence of age discrimination but is merely indicative of whether Eaton had adopted a wise policy. The reasons why Wilkins found the checklist to be inefficient and unsafe are the same reasons he felt it to be discriminatory. These arguments only reflect the value in Wilkins' refusal to abide by the checklist, and perhaps Eaton's poor judgment in dismissing Wilkins for this infraction, but are certainly not evidence of discriminatory intent.

Similarly, the graph prepared by Wilkins does not help him in reaching his ultimate production and persuasion burdens. The graph shows that the average age of pilots decreased during a certain period of time, but the graph completely lacks specificity. For instance, the decrease in age could have resulted because several pilots retired or voluntarily transferred to non-flying positions, requiring younger pilots to be hired. Although the graph arguably supports an inference of discrimination when establishing a prima facie case, it is insufficient circumstantial evidence to support the jury verdict in this case. Even when combined with the other pieces of evidence offered by the plaintiff, the result is a mere scintilla of evidence from which no rational jury could have found a violation of the ADEA.

The plaintiff has the burden of establishing by a preponderance of the evidence that age was the determining factor in his discharge. Wilkins did not meet this burden. We believe that the jury verdict resulted from mere speculation, and perhaps a dislike of Eaton's business judgment. However, the fact that a talented pilot was fired over a checklist which had questionable value cannot, by itself, form the basis of a finding of age discrimination. There must be evidence of discriminatory purpose and there must be evidence from which a reasonable jury could conclude that age was the more likely reason for Wilkins' discharge, rather than merely a speculative possibility. We are convinced that the evidence does not suffice to support as a reasonable probability the inference that but for claimant's age he would not have been discharged. Eaton's motion for judgment notwithstanding the verdict, therefore, should have been granted. Because of our disposition of this case, we do not reach the other issues raised by the appellant.

Accordingly, the judgment of the district court is Reversed and this case is Remanded with instructions to enter judgment notwithstanding the verdict in favor of the appellant.

Comments and Questions

1. In Chapter 1, you were given a number of different ways to read a procedural case. Continue to use those techniques as you consider the additional questions and comments that we provide.

2. What cause of action is Wilkins suing on, and what are its elements? How would you determine what the elements are in a statutory cause of action?

3. What does the court mean when it talks of Wilkins' prima facie case?

4. Does Wilkins lose this case because he fails to meet his production burden or his persuasion burden?

5. What evidence does Wilkins produce for each element? Do you find that Wilkins meets his initial production burden?

6. The court assumes that to win, the plaintiff must have evidence (meet his production burden) that he was dismissed, demoted, or not hired because of age (that is, he was discriminated against), and yet the court's rendition of the plaintiff's initial required prima facie case does not include this element. Why?

7. In this opinion, the court refers to the burden of the defendant. What is that burden? Is it a burden of production or a burden of persuasion? Does the defendant meet its burden? What happens next? What new burden (or burdens) does the plaintiff now have? Does the plaintiff meet this new burden?

8. In order to facilitate the goals of the Age Discrimination in Employment Act, do you think that the U.S. Court of Appeals for the Sixth Circuit does a good job in articulating the initial prima facie case, the defense, the ultimate prima facie case, and the burdens of proof? Would you do it differently if you had a free hand to interpret the statute? What factors are you considering when you make your decisions? What is the relationship of substantive law and procedural law in the decisions you make?

We want you to begin to integrate a sensitivity to causes of action and elements into your thinking. Much of your law school curriculum will deal with various causes of action from a wide variety of fields.

The lawyer can find various causes of action and their elements articulated in statutes and judicial opinions. Lawyers spend much of their creative energy trying to convince courts to expand older causes of action and to create new ones. Lawyers, lobbyists, and legislators try to create new causes of action through congressional statutes.

The library offers hundreds of places in which to research available causes of action, their elements, and the type of evidence one might find to meet both production and persuasion burdens. Each state, for instance, is likely to have at least one or more volumes in a "practice" series that explains causes of action in that state. What follows is a summary of a few (of among hundreds) of the causes of action listed in a multi-volume treatise by Shepard's/McGraw-Hill entitled *Causes of Action*, which is in the practicum section of the library. Please realize that this is a limited list with only a summary group of elements. Once you begin to prepare an actual case, you will gain sophistication in articulating the elements. It is also important to remember that your instructors may teach the elements of a claim or cause of action in a different manner than you see them here.

Breach of Implied Warranty of Habitability: sale of a residence by a builder-vendor; latent defects; breach of applicable standard of habitability; causation; notice of the defects; harm to the purchaser.

Defamation: defendant made defamatory statement; defendant published the statement; the statement was false; defendant was at fault in making the false statement; injury to plaintiff's reputation.

Defective Mechanism in Motor Vehicle: defective condition made operation of vehicle unreasonably dangerous; defect attributable to the defendant; proximate causation; vehicle was being used in a foreseeable manner at the time of the accident; defendant engaged in the business of manufacturing or selling vehicles.

Failure to Warn of Side Effects: identity of the manufacturer; duty to warn; failure to adhere to the standard of care in warning of side effects; proximate causation.

Failure to Warn of Road Construction or Repair Hazards: road construction or repair work performed by defendant that created hazard to motorists; duty to warn; failure to provide adequate signs, signals, or devices to warn; proximate causation.

Intentional Infliction of Emotional Distress: outrageous conduct; actions were intentional or reckless; severe emotional distress; proximate causation.

Interference with Prospective Business Advantage: business relationship with third party; reasonable expectancy of economic gain; conduct that has an adverse effect on the relationship; intention to cause the destruction of or harm to the relationship; proximate causation; damage or loss.

Malpractice: a duty to adhere to the accepted professional standard of care; failure to adhere to the standard; injury or loss; proximate causation.

Misrepresentation: misrepresentation in commercial advertising concerning goods, services, or commercial activities; deception or intended deception of recipients; likely influence of purchasing decisions; injury or likelihood of injuring plaintiff; misrepresentation in commerce.

Negligence: duty to harmed person; breach of the duty; injury; proximate causation.

Negligent Repair of Motor Vehicle: duty to exercise reasonable care in making repairs; breach of the duty; proximate causation.

Personal Injury: duty of reasonable care; breach of the duty; proximate causation; harm.

Premises Liability (business): owner sufficiently possessing or controlling property in question; actual or constructive knowledge of unreasonable risk of harm; owner's expectation that customers would fail to discover, realize, or avoid the danger.

Sexual Harassment: harassment because of plaintiff's sex; effect on term or condition of plaintiff's employment; substantial effect on plaintiff's employment.

Strict Liability for Harm Caused by Eating or Drinking Contaminated Food: defendant engaged in business of selling food; defective and unreasonably dangerous product; defective when it left defendant's control and in substantially unchanged condition when reaching the plaintiff; physical harm.

Practice Exercise No. 6:
Initial Strategy Session in *Carpenter*

Assume that you are an associate in a law firm and have received a memorandum in preparation for a strategy session. The memorandum on the potential client, which you should read for the exercise, is the first document in the case files for *Carpenter v. Dee*. (The documents relating to this case are printed at the end of your book in the section labeled Case Files.) Prepare to discuss with the senior partner the causes of action that may be available to Nancy Carpenter (and against whom) if the firm chooses to represent her. Consider each element of a potential claim and, using the facts of the case, note where you will need additional information. Of course, at this early stage in the litigation the memorandum is not a complete statement of the case; indeed, some important facts are missing. Although you do not know much about specific claims or causes of action yet, you can consult *Causes of Action*, which you just read, and also the three brief Massachusetts statutes in the Case Files that follow the initial memorandum.

2. The Purpose and Doctrine of Complaints

In this section, we introduce the civil complaint and modern-day pleading standards. As you read, consider the purposes of the complaint from the perspectives of parties, attorneys, judges and society. Please read

Fed. R. Civ. P. 1, 2, 3, 7(a), 8(a), 8(b), 8(e), 8(f), 9,12(b)(6),12(e), 84, and Fed. R. Civ. P. Form 9.

■ CONLEY v. GIBSON
355 U.S. 41 (1957)

Justice BLACK delivered the opinion of the Court:

Once again Negro employees are here under the Railway Labor Act asking that their collective bargaining agent be compelled to represent them fairly. In a series of cases beginning with *Steele v. Louisville & Nashville R. Co.*, 323 U.S. 192, this Court has emphatically and repeatedly ruled that an exclusive bargaining agent under the Railway Labor Act is obligated to represent all employees in the bargaining unit fairly and without discrimination because of race and has held that the courts have power to protect employees against such invidious discrimination.

This class suit was brought in a Federal District Court in Texas by certain Negro members of the Brotherhood of Railway and Steamship Clerks, petitioners here, on behalf of themselves and other Negro employees similarly situated against the Brotherhood, its Local Union No. 28 and certain officers of both. In summary, the complaint made the following allegations relevant to our decision: Petitioners were employees of the Texas and New Orleans Railroad at its Houston Freight House. Local 28 of the Brotherhood was the designated bargaining agent under the Railway Labor Act for the bargaining unit to which petitioners belonged. A contract existed between the Union and the Railroad which gave the employees in the bargaining unit certain protection from discharge and loss of seniority. In May 1954, the Railroad purported to abolish 45 jobs held by petitioners or other Negroes all of whom were either discharged or demoted. In truth the 45 jobs were not abolished at all but instead filled by whites as the Negroes were ousted, except for a few instances where Negroes were rehired to fill their old jobs but with loss of seniority. Despite repeated pleas by petitioners, the Union, acting according to plan, did nothing to protect them against these discriminatory discharges and refused to give them protection comparable to that given to white employees. The complaint then went on to allege that the Union had failed in general to represent Negro employees equally and in good faith. It charged that such discrimination constituted a violation of petitioners' right under the Railway Labor Act to fair representation from their bargaining agent. And it concluded by asking for relief in the nature of declaratory judgment, injunction and damages.

The respondents appeared and moved to dismiss the complaint on several grounds: (1) the National Railroad Adjustment Board had exclusive jurisdiction over the controversy; (2) the Texas and New Orleans Railroad, which had not been joined, was an indispensable party defendant;

and (3) the complaint failed to state a claim upon which relief could be given. The District Court granted the motion to dismiss holding that Congress had given the Adjustment Board exclusive jurisdiction over the controversy. The Court of Appeals for the Fifth Circuit, apparently relying on the same ground, affirmed. 229 F.2d 436. Since the case raised an important question concerning the protection of employee rights under the Railway Labor Act we granted certiorari.

[Justice Black then provided his rationale for overturning the district and circuit court determinations of the jurisdictional issue. Although "the District Court did not pass on the other reasons advanced for dismissal of the complaint," he thought it "timely and proper for" the Supreme Court to consider the other two arguments for dismissal. The "indispensable party" contention was swiftly rejected, and Black proceeded to address the 12(b)(6) motion.]

[W]e hold that . . . the complaint adequately set forth a claim upon which relief could be granted. In appraising the sufficiency of the complaint we follow, of course, the accepted rule that a complaint should not be dismissed for failure to state a claim unless it appears beyond doubt that the plaintiff can prove no set of facts in support of his claim which would entitle him to relief. Here, the complaint alleged, in part, that petitioners were discharged wrongfully by the Railroad and that the Union, acting according to plan, refused to protect their jobs as it did those of white employees or to help them with their grievances all because they were Negroes. If these allegations are proven there has been a manifest breach of the Union's statutory duty to represent fairly and without hostile discrimination all of the employees in the bargaining unit. This Court squarely held in *Steele* and subsequent cases that discrimination in representation because of race is prohibited by the Railway Labor Act. The bargaining representative's duty not to draw "irrelevant and invidious" distinctions among those it represents does not come to an abrupt end, as the respondents seem to contend, with the making of an agreement between union and employer. Collective bargaining is a continuing process. Among other things, it involves day-to-day adjustments in the contract and other working rules, resolution of new problems not covered by existing agreements, and the protection of employee rights already secured by contract. The bargaining representative can no more unfairly discriminate in carrying out these functions than it can in negotiating a collective agreement. A contract may be fair and impartial on its face yet administered in such a way, with the active or tacit consent of the union, as to be flagrantly discriminatory against some members of the bargaining unit.

The respondents point to the fact that under the Railway Labor Act aggrieved employees can file their own grievances with the Adjustment Board or sue the employer for breach of contract. Granting this, it still furnishes no sanction for the Union's alleged discrimination in refusing to represent petitioners. The Railway Labor Act, in an attempt to aid collective action by employees, conferred great power and protection on the bargaining agent chosen by a majority of them. As individuals or small groups the employees cannot begin to possess the bargaining power of their representative in negotiating with the employer or in presenting their grievances to him. Nor may a minority choose another agent to bargain in their behalf. We need not pass on the Union's claim that it was not obliged to handle any grievances at all because we are clear that once it undertook to bargain or present grievances for some of the employees it represented it could not refuse to take similar action in good faith for other employees just because they were Negroes.

The respondents also argue that the complaint failed to set forth specific facts to support its general allegations of discrimination and that its dismissal is therefore proper. The decisive answer to this is that the Federal Rules of Civil Procedure do not require a claimant to set out in detail the facts upon which he bases his claim. To the contrary, all the Rules require is "a short and plain statement of the claim" that will give the defendant fair notice of what the plaintiff's claim is and the grounds upon which it rests. The illustrative forms appended to the Rules plainly demonstrate this. Such simplified "notice pleading" is made possible by the liberal opportunity for discovery and the other pretrial procedures established by the Rules to disclose more precisely the basis of both claim and defense and to define more narrowly the disputed facts and issues. Following the simple guide of Rule 8(f) that "all pleadings shall be so construed as to do substantial justice," we have no doubt that petitioners' complaint adequately set forth a claim and gave the respondents fair notice of its basis. The Federal Rules reject the approach that pleading is a game of skill in which one misstep by counsel may be decisive to the outcome and accept the principle that the purpose of pleading is to facilitate a proper decision on the merits.

The judgment is reversed and the cause is remanded to the District Court for further proceedings not inconsistent with this opinion. . . .

■ BOWER v. WEISMAN
639 F. Supp. 532 (S.D.N.Y. 1986)

SWEET, District Judge.

. . . [I]n July, 1985, Bower and Weisman terminated a fifteen-year close personal and business relationship. According to Bower, in exchange for valuable business and social assistance which Bower rendered to Weisman during their relationship, Weisman promised to provide Bower with an economic interest in his affairs and to provide Bower and her daughter with financial security. Bower contends that Weisman agreed to provide these benefits even after their relationship terminated, as long as Bower, a Japanese citizen, did not remarry or leave the United States and that Weisman breached a series of written and oral agreements, codifying Weisman's promise of financial security.

Bower asserts that in the final version of this agreement dated July 6, 1985, Weisman agreed (1) to purchase a house in California for Bower at a cost of $6.5 million; (2) to provide Bower with an irrevocable trust in the amount of $3.9 million and $100,000 in trust for Bower's daughter; (3) to pay Bower an annual sum of $120,000 for ten years over and above a promissory note held by Frederick Weisman Company (FWC) dated November 1, 1983; (4) to pay Bower's living expenses until her remarriage or departure from the United States; (5) to provide rent-free possession of Weisman's New York townhouse until her remarriage or departure from the United States. Provision number (3) concerns a promissory note and consultant agreement executed on November 1, 1983 by FWC and Pre-ferred Capital International Inc. (Preferred Capital), a corporation wholly owned by Bower.

In mid-July, 1985, the Bower-Weisman relationship terminated, and according to Bower, Weisman reneged on this agreement and attempted to coerce her to leave the townhouse, which she asserts was purchased with her own money but which she sold to Weisman in 1980 at his request to accommodate his tax needs in reliance on his promises of a rent-free tenancy. In September and November, 1985, Weisman instructed his agents to enter the apartment, to strip it of artwork and furniture which was purportedly the property of Weisman, to change the locks on Bower's door when she was at work and her daughter was home ill, and to station three armed guards in the townhouse lobby, with instructions to prevent the entry of "unauthorized" individuals. Furthermore, Bower claims that Weisman's real estate agents and attorneys made unauthorized visits to the apartment and disturbed her personal belongings.

The complaint alleges seven claims arising from the July 6, 1985 agreement outlined above, each of which is challenged in [defendant's] motion. Claim One asserts tort and contract claims for money damages arising from the "breach of express agreements"; Claim Two alleges fraud, misrepresentation and deceit in connection with the agreement; Claim Three is for "breach of contract and conversion" and concerns Weisman's attempt to remove Bower from the townhouse and his alleged conversion of art and furniture. Claims Four and Five charge the defendants with trespass and false imprisonment in connection with the townhouse, and Claims Six and Seven concern intentional infliction of emotional distress, and private nuisance, also in connection with Weisman's actions to re-cover the townhouse. . . .

MOTION FOR A MORE DEFINITE STATEMENT

Weisman [next] argues that pursuant to Fed. R. Civ. P. 12(e), he is entitled to a more definite statement with respect to two aspects of the complaint. First, Weisman asserts that the complaint fails to disclose the specific provisions of the alleged agreements upon which plaintiff relies. Moreover, he argues that the complaint fails to reveal which parts of the agreements have been modified and which provisions remain in effect after these modifications. Second, Weisman urges that the complaint fails to identify which of the three defendants is charged with each act and merely discusses all as "defendant." . . . For the following reasons, this motion for a more definite statement is granted.

A motion for a more definite statement may be granted if "a pleading . . . is so vague and ambiguous that a party cannot reasonably be required to frame a responsive pleading. . . ." Fed. R. Civ. P. 12(e). A motion pursuant to Rule 12(e) should not be granted "unless the complaint is so excessively vague and ambiguous as to be unintelligible and as to prejudice the defendant seriously in attempting to answer it." *Boothe v. TRW Credit Data*, 523 F. Supp. 631, 635 (S.D.N.Y. 1981). With respect to Weisman's first assertion, Bower's complaint is not so unintelligible as to preclude Weisman from drafting a responsive pleading. The essence of a complaint is to inform the defendant as to the general nature of the action and as to the incident out of which a cause of action arose. *Id.* Bower's complaint satisfies this requirement as it clearly identifies the offending acts. The complaint traced in detail the interactions of Bower and Weisman which led to the first written agreement of July, 1983, and the series of subsequent modifications that occurred in September through November of 1983, September, 1984, October, 1984, culminating in the final agreement of July 6, 1985, embodied in paragraph 25. Moreover, paragraph 26 describes the provisions of the agreement that were allegedly violated by Weisman. Weisman has been given fair notice of the claims against him, and nothing prevents him from formulating a responsive pleading.

Weisman seeks to remove the ambiguity that is present in paragraphs 36, 40, 43-47, 50 and 52-55. These paragraphs employ the term "defendant" without specifying which particular defendant is referred to. Obviously, Weisman cannot effectively respond to Bower's complaint until he knows which claims Bower is asserting against him in his individual capacity. Although Rare Properties is a wholly owned subsidiary of FWC, of which Weisman is the sole owner, Bower has not produced any evidence that the proper corporate forms have not been observed with respect to these corporations. The motion for a more particular statement will be granted on this ground. . . .

MOTION TO DISMISS FOR FAILURE TO STATE FRAUD WITH PARTICULARITY

Fed. R. Civ. P. 9(b) requires that: "In all averments of fraud or mistake, the circumstances constituting fraud or mistake shall be stated with particularity." There is tension between the specificity required under Rule 9(b) and the liberal pleading allowances of Fed. R. Civ. P. 8(a)(2) which requires only a "short and plain statement of the claim showing that the pleader is entitled to relief." However, Rule 9(b) does not render Rule 8 meaningless in fraud cases. The two rules must be read in conjunction with each other. Courts have not struck a balance between these rules by devising an easily applied test. Thus, the degree of specificity required will be dependent upon the facts of each case.

Bower's allegations do no more than state generally that all three defendants intentionally misrepresented and defrauded the plaintiff by making promises and representations. In paragraph 32, Bower alleges that "[t]hose representations of the defendants were false and deceitful at the time they were made to the plaintiff. . . ." Such sweeping statements fail to clarify which alleged agreements form the basis of Bower's claim for fraud. "[A well-pleaded claim of fraud] normally includes the time, place, and content of the false representations, the facts misrepresented, and the nature of the detrimental reliance. . . ." *Elster v. Alexander*, 75 F.R.D. 458, 461 (N.D. Ga. 1977). Bower's claim fails with respect to all of these particulars. Moreover, Bower's failure to separate Weisman from the two corporate defendants involved in this case makes it impossible for Weisman to frame an effective response.

Rule 9(b) seeks, in part, to assure that defendants ". . . are given notice of the exact nature of the fraud claimed, sufficient to permit responsive measures." *Todd v. Oppenheimmer & Co., Inc.*, 78 F.R.D. 415, 419 (S.D.N.Y. 1978). Here, Bower's pleadings are vague and fail to provide the specificity required by Rule 9(b). Therefore, Bower's second claim for misrepresentation, fraud and deceit is dismissed with leave to replead.

When determining whether to grant a Rule 12(b)(6) motion, the court must primarily consider allegations in the complaint. However, at this early stage of the proceedings, a court's review of the sufficiency of the complaint is a very limited one. The allegations are accepted as true, and the complaint is construed in a light most favorable to the pleader. . . .

MOTION TO DISMISS FOR FAILURE TO STATE A CLAIM UPON WHICH RELIEF CAN BE GRANTED

The motion to dismiss for failure to state a claim is disfavored and is seldom granted. The reason for such a policy is two-fold. First, "[t]he salvaged minutes that may accrue from circumventing these procedures can turn to wasted hours if the appellate court feels constrained to reverse the dismissal of the action." *Rennie & Laughlin, Inc. v. Chrysler Corporation*, 242 F.2d 208, 213 (9th Cir. 1957). Second, courts are wary of dismissal in view of the policy of the federal rules which seeks to have determinations reached on the merits. *Id.* The test that is in accord with these goals is that ". . . a complaint should not be dismissed for failure to state a claim unless it appears beyond doubt that the plaintiff can prove no set of facts in support of his claim which would entitle him to relief." *Conley v. Gibson,* 355 U.S. 41, 45-46 (1957). Thus, this court must determine in the light most favorable to the plaintiff whether the following claims state any basis for relief.

A. TRESPASS

Plaintiff has alleged the necessary elements to sustain a cause of action in trespass. From July, 1983 to July, 1985, the agreements between Bower and Weisman contained a provision that in the event of the breakup of the parties' relationship, Bower would be permitted to reside rent-free at the 73rd Street townhouse so long as she paid all maintenance expenses and did not remarry or move out of the country. Upon termination of the relationship in August, 1985, plaintiff alleges that she was in actual possession of the townhouse and that she shared this residence only with her daughter, Teru. "Trespass is an action for injury to possession for which an action may be maintained even against an owner by the one entitled to possession." *Meadow Point Properties v. Nick Mazzoferro & Sons,* 219 N.Y.S.2d 908, 909 (Sup. Ct. Suffolk Co. 1961). Because Bower alleges to have been in actual (and exclusive) possession of the townhouse, she may maintain an action for trespass. . . .

Considering the allegations in the light most favorable to the plaintiff, Bower's complaint asserts a possessory interest in the townhouse beyond a licensing arrangement. . . .

Bower has also successfully pleaded the other requisite elements of trespass. . . . Bower asserts that Weisman, through his agents, intentionally entered the townhouse property without her consent. She alleges that artwork was removed from the premises by defendant and/or his agents. Bower also states that defendant changed her apartment locks and placed three armed guards at the entrance of the property. . . .

Defendant's motion to dismiss the trespass claim is denied.

B. FALSE IMPRISONMENT

The action for the tort of false imprisonment seeks to protect an individual's freedom from restraint of movement. The Court of Appeals of New York has set forth the following elements as constituting a cause of action for false imprisonment: (1) defendant intended to confine the plaintiff; (2) plaintiff was conscious of the confinement; (3) plaintiff did not consent to the confinement, and (4) confinement was not otherwise privileged.

Plaintiff's fifth claim for false imprisonment fails to set forth any facts which would support the allegation that plaintiff was confined at the 73rd Street townhouse. Bower alleges that due to the posting of three armed guards at the townhouse entrance, she "has been unable to freely enter and exit her home in the unfettered manner to which she is accustomed and . . . has become a prisoner by virtue of the defendant's acts." However, other paragraphs of Bower's Second Amended Complaint are entirely at odds with the proposition set forth above. Paragraph 42 states that on November 5, 1985, plaintiff left her house to go to work. Paragraph 44 states that the three armed guards were instructed "not to permit access to anyone other than the plaintiff, her daughter, or a person seeking access for emergency and/or medical purposes." This indicates that plaintiff was permitted ingress and egress from the townhouse. Moreover, paragraph 47 alleges that unauthorized persons entered the townhouse while Bower was not home. Plaintiff's own allegations support the conclusion that her movement was unrestrained. . . . Plaintiff's fifth claim for false imprisonment is dismissed with leave to replead within twenty (20) days.

C. INTENTIONAL INFLICTION OF EMOTIONAL DISTRESS

The following components form a claim for intentional infliction of emotion distress: (1) an extreme and outrageous act by the defendant; (2) an intent to cause severe emotional distress; (3) resulting severe emotion distress; (4) caused by the defendant's conduct. Plaintiff's complaint pleads each of the necessary elements of this cause of action to survive a 12(b)(6) challenge.

Paragraph 63 sets forth the "outrageous" acts by defendant that were directed at the plaintiff. First, three armed guards were placed in the lobby of the townhouse to prevent all persons except Bower, her child and medical personnel from entering or exiting from the townhouse. Second, the locks to Bower's apartment were changed without her consent which caused her to become "frightened and distraught." Third, Weisman, through his agents, entered plaintiff's apartment without her permission and removed artwork without her consent. Bower contends that defendant intended that such acts would cause her severe emotional distress, and that she has, in fact, "suffered severe mental anguish, anxiety, and unwarranted pain and suffering."

These allegations demonstrate that defendant embarked upon a course of conduct that was designed to intimidate, threaten and humiliate the plaintiff and which resulted in emotional upset. It will be for the trier of fact to determine whether defendant's conduct went beyond all reasonable bounds of decency, and would arouse resentment against the defendant as to cause the trier of fact to exclaim that such conduct was "outrageous." *Restatement (Second) of Torts* §46 comment (d) (1965).

D. PRIVATE NUISANCE

The elements of a private nuisance in New York are: (1) an interference substantial in nature, (2) intentional in origin, (3) unreasonable in character, (4) with a person's property right to use and enjoy land, (5) caused by another's conduct in acting or failure to act. Plaintiff's seventh claim for private nuisance must be dismissed since Bower has failed to allege an interference which is substantial in nature and unreasonable in character.

The "substantial" and "unreasonable" interference requirements distinguish an action for private nuisance from that of trespass. . . . The substantial interference requirement is to satisfy the need for a showing that the land is reduced in value because of the defendant's conduct. "The law does not concern itself with trifles and there must be a real and appreciable invasion of the plaintiff's interests before he can have an action for either a public or private nuisance." Restatement (Second) of Torts §821F comment c.

In paragraph 68, Bower asserts that defendant trespassed upon the townhouse, removed articles from the premises, changed locks and positioned guards in the lobby. However, plaintiff failed to allege that these acts caused a reduction in the value of the property. . . . Plaintiff's failure to plead a substantial and unreasonable interference with the land is fatal to her claim for private nuisance. . . .

In summary, Weisman's motion for a more definite statement pursuant to Fed. R. Civ. P. 12(e) and motion to dismiss the second claim in the Complaint for failure to state fraud with particularity pursuant to Rule 9(b) is granted, and Bower has leave to replead within thirty (30) days of this opinion. In addition, Bower's Fifth Claim for false imprisonment, and Seventh Claim for private nuisance are dismissed, as they fail to state a claim upon which relief can be granted, Fed. R. Civ. P. 12(b)(6). All other motions are denied. . . .

There is much dispute about whether the pleading requirements under the Federal Rules are too lenient to achieve the goal of screening out claims that lack merit. Some federal courts have reacted by requiring stricter pleading in some types of cases. The two *Leatherman* cases that follow exemplify the debate. We have printed the Fifth Circuit opinion first, although it has been reversed by the Supreme Court, because it gives more of the facts and provides insight into how some courts have required stricter pleading. The subtitles in the Fifth Circuit opinion are precisely as Judge Goldberg wrote them. A portion of the Supereme Court opinion follows the Circuit Court opinion.

■ LEATHERMAN v. TARRANT COUNTY NARCOTICS INTELLIGENCE AND COORDINATION UNIT
954 F.2d 1054 (5th Cir. 1992)

GOLDBERG, Circuit Judge.

After police shot and killed their two dogs during the execution of a search warrant, plaintiffs brought this section 1983 action against the municipal defendants employing the police officers involved. [The text of

42 U.S.C. §1983 is as follows: "Every person who, under color of any statute, ordinance, regulation, custom or usage, of any State or Territory or the District of Columbia, subjects, or causes to be subjected, any citizen of the United States or other person within the jurisdiction thereof to the deprivation of any rights, privileges, or immunities secured by the Constitution and laws, shall be liable to the party injured in an action at law, suit in equity, or other proper proceeding for redress. . . ."] They alleged that the municipalities had failed to adequately train their officers, and that such failure amounted to a municipal policy. The district court, 755 F. Supp. 726 (N.D. Tex. 1991), dismissed the complaint because it did not satisfy this circuit's "heightened pleading requirement." Under the heightened pleading standard, a complaint must allege with particularity all material facts establishing a plaintiff's right of recovery, including "detailed facts supporting the contention that [a] plea of immunity cannot be sustained," *Elliott v. Perez,* 751 F.2d 1472, 1482 (5th Cir. 1985), and, in cases like this one, facts that support the requisite allegation that the municipality engaged in a policy or custom for which it can be held responsible. Because plaintiffs' complaint does not satisfy the heightened pleading requirement, we affirm.

DOG DAY AFTERNOON

This civil rights case arose out of two separate incidents involving the execution of search warrants by law enforcement officers with the Tarrant County Narcotics Intelligence and Coordination Unit. One incident involved Charlene Leatherman, her son Travis, and her two dogs, Shakespeare and Ninja. Ms. Leatherman and Travis were driving in Fort Worth when they were suddenly stopped by police cars. Police officers surrounded the two of them, shouting instructions and threatening to shoot them. The officers informed Ms. Leatherman that other law enforcement officers were in the process of searching her residence. The officers also informed her that the search team had shot and killed their two dogs. Ms. Leatherman and Travis returned to their home to find Shakespeare lying dead some twenty-five feet from the front door. He had been shot three times, once in the stomach, once in the leg, and once in the head. Ninja was lying in a pool of blood on the bed in the master bedroom. He had been shot in the head at close range, evidently with a shotgun, and brain matter was splattered across the bed, against the wall, and on the floor around the bed. The officers found nothing in the home relevant to their investigation. Rather than departing with dispatch, they proceeded to lounge on the front lawn of the Leatherman home for over an hour, drinking, smoking, talking, and laughing, apparently celebrating their seemingly unbridled power.

The other incident alleged in plaintiffs' amended complaint involved a police raid of the home of Gerald Andert pursuant to a search warrant.

The warrant was issued on the basis that police officers had smelled odors associated with the manufacture of amphetamines emanating from the Andert home. At the time of the raid, Andert, a sixty-four year old grandfather, was at home with his family mourning the death of his wife; she had died after a three-year battle with cancer. Without knocking or identifying themselves, the officers burst into the home and, without provocation, began beating Andert. First, an unidentified officer knocked him backwards. When Andert turned, he was greeted by two swift blows to the head inflicted by a club, presumably of the billy-style. His head wound would require eleven stitches. Other officers, in the meantime, shouted obscenities at the family members, who were still unaware of the intruders' identities. At gun point, the officers forced the family members to lie face down on the floor. The officers did not relent: they continued to insult the residents and threatened to harm them. After searching the residence for one and one-half hours and finding nothing in the residence related to narcotics activity, the officers finally left.

Plaintiffs sued the Tarrant County Narcotics Intelligence and Coordination Unit ("TCNICU"), Tim Curry (in his official capacity as director of that unit), Tarrant County, Don Carpenter (sheriff of Tarrant County), the City of Lake Worth, Texas, and the City of Grapevine, Texas, in connection with these two incidents. Their amended complaint alleged generally that the municipalities failed to formulate and implement an adequate policy to train its officers on the proper manner to execute search warrants and respond when confronted by family dogs. The allegations were of the "boilerplate" variety, alleging no underlying facts other than the events described above to support the assertions that the municipalities had adopted policies, customs, and practices condoning the conduct of the officers involved. The complaint did not name any of the officers in their individual capacities as defendants.

TCNICU, Tim Curry, and Don Carpenter moved the district court to dismiss the complaint pursuant to Fed. R. Civ. P. 12(b)(6). . . . They argued . . . that the complaint did not adequately allege facts under this circuit's heightened pleading standard establishing that the municipality adopted a policy or custom countenancing the police conduct or that its failure to train amounted to deliberate indifference to the rights of the plaintiffs. . . .

The district court granted the motion and dismissed all of plaintiffs' claims against all of the defendants, movants and nonmovants alike. The district court held that the complaint did not satisfy the heightened pleading standard. . . . On appeal, plaintiffs urge this court to abandon the heightened pleading requirement, apparently conceding that their complaint does not satisfy that standard. . . . Finally, they contend that the district court's . . . dismissal of their claims against the nonmovants, defendants City of Grapevine and City of Lake Worth, was premature because the district court did not provide them with notice that it was contemplating dismissing their claims against those nonmoving defendants.

ALL BARK, NO BITE

In *Elliott v. Perez*, 751 F.2d 1472 (5th Cir. 1985), this circuit adopted the heightened pleading requirement for cases against state actors in their individual capacities. Reasoning that the doctrine of immunity should accord the defendant-official not only immunity from liability, but also immunity from defending against the lawsuit, *id.* at 1477-78, the *Elliott* court held that: In cases against government officials involving the likely defense of qualified immunity we require of trial judges that they demand that the plaintiff's complaint state with factual detail and particularity the basis for the claim which necessarily includes why the defendant-official cannot successfully maintain the defense of immunity. *Id.* at 1473.

Since *Elliott*, this circuit has, without fail, applied the heightened pleading requirement in cases in which the defendant-official can raise the immunity defense. We have written that "pleadings, replete with . . . conclusory statements, do not defeat the officers' qualified immunity defense." Other circuits have similarly applied the heightened pleading requirement. For a collection of cases, *see* Martin A. Schwartz and John E. Kirklin, *Section 1983 Litigation: Claims, Defenses and Fees*, Vol. I, §1.6 n.106 (1991).

In *Palmer v. City of San Antonio*, 810 F.2d 514, 516-17 (5th Cir. 1987), a panel of this court extended the heightened pleading requirement into the municipal liability context. The court assumed, sub silentio, that the heightened pleading requirement logically applied not only in cases against defendant-officials, but in all section 1983 cases, including cases brought against a municipality. The *Palmer* court did not explain why the heightened pleading requirement should be extended to defendant-municipalities, considering that municipalities cannot claim the immunity defense. A later panel of this court suggested that: [i]n view of the enormous expense involved today in litigation, . . . the heavy cost of responding to even a baseless legal action, and of Rule 11's new language requiring reasonable inquiry into the facts of the case by an attorney before he brings an action, applying the stated rule to all section 1983 actions has much to recommend it. *Rodriguez v. Avita*, 871 F.2d 552, 554 (5th Cir. 1989), *cert. denied*, 493 U.S. 854 (1989). Thus, under *Elliott* and *Palmer*, the heightened pleading requirement governs all section 1983 complaints brought in this circuit: If the complaint is all bark and no bite, a district court is constrained to dismiss it even before opening discovery.

With the heightened pleading requirement as our guide, we turn to the particulars of this case. Quite plainly, plaintiffs' complaint falls short of alleging the requisite facts to establish a policy of inadequate training. Where, as here, a lawsuit brought against a municipality is predicated on inadequate training of its police officers, this circuit has cautioned that "to make such a showing in such a case, there would have to be demonstrated 'at least a pattern of similar incidents in which the citizens were injured' . . . [in order] to establish the official policy requisite to municipal liability under section 1983." *Rodriguez*, 871 F.2d at 554-55. . . .

Although we are troubled by the absence of notice preceding the district court's *sua sponte* dismissal of the claims against the nonmovants, defendants City of Grapevine and City of Lake Worth, we nevertheless affirm the dismissal of those claims as well. Plaintiffs do not contend in this court that they are prepared to allege specific facts in an amended complaint so as to render it in compliance with our heightened pleading requirement. We conclude, therefore, that the district court's failure to notify plaintiffs of its intention to dismiss the claims against the nonmovants, in the context of this case, was harmless.

The judgment of the district court is Affirmed.

[We have omitted Judge Goldberg's opinion in which he concurs "specially." It also has subtitles: "These Dogs Want Their Day" and "Let Sleeping Dogs Lie." Judge Goldberg notes the strong arguments for not having heightened pleading requirements for Section 1983 cases, but feels "constrained to obey the command" of Fifth Circuit precedent.]

In 1993 the Supreme Court unanimously reversed the decision of the Fifth Circuit opinion you just read. Below is an excerpt from Justice Rehnquist's unanimous opinion for the Court.

■ LEATHERMAN v. TARRANT COUNTY NARCOTICS INTELLIGENCE AND COORDINATION UNIT
507 U.S. 163 (1992)

Chief Justice REHNQUIST delivered the opinion of the Court:

We granted certiorari to decide whether a federal court may apply a "heightened pleading standard"—more stringent than the usual pleading requirements of Rule 8(a) of the Federal Rules of Civil Procedure—in civil rights cases alleging municipal liability under Rev. Stat. §1979, 42 U.S.C. §1983. We hold it may not.

. . . We think that it is impossible to square the "heightened pleading standard" applied by the Fifth Circuit in this case with the liberal system of "notice pleading" set up by the Federal Rules. Rule 8(a)(2) requires that a complaint include only "a short and plain statement of the claim showing that the pleader is entitled to relief." In *Conley v. Gibson*, 355 U.S. 41, (1957), we said in effect that the Rule meant what it said: "[T]he Federal Rules of Civil Procedure do not require a claimant to set out in detail the facts upon which he bases his claim. To the contrary, all the Rules require is 'a short and plain statement of the claim' that will give the defendant fair notice of what the plaintiff's claim is and the grounds upon which it rests." *Id.*, at 47 (footnote omitted).

Rule 9(b) does impose a particularity requirement in two specific instances. It provides that "[i]n all averments of fraud or mistake, the circumstances constituting fraud or mistake shall be stated with particularity." Thus, the Federal Rules do address in Rule 9(b) the question of the need for greater particularity in pleading certain actions, but do not include among the enumerated actions any reference to complaints alleging municipal liability under §1983. *Expressio unius est exclusio alterius.*

The phenomenon of litigation against municipal corporations based on claimed constitutional violations by their employees dates from our decision in *Monell,* where we for the first time construed §1983 to allow such municipal liability. Perhaps if Rules 8 and 9 were rewritten today, claims against municipalities under §1983 might be subjected to the added specificity requirement of Rule 9(b). But that is a result which must be obtained by the process of amending the Federal Rules, and not by judicial interpretation. In the absence of such an amendment, federal courts and litigants must rely on summary judgment and control of discovery to weed out unmeritorious claims sooner rather than later.

The judgment of the Court of Appeals is reversed, and the case remanded for further proceedings consistent with this opinion.

Comments and Questions

1. In *Leatherman,* Chief Justice Rehnquist stated that the Court did not "consider whether [its] qualified immunity jurisprudence would require a heightened pleading in cases involving individual government officials[,]" as opposed to cases against a municipality in which the defense of qualified immunity is unavailable. The debate over this issue has become quite complicated and illustrates how creatively lawyers and judges use procedural rules and statutes. The Supreme Court has ruled that qualified immunity for governmental officials extends to their performance of discretionary functions "insofar as their conduct does not violate clearly established statutory or constitutional rights of which a reasonable person would have known." *Harlow v. Fitzgerald,* 457 U.S. 800, 818 (1982). This replaced a subjective good faith test for qualified immunity, which some felt led to both lengthy discovery and an inability to determine the qualified immunity defense without a full trial. Some courts hold that the heightened pleading standard still applies in Section 1983 cases involving individual government agents, and that since the Supreme Court in *Leatherman* did not rule on whether plaintiffs have to plead specific facts to negate the qualified immunity defense of official employees, they can require such specificity in pleading. *See, e.g., Harris v. Hayter,* 970 F. Supp. 500 (W.D. Va. 1997).

2. The Fifth Circuit has held that after an individual government official raises the qualified immunity defense in an answer, the trial court

can require a reply by the plaintiff under Fed. R. Civ. P. 7; that the lenient pleading requirements of Fed. R. Civ. P. 8(a) do not apply to a Rule 7 reply; and that "the reply must be tailored to the assertion of qualified immunity and fairly engage its allegations." *Shultea v. Wood*, 47 F.3d 1427 (5th Cir. 1995) (en banc). In *Crawford-El v. Britton*, 118 S. Ct. 1584, 1596 (1998), the majority opinion of Justice Stevens suggests that trial judges can order a reply under Fed. R. Civ. P. 7 or a more definite statement under Fed. R. Civ. P. 12(e) in order to force specificity upon plaintiffs alleging a claim that a public official has acted with a wrongful motive, regardless of whether the affirmative defense of qualified immunity has been pled.

A concurring opinion in *Shultea* suggests that the Supreme Court, which promulgates the Federal Rules under the authority of a congressional statute, must not interpret the Federal Rules in a way that permits vague pleading by a plaintiff to negate the defense of qualified immunity: "This substantive immunity afforded public officials to free them from the burdens of litigation cannot be abrogated by a rule of civil procedure. Under the Rules Enabling Act, the Federal Rules of Civil Procedure 'shall not abridge, enlarge or modify any substantive right.' 28 U.S.C. Sec. 2072(b)." 47 F.3d 1427, 1433 (Edith H. Jones, joined by three other judges). We will revisit the issue of heightened pleading standards in our later discussion of the history of procedure.

3. The language of Fed. R. Civ. P. 8(a)(2), requiring "a short and plain statement of the claim showing that the pleader is entitled to relief," carefully avoids using either the words "facts" or "causes of action," which are a part of some state pleading rules. The Federal Rule does not state that the pleader must identify facts for each element of the claim or cause of action. Nonetheless, it would be implausible were a complaint to just say that the defendant is liable without giving any hint about a theory of cognizability; nor is it likely that a complaint can tell so little about what happened that the defendant does not know enough to commence intelligent discovery. Here is one attempt to explain the ambiguity of federal pleading rules:

> The ambiguity of the Federal Rules' purpose has led to two lines of doctrine about pleading. One line, which seems more consistent with the drafter's intent, was that the pleaders did have to allege, if only in sketchy terms, the existence of circumstances that they had reason to believe were true and that, if true, would entitle them to relief of some kind. The other line is that expressed by the Supreme Court in *Conley v. Gibson*, and it asserts that a complaint under the Federal Rules is sufficient unless "it appears beyond doubt that the plaintiff can prove no set of facts in support of his claim which would entitle him to relief."
>
> A fundamental contradiction exists between these approaches. Under the first approach, the pleader can pursue the action into discovery only if the pleading establishes, as it were, probable cause. Under the second approach, the pleader can pursue the action beyond the pleading stage unless

the *pleading on its face* shows that the pleader has no cause. This would make pleading requirements rather pointless. Courts and commentators since *Conley v. Gibson* have therefore suggested that the Supreme Court could not literally have meant what it said. No doubt there is agreement that a complaint alleging only that "defendant wronged plaintiff" would not be sufficient, and to this extent *Conley v. Gibson*'s language is hyperbole. But the language is sufficiently undemanding so that the federal pleading rule can be boiled down to the following:

(1) The pleader may attempt to state the claim with sufficient clarity and in such detail as to pose at the pleading stage whether there is a legally valid claim on the facts he or she supposes to be true. If the pleader does so, and defendant moves to dismiss the claim, the court will give the pleader a ruling on the legal question. . . .

(2) Under *Conley v. Gibson*, the pleader may allege the claim in very general terms without specifying the facts. If the pleader does so, the action will continue into the discovery stage, and the legal sufficiency of the claim will not be determined until discovery is substantially completed.

Fleming James, Jr., Geoffrey C. Hazard, and John Leubsdorf, *Civil Procedure* (4th ed. 1992), §3.6, at 147-148.

4. Note that in *Conley v. Gibson*, the respondents are saying that the complaint fails to state a claim for which relief can be granted on two quite different grounds. Analytically, the Court's paragraph that begins "The respondents point to the fact that under the Railway Labor Act" is responding to a different argument from the one the Court discusses in the paragraph that begins "The respondents also argue that the complaint failed to set forth specific facts." Be prepared to explain the two different grounds. *Bower v. Weisman* shows still a third way that a portion of a claim may be deficient. How is it different from the other two?

Here is a summary of three different types of failure to state a claim upon which relief can be granted: (a) no such cause of action exists; (b) such a cause of action exists, but the plaintiff does not state even rudimentary information, such as that provided in Form 9 of the Federal Rules of Civil Procedure, to suggest that the plaintiff may conceivably have a cause of action; (c) there is a known cause of action, and the plaintiff states the facts with sufficient specificity to demonstrate that the facts alleged, even if true, do not correspond with the cause or causes of action that the plaintiff evidently has in mind.

5. Judges ordinarily do not look beyond the "four corners" of the complaint when ruling on a 12(b)(6) motion. Fed. R. Civ. P. 10(c) states, however, that "[a] copy of any written instrument which is an exhibit to a pleading is a part thereof for all purposes." Professor Marcus observes that "[c]ourts have energetically seized this opportunity and permitted defendants to bring a range of materials to bear on the complaint in support of motions to dismiss, even where not attached as exhibits." (His footnote 57 gives examples of courts' taking consideration of unattached

informational brochures, an unattached partnership agreement, and an EEOC charge that was not attached to the complaint.) Richard L. Marcus, *The Puzzling Persistence of Pleading Practice*, 76 Tex. L. Rev. 1749, 1757 (1998).

6. Rule 8(e)(2) provides that a party may state "as many separate claims or defenses as the party has *regardless of consistency*" (emphasis added). Judge Cabranes' opinion in the following case details the rationale for that rule.

■ HENRY v. DAYTOP VILLAGE, INC.
42 F.3d 89 (2nd Cir. 1994)

CABRANES, Circuit Judge.

We are asked to decide whether a Title VII plaintiff who brings arguably inconsistent claims is thereby precluded from challenging her employer's proffered legitimate nondiscriminatory reason for firing her. Because her claims are not inconsistent, and because the Federal Rules of Civil Procedure explicitly authorize pleading in the alternative, we hold that her second claim may not be construed as an admission against her first claim. Accordingly, we reverse in part and affirm in part. . . .

[Daytop Village's ("Daytop") employee health insurance plan provided health benefits to employees' spouses, but only to the extent that a spouse's own health plan would not cover medical expenses. All Daytop employees seeking reimbursement for spousal medical expenses were expected to provide written documentation of the spouse's health plan.

For a number of years, the plaintiff Celia Henry ("Henry") sought, and was granted reimbursement by Daytop for medical expenses of her husband, Ernesto. There was a dispute between Henry and Daytop as to what medical information she actually provided regarding Ernesto's health coverage. In 1989, Daytop's investigation of Ernesto's health insurance revealed that Daytop had overpaid Henry $760.53 for her husband's medical expenses, as a result of duplicative claims. Henry's supervisor confronted her with the company's findings. An argument ensued, and Henry was fired for employee misconduct.

In 1992, Henry filed a complaint in district court, claiming she was unlawfully fired under Title VII, because of her sex and race (black). She offered two theories in support of the discrimination claim: (1) she had not misrepresented her husband's medical coverage; therefore, Daytop's misconduct accusations were simply a pretext for firing her; (2) white male employees had received more lenient sanctions for similar misconduct. Daytop moved for summary judgment. It contended that the complaint failed to raise a genuine issue of material fact, because, as part in parcel of Henry's Title VII claim, she alleged that "similarly situated employees who were not black women had been punished less severely for similar violations of Daytop's disciplinary code." Daytop claimed that (1) Henry's allegations were, in effect, an admission of her conduct, and (2) were therefore inconsistent with her further allegations that she did not commit any misconduct. The district court granted Daytop's summary judgment motion. This appeal followed:]

The district court reasoned that Henry had admitted misconduct as a matter of law when she alleged that similarly situated white or male employees were treated less harshly for similar violations of Daytop's disciplinary code. Accordingly, the court concluded that neither Henry's personal affirmations nor the New York ALJ's finding that Henry had consistently informed Daytop of her husband's medical coverage raised an issue of material fact sufficient to defeat summary judgment.

The district court erred in two respects. First, Henry did not "admit" misconduct as a matter of law when she claimed disparate treatment. . . . [Rather,] Henry's claim is that regardless of whether she was guilty of the charged violations of Daytop's disciplinary code, the sanction imposed on her—immediate discharge—was more severe than sanctions imposed on similarly situated white or male employees. Far from being a conceded fact, the question of whether Henry in fact misrepresented her husband's insurance coverage is immaterial to whether Daytop treated her in the same way that it treated white or male employees who were accused of similar misconduct.

Second, even if Henry did concede her misconduct as a matter of law with respect to one claim, she did not concede that misconduct with respect to her other claims. . . . Henry's complaint presents two distinct claims. The first claim is that Daytop falsely accused Henry of violating the disciplinary code in order to fire her. The second claim, as stated above, is that regardless of whether Henry had in fact misrepresented her husband's medical insurance coverage to Daytop, the particular disciplinary sanction imposed on her—immediate discharge—was more severe than sanctions imposed on similarly situated white or male employees. . . . Under Rule 8(e)(2) of the Federal Rules of Civil Procedure, a plaintiff may plead two or more statements of a claim, even within the same count, regardless of consistency.

Common law and code practice condemned inconsistency in pleadings because it was believed that a pleading containing inconsistent allegations indicated falsehood on its face and was a sign of a chicanerous litigant seeking to subvert the judicial process. All too frequently, however, valid claims were sacrificed on the altar of technical consistency. In order to avoid the constrictions of the early practice, the draftsmen of the federal rules sought to liberate pleaders from the inhibiting requirement of technical consistency. The flexibility afforded by Rule 8(e)(2) is especially appropriate in civil rights cases, in which complex inquiries into the parties' intent may sometimes justify raising multiple, inconsistent claims.

Pursuant to Rule 8(e)(2), therefore, we may not construe Henry's first claim as an admission against another alternative or inconsistent claim. . . . Accordingly, even if Henry's claims were somehow inconsistent—which they are not, in our view—we could and would entertain them both. We now examine each claim in turn. . . .

Comments and Questions

1. Why, then, did Judge Sweet grant the defendant's 12(b)(6) motion as to the false imprisonment count in *Bower v. Weisman?*

2. You already have a good deal of information to help you consider the goals that pleading requirements should achieve. It is important that you understand these various goals, because they will help you make arguments for and against motions to dismiss, and they will also help you decide on your own strategy for drafting complaints in different types of cases. One way to consider goals is to think about the underlying values of a procedural system that we explored in Chapter 1. Another way to approach goals for a pleading system is to consider the relationship of the complaint to other stages of the litigation. What is the relationship of pleading requirements to discovery? To res judicata, in the claim preclusion sense? Finally, consider your various audiences. Are there times when you would plead more than is required by the pleading rules themselves? *See* the discussion of strategy considerations that follows.

3. Rule 9(b), which the court applied in *Bower v. Weisman,* required "particularity" in the pleading of the "circumstances constituting fraud or mistake." Why? Note that Rule 9(g) requires that "[w]hen items of special damage are claimed, they shall be specifically stated." The purpose of the rule is to notify the defendant when the type of loss is unusual for the type of claim being sued upon, so that the defendant is not unfairly surprised. For instance, the defendant might not know, absent specific pleading, that a plaintiff incurred expenses to minimize a loss. We have only provided one example here, because the question of what is a "special damage" for pleading purposes is just the type of question that gives you an opportunity to begin using the treatises we have described (or to find other sources in your school's library that might answer the question). If you were unsure whether a type of damage was "special," would you plead it?

4. We are blessed in the field of civil procedure with three exceptionally well written single-volume treatises: Jack H. Friedenthal, Mary Kay Kane, & Arthur R. Miller, *Civil Procedure* (3rd ed. 1999); Fleming James, Jr., Geoffrey C. Hazard, and John Leubsdorf, *Civil Procedure* (4th ed. 1992); and Charles A. Wright, *Law of Federal Courts* (5th ed. 1994). The Wright single volume, as its title connotes, concentrates almost exclusively on the federal court system. Wright also has a multi-volume treatise entitled *Federal Practice and Procedure.* Many of the volumes of this treatise were co-

authored with Arthur Miller, and the treatise thus is often referred to as *Wright & Miller*. The other most frequently cited multi-volume treatise in the federal procedure field is called *Moore's Federal Practice*, named after William Moore, who was its initial author. Find out where these books are in your law library. When you are stumped on a procedure question during this course, or want to know more about a given topic, take a look at these books. You can usually find an answer quickly—and it is great practice.

Practice Exercise No. 7: Analyzing 12(b)(6) and 12(e) Motions in *Carpenter*

After an initial client interview and strategy session, Attorney Carol Coblentz decided to represent Nancy Carpenter. Some legal research and factual investigation was done, and a complaint was filed. The defendants filed a 12(b)(6) motion to dismiss and a 12(e) motion for a more definite statement. You are a law clerk to a trial judge who soon will have to rule on the two motions. Consider what arguments both sides might make. What rulings do you suggest and why? Assume that the pleading rules applicable in the state courts of the Commonwealth of Massachusetts are identical to the Federal Rules of Civil Procedure. The complaint, relevant statutes and motions can be found (with the initial memorandum) in the *Carpenter v. Dee* Case Files.

3. Strategy Considerations

Many litigation decisions require the lawyer to consider three different questions: What must I do? What may I do? What should I do? As you have seen, the Federal Rules of Civil Procedure instruct the lawyer about the minimum requirements for a complaint. But lawyers can compose a much more comprehensive complaint if they choose. In addition to drafting a complaint so that it will survive a 12(b)(6) motion, a plaintiff's lawyer will have a number of audiences she may wish to persuade or influence. The obvious ones are the judge and the opposing party and her lawyer. But consider still other audiences.

In a 1995 article, brief portions of which are printed here, Professor Eastman urges that we make complaints more literary than the brief, simple allegations allowed by the Federal Rules. He suggests that we draw on other disciplines, such as literature, journalism, and history, in order to improve upon much of the sterility in legal drafting. We have printed the portion of the article in which he discusses many potential gains for drafting complaints as advocacy documents, as well as legally correct pleadings. We also print his literary revision of an amended complaint filed in a voting rights case that challenged the districting in Cairo, Illinois. The actual case settled, and a consent decree was entered and enforced by the court. After the article, we pose some of the questions that Professor Eastman considers at length.

■ HERBERT A. EASTMAN, SPEAKING TRUTH TO POWER: THE LANGUAGE OF CIVIL RIGHTS LITIGATORS
104 Yale L.J. 763 (1995)

I once had a client named Hattie Kendrick. She was a woman and an African-American, a school teacher and a civil rights warrior, spit upon, arrested, and tossed out of restaurants and clothing stores that did not "cater to the colored trade." She marched and spoke out for integration and against oppression. Her school fired her, but not before she had taught generations of black children in Cairo, Illinois, that participation in American democracy was their right and their duty. In the 1940's, she sued to win equal pay for black teachers, with Thurgood Marshall as her lawyer. And in the 1970's, she was a named plaintiff in a class action asserting the voting rights of black citizens in Cairo against a city electoral system rigged to reduce the value of their votes to nothingness. All she wanted was to cast a meaningful vote in a democratic election before she died—she was in her nineties, growing blind and weak. Such woman. Such a story. And such a voice. Listen to how she discerns the problems of her town: "Too long have the two races stood grinning in each other's faces, while they carry the fires of resentment and hate in their hearts, and with their hands hid behind their backs they carry the unsheathed sword." Yet here is how the complaint filed in federal court identifies the named plaintiffs, including Hattie Kendrick: "All plaintiffs are Blacks, citizens of the United States and of the State of Illinois, and residents of Cairo, Illinois registered to vote in Municipal Elections conducted in Cairo."

This Article springs from the recurring disappointment and frustration I have felt after consultation with clients in cases presenting outrages that, in a phrase loved by my mother, cried out to heaven. I have represented and continue to represent these clients in civil rights cases, broadly defined. . . .

My frustration and disappointment began when I reviewed the pleadings I drafted for them. I could barely see over the chasm separating what those clients told me about their lives and what I wrote to the court as factual allegations in the complaint—sterile recitations of dates and events that lost so much in the translation. What is lost in a description that identifies a woman like Hattie only as a registered voter? Details, of course. Passion, certainly, but more than that. We lose the identity of the person harmed, the story of her life. But even more is lost. This was a class action aimed at remedying a systemic problem harming thousands, over generations. The complaint omits the social chemistry underneath the events normally invisible to the law—events that create the injury or compound it. In this complaint, we lose the fullness of the harm done, the scale of the deprivations, the humiliation of the plaintiff class members, the damage to greater society, the significance of it all.

The complaint omits the frustration of the democratic process and the powerful metaphors that claim an exception to the rules restricting the court's involvement. The complaint leaves intact the walls between the clients and the court, the clients and the lawyer. In a strange way, it even effaces the lawyer by denying her the dynamic and creative role of responding to the tragedy witnessed.

I wondered how we, as lawyers, could plead the horror of wrong done on a mass scale. In reviewing the pleadings in other famous civil rights class actions, I found similar failings. This Article explores why we fail and wonders whether we can do better. . . .

The civil rights plaintiff may stand in the courtroom as an equal to her adversary, but she did not enter the courtroom in that condition and may leave with that inequality deepened. An adverse verdict can mean continued oppression, even death.

But this dramatic quality transcends the civil rights context. Every client has a story that deserves to be told—from the corporate client trying to survive in a harshly competitive climate, to a spouse embroiled in a bitter divorce. While the need to tell a story is present in many different kinds of litigation, the civil rights field is a good place to begin. . . .

What does it matter? What is wrong with a pleading that simply offers a short and concise statement of the claim, as the rules expect? Why are pleadings so important? . . .

Certainly, the persuasiveness of the stories lawyers tell for their clients matters. "People, including judges and jurors," Michael Tigar writes, "understand and restate events in terms of stories." Nevertheless, many lawyers view the complaint simply as the mechanism by which they get the case into a court and in front of a jury—irrelevant once defense motions attacking the pleading have been overcome. Viewed from their angle, the complaint only needs to meet legal sufficiencies; it need not tell a story. These lawyers might think that the trial, specifically the closing arguments, serves as a more appropriate vehicle for telling the tragic stories they seek to remedy.

Even so, civil rights pleadings in particular should tell stories, for these reasons: First, in civil rights cases seeking injunctions, there is no jury. The judge is the person who must be persuaded. She is the trier of fact who will then decide to issue an injunction or not. The complaint, while certainly not the only opportunity for persuasion, is the first in time and the one that frames the remaining discussion of the case. Second, not only will there be no jury, it is likely that there will be no trial. Years will be spent managing a complex discovery process, punctuated by scrimmages over various motions. Often the parties bypass trial by negotiating a consent decree, often with guidance from the court. While the parties may negotiate the relief, the court must approve of the terms and maintain a "continuing involvement in administration and implementation." Abram Chayes has noted that "[a]ll these factors thrust the trial judge into an active role in shaping, organizing and facilitating the litigation." When the decision maker shapes the development of the case and grants the relief without a trial, the complaint grows in significance. It is the first and perhaps the only means of communicating the client's story.

Third, even where a trial results, it will take years to get there. ["In Hattie Kendrick's case, settlement negotiations began in earnest on the eve of trial, six years after the initial complaint was filed. The case finally culminated in a consent decree six months later. . . . Even when clients are allowed to testify on their experiences during a preliminary injunction hearing, the narrative of their experiences may be lost once the court begins to focus more narrowly upon the more sterile legal issues raised by the complaints."] Erving Goffman has observed that in most personal encounters, one or the other of the participants in an interaction will shape that interaction, at the outset. In litigation, one participant—the judge—exercises much more power than the others in deciding who speaks, at what length, and at what time. The complaint—read by the judge, one would hope, before her first face-to-face interaction with plaintiffs' counsel—may present the lawyer with the sole means of shaping the continuing interaction "at the outset." The complaint may color the judge's perception throughout the trial and beyond—from motions, discovery disputes, and settlement conferences, through postdecree enforcement proceedings.

Fourth, the court's construction of the "real" problem dictates how the problem will be considered and addressed. For example, if a prison case is defined as a problem of resources rather than as a dispute over particular rights, the court may rule that it has no power to act. On the other hand, if the case is defined as a dispute over rights, then the lack of resources provides no defense. . . . Since we criticize judges who reach adverse decisions by using labels that misrepresent our client's reality, we should pause to consider how our complaints can educate the judge about that reality.

Fifth, federal judges who sit in isolation, economically and socially, from the problems of poor blacks in Cairo or of felons in maximum security prisons, need more vivid and complete pictures painted for them if they are to understand the problems sufficiently, to care about them enough to guide the litigation, and, ultimately, to remedy those problems. Beyond the personal life experiences of the judge, other obstacles restrict the view of the judge, e.g., the restraints of the role, limited resources, and even more limited access to the facts of a case. . . .

One federal judge has candidly written that

> [R]egardless of who appointed them, judges react negatively to the "gotcha" lawsuit. By that I mean the lawsuit based on some technical nonobservance of a law or regulation whose consequences are undocumented, or at best vague. We judges want to know the facts, the real-life conditions, the actual practices underlying a legal challenge. . . . Judges search for meaning in what we do. You need to convince us that the law or the regulation is important in poor people's lives.

Other judges—and their law clerks—have emphasized, in prisoner cases, that it is the "compelling" story that moves them to act.

Sixth, the complaint is even more important to lawyers who perceive themselves as representatives of a cause or constituency beyond the immediate client. Civil rights "litigation is itself an excellent constituency-building device." A lawyer can further her larger cause by drafting a pleading that serves as a "dramatic and decisive gesture, stating a claim in its most extreme and visible form—as a legal right." Impact litigation can give poor clients a chance to mobilize for change. Robert Jerome Glennon even argues that litigation contributed more to the success of the mid-1950's civil rights movement in Montgomery, Alabama, than did the bus boycott. The complaint, filed with the court and disseminated to clients or "constituents" and the media, communicates what the problem is all about.

Seventh, through the media, the complaint speaks to the greater community. That community includes the defendants, the defendants' superiors, and possibly their friends and colleagues. That community may come to see hidden problems in a new light, consider change, and press for settlement.

Eighth, the complaint offers the litigator the only chance to tell the client's story—a dramatic, compelling story—in a literary way. It is a rare chance for creativity. Civil rights lawyers should not resist this opportunity. Civil rights complaints, because they are of more recent vintage and so deeply fact sensitive, are rooted less often in common law pleading rules and techniques and written less frequently from formbooks. . . .

This complaint may not "crash through" the prejudices of a hostile audience with the power and skill of Abraham Lincoln. But it sure beats notice pleading. [Professor Eastman's revised complaint (which was never filed) was made all the more vivid by the inclusion of several photographs.]

IN THE UNITED STATES DISTRICT COURT
FOR THE SOUTHERN DISTRICT OF ILLINOIS

HATTIE KENDRICK, PRESTON EWING, JR., individually and on behalf of all others similarly situated, Plaintiffs, -vs- ALLEN MOSS, individually and as Mayor of the City of Cairo, Illinois; the CAIRO CITY COUNCIL; and the CITY OF CAIRO, a Municipal Corporation, Defendants	CIVIL ACTION NO. 73-19C EQUITABLE RELIEF REQUESTED

COMPLAINT

1. This is a class action brought before this Court by Hattie Kendrick and Preston Ewing, Jr., for the benefit of a class of all African-American citizens who are residents of Cairo, Illinois, and who are or will be entitled to vote in Cairo City Council elections. This action challenges, through 42 U.S.C. §1983, the at-large election basis for conducting City Council elections in Cairo as a violation of the Fourteenth and Fifteenth Amendments to the United States Constitution and the Voting Rights Act, 42 U.S.C. §1973.

2. Hattie Kendrick is an African-American, born in Mississippi, who moved to Cairo in the early 1920's. She has taught for decades in the racially segregated Cairo public schools, teaching generations of African-American children that participation in American democracy is their right and their duty. To set an example, she has worked throughout her life to better her community through neighborhood organization, peaceful demonstration, political activity, and litigation. She has paid a price for her dedication: She has been forced out of segregated business establishments, arrested by the police during peaceful marches, and fired by the school system. While many African-American leaders have advocated racial separatism, Ms. Kendrick has remained a fervent believer in peaceful integration with European-Americans living in Cairo.

3. Preston Ewing, Jr., a former student of Ms. Kendrick, is an African-American whose family has lived in Cairo for generations. Mr. Ewing's father worked to make his family economically secure through great personal sacrifice. When he worked as a postal deliverer, his supervisors forbade him from using the post office men's room. Mr. Ewing, Sr., therefore suffered the humiliation of asking people on his route to allow

him to use their bathrooms, keeping this secret from his wife and children for years to spare them the embarrassment. Mr. Ewing, Jr. has followed his father's example and dedicated his career to his community, organizing the local NAACP chapter and advocating for the educational needs of all children, both African-American and European-American. . . . Most of the photographs appearing in this complaint were taken by Mr. Ewing, Jr.

4. Hattie Kendrick, Preston Ewing, and the class they represent challenge the at-large form of voting for City Council because it denies them the right to vote. It does so through this formula: An at-large voting scheme for city council; racially polarized voting so extreme that European-American voters never vote for African-American candidates; a sixty-percent majority for European-American voters in the electorate; and a political system that excludes African-American citizens from participating. These factors together dilute the African-American vote to nothingness.

5. When she moved to Cairo from Mississippi, Ms. Kendrick found that Cairo government operates as a plantation democracy, nominally extending the vote to all citizens of age, yet enforcing an antidemocratic feudal system that keeps African-Americans, forty percent of the city population, in a state of poverty, dependence, and despair. It has been so for generations.

6. The median income for African-American families in Cairo is less than half that of European-American families and unemployment is much higher for African-Americans. As Preston Ewing says, "There is a job in Cairo for everyone who wants to work. But take a walk through the parking lots of the major employers. You'll see they are filled with license plates from Missouri and Kentucky. Cairo businesses would rather hire whites from across the Ohio and Mississippi Rivers than hire blacks who live here in the same town." Unions exclude African-Americans from membership. Predictably, this forces African-Americans onto welfare rolls. The welfare office has conspired with the local cotton growers so that while they are on welfare, African-Americans are forced to choose between picking cotton at substandard wages or forfeiting their welfare payments.

[illustration omitted]

7. African-American leaders in Cairo believe education is the straightest road to equality. Ms. Kendrick recalls that, "As far back as 1883 the Negro in Cairo tried to break up segregated schools, only to find the doors locked in their faces. Why has this been? How did this happen in Illinois, the Land of Lincoln?" Yet despite the repeated demands of Hattie Kendrick and others for equal and integrated schooling, schools were segregated until the late 1960's. When the federal government forced the inevitable desegregation upon the schools, European-Americans withdrew their children from the public schools and formed the private and racially pure Camelot Academy.

8. In virtually every aspect of life in Cairo, African-Americans have been told they have no place but down. Public housing is segregated. Until recently, only European-Americans were permitted to use the public

library, certain public parks, the National Guard Armory, and other public facilities.

9. In the mid-1960's, the Rotary Club closed the town's only swimming pool rather than integrate. Now all children of both races, out of school during Cairo's near-tropical summers, risk drowning in the treacherous currents of the Mississippi River. . . .

10. The City Council and Mayor jointly execute, under Illinois law, all legislative, administrative, and executive powers, controlling city finances, streets and public property, and public health and safety.

11. Although nominally nonpartisan, city elections are dominated by the Democratic and Republican parties. These parties have historically excluded African-Americans. The Republican Party did not open its membership until the 1960's. While the Democratic Party permitted African-American members in the 1940's, no African-American—in either party—has ever held a major leadership position. The only role the two parties have permitted to African-Americans has been that of precinct-committeeman, which, as we shall see later, has served only to solidify the racial monopoly on political power.

12. Successive city administrations have yet to appoint an African-American to almost all city boards. A few other public agencies have appointed only a few African-Americans who have been willing to submit to direction by the European-American majorities on those boards. One notable exception is the Reverend John Cobb, a leader of the African-American community, who was appointed to the police board, but was never told when or where meetings were to be held.

13. In recent citywide elections, African-American candidates have confronted newspaper advertisements urging the European-American majority to "vote for the white candidates" and to "save Cairo." Not surprisingly, the African-American candidates have lost. Mayor Moss and his City Council were elected as a slate openly organized and campaigned for by the United Citizens for Community Action (UCCA), a white supremacist group.

[illustration omitted]

14. As Ms. Kendrick has said, "many times has the Negro tried to emerge from his position of servitude, only to be pushed back into submission by his white brother." Believing that they have a right to participate in their own community, and pushed out of the democratic process, Cairo's African-American citizens have demonstrated against segregation in peaceful marches past the guns of police.

[illustration omitted]

15. Police and vigilantes have beaten the demonstrators. Pictured below is the current Mayor of Cairo swinging a movie camera at a picketer and a member of the City Council armed with a rifle and eyeing a march.

[illustrations omitted]

16. Vigilantes—known as White Hats because of their white helmets— have launched sniper attacks against African-American neighborhoods.

They have used clubs and chains to beat young African-Americans who wanted to skate in the Cairo roller rink in 1964. Among those beaten was 16-year-old Charles Koen, another of Ms. Kendrick's students who would later train for the Christian ministry and lead the United Front, an organization coordinating civil rights efforts in Cairo. He would become a lightning rod for the resistance of European-Americans to change. They would label him a criminal and anarchist.

[illustration omitted]

17. The Cairo police have done nothing to stop them. Not only have the Cairo police failed to protect African-American citizens, they have themselves laid siege to a Catholic Church in which African-Americans worshipped. African-American community leaders organized civil rights activities. . . . The City Council passed an ordinance making it illegal to picket or for two or more individuals to congregate. The Cairo Police Department organized the White Hats, and deputized them to help control the city.

18. Little has changed in Cairo since Ms. Kendrick arrived here in the 1920's. The at-large form of government was adopted in the early years of this century as a response to a public perception of widespread city corruption—connected by the contemporary press to the "criminal Negro element" in the community. Before the at-large system, African-Americans were elected to the City Council. Since its adoption, none have been elected. This at-large system has been maintained and used since its inception with the intent of discriminating against African-Americans in Cairo and denying them the vote.

19. Some African-Americans have despaired of change. Yet another of Ms. Kendrick's students, Anthony Patterson—and a member of this plaintiff class—was eight years old when the Rotary Club filled in the swimming pool. He survived the river and, now a man, he says, "This town is so far behind and backwards, it's really a shame. You don't think about staying and looking for a job. . . ."

20. With no chance to cast a vote for an electable candidate of their choice, some African-American voters have resorted to selling their votes on election day to whichever of the candidates standing some chance of victory—all European-American—pays the most. . . . The going rate is three to five dollars per vote, collected by the precinct committee chairmen. In the plantation democracy of Cairo, the fundamental American right, the right to vote, has been diluted to almost nothing, reduced in value to a few dollars.

21. This state of affairs suits the European-American men in power just fine. When asked if African-Americans in Cairo have any legitimate complaints, Tom Madra, the leader of the White Hats, has replied that "blacks from other states did gravitate here into Illinois because of the welfare programs. . . . They came here for the largesse." Presumably, the largesse he speaks of includes the privilege of picking cotton for slave

wages to protect their benefits. This leader insists that "[t]hey were unemployed and unemployable. They live by preference in a shanty." Pictured below is Riverlore, the home of William Wolters, a businessman owning one of Cairo's major employers, and next to that is a photograph of those shanties, which Mr. Wolters described to a Chicago Tribune reporter as "those nigger shacks."

[illustration omitted]

22. Madra and the White Hats believe that "[t]here's no good black leadership in this community." Public officials claim to agree and maintain a purported willingness to welcome African-American participation. But City Attorney John Holland has defended the absence of African-Americans from city government because "there are very few to choose from. . . ."

25. This suicidal leadership can only lead all of Cairo's citizens to ultimate disaster. The African-American community has struggled to save Cairo from the inevitable fate of all feudal societies throughout history—extinction. Their struggle has included marches to call attention to injustices, boycotts of businesses that discriminate, development of alternative economies, applications for federal grants, and litigation to desegregate public housing, win appointments to city boards and stop mistreatment by local police and prosecutors. This began in the mid-1940's when Ms. Kendrick and other African-American teachers sued for equal pay, with Thurgood Marshall as their lawyer. . . .

29. The plaintiff class has suffered and continues to suffer irreparable harm. Its members have no adequate remedy at law. As Plaintiff Hattie Kendrick says, "Too long have the two races stood grinning in each other's faces, while they carry the fires of resentment and hate in their hearts, and with their hands hid behind their backs they carry the unsheathed sword."

30. With one hand, Cairo's plantation democrats pay three dollars for a vote and, in the other, they wield that unsheathed sword against those who cannot be bought. Their fiefdom hurts black and white alike, denying a future to one race—the European-Americans—in order to control the future of the other race, just as it drives the children of both races into the muddy eddies of the Mississippi for a swim. The pretense of plantation democracy is that it is a democracy. The truth is that it is a plantation. Plaintiffs Hattie Kendrick and Preston Ewing come to this Court to ask it to protect their right to vote and to replace Cairo's plantation democracy with a real one.

31. Specifically, they ask the Court to declare that the at-large city council system in Cairo violates the Constitution and the Voting Rights Act and to enter an order dividing Cairo into aldermanic wards so that neighborhoods where African-Americans live have some chance of electing candidates of their choice.

32. . . . [I]t is critical that the Court order relief that will, at the earliest possible time, provide for a democratic election in which Hattie

Kendrick, who is over ninety years old and in poor health, may cast an equal, undiluted vote for a candidate of her choice.

WHEREFORE, plaintiffs ask that this Court:

(A) Declare that Cairo's at-large form of government violates the Fourteenth and Fifteenth Amendments to the United States Constitution and the Voting Rights Act; and

(B) Enter a preliminary and permanent injunction enjoining the operation of the at-large system and dividing the city into wards in a manner that does not again dilute the votes of the plaintiff class; and

(C) Order a new City Council election; and

(D) Award plaintiffs their reasonable attorney's fees and expenses; and

(E) Grant such further equitable and additional relief as the Court may deem equitable, just, and proper.

[handwritten margin note: demands]

Comments and Questions

1. You may wish to compare Professor Eastman's redrafted complaint with the more typical complaints that you have seen in *Goldberg v. Kelly* in Chapter 1 and in *Carpenter v. Dee* in the Case Files. What techniques does Eastman use in his new draft? Some of those he discusses in the article are metaphor, irony, poetry, homilies, and oxymorons.

2. Eastman also suggests that civil rights lawyers might draw inspiration from Cornel West's conception of "jazz": "I use the term 'jazz' here not so much as a term for a musical art form, as for a mode of being in the world, an improvisational mode of protean, fluid, and flexible dispositions toward reality suspicious of 'either/or' viewpoints, dogmatic pronouncements, or supremacist ideologies. To be a jazz freedom fighter is to attempt to galvanize and energize world-weary people into forms of organization with accountable leadership that promote critical exchange and broad reflection" (Eastman, *supra*, at 831, citing to Cornel West, *Race Matters* 105 (1993)). Eastman suggests that the influence of jazz can "open oneself to new paradigms for civil rights problems and new strategies to address, if not resolve, them—to lead the law, not follow it." *Id.* Can Eastman's literary complaint strategy be transported to areas of law other than civil rights? *[handwritten: Yes, probably many other areas]*

3. In reality, very few lawyers come close to pushing the bounds of literary pleading to the degree suggested by Eastman's redrafted complaint. What causes this inhibition? Is it justified? What potential pitfalls do you see for the lawyer who decides to move in the direction of more literary pleading? What are the potential gains for the client, the lawyer, the opposing client and lawyer, the decision maker, and society? Here is one of many gains suggested by Eastman: "Civil rights plaintiffs are not alone in yearning for change. Their lawyers do so as well. A thin, sterile complaint reflects the thin, sterile professional who slices away her fully human role.

[handwritten: Judge will think it takes too long to read]

Written differently, the complaint can serve as a way of integrating the two parts of the lawyer—the personal and the professional" (*Id.* at 851, citations omitted).

4. Looking at Eastman's complaint, what parts do you think would be susceptible to a motion to strike under Fed. R. Civ. P. 12(f)? Could the defense in this case argue that large portions of the complaint are "redundant, immaterial, impertinent, or scandalous"? *See* R. A. Givens, 1 *Manual of Federal Practice*, §4.21 (4th ed. 1991): "'Redundant' usually means verbose and repetitious; 'immaterial,' outside the scope of the action; 'impertinent,' containing elements of redundancy or immateriality or both; and 'scandalous,' as casting a gratuitously derogatory light on the moral character of a person, contrary to good manners, or unbecoming to the dignity of the court."

[handwritten marginalia: Court may strike any redundant, immaterial]

Practice Exercise No. 8:
Considering the *City of Cleveland* Complaint

As an associate in a law firm, you have received an initial memorandum introducing a case involving women firefighters in the City of Cleveland. The memorandum is printed in the Case Files, under *City of Cleveland Firefighters*. The senior partner in the firm wants you to read the memorandum in order to acquaint yourself with the facts and law in the case. The partner wants you to be prepared to talk with her and other partners and associates about the type of complaint to be drafted in this case. At the strategy session, the partner wants you to be prepared to explain the causes of action and their elements, and to discuss what audiences the complaint should be written for, what major problems you anticipate in drafting, what tone you would advise for the complaint, how specific the complaint should be, and what additional factual and legal information you think is needed. The partner has recently read the Eastman article, portions of which you have just read. She wants your advice on how much, if at all, she should be influenced by that article in drafting a complaint in this case.

4. Real Party in Interest

■ DM II, LTD. v. HOSPITAL CORPORATION OF AMERICA
130 F.R.D. 469 (N.D. Ga. 1989)

FORRESTER, District Judge.
This is an action for equitable relief brought by an assortment of Georgia corporations against two Tennessee corporations for breach of

fiduciary duties. These duties are alleged to exist by virtue of the parties' relationships in connection with their joint ownership of real property located in Columbus, Georgia. As to the ownership of this property, the parties are tenants in common. Less clear, however, is the nature of the parties' relationship in connection with the ownership and operation of Doctors Hospital which is located upon this property. It is plaintiffs' contention that they and defendants are partners in the ownership and operation of Doctors Hospital and that the existence of this partnership imposed certain fiduciary duties on each partner. Plaintiffs further contend that defendants breached duties owed to their partners by establishing a competing hospital in the Columbus area. By this action, plaintiffs seek an accounting of the profits earned by defendants at the expense of Doctors Hospital and the imposition of a constructive trust upon these funds or their proceeds. Defendants seek dismissal on the grounds that plaintiffs have failed to prosecute this action in the name of the real party in interest. . . .

A. Is There a Partnership?

The threshold question presented by defendants' motion concerns the nature of the parties' relationship in connection with the ownership and operation of Doctors Hospital. As just stated, plaintiffs contend a partnership exists. The court agrees. Georgia law defines a partnership as (1) an association of two or more persons (2) to carry on as co-owners (3) of a business for profit. O.C.G.A. §14-8-6(a). All three elements appear to be present here. The parties clearly constitute an unincorporated association and each has an ownership interest in Doctors Hospital and the property on which it is located. Finally, there can be no doubt that Doctors Hospital is operated by the parties as a business for profit. It is this latter element which distinguishes the partnership from the passive co-ownership of property; *i.e.,* joint tenancy, tenancy in common, etc. *See id.,* Note to Uniform Partnership Act. Accordingly, the court concludes that a partnership was formed and presently exists for the purpose of operating Doctors Hospital and that the parties together with several persons not joined in this action are members of this partnership.

B. Is the Partnership the Real Party in Interest?

Rule 17(a) requires that every action be prosecuted in the name of the real party in interest; *i.e.,* in the name of the party who, by the controlling substantive law, has the right sought to be enforced. Thus, while a real party in interest analysis is a matter of federal procedure, reference must be made to state substantive law to identify the true owner of the legal interest at issue. . . . [D]efendants argue that the Doctors Hospital partnership is the real party in interest to this action. In support of this argument, defendants show the court that plaintiffs represent but a portion of the partners alleged to have been harmed by defendants' conduct. It is defendants' position that under the controlling state substantive law, the claims asserted by plaintiffs belong to the partnership as a whole and thus must be brought by the partnership or by each partner in a single action. Plaintiffs, on the other hand, contend that the claims belong to each partner and therefore may be asserted individually or jointly. Thus, resolution of this issue depends on whether under the applicable Georgia law, the right to pursue this action is vested in the Doctors Hospital partnership or in each partner individually.

The answer to this question is found in the Georgia Partnership Act. . . . Under §14-8-21(a) of the Act, each partner is required to "account to the partnership for any benefit and hold as trustee for it any profits derived by him without the consent of the other partners from any transaction connected with the formation, conduct, or liquidation of the partnership or from any use by him of any property." In addition, any partner may bring an action against another to enforce this provision. O.C.G.A. §14-8-22(3).

In the case at hand, plaintiffs seek an accounting and imposition of a constructive trust on profits derived by defendants through wrongful competition with the partnership business. Because wrongful competition gives rise to an action for breach of fiduciary duties akin to wrongful conversion of partnership assets [a partner's share of partnership profits is considered personal property under the act. O.C.G.A. §14-8-22], the court finds §14-8-21(a) sufficiently broad to cover such actions. In addition, because §14-8-22 provides a cause of action to enforce §14-8-21 to "any partner," the court finds that the controlling substantive law vests the right of action in each partner independent of the partnership. The court therefore concludes that each partner is a real party in interest to this action and that Rule 17 does not require dismissal in this instance. . . .

Comments and Questions

1. Which party is claiming that the other is not the real party in interest, and what are the arguments on each side? Be precise.

2. What are the distinctions between capacity (Fed. R. Civ. P. 17(b)) and real party in interest (Fed. R. Civ. P. 17(a))?

3. Why doesn't the "real party in interest" Rule 17(a) cover defendants? Can you come up with a credible argument that such a rule is not needed for plaintiffs either?

4. Who is the appropriate plaintiff (or plaintiffs) in *Carpenter v. Dee*? What specific law or laws would you have to examine to be sure? In order to decide on the appropriate plaintiff or plaintiffs, is it necessary to consider real party in interest, capacity to sue, or both? Is Fed. R. Civ. P. 17(c) also relevant?

5. Anonymous Plaintiffs

■ DOE v. UNITED SERVICES LIFE INSURANCE COMPANY
No. 88-5630 (S.D.N.Y. 1988)

SWEET, District Judge.

Plaintiff "John Doe" ("Doe") has moved for an order granting him leave to prosecute this action under a pseudonym, sealing all court records in which his actual name, address, or employer appear and withholding this information from defendant United Services Life Insurance Company ("United Services") and any of United Services's witnesses unless they agree to a confidentiality order. United Services seeks to dismiss the complaint for failure to identify the plaintiff as Rule 10(a) of the Federal Rules of Civil Procedure requires. For the reasons set forth below, Doe's motion is granted to the extent set forth below and United Services's motion is denied.

Doe currently works as a law clerk to a federal judge. During Doe's last year of law school, Doe and his father agreed to obtain a life insurance policy on Doe's life to secure his father's obligations as guarantor of Doe's student loans. In November of 1987, Doe and his father allegedly applied to United Services to purchase a $100,000 life insurance policy on Doe's life, naming Doe's father as beneficiary.

As part of the application process, a United Services representative interviewed Doe and the company required that Doe undergo a physical examination. Doe alleges that United Services takes extra precautions in processing homosexuals' life insurance applications and that the company required the interview and blood test because as a single male living in Greenwich Village with another male at the time of his application—Doe fit a homosexual profile.

Because Doe allegedly admitted at the interview that he previously had been arrested for public intoxication and because his blood test revealed abnormally high levels of liver enzymes often associated with alcohol abuse, United Services added a $105 surcharge to Doe's premium, raising it from $155 to $260.

Upon learning of his abnormal blood test results, Doe offered to retake the blood test, but United Services declined. After undergoing an independent blood test that yielded no abnormal results, Doe brought this lawsuit. Doe alleges he is heterosexual.

Doe originally filed the complaint in this action in the Supreme Court of the State of New York, alleging violations of New York insurance law and discrimination based on sex, marital status, and sexual orientation. United Services removed the action and made the instant motion prior to answer.

Pursuant to a state court ex parte order authorizing service of the pleading under the name "John Doe," Doe served United Services with the complaint and an order to show cause returnable August 12, 1988, seeking leave to prosecute the action under a pseudonym and other protection of his identity. That motion was pending at the time United Services removed the case to federal court. Because motions pending in state court at the time of removal survive removal, this court made Doe's motion returnable September 16, 1988, upon the moving papers originally filed in state court.

After Doe initiated the lawsuit, United Services invited Doe to submit to another blood test and offered to issue him a standard rate policy if his liver enzyme tests were within normal range. Doe declined, presumably to defeat a mootness claim and to assert his rights as alleged in the complaint.

According to Doe, the public's interest in eliminating unfair practices in the sale of insurance, Doe's privacy interest in not being publicly identified as a homosexual, and Doe's concern for his status as a law clerk for a federal judge favor permitting him to proceed pseudonymously. United Services denies that this case will require Doe to reveal confidential information about his sexual preference or practices and characterizes the action as involving a challenge to the company's decision to charge Doe a higher premium "due to a health risk unrelated to sexual activities," not one regarding homosexuality or susceptibility to AIDS. United Services also argues that permitting Doe to proceed pseudonymously will injure it by involving it in a highly publicized case while denying it the ability to defend itself from publicity or to set the record straight by a full response.

"Generally, lawsuits are public events and the public has a legitimate interest in knowing the pertinent facts." *Free Market Compensation v. Commodity Exch.*, 98 F.R.D. 311, 312 (S.D.N.Y. 1983). Accordingly, parties to a lawsuit usually should proceed under their real names. *See* Fed. R. Civ. P. 10(a) ("In the complaint the title of the action shall include the names of all the parties. . . ."); Fed. R. Civ. P. 17 ("Every action shall be prosecuted in the name of the real party in interest."); *see also Coe v. United States Dist. Court for the Dist of Colo.*, 676 F.2d 411, 415 (10th Cir. 1982); *Southern Methodist Univ. Assn. v. Wynne & Jaffe*, 599 F.2d 707, 712 (5th Cir. 1979).

Under special circumstances, however, courts have allowed parties to use fictitious names, particularly where necessary to "protect privacy in a very private matter." *Doe v. Deschamps*, 64 F.R.D. 652, 653 (D. Mont. 1974); *see, e.g., Roe v. Wade*, 410 U.S. 113 (1973) (abortion); *Poe v. Ullman*, 367 U.S. 497 (1961) (birth control); *Doe v. Mundy*, 514 F.2d 1179 (7th Cir. 1975) (abortion); *Doe v. Alexander*, 510 F. Supp. 900 (D. Minn. 1981) (transsexuality); *Doe v. Harris*, 495 F. Supp. 1161 (S.D.N.Y. 1980) (mental illness); *Doe v. McConn*, 489 F. Supp. 76 (S.D. Tex. 1980) (transsexuality); *Doe v. Shapiro*, 302 F. Supp. 761 (D. Conn. 1969) (welfare rights of illegitimate children), *appeal dismissed*, 396 U.S. 488 (1970).

Cases where a party risks public identification as a homosexual also raise privacy concerns that have supported an exception to the general rule of disclosure. *See, e.g., Doe v. Weinberger*, 820 F.2d 1275 (D.C. Cir. 1987), *cert. granted,*—U.S.—, 108 S. Ct. 1073 (1988); *Doe v. United States Air Force*, 812 F.2d 738 (D.C. Cir. 1987); *Doe v. Commonwealth's Attorney for City of Richmond*, 403 F. Supp. 1199 (E.D. Va. 1975), *aff'd*, 425 U.S. 901 (1976); *Doe v. Chaffee*, 355 F. Supp. 112 (N.D. Cal. 1973). Concern to avoid public identification as a homosexual is heightened in light of widespread public fear engendered by the Acquired Immunodeficiency Syndrome ("AIDS") crisis. *Cf. Doe v. Rostker*, 89 F.R.D. 158, 161 (proceeding anonymously is appropriate where issues in case present a risk of "some social stigma").

Doe may well be publicly identified as homosexual, despite the fact that Doe contends—and United Services concedes—that he is heterosexual. Doe's complaint alleges that United Services discriminated against him because it suspected that he was homosexual, and by bringing this action Doe seeks to vindicate the rights of homosexuals. Moreover, Doe is represented in this case by attorneys cooperating with Lambda Legal Defense and Education Fund, Inc., an organization widely recognized for its efforts in defending the rights of lesbians and gay men. [In a footnote, the court stated, "One of the reasons Doe offers for prosecuting this case under a pseudonym involves the effect this case might have on his status as a law clerk to a federal judge. This court's decision to permit Doe to proceed pseudonymously reflects a concern for his public identification as a homosexual, not a concern for his employment status. Courts should not permit parties to proceed pseudonymously just to protect the parties' professional or economic life. *See Coe v. United States District Court for the District of Colo.*, 676 F.2d 411 (10th Cir. 1982); *Southern Methodist University Assn. v. Wynne & Jaffe*, 599 F.2d 707 (5th Cir. 1979)."]

Significantly, this is not a case in which permitting Doe to proceed pseudonymously will disadvantage United Services. United Services already knows Doe's true identity, it will have full discovery rights as the case progresses, and it will only be barred from using or disclosing the fruits of its discovery for purposes other than the defense of this action.

For the reasons set forth above, Doe's motion is granted upon the conditions set forth in connection with the denial of United Services's motion. It is so ordered.

Comments and Questions

1. What specific Federal Rules are relevant to the decision to be made by the court in this case? 10 A, 17 B
2. Where does the court get the authority to alter the clear language of the Rules, for instance, Rule 10(a)? *Case precedents*
3. Why is the plaintiff allowed to plead anonymously, when in most discrimination cases plaintiffs must reveal their true identities? Does the
reflects a concern for his public identification as a homosexual

court succeed in distinguishing the facts of this case from those in which courts have not permitted the plaintiffs to proceed anonymously?

4. Based on the values inherent in our procedural system, does it ever make sense to permit plaintiffs to proceed anonymously? Why do plaintiffs usually have to be named in complaints?

5. For the most part, the Federal Rules of Civil Procedure are trans-substantive in the sense that they apply to different types of cases, regardless of their substance. Do you think that anti-discrimination statutes such as Title VII (which deals with employment discrimination) should provide special rules for when plaintiffs have to reveal their identity? (Make a mental note that this would be an example of the Legislature's constructing non-trans-substantive or substance-specific procedure.) If Congress were presented with this issue, what would the arguments be in favor of and against such a proposal? Consider what language you would use in a statute to describe the conditions under which plaintiffs could or could not proceed anonymously.

6. You will find that "John Doe" parties appear in another context — where a plaintiff must name an unidentified defendant in a complaint in order to avoid a statute of limitations bar. These situations are often governed by statutes that provide a means of tolling (putting on hold) the statute of limitations while the plaintiff, often through discovery, attempts to uncover the identity of John Doe defendants named in the complaint. Once a plaintiff discovers the identity of defendants named fictitiously in the complaint, she must amend the complaint by naming the actual defendants in lieu of the John Doe defendants. Under the Federal Rules, as long as the amendments conform to requirements of Fed. R. Civ. P. 15(c), they will relate back to the time of the filing of the original complaint, thus avoiding the statute of limitations time bar. In *Jacobson v. Osborne*, 133 F. 2d 315 (5th Cir. 1998), however, the court would not permit the plaintiff to use Rule 15(c) in a situation where "John Doe" defendants were so named, because of the inability to identify them, rather than as a result of a mistake. For a critique of the federal approach to fictitious party pleading, *see* Carol M. Rice, *Meet John Doe: It Is Time for Federal Civil Procedure to Recognize John Doe Parties*, 57 U. Pitt. L. Rev. 883 (1996). Some states' statutes and decisions have allowed plaintiffs greater leeway in using fictitiously named defendants. California law is particularly liberal in allowing plaintiffs to plead John Doe defendants.

6. Answers, Motions, and Affirmative Defenses

a. Preliminary Motions

Assume that you are an attorney who has been told to deal with a complaint on behalf of a defendant who has been served. You will first note how much time is remaining in which you have to act, because you will not want your client to lose by *default* for failing to respond. If you were in federal district court, you would examine Rule 12(a) to determine the applicable time period. If you needed an extension, you would turn to Rule 6(b). You would also want to check the local rules of the court in question to determine if there were special rules for seeking an enlargement of time. Do not assume that you can deal with extensions by merely obtaining the consent of the plaintiff's lawyer, although such consent (in writing, when possible) is desirable. The safest course is to have the court grant a motion to extend time within the initial period allowed. Check with a knowledgable person in your office or with a clerk at the court in question to determine how gaining an extension of time is correctly accomplished in the court in question. It makes sense to satisfy yourself that not only are you in tune with the court's customs, but that you can back up your behavior with the specific language in a rule.

What are your options when faced with a complaint, assuming that you have now solved the timing question? In federal court, a good place to begin is Fed. R. Civ. P. 12 and 8, probably in that order.

A motion for a more definite statement (Fed. R. Civ. P. 12(e)) is available if the complaint is so vague or ambiguous that your client cannot reasonably be required to formulate a response. The rule mandates that the motion include a description of the "defects complained of and the details required." This motion must be made, as Rule 12(e) states, "before interposing a responsive pleading." You cannot answer and *then* successfully bring the motion. (There was a 12(e) Motion in Practice Exercise No. 7; you can find the motion in the *Carpenter v. Dee* Case Files.)

The courts have tried to prevent the motion for a more definite statement from being used as a substitute for discovery. Previous language in Federal Rule 12(e) permitted motions for a bill of particulars, but this method was deleted in 1946 because, according to the Advisory Committee, "[w]ith respect to the preparations for trial, the party is properly relegated to the various methods of examination and discovery provided in the rules for that purpose."

A motion to strike (Fed. R. Civ. P. 12(f)) asks the court to delete from a pleading "any insufficient defense or any redundant, immaterial, impertinent, or scandalous matter." Note that Rule 12(f) also imposes time limits, although the court can act on its "own initiative at any time" to strike the matters described in the rule. If a plaintiff lists several potential causes of action, and one of them "fails to state a claim upon which relief can be granted," the defendant can use Rule 12(f) on the ground that the particular count is "immaterial" or, more typically, can use a 12(b)(6) motion to seek the dismissal of that count. Assume you want examples of what courts have previously found to be insufficient defenses or "redundant, immaterial, impertinent, or scandalous" matters; name (or find) at least two different sources in the library where you could quickly find them.

b. Motions to Dismiss

Reread Federal Rule 12(b) to find the seven permitted motions to dismiss. Note that 12(b) gives you the choice of either raising these defenses as part of your answer, or by preliminary motions prior to filing an answer. You should consider as a matter of the defendant's strategy why you would choose to answer first, including your 12(b) defenses in the answer, rather than acting by motions and delaying your answer. One consideration is Rule 15(a) which permits a party to amend her pleading "once as a matter of course at any time before a responsive pleading is served." Since motions are not defined as pleadings (*see* Rule 7(a)), filing preliminary motions will not cut off the plaintiff's absolute right to amend, but filing an answer—even with (12)(b) motions as part of the answer—will. But this may not be a major consideration, given the historic ease of amendment under Federal Rule 15(a)—"leave shall be freely given when justice so requires." Can you come up with other strategic considerations for taking the answer or motion route?

You are already familiar with the *motion to dismiss for failure to state a claim* (12(b)(6)). Each of the other "12(b)'s" will be taken up when they are covered later in the course. For example, Chapters 7 and 8 deal with, among other things, jurisdictional issues and service of process. Consequently, the defenses (or motions to dismiss) based on *lack of jurisdiction over the subject matter* (12(b)(1)), *lack of jurisdiction over the person* (12(b)(2)), *improper venue* (12(b)(3)), *insufficiency of process* (12(b)(4)), and *insufficiency of service of process* (12(b)(5)) will be examined then. Perhaps you cannot wait to find out the difference between an "insufficiency of process" and an "insufficiency of service of process." In fact, lawyers often move under both subsections when they are challenging service of process. Technically, the former addresses a failure to conform the summons with the requirements of Rule 4(b), and the latter challenges a failure to properly serve the opponent. For instance, the form of a summons could be correct, but not served at all or not served correctly upon the defendant.

The final 12(b) defense, Fed. R. Civ. P. 12(b)(7), *failure to join a party under Rule 19*, refers to the failure to join an indispensable party in accordance with Rule 19, a topic we will discuss in detail when we come to more complex joinder problems in Chapter 11. You will later learn that defendants can use Rule 19 strategically to insist that an indispensable party be joined in circumstances where such joinder is impossible, because it would destroy subject matter jurisdiction or because the plaintiff is unable to obtain personal jurisdiction over the omitted Rule 19 party in the court where the case has been commenced. The net result may be dismissal.

Remember that although we are discussing the 12(b) defenses or motions in the context of a defendant's answering to a plaintiff's complaint, such defenses or motions will also have to be considered in other situations, such as by a plaintiff when she faces a counterclaim or a codefendant who faces a cross-claim. Rule 8(a) gives the requirements for all claims, "whether an original claim, counterclaim, cross-claim, or third-party claim," and Rule 8(b) requires defenses and admissions or denials to allegations when one is faced with an adverse claim (such as a plaintiff faced with a counterclaim).

Before moving on to the drafting of an answer (with admissions and denials and affirmative defenses), you should consider Rules 12(g) and 12(h), which deal with consolidating defenses in a motion and the waiver or preserving certain defenses. There are several ways that by omission you can lose the right to bring four of the 12(b) defenses or motions. (We will explain in a moment the "favored" three defenses, which receive greater protection against waiver.) One way to lose 12(b) defenses is to bring one 12(b) motion, but omit others. This is the purpose of 12(g). Let's say you, as defendant's counsel, bring a motion to dismiss for failure of personal jurisdiction (for instance, the defendant has never had any affiliation with the forum state and has not consented to be sued there), the motion is denied, and you then bring a motion to dismiss for lack of venue. Rule 12(h) forbids this, and you will have lost your challenge to venue by failure to consolidate the two motions.

Consider the same example, but this time you try to circumvent Rule 12(g) by filing an answer with your challenge to venue after losing the personal jurisdiction motion. Again, you will be stymied, but this time by Rule 12(h)(1); read it, and you will see why.

Or let's say that you do not raise any 12(b) defenses by motion, but instead put a 12(b)(2) defense — lack of jurisdiction over the person — in your answer. Later you try to add a challenge to venue. This is prohibited by Rule 12(h)(1). An amendment to add the defense will usually not save you from your waiver. Can you see why?

Another possibility is that you do not bring any 12(b) motions prior to answering, nor do you include any in your answer. You will have waived your personal jurisdiction (12(b)(2)), venue (12(b)(3)), and process (12(b)(4) and (12(b)(5)) defenses — the nonfavored defenses — by your inaction.

The long and short of it is this: (1) if you file a 12(b) motion prior to your answer, include any plausible less-favored defenses in your motion at the same time; and (2) if you answer, without having first brought 12(b) motions, include plausible less-favored defenses in your answer. Do these rules regarding consolidation and waiver of 12(b) defenses make sense to you? Why or why not?

We have yet to discuss why the defenses of failure to state a claim upon which relief can be granted, failure to join an indispensable party under Rule 19, and lack of subject matter jurisdiction are not waived by a failure to consolidate them with other 12(b) motions nor by failing to include them in your answer. Indeed, Rule 12(h)(3) goes even further, and states that "[w]henever it appears by suggestion of the parties or otherwise that the court lacks jurisdiction of the subject matter, the court shall dismiss the action."

We will discuss the sanctity of subject matter jurisdiction and indispensable party when we confront those concepts later. Similarly, we will discuss the common sense of having waiver provisions for personal jurisdiction, venue, and process issues when we reach those topics. But you are already equipped to figure out why 12(b)(6) is protected against waiver. Consider, for instance, what would happen at trial in a case where there was one alleged cause of action, but it was clear from the pleading that it did not cover the transaction in question. In other words, a 12(b)(6) motion would have been granted had it been filed or included in the answer as a defense. What if the court could not now consider the motion because of waiver? Would this make sense? Why or why not?

Rule 12(h) goes on to say that "an objection of failure to state a legal defense to a claim" may also "be made in any pleading permitted or ordered under Rule 7(a), or by a motion for judgment on the pleadings, or at the trial on the merits." Why is the plaintiff's objection—of failure to state a legal defense to a claim—also protected against waiver?

Although the favored 12(b) defenses relating to subject matter jurisdiction, Rule 19, and failure to state a claim are not waived by omission in the answer or failure to consolidate with other 12(b) motions, it is common practice for a defendant's lawyers to include them in their answer if applicable. Sometimes, however, defendants refrain from including such a defense. For instance, defense counsel may think that the plaintiff's counsel is lazy and will not realize the weakness of a particular element in its case if it does not have to defend against a 12(b)(6) motion. The defendant may omit the 12(b)(6) defense in its answer, knowing that it can raise it later or perhaps deciding to wait for the directed verdict stage—after it is usually too late for the plaintiff to cure an omission—before pointing out the failure to have any evidence of an element. (It is true that 12(b)(6) relates to the complaint and directed verdict to the evidence. However, since some courts have been reluctant to grant 12(b)(6) motions, or to grant them with leave to amend, a defendant's lawyer might wish not to draw attention to a potential weakness in the plaintiff's case, as demonstrated by a weakness in its complaint, at an early stage of the litigation.)

There is one final matter on the 12(b) defenses. Whether they are raised by preliminary motion, or in the answer, or—in the case of the "favored" defenses—after the answer, Rule 12(d) states that such defenses "shall be heard and determined before trial on application of any party, unless the court orders that the hearing and determination thereof be deferred until the trial." Why do the Rules encourage the early determination of the 12(b) defenses?

You should also be aware of the Rule 12(c) motion for judgment on the pleadings, although it is infrequently used. It is possible that upon considering all of the pleadings, which usually will be a complaint and an answer, it is clear that the plaintiff or defendant must win. An example of the latter would be a complaint in which the allegations, taken as true, show that the statute of limitations has run, coupled with an answer that raises the statute of limitations as an affirmative defense. An example of the former would be an answer that admits all of plaintiff's allegations and raises a nonapplicable defense, such as contributory negligence in a contract case. In this case, a plaintiff could win a motion for judgment on the pleadings.

c. Answers

It is now time to consider what you, as defense counsel, will put in your answer. Let us assume that you have decided not to bring 12(b) defenses by separate motion. Your answer will potentially contain four types of material, but you also have two more concerns. The four types of materials in the answer are: (1) *admissions* and *denials* to the averments in the plaintiff's complaint (Fed. R. Civ. P. 8(b)); (2) *12(b) defenses*; (3) *affirmative defenses* (Fed. R. Civ. P. 8(c)); and (4) *counterclaims* and *cross-claims* (Rule 13). These are often put on separate pieces of paper, even when filed at the same time as the answer. In addition, when filing their answer, defense counsel simultaneously consider whether they wish to *implead* a third party (Fed. R. Civ. P. 14) or *otherwise seek to add parties*. For instance, the defendant might consider adding an additional defendant to a counterclaim in accordance with Rule 13(h). Defense counsel might further attempt to enlarge the case through a motion to consolidate (Rule 42(a)), or by encouraging someone else to intervene (Rule 24). And defense counsel might seek to *reduce the number of parties* through a motion for misjoinder pursuant to Rule 21. Finally, defense counsel should also consider at the time of answering whether to *claim a jury trial*. The jury claim is often stated in the answer. We will discuss the topic of jury trials in Chapter 5.

d. Admissions and Denials

The doctrine on admissions and denials is fairly straightforward. Read Rule 8(b). The rule requires the admission or denial of each averment, except when "a party is without knowledge or information sufficient to form a belief as to the truth of an averment," a topic we explore in greater detail in a moment. A pleader may deny specific averments, paragraphs of the complaint, or the entire complaint, stating what is not denied, but the rule specifically states that such a general denial is "subject to the obligations set forth in Rule 11." All pleadings are subject to Rule 11, even without this specific reminder. You will study Rule 11 later. It is typical to deny entire paragraphs, as you will note by looking at the answers in the *Carpenter v. Dee* case. Rule 8(d) prescribes that when a responsive pleading is required, averments not denied are taken as admitted. One exception is "the amount of damages." Try thinking of an example of a pleading to which no responsive pleading is required. *See* Rule 7(a). When no responsive pleading is required or permitted, averments are "taken as denied or avoided."

A major purpose of an answer is to narrow the issues and to apprise the parties of what is still in dispute. Defense counsel are very careful not to admit anything that they in fact dispute, because once the defendant admits an averment, absent an amendment changing the admission to a denial, it will be taken as true for the remainder of the case. Consequently, admissions in pleadings are more binding than evidence given at a trial, which the fact finder can believe or disbelieve. Thus, it is very difficult to get a defendant to admit a legal conclusion, such as "duty" or "negligence," if there is *any* ground for denying the allegation. Sometimes, defense counsel state that the plaintiff has alleged a "legal conclusion" that does not require admission or denial, although the Rules do not specifically cover the situation. More frequently, the defendant will just deny the allegation. If a plaintiff desires to use the pleadings as a mechanism for reducing the legal battlefield, she is better off pleading very specific facts so that opposing counsel has more difficulty stating an unconditional denial.

Penalties exist for denying an entire group of averments when in fact the pleader denies only a portion (and could admit the remainder). A favorite example of casebooks is *Zielinski v. Philadelphia Piers, Inc.* 139 F. Supp. 408 (D.C. Pa. 1956), where the plaintiff alleged in the complaint that a vehicle owned, operated, and controlled by the defendant, its agents, servants, and employees was managed so negligently and carelessly that it came into contact with the plaintiff and caused him injuries. The defendant denied the entire paragraph of averments in the complaint, but could have admitted that (1) the accident happened; (2) it owned the vehicle that came into contact with the plaintiff; and (3) there was some injury to plaintiff. The defendant denied the group of allegations, however, presumably because it had leased the vehicle to another entity, which, in turn, had hired the allegedly negligent driver. The plaintiff thus had sued the wrong defendant, and the statute of limitations on its claim (against the proper defendant) had expired sometime after the defendant answered but before the plaintiff ascertained the identity of the correct defendant. Although the named defendant arguably was responsible under certain theories of agency, the court ruled that the defendant should be treated as if it had admitted operation and control of the vehicle, in part because it had not more carefully admitted and denied specific averments in the complaint. This is an unusual case, and in fact the court thought the plaintiff had been misled in additional ways. Nonetheless, the case is a reminder to defendants not to be casual in their admissions and denials.

Frequently, a defense lawyer has insufficient knowledge or information to form a belief about an allegation, and therefore wants to deny it. Although some courts have not required that the language in Rule 8(b) in this regard be precisely followed, others have required strict adherence and do not permit the language "neither admits nor denies." *See, e.g., Gilbert v. Johnston,* 127 F.R.D. 145 (D.C. Ill. 1989).

Some courts have insisted that parties not use the "without knowledge or information sufficient to form a belief" phrase of Rule 8(b) as an excuse to avoid making reasonable inquiry prior to admitting or denying averments. Consider the following excerpts:

■ GREENBAUM v. UNITED STATES
360 F. Supp. 784 (E.D. Pa. 1973)

Huyett, District Judge.

Plaintiff, Morey Greenbaum, filed suit against defendant, United States of America, under the Federal Tort Claims Act (FTCA), 28 U.S.C.A. §2671. Plaintiff seeks to recover two hundred thousand dollars ($200,000.00) for injuries suffered by him in a fall at defendant's Bustleton Post Office in Philadelphia, Pennsylvania. . . .

Plaintiff at the time of the accident, March 1, 1968, was an employee of the United States Post Office and worked out of the Bustleton station. The accident occurred on plaintiff's day off as he crossed the parking lot to enter the building through the rear employees' entrance. At trial it was established that one of the reasons he was going to the post office that day was to pick up his paycheck. The Federal Employees Compensation Act (FECA), 5 U.S.C.A. §8101 *et seq.,* provides that the United States will pay compensation for the disability of an employee resulting from personal injuries sustained while performing his duties. . . . This compensation is the exclusive remedy for anyone within its coverage. . . . The action of the Secretary of Labor in allowing or denying such compensation is final as to facts and law and is not reviewable by a court.

The Government claims that we are without jurisdiction to decide this case at this time and that we should either dismiss the action or hold it in abeyance pending a decision by the Secretary of Labor. . . . The Government asserts that there is a substantial question whether an employee who is injured on government property while coming to pick up his paycheck on his day off is covered by the FECA. Defendant alleges that the [court] has never ruled on the question but cites state court opinions which permit recovery in similar circumstances under state workmen's compensation laws. This case . . . is complicated by the long delay of the Government in asserting that this court lacks jurisdiction over the subject matter.

The accident occurred more than five years ago, on March 1, 1968. The plaintiff filed the claim required by the Federal Tort Claims Act, 28 U.S.C.A. §2675(a), with the Post Office Department on May 17, 1968. Suit was commenced on May 9, 1969, almost one year later. . . . In the intervening three and three-quarter years between the filing of the complaint and commencement of the trial defendant never raised the issue of jurisdiction or indicated in any manner that it challenged jurisdiction. There have been numerous pretrial conferences at which no question of jurisdiction was ever raised. Plaintiff prepared final pretrial orders, none of which were ever finally approved, but defendant never objected to the inclusion of a statement indicating that jurisdiction was proper.

The fact that defendant was merely late in raising the issue of jurisdiction, however, does not militate against its position. A defense of lack of jurisdiction is not waived because it is delayed. "[W]henever it appears by suggestion of the parties or otherwise that the court lacks jurisdiction of the subject matter, the court shall dismiss the action." Fed. R. Civ. P. 12(h)(3). . . .

Plaintiff never claimed that he was injured in the performance of his duties but always asserted that he was a business invitee who was on defendant's premises at the time of the accident to purchase postage stamps. . . . The problem in this action is the Government's long and inexcusable delay in discovering materials in its own possession which give rise to the issue of FECA coverage. There have been reports which indicated that plaintiff was at the post office to pick up his paycheck in Government files throughout the course of this litigation. The Government counsel who have been assigned to this case never discovered these reports until February, 1973. Even at that time, however, the Government gave no indication that it would dispute jurisdiction.

The preparation of this case by the Government has been quite casual. There have been delays in service of third-party complaints and answers. The Government sought no discovery from plaintiff until February, 1973, when it undertook trial preparation "with renewed vigor" because of an increase in the damages sought. Prior to that time it had not even found in Post Office Department files, which were clearly within its control and of great relevance, a statement and a report by James Esposito, Superintendent of the Bustleton Station at the time of the accident. These documents, executed shortly after the accident, indicate that the plaintiff was at the post office that day to pick up his paycheck, the very allegation on which defendant now bases its claim that there is no jurisdiction.

This failure to make reasonable investigation of even Government files in the preparation of this case prevented defendant from actually responding to plaintiff's allegation that he was a business invitee. In answer to that averment in plaintiff's original and amended complaints defendant stated that it lacked sufficient knowledge or information to admit or deny, in accord with Fed. R. Civ. P. 8(b).

An answer of lack of knowledge or information will usually be deemed a denial. A party, however, may be held to the duty to exert reasonable effort to obtain knowledge of a fact. . . . In the present case defendant failed to examine available, highly relevant Government documents which would have given a basis for the belief that plaintiff was not a business invitee and that the Court did not have jurisdiction under the FTCA. A fact which is denied for lack of knowledge or information may be deemed admitted if the matter is one to which the party does have knowledge or information. . . . The Government will be held to an admission that plaintiff was a business invitee at the time of the accident. . . .

This Court held at least five pretrial conferences and there was no hint of disagreement concerning this fact. It was only when the demand was increased that the Government took this case seriously and made the elementary discovery needed to make this motion. . . .

■ CONTROLLED ENVIRONMENT SYSTEMS v. SUN PROCESS CO., INC.
173 F.R.D. 509 (N.D. Ill. 1997)

SHADUR, Senior District Judge.

. . . [Controlled Environment Systems, the plaintiff, has stated in its answer to the counterclaim of the defendant, Sun Process Co., Inc.,] that it "lacks sufficient personal knowledge of the remaining allegations contained within paragraph 10 and therefore neither admits nor denies said allegations but demands strict proof thereof." That of course runs afoul of the second sentence of Rule 8(b), which specifically calls for a more demanding representation to entitle a responding party to the benefit of a deemed denial. It was obvious to the drafters of Rule 8(b), as it should be to everyone, that in light of what it takes for anyone to have real knowledge of a fact, it is entirely possible for someone to lack *knowledge* but still to have enough *information* to form a *belief.* . . . That is why Rule 8(b) also requires a disclaimer of both of those things, and that is why both Sun Process and this Court are entitled to have a representation from Controlled Environment Systems (if it can do so in objective good faith) as to its lack of information sufficient to form a belief regarding each of the Complaint's allegations in question. Accordingly . . . each of the Answer's paragraphs referred to in this opinion are stricken. Controlled Environment is granted until July 3, 1997 to file either an amendment to the Answer to cure the flaws identified here, or, if it wishes, a self-contained Amended Answer.

There is another thorny situation that often confronts defense counsel. The lawyer has been given some information about the plaintiff's averment that leads her to the belief it is false and should therefore be denied, but she is uncertain. This is not the situation where there is an insufficiency of knowledge or information, but rather an honest and justifiable hesitancy to express certainty in one's denial because of inability to test the reliability of sources. *Wright & Miller* put it this way:

> A party who lacks first-hand or personal knowledge of the validity of the allegations in the preceding pleading, but who has sufficient information to form a belief concerning the truth or falsity of those allegation may interpose a denial upon "information and belief." This form of denial is not authorized expressly by Rule 8(b), as is the denial based upon a lack of knowledge or information sufficient to form belief. However . . . federal courts have permitted allegations on information and belief, presumably because it was accepted under the codes and because of . . . [the] portion of Rule 11 stating that when an attorney signs the pleading that signature "constitutes the best of the signer's knowledge, information, and belief formed after reasonable inquiry. . . ."
>
> A denial upon information and belief is most appropriate when the pleader's denial is based upon information supplied by a third person, usually the attorney or another agent. . . .

Charles A. Wright & Arthur R. Miller, 5 *Federal Practice and Procedure* §1263.

e. Affirmative Defenses

Affirmative defenses are the counterpart to the "confession and avoidance" of the common law. In effect, the defendant is saying, "Even if you prove your cause of action (confession), I still win because of another rule or an exception (avoidance)." For instance, plaintiff might prove all of the elements of a negligence case, and yet lose because of the defense of statute of limitations or contributory negligence (if that is a complete defense under the applicable law). Usually, but not always, defendants have the burdens of pleading, production, and persuasion as to all elements of the affirmative defense, just as plaintiffs usually have the same burdens as to the elements of their causes of action.

Rule 8(c) lists nineteen matters as affirmative defenses, but makes clear that these are merely illustrative, and that the defendant has the obligation to plead "any other matter constituting an avoidance or an affirmative defense." One treatise for federal court practitioners helpfully lists some additional affirmative defenses:

> Other matters held to be affirmative defenses and thus to be affirmatively pleaded include comparative negligence, gift, rescission, election of remedies, bona fide purchase for value, mitigation of damages, discharge through extension of time of payment, exemption under the Fair Labor

Standards Act, Truth in Lending Act, or many other statutes, cost justification or meeting competition under the Robinson-Patman Act (15 U.S.C. §13a), multiplicity of suits, prematurity of action, truth, privilege, or retraction in a libel action, self-defense or other justification in an assault and battery action, exception to liability in or breach of insurance policy provision, and prior publications or prior use as a defense to patent infringement.

Richard A. Givens, 1 *Manual of Federal Practice* §3.35(1) (4th ed. 1991). The author suggests that "[i]f doubt exists as to the status of any defensive matter under a denial, it is proper, and certainly wise, to set it forth as an affirmative defense." The failure to specifically list an affirmative defense in the answer will normally mean that the defendant has waived it and cannot present evidence with respect to it at trial, unless an amendment is permitted.

Usually, lawyers know or are able to find out in advance and with certainty the elements of causes of action and the applicable affirmative defenses. The same sources that describe causes of action also usually describe affirmative defenses. On those rare occasions when a court must decide whether a circumstance should be part of the plaintiff's prima facie case or an affirmative defense of the defendant, the opinions discuss such matters as accessibility to the evidence, whether the potential defense is an exception to ordinary events, and whether the parties should be hampered or aided in proving their cases. If a statute is involved, the court will attempt to discern whether its language implies what is an affirmative defense (such as an "except" clause in the statute) or whether legislative intent helps resolve the question.

Sometimes, a court or legislature will wish to place some burden on a defendant, but not a total affirmative defense. For instance, consider the case where a plaintiff takes a suit to the dry cleaners for cleaning (a bailment) and it is not returned in as good condition as when the cleaner received it or it is not returned at all. Who has the burden of showing negligence or lack thereof? Some courts put the burden of proving negligence on the plaintiff, but then say that if the fact finder believes that the plaintiff took the suit to the dry cleaner in good condition and the dry cleaner accepted it and did not return it in at least as good condition (the triggering facts), then negligence is presumed, unless the defendant produces enough evidence to permit a finding that it was not negligent (production burden) and then the burden of persuasion is again on the plaintiff. Some courts use such a presumption to shift the entire burden of proof to the defendant, thus effectively creating an affirmative defense, but only after the plaintiff proves the triggering facts.

Another device courts occasionally use is to place the pleading burden on the plaintiff, but to require the defendant to plead the nonexistence of the element as an affirmative defense and to prove it. For instance, usually the plaintiff must allege nonpayment in a promissory note case, but the defendant must allege payment as an affirmative defense and has both the production and persuasion burdens with respect to payment. The following case discusses whether "qualified immunity" is an affirmative defense in a §1983 action. The debate about pleading "qualified immunity" and the extent of that immunity was also discussed in the Comments and Questions after the *Leatherman* cases earlier in this chapter.

■ GOMEZ v. TOLEDO
446 U.S. 635 (1980)

Justice MARSHALL delivered the opinion of the Court:

The question presented is whether, in an action brought under 42 U.S.C. §1983 against a public official whose position might entitle him to qualified immunity, a plaintiff must allege that the official has acted in bad faith in order to state a claim for relief or, alternatively, whether the defendant must plead good faith as an affirmative defense.

I

Petitioner Carlos Rivera Gomez brought this action against respondent, the Superintendent of the Police of the Commonwealth of Puerto Rico, contending that respondent had violated his right to procedural due process by discharging him from employment with the Police Department's Bureau of Criminal Investigation. Basing jurisdiction on 28 U.S.C. §1343(3) [that section grants the federal district courts jurisdiction "[t]o redress the deprivation, under color of any State law, statute, ordinance, regulation, custom or usage, of any right, privilege or immunity secured by the Constitution of the United States or by any Act of Congress providing for equal rights of citizens or of all persons within the jurisdiction of the United States"], petitioner alleged the following facts in his complaint. Petitioner had been employed as an agent with the Puerto Rican police since 1968. In April 1975, he submitted a sworn statement to his supervisor in which he asserted that two other agents had offered false evidence for use in a criminal case under their investigation. As a result of this statement, petitioner was immediately transferred from the Criminal Investigation Corps for the Southern Area to Police Headquarters in San Juan, and a few weeks later to the Police Academy in Gurabo, where he was given no investigative authority. In the meantime respondent ordered an investigation of petitioner's claims, and the Legal Division of the Police Department concluded that all of petitioner's factual allegations were true.

In April 1976, while still stationed at the Police Academy, petitioner was subpoenaed to give testimony in a criminal case arising out of the evidence that petitioner had alleged to be false. At the trial petitioner, appearing as a defense witness, testified that the evidence was in fact false. As a result of this testimony, criminal charges, filed on the basis of information furnished by respondent, were brought against petitioner for the allegedly unlawful wiretapping of the agents' telephones. Respondent suspended petitioner in May 1976 and discharged him without a hearing in July. In October, the District Court of Puerto Rico found no probable cause to believe that petitioner was guilty of the allegedly unlawful wiretapping and, upon appeal by the prosecution, the Superior Court affirmed. Petitioner in turn sought review of his discharge before the Investigation, Prosecution, and Appeals Commission of Puerto Rico, which, after a hearing, revoked the discharge order rendered by respondent and ordered that petitioner be reinstated with back pay.

Based on the foregoing factual allegations, petitioner brought this suit for damages, contending that his discharge violated his right to procedural due process, and that it had caused him anxiety, embarrassment, and injury to his reputation in the community. In his answer, respondent denied a number of petitioner's allegations of fact and asserted several affirmative defenses. Respondent then moved to dismiss the complaint for failure to state a cause of action, see Fed. R. Civ. P. 12(b)(6), and the District Court granted the motion. Observing that respondent was entitled to qualified immunity for acts done in good faith within the scope of his official duties, it concluded that petitioner was required to plead as part of his claim for relief that, in committing the actions alleged, respondent was motivated by bad faith. The absence of any such allegation, it held, required dismissal of the complaint. The United States Court of Appeals for the First Circuit affirmed. 602 F.2d 1018 (1979).

We granted certiorari to resolve a conflict among the Courts of Appeals. We now reverse.

II

Section 1983 provides a cause of action for "the deprivation of any rights, privileges, or immunities secured by the Constitution and laws" by any person acting "under color of any statute, ordinance, regulation, custom, or usage, or any State or Territory." 42 U.S.C. §1983. [Section 1983 provides in full: "Every person who, under color of any statute, ordinance, regulation, custom, or usage, of any State or Territory, subjects, or causes to be subjected, any citizen of the United States or other person within the jurisdiction thereof to the deprivation of any rights, privileges, or immunities secured by the Constitution and laws, shall be liable to the party injured in an action at law, suit in equity, or other proper proceeding for redress."] This statute, enacted to aid in "the preservation of human liberty and human rights," Owen v. City of Independence, 445 U.S. 622, 636, reflects a congressional judgment that a "damages remedy against the offending party is a vital component of any scheme for vindicating cherished constitutional guarantees," 445 U.S. at 651. As remedial legislation, §1983 is to be construed generously to further its primary purpose. See 445 U.S. at 636.

In certain limited circumstances, we have held that public officers are entitled to a qualified immunity from damages liability under §1983. This conclusion has been based on an unwillingness to infer from legislative silence a congressional intention to abrogate immunities that were both "well established at common law" and "compatible with the purposes of the Civil Rights Act." 445 U.S. at 638. Findings of immunity have thus been "predicated upon a considered inquiry into the immunity histori-cally accorded the relevant official at common law and the interests behind it." *Imbler v. Pachtman*, 424 U.S. 409, 421 (1976).

Nothing in the language or legislative history of §1983, however, suggests that in an action brought against a public official whose position might entitle him to immunity if he acted in good faith, a plaintiff must allege bad faith in order to state a claim for relief. By the plain terms of §1983, two—and only two—allegations are required in order to state a cause of action under that statute. First, the plaintiff must allege that some person has deprived him of a federal right. Second, he must allege that the person who has deprived him of that right acted under color of state or territorial law. Petitioner has made both of the required allegations. He alleged that his discharge by respondent violated his right to proce-dural due process . . . and that respondent acted under color of Puerto Rican law.

Moreover, this Court has never indicated that qualified immunity is relevant to the existence of the plaintiff's cause of action; instead we have described it as a defense available to the official in question. Since qualified immunity is a defense, the burden of pleading it rests with the defendant. See Fed. Civ. P. 8(c) (defendant must plead any "matter constituting an avoidance or affirmative defense"); Wright & Miller, 5 Federal Practice and Procedure §1271 (1969). It is for the official to claim that his conduct was justified by an objectively reasonable belief that it was lawful. We see no basis for imposing on the plaintiff an obligation to anticipate such a defense by stating in his complaint that the defendant acted in bad faith.

Our conclusion as to the allocation of the burden of pleading is sup-ported by the nature of the qualified immunity defense. As our decisions make clear, whether such immunity has been established depends on facts peculiarly within the knowledge and control of the defendant. Thus we have stated that "[i]t is the existence of reasonable grounds for the belief formed at the time and in light of all the circumstances, coupled with good-faith belief, that affords a basis for qualified immunity of executive officers for acts performed in the course of official conduct." *Scheuer v. Rhodes, supra,* 416 U.S. at 247-248. The applicable test focuses not only on whether the official has an objectively reasonable basis for that belief, but also on whether "[t]he official himself [is] acting sincerely and with a belief that he is doing right," *Wood v. Strickland, supra,* 420 U.S. at 321. There may be no way for a plaintiff to know in advance whether the official has such a belief or, indeed, whether he will even claim that he does. The existence of a subjective belief will frequently turn on factors which a plaintiff cannot reasonably be expected to know. . . .

The decision of the Court of Appeals is reversed, and the case is remanded to that court for further proceedings consistent with this opinion.

Mr. Justice REHNQUIST joins the opinion of the Court, reading it as he does to leave open the issue of the burden of persuasion, as opposed to the burden of pleading, with respect to a defense of qualified immunity.

Comments and Questions

1. As you have already read, the Supreme Court in 1982 stated that qualified immunity for government officials extends to their performance of discretionary functions "insofar as their conduct does not violate clearly established statutory or constitutional rights of which a reasonable person would have known." *Harlow v. Fitzgerald,* 457 U.S. 800, 818 (1982). This replaced the "good faith" test described in *Gomez.* If a case similar to *Gomez* arose today, should the result be the same?

2. What does Chief Justice Rehnquist accomplish in his one-sentence concurrence in *Gomez?* Burden on (D) for immunity

Practice Exercise No. 9:
Analyzing the Answer in *Carpenter*

The purpose of this exercise is to help you learn the differences among 12(b)(6) defenses, denials, and affirmative defenses. The Answer of Randall Dee to the initial Complaint is in the Case Files. Analyze the Answer in *Carpenter* in light of the Complaint. (Assume that the pleading rules in Massachusetts are the same as the Federal Rules of Civil Procedure.)

(a) What effect will the admissions in paragraphs four and five of Randall Dee's answer have on the trial?

(b) Assuming that the defendant has reasonable knowledge, is the answer to paragraph six in compliance with the applicable Massachusetts rules?

(c) What does the denial to the allegations in paragraph eleven put in issue? Assuming that further stages of this case (such as discovery, summary judgment, pretrial conference) do not bring closure to the issue and that it remains as defined by the pleadings, how will the judge instruct the jury on the question of conscious suffering, including instructions on burden of proof?

(d) Examine each of Randall Dee's defenses, and explain what type of defense it is. Is it a defense at all or a mislabeled "denial"?

(e) Notice that Randall Dee's counsel lumps different types of defenses together, rather than separating affirmative defenses from other types. This is common practice, although some lawyers divide their answer by making distinct categories, such as "12(b) defenses" and "affirmative defenses." Some lawyers begin their answers with affirmative defenses and thus take advantage of this opportunity for rhetoric. What order and method of labeling do the forms attached to the Federal Rules suggest? Which specific forms are you relying on in giving your answer?

(f) If you were a legislator or judge faced with the question, would you make the second defense an affirmative defense? Why or why not?

7. Amendments

When judges and lawyers want a quick introduction to a civil lawsuit, they often first look at the complaint and answer in order to educate themselves on the factual background of the case and the claims and defenses. Unless altered by a pretrial conference order, the pleadings also set the boundaries for the trial, confining the parties to the alleged claims and defenses and instructing the judge and the lawyers as to what facts have been admitted. But much of modern civil litigation revolves around discovery, and during that stage new facts, and consequently previously unpleaded causes of action and defenses, often emerge. It is true that the most plaintiff-friendly reading of Rule 8(a)(2) would permit the plaintiff simply to state a claim showing one cause of action, and that the plaintiff would then be able to prove at trial any cause of action within the story told in the complaint. But lawyers are cautious and want to be certain that at trial they can introduce evidence on their entire case. Since the trial judge may tell them that they cannot introduce evidence of causes of action and defenses absent from their pleadings (or outside the limits of a pretrial order under Rule 16 or a similar state rule), lawyers frequently want to amend their pleadings. In federal court civil litigation, Rule 15 controls whether one can amend a pleading, although sometimes local rules provide further requirements and limitations.

Rule 15 has four subparagraphs. The critical portions are (1) the sentence in 15(a) stating that leave to amend shall be "freely given when justice so requires" and (2) 15(c), which describes when an amendment "relates back to the date of the original pleading."

You should be aware, though, of the situations covered by Fed. R. Civ. P. 15(b) and 15(d). Rule 15(b) is there to help solve the problem of proffered or admitted evidence that seems to go beyond the confines of the pleadings. The first sentence to Rule 15(b) places trial lawyers in somewhat of a dilemma. It states: "When issues not raised by the pleadings are tried by express or implied consent of the parties, they shall be treated in all respects as if they had been raised by the pleadings." Consider defendant counsel's options when the plaintiff introduces a cause of action that is slightly different from what is explicit in the complaint. And similarly, consider the plaintiff's lawyers' predicament if the defendant raises an affirmative defense that was not pleaded. If one objects, the opponent will move to amend and "leave shall be freely given when justice so requires." (15(a)). If one doesn't object, the risk is that one has given "implied" consent.

In general, it is probably better to object when you think your opponent is introducing evidence beyond the pleadings. First, it is important to know whether a new issue has in fact been raised, so that you know whether you have to meet it through cross-examination or by introducing your own evidence. Sometimes it is not clear what your opponent is driving at when she introduces evidence, and you do not want to invite her to invent a new theory that perhaps she didn't see. So there may be occasions when you do not object because you do not want to educate the opposition. But the ambiguity may be resolved against you later (as a result of your "implied" consent by your not objecting to the admissibility of the evidence), so you are often better off knowing exactly where you and opposing counsel stand.

Second, you might win by your objection, and in fact keep a new cause of action, theory, or defense out of the case. Your arguments for keeping out evidence on a new theory will be similar to the arguments that you normally raise against an amendment. The stock ones (in addition to the argument that the statute of limitations has run, which we will take up later) are (1) the opponent has unreasonably delayed raising the issue, although this argument usually fails without an additional argument; (2) you have been prejudiced in your preparation of the case by the delay; (3) the new issue is raised in bad faith, such as for the purpose of clouding real issues or confusing the fact finder or making the other side look "bad" on a largely irrelevant question; or (4) the new issue is "futile" in the sense that the party pressing it cannot win on it. The last sentence of 15(b) permits the court to grant a continuance to the objecting party so she can prepare to meet the new issue without prejudice, but this option is particularly unappealing to judges in the middle of a jury trial or when the party introducing the new issue has had ample prior opportunity to raise the question by seeking a formal amendment.

Sometimes, events have happened since the date of the original pleading that are relevant to the case, but could not have been pleaded specifically at the time because they had not yet occurred. This is the reason for Fed. R. Civ. P. 15(d) on "Supplemental Pleadings." For instance, there may be subsequent breaches of the contract sued upon, or additional installment payments due, or patent, copyright, or trademark infringements that occurred after the initial complaint. A 1963 amendment to 15(d) makes clear that the trial court is empowered to grant a supplemental pleading even if the new material cures a defect in the original complaint. If a new claim is involved and the statute of limitations has now run, the pleader who seeks the supplemental pleading will have to rely on the provisions of 15(c) dealing with "relation back" of amendments.

Probably the most litigated provisions of Rule 15, or of any rules regarding amendments, concern statute of limitations problems and whether such a statute can be met by having the additional claim or defense relate back to the date of the original pleading. For example, if a plaintiff brought the initial cause of action within the statute of limitations, and the new claim or new cause of action to be "amended in" is now beyond the statutory period, the plaintiff will want the "amended in" claim or cause of action to "relate back" to the commencement date of the initial case. Can you see why it is the intersection of statutes of limitations and motions to amend that raise the most controversial amendment issues?

It is important to know clearly what a statute of limitations is. Most states have statutes requiring that certain causes of action be brought within a certain number of years from when the cause of action accrued. Some federal statutes provide limitations periods for specific federal claims.* Usually, the cause of action accrues when every element of the cause of action has taken place, and usually the last element to occur is the damage or harm. A typical tort statute of limitations is three years. Consequently, if an automobile accident happened on Day One, and the plaintiff was therefore injured on Day One, the plaintiff would have to bring her lawsuit within three years from Day One. (A typical contract statute of limitations is six years.)

Sometimes, potential parties will agree to stop the running of a statute of limitations. A defendant may not want a complaint to be filed and may be willing to agree to forestall the running of the period of time under the statute of limitations pending settlement negotiations. These are often called "tolling agreements."

Reasons for the existence of statutes of limitations include (1) giving potential parties a sense of repose or peace after time has expired (one shouldn't have to worry a lifetime about potential wrongdoing); (2) permitting accused parties to amass evidence while it is still fresh; (3) helping courts to avoid depleting their scarce resources on stale cases in which it will be difficult, if not impossible, to find out what happened. These rationales should help you see why the amendment doctrine becomes more complicated when amendments are sought after the expiration of a statute of limitations.

Consider the facts of *Carpenter v. Dee*. Let's say that *prior* to the running of the applicable statute of limitations, Nancy Carpenter's lawyer, who

---

*28 U.S.C. §1658, enacted in 1990, provides a general four-year statute of limitations (absent a specific limitations period in the applicable federal law) for all civil actions "arising under an Act of Congress enacted after the date of enactment of this section."

initially pleaded only a wrongful death count, decided that it was necessary to add a count for conscious suffering. Or assume that her lawyer, through discovery, found plausible defendants in addition to the Dee brothers, such as the retailer that sold the tires and the suspension lift kit. Such amendments normally will not cause parties or courts much trouble. Why? Then consider the same motions to amend *after* the applicable statute of limitations have expired. Why is it now more problematic?

Before reading an amendment/statute of limitations case, you should note two conceptual problems. One is whether the amendment concerns merely adding a claim or defense, as opposed to adding a party. Reread Fed. R. Civ. P. 15(c). Assume a federal cause of action that does not have any special "relationship back" law attached to it. (If you were in federal court and there were a claim grounded in state law, the federal court, by virtue of 15(c)(1), which was added in 1991, would apply the "relation back" doctrine of the state law if it were more lenient than the Federal Rules. This amendment changed language in 15(c)(3) and altered the doctrine and implications of *Schiavone v. Fortune*, 477 U.S. 21 (1986), a case that had required notice to a newly named defendant at an earlier time than that required for the initially named defendant.) If you sought to add a second federal claim to your first, after the statute of limitations had run, "relation back" would be governed by 15(c)(2). But if you sought to add a new party to your initial federal cause of action after the applicable statute of limitations had run, the more stringent provisions of 15(c)(3) would apply. Why are the provisions different?

The second conceptual problem arises from the fact that Fed. R. Civ. P. 15(a) and 15(c) impose different tests. Justice may require adding a claim, defense, or a party within the meaning of 15(a), but if the applicable statute of limitations has already expired, there may be a sound affirmative defense, unless the 15(c) "relation back" provisions save the amending party. A court could first grant the amendment and then, after the affirmative defense is raised in answer to the amended pleading, examine whether 15(c) permits the amender to surmount the defense. Or a court could decide not to permit the amendment unless it first determines that the amending party will be able to bring the amendment within the contours of the applicable statute of limitations. Some judges prefer the first route (decide the issues of amendment and relation back separately) and some prefer the second (deny the amendment if there is no relation back).

A practical point: careful lawyers often place the exact language to be amended (added or subtracted) within the motion to amend, and then attach the entire pleading in the form it would take if the amendment were granted. If you do this, the court can then merely ask the clerk to docket the amended pleading when the motion is granted. Often, local rules or special court rules will spell out the method you should use in seeking amendments.

As you read the following cases, see if you can articulate the subtle differences between the Massachusetts and Federal Rules on "relation back."

■ WORTHINGTON v. WILSON
8 F.3d 1253 (7th Cir. 1993)

MARION, Circuit Judge.

In his 42 U.S.C. §1983 complaint, Richard Worthington claimed that while being arrested the arresting officers purposely injured him. When he filed suit on the day the statute of limitations expired, he named "three unknown named police officers" as defendants. Worthington later sought to amend the complaint to substitute police officers Dave Wilson and Jeff Wall for the unknown officers. The district court concluded that the relation back doctrine of Fed. R. Civ. P. 15(c) did not apply, and dismissed the amended complaint. *Worthington v. Wilson*, 790 F. Supp. 829 (C.D. Ill. 1992). We affirm.

On February 25, 1989, Richard Worthington was arrested by a police officer in the Peoria Heights Police Department. At the time of his arrest, Worthington had an injured left hand, and he advised the arresting officer of his injury. According to Worthington's complaint, the arresting officer responded by grabbing Worthington's injured hand and twisting it, prompting Worthington to push the officer away and tell him to "take it easy." A second police officer arrived at the scene, and Worthington was wrestled to the ground and handcuffed. The police officers then hoisted Worthington from the ground by the handcuffs, which caused him to suffer broken bones in his left hand.

Exactly two years later, on February 25, 1991, Worthington filed a five-count complaint in the Circuit Court of Peoria County, Illinois, against the Village of Peoria Heights and "three unknown named police officers," stating the above facts and alleging that he was deprived of his constitutional rights in violation of 42 U.S.C. §1983. Counts one through three of the complaint named the police officers in their personal and official capacities, and alleged a variety of damages. Counts four and five named the Village of Peoria Heights, and alleged that it was liable for the police officers' conduct based on the doctrine of respondeat superior.

The Village removed the action to federal court and sought dismissal under Fed. R. Civ. P. 12(b)(6) for the reason that respondeat superior was not a valid basis for imposing liability against it under §1983. At a hearing on the motion to dismiss, Worthington voluntarily dismissed his claims against the Village and obtained leave to file an amended complaint. The Village thereafter moved for sanctions against Worthington and his counsel under Fed. R. Civ. P. 11. In the motion, the Village argued that Worthington's attempt to state a §1983 claim against it on the basis of respondeat superior was contrary to *Monell v. Department of Social Services*, 436 U.S. 658 (1978), and therefore in violation of Rule 11.

On June 17, 1991, Worthington filed an amended complaint in which he substituted as the defendants Dave Wilson and Jeff Wall, two of the twelve or so members of the Peoria Heights Police Department, for the "unknown named police officers" who arrested him on February 25, 1989. Wilson and Wall moved to dismiss the amended complaint primarily on grounds that Illinois' two-year statute of limitations expired, Ill. Ann. Stat. ch. 735, P 5/13-202 (Smith-Hurd 1993), and that the amendment did not relate back to the filing of the original complaint under Rule 15(c). Worthington responded to this motion, and a hearing was conducted before a magistrate judge on October 31, 1991.

On December 19, 1991, the magistrate judge recommended that Wilson's and Wall's motion to dismiss and the Village's motion for sanctions should be granted. Worthington filed objections to these recommendations, to which the defendants responded.

On March 17, 1992, the district judge held a hearing on the objections to the magistrate judge's recommendations. Prior to the hearing, the district judge notified the parties that Rule 15(c), on which Wilson and Wall based their argument, had been amended effective December 1, 1991, and asked them to address the effect of this amendment on the motion to dismiss.

On April 27, 1992, the district judge granted Wilson's and Wall's motion to dismiss the amended complaint under revised Rule 15(c) and denied the Village's motion for sanctions. *Worthington v. Wilson*, 790 F. Supp. 829 (C.D. Ill. 1992). Worthington appeals this dismissal. The Village cross-appeals the denial of sanctions.

Rule 15(c) was amended to provide broader "relation back" of pleadings when a plaintiff seeks to amend his complaint to change defendants. Rule 15(c) as amended December 1, 1991, provides, in pertinent part: An amendment of a pleading relates back to the date of the original pleading when (1) relation back is permitted by the law that provides the statute of limitations applicable to the action, or (2) the claim or defense asserted in the amended pleading arose out of the conduct, transaction, or occurrence set forth or attempted to be set forth in the original pleadings, or (3) the amendment changes the party or the naming of the party against whom a claim is asserted if the foregoing provision (2) is satisfied and, within the period provided by Rule 4(j) for service of the summons and complaint, the party to be brought in by amendment (A) has received such notice of the institution of the action that the party will not be prejudiced in maintaining a defense on the merits, and (B) knew or should have known that, but for a mistake concerning the identity of the proper party, the action would have been brought against the party.

Prior to this amendment, the standard for relation back under Rule 15(c) was set out in *Schiavone v. Fortune*, 477 U.S. 21 (1986): The four prerequisites to a "relation back" amendment under Rule 15(c) are: (1) the basic claim must have arisen out of the conduct set forth in the original pleading; (2) the party to be brought in must have received such notice that it will not be prejudiced in maintaining its defense; (3) that party must or should have known that, but for a mistake concerning identity, the action would have been brought against it; and (4) the second and third requirements must have been fulfilled within the proscribed [*sic*] limitations period. *Id.* at 29.

The Advisory Committee Notes to amended Rule 15(c) indicate that the amendment repudiates the holding in *Schiavone* that notice of a lawsuit's pendency must be given within the applicable statute of limitations period. The Advisory Committee stated: An intended defendant who is notified of an action within the period allowed by [current Rule 4(m)] for service of a summons and complaint may not under the revised rule defeat the action on account of a defect in the pleading with respect to the defendant's name, provided that the requirements of clauses (A) and (B) have been met. If the notice requirement is met within the [current Rule 4(m)] period, a complaint may be amended at any time to correct a formal defect such as a misnomer or misidentification. Fed. R. Civ. P. 15(c), Advisory Committee Notes (1991 Amendment).

In the order amending Rule 15(c), the Supreme Court expressed its intention that "insofar as just and practicable," the amendment governs cases pending in the district courts on December 1, 1991. Order Adopting Amendments to Federal Rules of Civil Procedure, 111 S. Ct. 813 (Apr. 30, 1991).

In this case, Wilson and Wall did not know of Worthington's action before the limitations period expired, as was required by *Schiavone*, but they were aware of its pendency within the extra 120 days provided by new Rule 15(c). *Worthington,* 790 F. Supp. at 833. Since the amendment was decisive to the issue of "notice," the district judge retroactively applied new Rule 15(c), finding it "just and practicable" to do so. *Id.* at 833-34. We have no need to consider the retroactivity of amended Rule 15(c) as it might apply in this case because Worthington's amended complaint did not relate back under either the old or new version of Rule 15(c).

Both versions of Rule 15(c) require that the new defendants "knew or should have known that, but for a mistake concerning the identity of the proper party, the action would have been brought against the party." In *Wood v. Worachek,* 618 F.2d 1225 (7th Cir. 1980), we construed the "mistake" requirement of Rule 15(c): A plaintiff may usually amend his complaint under Rule 15(c) to change the theory or statute under which recovery is sought; or to correct a misnomer of plaintiff where the proper party plaintiff is in court; or to change the capacity in which the plaintiff sues; or to substitute or add as plaintiff the real party interest; or to add additional plaintiffs where the action, as originally brought, was a class action. Thus, amendment with relation back is generally permitted in order to correct a misnomer of a defendant where the proper defendant is already before the court and the effect is merely to correct the name under which he is sued. But a new defendant cannot normally be substituted or added by amendment after the statute of limitations has run. . . .

Rule 15(c)(2) [current Rule 15(c)(3)] permits an amendment to relate back only where there has been an error made concerning the identity of the proper party and where that party is chargeable with knowledge of the mistake, but it does not permit relation back where, as here, there is a lack of knowledge of the proper party. Thus, in the absence of a mistake in the identification of the proper party, it is irrelevant for the purposes of Rule 15(c)(2) [current Rule 15(c)(3)] whether or not the purported substitute party knew or should have known that the action would have been brought against him. *Id.* at 1229 & 1230 (citation omitted). The record shows that there was no mistake concerning the identity of the police officers. At oral argument, counsel for Worthington indicated that he did not decide to file suit until one or two days before the statute of limitations had expired. At that point, neither Worthington nor his counsel knew the names of the two police officers who allegedly committed the offense. Thus, the complaint was filed against "unknown police officers." Because Worthington's failure to name Wilson and Wall was due to a lack of knowledge as to their identity, and not a mistake in their names, Worthington was prevented from availing himself of the relation back doctrine of Rule 15(c).

Worthington argues that the amended complaint should relate back based on the district judge's proposed reading of Rule 15(c) as not having a separate "mistake" requirement. The district judge construed the word "mistake" to mean "change the party or the naming of the party." *Worthington,* 790 F. Supp. at 835. This construction, however, ignores the continuing vitality of *Wood's* holding which interprets the "mistake" requirement under the old version of Rule 15(c). That holding remains unaffected by the 1991 amendment to Rule 15(c).

Worthington argues alternatively that equitable tolling should bar Wilson and Wall from asserting a statute of limitations defense because the officers fraudulently concealed their identity from him. Worthington concedes that he only mentioned the tolling argument obliquely in his pleadings. The district judge raised the tolling argument sua sponte at the hearing on the motion to dismiss. This appeal is the first time that the parties have had an opportunity to fully brief the tolling argument, so it is not waived.

Under Illinois law, a plaintiff who alleges fraudulent concealment to toll the statute of limitations must set forth affirmative acts or words by the defendants which prevented him from discovering their identity. Mere silence of the defendant and the mere failure on the part of the plaintiff to learn of a cause of action do not amount to fraudulent concealment. . . . [The court found no evidence of fraudulent concealment.]

On cross-appeal, the Village argues that Rule 11 sanctions were warranted against Worthington's counsel and should have been imposed. In denying Rule 11 sanctions, the district judge stated: " . . . [T]his court is without power to sanction [Worthington's lawyer's] conduct in this instance. While Rule 11 would authorize sanctions for such a filing in this court, it does not authorize sanctions for a pleading initially filed in state court which is later removed to federal court. . . . The amended complaint, which was filed in this court, contained no reference to respondeat superior." The Defendants' motion for sanctions is accordingly denied. *Worthington*, 790 F. Supp. at 838. . . .

[Accordingly, the court held that relationship back was precluded, and Rule 11 sanctions were denied.]

■ CHRISTOPHER v. DUFFY
28 Mass. App. Ct. 780 (1990)

KAPLAN, Justice.

A judge of the Superior Court denied the plaintiff's motion for leave to amend her complaint a second time to name five companies and a trade association as defendants and to assert against them fresh theories of liability. A single justice of this court denied the plaintiff's petition under G.L. c. 231, §118, first par., for relief from that interlocutory decision, but granted the plaintiff leave to appeal it to a panel of this court. We now affirm the decision on the principal ground that the judge did not abuse his discretion in denying leave.

The action was begun on May 27, 1982. The first amended complaint presented the following case. The Christopher family, mother, father, and five children, occupied an apartment at 117 Liberty Street, in Chelsea, since sometime in 1979. On June 4, 1981, a physician examining Janette Christopher, a child under the age of six, found that she was suffering from lead poisoning. He notified the appropriate State agency, which ordered the owners of the premises to "delead" the apartment. The owners hired one John Duffy to do the job, but he is alleged to have done it so improperly as to increase the exposure to lead poisoning. On July 1, it appeared Janette's condition had worsened. She was admitted to a hospital on July 9 for "chelation" treatment (neutralizing the lead by means of other substances) and discharged on July 15. She died of pneumonia on July 20, the result, allegedly, of an infection contracted at the hospital, which she had lost the capacity to resist.

The then plaintiffs in the action were the mother, as administratrix of Janette's estate, and the mother and father individually. Named as defendants were James and Bettina Pyne, owners of 117 Liberty Street since 1978; Alfonse J. Trulli, as trustee of School Street Trust, the former owner; and John Duffy. Various conventional theories of liability were set out applicable to particular defendants, including violation of the lead poisoning prevention statute (G.L. c. 111, §§191 *et seq.*) and regulations, negligence, wrongful death in violation of G.L. c. 229, intentional infliction of emotional distress (upon the parents), and unfair or deceptive practices in violation of G.L. c. 93A. Duffy, however, had not been served with process. [The original complaint reserved a "John Doe" place which was filled in by the name John Duffy in the first amended complaint. It is indicated that the plaintiffs conducted a deposition of Duffy.]

On January 12, 1987, agreements for judgment were executed in the action, by which the Pyne defendants paid $47,000 in settlement, and the trust defendant $5,000. Duffy was not involved in the settlements.

On November 6, 1987, the mother, as administratrix, now captioned as the sole plaintiff, moved to amend the first amended complaint so as to drop all the original defendants except Duffy, and to bring in as defendants five companies which manufacture lead for use in lead paint, together with their trade association. . . . The plaintiff withdrew her motion voluntarily on January 28, 1988, but renewed it on September 20, 1988. By the proposed amendment, intended by the plaintiff to have "relation back" to the original complaint, the companies would be charged with liability in the death of Janette on the alleged grounds that they had known or should have known since the 1920's of the dangerous qualities of their products and yet negligently produced and marketed them; that they were negligent in product design, and in failing to give warning; and that they were in breach of warranty. The companies, together with the association, would be further charged with "conspiracy" in concealing from the public the hazards associated with the products. And liability of the companies, according to the amendment, should be predicated, if necessary, on a "market share" basis. The judge denied leave to amend on December 30, 1988, filing a memorandum in which he laid stress on the prejudice to which the new defendants would be subjected by having to respond to the delayed claims now asserted against them. . . .

"[A] motion to amend should be allowed unless some good reason appears for denying it." *Castellucci v. United States Fid. & Guar. Co.*, 372 Mass. 288, 289, 361 N.E.2d 1264 (1977). Massachusetts Rule of Civil Procedure 15(c), 365 Mass. 762 (1974), together with the 1988 revision of G.L. c. 231, §51, by St. 1988, c. 141, §1, means that an amendment such as that proposed here—adding a party, sounding a new theory of liability, but claiming a remedy for the injury first sued on—should be allowed with relation back, unless there is good reason to deny it. As with any proffered amendment, the court decides whether a reason is good, and therein is bound to exercise a sound discretion.

We need not consider whether undue delay in seeking amendment can on occasion be itself sufficient to warrant a court's denying the leave. We assume, as did the judge below, that permission to amend turns, in discretion, on whether the opposing party will be unduly prejudiced by allowance of the amendment, recognizing, however, that delay may contribute, and even contribute seriously, to cause the prejudice. We assume, too, that it is up to the opposing party to point to the prejudice, whether that is apparent or requires demonstration.

In the present case, the judge, after noting the lengthy delay, observed on the question of prejudice: "[T]he plaintiff's cause of action alleges lead paint ingestion causing lead poisoning, causing hospitalization and heightened susceptibility, causing infection, causing pneumonia, causing eventual death. As . . . the proposed new defendants [were] served six years after the cause of action arose, to defend in a case which will necessitate extensive discovery and documentation of each link of the alleged causal chain is prejudicial to these defendants." It is evident, too, that what Duffy observed and did would be important for the new defendants' defense, but Duffy [who passed away on November 17, 1985] has been beyond recall since 1985. So also the defendants would be interested in the actual conditions, around the critical time, of the accessible places in the apartment to which paints were applied; the lapse of years almost necessarily would obscure those facts, as it would the actual identity of the companies furnishing the lead for any of the paints. (All this is apart from the defendants' likely defenses to the charges of negligence, conscious deception, etc.)

This is not the common case of a proposed amendment which will, if allowed, expose an existing party to a new theory of liability. Here we have parties, previously unconnected with the case, who are served long after the running of the relevant statute of limitations. The policies which support the extinguishment of claims after limitations periods speak against allowing such amendments against new defendants. They do not speak conclusively, but they are to be considered and weighed. For such reasons the decisions are especially sensitive to the likelihood of hardship where a tendered amendment would involve service upon and joinder of new parties. . . .

On the whole it cannot be said that the judge abused his discretion by acting capriciously or arbitrarily in rejecting the amendment, and his decision will be respected. Order affirmed.

Comments and Questions

1. The Massachusetts rule, Mass. R. Civ. P. 15, which was applied in *Christopher v. Duffy*, is identical to Fed. R. Civ. P. 15, except as to 15(c) which provides:

> Relation Back of Amendments. Whenever the claim or defense asserted in the amended pleading arose out of the conduct, transaction, or occurrence set forth or attempted to be set forth in the original pleading, the amendment (including an amendment changing a party) relates back to the original pleading.

2. There are, of course, many "holdings" for any particular case. What are the holdings for these two cases regarding the federal and state rules of civil procedure on amendments?

3. Some have criticized the leniency of the Massachusetts amendment rules concerning the addition of parties after the statute of limitations has run. What is your opinion of Mass. R. Civ. P. 15(c)?

4. Statutes of limitation, tolling, and the "discovery rule" (which states that a statute of limitations period should not commence until the cause of action is discovered) are creatures both of statute and of case law. For instance, a federal statute tolls the statute of limitations when a potential plaintiff is in the armed forces. *See* Soldiers and Sailors Relief Act, 50 App. U.S.C.A. §525. Also, states often have statutes that toll the statute of limitations for minors, so that the limitations period begins when the minor reaches majority, such as eighteen or twenty-one, depending on the applicable law. You will discover in your tort course that the statutes of limitations may not begin to run in circumstances where a reasonable potential plaintiff would not know she has been harmed. For example, in the situation in which a surgeon leaves a sponge in the patient's stomach, the statute may not begin running until the plaintiff becomes aware that the sponge was left in her stomach. The following case excerpt should give you a sense of how these issues arise, and how each inquiry may be fact-specific:

> Significantly, apathy, depression, posttraumatic neurosis, psychological trauma and repression therefrom, or mental illness alone have been held to be insufficient to invoke the tolling provisions of CPLR §208. Rather, the mental disability must be "severe and incapacitating." However, where repression, trauma or neurosis is "but one of a bundle of claimed injuries the totality of which, if established, would indicate an overall inability to function in society, then the Statute of Limitations will be tolled."

Wenzel v. Nassau County Police Dept., 914 F. Supp. 902, 904 (E.D.N.Y. 1996).

Practice Exercise No. 10: Argument on Plaintiff's Motion to Amend in *Carpenter*

Assume that the facts in the initial memo concerning *Carpenter v. Dee* are still the same (including that the plaintiff's lawyer did not know where Randall Dee bought the tires and suspension kit until she took Randall Dee's deposition). After discovery, the plaintiff moved to file an amended complaint. Assume the following timeline of relevant events: Randall Dee's deposition was first noticed by the plaintiff to be taken two months before the statute of limitations expired; the deposition of Randall Dee was then delayed several times, usually to meet Randall's needs (to meet his work schedule, a death in his family, and, on one occasion, his case of flu); the statute of limitations ran with respect to all defendants the week before the deposition was taken; at the deposition, Dee stated that he bought the oversized tires and suspension lift kit from Ultimate Auto; four weeks thereafter, the plaintiff's counsel received a transcript of the deposition; one week after receipt of the transcript, she moved to amend the complaint by adding Ultimate Auto and the City of Lowell as defendants. The day after Dee's deposition, Carpenter's lawyer notified the City of Lowell of their responsibility. Of course, Lowell police knew of the accident at the time it occurred and, according to the plaintiff, knew or should have known of statutory violations even before the accident occurred. Assume that according to Dee's deposition, he told the owner of Ultimate Auto about the accident a few days after it happened, and he also told him that he had been sued about a month after he was served (which was approximately three months before the applicable statutes of limitations expired). Assume that all applicable statutes in this case are three years.

When the motion to amend was first called to be heard, the judge postponed the hearing for two weeks and told the plaintiff's lawyer to notify immediately Ultimate Auto and the Legal Department of the City of Lowell in writing about the proposed amendment and the date for the continued hearing, which she has done. (Incidentally, it is not typical for the judge to mandate advance notice to those who will be added as defendants if the amendment is allowed.) At the hearing, which is about to take place, lawyers representing the plaintiff, Randall Dee, Ultimate Auto, and the City of Lowell are all present, but the lawyers for Ultimate Auto and City of Lowell have not yet filed appearances because they are not yet named parties.

The motion to amend will now be heard. Four months have passed since the statute of limitations ran. You know that the judge hearing this motion usually calls first on the moving party. The arguments to the court should be based on that rule, but remember that judges are human beings, with power to injure or help other real human beings. Consider what each party would lose or gain if the motion is granted or denied. Attached to the motion to amend (in the Case Files) is the amended complaint, which plaintiff seeks to file if the motion to amend is allowed. Reasonable inferences can be made about what records might be available to City of Lowell and Ultimate Auto.

The amended complaint, if allowed, mentions implied warranties and Mass. G.L.A. 90, §7P. Massachusetts has adopted the Uniform Commercial Code provisions on implied warranties, and those provisions follow the amended complaint, as does M.G.L.A. 90, §7P. You will find other relevant Massachusetts law (statutory provisions relating to wrongful death, conscious suffering, and fraudulent conveyance) also in the Case Files.

Important Instructions

If your last name begins with a letter from A through H, you are plaintiff's counsel and thus should prepare arguments in favor of the motion to amend. Last names beginning with the letters I and J should represent the defendants, Randall and Peter Dee. Last names beginning with K through P should represent Ultimate Auto, in opposition to the motion. Q through V should represent the City of Lowell, in opposition to the motion. Those with last names beginning with the letters W through Z should be prepared to act as clerks to the presiding judge. Judicial clerks ordinarily help the judge prepare for a motions session and sometimes offer suggestions about what questions to ask. Some judges even ask their clerks how they would decide the motion and why. *[handwritten: applying state statute]*

For purposes of discussion after the motion session ends, please consider the following questions: *[handwritten: ISC-1, even if fed ct, state law would use state rule]* *[handwritten: NOTICE + MISTAKE]*

(1) Would the issues be different had this been a diversity case brought in the federal district court for the District of Massachusetts? *[handwritten: yes, harder under the Federal Rule]*

(2) Would the issues be different had (1) Massachusetts adopted the same Rule 15 as is in the Federal Rules of Civil Procedure and (2) the case been a diversity case brought in the federal district court for the District of Massachusetts? In what ways, if any, would the arguments be different?

[handwritten: are quite liberal]

Note: Tips on Arguing Motions

It is not patronizing and, in fact, is good practice to assume that a judge in a motions session knows very little or even nothing about your case, the motion, or the applicable law. Judges at motions sessions, in those courts where oral arguments are permitted, often have to deal with many cases at one sitting, and may have just seen the relevant papers for the first time the minute before arguments begin. However, often you will have to make your argument quickly, for motions judges can be quite impatient. They have a lot to do.

Although there are many ways to try to persuade a judge at a motions session, here are a few clues that may be helpful. State who you are and whom you represent. Tell the judge the precise thing that must be decided (for instance, "this is a motion brought pursuant to Federal Rule 12(b)(6) to dismiss the first count of the plaintiff's complaint for failing to state a claim for which relief can be granted. I urge you to grant the motion for two major reasons"). If you are speaking first, tell the judge enough about the facts of the case and its procedural posture that she can easily follow your argument. If you rely on a rule (or statute), tell the judge precisely which provisions of which rule apply (give the exact words), and explain why what you seek is permitted, reasonable and fair, or compelled, if that is a plausible position, given the facts of your case. If you rely on case law, tell the judge enough about the facts of the case you rely upon so that she can understand its holding in context and can determine whether the case you rely upon is similar to the case she must decide. Answer the judge's questions, usually at the time she asks them. Do not ignore your opponent's arguments, or, if you are arguing first, the arguments you expect; briefly state your opponent's arguments and meet them head on.

Throughout, be polite but not obsequious. Usually, common sense arguments in plain English work the best. Make sure the judge knows what unfair impact will result if she rules against your client. End by again telling the judge precisely how you urge her to rule. (Judges are impatient when they do not know exactly what each side wants.)

D. THE HISTORICAL BACKGROUND OF CIVIL PROCEDURE

The next doctrine you will encounter in this course is Fed. R. Civ. P. 11, which has evolved through the years. We think it is important that you first get a sense of historical context to help you understand both the current procedural debates and the tensions that appear in most procedural systems. We hope that learning about the historical background of the Federal Rules, and the systems that preceded them, will help you make sense of the contradictions in, and problems confronting, current procedure. You will also be introduced to the Rules of Decision Act, Process and Conformity Acts, and the Enabling Act, all of which are critical to a thorough understanding of current procedural issues and debates. Early in the course you looked at procedural values, and now you can explore those same values in the historical context of actual people who, like you, had complex needs, ideologies and agendas that influenced their proposals and arguments.

1. Where Are We Heading?

Current American civil procedure is in a period of flux. Although we do not yet have sufficient perspective to be certain, it looks as if we are heading to, or are already in, a period of change as significant as that which took place after New York adopted a new procedural code in 1848 and the Federal Rules of Civil Procedure were adopted in 1938. You will be learning much of your civil procedure by reading and applying the Federal Rules of Civil Procedure. Those rules were based on a procedural philosophy that emphasized helping lawsuits get to their "merits," either through voluntary settlement or at a trial in open court. The ingredients of a good procedural system were thought to be procedural simplicity, uniformity of procedure from court to court and for all types of cases (called trans-substantive procedure), and flexible rules that give lawyers latitude to make choices and judges discretion to resolve disputes.

Judicial discretion is still emphasized; the other goals and principles have taken a severe beating, particularly since 1980. Consequently, you will be practicing under allegedly liberal procedural rules that in fact have become increasingly stringent and non-lawyer-friendly. Numerous indicia reflect this breakdown of the procedural order that dominated American law for fifty years. For example, review virtually any daily newspaper and observe the congressional hostility to lawyer-dominated civil litigation. When you get to the materials on discovery, in Chapter 4, you will find that the wide-open discovery of the original Federal Rules was constricted by amendments in 1980 (adding Rule 26(f) on discovery conferences) and in 1983 (amending Rule 26 and expanding the purposes of pretrial conference in Rule 16). In 1993, further amendments were made to the discovery rules, and still more reform appears on the horizon. Consequently, lawyers have less latitude in discovery, while the courts use a stronger hand. You will soon learn how Rule 11 was amended in 1983 specifically to curtail attorney freedom, bringing the Federal Rules a bit closer to the more restricted spirit of pleading under the nineteenth-century Field Code. Rule 11 was amended yet again in 1993, heading in a slightly different direction.

The idea of procedural uniformity from court to court has been eroded by the proliferation of local rules. *See* Fed. R. Civ. P. 83. The Local Rules Project of the Committee on Rules of Practice and Procedure of the Judicial Conference of the United States collected the local rules of all district courts, and reported in 1988:

> The ninety-four district courts currently have an aggregate of approximately 5,000 local rules, not including many "sub-rules," standing orders and standard operating procedures. These rules are extraordinarily diverse and their numbers continue to grow rapidly. To give one stark example, the Central District of California, based in Los Angeles, has about thirty-one local rules with 434 "sub-rules," supplemented by approximately 275 standing orders. At the other extreme, the Middle District of Georgia has only one local rule and just one standing order. These local rules cover the entire spectrum of federal practice, from attorney admission and discipline, through the various stages of trial, including pleading and filing requirements, pre-trial discovery procedures, and taxation of costs.

The Civil Justice Reform Act of 1990, P.L. 101-650, Title I, 28 U.S.C. §§471-482, virtually mandated procedural diversity from district court to district court, by obligating each district court to implement its own civil justice expense and delay reduction plan within three years after enactment of the legislation. A major purpose of the Act was to encourage courts to experiment with different types of case management systems and also to experiment with a variety of alternative dispute resolution (ADR) methods.

You have already learned something about the current unrest and instability in American civil procedure. Some federal courts of appeals have sanctioned even more stringent pleading for civil rights cases than one might anticipate by reading the federal pleading rules and their historical background. Congress also has attempted to curtail what are thought to be abuses inherent in the more open-textured federal procedural system, by passing the Private Securities Litigation Reform Act of 995 (PSLRA), Publ. 104-67, 109 Stat. 737 (1995). Written to address class-action lawsuits alleging fraud in the securities market, the PSLRA uses myriad procedural devices, including more stringent pleading requirements, to curtail what Congress has called "unmeritorious claims that were stifling free enterprise." New York Times, *Class-Action Lawsuits By Investors Are Not Turning Out Exactly As Congress Planned,* February 27, 1997, at D:8:3. For instance, in making a complaint, a plaintiff must specifically enumerate and explain each alleged misleading statement by a defendant. Further, the complaint must state with particularity facts giving rise to a strong inference that the defendant acted with the required state of mind.

The ongoing amendments to Rule 11 provide another example of the struggle over how much factual and legal information and certainty a lawyer and client should have prior to commencing suit. Once again, civil rights litigation provides an important battlefield, for the greater investigation and detail (and thus the cost) required in advance, the less likely a typical civil rights plaintiff and her lawyers will be willing or able to commence suit.

These examples reveal two conflicting themes that seem to prevail in each period of Anglo-American civil procedure. First, procedure is looked at as a formal means of containing civil disputes. Procedural law is seen as a means, along with substantive law, of reducing the number of variables that the decision maker will consider. It is also seen as a means of providing definition, focus, and constraints of time. Some would say that the very purpose of law is to provide such formalized definition and restraint. Justice Harlan put it this way in *Boddie v. Connecticut,* 401 U.S. 371, 374 (1971):

> Perhaps no characteristic of an organized and cohesive society is more fundamental than its erection and enforcement of a system of rules defining the various rights and duties of its members, enabling them to govern their affairs and definitively settle their differences in an orderly predictable manner. Without such a "legal system," social organization and cohesion are virtually impossible. . . . Put more succinctly, it is this injection of the rule of law that allows society to reap the benefits of rejecting what political theorists call "the state of nature."

The second theme is that human situations and particularly human disputes do not easily lend themselves to rigidity and formalism. The story, what many now call the "narrative," inevitably seeps beyond the narrowness of causes of actions and their elements. Indeed, it may be impossible to understand a claim without knowing the full story that gives rise to it; one meaning of "claim" under the federal rules is the entirety of a transaction or occurrence, and you will find out later in the course that principles of *res judicata* and preclusion law track this understanding. Professor James White, a professor of both law and English at the University of Michigan, has argued that the discipline of law is not unique in its inability to reduce life's circumstances to a selected set of variables captured in words that mean exactly what they say. *See* James B. White, *The Legal Imagination: Studies in the Nature of Legal Thought* (1973). Lawyers, like poets, novelists, and historians, are inevitably telling a story larger than the precise meaning of words. Trial lawyers know that the art of persuasion is in large measure the art of creating and telling stories. As you will soon see, this tension between the story confined by substantive law and procedure, and the need to tell larger stories, is played out in some measure in the history of the different procedures of law courts and equity courts dating back to the middle ages.

The formalism/narrative tension does not take place in a human vacuum. As you saw from your first case in this civil procedure book, issues of power underlie many of the most perplexing questions of civil procedure. This is not a recent phenomenon. As you read about the use of jury in the common law courts, it is important to realize that by establishing the jury in common law courts, the King sought to gain the loyalty of the citizens of England. And by requiring that land disputes be resolved in his courts, rather than in those of barons or the county, the King sought to centralize his emerging nation and bring power to himself. The emerging power of the entrepreneurial class and the desire of lawyers to earn a better living (an issue of professional power) were important factors in the mid-nineteenth-century American procedural reform called the "Field Code."

As you read the following materials on equity and the common law, the Field Code, and the Federal Rules, bear in mind these themes of the formalism/narrative tension and how the quest for power influenced civil procedure in the past; surely, both themes will influence current and future reform movements as well. As you proceed through the various stages of litigation in this course and you consider the choices that former and current procedural reformers have made, and continue to make, the theme of formalism in tension with narrative, and the theme of power (with its own tensions: judge and jury; client and lawyer; lawyer and judge; judiciary and legislature) should provide lenses through which you can begin to understand what was and is at stake at both conceptual and political levels. And, of course, the formalism/narrative and power themes are themselves related. Formal procedural rules are often an attempt to confine power, just as narrative may be a means of broadening discretion or democratizing the procedural system.

2. The Common Law and Equity*

"Common law" has several meanings. It describes the English system of judge-made law, as opposed to the Continental system (such as in France and Germany) contained primarily in Codes. "Common law" is also used in the United States to distinguish law developed through judicial opinions from that enacted by legislative statutes. In addition, it is used to describe one of the two sets of courts in which formal litigation took place in England at least as early as the thirteenth century. On one hand, there were the three central law courts, King's Bench, Exchequer, and Common Pleas, which used "common law" procedures. On the other, there was the Chancery or equity court, which had its own procedures.

The law courts and equity court each had its own distinct procedural system, jurisprudence, and outlook; it is difficult to understand the development of American procedure without considering the differences.

Common Law Procedure

The law courts had three major characteristics: the writs, single-issue pleading, and the jury. Ironically, the writ system developed in Chancery, which later housed the equity court. As early as the thirteenth century, subjects of the King would bring grievances to the Chancellor, who served as the King's secretary, adviser, and agent. The Chancellor's staff sold writs, royal orders that authorized a court to hear a case and instructed a sheriff to secure the defendant's attendance. Over time, the writs became organized into categories of often-used complaints. They became formalized, so that a plaintiff could not get into court without fitting into a specific category, such as trespass, replevin, or covenant. Each writ implied a range of procedural, remedial, and evidentiary incidents, such as subject matter and personal jurisdiction, burden of proof, and method of execution. Writs began to connote what events would permit what remedy; a body of substantive law ultimately evolved.

Accompanying the writ system was a process that we would call "single-issue pleading." At an earlier time, pleading designed to reduce cases to a single issue took place orally before a judge in London. Later, this developed into exchanges of documents. A defendant could plead

---

*Stephen N. Subrin has described the development of nineteenth- and twentieth-century civil procedure in the United States, and the antecedents to that procedure in England, in two articles: Stephen N. Subrin, *How Equity Conquered Common Law: The Federal Rules of Civil Procedure in Historical Perspective,* 135 U. Pa. L. Rev. 909 (1987), and Stephen N. Subrin, *David Dudley Field and the Field Code: An Historical Analysis of an Earlier Procedural Vision,* 6 L. & Hist. Rev. 311 (1988). Much of the history contained in the following pages borrows from those articles.

jurisdictional defenses, demur to test a legal question, or traverse to raise a factual dispute. Alternatively, the defendant could plead a "confession and avoidance," today's affirmative defense. Unless a jurisdictional plea was granted, the parties pleaded back and forth until one side either demurred, resulting in a legal issue, or traversed, requiring the resolution of a factual dispute.

A factual dispute would be brought to a jury. The jury replaced earlier common law trial methods by which the parties were tested before God through ordeal, battle, or the swearing of neighbors ("compurgators") that they believed the parties. Like the writ system and single-issue pleading, the jury evolved as an attempt to make the resolution of human disputes more rational and predictable. Because human beings, instead of God, were to hear and decide cases, it became advantageous for parties to present facts that could change the minds of the now-human dispute resolvers.

The technicality and rigidity of the common law writ and single-issue system drew ridicule. To be called a "special pleader" was an insult. But given the complexity of many lawsuits today, with so many legal issues and so much discovery, one can perhaps sympathize with our procedural ancestors' attempts to reduce and focus cases, achieve a degree of predictability, and, through the writ system, use defined procedures to integrate the ends sought and means used. Moreover, today one can perhaps appreciate the historical development of the lay jury, for most current citizens have few opportunities other than jury service to partake in government.

Equity Procedure

By the early sixteenth century it was apparent that the common law system was accompanied by a substantially different one called equity, probably based on the historic power of the Chancellor to fashion new writs. The formulary writ system's defined cubbyholes did not readily allow for individual assistance in unusual and unfair circumstances, such as a contract based on mistake or fraud, or a beneficiary's being deprived of the benefits of property where title was in the name of another. Bills in equity were written to persuade the Chancellor to relieve the petitioner from an alleged injustice that would result from the rigorous application of the common law. One could turn to equity only if there was no adequate remedy at law.

The equity court and its procedure were distinguishable from that of the common law courts in several ways. The bill in equity permitted, and often required, the joinder of multiple parties. While in the law courts the self-interest of the parties was thought too great to permit them to testify, the Chancellor in equity compelled the defendant personally to come before him to answer under oath each sentence of the petitioner's bill. As a precursor to modern pretrial discovery, a petitioner in equity could attach interrogatories to the petition, requiring answers from the defendant. The Chancellor did not take testimony in open court, but relied on documents to decide a case. The Chancellor, not juries, decided equity cases. The Chancellor was able to fashion injunctive relief, such as compelling a defendant to give the use and profit of a property to a beneficiary, rather than being limited to awarding a specific amount of damages, as in common law courts. Finally, a Chancellor was less bound by the rigidity of the common law writ and pleading system, and could exercise more discretion in an attempt to do justice in the particular case.

The Common Law Mentality in Pre-Twentieth-Century America

Just as the common law system provoked ridicule for injustice through technicality, the equity system brought complaints arising from the burdens of too many parties, issues, and papers. Many colonists in the new world brought with them a deep distrust of the royal Chancellor, who for them symbolized the unjust King. To them equity represented uncontrolled discretion, arbitrariness, and needless delay and expense. *Jarndyce v. Jarndyce* in Charles Dickens' *Bleak House* comes to mind.

Some of the earliest colonial courts had jurisdiction over disputes and lawmaking functions that in England would have fallen to several different courts and even to legislators. From 1680 to 1820, there was a gradual movement from the relatively unstructured, nontechnical procedural systems of the early colonists to a greater reliance on common law forms and procedures. Pleadings were usually limited to a few simple steps; joinder was restricted; and only a single form of action was allowed. Ironically, after the Revolution brought victory over the British, many states more formally followed the British system not only in pleading requirements, but in establishing separate equity courts or permitting common law judges to hear equity cases and grant equitable remedies.

Through the entire colonial period, great confidence was reposed in juries. Upon attaining statehood, each of the thirteen original colonies, as well as the federal government, provided citizens with the right to a jury trial in both criminal and civil cases. The jury was viewed as a means of permitting laymen to partake in governing themselves, educating the citizenry, and controlling the discretion and possible arbitrariness of judges. But by the beginning of the nineteenth century, American judges had begun to fashion ways for constricting and controlling the role of juries. Over time, many lawyers and judges began to view the jury as a cumbersome and unreliable mode of dispute resolution, rather than as an integral part of democratic government.

Comments and Questions

1. This may be a good occasion for you to browse through the historical section of the law library. There exist several fine descriptions of the historic English bifurcated common law—equity system. The two courses of lectures of Frederick W. Maitland, *Equity and The Forms of Action at Common Law* (1913) and Stroud Francis Charles Milsom, *Historical Foundation of the Common Law* (1969) deserve special mention. The latter requires careful reading and re-reading. An easier and more comprehensive single volume is T. Plucknett, *A Concise History of the Common Law* 139-156 (5th ed. 1956). Two well-regarded multivolume histories of the law in England are William S. Holdsworth, *A History of the Common Law* (2d ed. 1937) and Frederick Pollock and Frederick W. Maitland, *History of English Law* (2d ed. 1905). For copies of common law documents (such as writs), see a set of volumes published through the years by the Selden Society. Perhaps the most engaging way to learn about the Chancery Court in England, however, is to read *Bleak House* (1853), a classic by Charles Dickens. (Do you see how the formalism/narrative tension exists even in our assignments?)

2. The most cited, if not the best, single-volume history of American law is the extremely readable *A History of American Law*, by Lawrence M. Friedman (2d ed. 1985). This is available in paperback. A useful single volume on early American law is the compilation of essays reprinted in *Essays in the History of Early American Law* (David H. Flaherty, ed. 1969). On the colonial experience, and the early faith in juries, William Nelson, *Americanization of the Common Law* (1975) is extremely useful. Morton J. Horwitz, *The Transformation of American Law 1780-1860* (1977), and Morton J. Horwitz, *The Transformation of American Law, 1870-1960: The Crisis of Legal Orthodoxy* (1993), invite one to think about the socio-economic agendas of those who developed American law. For a light and very entertaining account of the evolution of American civil procedure, *see* Charles Rembar, *The Law of the Land: The Evolution of Our Legal System* (1980). It is available in paperback and will also provide context for other first-year courses.

3. Consider this paragraph from Frederick W. Maitland, *Selected Essays* 19 (H.D. Hazeltine et al. eds. 1936):

> We ought not to think of common law and equity as of two rival systems. Equity was not a self-sufficient system, at every point it presupposed the existence of common law. Common law was a self-sufficient system. I mean this: that if the legislature had passed a short act saying "Equity is hereby abolished," we might still have got on fairly well; in some respects our law would have been barbarous, unjust, absurd, but still the great elementary rights, the right to immunity from violence, the right to one's good name, the rights of ownership and of possession would have been decently protected and contract would have been enforced. On the other hand had the legislature said, "Common Law is hereby abolished," this decree if obeyed would have meant anarchy. At every point equity presupposed the existence of

common law. Take the case of the trust. It's of no use for Equity to say that A is a trustee of Blackacre for B, unless there by some court that can say that A is the owner of Blackacre. Equity without common law would have been a castle in the air, an impossibility.

What is Maitland talking about? Could you explain to another person why he found equity standing alone "anarchy" or "a castle in the air"? Maitland is apparently talking about equity as a repository of substantive law. Would his insight retain force with respect to procedural law?

Maitland sees common law and equity as complementary. In terms of procedure, how do common law and equity perspectives relate to each other? What are the advantages and disadvantages of each?

3. David Dudley Field and the Field Code: The Multiple Agendas of Procedural Reformers

During the first half of the nineteenth century, objections developed to the common law-equity system that the United States had inherited from the English. In 1846, a new constitution in New York eliminated the chancery court and created a court "having general jurisdiction in law and equity." It also provided for the legislature to appoint a commission of three members to "revise, reform, simplify, and abridge the rules of practice, pleading, forms, and proceeding of the courts of record of this state, and to report thereon to the legislature." This commission became known as the Practice Commission.

David Dudley Field (1805-1894) was an enormously talented and successful trial lawyer in New York City who participated in some of the most important litigation of his day. For instance, he represented Jim Fisk and Jay Gould in their struggle for control of the Erie Railroad and also represented Boss Tweed. Later in his career, in unpublished notes for an autobiography he contemplated writing, he concluded, probably accurately: "My practice was the largest and my income from it the most that any lawyer had at the New York Bar, and probably at any Bar in the country." His firm, Field and Shearman, later became the prestigious firm of Shearman and Sterling.

Although not among the original members of the Practice Commission, Field was appointed to replace an original member in 1847 and became the most dominant and well known commissioner. The New York procedural code, adopted in that state in 1848, became known as the Field Code. It eventually was adopted in twenty-seven states, including such populous states as California and Ohio. As of 1890, 38,000,000 Americans out of 63,000,000 (60 percent of the population) lived in Field Code States. Field also wrote codes for almost all substantive law, but those codes were not adopted in New York nor in many other states.

The Field Code eliminated the forms of action and, for the most part, provided the same procedure for all types of cases. It reduced the number of pleadings to the complaint, answer, reply, and demurrer, and discarded the stylized search for a single issue. It required that complaints contain: "A statement of the facts constituting the cause of action in ordinary and concise language, without repetition, and in such a manner as to enable a person of common understanding to know what is intended." (N.Y. Laws 1848, c. 379, §120 (2)). In 1851, this was amended to read: "A plain and concise statement of the facts constituting a cause of action without unnecessary repetition." (N.Y. Laws 1851, c. 479, §1.)

The Code liberalized a party's ability to amend pleadings and to enter evidence at variance with a pleading. It expanded — but not to the same degree as the Federal Rules later would — the number of potential parties, causes of action, and defenses that could be joined in one suit. The Field Code eliminated equitable bills of discovery and interrogatories, but provided for limited discovery through requests to inspect and copy "a paper" in the other's possession or control "relating to the merits of the action, or the defense therein" (§342), and for limited requests to admit the genuineness of writings (§341). The Code permitted oral depositions of the opposing party. But unlike the Federal Rules, the Code deposition was in lieu of calling the adverse party at the trial; the deposition was before a judge, who would rule on evidence objections (§345). The Code permitted the court to grant the plaintiff "any relief consistent with the case made by the complaint, and embraced within the issue" (§231).

Procedural reform has recurrent themes. To understand this better, try to isolate the rationale of the Field Code reformers and compare it to the reform purposes behind the Federal Rules of Civil Procedure as well as those undercurrents of present-day reform efforts. The following are portions of an essay on procedural reform written by David Dudley Field on January 1, 1847.

■ DAVID DUDLEY FIELD, WHAT SHALL BE DONE WITH THE PRACTICE OF THE COURTS? SPEECHES, ARGUMENTS AND MISCELLANEOUS PAPERS OF DAVID DUDLEY FIELD
226-260 (A. P. Sprague, ed. 1884)

The Constitution of this State, which goes into effect today, will render great changes necessary in our system of legal procedure. It remodels our Courts; unites the administration of law and equity in the same tribunal; directs testimony to be taken in like manner in both classes of cases; abolishes the offices of Master and Examiner in Chancery, hitherto important parts of our equity system; and, finally, directs that the next

Legislature shall provide for the appointment of three commissioners, "whose duty it shall be to revise, reform, simplify, and abridge the rules and practice, pleadings, forms, and proceedings of the courts of record," and report thereon to the Legislature for its action. . . .

What I propose . . . in respect to cases of legal cognizance, is this: that the present forms of action be abolished, and in their stead a complaint and answer required, each setting forth the real claim and defense of the parties. Such pleadings would be precisely similar to those proposed for equity cases, *and we should thus have a uniform course of pleading for all cases, legal and equitable.* The distinction between the two classes of cases is now merely a distinction in the forms of proceeding. . . .

Let the plaintiff set forth his cause of action in his complaint briefly, in ordinary language, and without repetition; and let the defendant make his answer in the same way. Let each party verify his allegation by making oath that he believes it to be true. The complaint will then acquaint the defendant with the real charge, while the answer will inform the plaintiff of the real defense. The disputed facts will be sifted from the undisputed, and the parties will go to trial knowing what they have to answer. The plaintiff will state his case as he believes it, and as he expects to prove it. The defendant, on his part, will set forth what he believes and expects to establish, and he need set forth no more. He will not be likely to aver what he does not believe. His answer will disclose the whole of his defense, because he will not be allowed to prove anything which the answer does not contain. He will not be perplexed with questions of double pleading, nor shackled by ancient technical rules. . . .

The most ample power of amendment should likewise be given to the Courts. . . .

The legitimate end of every administration of law is to do justice, with the least possible delay and expense. Every system of pleading is useful only as it tends to this end. This it can do but in one of two ways: *either by enabling the parties the better to prepare for trial, or by assisting the jury and the court in judging the cause.* Let us consider it, then, in these two aspects:

First, as it enables the parties to prepare for trial. This it can only do by informing them of each other's case. To make them settle beforehand wherein they disagree, so as to enable them to dispense with unnecessary proofs, and to be prepared with those which are necessary, is the legitimate end of pleadings, so far as the parties are concerned. Now, no system could accomplish this more effectually than the one proposed. The plaintiff's whole case is stated in his complaint, the defendant's whole case in his answer; and nothing beyond what is contained in one of these is to be received in evidence, except, perhaps, such rebutting proof as may have been specified in written points, filed a certain number of days before the trial. . . .

Second, as it assists the jury and the Court in performing their functions. An opinion prevails that nothing but common-law issues are fit for a jury.

Many lawyers are wedded to the system of pleading according to the ancient rules, though they admit and deplore the imperfections of our present practice. It is said that the production of the issue disentangles the case, lessens the number of questions of fact, and separates them from the questions of law.

Now, I deny, in the first place, that the production of an issue, according to the course of the common law, does really lessen the number of questions of fact. The declaration may contain any number of counts, each setting forth different causes of action, or the same cause of action in different forms. If the same plea is put into all the counts, there will be as many issues as there are counts. But the defendant may plead as many pleas to each count as he likes; and the plaintiff, with leave of the Court, may put in as many replications to each plea as he may happen to have answers to it. Suppose, now, a declaration containing five counts—no uncommon thing—three pleas to each count, and a single replication to each plea. Here are fifteen issues; and, if there be two replications to each plea, there will be thirty. . . .

The attempt to reduce questions to all their elements before trial, must commonly fail. What subordinate ones may arise can scarcely be known till the evidence is all disclosed. The greatest diligence and skill will lead only to an approximation, greater or less according to the nature of the original questions. The first one is always this: Has the plaintiff the right, or the defendant? This depends upon others. You may go on, if you please, to reduce them as far as possible, but you will scarcely ever reach the elementary ones till the cause is brought to trial, and the evidence produced. Then, by a strict analysis, they are rapidly sifted; and the cause turns at last upon two or three. . . .

Comments and Questions

1. Common law procedure emphasized pleading. What stage of the litigation was most important to Field?

2. Most procedural reformers tend to ignore potential problems in their own proposals; consequently, most procedural reform gives way to later reform. What miscalculations, if any, do you think Field made?

3. The Field siblings may rank with the Adams and James families among the most productive and important in the early history of our country: Henry was the editor of a Presbyterian newspaper for forty-four years; Jonathan was a leader in the Massachusetts legislature; Matthew built the longest suspension bridge of his time; Cyrus laid the first transatlantic cable; and Stephen became a United States Supreme Court justice. Not many women were allowed to progress in the legal profession (or any other) at the time, but Field's only sister,

Emelia, gave birth to David Brewer, who joined his uncle on the Supreme Court.

4. Usually, sound procedural reasons support procedural reform. But procedural reform has many faces. Field and his reforms had several progressive elements. He wanted litigation to be less costly and more efficient, and strove to make law understandable and accessible to ordinary people. He fervently believed in equality of opportunity. One law professor summarized the progressive elements in Field and his work, concluding that Field had worked for "scientific law reform, international peace, feminism, and abolition of slavery."* But at the same time, there were several less liberal aspects undergirding Field's reforms.† At a time of mounting complaints about the technicality of law and a movement to eliminate the legal profession, Field stressed the need of well-trained legal experts both to represent clients and to "reform" the law. His reforms eliminated state regulation of lawyer's litigation fees and permitted Field and his extremely wealthy clients to make their own fee arrangements. At a time when a farmers' rebellion in the state of New York questioned the entire socio-economic fabric of the country, Field emphasized a need to reform the judicial system and civil procedure. He wanted a well-defined substantive and procedural law that would both tie the hands of judges and permit clients to act freely, except where the law specifically prohibited such activity.

5. The American Law Institute has a project on Transnational Rules of Civil Procedure. In the Preface to the April 1, 1999 Discussion Draft, the Reporters, Michele Taruffo and Geoffrey C. Hazard, Jr. (self-described as "one of whom has a European civil-law background and the other a North American common-law background") explain that "[t]he basic pattern in the Discussion Draft is approximately that of civil procedure in the Commonwealth countries, particularly England (and Wales), Canada, and Australia. . . . The U.S. system is unique among common-law systems in having broad discovery and jury trial and the more so in having the combination of these procedures." American Law Institute, *Transnational Rules of Civil Procedure, Discussion Draft* (April 1, 1999), Preface (March 26, 1999, xi-xiii). The scope of the proposed Transnational Civil Rules "is now conceived in terms of 'business disputes.'" *Id.*, at xii. David Dudley Field's influence continues in the Draft's pleading requirements: "8. Statements of Claim (a) The plaintiff shall state the facts on which the claim is based, the legal grounds that support the claim, and the basis upon which the

---

*Peggy A. Rabkin, *The Origins of Law Reform: The Social Significance of the Nineteenth Century Codification Movement and Its Early Contribution to the Passage of the Early Married Women's Property Acts,* 24 Buffalo L. Rev. 683, 714 (1974).

†For a fuller exploration of the conservative aspects of Field's philosophy and reform efforts, see Stephen N. Subrin, *David Dudley Field and the Field Code: A Historical Analysis of an Earlier Procedural Vision,* 6 L. and Hist. Rev. 311, 319-327 (1988) (Subrin defends aspects of Field's procedural philosophy at 328-345).

claim is brought under these Rules. The statement of facts shall, so far as reasonably practicable, set forth detail as to time, place, participants, and events. . . ." *Id.* at 56. The Reporters explain that the "Rule calls for particularity of statement, such as that required in most civil-law and most common-law jurisdictions and traditionally required in American 'code pleading.' In contrast, some American systems, notably those employing the Federal Rules of Civil Procedure, permit very general allegations. . . ." Comment, 8.1, *id.* at 57.

4. The Historical Background of the Federal Rules of Civil Procedure

The Rules of Decision Act, Process and Conformity Acts, and the Enabling Act

A major decision to be made in a federal system is what law should apply in the state and federal courts. In 1789, the same year as the first presidential election, the Federal Judiciary Act provided for the establishment of the Supreme Court, as well as thirteen district and three circuit courts. Section 34 of the Judiciary Act of 1789 provided "that the laws of the several states, except where the constitution, treaties, or statutes of the United States shall otherwise require or provide, shall be regarded as the rules of decision in trials at common law in the courts of the United States in cases where they apply." This section became known as the "Rules of Decision Act" and is now found, in slightly different form, in 28 U.S.C. §1652. The exception clause in the Rules of Decision Act tracks the Supremacy Clause in Article VI of the Constitution.

It was unclear whether the Rules of Decision section of the Judiciary Act of 1789 covered procedural law, but the Process Act of the same year supplied the same basic formula: apply state law in federal court, unless a federal law provides otherwise. Act of Sept. 29, 1789, ch. 21, §2, 1 Stat. 93 (Process Act). Subsequent process and conformity acts repeated the pattern of requiring federal trial courts, for the most part, to apply the procedure of the state in which the federal court sat. Therefore, absent applicable federal law, state substantive and procedural law applied in both state and federal courts.

Until 1872, the Conformity Acts were what have been called "static conformity acts," for they required the federal courts to apply the state procedural law in existence at the time the federal act was passed. It was thought to be unwise, if not unconstitutional, to permit the states to effectively pass laws that would become federal laws of procedure. The problem was thought to be mitigated if Congress could look at the procedure of the states at the time of any one conformity act, and then vote to conform the federal procedure to the state procedure in a static way as of that date.

By 1872, it was clear that the static conformity acts presented some severe problems for practitioners. Most lawyers were applying procedural provisions similar to the Field Code in their state courts, but were required to apply previous common law procedures in federal court, because static conformity required the federal court to apply the state procedural law as of the time the federal conformity act was passed. In the Conformity Act of 1872, Congress moved to what is called "dynamic conformity," requiring federal courts, for the most part, to apply the same procedural law of the state that the state courts would then apply, thus keeping the federal courts up to date — in a dynamic way — with the then current state procedures.

Yet for several practical reasons, lawyers in federal court in their own state could not just apply the state procedural law with which they were familiar. The Conformity Act of 1872 provided that the federal trial judges should conform the federal procedure to state procedure "as near as may be." Federal judges used this language to apply some federal procedures that they favored, such as rules permitting them to supervise, if not control, juries through instructions and the granting of new trial motions. The Conformity Act (along with the Supremacy Clause and the exception clause of the Rules of Decision Act) also obligated federal trial judges to apply any specific procedural laws that Congress had passed for the federal courts.

The potential for state-federal court procedural uniformity was further eroded by equity practice in the federal courts. In 1789, when the first process act was passed, equity jurisdiction, jurisprudence, and procedure either did not exist or were underdeveloped in many state courts. Therefore, in some states, there would be little or no distinct equity law to conform to. The solution in the succession of process and conformity acts was to have federal courts apply historic equity law, and not state law, in equity cases. The Supreme Court adopted specific procedural rules for equity cases to be applied in the federal trial courts. The Supreme Court adopted the Federal Equity Rules of 1912, which became effective in 1913, to replace the outdated Equity Rules of 1842, which had been drafted to operate in the context of historic equity practice. Drawing heavily upon simplified practice under the English Judicature Acts of 1873 and 1875, technical pleadings and demurrers were eliminated, and the right to amend was liberalized. Although not unanimous, the opinion of most contemporaneous commentators was that the Equity Rules of 1912 were simple and efficient, and greatly improved equity practice by appropriately freeing judges from procedural technicalities.

Many of those who argued for uniform federal rules to be applied in all federal district courts premised their position on the failure of the conformity acts to provide true procedural uniformity between state and federal courts, and on the efficacy of the Equity Rules of 1913 as a model for uniform federal rules of procedure. Proponents of uniform federal procedural rules further argued that once the Supreme Court had provided simple, flexible, uniform rules for the federal courts, the states would follow suit, thus finally achieving the conformity of state and federal practice that had failed to be accomplished under the series of process and conformity acts.

Starting in 1911, the American Bar Association (ABA), at the urging of a Virginia lawyer, Thomas Wall Shelton, lobbied in Congress for a bill that would enable the Supreme Court to promulgate uniform procedural rules for all district courts—an "Enabling Act." Many of the arguments were based on the often cited, and little read, 1906 address of Roscoe Pound, then Dean of the Nebraska College of Law School, to the annual meeting of the ABA. In his historic address on *The Causes of Popular Dissatisfaction with the Administration of Justice,* 29 A.B.A. Rep. 395, 409-413 (1906), Pound—in addressing the topic suggested by the title of his speech—argued that the public was mistaken in its criticisms of the judiciary. The problem was not the power of judges under our constitutional system to hold legislative enactments unconstitutional, nor was it that judges were inevitably thrown into political controversy as a result of our tripartite government. According to Pound, much of the real fault was procedure, particularly "contentious procedure," and the "sporting theory of justice" whereby lawyers took advantage of procedural technicalities that stood in the way of justice. During the decade starting in 1905, he argued that it was the formalism of the common law writ system (which in his view survived the Field Code) and its rigid and inflexible procedural steps that hindered the just application of substantive law and the adjustment of law to modern circumstances. Pound complained that American judges were unduly hemmed in by procedural rules designed to control them and handicapped by their role as umpires who could not "search independently for truth and justice."

Pound turned to equity as a model for expanded judicial discretion and for more liberal principles of pleading and joinder in order to meet the needs of modern jurisprudence. In this argument, he was later joined by Charles E. Clark, a professor and later dean at the Yale Law School. In 1935, Clark became the Reporter (the chief drafter) to the Advisory Committee appointed by the Supreme Court to draft the initial Federal Rules. He consistently turned to equity as the model for modern procedure.

Pound and Clark stressed the waste of time and the injustices that were perpetrated by having two types of jurisdiction—law and equity—in federal courts and in some state systems. Some litigants were thrown out of court because they mistakenly chose law or equity, and the statute of limitations had then run. Clark and other proponents complained at how complicated and lengthy the Field Code had become because of unsound legislative amendments. They complained that judges had made the Field Code too technical by insisting on precision in "fact" pleading, by narrowing the potential joinder of parties, and by allowing plaintiffs only a single theory of recovery in any one case.

Between 1912 and 1932, the ABA succeeded in creating a bill for an Enabling Act to authorize the Supreme Court to draft uniform federal rules proposed in almost every session of Congress. President and later Chief Justice William Howard Taft, presidential candidate and later Chief Justice Charles Evan Hughes, virtually every luminary in the American Bar Association, and legions of local bar leaders and law school scholars supported the ABA effort. But for twenty years the bill was usually held up in the Senate Judiciary Committee, and on one occasion killed on the floor, because of the determined opposition of Senator Thomas Walsh. Walsh was a Montana Progressive Democrat who was first elected to the Senate in 1912, at the same time Woodrow Wilson was elected President. Walsh was a brilliant constitutional and trial lawyer, who argued and wrote passionately for the confirmation of Louis D. Brandeis to the Supreme Court, for judicial recall, against judicial control of juries, and for enhancing jury power in labor disputes.

Walsh had many objections to proposals for an Enabling Act that would empower the Supreme Court to promulgate uniform federal procedural rules.* A trip to England and its courts had convinced him that legal culture was considerably more influential than procedural rules on the professional conduct of lawyers. He thought, based on his own experience as a trial lawyer in Montana, that the Conformity Act rarely caused procedural uncertainty and that the Field Code, which had been adopted in his state, worked well. He argued that uniform federal rules, as opposed to conforming to state practice, would prejudice the vast majority of lawyers because, although they knew their state procedure, they rarely appeared in federal court. Walsh thought that Supreme Court members, far removed from the trial of cases, were ill-adapted for what he saw as the legislative function of procedural rule making. Finally, he urged that equity rules, which he correctly assumed would form the basis for new uniform federal rules, were complex in practice and would not lead to uniformity and simplicity as the Enabling Act proponents contended. Walsh's death on the way to President Franklin Roosevelt's inauguration in 1933, after which Walsh was to have been sworn in as Attorney General, removed the major opponent to uniform federal procedural rules.

The Enabling Act and the Drafting of the Federal Rules of Civil Procedure

In 1932, the ABA gave up trying to get Congress to pass an Enabling Act. Homer Cummings, Franklin Roosevelt's first Attorney General, was perfectly typecast to resubmit the Enabling Act to Congress in 1934, after

---

*For a more detailed description of Walsh's opposition to the Enabling Act, see Stephen N. Subrin, *How Equity Conquered Common Law: The Federal Rules of Civil Procedure in Historical Perspective*, 135 U. Pa. L. Rev. 909, 996-998 (1987).

conservatives had failed to accomplish its passage for twenty years. This Democratic liberal spokesperson was, like Taft and Hughes, familiar with big cases and with clients that were major banks, corporations, and utilities. When he sponsored the Act in 1934, he echoed the themes already developed by Pound and Clark: now was the time for lawyers to give up their technical rules and to aid the government in drafting and implementing new legislation to solve national problems.

In 1934, the Enabling Act was passed with only modest resistance. It is now found in 28 U.S.C. §2072. At first, the Supreme Court seemed reluctant to centralize the drafting of uniform federal rules or to take advantage of a provision in the Enabling Act that permitted the Court to merge law and equity procedure. During the first six months of 1935, Clark lobbied vigorously and effectively to have the Supreme Court exercise its authority under the Enabling Act to adopt the same procedural rules for both law and equity cases, to have those rules patterned on equity practice (particularly on the Federal Equity Rules of 1913), and to have a centralized drafting committee of experts to accomplish these aims. Later in 1935, the Supreme Court appointed a fourteen-person committee "to Draft Unified System of Equity and Law Rules," which became known as the Advisory Committee. 295 U.S. 774 (1935).

The composition of the Advisory Committee reflected both the political conservatives and the academic liberals who had joined in supporting uniform federal rules. Clark, Professor Edson Sunderland of the University of Michigan Law School (who was primarily responsible for drafting the liberal discovery provisions), Professor Edmund Morgan of Harvard Law School, the Dean of the University of Virginia Law School, and a Professor of Law at the University of Minnesota were joined by nine lawyers, most of whom were in large firm practice or were active participants in the ABA, and, in most cases, both. The chairman of the committee, William D. Mitchell, had been Solicitor General under President Coolidge and Attorney General under President Hoover before setting up his partnership in New York. The firms with partners on the committee, such as Cadwalader, Wickersham & Taft in New York City and Palmer, Dodge, Gardner & Bradford in Boston, represented leading banks, insurance companies, industries, railroads, and utilities in their communities throughout the country. Nevertheless, the original Federal Rules drafted by the Advisory Committee appear to have been conducive to the needs of plaintiffs, to the activism of liberal federal judges, and to the creation of new rights that have helped minorities, the poor, and the underrepresented, along with other citizens.

During the drafting process, the Pound-Clark equity-based vision prevailed, as you will see throughout the remainder of this course. Perhaps the predominant theme was that procedure should be subordinate to and should not interfere with substance. The rules became law in 1938 by congressional inaction. A later comment will explain how amendments to the rules are accomplished today.

Comments and Questions

1. Before continuing, please have clear in your mind the major purpose and gist of the Rules of Decision Act, the Supremacy Clause, the Process and Conformity Acts, and the Enabling Act. These provisions recur throughout a civil procedure course. We will cover the precise provisions of the Enabling Act in more detail in the second half of the course, particularly when we cover *Erie* and *Hanna v. Plumer.*

2. The most comprehensive history of the Enabling Act is Stephen Burbank, *The Rules Enabling Act of 1934,* 130 U. Pa. L. Rev. 1015 (1982). This meticulously researched and reasoned article also provides in its footnotes exhaustive cites to historical material on the Process and Conformity Acts. For a thorough exploration of the early process acts and the Rules of Decision Act, *see* J. Goebel, *History of the Supreme Court of the United States: Antecedents and Beginnings to 1801* (1971).

3. Consider now the views of Clark on the Rules he drafted as Reporter.

■ CHARLES E. CLARK, COMMENTS
Proceedings of the Institute at Washington, D.C. on
the Federal Rules of Civil Procedure
(American Bar Association, Oct. 6, 1938), at 34-44

. . . I have the function here this afternoon of discussing particularly Rules 7 to 25, and I am glad to do that because in some ways these seem to me the quintessence of the whole system we are here planning. I think that if you follow the general plans and principles that we have in mind here you will agree with all the other rules. In fact, I might put it this way, that if you are likely to be shocked at all by the new rules I think that it probably is in this material that the shock will come. . . .

[T]here should be a considerable amount of flexibility permitted in the way in which lawyers present cases to the court. In fact, I think if there is one advance we have made it is that we realize there are more ways than one of telling a story, and so long as we get it out clearly and forcefully and simply to the court, the court ought not to try to tell the lawyers that they should have told the story in a different way. In other words, at the present time there are possibilities of various differences in statement, and that is going to be true under the new system just as before. Hence, if there are garrulous lawyers (and I am informed there are) they may still—probably with impunity—be garrulous in their pleadings. Therefore you have a good deal of opportunity of following your own previous plans and practices as before. After all, you are writing the story of your case for the court, and just as there should be a choice if you were writing any other type of essay—for, as I like to tell my class, the making of pleadings is one type of essay writing, a particular type, of course, where you should be above all else direct and forceful and see that you get your point over—so, since there is a choice here, you are entitled to make it.

But beyond that I would say this, that I think you will see at once these pleadings follow a general philosophy which is that detail, fine detail, in statement is not required and is in general not very helpful. . . .

I suggest that it is not the function of the pleadings to supply the place of evidence. It is not the function of the pleadings to give you admissions on the case except in a very broad way, except as to things that the parties or their counsel are perfectly ready to admit at any time, at the opening of the trial and so on. The function of the pleadings, as it now develops, is other than this. It is, in the first place, to distinguish the case from all others so that you can properly send it through the processes of the court, send it to the proper tribunals for trial, decide on such preliminary steps as may be necessary, the taking of depositions, reference to a Master, claim of jury trial, and so forth; in other words, to determine the proper routing of the case through the tribunal; and then secondly to serve as a basis for the binding force of the judgment, that is, for the application of the principle of *res adjudicata*.

For that purpose the more general pleadings are amply sufficient. Let me say that if any of you feel you need more information to develop your own case, if you need more information from your opponent, we have provided for that, and I think have provided for that much more directly and simply than ever you will obtain by attempting to force the correction of the pleadings. That is in the section on Deposition and Discovery. I think that is the device you should use to secure that information. Those rules will be explained to you tomorrow. . . .

In order to give you a concrete example of what I am talking about before I go to the separate rules, let us turn, if you will, to the appendix of forms. Let me say just a moment what those forms are intended to do. Those forms are not intended to be a desk manual so that whenever you have a case you won't have to do any thinking but simply say to your secretary, "Use official form No. So-and-so." That is not the purpose. The purpose is to illustrate the rules. These are the pictures that we hope will make the rules alive to you, and it seems to me if you look at the forms with that in mind you will get a great deal of the general philosophy which I am trying to state. . . . [Clark then used the Fed. R. Civ. P. Form 9 complaint for negligence as his example.]

Now I find that a great many lawyers feel, "Why, that is a very skinny statement. That is not the kind of thing to which we are accustomed." But I ask you, if you have in mind what I was suggesting before, that you are not looking for admissions or for something that will take the place of proof, if you are looking for a general statement which will send the case through the proper channels of the court and eventually provide for *res judicata*, how could you ask anything more? You have the case here differentiated from all the other situations giving rise to legal relations requiring court action. It is the case of the pedestrian-automobile accident. . . .

I think anyone who has had experience with the sort of case will know what to expect, and the addition of all those details will really add nothing to the real picture you have. . . .

Comments and Questions

1. How would you summarize Clark's procedural philosophy? Now would be a good time to look again at some rules you have already studied, such as Fed. R. Civ. P. 7(a), 7(c), 8(a), 8(e), and 12(b)(6). Consider the historical context in which the Advisory Committee was drafting.

2. Clark's procedural philosophy is manifest in his opinion in *Dioguardi v. Durning*, 139 F. 2d 774 (2d Cir. 1944), written during his tenure as a judge for the United States Court of Appeals. In *Dioguardi*, the plaintiff submitted an "obviously home drawn" complaint that alleged— in broken English—that the Collector of Customs at the Port of New York had stolen and converted two cases of Mr. Dioguardi's "medicinal extracts." The district court dismissed the complaint on the ground that it "[failed] to state sufficient facts to constitute a cause of action." Clark, writing for the court, reversed the dismissal. He emphasized the liberal nature of pleading allowed by Rule 8(a): "however inartistically they may be stated, the plaintiff has disclosed his claims. . . ." He then went on to chastise the lower court's ruling as "another instance of judicial haste which in the long run makes waste."

3. You were previously asked what misconceptions Field might have had in drafting his code. What about the proponents of the Enabling Act and its drafters, such as Clark?

4. How is it that Clark, who was appointed by President Roosevelt to be a judge on the illustrious Second Circuit Court in 1939, could have ended up agreeing basically with Pound, Taft, Shelton, and the A.B.A. leadership on procedural reform, and how did he end up in the opposite camp from Tom Walsh? After all, Clark and Walsh would have been considered political allies. Did the conservative and liberal supporters of the Enabling Act and the Federal Rules in fact have a great deal in common?

5. In the debate over the Enabling Act and in discussions surrounding the drafting of the Federal Rules, there was very little explicit talk about the fact that the rules (or procedural options within the rules) were the same for all cases (trans-substantive civil procedure). There was, of course, a good deal of discussion concerning the merger of law and

equity. How, then, did this procedural choice of trans-substantive rules come about? Was it inherent in the proponents' other assumptions about civil procedure?

6. Two related debates are now raging about the appropriate direction for civil procedure. One is whether current procedure is or should be non-trans-substantive. In other words, should some procedures be specifically developed for given types of cases? A related question is how much civil procedure knowingly favors some types of litigants or some types of cases, and to what extent this is purposeful. For a discussion of these issues on the occasion of the fiftieth anniversary of the Federal Rules of Civil Procedure, *see* Stephen N. Subrin, *Fireworks on the Fiftieth Anniversary of the Federal Rules of Civil Procedure*, 73 Judicature 4 (1989). *See also* 137 U. Pa. L. Rev. 1873-2257 (1989) (symposium issue).

7. The current procedural rule-making provisions are contained in 28 U.S.C. §§2071, 2072. Proposals for amendments to the Federal Rules of Civil Procedure are first considered and drafted in the Advisory Committee on Civil Rules and are then reviewed, with the power to change them, in the Standing Committee on Rules of Practice and Procedure. There are also Advisory Committees on Criminal, Bankruptcy, Evidence, and Appellate Rules. The Chief Justice appoints members to the Advisory Committees and the Standing Committee.

The Standing Committee proposes rules to the Judicial Conference of the United States, which in turn proposes rules to the Supreme Court. The Judicial Conference of the United States is defined in 28 U.S.C. §331. It begins:

> The Chief Justice of the United States shall summon annually the chief judge of each judicial circuit, the chief judge of the Court of International Trade and a district judge from each judicial circuit to a conference at such time and place in the United States as he may designate. He shall preside at such conference which shall be known as the Judicial Conference of the United States.

The Supreme Court decides what, if any, rules to present to Congress. In accordance with Title 28, §2072, "[s]uch rules shall not take effect until they have been reported to Congress by the Chief Justice at or after the beginning of a regular session thereof but not later than the first day of May, and until the expiration of ninety days after they have been thus reported." Congress has specifically refused to allow some amendments to become law by this method of inaction, and, although infrequently, have even passed their own rule. Given these exceptions, Federal Rules of Civil Procedure are not actually statutes, for they have not gone through the normal Congressional committee process, been voted on by both houses, nor signed by the President. Section 2072, however, does state that "all laws in conflict with such rules shall be of no further force or effect after such rules have taken effect."

E. SANCTIONS

You have now learned about the liberalizing aspects of the pleading rules, which were an important part of the 1938 Federal Rules of Civil Procedure. You have seen that in procedure, revolutions seem to bring counterrevolutions. Scholars, judges, and lawyers now question whether the Federal Rules make it too easy to commence litigation. In the face of allegations that frivolous litigation is facilitated, if not invited, by the ease of pleading under Fed. R. Civ. P. 8(a), some advocate a return to more fact-specific pleading requirements. Others question whether Fed. R. Civ. P. 11's sanctions effectively discourage lawyers from making ungrounded allegations in their complaints.

Since its inception in 1938, Fed. R. Civ. P. 11 has been substantively changed twice. The original Fed. R. Civ. P. 11 remained in effect from 1938 until 1983. The 1983 amendment used mandatory sanctions as a means of forcing lawyers to conduct adequate factual and legal investigations prior to commencing suit. Many thought that this change pitted judges against lawyers and lawyers against lawyers in undesirable ways. They felt that it overly chilled litigation, especially in the civil rights arena. Others thought the 1983 amendment worked well and achieved the goals for which it was passed. Although the 1993 amendment eased the stringency of the 1983 rule, the Supreme Court continues to think that Fed. R. Civ. P. 11 will deter frivolous litigation. Referring to Fed. R. Civ. P. 11 and 28 U.S.C. §1927, the Court has stated that "the availability of sanctions provides a significant deterrent to litigation directed at the president in his unofficial capacity for purposes of political gain or harassment." *Clinton v. Jones,* 117 S. Ct. 1636, 1651 (1997).

In the following pages, you will read about these amendments. Having read about the evolution of this one rule, think about which iteration of Rule 11 you would adopt for state practice.

Excerpts from the Fifth Circuit's 1988 opinion in *Thomas* explain the history of the background of the 1983 amendments to Rule 11 and how that court interpreted those amendments. *Thomas* was a Title VII class action, which the court remanded for more explicit findings as to whether there were any violations of Rule 11 and, if there were any such violations, for the mandatory imposition of sanctions.

■ THOMAS v. CAPITAL SECURITY SERVICES, INC.
836 F.2d 866 (5th Cir. 1988)

JOHNSON, Circuit Judge.

. . . A. AMENDED RULE 11

In recent years, Fed. R. Civ. P. 11 has generated extensive debate and controversy among legal scholars, jurists, and practitioners. Originally enacted in 1937, Rule 11, as amended in 1983, currently provides in pertinent part:

> Every pleading, motion, and other paper of a party represented by an attorney shall be signed by at least one attorney of record in the attorney's individual name, whose address shall be stated. . . . The signature of an attorney or party constitutes a certificate by the signer that the signer has read the pleading, motion, or other paper; that to the best of the signer's knowledge, information, and belief formed after reasonable inquiry it is well grounded in fact and is warranted by existing law or a good faith argument for the extension, modification, or reversal of existing law, and that it is not interposed for any improper purpose, such as to harass or to cause unnecessary delay or needless increase in the cost of litigation. . . . If a pleading, motion, or other paper is signed in violation of this rule, the court, upon motion or upon its own initiative, shall impose upon the person who signed it, a represented party, or both, an appropriate sanction, which may include an order to pay to the other party or parties the amount of the reasonable expenses incurred because of the filing of the pleading, motion, or other paper, including a reasonable attorney's fee.

Fed. R. Civ. P. 11 [1983].

Despite its laudable goals, Rule 11 was rarely applied before its amendment in 1983. Growing concern over misuse and abuse of the litigation process prompted rulemakers to amend Rule 11 in 1983 to reduce the reluctance of courts to impose sanctions by emphasizing the responsibilities of attorneys and reinforcing those obligations through the imposition of sanctions. Fed. R. Civ. P. 11 advisory committee notes. Former Rule 11 provided that an attorney's signature acted as a certificate by the attorney "that to the best of his knowledge, information, and belief there is good ground to support [the motion]," and the standard by which to assess attorney conduct for Rule 11 purposes was a subjective good faith standard, contemplating sanctions only when there was a showing of bad faith on the part of the attorney. Amended Rule 11 changed the rule by requiring that the attorney's certification must be formed "after reasonable inquiry," thereby defining a standard of reasonableness under the circumstances by which to measure attorney conduct.

In addition to the requirement of a reasonable prefiling inquiry, Judge Schwarzer, in his article *Sanctions Under the New Federal Rule 11—A Closer Look,* 104 F.R.D. 181 (1985), notes further changes effected by amended Rule 11 from its predecessor, including: (1) the rule now applies to all papers filed in court, not only pleadings; (2) the rule applies to persons appearing pro se as well as to attorneys and parties; (3) the rule specifies that papers filed must be well grounded in fact and warranted by existing law or by a good faith argument for the extension, modification or reversal of existing law; and (4) the rule specifies that papers may not be interposed for any improper purpose such as to harass or to cause unnecessary delay or needless increase in the cost of litigation. *Id.* at 184-85. One further important difference between former Rule 11 and Rule 11, as amended in 1983, is the latter's mandatory character, directing district courts to impose a sanction once a violation of Rule 11 has occurred. While the type of sanction imposed lies within the discretion of the district court, amended Rule 11 expressly authorizes an award of reasonable expenses, including attorney's fees, as an appropriate sanction. [In a footnote, the court added "In addition to Rule 11, several other statutory and procedural provisions exist whereby a court may deter litigation abuse. For instance, 28 U.S.C. §1927 permits a court to assess against an attorney who so multiplies the proceedings in any case unreasonably and vexatiously the excess costs, expenses, and attorney's fees incurred as a result of such conduct. Further, Fed. R. Civ. P. 37 provides generally for sanctions against parties or persons unjustifiably resisting discovery. In civil rights actions, a court, in its discretion, may award the prevailing party a reasonable attorney's fee as part of the costs pursuant to 42 U.S.C. §1988. Furthermore, as previously noted, Rules 16 and 26 deter abuse in litigation by providing procedures for effective judicial management of pretrial and discovery. Finally, under its inherent power, a district court may award to the prevailing party reasonable attorney's fees upon a showing that an attorney has acted in bad faith, vexatiously, wantonly, or for oppressive reasons. *Batson v. Neal Spelce Associates,* 805 F.2d 546, 550 (5th Cir. 1986). In addition to district courts, appellate courts may also impose sanctions in the form of single or double costs against an appellant who brings a frivolous appeal. Fed. R. App. P. 38. Tax courts also possess the power to deter abuse by imposing damages, not to exceed $5,000.00, against taxpayers who have asserted a frivolous or baseless claim, or have filed a claim only for purposes of delay. 26 U.S.C. §6673."]

As Rule 11 cases begin to emerge in the wake of the 1983 amendments it is apparent that courts are no longer reluctant to impose sanctions on attorneys and litigants who stray from their obligations under the rule. However, Rule 11 decisions by courts have not always been consistent, producing confusion among the bench and bar, as well as inequitable results. By our opinion today, we seek to ameliorate this confusion and modify existing inequities to the extent possible by clarifying some of the more important issues presented by the application of Rule 11 in this case. . . .

C. Attorneys' Obligations Under Rule 11

Having determined the appropriate standard of review in Rule 11 cases [abuse of discretion], we now turn to the obligations imposed upon litigants and their counsel under the amended rule. Consistent with the purpose of the 1983 amendments, this Court has held that Rule 11 compliance is now measured by an objective, not subjective, standard of reasonableness under the circumstances. *Robinson v. National Cash Register Co.*, 808 F.2d 1119, 1127 (5th Cir. 1987); *Davis v. Veslan Enterprises*, 765 F.2d 494, 497 (5th Cir. 1985). "An attorney's good faith is no longer enough to protect him from rule 11 sanctions." *Robinson*, 808 F.2d at 1127.

It is well established that Rule 11 imposes the following affirmative duties with which an attorney or litigant certifies he has complied by signing a pleading, motion, or other document: (1) that the attorney has conducted a reasonable inquiry into the facts which support the document; (2) that the attorney has conducted a reasonable inquiry into the law such that the document embodies existing legal principles or a good faith argument "for the extension, modification, or reversal of existing law;" and (3) that the motion is not interposed for purposes of delay, harassment, or increasing costs of litigation. In addition to the aforementioned duties, the instant panel imposed upon a certifying attorney the continuing obligation to review and reevaluate his position as a case develops.

While sympathizing with the concerns that prompted previous panels in our Circuit to hold to the contrary, we depart from language in the instant panel's opinion and earlier decisions by this Court that impose upon an attorney a continuing obligation under Rule 11. Instead, we believe that a construction of Rule 11 which evaluates an attorney's conduct at the time a "pleading, motion, or other paper" is signed is consistent with the intent of the rulemakers and the plain meaning of the language contained in the rule. Like a snapshot, Rule 11 review focuses upon the instant when the picture is taken—when the signature is placed on the document. Rule 11 was promulgated for a particular purpose—to check abuses in the signing of pleadings. . . .

D. Mandatory Application of Sanctions

Rule 11 provides that "[i]f a pleading, motion, or other paper is signed in violation of this rule, the court, upon motion or upon its own initiative, shall impose . . . an appropriate sanction. . . ." Fed. R. Civ. P. 11 (emphasis added). In *Bell v. Bell,* a panel of this Court found no abuse of discretion on the part of the district court in finding no sanction as the appropriate sanction for a Rule 11 violation. The *Bell* Court stated "[w]e are not constrained to say that the district court must, upon the establishment of a violation of the rules at issue here, impose some sort of sanction however nominal." . . . Another panel of this Circuit found that where a district court determines an attorney's conduct to be violative of Rule 11, that court must then fashion an appropriate sanction in accordance with the dictates of Rule 11. *Robinson*, 808 F.2d at 1130-31. We adopt the *Robinson* rule. There are no longer any "free passes" for attorneys and litigants who violate Rule 11. Once a violation of Rule 11 is established, the rule mandates the application of sanctions. This appears to be the only construction consistent with the plain language of the rule.

When Rule 11 was amended in 1983 to include the mandatory "shall" language regarding the imposition of sanctions, the rulemakers inserted such language in an attempt to combat the reluctance of judges to impose sanctions on their fellow professionals. This reluctance on the part of the judiciary to impose sanctions has been explained as stemming from judges' sympathy, as former practitioners, for the pressures on lawyers in the adversarial system, concern that available sanctions would punish the client, and uncertainty as to whether judges could impose sanctions on their own initiative. Melissa L. Nelken, *Sanctions Under Amended Federal Rule 11 — Some "Chilling" Problems in the Struggle Between Compensation and Punishment,* 74 Geo. L.J. 1313, 1321-22 (1986). [The court added in a footnote, "The extent to which judges were reluctant to impose sanctions prior to the 1983 amendments to Rule 11 is evidenced by the fact that between 1938 and 1976, Rule 11 motions had been filed in only nineteen reported cases. Among those cases, violations were found in only eleven instances, and attorneys sanctioned in only three. Saul M. Kassin, *An Empirical Study of Rule 11 Sanctions* 2 (Fed. Jud. Center 1985). Through 1979, there was only one additional reported opinion in which a sanction was imposed pursuant to Rule 11. *Id.* In contrast, after Rule 11 was amended in 1983, there were, between August 1, 1983 and August 1, 1985, more than 200 reported cases involving Rule 11 sanctions. Nelken, 74 Geo. L.J. at 1326 (1986)."]

In concluding that Rule 11 requires the imposition of sanctions once a violation has been found, however, we stress that the district court is vested with considerable discretion in determining the "appropriate" sanction to impose upon the violating party. . . .

An examination of the history behind the 1983 amendments to Rule 11 indicates that the rulemakers inserted the discretionary language in Rule 11 in response to concerns that mandatory sanctions would chill the adversarial process. . . . Thus, it can be inferred that the broad discretion given district courts in determining sanctions was intended as a "safety valve" to reduce the pressure of mandatory sanctions.

The broad discretion afforded district courts is reflected in the numerous types of sanctions that may be imposed under Rule 11. As attorneys' fees and reasonable costs are expressly provided for by Rule 11, we recognize the natural tendency of district courts to gravitate toward imposing these types of sanctions. However, we would caution that:

> [w]hether sanctions are viewed as a form of cost-shifting, compensating opposing parties injured by the vexatious or frivolous litigation forbidden by Rule 11, or as a form of punishment imposed on those who violate the rule, *the imposition of sanctions pursuant to Rule 11 is meant to deter attorneys from violating the rule.*

Donaldson v. Clark, 819 F.2d 1551, 1556 (emphasis added). Sanctions should also be educational and rehabilitative in character and, as such, tailored to the particular wrong. . . .

While monetary sanctions are appropriate under Rule 11, it is noted that this Court has previously held that the basic principle governing the choice of sanctions is that the least severe sanction adequate to serve the purpose should be imposed. *Boazman v. Economics Laboratory, Inc.* 537 F.2d 210, 212-12 (5th Cir. 1976). *See also Reizakais v. Loy,* 490 F.2d 1132, 1136 (4th Cir. 1974); *Industrial Building Materials, Inc. v. Interchemical Corp.,* 437 F.2d 1336, 1339 (9th Cir. 1970). We specifically adopt the principle that the sanction imposed should be the least severe sanction adequate to the purpose of Rule 11. Therefore, as a less severe alternative to monetary sanctions, district courts may choose to admonish or reprimand attorneys who violate Rule 11. . . . In an innovative approach, one district court required the errant attorney to circulate the court's opinion criticizing his conduct throughout his firm. *Heuttig & Schromm, Inc. v. Landscape Contractors Council,* 582 F. Supp. 1519 (N.D. Cal. 1984), *aff'd,* 790 F.2d 1421 (9th Cir. 1986). The educational effect of sanctions might be enhanced even by requiring some form of legal education. . . .

In sum, a district court must impose sanctions once a violation of Rule 11 is found, but the district court retains broad discretion in determining the "appropriate" sanction under the rule. What is "appropriate" may be a warm friendly discussion on the record, a hard-nosed reprimand in open court, compulsory legal education, monetary sanctions, or other measures appropriate to the circumstances. Whatever the ultimate sanction imposed, the district court should utilize the sanction that furthers the purposes of Rule 11 and is the least severe sanction adequate to such purpose. . . .

At the time the following letter was written, Judge Keeton was the Chairman for the Standing Committee on Rule of Practice and Procedure. In addition to being the Chairperson for this committee, Judge Keeton is a United States Federal District Court Judge in Massachusetts. Before being appointed to the bench in 1979, Judge Keeton was a Harvard Law Professor for over forty years. Judge Pointer is the Chief Judge for the United States District Court for the Northern District of Alabama.

■ ATTACHMENT B TO LETTER TO HON. ROBERT E. KEETON FROM HON. SAM C. POINTER, JR., CHAIR OF THE ADVISORY COMM. ON CIVIL RULES
146 F.R.D. 401, 522-525 (1993)

The proposed amendment of Rule 11 is controversial. It has provoked extensive comment from the bench, bar, and public. . . .

The goal of the 1983 version remains a proper and legitimate one, and its insistence that litigants "stop-and-think" before filing pleadings, motions, and other papers should, in the opinion of the Committee, be retained. Many of the initial difficulties have been resolved through case law over the past nine years. Nevertheless, there was support for the following propositions: (1) Rule 11, in conjunction with other rules, has tended to impact plaintiffs more frequently and severely than defendants; (2) it occasionally has created problems for a party which seeks to assert novel legal contentions or which needs discovery from other persons to determine if the party's belief about the facts can be supported with evidence; (3) it has too rarely been enforced through nonmonetary sanctions, with cost-shifting having become the normative sanction; (4) it provides little incentive, and perhaps a disincentive, for a party to abandon positions after determining they are no longer supportable in fact or law; and (5) it sometimes has produced unfortunate conflicts between attorney and client, and exacerbated contentious behavior between counsel. In addition, although the great majority of Rule 11 motions have not been granted, the time spent by litigants and the courts in dealing with such motions has not been insignificant.

The Committee [has] drafted a proposed amendment with the objective of increasing the fairness and effectiveness of the rule as a means to deter presentation and maintenance of frivolous positions, while also reducing the frequency of Rule 11 motions. The proposed amendment was published in August 1991 and has generated many comments, written and oral. ·

Summarized below are the principal criticism and suggestions that the Committee has received [regarding the proposed amendment to Rule 11]. Several of these, it may be noted, are embodied in an alternative proposal for amendment of Rule 11 sponsored by Attorney John Frank and others, which has gained significant support from various judges, lawyers, and organizations.

Opposition to this revision as "weakening" the rule. It is correct that, given the "safe harbor" provisions and those affecting the type of sanction to be imposed, the amendment should reduce the number of Rule 11 motions and the severity of some sanctions. The Advisory Committee is unanimous that, to the extent these changes may be viewed as "weakening" the rule, they are nevertheless desirable.

Opposition to any amendment as "premature." While several problem areas encountered under the 1983 version of Rule 11 have been corrected by case law, others remain and cannot be cured by greater experience within the bench and bar. By the time the new amendments can become effective, a period of ten years will have elapsed since the prior revision. The Advisory Committee is unanimous that changes should not be deferred for additional time and study.

Application to discovery documents. Notes to the published draft asked for comments on whether Rule 11 should be made explicitly inapplicable to discovery documents, and indicated that the Advisory Committee would be considering such a change without additional publication. The comments received support this change. The Advisory Committee is unanimous that this change should be made and has done so through the addition of subdivision (d).

Continuing duty to withdraw unsupportable contentions. The published draft abandoned the "signer snapshot" approach of the current rule that imposes obligations solely on the persons signing a paper and measures those obligations solely as of the time the paper is filed. It provided that litigants have a duty not to maintain a contention that, though perhaps initially believed to be meritorious, is no longer supportable in fact or law. Several comments expressed concern that, at least as drafted, the revision might lead to disruptive and wasteful activities based on a mere failure to re-read and amend previously filed pleadings, motions, or briefs. The Advisory Committee believes that this latter criticism is well taken and has made several modifications to the published language of the text and limited the expansion to non-signers to persons who "pursue" a previously filed paper. These changes, coupled with the "safe harbor" provisions, should minimize these concerns.

Duty to conduct pre-filing investigation. Some critics express skepticism regarding the obligation to conduct an appropriate pre-filing investigation in view of the provisions allowing pleading on "information and belief" and affording a "safe harbor" against the filing of Rule 11 motions if unsupportable contentions are withdrawn. The basic requirement for pre-filing investigation is retained in the text of the rule, and, as the Committee Notes make clear, pleading on information and belief must be preceded by an inquiry reasonable under the circumstances. The revision is not a license to join parties, make claims, or present defenses without any factual basis or justification. However, it must be acknowledged that, with these changes, some litigants may be tempted to conduct less of a pre-filing investigation than under the current rule. The Advisory Committee believes that this risk is justified, on balance, by the benefits from the changes.

Pleading "as a whole." Several comments urged that the revision of Rule 11 incorporate the approach adopted in some decisions, permitting sanctions only if, taken "as a whole," the paper violated the standards of the rule. The Advisory Committee continues to believe that the "stop-and-think" obligations apply to all of the allegations and assertions, not just to a majority of them. Nevertheless, the language of the published draft might have inappropriately encouraged an excessive number of Rule 11 motions premised upon a detailed parsing of pleadings and motions. The Advisory Committee has changed the text of subdivision (b) to eliminate the specific reference to a "claim, defense, request, demand, objection, contention, or argument" and has also modified the accompanying Notes to emphasize that Rule 11 motions should not be prepared—or threatened—for minor, inconsequential violations or as a substitute for traditional motions specifically designed to enable parties to challenge the sufficiency of pleadings. These changes, coupled with the opportunity to correct allegations under the "safe harbor" provisions, should eliminate the need for court consideration of Rule 11 motions directed at insignificant aspects of a complaint or answer.

"Mandatory" sanctions. The most frequent criticism has been that revision leaves in place the current mandate that some sanction be imposed if the court determines that the rule has been violated. The suggestion is that, even if a violation is found, the district court should have discretion not to impose any sanction. Two members of the Advisory Committee prefer this approach, though do not request that this view be expressed as a formal minority view in the Committee Notes. The other members of the Advisory Committee believe that, particularly given the opportunity through the "safe harbor" provisions to withdraw an unsupportable contention before a Rule 11 motion is even filed, some sanction should be imposed if the court is called upon to determine, and does determine, that the rule has been violated. As under the current rule, the court retains discretion as to the particular sanction to be imposed, subject however to the principle that it not be more severe than needed for effective deterrence, and the court's decision whether a violation has occurred is reviewed on appeal for abuse of discretion. [Note that the wording of the 1993 amendment to Rule 11 changed after it was initially drafted by the Advisory Committee and sent to the Standing Committee on Rules of Practice and Procedure. In the version drafted by the Advisory Committee, subsection (c) read: "If, after notice and a reasonable opportunity to respond, the court determines that subdivision (b) has been violated, the court *shall*, subject to the conditions stated below, impose an appropriate sanction. . . ." (emphasis added). Subsequently, the "shall" was changed to "may".]

Payment of monetary sanctions to an adversary. Another frequent criticism is that the draft continues to permit a monetary award to be paid to an adversary for damages resulting from a Rule 11 violation, rather than limiting monetary awards to penalties paid into court. The Advisory Committee agrees with the premise that cost-shifting has created the incentive for many unnecessary Rule 11 motions, has too frequently been selected as the sanction, and, indeed, has led to the large awards most often cited by critics of the 1983 rule. Both in the text and the Committee Notes, the published draft contained language that, while continuing to permit cost-shifting awards, explicitly recited the deterrent purpose of Rule 11 sanctions and the potential for non-monetary sanctions. The Advisory Committee remains convinced that there are situations—particularly when unsupportable contentions are filed to harass or intimidate an adversary in some cases involving litigants with greatly disparate financial resources—in which cost-shifting may be needed for effective deterrence. The Committee has, however, made a further change in the text of subdivision (c)(2) to emphasize that cost-shifting awards should be the exception, rather than the norm, for sanctions. As to the expenses incurred in presenting or opposing a Rule 11 motion, the published draft provides the court with discretion to award fees to the prevailing party: this is needed to discourage non-meritorious Rule 11 motions without creating a disincentive to the presentation of motions that should be filed.

Protection of represented parties (as distinguished from attorneys) from sanctions. The current rule permits the court to impose a sanction upon the person who signed the paper, "a represented party, or both." The published draft would have restricted the imposition of monetary sanctions upon a represented party to situations in which the party was responsible for a violation of Rule 11(b)(1) (papers filed to harass or for other improper purpose). Comments have been mixed: some opposing any such restriction; others opposing any monetary sanctions on represented parties; others suggesting variants on the language in the draft. Upon further reflection and consideration of the comments, the Advisory Committee believes that the prohibition of monetary sanctions against a represented party should be limited to violations of Rule 11(b)(2) (frivolous legal arguments), and has changed the language of subdivision (c)(2)(A) accordingly.

Sanctions against law firms. The published draft contained provisions designed to remove the restrictions of the current rule respecting sanctions upon law firms. *See Pavelic & LeFlore v. Marvel Entertainment Group,* 493 U.S. 120 (1989) (1983 version of Rule 11 does not permit sanctions against law firm of attorney signing groundless complaint). While many comments supported this change others opposed it, urging that sanctions be imposed only on the individual attorney found to have violated the rule. The Advisory Committee believes that, consistent with general principles of agency, it is often appropriate for a law firm to be held jointly responsible for violations by its partners, associates, and employees. Given the opportunity under the "safe harbor" provisions to avoid sanctions imposed on a motion, coupled with the changes designed to reduce the frequency of "fee-shifting" sanctions that have produced the largest monetary sanctions, the Committee has added to the published draft in subdivision (c)(1)(A) language clarifying that a law firm should ordinarily be held jointly accountable in such circumstances.

Court-initiated sanctions after case dismissed. Several groups have suggested that the safe harbor provisions, which under the published draft apply only to motions filed by other litigants, should apply also to show cause orders issued at the court's own initiative. The Advisory Committee continues to believe that court-initiated show cause orders—which typically relate to matters that are akin to contempt of court—are properly treated somewhat differently from party-initiated motions. The published draft does, however, contain provisions in subdivision (c)(2)(B) protecting a litigant from monetary sanctions imposed under a show cause order not issued until after the claims made by or against it have been voluntarily dismissed or settled.

Standards for appellate review. Some of the comments have urged that the revision contain language modifying the standard for appellate review announced in *Cooter & Gell v. Hartmarx Corp.* The Advisory Committee concludes that the arguments are not sufficiently compelling to justify a deviation from the principle that ordinarily the rules should not attempt to prescribe standards for appellate review.

The Advisory Committee has carefully considered the various criticisms and suggestions, as well as those comments favoring the published proposal. Ultimately the only disagreement within the Committee related, as noted above, to whether imposition of sanctions should be mandatory or discretionary. The two members who favored the discretionary standard nevertheless believe that proposed amendment is preferable to the current rule, and accordingly the Committee is unanimous in recommending adoption of the proposed amendment of Rule 11. . . .

The safe harbor provision of the new Rule, albeit a procedural technicality of sorts, has generated a substantial amount of litigation. The dispute in the following case centers on this provision.

■ PROGRESS FEDERAL SAVINGS BANK v. NATIONAL WEST LENDERS ASSOCIATION, INC.
1996 WL 57942 (E.D. Pa. Feb. 12, 1996)

YOHN, District Judge.

[Plaintiff Progress Federal Savings Bank ("Progress") sued Defendant National West Lenders Association, Inc. ("NatWest") in breach of contract. Its claims against NatWest were fraud, misrepresentation, intentional interference with contractual relations, and civil conspiracy. The court dismissed the fraud and misrepresentation counts for failing to state claims upon which relief could be granted. Five months later, the court granted NatWest's motion for summary judgment on the remaining counts. Three months after being dismissed from the litigation, NatWest filed a Rule 11 motion for sanctions on Progress. After waiting the twenty-one days required by Rule 11, NatWest filed a motion for sanctions with the court. Without addressing the merits, Progress responded with a motion to strike the sanctions because NatWest failed to comply with the procedural requirements of Rule 11. After explaining in a footnote that the Federal Rules of Civil Procedure do not provide for motions to strike motions, the court treated the motion to strike as a brief in opposition to the sanctions and denied NatWest's request for sanctions.]

. . . The court must give [Rule 11] its plain meaning, as its task is to apply the text rather than to improve upon it. *Pavelic & LeFlore v. Marvel Group*, 493 U.S. 120, 123, 126 (1989). When interpretation is necessary, the court must consider the purposes of the rule, including the deficiencies in its prior form that the 1993 revision was meant to address. *See, Cooter & Gell v. Hartmarx Corp.*, 496 U.S. 384, 392 (1990).

The primary purpose of Rule 11 is to deter groundless proceedings and abusive litigation practices. *Business Guides, Inc. v. Chromatic Communications Enters., Inc.*, 498 U.S. 533, 553 (1991). However, the 1993 changes to Rule 11 were intended to strike a new balance between this goal and the unintended effects of the 1983 revision. The 1983 version of Rule 11 was widely criticized for spurring extensive satellite litigation, for eroding civility among lawyers, and for chilling zealous advocacy on behalf of civil rights plaintiffs and others with limited resources. Howard A. Cutler, *Comment, A Practitioner's Guide to the 1993 Amendment to Federal Rule of Civil Procedure 11*, 67 Temp. L. Rev. 265, 268 (1994). The 1993 revision constituted a significant shift and the "safe harbor" provision is a major element of the new rule's structure. The Advisory Committee on Rules adopted the "safe harbor" provision knowing that it could diminish attorneys' incentives to make good faith inquiries before filing. . . .

I. Application of the "Safe Harbor" Provision

The parties dispute whether NatWest has complied with Rule 11's procedural requirements. NatWest argues that it repeatedly told Progress that its claims were groundless, providing ample time for corrective action, and that it gave Progress the required twenty-one day formal notice before filing for sanctions with the court. Progress counters that NatWest simply prepared and served its motion too late. Progress has the better of this argument.

Throughout the litigation, NatWest apparently gave Progress a number of informal warnings that its conduct was in violation of Rule 11. Therefore, according to NatWest, no "safe harbor" period was necessary once the motion for sanctions was actually filed. However, Progress is correct in arguing that "An informal notice, either by letter or other means, does not trigger the commencement of the 21 day period."

NatWest did give Progress twenty-one days' notice of the filing of its motion. However, NatWest did not serve Progress with a motion for sanctions until all of the claims against NatWest had already been dismissed and the balance of the action, a dispute between Progress and Lenders, had been settled. This timing is antithetical to the purposes of the twenty-one day "safe harbor" period. In other words, the "safe harbor" presumes the motion's timeliness; as stated in the Notes, "Given the 'safe harbor' provisions . . . a party cannot delay serving its Rule 11 motion until conclusion of the case (or judicial rejection of the offending contention)." This notation fits precisely with the language of the Rule, which prohibits the filing of the sanctions motion with the court unless the "challenged paper, claim, defense, contention, allegation, or denial is not withdrawn or appropriately corrected." After the claims against NatWest had been rejected through the court's granting of the motion to dismiss as to some and the motion for summary judgment as to the others, and after all other parties to the case had settled their dispute, there was nothing for Progress to withdraw or correct.

As the United States Court of Appeals for the Third Circuit has written, "Promptness in filing valid motions will serve not only to foster efficiency [of appeals], but in many instances will deter further violations of Rule 11 which might otherwise occur during the remainder of the litigation." *Mary Ann Pensiero, Inc. v. Lingle*, 847 F.2d 90, 99 (3rd Cir. 1988). The Third Circuit's 1988 instruction that motions for sanctions be filed "as soon as practicable after discovery of the Rule 11 violation," *id.* at 100, retains its authority, as the 1993 revisions do not address when, in the context of the litigation as a whole, a party must initiate the Rule 11 procedures. Rather, the 1993 revisions merely require a delay between serving and filing the motion.

II. PROPOSED EXCEPTIONS TO THE "SAFE HARBOR" PROVISION

In the alternative to arguing that it has satisfied Rule 11, NatWest argues, in essence, that an exception to the "safe harbor" provision is warranted for three reasons: (1) Progress waived the "safe harbor" provision and is estopped from relying upon it now; (2) Progress has failed to state that it would have withdrawn its claims had a motion for sanctions been filed earlier—and in fact has demonstrated the opposite through its conduct; and (3) at least for the Rule 11 claim based on Progress's opposition to summary judgment, compliance with the "safe harbor" provision was impossible. However, the court is not persuaded.

First, NatWest claims that Progress's counsel "should be estopped from seeking enforcement of the safe harbor provision" because it asked NatWest to wait until after the court had ruled on summary judgment to file its sanctions motion. Progress disputes that this occurred. However, even were it to take NatWest's account as true, the court could not find estoppel. The record contains no evidence that Progress gave NatWest reason to believe that it would not oppose a motion for sanctions, whenever filed, on all available grounds. Furthermore, Rule 11 is binding on the court as well as on the parties; no party has a right to rely (and no party may reasonably rely) on its adversary's representations that the Federal Rules of Civil Procedure will not apply to a given situation. Therefore, Progress did not and could not have waived its rights to the procedural protections of Rule 11.

Second, NatWest argues that the "safe harbor" rule should not apply because Progress would not have withdrawn its papers even if served with a timely motion. To encourage the court to reason in this way, NatWest points to *Silva v. Witschen*, 19 F.3d 725 (1st Cir. 1994). However, *Silva* was ultimately decided under the pre-1993 Rule 11. The *Silva* court, in determining not to apply the amendments to a case pending on their effective date, merely considered how the offending party might have fared had the 1993 "safe harbor" provision applied. The court found that the litigant would likely have ignored formal warnings that his claims could lead to sanctions, just as he had ignored informal ones. This type of speculation, however, is not endorsed by the text of the new Rule 11.

Finally, NatWest argues that, since the court ruled on its motion for summary judgment within nineteen days of the filing of Progress's brief in opposition, "it was impossible for NatWest to have complied with the safe harbor provisions of Rule 11" with respect to its claim that the brief in opposition to summary judgment was frivolous. While this does present an interesting question in theory, the fact is that NatWest was not actually prejudiced by this turn of events. If NatWest had served its motion for sanctions in the weeks immediately following its receipt of the opposition brief, then an exception to the "safe harbor" provision would perhaps be warranted. However, NatWest waited three months to take action. As already discussed, the Third Circuit has urged the district courts to discourage delay in the filing of motions for sanctions. Furthermore, the 1993 Advisory Committee Notes support the Third Circuit's approach: "Ordinarily the motion should be served promptly after the inappropriate paper is filed, and, if delayed too long, may be viewed as untimely."

III. CONSIDERATION OF COURT-INITIATED SANCTIONS

The "safe harbor" provision of Rule 11 does not apply when the court rather than a party initiates the consideration of sanctions. The Notes explain this discrepancy by pointing out that "show cause orders will ordinarily be issued only in situations that are akin to a contempt of court." The Notes also encourage courts to consider corrective action taken following the issuance of a show cause order when deciding what, if any, sanction to impose. Therefore, the separate provisions of Rule 11 now embody a consistent policy: whenever possible, to address abuses as they occur.

It is hereby ordered that both the Motion for Sanctions and the Motion to Strike are denied.

Comments and Questions

1. What effect, if any, does Rule 11 have on the pleading requirements under Rule 8(a)?

2. Several studies might be read to indicate that Rule 11 (or, at least, the 1983-1993 version) is dramatically pro-defendant and particularly detrimental to plaintiffs in civil rights cases. Some are summarized in Georgene M. Vairo, *Rule 11: Where We Are and Where We Are Going*, 60 Fordham L. Rev. 475 (1991). Perhaps the most thorough study of the operation of Rule 11 is the report of a task force of the U.S. Court of Appeals for the Third Circuit published by the American Judicature Society in *Rule 11 in Transition: The Report of the Third Circuit Task Force on Federal Rule of Civil Procedure 11* (Stephen B. Burbank, Reporter, 1989). Among other things, the Third Circuit study examined all Rule 11 motions in the Third Circuit for one year, and found that "motions for sanctions under the Rule were made in only approximately one half of one percent of the civil cases in the district courts of the Third Circuit . . . " *Id.* at xiii. "In assessing the costs and benefits of Rule 11 in the Third Circuit, the Task Force found evidence in responses to its attorney questionnaire and in interviews with attorneys that the Rule has had widespread effects on conduct of the sort hoped for by the rulemakers and other evidence that it has yielded benefits (*e.g.*, contributing to case dismissal or settlement). . . . It also found that directly associated costs (such as, the costs of litigating Rule 11 issues to litigants and courts) do not appear to be clearly incommensurate with probable benefits. . . ." *Id.* at xiv.

But the Third Circuit Task Force also reported:

> According to the data from our survey, sanctions are imposed pursuant to 13.6% (18/132) of Rule 11 motions. . . . Plaintiffs (and/or their counsel) are the "targets" of 66.7% (88/132) of such motions . . . ; defendants (and/or their counsel) of 33.3% (44/132). Plaintiffs are sanctioned pursuant to 15.9% (14/88) of the motions made against them . . . ; defendants pursuant to 9.1% (4/44) of the motions made against them. . . . Civil rights and employment discrimination cases account for 18.2% (24/132) of the Rule 11 motions in the survey. . . . Plaintiffs are the "targets" of 70.8% (17/24) of the motions in such cases. . . . , and they are sanctioned pursuant to 47.1% (8/17) of such motions. . . .

Id. at 57. It is important to note that the Third Circuit Task Force found that "[r]equests for sanctions in civil rights cases constituted only a slightly larger slice of our pie (24/132 or 18.2%) than one would expect on the basis of civil filings in this circuit (16% of civil filings in the period [were civil rights cases]. . . ." *Id.* at 69.

What might be the reasons that Rule 11 sanctions are sought more frequently against plaintiffs than defendants, and that civil rights plaintiffs may be sanctioned substantially more frequently (47.1% compared to 8.45% in the Third Circuit for one year) than other plaintiffs? *Id.* at 69. Are there possible legitimate reasons? If a reformer were (1) concerned about an adverse chilling effect on civil rights plaintiffs, but (2) thought Rule 11 was generally salutary, what changes would she propose? To whom should such a proposal be made? This might be a good time for you to review the exact language of the current rendition of the Rules Enabling Act.

3. Why is the Advisory Committee reluctant to see Rule 11 as a fee-shifting device? What is wrong with the goal of compensation in addition to that of deterrence? Is the Committee afraid that attorneys will bring questionable Rule 11 motions? Wouldn't the threat of a countermotion under Rule 11 take care of that?

4. A few years ago the Judicial Conference of the United States recommended that the amendments to Rule 11 (and other rules) be approved by the Supreme Court and transmitted to Congress. The Supreme Court submitted the amendments (without change) to the Congress, but noted that the transmittal did not "necessarily indicate that the Court itself would have proposed these amendments in the form submitted." Letter from William H. Rehnquist, Chief Justice of the United States Supreme Court, to Thomas S. Foley, Speaker of the House of Representatives (April 22, 1993), reprinted in 146 F.R.D. 403 (1993). The transmittal of the Promulgated Rules was accompanied by a statement from Justice White challenging the wisdom of the current rule-making process, and a dissent from Justice Scalia (joined by Justice Thomas with respect to amendments to Rule 11) challenging the wisdom of the proposed amendments. *Id.* at 507. With regard to the 1993 amendment to Rule 11, Justice Scalia wrote:

It is undeniably important to the Rules' goal of "the just, speedy, and inexpensive determination of every action," Fed. R. Civ. P. 1, that frivolous pleadings and motions be deterred. The current [1983-1993] Rule 11 achieves that objective by requiring sanctions when its standards are violated (though leaving the court broad discretion as to the manner of sanction), and by allowing compensation for the moving party's expenses and attorney's fees. The proposed revision would render the Rule toothless, by allowing judges to dispense with sanction, by disfavoring compensation for litigation expenses, and by providing a 21-day "safe harbor" within which, if the party accused of a frivolous filing withdraws the filing, he is entitled to escape with no sanction at all.

To take the last first: In my view, those who file frivolous suits and pleadings should have no "safe harbor." The Rules should be solicitous of the abused (the courts and the opposing party), and not of the abuser. Under the revised Rule, parties will be able to file thoughtless, reckless, and harassing pleadings, secure in the knowledge that they have nothing to lose: If objection is raised, they can retreat without penalty. The proposed revision contradicts what this Court said only three years ago: "Baseless filing puts the machinery of justice in motion, burdening courts and individuals alike with needless expense and delay. Even if the careless litigant quickly dismisses the action, the harm triggering Rule 11's concerns has already occurred. Therefore a litigant who violates Rule 11 merits sanctions even after a dismissal." *Cooter & Gell v. Hartmarx Corp.*, 496 U.S. 384, 398 (1990). The advisory committee itself was formerly of the same view. *Ibid.* (quoting Letter from Chairman, Advisory Committee on Civil Rules).

The proposed Rule also decreases both the likelihood and the severity of punishment for those foolish enough not to seek refuge in the safe harbor after an objection is raised. Proposed subsection (c) makes the issuance of any sanction discretionary, whereas currently it is *required.* Judges, like other human beings, do not like imposing punishment when their duty does not require it, especially upon their own acquaintances and members of their own profession. They do not immediately see, moreover, the system-wide benefits of serious Rule 11 sanctions, though they are intensely aware of the amount of their own time it would take to consider and apply sanctions in the case before them. For these reasons, I think it important to the effectiveness of the scheme that the sanctions remain mandatory.

Finally, the likelihood that frivolousness will even be *challenged* is diminished by the proposed Rule, which restricts the award of compensation to "unusual circumstances," with monetary sanctions "ordinarily" to be payable to the court. Advisory Committee Notes to Proposed Rule 11, pp 53-54. Under Proposed Rule 11(c)(2), a court may order payment for "some or all of the reasonable attorneys' fees and other expenses incurred as a direct result of the violation" only when that is "warranted for effective deterrence." Since the deterrent effect of a fine is rarely increased by altering the identity of the payee, it takes imagination to conceive of instances in which this provision will ever apply. And the commentary makes it clear that even when compensation is granted it should be granted stingily—only for costs "directly and unavoidably caused by the violation." *Id.* at 54. As seen from the viewpoint of the victim of an abusive litigator, these revisions convert Rule 11 from a means of obtaining compensation to an invitation to throw good money after bad. The net effect is to decrease the incentive on the part of the person best situated to alert the court to perversion of our civil justice system.

I would not have registered this dissent if there were convincing indication that the current Rule 11 regime is ineffective, or encourages excessive satellite litigation. But there appears to be general agreement, reflected in a recent report of the advisory committee itself, that Rule 11, as written, basically works. According to that report, a Federal Judicial Center survey showed that 80% of district judges believe Rule 11 has had an overall positive effect and should be retained in its present form, 95% believed the Rule had not impeded development of the law, and about 75% said the benefits justify the expenditure of judicial time. *See* "Interim Report on Rule 11, Advisory Committee on Civil Rules," reprinted in Georgene M. Vairo, *Rule 11 Sanctions:*

Case Law Perspectives and Preventive Measures, App. I-8-I-10 (2d ed. 1991). True, many lawyers do not like Rule 11. It may cause them financial liability, it may damage their professional reputation in front of important clients, and the cost-of-litigation savings it produces are savings not to lawyers but to litigants. But the overwhelming approval of the Rule by the federal district judges who daily grapple with the problem of litigation abuse is enough to persuade me that it should not be gutted as the proposed revision suggests. . . .

5. Recent federal reform efforts, including the Contract with America, have sought to repeal the 1993 amendment to Rule 11. These reformers argue that the safe-harbor provisions and discretionary sanctions have eviscerated the Rule. *See* Republican National Committee, Contract with America: The Bold Plan by Newt Gingrich, Rep. Dick Armey, and the House Republicans to Change the Nation (Ed Gillespie & Bob Schellhas eds., 1994).

6. Would Randall Dee's Motion to Dismiss for failure to state a claim be sanctionable under any of the three versions of Rule 11?

7. In 1982, Professor John Oakley of the University of California used a nine-variable test to determine which states had procedural rules that "replicated" the Federal Rules. He found that in 1975, Massachusetts became the last of twenty-two states plus the District of Columbia to conform its procedure substantially to the Federal Rules through judicially promulgated rules; if one included statutorily adopted versions of the Federal Rules, there were four additional states, making a total of twenty-six. However, of the ten most populous states, only Ohio was a replica state. John B. Oakley & Arthur F. Coon, *The Federal Rules in State Courts: A Survey of State Court Systems of Civil Procedure*, 61 Wash. L. Rev. 1367 (1986).

The influence of the Federal Rules procedural system is even more widespread, however. The most important attributes of the Federal Rules—merger of law and equity, relative ease of pleading and amendment, liberal joinder of parties and theories, broad discovery, and summary judgment—are part of the rules governing civil litigation in courts of general jurisdiction in virtually every state.

Because many states have replicated the federal model for their own state rules of civil procedure, these states must decide with every amendment to the Federal Rules whether also to adopt the federal amendments. If you were a member of a state Advisory Committee on Civil Rules, would you urge adoption of the recent amendment to Rule 11? Is amending Rule 8(a) a better means to achieve the ends sought by the recent amendment to Rule 11? What are the advantages of uniform state and federal rules? Does intra-state procedural uniformity compromise other procedural values?

8. The materials in this chapter lend the impression that there is an abundance of frivolous litigation in the present court system. This may or may not be true. Because there has been little data collected regarding the behavior of the court system, no one really knows. Michael Saks, a law professor at the University of Iowa, summarized much of the literature on this subject in the seminal law review article, *Do We Really Know Anything About*

the Behavior of the Tort Litigation System—And Why Not?, 140 U. Pa. L. Rev. 1147 (1992). His introductory words epitomize the article: "Much of what we know about the tort litigation system is untrue, unknown, or unknowable." *Id.*

9. Rule 11 is not the only means to sanction improper conduct in the federal courts. Because Rule 11 is inapplicable to discovery disputes (*see* Rule 11(d)), courts use Rule 37 to enforce the discovery rules. Further, 28 U.S.C. §1927 permits the court to make attorneys liable for excessive "costs, expenses and attorneys fees reasonably incurred because of such unreasonable and vexatious conduct." *Id.* A court can also "rely on its inherent power" to impose appropriate sanctions to control its proceedings. *Chambers v. NASCO, Inc.* 501 U.S. 32, 50 (1991).

10. A misrepresentation during oral argument can trigger a Rule 11 violation and sanction. While the Advisory Committee report on the 1993 amendment stated that Rule 11 applies only to assertions contained in papers filed or submitted to the court, the Second Circuit has held that the phrase "or later advocating" in Rule 11(b) is sufficiently broad to allow a court to impose sanctions for oral misrepresentations if the misrepresentation has a "substantial connection" to a signed document that is presented to the court. *O'Brien v. Alexander*, 101 F. 3d 1479 (2d Cir. 1996).

11. Courts have become very creative when imposing sanctions under Rule 11. One district court required an attorney to obtain at least forty hours of individual instruction on federal and applicable rules of procedure from a professor at an accredited law school. *Bergeron v. Northwest Publications, Inc.* 165 F.R.D. 518 (D. Minn. 1996). Another court ordered an attorney who had improperly attempted to remove a case from state to federal court to copy, in his own handwriting, text on removal procedure from a federal practice book. *Curran v. Price*, 150 F.R.D. 85 (D. Md. 1993).

Practice Exercise No. 11: Reviewing the *City of Cleveland* Complaint Under Rule 11

Re-read the introductory memorandum in the *City of Cleveland* Case Files and prepare to discuss at a firm strategy session whether a partner can safely sign and file the complaint (in the *Case Files*) in light of the requirements of current Rule 11. Consider all four counts of the complaint, and be prepared to advise what, if any, additional factual or legal investigation is needed as to any count. The partner realizes that current Fed. R. Civ. P. 11 has a "safe harbor" provision, but she does not want to be forced to withdraw or amend portions of the complaint if the defendants make a Rule 11 motion for sanctions. Are there any allegations in the complaint for which the partner should use the "hedging" language permitted by Fed. R. Civ. P. 11(b)(3)? Do not concern yourself at this time with the class action aspects of the complaint. Assume that both the specific factual information in the introductory memorandum and the specific factual allegations in the complaint are true and have ample evidentiary support.

F. SIMPLE JOINDER

Some obvious considerations in drafting a complaint are who can be sued and on what causes of actions. Rules 18 and 20 provide guidance: the former addressing joinder of multiple claims and the latter joinder of parties. However, Rule 20 is but one end of the "joinder" spectrum; it addresses only who *may* be included as parties to the suit. The complement to Rule 20 is Rule 19, which we address in the final chapter. Rule 19 regulates the *mandatory* inclusion of parties that are necessary to the suit.

Another Rule associated with these Rules, Rule 21, permits the court to drop or add any dispensable party on its own initiative or as a result of a motion by any party. Because this rule is very straightforward, this chapter does not provide a case for illustration. Simply put, Rule 21 permits the court to drop or add any non-necessary party at any stage in the action on any terms "as are just." Further, the court may sever any claim against any party and proceed with the severed claim separately.

However, this chapter does consider several of the simpler ways in which claims and parties are added: counterclaims (Fed. R. Civ. P. 13(a,b)), cross-claims (Fed. R. Civ. P. 13(g)), joinder of additional parties to counterclaims and cross-claims (Fed. R. Civ. P. 13(h)), and impleaders, also known as third-party practice (Fed. R. Civ. P. 14). The more exotic joinder rules, Interpleader (Fed. R. Civ. P. 22), Class Action (Fed. R. Civ. P. 23), and Intervention (Fed. R. Civ. P. 24), appear in the final chapter, along with Rule 19. The case that follows addresses issues regarding Rules 18 and 20.

■ KEDRA v. CITY OF PHILADELPHIA
454 F. Supp. 652 (E.D. Pa. 1978)

LUONGO, District Judge.

This civil rights action arises out of an alleged series of brutal acts committed by Philadelphia policemen against the plaintiffs. The events set forth in the complaint span one and one-half years, from December 1975 to February or March 1977. . . .

I. THE FACTUAL ALLEGATIONS

Plaintiffs are Dolores M. Kedra; her children, Elizabeth, Patricia, Teresa, Kenneth, Joseph, Michael, Robert, and James; and Elizabeth's husband, Richard J. Rozanski. Michael, Robert, and James Kedra are minors, and their mother sues on their behalf as parent and natural guardian.

Defendants are the City of Philadelphia; Police Commissioner Joseph J. O'Neill; officials of the Police Department's Homicide Division, Chief Donald Patterson, Chief Inspector Joseph Golden, Lieutenant Leslie Simmins, and Sergeant John Tiers; Homicide Detectives Richard Strohm, James Richardson, George Cassidy, and Michael Gannon; Police Lieutenant Augustus C. Miller; Police Officers James Brady, Robert Pitney, Jessie Vassor, and John J. D'Amico; an officer surnamed Tuffo; and other unidentified members of the Police Department. It is alleged that "at all times material to plaintiffs' cause of action (the City of Philadelphia) employed all of the individual defendants." It is further alleged that each of the individual defendants, "separately and in concert," acted under color of Pennsylvania law and, "pursuant to their authority as agents, servants, and employees of defendant City of Philadelphia, intentionally and deliberately engaged in the unlawful conduct described. . . ." They are sued "individually and in their official capacity" and "jointly and severally."

The series of events set forth in the complaint dates from December 22, 1975. On that evening, Richard Rozanski and Joseph and Michael Kedra were arrested at gun point without probable cause by defendants Vassor and D'Amico and taken to Philadelphia Police Headquarters (the Roundhouse). At the Roundhouse, they were separated and questioned for seventeen hours by defendants Strohm, Richardson, Cassidy, and Gannon. They were not informed of their constitutional rights and were refused requests for counsel. The complaint states

> During the course of the interrogation, plaintiffs Richard Rozanski, Michael Kedra and Joseph Kedra were handcuffed, struck about the head, face, stomach, abdomen, arms and legs with fists and physical objects, were harassed and threatened with further physical violence by defendants Strohm, Richardson, Cassidy and Gannon; during the course of this interrogation, plaintiff Richard Rozanski's legs were held apart by two of the defendant detectives while he was kicked in the testicles, groin, buttocks and legs by defendant Strohm." Rozanski, and Michael and Joseph Kedra each sustained serious injuries as a result of the beatings.

Meanwhile, defendant Richardson forcibly took Elizabeth Rozanski from her mother's house to the Roundhouse, where she was detained and questioned for seventeen hours by defendants Strohm, Gannon, Richardson, and Simmins. She was not advised of her rights. She was shown her husband, who had been beaten badly, and "was threatened with arrest in an attempt to coerce a false statement from her." A warrantless search of her bedroom was conducted by defendant Strohm "and others" without her consent and without probable cause.

On that same evening, Dolores Kedra voluntarily went to the Roundhouse "where she was illegally interrogated, coerced into signing a release authorizing the search of her house and forcibly detained" for nine hours by Strohm, Richardson, Cassidy, Gannon, "and other unidentified defendants."

Seven days later, on the morning of December 29, 1975, defendants Brady and Pitney went to the Kedra home, demanding to see Richard Rozanski and "falsely stating that they had papers for his appearance in Court on the following day." All of the plaintiffs except Dolores Kedra, the mother, were at home at the time. The policemen "attempted to drag (Rozanski) out of the house," but Rozanski and Kenneth Kedra shut and locked the door. Rozanski asked to see a warrant, but Brady and Pitney did not have one. Brady and Pitney then secured the aid of other policemen who, without a warrant or probable cause and "through the use of excessive force," "broke open the door with the butt end of a shotgun and forced their way into the house with shotguns, handguns, blackjacks, and nightsticks in hand." Defendants Brady, Pitney, Miller, Tiers, "and ten to fifteen other defendant members of the Philadelphia Police Department" conducted a thorough search of the house and, while doing so, physically assaulted Patricia, Joseph, Michael, and Kenneth Kedra, inflicting serious injuries. They also attempted to confiscate a camera and note pad being used by Joseph Kedra. It is alleged further that

> [T]he defendants unlawfully detained plaintiffs within the house by blocking off both the front and rear doors, holding plaintiffs in fear of life and limb by visibly displaying shotguns, handguns and nightsticks, and through threats of violence, coercion and abusive language.

Rozanski and Joseph, Michael, and Kenneth Kedra were taken to the Roundhouse in a police van, and Kenneth was beaten while being led to the van. At the Roundhouse, Michael and Kenneth were "unlawfully detained" for twenty-four hours, and Rozanski "was struck in the face by defendant Strohm" and was denied repeated requests for counsel. "[W]ithout just or probable cause," Rozanski was charged with murder, burglary, and receiving stolen goods, and Kenneth and Joseph were charged with assault and battery, harboring a fugitive, and resisting arrest. In defending these charges, they incurred attorney's fees. All three later were acquitted on all counts.

With respect to the December 1975 events, the complaint sets forth the following general allegations:

> 1. At all times material to plaintiffs' cause of action, plaintiff Richard Rozanski, through his attorney, offered to voluntarily surrender to the Philadelphia Police; the defendants chose, however, to engage in the course of conduct described in detail above, the purpose and effect of which was to

knowingly, intentionally and deliberately deprive plaintiffs of rights secured by the Constitution of the United States.

2. All of the aforementioned acts were committed by defendants intentionally, deliberately and maliciously, pursuant to their authority as agents, servants and employees of the Police Department of the City of Philadelphia.

3. The aforementioned acts were committed with the consent and knowledge and at the direction of defendant Joseph F. O'Neill in his capacity as Police Commissioner of the City of Philadelphia.

4. The aforementioned acts were committed with the knowledge and consent and at the direction of defendant Joseph Golden in his official capacity as Chief Inspector of the Homicide Division of the Police Department of the City of Philadelphia.

5. The aforementioned acts were committed with the knowledge and consent and at the direction of Captain Donald Patterson, Chief of the Homicide Division of the Philadelphia Police Department, Lieutenant Lesley Simmins and Sergeant John Tiers, in their official capacities as supervisory officials of the Philadelphia Police Department.

6. The defendants named in Paragraphs 18, 19, 20 and 21 are and were at all times material to plaintiffs' cause of action in a position to exercise direct supervision of the defendant officers and detectives and did in fact exercise such control and supervision at all times material to plaintiffs' cause of action.

7. All of the aforementioned acts were committed without just or probable cause with regard to each of the plaintiffs.

The complaint alleges further that "defendants have engaged and continue to engage in a systematic pattern of harassment, threats and coercion with the intention of, and having the effect of depriving plaintiffs of . . . rights and privileges. . . ." As part of this "pattern," Michael Kedra was arrested in June 1976 and was beaten by defendant Strohm, "who handcuffed plaintiff's hands behind his back, and struck him in the chest and stomach with a nightstick and fist." James Kedra has been "harassed and threatened without cause" by defendants D'Amico, Brady and Pitney, and in February or March 1977 "was grabbed by the shirt" by Tuffo and Pitney "and threatened with physical violence."

The complaint asserts that "as a result of the aforementioned actions, plaintiffs have suffered and continue to suffer severe emotional distress."

II. THE SUIT AND THE MOTION

Plaintiffs' complaint was filed on November 23, 1977. The action is brought under the Constitution and the Civil Rights Act of 1871, 42 U.S.C. §§1983, 1985, 1986. Jurisdiction is based on 28 U.S.C. §§1331 and 1343. As a basis for their civil rights claims, the plaintiffs assert that defendants' actions deprived them of the following federal "rights, privileges and immunities":

(a) The right of free speech and the right to peacably [*sic*] assemble under the First and Fourteenth Amendments. (b) The right to be secure in their persons, houses, papers, and effects against unreasonable searches and seizures under the Fourth and Fourteenth Amendments. (c) The prohibition against compulsory self-incrimination under the Fifth and Fourteenth Amendments. (d) The right to be free from deprivation of life, liberty or property without due process of law under the Fifth and Fourteenth Amendments. (e) The prohibition against cruel and unusual punishment under the Eighth and Fourteenth Amendments.

Without explanation, the complaint also cites the Equal Protection Clause of the Fourteenth Amendment and Article 1, §§1, 8, and 9 of the Pennsylvania Constitution. Plaintiffs also invoke the pendent jurisdiction doctrine to assert additional claims under Pennsylvania law "for false arrest, false imprisonment, malicious prosecution, assault and battery, trespass to real and personal property and negligent and intentional infliction of emotional distress." Plaintiffs seek compensatory and punitive damages in excess of $10,000 and attorneys' fees and costs.

All of the named defendants have filed the motion to dismiss. It is based on several grounds and raises questions of procedure as well as jurisdictional and substantive issues under the civil rights laws. In addition, the pendent state claims raise jurisdictional issues not discussed in the motion which should be examined in this opinion.

III. PROCEDURAL QUESTIONS

. . . Defendants contend that there has been an improper joinder of parties under Federal Rule of Civil Procedure 20(a). . . . Defendants argue that plaintiffs' claims against them do not "aris[e] out of the same transaction, occurrence, or series of transactions or occurrences" because they stem from events spanning a fourteen or fifteen month period. [A footnote states that the Federal Rules permit unlimited joinder of claims against an opposing party (Fed. R. Civ. P. 18(a)), but in multiparty cases joinder is limited by the requirement of Rule 20(a) that plaintiffs or defendants may not be joined in the same case unless some of the claims by or against each party arise out of common events and contain common factual or legal questions. Defendants have not argued that common factual and legal questions are not present in this case; the similarity of the claims against each defendant makes it abundantly clear that there are common issues. Once parties are joined under Rule 20(a), Rule 18(a)'s allowance of unlimited joinder of claims against those parties is fully applicable. *See* Advisory Committee on Rules, Note to 1966 Amendment to Rule 18.] The joinder provisions of the Federal Rules are very liberal. As the Supreme Court noted in *United Mine Workers v. Gibbs*, 383 U.S. 715, (1966), "Under the Rules, the impulse is toward entertaining the broadest possible scope of action consistent with fairness to the parties; joinder of claims, parties and remedies is strongly encouraged." 383 U.S. at 724 (footnote omitted). The reason for the liberality is that unification of claims in a single action is more convenient and less expensive and time-consuming for the parties and the court. *Mosley v. General Motors Corp.*, 497 F.2d 1330, 1332 (8th Cir. 1974). In recognition of this attitude, the "transaction or occurrence" language of Rule 20 has been interpreted to "permit all reasonably related claims for relief by or against different parties to be tried in a single proceeding. Absolute identity of all events is unnecessary." *Id.*, at 1333.

Although the events giving rise to plaintiffs' claims in this case occurred over a lengthy time period, they all are "reasonably related." The complaint sets forth a series of alleged unlawful detentions, searches, beatings and similar occurrences and charges defendants with "engag[ing] in a systematic pattern of harassment, threats and coercion with the intention of . . . depriving plaintiffs of [their] rights"; each of the incidents set forth is encompassed within the "systematic pattern." There is no logical reason why the systematic conduct alleged could not extend over a lengthy time period and, on the face of these allegations, there is nothing about the extended time span that attenuates the factual relationship among all of these events. The claims against the defendants "aris[e] out of the same transaction, occurrence, or series of transactions or occurrences" for purposes of Rule 20(a), and therefore joinder of defendants in this case is proper.

Apart from the procedural propriety of the joinder under Rule 20(a), however, there is a question whether a single trial of all claims against all defendants will prejudice some of the defendants. Some of the defendants were involved in only one of the several incidents alleged, and lumping them together with other defendants who were involved in more than one incident may be unfair. This problem is of particular concern with respect to the December 29, 1975 incident, which, apart from the allegations of direction, supervision, and control, appears to involve different actors than the other incidents alleged. Federal Rule 20(b) provides the court with power to remedy this situation: "The court may make such orders as will prevent a party from being embarrassed, delayed, or put to expense by the inclusion of a party against whom he asserts no claim and who asserts no claim against him, and may order separate trials or make other orders to prevent delay or prejudice." At oral argument, counsel for both sides recognized the potential prejudicial effect of the joinder in this case and suggested formulation of a stipulation which would attempt to remedy the problem. It appears, however, that it will be better to deal with the problem after discovery has been completed and the case is ready for trial. At that time, the degree of involvement of each of the defendants will be more clear and potential prejudice will be easier to assess. I therefore shall defer decision of this aspect of the case. I shall retain flexibility to sever portions of it or to take other remedial actions, if necessary, once the prejudice issue is more clearly focused.

[We have omitted a lengthy portion of this case that deals with 12(b)(6) motions.]

Comments and Questions

1. Use *Kedra* as an opportunity to truly "get your hands dirty" with facts and with the precise application of doctrine to those facts. Exactly why could the Kedras all be joined as plaintiffs along with the Rozanskis? Why could all of the quite different types of defendants be joined? And why could the various claims and theories of recovery be joined? A major difference between good and sloppy legal analysis is whether the lawyer is excruciatingly precise with what particular facts make the doctrine apply. For example, don't just say that it's the "same transaction, occurrence, or series of transactions or occurrences," and that there is a "question of law or fact common to all" the persons who have been joined. Prove your points to a skeptic by including the particular facts in the case. Much of civil procedure is proving the commonality of events that happened to different people. One way to focus your analysis is to ask which particular facts and legal questions are relevant to each element of each cause of action that applies to each party. For instance, think about the case of *Joe v. Sally* from the beginning of this chapter. Assume that Sally allegedly tripped Mary the following day. It is difficult to come up with any overlapping questions of law or fact, or any commonality of transaction, without going to such a level of generality that a judge would dismiss the commonality out of hand. You could argue that a common question of law is whether tripping can ever be intentional (or an act of unreasonable care), but surely a more precise bit of commonality is required by either the same transaction test or the "common question of law or fact" test in Rule 20.

One reason we have given you *Carpenter v. Dee* is to provide you a set of facts that you can return to in order to prove to yourself that you can apply procedural rules. Can Nancy Carpenter join the various causes of action and theories you came up with in former assignments? What if Randall Dee owed Charlie Carpenter $1000 on a debt unrelated to the Jeep or the accident? Could the plaintiff join that claim? What if Randall Dee had borrowed $1000 from Nancy Carpenter after the accident and now refuses to repay that debt. Can she join that claim in her complaint? Can she join Randall Dee, his brother, Ultimate Auto (where Dee bought the oversize tires and suspension lift kit), McGill's Garage, Inc. (where the jeep passed inspection), the City of Lowell (whose police evidently let the infractions relating to height pass without comment), and the manufacturer of the tires (assuming you can come up with a cause of action) as defendants in the same case? Prove your conclusion—using specific facts! What if Scott was injured in a similar incident a week later by Keefe, who also bought tires and a suspension lift kit from Ultimate Auto and lifted his jeep in the same manner? Can Carpenter and Scott draft one complaint against Ultimate Auto—a joinder of plaintiffs? What if Randall Dee and Keefe were racing their jeeps against each other when each tipped, injuring Charlie Carpenter and Scott? Could Nancy Carpenter and Scott join in a suit against Dee, Keefe, and Ultimate Auto? At the beginning of the course, we wrote that learning procedure permits you to exercise a great deal of imagination by considering "what ifs." Get in the habit of constructing your own hypotheticals to analyze alone or with your study group. The facts of the jeep case and the Cleveland firefighters case are rich with potential hypotheticals.

2. Rules 18 and 20 do not mention other procedural rules, concepts, and laws that might impose their own restraints, but those restraints are present. For instance, the Advisory Committee Notes to Subdivision (a)(1) of Rule 18 remind lawyers that jurisdictional and venue requirements must still be met. Issues of subject matter jurisdiction, personal jurisdiction, venue, and notice would of course apply to each party joined under Rule 20 as well. These topics are covered elsewhere in the course. Moreover, although Rule 18 (joinder of claims) is permissive, you must consider another field of civil procedure to decide what causes of action or theories to join. For example, in the case of *Joe v. Sally*, what would happen if Joe sued for battery and omitted negligence? Let's say Sally wins, and the case goes to final judgment. Could Joe then sue Sally again in negligence for the same tripping? Maybe you should put *res judicata* or *preclusion* in the margin of Rule 18 to remind yourself that the law does not allow as much permissiveness as Rule 18 would lead you to believe.

3. Throughout the course you should keep a very close watch on the expression "transaction or occurrence"—the phrase is a malleable guideline, but it is also a favorite of the drafters of the Federal Rules. Pay special attention to *which* rules use the phrase and notice *how* (as explained in the appellate holdings). Why did Charles Clark use a concept such as "transaction" as his unit of measure for the limits of joinder? What role does this "transactional" approach play in the overall philosophy of the Federal Rules? Why did the common law procedure inherently have much more limited joinder of claims and parties? Why would Field have wanted less joinder, particularly if he knew the types of cases brought today? When making arguments to courts, lawyers often go to the rationale of a rule in order to convince the court of the rule/application they want on the facts of the case. In *Kedra*, do the plaintiffs have policy arguments that would help them convince the court of a broad meaning for "transaction, occurrence, or series of transactions or occurrences"?

4. Strategic considerations matter in deciding how many claims and parties to try to put in any one lawsuit. For example, the size of the lawsuit will have a tremendous impact on (1) discovery (e.g., interrogatories can only be sent to actual parties of the suit); (2) costs (e.g., the more parties and theories, the more discovery and the more costs to your client); (3) evidence (e.g., different hearsay restrictions and altering what is relevant evidence depend on what claims and parties you have joined); (4) the jury (e.g., you may or may not want several defendants all pointing at each other, or you may or may not want to associate yourself with another party whose case or personality may rub off on your client); (5) *res judicata* (e.g.,

you may not want all of your eggs in one basket, but you don't want to be barred from plausible claims); and (6) control (e.g., with more parties it may or may not be harder to settle, depending on how you assess the situation; more defendants mean more pockets from which to pay your client, but may also mean that no one of them will want to give very much; more parties may also mean more lawyers who want to control the litigation in various ways). Use *Kedra* and *Carpenter v. Dee* to assess some of the strategic concerns relating to joinder.

5. Do the values "codified" in Rules 18 and 20 further the goal of making remedial justice more accessible? The goal of efficiency? Are these goals a zero-sum trade-off? For example, in *Kedra*, what do the plaintiffs and defendants gain or lose by broad joinder rules? What does society gain or lose? What about the values inherent in the tremendous discretion offered the trial judge by Rule 20(b) and Rule 42? If you were drafting the joinder provisions, would you grant this discretion to judges? In all cases?

6. How and why is the rule for consolidation (Fed. R. Civ. P. 42(a)) different from the rule for joinder of parties (Fed. R. Civ. P. 20(a))?

G. COUNTERCLAIMS AND CROSS-CLAIMS

A counterclaim is a claim asserted by a defendant against a plaintiff. A counterclaim may seek any kind of relief that the court is competent to give. The relief may or may not be related to the plaintiff's claim. A counterclaim may ask for relief that merely neutralizes or cancels out the plaintiff's claim, or it may seek relief that exceeds the plaintiff's desired relief. A cross-claim is a claim between co-parties, usually defendants.

In contrast to the blanket permissiveness of the counterclaim, a cross-claim may not assert every claim that possibly exists between co-parties. Instead, a cross-claim must be closely related to at least one other claim between co-parties. (However, once a cross-claim has been legitimately asserted, consider the expansiveness permitted by Rule 18(a).)

Under the Federal Rules, counterclaims can be either compulsory or permissive. *See* Fed. R. Civ. P. 13. The following case, *Banque Indosuez v. Trifinery*, introduces both types of counterclaims, and raises an interesting issue about Rule 11. Cross-claims, on the other hand, are always permissive. A party who does not bring a claim under 13(g) will not be barred by *res judicata*, waiver, or estoppel from asserting the claim at another time.

■ BANQUE INDOSUEZ v. TRIFINERY
817 F. Supp. 386 (S.D.N.Y. 1993)

HAIGHT, District Judge.

This case is before the Court on plaintiff's motion for partial summary judgment pursuant to Fed. R. Civ. P. 56. For the reasons discussed below, plaintiff's motion is granted.

BACKGROUND

This case arises out of a promissory note executed by defendant Trifinery and guaranteed by defendant Brass. Defendants do not dispute that they are liable under the note, but contend that summary judgment is inappropriate in that they have a viable claim for set-off, which they have brought as a counterclaim in this action. [Defendants asserted that they had paid plaintiff $963,183.36, which represented the amount of the note ($1,404,420.00) less the amount of their set-off ($461,236.64).]

Since there is no dispute as to liability under the promissory note, the only issue presented is whether defendants' assertion of a counterclaim is valid, and would therefore bar the entry of summary judgment on the note.

DISCUSSION

Defendants claim that the entry of summary judgment is inappropriate where the value of the counterclaim is uncertain. Plaintiff argues, however, that neither Trifinery as maker of the note, nor Brass as it[s] guarantor has the right to assert a counterclaim in this action, since a clause in the promissory note provides: "[Trifinery] further waives trial by jury and the right to interpose any counterclaim or set-offs of any kind in any litigation relating to this note or any such other liabilities." Plaintiff contends that by this provision, defendants waived any right to assert a counterclaim; accordingly, nothing stands in the way of the entry of summary judgment.

Defendants argue that this provision is not enforceable in a federal court, since the counterclaim is compulsory, and Fed. R. Civ. P. 13(a) requires a party to assert all compulsory counterclaims in this action, or waive them. In support of their argument that the clause is unenforceable, defendants cite *Loader Leasing Corp. v. Kearns*, 83 F.R.D. 202 (W.D. Pa. 1979). *Loader Leasing* also involved a contract provision which purportedly waived defendant's right to set-off any claims he might have against plaintiff. The court held that although the waiver provision would be enforceable in state court, it could not "unreasonably restrict[] the privilege of litigating an issue in a court of law . . . or unreasonably restrict[] the jurisdiction of a federal court," *id.*, at 203. Those problems arose in *Loader* because, in part, defendant's counterclaim was compulsory under Rule 13(a); and "[t]he failure to assert a compulsory counterclaim is a bar to a subsequent action in either a federal or state court." *Id.*, at 203-04. The district court in *Loader* enforced the waiver provision as to the defendant's second counterclaim which was permissive, but refused to do so as to the first, compulsory counterclaim.

In their briefs, the parties assume the applicability of New York law. New York law enforces waivers of the right to assert affirmative defenses, set-offs or counterclaims. *See Bank of New York v. Cariello,* 69 A.D.2d 805, 415 N.Y.S.2d 65 (2d Dept. 1979); *FDIC v. Frank Marino Corp.,* 74 A.D.2d 620, 425 N.Y.S.2d 34 (2d Dept. 1980). Courts in this circuit, applying New York law, generally hold that contractual agreements not to assert defenses, set-offs or counterclaims in subsequent litigation do not contravene public policy and are enforceable. *See Bankers Trust Co. v. Litton Systems,* 599 F.2d 488, 490 (2d Cir. 1979); *In re Gas Reclamation, Inc. Securities Litigation,* 741 F. Supp. 1094, 1102 (S.D.N.Y. 1990); *FDIC v. Borne,* 599 F. Supp. 891, 894-95 (E.D.N.Y. 1984). The waiver will not be enforced so as to bar a viable set-off or counterclaim sounding in fraud, but defendants at bar do not allege fraudulent conduct on the part of plaintiff.

Under New York law, all counterclaims are permissive. *See* N.Y.CPLR §3019 (McKinney's 1991), and practice commentary at 205. This contrasts with federal practice, where a counterclaim may be compulsory under Rule 13(a) or permissive under Rule 13(b), depending on the circumstances.

The question of fairness posed by *Loader Leasing Corp. v. Kearns, supra,* arises because plaintiff chose to file its action in federal court. It is not fair to enforce the contractual waiver of defendants' counterclaim if that counterclaim is compulsory under Rule 13(a). Were it otherwise, a party to a contract containing such a waiver provision could, by choice of a federal over state forum, prevent its adversary's counterclaim from ever being reached on the merits.

Accordingly, defendants' right to assert a counterclaim in this action turns on whether defendants' claim is permissive or compulsory under Rule 13. If the counterclaim is compulsory, the waiver clause is not enforceable since it would preclude defendants from ever raising the issue in this or any other court. If the counterclaim is permissive, however, the waiver clause is enforceable, and defendants would have to bring their claims in a separate action.

The test for determining whether a counterclaim is permissive or compulsory is set forth in *McCaffrey v. Rex Motor Transp., Inc.,* 672 F.2d 246, 248 (1st Cir. 1982):

(1) Are the issues of fact and law raised by the claim and the counterclaim largely the same; (2) would res judicata bar a subsequent suit on defendants' claims absent a compulsory counterclaim; (3) will substantially the same

evidence support or refute plaintiff's claim as well as defendants' counter-claims; and (4) is there any logical relationship between the claim and the counterclaim?

Plaintiff's claim is for payment on a promissory note. Defendants' counterclaims allege, in substance, that plaintiff negligently delayed the processing and delivery of letters of credit.

It is clear that the issues raised are not sufficiently interrelated to render defendants' counterclaim compulsory. The issues of fact and law are not substantially the same: breach of an implied duty of care in letter of transactions and liability under a promissory note present a host of different issues. In fact, plaintiff's claim, which involves two letters of credit, and defendants' claim, which involves three letters of credit, overlap as to only one letter of credit.

Moreover, because the issues are not sufficiently similar, there would be no res judicata bar if plaintiff's claim were decided before defendants' counterclaim. Although both claims do arise out of the same business relationship, this alone is insufficient to make the counterclaim compulsory.

Since defendants' counterclaim is permissive under Rule 13(b), the clause waiving defendants' right to assert a counterclaim or set-off is enforceable. Accordingly, defendants may not assert a counterclaim in this action, and that claim will be dismissed without prejudice.

Comments and Questions

1. What precise facts would you use to prove or disprove whether this case presents a Rule 13(a) or 13(b) counterclaim?

2. *Wright and Miller* also describe four tests for applying the words "transaction or occurrence" within the meaning of Rule 13(a). They are:

(1) Are the issues of fact and law raised by the claim and counterclaim largely the same?

(2) Would *res judicata* bar a subsequent suit on defendant's claim absent the compulsory counterclaim rule?

(3) Will substantially the same evidence support or refute plaintiff's claim as well as defendant's counterclaim?

(4) Is there any logical relation between the claim and the counterclaim?

Charles A. Wright, Arthur R. Miller & Mary Kay Kane, *Federal Practice and Procedure* §1410 (2d ed. 1990).

3. You have now seen the terms "transaction" or "occurrence" as a portion of different rules: Fed. R. Civ. P. 20 (permissive joinder of parties); Fed. R. Civ. P. 15(c) (relation back of amendments); Fed. R. Civ. P. 13(a) (compulsory counterclaims); Fed. R. Civ. P. 13(g) (cross-claims against a

co-party). Should the words be interpreted the same way, regardless of these different contexts, or might their interpretations take on slightly different shades of meaning? One way to approach such a question is to consider the purposes for using the terms in each context. Why are "transaction" and "occurrence" relevant to relationship back? Why are they relevant to joinder of parties or whether a counterclaim is compulsory? Would such a functional analysis lead one to different meanings? Professor Kane has explained how the term "transaction" has been used in the Federal Rules and elsewhere for differing purposes, and argues that those divergent purposes lead to different interpretations of the same word. Mary Kay Kane, *Original Sin and the Transaction in Federal Civil Procedure,* 76 Tex. L. Rev. 1723 (1998).

4. What does it mean to say that a counterclaim is "compulsory" or "permissive"? In what circumstances will the question of whether a potential counterclaim was compulsory normally be raised? For instance, assume that A and B are in a motor vehicle accident, each potentially having driven negligently into the other. A sues B. Will a court have to face the issue of whether B should have counterclaimed against A in the first suit, or in a later suit? As a defendant, how will you plead if you are in doubt as to whether a counterclaim is compulsory?

5. What place would Rule 13(a) counterclaims play in the overall procedural philosophy of Charles Clark? If you were on a committee drafting procedural rules, would you consider that a compulsory counterclaim provision would lead to "efficiency" or "inefficiency" or both? Consider the viewpoints of the court system, litigants, and their attorneys.

6. What are the reasons for the two exceptions in the second sentence of Rule 13(a)?

7. The courts are in disagreement as to why there is a bar of the compulsory counterclaim that had not been brought in the first case. Some say it is a result of waiver, and others apply *res judicata* or estoppel doctrine. From the point of view of the defendant in the first case, whose attorney neglected to bring the compulsory counterclaim (such that she cannot bring that claim in a subsequent case), it is difficult to see how it matters which theory causes the inability to now bring the claim.

8. Cross-claims must be closely related to at least one claim in the action. Consider the purpose of this requirement:

> When plaintiff brings suit against defendant, he is not free to object at some later time if defendant utilizes the forum to assert some unrelated claim against him in the forum of his own choice. But plaintiff's suit could become unduly complicated and prejudice might result to him if defendant is allowed to raise a claim against a co-defendant in which the original plaintiff has no interest.

Charles A. Wright, Arthur R. Miller & Mary Kay Kane, *Federal Practice and Procedure* §1431 (2d ed. 1990).

9. Make up a hypothetical involving a potential cross-claim. Why aren't cross-claims compulsory?

Practice Exercise No. 12: Considering Counterclaims, Cross-Claims, and Rule 13(h) Additional Parties in *Carpenter*

Counterclaims. Consider the following possible counterclaim in the *Carpenter* case. Shortly after the accident in which her husband was killed, Nancy Carpenter calls a friend of the family who works at Raytheon (where Randall Dee was and is employed) and tells her that Randall Dee is an alcoholic. Randall Dee is then fired from his job. Does Randall Dee have a defamation claim against Nancy Carpenter for slander? Would this be a compulsory counterclaim? A permissive counterclaim? Would you need to do some legal research before you could answer this question?

Cross-claims. Assume that the judge in the motions session in the previous class has granted the motion of Nancy Carpenter to add Ultimate Auto, Inc. and the City of Lowell as named defendants, and the complaint is now filed as amended. Assume further that you represent the defendant driver of the jeep in question, Randall Dee. Do you have a plausible cross-claim? Prove it. Focus on the language of Mass. R. Civ. P. 13(g), which is the same as Fed. R. Civ. P. 13(g). If you do have a plausible cross-claim, how many counts would it have? What are the strategic reasons for filing it or not filing it? Regardless, try your hand at drafting such a cross-claim. Will you draft *de novo*, or can you get some help from a form somewhere near at hand?

You should also now look at the Massachusetts Contribution Statute in the Case Files. Consider other possible cross-claims, as well as Mass. R. Civ. P. 13(h). Are there parties you might wish to bring in through the 13(h) route? Would you be able to?

H. THIRD-PARTY PRACTICE

Rule 14 governs the procedure through which a defendant can bring a third party into the action. The rule permits the court to allow a defendant to *implead* a person not already a party to the action who is purportedly liable to the defendant for all or part of the defendant's liability to the plaintiff. In such an instance, the original defendant, now acting as a *third-party plaintiff*, impleads a *third-party defendant*. The case below illustrates.

■ GROSS v. HANOVER INS. CO.
138 F.R.D. 53 (S.D.N.Y. 1991)

LEISURE, District Judge.

This is an action arising out of an insurance claim following the alleged loss of a substantial amount of jewelry. Defendant Hanover Insurance Company has now moved, pursuant to Federal Rule of Civil Procedure 14(a), to implead as third-party defendants Joseph Rizzo and Anthony Rizzo. For the reasons stated below, defendant's motion is granted.

BACKGROUND

The facts necessary to decide the instant motion are not complex. Plaintiff alleges that he suffered a loss consisting of approximately $217,800 worth of diamonds consigned to one "3-R Jewelers" ("3-R"), a retail jewelry store, and approximately $48,000 worth of diamonds and emeralds left by plaintiff at 3-R for safekeeping. 3-R was at the relevant time owned by one Anthony Rizzo ("Anthony"), who employed his brother Joseph Rizzo ("Joseph") at the store. Plaintiff thereafter made a claim under a jewelers' block insurance policy issued to him by defendant, seeking $50,000 for loss of consignment goods and $25,000 for loss of goods left for safekeeping. The parties agree that the loss of the jewels was the result of a theft that occurred at the 3-R store.

Defendant alleges, however, that on December 16, 1989, the evening of the theft, a witness observed a man enter the 3-R store and begin talking to Joseph. Shortly thereafter, the man talking with Joseph walked out, then returned with a paper bag and proceeded to walk behind the counter and into a back room. When the witness left 3-R, the man was still in the store. Affidavit of Stephen H. Marcus, Esq., sworn to on June 28, 1991 ("Marcus Aff."), Exhibit H. In a statement he gave to the police, Joseph stated that he was in the store preparing to close for the night when two men entered and asked to purchase a watch. Joseph stated that he left the two men in the front of the store and went to the back to get a warranty card for the watch. He stated that he then heard the front door slam. When he returned to the front of the store the men were gone and a box and case of jewels were missing from the safe, which he had left open. Marcus Aff., Exhibit G. Defendant also claims that Joseph was addicted to cocaine, and that Anthony was aware of this fact but nevertheless continued to employ Joseph at 3-R. The police report includes statements from Anthony that Joseph had a cocaine habit, that he thought the habit was under control, but "guess bigger problem than he [Anthony] thought," and that it "Looked like Joey was setting place up." Marcus Aff., Exhibit F.

Defendant's proposed third-party complaint thus seeks to implead Joseph and Anthony on the ground that they will be liable to defendant, should defendant be found to be liable to plaintiff. Marcus Aff., Exhibit E. Specifically, the proposed third-party complaint asserts claims against Joseph for negligent handling of the jewels as plaintiff's consignee or bailee, or as the agent of 3-R; against Joseph for actual conversion of the jewels; and against Anthony for the negligent hiring, retention and super-vision of Joseph.

DISCUSSION

Rule 14(a) provides in relevant part that "[a]t any time after com-mencement of the action a defending party, as a third-party plaintiff, may cause a summons and complaint to be served upon a person not a party to the action who is or may be liable to the third-party plaintiff for all or part of the plaintiff's claim against the third-party plaintiff." Fed. R. Civ. P. 14(a). Where, as here, the defendant seeks to file the third-party com-plaint more than ten days after serving its original answer, the defendant "must obtain leave on motion upon notice to all parties to the action." Fed. R. Civ. P. 14(a). "The purpose of this rule is to promote judicial effi-ciency by eliminating the necessity for the defendant to bring a separate action against a third individual who may be secondarily or derivatively liable to the defendant for all or part of the plaintiff's original claim." *McLaughlin v. Biasucci*, 688 F. Supp. 965, 967 (S.D.N.Y. 1988). Accordingly, the district court has considerable discretion in deciding whether to per-mit a third-party complaint. *See Consolidated Rail Corp. v. Metz*, 115 F.R.D. 216, 218 (S.D.N.Y. 1987); *Old Republic Insurance Co. Concast.*, 99 F.R.D. 566, 568 (S.D.N.Y. 1983). "The court must balance the benefits derived from impleader—that is, the benefits of settling related matters in one suit— against the potential prejudice to the plaintiff and third-party defendants." *Oliner v. McBride's Industries, Inc.*, 106 F.R.D. 14, 20 (S.D.N.Y. 1985).

In the case at bar, defendant's proposed third-party claims arise from "'the same aggregate or core of facts which is determinative of the plain-tiff's claim,'" and thus the interest in judicial economy would be served by permitting those claims to proceed in the instant action. *National Bank of Canada v. Artex Industries, Inc.*, 627 F. Supp. 610, 613 (S.D.N.Y. 1986) (quot-ing *Dery v. Wyer*, 265 F.2d 804, 807 (2d Cir. 1959)). Plaintiff argues, however, that the proposed third-party claims are "speculative," and thus the motion to implead should be denied. This argument fails for several reasons.

First, there is some question as to whether plaintiff may attack the merits of the proposed third-party claims at this stage of the proceedings. Second, it is well established that the words "is or may be liable" in Rule 14(a) make it clear that impleader is proper even though the third-party defendant's liability is not automatically established once the third-party plaintiff's liability to the original plaintiff has been determined. . . . Finally, the proposed third-party claims are sufficiently alleged, for Rule

14(a) purposes. "The federal and New York state court decisions hold that third-party impleader practice encompasses subrogation claims." . . .

Plaintiff's second argument in opposition to the instant motion consists of a claim that defendant has been dilatory in seeking to implead, and that plaintiff will suffer prejudice if discovery is expanded to include the third-party claims. There is, however, little evidence to suggest that defendant was so slow in bringing its Rule 14(a) motion that that motion should be denied. More importantly, the Court believes that the prejudice to be felt by plaintiff—if any—due to the need for additional discovery, is sufficiently outweighed by the benefits of more efficient litigation to be gained by permitting impleader. . . . If, in the future, plaintiff believes that defendant is using its third-party claims to delay the progress of the principal complaint in this action, he should so inform the Court. Needless to say, the Court would not countenance such tactics. . . .

CONCLUSION

For the reasons stated above, defendant's motion to implead Joseph Rizzo and Anthony Rizzo, pursuant to Federal Rule of Civil Procedure 14(a), is granted. SO ORDERED.

Comments and Questions

1. Perhaps the most difficult language to apply in Rule 14 is the description in the first sentence of the type of person who is not a party who can be brought in as a third-party defendant. Note the following words carefully: "who is or may be liable to the third-party plaintiff for all or part of the plaintiff's claim against the third-party plaintiff." Consequently, in order for a defendant (third-party plaintiff) to implead a new party (the third-party defendant), three conditions must be met (leaving out for now jurisdiction and notice problems, which will come later in the course). First, and easiest, impleader can be used only in order to bring in one who is not already a party. Second, the defendant (third-party plaintiff) has to have a claim against the new party it is trying to implead (the third-party defendant). In other words, if A sues B, and B says, in effect, "It's not my fault, it is C's fault," that alone does *not* a good impleader make. Instead, B needs a theory of liability *against* C. By the way, nothing prevents B from pointing the finger at C throughout the trial, or even subpoenaing C to testify at the trial. C doesn't have to be a party in order for one side to blame C, assuming the evidence is relevant.

Third, for B to have a valid impleader against C, B not only needs a theory of liability against C, but it has to be "for all or part of" A's claim against B. Here is an example of a good impleader. A lent money to C, and B agreed to be C's guarantor. Under guaranty or surety law, if the guarantor or surety has to pay the lender, then the guarantor ordinarily has a claim against the borrower for what the guarantor was forced to pay the lender because of the borrower's debt. Therefore, if A (lender) sues B (guarantor), then B could implead C (borrower) because B will have a claim against C for all of what B will have to pay A.

2. The Rule 8(a) pleading requirements explicitly apply to a Rule 14 third-party complaint. Rule 7 makes clear that a third-party complaint is ordinarily a "pleading" and that a third-party answer is required if a "third-party complaint is served." An answer by the third-party defendant should include Rule 8(b) admissions and denials and 8(c) affirmative defenses. Moreover, Rule 12(b) requires that all defenses to a "claim for relief in any pleading," explicitly including third-party claims, "shall be asserted in the responsive pleading thereto if one is required," and then excepts the 12(b) defenses that can be made by motion. Therefore, the third-party defendant should raise 12(b) defenses against the third-party plaintiff either by answer or motion. (However, 12(b)(1) and 12(b)(3) defenses generally will be unsuccessful, as will be explored in a later chapter.) The third-party defendant may also, according to Rule 14, "assert against the plaintiff any defenses which the third-party plaintiff has to the plaintiff's claim." Why should the third-party defendant be able to assert the initial defendant's defenses against the plaintiff?

3. As you read the following excerpt from *United States v. Olavarrieta,* 812 F.2d 640 (11th Cir. 1987), see if you agree with the court that it is an improper impleader, and consider the tactical issues facing a litigator who has the the option of impleader versus separate trials. Assuming Olavarrieta's impleader against the Board of Regents was proper, could Olavarrieta claim more from the Board of Regents than the United States was claiming from him? Precisely where would you look to find an answer to this?

The United States, as guarantor of Jose Olavarrieta's federally insured student loans totaling $4,000, filed suit against Olavarrieta in order to collect the unpaid balance and interest on the loans. Inter-National Bank of Miami made the loans to Olavarrieta under the Federal Insured Student Loan Program, Title IV-B of the Higher Education Act of 1965, 20 U.S.C.A. §§1071-88. After Olavarrieta defaulted on the loans, the bank sought payment from the government. The government paid off Olavarrieta's liability to the bank and then sought reimbursement from Olavarrieta by filing this suit.

Olavarrieta filed a third party complaint against the University of Florida, claiming that it had violated the Higher Education Act of 1965 and had breached its contract with him by failing to award him a J.D. degree. Olavarrieta amended this complaint to add the Board of Regents of the Division of Universities of the Florida Department of Education as a third party defendant and to add a claim for indemnification by the third party defendants for any sums he was found to owe the government. The district court granted the University of Florida's motion to dismiss. . . .

[W]e hold that the district court properly dismissed the third party complaint against the University of Florida. The capacity to be sued is determined by state law. Fed. R. Civ. P. 17(b). Under Florida law, the University of Florida is not endowed with an independent corporate existence or the capacity to be sued in its own name. Rather, those characteristics are bestowed on the Board of Regents as the head of Florida's university system. Therefore, the University of Florida is not a proper party in this action, and the district court was correct in dismissing the third party complaint asserted against it.

The district court was also correct in dismissing the third party complaint against the Board of Regents. Olavarrieta simply has failed to state any legal or factual grounds for indemnification. Furthermore, to the extent the third party complaint seeks relief on account of the University's failure to award Olavarrieta a J.D. degree as promised, it does not set forth proper grounds for a third party claim under Fed. R. Civ. P. 14(a). Rule 14(a) allows a defendant to assert a claim against any person not a party to the main action only if that third person's liability on that claim is in some way dependent upon the outcome of the main claim. Rule 14(a) does not allow the defendant to assert a separate and independent claim even though the claim arises out of the same general set of facts as the main claim. . . . Olavarrieta's third party claim alleging breach of contract or fraud on account of the University of Florida's failure to award him a J.D. degree as promised is a separate and independent action from the government's action against him. Whether Olavarrieta is entitled to any relief on this claim is wholly independent of his liability to the government for defaulting on his student loans. Therefore, Olavarrieta has failed to state any appropriate grounds for maintaining a third party complaint against the Board of Regents.

4. Be sure to read all of Rule 14. It contains some details regarding transactions or occurrences that you should know. For instance, the third-party defendant may, but is not required to, assert any claims arising out of the same transaction or occurrence against the plaintiff. Also, the (original) plaintiff may assert a claim against the third-party defendant if the claim arises out of the same transaction or occurrence.

5. Note how third-party plaintiffs may implead someone whom plaintiff could not have sued directly; also, note how they might implead someone whom plaintiff could have sued directly (but chose not to).

Practice Exercise No. 13: Considering Impleader and Settlement in *Carpenter*

For a complex application of what you learned in this assignment, now assume that your success and familiarity with *Carpenter* has led the senior partner of the firm representing the defendant, Ultimate Auto, to approach you with the latest developments in this tort case. She informs you that the plaintiff, Nancy Carpenter, is interested in reaching a settlement with our client (Ultimate Auto) and has already reached a settlement with the City of Lowell for $15,000. The firm will, of course, settle this case if it is in the best interest of our client. The partner also informs you, however, that last night she commissioned a draft of a third-party complaint from one of her budding associates. The motion to bring the third-party complaint against the garage that had passed the Dee Jeep for inspection (and against the garage's owner), and the third-party complaint, are in the Case Files. The issues for your resolution are as follows:

(a) Is the third-party complaint properly drafted?
(b) Since the plaintiff has settled with the City, can Ultimate Auto still implead the garage?
(c) If Carpenter settles her claims against Ultimate Auto, can our client still recover on the third-party claim against McGill's Garage? If so, what will Ultimate Auto have to prove in such a lawsuit? (In order to answer this question, you must read the contribution statute very carefully. Pay particular attention to each word in part 3(d).)
(d) What are the overall strategic gains and losses by settling or not settling? How substantial are the risks of each?

In this assignment you will need to use (and meticulously apply) the text of Rule 14 and the Massachusetts Contribution Statute, which is in the Case Files.

Contribution is an action in tort. When two or more parties are jointly liable for the same injury and the injured party has recovered for the losses from one of the parties, contribution statutes permit that paying party to seek contribution from the other tortfeasors. As the Massachusetts Contribution Statute suggests, settlements substantially complicate the situation.

I. REVIEW

This is a good time to review the materials in this chapter. After doing so, answer this review question.

Instructions: Complete the opinion of the trial court in the following case. Assume that the Federal Rules of Civil Procedure apply. Be a careful judge, who explains her or his actions. This question should take the *full* 90 minutes to answer completely; use at least half the time thinking, not writing. Your Rules Supplement is the only source you should require (though you may cite to cases that we have studied).

Flannel v. J. C. Penny*

Justice, J.:

The facts that underlie this lawsuit for $2.8 million are traceable to a dispute over $2.00 between a customer and the management of a retail store. Ms. Flannel seeks to "make a federal case"—as certainly is her right under the existing statutes—out of the circumstances that befell her after she purchased a pair of blue jeans for eight dollars at the J. C. Penny store in Capital City, Northeastern. The following facts are alleged in her complaint filed in district court.

The day after she purchased the jeans, she discovered that the jeans were defective and returned them to the store. She requested that they give her a new pair or that they refund her the purchase price, which she had paid by personal check. The store refused. Ms. Flannel left the store with the jeans and then did two things: she stopped payment on her check and went and had the zipper replaced at the local cleaners at a cost of $2.00. With the repair bill in hand, she then returned to the store and demanded that the store pay her back for the cost of the repair. The customer-returns employee, Isabel Duffey, refused. Instead she made an oral demand of Ms. Flannel for $13.25 representing the original purchase price and the bank service handling charge for the stopped check. Ms. Flannel refused to honor this demand for payment in rather colorful language. The next day, the store's assistant manager, Douglas A. Stauffer, filed a criminal complaint against her, charging her with a violation of the bad check statute. 18 N.G.L. §4195.11.†

After the criminal complaint was filed, Ms. Flannel returned to the store and offered to pay the eight dollars; the offer was refused. Ms. Flannel went to see the store manager, Robert Boyd, who told Ms. Flannel that he had authorized the complaint because "you attempted fraud on my store." He also stated that he would not drop the complaint because "then the store would have to pay court costs and we want to make an example of you

---

*This question is based on a Third Circuit case decided by Chief Judge Ruggero J. Aldisert, *Rannels v. S. E. Nichols, Inc.*, 591 F.2d 242 (3rd Cir. 1979).

†18 N.G.L. §4195.11 provides:

> (a) Offense defined. A person commits an offense if s/he issues or passes a check or similar order for the payment of money, knowing that it will not be honored by the drawee.
>
> (b) Presumption. For the purposes of this section as well as in any prosecution for theft committed by means of a bad check, an issuer is presumed to know that the check or order (other than a post-dated check or order) would not be paid, if (1) the issuer had no account with the drawee at the time the check or order was issued; or (2) payment was refused by the drawee for lack of funds, upon presentation within thirty days after issue, and the issuer failed to make good within ten days after receiving notice of that refusal.
>
> (c) Grading. An offense under this section is a misdemeanor of the second degree if the amount of the check or order exceeds $200.00; otherwise it is a summary offense.

so that people don't try to stop checks on us and keep the goods." These remarks were made in the presence of Ms. Flannel, her son and other customers.

Ms. Flannel then wrote to the corporate president, Manfred Brecker, at the head office in New Jersey, explaining the history of the transaction asking him to intervene and order his subordinates to drop the criminal complaint. She also told him that she was concerned about the defamation to her character and good standing in the community as she was the local PTA president and an elder in her church. His letter in response, as described in her complaint, shows that he was informed as to the facts of the transaction and that he supported the actions of his employees at the Capital City store in filing the criminal charges against her.

Ms. Flannel was tried and acquitted of the bad check charge and later voluntarily paid the Capital City store $6.00 "in full satisfaction and settlement of her debt."

Ms. Flannel then filed suit in this court for $2.8 million in damages for malicious prosecution. The elements of the relevant Northeastern law on malicious prosecution are: (1) the termination in the complainant's favor of the criminal proceedings; (2) want of probable cause for the criminal proceedings; and (3) malice. Probable cause has been defined as "a reasonable ground of suspicion supported by circumstances sufficiently strong in themselves as to make a cautious person believe that the person accused is guilty of the charged offense." Malice has been defined as "the intentional doing of a wrongful act without just cause or excuse, with an intent to inflict an injury or under circumstances that the law will imply an evil intent."

The defendants have filed a 12(b)(6) motion to dismiss, claiming that the allegations in the plaintiff's complaint fall short of making out a claim for relief under Northeastern law. We rule that . . .

[Students: Complete the opinion, giving your ruling and your reasoning.]

4

Discovery

A. INTRODUCTION

The primary function of the discovery process is to provide litigants with an opportunity to review all of the pertinent evidence prior to trial. This function is thought to be consistent with the pursuit of justice for at least three reasons. First, it reduces the chances of trial by ambush and facilitates determination upon the merits of the case. Second, it promotes settlement because it enables parties to assess the merits of their case well before trial. And third, it reduces the drain on the resources of the court because discovery educates the parties and often narrows the scope of issues in dispute.

Perhaps you associate the discovery process, however, not with the pursuit of justice, but rather with its notorious reputation for cost and abuse. Indeed, the discovery process has become a focal point of considerable criticism in the popular media. And to be sure, some litigants impose onerous burdens upon their adversaries, whether through excessive discovery requests to the other side or through production of an avalanche of documents to hide the proverbial needle in a haystack. In these circumstances, instead of being an essential element in the pursuit of justice, discovery proves to be a crippling obstacle. But we ask you to keep an open mind about the true dimensions of discovery abuse problems. You will learn by the end of this chapter that, in most cases, albeit not the most publicized ones, discovery is used rather sparingly.

In this chapter, we explore the process of discovery from a variety of angles to understand its role in the jurisprudence of procedure. The chapter introduces the techniques of discovery under the Federal Rules in their historical context. In a Practice Exercise and in the Case Files, we then invite you to consider the strategy and efficacy of various types of discovery in an actual case. In order to facilitate your understanding of the operation of discovery (and other procedural) rules, we also offer a short primer on some of the rules of evidence. And, finally, we take a step back to review the goals, use (and abuse), and effect of the discovery rules in the context of (1) the lawyer's role as zealous advocate and (2) recent and proposed reforms.

B. THE ROLE OF DISCOVERY   G

The message from practicing lawyers to law students is clear and unambiguous:

> Make no mistake: it is not trials, but discovery, that is the work of today's litigator (yesterday's "trial lawyer").

You may already be familiar with the laments of the young lawyer: "I practiced four years before I had the opportunity even to second-chair a trial." "There are young partners around here that still don't have any real trial experience." "Even when there is a trial, the partners always handle them." "I've never lost a trial—but, unfortunately, for all the wrong reasons." And the chorus from senior lawyers strikes a similar chord: "We're ready for trial, but the court is booked for the next six months; we'll probably settle first." "My client can't afford a trial." "It's rare that cases actually go to trial these days." This phenomenon about which lawyers complain is real:

> The dream, of course, is to be called two weeks before trial to try the case. That's just enough time to master the facts, learn the law, and not be bored by hundreds of documents and depositions. A masterful opening ensues, then a killer cross, leaving the expert to slither in shame from the stand. The brilliant closing is almost unnecessary. The jury verdict in your favor is returned in only the time it takes the jury to eat a corned beef on rye.
>
> Reality, however, is different. Most cases settle, and victory is not in the scathing cross, but in the tedious review of documents. Success is in the details, the expertly drafted interrogatories or request for records, and in the ingenious strategy to obtain the statement allegedly protected by privilege.
>
> For it is Discovery which we do. The motions, the papers, the depositions. This is the numbing, ditch digging work that determines the winner. . . .

[W]e know without devoting our time and sweat to discovery, the thought of a favorable jury verdict is a mere dream.

American Bar Association, *Discovery*, Litigation (Winter 1997).

The predominant and all-consuming role of discovery in American civil procedure, however, is neither inevitable nor unavoidable. Indeed, it is largely a product of our own creation—and even a fairly recent one. Prior to the Federal Rules of Civil Procedure, discovery in civil cases in federal court was severely limited.* At common law, and even under the Field Code, pleadings were the primary mechanism for divulging and clarifying the issues and facts that would define the controversy at trial and determine the results.

Under the common law, the federal courts had no general inherent power to order discovery and were only invested with that power by two statutes dealing with depositions. (Depositions are used by attorneys to question potential witnesses under oath about their knowledge and participation in the events surrounding a lawsuit.) The first of these statutes permitted depositions only "when the witness lived more than one hundred miles from the place of trial, or was on a voyage at sea, or about to go out of the United States, or when the witness was aged or infirm."† Depositions were permitted under the second statute only when "necessary to prevent a failure or delay of justice."†† Both statutes were designed to record the testimony of witnesses who were unavailable for trial, not merely to discover facts. There were two additional rules that applied only in equity cases, but even these rules permitted discovery only of facts or documents necessary to prove one's own case; parties were not permitted to "discover" their opponent's claims or defenses.

Even today, in other countries, discovery of an opponent's claims or defenses is not widely recognized as a right. Many of the European continental systems have no discovery. In Germany, for example, the plaintiff typically attaches to his complaint all of the major documents that support his claim, and the defendant follows the same pattern in his answer. Neither counsel seeks to discover evidence unknown to her or his client, because digging for the facts is the province of the court. *See* J. H. Langbein, *The German Advantage in Civil Procedure*, 52 U. Chicago L. Rev. 823, 827 (1985). Japan, another civil law country, takes a different tack. Before

---

*Prior to 1938, some of the states had experimented in various degrees with the discovery devices, which became central to federal practice. However, no single state went as far as the federal rules in opening up discovery.

†Stephen N. Subrin, *Fishing Expeditions Allowed: The Historical Background of the 1938 Federal Discovery Rules*, 34 B.C. L. Rev. (1998) 691, 698 (quoting Edson R. Sunderland, The New Federal Rules, 45 W. Va. L. Q. 5, 19 (1938)).

††*Id.* (quoting Sunderland, 45 W. Va. L. Q. at 19); *see also id.* at 698-699 ("In order to warrant the taking of such a deposition it was necessary to show . . . that the application was made in good faith and not merely for discovery purposes.") (quoting 6 James Wm. Moore, *Moore's Federal Practice* §26 App. 100 (citations omitted)).

bringing a case to trial, attorneys are expected to conduct intensive pre-trial investigations, such as interviewing witnesses and examining other evidence. All interviewing must be voluntary, and there is no formal method for seeking written replies under oath or admissions. Attorneys may request specific categories of documents from the other party if there is a risk that the evidence will be altered or destroyed after the complaint is filed. All requests must specifically identify the document, must summarize the contents, and must specify the facts to be proven.

The Federal Rules revolutionized American procedure by establishing a broad scope for what may be obtained through discovery. Read Fed. R. Civ. P. 26(b). Generally speaking, a party is *entitled* to demand the discovery of any matter that

- is relevant to the subject matter;
- is not unreasonably cumulative or burdensome; and
- is not privileged.

See Fed. R. Civ. P. 26(b).

Given the capacity of the human imagination, the relevancy criterion is virtually without boundary. Moreover, a party is entitled to discovery not only of material that is relevant and admissible at trial, but also of information that "appears reasonably calculated to lead to the discovery of admissible evidence." Fed. R. Civ. P. 26(b)(1). Accordingly, it is an uphill battle to convince a court that discovery sought by opposing counsel is so unrelated to the subject matter of any claim, defense, issue, statement, document, or other discoverable matter in the case that it cannot be said to be "relevant" within the expansive meaning of that term in Rule 26.

The second discovery criterion is the product of a 1983 amendment to Rule 26. Prior to the amendment, Rule 26 provided for unlimited discovery "[u]nless the court orders otherwise." As amended, the Rule now provides that the court may limit the frequency of discovery when the information sought is "unreasonably cumulative or duplicative, or is obtainable from some other source that is more convenient." Naturally, good lawyers will usually have an argument why even multiple identical versions of a document need to be produced in order for them to prepare their case.

The third discovery criterion exempts privileged material from discovery—even if it is "relevant." The most frequently invoked privilege is the attorney-client privilege, which precludes the discovery of confidential communications between an attorney and her client. By virtue of a 1970 amendment to Rule 26, limitations were placed on the discovery of trial preparation materials and on the methods for obtaining information about experts and their opinions. The following is an excerpt from a 1947 Supreme Court decision that deals with the issue of an attorney's trial preparation and the protection of his work product. The excerpt is included here primarily because it outlines the Court's general attitude toward the purpose of the new paradigm of open-handed, party-controlled discovery. This was the Court's first major decision discussing discovery following the 1938 enactment of the Federal Rules.

■ HICKMAN v. TAYLOR
329 U.S. 495 (1947)

Justice MURPHY delivered the opinion of the Court:

This Case presents an important problem under the Federal Rules of Civil Procedure . . . as to the extent to which a party may inquire into oral and written statements of witnesses, or other information, secured by an adverse party's counsel in the course of preparation for possible litigation after a claim has arisen. Examination into a person's files and records, including those resulting from the professional activities of an attorney, must be judged with care. It is not without reason that various safeguards have been established to preclude unwarranted excursions into the privacy of a man's work. At the same time, public policy supports reasonable and necessary inquiries. Properly to balance these competing interests is a delicate and difficult task. . . .

[The facts of the case are summarized as follows: The *J. M. Taylor* tug sank while towing a Baltimore & Ohio Railroad car float across the Delaware River. Five crewmembers drowned; four survived. Two months after the accident, the United States Steamboat Inspectors held a public hearing where the four survivors were examined. Shortly thereafter, counsel for the tug owners, Fortenbaugh, took statements privately from survivors and witnesses in anticipation of possible litigation from the families of the deceased. Eventually, families of each of the deceased brought claims against the tug owners. All but one of the claims settled without litigation. About nine months after the accident, the fifth claimant (Petitioner) brought suit in the federal district court suing the tug owners and the railroad (Defendants).]

One year later, petitioner filed 39 interrogatories directed to the tug owners. The 38th interrogatory read:

> State whether any statements of the members of the crews of the Tugs *J. M. Taylor* and *Philadelphia* or of any other vessel were taken in connection with the towing of the car float and the sinking of the Tug *John M. Taylor.*
>
> Attach hereto exact copies of all such statements if in writing, and if oral, set forth in detail the exact provisions of any such oral statements or reports.

Supplemental interrogatories asked whether any oral or written statements, records, reports or other memoranda had been made concerning any matter relative to the towing operation, the sinking of the tug, the salvaging and repair of the tug, and the death of the deceased. If the answer was in the affirmative, the tug owners were then requested to set forth the nature of all such records, reports, statements or other memoranda.

The tug owners, through Fortenbaugh, answered all of the interrogatories except No. 38 and the supplemental ones just described. While admitting that statements of the survivors had been taken, they declined to summarize or set forth the contents. They did so on the ground that such requests called "for privileged matter obtained in preparation for litigation" and constituted "an attempt to obtain indirectly counsel's private files." It was claimed that answering these requests "would involve practically turning over not only the complete files, but also the telephone records and, almost, the thoughts of counsel."

In connection with the hearing on these objections, Fortenbaugh made a written statement and gave an informal oral deposition explaining the circumstances under which he had taken the statements. But he was not expressly asked in the deposition to produce the statements. . . . [The District Court held that petitioner's requests were not privileged and ordered counsel to answer the interrogatory and the supplemental interrogatories, produce all of the witnesses' statements, and state any facts concerning the case that Defendants learned through the witnesses, and to] produce Mr. Fortenbaugh's memoranda containing statements of fact by witnesses or to submit these memoranda to the Court for determination of those portions which should be revealed to Plaintiff." Upon their refusal, the court adjudged them in contempt and ordered them imprisoned until they complied.

The Third Circuit Court of Appeals, also sitting *en banc*, reversed the judgment of the District Court. It held that the information here sought was part of the "work product of the lawyer" and hence privileged from discovery under the Federal Rules of Civil Procedure. The importance of the problem, which has engendered a great divergence of views among district courts, led us to grant certiorari. . . .

The pre-trial deposition-discovery mechanism established by Rules 26 to 37 is one of the most significant innovations of the Federal Rules of Civil Procedure. Under the prior federal practice, the pre-trial functions of notice-giving issue-formulation and fact-revelation were performed primarily and inadequately by the pleadings. Inquiry into the issues and the facts before trial was narrowly confined and was often cumbersome in method. The new rules, however, restrict the pleadings to the task of general notice-giving and invest the deposition-discovery process with a vital role in the preparation for trial. The various instruments of discovery now serve (1) as a device, along with the pre-trial hearing under Rule 16, to narrow and clarify the basic issues between the parties, and (2) as a device for ascertaining the facts, or information as to the existence or whereabouts of facts, relative to those issues. Thus civil trials in the federal courts no longer need be carried on in the dark. The way is now clear, consistent with recognized privileges, for the parties to obtain the fullest possible knowledge of the issues and facts before trial. . . .

[T]he basic question at stake is whether [discovery] may be used to inquire into materials collected by an adverse party's counsel in the course of preparing for possible litigation. . . .

In urging that he has a right to inquire into the materials secured and prepared by Fortenbaugh, petitioner emphasizes that the deposition-discovery portions of the Federal Rules of Civil Procedure are designed to enable the parties to discover the true facts and to compel their disclosure wherever they may be found. It is said that inquiry may be made under these rules, epitomized by Rule 26[b], as to any relevant matter which is not privileged; and since the discovery provisions are to be applied as broadly and liberally as possible, the privilege limitation must be restricted to its narrowest bounds. On the premise that the attorney-client privilege is the one involved in this case, petitioner argues that it must be strictly confined to confidential communications made by a client to his attorney. And since the materials here in issue were secured by Fortenbaugh from third persons rather than from his clients, the tug owners, the conclusion is reached that these materials are proper subjects for discovery under Rule 26[b].

As additional support for this result, petitioner claims that to prohibit discovery under these circumstances would give a corporate defendant a tremendous advantage in a suit by an individual plaintiff. Thus in a suit by an injured employee against a railroad or in a suit by an insured person against an insurance company the corporate defendant could pull a dark veil of secrecy over all the pertinent facts it can collect after the claim arises merely on the assertion that such facts were gathered by its large staff of attorneys and claim agents. At the same time, the individual plaintiff, who often has direct knowledge of the matter in issue and has no counsel until some time after his claim arises could be compelled to disclose all the intimate details of his case. By endowing with immunity from disclosure all that a lawyer discovers in the course of his duties, it is said, the rights of individual litigants in such cases are drained of vitality and the lawsuit becomes more of a battle of deception than a search for truth.

But framing the problem in terms of assisting individual plaintiffs in their suits against corporate defendants is unsatisfactory. Discovery concededly may work to the disadvantage as well as to the advantage of individual plaintiffs. Discovery, in other words, is not a one-way proposition. It is available in all types of cases at the behest of any party, individual or corporate, plaintiff or defendant. The problem thus far transcends the situation confronting this petitioner. And we must view that problem in light of the limitless situations where the particular kind of discovery sought by petitioner might be used.

We agree, of course, that the deposition-discovery rules are to be accorded a broad and liberal treatment. No longer can the time-honored cry of 'fishing expedition' serve to preclude a party from inquiring into the facts underlying his opponent's case. Mutual knowledge of all the relevant facts gathered by both parties is essential to proper litigation. To that end, either party may compel the other to disgorge whatever facts he has in his possession. The deposition-discovery procedure simply advances the stage at which the disclosure can be compelled from the time of trial to the period preceding it, thus reducing the possibility of surprise. But discovery, like all matters of procedure, has ultimate and necessary boundaries. [*See* Rules 26(b) and (c).] . . .

But the impropriety of invoking that privilege does not provide an answer to the problem before us. Petitioner has made more than an ordinary request for relevant, non-privileged facts in the possession of his adversaries or their counsel. He has sought discovery as of right of oral and written statements of witnesses whose identity is well known and whose availability to petitioner appears unimpaired. He has sought production of these matters after making the most searching inquiries of his opponents as to the circumstances surrounding the fatal accident, which inquiries were sworn to have been answered to the best of their information and belief. Interrogatories were directed toward all the events prior to, during and subsequent to the sinking of the tug. Full and honest answers to such broad inquiries would necessarily have included all pertinent information gleaned by Fortenbaugh through his interviews with the witnesses. Petitioner makes no suggestion, and we cannot assume, that the tug owners or Fortenbaugh were incomplete or dishonest in the framing of their answers. In addition, petitioner was free to examine the public testimony of the witnesses taken before the United States Steamboat Inspectors. We are thus dealing with an attempt to secure the production of written statements and mental impressions contained in the files and the mind of the attorney Fortenbaugh without any showing of necessity or any indication or claim that denial of such production would unduly prejudice the preparation of petitioner's case or cause him any hardship or injustice. For aught that appears, the essence of what petitioner seeks either has been revealed to him already through the interrogatories or is readily available to him direct from the witnesses for the asking. . . .

In our opinion, neither Rule 26 nor any other rule dealing with discovery contemplates production under such circumstances. That is not because the subject matter is privileged or irrelevant, as those concepts are used in these rules. Here is simply an attempt, without purported necessity or justification, to secure written statements, private memoranda and personal recollections prepared or formed by an adverse party's counsel in the course of his legal duties. As such, it falls outside the arena of discovery and contravenes the public policy underlying the orderly prosecution and defense of legal claims. Not even the most liberal of discovery theories can justify unwarranted inquiries into the files and the mental impressions of an attorney.

Historically, a lawyer is an officer of the court and is bound to work for the advancement of justice while faithfully protecting the rightful interests of his clients. In performing his various duties, however, it is essential that a lawyer work with a certain degree of privacy, free from unnecessary intrusion by opposing parties and their counsel. Proper preparation of a client's case demands that he assemble information, sift what he considers to be the relevant from the irrelevant facts, prepare his legal theories and plan his strategy without undue and needless interference. That is the historical and the necessary way in which lawyers act within the framework of our system of jurisprudence to promote justice and to protect their clients' interests. This work is reflected, of course, in interviews, statements, memoranda, correspondence, briefs, mental impressions, personal beliefs, and countless other tangible and intangible ways—aptly though roughly termed by the Circuit Court of Appeals in this case (153 F.2d 212, 223) as the "Work product of the lawyer." Were such materials open to opposing counsel on mere demand, much of what is now put down in writing would remain unwritten. An attorney's thoughts, heretofore inviolate, would not be his own. Inefficiency, unfairness and sharp practices would inevitably develop in the giving of legal advice and in the preparation of cases for trial. The effect on the legal profession would be demoralizing. And the interests of the clients and the cause of justice would be poorly served.

We do not mean to say that all written materials obtained or prepared by an adversary's counsel with an eye toward litigation are necessarily free from discovery in all cases. Where relevant and non-privileged facts remain hidden in an attorney's file and where production of those facts is essential to the preparation of one's case, discovery may properly be had. Such written statements and documents might, under certain circumstances, be admissible in evidence or give clues as to the existence or location of relevant facts. Or they might be useful for purposes of impeachment or corroboration. And production might be justified where the witnesses are no longer available or can be reached only with difficulty. Were production of written statements and documents to be precluded under such circumstances, the liberal ideals of the deposition-discovery portions of the Federal Rules of Civil Procedure would be stripped of much of their meaning. But the general policy against invading the privacy of an attorney's course of preparation is so well recognized and so essential to an orderly working of our system of legal procedure that a burden rests on the one who would invade that privacy to establish adequate reasons to justify production through a subpoena or court order. That burden, we believe, is necessarily implicit in the rules as now constituted.

[Rule 26(b)(3)] gives the trial judge the requisite discretion to make a judgment as to whether discovery should be allowed as to written statements secured from witnesses. But in the instant case there was no room for that discretion to operate in favor of the petitioner. No attempt was made to establish any reason why Fortenbaugh should be forced to produce the written statements. There was only a naked, general demand for these materials as of right and a finding by the District Court that no recognizable privilege was involved. That was insufficient to justify discovery under these circumstances and the court should have sustained the refusal of the tug owners and Fortenbaugh to produce.

But as to oral statements made by witnesses to Fortenbaugh, whether presently in the form of his mental impressions or memoranda, we do not believe that any showing of necessity can be made under the circumstances of this case so as to justify production. Under ordinary conditions, forcing an attorney to repeat or write out all that witnesses have told him and to deliver the account to his adversary gives rise to grave dangers of inaccuracy and untrustworthiness. No legitimate purpose is served by such production. The practice forces the attorney to testify as to what he remembers or what he saw fit to write down regarding witnesses' remarks. Such testimony could not qualify as evidence; and to use it for impeachment or corroborative purposes would make the attorney much less an officer of the court and much more an ordinary witness. The standards of the profession would thereby suffer.

Denial of production of this nature does not mean that any material, non-privileged facts can be hidden from the petitioner in this case. He need not be unduly hindered in the preparation of his case, in the discovery of facts or in his anticipation of his opponents' position. Searching interrogatories directed to Fortenbaugh and the tug owners, production of written documents and statements upon a proper showing and direct interviews with the witnesses themselves all serve to reveal the facts in Fortenbaugh's possession to the fullest possible extent consistent with public policy. Petitioner's counsel frankly admits that he wants the oral statements only to help prepare himself to examine witnesses and to make sure that he has overlooked nothing. That is insufficient under the circumstances to permit him an exception to the policy underlying the privacy of Fortenbaugh's professional activities. If there should be a rare situation justifying production of these matters, petitioner's case is not of that type.

We fully appreciate the wide-spread controversy among the members of the legal profession over the problem raised by this case. It is a problem that rests on what has been one of the most hazy frontiers of the discovery process. But until some rule or statute definitely prescribes otherwise, we are not justified in permitting discovery in a situation of this nature as a matter of unqualified right. When Rule 26 and the other discovery rules were adopted, this Court and the members of the bar in general certainly did not believe or contemplate that all the files and mental processes of lawyers were thereby opened to the free scrutiny of their adversaries. And we refuse to interpret the rules at this time so as to reach so harsh and unwarranted a result.

We therefore affirm the judgment of the Circuit Court of Appeals.

Justice JACKSON, concurring:

. . . Counsel for the petitioner candidly said on argument that he wanted this information to help prepare himself to examine witnesses, to make sure he overlooked nothing. He bases his claim to it in his brief on the view that the Rules were to do away with the old situation where a law suit developed into "a battle of wits between counsel." But a common law trial is and always should be an adversary proceeding. Discovery was hardly intended to enable a learned profession to perform its functions either without wits or on wits borrowed from the adversary.

The real purpose and the probable effect of the practice ordered by the district court would be to put trials on a level even lower than a "battle of wits." I can conceive of no practice more demoralizing to the Bar than to require a lawyer to write out and deliver to his adversary an account of what witnesses have told him. Even if his recollection were perfect, the statement would be his language permeated with his inferences. Every one who has tried it knows that it is almost impossible so fairly to record the expressions and emphasis of a witness that when he testifies in the environment of the court and under the influence of the leading question there will not be departures in some respects. Whenever the testimony of the witness would differ from the "exact" statement the lawyer had delivered, the lawyer's statement would be whipped out to impeach the witness. Counsel producing his adversary's "inexact" statement could lose nothing by saying, "Here is a contradiction, gentlemen of the jury. I do not know whether it is my adversary or his witness who is not telling the truth, but one is not." Of course, if this practice were adopted, that scene would be repeated over and over again. The lawyer who delivers such statements often would find himself branded a deceiver afraid to take the stand to support his own version of the witness' conversation with him, or else he will have to go on the stand to defend his own credibility—perhaps against that of his chief witness, or possibly even his client.

Every lawyer dislikes to take the witness stand and will do so only for grave reasons. This is partly because it is not his role; he is almost invariably a poor witness. But he steps out of professional character to do it. He regrets it; the profession discourages it. But the practice advocated here is one which would force him to be a witness, not as to what he has seen or done but as to other witnesses' stories, and not because he wants to do so but in self-defense. . . .

Comments and Questions

1. Permitting parties to obtain information through affirmative discovery about issues only hinted at in the pleadings (whether their own

or their opponents') may be a natural complement to the liberalized procedure of "notice pleading." Is it also a necessary complement?

2. The drafters of the Federal Rules thought that broad discovery would help get the relevant facts into the open before trial, thereby reducing the possibility of surprise and producing a more just result. Why, then, offer protection to an attorney's work product? Put another way, why preserve this particular element of surprise?

3. Does the element of surprise necessarily run counter to the pursuit of justice? As one federal judge puts it, "A certain amount of surprise is often a catalyst which precipitates the truth." *Margeson v. Boston & Maine R.R.*, 16 F.R.D. 200, 201 (D. Mass. 1954).

C. DISCOVERY TECHNIQUES   Ⓓ Ⓟ

Federal Rules 26 through 37 govern discovery practice and outline the methods by which parties may obtain discovery. Below, we identify the most commonly used types of discovery, describing some of the advantages and disadvantages of each.

1. Informal Discovery

The Federal Rules do not discuss what are perhaps the most commonly used methods for discovering information. Informal discovery techniques include (1) nonparty interviews; (2) site visits; (3) exchange of information (for instance, with other attorneys who have handled cases against the same defendants or regarding similar events); (4) requests for information from government agencies (under the Freedom of Information Act or other procedures); and (5) records requests from other institutions and courts (including criminal, probate, tax and land courts and directories). In sum, informal discovery refers to any form of extrajudicial research or inquiry that attempts to obtain facts relevant to the case.

There are two primary advantages to informal discovery techniques. First, informal discovery may cost less. Indeed, in certain circumstances the party may be able to perform the discovery for or in concert with the attorney, and thereby limit the fees incurred. In some cases, a private investigator may also be able to discover certain information quickly and efficiently. A second advantage to informal discovery is that its informality offers no notice to opposing parties. This may be particularly useful to an attorney who wishes to develop elements of her case without alerting her opponents to theories she may pursue. It bears noting here that some institutions, such as hospitals, will release records only upon authorization from the party whose information is sought. Under these circumstances, then, the opposing party would likely be notified of your informal discovery efforts.

2. Required Disclosures

Save certain exceptions, parties are required to disclose some information as a matter of course. Fed. R. Civ. P. 26 provides for three stages of mandatory disclosure: initial, expert, and pretrial.

"Except to the extent otherwise stipulated or directed by order or local rule . . ."* an initial disclosure must occur within ten days after the parties first meet and confer. *See* Fed. R. Civ. P. 26(a)(1) and 26(f). At this stage, the Rule requires that a party provide to the other parties (without awaiting a discovery request):

- the name, address and telephone number of each individual likely to have discoverable information "relevant to disputed facts alleged with particularity in the pleadings";
- a copy or description of documents "that are relevant to the disputed facts alleged with particularity in the pleadings"; and
- a computation of damages.

Parties likewise are obliged then to make available for inspection and copying (1) supporting documentation for the computation of damages and (2) any insurance agreement under which any carrier may be liable to satisfy part or all of a judgment.

Expert testimony, absent certain exceptions, is required to be disclosed as directed by the court, and in any event at least 90 days before the trial date. *See* Fed. R. Civ. P. 26(d)(2). Parties then are required to disclose

- the identity of any expert to be used at trial;
- an expert report, signed by the expert, setting forth the opinions to which the expert will testify and the underlying basis and reasons for those opinions; and
- biographical information setting forth the expert's qualifications, publications, and other cases where the expert testified.

A third stage of required disclosures is to occur at least 30 days prior to trial. *See* Fed. R. Civ. P. 26(d)(3). At this stage, the parties must disclose the identity of each witness the party expects to call (or whose testimony is expected to be presented by means of deposition), the identity of witnesses the party will call if the need arises, and the identity of documents to be introduced into evidence.

As a practice note, remember that Fed. R. Civ. P. 26(e) imposes a continuing duty to supplement these mandatory disclosures.

---

*Under the discretionary provision of the rule, approximately one-third of the federal district courts opted out of the mandatory disclosure provisions, while another third opted for a disclosure plan of their own making, formulated under the Civil Justice Reform Act instead of under Rule 26(a).

3. Methods to Discover Additional Matter

Fed. R. Civ. P. 26(a)(5) provides that parties may obtain discovery by one or more of the following methods.

a. Depositions

Depositions are used by attorneys to question potential witnesses (both parties and nonparties) under oath about their knowledge and participation of certain events or circumstances concerning the underlying action. Depositions typically are conducted orally, and every word that is spoken is recorded *verbatim* by a court reporter (or by mechanical means) and is transcribed. The witness (called the deponent) is given an opportunity to review the transcript and make technical corrections. Fed. R. Civ. P. 30(e).

Depositions are widely thought to be the most important step of the formal discovery process. It is perhaps no surprise, then, that half of the twelve discovery rules pertain solely to deposition practice. Read Fed. R. Civ. P. 27 through 32, which address a range of technicalities, including how depositions should be noticed, under what circumstances a witness may be deposed, before whom a deposition may be taken, and how a deposition transcript may be used.

A deposition may be scheduled on "reasonable notice" in writing. The noticing party may ask the witness to bring documents along, but that invokes the time limits of Fed. R. Civ. P. 34; *see* Fed. R. Civ. P. 30(b)(5). If the deponent is a nonparty, the noticing party must also provide for the attendance of the witness, usually by serving him with a subpoena. *See* Fed. R. Civ. P. 45. If a witness (whether a party or nonparty) fails to show up for the deposition, she may be assessed to pay the expenses and fees of the noticing party under Rule 30(g).

The noticing party schedules the location of the deposition and usually identifies her own law office as the situs. Depositions typically resemble a business meeting, with the deponent and his counsel on one side of the table and opposing counsel on the other side. Parties are entitled to attend any depositions taken in their case, and it is often a matter of strategy who, from each side, appears to observe a given deposition. Deponent's counsel may object to questions during the deposition, but the only objections that may preclude the deponent from answering the question posed are an objection as to the form of the question and an objection that to answer would reveal privileged information. All other answers are required and recorded, but remain "subject to the objection." Fed. R. Civ. P. 30(c).

There are at least five fundamental advantages to oral depositions. First, an oral deposition gives an attorney a chance to question potential witnesses under oath, in a manner similar to trial. This may be particularly useful as a means of assessing the demeanor of a witness under a variety of questioning styles. Second, while it is true that nearly all deponents will have been coached by an attorney prior to a deposition, responses to questions will have a degree of spontaneity unavailable under other discovery methods. Third, in a deposition an attorney has the opportunity to follow up on information revealed in answers and to take the questioning in any new direction that may reveal itself. Fourth, subject to the rules of evidence, anything recorded in a deposition is available for use at trial. Portions of depositions are often used to impeach a witness's testimony and can substitute for live testimony in cases where a witness is unavailable for trial. Fifth, nonparties may be deposed. Indeed, nonparties may also be subpoenaed to bring documents or other tangible items to the deposition and, thus, otherwise undiscoverable evidence may be obtained through questioning regarding those documents or items.

The most significant disadvantage to taking depositions is the expense. The party requesting the deposition must spend a significant amount of time preparing for each deposition. Counsel must also hire a court reporter, who charges approximately $20 per hour to attend the deposition, and later, approximately $5 per page for transcription. Depending on the pace of the deposition, court reporters can generate as many as fifty pages per hour. The recording expenses, combined with the legal fees, mean that an eight-hour deposition can easily cost the requesting party approximately $5,000. In addition to these expenses, parties must also pay travel expenses when the deponent is not local. Deponents also suffer costs, including preparation time spent with their counsel, and often lost time from work. Since 1993, there has been a limitation on the numbers of depositions parties may take as a matter of right, *see* Fed. R. Civ. P. 30(a)(2)(A); and local rules may limit still further, *see* Fed. R. Civ. P. 26(b)(2). In some cases, a lawyer contemplating the taking of a deposition may decide not to do so because she does not want the deponent (or the deponent's lawyer) to be able to infer anything about her theories of the case; similarly, she may not want the putative deponent to be confronted until the trial.

b. Written Interrogatories

Under Fed. R. Civ. P. 33, written questions may be submitted to an opposing party and must be answered in writing, under oath and returned within the specified time period. Read Fed. R. Civ. P. 33. Notice that Rule 33(a) specifies agency concepts for interrogating corporations and partnerships. Questions may seek any information discoverable under the scope of discovery standard of Rule 26(b)(1).

There are at least three advantages to using written interrogatories. First, interrogatories are usually the most useful mechanism for obtaining detailed and/or noncontroversial information from an adversary. If served early in the case, interrogatories can be very useful in obtaining names, addresses, dates, employers, relationships, histories, lists, numbers, or other technical information that a party may be required to assemble. Second, interrogatories are inexpensive to prepare and serve (or "propound") upon the opposing party. In fact, most lawyers (and many practice books) have pattern interrogatories for specific types of cases. Third, interrogatories are available for use at trial. Interrogatory answers are statements of an opposing party, and thus may be admitted as an admission under the Rules of Evidence over a hearsay objection.

The unfortunate downside to interrogatories, however, is that the answers are almost always drafted by lawyers and, thus, typically are crafted to contain as little useful information as possible. The answers are not spontaneously offered, and there is no opportunity for a timely follow-up question for clarification. Moreover, some lawyers delay the answering of interrogatories until their client is compelled to answer by the judge or will make every conceivable objection to the wording and scope of the interrogatories. As with depositions, there is a limit on the numbers of interrogatories that parties may serve as a matter of right. Fed. R. Civ. P. 33(a) now has a presumptive limit of 25, and local rules may limit still further, *see* Fed. R. Civ. P. 26(b)(2).

An important strategic consideration that is part of both drafting and answering interrogatories is the extent to which you choose to inform the party of your theories of the case. On the one hand, the interrogatory is a subtle rhetorical device, an opportunity for advocacy; on the other hand, detail sufficient to persuade will necessarily inform the other party of your line of thinking and may give your opponent ample time to formulate a responsive theory.

Once again, remember that Fed. R. Civ. P. 26(e) imposes a continuing duty to supplement your discovery responses.

c. Production of Documents and Things

Under Fed. R. Civ. P. 34, any party may request another party to produce documents and things and may then inspect and copy those documents and things before returning them to the producing party. Read Fed. R. Civ. P. 34. "Production" can include turning over a copy of the requested information or making it available at a specified time and place.

One advantage of what commonly is referred to as a document request is that the term "documents" is construed widely (as the listed items in the rule itself imply) to mean almost any type of written, recorded, or digitized item of information. A document request may also include a request for things, which may include the physical inspection of real or personal property, including equipment, devices, vehicles, and the like.

The broad scope of the definition of document works in tandem with the broad scope of discovery under Fed. R. Civ. P. 26(b).

One primary disadvantage of a document request is that it is difficult to strike a balance between over- and under-inclusiveness. On the one hand, a certain level of specificity is required, because a requesting party must request with specificity sufficient to ensure that the opposing party will deliver the sought documents. However, casting the request too broadly can result in an avalanche of documents that are responsive to the request but will bury the desired document(s).

One historical disadvantage to use of a discovery request was that Rule 34 was limited to parties and, even as to parties, to items only within their "possession, custody, or control." Recent amendments to the Federal Rules, however, have relaxed the requirement that the request be directed to a party. Part (c) of Rule 34 permits a party to subpoena documents even from a nonparty in conformity with the requirements for a subpoena in Rule 45.

Again, remember that Fed. R. Civ. P. 26(e) imposes a continuing duty to supplement your discovery responses.

d. Physical and Mental Examinations

Under Fed. R. Civ. P. 35, a physical and/or mental examination of a person may be requested when the person's condition is in controversy and the person to be examined is given proper notice. Read Fed. R. Civ. P. 35. Medical examinations are the only discovery tools for which advance court approval is required, and the court requires a showing of "good cause" for the examination.

This device applies only to a relatively narrow subset of cases, where the condition of the putative examinee is truly "in controversy." The Supreme Court has made clear that the Rule requires more than "mere conclusory allegations of the pleadings" or even "mere relevance to the case." Instead, there must be "an affirmative showing by the movant that each condition as to which examination is sought is really and genuinely in controversy." *Schlagenhauf v. Holder*, 379 U.S. 104 (1964).

When an examination is permitted, the court orders the time and place. Counsel for the party being examined typically is not permitted to attend. Reread Fed. R. Civ. P. 35(b)(1), and you will see what, in addition to expense, may be viewed as a disadvantage of this device.

e. Requests for Admissions

Under Fed. R. Civ. P. 36, a party may serve upon any other party a request for admission of any matter within the scope of discovery. Read Fed. R. Civ. P. 36. Requests for admissions typically are "question and answer" statements that are used by either party to further explore specific contentions. The requesting party formulates a "question" in the form of a statement, which the answering party is requested to admit or deny. For example, a defense attorney may incorporate a request such as "Admit or deny: Randall Dee was not wearing a seat belt at the time of his fatal accident." This type of request may be intended to determine whether certain affirmative defenses will be available at trial.

The primary benefits of requests for admission is that they provide an opportunity to "lock in" particular admissions or denials of fact. Unlike evidence at trial, which may be rebutted and refuted, once admitted, the fact must be taken as true in the pending action, unless the court permits "withdrawal or amendment." Fed. R. Civ. P. 36(b). Importantly, under the Federal Rules, there is no limit on the number of allowable requests a party can make. Accordingly, the device may be especially helpful as a pretrial device to obviate the need for certain presentations of proof, including, for example, establishing the foundations for the admissibility of documents.

Comments and Questions

1. What is a plaintiff's obligation under the mandatory disclosure rule if the complaint contains a short and plain statement of a claim, but no facts are alleged with particularity? What is the defendant's obligation?

2. By what criterion (or criteria) would you establish whether a fact is alleged with particularity sufficient to trigger a disclosure obligation? To demonstrate where you draw the line, draft two versions of an allegation (on any matter) that straddle the margin of what you think is "particular."

3. Consider the arguments for and against the provision of Fed. R. Civ. P. 26(a)(1), which permits local defection by local rule.

4. Could the petitioner in *Hickman v. Taylor* have noticed the deposition of Attorney Fortenbaugh? Could the petitioner force Fortenbaugh to answer Rule 33 interrogatories?

5. The discovery system requires cooperation between the parties, but the required cooperation exists against the backdrop of our adversarial system. Reread Fed. R. Civ. 26(g) and 30(g); read Fed. R. Civ. P. 37.

6. A party must demonstrate good cause under Fed. R. Civ. P. 26(c) in order to obtain an order to protect it against a discovery request. When sensitive materials are the subject of discovery, a judge may conduct an in camera review to weigh the sensitivity of documents subject to the request. Sensitive (or privileged) portions of documents also may be *redacted* to prevent the disclosure of certain information.

7. Discovery orders are not final orders and thus are seldom reviewed on appeal. Even when a discovery order is subject to review by an appellate court (after final judgment), the trial judge's decision is reviewed only for an "abuse of discretion" and thus is very seldom reversed.

8. Start your own list of ways to defend against discovery. Here are some of the methods you might include in a list: objections to answering (such as objections to interrogatories or instructing a witness at a deposition not to answer); seeking continuances; restricting an answer or compliance to a request to the most narrow possible reading of the question or request; seeking a limiting order or a protective order; moving to quash; reading a request in the broadest possible light, providing so much information that the most relevant information may become lost in the shuffle; claiming that the opponent has not complied with the required disclosure, meeting, planning and certification requirements *prior* to commencing additional discovery. Find the corresponding Rules provision that authorize each of the above (and all of those you add to the list).

9. Start your own list of ways to compel discovery. Begin with the following, and again find the corresponding Rules provision(s) that authorize all of the techniques on your list: seeking an order to force compliance; seeking the assistance of the court through case management; seeking sanctions; seeking a contempt order; defending and then trying to reach a voluntary and explicit agreement with opposing counsel on how discovery will be sensibly and fairly conducted, with very precise commitments included (it would be best to have such an agreement incorporated in an order of the court). You can also move to force your opponent to comply with required disclosure requirements or a discovery plan, or to supplement disclosures.

10. We are not endorsing obstreperous behavior; in fact, later in this chapter you will be dealing with a host of ethical questions implicated by the discovery rules. Please also consider that discovery "is a long road that doesn't turn." In other words, the attorney you push to the limits this time will have his or her chance later. Judges talk to one another, as do lawyers. Thus, your behavior and reputation help define how you will be treated by others and how your words or your arguments will be accepted—now and later. And, of course, the ancient art of rhetoric has always considered the speaker—as well as the words—critical to whether the audience is persuaded.

11. Conducting discovery abroad for use in civil litigation in the United States raises a host of thorny problems. No other country in the world allows as much discovery as the United States, and many countries have passed legislation in the form of "blocking" statutes that limit the ability of foreign parties to conduct discovery within their borders. Perhaps the most famous of such measures is the French blocking statute, which prohibits parties within its jurisdictional reach from requesting or producing evidence for use in foreign judicial proceedings other than through the procedures provided for by the Hague Convention, other international treaties, or express provisions of French law. *See* Vincent Mercier & Drake D. McKenney, *Obtaining Evidence in France for Use in United States Litigation*, 2 Tul. J. Int'l & Comp. L. 91, 92 (1994).

In the United States, three principal sources of procedural rules govern the gathering of evidence abroad: (1) If the person from whom discovery is sought is subject to personal jurisdiction in United States courts, then several of the Federal Rules assist with foreign discovery, *see, e.g.,* Fed. R. Civ. P. 28(b), 34, 45(b)(2); (2) similarly, if personal jurisdiction requirements are met, state procedural rules may be of assistance in state court proceedings; and (3) the Hague Convention on the Taking of Evidence Abroad in Civil and Commercial Matters, reprinted at 28 U.S.C. §1781. The discovery rules under the Hague Convention are available to civil and commercial law litigants in both federal and state trial courts when the evidence sought to be discovered is located in a country that is a signatory to the Convention. Whether discovery abroad is carried out pursuant to the Hague Convention or procedural rule is a question left to the discretion of the trial court. *See Société Nationale Industrielle Aerospatiale v. United States District Court for the Southern District of Iowa,* 482 U.S. 522 (1987); *see also* Gary B. Born & Scott Hoing, *Comity and the Lower Courts: Post* Aerospatiale *Applications of the Hague Evidence Convention,* 24 Int'l Law 393, 394 (1990).

Practice Exercise No. 14: Discovery Planning in *Carpenter*

You are an associate in the firm that represents Nancy Carpenter. Assume that the plaintiff, Nancy Carpenter, as administratrix, has added Ultimate Auto, Inc., to Randall Dee and Peter Dee as defendants. As a result, Ultimate Auto has cross-claimed against Randall Dee for contribution. Assume further that the preliminary injunctions sought in the initial complaint (paragraphs 4, 6, 9) were granted and are still in effect.

Review the initial interview with Nancy Carpenter, the original complaint and the answer of the Dees to that complaint, the amended complaint, and the answer and cross-claim of Ultimate Auto, which are all in the Case Files. Assume that the only discovery to date by your firm has been private investigation and a telephone conversation with Randall and Peter Dee's lawyer, which prompted your firm to move to amend the complaint to add Ultimate Auto as another defendant.

You have received the following memorandum from a junior partner of the firm where you are a summer associate.

Memorandum

To: Summer Associate
Re: *Carpenter v. Dee* / Discovery Plan

I need a sense of where we are heading with discovery in the *Carpenter* case because I am scheduled to meet with opposing counsel tomorrow morning. Please review the complaint and the file to date, and then outline a discovery plan for this case. In particular, I am interested in your assessment of which discovery techniques we should use, which witnesses we should depose, and in which order all of these discovery techniques should be deployed, given the facts as we presently know them. (Don't forget the informal techniques nor our required disclosures.) Assume for purposes of this exercise (although it is not reality) that Massachusetts state courts apply the current version of all of the federal discovery rules. (And assume further that there has been no opt-out from Fed. R. Civ. P. 26(a).)

As you consider whether and when to depose particular witnesses, I'll give you my thoughts (although there are always exceptions—and many great attorneys might disagree with some of these):

1. I always want to depose the adverse part(ies).

2. I usually like to depose adverse nonparty witnesses because I need to know exactly how they are going to testify. Nevertheless, I usually wait to notice the deposition until I'm sure that my opponent has found that witness too; I wouldn't want to lead them to a witness they didn't know about. I also try to make some judgment about whether I think the unfavorable witness will be unavailable for trial.

3. The question whether to depose a nonparty witness (who is not adverse) has always been a tricky call for me. I've seen catastrophes where favorable witnesses were unavailable for trial and there was no substitute deposition testimony. I've also seen friendly witnesses turn unfriendly before I could take their deposition and lock them in. At the same time, though, I always enjoy the tactical advantage of calling witnesses at trial who were not deposed—especially when my opponents may otherwise learn something at the deposition (including even how best to question the witness) that they then exploit at trial.

4. Don't forget that depositions are expensive. Consider whether we might be able to accomplish the same result with a telephone call or an informal interview.

For your information, in cases where I don't have substantial knowledge about the claims or the underlying facts at the outset of litigation, I usually start with a set of general interrogatories and document requests. Shortly after we receive the responses to these general requests, I usually depose secondary witnesses and use information gained from them to issue a second set of interrogatories and document requests to get what we really need. With the benefit of this second round of written discovery, I then usually depose the key witnesses, including the other party. I then typically depose the experts and serve a few requests for admission to clean up any outstanding matters.

But I wonder if this case is different. I haven't done many cases like this, and now I'm wondering if we should take Mr. Dee's deposition right away.

Please give this some thought and prepare an outline of discovery plan for my review.

N.B. You will notice in the Case Files that we received illustrations and an explanation of "Lifting a Truck." Some photographs of the accident scene also were recently added.

You may look at the selected *Carpenter* discovery materials that are in the Case Files either before or after you attempt this exercise. For purposes of the Practice Exercise, however, assume that no discovery has yet taken place. Can you identify the strategy of Nancy Carpenter's actual lawyer? Do you think that lawyer did a good job?

D. A BRIEF INTRODUCTION TO   𝔻 ℙ
THE RULES OF EVIDENCE

It is important to realize, in the words of one trial lawyer, that "the courtroom is its own reality": if evidence is not admitted into the record of that case by one of the established techniques, then it cannot be considered by the fact finder. Put another way, the evidence necessary to support a verdict must be *on the record*; the attorney thus must ensure that all pieces of the evidence that she wants the fact finder to consider are properly admitted lest they be ignored. Importantly, facts alleged in a pleading, discovery materials produced or held, statements or arguments made in pretrial proceedings are not evidence and cannot support a verdict. Evidence is only that information that was introduced by the parties at trial (whether through testimony or documents or things) and was admitted by the court onto the record.* The rules of evidence govern what evidence is admissible for parties to submit for the record.

Most cases are not proven with "the smoking gun," that is, *direct evidence* of an issue. Direct evidence is evidence that is precisely on point. For example, in *Carpenter*, a witness on the stand can testify that she saw the jeep tip over to prove that it in fact tipped. Why it tipped will probably require *circumstantial evidence*, which is evidence relating to a series of facts other than those directly at issue in order to prove a fact at issue. An expert may take the stand in order to testify as to how raising a vehicle will alter its center of gravity and destabilize it when it turns a corner. This, along with other evidence, may permit an *inference* that the sale of the oversize tires and elevation kit without a warning was (1) negligent,

---

*There are a few methods of providing evidence that are often overlooked, such as asking the court to take judicial notice of a particular fact or by the submission of facts stipulated by the parties.

(2) the cause in fact, and/or (3) the proximate cause of the death of Charlie Carpenter. A good deal of the civil litigator's skill and art relates to creatively getting facts into evidence that will later permit the drawing of desired inferences.

When one is in federal court, the admissibility of evidence is governed by the Federal Rules of Evidence, which likely are printed in your rules supplement. In state court, admissibility is governed by either a written code or statute of evidence rules, often patterned after the federal rules, or common law rules of evidence, often supplemented by statutes. For purposes of our exercises in *Carpenter* and *City of Cleveland,* assume that the Federal Rules are the operative evidence rules. They are usually fairly representative of the common law of evidence, although in many instances they are weighted more toward admitting evidence than the corresponding common law rule.

It might be helpful to you, even at this early stage, to be familiar with a few rules of evidence—namely, some of the rules concerning relevance, hearsay, opinion, and privileges. Of course, there is an upper level course on (all of) the rules of evidence, so this is but an introduction.

Relevant evidence, according to Rule 401, "means evidence having any tendency to make the existence of any fact that is of consequence to the determination of the action more probable or less probable than it would be without the evidence." Fed. R. Evid. 401. In order to make a relevancy argument, one must usually turn to the concepts that you learned early in the course: causes of action and elements. After all, how does one know whether a fact is "of consequence to the determination of the action" unless one knows the cause of action relied upon, its elements, defenses and their elements, and the theories propounded by each side?

Consider *Carpenter v. Dee* again. If the sole theory in a negligence case was that the driver failed to wear his prescription glasses and therefore didn't see the pedestrian whom he hit, then evidence of unusually large tires on the vehicle would probably be irrelevant. (We say probably, because maybe the high tires are relevant to line of vision, and perhaps you can come up with another "relevancy" argument.) But when the theories against a driver are that it was negligent to alter a jeep by lifting it with unusually large tires and a suspension kit (plus hockey pucks!) and to drive the jeep in that condition, otherwise irrelevant evidence suddenly becomes relevant.

The more remote the relationship between the proffered evidence and the issue in question, the less likely the judge will be to find it relevant. In our firefighters case, maybe it's a little relevant that in Paris ten years ago one engine company had a woman driver for one day, but it seems quite remote from the issues in the Cleveland case, and in all likelihood would be excluded on an evidence objection. In evidence parlance, the party trying to exclude evidence makes an *objection.* If the judge agrees with the objection, she *sustains* it. If the judge decides it's a bad objection, she *overrules* it. If the objection is overruled, that means that the witness will be ordered to answer the question or, if pertaining to physical evidence, the proffered exhibit will be admitted.

A witness's credibility is always relevant. The evidence rules permit a number of ways to *impeach* credibility, such as through *bias*, a *contradictory statement*, what is called *bad reputation for truth and veracity*, or documentation of a *conviction for a felony or for a crime involving dishonesty or false statement*. In unusual cases, otherwise relevant evidence might be excluded because it is *prejudicial* (*see* Rule 403). For instance, if the deceased in the *Carpenter* case was under indictment for burglary at the time of the accident, one could argue that the deceased was distracted at the time, and therefore consented to accompany Randall Dee in the jeep when he should have refused because of its altered construction. One might also argue that this testimony is relevant to the deceased's earning capacity. Whether or not this information is slightly probative of comparative negligence, or somewhat relevant to damage issues, some judges would consider the relevancy of such information to be sufficiently attenuated and thus outweighed by the potential prejudice.

Hearsay according to Rule 801(c) is "a statement, other than one made by the declarant [the person who makes a statement] at the trial or hearing, offered in evidence to prove the truth of the matter asserted." Fed. R. Evid. 801(c). Hearsay includes both oral and written statements. In general, even if an out of court statement introduced to prove the truth of its contents is signed or under oath, it is still hearsay. Hearsay is perhaps the most elusive of evidentiary concepts and takes many forms. Hearsay is generally inadmissible, unless one can find an exception to the hearsay rule.

Some hearsay examples are relatively easy. In *Carpenter*, if Melissa takes the stand in order to testify to what Lee told her about the jeep accident he witnessed, such testimony would ordinarily be hearsay. The fact finder would have to determine whether Lee's rendition of the accident was true, although Lee was not on the stand to be cross-examined. If Melissa were asked where Lee was standing at the time he allegedly saw the accident, she would probably answer "I don't know." She might say, "Ask Lee." That's the point; it is the person who actually witnessed the event who should testify, as opposed to the person to whom he or she told the story.

Sometimes an out-of-court statement is not being introduced for a hearsay purpose (that is, the truth of the matter asserted), and therefore it is admissible. In an oral contract case in which A says that B made an oral promise, the words of the contract are themselves relevant and admissible over a hearsay objection. If C takes the stand and says that he heard "A tell B that he would take care of her mother for $500 a week, and B said she'd pay that amount," then that is not hearsay in a lawsuit based on that contract. The words spoken are themselves relevant, and one doesn't need to cross-examine the speakers (A and B). It is enough that C can be cross-examined about where C was standing, and about C's ability to hear or C's bias. Indeed, for the same reasons, A and B could also testify to the words of contract which were spoken between them. The concept of "nonhearsay purpose" is tricky, and it takes many students enrolled in an evidence course (and many practicing attorneys) time to catch on.

Even if offered testimony is hearsay, it may be subject to an exception and thus admissible as evidence in court. Probably the most common way of getting around what would otherwise be hearsay is through what historically was called the *admissions* exception. Fed. R. Evid. 801(d)(2). For evidence purposes, an "admission" is any statement made by the party-opponent. It doesn't matter whether the opponent is in fact admitting anything. If your opponent said it or wrote it, it will not be excluded on hearsay grounds. In other words, if in a motor vehicle personal injury negligence case the defendant said that "the roads were slippery the night of the accident," the plaintiff could put a witness on the stand to testify she heard what the defendant had said. It will be admitted against the defendant without any analysis of whether defendant thought he was admitting anything. If your opponent (the opposing party) said it or wrote it, and it's relevant, it normally will be admitted. For a very sophisticated reason, which we won't consider here, the drafters of the federal rules made "admissions" nonhearsay, rather than an exception (*see* Rule 801(d)(2)). But the result is the same: statements of a party-opponent will be admitted over a hearsay objection.

The many hearsay exceptions are divided among those in which it matters whether or not the out-of-court declarant is available to testify because of reasons such as death, illness, refusal, or memory problems. Rule 804 lists the exceptions that require the proponent of what would otherwise be hearsay to show that the declarant is unavailable.

The *opinion* rule normally makes opinions by lay persons inadmissible. *See* Fed. R. Evid. 701. In a discrimination case, the plaintiff could not ordinarily say that in her opinion she was discriminated against. She would be permitted to describe how she was treated by the defendant-employer so that the fact finder can conclude whether there was discrimination in violation of the law. If a witness is shown through questions (or by stipulation of the parties) to be an expert (this is often called *qualification*) and seeks to give an opinion in her field of expertise that will aid the fact finder on a relevant point, than such *expert opinion* is normally admissible (*see* Fed. R. Evid. 702). There are occasions when a party needs experts in order to meet the production burden. For example, in a medical malpractice case the plaintiff will usually have trouble surviving a directed verdict without evidence from at least one expert on the standard of medical care that was allegedly breached and on the question of whether the alleged negligence was the cause of the alleged injury.

Another group of evidence rules relate to *privileges*. You have probably heard of the Fifth Amendment Constitutional privilege against "self-incrimination." But several other privileges, frequently statutory, identify and protect confidential communications between certain people. Perhaps the most frequently used in litigation is the *attorney-client* privilege, which was developed at common law, but is now statutory in many states. If a protected professional relationship exists, such as that between attorney and client, it is the client who controls the privilege. The client, not the attorney, can waive the right to exclude oral and written communications between them that are related to their professional relationship. The rationale here is that without such a privilege, clients would not reveal information that their lawyers need to know in order to give good sound legal advice.

Many states also have some combination of the following privileges: *priest-penitent, doctor-patient, spousal (husband-wife), psychotherapist-patient.* Various rationales support these and other privileges that you will read about in your evidence class. The drafters of the Federal Rules were unable to reach agreement on privileges that would also satisfy Congress. This was particularly true with privileges relating to state secrets. Consequently, Fed. R. Evid. 501 is the only portion of the Federal Rules of Evidence on privileges in federal courts. Thus, the federal courts look to other sources (such as the Constitution, congressional statutes, and the common law developed in the federal courts or state evidence law, especially in diversity of citizenship cases) for the applicable evidence rules.

When lawyers need more guidance in evidence matters, they often look to a treatise called *McCormick on Evidence.* Lawyers also refer to *Wright and Miller,* which covers the Federal Rules of Evidence as well as the Federal Rules of Civil Procedure. In addition, the annotated version of the Federal Rules of Evidence provides relevant case law after every rule. Lawyers often use this case law to supplement their arguments regarding the admissibility of a particular piece of evidence. The Advisory Committee Notes to the Federal Rules of Evidence are also quite helpful in this respect. There also exist Uniform Rules of Evidence, which some states have adopted in whole or in part. Lawyers in state court often use a handbook on the rules of evidence in their state. For direction with respect to a particular state evidence issue, lawyers often refer to state treatises that specifically discuss the particular state's evidence law.

E. ZEALOUS ADVOCACY AND ETHICAL CONSIDERATIONS

Lawyers often attempt to keep evidence from opposing counsel, while diligently seeking information on behalf of their clients. Even well intentioned counsel are likely to read a request for information as narrowly as possible in order to protect their clients. It may, in fact, be considered malpractice—or at least bad lawyering—not to do so. In this section, we explore the tension between zealous advocacy for your client and your ethical obligations as an officer of the court. Both types of obligations are found in the Model Code and Model Rules of Professional Responsibility, portions of which are reprinted later in this section.

These readings are offered to acquaint you with the relationship between zealous advocacy and other ethical obligations in the discovery context. As you read the *Bleak House* article by Professor Schrag, here are some questions you might want to consider:

1. Do you think Schrag did a good job representing his clients in his cases? What, if anything, would you have done differently?

2. What do you think the defendants' lawyer thought about Schrag and the cases he was bringing?

3. Was discovery improperly used by either side in the case?

4. To what extent were discovery problems the fault of the New York state system of civil justice? What changes in the New York system would you suggest for discovery rules or other procedural rules?

5. If discovery had been governed by the current Federal Rules of Civil Procedure, how would it have transpired differently? What steps could Schrag have taken to improve the process if he were in federal court today? Be precise, and consider Fed. R. Civ. P. 16, as well as the discovery rules.

6. Overall, what were Schrag's achievements? Were his personality traits and his lack of experience benefits, burdens, or both?

■ PHILIP G. SCHRAG, BLEAK HOUSE 1968: A REPORT ON CONSUMER TEST LITIGATION
44 N.Y.U. L. Rev. 115 (1969)

> This is the Court of Chancery, which has its decaying houses and its blighted lands in every shire, which has its worn-out lunatic in every madhouse and its dead in every churchyard, which has its ruined suitor with his slipshod heels and threadbare dress borrowing and begging through the round of every man's acquaintance, which gives to monied might the means abundantly of wearying out the right, which so exhausts finances, patience, courage, hope, so overthrows the brain and breaks the heart, that there is not an honourable man among its practitioners who would not give—who does not often give—the warning, "Suffer any wrong that can be done you rather than come here!"
>
> —Charles Dickens, *Bleak House*

. . . During 1968, I spent most of my time as a staff attorney of the National Office for the Rights of the Indigent (NORI), the poverty-law affiliate of the NAACP Legal Defense Fund, trying to bring test cases to challenge some unjust doctrines of consumer law. This article is a chronicle of my attempt. For law student readers, I hope that it is also a picture both of what test litigation is like, day-by-day, and of the interaction between legal theory and litigation strategy, because I know of no similar literature available to students considering employment with a test-case organization. What follows is not a happy tale, as I have found the courts to be so insensitive—not only to the need for substantive law reform but even to the need for a semblance of expeditious justice—that the passage quoted above from Dickens is the only one I could find to describe accurately the lower and middle echelons of our modern judicial system.

I THE SETTLEMENT SYSTEM

. . . New York has thousands of retail sellers operating so close to the margin that many will engage in any degree of chicanery to make a sale. Thousands of fraudulent or unconscionable sales are made every day; thousands of warranties are breached. Customers who complain are put off indefinitely. Second, New York has a dozen finance companies which immediately buy up contracts signed by low-income consumers from the sellers. When a finance company buys a consumer contract, the buyer becomes a cipher in an IBM computer. The computer mails the buyer a coupon book and instructs him to mail to it one coupon each month along with his check or money order. With the coupon book, the buyer receives a notice that if he has any complaints about the goods he bought, he must notify the finance company of them within ten days or lose forever his claims and defenses. (I have never met a consumer who read the notice when he received it, nor have I met one who understood it when I read it to him.) If the buyer later has a problem (e.g., a leg falls off his table a month after he bought it), and calls the store, they tell him: "We sold your contract to the credit company—we have nothing to do with you anymore." And if he calls the credit company, he is told: "All we do is collect your payments; we're not responsible for the quality of the merchandise."

As everywhere, buyers confronted with this kind of treatment often stop paying; they think this will force someone to pay attention to their complaint, or at least effect rough justice. But as soon as a payment is missed, the computer starts spitting out dunning letters, and even letters over the signatures of the collection attorney threatening suit.

The consumer may then be informed that a suit has been commenced against him, but more often, the finance company's collection attorney fills in a standard form complaint and gives it to a process server or city marshal who destroys it and files a perjured affidavit of service; "sewer service," as it is called, is widespread. So a buyer first learns that a default judgment has been entered against him when his employer notifies him of a garnishment and warns him that more than one wage garnishment is cause for dismissal. It is at this point that the consumer typically visits

Legal Aid, if he sees a lawyer at all. Thus, when the settlement process begins in New York, the Legal Aid lawyer has to try to reopen a default judgment and has to face a finance company considered by the law to be a bona fide purchaser, immune from any defenses.

One nice thing about NORI is that when you get mad about a problem, you are pretty free to take a whack at it. So, in December 1967, I decided to bring a series of consumer test cases to shake up the system, or at least to strengthen the bargaining power of the consumers' representatives. . . . I notified Legal Aid that I was willing to take two or three interesting cases from them, to litigate rather than to settle; it was not long before I had a consumer client.

II MR. ALLEN'S FREEZER

Frank Allen is a Negro in his twenties. He has a tenth grade education, lives in a city housing project, and earns about $5000 a year. . . . He told me of his encounter with a salesman in March 1966. The salesman, "Richard" (he never gave his last name), came to see the Allens, said he had been referred by a friend of Mr. Allen, and made them an appealing offer. He represented Quality Furniture, Inc., a large Harlem store, in business for 133 years. For less than twenty dollars a week, he would provide them with all the food they and their four-year-old daughter needed, so they would not have to fritter away their budget at grocery stores or supermarkets. . . . He noted that the Allens would still have to buy milk and fresh vegetables in the store but that his plan would supply everything else they needed. "This food will be delivered monthly," he said, "and you will need someplace to store it, so I will also provide you with a fine freezer, which will be less than $8.00 a week, but the savings on the food will be so great that the freezer pays for itself and is essentially free."

. . . A week later, a great volume of food arrived, along with a freezer. The food was not the high quality Mr. Allen expected, but it was tolerable. The quantity, however, was so small that it ran out long before the four months it was supposed to last; and the Allens had to buy as much from stores in the final weeks of the four months as they did before they started the plan.

A week after the food and freezer came, Mr. Allen received from Budget Finance, Inc. two coupon books, one for the food and one for the freezer. One required him to pay $30.22 a month; the other required him to pay $74.83 per month. Mr. Allen looked at the books, saw that he did not have to make his first payment for about four weeks, and threw the books—along with some accompanying forms—into a drawer until the first payments were due. (At this point, he wasn't sure whether the food supply would last or not.)

After grumbling for four months, but making all payments on time, Mr. Allen called Richard at a number the salesman had left and told him that he was not reordering because he was dissatisfied with the inadequate quantity of food supplied. "You can pick up the freezer any time," he said. "Oh no," said Richard, "you can cancel the food, but you may not cancel payments on the freezer. You signed a contract to buy it, by paying $30.22 a month for three years. Look at your copy of the contract."

Mr. Allen looked at the contract and saw for the first time that he had agreed in writing, not to rent a freezer, but to buy one at a price of $1087 over three years. He was shocked by the price because he had never heard of a freezer costing more than three or four hundred dollars. "I'm going to talk to a lawyer," he told Richard. "Don't do that," said Richard. "I'll straighten this out and call you back." He never did.

Mr. Allen went to see his union's lawyer, who told him that contracts were binding and that once he signed, there was nothing he could do. "Besides," said the lawyer, "it appears that a credit company bought your contract; and if you don't keep up your payments, they'll garnishee your wages and you may be fired."

Mr. Allen kept up his payments for fourteen months, becoming angrier with each payment. Finally he went to Legal Aid and was referred to me.

I was very pleased to have a client who was in the rare position of not having defaulted, much less not having lost a default judgment. It seemed like a fine opportunity to test an affirmative strategy—suing rather than being sued. I told Mr. Allen that my organization was in the test-case business—and that if we represented him, his case might take a long time to litigate, although the potential payoff was great, for others as well as for himself. I said that if he preferred to try for a quick compromise settlement, I would find a good lawyer to represent him. He said he would stick with me, and we started to draft a complaint.

[They decided to sue Richard Lewis (the salesman), Quality Furniture (Lewis' employer) and Budget Finance (the company that purchased the finance agreement). They alleged: (1) that the contract was unconscionable and, thus unenforceable, because the price of the freezer was "outrageously high"; (2) fraud, because Lewis led Allen to believe he was renting a freezer and had made assurances that the food would last for four months; and (3) violations of New York's Retail Installment Sales Act.]

There remained the issue of the holder in due course. Among the papers received by Mr. Allen with his coupon book was a document he had never read or tried to read—the notice which under New York law enables a credit company to become a bona fide purchaser of a consumer contract. It consisted of a single 125-word sentence, to wit:

1. If the within statement of your transaction with the seller is not correct in every respect; or 2. if the vehicle or goods described in or in an enclosure with this notice have not been delivered to you by the seller or are not now

in your possession; or 3. if the seller has not fully performed all his agreements with you; you must notify the assignee in writing at the address indicated at right in [*sic*] or in an enclosure with this notice within ten days from the date of the mailing of this notice; otherwise, you will have no right to assert against the assignee any right of action or defense arising out of the sale which you might otherwise have against the seller.

I had two possible attacks on Budget's status. One was to show that they had not acquired the contract "in good faith" and "without notice of a claim or defense." This would require proving a course of dealing between them and Quality Furniture or some other proof indicating they had knowledge of overreaching. Perhaps the price of $1087 for a freezer—apparent on the face of the contract—would be sufficient. The other strategy was to argue that . . . the Uniform Commercial Code left the court free to abolish holder-in-due-course status for all purchasers of consumer paper. I decided to allege all of these theories and to elect among them only after I had used discovery to learn more of the relations between the companies.

I instructed Mr. Allen to keep up his monthly payments, but to put them into a savings account rather than sending them to Budget. . . .

JANUARY

. . . I first heard from Budget's collection attorney—how much would I settle for? In expectation of such an offer, I had discussed settlement with Mr. Allen, and we agreed that under no conditions would we accept settlement that did not include some punitive damages. Such a settlement would have been so unusual that it could itself have been publicized and would have demonstrated that an aggressive complaint was enough to improve upon the settlement system. This was equally evident to Budget, so a settlement was out of the question. The collection attorney requested an extension of time to answer; he told me that Budget did not consider him capable of managing contested litigation. Although I was anxious to get on with the case, particularly in light of inevitable delays due to court congestion, I agreed to the extension, as it is the general custom to do so.

On January 10, I received Budget's answer from Bender, Segal, Parker & Lochinger, their Wall Street counsel. Budget denied or had no knowledge of most of the allegations in the complaint and claimed that, in any event, it was a holder in due course of the contract, having sent Mr. Allen a notice. Along with the answer came a notice to take the oral deposition of Mr. Allen on January 23. . . .

Along with Budget's answer and notice came the combined answer of Richard Lewis and Quality Furniture, who had hired the same lawyer, a sole practitioner named Alfred Stone, to represent them. (I later learned that Stone was one of the city's leading collection attorneys, and worked for several small finance companies as well as for Quality.) This was curious, because the joint answer denied an agency relationship between Lewis and the store; such a denial would be in the interest of the store but not of the salesman. My hunch is that the store agreed to hire the lawyer and gave the salesman a free ride. In any event, the agency relation was easy to prove, so I was more intrigued than concerned about the denial.

Their answer included a demand that I amend my complaint to add as co-plaintiff and necessary party Mrs. Allen, whose name was on the contract. I had indeed overlooked this detail. I had no objection to doing so, except for the vague feeling that at some point, a defendant might demand to examine Mrs. Allen, as they would have a right to do if she were a party.* A seller obtaining a wife's signature to a contract gets more than additional security—it gets an extra opportunity to make life difficult for the buyer if either side wishes to threaten litigation. [Schrag notes "Of course, a court can enjoin discovery to prevent harassment. But how can one prove, before the fact, that a proposed deposition is not in good faith? And how can one prove it even after the fact, if the examiner is clever enough to ask relevant but essentially unnecessary questions?"]

The day before Mr. Allen's examination began, I went over his case with him again. He had little to add that was not in his complaint, so I felt reasonably confident that the questioning would be brief.

We arrived at Bender, Segal's for the examination at 10:30, as required by the notice, but Bender, Segal kept us waiting until 11:00. Finally a young lawyer emerged into the waiting room and introduced himself as Jack Schwartz; he would conduct the examination in the conference room. Alfred Stone did not show up, and at 11:15 we began. Although the traditional New York practice is to object to every possible question, I had resolved not to object even to improper questions unless Mr. Allen felt really harassed; objections would take more time, and litigation over their propriety would delay the lawsuit and waste my time. Yet Schwartz's first questions almost provoked me, for he launched into an inquiry into Allen's finances—his earnings and that of his wife. But after a while, he got back on the track and asked about Mr. Allen's discussions with Richard. His questions covered every facet of the sale: how Allen knew who Richard was and whom he represented; who had made the referral; what his friend who referred him had said; what Richard had said about the food and the freezer; what Richard had shown him (the list of foods to be supplied, which Allen brought to the examination, as required); what papers Allen had signed; and what Allen had said when he called Richard to cancel. Schwartz's style of questioning was so detailed and so nearly repetitive (but not truly duplicative and therefore not objectionable) that the examination seemed hardly to be progressing. One brief sample:

---

* *Eds. Note:* Under the Federal Rules, a party can depose any witness, whether or not a party. *See* Fed. R. Civ. P. 30(a)(1).

Q. Did Mr. Lewis give you the freezer contract to look at during your discussion?

A. Are you referring to giving it to me to read?

Q. Yes.

A. No.

Q. Did you ask him to see it?

A. No.

Q. Did he explain to you what its contents were? What it said?

A. No.

Q. When was the first time that you saw it?

A. I think that night.

Q. More specifically, when during the course of this discussion or conversation with Mr. Lewis did he first present you with or hand to you this document, or the original?

A. I don't recall.

Q. Was it after he had done all his figuring on the yellow paper, as you testified before?

A. Yes.

Q. Was it already filled in the way it is now?

A. I don't recall.

Q. To your knowledge or to your recollection did Mr. Lewis fill in anything after he handed it to you?

A. I don't recall. I was just asked to sign it.

Q. Did you ask any questions when he asked you to sign this?

A. No.

Q. Had you already agreed to purchase the freezer?

A. Purchase? No, rent.

Q. Is your signature on it?

A. Yes.

Q. Is your wife's?

A. Yes.

Q. Did you both sign that, the evening of your first visit from Mr. Lewis?

A. I think so.

Q. At the time you signed it, were all of the writings now on it filled in?

A. I don't recall.

Q. Did you read it before you signed it?

A. No.

Q. Did your wife?

A. No.

Q. Were you given an opportunity to do so?

A. I don't understand you.

Q. Could you have read it?

A. Could I have read it?

Q. Yes.

A. Possibly.

Q. When you say possibly, what do you mean?
A. I was just asked to sign it.
Q. Were you told you could not read it?
A. No.

The examination became even more tedious as Schwartz began questioning Allen about each of the many papers that he had at some point received from Richard or Quality—forms to refer other customers, lists of groceries, invoices which came with the food, envelopes in which other papers had been place, etc. When did Allen first see each paper? Where? Whose writing was on it? What had Allen scribbled on the back? When? What did Richard say about it? And so on.

Shortly after 1:00 P.M., Schwartz announced that he had much questioning left to do. Somewhat angry about the pace, but anxious to get the examination over with, we broke for lunch. After lunch, the same slow process was repeated: What had Mr. Allen signed on Richard's second visit? Had he read the papers? When was this visit? Who was present? What was said? Another hour passed. Mr. Allen began to get confused about all the papers; occasionally he contradicted himself. Still, objections would only prolong the examination, and the contradictions were about trivial details. Finally Schwartz concluded his questions about the transactions. Surely we must be finished. But:

Q. You say the contract was unconscionable.
A. What do you mean by unconscionable?
Q. That is your word.
Schrag: Can you rephrase the question? Obviously his attorneys drafted the complaint.
Schwartz: I am afraid I cannot rephrase the question because I do not know any other word to ask him. I cannot define unconscionable in your complaint. . . .
Q. Are you familiar with Section 2-302 of the Uniform Commercial Code?
A. No, I'm not.
Q. Can you tell me what unconscionable means in your complaint?

I was sure that my client would say "no," and that would be an end to this line of questioning, but he said, "yes."

So here I had a problem. Of course I wanted my complaint to be read as broadly as it could be, so that it would not limit my proof at trial. But if my client discussed his understanding of the complaint, would that limit my proof? On the other hand, if I objected, would we have to spend weeks litigating the issue? I objected, and Schwartz defended his question on the ground that "the purpose of discovery is to enable me not to be surprised when I come into court." Finally, though his reason was preposterous, I decided to see how my client would field the question before cutting off further questioning and provoking a delay. Fortunately, Mr. Allen said that he had no personal knowledge about unconscionability and that any information he had about it was on the advice of counsel.

But Schwartz had begun a whole new line of questions—and he began reading down the complaint, paragraph by paragraph, asking Mr. Allen about his legal claims: Just which part of Richard's statements was fraudulent? How do you know that the representations were false? What do you mean by an exorbitant price? Is that just a high price? High with relation to what? I constantly expected my client to say that he didn't know or understand, but each time, he attempted to explain the complaint I had drafted as best he could, even after some dialogue between Schwartz and myself about how the witness could not know such things.

And now it was 5:00 P.M., and although Mr. Allen had been answering questions for a full day, Schwartz announced that he had many more questions—that he had not even begun to ask about Mr. Allen's relation to Budget Finance. "Of course you are free to seek a protective order from the Court," he said, "but my questioning has been relevant and you will not win" (a forecast concurred in by neutral sources). Reluctantly, I agreed that if I did not seek such an order, I would produce Mr. Allen again after we both had the transcript of the first session.

Meanwhile, I had begun my investigation. On January 19, to lay the groundwork for an oral deposition, I served Richard Lewis's lawyer with a demand to see all of the documents which might lie in the background of the case: contracts between Lewis and Quality Furniture; agreements between Quality and Budget, invoices showing the price Quality paid for freezers, lists of other freezer customers (relevant because such customers were witnesses to the pattern of Lewis's selling techniques), etc. I demanded that these documents be produced in my office on February 1.

Early in January, a Harlem newspaper had carried some publicity about the institution of a consumers' test case, and as a result I received many requests for help from the community. From these, I selected three other cases, which I commenced in rapid succession while I awaited discovery. . . .

[Schrag describes additional cases he commenced against Lewis, Quality, and Budget and another case he started against a different credit company engaged in similar practices. Although it took some months, in one case he was able to get a deposition set at a more convenient time for his working client; in another, he ultimately was able to convince a court to determine that his opposing defendants had been properly served, despite their using extremely questionable evasive tactics to avoid service; in another case, he eventually persuaded a court to permit him to see all of a finance company's contracts.]

FEBRUARY

There were times during February and March when I felt as though I shared offices with Messrs. Bender, Segal, Parker & Lochinger. Their oral examinations of my clients seemed endless. Mr. Allen was brought back, and his testimony consumed a total of 247 pages. . . . When I joined Mrs. Allen as a party plaintiff, Budget's attorneys, as I feared they would, exercised their right to require her to be questioned; and she had to submit to a day of examination. . . .

Any further quotation of the questioning would render this article too tedious to bear. Suffice it to say that I found myself continually apologizing to my clients for causing them to be subjected to the length and difficulty of the questioning; its infliction upon clients is a very real cost of making a test case out of a dispute which could be routinely settled in an hour— though such a settlement also has costs, which are, however, less tangible. Schwartz's questions continued to be very nearly repetitive, although he was careful never to ask precisely the same question a second time, unless the witness gave an ambiguous answer. The trouble was that my clients had great difficulty recalling precisely the events in a sale which had taken place two years earlier, and each minor uncertainty provided Schwartz with fuel for an additional half-hour of questioning. In two or three days of questioning, there were also inevitable self-contradictions; and these often occasioned an attempt by Schwartz to go over the same ground again, to "straighten it out." . . .

These examinations became an enormous burden on my time and effectively precluded me from initiating any new cases. Between the time it took to prepare my clients for examination, attend day after day of questioning with client after client, and read through the transcripts with my clients, several man-weeks were expended. (Of course, I received some satisfaction at the thought that whatever my time cost NORI, Bender, Segal would be billing Budget many, many times as much.) I was still opposed to making motions to halt the questioning, both because the courts are generally reluctant to restrict disclosure (or so say the reported cases) and because I wanted to go to trial as soon as possible. One cannot get on the trial calendar until all discovery is completed. . . .

Meanwhile, I attempted to proceed with my side of the cases. On the morning of February 1, I expected Richard Lewis's attorney, Alfred Stone, to appear in my office with the documents I had demanded relating to Mr. Allen's case. But when no one arrived at the appointed hour, I called Mr. Stone. "Didn't you get my motion papers?" he asked. "I sent them out the day before yesterday." The making of a motion to prevent discovery stays the disclosure until the motion is decided.

The next day, I received Mr. Stone's motion papers. I noticed that although a movant may make his motion returnable in eight days, Mr. Stone had "noticed" his motion for February 18, nearly three weeks away, and had thus prolonged the period that my discovery was stayed, even if he lost his motion. For grounds, Mr. Stone argued that the notice served "does not specifically designate the documents to be produced, and furthermore the items demanded clearly indicate that the plaintiffs have embarked on a fishing expedition. . . ." This was surprising to me, since I thought my descriptions had been extraordinarily particular. In my papers, I pointed out how specific each of my descriptions was and that Mr. Stone had made no claim that he did not know what I was referring to. In addition, I explained the relevance of each category of papers I demanded to see to my theory of the case.

On February 18, I appeared in court, fully expecting to argue this motion so that I could get on with the case (having lost three weeks) and perhaps encourage the court to write a short opinion on the relevance of the documents I'd asked for, which might suggest some movement in the law. My first shock was the discovery that two hundred and fifty motions were scheduled to be heard that day and that this was an average calendar. My second shock was the sight of the courtroom; as the clerk called the calendar, he could hardly be heard over the hubbub, as dozens of attorneys engaged in last-minute negotiations. And after the clerk called "Oyez oyez, all those with business for this honorable court, step forward and be heard," I received my third shock of the day: I stepped forward to announce myself ready for argument and the judge said, "You should know we don't allow argument on discovery motions; submit your papers."

My fourth shock occurred later that day, when another lawyer informed me, in response to my story of what had occurred, that not only do the judges not allow argument, but that the docket is so crowded that they do not read the motion papers; the papers are usually read by someone from a pool of law assistants who writes a short decision to which the judge assigned to motions puts his name. And my fifth shock came three weeks later when, having waited all that time for some decision, the court ruled:

> Motion for a protective order vacating the notice of discovery and inspection is denied without prejudice to renewal upon proper papers, including a copy of the complaint, without which the court cannot determine the propriety of the items objected to, which defendants maintain go beyond the scope of the transaction involving plaintiff.

In other words, my adversary had lost because he had not filed enough papers (the complaint had been filed in the court clerk's office, but the motions judge and clerks evidently do not pull papers from their own court files—the complaint must also be annexed to motion papers). But in reality, since my adversary was free to start all over again, I had lost many hours in preparing papers and had lost six weeks' time.

[In order to expedite the discovery process, Schrag made two motions—a motion to commence Lewis' oral examination and a motion to inspect documents relating to the case. In response, Stone served Schrag with a motion for a protective order, staying discovery.]

. . . The ground for Mr. Stone's motion was simply that the deposition of Mr. Allen, which Budget was taking, had been recessed indefinitely, and "it is elementary that the right of defendants to examine the plaintiffs has priority and the examination of the defendant may not go forward until the examination of the plaintiffs has been completed." * . . .

MARCH

[Schrag spent most of March preparing for and attending examinations. The court responded to Stone's motion, requiring Lewis to appear for examination ten days after defendants finished examining the plaintiffs. Instead of producing the documents for Schrag's inspection, Stone made another motion for a protective order, complaining that Schrag had not described the documents with sufficient specificity and arguing that the documents in issue would be "more readily determinable after defendants completed their examination of the plaintiffs."]

APRIL

[Schrag learned that the court had granted Stone's motion for a protective order. Fortunately, however, defendants completed their examination of the Allens by mid-April.] Thus, on April 17, I called Mr. Stone and told him that the examinations were completed. But he took the position that the examinations of the Allens were not "completed" until the transcripts were typed and signed by the Allens.

I had no choice but to accept his interpretation, because it would take longer for me to make a motion to the court (on eight days' notice) to order the examination scheduled and to wait for the decision, than to wait for the transcripts and have my clients read and correct and sign them. . . .

MAY

. . . I expected real progress towards examining Richard Lewis. The transcripts of the examinations of the Allens were signed May 3, and I notified Mr. Stone of the event, saying that I expected to examine his client by May 13, in conformity with the court's order. He said he would talk to his client about a date and call me back. But by May 7, he had not called me back, so I called him again. He said he had not been able to reach his client who "didn't have a telephone," and he would call me in "a couple of days." [In a footnote, Schrag adds, "Very shortly after I began my suit, Quality Furniture ended its relationship with Lewis; and their particular freezer racket came to an end. Chalk up three points for the strategy of affirmative suits for damages."] Since that would take us almost to the tenth day after May 3, I sent him a hand-delivered letter notifying him that I would conduct the examination on May 13, at 10:00 A.M.

[When neither Mr. Stone nor Mr. Lewis appeared for the examination, Schrag called Mr. Stone at his office.] He said that he hadn't reached his

_____

* *Eds. Note:* This is not the case under Fed. R. Civ. P. 26(d).

client, that he thought his client might get in touch with him "any day now" and that he hadn't called me the day before because that "was a very hectic day for me."

I was extremely angry, both because I was getting nothing in return for having subjected my clients to questioning, and because I was getting no closer to testing the legal issues I had set out to challenge. So once again I went back to my typewriter, this time to write a motion to strike the answer of Richard Lewis for his failure to appear or alternatively to order him to appear and to pay the stenographer's bill and reasonable attorney's fees for the time I had to spend writing motions to make him appear.

Stone answered by saying that "we could not possibly communicate with our client. . . . on such short notice. [Schrag is trying to have this court impose] costs on the defendant Lewis who was completely unaware of these conversations between counsel and who is certainly not avoiding any examination. [We do not] understand the reasons for this apparent zeal on the part of the moving attorney. . . . [T]here is no particular urgency to the proceedings herein." He concluded by requesting that the court merely fix a date and time for Lewis to be examined at the court house, which struck me as an odd request since the examining party is supposed to have his choice of where to conduct the examination.

JUNE

On the third day of June, my motion to punish Lewis was granted only to the extent of requiring Lewis to appear for examination on the 17th. No mention was made in the decision of my request for costs or counsel fees. The court set the court house as the place of examination. So by failing to appear within ten days as the court had earlier ordered, Stone was able both to delay the case by a month and four days and to have the examination switched from my office to the court house across the street from his office, with no penalty whatsoever.

But Stone and Lewis did appear on the 17th, and the examination must be reckoned a success. Lewis denied making any guarantees that the food would last four months but gave evidence going beyond my expectations about his close relationship with Budget Finance. He testified, for example, that when a customer gave him an order, he made the customer fill out a credit application (on a Budget form) which was then sent to the finance company. If Budget approved the credit, the customer was notified that the sale was final, but if Budget rejected the credit application, the customer was told the deal was off; Lewis made no effort to finance his sales except through Budget.

At noon, Stone flatly refused to come back after eating. He said he was a busy man with other things to do, nor could he come back to complete the examination during the next few weeks. I thought I had a right to insist on a continuation reasonably promptly, but given the inevitable month's delay between the making of a motion and its resolution, I had no way to enforce any demand for an earlier date. I therefore agreed to the setting of July 15 as an adjourned date. . . .

JULY

. . . On July 15, I completed my examination of Richard Lewis. This second session was less successful than the first. I asked him about other customers to whom he had sold freezers, pointing out that these questions were relevant because I had to prove a pattern or practice of fraudulent dealings in order to collect punitive damages. But Stone directed Lewis not to answer these questions nor to reveal the names of other buyers, on the ground that they were not relevant to any valid action I might have.[*] In addition, Lewis did not produce any of his business records, claiming that he had gone out of business shortly before my suit was instituted and had destroyed all his records at that time because he no longer needed them. I felt certain that he was not telling the truth but had no way to prove that he had not destroyed his records.

At the beginning of July, contemplating the completion of the examination of Richard Lewis on July 15, I served Stone with a notice to examine the president of Quality Furniture on July 16. I had not wanted to examine him earlier, because I assumed that information revealed by Lewis would be of help in questioning officers of Quality. But on the 15th, Stone again announced that he would not comply with my demand, and I was relegated to choosing between the adjourned date he offered me—August 13—or moving to punish his client, a motion which, in the light of the history of the case, I felt no confidence about winning. I accepted his August 13 date.

AUGUST

But on August 9th, he wrote me:

Dear Sir:

Please be advised that our client Quality Furniture, Inc., has filed a petition in bankruptcy under Chapter 11. Under the circumstances all proceedings against it are stayed until disposition of that proceeding. The examination scheduled for August 13th will therefore have to be delayed to some future date.

Ah, the regretful tone of his letter, Ah, the law. At this point I started thinking seriously about some other career.

A little research confirmed the fact that the federal bankruptcy court had indeed stayed all state court proceedings against Quality (to preserve the estate for the creditors) and that it was virtually impossible to have such a stay vacated. Yet this might delay my suits against them indefinitely.

---

[*] *Eds. Note: Cf.* Fed. R. Civ. P. 30(c).

With no particular plan in mind, however, I resolved to attend the first hearing in the case in federal bankruptcy court and do what I could for my clients. That hearing was set for August 27.

Meanwhile, I invented a tort. I served an amended complaint on behalf of [clients in another case] accusing [Quality Furniture's credit company] of engaging in a pattern and practice of purchasing unconscionable contracts, which on their face were exorbitant, and alleging that such conduct subjected them to liability for punitive damages. I hoped that this claim would seem so outrageous to them that they would move to dismiss, but they did not. They merely answered. So to provoke the issue, I served them with a notice to inspect all of the freezer contracts they had bought during the last three years. I knew they could not comply with this demand because they would have to fear that I would peruse the contracts to solicit new plaintiffs to sue them. Little did they know that I had my hands full with a half a dozen cases. They had to object to the notice on the ground that my tort was unknown to the law. And they did, by a motion returnable August 23. They did me the favors of informing the court that this was an important test case and of arguing squarely on the merits rather than on some obscure technical ground. In my response, I too argued the merits, presenting the court with a somewhat academic analysis of the role of tort law in regulating merchant-consumer relations. . . . At last, after seven months, this was test case litigation as I had imagined it as a law student. I expected to lose, but at least I would have an appealable decision, and I would be able to present an issue of some significance to an appellate court. I looked forward to September for a square ruling on the merits, one way or the other.

[Schrag attended one of Quality's bankruptcy hearings, where he moved to vacate the automatic stay so that he could continue to litigate his claims against Quality Furniture. Two months after learning about the bankruptcy, the court granted Schrag's motion, vacating the stay only as to the discovery and requiring Schrag to apply for further relief if and when he went on the state court trial calendar.]

SEPTEMBER

At the beginning of September I left for a three-week vacation. I returned to find that I had won more little victories while I was away than during any comparable period while at work.

For one thing, the court had granted my motion to require Lewis to produce the names and addresses of his other customers. Unfortunately, it reached this decision without any opinion whatsoever, so the precedential value was limited. And, as I expected, even the immediate impact of the decision was slight. While I was still away, another NORI attorney interrogated Lewis (pursuant to the order) about his business records, but Lewis stuck to his story that "I never kept any books of account" and that "I threw away most of the things [records] that I had, being that I had no more interest in the business. . . . What am I going to do with them? . . . Of course, to me it was garbage." . . .

My final effort in September was the drafting of a third set of interrogatories in [another] case. A staff attorney older and wiser than I concluded that although the court had never said so either time, what it really found offensive in my first two sets of interrogatories was their sheer length—that 90 written questions was simply too much for the court, regardless of their relevance or of the equities. So I chopped them down to the 19 most important questions, those which I considered to be most essentially directed to the evidence I would need to establish. . . .

OCTOBER

On October 7, I sent Mr. Stone a copy of the freshly signed order of the federal court permitting my interrogation of Quality's officers to proceed. I asked him to select a date convenient for him so that he would not make a motion on the excuse that I had picked an impossible date. Not having heard from him, I called him a week later, and he said that he had not asked his client about a date, but he would do so the next week. Of course, the next week, when I called again, he said that he would not have time to contact his client until the following week. Having no choice but to set a date myself, I sent him a notice demanding examinations of Quality's president and treasurer on October 31, and requiring them to bring with them their lists, if they had any, of Lewis's other freezer customers.

As usual, at the last possible moment Stone served me with a motion (returnable three weeks hence) for a protective order, claiming that I had no right to examine both officers until I first demonstrated that one did not have all the requisite knowledge and that I was seeking the production of improper and irrelevant documents, such as the list of the other freezer customers. I pointed out that we had already been through the issue of the lists of customers and that the law of the case had been resolved in my favor.

NOVEMBER

Or so I thought. Without further explanation, the court in November permitted the examination to proceed (at the court house, as Stone had again requested), but my demand to see the customer lists was stricken "as improper." Since I didn't think that Quality would produce such lists in any event, I did not bother wasting six months on an appeal. . . . Shortly thereafter, the court struck my third set of . . . interrogatories. Once again, its reasoning made little contact with the questions asked or the facts in the record. . . .

The court granted me permission to submit proper interrogatories to another judge, for approval by the court, so I drafted still a fourth set of questions. This fourth set (now down to 17 questions) was very much like the third; I cut out demands for some of the papers to be duplicated and now asked for copies of only nine pieces of paper. . . . As the year 1968 ran out, the court had not yet ruled on the fourth set of [these] interrogatories.

DECEMBER

[At the next bankruptcy proceeding, the court granted Schrag's motion to add Schyleur Barrack, an attorney for the legal aid society, to the creditors' committee. The next week, Schrag, Shyleur Barrack, and another attorney from the Legal Aid Society, Susan Frieman, attended the creditors' meeting.] Quality's owners simply could not reach a suitable arrangement with the creditors and were ready to consent to an adjudication of bankruptcy. The store would be closed down and sold at auction for the benefit of creditors.

But the consumers' representatives still had a role to play. We listened in silent amazement as the creditors decided not to close the store at once, but to obtain an adjudication of bankruptcy to take effect just before Christmas. Christmas sales would swell the pot which they would eventually divide; contracts for the merchandise sold would quickly be assigned to Budget for cash. No one mentioned the fact that each sale would involve express and implied warranties to consumers which would be meaningless because Quality would be out of business and Budget would claim to be a bona fide purchaser.

Back in court three days later, the creditors and Quality made a joint application for an adjudication of bankruptcy to take effect just before Christmas. Once again there was a stirring in the back of the court. "Before you sign that order, your Honor," said Miss Frieman in a tiny voice, "I think that there is something that you should know."

"What's that?" asked his Honor. And she told him about the warranties that would be valid for four years under the Uniform Commercial Code, or until Christmas, whichever came sooner.

"Are you suggesting that I close down the store at once?" he asked.

"I suppose I am," she said.

"So ordered," replied his Honor. And he ordered Quality's lawyer immediately to telephone the store and instruct the management to stop selling, to send home the employees, and to lock the door.

The lawyers for Quality and the creditors simply lost control over themselves. Flailing their arms, they demanded to know from Miss Frieman who she was and whom she thought she represented. "She doesn't represent any potential buyer; she has no standing to make a motion," yelled one of the lawyers. "I doubt she's even a lawyer."

But Miss Frieman, who did not represent a potential buyer, stood mute, and after the room was again calm, the referee said quietly, "I guess you gentlemen will simply have to accept her as the representative of the community."

III CONCLUSION

My involvement in the bankruptcy proceedings was one of the high and even humorous spots in what was otherwise a disillusioning year. Disillusioning because I learned how time-consuming and how costly test cases are, but most of all because I had thought that poverty lawyers and the judiciary—at least in the North—would be partners in reforming the law as quickly as possible. I learned, instead, that the lower state courts—on which so much really depends—are neither friendly nor hostile to law reform. Instead, they are totally indifferent. . . .

In ordinary times, a Court of Chancery as deaf to the need for expeditious justice as the court Dickens described would be a tragic mockery of the origin and theory of Equity. Today it forebodes disaster. . . .

Comments and Questions

1. One of the biggest problems faced by Schrag and other legal aid lawyers was that neither the company who sold the goods on credit nor the credit company that purchased the credit was responsible for the warranty. This problem was solved in 1975, when the Federal Trade Commission passed a regulation known as the Holder in Due Course Rule. Prior to the promulgation of this rule, Article 3 of the U.C.C. generally permitted a holder in due course to take a negotiable instrument free of most claims and defenses. The U.C.C. now requires that the holder of a credit instrument be subject to all of the claims and defenses that the claimant could assert against the original seller.

2. Currently, in the United States, disciplinary rules are embodied in two "model" forms, The Model Code of Professional Responsibility and The Model Rules of Professional Conduct. The Model Code of Professional Responsibility was created in 1969, when the ABA grouped and adopted nearly 50 canons from various state bar associations. In 1983, the ABA adopted the Model Rules of Professional Conduct to replace the Model Code. In general, the Model Rules are more legally concrete and less abstract than the Model Code. Nearly all of the states have moved from the Model Code to the Model Rules. When you read the following excerpts, consider whether the lawyers' behavior in *Bleak House* violated the Model Rules and/or the Model Code.

■ ABA MODEL CODE OF PROFESSIONAL RESPONSIBILITY

CANON 7

A Lawyer Should Represent a Client Zealously Within the Bounds of the Law

DISCIPLINARY RULE 7-101. REPRESENTING A CLIENT ZEALOUSLY.

(A) A lawyer shall not intentionally:

(1) Fail to seek the lawful objectives of his client through reasonably available means permitted by law and the Disciplinary Rules, except as provided by DR 7-101(B). A lawyer does not violate this Disciplinary Rule, however, by acceding to reasonable requests of opposing counsel which do not prejudice the rights of his client, by being punctual to fulfilling all professional commitments, by avoiding offensive tactics, or by treating with courtesy and consideration all persons involved in the legal process.

(2) Fail to carry out a contract of employment entered into with a client for professional services, but he may withdraw as permitted under DR 2-110, DR 5-102, and DR 5-105.

(3) Prejudice or damage his client during the course of the professional relationship, except as required under DR 7-102 (B).

(B) In his representation of a client, a lawyer may:

(1) Where permissible, exercise his professional judgment to waive or fail to assert a right or position of his client.

(2) Refuse to aid or participate in conduct that he believes to be unlawful, even though there is some support for an argument that the conduct is legal.

DISCIPLINARY RULE 7-102. REPRESENTING A CLIENT WITHIN THE BOUNDS OF THE LAW.

(A) In his representation of a client, a lawyer shall not:

(1) File a suit, assert a position, conduct a defense, delay a trial, or take other action on behalf of his client when he knows or when it is obvious that such action would serve merely to harass or maliciously injure another.

(2) Knowingly advance a claim or defense that is unwarranted under existing law, except that he may advance such claim or defense if it can be supported by good faith argument for an extension, modification, or reversal of existing law.

(3) Conceal or knowingly fail to disclose that which he is required by law to reveal.

(4) Knowingly use perjured testimony or false evidence.

(5) Knowingly make a false statement of law or fact.

(6) Participate in the creation or preservation of evidence when he knows or it is obvious that the evidence is false.

(7) Counsel or assist his client in conduct that the lawyer knows to be illegal or fraudulent.

(8) Knowingly engage in other illegal conduct or conduct contrary to a Disciplinary Rule.

(B) A lawyer who receives information clearly established that:

(1) His client has, in the course of the representation, perpetrated a fraud upon a person or tribunal shall promptly call upon his client to rectify the same, and if his client refuses or is unable to do so, he shall reveal the fraud to the affected person or tribunal, except when the information is protected as a privileged communication.

(2) A person other than his client has perpetrated a fraud upon a tribunal shall promptly reveal the fraud to the tribunal.

■ ABA MODEL RULES OF PROFESSIONAL CONDUCT

RULE 1.1 COMPETENCE

A lawyer shall provide competent representation to a client. Competent representation requires the legal knowledge, skill, thoroughness and preparation reasonably necessary for the representation.

COMMENT:

Legal Knowledge and Skill. In determining whether a lawyer employs the requisite knowledge and skill in a particular matter, relevant factors include the relative complexity and specialized nature of the matter, the lawyer's general experience, the lawyer's training and experience in the field in question, the preparation and study the lawyer is able to give the matter and whether it is feasible to refer the matter to, or associate or consult with, a lawyer of established competence in the field in question. In many instances, the required proficiency is that of a general practitioner. Experience in a particular field of law may be required in some circumstances. . . .

Thoroughness and Preparation. Competent handling of a particular matter includes inquiry into and analysis of the factual and legal elements of the problem, and use of methods and procedures meeting the standards of competent practitioners. It also includes adequate preparation. The required attention and preparation are determined in part by what is at stake; major litigation and complex transactions ordinarily require more elaborate treatment than matters of lesser consequence. . . .

RULE 1.3 DILIGENCE

A lawyer shall act with reasonable diligence and promptness in representing a client.

COMMENT:

A lawyer should pursue a matter on behalf of a client despite opposition, obstruction or personal inconvenience to the lawyer, and may take whatever lawful and ethical measures are required to vindicate a client's cause or endeavor. A lawyer should act with commitment and dedication to the interests of the client and with zeal in advocacy upon the client's behalf. However, a lawyer is not bound to press for every advantage that might be realized for a client. A lawyer has professional discretion in determining the means by which a matter should be pursued. *See* Rule 1.2. A lawyer's workload should be controlled so that each matter can be handled adequately. . . .

RULE 3.2 EXPEDITING LITIGATION

A lawyer shall make reasonable efforts to expedite litigation consistent with the interests of the client.

COMMENT:

Dilatory practices bring the administration of justice into disrepute. Delay should not be indulged merely for the convenience of the advocates, or for the purpose of frustrating an opposing party's attempt to obtain rightful redress or repose. It is not a justification that similar conduct is often tolerated by the bench and bar. The question is whether a competent lawyer acting in good faith would regard the course of action as having some substantial purpose other than delay. Realizing financial or other benefit from otherwise improper delay in litigation is not a legitimate interest of the client.

Comments and Questions

1. Schrag's article *Bleak House* leaves many with the impression that there is a lack of civility in the discovery process as well as in other aspects of litigation. Examples of this problem abound. In the following excerpts, Judge Marvin E. Aspen, a U.S. District Judge in the Northern District of Illinois, describes some of these problems:

> These are troubled times for lawyers. Not only is the practice of law suffering from the current economic malaise, but lawyer bashing has become our new national pastime. . . . Most of this public derision and media abuse is, of course, unjustified. But is some of it self-inflicted? Just how much has the legal profession contributed to the public's misperception of lawyers as heartless, self-interested, parasites, flourishing only by virtue of others' misery and misfortune?
> Let us, for example, look at the following exchange during a deposition taken in Madison, Wisconsin, this year by two veteran Chicago trial lawyers.

Attorney V had just asked Attorney A for a copy of a document he was using to question the witness:

"*Mr. V:* Please don't throw it at me.

Mr. A: Take it.

Mr. V: Don't throw it at me.

Mr. A: Don't be a child, Mr. V. You look like a slob the way you're dressed, but you don't have to act like a slob.

Mr. V: Stop yelling at me. Let's get on with it.

Mr. A: Have you not? You deny I have given you a copy of every document?

Mr. V: You just refused to give it to me.

Mr. A: Do you deny it?

Mr. V: Eventually you threw it at me.

Mr. A: Oh, Mr. V, you're about as childish as you can get. You look like a slob, you act like a slob.

Mr. V: Keep it up.

Mr. A: Your mind belongs in the gutter."

Although obviously an extreme incident of lawyer incivility, this interaction of attorneys during a multi-billion dollar case nonetheless exemplifies the erosion of professionalism in attorney relationships. . . .

Marvin E. Aspen, *The Search for Renewed Civility in Litigation*, 28 Val. U.L. Rev. 513, 513-514 (1994).

Later in this article, Judge Aspen lists some standards to improve professional conduct that then were under consideration by the Seventh Federal Judicial Circuit:

10. We will not use any form of discovery or discovery scheduling as a means of harassment. . . .

13. We will not request an extension of time solely for the purpose of unjustified delay or to obtain a tactical advantage. . . .

19. We will take depositions only when actually needed to ascertain facts or information or to perpetuate testimony. We will not take depositions for the purposes of harassment or to increase litigation expenses.

20. We will not engage in any conduct during a deposition that would not be appropriate in the presence of a judge. . . .

22. During depositions we will ask only those questions we reasonably believe are necessary for the prosecution or defense of an action. . . .

26. We will respond to interrogatories reasonably and will not strain to interpret them in an artificially restrictive manner to avoid disclosure of relevant and non-privileged information.

Id. at 524-527.

A preamble to the proposed standards states: "These standards shall not be used as a basis for litigation or for sanctions or penalties. Nothing in these standards supersedes or detracts from existing disciplinary codes or alters existing standards of conduct against which lawyer negligence would be determined." *Id.* at 524.

Do you think such standards will improve the civility of lawyers? How and why?

2. Do you have any suggestions for improving the civility of lawyers in litigation? What effect is your legal education having on your civility in law school or in daily life? What effect do you think your legal education will have on your civility in practicing law? What do you think the causes are of a lack of civility in litigation?

Practice Exercise No. 15: Ethical Issues in Discovery

The following two fact patterns present issues that may arise in the context of discovery. We are interested in finding out how you would respond under each of these circumstances (assume that you are an attorney with the power to make these choices). Remember that you have a duty both to zealously (or "competently" and "diligently" under the Model Rules) represent your clients and to behave ethically. You may want to consider the potential effect your decision will have on your client and their case, on the opposing party and its case, on your practice, and on the legal system generally. You may, of course, consider other factors as you see fit.

Scenario No. 1

Your clients, the City Police Department, its Chief, and members of the Department, are defendants in a civil rights case. Plaintiff claims that two policemen stood by and watched her husband brutally beat her, and that their failure to stop the beating was part of a pattern and practice of refusing to come to the aid of victims of domestic violence. Plaintiff is represented by a solo practitioner who recently graduated from law school and (you know from a friend) has lots of debt and almost no assets. She is representing the plaintiff on a pro bono basis and (you have heard) has volunteered to front the costs for her client, pending settlement or a favorable verdict. You are a third-year associate in a successful, respected firm. Defendants pay (through the City) $175 per hour for your services, plus costs.

Plaintiff has sent you a request for production of the following documents:

> Any and all records from the period 1/1/89-10/31/99 of or pertaining to any and all complaints, formal and/or informal, made by women to the City Police Department, regarding violence, abuse, forced sexual relations, and/or any other injury, act, or practice perpetrated upon them by a present or past husband, a present or past "boyfriend," and/or a present or past lover, and/or any other person known to them.

Any and all statements, memoranda, reports, or internal policy guidelines, in whatever form, pertaining to the period 1/1/89-10/31/99 of or
pertaining to the handling of complaints formal and/or informal, made
by women to the City Police Department, regarding violence, abuse,
forced sexual relations, and/or any other injury, act or practice perpetrated upon them by a present or past husband, a present or past
"boyfriend," and/or a present or past lover, and/or any other person
known to them.

With no further investigation (based on conversations you have had
with some of the defendants), you know that some items exist that
arguably would fit into each category requested by the plaintiff. You also
know that considerable time and expense (on the part of the Police
Department) would be involved in fairly compiling all of the materials
requested. From what you know so far, it could go a long way to proving
Plaintiff's claims if the request is read with any liberality. You fear that
there may even be some particularly damaging written memoranda signed
by the Chief calling domestic violence cases "none of our damn business,"
and similar statements by others in the department.

You consider the following responses to the request (or any others
that make sense to you):

(1) complying with what you understand to be the spirit of the
    request in as direct a manner as possible;
(2) producing nothing and saying these "requests are overly broad,
    unduly burdensome, and request materials beyond the scope of
    discovery";
(3) offering to make the materials available to the plaintiff "as they
    are kept," which would force them to go through the more than
    3,000 boxes of stored complaints, memoranda, etc., in the City
    Police Department basement;
(4) informing the Defendants (your clients) that you will need to
    look through the same 3,000 boxes yourself to determine what
    to produce (at your usual hourly rate);
(5) asking the Chief to provide you with whatever he thinks fits the
    request (you're pretty sure that his "eyesight is poor") and review-
    ing his production (at your hourly rate) to determine what must
    be produced;
(6) sending a photocopy of records of all complaints made by
    women—including the many which are not related to domestic
    violence, even those made by women on behalf of children,
    friends, etc., since the sweeping wording of the requests includes
    those items.

Which, if any, of these responses would be appropriate? Give a quick
assessment of each one and sketch your own course of action.

Scenario No. 2

Continuing with the same facts as above, the Chief comes to your office to prepare for his deposition, which is to occur next week. Upon his arrival, he says, "Hey, I know I told you I hadn't exactly established a firm policy for how to handle domestic violence cases, but you know what? I forgot about this memo I sent around a couple of years ago. One of my best officers just gave me his copy this morning. I'm sure you'll love it because I took all of the ideas from a great civil rights lawyer on how police departments ought to handle these cases. Before I left the station this morning, I talked with a bunch of my veteran cops and they all said they have copies in their procedures files and distinctly remember my long lecture to them on handling these cases seriously. I can't believe that it slipped my mind earlier, but I've been under a lot of pressure, you know. I'm really feeling better about my deposition testimony already."

What are you going to ask or say to the Chief? And what will you do at the deposition if he has the opportunity to testify according to what you have just heard?

The tension between zealous advocacy and other ethical considerations is the subject of much scholarly study. Consider the following excerpts on the adversarial process generally, especially in the context of discovery.

■ STEPHEN LANDSMAN, DEFENSE OF THE ADVERSARIAL PROCESS: READINGS ON ADVERSARIAL JUSTICE: THE AMERICAN APPROACH TO ADJUDICATION
33-39 (1988)

A fundamental lesson of Anglo-American legal history is that traditional methods of resolving disputes have served as a rampart against government tyranny. In light of this insight, reform of the judicial machinery should be approached with caution. The historical evidence will not support a flat refusal to change (innovation has been an important element in English and American law since the medieval period), but it does counsel caution where significant departures from previous practices are contemplated. Therefore, even if there were little good to say about the adversary system, those who argue for change would still face a significant burden of persuasion.

BENEFITS OF PARTY CONTROL OF LITIGATION

A number of reasons, apart from the historical, warrant reliance on adversarial methods. The adversary process provides litigants with the means to control their lawsuits. The parties are preeminent in choosing the forum, designating the proofs, and running the process. The courts, as a general rule, pursue the questions the parties propound. Ultimately, the whole procedure yields results tailored to the litigants' needs and in this way reinforces individual rights. As already noted, this sort of procedure also enhances the economic efficiency of adjudication by sharply reducing impositional costs.

Party control yields other benefits as well. Perhaps most important, it promotes litigant and societal acceptance of decisions rendered by the courts. Adversary theory holds that if a party is intimately involved in the adjudicatory process and feels that he has been given a fair opportunity to present his case, he is likely to accept the results whether favorable or not. Assuming this theory is correct, the adversary process will serve to reduce post-litigation friction and to increase compliance with judicial mandates.

Adversary theory identifies litigant control as important to satisfy not only the parties but society as well. When litigants direct the proceedings, there is little opportunity for the judge to pursue her own agenda or to act on her biases. Because the judge seldom takes the lead in conducting the proceedings, she is unlikely to appear to be partisan or to become embroiled in the contest. Her detachment preserves the appearance of fairness as well as fairness itself. In legal proceedings, as the United States Supreme Court stated in *Offutt v. United States* [384 U.S. 11, 14 (1954)], "justice must satisfy the appearance of justice." When it fails to do so, social credibility is eroded and distrust introduced. There is little direct evidence of the extent of personal or societal acceptance of adversarial processes as contrasted with other adjudicatory methodologies. A number of multinational surveys, however, including those conducted by Professors John Thibaut and Laurens Walker, have found that a majority of subjects will designate adversary procedure as the fairest for resolving disputes. This finding lends support to the argument that adversary procedures are perceived as fairest and are more likely to satisfy litigants and onlookers than nonadversary alternatives.

Thibaut and Walker have provided empirical evidence that litigant control produces other sorts of benefits. First, it tends to encourage desirable conduct on the part of litigants and their counsel. Psychological experimentation has shown that an advocate working in an adversarial context who finds his client at a factual disadvantage will expend significant effort to improve his client's position. This is to be contrasted with the behavior of the advocate working in an inquisitorial setting who will seldom undertake an extensive search for better evidence to bolster a weak case. The adversary process appears to encourage advocates to protect parties facing an initial disadvantage and hence to improve the overall quality of the evidence upon which adjudication will be based.

Thibaut and Walker have also found that adversarial emphasis on party presentation tends to counteract the bias of the decision maker more effectively than does an approach requiring the active participation of the trier in marshaling the proof. This finding provides tangible support for the theoretical assertion that the best decision maker is one whose sole function is adjudication. Because the adversary process assigns the prosecutorial function to the parties, it serves to increase the likelihood that the trier will be able to devote her full attention to the neutral adjudication of the case.

The adversary process assigns each participant a single function. The judge is to serve as neutral and passive arbiter. Counsel are to act as zealous advocates. According to adversary theory, when each actor performs only a single function the dispute before the court will be resolved in the fairest and most efficient way. The strength of such a division of labor is that individual responsibilities are clear. The possibility that a participant in the system will face conflicting responsibility is minimized. Each knows what is expected of him and can work conscientiously to achieve a specifically defined goal. When participants in the judicial process are confronted with conflicting obligations, it becomes difficult for them to discharge any of their duties satisfactorily. The more frequently they face conflict, the more likely it is that they will not perform their assigned part or will not perform it in a way that minimizes conflict rather than fully discharging their responsibilities. Among the greatest dangers in this regard are that the judge will abandon neutrality if encouraged to search for material truth and that the attorney will compromise his client's interests if compelled to serve as an officer of the court rather than as an advocate. In either case the probity of the process is seriously undermined.

Party control has another beneficial effect as well. It affirms human individuality. It mandates respect for the opinions of each party rather than those of his attorney, of the court, or of society at large. It provides the litigant a neutral forum in which to air his views and promises that those views will be heard and considered. The individualizing effect of adversary procedure has important implications besides those involving individual satisfaction. The receptiveness of adversary procedure to individual claims implies that an adversarial court will take a sympathetic view of the claims of individuals against the state. The prospects for sympathetic hearing are increased because the judge and, to an even greater extent, the jury are beyond governmental control and cannot be taken to task for their decisions.

These propositions concerning the receptiveness of adversarial courts to the claims of individual citizens are, at least in part, borne out by historical evidence. For centuries adversarial courts have served as a counterbalance to official tyranny and have worked to broaden the scope of individual rights. The steady expansion of doctrines protecting minorities both in England and in the United States reflects this fact. When adversarial process has been ignored in the operation of the courts, as in the days of the Star Chamber, human rights diminished and governmental repression increased.

We live in an era of expanding government power. The urgency of social problems, including the scarcity of resources and the exigencies of national defense, tends to lead the government to exert pressure on the citizenry to cooperate in ensuring the efficient operation of society as a whole. This pressure poses a keen threat to the maintenance of individual rights. In these circumstances, there is a need to preserve the kind of institution that will sympathetically review claims based on individual rights rather than on governmental necessity or the common good. Because the adversarial courts are primarily committed to hearing and to upholding the claims of individuals, they are most likely to be capable of handling this task.

Comments and Questions

1. Landsman offers a persuasive apology for the adversary process. Does it follow that each segment of the litigation process—such as discovery—should likewise be founded on these time-tested precepts?

2. Would the adversary nature of adjudication be compromised if fact development were left to the judge? See John H. Langbein, *The German Advantage in Civil Procedure*, 52 U. Chi. L. Rev. 823 (1985).

3. Landsman speaks eloquently in defense of the adversary process as a guarantor of individual rights. What "rights," loosely defined, should an individual have (or expect) in discovery in the course of litigation?

4. Landsman has compiled a number of excerpts from writings that criticize or defend the adversary system. The portion printed above is from his introductory essay to the readings, which is largely laudatory of the adversary system. The book was produced under the sponsorship of the American Bar Association Section of Litigation.

■ WAYNE BRAZIL, THE ADVERSARY CHARACTER OF CIVIL DISCOVERY: A CRITIQUE AND PROPOSALS FOR CHANGE
37 Vand. L. Rev. 1295 (1978)

> [W]e need to study whether our elaborate struggles over discovery . . . may be incurable symptoms of pathology inherent in our rigid insistence that the parties control the evidence until it is all "prepared" and packaged for competitive manipulation at the eventual continuous trial [Marvin E. Frankel, *The Search for Truth: An Umpireal View*, 123 U. Pa. L. Rev. 1031, 1054 (1975)].

I. INTRODUCTION

. . . The thesis I explore is that the adversary character of civil discovery, with substantial reinforcement from the economic structure of our legal system, promotes practices that systematically impede the attainment of the principal purpose for which discovery was designed. The adversary structure of the discovery machinery creates significant functional difficulties for, and imposes costly economic burdens on, our system of dispute resolution. Because these difficulties and burdens are an inevitable consequence of adversary relationships and competitive economic pressures, they cannot be removed by the kind of limited, nonstructural discovery reforms that have been made in the past and are once again under consideration. To come to terms with these problems will require an assault on their sources; effective reform consequently must include institutional changes that will curtail substantially the impact of adversary forces in the pretrial stage of litigation. . . .

II. THE PURPOSES OF DISCOVERY

The purposes that modern civil discovery is designed to accomplish are crucial to a system of dispute resolution committed to justice. In its seminal opinion about the scope of discovery, the United States Supreme Court declared that "[m]utual knowledge of all the relevant facts gathered by both parties is essential to proper litigation." Discovery is designed to serve as the principal mechanism by which such "[m]utual knowledge of all the relevant facts" will be achieved. As the Supreme Court of Illinois forthrightly stated, the overriding purpose of discovery is nothing less than to promote "the ascertainment of the truth and ultimate disposition of the lawsuit in accordance therewith. . . ." . . .

Minimal reflection reveals a fundamental antagonism between the goal of truth through disclosure and the protective and competitive impulses that are at the center of the traditional adversary system of dispute resolution. While drafters and early proponents of the rules of discovery were not oblivious to that antagonism, they seem to have assumed that the rules themselves would reduce the size of the litigation arena in which adversary pressures and tactics in the pretrial process of gathering relevant evidentiary data.

The literature that emanated from the academic and judicial proponents of discovery during the decades surrounding the 1938 adoption of the Federal Rules of Civil Procedure is replete with optimistic forecasts about the beneficial changes discovery would bring to the adversary system. Edson R. Sunderland, who is credited with drafting the discovery components of the 1938 Federal Rules, wrote that the new procedural rules: "mark the highest point so far reached in the English speaking world in the elimination of secrecy in the preparation for trial. Each party may in effect be called upon by his adversary or by the judge to lay all his cards upon the table, the important consideration being who has the stronger hand, not who can play the cleverer game."

Six years earlier, while advocating the discovery reforms that culminated in the Federal Rules, Sunderland had declared that:

> Lawyers who constantly employ [discovery] in their practice find it an exceedingly valuable aid in promoting justice. Discovery procedure serves much the same function in the field of law as the x-ray in the field of medicine and surgery; and if its use can be sufficiently extended and its methods simplified, litigation will largely cease to be a game of chance. . . .
>
> [T]he primary purpose of the modern rules of discovery was to secure complete disclosure of all relevant evidentiary information and to do so by altering the nature of the relationship between the parties during the trial preparation period. . . . The unarticulated premise that seems to underlie much of the work of discovery's most vocal proponents is that the process of gathering, organizing, and sharing evidentiary information should take place in an essentially nonadversarial context. . . .

III. Adversary Instincts and the Undoing of the Nonadversarial Assumption

The academic and judicial proponents of the modern rules of discovery apparently failed to appreciate how tenaciously litigators would hold to their adversarial ways and the magnitude of the antagonism between the principal purpose of discovery (the ascertainment of truth through disclosure) and the protective and competitive instincts that dominate adversary litigation. . . .

Instead of reducing the sway of adversary forces in litigation and confining them to the trial stage, discovery has greatly expanded the arenas in which those forces can operate. It also has provided attorneys with new weapons, devices, and incentives for the adversary gamesmanship that discovery was designed to curtail. Rather than discourage "the sporting or game theory of justice," discovery has expanded both the scope and the complexity of the sport. Modern discovery also has removed most of the decisive plays from the scrutiny of the court. Because so many civil cases are settled before trial and because the conduct of attorneys is subject only to fitful and superficial judicial review during the discovery stage, much of the decisive gamesmanship of modern litigation takes place in private settings.

Such factors as traditional professional loyalties, deeply ingrained lawyering instincts, and competitive economic pressures assured that the process of gathering and organizing evidence would not take place in an essentially nonadversarial context. Escape from this outcome would have required substantial changes in the institutional context within which discovery is conducted. However, no such changes have been made.

Attorneys conducting discovery still are commanded by the rules of professional responsibility and by their own economic self-interest to commit their highest loyalty to their client's best interests. By contrast, there is generally no ethical pressure or financial incentive for attorneys voluntarily to disclose the fruits of their investigations or in any way make ascertainment of the truth easier for opposing counsel or the trier of fact. In short, all the well-established institutional pressures that for generations have operated to make attorneys partisan advocates and to make them view each other as committed adversaries have remained intact. In this context, it is indeed naive to expect that discovery, armed only with its own executional rules, could somehow resist the inroads of the adversarial and competitive pressures that dominate its surroundings. . . .

V. DISCOVERY'S PSYCHOLOGICAL AND INSTITUTIONAL ENVIRONMENT

An appropriate way to begin an examination of the psychological and institutional environment within which discovery is conducted is by identifying the goals that motivate the attorneys who use discovery procedures. The process of identifying those goals must begin with acknowledgment of one controlling fact: attorneys who use discovery procedures are attorneys engaged in litigation. Discovery is a tool whose purposes are fixed by the purposes of the larger process of which it is a part. That larger process is litigation. Attorneys in litigation have five primary objectives: (1) to win; (2) to make money; (3) to avoid being sued for malpractice; (4) to earn the admiration of the professional community; and (5) to develop self-esteem for the quality of their performances. These objectives are not born simply of cynicism and selfishness. They are institutionalized commands that emanate from a system of combat within a competitive economic structure. It is not difficult to perceive that these goals make the purposes of discovery for individual litigators quite different from the purposes which the architects of the discovery system contemplated. . . .

[A]dversary litigation and competitive economics offer no institutionalized rewards for disclosure of potentially relevant data. They instead offer many institutional deterrents to full disclosure. Review of the primary means by which litigators seek to earn the rewards of the legal system graphically illustrates this generalization. Litigators generally believe they will win the primary forms of recognition our system offers not through full disclosure, not through relentless efforts to secure just results, not through honesty, openness, and uncalculating cooperation, nor even necessarily through efficiency and superior work quality, but rather by tailoring the most clever package of tactics and stratagems to fit the needs of a given case.

The means employed by litigators to achieve victory for their clients regularly involve manipulating people and the flow of information in order to present their client's positions as persuasively and favorably as possible. This manipulation may involve any or all of the following general techniques: not disclosing evidence that could be damaging to the client or helpful to an opposing party; not disclosing persuasive legal precedents that could be damaging to the client; undermining or deflating persuasive evidence and precedents that are damaging to the client and are intro- duced by opposing counsel, by such means as upsetting or discrediting honest and reliable witnesses or by burying adverse evidence under mounds of obfuscating evidentiary debris; overemphasizing and present- ing out of context evidence and precedents that appear favorable to the client; pressuring or cajoling witnesses, jurors, and judges into adopting views that support the client's position; deceiving opposing counsel and parties about the weaknesses of the client's case and the strengths of opposing cases; aggravating and exploiting to the fullest extent possible vulnerabilities of the opposing party and counsel that have nothing to do with the merits of a given dispute by such means as intimidating an anx- ious opponent, spending a poor opponent into submission, or "soaking" in settlement an opponent who has public image problems or who for other reasons cannot endure the risk and public exposure of a trial. None of these techniques is illegal or violates the letter of the ethical rules of the profession. Indeed, the refusal to resort to at least some of these devices may be construed as a breach of an attorney's obligation "to represent his client zealously within the bounds of the law." . . .

[In part VI, the author discusses in detail "how attorneys, responding to the adversarial and economic pressures discussed above, can use specific discovery tools to limit and distort the flow of relevant data to their opponents and to the trier of fact, to increase the cost of gathering and organizing that data, and to reduce the likelihood that settlements and judgments after trial will be just. . . ." He emphasizes how some lawyers over-supply documents in responding to discovery requests, in the hope that relevant information will become an unfound needle in the haystack, or read discovery requests in the most narrow fashion, again hoping to conceal relevant information that is detrimental to their case.]

VIII. TOWARD AN ALTERNATIVE

As the foregoing discussion makes clear, I believe that discovery cannot serve effectively its intended purposes unless substantial changes are made both in the extent and quality of judicial control over its processes. While I venture some suggestions for such changes, I cannot pretend to offer a fully refined blueprint for an alternative discovery system. Nor have I been able to explore all the ramifications that might accompany the changes I propose. My hope, rather, is that these recom- mendations will provoke within the profession a spirited and constructive debate about the fundamental structure of civil discovery. . . .

The core of the changes I propose to combat these problems can be summarized as follows: shifting counsel's principal obligation during the investigation and discovery stage away from partisan pursuit of clients' interests and towards the court; imposing a duty on counsel to investigate thoroughly the factual background of disputes; imposing a duty on both counsel and client to disclose voluntarily, and at all stages of trial preparation, all potentially relevant evidence and information; narrowing the reach of the attorney-client privilege and the work product doctrine; making early discovery conferences mandatory; substantially expanding the role of the court in monitoring the execution of discovery; and requiring thorough judicial review of, or participation in, all settlements that exceed a specified dollar amount.

These reform proposals are logical derivatives of the basic premise of this essay—that because the pressures generated and the loyalties commanded by the adversary relationships currently dominating litigation are largely responsible for the frustration of the purposes of discovery, meaningful reform does not seem possible without changing these pressures and shifting these loyalties. Toward that end I recommend major changes in the Federal Rules of Civil Procedure and in the Code of Professional Responsibility, changes designed to reduce as much as possible the sway of adversary forces in the discovery process. The Code of Professional Responsibility, for example, currently treats litigation almost monolithically, making few significant distinctions between criminal and civil actions or between the various stages of lawsuits. A breakdown of this monolithic approach is required. Canons and disciplinary rules especially tailored to civil matters should be drafted. Moreover, ethical standards should be refined in order to distinguish between the different requirements of the investigative and discovery stages, on the one hand, and the trial and post-trial stages on the other.

In particular, new rules of professional responsibility and civil procedure should be fashioned for the investigative and discovery stages. During these stages, counsel should be directed to view themselves primarily as officers of the court rather than partisan advocates. As officers of the court, counsel should be commanded by new ethical directives and civil rules to search diligently for all data that might help resolve disputes fairly and to share voluntarily the results of their searches with both the court and the other parties to the action. Under this new system, the court would determine at discovery conferences how much investigation counsel would have to undertake in given cases to comply with this general obligation. In making this determination at the outset of the litigation and in refining it over the course of the pretrial period, the court would strive to balance the investigative burden equitably among all participating counsel. Under the changes proposed here, counsel's primary loyalties during the trial and post-trial stages would remain where they are today: to their clients. . . .

This proposed shift during the discovery stage of counsel's primary obligation away from purely partisan advocacy and toward full disclosure has some potentially troublesome implications for the traditional relationship between counsel and client. For example, clients might feel more pressure not to divulge to their attorney evidence they fear could damage their case. Clients also might feel that it is unfair to ask them to pay an attorney whose loyalties are divided between serving a public interest in justice and the clients' private interest in victory. While these problems could be significant, their dimensions are readily subject to exaggeration, and they probably are not insurmountable. Even under current rules, for example, clients frequently are reluctant to share clearly inculpating evidence with their attorneys. Such reluctance may stem from clients' failure to understand the ways the rules of professional responsibility and evidence can work to protect them, from their fear of being morally condemned by their lawyer, or from cynical appreciation that if they share certain information with their attorney they lose control over whether it will be disclosed. In short, it simply is not clear that the changes I propose would alter to a considerable extent the way most clients share information with their counsel. It seems reasonable to predict that clients who are predisposed to be honest with their attorneys probably would continue to do so, and that clients who are not so predisposed probably would not change their behavior in significant ways. . . .

This mandate to disclose would not be fully effective, however, without establishing the procedural machinery for making disclosures and for enforcing the duty to disclose. There probably are several different procedural forms that could be devised to act as the principal vehicle for disclosure. Certain minimum features, however, should be included. One is to reduce the disclosed information as completely as possible to some permanently recorded form. This requirement is essential in order to assure the reliable sharing of information between all parties and the court, to preserve the shared information, to establish the record necessary to control the presentation of evidence at trial, and to evaluate the propriety of imposing sanctions for breaching the duty to disclose. Another requirement that should be built into the disclosure procedure calls for periodic updating and supplementing of the information provided at the initial stages of the litigation process. There are two junctures at which some formal disclosure should be required in every civil action: (1) immediately after the issues have been joined through the filing of pleadings; and (2) at the close of the first major investigative period. New rules also should make some provision, however, for subsequent periodic disclosures, the precise timing of which might best be left for determination by the judge presiding over the discovery conferences.

Since the duty to disclose is a central feature of the procedures I am proposing, devising a set of controls, encouragements, and sanctions that would maximize compliance with this duty is critically important. Candor compels acknowledgment, however, that designing a just and effective system of incentive and enforcement for this purpose would be a most difficult task. No such system could eliminate the possibility of abuse or thwart every evasive effort by the intentionally dishonest. There are, however, several measures whose implementation could reduce substantially the likelihood of certain repeated breaches of this duty to disclose that would jeopardize most seriously the fairness of the proposed procedures.

One such measure would be to require both counsel and client to swear under oath on every disclosure occasion and at the close of the pretrial period that they had searched diligently for and disclosed all information that arguably might be relevant to the dispute in question. . . .

Another device that might prove useful in enforcing the duty to disclose would be to require counsel and client to identify for the court and other parties all the sources from which information or evidence was sought. . . .

A series of mandatory discovery conferences would be essential, at least in the more complex cases, in order to achieve all the objectives of this alternative system for gathering and sharing data. . . .

This alternative system for gathering and organizing information obviously contemplates a much larger and more aggressive pretrial role for the judiciary. In addition to the functions described in the preceding paragraphs, this expanded role should include the power to participate directly in both the investigation and discovery stages of litigation. A court should be empowered, for example, to pose written or oral questions to parties, witnesses, or attorneys whenever the court is unsatisfied with the quality or comprehensiveness of questions propounded by counsel. Similarly, a court on its own initiative should be able to request admissions of fact and the production of documents from parties. It also should be permitted to participate in depositions directly or through a magistrate or clerk. While these kinds of powers should exist to improve the likelihood that neither the incompetence nor the adversary motives of counsel will leave major holes in the evidentiary record, judges should be directed to employ these tools sparingly and only when required to do so in the interests of justice. . . .

Comments and Questions

1. Wayne D. Brazil has been a Magistrate Judge in the U.S. District Court for the Northern District of California since 1984. He had been a professor of law at the University of California, Hastings College of the Law, and since 1988 has been a member of the Judicial Conference of the United States Advisory Committee on the Civil Rules.

2. Brazil hypothesizes that the adversary character of civil discovery promotes practices that systematically obstruct the basic system of dispute

resolution. Part of Brazil's proposal involves mandatory disclosure of certain discovery by the parties. Although then more than a decade old, this article was very important in the movement for reform that led to the 1993 amendments requiring mandatory disclosures. Indeed, this article was cited in the Advisory Committee Notes to those amendments; the Advisory Committee stated that this article sets forth the "concepts of imposing a duty of disclosure." What are those "concepts"?

3. The wisdom of mandatory disclosure was (and remains) a hotly contested reform measure. Consider the following excerpt from Justice Scalia's dissent to the Court's transmittal of the 1993 discovery amendments:

> . . . The proposed radical reforms to the discovery process are potentially disastrous and certainly premature—particularly the imposition on litigants of a continuing duty to disclose to opposing counsel. . . .
>
> The proposed new regime does not fit comfortably within the American judicial system, which relies on adversarial litigation to develop the facts before a neutral decisionmaker. By placing upon lawyers the obligation to disclose information damaging to their clients—on their own initiative, and in a context where the lines between what must be disclosed and what need not be disclosed are not clear but require the exercise of considerable judgment—the new Rule would place intolerable strain upon lawyers' ethical duty to represent their clients and not to assist the opposing side. . . .
>
> It seems to me most imprudent to embrace such a radical alteration that has not, as the advisory committee notes, *see id.*, at 94, been subjected to any significant testing on a local level. . . . Any major reform of the discovery rules should await completion of the pilot programs authorized by Congress, especially since courts already have substantial discretion to control discovery. *See* Fed. Rule. Civ. P. 26.
>
> I am also concerned that this revision has been recommended in the face of nearly universal criticism from every conceivable sector of our judicial system, including judges, practitioners, litigants, academics, public interest groups, and national, state and local bar and professional associations. . . . Indeed, after the proposed rule in essentially its present form was published to comply with the notice-and-comment requirement of 28 U.S.C. §2071(b), public criticism was so severe that the advisory committee announced abandonment of its duty-to-disclose regime (in favor of limited pilot experiments), but then, without further public comment or explanation, decided six weeks later to recommend the rule. . . .

4. Would you expect Brazil to defend, revise, and/or distinguish his proposal(s) for mandatory disclosure in light of current discovery practice?

5. The discovery process (by design) contributes to the current environment in which well over 90 percent of all cases settle or are otherwise disposed of without a full-scale trial. The information obtained in discovery allows counsel to assess the evidence that would be available at trial. Oral depositions give an opportunity to see witnesses' demeanor under questioning. This information is extremely useful in settlement negotiations,

since opposing counsel will have seen and heard the same depositions. Moreover, the cost of discovery may help precipitate settlement.

6. In considering the process of discovery, it is important to remember that certain causes of action, such as products liability, antitrust, and employment discrimination, are extremely difficult or impossible to win (even when the facts, if known, would establish liability) without broad access to information held by opponents and other witnesses. Thus, good arguments exist for the discovery rules to provide sufficient means to discourage or prevent the abuses of unjustified burdensome discovery and the obstreperous blocking of legitimate discovery, while preserving the basic nature of an open discovery system. In light of this concern, consider how the current system works and doesn't work, and how changing discovery rules to prevent unreasonable obstruction might affect our legal system as a whole.

F. CRITICISM: RECENT AND PROPOSED REFORM

Notwithstanding waves of reforms to the discovery rules throughout the past two decades, there remains a belief, widely held by members both inside and outside of the legal community, that the discovery process still is choking our legal system. As you read the following excerpts, focus on how that argument is treated.

■ LOREN KIEVE, DISCOVERY REFORM
A.B.A. J. 81-86 (Dec. 1991)

There has been almost universal agreement that discovery has become a nightmare. It has provoked local rules limiting discovery, proposals by Vice President Quayle's Council on Competitiveness, and most recently proposals to amend the Federal Rules of Civil Procedure themselves.

A federal district judge, William Schwarzer, who is also currently director of the Federal Judicial Center, has written a thought-provoking article on the subject entitled, "Slaying the Monsters of Cost and Delay: Would Disclosure Be More Effective Than Discovery?" in the December-January '91 issue of Judicature magazine.

Schwarzer's proposal, which legal columnist Stuart Taylor has called a "lifeline for [a] system drowning in discovery," calls for mandatory disclosure—requiring both sides to a lawsuit disclose at the very beginning of a case any material that is "relevant" to the issues.

The disclosure concept has most recently been embraced by the Judicial Conference Advisory Committee on Civil Rules in its August 1991

Preliminary Draft of proposed rule amendments (now being circulated for comment). [Mandatory disclosure was incorporated into Rule 26 by virtue of a 1993 amendment.]

. . . In sharp contrast to Judge Schwarzer's original proposal, however, the draft would continue to allow the parties to use the traditional discovery devices—although it would place not terribly restrictive limits on their number and length (15 interrogatories and 10 depositions, no more than six-hours long per side)—unless the parties otherwise agreed or the court directed for good cause.

Although superficially appealing, the disclosure concept is far from a lifeline. It may be more like taking a drowning victim out of one river only to throw her into another.

If discovery is overwhelming litigation (as I and many others believe), then the answer is not a mutated form of discovery—one that requires each party immediately after a lawsuit is filed to guess what documents, etc., the other side might find relevant or that "bear significantly" on the issues (or, to use Taylor's term, are "damaging") and turn them over to the adversary. This simply would compound the problem by adding confusion to an already overburdened system.

Our legal system is predicated on the curious notion that a lawyer can file a lawsuit with only a bare idea of what the case—much less the trial— will look like, and then require the opposition and its lawyers to go through the cumbersome, expensive procedure of sifting through its files to turn over a vast array of material that is not merely relevant but that may "lead to the discovery" of relevant evidence.

I am in full agreement with Judge Schwarzer's bottom line. The current discovery process is a monster out of control. As Taylor so aptly put it, discovery "devours millions of dollars and countless hours of a lawyer's time in cases that would be better settled or tried with far less ado." . . .

Some have suggested cynically that lawyers have glommed onto discovery because it is has become the ideal way to rack up billable hours—with legions of leveraged associates reinventing new forms of multipart interrogatories, and document requests spewing forth from word processors like the multi-headed Hydra of mythology. As soon as one discovery head is cut off, two more appear in its place.

When the other side responds in kind by launching its retaliatory first, second and third waves, the lawyers then can generate even more billables by dispatching another team to sift through every nook and cranny of the client's files. The object is to find the smoking gun the other side just knows has to be there.

Of course, all the while, both sides have to fight about the scope of discovery, privilege, protective orders, the length (and place) of depositions, and so on—generating even more revenue.

The truth is that the system itself is the root evil. Like Mount Everest, a lawyer uses discovery "because it is there." It is one of the tools (choose your own metaphor—chainsaw, axe) the rules give us.

If you know your opponent has this tool, and is going to use it, then you risk 1) loss of the case; 2) a malpractice suit; and 3) the wrath of your client by not using discovery—either aggressively or defensively.

The proposal to substitute disclosure for discovery hopes to do away with this. It is certainly a step in the right direction, but it does not go far enough, and may actually exacerbate the problem.

The theory behind disclosure is that it will require the parties, at the beginning of a case, to produce all relevant materials and the names of people who may know something about it. The lawyers will then know enough about the case to settle, file a dispositive (or partially dispositive) motion, or go to trial.

If disclosure actually stopped there, it might do some good. But current proposals allow for traditional discovery as well and also contemplate, upon a showing of good cause, even more depositions, interrogatories and document requests—the grist of the traditional discovery mill. . . .

The twin premises underlying the disclosure model are that it will require federal trial judges to take a more active role in managing their cases and substantially reduce discovery battles. If a party is unsure of what it should disclose, it will file a motion to clarify its obligation, and the judge will take charge.

This all but guarantees the same kind (if not more) of the motion practice that now permeates our oldfangled discovery system—but shifts it right up front. . . .

Federal trial judges are for the most part extremely busy and do not have the time (assuming they have the inclination) to supervise disclosure any more than they have had the time to supervise discovery. . . .

The obvious solution is one the rest of the civilized world (or at least the English and civil law systems) has long used: No discovery.

Lawyers in England and on the Continent investigate the case before it is filed (presumably trying all the while to settle it), obtain the documents and witnesses they need to try it, and, only then, file a lawsuit. At that point they are ready to try it.

Once the suit is filed, preliminary pleadings are filed to see if the case has legal merit. If it passes this test, a trial date is set. Before trial, the parties exchange lists of witnesses and a short statement of what they will say, and turn over copies of the exhibits they plan to use. Then they go to trial. If a witness is unavailable because he is in another jurisdiction or on his deathbed, then his deposition can be taken, but this is the only exception.

Not only do lawyers in England and Europe do this every day, so do U.S. criminal defense lawyers and those who try arbitrations.

I know of no empirical study or scientific proof that suggests that this produces a result that is less fair. Nor do I know of any study or proof to indicate that our unique, over-burdened system is better.

I do know, though, that there are very few actual litigants—those who have been through the crucible of American discovery—who think that our discovery system is worth the time and expense it has engendered. . . .

Eliminating discovery entirely would streamline cases and require lawyers and clients to think seriously about the merits of a suit before filing or defending one. (Requiring the losing side to pay the other's attorney fees and expenses also might go a long way toward reducing our over-loaded civil litigation, but that is a different, although related, subject.)

There may be a few types of cases where some limited discovery would be appropriate because of the nature of the issues—employment discrimi-nation, for example, where the plaintiff needs to have access to the employer's statistical employment information—but these should be a narrow exception.

Doing away with discovery probably would require pleading with greater particularity than under the current (but not terribly informative) system of notice pleading—where, for example, a lawyer only has to allege that one of three defendants, or perhaps all three, negligently drove or caused to be driven a motor vehicle against plaintiff to state a claim. But more particularity certainly would help frame the issues better and might even eliminate meritless cases early on.

I have tried cases under both the American and English systems, and have concluded that the U.S. discovery system is not worth it.

The great experiment of discovery—and the notion that it would allow a fairer trial at less expense to the litigants—is demonstrably an abject failure. It should be eliminated, period, and not replaced by another system that does not solve the problem, and may compound it.

If discovery is not simply abolished, then it has to be severely trun-cated; both in scope and in the time it takes. The Eastern District of Virginia—the "rocket docket"—has such a system. It is not as good as no discovery, but it is certainly better than what exists in most courts today.

Firm discovery deadlines (usually in the three- to four-month range) and firm dates for a final pretrial conference (normally a month or so after the discovery cutoff date) are automatically set in every case. They can be extended only for good cause (and never merely by agreement of counsel). Trial is set within three to eight weeks of the final pretrial conference. The judges operate on a master calendar, so if one judge is not available, another will try the case.

Unless they obtain a court order based on good cause, the parties are limited to 30 interrogatories—including subparts—and five depositions of non-parties. Objections to discovery must be made within 15 days. And the parties are required to consult in good faith before filing any motion.

Motions are noticed to the nearest Friday, when all of the judges sit to hear both criminal and civil motions. Most motions are decided from the bench; those that are not usually come down the following week. Written decisions are typically not very long, but the parties know why the court has ruled the way it has.

More importantly, they obtain a result that moves them toward trial, or disposes of the case entirely. And how many lawyers can honestly say that their case was hurt because they did not get a crack at a particular document, or could not take seven more depositions?

Lawyers who practice in the Eastern District of Virginia know that they have to be ready to go to trial. More than 90 percent of all civil cases, however, settle. The judges I have spoken to are unanimous that the way to make sure cases settle earlier is to have firm deadlines, both for discovery and for trial. That is why the Eastern Division of Virginia has among the highest and fastest disposition rates of any federal trial court. . . .

■ WALTER OLSON, DENTISTS, BARTENDERS, AND LAWYER UNPOPULARITY
Manhattan Institute, Civil Justice Memo No. 37 (April 1999)

The current unpopularity of lawyers has been the subject of much hand-wringing, and no little indignation, on the part of such groups as the American Bar Association (ABA). . . . According to the ABA view, the prevailing low regard for lawyers has nothing whatsoever to do with the public's having noticed and reacted against any misconduct or hubris or overreaching by the legal profession or the legal system itself. Certainly not. Lawyers have plummeted in the occupational-esteem standing not because lawyers do more destructive or useless things than they used to, not because people think they've nosed into too many areas of American life, not because the system gives attorneys too much power to inflict injury on their opponents, their clients and third parties. No, it's that the public has been terribly misled. If it only knew more about how the American legal system worked, it would not be so upset with lawyers. Its unfavorable view of lawyers arises from misunderstanding, or, if you will, false consciousness. . . .

[L]awyers, I submit, are so widely disliked in this country because they are so very widely, and correctly, feared for the power without responsibility they wield. . . . Nowhere else can a lawyer show up, dump a pile of papers on your front lawn, tie you up for years, responding to untold damage to your business and reputation, and then walk away with so few consequences if he is proven wrong. . . .

So the question I leave for the bar associations is: is your profession mistrusted because it's not understood? Or because it's understood too well?

Comments and Questions

1. Loren Kieve is a partner in the Washington, D.C., office of Debevoise & Plimpton. William W. Schwarzer is the former director of the Federal Judicial Center, the research arm of the federal judiciary. He is now a Senior Judge of the U.S. District Court for the Northern District

of California. Walter Olson is the author of the 1991 best-seller *The Litigation Explosion.*

2. Why does American society give litigators so much power, yet provide so little control over how they use it? Does Landsman answer this question? One popular answer to the question is the theory of the "private attorney general." Under this theory, the litigation process uncovers and punishes unreasonable or unethical conduct, and thereby benefits all of us. But in the case of actual public prosecutors and regulatory agencies, we expect (and are entitled to) a close public accounting of both costs and results. We may obtain information about their salaries and have the benefit of freedom of information, open records, and sunshine laws. Agencies routinely provide status reports and also are subject to investigations. Banks, airlines, utilities, hospitals, and other private enterprises are likewise subject to public inquiry whenever some component of the public interest is implicated. And securities regulations ensure that most other large enterprises disclose salient information, including balance sheets, income data, and executive salaries. Official data collection about the litigation business is virtually nonexistent. Why? Does this lack of public disclosure undermine the "private attorney general" theory? Explain.

In August 1998, the Standing Committee on Rules of Practice and Procedure released for public comment a package of amendments developed by the Advisory Committee on Civil Rules. This set of amendments proposes still more changes to the discovery rules, which have seen far more than their fair share of revision in the past two decades. Still, these most recent proposed amendments provide an excellent opportunity to focus on the contours of these recurring reforms and the efforts of rule-makers to cure the ills of discovery with textual amendments. In the following excerpt, Professor Marcus, a professor of law at the University of California, Hastings College of Law, establishes some historical context for a better understanding of the proposed 1998 reforms, and Professor Thornburg, a professor of law at Southern Methodist University School of Law, responds to Professor Marcus's analysis. As you read this "conversation" on the evolution of discovery reform, consider whether you think the reform is moving in the right direction and whether the debate is focusing on the right questions.

■ RICHARD L. MARCUS,
DISCOVERY CONTAINMENT REDUX
39 B.C. L. Rev. 747 (1998)

. . .

I. THE WAY THINGS WERE

Much as the Federal Rules of Civil Procedure broke new ground in allowing broad discovery, they did not, as adopted in 1938, make it entirely open. Document discovery, in particular, was until 1946 subject to a narrow scope permitting discovery of documents "which constitute or contain evidence material to any matter involved in the action," and until 1970 available only on motion based on a showing of "good cause." More generally, the rules provided separately for the different discovery devices rather than combining coverage of general provisions concerning relevancy and the like. . . .

Much as discovery had thus become central to American litigation, it is equally clear that very broad opposition to the liberality of discovery grew in the early 1970's. Many complained that the rule amendments of the 1960's created procedural tools that eclipsed, or even subverted, the substantive law. . . . Such pervasive concern about discovery abuse is striking from twenty years' remove, and was sufficient to fuel two rounds of rule changes designed to contain discovery.

II. THE FIRST ROUND OF DISCOVERY CONTAINMENT . . .

[This section explains that the ABA formed the ABA Special Committee in order to study and recommend solutions to the various discovery concerns. After reviewing the Federal Rules of Civil Procedure for almost a year (from August 1976 to April 1977), the committee announced its three major recommendations: (1) narrowing the scope of discovery material to those issues relevant to the issues raised by the claims or defenses of the parties in the dispute; (2) providing that the court should hold a discovery conference if requested by any party in a dispute; and (3) limiting interrogatories to thirty.]

A. THE 1980 AMENDMENTS—FLIRTING WITH CHANGING THE SCOPE OF DISCOVERY

[After much debate over the ABA Special Committee's recommendations, the Advisory Committee to the 1980 Amendments decided not to follow the ABA committee's recommendations. It refused both narrowing the scope of discovery and adopting a national limit on the number of interrogatories. The Advisory Committee did, however, propose a new Rule 26(f) incorporating the ABA Special Committee's recommendation on the discovery conference. It also recommended an addition to Rule 37 that would authorize a court to impose sanctions against parties who fail to obey a court order under Rule 26(f).]

. . . In its comments [to the 1980 Amendments to Rule 26, the Advisory Committee] explained that it "believes that abuse of discovery, while very serious in certain cases, is not so general as to require such basic changes." [Advisory Committee Notes to 1980 Amendments to Fed. R. Civ. P. 26.] In February 1979, the ABA Special Committee issued a long memorandum supporting its original proposals and denouncing the revised amendments as too cautious. The amendments nevertheless went forward in 1980. Justice Powell (a former President of the ABA), joined by Justices Stewart and Rehnquist, dissented on the ground that the amendments did not go far enough, and that "acceptance of these tinkering changes will delay for years the adoption of genuinely effective reforms" [Amendments to the Federal Rules of Civil Procedure, 85 F.R.D. 521, 523 (1980) (Powell, J., dissenting)].

B. THE 1983 AMENDMENTS — THE SHIFT TO CASE MANAGEMENT AND PROPORTIONALITY

Justice Powell need not have worried, for even before he issued his dissent the seeds of more aggressive changes were being sown. . . .

In 1981, the [Advisory Committee] circulated a set of proposed amendments building on [a] background that contained a number of features not bearing directly on discovery. Most notable of these were a substantial expansion of Rule 11 and comprehensive revision of Rule 16 to make scheduling orders and further case management much more prevalent. It also proposed three changes to Rule 26: (1) deleting the final sentence of Rule 26(a), which had said "[u]nless the court orders otherwise under subdivision (c) of this rule, the frequency and use of these methods is not limited"; (2) adding a paragraph to Rule 26(b) directing the court to limit disproportionate discovery, and (3) adding Rule 26(g) requiring the signing of discovery requests as certification of their bona fides and permitting sanctions for violation. The Advisory Committee Notes explained that the changes contemplated "greater judicial involvement in the discovery process," and that the sanctions provision paralleled the contemporaneous amendment to Rule 11. The ABA Special Committee generally favored these amendments but proposed clarifications. . . . At the completion of the commentary period, the Advisory Committee fortified Rule 26(g) by changing the authorization for sanctions from "may" to "shall" and the amendments went into effect in 1983. The ABA Special Committee, believing its work to be finished, disbanded after five years of activity. . . .

III. THE SECOND ROUND OF DISCOVERY CONTAINMENT — THE 1993 AMENDMENTS

If the first round was characterized by a possible failure of resolve by the Advisory Committee in 1979 regarding scope of discovery, the second round might be characterized as involving too much resolve by the Committee. . . . In 1991, the Advisory Committee brought out an array of proposed amendments: (1) requiring initial disclosure of the identity of any witness or document with information "that bears significantly on any claim or defense"; (2) precluding formal discovery until after this initial disclosure; (3) directing exclusion of any evidence not disclosed as required; (4) requiring preparation of a report detailing the testimony and background of any expert trial witness; (5) expanding the duty to supplement discovery responses and applying this expanding duty to disclosures as well; (6) placing presumptive numerical limits on both interrogatories and depositions; (7) limiting depositions to six hours; (8) authorizing videotaping of depositions without advance court approval; and (9) requiring that parties who withhold material on grounds of privilege supply details about the withheld materials sufficient to permit evaluation of the claim of privilege. . . . [Other minor amendments were proposed but not mentioned in this list.]

The acrimonious general reception of some of these proposals is well known and not worth mentioning here. But it is worth pausing to reflect a moment on what the initial disclosure proposal seemed to be on its face. To begin with, the limit on initial disclosure to material that "bears significantly on any claim or defense" sounds like an effort to narrow the scope of this obligation compared to the general scope of discovery. Thus, it does not involve the much-reviled "subject matter" terminology of Rule 26(b)(1), and might have been taken as a step toward narrowing the scope of discovery to claims and defenses. Requiring that the material "bear significantly" on claims and defenses seems to narrow the obligation further and to avoid incursion into peripheral matters. Certainly the direction is consistent with the claimed limitation of disclosure to "core information."

Additionally, the amendments seemed designed to give teeth to the proportionality provisions added in 1983. Thus, a court asked to permit a party to exceed the numerical or time limitations prescribed should determine whether that would be "consistent with the principles stated in Rule 26(b)(2)."

Given the "flood of objections unprecedented in fifty plus years of rule making," the Advisory Committee reconsidered the disclosure requirement. First it decided to withdraw the proposal altogether, much as it had done with narrowing the scope of discovery in 1979. But a number of districts had adopted disclosure provisions modeled after the draft amendments pursuant to the Civil Justice Reform Act, and we are told that there seemed some need to "put the sidewalks where the people are walking." On reconsideration, the Advisory Committee adopted a revised approach to disclosure. It permitted any district to opt out, and permitted the parties to stipulate not to disclose. Additionally, although disclosure would apply to the full scope of discovery, it would only apply as to disputed facts alleged with particularity, thereby reducing the burden resulting from vague complaints. In addition, there should be a conference between counsel early in the case to develop a discovery plan before the Rule 16 conference with the court. The Committee also deleted the six-hour limitation on depositions, but it added further limitations on conduct during them, forbidding instructions that a witness refuse to answer unless based on a privilege or limitation on discovery imposed by the judge in the case.

With a less ambitious disclosure plank, the amendments were cautiously adopted by the Supreme Court. The disclosure provision almost did not go into effect. The ABA opposed it, the Clinton Administration opposed it, the House of Representatives passed a bill deleting it from the package of amendments, and the bill failed to pass the Senate only because of a last-minute concern about other aspects of the package. Virtually nobody believes that disclosure would have survived an actual vote.

■ ELIZABETH G. THORNBURG, GIVING THE "HAVES" A LITTLE MORE: CONSIDERING THE 1998 DISCOVERY PROPOSALS
52 SMU L. Rev. 229, 246-249 (1999)

A. WHO WANTS TO LIMIT DISCOVERY?

As Professor Marcus has recently reminded us, "in a world in which proposals do emanate from interest groups and some players are focused on their private advantage, it would be foolish to disregard motivation as a hint about both the desirability and likely impact of proposals for change." While this is not the only question to ask, it is important to consider which groups have been lobbying (literally) for limits on the extent of civil discovery.

It is no secret that the anti-discovery pressure has come from defendants, especially defendants in product liability, securities, and antitrust cases. The most recent push for limits resembles the proposals of then-Vice-President Quayle and the President's Council on Competitiveness. In a 1991 speech to the American Bar Association, Vice-President Quayle announced the Council's recommendations for changing the civil litigation system, with a focus on discovery. The Council's Report, called Agenda for Civil Justice Reform in America, attacked discovery, conflating tort liability and procedural issues, claiming that the decline of the American economy was caused by the tort and products liability system, which was caused by litigation transaction costs, which were caused by the failing of the procedural rules. The Agenda "proposed revamping tort litigation and procedural rules in order to provide advantages to business and the insurance industry. The Agenda expressed little concern with whether or not potential claims might be meritorious; rather, it embodied a blatant attempt to modify the rules in order to frustrate plaintiffs' litigation."

Meanwhile, back in Congress, a crisis-slanted opinion poll conducted by Louis Harris became the basis for the Brookings-Biden Report.

> Underwritten by business and insurance concerns, neither the Harris survey nor the Brookings-Biden report considered alternative views of the purposes of the federal justice system; instead, both concentrated on portraying procedural rules as mere adjuncts to the concerns of American

businessmen and insurance companies seeking to secure the position of the United States within the global economy.[92]

The business community then appeared to testify in support of the Civil Justice Reform Act (CJRA). When the CJRA was passed by Congress, pilot district advisory groups were directed to study discovery abuse and were provided with copies of the Council's *Agenda.*

The Advisory Committee's current interest in discovery is a reflection of the continued complaints from corporate constituents. Judge Paul V. Niemeyer, of the Fourth Circuit Court of Appeals, chaired his first meeting of the Advisory Committee in October of 1996. Judge Niemeyer made review of discovery the highest priority for the Committee. He acted in response to "longstanding concerns" about discovery abuse. Judge Niemeyer also "spoke eloquently about the depth of dissatisfaction with discovery" and repeated the claim that discovery "accounts for 80 percent of litigation costs." Reflecting on his own experience as an attorney, Niemeyer reported that he "knew all the tricks" and that "we used to shuffle the documents."

At a conference at Boston College Law School in the fall of 1997, the Committee had the chance to consider reports from various groups on the issue of discovery reform. The plaintiff-based Association of Trial Lawyers of America reported that discovery abuse is "rare" and recommended against changes in the rules and Trial Lawyers for Public Justice asserted that "there is no serious, scholarly empirical work to justify system-wide restrictions upon discovery." The American College of Trial Lawyers, on the other hand, proposed narrowing the scope of discovery in the way that the Committee had recommended. This proposal was backed by the Defense Research Institute, which also called for replacing automatic disclosure with an exchange of information such as a narrative of the incident that led to the suit, legal claims and defenses, and associated documents.

The kinds of amendments proposed by the Advisory Committee, then, are those sought by groups that tend to appear in court as defendants and by their lawyers. It is, however, possible that "a given proposal could, regardless of its origin and its supporters, actually be justified on more neutral grounds . . . .".

B. Empirical Data and the Need for Change

. . . Outcry about the cost and abuses of discovery is intimately connected with outcry about the "litigation explosion." The notion that we

---

92. Linda S. Mullenix, *Discovery in Disarray: The Pervasive Myth of Pervasive Discovery Abuse and the Consequences for Unfounded Rulemaking,* 46 Stan. L. Rev. 1393, 1416-1417 (1994).

are experiencing a crisis in civil caseload was popularized by Walter K. Olson's 1991 [*The Litigation Explosion*], politicized by the President's Council on Competitiveness and fed by the media and by lawyers themselves. Careful empirical analysis, particularly that of professor Marc Gallanter, has demonstrated that no such crisis exists.[107] This scholarly rebuttal, however, does not seem to have made a dent in public perception. The same seems to be true of concerns about problems with discovery. Public outcry and media coverage continue to send the message that discovery is a gigantic and pervasive problem. This . . . Article examines what empirical research in fact indicates about discovery and the need, if any, for rule changes.

The most recent study by the Federal Judicial Center succinctly summarizes the findings of empirical researchers: "[T]he typical case has relatively little discovery, conducted at costs that are proportionate to the stakes of the litigation, and . . . discovery generally—but with notable exceptions—yields information that aids in the just disposition of cases."[108] This conclusion is supported by numerous studies going back thirty years. The Columbia Project for Effective Justice, working in the 1960s, deliberately chose cases to maximize the likelihood of finding discovery activity. Even within this group, only two-thirds of attorneys reported using formal discovery. The researchers further concluded that "the costs of discovery were not oppressive, either in relation to ability to pay or to the stakes of litigaiton."[110] Ten years later, the Federal Judicial Center (FJC) completed a significant study of discovery practices. This project studied 3,000 federal civil cases from six metropolitan districts.[111] The FJC found that in 52% of the cases, there was *no discovery at all*. In 72% of the cases, there were no more than *two* discovery events. At about the same time, the Civil Litigation Research Project (CLRP) at the University of Wisconsin studied "ordinary litigation": cases in which more than $1,000 is in controversy but excluding "mega" cases. The CLRP found that "relatively little discovery occurs in the ordinary lawsuit. We found no evidence of discovery in over half our cases. Rarely did the records reveal more than five separate discovery events."[113]

107. *See generally* Marc S. Galanter, *Real World Torts: An Antidote to Anecdote*, 55 Md. L. Rev. 1093 (1996); Marc S. Galanter, *News from Nowhere: The Debased Debate on Civil Justice*, 71 Denv. U. L. Rev. 77 (1993); Marc S. Galanter, *The Day After the Litigation Explosion*, 46 Md. L. Rev. 3 (1986); Marc S. Galanter, *Reading the Landscape of Disputes: What We Know and Don't Know (and Think We Know) About Our Allegedly Contentious and Litigious Society*, 31 UCLA L. Rev. 2 (1983).

108. Thomas E. Willging et al., *An Empirical Study of Discovery and Disclosure Practice Under the 1993 Federal Rule Amendments*, 39 B.C. L. Rev. 525, 527 (1998).

110. Judith A. McKenna & Elizabeth C. Wiggins, *Empirical Research on Civil Discovery*, 39 B.C. L. Rev. 785, 787 (citing Columbia Project for Effective Justice).

111. *See generally* Paul R. Connolly et al., *Federal Judicial Center, Judicial Controls and the Civil Litigative Process: Discovery* (1978).

113. David M. Trubek et al., *The Costs of Ordinary Litigation*, 31 UCLA L. Rev. 72, 90 (1983).

These studies were consistent but dated. The Advisory Committee therefore wisely looked to the RAND Institute for Civil Justice[114] and the Federal Judicial Center[115] for information about the current discovery environment. The findings of both groups were consistent with the older studies. The RAND study was based on 5,222 cases filed in 1992-1993 in twenty federal districts. RAND excluded from its sample cases that usually involve little or no discovery or management.[117] In cases that closed before issue was joined (28% of the sample), there was no discovery at all. In cases that closed after issue was joined but in 270 days or less (27% of the sample), the median lawyer work hours on discovery per litigant was a whopping three hours. Even in cases that closed more than 270 days after filing (45% of the sample), lawyers worked a median of twenty hours on discovery per litigant. Fifty-five percent of the RAND sample, then, involved little or no discovery. For 38% of general civil cases, lawyer work hours for discovery were zero.

The FJC studied 1000 cases closed in the last quarter of 1996 and strove to sample cases likely to involve discovery. The FJC focused on costs as reported by the attorneys in the cases studied. They found that the median cost of discovery was about $6,500 per client (about half of median litigation costs). Relative to stakes, the FJC found that discovery expenses were quite low. The median percentage was 3% of the stakes.

Despite consistent findings of low discovery cost and a functioning system, however, the studies are also consistent in finding a small percentage of cases in which there is a larger volume of discovery activity and discovery disputes. The 1978 FJC study concluded that a few cases—less than five percent—had more than ten discovery requests. The two modern studies also discovered a large amount of discovery concentrated in a small number of cases. For example, in the RAND study, the median number of discovery hours in the top 10% of cases was 300—fifteen times the median for discovery of the active cases. In the FJC study, while the median percentage of discovery expenses to stakes was quite low (3%), about 5% of attorneys estimated discovery expenses at 32% or more of the amount at stake. As the Director of the American Bar Foundation reminds us, "[a] rather small number of cases thus generated a very large amount of discovery."[125]

At least at a level of generality, the research has also identified characteristics that tend to be associated with this small percentage of problematic cases. These include amount at stake, case complexity, case contentiousness, subject matter of the lawsuit, size of law firm, number of

114. *See* James S. Kakalik et al., *Discovery Management: Further Analysis of the Civil Justice Reform Act Evaluation Data*, 39 B.C. L. Rev. 613, 615 (1998).

115. See Willging, *supra* note 108 (reporting the FJC findings).

117. They excluded prisoner cases, administrative review of social security cases, bankruptcy appeals, foreclosures, forfeiture and penalty cases, and debt recovery....

125. Bryant G. Garth, *Two Worlds of Civil Discovery: From Studies of Cost and Delay to the Markets in Legal Services and Legal Reform*, 39 B.C. L. Rev. 597, 600 (1998).

parties, and number of claims, with the amount at stake having the strongest correlation with discovery problems. The consistency of these findings led the RAND researchers to recommend special attention to the small number of problem cases. . . .

These findings suggest that policymakers should consider focusing discovery rule changes and discovery management on the types of cases likely to have high discovery costs, and the discovery practices that are likely to generate those high costs. More attention and research is clearly needed on how to identify those high discovery cost cases early in their life, and how best to manage discovery on those cases.

Similarly, the FJC researchers were led by their data to theorize that "there may be problem cases rather than isolated problems with each separate form of discovery."

What we do *not* know is why these particular cases generate a large volume of discovery and discovery disputes. What exactly are the problems? And are the problems caused by the rules or by forces outside the rules? What are the incentives for lawyers, clients, and judges that cause problems to arise and to have persisted over time? Can these situations be addressed by rule changes? . . .

Comments and Questions

1. Despite the criticisms you have read about wide-open discovery, it is important to remember that discovery seems to work as intended in most cases and that discovery has become important in ferreting out illegal behavior through private litigation. The alternative would probably be substantially expanded government regulation and government prosecution. Would this be an improvement? In summarizing what he distilled from a conference of experts on discovery rules, the current Chair of the Civil Rules Advisory Committee started with these three conclusions:

> 1. The desire for information in connection with the resolution of civil disputes was nearly universal. No one at the Conference seemed to advocate the elimination of requiring full disclosure of relevant information.
> 2. Discovery is now working effectively and efficiently in a majority of the cases, which represent "routine" cases.
> 3. In cases where discovery was actively used, it was thought to be unnecessarily expensive and burdensome. . . .

Paul V. Niemeyer, *Here We Go Again: Are the Federal Discovery Rules Really in Need of Amendment?* 39 B.C. L. Rev. 517 (1998). Are these observations encouraging? Why or why not?

2. The proposed 1998 amendments propose significant changes to Fed. R. Civ. P. 26(a)(1), 26(b)(1), 30(d)(2), and 34(b). Due to the relatively

long amendment process, the earliest possible effective date for these proposed modifications would be December 1, 2000. The four most significant changes in the proposed 1998 amendments are

(a) Instead of mandating disclosure of any material "relevant to the subject matter involved in the pending action" the changes to Fed. R. Civ. P. 26(a)(1) would require disclosure of any material "tending to support the position of the disclosing party." In addition to severely limiting the scope of mandatory discovery, the Advisory Committee also proposed to eliminate the opt-out provision by local rule and thus require this scaled-back version in every jurisdiction. (However, the amendment would not, as currently drafted, eliminate the parties' ability to stipulate out of their mandatory initial disclosure requirements.)

(b) Fed. R. Civ. P. 26(b)(1) would be modified and "which is relevant to the subject matter involved in the pending action" would be stricken from the definition of the scope of discovery. With this change, the scope of discovery would be limited to the claims or defenses of the parties. The Advisory Committee proposed this modification in order to control discovery in cases particularly vulnerable to extremely broad discovery requests, such as products liability suits.

(c) Specific language would be added to Fed. R. Civ. P. 34(b) empowering courts to require a requesting party to pay the reasonable cost of any discovery request that is duplicative, unduly burdensome or unduly expensive. This amendment would validate a current practice in many jurisdictions and establish it in the others.

(d) Depositions would be presumptively limited to one seven-hour day under an amendment to Fed. R. Civ. P. 30. If a party wishes to depose a witness for longer than seven hours, the party must obtain authorization from the court or both parties, and the deponent must stipulate to an increase in the deposition limit.

3. The 1998 proposed amendments are a product of the Civil Rules Advisory Committee. When Paul Niemeyer convened that committee in the mid-1990s, he focused the committee's attention on the discovery rules by posing three questions:

(a) When fully used, is the discovery process too expensive for what it contributes to the dispute resolution process?

(b) Are there rule changes that can be made which might reduce the cost and delay of discovery without undermining a policy of full disclosure?

(c) Should the federal rules for discovery, applying to cases involving national substantive law and procedure, as well as to cases involving state law, be made uniform throughout the United States?

How do the 1998 proposed amendments suggest that the Advisory Committee members answered those questions? What are your answers to these questions? What three questions would you pose to frame a discussion on discovery reform?

4. If discovery is not a systemic problem for the ordinary lawyer with the ordinary case, as the empirical data suggests, why isn't the existing large group of ordinary lawyers trying this large majority of ordinary cases? Why, in light of the empirical data suggesting a relative normalcy of discovery, do so many attorneys nevertheless want significant changes made to the discovery process?

5. Some scholars have argued that discovery reforms are targeted almost exclusively at over-discovery—that is, parties trying to extract from their opponents more than that to which they are entitled (and more than a cost/benefit analysis could justify). Indeed, few proposals are instead targeted at abusive resistance to discovery. What are possible explanations for this difference? Consider also that empirical research commissioned by the Advisory Committee and done by the Federal Judicial Center suggests that the most common problems in document production are failure to respond adequately and failure to respond in a timely fashion. *See* Thomas E. Willging et al., *An Empirical Study of Discovery and Disclosure Practice Under the 1993 Federal Rule Amendments*, 39 B.C. L. Rev. 525, 540 (1998).

Practice Exercise No. 16: Procedural Rulemaking

You are a participant in an open forum assembled to address the following resolution:

RESOLVED: That the Supreme Court is well-suited for the rulemaking role that Congress has assigned to it under 28 USC §§2072 and 2074.

The materials for the conference make clear that a primary focus of debate will be the discovery rules, and particularly (1) the proliferation of amendments to the discovery rules, generally, over the course of the past two decades; and (2) the 1993 Amendments, which were enacted without substantial consideration or debate by the Congress. Broader issues flagged in the conference materials suggest that the following may also be addressed: (1) non-trans-substantive procedure, (2) efficiency in the judicial system, (3) separation of powers, and (4) allocation of competence.

Prepare to be called upon to share your thoughts with regard to the Supreme Court's role in the above matters. Naturally, you should prepare to defend any reforms suggested in your remarks.

As part of this Practice Exercise, read a portion of the Supreme Court's transmittal letter to Congress of the 1993 amendments (as well as Justice White's opinion), which follows.

Supreme Court of the United States
Washington, D.C. 20543

Chambers of
THE CHIEF JUSTICE

April 22, 1993
Dear Mr. Speaker [of the House of Representatives]:

By direction of the Supreme Court of the United States, I have the honor to submit to the Congress amendments to the Federal Rules of Civil Procedure that have been adopted by the Supreme Court pursuant to Section 2072 of Title 28, United States Code. While the Court is satisfied that the required procedures have been observed, this transmittal does not necessarily indicate that the Court itself would have proposed these amendments in the form submitted.

Justice White has issued a separate statement. Justice Scalia has issued a dissenting statement, which Justice Thomas joins and Justice Souter joins in part. . . .

Sincerely,
/s/
William H. Rehnquist

[The order transmitting the amendments has been omitted.]

SUPREME COURT OF THE UNITED STATES
AMENDMENTS TO THE FEDERAL RULES OF CIVIL PROCEDURE
[April 22, 1993]

WHITE, Justice:

28 U.S.C. §2072 empowers the Supreme Court to prescribe general rules of practice and procedure and rules of evidence for cases in the federal courts, including proceedings before magistrates and courts of appeals. But the Court does not itself draft and initially propose these rules. Section 2073 directs the Judicial Conference to prescribe the procedures for proposing the rules mentioned in §2072. The Conference is authorized to appoint committees to propose such rules. These rules advisory committees are to be made up of members of the professional bar and trial and appellate judges. The Conference is also to appoint a standing committee on rules of practice and evidence to review the recommendations of the advisory committees and to recommend to the Conference such rules and amendments to those rules "as may be necessary to maintain consistency and otherwise promote the interest of justice."

§2073(b). Any rules approved by the Conference are transmitted to the Supreme Court, which in turn transmits any rules "prescribed" pursuant to §2072 to the Congress. Except as provided in §2074(b), such rules become effective at a specified time unless Congress otherwise provides.

The members of the advisory and standing committees are carefully named by The Chief Justice, and I am quite sure that these experienced judges and lawyers take their work very seriously. It is also quite evident that neither the standing committee nor the Judicial Conference merely rubber stamps the proposals recommended to it. It is not at all rare that advisory committee proposals are returned to the originating committee for further study.

During my 31 years on the Court, the number of advisory committees has grown as necessitated by statutory changes. During that time, by my count at least, on some 64 occasions we have "prescribed" and transmitted to Congress a new set of rules or amendments to certain rules. Some of the transmissions have been minor, but many of them have been extensive. Over this time, Justices Black and Douglas, either together or separately, dissented 13 times on the ground that it was inappropriate for the Court to pass on the merits of the rules before it. Aside from those two Justices, Justices Powell, Stewart and then-Justice Rehnquist dissented on one occasion and Justice O'Connor on another as to the substance of proposed rules. . . . Only once in my memory did the Court refuse to transmit some of the rule changes proposed by the Judicial Conference. . . .

That the Justices have hardly ever refused to transmit the rules submitted by the Judicial Conference and the fact that, aside from Justices Black and Douglas, it has been quite rare for any Justice to dissent from transmitting any such rule, suggest that a sizable majority of the 21 Justices who sat during this period concluded that Congress intended them to have a rather limited role in the rulemaking process. The vast majority (including myself) obviously have not explicitly subscribed to the Black-Douglas view that many of the rules proposed dealt with substantive matters that the Constitution reserved to Congress and that in any event were prohibited by §2072's injunction against abridging, enlarging or modifying substantive rights.

Some of us, however, have silently shared Justice Black's and Justice Douglas' suggestion that the enabling statutes be amended to place the responsibility upon the Judicial Conference rather than upon this Court. Since the statute was first enacted in 1934, 48 Stat. 1064, the Judicial Conference has been enlarged and improved and is now very active in its surveillance of the work of the federal courts and in recommending appropriate legislation to Congress. The present rules produced under 28 U.S.C. §2072 are not prepared by us but by Committees of the Judicial Conference designated by The Chief Justice, and before coming to us they are approved by the Judicial Conference pursuant to 28 U.S.C. §331. The Committees and the Conference are composed of able and distinguished members and they render a high public service. It is they, however, who do the work, not we, and the rules have only our imprimatur. The only contribution that we actually make is an occasional exercise of a veto power. If the rule-making for Federal District Courts is to continue under the present plan, we believe that the Supreme Court should not have any part in the task; rather, the statute should be amended to substitute the Judicial Conference. The Judicial Conference can participate more actively in fashioning the rules and affirmatively contribute to their content and design better than we can. Transfer of the function to the Judicial Conference would relieve us of the embarrassment of having to sit in judgment on the constitutionality of rules which we have approved and which as applied in given situations might have to be declared invalid. 374 U.S. 865, 869-80 (1963) [footnote omitted].

Despite the repeated protestations of both or one of those Justices, Congress did not eliminate our participation in the rulemaking process. Indeed, our statutory role was continued as the coverage of §2072 was extended to the rules of evidence and to proceedings before magistrates. Congress clearly continued to direct us to "prescribe" specified rules. But most of us concluded that for at least two reasons Congress could not have intended us to provide another layer of review equivalent to that of the standing committee and the Judicial Conference. First, to perform such a function would take an inordinate amount of time, the expenditure of which would be inconsistent with the demands of a growing caseload. Second, some of us, and I remain of this view, were quite sure that the Judicial Conference and its committees, "being in large part judges of the lower courts and attorneys who are using the Rules day in and day out, are in a far better position to make a practical judgment upon their utility or inutility than we." 383 U.S. 1089, 1090 (1966) (Douglas, J., dissenting).

I did my share of litigating when in practice and once served on the Advisory Committee for the Civil Rules, but the trial practice is a dynamic profession, and the longer one is away from it the less likely it is that he or she should presume to second-guess the careful work of the active professionals manning the rulemaking committees, work that the Judicial Conference has approved. At the very least, we should not perform a *de novo* review and should defer to the Judicial Conference and its committees as long as they have some rational basis for their proposed amendments.

Hence, as I have seen the Court's role over the years, it is to transmit the Judicial Conference's recommendations without change and without careful study, as long as there is no suggestion that the committee system has not operated with integrity. If it has not, such a fact, or even such a claim, about a body so open to public inspection would inevitably surface. This has been my practice, even though on several occasions, based perhaps on out-of-date conceptions, I had serious questions about the wisdom of particular proposals to amend certain rules.

In connection with the proposed rule changes now before us, there is no suggestion that the rulemaking process has failed to function properly. No doubt the proposed changes do not please everyone, as letters I have received indicate. But I assume that such opposing views have been before the committees and have been rejected on the merits. That is enough for me.

Justice Douglas thought that the Court should be taken out of the rulemaking process entirely, but as long as Congress insisted on our "prescribing" rules, he refused to be a mere conduit and would dissent to forwarding rule changes with which he disagreed. I note that Justice Scalia seems to follow that example. But I also note that as time went on, Justice Douglas confessed to insufficient familiarity with the context in which new rules would operate to pass judgment on their merits.

In conclusion, I suggest that it would be a mistake for the bench, the bar, or the Congress to assume that we are duplicating the function performed by the standing committee or the Judicial Conference with respect to changes in the various rules which come to us for transmittal. As I have said, over the years our role has been a much more limited one.

5

■

The Right to Jury Trial and Judicial Control of Results

This chapter will explore the debate over the civil jury, as well as the doctrine of the right to jury trial and the many methods for controlling the jury or preventing cases from reaching a trial, such as summary judgment, judgment as a matter of law (directed verdict and judgment n.o.v.), jury instructions, motions for new trial, and remittitur and additur. The chapter ends with sections on closing arguments and appeals.

A. VALUES AND HISTORICAL BACKGROUND

1. Introduction

Why would a course in civil procedure have a whole chapter on "The Right to Jury Trial and Judicial Control of Results"? "Less than 6% of all civil cases filed are resolved at trial, and less than one-third of those are tried by a jury."* Despite the relative paucity of actual civil jury trials, or of

---

*Paula L. Hannaford, B. Michael Dann, and G. Thomas Munsterman, *How Judges View Civil Juries*, 48 DePaul L. Rev. 247, 253 (1998) (citing Carol J. DeFrances et al., *Civil Jury Cases and Verdicts in Large Counties*, *Bureau of Just. Stat. Special Rep.* (U.S. Dept. of Just., Washington, D.C.), July 1995, at 2.

civil trials of any kind, the right to jury trial is claimed in a substantial percentage of cases, and the filing, preparation, and settlement of lawsuits is often done "in the shadow" of educated guesses about what a jury would ultimately decide if a jury trial did take place. Moreover, it is difficult to understand much of current civil procedure, and of the development of American law generally (particularly in the field of evidence), without taking account of the historical ambivalence in our country about juries. As you will see as this chapter unfolds, there is a good deal of procedural doctrine defining and protecting the right to civil jury trial, accompanied by many different procedures to control juries and their verdicts, developed as a result of judicial distrust of lay people's ability to act without prejudice.

Major tensions in American civil procedure emerge in debates about the civil jury and in the doctrine that has developed both to protect and to control the jury: formalism and definition versus narrative and less constraint; experts versus lay people. Heated disputes in our society on issues of race and gender come to the fore in doctrinal battles about the selection and composition of juries. Political views influence whether one reads the right to jury trial more or less broadly and whether one would restrict or liberate the jury in the evidence they hear, the manner in which they are instructed, and the deference given to their decisions.

This chapter begins with two orientation sections, the first providing excerpts from the ongoing debate about the American civil jury, and the second outlining a brief history of the development of the jury. You will then read about the constitutional right to trial by jury in civil cases and the quite complicated case law that has attempted to define that right. The Seventh Amendment to the United States Constitution states:

> In Suits at common law, where the value in controversy shall exceed twenty dollars, the right of trial by jury shall be preserved, and no fact tried by a jury shall be otherwise re-examined in any Court of the United States, than according to the rules of the common law.

The language "shall be preserved" has caused the Supreme Court to consider the extent to which one had the right to a civil jury as of 1791, when the Bill of Rights became part of the Constitution. Consequently, history is important not only to understand the context of another element of civil procedure, the jury, but also because courts turn to history in attempting to define the right.

Part C of this chapter covers the doctrine and practice that has developed around jury selection. You will see once again how a procedural issue becomes a lightning rod for ongoing cultural arguments about race and gender. The remainder of the chapter covers many different ways that have developed to influence, control, and overturn jury verdicts. Issues that you have previously heard about, such as summary judgment and directed verdict (now called judgment as a matter of law), will now be covered in more detail. And you will learn that some of this doctrine, such as ending a case early because there is insufficient evidence to permit the plaintiff to win, also governs cases in which the judge—not the jury—is the trier of fact, with permutations to take account of that difference.

As you read the following passages favoring or opposing the American civil jury, along with the remainder of the chapter, which explores jury composition and jury control, try to formulate and defend your own opinions about the continued utility (or lack thereof) of the civil jury. What are the most compelling arguments, pro and con?

2. The Debate Over the American Civil Jury

What do modern juries do in the United States? In civil cases, they are instructed to impartially weigh the evidence, to decide what actually happened in the dispute ("the facts"), and to apply the law (as given by the judge) to those facts. The strategic importance of the jury in modern legal practice, then, is unquestioned, both in those cases actually decided by a jury and those settled in their "shadow." But the jury as an institution has been a target of sustained criticism for centuries. At the present time, about 80 percent of the jury trials in the world are conducted in the United States, a fact not lost on opponents of the jury concept: "Some opponents of the civil jury cite its abolition in other legal systems as evidence that civil juries are outmoded. Indeed, the use of civil juries has declined significantly in Canada and Australia and has effectively disappeared in England, their country of origin."*

Those who oppose the use of the civil jury usually make efficiency arguments, emphasize the amateurish nature of lay jurors, and aver that jurors are influenced by prejudice and passion. Supporters, increasingly relying on empirical data, dispute such assumptions about inefficiency and incompetence. Moreover, they argue that the civil jury plays critical roles in a democracy—legitimizing the process, curbing arbitrary judicial behavior, inculcating community values, and permitting citizen participation and education, in addition to providing neutral, fair, and accurate dispute-resolution. Consider the following voices from the debate, past and present, and draw your own conclusions:

> The jury system puts a ban upon intelligence and honesty, and a premium upon ignorance, stupidity, and perjury. It is a shame that we must continue to use a worthless system because it was good a thousand years ago.

---

* *The Civil Jury (Developments in the Law)*, 110 Harv. L. Rev. 1408, 1411 (1997) (citations omitted).

Mark Twain, *Roughing It* 309 (1872).

Even in the best of cases trial by jury is the apotheosis of amateurs. How can anyone think that 12 people selected at random in twelve different ways with the only criterion being a complete lack of general qualification, would have special ability to decide on disputes between people?

Erwin N. Griswold, Harvard Law School, Dean's Report 5-6 (1962-1963).

[W]e live in a different age now and our society has grown increasingly complex, as has our legal system. In earlier times, a jury might have been called upon to sit for a day or two to consider a simple dispute between neighbors. Today, however, a jury often finds itself sitting for many months, attempting to assimilate mountains of evidence in controversies pitting large corporations against each other in complicated cases involving antitrust, securities, tax, patent, and similar business related issues. . . .

A lengthy trial . . . may make it impossible to impanel a jury of impartial minds of diverse backgrounds. It is unrealistic to suppose that employed persons, who compose the group most likely to have any familiarity with business matters of the type frequently at issue in lengthy litigation, would be available for jury service in lengthy trials. Judge Charles L. Brieant of the Southern District of New York aptly put it: "[M]ust litigants be left with a panel consisting solely of retired people, the idle rich, those on welfare, and housewives whose children are grown? Hardly a 'fair cross section of the community wherein the court convenes.'" . . .

Studies of this subject suggest that factual issues presented in a case can be considered complex, either when the facts needing resolution are conceptually difficult for a non-specialist to understand, or when the facts are made difficult by the volume of evidentiary material needed to establish them. It also has been suggested that legal issues can be considered complex when they are multiple, overlapping, ambiguous, or pose issues requiring instructions on close questions of statutory interpretation. Even with instructions carefully crafted with an eye toward clarity and simplicity, it is practically impossible in some specialized fields of law to guide a jury through the awesome job of rationally applying complex instructions to a huge volume of technical evidence.

Edward J. Devitt, *Should Jury Trial Be Required in Civil Cases? A Challenge to the Seventh Amendment,* 47 J. Air L. & Comm. 495, 497, 498, 500 (1982).

■ JEROME T. FRANK, COURTS ON TRIAL
110-111, 129-130 (1949)

. . . There are three theories of the jury's function:

(1) The naive theory is that the jury merely finds the facts; that it must not, and does not, concern itself with the legal rules, but faithfully accepts the rules as stated to them by the trial judge.

(2) A more sophisticated theory has it that the jury not only finds that facts but, in its deliberation in the jury-room, uses legal reasoning to apply to those facts the legal rules it learned from the judge. . . .

On the basis of this sophisticated theory, the jury system has been criticized. It is said that juries often do not find the facts in accordance with the evidence, but distort—or "fudge"—the facts, and find them in such a manner that (by applying the legal rules laid down by the judge to the facts thus deliberately misfound) the jury is able to produce the result which it desires, in favor of one party or the other. "The facts," we are told, "are found in order to reach the result."

This theory ascribes to jurors a serpentine wisdom. It assumes that they thoroughly understand what the judge tells them about the rules, and that they circumvent the rules by falsely contriving—with consummate skill and cunning—the exact findings of fact which, correlated with those rules, will logically compel the result they desire.

(3) We come now to a third theory which may be called the "realistic" theory. It is based on what anyone can discover by questioning the average person who has served as a juror—namely that often the jury are neither able to, nor do they attempt to, apply the instructions of the court. The jury are more brutally direct. They determine that they want Jones to collect $5,000 from the railroad company, or that they don't want pretty Nellie Brown to go to jail for killing her husband; and they bring in their general verdict accordingly. Often, to all practical intents and purposes, the judge's statement of the legal rules might just as well never have been expressed. "Nor can we," writes Clemenston, "cut away the mantle of mystery in which the general verdict is enveloped, to see how the principle facts were determined, and whether the law was applied under the judge's instructions. . . . It is a matter of common knowledge that the general verdict may be the result of anything but the calm deliberation, exchange of impressions and opinions, resolution of doubts, and final intelligent concurrence which, theoretically, produced it. It comes into court unexplained and impenetrable."

The "realistic" theory, then, is that, in many cases, the jury, often without heeding the legal rules, determine, not the "facts," but the respective legal rights and duties of the parties to the suit. For the judgment of the court usually follows the general verdict of the jury, so that the verdict results in a decision which determines those rights and duties. . . .

The [pro-jury] argument that juries make better rules than judges do has at least the virtue of honestly admitting the realities—of conceding that jurors often disregard what the trial judge tells the jurors about the [rules]. But as a rational defense of the jury system, it is surely curious. It asserts that, desirably, each jury is a twelve-man ephemeral legislature, not elected by the voters, but empowered to destroy what the elected legislators have enacted or authorized. Each jury is thus a legislative assembly, legislating independently of all others. For even if a jury does no more than nullify a legal rule by refusing to apply it in a particular lawsuit, yet it is legislating, since the power to destroy legal rules is legislative power. This argument for the jury should lead to a revised description of our legislative system to show that it consists, in the case of our federal government for instance, of (1) a Senate, (2) a House of Representatives, and (3) a multitude of juries.

I have one objection to such a description: I think it too sophisticated. It implies that the members of the ordinary jury say to themselves, "We don't like this legal rule of which the judge told us, and we won't apply it but will apply one of our own making." But when, as often happens, juries do not understand what the judge said to them about the applicable rule, it simply is not true that they refuse to follow it because they dislike it. Many juries in reaching their verdicts act on their emotional responses to the lawyers and the witnesses; they like or dislike, not any legal rule, but they do like an artful lawyer for the plaintiff, the poor widow, the brunette with the soulful eyes, and they do dislike the big corporation, the Italian with the thick, foreign accent. We do not have uniform jury nullification of harsh rules; we have juries avoiding—often in ignorance that they are so doing—excellent as well as bad rules, and in capricious fashion.

■ HARRY KALVEN, THE DIGNITY OF THE CIVIL JURY
50 U. Va. L. Rev. 1055, 1059-1067 (1964)

How much longer is a jury trial than a bench trial? Estimates by experienced judges and lawyers have varied widely; and it is surprisingly difficult to arrive at a satisfactory answer since we cannot try *the same case* by each method with a stopwatch in hand. Further, since there is good reason to believe that cases tried to a jury are in many respects different and more complex than cases in which a jury is waived, we cannot arrive at an answer simply by comparing a sample of jury trials and a sample of bench trials. . . . By using a series of estimates, we reached the conclusion that on the average a bench trial would be 40 percent less time consuming than a jury trial of the same case. . . .

As we come to the merits of the institution, it may be useful to sketch three main heads under which criticism and defense of the jury have fallen.

First, there is a series of collateral advantages and disadvantages such as the fact that the jury provides an important civic experience for the citizen; that, because of popular participation the jury makes tolerable the stringency of certain decisions; or that because of its transient personnel the jury acts as a lightning rod for animosity and suspicion which might otherwise center on the more exposed judge; or that the jury is a guarantor of integrity since it is said to be more difficult to reach twelve men than one. On the negative side it is urged that jury fees are an added expense to the administration of justice; that jury service often imposes an unfair economic and social burden on those forced to serve; and that exposure to jury service disenchants the citizen and leads him to lose confidence in the administration of justice.

Although many of these considerations loom large in the tradition of jury debate, they are unamenable to research and will not concern us here. We have, however, collected considerable data bearing on the reaction of jurors to services. It will suffice for present purposes simply to state that there is much evidence that most people, once actually serving in a trial, become highly serious and responsible toward their task and toward the joint effort to deliberate to a verdict. . . . The heart of the matter, the trial itself and deliberation, is very often a major and moving experience in the life of the citizen-juror.

The second cluster of issues goes to the competence of the jury. Can it follow and remember the presentation of the facts and weigh the conflicting evidence? Can it follow and remember the law? Can it deliberate effectively?

The third cluster of issues goes to the adherence of the jury to the law, to what its admirers call its sense of equity and what its detractors view as its taste for anarchy.

The latter two issues go to the heart of the debate and have long been the occasion for a heated exchange of proverbs. Further, they may seem so heavily enmeshed in difficult value judgments as to make further discussion unpromising. Yet it is precisely here that our empirical studies can offer some insight, although they too cannot fully dispose of the issues.

When one asserts that jury adjudication is of low quality, he must be asserting that jury decisions vary in some significant degree from those a judge would have made in the same cases. If he denies this and wishes to include the judge, he has lost any baseline, and with it any force, for his criticism. While it is possible to say that even those juries whose decision patterns coincide with those of judges are nevertheless given to caprice, lack of understanding, and sheer anarchic disobedience to law, it is not likely that the critic means to go this far. If he does, he may have an interesting point to make about the legal order as a whole, but he has lost any distinctive point about the jury as a mode of trial. Further, trial by judge is the relevant and obvious alternative to trial by jury. To argue against jury trial is, therefore, to argue for bench trial.

[The University of Chicago Jury Project found that, in a study of several thousand personal injury cases, judges and juries agreed on liability in 79 percent of cases. "The judge disagrees with the jury because he is more pro-plaintiff about as often as the jury disagrees with him because it is more pro-plaintiff." In awarding damages, there is more disagreement. Of the 44 percent of cases where both judge and jury agreed, the jury gave the higher award in 23 percent, the judge gave a higher award in 17 percent, and the awards were approximately equal in 4 percent of cases. Jury awards averaged about 20 percent higher than those of the judge.]

There are . . . some further observations about the issue of jury competence. We have been told often enough that the jury trial is a process whereby twelve inexperienced laymen, who are probably strangers to each other, are invited to apply law which they will not understand to facts which they will not get straight and by secret deliberation arrive at a group decision. We are told also that heroic feats of learning law, remembering facts, and running an orderly discussion as a group are called for in every jury trial. . . .

In the judge-jury survey the trial judge, among other things, classified each case as to whether it was "difficult to understand" or "easy." We can therefore spell out the following hypothesis to test against the judge jury data. If the jury has a propensity not to understand, that propensity should be more evident in the cases rated by the judges as difficult than in those rated as easy. Further, disagreement should be higher in cases which the jury does not understand than in cases which they do understand since, where the jury misunderstands the case, it must be deciding on a different basis than the judge. We reach, then, the decisive hypothesis to test, namely, that the jury should disagree more often with the judges in difficult cases than in easy ones. However, when we compare the decision patterns in easy cases with those in difficult cases we find that the level of disagreement remains the same. . . .

Any mystery as to why the plausible *a priori* surmises of jury incompetence should prove so wrong is considerably reduced when we take a closer look at the dynamics of the jury process, a look we have been able to take as a result of intensive and extensive post-trial juror interviews in actual cases and as a result of complete observation of jury deliberations in mock experimental cases, a technique used widely in the project. We observed that the trial had structured the communication to the jury far more than the usual comment recognizes and had made certain points quite salient. A more important point is that the jury can operate by *collective* recall. Different jurors remember, and make available to all, different items of the trial so that the jury as a group remembers far more than most of its members could as individuals. It tends, in this connection, to be as strong as its strongest link. The conclusion, therefore, is that the jury understands well enough for its purposes and that its intellectual incompetence has been vastly exaggerated. . . .

■ VALERIE P. HANS AND NEIL VIDMAR, JUDGING THE JURY
247-249 (1986)

In judging the jury there are some other issues to consider. The first concerns the alternatives to the jury. In France, West Germany, and some other European countries, mixed tribunals composed of a judge and prominent laypersons decide legal cases. In Britain, minor crimes are tried in a magistrate's courts by tribunals of laypersons. However, in most instances those who advocate abolition of the jury propose that the jury's work should be done by a judge. The question then becomes, are judges really superior to juries? Unfortunately, we have little data about the competency of judges, though . . . we know that the jury would agree with their decisions in four cases out of five. To be sure, judges have training in law, and perhaps, as Judge Frank claimed, they attempt to be more scientific in their approach to the evidence. On the other hand, many knowledgeable legal commentators have argued that judges are not necessarily better triers of fact. A jury which contains one or more persons proficient in automobile repair might be far better at assessing evidence in a products liability case involving a car manufacturer than a judge whose experience with things mechanical is limited to changing a spare tire. Even if one argues that the average judge is smarter in discerning legal facts than the average juror, is the judge as smart as twelve jurors?

We must also consider the fact that trials are about justice as well as law. The inescapable fact is that despite attempts in recent years to recruit minority group members and women into the judiciary, the overwhelming majority of judges are still white males who come from a privileged sector of our society. Often their views of the world reflect their backgrounds. Some rather rigidly adhere to a narrow perspective of justice and fairness that is not consistent with that of the general community. . . .

There are two other aspects to the political side of the jury. One is its "legitimating" function. In a democracy the average citizen obeys the law not so much because of its threat but because he or she grants it legitimacy, that is, accepts it as a body of rules to be followed. It may be true that democracies can survive without juries. Many Western democracies do not have juries and seem to function quite well. Yet, in the United States, Canada and Great Britain, the jury is an important symbol that helps to confer legitimacy to law.

The remaining political aspect of the jury concerns its socializing function. Not only does the jury system allow the people to contribute to the legal system, but the legal system, through the jury, contributes to the education of the people.

■ ALEXIS DE TOCQUEVILLE, DEMOCRACY IN AMERICA
Pt II, Ch. B (1835)

. . . The jury is pre-eminently a political institution; it must be regarded as one form of the sovereignty of the people; when that sovereignty is repudiated, it must be rejected; or it must be adapted to the laws by which that sovereignty is established. The jury is that portion of the nation to which the execution of the laws is intrusted, as the houses of parliament constitute that part of the nation which makes the laws. . . .

The institution of the jury, if confined to criminal causes, is always in danger; but when once it is introduced into civil proceedings, it defies the aggressions of time and man. . . . The jury, and more especially the civil jury, serves to communicate the spirit of the judges to the minds of all the citizens; and this spirit, with the habits which attend it, is the soundest preparation for free institutions. It imbues all classes with a respect for the thing judged and with the notion of right. If these two elements be removed, the love of independence becomes a mere destructive passion. It teaches men to practice equity; every man learns to judge his neighbor as he would himself be judged. And this is especially true of the jury in civil causes; for while the number of persons who have reason to apprehend a criminal prosecution is small, everyone is liable to have a lawsuit. . . . It invests each citizen with a kind of magistracy; it makes them all feel the duties which they are bound to discharge towards society and the part which they take in its government. By obliging men to turn their attention to other affairs than their own, it rubs off that private selfishness which is the rust of society. . . .

The jury contributes most powerfully to form the judgment, and to increase the natural intelligence of a people; and this is, in my opinion, its greatest advantage. It may be regarded as a gratuitous public school ever open, in which every juror learns to exercise his rights . . . and becomes practically acquainted with the laws of this country, which are brought within the reach of his capacity by the efforts of the bar, the advice of the judge, and even by the passions of the parties. I think that the practical intelligence and political good sense of the Americans are mainly attributable to the long use which they have made of the jury in civil causes.

Comments and Questions

1. There is widespread agreement that jury verdicts help lawyers and their clients assess the value of cases for settlement purposes. Moreover, jury verdicts influence behavior, particularly when the parties are informed professionals or employed in a business in which profit is influenced by financial losses, real or potential. Indeed, one purpose of the tort liability system is to deter unreasonable behavior, and the jury often determines what is reasonable. There are, though, fewer jury trials than one might expect. In 1990, for example, there were 4,765 civil jury trials in the U.S. district courts (a little over 25 percent of all trials in those courts). "[R]esearchers for the National Center for State courts estimate that the total number of state jury trials annually is in the vicinity of 150,000." Jeffrey Abramson, We, the Jury 251 (1994).

Still, many Americans participate each year in the jury process: "In the federal district courts, over 400,000 persons were present for voir dire in jury trials during 1990. From this number, the total selected for actual jury service was 115,877. The sum of individual days served by all federal trial jurors was 825,020." (citations omitted). *Id.* at 252.

Those who serve on juries usually find it a positive and important experience:

> [F]or many of the millions of Americans who have exercised the power and experienced the responsibility, jury service turns out to be an unforgettable, even transforming experience. Although a majority of people try to avoid service, nearly three quarters of those who do serve come away with a more favorable view of the system than they had before. They eagerly tell war stories from the jury room: many decide to write about what they saw and accomplished. Nearly every juror interviewed for this book is proud of the job he or she did, proud of the seriousness of deliberations, proud of having exercised power soberly, proud—rightly or wrongly—of the verdicts that were reached. More than when they vote, or pay taxes, or attend a parade, they are realizing the democratic vision that still sustains our nation: They are governing themselves.
>
> There's disorder in the court but not despair. The jury system can be saved and is, for all our disappointments, well worth saving.

Stephen J. Adler, *Trial and Error in the American Courtroom* 242 (1994).

2. You have read about the famous Kalven and Zeisel University of Chicago Jury project, conducted in the 1950s, which found that judges and juries agreed on liability approximately 80 percent of the time in personal injury cases. More recent studies continue to find that by any measure, juries appear to act competently most of the time. The accusations that they are pro-plaintiff, that they irrationally inflate damages, or that they tend to give huge punitive damages are not borne out by data, although, of course, on occasion juries act in ways that appear aberrant. In 1986, Valerie P. Hans and Neil Vidmar published *Judging the Jury*, which analyzes empirical data about juries. Here are some of their conclusions:

> Based on the various studies examining different aspects of the jury, we can conclude that the jury has not been shown, as a general matter, to be incompetent. . . . No doubt some juries are. Yet, the data from studies of hundreds of jury trials and jury simulations suggest that actual incompetence is a rare phenomenon. Juries do differ sometimes from the way judges would have decided, but it is on grounds other than incompetence.
>
>   . . . Sometimes the jury is at war with the law, but for the most part it is, in Kalven and Zeisel's phrase, a "modest war." There are very few instances in which the jury rejects the law outright. Rather it sometimes bends

the law to comport with its own sense of what is just, fair, and equitable. Some will argue that this is still wrong; the law should always be followed. Others will say that the jury is doing exactly what it was intended that it should do. Regardless, the hard facts indicate that on the whole the jury behaves responsibly and rationally.

Id. at 120 and 163. And a recent study by the National Center for State Courts and the Bureau of Justice Standards reached these conclusions about state court civil jury litigation:

> Overall, plaintiffs are successful in 49% of tort jury trials. . . . The distribution of successful plaintiffs in medical malpractice cases . . . is concentrated around the national average of 30 percent. The median jury award is $52,000, a relatively modest sum in light of the estimated legal costs of taking a case through to a jury verdict. . . . Punitive damages are included in 6 percent of all general civil cases with a monetary award. . . . For all cases with a punitive award, the median is $50,000, but the mean is 17 times larger ($859,000). . . . During 1992 state court juries in the 75 most populous counties awarded an estimated $327,300,000 in punitive damages. Overall, tort cases account for just over a third of all dollars awarded as punitive damages, while contract-related cases account for 63 percent. Employment cases with punitive damages, most of which are employment discrimination cases, account for 40 percent of all the money awarded in punitive damages. . . . None of the punitive damages awards in medical malpractice or product liability cases (excluding toxic substance cases) were more than twice the compensatory damages (citations omitted). . . .

Brian J. Ostrom, David B. Rottman, and John A. Goerdt, *A Step Above Anecdote: A Profile of the Civil Jury in the 1990s,* 79 Judicature 233, 235-240 (March-April, 1996).

A 1998 symposium focused on "The American Civil Jury: Illusion and Reality." The papers, many of which were empirical studies, are printed in 48 DePaul L. Rev. No. 2 (Winter, 1998). Most of the articles stress data similar to that described above and conclude that attacks on the American jury—allegations of exorbitant and irrational verdicts and jury-prejudice, particularly against business or corporations—are largely mythology, unsupported by the data. *In Public Opinion about the Civil Jury: Can Reality Be Found in the Illusions?,* Michael J. Saks attacks the myths of "too many frivolous suits"; of "[j]urors are biased in favor of plaintiffs, out of sympathy toward victims of injury"; and of excessive jury awards of both compensatory and punitive damages. 48 DePaul L. Rev. 221, 229-231 (1998). Other papers argued that trial judges throughout the country are generally very positive about the role of juries in our civil justice system (Paula L. Hannaford, B. Michael Dann and G. Thomas Munsterman, *How Judges View Civil Juries,* 48 DePaul L. Rev. 247 (1998)) and that "the simplistic illusion of the antibusiness jury fails to accord with a much more complex reality."

Valerie P. Hans, *The Illusions and Realities of Jurors' Treatment of Corporate Defendants,* 48 DePaul L. Rev. 327 (1998). That both judges and jurors hold corporations more responsible than individuals conducting similar activity seems to come not from an antibusiness bias or a desire to redistribute wealth from deep to shallow pockets, but from the rational perception that corporations should be held to a higher standard because of their greater knowledge of potential harms and their greater ability to reduce risks. *Id.* And in responding to the Saks article, Professor Alschuler argues that the public's allegedly negative perceptions of juries may not in fact be antijury. Albert W. Alschuler, *Explaining the Public Wariness of Juries,* 48 DePaul L. Rev. 407 (1998).

3. Which pro-jury arguments do you find the strongest? Which antijury arguments are most persuasive? What other arguments can you imagine for and against the use of juries in particular cases?

4. Three current debates about the jury are especially worth noting:

a. *Size.* "In a series of decisions in the 1970s [*Williams v. Florida,* 399 U.S. 78 (1970); *Colgrove v. Battin,* 413 U.S. 149 (1973); *Ballew v. Georgia,* 435 U.S. 223 (1978)], the U.S. Supreme Court set aside 600 years of settled common law tradition and two centuries of constitutional history, including the reversal of its own precedents to the contrary, in holding that both criminal and civil juries smaller than 12 do not violate constitutional requirements. Many states and federal districts took advantage of the permission that the Court, in effect, granted them to reduce the size of their juries. . . . [T]he majority of justices concluded that the size of the jury made no difference, at least down to sizes as small as six." (Footnotes omitted.) Michael J. Saks, *The Smaller the Jury, the Greater the Unpredictability,* 79 Judicature 263 (March-April, 1996). There is now a great deal of theory and empirical data suggesting that the Supreme Court was mistaken and that in fact the reduction of the size of the jury to six increases the unpredictability of verdicts and awards, reduces the likelihood of representation on the jury by minority groups, makes it more difficult for a dissenting member of the jury to argue her position (because of the reduced chance of having an ally), and reduces the collective memory and experience of the group. *Id.* In 1996, the Judicial Conference's Standing Committee on Rules of Practice and Procedure voted overwhelmingly to submit a proposal to amend Fed. R. Civ. P. 48 to restore twelve-member jurors, but the recommendation was not adopted by the Judicial Conference. *See The Civil Jury (Developments in the Law),* 110 Harv. L. Rev. 1408, 1487 (1997).

b. *Unanimity.* "The Seventh Amendment was held to require a unanimous verdict in *American Pub. Co. v. Fisher,* 1897, 166 U.S. 468. More recently the Court has held that the Fourteenth Amendment does not require a unanimous verdict in a state criminal case. *Apodaca v. Oregon,* 1972, 406 U.S. 404, but that the Sixth Amendment requires a unanimous verdict in a federal prosecution. 406 U.S. at 366 (Powell, J., concurring.)

There are no recent opinions on the requirement of unanimity in civil cases, but if the issue should arise, it seems very likely that the Court would hold that unanimity is not required." Charles A. Wright, *Law of Federal Courts* 671-672 n.5 (5th ed. 1994). Fed. R. Civ. P. 48 requires a unanimous verdict "[u]nless the parties otherwise stipulate." Some jury simulation studies suggest that moving to non-unanimity in jury verdicts may have some unfortunate consequences. For example, when unanimity is required, deliberations may last longer, but evaluation of the evidence and the law may be more thorough, jurors in the minority may participate more actively in the discussion and be more listened to, and jurors may be more satisfied with the final verdict. Valerie P. Hans and Neil Vidmar, *Judging the Jury* 175 (1986). In *Apodaca,* Justice Douglas vigorously dissented, suggesting that ". . . human experience teaches that polite and academic conversation is no substitute for the earnest and robust argument necessary to reach unanimity."

    c. *Complexity.* Some argue that in complex civil cases that are apt to last a long time, the Constitution does not require a jury trial. In an enigmatic footnote in *Ross v. Bernard,* 396 U.S. 531, 538 n.10 (1970), the Supreme Court mentioned a new factor, in addition to custom and remedy sought, as relevant to whether a party is entitled to a jury trial under the Seventh Amendment: "the practical abilities and limitations of juries." Some have also argued that there exist English precedents before 1791 for an exception to the Seventh Amendment for complex cases. Others have made a similar argument, relying on the Due Process Clause of the Fifth Amendment. However, "[t]he Ninth Circuit has rejected all of these arguments and held that there is no complexity exception. The Third Circuit rejected the historical argument and the argument from the *Ross* footnote, but accepted, in guarded form, a complexity exception based on the due process argument. Finally, the Fifth Circuit has expressed no opinion on whether there can be a complexity exception, but has held that if such an exception exists, it cannot reach a case where the trial court finds only that 'it would be most difficult, if not impossible, for a jury to reach a rational decision (citations omitted).'" Charles A. Wright, *Law of Federal Courts* 659-660 (5th ed. 1994). You may recall from the famous Kalven Chicago jury study that juries do not disagree with judges more in difficult cases than they do in easier ones.

    5. The modern jury debate has revolved less around abolishing the jury altogether than around possible modifications of the jury system. Consider the following proposed modifications in light of the values discussed above, as well as the "notice and the right to be heard" values discussed earlier in the book:

    (i) allowing jurors to take notes during all or parts of the trial; *yes*

    (ii) allowing jurors to ask questions of the witnesses; *- NO*

    (iii) rewriting jury instructions in simpler language (jury instructions ordinarily are given only orally, can be several hours long, and are often complex); Yes
    (iv) giving legal instructions to the jury before the evidence is heard; Yes
    (v) permitting jurors to have written copies of the instructions; Yes
    (vi) increasing juror fees; NO
    (vii) reducing juror "down time" by scheduling attorney-judge conferences when jurors are not present. Ø

Many of these modifications are already present in some jurisdictions. What impact would these modifications have on the jury?

3. The Historical Background of the Modern American Civil Jury

    While some historians trace the modern American civil jury back to the ancient civilizations of Greece and Rome or to the Scandinavians who settled England before A.D. 1000, most modern scholars begin the story of the jury at the time of the Norman Conquest of England in 1066. Those early juries were committees assembled by William the Conqueror to determine who owned the various tracts of land in a given area. Later, trial by jury became an alternative to the other forms of trial available, which involved various forms of battle or ordeal, or compurgation, and in which each side would bring forth friends to swear to the truth of his position. Jurors were selected from the local community where the dispute arose and were required to have some familiarity with the facts of the case. In a sense, then, the earliest juries were groups of witnesses, who discussed the case among themselves and arrived at a verdict. The judge's role in such a case was to tell the jurors the law that applied to the dispute. *See* Lloyd E. Moore, *The Jury: Tool of Kings, Palladium of Liberty*, 2d ed. (1985).

    In the centuries that followed, the distinction between juror and witness became more pronounced. In one intermediary phase, jurors who had personal knowledge of the case were required to testify in open court as witnesses and then to return to the jury box. Gradually, courts recognized the need for jurors who based their verdict not on personal knowledge, but only on the evidence presented in court. Elaborate procedures developed to ensure that only disinterested persons sat on juries. *See* John Marshall Mitnick, *From Neighbor-Witness to Judge of Proofs: The Transformation of the English Civil Juror*, 32 Am. J. Legal Hist. 201 (1988).

    When the first English colonists brought trial by jury to America, it was still in flux. As late as 1670, in *Bushell*'s case, an English judge declared that jurors had the right to use their personal knowledge to decide the verdict. In colonial America, jurors often heard three different versions of the law from three different judges. In such cases, the jury could decide both fact and law, a situation that prevailed in some colonies, such as Massachusetts, until the Revolution. *See* William E. Nelson, *Americanization of the Common Law* (1975).

During the colonial period, juries were perceived to be guardians of local community values against outsider judges appointed by the royal governor. They were also seen as bulwarks of integrity against corrupt public officials, and, finally, as revolution drew near, as wellsprings of patriotism in the fight against imperialist injustices. British attempts to constrain the use of jury trial were among the foremost complaints of the founders of the movement for American independence and were mentioned in the Declaration of Independence.

When the British presence was eradicated and American judges were placed at the head of the various courts, some leaders of the new nation sought to restrain the influence of juries, who, they believed, were thwarting creditors from collecting on their debts and jeopardizing the economic stability of the new nation. At the Constitutional Convention, which was dominated by pro-creditor Federalists, no provision for civil jury trial was adopted in the original document. Indeed, in Federalist No. 83, Alexander Hamilton argued that the right to civil jury trial was not fundamental to liberty and that, given the diversity of practice throughout the states, it would be impossible to draft a provision that would satisfy all factions.

The omission of a right to jury trial in civil cases, as well as a provision that would have allowed the Supreme Court to reconsider factual issues decided by a jury, were among the chief rallying cries of the pro-debtor Anti-Federalists, whose impassioned pleas in state legislatures' ratification debates called for a guarantee of civil jury trial in all common law cases. In the end, the Anti-Federalists won the debate. The Seventh Amendment to the Constitution, adopted in 1791, provides that "In suits at common law, where the amount in controversy exceeds twenty dollars, the right to trial by jury shall be preserved. . . ." For a complete discussion of the Federalist/Anti-Federalist debate over the Seventh Amendment, *see* Charles W. Wolfram, *The Constitutional History of the Seventh Amendment*, 57 Minn. L. Rev. 639 (1973).

B. THE RIGHT TO JURY TRIAL IN CIVIL CASES IN FEDERAL COURT

Read the language of the Seventh Amendment. In its earliest review of the Seventh Amendment, the Supreme Court, under Justice Story, declared that the "common law" referred to in the Constitution should be determined by looking at the common law of England. *United States v.*

Wonson, 28 F. Cas. 745. Later courts refined the analysis, focusing on the historical implications of the word "preserved" to require looking at the common law of England in 1791—when the Seventh Amendment was adopted.

Two complications arose, one almost immediately and the other after the merger of law and equity in federal practice. First, what about civil causes of action created by statute after 1791? Were these actions automatically exempted from the Seventh Amendment because they were not part of the "common law"? Second, after the merger of law and equity, what are the rights of parties who raise both equitable and legal (or common law) claims? Justice Story began to answer these questions in the 1830 Supreme Court case *Parsons v. Bedford,* 28 U.S. 433, 447:

> By *common law,* [the framers of the Seventh Amendment] meant . . . not merely suits, which the *common* law recognized among its old and settled proceedings, but suits in which *legal* rights were to be ascertained and determined, in contradistinction to those where equitable rights alone were recognized, and equitable remedies were administered. . . .

In recent history, beginning with *Beacon Theaters v. Westover,* 359 U.S. 500 (1959), and continuing until the present day, the Supreme Court has continued to wrestle with the answers to these questions.

■ CHAUFFEURS, TEAMSTERS AND HELPERS, LOCAL NO. 391 v. TERRY
494 U.S. 558 (1990)

Justice MARSHALL delivered the opinion of the Court, except as to Part III-A:

This case presents the question whether an employee who seeks relief in the form of back pay for a union's alleged breach of its duty of fair representation has a right to trial by jury. We hold that the Seventh Amendment entitles such a plaintiff to a jury trial.

I

McLean Trucking Company and the Chauffeurs, Teamsters and Helpers Local Union No. 391 were parties to a collective-bargaining agreement that governed the terms and conditions of employment at McLean's terminals. The 27 respondents were employed by McLean as truckdrivers in bargaining units covered by the agreement, and all were members of the Union. In 1982 McLean implemented a change in operations that resulted in the elimination of some of its terminals and the reorganization of others. As part of that change, McLean transferred respondents to the terminal located in Winston-Salem and agreed to give them special seniority rights in relation to "inactive" employees in Winston-Salem who had been laid off temporarily.

After working in Winston-Salem for approximately six weeks, respondents were alternately laid off and recalled several times. Respondents filed a grievance with the Union, contesting the order of the layoffs and recalls. Respondents also challenged McLean's policy of stripping any driver who was laid off of his special seniority rights. Respondents claimed that McLean breached the collective-bargaining agreement by giving inactive drivers preference over respondents. After these proceedings, the grievance committee ordered McLean to recall any respondent who was then laid off and to lay off any inactive driver who had been recalled; in addition, the committee ordered McLean to recognize respondents' special seniority rights until the inactive employees were properly recalled.

On the basis of this decision, McLean recalled respondents and laid off the drivers who had been on the inactive list when respondents transferred to Winston-Salem. Soon after this, though, McLean recalled the inactive employees, thereby allowing them to regain seniority rights over respondents. In the next round of layoffs, then, respondents had lower priority than inactive drivers and were laid off first. Accordingly, respondents filed another grievance, alleging that McLean's actions were designed to circumvent the initial decision of the grievance committee. The Union representative appeared before the grievance committee and presented the contentions of respondents and those of the inactive truckdrivers. At the conclusion of the hearing, the committee held that McLean had not violated the committee's first decision.

McLean continued to engage in periodic layoffs and recalls of the workers at the Winston-Salem terminal. Respondents filed a third grievance with the Union, but the Union declined to refer the charges to a grievance committee on the ground that the relevant issues had been determined in the prior proceedings.

In July 1983, respondents filed an action in District Court, alleging that McLean had breached the collective-bargaining agreement in violation of §301 of the Labor Management Relations Act, 1947, 61 Stat. 156, 29 U.S.C. §185 (1982 ed.) and that the Union had violated its duty of fair representation. [Section 301(a) of the Labor Management Relations Act, 1947, provides for suits by and against labor unions: "Suits for violation of contracts between an employer and a labor organization representing employees in an industry affecting commerce as defined in this chapter, or between any such labor organizations, may be brought in any district court of the United States having jurisdiction of the parties, without respect to the amount in controversy or without regard to the citizenship of the parties." 61 Stat. 156, 29 U.S.C. §185(a) (1982).] Respondents requested a permanent injunction requiring the defendants to cease their illegal acts and to reinstate them to their proper seniority status; in addition, they sought, inter alia, compensatory damages for lost wages and health benefits. In 1986 McLean filed for bankruptcy; subsequently, the action against it was voluntarily dismissed, along with all claims for injunctive relief.

Respondents had requested a jury trial in their pleadings. The Union moved to strike the jury demand on the ground that no right to a jury trial exists in a duty of fair representation suit. The District Court denied the motion to strike. After an interlocutory appeal, the Fourth Circuit affirmed the trial court, holding that the Seventh Amendment entitled respondents to a jury trial of their claim for monetary relief. We granted the petition for certiorari to resolve a circuit conflict on this issue, and now affirm the judgment of the Fourth Circuit.

II

. . . [Employees] must prove the same two facts to recover money damages: that the employer's action violated the terms of the collective-bargaining agreement and that the union breached its duty of fair representation.

III

We turn now to the constitutional issue presented in this case — whether respondents are entitled to a jury trial. The Seventh Amendment provides that "[i]n Suits at common law, where the value in controversy shall exceed twenty dollars, the right of trial by jury shall be preserved." The right to a jury trial includes more than the common-law forms of action recognized in 1791; the phrase "Suits at common law" refers to "suits in which legal rights [are] to be ascertained and determined, in contradistinction to those where equitable rights alone [are] recognized, and equitable remedies [are] administered." *Parsons v. Bedford*, 3 Pet. 433, 447, 7 L. Ed. 732 (1830) ("[T]he amendment then may well be construed to embrace all suits which are not of equity and admiralty jurisdiction, whatever may be the peculiar form which they may assume to settle legal rights"). The right extends to causes of action created by Congress. Since the merger of the systems of law and equity, *see* Fed. R. Civ. P. 2, this Court has carefully preserved the right to trial by jury where legal rights are at stake. As the Court noted in *Beacon Theatres, Inc. v. Westover*, "Maintenance of the jury as a fact-finding body is of such importance and occupies so firm a place in our history and jurisprudence that any seeming curtailment of the right to a jury trial should be scrutinized with the utmost care." 359 U.S. 500, 501 (1959).

To determine whether a particular action will resolve legal rights, we examine both the nature of the issues involved and the remedy sought. "First, we compare the statutory action to 18th-century actions brought in the courts of England prior to the merger of the courts of law and equity. Second, we examine the remedy sought and determine whether it is legal or equitable in nature." 481 U.S., at 417-418. The second inquiry is the more important in our analysis.

A

An action for breach of a union's duty of fair representation was unknown in 18th-century England; in fact, collective-bargaining was unlawful. We must therefore look for an analogous cause of action that existed in the 18th century to determine whether the nature of this duty of fair representation suit is legal or equitable.

The Union contends that this duty of fair representation action resembles a suit brought to vacate an arbitration award because respondents seek to set aside the result of the grievance process. In the 18th century, an action to set aside an arbitration award was considered equitable. 2 Joseph Story, *Commentaries on Equity Jurisprudence* §1452, pp. 789-790 (13th ed. 1886) (equity courts had jurisdiction over claims that an award should be set aside on the ground of "mistake of the arbitrators"). . . .

The arbitration analogy is inapposite, however, to the Seventh Amendment question posed in this case. No grievance committee has considered respondents' claim that the Union violated its duty of fair representation; the grievance process was concerned only with the employer's alleged breach of the collective-bargaining agreement. Thus, respondents' claim against the Union cannot be characterized as an action to vacate an arbitration award. . . .

The Union next argues that respondents' duty of fair representation action is comparable to an action by a trust beneficiary against a trustee for breach of fiduciary duty. Such actions were within the exclusive jurisdiction of courts of equity. This analogy is far more persuasive than the arbitration analogy. Just as a trustee must act in the best interests of the beneficiaries, a union, as the exclusive representative of the workers, must exercise its power to act on behalf of the employees in good faith, *Vaca v. Sipes*, [386 U.S., 171, 177 (1967)]. Moreover, just as a beneficiary does not directly control the actions of a trustee, an individual employee lacks direct control over a union's actions taken on his behalf. . . .

Respondents contend that their duty of fair representation suit is less like a trust action than an attorney malpractice action, which was historically an action at law. . . . [W]e find that, in the context of the Seventh Amendment inquiry, the attorney malpractice analogy does not capture the relationship between the union and the represented employees as fully as the trust analogy does.

The attorney malpractice analogy is inadequate in several respects. Although an attorney malpractice suit is in some ways similar to a suit alleging a union's breach of its fiduciary duty, the two actions are fundamentally different. The nature of an action is in large part controlled by the nature of the underlying relationship between the parties. Unlike employees represented by a union, a client controls the significant decisions concerning his representation. Moreover, a client can fire his attorney if he is dissatisfied with his attorney's performance. . . . Thus, we find the malpractice analogy less convincing than the trust analogy.

Nevertheless, the trust analogy does not persuade us to characterize respondents' claim as wholly equitable. The Union's argument mischaracterizes the nature of our comparison of the action before us to 18th-century forms of action. As we observed in *Ross v. Bernhard*, 396 U.S. 531 (1970), "The Seventh Amendment question depends on the nature of the issue to be tried rather than the character of the overall action." *Id.*, at 538 (finding a right to jury trial in a shareholder's derivative suit, a type of suit traditionally brought in courts of equity, because plaintiffs' case presented legal issues of breach of contract and negligence). As discussed above, . . . to recover from the Union here, respondents must prove both that McLean violated §301 by breaching the collective-bargaining agreement and that the Union breached its duty of fair representation. When viewed in isolation, the duty of fair representation issue is analogous to a claim against a trustee for breach of fiduciary duty. The §301 issue, however, is comparable to a breach of contract claim—a legal issue.

Respondents' action against the Union thus encompasses both equitable and legal issues. The first part of our Seventh Amendment inquiry, then, leaves us in equipoise as to whether respondents are entitled to a jury trial.

B

Our determination under the first part of the Seventh Amendment analysis is only preliminary. In this case, the only remedy sought is a request for compensatory damages representing back pay and benefits. Generally, an action for money damages was "the traditional form of relief offered in the courts of law." *Curtis v. Loether*, 415 U.S. 189, 196 (1974). This Court has not, however, held that "any award of monetary relief must necessarily be 'legal' relief." *Ibid.* (emphasis added). Nonetheless, because we conclude that the remedy respondents seek has none of the attributes that must be present before we will find an exception to the general rule and characterize damages as equitable, we find that the remedy sought by respondents is legal.

First, we have characterized damages as equitable where they are restitutionary, such as in "action[s] for disgorgement of improper profits," *Tull*, 481 U.S. at 424. The back pay sought by respondents is not money wrongfully held by the Union, but wages and benefits they would have received from McLean had the Union processed the employees' grievances properly. Such relief is not restitutionary.

Second, a monetary award "incidental to or intertwined with injunctive relief" may be equitable. *Tull*, 481 U.S. at 424. *See, e.g., Mitchell v.*

DeMario Jewelry, Inc., 361 U.S. 288, 291-292 (1960) (district court had power, incident to its injunctive powers, to award back pay under the Fair Labor Standards Act; also back pay in that case was restitutionary). Because respondents seek only money damages, this characteristic is clearly absent from the case.

The Union argues that the back pay relief sought here must nonetheless be considered equitable because this Court has labeled back pay awarded under Title VII, 42 U.S.C. §2000e et seq. (1982 ed.), as equitable. *See Albemarle Paper Co. v. Moody*, 422 U.S. 405, 415-418 (1975) (characterizing back pay awarded against employer under Title VII as equitable in context of assessing whether judge erred in refusing to award such relief). It contends that the Title VII analogy is compelling in the context of the duty of fair representation because its back pay provision was based on the NLRA provision governing back pay awards for unfair labor practices, 29 U.S.C. §160(c) (1982 ed.). ("[W]here an order directs reinstatement of an employee, back pay may be required of the employer or labor organization"). We are not convinced.

The Court has never held that a plaintiff seeking back pay under Title VII has a right to a jury trial. *See Lorillard v. Pons*, 434 U.S. 575, 581-582 (1978). Assuming, without deciding, that such a Title VII plaintiff has no right to a jury trial, the Union's argument does not persuade us that respondents are not entitled to a jury trial here. Congress specifically characterized back pay under Title VII as a form of "equitable relief." 42 U.S.C. §2000e-5(g) (1982 ed.). . . . Congress made no similar pronouncement regarding the duty of fair representation. Furthermore, the Court has noted that back pay sought from an employer under Title VII would generally be restitutionary in nature, *see Curtis v. Loether*, at 197, in contrast to the damages sought here from the Union. Thus, the remedy sought in this duty of fair representation case is clearly different from back pay sought for violations of Title VII. . . .

We hold, then, that the remedy of back pay sought in this duty of fair representation action is legal in nature. Considering both parts of the Seventh Amendment inquiry, we find that respondents are entitled to a jury trial on all issues presented in their suit.

IV

On balance, our analysis of the nature of respondents' duty of fair representation action and the remedy they seek convinces us that this action is a legal one. Although the search for an adequate 18th-century analog revealed that the claim includes both legal and equitable issues, the money damages respondents seek are the type of relief traditionally awarded by courts of law. Thus, the Seventh Amendment entitles respondents to a jury trial, and we therefore affirm the judgment of the Court of Appeals.

Justice BRENNAN, concurring in part and concurring in the judgment:

I agree with the Court that respondents seek a remedy that is legal in nature and that the Seventh Amendment entitles respondents to a jury trial on their duty of fair representation claims. I therefore join Parts I, II, III-B, and IV of the Court's opinion. I do not join that part of the opinion which reprises the particular historical analysis this Court has employed to determine whether a claim is a "Suit at common law" under the Seventh Amendment, . . . because I believe the historical test can and should be simplified. . . .

I believe that our insistence that the jury trial right hinges in part on a comparison of the substantive right at issue to forms of action used in English courts 200 years ago needlessly convolutes our Seventh Amendment jurisprudence. For the past decade and a half, this Court has explained that the two parts of the historical test are not equal in weight, that the nature of the remedy is more important than the nature of the right. Since the existence of a right to jury trial therefore turns on the nature of the remedy, absent congressional delegation to a specialized decisionmaker, there remains little purpose to our rattling through dusty attics of ancient writs. The time has come to borrow William of Occam's razor and sever this portion of our analysis. . . .

Requiring judges, with neither the training nor time necessary for reputable historical scholarship, to root through the tangle of primary and secondary sources to determine which of a hundred or so writs is analogous to the right at issue has embroiled courts in recondite controversies better left to legal historians. . . .

Furthermore, inquiries into the appropriate historical analogs for the rights at issue are not necessarily susceptible of sound resolution under the best of circumstances. . . .

In addition, modern statutory rights did not exist in the 18th-century and even the most exacting historical research may not elicit a clear historical analog. The right at issue here, for example, is a creature of modern labor law quite foreign to Georgian England. . . .

To rest the historical test required by the Seventh Amendment solely on the nature of the relief sought would not, of course, offer the federal courts a rule that is in all cases self-executing. Courts will still be required to ask which remedies were traditionally available at law and which only in equity. But this inquiry involves fewer variables and simpler choices, on the whole, and is far more manageable than the scholasticist debates in which we have been engaged. Moreover, the rule I propose would remain true to the Seventh Amendment, as it is undisputed that, historically, "[j]urisdictional lines [between law and equity] were primarily a matter of remedy." John C. McCoid, II, *Procedural Reform and the Right to Jury Trial: A Study of Beacon Theatres, Inc. v. Westover,* 116 U. Pa. L. Rev. 1 (1967). . . .

The encroachment on civil jury trial by colonial administrators was a "deeply divisive issue in the years just preceding the outbreak of hostilities between the colonies and England," and all thirteen States reinstituted the right after hostilities ensued. Charles W. Wolfram, *The Constitutional History of the Seventh Amendment*, 57 Minn. L. Rev. 639, 654-655 (1973). . . .

We can guard this right and save our courts from needless and intractable excursions into increasingly unfamiliar territory simply by retiring that prong of our Seventh Amendment test which we have already cast into a certain doubt. If we are not prepared to accord the nature of the historical analog sufficient weight for this factor to affect the outcome of our inquiry, except in the rarest of hypothetical cases, what reason do we have for insisting that federal judges proceed with this arduous inquiry? It is time we read the writing on the wall, especially as we ourselves put it there.

[The opinion of Justice STEVENS, concurring in part and concurring in the judgment, is omitted.]

Justice KENNEDY, with whom Justice O'CONNOR and Justice SCALIA join, dissenting:

. . . To determine whether rights and remedies in a duty of fair representation action are legal in character, we must compare the action to the 18th-century cases permitted in the law courts of England, and we must examine the nature of the relief sought. I agree also with those Members of the Court who find that the duty of fair representation action resembles an equitable trust action more than a suit for malpractice.

I disagree with the analytic innovation of the Court that identification of the trust action as a model for modern duty of fair representation actions is insufficient to decide the case. The Seventh Amendment requires us to determine whether the duty of fair representation action "is more similar to cases that were tried in courts of law than to suits tried in courts of equity." *Tull v. United States*, 481 U.S. 412, 417 (1987). Having made this decision in favor of an equitable action, our inquiry should end. Because the Court disagrees with this proposition, I dissent.

I

[Justice Kennedy explains that he finds the analogy to an equitable suit by a beneficiary against a trustee more persuasive, largely because a trustee is required to serve all beneficiaries with impartiality and may not ordinarily be directed to act by a beneficiary. He notes that this is unlike an action by a client against an attorney because the attorney is entrusted with representing the sole interests of the client and acts as an agent on the client's behalf. Moreover, Justice Kennedy states that the remedies available to employees in claims for breach of the duty of fair representation are equitable in nature and are therefore more like the remedies available in an action against a trustee. On the other hand, in an action by a client against an attorney, compensatory damages are often the appropriate remedy.]

II

The Court relies on two lines of precedents to overcome the conclusion that the trust action should serve as the controlling model. The first consists of cases in which the Court has considered simplifications in litigation resulting from modern procedural reforms in the federal courts. Justice Marshall asserts that these cases show that the Court must look at the character of individual issues rather than claims as a whole. The second line addresses the significance of the remedy in determining the equitable or legal nature of an action for the purpose of choosing the most appropriate analogy. Under these cases, the Court decides that the respondents have a right to a jury because they seek money damages. These authorities do not support the Court's holding.

A

In three cases we have found a right to trial by jury where there are legal claims that, for procedural reasons, a plaintiff could have or must have raised in the courts of equity before the systems merged. In *Beacon Theatres, Inc. v. Westover*, 359 U.S. 500 (1959), Fox, a potential defendant threatened with legal antitrust claims, brought an action for declaratory and injunctive relief against Beacon, the likely plaintiff. Because only the courts of equity had offered such relief prior to the merger of the two court systems, Fox had thought that it could deprive Beacon of a jury trial. Beacon, however, raised the antitrust issues as counterclaims and sought a jury. We ruled that, because Beacon would have had a right to a jury trial on its antitrust claims, Fox could not deprive it of a jury merely by taking advantage of modern declaratory procedures to sue first. The result was consistent with the spirit of the Federal Rules of Civil Procedure, which allow liberal joinder of legal and equitable actions, and the Declaratory Judgment Act, 28 U.S.C. §§2201, 2202 (1982 ed.), which preserves the right to jury trial to both parties. See 359 U.S., at 509-510.

In *Dairy Queen, Inc. v. Wood*, 369 U.S. 469 (1962), we held, in a similar manner, that a plaintiff, by asking in his complaint for an equitable accounting for trademark infringement, could not deprive the defendant of a jury trial on contract claims subsumed within the accounting. Although a court of equity would have heard the contract claims as part of the accounting suit, we found them severable under modern procedure. See *id.*, at 477-479.

In *Ross v. Bernhard*, 396 U.S. 531 (1970), a shareholder-plaintiff demanded a jury trial in a derivative action asserting a legal claim on behalf of his corporation. The defendant opposed a jury trial. In deciding the case, we recognized that only the courts of equity had procedural devices allowing shareholders to raise a corporation's claims. We nonetheless again ruled that modern procedure allowed trial of the legal claim to a jury. *See id.* at 542.

These three cases responded to the difficulties created by a merged court system. *See* John C. McCoid, II, *Procedural Reform and the Right to Jury Trial: A Study of Beacon Theatres, Inc. v. Westover,* 116 U. Pa. L. Rev. 1 (1967). They stand for the proposition that, because distinct courts of equity no longer exist, the possibility or necessity of using former equitable procedures to press a legal claim no longer will determine the right to a jury. Justice Marshall reads these cases to require a jury trial whenever a cause of action contains legal issues and would require a jury trial in this case because the respondents must prove a breach of the collective-bargaining agreement as one element of their claim.

I disagree. The respondents, as shown above, are asserting an equitable claim. Having reached this conclusion, the *Beacon, Dairy Queen,* and *Ross* cases are inapplicable. . . .

B

The Court also rules that, despite the appropriateness of the trust analogy as a whole, the respondents have a right to a jury trial because they seek money damages. The nature of the remedy remains a factor of considerable importance in determining whether a statutory action had a legal or equitable analog in 1791, but we have not adopted a rule that a statutory action permitting damages is by definition more analogous to a legal action than to any equitable suit. In each case, we look to the remedy to determine whether, taken with other factors, it places an action within the definition of "suits at common law." . . .

III

The Court must adhere to the historical test in determining the right to a jury because the language of the Constitution requires it. The Seventh Amendment "preserves" the right to jury trial in civil cases. We cannot preserve a right existing in 1791 unless we look to history to identify it. Our precedents are in full agreement with this reasoning and insist on adherence to the historical test. No alternatives short of rewriting the Constitution exist. . . .

If Congress has not provided for a jury trial, we are confined to the Seventh Amendment to determine whether one is required. Our own views respecting the wisdom of using a jury should be put aside. Like Justice Brennan, I admire the jury process. Other judges have taken the opposite view. *See, e.g.,* Jerome Frank, *Law and the Modern Mind* 170-185 (1931). But the judgment of our own times is not always preferable to the lessons of history. Our whole constitutional experience teaches that history must inform the judicial inquiry. Our obligation to the Constitution and its Bill of Rights, no less than the compact we have with the generation that wrote them for us, do not permit us to disregard provisions that some may think to be mere matters of historical form. . . .

Comments and Questions

1. Articulate the current test as interpreted by Justice Marshall writing for the majority and by Justice Kennedy in his dissent. How does Justice Brennan seek to change the test?

2. Although the Supreme Court continues to apply the historical test, it made room for consideration of functional criteria and policy in a 1996 Seventh Amendment case. In *Markman v. Westview Instruments, Inc.*, 517 U.S. 370 (1996), a unanimous Court agreed that the interpretation of a patent in a patent infringement claim is a matter of law to be decided by the court, not a jury. After finding the historical evidence equivocal, the Court took into consideration "the relative interpretative skills of judges and juries and the statutory policies that ought to be furthered" in allocating the interpretation to either judge or jury.

3. Does the historical test make sense? Does it really work? Consider these alternative views:

[T]he term "common law" in the Seventh Amendment was probably intended to refer to a process of legal development, rather than to an immutable and changeless state of the law. . . . I wish to suggest, therefore, that the Seventh Amendment . . . could justifiably be read to refer neither to the law of England nor to the law of any of the states and certainly not to an arbitrary point in time, but rather to the distinctive common-law process of adjudication and law-making that then and now, in England and in the United States, was recognized as flexible and changing. [Under such a "dynamic" reading of the Seventh Amendment, which presumes that "future development was contemplated" and that that development was "largely one of the expansion of the remedies available at 'common law'"], one possibility would be to recognize as constitutionally valid only those post-1791 changes in common law remedies and practices that would have the effect of enlarging the occasions for civil jury trial and the prerogatives of the civil jury. . . .

Charles W. Wolfram, *The Constitutional History of the Seventh Amendment*, 57 Minn. L. Rev. 639, 744-747 (1973).

The seemingly flexible rational approach [taken by the Supreme Court in its Seventh Amendment cases] does take account of changing social conditions, but only to a limited extent. For the approach asks only how the broad purposes of the constitutional provision can best be accomplished in modern society. Its analysis is thus fatally incomplete, since it does not ask the further question of whether those broad purposes are advisable or feasible in modern society. . . . The Seventh Amendment, however, . . . permits the judiciary to take into account what many consider the questionable advisability of the constitutional right . . . , while not overstepping its proper role. The amendment's use of the term "preserved" at least arguably authorizes an exact replication of the historical right, regardless of how irrational those practices may appear under modern merged procedures. Such an approach would . . .[,] when taken to its fullest extent, free any cause of action created after 1791 from the jury trial dictate.

Martin Redish, *Seventh Amendment Right to Jury Trial: A Study in the Irrationality of Decision Making*, 70 Nw. U. L. Rev. 486, 530-531 (1975).

4. In determining whether statutorily created causes of action deserve a jury trial, the Supreme Court applies the general Seventh Amendment test quite differently. First, it looks to legislative purpose: if Congress has created an administrative scheme for adjudicating disputes outside the traditional courts, or has delegated dispute resolution to a specialty court, then there is likely no right to jury trial. *See, e.g., NLRB v. Jones & Laughlin,* 57 301 U.S.1 (1937) (jury trial would subvert purpose of Congress in creating separate administrative agency for labor disputes); *Katchen v. Landy,* 382 U.S. 323 (1966) (Bankruptcy Court is special, Chancery-like court for resolving complex disputes; jury trial would subvert Congress' intent as expressed by Bankruptcy Act). Second, the Court looks to whether the statute creates a mechanism for enforcing rights that are primarily public or private. If the rights are public, then jury trial is often not necessary. If the statute creates a private rights enforcement scheme, then jury trial may be available for adjudication of those private rights. *See Granfinanciera v. Nordberg,* 492 U.S. 33 (1989) (certain rights under Bankruptcy Act are private and require jury trial right). Third, the Court looks at the remedies provided in the statute. If they are traditional "legal" remedies, then jury trial may be available. If the remedies are "equitable" in nature, then trial by jury may be denied without violating the Seventh Amendment.

Regarding discrimination suits under the Civil Rights Acts, the Court has split its decisions. In *Curtis v. Loether,* 415 U.S. 189 (1974), it held that litigants in a Title VIII housing discrimination lawsuit were entitled to trial by jury. In cases of intentional discrimination on the basis of race, the Court has provided trial by jury in suits brought under §1981, but not those under Title VII; courts have the option of severing the jury and non-jury aspects of the case. The 1991 Civil Rights Act, however, specifically provides for trial by jury in intentional discrimination cases on the basis of race, gender, and religion. The Supreme Court has not specifically ruled on the issue, but most lower courts have agreed that there is no right to jury trial for nonintentional, or "disparate impact" discrimination cases under Title VII.

5. In *Beacon Theatres, Inc. v. Westover,* 359 U.S. 500 (1959), *Dairy Queen, Inc. v. Wood,* 369 U.S. 469 (1962); and *Ross v. Bernhard,* 396 U.S. 531 (1970), the Supreme Court said unequivocally that, where equitable and legal claims are joined in the same action, the legal claims must be tried to a jury before the court resolves any equitable issues. These cases involved legal

and equitable claims originally joined in the same civil lawsuit. At least one federal circuit court has ruled that a judge may determine an issue common to equitable and legal claims prior to a jury trial when the claims were originally brought separately and have since been consolidated under Fed. R. Civ. P. 42(a). *Newfound Management Corp. v. Lewis*, 131 F.3d 108 (3d Cir. 1997). Why should consolidated claims be treated differently?

6. As you will learn in Constitutional Law, the Seventh Amendment is one of the few Bill of Rights guarantees that has not been applied to the states through the Fourteenth Amendment's Due Process Clause. Most state constitutions provide a right to trial by jury, although the form of the right varies from state to state, with some providing greater right to jury trial than the federal courts, and others providing a restricted right. How would you write a Constitutional amendment to guarantee the right to trial by jury? Would you seek to expand or constrict the right as currently provided at the federal level? What other purposes would your amendment serve?

Practice Exercise No. 17:
Legislative Exercise re Right to Jury Trial

You are a politician assigned to a legislative committee that is deciding whether to allow jury trials for Title VII disparate impact discrimination suits, such as the Cleveland Firefighters lawsuit. Using *Terry* and the other materials in this section, try to decide whether the Seventh Amendment requires (or should require) the right to trial by jury in such cases. Regardless of whether the Seventh Amendment requires it, should Congress provide for juries as a matter of right in Title VII disparate impact cases?

Practice Exercise No. 18: Law Firm Strategy Session
re Jury Trial in *City of Cleveland*

You are an associate at a staff meeting of the attorneys in the *City of Cleveland* case. The task of this meeting is limited to one question: whether or not to demand a jury trial. If your last name begins with the letters A-L, you are counsel for the plaintiffs; all others represent the defendants.

C. JURY SELECTION: TECHNIQUES
AND PURPOSES, INCLUDING
PEREMPTORY CHALLENGES

In this section, you will learn the basic premises and techniques of modern jury selection, explore the need for a fair representation of the community in the jury pool, and examine current attempts to curb discrimination in jury selection. You begin with an orientation essay, followed by the federal jury statutes and two recent Supreme Court cases, *Edmonson v. Leesville Concrete* and *J. E. B. v. Alabama.*

1. Attorney Behavior   **D** **P**

In most courts a "pool" or "panel" of potential jurors has been selected by lottery in advance. In some instances, prior to their encounter with any attorneys, the jurors are shown a film or are simply told about the duties of a juror. Prospective jurors are often given a pamphlet describing the obligations of jurors and detailing what will go on in the courtroom. In most courts, the lawyers are given a list of basic information about who is in the pool. In federal court, the lawyers are given a list that contains the pool members' names, addresses, occupations, and spouses' occupations. Normally, lawyers would not see the list of who is in the pool until right before the jury is selected.

Next, there is what is called a voir dire examination of the prospective jurors as part of the selection process. The stated purpose is to disqualify jurors who cannot be impartial and fair. For instance, a prospective juror may know one of the parties or lawyers, or have previous information about the lawsuit. But lawyers also use the process to begin establishing a rapport with the jury and advocating their view of the case through the questions that they ask.

Depending on the section of the country and the particular court, the voir dire is conducted in different ways. It used to be that the voir dire was conducted primarily by the lawyers, who asked the potential jurors a number of questions. It is probably more typical today, particularly in federal court, for the judge to do the bulk of the questioning. In some courts, the judge asks preliminary questions, and the attorneys are permitted to add a few questions of their own.

Of course, good lawyering calls for finding out in advance how the voir dire will be conducted in your particular case. In some courts, the entire panel is questioned. In others, a smaller number of potential jurors are randomly picked from the panel to be questioned. Sometimes, the whole panel gets general questions, with more particular questions reserved for the chosen portion of the pool.

Most young lawyers spend a lot of time seeking information about local practices and customs from older lawyers and clerks. One needs to know how many jurors will hear the case and how many alternates. Who asks the questions at voir dire? Who picks the jury foreperson, and where will she be seated? Must the jury return a unanimous vote? Can they ask questions or take notes? It may be important for the lawyers to read any pamphlet and view any instructional film that is given or shown to the jurors. The jurors are the audience, and it is crucial for the advocate to know the common information base.

Lawyers can challenge jurors either for cause or with peremptory challenges, for which a cause is not given. The number of challenges for cause are unlimited; sometimes statutes list the "for cause" reasons. Statutes normally also list the number of permitted peremptory challenges. Some statutes permit the judge to add to the number of peremptory challenges. You will also want to know in advance such things as whether you have a second chance to strike jurors once a full jury has been selected and whether you will have to state in open court the name of the juror you have challenged, as well as the reason for the strike.

Lawyers vary on their theories of jury selection; naturally, the court, locale, jury pool, type of case, local customs, and similar matters are relevant. For instance, in some courts the panel sits for an entire month. If it is nearer to the end of the month, some lawyers are reluctant to ever strike a potential juror, except for obvious and noncontroversial cause. The person one strikes may have become a luncheon companion of a juror—now resentful—who later sits on the jury. This concern is heightened if the lawyer has had to publicly challenge or strike a juror; but even if the process is secret, some lawyers are hesitant to have the jurors guessing about who made the challenge. Some lawyers, if permitted, like to say in open court: "No challenges; I am content." Perhaps they believe that this advertises that they have such a strong case that it does not matter which jurors are selected.

As you think about the jurors whom you would challenge or strike, to probe your own reasoning and prejudices. Some lawyers seek jurors who have certain ethnic or professional characteristics. Some very good lawyers doubt their own ability—or anyone's ability—to strike jurors rationally, and they very rarely challenge a juror. For instance, it used to be folklore that employees of insurance companies were defense-prone in civil cases; some attorneys now think that it is equally likely that an employee of large companies could be hostile to other large entities. One's sense of such matters may change from decade to decade. It has remained a constant, however, that lawyers are reluctant to use up their peremptory challenges unless they absolutely have to; they are afraid that a subsequently selected juror may be worse than the one they already "bumped."

Regardless of the philosophy that you develop for jury selection, remember that every time you appear before a judge or jury, you too are on trial. The judge and jurors who will sit in your case are watching and listening. This does not mean that you should change your personality for the voir dire or trial; often who we really are comes out during the pressure of a trial anyway. It does mean you should consider how best to present the "you" who you are during each stage of litigation.

Comments and Questions

1. What assumptions, if any, do you have about potential jurors? How would you go about testing whether they are true or false?

2. How do attorneys know when their jury selection techniques have worked? How do they know if they have failed? What other factors might influence the outcome of a case? In Great Britain, attorneys have extremely limited rights to challenge jurors and have little or no opportunity to ask them questions. Are you inclined to think that their system is better or worse? In federal court, Fed. R. Civ. P. 47(a) leaves to the judge's discretion whether to conduct examination of potential jurors herself or permit the parties or their attorneys to conduct the examination. Consider the results of at least one study, which indicates that the verdicts of juries selected according to the current procedure and those selected at random with no attorney input do not differ significantly. Hans and Vidmar, *Judging the Jury* (1986).

3. Techniques for selecting jurors have become increasingly complex in the past decade or so, with an entire cottage industry of jury consultants available to clients with adequate means to pay for their services. Consider the following account, taken from Hans and Vidmar's *Judging the Jury* and based on contemporary newspaper accounts. As you read it, think about the techniques M.C.I. used. Would justice be served by widespread use of such methods? What are the potential drawbacks, if any?

■ VALERIE P. HANS AND NEIL VIDMAR, JUDGING THE JURY
79-80 (1986)

In June of 1980, after 15 weeks of testimony, a federal jury deciding an antitrust suit awarded M.C.I. Communications Corporation $600 million, to be paid by the American Telephone and Telegraph Company. Antitrust awards are automatically tripled for punitive purposes, which meant that M.C.I. was to receive the largest antitrust judgment ever—the stunning amount of $1.8 billion. Although the attorneys for the winning side were jubilant, they were not really surprised by the decision. Before the trial, they had engaged jury researchers who used sophisticated social science techniques to determine which jurors would be most favorable to M.C.I., and to predict how jurors would react to the evidence.

A Chicago research firm conducted a telephone poll of local residents and supplemented it by personal interviews. In their interview they asked questions designed to reveal whether the respondents, if they were jurors, would be likely to side with M.C.I. or AT&T. They also obtained the demographic characteristics of these individuals. With computer analyses of these responses, the researchers developed demographic profiles of people who were favorable and unfavorable to M.C.I.'s case, knowledge that would later be of benefit in selecting jurors for the trial.

Next, the firm paid individuals of varying sympathy toward M.C.I. to meet on three successive evenings. On each evening, a mock jury composed of eight of these individuals listened to M.C.I.'s attorneys present abbreviated versions of both M.C.I.'s and AT&T's sides of the dispute in a minitrial. The researchers and attorneys then watched the mock jurors deliberate on the case through a one-way mirror. What they learned from behind the one-way mirror affected how the attorneys presented their side before the real jury.

M.C.I. was suing AT&T for damages they alleged were due to AT&T's monopolistic practices. By law, AT&T was required to share its long lines with other communication companies, and this information was presented to the simulated juries. The first evening, from behind the one-way mirror, the observers watched while the mock jurors debated heatedly about the fairness of this law. After all, some jurors argued, why should AT&T have to share its lines with competitors if it owned the lines? The attorneys learned from their experiences. The next evening, they emphasized to the mock jury that they were to decide the M.C.I.-AT&T case according to the letter of the law, regardless of their personal views about its fairness. That night, the jurors did not have much trouble accepting the law.

Another lesson from the observations may have played a role in netting M.C.I. the largest antitrust award in history. In the first evening's presentation, the attorney representing M.C.I.'s side argued that M.C.I. had suffered $100 million in lost profit from AT&T's monopolistic behavior. The first mock jury decided in M.C.I.'s favor and awarded it exactly $100 million. Noting the similarity, the attorneys wondered what would happen if they avoided mentioning a specific figure. The next night they experimented, and left it to the jury's speculation how much AT&T had cost M.C.I. With no exact dollar amounts to guide or constrain them, the second mock jury's award was $900 million.

Thus, from the community surveys and the mock juries, the M.C.I. attorneys learned what kinds of jurors to look for and to eliminate during the selection process. They also obtained tactical clues about how to present their case to different types of individuals. Morton Hunt, a journalist who has written about the M.C.I. case, likened it to "putting juries on the couch." In a sense, though, in M.C.I.'s attempt to put its jury on the couch, the M.C.I. team was doing more precisely and with scientific assistance what lawyers have tried to do for centuries: stack the jury in their favor. The M.C.I. team may have been *too* successful. The jury award was judged to be excessive and on appeal it was overturned. A second jury evaluating the damages awarded M.C.I. only $37.8 million.

■ FEDERAL JURY SELECTION STATUTES

28 U.S.C. §1861 Declaration of Policy

It is the policy of the United States that all litigants in Federal courts entitled to trial by jury shall have the right to grand and petit juries selected at random from a fair cross section of the community in the district or division wherein the court convenes. It is further the policy of the United States that all citizens shall have the opportunity to be considered for service on grand and petit juries in the district courts of the United States, and shall have an obligation to serve as jurors when summoned for that purpose.

28 U.S.C. §1862 Exemptions

No citizen shall be excluded from service as a grand or petit juror in the district courts of the United States or in the Court of International Trade on account of race, color, religion, sex, national origin, or economic status.

28 U.S.C. §1865 Qualification for Jury Service

(a) The chief judge of the district court, or such other district court judge as the plan may provide, on his initiative or upon recommendation of the clerk or jury commission, shall determine solely on the basis of information provided on the juror qualification form and other competent evidence whether a person is unqualified for, or exempt, or to be excused from jury service. The clerk shall enter such determination in the space provided on the juror qualification form and in any alphabetical list of names drawn from the master jury wheel. If a person did not appear in response to a summons, such fact shall be noted on said list.

(b) In making such determination the chief judge of the district court, or such other district court judge as the plan may provide, shall deem any person qualified to serve on grand and petit juries in the district court unless he—

(1) is not a citizen of the United States eighteen years old who has resided for a period of one year within the judicial district;

(2) is unable to read, write, and understand the English language with a degree of proficiency sufficient to fill out satisfactorily the juror qualification form;

(3) is unable to speak the English language;

(4) is incapable, by reason of mental or physical infirmity, to render satisfactory jury service; or

(5) has a charge pending against him for the commission of, or has been convicted in a State or Federal court of record of, a crime

punishable by imprisonment for more than one year and his civil rights have not been restored.

Comments and Questions

1. What is a "fair cross section of the community"? Should diversity be based on race and ethnicity, religion, age, gender, political views or some other criteria? The most common method of juror selection is the use of voter registration lists covering the district or division in which the court resides. Does a collection of registered voters represent a "fair cross section of the community"? What groups might be excluded or under-represented when jurors are drawn solely from voter registration lists?

2. The Supreme Court has ruled that the requirement of a "fair cross section of the community" applies only to the jury pool or panel as a whole, not to any one particular jury. What are the practical and philo-sophical reasons for such a distinction? What are its likely results?

2. Peremptory Challenges and Discrimination

Traditionally, attorneys have used their peremptory challenges to re-move jurors on grounds that did not amount to "cause." These grounds range from "gut" feelings to the systematic exclusion of certain types of people. Clarence Darrow advised criminal defense lawyers to exclude women from juries; Melvin Belli, in contrast, suggests in his books on trial technique that the defense should seek to include women, because of their alleged "sympathy" for defendants. The most notorious uses of peremptories—to exclude members of a single race, ethnic group or gen-der on the basis of often unproved assumptions and beliefs—have been under attack in recent years.

In *Batson v. Kentucky*, 476 U.S. 79 (1986), a criminal case, the Supreme Court ruled that the use of peremptory challenges by the government to systematically exclude black jurors violated the Fourteenth Amendment Equal Protection rights of a black defendant. Under *Batson* and its prog-eny, once the defendant makes a *prima facie* showing that the prosecution used peremptory challenges to exclude members of a particular racial or ethnic group from the jury, the burden shifts to the government to come forward with a race-neutral explanation for challenging the jurors.

In *Powers v. Ohio*, 499 U.S. 400 (1991), the Court extended the right to a white criminal defendant who protested the prosecution's exclusion of blacks from the jury. Several questions remained, however. One of the most pressing was, did the *Batson* rule apply to civil cases, where the gov-ernment was not a litigant? The key doctrinal question revolved around the constitutional law concept of "state action." Under the Fourteenth

Amendment, from which *Batson* and *Powers* rights are derived, only the government is prohibited from taking away an individual's equal protection of the law. Can private plaintiffs and defendants be characterized as "state actors" when they challenge jurors? As you read the following case, consider whether the majority or dissenting opinion is the more persuasive on the question of state action.

■ EDMONSON v. LEESVILLE CONCRETE CO., INC.
500 U.S. 614 (1991)

Justice KENNEDY delivered the opinion of the Court:

We must decide in the case before us whether a private litigant in a civil case may use peremptory challenges to exclude jurors on account of their race. Recognizing the impropriety of racial bias in the courtroom, we hold the race-based exclusion violates the equal protection rights of the challenged jurors. This civil case originated in a United States District Court, and we apply the equal protection component of the Fifth Amendment's Due Process Clause. *See Bolling v. Sharpe*, 347 U.S. 497 (1954).

I

Thaddeus Donald Edmonson, a construction worker, was injured in a job-site accident at Fort Polk, Louisiana, a federal enclave. Edmonson sued Leesville Concrete Company for negligence in the United States District Court for the Western District of Louisiana, claiming that a Leesville employee permitted one of the company's trucks to roll backward and pin him against some construction equipment. Edmonson invoked his Seventh Amendment right to a trial by jury.

During voir dire, Leesville used two of its three peremptory challenges authorized by statute to remove black persons from the prospective jury. Citing our decision in *Batson v. Kentucky*, 476 U.S. 79 (1986), Edmonson, who is himself black, requested that the District Court require Leesville to articulate a race-neutral explanation for striking the two jurors. The District Court denied the request on the ground that *Batson* does not apply in civil proceedings. As impaneled, the jury included 11 white persons and 1 black person. The jury rendered a verdict for Edmonson, assessing his total damages at $90,000. It also attributed 80% of the fault to Edmonson's contributory negligence, however, and awarded him the sum of $18,000.

Edmonson appealed, and a divided panel of the Court of Appeals for the Fifth Circuit reversed, holding that our opinion in *Batson* applies to a private attorney representing a private litigant and that peremptory challenges may not be used in a civil trial for the purpose of excluding jurors on the basis of race. The Court of Appeals panel held that private parties become state actors when they exercise peremptory challenges and that to limit *Batson* to criminal cases "would betray *Batson's* fundamental principle [that] the state's use, toleration, and approval of peremptory challenges based on race violates the equal protection clause." The panel remanded to the trial court to consider whether Edmonson had established a prima facie case of racial discrimination under *Batson*.

The full court then ordered rehearing en banc. A divided en banc panel affirmed the judgment of the District Court, holding that a private litigant in a civil case can exercise peremptory challenges without accountability for alleged racial classifications. The court concluded that the use of peremptories by private litigants does not constitute state action and, as a result, does not implicate constitutional guarantees. The dissent reiterated the arguments of the vacated panel opinion. The courts of appeals have divided on the issue. . . .

II

A

In *Powers v. Ohio*, 499 U.S. 400 (1991), we held that a criminal defendant, regardless of his or her race, may object to a prosecutor's race-based exclusion of persons from the petit jury. Our conclusion rested on a two-part analysis. First, following our opinions in *Batson* and in *Carter v. Jury Commission of Greene County*, 396 U.S. 320 (1970), we made clear that a prosecutor's race-based peremptory challenge violates the equal protection rights of those excluded from jury service. 499 U.S. at 407-409. Second, we relied on well-established rules of third-party standing to hold that a defendant may raise the excluded jurors' equal protection rights. *Id.* at 410-415.

Powers relied upon over a century of jurisprudence dedicated to the elimination of race prejudice within the jury selection process. *See, e.g., Batson, supra,* 476 U.S., at 84; *Swain v. Alabama,* 380 U.S. 202, 203-204 (1965); *Carter, supra,* 396 U.S., at 329-330; *Neal v. Delaware,* 103 U.S. 370, 386 (1881); *Strauder v. West Virginia,* 100 U.S. 303 (1880). While these decisions were for the most part directed at discrimination by a prosecutor or other government officials in the context of criminal proceedings, we have not intimated that race discrimination is permissible in civil proceedings. Indeed, discrimination on the basis of race in selecting a jury in a civil proceeding harms the excluded juror no less than discrimination in a criminal trial. In either case, race is the sole reason for denying the excluded venireperson the honor and privilege of participating in our system of justice.

That an act violates the Constitution when committed by a government official, however, does not answer the question whether the same act offends constitutional guarantees if committed by a private litigant or his attorney. The Constitution's protections of individual liberty and equal protection apply in general only to action by the government. *National Collegiate Athletic Assn. v. Tarkanian,* 488 U.S. 179, 191 (1988). Racial discrimination, though invidious in all contexts, violates the Constitution only when it may be attributed to state action. . . .

We begin our discussion within the framework for state action analysis set forth in *Lugar, supra,* 457 U.S., at 937. There we considered the state action question in the context of a due process challenge to a State's procedure allowing private parties to obtain prejudgment attachments. We asked first whether the claimed constitutional deprivation resulted from the exercise of a right or privilege having its source in state authority, 457 U.S., at 939-941; and second, whether the private party charged with the deprivation could be described in all fairness as a state actor, *id.,* at 941-942.

There can be no question that the first part of the *Lugar* inquiry is satisfied here. By their very nature, peremptory challenges have no significance outside a court of law. Their sole purpose is to permit litigants to assist the government in the selection of an impartial trier of fact. . . . Peremptory challenges are permitted only when the government, by statute or decisional law, deems it appropriate to allow parties to exclude a given number of persons who otherwise would satisfy the requirements for service on the petit jury.

Legislative authorizations, as well as limitations, for the use of peremptory challenges date as far back as the founding of the Republic; and the common-law origins of peremptories predate that. *See Holland v. Illinois,* 493 U.S. 474, 481 (1990); *Swain,* 380 U.S., at 212-217. Today in most jurisdictions, statutes or rules make a limited number of peremptory challenges available to parties in both civil and criminal proceedings. In the case before us, the challenges were exercised under a federal statute that provides, inter alia: "In civil cases, each party shall be entitled to three peremptory challenges. Several defendants or several plaintiffs may be considered as a single party for the purposes of making challenges, or the court may allow additional peremptory challenges and permit them to be exercised separately or jointly." 28 U.S.C. §1870. Without this authorization, granted by an Act of Congress itself, Leesville would not have been able to engage in the alleged discriminatory acts.

Given that the statutory authorization for the challenges exercised in this case is clear, the remainder of our state action analysis centers around the second part of the *Lugar* test, whether a private litigant in all fairness must be deemed a government actor in the use of peremptory challenges. Although we have recognized that this aspect of the analysis is often a fact-bound inquiry, *see Lugar, supra,* 457 U.S., at 939, our cases disclose certain principles of general application. Our precedents establish that, in determining whether a particular action or course of conduct is governmental in character, it is relevant to examine the following: the extent to which the actor relies on governmental assistance and benefits, *see Tulsa Professional Collection Services, Inc. v. Pope*, 485 U.S. 478 (1988); *Burton v. Wilmington Parking Authority*, 365 U.S. 715 (1961); whether the actor is performing a traditional governmental function, *see Terry v. Adams*, 345 U.S. 461 (1953); *Marsh v. Alabama*, 326 U.S. 501; *cf. San Francisco Arts & Athletics, Inc. v. United States Olympic Committee*, 483 U.S. 522, 544-545 (1987); and whether the injury caused is aggravated in a unique way by the incidents of governmental authority, *see Shelley v. Kraemer*, 334 U.S. 1 (1948). Based on our application of these three principles to the circumstances here, we hold that the exercise of peremptory challenges by the defendant in the District Court was pursuant to a course of state action.

Although private use of state-sanctioned private remedies or procedures does not rise, by itself, to the level of state action, *Tulsa Professional, supra*, 485 U.S., at 485, our cases have found state action when private parties make extensive use of state procedures with "the overt, significant assistance of state officials." 485 U.S., at 486; *see Lugar v. Edmondson Oil Co.*, 457 U.S. 922 (1982); *Sniadach v. Family Finance Corp.*, 395 U.S. 337 (1969). . . .

. . . [A] private party could not exercise its peremptory challenges absent the overt, significant assistance of the court. The government summons jurors, constrains their freedom of movement, and subjects them to public scrutiny and examination. The party who exercises a challenge invokes the formal authority of the court, which must discharge the prospective juror, thus effecting the "final and practical denial" of the excluded individual's opportunity to serve on the petit jury. *Virginia v. Rives*, 100 U.S. 313, 322 (1880). Without the direct and indispensable participation of the judge, who beyond all question is a state actor, the peremptory challenge system would serve no purpose. . . .

In determining Leesville's state-actor status, we next consider whether the action in question involves the performance of a traditional function of the government. A traditional function of government is evident here. The peremptory challenge is used in selecting an entity that is a quintessential governmental body, having no attributes of a private actor. The jury exercises the power of the court and of the government that confers the court's jurisdiction. . . .

Finally, we note that the injury caused by the discrimination is made more severe because the government permits it to occur within the courthouse itself. Few places are a more real expression of the constitutional authority of the government than a courtroom, where the law itself unfolds. . . .

Race discrimination within the courtroom raises serious questions as to the fairness of the proceedings conducted there. Racial bias mars the integrity of the judicial system and prevents the idea of democratic government from becoming a reality. . . .

B

Having held that in a civil trial exclusion on account of race violates a prospective juror's equal protection rights, we consider whether an opposing litigant may raise the excluded person's rights on his or her behalf. As we noted in *Powers*: "[I]n the ordinary course, a litigant must assert his or her own legal rights and interests, and cannot rest a claim to relief on the legal rights or interests of third parties." *Id.*, at 410. We also noted, however, that this fundamental restriction on judicial authority admits of "certain, limited exceptions," *ibid.*, and that a litigant may raise a claim on behalf of a third party if the litigant can demonstrate that he or she has suffered a concrete, redressable injury, that he or she has a close relation with the third party, and that there exists some hindrance to the third party's ability to protect his or her own interests. All three of these requirements for third-party standing were held satisfied in the criminal context, and they are satisfied in the civil context as well.

Our conclusion in *Powers* that persons excluded from jury service will be unable to protect their own rights applies with equal force in a civil trial. . . .

We believe the only issue that warrants further consideration in this case is whether a civil litigant can demonstrate a sufficient interest in challenging the exclusion of jurors on account of race. In *Powers*, we held: "The discriminatory use of peremptory challenges by the prosecution causes a criminal defendant cognizable injury, and the defendant has a concrete interest in challenging the practice. *See Allen v. Hardy*, 478 U.S., [255], at 259 [(1986)] (recognizing a defendant's interest in 'neutral jury selection procedures'). This is not because the individual jurors dismissed by the prosecution may have been predisposed to favor the defendant; if that were true, the jurors might have been excused for cause. Rather, it is because racial discrimination in the selection of jurors 'casts doubt on the integrity of the judicial process,' *Rose v. Mitchell* [*supra*, at 556], and places the fairness of a criminal proceeding in doubt."

III

It remains to consider whether a prima facie case of racial discrimination has been established in the case before us, requiring Leesville to offer race-neutral explanations for its peremptory challenges. In *Batson*, we held that determining whether a prima facie case has been established requires consideration of all relevant circumstances, including whether there has been a pattern of strikes against members of a particular race. 476 U.S., at 96-97. The same approach applies in the civil context, and we leave it to the trial courts in the first instance to develop evidentiary rules for implementing our decision.

The judgment is reversed, and the case is remanded for further proceedings consistent with our opinion.

Justice O'CONNOR, with whom the CHIEF JUSTICE and Justice SCALIA join, dissenting:

The Court concludes that the action of a private attorney exercising a peremptory challenge is attributable to the government and therefore may compose a constitutional violation. This conclusion is based on little more than that the challenge occurs in the course of a trial. Not everything that happens in a courtroom is state action. A trial, particularly a civil trial, is by design largely a stage on which private parties may act; it is a forum through which they can resolve their disputes in a peaceful and ordered manner. The government erects the platform; it does not thereby become responsible for all that occurs upon it. As much as we would like to eliminate completely from the courtroom the specter of racial discrimination, the Constitution does not sweep that broadly. Because I believe that a peremptory strike by a private litigant is fundamentally a matter of private choice and not state action, I dissent.

I

In order to establish a constitutional violation, Edmonson must first demonstrate that Leesville's use of a peremptory challenge can fairly be attributed to the government. . . .

The Court concludes that this standard is met in the present case. It rests this conclusion primarily on two empirical assertions. First, that private parties use peremptory challenges with the "overt, significant participation of the government." Second, that the use of a peremptory challenge by a private party "involves the performance of a traditional function of the government." Neither of these assertions is correct.

A

The Court begins with a perfectly accurate definition of the peremptory challenge. Peremptory challenges "allow parties to exclude a given number of persons who otherwise would satisfy the requirements for service on the petit jury." This description is worth more careful analysis, for it belies the Court's later conclusions about the peremptory.

The peremptory challenge "allow[s] parties," in this case private parties, to exclude potential jurors. It is the nature of a peremptory that its exercise is left wholly within the discretion of the litigant. . . . The peremptory is, by design, an enclave of private action in a government-managed proceeding. . . .

B

The Court errs also when it concludes that the exercise of a peremptory challenge is a traditional government function. In its definition of the peremptory challenge, the Court asserts, correctly, that jurors struck via peremptories "otherwise . . . satisfy the requirements for service on the petit jury." Whatever reason a private litigant may have for using a peremptory challenge, it is not the government's reason. The government otherwise establishes its requirements for jury service, leaving to the private litigant the unfettered discretion to use the strike for any reason. This is not part of the government's function in establishing the requirements for jury service. . . .

Peremptory challenges are not a traditional government function; the "tradition" is one of unguided private choice. . . .

C

None of this should be news, as this case is fairly well controlled by *Polk County v. Dodson*, 454 U.S. 312 (1981). We there held that a public defender, employed by the State, does not act under color of state law when representing a defendant in a criminal trial. In such a circumstance, government employment is not sufficient to create state action. More important for present purposes, neither is the performance of a lawyer's duties in a courtroom. This is because a lawyer, when representing a private client, cannot at the same time represent the government. . . .

II

Beyond "significant participation" and "traditional function," the Court's final argument is that the exercise of a peremptory challenge by a private litigant is state action because it takes place in a courtroom. In the end, this is all the Court is left with; peremptories do not involve the "overt, significant participation of the government," nor do they constitute a "traditional function of the government." The Court is also wrong in its ultimate claim. If *Dodson* stands for anything, it is that the actions of a lawyer in a courtroom do not become those of the government by virtue of their location. This is true even if those actions are based on race.

Racism is a terrible thing. It is irrational, destructive, and mean. Arbitrary discrimination based on race is particularly abhorrent when manifest in a courtroom, a forum established by the government for the resolution of disputes through "quiet rationality." But not every opprobrious and inequitable act is a constitutional violation. The Fifth Amendment's Due Process Clause prohibits only actions for which the Government can be held responsible. The Government is not responsible for everything that occurs in a courtroom. The Government is not responsible for a peremptory challenge by a private litigant. I respectfully dissent.

Justice SCALIA, dissenting:

I join Justice O'Connor's dissent, which demonstrates that today's opinion is wrong in principle. I write to observe that it is also unfortunate in its consequences.

The concrete benefits of the Court's newly discovered constitutional rule are problematic. It will not necessarily be a net help rather than hindrance to minority litigants in obtaining racially diverse juries. . . . Both sides have peremptory challenges, and they are sometimes used to assure rather than to prevent a racially diverse jury.

The concrete costs of today's decision, on the other hand, are not at all doubtful; and they are enormous. We have now added to the duties of already-submerged state and federal trial courts the obligation to assure that race is not included among the other factors (sex, age, religion, political views, economic status) used by private parties in exercising their peremptory challenges. That responsibility would be burden enough if it were not to be discharged through the adversary process; but of course it is. When combined with our decision this Term in *Powers v. Ohio*, which held that the party objecting to an allegedly race-based peremptory challenge need not be of the same race as the challenged juror, today's decision means that both sides, in all civil jury cases, no matter what their race (and indeed, even if they are artificial entities such as corporations), may lodge racial-challenge objections and, after those objections have been considered and denied, appeal the denials—with the consequence, if they are successful, of having the judgments against them overturned. Thus, yet another complexity is added to an increasingly Byzantine system of justice that devotes more and more of its energy to sideshows and less and less to the merits of the case.

Comments and Questions

1. Even in cases where the Seventh Amendment (or a state constitution) guarantees the right to jury trial in a particular case, both parties may waive the right and choose instead to try the case before a single judge. Fed. R. Civ. P. 38(b) requires a party with the right to try an issue to a jury to serve upon the other parties a written jury demand "at any time after the commencement of the action and not later than 10 days after the service of the last pleading directed to such issue," and to file the demand in court in accordance with Rule 5(d). Otherwise, the right is waived. Fed. R. Civ. P. 38(d). (Recall that many lawyers put their demand in their complaint or answer in order not to waive their right by inadvertence.) In other words, the Seventh Amendment does not *require* jury trial in any civil case. Should it? Why or why not?

2. Although the Court in *Batson* relied on the rights of the criminal defendant to forbid racially based challenges, the *Edmonson* Court locates the rights in a different player. Whose rights are being protected in *Edmonson*? The results of the Court's *Batson* decision influenced the criminal arena as well. In *Georgia v. McCollum*, 505 U.S. 42 (1992) the Court extended *Batson* to allow the prosecution to assert the Equal Protection

rights of the jurors against a criminal defendant who has excluded black jurors.

3. *Batson* articulated a three-part test to detect race-based uses of peremptory strikes; that test continues to be used today. First, the party opposing the strike must show that circumstances surrounding a particular strike create a prima facie case that the proponent of the strike challenged the potential juror on the basis of race. For instance, a party may satisfy the first part of the test by proving that the opposing party excluded all members of a cognizable racial group. Second, the burden shifts to the proponent of the challenge to provide a race-neutral reason for exercising the strike. Third, it is then incumbent upon the party opposing the strike to prove to the court that use of the strike was motivated by purposeful discrimination. Presumably, if the race-neutral reason for the striking of a juror applies equally to a juror who was impaneled, than that is evidence that the proffered reason for striking was pretext and that instead there was purposeful discrimination. The circuit courts are split on the issue. *Compare Turner v. Marshall,* 121 F.3d 1248, 1251-1252 (9th Cir. 1997) (race-neutral reasons are pretextual when impaneled nonminority juror shared characteristics of struck minority juror), *with Dudley v. Wal-Mart Stores, Inc.,* 166 F.3d 1317, 1321 (11th Cir. 1999) (striking juror who shared similar trait with impaneled juror "does not automatically prove discrimination").

4. In *Purkett v. Elem,* 514 U.S. 765 (1995), the majority held in a *per curiam* opinion (Justice Stevens, joined by Justice Breyer, dissenting) that a race-neutral explanation tendered by the proponent of a peremptory challenge need not be "persuasive, or even plausible." In this case, the prosecutor said that he challenged one black male because he " 'had long curly hair, . . . the longest hair on anybody on the panel by far'" and " 'he had a mustache and goatee type beard.'" He challenged a second black male because he " 'also has a mustache and goatee type beard. Those are the only two people on the jury . . . with facial hair. . . . And I don't like the way they looked, with the way the hair is cut, both of them. And the mustaches and the beards look suspicious to me.'" He added that he feared that the second struck juror, who had had a sawed-off shotgun pointed at him during a supermarket robbery, would believe that " 'to have a robbery you have to have a gun, and there is no gun in this case.'" The Supreme Court upheld the challenges, reversing the Court of Appeals for the Eighth Circuit, which had found that the prosecution's explanation for striking the first of the two black males was "pretextual." The Court stated that all that is required under the second step in *Batson* is a "legitimate reason . . . not a reason that makes sense, but a reason that does not deny equal protection." One lawyer has concluded that the *Batson* attempt to eliminate challenges based on race or gender (*see J.E.B. v. Alabama,* which follows) "may be of marginal utility, because almost any lawyer worth her salt can come up with some plausible protected class-neutral explanation for the strike." Andrew T. Berry, *Selecting Jurors,* 24 Litigation 8, 9 (1997).

5. Notwithstanding the Supreme Court's holding that racially based challenges are unconstitutional, empirical data indicates that people of color are underrepresented in both the jury pool and in the jury as finally constituted. Professor Deborah Ramirez has summarized the data and explained why it is disturbing:

> In judicial districts in which minorities comprise a relatively small percentage of the population, even a jury venire that fairly reflects the population of the district would produce some juries that contain no minority jurors. Furthermore, jury venires often do not fairly reflect the percentage of minorities in the general population, thereby exacerbating the problem. In both federal and state courts, in cities and towns across the nation, the percentage of minority jurors remains significantly lower than the percentage of minority adults living in the communities from which these jurors are selected.
>
> When a jury that is not racially mixed must pass judgment in a case involving minority defendants or victims, the fairness of its judgment is often met with skepticism, rightly or wrongly. Both minority defendants and victims, having experienced prejudice among citizens outside the courts, fear that prejudice may be carried into the jury room. They believe that some minority representation on the jury is critical to a fair outcome. As a result, the failure to secure a multiracial jury may diminish the credibility and legitimacy of the jury's verdict and, in certain highly publicized cases, shatter the public confidence needed to preserve peace following the verdict [citations omitted].

Deborah Ramirez, *The Mixed Jury and the Ancient Custom of Trial by Jury de Linguae: A History and a Proposal for Change*, 74 B.U. L. Rev. 777, 780-781 (1994).

There are many reasons why minorities are frequently underrepresented in both the jury pool and the jury. Local residency requirements and standards requiring the ability to read, write, speak, and understand English, or excluding members of the court or a law enforcement agency, can all be factors. The source lists, often reliant on voting lists, tip prospective jurors to the elderly, the relatively affluent, the self-employed, and government workers, and away from minorities, including blacks, Hispanics, and women. Those who frequently change residence, who often happen to be citizens of color, are less likely to register to vote. Even when other lists are used, such as driver's registration lists, the manner in which duplicate names remain can lead to underrepresentation. Some states have subjective tests, such as "good character," "sound judgment," "mentally sound," and "intelligence," that can result in discriminatory exclusion. Language requirements, lack of follow-up of qualification questionnaires sent to prospective jurors, and excuses from jury duty based on travel difficulties and the loss of wages are additional factors. Hiroshi Fukurai and Edgar W. Butler, *Sources of Racial Disenfranchisement in the Jury and Jury Selection System*, 13 Natl. Black L.J. 238 (1994). The use of race-based peremptory challenges, hiding under the pretense of "neutral reasons," also may be a critical factor: "[A] statistical analysis of the results of federal lower court decisions . . . reveals that the federal courts rarely find *Batson* violations and overwhelmingly accept proffered 'neutral reasons.'" Jeffrey Brand, *The Supreme Court, Equal Protection, and Jury Selection: Denying that Race Still Matters,* 1994 Wis. L. Rev. 511, 584.

6. Professor Ramirez has explained that the problem of achieving juries with a diverse mix of participants is by no means a new one, and that "for 600 years English law used quotas to create mixed juries. Beginning in the Twelfth Century, the legal principle called *de medietate linguae* or 'the jury of the half tongue' guaranteed Jewish civil and criminal defendants in England that one-half of their jurors would be fellow Jews." Deborah Ramirez, *Affirmative Jury Selection: A Proposal to Advance Both the Deliberative Ideal and Jury Diversity,* 1998 U. Chi. Legal F. 161, 167-168 (citations omitted). Later, the same right was extended to alien merchants, "eventually becoming a right enjoyed by all aliens to a jury divided equally between English nationals and fellow countrymen. When the English colonized the New World, they brought with them this principle." *Id.* (Ramirez does not, however, propose quotas as a solution for achieving more diverse juries.)

7. Some recent suggestions to achieve interracial juries, especially when people of color are parties, are (1) to eliminate peremptory challenges; (2) treat challenges differently when they operate to the detriment of a minority group; (3) affirmatively add a quota of minorities to the jury pool or the jury; and (4) allow peremptory additions of each party's choice to the qualified jury pool from which the ultimate jury will be picked. In addition to the previously cited articles by Jeffrey Brand and Deborah Ramirez, *see* Albert W. Alschuler, *Racial Quotas and the Jury,* 44 Duke L.J. 704 (1995).

8. You should not be left with the impression that only jurors, and not judges or court personnel, have prejudices that are difficult, if not impossible, to put aside. Justice Cardozo put it this way: "[E]very day there is borne in on me a new conviction of the inescapable relation between the truth without us and the truth within. The spirit of the age, as it is to each of us, is too often only the spirit of the group in which the accidents of birth or education or occupation or fellowship have given us a place. No effort or revolution of the mind will overthrow utterly and at all times the empire of these subconscious loyalties." Benjamin N. Cardozo, *The Nature of the Judicial Process* 174-175 (1921). Justice Holmes made a similar point: "What we most love and revere generally is determined by early associations. I love granite rocks and barberry bushes, no doubt because with them were my earliest joys that reach back through the past eternity of my life. But while one's experience thus makes certain preferences dogmatic for oneself, recognition of how they came to be so leaves one able to see that others, poor souls, may be equally dogmatic about something

else. And this again means skepticism." Oliver Wendell Holmes, *Natural Law*, 32 Harv. L. Rev. 40, 41 (1918). That judges and other court personnel, yet alone other lawyers, may be unable to put aside their prejudices with respect to race and gender is the topic of numerous state and federal court race and gender bias studies. *See, e.g.,* Todd D. Peterson, *Studying the Impact of Race and Ethnicity in the Federal Courts*, 64 Geo. Wash. L. Rev. 173, 178 (1996): "Forty-three percent of minority lawyers reported that they had been ignored or not listened to by a federal judge because of gender, race, or ethnicity, while only seven percent of white lawyers reported such experiences. Female minority litigators reported such experiences in even higher numbers. . . . Forty percent of African American respondents believed that they were at a disadvantage compared to white attorneys in a bench trial, while only two percent of white attorneys believed that African American litigators suffer such a disadvantage." (citations omitted) (This article describes a Federal D.C. Circuit study and report on Race and Ethnicity (which is reprinted in the same issue of the George Washington Law Review), and in note 4, page 174, lists a number of other court bias studies.) Here are conclusions of Massachusetts state court studies: "Minority attorneys often receive poor treatment from other attorneys, court-room personnel and some judges because of their race and ethnicity. Such conduct ranges from a negative perception of the attorneys' professionalism to discourteous and discriminatory comments and actions." Commission to Study Racial and Ethnic Bias in the Courts, Massachusetts Supreme Judicial Court, Final Report, Equal Justice 117 (September 1994); "Gender bias exists in many forms throughout the Massachusetts court system. Sexist language and behavior are still common. Beyond these overt signs of bias, many practices and procedures exist that may not appear motivated by bias but nonetheless produce biased results." *Report of the Gender Bias Study of The Supreme Judicial Court, Commonwealth of Massachusetts* 1 (1989).

9. In the 1994 case of *J.E.B. v. Alabama*, the Supreme Court addressed the question of whether peremptory challenges based on gender are permissible under *Batson* and *Edmonson*. Read that case, which follows, paying special attention to possible future extensions of the doctrine. Has the Court foreclosed any extension? What about peremptory challenges based solely on jurors' sexual orientation?

■ J.E.B. v. ALABAMA
511 U.S. 127 (1994)

Justice BLACKMUN delivered the opinion of the Court:
. . . Today we are faced with the question whether the Equal Protection Clause forbids intentional discrimination on the basis of gender, just as it prohibits discrimination on the basis of race. We hold that

gender, like race, is an unconstitutional proxy for juror competence and impartiality.

On behalf of relator T. B., the mother of a minor child, respondent State of Alabama filed a complaint for paternity and child support against petitioner J. E. B. in the District Court of Jackson County, Alabama. On October 21, 1991, the matter was called for trial and jury selection began. The trial court assembled a panel of 36 potential jurors, 12 males and 24 females. After the court excused three jurors for cause, only 10 of the remaining 33 jurors were male. The State then used 9 of its 10 peremptory strikes to remove male jurors; petitioner used all but one of his strikes to remove female jurors. As a result, all the selected jurors were female.

Before the jury was impaneled, petitioner objected to the State's peremptory challenges on the ground that they were exercised against male jurors solely on the basis of gender, in violation of the Equal Protection Clause of the Fourteenth Amendment. Petitioner argued that the logic and reasoning of *Batson v. Kentucky*, which prohibits peremptory strikes solely on the basis of race, similarly forbids intentional discrimination on the basis of gender. The court rejected petitioner's claim and impaneled the all-female jury. The jury found petitioner to be the father of the child and the court entered an order directing him to pay child support. On post-judgment motion, the court reaffirmed its ruling that *Batson* does not extend to gender-based peremptory challenges. The Alabama Court of Civil Appeals affirmed. The Supreme Court of Alabama denied certiorari.

We granted certiorari to resolve a question that has created a conflict of authority—whether the Equal Protection Clause forbids peremptory challenges on the basis of gender as well as on the basis of race. Today we reaffirm what, by now, should be axiomatic: Intentional discrimination on the basis of gender by state actors violates the Equal Protection Clause, particularly where, as here, the discrimination serves to ratify and perpetuate invidious, archaic, and overbroad stereotypes about the relative abilities of men and women.

Discrimination on the basis of gender in the exercise of peremptory challenges is a relatively recent phenomenon. Gender-based peremptory strikes were hardly practicable for most of our country's existence, since, until the 19th century, women were completely excluded from jury service. So well-entrenched was this exclusion of women that in 1880 this Court, while finding that the exclusion of African-American men from juries violated the Fourteenth Amendment, expressed no doubt that a State "may confine the selection [of jurors] to males." *Strauder v. West Virginia*, 100 U.S. 303, 310. . . .

Many States continued to exclude women from jury service well into the present century, despite the fact that women attained suffrage upon ratification of the Nineteenth Amendment in 1920. [In a footnote, the Court notes that in 1947, women still had not been granted the right to serve on juries in 16 States. *See* Wallace M. Rudolph, *Women on the Jury—Voluntary or*

Compulsory?, 44 J. Am. Jud. Soc. 206 (1961). As late as 1961, three States, Alabama, Mississippi, and South Carolina, continued to exclude women from jury service.] States that did permit women to serve on juries often erected other barriers, such as registration requirements and automatic exemptions, designed to deter women from exercising their right to jury service. *See, e.g., Fay v. New York*, 332 U.S., at 289 ("[I]n 15 of the 28 states which permitted women to serve [on juries in 1942], they might claim exemption because of their sex"); *Hoyt v. Florida*, 368 U.S. 57 (1961) (upholding affirmative registration statute that exempted women from mandatory jury service). . . .

Since *Reed v. Reed*, 404 U.S. 71 (1971), this Court consistently has subjected gender-based classifications to heightened scrutiny in recognition of the real danger that government policies that professedly are based on reasonable considerations in fact may be reflective of "archaic and overbroad" generalizations about gender, . . . or based on "outdated misconceptions concerning the role of females in the home rather than in the 'marketplace and world of ideas.'" *Craig v. Boren*, 429 U.S. 190, 198-199 (1976). Despite the heightened scrutiny afforded distinctions based on gender, respondent argues that gender discrimination in the selection of the petit jury should be permitted, though discrimination on the basis of race is not.

Respondent suggests that "gender discrimination in this country . . . has never reached the level of discrimination" against African-Americans, and therefore gender discrimination, unlike racial discrimination, is tolerable in the courtroom. While the prejudicial attitudes toward women in this country have not been identical to those held toward racial minorities, the similarities between the experiences of racial minorities and women, in some contexts, "overpower those differences." Note, *Beyond Batson: Eliminating Gender-Based Peremptory Challenges*, 105 Harv. L. Rev. 1920, 1921 (1992). As a plurality of this Court observed in *Frontiero v. Richardson*, 411 U.S. 677, 685 (1973):

> [T]hroughout much of the 19th century the position of women in our society was, in many respects, comparable to that of blacks under the pre-Civil War slave codes. Neither slaves nor women could hold office, serve on juries, or bring suit in their own names, and married women traditionally were denied the legal capacity to hold or convey property or to serve as legal guardians of their own children. . . . And although blacks were guaranteed the right to vote in 1870, women were denied even that right—which is itself "preservative of other basic civil and political rights"—until adoption of the Nineteenth Amendment half a century later. (Footnotes omitted.)

Certainly, with respect to jury service, African-Americans and women share a history of total exclusion, a history which came to an end for women many years after the embarrassing chapter in our history came to an end for African-Americans. . . .

Under our equal protection jurisprudence, gender-based classifications require "an exceedingly persuasive justification" in order to survive
constitutional scrutiny. Thus, the only question is whether discrimination
on the basis of gender in jury selection substantially furthers the State's
legitimate interest in achieving a fair and impartial trial. . . .

Far from proffering an exceptionally persuasive justification for its
gender-based peremptory challenges, respondent maintains that its decision to strike virtually all the males from the jury in this case "may reasonably have been based upon the perception, supported by history, that men
otherwise totally qualified to serve upon a jury might be more sympathetic
and receptive to the arguments of a man alleged in a paternity action to
be the father of an out-of-wedlock child, while women equally qualified to
serve upon a jury might be more sympathetic and receptive to the
arguments of the complaining witness who bore the child." Brief for
Respondent 10.

We shall not accept as a defense to gender-based peremptory challenges "the very stereotype the law condemns." *Powers v. Ohio*, 499 U.S.
400, 410 (1991). Respondent's rationale, not unlike those regularly
expressed for gender-based strikes, is reminiscent of the arguments
advanced to justify the total exclusion of women from juries. [Justice
Blackmun further notes: "A manual formerly used to instruct prosecutors
in Dallas, Texas, provided the following advice: 'I don't like women jurors
because I can't trust them. They do, however, make the best jurors in cases
involving crimes against children. It is possible that their "women's intuition" can help you if you can't win your case with the facts.'" Albert W.
Alschuler, *The Supreme Court and the Jury: Voir Dire, Peremptory Challenges,
and the Review of Jury Verdicts*, 56 U. Chi. L. Rev. 153, 210 (1989).] . . .

Discrimination in jury selection, whether based on race or on gender,
causes harm to the litigants, the community, and the individual jurors who
are wrongfully excluded from participation in the judicial process. The
litigants are harmed by the risk that the prejudice which motivated the
discriminatory selection of the jury will infect the entire proceedings. . . .
The community is harmed by the State's participation in the perpetuation
of invidious group stereotypes and the inevitable loss of confidence in our
judicial system that state-sanctioned discrimination in the courtroom
engenders.

When state actors exercise peremptory challenges in reliance on gender stereotypes, they ratify and reinforce prejudicial views of the relative
abilities of men and women. Because these stereotypes have wreaked
injustice in so many other spheres of our country's public life, active discrimination by litigants on the basis of gender during jury selection
"invites cynicism respecting the jury's neutrality and its obligation to
adhere to the law." *Powers v. Ohio*, 499 U.S., at 412. The potential for
cynicism is particularly acute in cases where gender-related issues are
prominent, such as cases involving rape, sexual harassment, or paternity.

Discriminatory use of peremptory challenges may create the impression that the judicial system has acquiesced in suppressing full participation by one gender or that the "deck has been stacked" in favor of one side. . . .

In view of these concerns, the Equal Protection Clause prohibits discrimination in jury selection on the basis of gender, or on the assumption that an individual will be biased in a particular case for no reason other than the fact that the person happens to be a woman or happens to be a man. . . . The judgment of the Court of Civil Appeals of Alabama is reversed and the case is remanded to that court for further proceedings not inconsistent with this opinion.

[We have omitted the concurring opinions of Justice O'CONNOR and Justice KENNEDY, the dissenting opinion of Chief Justice REHNQUIST, and the dissenting opinion of Justice SCALIA in which Chief Justice REHNQUIST and Justice THOMAS joined.]

Comments and Questions

1. *J.E.B. v. Alabama* prompts the question of what other groups should be entitled to *Batson* protection. In *Hernandez v. New York*, 500 U.S. 352 (1991), the Supreme Court found that peremptory challenges based on ethnic origin (the struck jurors were Hispanic) were illegal, but upheld challenges based on whether the jurors could speak English. A number of states have indicated that religion-based peremptories would violate state law. Some commentators (and at least one court) have taken the position that peremptory challenges based on disability also are illegal. *See* Andrew Weis, *Peremptory Challenges: The Last Barrier to Jury Service for People with Disabilities*, 33 Willamette L. Rev. 1 (Winter 1997), and *People v. Green*, 561 N.Y.S.2d 130 (N.Y. Co. Ct. 1990) (involving challenges to deaf jurors).

2. One of the authors of this casebook has invited readers to "invent ways to achieve governmental purposes that do not deploy the group-based identities yet again." Martha Minow, *Not Only for Myself—Identity, Politics and the Law* (1997). One of her three examples is the elimination of peremptory challenges. Consider whether you are convinced by her argument, which follows:

> Several benefits could emerge from this elimination of the peremptory challenge. The messy administration of the Equal Protection challenges and the strategic gamesmanship surrounding jury selection would end, or at least be forced into the "for cause" exclusions, which require reasons and judicial approval. Eliminating peremptory challenges would reduce the parties' (and lawyers') abilities to shape the jury and seek to influence their results, which could both help but also significantly hurt members of disadvantaged groups. The very practice of trying to shape the jury through

peremptory challenges has been deeply characterized by stereotypic predictions about how members of particular groups would respond to the topics
on trial. Ending the peremptory challenge would, at least symbolically, rule
all such thinking out of bounds, at least in this setting.

Indeed, parties, and lawyers, commonly seek to remove jurors based on
their group characteristics because they load many presumptions—and
prejudices—onto those identities. The prosecution tries to exclude people
who look like the defendant on the assumption of undue sympathy; the defense tries to exclude those whose racial and ethnic membership differs
from that of the defendant. Why permit peremptory challenges that presume that people *cannot* empathize across lines of difference? Not only is
such a rule untrue to human possibilities, it might also be a self-fulfilling
prophecy.

Eliminating peremptory challenges would not halt attention to group-
based categories, for aggressive anti-discrimination enforcement would still
be needed at the systemic levels defining the pool of available jurors and
calling specific people to serve. Eliminating peremptory challenges would
afford one way to restrict the use of governmentally imposed group-based
categories while still achieving the underlying governmental purpose. It
would send a signal that a practice must end if it plays into or reinforces
group stereotyping.

Id. at 99-100.

3. What effect(s), if any, do you think the elimination of peremptory
challenges would have on the behavior of lawyers, judges, and prospective
jurors?

_____

Take a moment to assess your feelings about juries. The next subjects
you will learn include how a judge can take cases away from the jury at
various points before, during, and after the trial. Try to evaluate
these powerful jury-controlling tools in light of what you believe about
the jury.

D. SUMMARY JUDGMENT

The beginning of this chapter has been about the role and composition of the American jury. The remainder of the chapter covers several
judicial methods for controlling and limiting the power of the jury.
Throughout this chapter, you will want to consider the advantages and
disadvantages of each method and the extent to which they improve or
hinder the benefits of jury trial.

Although our focus will frequently be on the relationship of these
procedural steps to the right and substance of jury trial, you should keep

in mind that some of the procedural incidents we discuss also apply to nonjury cases. For instance, summary judgment applies both to jury and nonjury cases.

You can probably figure out on your own why the drafters of the Federal Rules made available a motion for summary judgment at a point after discovery and before trial. Bear in mind that as originally construed, Rules 8(a) and 12(b)(6) made it relatively easy for a plaintiff to survive to the discovery stage. Charles Clark and his colleagues on the Advisory Committee did not think it made much sense to try to weed out many cases at the pleading stage. But since the pleadings alone would strain out few meritless cases, some mechanism was needed after discovery to weed out cases in which it was clear what the result at trial would be. It does not make sense to force the parties to try a case in which the result is a foregone conclusion. For instance, if you as a judge knew in a negligence case that the plaintiff was incapable of producing evidence at trial of unreasonable care, why put the parties and the court system to the expense of a trial? To put it another way, assume that you as a judge could predict with certainty that at the trial in a given case, a directed verdict (now called "judgment as a matter of law," Fed. R. Civ. P. 50(a)) would have to be granted in favor of the defendant because the plaintiff had not entered sufficient evidence to permit the jury to find one or more elements of the plaintiff's cause of action. Wouldn't it be both fair and efficient to enter a judgment prior to trial, rather than go through the time, expense, and anguish to the parties and witnesses (if not the jurors) of a futile jury trial?

But, as is typical in devising and interpreting procedures, there are dangers in whatever tack one takes. If it is too easy for a moving party to gain a judgment on what, after all, is only a prediction of what the evidence will be at trial, then the right to jury trial can be seriously impaired. If, on the other hand, courts are too reluctant to grant a summary judgment in cases that will later be determined by the granting of a directed verdict, that is wasteful to the parties and the public, and unfair to the party who ultimately wins. Even when there will be no jury, the judge considering a summary judgment motion must be careful not to deprive a party of what might have been a different result if witnesses had to appear before the judge in person, with the added formality of a full trial, cross-examination, and opening and closing arguments.

Four additional points bear mention. First, keep in mind the differences that a judge must consider among a 12(b)(6) motion, a motion for summary judgment, and a motion for a directed verdict. In a 12(b)(6), there exist only the allegations in the complaint. In summary judgment, the judge, in trying to predict what the evidence will be at trial, can consider the pleadings, affidavits, and discovery. (The mention of pleadings in Rule 56(c) is a bit misleading. Since, as you will see, the judge is trying to predict at the summary judgment stage what evidence will have been admitted by the time of a motion for directed verdict, a mere allegation in an unverified pleading would not aid a party trying to show that she will adduce evidence at the trial.) Unlike the 12(b)(6) motion (based on allegations alone) or the summary judgment motion (primarily based on affidavits and discovery), the directed verdict motion will be based on the evidence actually admitted at the trial (plus evidence taken to be true by virtue of admissions, stipulations, or otherwise).

Second, most motions for summary judgment or directed verdict that result in a final judgment for the moving party are motions made by the defendant. Can you see why? For a plaintiff to win at summary judgment, she would have to convince the judge that she will have admissible, persuasive, noncontroverted evidence to prove every element of her cause of action. In a negligence case, for example, a plaintiff moving for a summary judgment would have to persuade the judge through affidavits and discovery (and facts admitted by the defendant to be true) that reasonable people would have to believe that there was a duty, a breach of duty or unreasonable care, cause in fact, proximate cause, and a certain amount of damages. The plaintiff moving for summary judgment would have to convince the judge that there was no credibility issue and no task to be performed by the jury on any of the elements. In short, the moving plaintiff would have to convince the judge that she has met both her production and persuasion burdens in a manner permitting no reasonable argument. On the other hand, the defendant in a negligence case who seeks a summary judgment (or directed verdict) would have to poke a hole in only one of the elements, and as to that, she would have to show only that the plaintiff's production burden cannot be met. It is considerably easier to show a lack of potential evidence as to one element, than to convince a judge that all elements must be taken as true.

Third, study the critical language in Rule 56(c), which states that the moving party is entitled to a summary judgment if the listed materials "show that there is no genuine issue as to any material fact and that the moving party is entitled to a judgment as a matter of law." The term *material fact* has a rather specialized meaning in this context—a meaning that embodies some notion of relevance, but goes beyond merely that. Let's say in the *Carpenter* case that genuine disputes exist as to unreasonable care, causation, and the amount of damages. But assume further that there is uncontroverted evidence leading to the inescapable conclusion that the statute of limitations has already run. If the defendant can persuade the judge at the summary judgment stage that, at a trial, it (the defendant) necessarily would win on this affirmative defense (in effect, a verdict would have to be directed on the statute of limitations in favor of the defendant), then this would render the issues of unreasonable care, causation, and the amount of damages "immaterial." Similarly, if a defendant convinces a judge that at trial the plaintiff will have no admissible evidence to permit a finding as to any one of the plaintiff's elements, that would render dispute as to facts with respect any other element "immaterial."

Put another way, a judge could believe at the summary judgment stage that there are loads of disputed facts (as to the color of the jeep, the sobriety of the driver, the amount of damages), but if the plaintiff still will have to lose because of a failure of evidence as to one element (or if an affirmative defense must be taken as true), that renders all other disputes immaterial. In these instances, summary judgment should be granted even though there are disputes of fact.

Fourth, it is a bit awkward conceptually when the moving party at summary judgment is not the party with the burden of production and persuasion at the trial. Regrettably, this is in fact the typical situation: the defendant has the burden of convincing the judge to grant a summary judgment motion based on the argument that the plaintiff will have an insufficiency of evidence to meet its production burden on at least one element at the trial. In these cases, the moving party (the defendant) has a positive burden to do something to win on the motion, but it is with respect to a negative: that the plaintiff will not have a sufficiency of evidence to survive a directed verdict.

Read Fed. R. Civ. P. 56(e), particularly the penultimate sentence, and you will see a problem that has plagued judges and lawyers: "*When a motion for summary judgment is made and supported as provided in this rule*, an adverse party may not rest upon the mere allegations or denials of the adverse party's pleading, but the adverse party's response, by affidavits or otherwise or as otherwise provided in this rule, must set forth specific facts showing that there is a genuine issue for trial" (emphasis added). What does the moving party on the motion (again, typically the defendant) have to do in order to require the nonmoving party to show that she will have a sufficiency of evidence to meet its production burden? For example, if there has been no discovery, can the defendant merely move for summary judgment, thus forcing the plaintiff to reveal the supporting evidence for each element of plaintiff's case? *Adickes* and *Celotex*, which follow in this chapter, are probably the most important cases decided so far on this question of the moving party's initial burden on a summary judgment motion.

You should read Rule 56 with great care, and, as you read the two following cases, keep asking yourself, what are the roles of the moving party, the nonmoving party, and the judge when there is a summary judgment motion? What are the duties of each of these actors in the process? Can *Adickes* and *Celotex* be reconciled? To what extent have *Celotex* and other post-*Adickes* Supreme Court cases moved summary judgment in new directions?

1. *The Legal Standard: From* Adickes *to* Celotex

■ADICKES v. S. H. KRESS & CO.*
398 U.S. 144 (1970)

Justice HARLAN delivered the opinion of the Court:

Petitioner, Sandra Adickes, a white school teacher from New York, brought this suit in the United States District Court for the Southern District of New York against respondent S. H. Kress & Co. ("Kress") to recover damages under 42 U.S.C. §1983 for an alleged violation of her constitutional rights under the Equal Protection Clause of the Fourteenth Amendment. The suit arises out of Kress' refusal to serve lunch to Miss Adickes at its restaurant facilities in its Hattiesburg, Mississippi, store on August 14, 1964, and Miss Adickes' subsequent arrest upon her departure from the store by the Hattiesburg police on a charge of vagrancy. At the time of both the refusal to serve and the arrest, Miss Adickes was with six young people, all Negroes, who were her students in a Mississippi "Freedom School" where she was teaching that summer. Unlike Miss Adickes, the students were offered service, and were not arrested.

Petitioner's complaint had two counts, each bottomed on §1983, and each alleging that Kress had deprived her of the right under the Equal Protection Clause of the Fourteenth Amendment not to be discriminated against on the basis of race. The first count charged that Miss Adickes had been refused service by Kress because she was a "Caucasian in the company of Negroes." Petitioner sought, inter alia, to prove that the refusal to serve her was pursuant to a "custom of the community to segregate the races in public eating places." However, in a pretrial decision, 252 F. Supp. 140 (1966), the District Court ruled that to recover under this court, Miss Adickes would have to prove that at the time she was refused service, there was a specific "custom . . . of refusing service to whites in the company of Negroes" and that this custom was "enforced by the State" under Mississippi's criminal trespass statute. Because petitioner was unable to prove at the trial that there were other instances in Hattiesburg of a white person having been refused service while in the company of Negroes, the District Court directed a verdict in favor of respondent. A divided panel of the Court of Appeals affirmed on this ground, also holding that §1983 "requires that the discriminatory custom or usage be proved to exist in the locale where the discrimination took place, and in the State generally," and that petitioner's "proof on both points was deficient."

The second count of her complaint, alleging that both the refusal of service and her subsequent arrest were the product of a conspiracy between Kress and the Hattiesburg police, was dismissed before trial on a

---

* *Eds. Note*: There is historical background on this case following the opinion. Some students may prefer to read the history first.

motion for summary judgment. The District Court ruled that petitioner had "failed to allege any facts from which a conspiracy might be inferred." 252 F. Supp., at 144. This determination was unanimously affirmed by the Court of Appeals, 409 F.2d, at 126-127.

Miss Adickes, in seeking review here, claims that the District Court erred both in directing a verdict on the substantive count, and in granting summary judgment on the conspiracy count. Last Term we granted certiorari, 394 U.S. 1011 (1969), and we now reverse and remand for further proceedings on each of the two counts.

As explained in Part I, because the respondent failed to show the absence of any disputed material fact, we think the District Court erred in granting summary judgment. With respect to the substantive count, for reasons explained in Part II, we think petitioner will have made out a claim under §1983 for violation of her equal protection rights if she proves that she was refused service by Kress because of a state-enforced custom requiring racial segregation in Hattiesburg restaurants. We think the courts below erred (1) in assuming that the only proof relevant to showing that a custom was state-enforced related to the Mississippi criminal trespass statute; (2) in defining the relevant state-enforced custom as requiring proof of a practice both in Hattiesburg and throughout Mississippi, of refusing to serve white persons in the company of Negroes rather than simply proof of state-enforced segregation of the races in Hattiesburg restaurants.

I

Briefly stated, the conspiracy count of petitioner's complaint made the following allegations: While serving as a volunteer teacher at a "Freedom School" for Negro children in Hattiesburg, Mississippi, petitioner went with six of her students to the Hattiesburg Public Library at about noon on August 14, 1964. The librarian refused to allow the Negro students to use the library, and asked them to leave. Because they did not leave, the librarian called the Hattiesburg chief of police who told petitioner and her students that the library was closed, and ordered them to leave. From the library, petitioner and the students proceeded to respondent's store where they wished to eat lunch. According to the complaint, after the group sat down to eat, a policeman came into the store "and observed [Miss Adickes] in the company of the Negro students." A waitress then came to the booth where petitioner was sitting, took the orders of the Negro students, but refused to serve petitioner because she was a white person "in the company of Negroes." The complaint goes on to allege that after this refusal of service, petitioner and her students left the Kress store. When the group reached the sidewalk outside the store, "the Officer of the Law who had previously entered [the] store" arrested petitioner on a groundless charge of vagrancy and took her into custody.

Consp Claim

On the basis of these underlying facts petitioner alleged that Kress and the Hattiesburg police had conspired (1) "to deprive [her] of her right to enjoy equal treatment and service in a place of public accommodation"; and (2) to cause her arrest "on the false charge of vagrancy."

A. CONSPIRACIES BETWEEN PUBLIC OFFICIALS AND PRIVATE PERSONS — GOVERNING PRINCIPLES

The terms of §1983 make plain two elements that are necessary for recovery. First, the plaintiff must prove that the defendant has deprived him of a right secured by the "Constitution and laws" of the United States. Second, the plaintiff must show that the defendant deprived him of this constitutional right "under color of any statute, ordinance, regulation, custom, or usage, of any State or Territory." This second element requires that the plaintiff show that the defendant acted "under color of law."

As noted earlier we read both counts of petitioner's complaint to allege discrimination based on race in violation of petitioner's equal protection rights. Few principles of law are more firmly stitched into our constitutional fabric than the proposition that a State must not discriminate against a person because of his race or the race of his companions, or in any way act to compel or encourage racial segregation. Although this is a lawsuit against a private party, not the State or one of its officials, our cases make clear that petitioner will have made out a violation of her Fourteenth Amendment rights and will be entitled to relief under §1983 if she can prove that a Kress employee, in the course of employment, and a Hattiesburg policeman somehow reached an understanding to deny Miss Adickes service in the Kress store, or to cause her subsequent arrest because she was a white person in the company of Negroes.

The involvement of a state official in such a conspiracy plainly provides the state action essential to show a direct violation of petitioner's Fourteenth Amendment equal protection rights, whether or not the actions of the police were officially authorized, or lawful; [citations omitted]. Moreover, a private party involved in such a conspiracy, even though not an official of the State, can be liable under §1983. "Private persons, jointly engaged with state officials in the prohibited action, are acting 'under color' of law for purposes of the statute. To act 'under color' of law does not require that the accused be an officer of the State. It is enough that he is a willful participant in joint activity with the State or its agents," *United States v. Price*, 383 U.S. 787, 794 (1966).

B. SUMMARY JUDGMENT

We now proceed to consider whether the District Court erred in granting summary judgment on the conspiracy count. In granting respondent's motion, the District Court simply stated that there was "no evidence in the complaint or in the affidavits and other papers from which a 'reasonably-minded person' might draw an inference of conspiracy," 252

·F. Supp., at 144, *aff'd,* 409 F.2d at 126-127. Our own scrutiny of the factual allegations of petitioner's complaint, as well as the material found in the affidavits and depositions presented by Kress to the District Court, however, convinces us that summary judgment was improper here, for we think respondent failed to carry its burden of showing the absence of any genuine issue of fact. Before explaining why this is so, it is useful to state the factual arguments, made by the parties concerning summary judgment, and the reasoning of the courts below.

In moving for summary judgment, Kress argued that "uncontested facts" established that no conspiracy existed between any Kress employee and the police. To support this assertion, Kress pointed first to the statements in the deposition of the store manager (Mr. Powell) that (a) he had not communicated with the police,[8] and that (b) he had, by a prearranged tacit signal,[9] ordered the food counter supervisor to see that Miss Adickes was refused service only because he was fearful of a riot in the store by customers angered at seeing a "mixed group" of whites and blacks eating together.[10] Kress also relied on affidavits from the Hattiesburg chief of

8. In his deposition, Powell admitted knowing Hugh Herring, chief of police of Hattiesburg, and said that he had seen and talked to him on two occasions in 1964 prior to the incident with Miss Adickes. (App. 123-126). When asked how often the arresting officer, Ralph Hillman, came into the store, Powell stated that he didn't know precisely but "Maybe every day." However, Powell said that on August 14 he didn't recall seeing any policemen either inside or outside the store (App. 136, and he denied (1) that he had called the police, (2) that he had agreed with any public official to deny Miss Adickes the use of the library, (3) that he had agreed with any public official to refuse Miss Adickes service in the Kress store on the day in question, or (4) that he had asked any public official to have Miss Adickes arrested. App. 154-155.

9. The signal, according to Powell, was a nod of his head. Powell claimed that at a meeting about a month earlier with Miss Baggett, the food counter supervisor, he "told her not to serve the white person in the group if I . . . shook my head no. But, if I didn't give her any sign, to go ahead and serve anybody." App. 135. Powell stated that he had prearranged this tacit signal with Miss Baggett because "there was quite a lot of violence . . . in Hattiesburg" directed towards whites "with colored people, in what you call a mixed group." App. 131.

10. Powell described the circumstances of his refusal as follows: "On this particular day, just shortly after 12 o'clock, I estimate there was 75 to 100 people in the store, and the lunch counter was pretty—was pretty well to capacity there, full, and I was going up towards the front of the store in one of the aisles, and looking towards the front of the store, and there was a group of colored girls, and a white woman who came into the north door, which was next to the lunch counter. And the one thing that really stopped me and called my attention to this group, was the fact that they were dressed alike. They all had on, what looked like a light blue denim skirt. And the best I can remember is that they were—they were almost identical, all of them. And they came into the door, and people coming in stopped to look, and they went on to the booths. And there happened to be two empty there. And one group of them and the white woman sat down in one, and the rest of them sat in the second group. And, almost immediately there—I mean this, it didn't take just a few seconds from the time they came into the door to sit down, but, already the people began to mill around the store and started coming over towards the lunch counter. And, by that time I was up close to the candy counter, and I had a wide open view there. And the people had real sour looks on their faces, nobody was joking, or being corny, or carrying on. They looked like a frightened mob. They really did. I have seen mobs before. I was in Korea during the riots in 1954 and 1955. And I know what they are. And this actually got me. I looked out towards the front, and we have what they call see-through windows. There is no backs to them. You can look out of the store right into the street. And the north window, it looks right into the lunch counter.

police,[11] and the two arresting officers,[12] to the effect that store manager Powell had not requested that petitioner be arrested. Finally, Kress pointed to the statements in petitioner's own deposition that she had no knowledge of any communication between any Kress employee and any member of the Hattiesburg police, and was relying on circumstantial evidence to support her contention that there was an arrangement between Kress and the police.

Petitioner, in opposing summary judgment, pointed out that respondent had failed in its moving papers to dispute the allegation in petitioner's complaint, a statement at her deposition,[13] and an unsworn statement by a Kress employee,[14] all to the effect that there was a policeman in the store at the time of the refusal to serve her, and that this was

---

25 or 30 people were standing there looking in, and across the street even, in a jewelry store, people were standing there, and it looked really bad to me. It looked like one person could have yelled 'Let's get them,' which has happened before, and cause this group to turn into a mob. And, so, quickly I just made up my mind to avoid the riot, and protect the people that were in the store, and my employees, as far as the people in the mob who were going to get hurt themselves. I just knew that something was going to break loose there." App. 133-134.

11. The affidavit of the chief of police, who it appears was not present at the arrest, states in relevant part: "Mr. Powell had made no request of me to arrest Miss Sandra Adickes or any other person, in fact, I did not know Mr. Powell personally until the day of this statement. (*But cf.* Powell's statement at his deposition, n.8, *supra.*) Mr. Powell and I had not discussed the arrest of this person until the day of this statement and we had never previously discussed her in any way." (App. 107.)

12. The affidavits of Sergeant Boone and Officer Hillman each state, in identical language: "I was contacted on this date by Mr. John H. Williams, Jr., a representative of Genesco, owners of S. H. Kress and Company, who requested that I make a statement concerning alleged conspiracy in connection with the aforesaid arrest. This arrest was made on the public streets of Hattiesburg, Mississippi, and was an officers discretion arrest. I had not consulted with Mr. G. T. Powell, Manager of S. H. Kress and Company in Hattiesburg, and did not know his name until this date. No one at the Kress store asked that the arrest be made and I did not consult with anyone prior to the arrest." (App. 110, 112.)

13. When asked whether she saw any policeman in the store up to the time of the refusal of service, Miss Adickes answered: "My back was to the door, but one of my students saw a policeman come in." (App. 75.) She went on to identify the student as "Carolyn." At the trial, Carolyn Moncure, one of the students who was with petitioner, testified that "about five minutes" after the group had sat down and while they were still waiting for service, she saw a policeman come in the store. She stated: "(H)e came in the store, my face was facing the front of the store, and he came in the store and he passed, and he stopped right at the end of our booth, and he stood up and he looked around and he smiled, and he went to the back of the store, he came right back and he left out." (App. 302.) This testimony was corroborated by that of Dianne Moncure, Carolyn's sister, who was also part of the group. She testified that while the group was waiting for service, a policeman entered the store, stood "for awhile" looking at the group, and then "walked to the back of the store." (App. 291.)

14. During discovery, respondent gave to petitioner an unsworn statement by Miss Irene Sullivan, a check-out girl. In this statement Miss Sullivan said that she had seen Patrolman Hillman come into the store "(s)hortly after 12:00 noon," while petitioner's group was in the store. She said that he had traded a "hello greeting" with her, and then walked past her check-out counter toward the back of the store "out of (her) line of vision." She went on: "A few minutes later Patrolman Hillman left our store by the northerly front door just slightly ahead of a group composed of several Negroes accompanied by a white woman. As Hillman stepped onto the sidewalk outside our store the police car pulled across the street and into an alley that is alongside our store. The police car stopped and Patrolman Hillman escorted the white woman away from the Negroes and into the police car." (App. 178.)

the policeman who subsequently arrested her. Petitioner argued that although she had no knowledge of an agreement between Kress and the police, the sequence of events created a substantial enough possibility of a conspiracy to allow her to proceed to trial, especially given the fact that the noncircumstantial evidence of the conspiracy could only come from adverse witnesses. Further, she submitted an affidavit specifically disputing the manager's assertion that the situation in the store at the time of the refusal was "explosive," thus creating an issue of fact as to what his motives might have been in ordering the refusal of service.

We think that on the basis of this record, it was error to grant summary judgment. As the moving party, respondent had the burden of showing the absence of a genuine issue as to any material fact, and for these purposes the material it lodged must be viewed in the light most favorable to the opposing party. Respondent here did not carry its burden because of its failure to foreclose the possibility that there was a policeman in the Kress store while petitioner was awaiting service, and that this policeman reached an understanding with some Kress employee that petitioner not be served.

It is true that Mr. Powell, the store manager, claimed in his deposition that he had not seen or communicated with a policeman prior to his tacit signal to Miss Baggett, the supervisor of the food counter. But respondent did not submit any affidavits from Miss Baggett,[16] or from Miss Freeman,[17] the waitress who actually refused petitioner service, either of whom might well have seen and communicated with a policeman in the store. Further, we find it particularly noteworthy that the two officers involved in the arrest each failed in his affidavit to foreclose the possibility (1) that he was in the store while petitioner was there; and (2) that, upon seeing petitioner with Negroes, he communicated his disapproval to a Kress employee, thereby influencing the decision not to serve petitioner.

Given these unexplained gaps in the materials submitted by respondent, we conclude that respondent failed to fulfill its initial burden of demonstrating what is a critical element in this aspect of the case—that

---

16. In a supplemental brief filed in this Court respondent lodged a copy of an unsworn statement by Miss Baggett denying any contact with the police on the day in question. Apart from the fact that the statement is unsworn, see Fed. R. Civ. P. 56(e), the statement itself is not in the record of the proceedings below and therefore could not have been considered by the trial court. Manifestly, it cannot be properly considered by us in the disposition of the case. During discovery, petitioner attempted to depose Miss Baggett. However, Kress successfully resisted this by convincing the District Court that Miss Baggett was not a "managing agent," and "was without power to make managerial decisions."

17. The record does contain an unsworn statement by Miss Freeman in which she states that she "did not contact the police or ask anyone else to contact the police to make the arrest which subsequently occurred." (App. 177.) (Emphasis added.) This statement, being unsworn, does not meet the requirements of Fed. R. Civ. P. 56(e), and was not relied on by respondent in moving for summary judgment. Moreover, it does not foreclose the possibility that Miss Freeman was influenced in her refusal to serve Miss Adickes by some contact with a policeman present in the store.

there was no policeman in the store. If a policeman were present, we think it would be open to a jury, in light of the sequence that followed, to infer from the circumstances that the policeman and a Kress employee had a "meeting of the minds" and thus reached an understanding that petitioner should be refused service. Because "[o]n summary judgment the inferences to be drawn from the underlying facts contained in [the moving party's] materials must be viewed in the light most favorable to the party opposing the motion," *United States v. Diebold, Inc.*, 369 U.S. 654, 655 (1962), we think respondent's failure to show there was no policeman in the store requires reversal.

Pointing to Rule 56(e), as amended in 1963,[18] respondent argues that it was incumbent on petitioner to come forward with an affidavit properly asserting the presence of the policeman in the store, if she were to rely on that fact to avoid summary judgment. Respondent notes in this regard that none of the materials upon which petitioner relied met the requirements of Rule 56(e).

This argument does not withstand scrutiny, however, for both the commentary on and background of the 1963 amendment conclusively show that it was not intended to modify the burden of the moving party under Rule 56(c) to show initially the absence of a genuine issue concerning any material fact. The Advisory Committee note on the amendment states that the changes were not designed to "affect the ordinary standards applicable to the summary judgment." And, in a comment directed specifically to a contention like respondent's, the Committee stated that "[w]here the evidentiary matter in support of the motion does not establish the absence of a genuine issue, summary judgment must be denied even if no opposing evidentiary matter is presented." Because respondent did not meet its initial burden of establishing the absence of a policeman in the store, petitioner here was not required to come forward with suitable opposing affidavits.

If respondent had met its initial burden by, for example, submitting affidavits from the policemen denying their presence in the store at the time in question, Rule 56(e) would then have required petitioner to have done more than simply rely on the contrary allegation in her complaint. To have avoided conceding this fact for purposes of summary judgment, petitioner would have had to come forward with either (1) the affidavit of someone who saw the policeman in the store or (2) an affidavit under Rule 56(f) explaining why at that time it was impractical to do so. Even though not essential here to defeat respondent's motion, the submission

18. The amendment added the following to Rule 56(e): "When a motion for summary judgment is made and supported as provided in this rule, an adverse party may not rest upon the mere allegations or denials of his pleading, but his response, by affidavits or as otherwise provided in this rule, must set forth specific facts showing that there is a genuine issue for trial. If he does not so respond, summary judgment, if appropriate, shall be entered against him."

of such an affidavit would have been the preferable course for petitioner's counsel to have followed. As one commentator has said: "It has always been perilous for the opposing party neither to proffer any countering evidentiary materials nor file a 56(f) affidavit. And the peril rightly continues (after the amendment to Rule 56(e)). Yet the party moving for summary judgment has the burden to show that he is entitled to judgment under established principles; and if he does not discharge that burden then he is not entitled to judgment. No defense to an insufficient showing is required." 6 James Moore, *Federal Practice*, 6.22(2), pp. 2824-2825 (2d ed. 1966). . . .

[We have omitted Part II of Justice Harlan's opinion, which addresses the meaning of "custom" for purposes of §1983 and the substance of the alleged Fourteenth Amendment violation. We also have omitted Justice Black's concurring opinion; the opinion of Justice Douglas, dissenting in part; and the opinion of Justice Brennan, concurring in part and dissenting in part.]

As you read the historical background that follows, consider whether it helps explain this case. This background may also be relevant in helping you reconcile *Adickes* with *Celotex*, which follows this historical account.

2. *Background of* Adickes v. S. H. Kress & Co. *

In Mississippi in 1964, no one could have foreseen that this story—among all that was happening—would have such a far-ranging effect. Mississippi was a state at war with itself. In the four months after Sandra Adickes arrived in Mississippi, three persons would be killed, "80 beaten, three wounded by gunfire in 35 shootings, more than 1,000 arrested, 35 Negro churches burned . . . and 31 homes and other buildings bombed. In addition [there would be] several unsolved murders of Negroes that may have been connected with the racial conflict." John Herbers, *Communique From the Mississippi Front*, N.Y. Times Magazine, October 8, 1964, at 34.

Barely a year before, federal troops had faced down a mob of armed whites as James Meredith became the first black to register at the University of Mississippi. In the ensuing disturbance, two journalists were killed.

Black rhetoric, though mild compared to what would follow in the late sixties, had taken on an undertone of violence. Pulitzer Prize winner Hodding Carter wrote, "Attitudes on both sides have been hardening. A fatalistic belief in an eventual and inevitable showdown has animated

*Thanks to Joel Rosen, a 1994 graduate of Northeastern University School of Law, for research and writing.

many members of both races. . . . The hatred of the Negro for the white man is stark, naked and openly expressed to anyone to whom a Negro is willing to talk." Hodding Carter, *Mississippi Now—Hate and Fear,* N.Y. Times Magazine, June 23, 1963, at 11, 24. Mississippians feared race riots like those that had occurred in Washington, New York, Chicago, and Detroit.

Frightened by unprecedented black militancy, whites girded themselves for war. Rumors flew. It was said that black men, designated with white Bandaids on their throats, had been assigned to rape white women; black cooks were poisoning the food at local restaurants; black maids had been instructed to harass their white mistresses by hiding valuables so that their owners would briefly be terrified that they had been stolen.

The whites' response was terrible. Medgar Evers, the Mississippi-born field secretary for the NAACP was shot to death in an ambush. The Ku Klux Klan "airforce" used light planes to drop bombs on black churches and meeting places. Others drove by in cars, spraying community centers with a hail of bullets. In the arrest of men accused of bombing black homes in southwestern Mississippi, police uncovered a cache of high-powered rifles, carbines and pistols, dynamite bombs, several thousand rounds of ammunition, hand grenades, clubs, and blackjacks.

Northern liberals, seeking to help African Americans join the mainstream of the country, concentrated on two areas. One was the overthrow of segregation imposed by Mississippi law. The other was to get blacks to vote.

Voter registration was the most obvious and immediate means of power sharing. The 900,000 blacks in Mississippi made up 42 percent of the state's population; their potential political power was enormous. Getting them to seize that power, however, was difficult in the face of white resistance. Blacks, dependent on whites for jobs, were afraid to risk their survival by antagonizing the power structure. Behind the threat of starvation loomed that of violence.

As if these barriers to participation were not enough, the state required that prospective voters be of "good moral character," pass a literacy test, and interpret two sections of the state constitution. Robert Kennedy's Justice Department challenged these arbitrary testing procedures as discriminatory, particularly as applied to uneducated blacks. But in March, 1964, a federal court upheld the constitutionality of those laws. Clearly, then, if black voters were to be registered, they must first be educated.

The two-tiered program of education and registration was the goal of the Freedom Schools, a project underwritten by the Council of Federated Organizations (COFO) and run by a Yale historian named Staughton Lynd. COFO set up 47 schools throughout Mississippi in churches, dance halls, and panel trucks. They were a welcome supplement to the sixth-grade education of the average Mississippi black. The black schools were typically underfunded, and black children were expected to help pay for their education by spending one day a year picking cotton.

The Freedom Schools were ad hoc gatherings that specialized in African-American history and American government. They allowed a free range of ideas, and classes discussed topics like skepticism, power sharing, and the right to vote. Teachers and students canvassed the black neighborhoods, signing up voters and talking about new ideas. Predictably, the white reaction to these schools was sometimes deprecatory, sometimes violent. *See* Pat Waters, *Their Text is a Civil Rights Primer,* N.Y. Times Magazine, December 20, 1964, at 44.

In the early months of 1964, Sandra Adickes was in New York, training for her work at the Freedom Schools. She learned that she would not be merely making lesson plans and teaching classes. Rather, she would live among the poor blacks and participate in the life of their community. "If we were called upon to chop cotton, if that is the thing people did in the community, and we wanted to be good Freedom School teachers, that . . . is what we would do." Brief for Petitioner (*Adickes v. Kress*) at 44. The trainees were instructed never to resist arrest, never to provoke incidents. "If we were insulted we were . . . not to respond to abuse. . . . We were advised not to travel alone, so in case one of us is arrested, the other could at least report, or if we were both arrested . . . we would offer some sort of comfort to each other." *Id.* at 50. Adickes had no illusions about how white Mississippians would see the Freedom School teachers. "They think of themselves as God-fearing, law-abiding, good citizens, and you are atheists and communists, and you are there to . . . destroy their way of life." *Id.* at 51.

On July 4, two days after Congress passed the Civil Rights Act of 1964, Sandra Adickes left New York for a Freedom School in Hattiesburg, Mississippi.

Hattiesburg, the seat of Forrest County, was a city of 35,000, largely black. Civil rights leaders had targeted the city for voter-registration efforts. The city stepped up harassment of the northern agitators. In March, ten clergymen were arrested and fined in the registration drive. In May, another seven demonstrators were arrested for unlawful picketing. On July 10, a rabbi and two other whites were beaten by segregationists. By then, Sandra Adickes had finished her orientation and begun teaching at the local Freedom School.

Adickes lived with a black family in Palmer's Crossing, a rural, black community on the outskirts of Hattiesburg. She joined approximately seven other teachers at the Priest Creek Baptist Church, instructing 80 African-American students in The History of the American Negro, American Social Ideals, and Current Events, including the passage of the 1964 Civil Rights Act.

In early August, the class was discussing what new freedoms the Civil Rights Act provided. The conversation turned to immediate, simple freedoms. What the students really wanted was to go to the Holiday Inn, the white schools, the public library, and the movies. Only one movie theater had admitted blacks until that time, and that was in a small roped-off section. Some of the students said that since the Civil Rights Act had passed, they had eaten at lunch counters at local Woolworth and Kress department stores but that service had been deliberately slow and other customers had insulted them while they were eating. The class was determined to go on a simple field trip, to a place to which they had never been admitted, although their parents paid taxes to support it: the Hattiesburg Public Library. Then they would have lunch.

Adickes, along with five black girls and one boy, took the bus from Palmer's Crossing into the white section of town and walked to the library. A young woman at the desk was on the phone when the group walked in. She hung up, buzzed her supervisor, and then turned to the members of the group, who were asking for library cards. "We are not giving any cards right now," she said.

The supervisor arrived and suggested that the children try a branch of the library that served blacks. The students replied that they had been there, but the branch did not have the books they wanted. The supervisor told the students that she was a Yankee and was sympathetic to their cause; in fact she had tried to get the trustees to integrate the library. The trustees, she said, had told her they would close the library if that were to happen. Didn't the students agree that a segregated library was better than no library at all?

When it turned out that the students did not agree, the librarian said, "Close your mouths and open your minds." Finally, this sympathetic Yankee threw up her hands. "I can't make you go," she said, "but if you insist on staying, I will have to close the library and call the police."

The party refused. In several minutes the chief of police arrived and closed the library.

Following this object lesson on the effect of federal law on their everyday civil rights, the party decided to have lunch. They started for the lunch counter at Woolworth's, but when that was crowded, they decided on the nearby S. H. Kress store. While the group waited for a table, Hattiesburg patrolman Ralph Hillman entered the store and then left. A waitress then took the students' orders for hamburgers and Cokes. Adickes asked if the waitress had forgotten about her.

"No," the waitress said, "I am not serving you."

Adickes asked why.

"We have to serve Negroes," the waitress said, "but we are not serving whites who come in with them."

"Do you realize," asked Adickes, continuing the civics lesson, "this is a violation of the Civil Rights Bill [*sic*]?"

The waitress said she was acting under orders from her manager, Mr. G. T. Powell, who later testified that he gave those orders because he feared the "explosive situation" in the store.

The group left without eating. As Adickes stepped out onto the sidewalk, a police car pulled out of an alley and stopped on the street in front of her. In it were patrolman Hillman and a sergeant. They arrested her on a charge of vagrancy. Adickes had over fifty dollars with her and had a job making $2,200 a year as a New York City schoolteacher. She did not fit the definition of a vagrant who is "without regular employment or any visible means of support," and told the officers so. One replied, "We have orders to pick you up." Then he took her arm, saying, "Don't resist," and she got into the back of the cruiser.

On the way down, one of the officers taunted her, asking repeatedly, "Are you a nigger? You with the Liberace glasses, are you a nigger?"

The ride took five minutes, after which she was booked, fingerprinted, and placed in a cell. After about an hour, three lawyers came down to bail her out.

Adickes did not take the case to trial again after the Supreme Court decision in her favor.

Sandra Adickes did not drop out of the legal limelight, though. She turned up again in federal court against New York City in 1969. The suit involved a scuffle during a teachers' strike in which she allegedly kicked a policeman in the groin. When she was arrested for interfering with the arrest of another teacher, she sued the city, also under 42 U.S.C. §1983, for depriving her of her constitutional provision for such a right, and although Adickes ultimately did not win, legal scholars will be glad to know that she is still alive and kicking.

3. The Trilogy Cases

As you have seen, by the mid-1980s there had been a good deal of criticism about alleged abuses of the wide-open, permissive Federal Rules. Amendments to the discovery rules and Rule 11 were one reaction. Allegations about frivolous lawsuits also brought demands for more judicial responsiveness to summary judgment motions. *Celotex* and two other cases decided in the same term (*see* the notes following *Celotex*) were read by most commentators as an attempt to dissuade and terminate what the majority of the Supreme Court thought was a growing number of meritless lawsuits.

■ CELOTEX CORP. v. CATRETT
477 U.S. 317 (1986)

Justice REHNQUIST delivered the opinion of the Court:

The United States District Court for the District of Columbia granted the motion of petitioner Celotex Corporation for summary judgment against respondent Catrett because the latter was unable to produce evidence in support of her allegation in her wrongful-death complaint that the decedent had been exposed to petitioner's asbestos products. A divided panel of the Court of Appeals for the District of Columbia Circuit reversed, however, holding that petitioner's failure to support its motion with evidence tending to negate such exposure precluded the entry of summary judgment in its favor. *Catrett v. Johns-Manville Sales Corp.*, 244 U.S. App. D.C. 160, 756 F.2d 181 (1985). This view conflicted with that of the Third Circuit in *In re Japanese Electronic Products*, 723 F.2d 238 (1983), *rev'd on other grounds sub nom. Matsushita Electric Industrial Co. v. Zenith Radio Corp.*, 475 U.S. 574 (1986). We granted certiorari to resolve the conflict, and now reverse the decision of the District of Columbia Circuit.

Respondent commenced this lawsuit in September 1980, alleging that the death in 1979 of her husband, Louis H. Catrett, resulted from his exposure to products containing asbestos manufactured or distributed by 15 named corporations. Respondent's complaint sounded in negligence, breach of warranty, and strict liability. Two of the defendants filed motions challenging the District Court's in personam jurisdiction, and the remaining 13, including petitioner, filed motions for summary judgment. Petitioner's motion, which was first filed in September 1981, argued that summary judgment was proper because respondent had "failed to produce evidence that any [Celotex] product . . . was the proximate cause of the injuries alleged within the jurisdictional limits of [the District] Court." In particular, petitioner noted that respondent had failed to identify, in answering interrogatories specifically requesting such information, any witnesses who could testify about the decedent's exposure to petitioner's asbestos products. In response to petitioner's summary judgment motion, respondent then produced three documents which she claimed "demonstrate that there is a genuine material factual dispute" as to whether the decedent had ever been exposed to petitioner's asbestos products. The three documents included a transcript of a deposition of the decedent, a letter from an official of one of the decedent's former employers whom petitioner planned to call as a trial witness, and a letter from an insurance company to respondent's attorney, all tending to establish that the decedent had been exposed to petitioner's asbestos products in Chicago during 1970-1971. Petitioner, in turn, argued that the three documents were inadmissible hearsay and thus could not be considered in opposition to the summary judgment motion.

In July 1982, almost two years after the commencement of the lawsuit, the District Court granted all of the motions filed by the various defendants. The court explained that it was granting petitioner's summary judgment motion because "there [was] no showing that the plaintiff was exposed to the defendant Celotex's product in the District of Columbia or elsewhere within the statutory period." Respondent appealed only the grant of summary judgment in favor of petitioner, and a divided panel of the District of Columbia Circuit reversed. The majority of the Court of

Appeals held that petitioner's summary judgment motion was rendered "fatally defective" by the fact that petitioner "made no effort to adduce *any evidence*, in the form of affidavits or otherwise, to support its motion." 244 U.S. App. D.C., at 163, 756 F.2d, at 184 (emphasis in original). According to the majority, Rule 56(e) of the Federal Rules of Civil Procedure, and this Court's decision in *Adickes v. S. H. Kress & Co.*, 398 U.S. 144, 159 (1970), establish that "the party opposing the motion for summary judgment bears the burden of responding only after the moving party has met its burden of coming forward with proof of the absence of any genuine issues of material fact." The majority therefore declined to consider petitioner's argument that none of the evidence produced by respondent in opposition to the motion for summary judgment would have been admissible at trial. *Ibid.* The dissenting judge argued that "[t]he majority errs in supposing that a party seeking summary judgment must always make an affirmative evidentiary showing, even in cases where there is not a triable, factual dispute." According to the dissenting judge, the majority's decision "undermines the traditional authority of trial judges to grant summary judgment in meritless cases."

We think that the position taken by the majority of the Court of Appeals is inconsistent with the standard for summary judgment set forth in Rule 56(c) of the Federal Rules of Civil Procedure. Under Rule 56(c), summary judgment is proper "if the pleadings, depositions, answers to interrogatories, and admissions on file, together with the affidavits, if any, show that there is no genuine issue as to any material fact and that the moving party is entitled to a judgment as a matter of law." In our view, the plain language of Rule 56(c) mandates the entry of summary judgment, after adequate time for discovery and upon motion, against a party who fails to make a showing sufficient to establish the existence of an element essential to that party's case, and on which that party will bear the burden of proof at trial. In such a situation, there can be "no genuine issue as to any material fact," since a complete failure of proof concerning an essential element of the nonmoving party's case necessarily renders all other facts immaterial. The moving party is "entitled to a judgment as a matter of law" because the nonmoving party has failed to make a sufficient showing on an essential element of her case with respect to which she has the burden of proof. "[T]h[e] standard [for granting summary judgment] mirrors the standard for a directed verdict under Federal Rule of Civil Procedure 50(a). . . ." *Anderson v. Liberty Lobby, Inc.*, 477 U.S. 242, 250 (1986).

Of course, a party seeking summary judgment always bears the initial responsibility of informing the district court of the basis for its motion, and identifying those portions of "the pleadings, depositions, answers to interrogatories, and admissions on file, together with the affidavits, if any," which it believes demonstrate the absence of a genuine issue of material fact. But unlike the Court of Appeals, we find no express or implied requirement in Rule 56 that the moving party support its motion with affidavits or other similar materials negating the opponent's claim. On the contrary, Rule 56(c), which refers to "*the affidavits, if any . . .*" (emphasis added), suggests the absence of such a requirement. And if there were any doubt about the meaning of Rule 56(c) in this regard, such doubt is clearly removed by Rules 56(a) and (b), which provide that claimants and defendants, respectively, may move for summary judgment "with or without supporting affidavits." . . .

Respondent argues, however, that Rule 56(e), by its terms, places on the nonmoving party the burden of coming forward with rebuttal affidavits, or other specified kinds of materials, only in response to a motion for summary judgment "made and supported as provided in this rule." According to respondent's argument, since petitioner did not "support" its motion with affidavits, summary judgment was improper in this case. But as we have already explained, a motion for summary judgment may be made pursuant to Rule 56 "with or without supporting affidavits." In cases like the instant one, where the nonmoving party will bear the burden of proof at trial on a dispositive issue, a summary judgment motion may properly be made in reliance solely on the "pleadings, depositions, answers to interrogatories, and admissions on file." Such a motion, whether or not accompanied by affidavits, will be "made and supported as provided in this rule," and Rule 56(e) therefore requires the nonmoving party to go beyond the pleadings and by her own affidavits, or by the "depositions, answers to interrogatories, and admissions on file," designate "specific facts showing that there is a genuine issue for trial."

We do not mean that the nonmoving party must produce evidence in a form that would be admissible at trial in order to avoid summary judgment. Obviously, Rule 56 does not require the nonmoving party to depose her own witnesses. Rule 56(e) permits a proper summary judgment motion to be opposed by any of the kinds of evidentiary materials listed in Rule 56(c), except the mere pleadings themselves, and it is from this list that one would normally expect the nonmoving party to make the showing to which we have referred.

The Court of Appeals in this case felt itself constrained, however, by language in our decision in *Adickes v. S. H. Kress & Co.*, 398 U.S. 144 (1970). There we held that summary judgment had been improperly entered in favor of the defendant restaurant in an action brought under 42 U.S.C. §1983. In the course of its opinion, the *Adickes* Court said that "both the commentary on and the background of the 1963 amendment conclusively show that it was not intended to modify the burden of the moving party . . . to show initially the absence of a genuine issue concerning any material fact." *Id.* at 159. We think that this statement is accurate in a literal sense, since we fully agree with the *Adickes* Court that the 1963 amendment to Rule 56(e) was not designed to modify the burden of making the showing generally required by Rule 56(c). It also appears to us that, on the basis of the showing before the Court in *Adickes*, the motion for summary judgment in that case should have been denied. But we do not think the *Adickes* language quoted above should be construed to mean that the burden is on the party moving for summary judgment to produce evidence showing the absence of a genuine issue of material fact, even with respect to an issue on which the nonmoving party bears the burden of proof. Instead, as we have explained, the burden on the moving party may be discharged by "showing"—that is, pointing out to the district court—that there is an absence of evidence to support the non-moving party's case.

The last two sentences of Rule 56(e) were added, as this Court indicated in *Adickes*, to disapprove a line of cases allowing a party opposing summary judgment to resist a properly made motion by reference only to its pleadings. While the *Adickes* Court was undoubtedly correct in concluding that these two sentences were not intended to reduce the burden of the moving party, it is also obvious that they were not adopted to add to that burden. . . .

In this Court, respondent's brief and oral argument have been devoted as much to the proposition that an adequate showing of exposure to petitioner's asbestos products was made as to the proposition that no such showing should have been required. But the Court of Appeals declined to address either the adequacy of the showing made by respondent in opposition to petitioner's motion for summary judgment, or the question whether such a showing, if reduced to admissible evidence, would be sufficient to carry respondent's burden of proof at trial. We think the Court of Appeals with its superior knowledge of local law is better suited than we are to make these determinations in the first instance.

The Federal Rules of Civil Procedure have for almost 50 years authorized motions for summary judgment upon proper showings of the lack of a genuine, triable issue of material fact. Summary judgment procedure is properly regarded not as a disfavored procedural shortcut, but rather as an integral part of the Federal Rules as a whole, which are designed "to secure the just, speedy and inexpensive determination of every action." Fed. R. Civ. Proc. 1; *see* William Schwarzer, *Summary Judgment Under the Federal Rules: Defining Genuine Issues of Material Fact*, 99 F.R.D. 465, 467 (1984). Before the shift to "notice pleading" accomplished by the Federal Rules, motions to dismiss a complaint or to strike a defense were the principal tools by which factually insufficient claims or defenses could be isolated and prevented from going to trial with the attendant unwarranted consumption of public and private resources. But with the advent of "notice pleading," the motion to dismiss seldom fulfills this function anymore, and its place has been taken by the motion for summary judgment. Rule 56 must be construed with due regard not only for the rights of persons asserting claims and defenses that are adequately based in fact to have those claims and defenses tried to a jury, but also for the rights of persons opposing such claims and defenses to demonstrate in the manner provided by the Rule, prior to trial, that the claims and defenses have no factual basis.

The judgment of the Court of Appeals is accordingly reversed, and the case is remanded for further proceedings consistent with this opinion.

Justice WHITE, concurring:

I agree that the Court of Appeals was wrong in holding that the moving defendant must always support his motion with evidence or affidavits showing the absence of a genuine dispute about a material fact. I also agree that the movant may rely on depositions, answers to interrogatories, and the like, to demonstrate that the plaintiff has no evidence to prove his case and hence that there can be no factual dispute. But the movant must discharge the burden the Rules place upon him: It is not enough to move for summary judgment without supporting the motion in any way or with a conclusory assertion that the plaintiff has no evidence to prove his case.

A plaintiff need not initiate any discovery or reveal his witnesses or evidence unless required to do so under the discovery Rules or by court order. Of course, he must respond if required to do so; but he need not also depose his witnesses or obtain their affidavits to defeat a summary judgment motion asserting only that he has failed to produce any support for his case. It is the defendant's task to negate, if he can, the claimed basis for the suit. . . .

Justice BRENNAN, with whom the CHIEF JUSTICE and Justice BLACKMUN join, dissenting:

This case requires the Court to determine whether Celotex satisfied its initial burden of production in moving for summary judgment on the ground that the plaintiff lacked evidence to establish an essential element of her case at trial. I do not disagree with the Court's legal analysis. The Court clearly rejects the ruling of the Court of Appeals that the defendant must provide affirmative evidence disproving the plaintiff's case. Beyond this, however, the Court has not clearly explained what is required of a moving party seeking summary judgment on the ground that the nonmoving party cannot prove its case. This lack of clarity is unfortunate: district courts must routinely decide summary judgment motions, and the Court's opinion will very likely create confusion. For this reason, even if I agreed with the Court's result, I would have written separately to explain more clearly the law in this area. However, because I believe that Celotex did not meet its burden of production under Federal Rule of Civil Procedure 56, I respectfully dissent from the Court's judgment.

I

Summary judgment is appropriate where the Court is satisfied "that there is no genuine issue as to any material fact and that the moving party is entitled to a judgment as a matter of law." Fed. R. Civ. P. 56(c). The burden of establishing the nonexistence of a "genuine issue" is on the party moving for summary judgment. This burden has two distinct components: an initial burden of production, which shifts to the nonmoving party if satisfied by the moving party; and an ultimate burden of persuasion, which always remains on the moving party. The court need not decide whether the moving party has satisfied its ultimate burden of persuasion unless and until the Court finds that the moving party has discharged its initial burden of production. *Adickes v. S. H. Kress & Co.*, 398 U.S. 144, 157-161 (1970); 1963 Advisory Committee's Notes on Fed. R. Civ. P. 56(e).

The burden of production imposed by Rule 56 requires the moving party to make a prima facie showing that it is entitled to summary judgment. The manner in which this showing can be made depends upon which party will bear the burden of persuasion on the challenged claim at trial. If the moving party will bear the burden of persuasion at trial, that party must support its motion with credible evidence—using any of the materials specified in Rule 56(c)—that would entitle it to a directed verdict if not controverted at trial. *Ibid.* Such an affirmative showing shifts the burden of production to the party opposing the motion and requires that party either to produce evidentiary materials that demonstrate the existence of a "genuine issue" for trial or to submit an affidavit requesting additional time for discovery. *Ibid.*; Fed. R. Civ. P. 56(e), (f).

If the burden of persuasion at trial would be on the non-moving party, the party moving for summary judgment may satisfy Rule 56's burden of production in either of two ways. First, the moving party may submit affirmative evidence that negates an essential element of the nonmoving party's claim. Second, the moving party may demonstrate to the Court that the nonmoving party's evidence is insufficient to establish an essential element of the nonmoving party's claim. If the nonmoving party cannot muster sufficient evidence to make out its claim, a trial would be useless and the moving party is entitled to summary judgment as a matter of law. *Anderson v. Liberty Lobby, Inc.*, 477 U.S. 242, 249 (1986).

Where the moving party adopts this second option and seeks summary judgment on the ground that the nonmoving party—who will bear the burden of persuasion at trial—has no evidence, the mechanics of discharging Rule 56's burden of production are somewhat trickier. Plainly, a conclusory assertion that the nonmoving party has no evidence is insufficient. Such a "burden" of production is no burden at all and would simply permit summary judgment procedure to be converted into a tool for harassment. Rather, as the Court confirms, a party who moves for summary judgment on the ground that the nonmoving party has no evidence must affirmatively show the absence of evidence in the record. This may require the moving party to depose the non-moving party's witnesses or to establish the inadequacy of documentary evidence. If there is literally no evidence in the record, the moving party may demonstrate this by reviewing for the court the admissions, interrogatories, and other exchanges between the parties that are in the record. Either way, however, the moving party must affirmatively demonstrate that there is no evidence in the record to support a judgment for the nonmoving party.

If the moving party has not fully discharged this initial burden of production, its motion for summary judgment must be denied, and the Court need not consider whether the moving party has met its ultimate burden of persuasion. Accordingly, the nonmoving party may defeat a motion for summary judgment that asserts that the nonmoving party has no evidence by calling the Court's attention to supporting evidence already in the record that was overlooked or ignored by the moving party. In that event, the moving party must respond by making an attempt to demonstrate the inadequacy of this evidence, for it is only by attacking all the record evidence allegedly supporting the nonmoving party that a party seeking summary judgment satisfies Rule 56's burden of production. Thus, if the record disclosed that the moving party had overlooked a witness who would provide relevant testimony for the nonmoving party at trial, the Court could not find that the moving party had discharged its initial burden of production unless the moving party sought to demonstrate the inadequacy of this witness' testimony. Absent such a demonstration, summary judgment would have to be denied on the ground that the moving party had failed to meet its burden of production under Rule 56.

The result in *Adickes v. S. H. Kress & Co., supra,* is fully consistent with these principles. In that case, petitioner was refused service in respondent's lunchroom and then was arrested for vagrancy by a local policeman as she left. Petitioner brought an action under 42 U.S.C. §1983 claiming that the refusal of service and subsequent arrest were the product of a conspiracy between respondent and the police; as proof of this conspiracy, petitioner's complaint alleged that the arresting officer was in respondent's store at the time service was refused. Respondent subsequently moved for summary judgment on the ground that there was no actual evidence in the record from which a jury could draw an inference of conspiracy. In response, petitioner pointed to a statement from her own deposition and an unsworn statement by a Kress employee, both already in the record and both ignored by respondent, that the policeman who arrested petitioner was in the store at the time she was refused service. We agreed that "[i]f a policeman were present, . . . it would be open to a jury, in light of the sequence that followed, to infer from the circumstances that the policeman and Kress employee had a 'meeting of the minds' and thus reached an understanding that petitioner should be refused service." 398 U.S., at 158. Consequently, we held that it was error to grant summary judgment "on the basis of this record" because respondent had "failed to fulfill its initial burden" of demonstrating that there was no evidence that there was a policeman in the store. *Id.,* at 157-158.

The opinion in *Adickes* has sometimes been read to hold that summary judgment was inappropriate because the respondent had not submitted affirmative evidence to negate the possibility that there was a policeman in the store. The Court of Appeals apparently read *Adickes* this way and therefore required Celotex to submit evidence establishing that plaintiff's decedent had not been exposed to Celotex asbestos. I agree with the Court that this reading of *Adickes* was erroneous and that Celotex could seek summary judgment on the ground that plaintiff could not prove exposure to Celotex asbestos at trial. However, Celotex was still required to satisfy its initial burden of production.

II

I do not read the Court's opinion to say anything inconsistent with or different than the preceding discussion. My disagreement with the Court concerns the application of these principles to the facts of this case.

Defendant Celotex sought summary judgment on the ground that plaintiff had "failed to produce" any evidence that her decedent had ever been exposed to Celotex asbestos. Celotex supported this motion with a two-page "Statement of Material Facts as to Which There is No Genuine Issue" and a three-page "Memorandum of Points and Authorities" which asserted that the plaintiff had failed to identify any evidence in responding to two sets of interrogatories propounded by Celotex and that therefore the record was "totally devoid" of evidence to support plaintiff's claim.

Approximately three months earlier, Celotex had filed an essentially identical motion. Plaintiff responded to this earlier motion by producing three pieces of evidence which she claimed "[a]t the very least . . . demonstrate that there is a genuine factual dispute for trial,": (1) a letter from an insurance representative of another defendant describing asbestos products to which plaintiff's decedent had been exposed; (2) a letter from T. R. Hoff, a former supervisor of decedent, describing asbestos products to which decedent had been exposed; and (3) a copy of decedent's deposition from earlier workmen's compensation proceedings. Plaintiff also apparently indicated at that time that she intended to call Mr. Hoff as a witness at trial.

Celotex subsequently withdrew its first motion for summary judgment. However, as a result of this motion, when Celotex filed its second summary judgment motion, the record did contain evidence—including at least one witness—supporting plaintiff's claim. Indeed, counsel for Celotex admitted to this Court at oral argument that Celotex was aware of this evidence and of plaintiff's intention to call Mr. Hoff as a witness at trial when the second summary judgment motion was filed. Moreover, plaintiff's response to Celotex' second motion pointed to this evidence—noting that it had already been provided to counsel for Celotex in connection with the first motion—and argued that Celotex had failed to "meet its burden of proving that there is no genuine factual dispute for trial."

On these facts, there is simply no question that Celotex failed to discharge its initial burden of production. Having chosen to base its motion on the argument that there was no evidence in the record to support plaintiff's claim, Celotex was not free to ignore supporting evidence that the record clearly contained. Rather, Celotex was required, as an initial matter, to attack the adequacy of this evidence. Celotex' failure to fulfill this simple requirement constituted a failure to discharge its initial burden of production under Rule 56, and thereby rendered summary judgment improper.

This case [therefore] is indistinguishable from *Adickes*. . . .

[The dissenting opinion of Justice STEVENS is omitted.]

Comments and Questions

1. In *Celotex*, the plaintiff defeated the summary judgment motion on remand to the appeals court that had earlier heard the case. Judge Kenneth Starr, a judge on that appeals court, wrote an opinion denying defendant's summary judgment motion. *Catrett v. Johns-Mansville*, 826 F.2d 33 (D.C. Cir. 1987).

2. Do you agree with Justice Brennan that *Adickes* and *Celotex* are reconcilable? Does each case approach summary judgment the same way? What was Justice White's concern that precipitated a separate opinion? What is the burden on a defendant who moves for summary judgment after *Celotex*?

3. The Supreme Court ruled on two other summary judgment cases during the same term as *Celotex*; the three cases are frequently referred to as the "trilogy" of summary judgment cases. Most commentators at the time read the trilogy as signaling that the federal courts would be more favorably disposed to summary judgment motions than before. For instance, a partner at Skadden, Arps, Slate, Meagher & Flom, a large New York City law firm, already noted this tendency a year after the trilogy: "There is no question that the courts are more hospitable toward summary judgment. The attitude throughout the country has been changing toward them. Judges want more than ever to dispose of cases if they can at an early stage." Stephen Labaton, *The Summary Judgment Rule*, N.Y. Times, Aug. 17, 1987, at 22. For a more recent assessment of summary judgment practice subsequent to the 1986 trilogy of cases, *see* Patricia M. Wald, *Summary Judgment at Sixty*, 76 Tex. L. Rev. 1897 (1998). Judge Wald reports that in calendar year 1996, 22 percent of the terminations in the United States District Court for the District of Columbia were by summary judgment, and only 3 percent by trial. "We are approaching a time when a civil trial will be

thought of as a 'pathological event.'" *Id.* at 1915. "While judges appear to be requiring plaintiffs to plead facts with ever greater detail in order to survive motions to dismiss, they also seem reluctant to find genuine issues of material fact meriting a trial, often declaring that the factual issues are immaterial, or requiring a higher standard of proof at summary judgment that a fact [is] in dispute than had traditionally been thought necessary." *Id.* at 1942.

4. The second case in the trilogy was *Anderson v. Liberty Lobby, Inc.*, 477 U.S. 242 (1986). In *Liberty Lobby*, the district court had granted summary judgment on the grounds that in libel suits of this nature, the plaintiff needed to prove actual malice, and the plaintiff did not show that it would have evidence at the trial permitting such a finding. The appellate court reversed, saying that the plaintiff's obligation to prove actual malice at the trial by clear and convincing evidence did not apply at the summary judgment stage. Justice White, writing for the majority, is explicit that the summary judgment motion requires the court to predict what would happen to the case at the directed verdict stage: "The petitioners suggest, and we agree, that this standard [for summary judgment under Rule 56(c)] mirrors the standard for a directed verdict under Federal Rules of Civil Procedure 50(a), which is that the trial judge must direct a verdict if, under the governing law, there can be but one reasonable conclusion as to the verdict." *Id.* at 250.

Justice White further stated, "Our holding that the clear-and-convincing standard of proof should be taken into account in ruling on summary judgment motions does not denigrate the role of the jury." *Id.* at 255. But Justice Brennan argued in dissent that when trial judges try to apply a "clear-and-convincing" standard at the summary judgment stage, they cannot avoid weighing evidence, and thus improperly infringing on the province of the jury. Justice Brennan complained that the Court's opinion did not explain how a judge should "assess how one-sided evidence is, or what a 'fair-minded' jury could 'reasonably' decide. . . . I simply cannot square the direction that the judge 'is not himself to weigh the evidence' with the direction that the judge also bear in mind the 'quantum' of proof required and consider whether the evidence is of sufficient 'caliber or quantity' to meet that 'quantum.' I would have thought that a determination of the 'caliber and quantity,' i.e., the importance and value, of the evidence in light of the 'quantum,' i.e., amount 'required,' could *only* be performed by weighing the evidence." *Id.* at 265-66 (emphasis in original).

Justice Rehnquist, joined by Chief Justice Burger, argued in dissent that the majority's test would be difficult to apply. If the plaintiff could show that it had evidence of malice at the summary judgment stage, Justice Rehnquist did not see how a judge ruling on a summary judgment motion could determine that it would be insufficient evidence for the jury to find malice at the trial itself, unless the judge made a credibility determination. Justice Rehnquist concluded: "The primary effect of the Court's opinion today will likely be to cause the decisions of trial judges on summary judgment motions in libel cases to be more erratic and inconsistent than before. This is largely because the Court has created a standard that is different from the standard traditionally applied in summary judgment motions without even hinting as to how its new standard will be applied to particular cases." *Id.* at 272-273.

On remand, the federal district court applied the "clear and convincing evidence of actual malice" standard and granted summary judgment on seven of the nine counts remanded. *Liberty Lobby v. Anderson,* 1991 WL 186998 (D.D.C. May 1, 1991).

5. The third case of the trilogy, *Matsushita v. Zenith,* 475 U.S. 574 (1986), dealt with a claim by Zenith Co. against 21 Japanese companies manufacturing or selling consumer electronics products in America or controlling American firms that sell the products. Zenith alleged that the Japanese companies had conspired, in violation of the Sherman Antitrust Act and other statutes, to keep prices artificially high in Japan in order to subsidize artificially low prices in the United States, in order to push American companies out of the market. The case focused on a "Five Company Rule"—an agreement that defendants had made with each other that no one company would have more than five distributors.

The district court, finding that Zenith's theory did not make economic sense, granted summary judgment to the defendants. The appeals court reversed summary judgment with respect to some of the defendants, finding sufficient evidence from which a jury could infer a conspiracy. The Supreme Court reversed and remanded, with Justice Powell writing the majority opinion, in which Justices Burger, Marshall, Rehnquist, and O'Connor joined.

The Court ruled that "where the record taken as a whole could not lead a rational trier of fact to find for the non-moving party, there is no genuine issue for trial." *Id.* at 587. On the facts of the *Matsushita* case, the Court held that Zenith, the non-mover with the burden of proof at trial, had failed to present evidence at the summary judgment stage that "tends to exclude the possibility that the alleged conspirators acted independently." *Id.* at 588. The Court reasoned that the plaintiff's theory did not make economic sense and that the Five Company Rule would tend to raise, not lower, prices. Nor would the court allow the plaintiff to survive summary judgment based on the proposed testimony of plaintiff's expert that there was a conspiracy; the Court found that the expert's opinion was "implausible" and inconsistent with other evidence in the record.

Justice White, joined by Justices Brennan, Blackmun, and Stevens, dissented, arguing that the majority had disregarded traditional summary judgment doctrine. They found the majority's disregard for the expert's proposed testimony a clear violation of the judicial obligation not to weigh evidence and assess credibility when ruling on a summary judgment motion: "If the Court intends to give every judge hearing a motion for summary judgment in an antitrust case the job of determining if the evidence makes the inference of conspiracy more probable than not, it is overturning settled law. If the Court does not intend such a pronouncement, it should refrain from using unnecessarily broad and confusing language." *Id.* at 598, 601. With respect to the majority's rejection of the opinion of the plaintiff's proposed expert, the dissent concluded: "No doubt the Court prefers its own economic theorizing to Dr. DePodwin's, but that is not a reason to deny the factfinder an opportunity to consider Dr. DePodwin's views on how petitioners' alleged collusion harmed respondents." *Id.* at 598, 603. Indeed, from our current knowledge of how Japanese electronics firms have employed long-term pricing strategies to maximize efficiency, we may wonder whether DePodwin's testimony would have struck fact finders as unbelievable. Isn't a court's judgment that there is no evidence different from its refusal to believe evidence that will be presented?

6. During your law career, you will hear many times that issues of fact are for the jury and issues of law are for the judge. And yet, the very notion of summary judgment and directed verdict presupposes that judges are permitted to enter the domain of factual issues. Hence, this can be confusing. In order to ensure that juries do not act irrationally, the theory goes, judges must be certain that before the jury can decide a factual issue on behalf of the party with the burden of production, there is sufficient evidence to permit reasonable people to make such a finding. Thus, the judiciary has created a threshold legal issue in order to decide the factual issue: it is deemed a legal question whether there is sufficient evidence to make a rational factual determination.

When a judge says that something is a question of law, this is a shorthand for saying, "I have determined that the jury should not hear the issue." When a judge grants a summary judgment motion on behalf of a defendant because of a failure in the plaintiff's prima facie case, she is saying, "As a matter of law, I have determined that the plaintiff has not shown it will have sufficient evidence at the trial to permit a jury to find for the plaintiff on all of its elements."

It is by no means written in concrete which issues the judge will turn into "law" questions, and which will be treated as "factual" issues for the jury. Perhaps it is best to see "as a matter of law" as shorthand for saying that, based on policy considerations, a judge thinks the judiciary is better at deciding the question than a jury of lay people.

In cases such as *Adickes* or *Celotex*, the Supreme Court assumed that the questions of whether there was a conspiracy between a store and the police, or whether someone was exposed to asbestos manufactured by a defendant, were fact questions for the jury, and the legal question was whether there was a sufficiency of evidence to permit the jury to decide those questions. William W. Schwarzer, a Senior United States District Judge for the Northern District of California and a former Director of the Federal Judicial Center, has pointed out that the fact/law distinction takes place at another level as well: the initial question of whether the issue to be decided, often a mixed question of law and fact, should be decided by the jury at all. In the following article, Senior Judge Schwarzer explains this level of decision and gives examples.

■ WILLIAM SCHWARZER, SUMMARY JUDGMENT UNDER THE FEDERAL RULES: DEFINING GENUINE ISSUES OF MATERIAL FACT
99 F.R.D. 465, 471-474 (1984)

Thus the court should first consider whether the disputed issue, as a matter of precedent or policy, should be decided by the jury or by the court. That approach should present no difficulty with respect to a large category of issues traditionally tried to juries. Whether a defendant has failed to use due care in the operation of his vehicle, whether he was driving in the course of his employment, and whether the injuries suffered by plaintiff were proximately caused by the defendant's operation of the vehicle are issues of ultimate fact for the jury. Similarly, whether a person had reasonable cause, acted within a reasonable time or can be charged with notice are jury issues. All are ultimate facts turning on examination and assessment of human behavior within the common experience of jurors. Concerning issues of this sort, "[i]t is assumed that twelve men know more of the common affairs of life than does one man, that they can draw wiser and safer conclusions from admitted facts thus occurring than can a single judge." Decisions of such issues, moreover, are generally ad hoc, with little resort to policy, with precedent playing a minor part, and with no compelling need for uniform or predictable outcomes. Of such mixed issues of fact and law, one can say that their law content is relatively low.

This does not mean that every such issue must be submitted to the jury, i.e. that summary judgment is precluded. That will turn on the second prong of the test—whether the motion or the opposition is sufficient to establish that the proponent of the issue could survive a motion for directed verdict or for judgment n.o.v. . . .

A second category of ultimate fact issues consists of those which involve the application of predominantly legal standards to undisputed historical facts. The decision here turns not so much on factors within the common experience of jurors as on matters of law and policy and on technical questions underlying the particular legal scheme. It should not be made ad hoc; consistency, uniformity and predictability here are important to the administration of the underlying laws. Issues of this sort arise most frequently in the application of legislation or of public policies. Examples include whether a union breached its duty of fair representation, whether a controlling person acted in good faith within the meaning of the securities laws, whether location restrictions in a dealer agreement were an unreasonable restraint in violation of the antitrust laws. . . . Of mixed questions such as these, it is fair to say that their law content predominates.

Ultimate fact issues of this sort are properly decided by the court and are therefore appropriate for summary judgment if the underlying historical facts are not disputed. That is true even though the process of decision requires the trial court to "weigh the evidence" on both sides of the argument in deciding what ultimate fact to derive. . . .

A third category consists of those issues of ultimate fact which may be appropriate for jury determination in some cases but not in others. One example of such a variable issue is the existence of a conspiracy under the antitrust laws. In certain conspiracy cases the lawfulness of joint conduct of defendants can turn on their purpose and intent, a question of fact usually disputed and well within the conventional sphere of the jury. In other cases, the conspiracy issue may turn on whether, as a matter of law and policy, a particular relationship among parties, the historical facts of which are not disputed, should be treated as an unlawful conspiracy. . . .

Comments and Questions

Portions of Rule 56 make clear that a judge may order a partial summary judgment. This would mean that at trial, some facts or some elements will be treated as true, leaving the fact finder with only the remaining facts and elements to consider. As you study Rule 56, note the last five words of 56(a) and the last sentences of 56(c) and 56(d), each of which permits partial summary judgments.

4. Strategic Considerations

Like all motions, there are strategic matters to consider before filing a summary judgment motion. This is not just a matter of avoiding sanctions or avoiding a likely waste of time and money, although these are important considerations. To file a summary judgment motion and memorandum or brief in support thereof means educating opposing counsel about your view of their case and, in some instances, of your own case. On the other hand, it may be a way of smoking out opposing counsel's best case in advance of trial. But even this is more complicated. If a party against whom the motion is brought thinks she can easily defeat it without revealing all of her cards, she may do so. For instance, a plaintiff may have many theories of recovery or cumulative potential evidence, but reveal at the summary judgment stage only enough to survive the motion. This, too, is complex. It would be embarrassing—if not malpractice—for counsel defending against a summary judgment to hold back in order not to educate an opponent, only to find out that her client loses at the summary judgment stage.

Bear in mind that winning or losing the motion is not the only issue and that there are audiences other than opposing counsel. One must consider who the judge is likely to be and whether the summary judgment motion is a good means of early education for the judge. Will the judge who hears the motion be the same judge who sits at trial? There also looms the question of settlement. Will it be easier or harder to settle the case once the outcome of your motion is known? Do you want to run that risk?

Some cases look stronger or weaker depending on whether they are decided on a written record or with live testimony. Some cases simply look different when you consider whether a judge or a jury will be the fact finder. Even though a summary judgment motion is in large measure a prediction of what would happen at the directed verdict stage at trial, the situations are different psychologically. Many cases demand the drawing of inferences, for example, and sympathetic testimony for one side or another may contract or expand the inferences that a judge is willing to draw or to permit a jury to draw.

Finally, consider these questions. Will the filing of a summary judgment motion delay your trial date? Is delay good or bad for your client? Is a swift decision—even if it is a negative one—a priority for your client? Perhaps you and your client are trying to establish a new cause of action in your jurisdiction, and you want an appellate court to hear the question as soon as possible. But, then again, you may want to attempt to convince appellate judges to stretch current precedent with the aid of an entire trial record.

Litigation is a human enterprise in which experience means a great deal; lawyers tend to become more valuable with age and practice. If you choose to do trial work, over time you will work out your own sense of litigation strategy. You will become more skilled at deciding which variables are most important to you and your client—and, if your client is lucky, your mind will remain open to new variables and new assessments of the old variables.

Practice Exercise No. 19: Summary Judgment Motion Session in *Carpenter*

This practice exercise has two parts. You may be assigned either or both. For each part, read the summary judgment motion of the third-party defendants, the memorandum in support of the motion, the Regulations, the stipulation of all parties, the *Restatement* excerpts, and the *Pederson v. Time, Inc.* case, which are in the Case Files, as well as any other materials in the *Carpenter v. Dee* case that you feel are relevant to the exercise. (There is absolutely no need to go beyond the pages of this textbook, including the Case Files, in order to do a first-rate job on these exercises.) As you read the materials, consider how, if you represented Dale McGill and McGill's Garage, you would attempt to convince a judge that there is no material issue of fact for the jury to decide and that this is a case that can be decided at summary judgment as a matter of law. Is it your position that the issue to be decided at summary judgment is for the court and not the jury, or that as to one or more elements, Ultimate Auto will have insufficient evidence for the court to find for it—or that both are true?

For purposes of both the written and oral portion of the exercise, assume that this is the structure of the case. Nancy Carpenter sued the Dees. She then amended to add Ultimate Auto and the City as defendants. Ultimate Auto impleaded McGill and his Garage. The Dees, Ultimate Auto, and the City each filed cross-claims against each other. After discovery, and before any amendment by Carpenter to claim against McGill and his Garage, McGill and his Garage moved for summary judgment against Ultimate Auto, and Ultimate Auto opposed this motion. It is the McGill and McGill Garage summary judgment motion against Ultimate Auto that you will address in both the written and oral portions of the Exercise.

In the actual case, the City also moved for summary judgment, and that motion was denied. As a matter of trial strategy, however, the plaintiff's counsel later dropped the allegations against the City, because of (a) concern for the feelings a jury might have about blaming police officers for failing to get the jeep off the road (or otherwise warn), which might in turn prejudice a jury against the plaintiff's strong claim against Ultimate Auto; (b) concern about the reaction of jurors as taxpayers who might not want to cost the City money which, in turn, might somehow poison them against the plaintiff generally; (c) concern that juries think a plaintiff's case is weaker when a shotgun approach is used of suing everyone in sight; (d) belief that the City was largely judgment-proof; and (e) belief that the case against the City was not very strong anyway. In fact, after the actual lawsuit, the Massachusetts legislature passed a statute making it very unlikely that a case such as this could be successfully sustained against a Massachusetts municipality.

A. Written Exercise. *As counsel for Ultimate Auto, prepare a Memorandum for the Court in Opposition to the Third Party Motion for Summary Judgment.* The memorandum should not exceed four double-spaced pages (including the caption). The memoranda will be collected at the end of class. Before you prepare your memorandum, make sure you are clear on how many arguments you have. You may wish first to make an outline. For instance, are you arguing that the law requires a broader duty than the third-party defendants suggest, or that there are underlying factual disputes, or both? Or do you have other arguments? As to each argument, make subarguments or a list of reasons. Definition and clarity are essential in constructing effective legal arguments.

B. Oral Exercise. *As counsel for Ultimate Auto or the Garage, prepare an oral argument for or against the summary judgment motion.* A motion session judge will hear argument from both sides on the summary judgment motion of McGill and the Garage against Ultimate Auto. If your last name begins with any letter from H through T, be prepared to argue orally on behalf of Ultimate Auto. If your last name begins with any other letter, be prepared to argue for Dale McGill and McGill's Garage in favor of the summary judgment motion. Assume that the judge will ask to hear first from the moving party. Also assume that the judge was recently appointed to the bench, and is unfamiliar with the details of your case.

E. DISMISSALS, DIRECTED VERDICTS, JUDGMENTS N.O.V., NEW TRIAL MOTIONS, AND MOTION TO VACATE JUDGMENT

You have now studied summary judgment, which takes places prior to trials. We next want to teach you about three jury-control mechanisms — directed verdict, judgment n.o.v., and new trial motions — and about methods for dismissing cases and having judgments vacated. If we were going in chronological order, a time-line for a typical federal jury case might look something like the following. Don't take the time-line too literally; not every step must take place, and many steps overlap or could happen in a different order for any of a number of good reasons.

Complaint

12(b) motions

Answer

Motions for voluntary or involuntary dismissal

Rule 16 scheduling conference and order (*see* Chapter 6)

Discovery

Motions to amend

Settlement discussion

Motions for summary judgment

Rule 16 pretrial conference

Trial

Motions for directed verdict / judgment as a matter of law

Verdict

Entry of judgment

Motions for judgment n.o.v. / judgment as a matter of law

Motions for new trial

Appeals

Motions to vacate judgment

Execution of judgment

You should also have some picture in your mind of what goes on at a trial. A jury trial begins with impaneling a jury, including voir dire and challenges of jurors for cause and peremptory challenges, topics that we have already covered. Whether there is a jury or not, the next stage is for the plaintiff and the defendant to give opening statements, with the plaintiff ordinarily going first. The parties then present their evidence through witnesses and exhibits. As each party presents its evidence, the opposing parties may object on the grounds that the evidence is inadmissible. The defendant's lawyer has an opportunity to cross-examine each of the plaintiff's witnesses, usually followed by re-direct and re-cross. After the plaintiff rests, and assuming that there is not a directed verdict motion or that such a motion has been denied, the defendant presents its case in the same manner that the plaintiff did (with direct and cross-examination). The plaintiff can then present rebuttal evidence, and then the defendant can do the same. Assuming that the case is not disposed of by directed verdict motions after all parties have rested, there are then final arguments by each side. In many courts, the defendant closes first, followed by the plaintiff. In others, the plaintiff is permitted to have the first and final closing arguments, with the defendant's closing argument in between. If there is a jury, the judge will usually instruct it on the law after all of the closing arguments. Some judges choose to instruct at the beginning of the case and at the end, while others instruct the jury immediately before the lawyers give their closing arguments. The jury then deliberates and returns a verdict, filling in the verdict slip or answering the questions presented by the judge, sometimes both. (*See* Fed. R. Civ. P. 49.)

We next discuss the current ground rules on dismissals, directed verdict motions, and the like.

1. Voluntary Dismissal

Fed. R. Civ. P. 41(a)(1) prescribes when a plaintiff has a right to dismiss a case voluntarily, and 41(b)(1) describes the court's power to permit a plaintiff to dismiss a case voluntarily. Note that in the normal case, the plaintiff has an absolute right to dismiss voluntarily prior to the adverse party's filing an answer or a motion for summary judgment. Unless otherwise stated in the court's notice of dismissal or in a stipulation of dismissal signed by all parties who have appeared in the action, or unless the plaintiff has previously filed and dismissed the same claim in a state or federal court, then such voluntary dismissal will be *without prejudice*. That means that it is without prejudice to bring the claim again; put another way, it means the dismissal will *not* have a *res judicata* effect.

Under Fed. R. Civ. P. 41(a)(2), the plaintiff, in situations not covered by 41(a)(1), can apply to the court for a voluntary dismissal, and the court, upon "such terms and conditions as the court deems proper," has the power to grant it. Unless the court otherwise states, this dismissal will also be "without prejudice." The "terms and conditions" phrase is an invitation to the court to condition the dismissal on the plaintiff's paying all or part of the defendant's expenses to date in defending the suit. The court can also decide only to permit the voluntary dismissal *with prejudice*. If the case has proceeded very far, and the court and the other party have already expended significant resources and time on the case, the court will likely dismiss with prejudice or dismiss without prejudice on the condition that plaintiff pay defendant's expenses to defend to date. Fed. R. Civ. P. 41(d) covers a lacuna in 41(a)(1): the situation in which a plaintiff has an absolute right to voluntarily dismiss "without prejudice," but this is not the first time the plaintiff has had the same claim dismissed. In this situation, the court can award the costs of the action previously dismissed to the opposing party and "may stay the action until the plaintiff has complied with the order."

Notice that Fed. R. Civ. P. 41(c) permits claimants other than plaintiffs to seek dismissals. This is because counterclaims, cross-claims, and third-party claims put the defendant in a plaintiff's posture for those aspects of the case.

2. Involuntary Dismissal

Often a court orders a case dismissed even though the plaintiff would very much like it to continue. For instance, you have already seen dismissals for failure to state a claim or for failure to survive a summary judgment motion. Pursuant to Fed. R. Civ. P. 41(b), unless the court otherwise orders, these and other involuntary dismissals operate "as an adjudication on the merits," which is another way of saying the dismissal has a *res judicata* effect. When we reach the sections on jurisdictional matters and Rule 19 (necessary and indispensable parties), we will consider why dismissals for lack of subject matter jurisdiction, personal jurisdiction, venue, or failure to join a necessary party do not have a *res judicata* effect, although the answer may well be obvious.

It is probably also obvious why involuntary dismissals for failing to comply with a court order operate "as an adjudication on the merits." It would be a very inefficient system, if not an unfair one, that permitted a plaintiff or its attorney to fail to comply with a discovery order, an order relating to pretrial conferences, or other orders of the court, without the ultimate available sanction of dismissal with prejudice.

The next three procedural devices we will describe are more in keeping with the major themes of this chapter: the right to trial by jury and judicial control of juries.

3. Directed Verdict (Judgment as a Matter of Law)

We have been anticipating this device ever since Chapter 3, when you were first exposed to the burden of production, and you have met the concept again in our classes on summary judgment. To refresh your recollection, the party with the burden of production on an issue (we have been using the word *element* previously, for that is usually what is at stake) has the obligation to enter sufficient evidence on that issue to permit a reasonable fact finder to find for that party. Otherwise, as to that issue, and upon proper motion by the opposition, the party with the production burden will lose. If losing on that issue means the party cannot win on the claim, it will lose the case.

It is probably obvious to you by now that, just as in summary judgment, the judge deciding a directed verdict motion is obligated to consider the evidence of the nonmoving party in the light most favorable to that party, taking the nonmover's conceivably believable evidence as true and giving the nonmover the benefit of all reasonable inferences. This procedural mechanism is usually used by a defendant to defeat a plaintiff, before the fact finder even deliberates on the evidence, on the ground that, on at least one element of the plaintiff's cause of action, no reasonable fact finder could find for the plaintiff. We will consider after *Galloway* the less typical situation of a plaintiff's seeking and receiving a directed verdict or "judgment as a matter of law."

As the new version of Fed. R. Civ. P. 50 puts it, in cases tried before a jury, if a claim cannot be maintained without a party's having "a legally sufficient evidentiary basis for a jury to have found for that party with respect to that issue," and if such evidence was not presented—and if the party has been fully heard with respect to that issue—then the court "may grant a motion for judgment as a matter of law" on that claim.

Fed. R. Civ. P. 50(a)(1). Re-read Fed. R. Civ. P. 50(a)(1), and challenge yourself to try to understand the actual language of the newly amended rule.

As the new rule is worded, a party may move for judgment as a matter of law at any time before submission to the jury. Fed. R. Civ. P. 50(a)(2). According to the Advisory Committee Notes on the amendment, this means that a judge could, for instance, require a plaintiff to introduce all of her evidence on a necessary element early in a case (such as duty or un-reasonable care in a negligence case) and then, prior to the plaintiff's resting on the entire case, permit the defendant to move for judgment as a matter of law on the grounds of insufficient evidence on the one ele-ment. Please read the Advisory Committee Notes on the 1991 amend-ments to the Federal Rules to discover why the language was changed from "directed verdict" to "judgment as a matter of law," even though the Advisory Committee hastened to add that the new rule "effects no change in the existing standard" that has been "articulated in long-standing case law."

As you think about the dissenters' position in *Galloway*, that there has been a gradual erosion in civil cases involving the Seventh Amendment right to jury trial, consider whether the amendments to Rule 50 continue that erosion. For instance, what effect does the parties' ability to move for "judgment as a matter of law" any time before submission to the jury have on the right to (or quality of) jury trial? Compare the language to the previous rendition of Fed. R. Civ. P. 50(a).

The concept of "sufficiency of evidence to permit a finding on an ele-ment of the case" (put another way, the idea of a "production burden") is also applicable in cases without a jury. For instance, if in a Title VII case without a jury the plaintiff had no evidence of discrimination (either through adverse impact or adverse treatment), then it would not make sense to force the defendant to present evidence or for the judge to hear it. Rule 52(c) covers this situation, and permits the judge to enter judg-ment as a matter of law against a party on a claim that the party cannot win, so long as that party "has been fully heard with respect to" the issue that cannot be won, and that is dispositive of the case.

Notice that Rule 52(c), which deals with actions without a jury, does not use the Rule 50(a) language about "legally sufficient evidentiary basis." Can you see why? Assume in *Carpenter*, for example, that the parties chose to try the case on a jury-waived basis. Assume further that the plain-tiff introduced evidence that would be sufficient to permit a finding of unreasonable care against Ultimate Auto, the retailer, but that the judge does not believe the plaintiff's evidence, and the judge knows this even before the defendant has put on any evidence of its own. Could the judge enter judgment as a matter of law against the plaintiff, even though she could not have done so had there been a jury? Does the difference in language between Rules 50(a) and 52(c) make sense? In both jury cases and nonjury cases, could the plaintiff achieve a judgment as a matter of law prior to the defendant's having an opportunity to put on its case?

4. Judgment Notwithstanding the Verdict
   (Judgment n.o.v./Judgment as a Matter of Law)

Even after the jury has rendered a verdict, a judge—having previously denied a directed verdict motion on the same grounds—can grant the party against whom the judgment was rendered a judgment notwithstanding the verdict. The test is identical to that of directed verdict (or the test for judgment as a matter of law, under Fed. R. Civ. P. 50(a)). For the federal rendition of this concept, *see* Fed. R. Civ. P. 50(b).

Consider a simple motor vehicle negligence case. Assume the plaintiff, a pedestrian, has introduced its evidence, and rested. The defendant, driver of a car, moves for directed verdict on the ground that there is insufficient evidence for the jury to find for the plaintiff on the element of unreasonable care. The judge may think the defendant is correct about the insufficiency of evidence, and be tempted to grant the motion, but remain uncertain. Since it is a close question—for example, one based on the inferences that can be drawn from a skid mark—the judge thinks that an appellate court may disagree. Can you see two reasons why it may make sense for the judge to deny the initial motion for directed verdict, and, then, if the jury finds for the plaintiff, grant the motion for judgment n.o.v.? If you need help, or just want to check your instincts, the Advisory Committee Notes to the 1991 amendments to Fed. R. Civ. P. 50(b) discuss this issue.

Reread the Seventh Amendment to the United States Constitution carefully, concentrating on the language about "no fact tried by a jury," and you will see why judgment n.o.v. was constitutionally problematic. (Judgment n.o.v. is shorthand for a somewhat different common law motion which, using Latin, was *called judgment non-obstante veredicto.)* The motion was held unconstitutional by a bare majority in *Slocum v. New York Insurance Co.*, 228 U.S. 364 (1913). In *Baltimore & Carolina Line, Inc. v. Redman*, 295 U.S. 654 (1935), the Court allowed such a motion in a case in which the trial judge had reserved decision on the directed verdict motion until after the verdict was rendered. The Court seized upon the "reservation" to distinguish *Slocum*. The original drafters of the Federal Rules went one step further in Fed. R. Civ. P. 52(b) and said that if a party seeks directed verdict at the close of *all* of the evidence and it is denied or not granted, "the court is deemed to have submitted the action to the jury subject to a later determination of the legal questions raised by the motion." This fiction, which also remains in the current version, has been held sufficient to render the Rule and the practice constitutional. *Neely v. Martin K. Eby Construction Co.*, 386 U.S. 317, 321 (1967).

Courts have affirmed the requirement that a party move for directed verdict at the close of all of the evidence in order to bring a motion for judgment n.o.v. *See* 9A Charles A. Wright & Arthur R. Miller, *Federal Practice and Procedure* §2537. When such motions are plausible (remembering the applicability of Rule 11 to motions as a result of Rule 7(b)(3)), defense counsel normally moves for directed verdict after the plaintiff rests, and then, if denied, again after all parties rest. In all motions under Fed. R. Civ. P. 50, Rule 50(a)(2) requires the moving party "to specify the judgment sought and the law and the facts on which the moving party is entitled to the judgment." In federal court, Fed. R. Civ. P. 7(b)(1) mandates which motions must be in writing. Read the Rule to see whether motions in federal court for directed verdict or judgment n.o.v. must be in writing.

5. Motions for New Trial

Even after the jury renders its verdict (or a judge without a jury, for that matter), the losing side can still move for a new trial. *See* Fed. R. Civ. P. 59(a)(1) and (a)(2). In fact, in federal court, pursuant to Rule 59(d), the judge is explicitly empowered to grant a new trial on the judge's own initiative. Students often find the notion of new trial motions the "straw that breaks the camel's back" when it comes to judicial control of juries. But before you draw that conclusion, give it some thought.

Consider first the language of the Rule itself, which says that a new trial may be granted in jury cases "for any of the reasons for which new trials have heretofore been granted in actions at law in the courts of the United States." Fed. R. Civ. P. 59(a)(1). Many states have similar language, although the state rule would instead look to the historic practice in the courts of the state in question. Other states, by statute or rule, list the grounds for new trial motions; but these are often quite similar to the grounds that would be permissible in federal court or in a state that merely looks to precedents.

One type of new trial motion should not be problematic at all. Assume that after the jury has rendered its verdict (or even during a case), a judge becomes convinced that she has made a mistake that would be reversible error if considered by an appellate court, and that there is no way to correct the error. Say, for instance, the judge realizes after the jury has rendered its verdict and has been released that she mistakenly admitted evidence over correct objection, and that this was not "harmless" within the meaning of Fed. R. Civ. P. 61. Or assume that she was incorrect in her charge to the jury in a material way, even though the losing party had tried to save the court from error by complying with Fed. R. Civ. P. 51 ("Instruction to Jury; Objection"). If the losing party moves for a new trial on grounds for which an appellate court would grant a new trial on appeal, then surely it makes sense for the new trial to be granted by the trial judge if she is now aware of the reversible error. Would not any other solution be wasteful, if not cruel, because it would force parties into the time, expense, and anxiety of an appeal in which the result is known? We realize that it is rare that a trial judge will be sure she has committed reversible error, but, nonetheless, trial judges should (and thus likely do) try to do justice by granting new trials when they are fairly certain an appellate court would do the same.

Perhaps a bit more problematic, but nonetheless well-established law in many jurisdictions, is the granting of new trial motions on grounds that the a jury verdict is so excessive or inadequate as to demonstrate that the jury has misunderstood their duty or acted with extreme prejudice. The situation is most clear when the damages are liquidated, as in a written contract case with a specified monetary amount, and the jury finds for the plaintiff in an amount unrelated to the contractual provision. A tort verdict that contains an amount for "pain and suffering" or "disfigurement" is by its very nature discretionary. Consequently, the grant of a new trial because of the excessiveness or inadequacy of the award has a discretionary element. But even here, some awards would to most reasonable people seem "unsupported by the evidence." Consider a negligently caused scratch, without any sign of malice or realistically increased risk to the plaintiff, which results in a multimillion dollar award. Shouldn't a trial judge, who, like the jury, has taken an oath to do justice, grant a new trial? The courts are not in agreement on how far appellate courts should exercise authority over trial courts in granting or denying motions for a new trial based on the amount of damages.

Later, we will take up other questions related to damages and jury control, such as whether a judge can threaten to grant a new trial unless the plaintiff agrees to take less money (*remittitur*) or unless the defendant agrees to pay more (*additur*). Also can a trial, or a new trial, appropriately be held on only damages, if the judge believes the jury was right on liability but wrong on damages? We will also consider new trial motions on the grounds of "jury misconduct." Here again, even the most enthusiastic proponent of civil juries would want some judicial control. Thus, "[d]runkenness of a juror, bribery, private communication with a party, improper remarks made in the juror's presence by a court officer or other outsider, the consulting of documents not in evidence, and the like, are sufficient grounds for setting aside a verdict. (citations omitted)" Flemming James Jr., Geoffrey Hazard, & John Leubsdorf, *Civil Procedure* §7.27 at 389 (4th ed. 1992).

More difficult questions arise when the alleged jury misconduct relates to the deliberative process of the jury. For example, should a verdict be set aside because a juror incorrectly remembered the testimony of a witness or misinterpreted the judge's instructions, although one could not infer these mistakes by examining the verdict? Such examples, which reflect the imperfection of human beings and social structures rather than perversion of the entire process, are usually handled by evidentiary rules that protect against intrusion into the jury's deliberations while at the same time admitting evidence of gross misconduct.

Let's consider several compelling policy issues. If lawyers, and then judges, were permitted to delve frequently and deeply into the deliberation of jurors, then perhaps few jury verdicts could stand. It is unlikely that twelve or six people could behave perfectly, hard as they might try. (Of course, the same could be said of a judge acting alone.) Indeed, if it were easy to attack jury verdicts because of faults in the deliberations, and if all that is said in the jury room were made admissible through the testimony of jurors, then (1) an attorney who has lost a case would feel obligated to question each juror at length, and (2) some jurors would not want to speak (or at least not say what they think) during deliberations. This would create real potential for juror silence during deliberations, and for juror harassment after verdict. (This leaves aside those intrusions on the jury, such as bribery or private conversations with one of the parties, that already are clearly forbidden and certainly should be.)

The Federal Rules of Evidence provide one attempt to find a healthy balance on this issue. This federal solution incorporates much of the common law rule that a jury verdict cannot be impeached by the testimony of the jurors themselves, but tries to draw a line between the normal deliberative process and unfair external intrusions upon it:

> Fed. R. Evid. 606(b) *Inquiry into the validity of verdict or indictment.* Upon an inquiry into the validity of a verdict or indictment, a juror may not testify as to any matter or statement occurring during the course of the jury's deliberations or to the effect of anything upon that or any other juror's mind or emotions as influencing the juror to assent to or dissent from the verdict or indictment or concerning the juror's mental processes in connection therewith, except that a juror may testify on the question whether extraneous prejudicial information was improperly brought to the jury's attention or whether any outside influence was improperly brought to bear upon any juror. Nor may a juror's affidavit or evidence of any statement by the juror concerning a matter about which the juror be precluded from testifying be received for these purposes.

Sometimes, behavior by the jury as a whole seems reprehensible but does not involve external influence. For example, Professors Hazard, James, and Leubsdorf describe the cases of "reaching of a verdict by flipping a coin, agreeing to abide by the vote of a majority when a unanimous verdict is required, and averaging the sums put down by each juror (the quotient verdict)." Flemming James, Jr., Geoffrey Hazard, & John Leubsdorf, *Civil Procedure* §7.27 at 389, 390. Courts disagree about how to handle these improprieties. One solution is to treat the behavior as substantive grounds for a new trial, but, in keeping with Fed. R. Evid. 606(b), to permit the behavior to be proven only by competent evidence other than the testimony of the jurors themselves. Such testimony might be given by an eavesdropper or a court official who finds a document in the jury room that indicates a quotient verdict.

Finally, we have arrived at the motion for new trial that you may find the most problematic: a motion for a new trial on the grounds that the verdict "is against the weight of the evidence." In federal courts, and in most state courts, the losing attorney can appeal to the discretion of the trial judge to grant a new trial motion, *not* because there is insufficient evidence to support the jury verdict (that is, the directed verdict or judgment n.o.v. standard), but because the verdict is clearly wrong: the jury made a horrible mistake; there has been a gross miscarriage of justice. We will later raise issues about this motion after you have read *Galloway*, but before forming your opinion, consider the words of one state supreme court judge:

> The authority of the common pleas in the control and revision of excessive verdicts through the means of new trials was firmly settled in England before the foundation of this colony, and has always existed here without challenge under any of our constitutions. It is a power to examine the whole case on the law and the evidence, with a view to securing a result, not merely legal, but also not manifestly against justice, without which the jury system would be a capricious and intolerable tyranny, which no people could long endure. This court has had occasion more than once recently to say that it was a power the courts ought to exercise unflinchingly.

Smith v. Times Publishing Co., 178 Pa. 481 (1897).

In *Aetna Casualty & Surety Co. v. Yeatts*, 122 F.2d 350 (4th Cir. 1941), which relies on the above quote, Judge Parker stated the position of most state and federal courts on the motion for a new trial on the ground that the verdict is *against the weight of the evidence*:

> On such a motion it is the duty of the trial judge to set aside the verdict and grant a new trial, if he is of the opinion that the verdict is against the clear weight of the evidence, or is based upon evidence that is false, or will result in a miscarriage of justice, even though there may be substantial evidence which would prevent the direction of a verdict.

Most appellate courts, including the federal, tend to leave this motion to the discretion of the trial judge, and almost always refuse to upset either the grant or the denial of the motion. It seems clear that the motion is brought far more often than it is allowed. Moreover, it is rare that a party loses the same jury case twice and is granted yet a third jury trial on successive motions that call upon the judge to exercise this discretionary power.

If you were a judge, under what circumstances would you grant a motion for a new trial on the ground that the verdict is against the weight of the evidence? Do you think the judge should be required to state the reasons for granting such a motion? When denying such a motion? (Judges frequently deny or grant these motions, like other motions, without explanation.)

This would be a logical place to introduce you to motions to *vacate judgment* (Fed. R. Civ. P. 60), for such motions permit the correction of error in much the same way as motions for a new trial, except they usually are filed later. For pedagogical reasons, however, it makes more sense for you to now read *Galloway*, which is more directly related to directed verdict and the common law motion for a new trial. We will cover Rule 60 at the end of the comments.

6. Directed Verdict, Judgment n.o.v., and New Trial Motions in More Detail

■ GALLOWAY V. UNITED STATES
319 U.S. 372 (1943)

Justice RUTLEDGE delivered the opinion of the Court:

Petitioner seeks benefits for total and permanent disability by reason of insanity he claims existed May 31, 1919. On that day his policy of yearly renewable term insurance lapsed for nonpayment of premium.

The suit was filed June 15, 1938. At the close of all the evidence the District Court granted the Government's motion for a directed verdict. Judgment was entered accordingly. The Circuit Court of Appeals affirmed. Both courts held the evidence legally insufficient to sustain a verdict for petitioner. He says this was erroneous and, in effect, deprived him of trial by jury, contrary to the Seventh Amendment.

The constitutional argument, as petitioner has made it, does not challenge generally the power of federal courts to withhold or withdraw from the jury cases in which the claimant puts forward insufficient evidence to support a verdict. The contention is merely that his case as made was substantial, the courts' decisions to the contrary were wrong, and therefore their effect has been to deprive him of a jury trial. . . . [T]he only question is whether the evidence was sufficient to sustain a verdict for petitioner. On that basis, we think the judgments must be affirmed.

I

Certain facts are undisputed. Petitioner worked as a longshoreman in Philadelphia and elsewhere prior to enlistment in the Army November 1, 1917. [The record does not show whether this employment was steady and continuous or was spotty and erratic. But there is no contention that petitioner's behavior was abnormal before he arrived in France in April, 1918.] He became a cook in a machine gun battalion. His unit arrived in France in April, 1918. He served actively until September 24. From then to the following January he was in a hospital with influenza. He then returned to active duty. He came back to the United States, and received honorable discharge April 29, 1919. He enlisted in the Navy January 15, 1920, and was discharged for bad conduct in July. The following December he again enlisted in the Army and served until May, 1922, when he deserted. Thereafter he was carried on the Army records as a deserter.

In 1930 began a series of medical examinations by Veterans' Bureau physicians. On May 19 that year his condition was diagnosed as "Moron, low grade; observation, dementia praecox, simple type." In November, 1931, further examination gave the diagnosis, "Psychosis with other diseases or conditions (organic disease of the central nervous system—type undetermined)." In July, 1934, still another examination was made, with diagnosis: "Psychosis manic and depressive insanity incompetent; hypertension, moderate; otitis media, chronic, left; varicose veins left, mild; abscessed teeth roots; myocarditis, mild."

Petitioner's wife, the nominal party in this suit, was appointed guardian of his person and estate in February, 1932. Claim for insurance benefits was made in June, 1934, and was finally denied by the Board of Veterans' Appeals in January, 1936. This suit followed two and a half years later.

Petitioner concededly is now totally and permanently disabled by reason of insanity and has been for some time prior to institution of this suit. It is conceded also that he was sound in mind and body until he arrived in France in April, 1918.

The theory of his case is that the strain of active service abroad brought on an immediate change, which was the beginning of a mental breakdown that has grown worse continuously through all the later years. Essential in this is the view it had become a total and permanent disability not later than May 31, 1919.

The evidence to support this theory falls naturally into three periods, namely, that prior to 1923; the interval from then to 1930; and that following 1930. It consists in proof of incidents occurring in France to show the beginnings of change; testimony of changed appearance and behavior in the years immediately following petitioner's return to the United States as compared with those prior to his departure; the medical evidence of insanity accumulated in the years following 1930; and finally the evidence of a physician, given largely as medical opinion, which seeks to tie all the other evidence together as foundation for the conclusion, expressed as of 1941, that petitioner's disability was total and permanent as of a time not later than May of 1919.

Documentary exhibits included military, naval and Veterans' Bureau records. Testimony was given by deposition or at the trial chiefly by five witnesses. One, O'Neill, was a fellow worker and friend from boyhood; two, Wells and Tanikawa, served with petitioner overseas; Lt. Col. Albert K. Mathews, who was an Army chaplain, observed him or another person of the same name at an Army hospital in California during early 1920; and Dr. Wilder, a physician, examined him shortly before the trial and supplied the only expert testimony in his behalf. The petitioner also put into evidence the depositions of Commander Platt and Lt. Col. James E. Matthews, his superior officers in the Navy and the Army, respectively, during 1920-22.

What happened in France during 1918-19 is shown chiefly by Wells and Tanikawa. Wells testified to an incident at Aisonville, where the unit was billeted shortly after reaching France and before going into action. Late at night petitioner created a disturbance, "hollering, screeching, swearing. . . . The men poured out from the whole section." Wells did not see the incident, but heard petitioner swearing at his superior officers and saw "the result, a black eye for Lt. Warner." However, he did not see "who gave it to him." Wells personally observed no infraction of discipline except this incident, and did not know what brought it on. Petitioner's physical appearance was good, he "carried on his duties as a cook all right," and the witness did not see him after June 1, except for about three days in July when he observed petitioner several times at work feeding stragglers.

Tanikawa, Hawaiian-born citizen, served with petitioner from the latter's enlistment until September, 1918, when Galloway was hospitalized, although the witness thought they had fought together and petitioner was "acting queer" at the Battle of the Argonne in October. At Camp Greene, North Carolina, petitioner was "just a regular soldier, very normal, . . . pretty neat." After reaching France "he was getting nervous . . . , kind of irritable, always picking a fight with other soldier." This began at Aisonville. Tanikawa saw Galloway in jail, apparently before June. It is not clear whether these are references to the incident Wells described.

Tanikawa described another incident in June "when we were on the Marne," the Germans "were on the other side and we were on this side." It was a new front, without trenches. The witness and petitioner were on guard duty with others. Tanikawa understood the Germans were getting ready for a big drive. "One night he (petitioner) screamed. He said, 'The Germans are coming' and we all gagged him." There was no shooting, the Germans were not coming, and there was nothing to lead the witness to believe they were. Petitioner was court martialed for the matter, but Tanikawa did not know "what they did with him." He did not talk with Galloway that night, because "he was out of his mind" and appeared insane. Tanikawa did not know when petitioner left the battalion or what happened to him after (as the witness put it) the Argonne fight, but heard he went to the hospital, "just dressing station I guess." The witness next saw Galloway in 1936, at a disabled veterans' post meeting in Sacramento, California. Petitioner then "looked to me like he wasn't all there. Insane.

About the same . . . as compared to the way he acted in France, particularly when they gagged him. . . ."

O'Neill was "born and raised with" petitioner, worked with him as a longshoreman, and knew him "from when he come out of the army for seven years, . . . I would say five or six years." When petitioner returned in April or May, 1919, "he was a wreck compared to what he was when he went away. The fellow's mind was evidently unbalanced." Symptoms specified were withdrawing to himself; crying spells; alternate periods of normal behavior and nonsensical talk; expression of fears that good friends wanted "to beat him up"; spitting blood and remarking about it in vulgar terms. Once petitioner said, "G—d—it, I must be a Doctor Jekyll and Mr. Hyde."

O'Neill testified these symptoms and this condition continued practically the same for about five years. In his opinion petitioner was "competent at times and others was incompetent." The intervals might be "a couple of days, a couple of months." In his normal periods Galloway "would be his old self . . . absolutely O.K."

O'Neill was definite in recalling petitioner's condition and having seen him frequently in 1919, chiefly however, and briefly, on the street during lunch hour. He was not sure Galloway was working and was "surprised he got in the Navy, I think in the Navy or in the Government service."

O'Neill maintained he saw petitioner "right on from that (1920) at times." But his recollection of dates, number of opportunities for observation, and concrete events was wholly indefinite. He would fix no estimate for the number of times he had seen petitioner: "In 1920 I couldn't recall whether it was one or a thousand." For later years he would not say whether it was "five times or more or less." When he was pinned down by cross-examination, the effect of his testimony was that he recalled petitioner clearly in 1919 "because there was such a vast contrast in the man," but for later years he could give little or no definite information. [The Court reprinted the following excerpt from the testimony in a footnote:

"X Can you tell us approximately how many times you saw him in 1919?" "A. No; I seen him so often that it would be hard to give any estimate." "X And the same goes for 1920?" "A. I wouldn't be sure about 1920. I remember him more when he first came home because there was such a vast contrast in the man. Otherwise, if nothing unusual happened, I wouldn't probably recall him at all, you know, that is, recall the particular time and all." "X Well, do you recall him at all in 1920?" "A. I can't say." "X And could you swear whether or not you ever saw him in 1921?" "A. I think I seen him both in 1921 and 1920 and 1921 and right on. I might not see him for a few weeks or months at a time, but I think I saw him a few times in all the years right up to, as I say, at least five years after." "X Can you give us an estimate as to the number of times you saw him in 1920?" "A. No, I would not." "X Was it more than five times or less?" "A. In 1920 I couldn't recall whether it was one or a thousand. The time I recall him well is when he first come home, but I know that I seen him right on from that at times." "X And the same goes for 1921, 1922, 1923 and 1924?" "A. I would say for five years afterwards, but I don't know just when or how often I seen him except when he first come home for the first couple of months." "X But for years after his return you couldn't say definitely whether you saw him five times or more or less, could you?" "A. No, because it was a thing that there was a vast contrast when he first come home and everybody noticed it and remarked about it and it was more liable to be remembered. You could ask me about some more friends I knew during those years and I wouldn't know except there was something unusual." [The Court further noted that "Petitioner's own evidence shows without dispute he was on active duty in the Navy from January 15, 1920, to July of that year and in the Army from December, 1920, to May 6, 1922. As is noted in the text, O'Neill was not sure he was working and 'was surprised he got in the Navy, I think in the Navy or in the Government service.' He only 'heard some talk' of petitioner's having reenlisted in the Army, but 'if it was the fact, I would be surprised that he could do it owing to his mental condition.' O'Neill was not certain that he saw Galloway in uniform after the first week of his return to Philadelphia from overseas, although he said he saw petitioner during 'the periods of those reenlistments . . . but I can't recall about it.'"] O'Neill recalled one specific occasion after 1919 when petitioner returned to Philadelphia, "around 1920 or 1921, but I couldn't be sure," to testify in a criminal proceeding. He also said, "After he was away for five or six years, he came back to Philadelphia, but I wouldn't know nothing about dates on that. He was back in Philadelphia for five or six months or so, and he was still just evidently all right, and then he would be off."]

Lt. Col. (Chaplain) Mathews said he observed a Private Joseph Galloway, who was a prisoner for desertion and a patient in the mental ward at Fort MacArthur Station Hospital, California, during a six weeks period early in 1920. The chaplain's testimony gives strong evidence the man he observed was insane. However, there is a fatal weakness in this evidence. In his direct testimony, which was taken by deposition, the chaplain said he was certain that the soldier was petitioner. When confronted with the undisputed fact that petitioner was on active duty in the Navy during the first half of 1920, the witness at first stated that he might have been mistaken as to the time of his observation. Subsequently he reasserted the accuracy of his original statement as to the time of observation, but admitted that he might have been mistaken in believing that the patient-prisoner was petitioner. In this connection he volunteered the statement, "Might I add, sir, that I could not now identify that soldier if I were to meet him face to face, and that is because of the long lapse of time." The patient whom the witness saw was confined to his bed. The record is barren of other evidence, whether by the hospital's or the Army's records or otherwise, to show that petitioner was either patient or prisoner at Fort MacArthur in 1920 or at any other time.

Commander Platt testified that petitioner caused considerable trouble by disobedience and leaving ship without permission during his naval service in the first half of 1920. After "repeated warnings and punishments, leading to court martials," he was sentenced to a bad conduct discharge.

Lt. Col. James E. Matthews (not the chaplain) testified by deposition which petitioner's attorney interrupted Dr. Wilder's testimony to read into evidence. The witness was Galloway's commanding officer from early 1921 to the summer of that year, when petitioner was transferred with other soldiers to another unit. At first Colonel Matthews considered making petitioner a corporal, but found him unreliable and had to discipline him. Petitioner "drank considerably," was "what we called a bolshevik," did not seem loyal, and "acted as if he was not getting a square deal." The officer concluded "he was a moral pervert and probably used narcotics," but could not secure proof of this. Galloway was court martialed for public drunkenness and disorderly conduct, served a month at hard labor, and returned to active duty. At times he "was one of the very best soldiers I had," at others undependable. He was physically sound, able to do his work, perform close order drill, etc., "very well." He had alternate periods of gaiety and depression, talked incoherently at times, gave the impression he would fight readily, but did not resent orders and seemed to get along well with other soldiers. The officer attributed petitioner's behavior to alcohol and narcotics and it occurred to him at no time to question his sanity.

Dr. Wilder was the key witness. He disclaimed specializing in mental disease, but qualified as having given it "special attention." He first saw petitioner shortly before the trial, examined him "several times." He concluded petitioner's ailment "is a schizophrenic branch or form of praecox." Dr. Wilder heard the testimony and read the depositions of the other witnesses, and examined the documentary evidence. Basing his judgment upon this material, with inferences drawn from it, he concluded petitioner was born with "an inherent instability," though he remained normal until he went to France; began there "to be subjected to the strain of military life, then he began to go to pieces." In May, 1919, petitioner "was still suffering from the acuteness of the breakdown. . . . He is going down hill still, but the thing began with the breakdown. . . ." Petitioner was "definitely insane, yes, sir," in 1920 and "has been insane at all times, at least since July, 1918, the time of this episode on the Marne"; that is, "to the point that he was unable to adapt himself. I don't mean he has not had moments when he could not perform some routine tasks," but "from an occupational standpoint . . . he has been insane." He could follow "a mere matter of routine," but would have no incentive, would not keep a steady job, come to work on time, or do anything he didn't want to do. Dr. Wilder pointed to petitioner's work record before he entered the service and observed: "At no time after he went into the war do we find him able to hold any kind of a job. He broke right down." He explained petitioner's enlistment in the Navy and later in the Army by saying, "It would have been no trick at all *for a man who was reasonably conforming* to get into the Service." (Emphasis added.)

However, the witness knew "nothing whatever except his getting married" about petitioner's activities between 1925 and 1930, and what he knew of them between 1922 and 1925 was based entirely on O'Neill's testimony and a paper not of record here. Dr. Wilder at first regarded knowledge concerning what petitioner was doing between 1925 and 1930 as not essential. "We have a continuing disease, quite obviously beginning during his military service, and quite obviously continuing in 1930, and the minor incidents don't seem to me. . . ." Counsel for the government interrupted to inquire, "Well, if he was continuously employed for eight hours a day from 1925 to 1930 would that have any bearing?" The witness replied, "It would have a great deal." Upon further questioning, however, he reverted to his first position, stating it would not be necessary or helpful for him to know what petitioner was doing from 1925 to 1930: "I testified from the information I had."

II

This, we think, is the crux of the case and distinguishes it from the cases on which petitioner has relied. His burden was to prove total and permanent disability as of a date not later than May 31, 1919. He has undertaken to do this by showing incipience of mental disability shortly before that time and its continuance and progression throughout the succeeding years. He has clearly established incidence of total and permanent disability as of some period prior to 1938, when he began this suit. For our purposes this may be taken as medically established by the Veterans' Bureau examination and diagnosis of July, 1934.

But if the record is taken to show that some form of mental disability existed in 1930, which later became total and permanent, petitioner's problem remains to demonstrate by more than speculative inference that this condition itself began on or before May 31, 1919 and continuously existed or progressed through the intervening years to 1930.

To show origin before the crucial date, he gives evidence of two abnormal incidents occurring while he was in France, one creating the disturbance before he came near the fighting front, the other yelling that the Germans were coming when he was on guard duty at the Marne. There is no other evidence of abnormal behavior during his entire service of more than a year abroad.

That he was court martialed for these sporadic acts and bound and gagged for one does not prove he was insane or had then a general breakdown in "an already fragile mental constitution," which the vicissitudes of a longshoreman's life had not been able to crack.

To these two incidents petitioner adds the testimony of O'Neill that he looked and acted like a wreck, compared with his former self, when he returned from France about a month before the crucial date, and O'Neill's vague recollections that this condition continued through the next two, three, four or five years.

O'Neill's testimony apparently takes no account of petitioner's having spent 101 days in a hospital in France with influenza just before he came home. But, given the utmost credence, as is required, it does no more than show that petitioner was subject to alternating periods of gaiety and depression for some indefinite period after his return, extending perhaps as late as 1922. But because of its vagueness as to time, dates, frequency of opportunity for observation, and specific incident, O'Neill's testimony concerning the period from 1922 to 1925 is hardly more than speculative.

We have then the two incidents in France followed by O'Neill's testimony of petitioner's changed condition in 1919 and its continuance to 1922. There is also the testimony of Commander Platt and Lt. Col. James E. Matthews as to his service in the Navy and the Army, respectively, during 1920-1922. Neither thought petitioner was insane or that his conduct indicated insanity. Then follows a chasm of eight years. The only evidence we have concerning this period is the fact that petitioner married his present guardian at some time within it, an act from which in the legal sense no inference of insanity can be drawn.

This period was eight years of continuous insanity, according to the inference petitioner would be allowed to have drawn. If so, he should have no need of inference. Insanity so long and continuously sustained does not hide itself from the eyes and ears of witnesses. The assiduity which produced the evidence of two "crazy" incidents during a year and a half in France should produce one during eight years or, for that matter, five years in the United States.

Inference is capable of bridging many gaps. But not, in these circumstances, one so wide and deep as this. Knowledge of petitioner's activities and behavior from 1922 or 1925 to 1930 was peculiarly within his ken and that of his wife, who has litigated this cause in his and presumably, though indirectly, in her own behalf. His was the burden to show continuous disability. What he did in this time, or did not do, was vital to his case. Apart from the mere fact of his marriage, the record is blank for five years and almost blank for eight. For all that appears, he may have worked full time and continuously for five and perhaps for eight, with only a possible single interruption.

No favorable inference can be drawn from the omission. It was not one of oversight or inability to secure proof. That is shown by the thoroughness with which the record was prepared for all other periods, before and after this one, and by the fact petitioner's wife, though she married him during the period and was available, did not testify. The only reasonable conclusion is that petitioner, or those who acted for him, deliberately chose, for reasons no doubt considered sufficient (and which we do not criticize, since such matters including tactical ones, are for the judgment of counsel) to present no evidence or perhaps to withhold evidence readily available concerning this long interval, and to trust to the genius of expert medical inference and judicial laxity to bridge this canyon.

In the circumstances exhibited, the former is not equal to the feat, and the latter will not permit it. No case has been cited and none has been found in which inference, however expert, has been permitted to make so broad a leap and take the place of evidence which, according to all reason, must have been at hand. To allow this would permit the substitution of inference, tenuous at best, not merely for evidence absent because impossible or difficult to secure, but for evidence disclosed to be available and not produced. This would substitute speculation for proof. Furthermore, the inference would be more plausible perhaps if the evidence of insanity as of May, 1919, were stronger than it is, such for instance as Chaplain Mathews' testimony would have furnished if it could be taken as applying to petitioner. But, on this record, the evidence of insanity as of that time is thin at best, if it can be regarded as at all more than speculative.

Beyond this, there is nothing to show totality or permanence. These come only by what the Circuit Court of Appeals rightly characterized as "long-range retroactive diagnosis." That might suffice, notwithstanding this crucial inference was a matter of opinion, if there were factual evidence over which the medical eye could travel and find continuity through the intervening years. . . . But eight years are too many to permit it to skip, when the bridgeheads (if the figure may be changed) at each end are no stronger than they are here, and when the seer first denies, then admits, then denies again, that what took place in this time would make "a great deal" of difference in what he saw. Expert medical inference rightly can do much. But we think the feat attempted here too large for its accomplishment. . . .

III

What has been said disposes of the case as the parties have made it. For that reason perhaps nothing more need be said. But objection has been advanced that, in some manner not wholly clear, the directed verdict practice offends the Seventh Amendment.

It may be noted, first, that the Amendment has no application of its own force to this case. The suit is one to enforce a monetary claim against the United States. It hardly can be maintained that under the common law in 1791 jury trial was a matter of right for persons asserting claims against the sovereign. Whatever force the Amendment has therefore is derived because Congress in the legislation cited, has made it applicable. Even so, the objection made on the score of its requirements is untenable.

If the intention is to claim generally that the Amendment deprives the federal courts of power to direct a verdict for insufficiency of evidence, the short answer is the contention has been foreclosed by repeated decisions made here consistently for nearly a century. More recently the practice has been approved explicitly in the promulgation of the Federal Rules of Civil Procedure. *Cf.* Rule 50. The objection therefore comes too late.

Furthermore, the argument from history is not convincing. It is not that "the rules of the common law" in 1791 deprived trial courts of power to withdraw cases from the jury, because not made out, or appellate courts of power to review such determinations. The jury was not absolute master of fact in 1791. Then as now courts excluded evidence for irrelevancy and relevant proof for other reasons. The argument concedes they weighed the evidence, not only piecemeal but in toto for submission to the jury, by at least two procedures, the demurrer to the evidence and the motion for a new trial. The objection is not therefore to the basic thing, which is the power of the court to withhold cases from the jury or set aside the verdict for insufficiency of the evidence. It is rather to incidental or collateral effects, namely, that the directed verdict as now administered differs from both those procedures because, on the one hand, allegedly higher standards of proof are required and, on the other, different consequences follow as to further maintenance of the litigation. Apart from the standards of proof, the argument appears to urge that in 1791, a litigant could challenge his opponent's evidence, either by the demurrer, which when determined ended the litigation, or by motion for a new trial which if successful, gave the adversary another chance to prove his case; and therefore the Amendment excluded any challenge to which one or the other of these consequences does not attach.

The Amendment did not bind the federal courts to the exact procedural incidents or details of jury trial according to the common law in 1791, any more than it tied them to the common-law system of pleading or the specific rules of evidence then prevailing. . . .

Each of the classical modes of challenge [that is, demurrer to the evidence and new trial motions] disproves the notion that the characteristic feature of the other, for effect upon continuing the litigation, became a part of the Seventh Amendment's guaranty to the exclusion of all others. That guaranty did not incorporate conflicting constitutional policies, that challenge to an opposing case must be made with the effect of terminating the litigation finally and, at the same time, with the opposite effect of requiring another trial. Alternatives so contradictory give room, not for the inference that one or the other is required, but rather for the view that neither is essential.

Finally, the objection appears to be directed generally at the standards of proof judges have required for submission of evidence to the jury. . . . Whatever may be the general formulation, the essential requirement is that mere speculation be not allowed to do duty for probative facts, after making due allowance for all reasonably possible inferences favoring the party whose case is attacked. . . . .

Judged by this requirement, or by any standard other than sheer speculation, we are unable to conclude that one whose burden, by the nature of his claim, is to show continuing and total disability for nearly twenty years supplies the essential proof of continuity when he wholly omits to show his whereabouts, activities or condition for five years, although the record discloses evidence must have been available, and, further, throws no light upon three additional years, except for one vaguely described and dated visit to his former home. . . . The words "total and permanent" are the statute's, not our own. They mean something more than incipient or occasional disability. We hardly need add that we give full credence to all of the testimony. But that cannot cure its inherent vagueness or supply essential elements omitted or withheld.

Accordingly, the judgment is Affirmed.

Justice BLACK, with whom Justice DOUGLAS and Justice MURPHY concur, dissenting:

The Seventh Amendment to the Constitution provides:

> In suits at common law, where the value in controversy shall exceed twenty dollars, the right of trial by jury shall be preserved, and no fact tried by a jury shall be otherwise re-examined in any Court of the United States, than according to the rules of the common law.

The Court here re-examines testimony offered in a common law suit, weighs conflicting evidence, and holds that the litigant may never take this case to a jury. The founders of our government thought that trial of fact by juries rather than by judges was an essential bulwark of civil liberty. For this reason, among others, they adopted Article III, §2 of the Constitution, and the Sixth and Seventh Amendments. Today's decision marks a continuation of the gradual process of judicial erosion which in one hundred fifty years has slowly worn away a major portion of the essential guarantee of the Seventh Amendment.

I

. . . In 1789, juries occupied the principal place in the administration of justice. They were frequently in both criminal and civil cases the arbiters not only of fact but of law. Less than three years after the ratification of the Seventh Amendment, this Court called a jury in a civil case brought under our original jurisdiction. There was no disagreement as to the facts of the case. Chief Justice Jay, charging the jury for a unanimous Court, three of whose members had sat in the Constitutional Convention, said: "For as, on the one hand, it is presumed, that juries are the best judges of facts; it is, on the other hand, presumable, that the court[s] are the best judges of law. But still, both objects are lawfully within your power of decision." *State of Georgia v. Brailsford*, 3 Dall. 1, 4, 1 L. Ed. 483. Similar views were held by state courts in Connecticut, Massachusetts, Illinois, Louisiana and presumably elsewhere. . . .

As Hamilton had declared in The Federalist, the basic judicial control of the jury function was in the court's power to order a new trial. In 1830, this Court said: "The only modes known to the common law to re-examine such facts, are the granting of a new trial by the court where the issue was tried, or to which the record was properly returnable; or the award of a venire facias de novo, by an appellate court, for some error of law which intervened in the proceedings." *Parsons v. Bedford, supra*, 3 Pet. at page 448, 7 L. Ed. 732. That retrial by a new jury rather than factual reevaluation by a court is a constitutional right of genuine value was restated as recently as *Slocum v. New York Life Insurance Co.*, 228 U.S. 364.

A long step toward the determination of fact by judges instead of by juries was the invention of the directed verdict. In 1850, what seems to have been the first directed verdict case considered by this Court, *Parks v. Ross*, 11 How. 362, 374, was presented for decision. The Court held that the directed verdict serves the same purpose as the demurrer to the evidence, and that since there was "no evidence whatever" on the critical issue in the case, the directed verdict was approved. The decision was an innovation, a departure from the traditional rule restated only fifteen years before in *Greenleaf v. Birth*, 1835, 9 Pet. 292, 299, in which this Court had said: "Where there is no evidence tending to prove a particular fact, the court[s] are bound so to instruct the jury, when requested; but they cannot legally give any instruction which shall take from the jury the right of weighing the evidence and determining what effect it shall have."

This new device contained potentialities for judicial control of the jury which had not existed in the demurrer to the evidence. In the first place, demurring to the evidence was risky business, for in so doing the party not only admitted the truth of all the testimony against him but also all reasonable inferences which might be drawn from it; and upon joinder in demurrer the case was withdrawn from the jury while the court proceeded to give final judgment either for or against the demurrant. Imposition of this risk was no mere technicality; for by making withdrawal of a case from the jury dangerous to the moving litigant's cause, the early law went far to assure that facts would never be examined except by a jury. Under the directed verdict practice the moving party takes no such chance, for if his motion is denied, instead of suffering a directed verdict against him, his case merely continues into the hands of the jury. The litigant not only takes no risk by a motion for a directed verdict, but in making such a motion gives himself two opportunities to avoid the jury's decision; for under the federal variant of judgment notwithstanding the verdict, the judge may reserve opinion on the motion for a directed verdict and then give judgment for the moving party after the jury was formally found against him. In the second place, under the directed verdict practice the courts soon abandoned the "admission of all facts and reasonable inferences" standard referred to, and created the so-called "substantial evidence" rule which permitted directed verdicts even though there was far more evidence in the case than a plaintiff would have needed to withstand a demurrer.

The substantial evidence rule did not spring into existence immediately upon the adoption of the directed verdict device. For a few more years federal judges held to the traditional rule that juries might pass finally on facts if there was "any evidence" to support a party's contention. The rule that a case must go to the jury unless there was "no evidence" was completely repudiated in *Schuylkill and Dauphin Improvement Co. v. Munson*, 14 Wall. 442, 447, 448 (1871), upon which the Court today relies in part. There the Court declared that "some" evidence was not enough—there must be evidence sufficiently persuasive to the judge so that he thinks "a jury can properly proceed." The traditional rule was given an ugly name, "the scintilla rule," to hasten its demise.

Later cases permitted the development of added judicial control. New and totally unwarranted formulas, which should surely be eradicated from the law at the first opportunity, were added as recently as 1929 in *Gunning v. Cooley*, 281 U.S. 90, which, by sheerest dictum, made new encroachments on the jury's constitutional functions. There it was announced that a judge might weigh the evidence to determine whether he, and not the jury, thought it was "overwhelming" for either party, and then direct a verdict. [The case] also suggests quite unnecessarily for its decision, that "When a plaintiff produces evidence that is consistent with an hypothesis that the defendant is not negligent, and also with one that he is, his proof tends to establish neither." This dictum . . . assumes that a judge can weigh conflicting evidence with mathematical precision and which wholly deprives the jury of the right to resolve that conflict. . . . With it, and other tools, jury verdicts on disputed facts have been set aside or directed verdicts authorized so regularly as to make the practice commonplace while the motion for directed verdict itself has become routine. . . .

Even *Gunning v. Cooley*, 281 U.S. at page 94, acknowledged that "issues that depend on the credibility of witnesses . . . are to be decided by the jury." Today the Court comes dangerously close to weighing the credibility of a witness and rejecting his testimony because the majority do not believe it.

The story thus briefly told depicts the constriction of a constitutional civil right and should not be continued. . . .

The language of the Seventh Amendment cannot easily be improved by formulas. The statement of a district judge in *Tarter v. United States*, D.C., 17 F. Supp. 691, 692, 693, represents, in my opinion, the minimum meaning of the Seventh Amendment:

The Seventh Amendment to the Constitution guarantees a jury trial in law cases, where there is substantial evidence to support the claim of the plaintiff in an action. If a single witness testifies to a fact sustaining the issue between the parties, or if reasoning minds might reach different conclusions from the testimony of a single witness, one of which would substantially support the issue of the contending party, the issue must be left to the jury. Trial by jury is a fundamental guaranty of the rights of the people, and judges should not search the evidence with meticulous care to deprive litigants of jury trials.

The call for the true application of the Seventh Amendment is not to words, but to the spirit of honest desire to see that Constitutional right preserved. Either the judge or the jury must decide facts and to the extent that we take this responsibility, we lessen the jury function. Our duty to preserve this one of the Bill of Rights may be peculiarly difficult, for here it is our own power which we must restrain . . . . As for myself, I believe that a verdict should be directed, if at all, only when, without weighing the credibility of the witnesses, there is in the evidence no room whatever for honest difference of opinion over the factual issue in controversy . . . .

II

The factual issue for determination here is whether the petitioner incurred a total and permanent disability not later than May 31, 1919. It is undisputed that the petitioner's health was sound in 1918, and it is evidently conceded that he was disabled at least since 1930. When in the intervening period, did the disability take place?

A doctor who testified diagnosed the petitioner's case as a schizophrenic form of dementia praecox. He declared it to be sound medical theory that while a normal man can retain his sanity in the face of severe mental or physical shock, some persons are born with an inherent instability so that they are mentally unable to stand sudden and severe strain. The medical testimony was that this petitioner belongs to the latter class and that the shock of actual conflict on the battle front brought on the incurable affliction from which he now suffers. The medical witness testified that the dominant symptoms of the condition are extreme introversion and preoccupation with personal interests, a persecution complex, and an emotional instability which may be manifested by extreme exhilaration alternating with unusual depression or irrational outbursts. Persons suffering from this disease are therefore unable to engage in continuous employment.

The petitioner relies on the testimony of wartime and post war companions and superiors to show that his present mental condition existed on the crucial date. There is substantial testimony from which reasonable men might conclude that the petitioner was insane from the date claimed. [Justice Black then summarized that testimony.]

. . . All of this evidence, if believed, showed a man healthy and normal before he went to the war suffering for several years after he came back from a disease which had the symptoms attributed to schizophrenia and who was insane from 1930 until his trial. Under these circumstances, I think that the physician's testimony of total and permanent disability by reason of continuous insanity from 1918 to 1938 was reasonable. The fact that there was no direct testimony for a period of five years, while it might be the basis of fair argument to the jury by the government, does not, as the Court seems to believe, create a presumption against the petitioner so strong that his case must be excluded from the jury entirely. Even if during these five years the petitioner was spasmodically employed, we could not conclude that he was not totally and permanently disabled. . . . It is not doubted that schizophrenia is permanent even though there may be a momentary appearance of recovery. . . .

This case graphically illustrates the injustice resulting from permitting judges to direct verdicts instead of requiring them to await a jury decision and then, if necessary, allow a new trial. The chief reason given for approving a directed verdict against this petitioner is that no evidence except expert medical testimony was offered for a five to eight year period. Perhaps, now that the petitioner knows he has insufficient evidence to satisfy a judge even though he may have enough to satisfy a jury, he would be able to fill this time gap to meet any judge's demand. If a court would point out on a motion for new trial that the evidence as to this particular period was too weak, the petitioner would be given an opportunity to buttress the physician's evidence. If, as the Court believes, insufficient evidence has been offered to sustain a jury verdict for the petitioner, we should at least authorize a new trial. . . .

I believe that there is a reasonable difference of opinion as to whether the petitioner was totally and permanently disabled by reason of insanity on May 31, 1919, and that his case therefore should have been allowed to go to the jury. The testimony of fellow soldiers, friends, supervisors, and of a medical expert whose integrity and ability is not challenged cannot be rejected by any process available to me as a judge.

Comments and Questions

1. For class, please be prepared to answer these questions about *Galloway*:

(a) What is the cause of action and its elements?

(b) Which of the elements are not disputed? Explain how you know this.

(c) In advance of trial, what methods could Galloway's lawyer have used to make certain that the points of common agreement were taken as true at the trial? (Do not yet consider Rule 16 or case management. We will do that later.) Could either side have gained a victory using Fed. R. Civ. P. 12(b)(6) or 12(c)?

(d) Assume that you are Galloway's lawyer and that after you, representing the plaintiff, have rested, defense counsel moves for directed verdict (or "judgment sas a matter of law" under Rule 50). The judge will call on you to explain precisely how you have met your production burden as to each disputed element. Be precise with the evidence. The judge will also ask you: "To what extent can I use the fact that you did not put plaintiff's wife on the stand? Do you have any reasons for not doing so other than the risk that her evidence would destroy your case? Tell me honestly, do I have a right to ask you that question?"

(e) Assume that you represent the government. Explain the failure of evidence as to any element for which you think there is an insufficiency of evidence to permit a plaintiff's verdict. Among other questions, the trial judge will ask you: "Are you not asking me to engage in assessing credibility and weighing the evidence? I'm not allowed to do that, am I?"

(f) Assume now that you are a clerk to the trial judge, who turns to you:. "Clerk, I think the plaintiff's evidence is extremely weak and perhaps even nonexistent as to one element. Would this be a good case for me to let the case go to the jury, and then to grant a judgment n.o.v., rather than granting the directed verdict motion?" Why and why not? Consider the strategic considerations for the lawyers, their clients, the jurors, and the court system. What are the consequences if the judge goes the n.o.v. route as opposed to the directed verdict? Which method is more efficient? Are you sure? Explain.

(g) You represent the defendant. Assume that on February 1, a Thursday, the jury comes in with a plaintiff's verdict in *Galloway* and judgment is entered the same day. You wish to move for a judgment n.o.v. and a new trial. You are awaiting a copy of the transcript, and therefore want the most time possible. Absent a snow storm, when is the latest you can file your motions? Can you get an enlargement of time under Rule 6? Do the lengths of time for the making of such motions make sense?

(h) You are a member of a new organization ("S.A.J."—Save American Juries—pronounced "SAGE") of lawyers, judges, and legal scholars who have organized to find ways to engender new respect for the right to jury trial in civil cases and to lobby state and federal legislators to invigorate that right. Take realistic positions on the motions for directed verdict, judgment n.o.v., and for a new trial because the verdict is against the weight of the evidence, and be prepared to defend those positions.

2. Defendants make motions for directed verdict based on many different theories. Many of the arguments overlap. Here are some:

(a) There is insufficient evidence of one or more elements to permit reasonable people to find that it is true. This is often a matter of arguing that inferences do not stretch so far as the plaintiff claims. You have seen the argument in *Galloway*. If you have occasion to do research on directed verdict cases in federal court, particularly those in which it matters how little evidence can suffice in order for a plaintiff to survive a directed verdict motion and how far inferences can be stretched, you should appraise the case law with caution. The many Supreme Court Federal Employment Liability Act (FELA) cases supporting plaintiffs' verdicts may be idiosyncratic to that field for a number of historic and policy reasons. *See, e.g.*, 9A Charles A. Wright & Arthur R. Miller, *Federal Practice and Procedure* §2526.

(b) The facts are in a "fog." No one knows what happened. Therefore the plaintiff cannot make out a prima facie case. Sometimes, this is a literal argument, as in the motor vehicle accident in which both drivers are killed, no witnesses exist (perhaps because it happened in a fog), and no reconstruction is possible, based on the remaining physical evidence. In these and similar circumstances, defendants argue that a jury would have to engage in "mere speculation" or that a plaintiff's finding would be only "guesswork."

(c) We know what happened, but reasonable people cannot find that it meets the legal standard. For instance, the plaintiff might describe the defendant's activity in great detail, but as a matter of law there was "no duty" or the activity does not add up to negligence or whatever wrongdoing is alleged. In a contract case, the defendant may ask the court to interpret a written contract such that the plaintiff's rendition of factual events, even if believed, cannot rationally be found to be a breach of anything the defendant promised to do.

(d) The defendant may concede that the plaintiff has presented evidence of an element, but argues that no reasonable person could believe that evidence because it is not credible on its face. This is one way to read *Galloway*, or the *Matsushita* case, which we addressed in our discussion of summary judgment.

(e) There may be another kind of case in which the evidence seems to permit two equal but inconsistent inferences, and the defendant argues that the jury would only be guessing which one is true. The classic example of this in federal court is *Pennsylvania Railroad Co. v. Chamberlain*, 288 U.S. 333 (1933), but that case is probably no longer the rule in federal court. "The courts recognize that they lack the ability to say whether two or more inferences are equal." 9A Charles A. Wright & Arthur R. Miller, *Federal Practice and Procedure* §2528 (citation omitted).

(f) Sometimes plaintiffs try to survive a directed verdict motion by arguing that the evidence is in the defendant's hands and that the jury, in judging the demeanor of the defendant or another witness, should find that the defendant or the witness is so unbelievable that the opposite is true: "Since the defendant denies he did it, and you can see what a rascal and liar he is, you should believe the opposite." This argument will not usually wash. Indeed, if it did, it would be difficult for defendants ever to win a directed verdict or for appellate courts to know whether a motion for directed verdict was incorrectly denied, for the jury might always believe the opposite of what they heard. If you want to research this issue, find where *Dyer v. MacDougall,* 201 F.2d 265 (2d Cir. 1952), is included in the procedural treatise or hornbook of your choice, for that is the opinion (rendered by Justice Learned Hand) that scholars frequently invoke when discussing this topic. We put the issue here because once a defendant defeats the plaintiff's argument to draw the positive inference from disbelief of a denial, the plaintiff may be left with no evidence of a particular element.

(g) A defendant can seek a directed verdict by using evidence that must be believed. This could help a defendant in two ways. Perhaps evidence that must be believed will defeat one of plaintiff's necessary elements. Or perhaps an affirmative defense that must be taken as true will defeat the plaintiff "as a matter of law." Some courts say that whenever the testimony of a witness is involved, the issue must go to the jury, for the jury might disbelieve the testimony based on credibility. The prevailing view, however, regards the clear, uncontradicted, consistent, unimpeached testimony of even interested witnesses as evidence that must be taken as true, and therefore as sufficient basis for a directed verdict in favor of the party having the persuasion burden as well as the initial production burden. This amounts to a holding that reasonable men could not disbelieve such testimony on the basis of demeanor evidence. Flemming James, Jr., Geoffrey Hazard, & John Leubsdorf, *Civil Procedure* §7.20 at 364-365 (4th ed. 1992).

3. The Federal Rules of Evidence play an important role in directed verdict, and consequently, in summary judgment. As the federal courts have taken a more active role in excluding expert testimony that they believe is unreliable (*see Daubert v. Merrill Dow Pharmaceuticals, Inc.,* 509 U.S. 579 (1993), and *Kumho Tire Co. Ltd. v. Carmichael,* No. 97-1709, 1999 U.S. LEXIS 2189 (March 23, 1999)), this in turn has led to increased restriction of what cases are permitted to reach a jury, and, if they do survive a directed verdict motion, what testimony the jury can consider.

4. Plaintiffs do, on occasion, win directed verdicts, even though they have the burden of both production and persuasion. We have discussed this possibility previously, and it should now be clear to you why it is usually more unlikely for a plaintiff to win a directed verdict than for a defendant. Still, some cases are ripe for a plaintiff's directed verdict, such as a promissory note case in which the defendant has no defense and the damages are liquidated. Bear in mind also that a plaintiff can frequently win on some of its elements "as a matter of law." For example, if a defendant admits an element in the pleading, or through answering positively or neglecting to answer a request for an admission (Fed. R. Civ. P. 36), or through stipulation or a blanket admission on the stand, the judge can instruct the jury that the element must be believed. In the alternative, the judge can just omit such an element from those that the jury is instructed to consider.

5. You should understand that it is a *legal* question whether or not to grant a directed verdict—even though that determination necessarily involves factual issues. Another way to think of this is that a judge must decide the legal question of whether or not there are facts sufficient to let the jury deliberate on the matter.

6. Shortly after the Federal Rules of Civil Procedure became law, the Supreme Court, in *Montgomery Ward & Co. v. Duncan*, 311 U.S. 243 (1940), was called upon to interpret the relationship between a motion for-judgment n.o.v. and a motion for new trial (Fed. R. Civ. P. 59). An amendment to Rule 50 in 1963 sought to clarify what a trial judge should do when confronted with both motions, and subsequent amendments have attempted to give further guidance. What is the trial judge now obligated to do do when she grants a judgment n.o.v. and has also been requested to grant a new trial? Consider why, from the defendant's point of view, it may be important to have an opportunity to argue the motion for a new trial in front of the same judge who heard argument for the motion for judgment n.o.v.. Under what circumstances would it become relevant whether the trial judge decides both judgment n.o.v. and new trial motions? Does this suggest potential unfairness to the nonmoving party, normally the plaintiff?

Practice Exercise No. 20: Ruling Upon a Motion for Directed Verdict in *City of Cleveland*

You are a law clerk in a judge's chambers discussing the *City of Cleveland* case. Read the judge's memorandum on directed verdict and the portions of the judge's Trial Notebook, which are in the Case Files. Assume that the plaintiffs' counsel have now rested and that the defendant has moved for a directed verdict on all four counts. The defendant's counsel must be told on which counts the case will proceed. The judge is in a hurry, not wanting to leave the jury out for an extended recess. Although the judge will hear argument by counsel, the judge wants your advice as to whether you would grant directed verdict on any of the counts. As you will see from the memorandum, the judge is sure how to rule on one of the counts. Of course, the judge may also consider whether to go the judgment n.o.v. route. The memorandum will tell you which count you should be most prepared on. Prepare to give informed advice.

7. *Motion to Vacate Judgment*   D

Reread Fed. R. Civ. P. 60, which gives the ground rules for moving to vacate a judgment in federal court. These rules are typical of what applies in most states as well. Rule 60 is mostly used subsequent to the time period that is permitted for making motions for judgment n.o.v. or for new trial motions, but nothing prevents a losing party from making all three motions together if the time periods permit.

Fed. R. Civ. P. 60 requires the lawyer to do additional research before relying upon it. For example, many of the categories in Rule 60(b) have been interpreted in ways that one would be unlikely to infer by only reading the rule; the interpretations generally narrow the application of the Rule. Here are some examples, by no means exhaustive:

(1) The "mistake, inadvertence, surprise, or excusable neglect" language in Rule 60(b)(1) has been severely limited by case law. In most of the cases in which a judgment is vacated under this provision, the losing party is unable to have any trial because of a default judgment or similar reason.

(2) The "newly discovered evidence" cases (60(b)(2)) tend to tack on a number of additional requirements. Some cases say, for example, that the evidence must not be merely cumulative or impeaching, and that such evidence must relate to facts that were in existence at the time of trial. The provision itself requires that the matter could not have been discovered "by due diligence" in time to move for a Rule 59(b) new trial, which is a difficult condition to meet, given the many discovery devices.

(3) Cases applying the "fraud . . . , misrepresentation, or other misconduct of adverse party" category in Rule 60(b)(3) tend to look into a number of factors, such as the opportunities for detection of the misconduct, before or during trial, and the strength of the proof of the misconduct. These interpretive factors are complicated by the fact that fraud can also be a reason for voiding a judgment under 60(b)(4) and that the Rule explicitly "does not limit the power of a court . . . to set aside a judgment for fraud upon a court" through an independent action. That there are several subcategories of fraud cases under Rule 60(b) is not merely a matter of academic concern, for the motions under 60(b)(1), (2), and (3) must be made within a year, and other motions must be made "within a reasonable time." Since the independent action is not a motion, it may have a different time period.

(4) Rule 60(b)(6) establishes the category "any other reason justifying relief from the operation of the judgment." Since this category is not subject to the "within one year after the judgment" limitation, lawyers frequently try to recast a motion that would ordinarily be brought under (b)(1), (2), and (3) into a reason not covered by those provisions. The courts tend to rule, however, that if the case could have been covered by the 60(b)(1) through (3) categories, then litigants cannot avoid the one-year limitation by seeking refuge in the catch all language of 60(b)(6).

———

The following case considers the application of the language of Fed. R. Civ. P. 60(b)(1). As you read the case, ask yourself how you would have decided. Are you surprised by the court's result? Could you write an equally convincing opinion reaching a different conclusion?

■ INFORMATION SYSTEMS & NETWORKS CORP. v. UNITED STATES
994 F.2d 792 (Fed. Cir. 1993)

LOURIE, Circuit Judge.

Information Systems and Networks Corporation (ISN) appeals from the June 16, 1992 order of the United States Claims Court denying its motion for relief from default judgment. Because we conclude that the Claims Court abused its discretion in denying ISN's motion, we reverse.

BACKGROUND

In September, 1988 the United States Air Force and ISN entered into a contract under which ISN was required to, inter alia, convert certain Air Force computer operations from Honeywell equipment to IBM equipment. On May 21, 1991, the Contracting Officer (CO) issued a final decision terminating the contract for default and asserting a government claim for $385,211.32 in damages incurred by the Air Force as a result of ISN's alleged failure to properly complete the required conversions. ISN subsequently filed a complaint with the Claims Court alleging that the government was in breach and that the termination for default was wrongful. ISN then filed a joinder motion . . . to join its subcontractors as parties in the action.

The government filed an answer to ISN's complaint on January 27, 1992 and an amended answer and counterclaim on January 31. The counterclaim was based on the CO's final decision and it reasserted the government's claim for damages. ISN did not file an answer to the counterclaim and on February 28, 1992, the Clerk entered default pursuant to RUSCC 55(a).* On March 20, 1992 the government moved for default judgment, which the Claims Court entered on March 31 for the amount of the counterclaim.

Following the entry of default judgment, ISN, which had been pursuing the case through house counsel, immediately hired outside counsel, who filed a motion for relief pursuant to RUSCC 55(c), which provides: "For good cause shown the court may set aside an entry of default and, if a judgment by default has been entered, may likewise set it aside in accordance with RUSCC 60(b)." RUSCC 60(b) provides in pertinent part: "On motion and upon such terms as are just, the court may relieve a party or his legal representative from a final judgment, order, or proceeding for the following reasons: (1) mistake, inadvertence, surprise, or excusable neglect." ISN supported its motion with an affidavit of house counsel stating that he mistakenly believed the joinder motion suspended the requirement to file an answer and that, following the entry of default, he met with government counsel during preparation of the joint preliminary status report and was under the impression that the government did not intend to move

---

*RUSCC refers to the procedural rules for the United States Claims Court.

for default judgment. Accordingly, ISN argued that its failure to file an answer to the counterclaim was the result of excusable neglect.

The Claims Court denied ISN's motion. The court found both that the government would not be prejudiced if it granted ISN's motion and that ISN's complaint established a meritorious defense to the counterclaim, since ISN disputed its liability by alleging that the government breached the contract. *Id.* at 317. The court concluded, however, that ISN's failure to file an answer after receiving notice of the government's counterclaim constituted "culpable" conduct which was not the excusable neglect required by RUSCC 60(b)(1).

The sole issue before us is whether the court properly denied ISN's motion for relief under RUSCC 60(b)(1). Since the government does not dispute the court's findings regarding the absence of prejudice and the presence of a meritorious defense, this appeal hinges on the definition of "culpable" conduct and its relationship to the criteria for excusable neglect.

DISCUSSION

We review a trial court's denial of a motion for relief under Rule 60(b)* for abuse of discretion. . . .

Our review is guided by the well-established principles that a trial on the merits is favored over default judgment and that close cases should be resolved in favor of the party seeking to set aside default judgment. . . .

When a court has denied a party's motion to be relieved from default judgment, "a 'glaring abuse' of discretion [has] not [been] required for reversal of a court's refusal to relieve a party of the harsh sanction of default," . . . and "even a slight abuse [of discretion] may justify reversal." It has been stated that Rule 60(b) "is applied most liberally to judgments in default."

Other circuits that have considered the issue of excusable neglect for purposes of Rule 60(b)(1) have held that a court should consider three factors: (1) whether the non-defaulting party will be prejudiced; (2) whether the defaulting party has a meritorious defense; and (3) whether culpable conduct of the defaulting party led to the default. The Claims Court utilized these factors and we adopt them as well.

The court stated that the three factors are "disjunctive" such that a finding that any one of the factors is unfavorable to the defaulting party requires denial of the motion for relief. The court found that the first two factors favored ISN, and the government does not dispute those findings. The court further found that ISN's failure to file an answer to the government's counterclaim was "culpable" conduct. Regarding the standard of culpability, the court stated that "[a] party's conduct is culpable if

---

* *Eds. Note:* Rule 60(b) of the Claims Court is a virtual duplicate of Federal Rule of Civil Procedure 60(b).

that party has received 'actual or constructive notice of the filing of the action and failed to answer the complaint.'" The court stated that "[e]ven allowing for [ISN's] confusion in responding to the counterclaim, there was sufficient time between the date [ISN] received notice of the default and both the filing of the motion for entry of default and the entry of the default judgment for [ISN] to respond in some fashion."

ISN argues that the Claims Court's approach to evaluating its RUSCC 60(b)(1) motion was incorrect. It argues that application of the three factors in the disjunctive was unsound and that, in light of its meritorious defense and the lack of prejudice to the government, the court abused its discretion in refusing to set aside the default judgment for excusable neglect.

We agree. First, the court incorrectly relied on *Ackermann v. United States*, 340 U.S. 193 (1950), for the proposition that subsection (1) of Rule 60(b) requires a showing of "extraordinary circumstances." The court's reliance on *Ackermann* was misplaced because that case did not apply the "extraordinary circumstances" criterion to excusable neglect under subsection (1), but to subsection (6), the residual clause of Rule 60(b) authorizing relief from a judgment for "any other reason justifying relief from the operation of the judgment." While subsection (6) requires a showing of "extraordinary circumstances," *Ackermann*, 340 U.S. at 202, subsections (1) and (6) of Rule 60(b) "are mutually exclusive," *Pioneer Inv. Services Co. v. Brunswick Assoc. Ltd. Partnership*, 113 S. Ct. 1489, 1497 (1993), and the required showing of extraordinary circumstances under subsection (6) does not apply to excusable neglect under subsection (1).

Furthermore, the court erred in applying the three factors disjunctively. The majority of circuits balance the three factors in determining whether to grant relief for excusable neglect under Rule 60(b)(1). In *Pioneer*, which dealt with "excusable neglect" under Bankruptcy Rule 9006(b)(1), the Supreme Court adopted a balancing approach, "taking account of all relevant circumstances surrounding the party's omission." 113 S. Ct. at 1498. . . . We adopt the balancing approach since it best enables a court to weigh the facts and use its discretion to determine whether a party is deserving of the harsh sanction of default judgment.

We also reject the trial court's standard of culpability. The majority of circuits focus on the willfulness of the defaulting party and consider whether that party intended to violate court rules and procedures. . . .

We favor the majority approach. Under the [minority approach], a party may never be relieved from a default judgment once it has notice of a claim against it and fails to answer. We find that result inconsistent with Rule 60(b)(1), which authorizes relief from a judgment when the failure to file an answer is the result of excusable neglect. Indeed, the Supreme Court recently considered the meaning of "excusable neglect" under Rule 60(b)(1) in the context of construing the same language in Bankruptcy Rule 9006(b)(1), which permits late filings in cases of "excusable neglect." *Pioneer*, 113 S. Ct. at 1489. The Court stated that "at least for purposes of Rule 60(b), 'excusable neglect' is understood to encompass situations in which the failure to comply with a filing deadline is attributable to negligence." *Id.* at 1497. If negligence can come within the definition of excusable neglect, mere failure to answer after receiving notice of a counterclaim can also. Thus, one should inquire whether the defaulting party willfully declined to follow a court's rules and procedures.

We conclude that the trial court abused its discretion in determining that ISN's failure to file an answer constituted culpable conduct. Under the standard of culpability we have adopted, the undisputed facts do not establish a willful disregard for the court's rules and procedures, merely negligence. The government repeatedly states that the facts show "a willful pattern of disregard for the Claims Court's rules." However, the only facts that the government points to are ISN's failure to file an answer after receiving notice of its counterclaim and ISN's failure to move to vacate the entry of default prior to the entry of default judgment. The government emphasizes only the number of days that elapsed between the time the government filed its counterclaim and the time the clerk entered default judgment.

These facts do not show a willful disregard for the court's rules and procedures. ISN's house counsel stated that he believed he was not required to file an answer to the government's counterclaim, and ISN has diligently pursued the action in every other regard. "Judgment by default is a drastic step which should be resorted to only in the most extreme cases." This case is not an "extreme" one deserving of the "drastic step" of default judgment.

Another factor negating any idea of willfulness is that ISN's failure to file an answer to the counterclaim has little, if any, substantive significance. As the Claims Court found, ISN's complaint was essentially a defense to the government's counterclaim since it disputed ISN's liability and alleged that the government, not ISN, had breached the contract. . . .

Since we conclude that, lacking any element of willfulness, ISN has not been shown to be culpable, and no challenge has been made to the court's findings in favor of ISN on the other two factors relating to excusable neglect, it is clear that remand is not necessary in this case.

Conclusion

In view of the lack of prejudice to the government and the presence of a meritorious defense, as well as ISN's lack of culpability, we conclude that the Claims Court abused its discretion in refusing to relieve ISN from default judgment for excusable neglect under RUSCC 60(b)(1). . . .

F. INSTRUCTIONS, BIFURCATION/ TRIFURCATION, TYPES OF VERDICTS, REMITTITUR AND ADDITUR

In this section we introduce the rationale, doctrine, and strategic concerns of jury instructions, bifurcation and trifurcation, types of verdict, and remittitur and additur. Are these ways of helping the jury to be just and rational, or do they invade the jury's fact-finding province?

Traditionally, juries rendered general verdicts. In civil cases, juries were asked only to find for the plaintiff or for the defendant, and if for the plaintiff, to state the amount of monetary damages. One procedural device already available in federal and state courts is the *special verdict,* which provides means by which trial judges can structure a jury's reasoning process. Under the Federal Rules of Civil Procedure, the trial judge can submit written questions to the jury, and the jury returns a special verdict in the form of written findings of fact. Alternatively, the judge can have the jury return a general verdict, but answer interrogatories that have been posed to it by the judge. With either method, the judge is outlining the way the jury should approach the issue, step by step. Read Fed. R. Civ. P. 49.

Some of the traditional arguments for special verdicts are that restricting the decision-making functions of the jury would "improve the deliberation process by packaging the dispute in distinct, manageable components," "concentrat[e] juror attention on certain matters," "aid the jurors in sorting out the facts and avoiding confusion," "ensure a truly unanimous decision," "facilitate the appellate process by spelling out the premises underlying the jury's ultimate conclusions," and "[be] extremely helpful in the application of collateral estoppel (issue preclusion)." *See* Mark Brodin, *Accuracy, Efficiency, and Accountability in the Litigation Process— The Case for the Fact Verdict,* 59 U. Cinn. L. Rev. 15 (1990). These arguments all imply that the jury is either not to be trusted or is overtaxed by being asked to do more than decide the facts. What is your visceral reaction to this so-called interference with the deliberative process?

Another reform is splitting trials into stages (for instance, separating liability from damages and first trying the liability portion, or otherwise separating elements for successive trials, unless the plaintiff loses at a prior trial on an element). Such procedure has become particularly attractive to judges in mass tort cases. Again, some scholars have been critical of the increased use of such devices, claiming that they distort the jury process and alter substantive results, usually in a manner that is pro-defendant. The following is one example of such criticism.

■ ROGER H. TRANGSRUD, MASS TRIALS IN MASS TORT CASES: A DISSENT
1989 U. Ill. L. Rev. 69

. . . The professors and federal judges who have urged or ordered the use of mass trials in mass tort cases have ignored or declined to address the unintended consequences of this extraordinary procedure. Mass trials in mass tort cases involving substantial personal injury or wrongful death claims result in a compromised due process to all of the litigants, but in particular to the plaintiffs. As the Bendectin litigation illustrates, mass trials typically require the trifurcation* of issues, the use of special verdict forms, and other extraordinary amendments to the usual procedure followed in ordinary tort cases. These devices have an intangible, but significant, adverse effect on the fairness of the proceedings. The unusual conditions present in mass trials also encourage shaded rulings on substantive law issues by the trial judge, improper judicial involvement in the settlement process, and troubling distortions in the attorney-client relationship.

Trifurcation of issues in a mass tort case is neither fair nor efficient. It is not fair because it robs the jury of its traditional flexibility in tort cases to balance uncertainties in the plaintiff's case on liability against strengths in the plaintiff's case on damages. Trifurcation of issues also inevitably leads to the sterile trial of technical issues related to causation divorced from the fact of the plaintiff's injury and a full account of the defendant's role in the tragedy.

Appellate courts have expressed anxiety about the trifurcation of mass tort claims but have stopped short of reversing such orders. In the litigation following the Beverly Hills Supper Club fire, the trial judge, over the plaintiffs' objections, severed the issue of causation from the remainder of the case against the defendant aluminum wire manufacturers. After a mass trial limited to the question of causation, the jury returned a special verdict finding that aluminum wire had not caused the fire. On appeal, the Sixth Circuit ordered a new trial on other grounds and stated that on remand the trial judge should consider conducting the retrial in a different manner. The Sixth Circuit noted that "[t]here is a danger that bifurcation may deprive plaintiffs of their legitimate right to place before the jury circumstances and atmosphere of the entire cause of action . . . replacing it with a sterile or laboratory atmosphere in which causation is parted from the reality of injury." The Sixth Circuit's concerns about this approach were allayed to some extent by its assumption that the fire had been such a well-publicized incident that the jury would likely be aware of the nature of the plaintiffs' injuries and deaths.

The issue of special verdict forms and split trials returned to the Sixth Circuit when a panel affirmed the judgment entered after a trifurcated mass trial in the Bendectin litigation. Although the court did not reverse based on the trifurcation order, all three judges on the panel were very concerned by this procedure. Two of the judges stated that it was the most "troubling" question on appeal, while a third seemingly disapproved of

---

* *Eds. Note:* Trifurcation divides a case into three parts for purposes of trial, usually causation, liability, and damages. Bifurcation ordinarily separates a case into two trials, usually liability, followed by damages. Of course, if the fact finder finds for the defendant on causation or liability, there is no need for a further trial. In the *Bendectin* litigation, in which liability was divided between causation and other liability issues, causation was tried first. "Fearing undue prejudice to the defendant, the trial court also excluded from the courtroom all visibly deformed plaintiffs and all plaintiffs under the age of ten." *In re Bendectin Litigation,* 857 F.2d 290 (6th Cir. 1988).

the order, but felt it was within the permissible discretion of the trial judge to proceed in this way. Shrugging off constitutional concerns about whether the issue of "general causation" was sufficiently "distinct and separable" from the other liability issues to permit it to be tried separately under the Seventh Amendment, the Sixth Circuit upheld the trifurcation order, finding it was entered to conserve judicial resources and was within the broad latitude allowed trial judges in conducting trials.

The plaintiffs' argument that trifurcation had transformed an ordinary tort suit into a sterile and laboratory inquiry into causation was rejected on grounds that appear to be utterly implausible. The Sixth Circuit stated that this concern was adequately allayed by the trial judge's instruction to the jury that "[t]his is a significant case. It involves a lot of people" and by the closing argument of plaintiffs' counsel that the trial was "not an academic exercise" and "involved many real people who sought justice." The suggestion that such remarks are an adequate substitute for the presence and testimony of the injured plaintiff and a full presentation of all of the alleged misconduct of the defendant pharmaceutical company is incredible on its face. This Bendectin jury was deprived of the evidence most tort juries would routinely hear regarding the totality of circumstances surrounding the plaintiff's injury in a manner likely to affect their deliberations in a substantial way.

Some commentators have argued all tort cases should be routinely bifurcated so that jury deliberation on liability issues would be unswayed by evidence of the nature and severity of the plaintiff's injury. Despite the apparent appeal of separating these issues, bifurcation is rare in ordinary tort litigation because for decades most courts have felt that the fusion of liability and damage issues by a tort jury is necessary to allow the jury to play its proper and traditional role as an institution that directly reflects current norms, concerns, and thinking. Sometimes legal doctrine falls behind jury wisdom. In contributory negligence states it was suspected for many years that juries "improperly" discounted plaintiff recoveries to the extent the plaintiff was negligent rather than holding for the defendant based upon the plaintiff's contributory negligence. Today, legal doctrine formally endorses such discounting through the comparative negligence formulas widely used in many states.

If the Bendectin claims had been tried separately, it is possible that the defendant would have consistently prevailed. It is also possible, however, that juries presented with the entire case against the manufacturer of this drug would have awarded discounted damages to the plaintiffs before them, mindful of the serious character of the plaintiffs' injuries and the inconclusive evidence that the injuries were caused by the defendant's drug. Such an outcome would seem to be at odds with our current law of causation, but might anticipate reform of that law in the future. Perhaps the law is moving to allow a discounted recovery when a defendant's product increases the risk of disease or injury beyond natural levels, but strict causation cannot be proven due to the passage of time or the imperfect nature of our science.

In any event, it is wrong to take such options and flexibility away from those juries that hear mass tort trials and leave them only with the opportunity to give an opinion on an abstract question of causation. The plaintiffs in such cases are no less deserving of and entitled to full jury consideration of their case than are the victims of isolated torts. . . .

Procedural rules are intended to facilitate the fair disposition of substantive disputes. One meaning of fairness in this context is that similar claims should be treated similarly in all respects likely to affect the outcome of the case. The lone victim of a doctor's alleged negligence is entitled to no better and no worse process than the many victims of an intrauterine device alleged to be defective and hazardous. Accordingly, special procedural rules or practices that are likely to have a significant effect on the probable outcome of a case should not be used in mass tort cases when they are shunned in ordinary tort cases, unless compelling justification exists for their use.

Many federal laws and doctrines reflect this principle of substantive neutrality. For example, in diversity cases federal courts are allowed some latitude in the procedures and practices they follow but may not pursue policies or follow rules that are likely to be "outcome determinative" or to affect the substantive rights of the litigants. The object of the *Erie* limitations on federal procedure and practice is to assure that the outcome of the case will not depend on the court where the claim is filed.

This same principle of substantive neutrality is found elsewhere in federal law. When a diversity case is transferred from one federal venue to another for the convenience of the parties and the witnesses, the Supreme Court has held that the transferee court is to apply the same choice of law principles applicable in the transferor court. The evident purpose of this rule is to avoid any impact on the likely outcome of the case due to the change of venue. Although federal trial courts have the authority to bifurcate ordinary tort cases, they do so very infrequently out of concern for the impact of trying the liability issue without having the nature and severity of the plaintiff's injury before the jury. In fact, the authors of Federal Rule of Civil Procedure 42 stated explicitly that severance and bifurcation should be used infrequently. This is because in tort cases there is substantial evidence that the probable outcome of cases varies dramatically depending upon whether the entire case or only part of the case is presented to the jury.

As explained above, the principle of substantive neutrality has been widely violated in mass tort cases where mass trials have been ordered. Trial judges employ special verdict forms and trifurcation with seeming disregard for their impact on the fairness or probable outcome of the trial. They decide substantive or choice of law issues in indefensible ways to skirt procedural obstacles to mass trials. The trial judges sometimes collaborate with counsel in fashioning and approving a settlement and an award of attorneys fees on one set of assumptions and then dismiss remaining claims on an inconsistent set of assumptions. . . . All this extraordinary behavior and recent experimentation has been done in the name of efficiency and preserving scarce judicial resources even though it remains unclear to this day whether such procedures are actually likely to achieve this goal in any significant measure.

Practice Exercise No. 21: Motion to Bifurcate in *City of Cleveland*

Review the motion to bifurcate and the accompanying brief in the *City of Cleveland* Case Files. In the actual firefighters litigation, two companion cases had been consolidated for trial. One was brought by the United States of America, solely on the Title VII cause of action. The other is the private class action that you have been following in the Case Files. Assume that the motion to bifurcate and the accompanying memorandum were filed about half-way through the discovery process and that the United States of America is correct in its assertion that little or no discovery on individualized damages has taken place at this point. If you represented the plaintiffs in the private class action, would you oppose the motion? Why or why not? How would you advise a judge to rule on the motion?

Comments and Questions

1. The controversy over bifurcation of mass tort claims dramatizes a theme running throughout this text: the tension between narrative and formal legal reasoning. That is, while an advocate of formal legal reasoning might favor having elements of a claim tried in separate trials, such a separation tends to destroy the narrative force of the story that an injured plaintiff wants to tell a jury. For an example of an argument favoring the judicious application of issue-separation in mass tort cases, *see* James A. Henderson et al., *Optimal Issue Separation in Modern Products Liability Litigation*, 73 Tex. L. Rev. 1653 (1995).

2. If you are more pro-jury than skeptical of the jury process, we want your honest opinion on the practice of instructing juries. In the *City of Cleveland* Case Files, you will find the judge's instructions on the §1983 count of the class action plaintiffs against the city. As you read those instructions, consider whether you agree that a jury should be instructed at all. If you are generally wary of the court's controlling the jury, are you willing to concede that instructions of some kind are necessary? Be prepared to defend your opinion.

If you generally think juries need a good deal of guidance, be prepared to give your assessment of the judge's instructions in this case. Are they helpful to the jurors in making a rational, law-based decision? In what ways, if any, would you have framed the instructions differently? We are not asking you at this time to comment on the correctness of the law stated, but to consider such matters as the tone, clarity, and degree of specificity of the instructions. Was there too much "legalese"? Would commenting on the evidence itself, or describing some of the evidence, have been helpful to the jury?

3. It is common in federal courts, and in some states, for judges to comment on the evidence. It is improper for a judge, of course, to actually tell a jury who should win, but when commenting on the evidence is allowed, the trial judge can summarize particular evidence, or inform the jury of the types of things they may wish to consider. Naturally, sometimes the summary or comment is not as neutral as one party or the other would like.

4. Assume that the judge showed you the instructions, which are in the Case Files, before giving them to the jury. The judge has asked for your comments, if any.

(a) Assume that you represent the City of Cleveland. Do you approve of the type of verdict that the judge has chosen, of the judge's language in the question he posed, and of his explanation of what the jury should do with the question and the verdict slips? (Does the judge have authority in the Rules to use this method? Which method is it?) What changes would you suggest, especially on the verdict method and on the judge's instructions about that method?

(b) Assume that you represent the plaintiffs. Answer the same questions as in (a) above, making concrete suggestions for changes if you want them.

5. Assume now that the defendant City in the *City of Cleveland* case has rested much sooner than either side actually expected, because its evidence went in smoothly and quickly. The judge turns to both sides, tells them generally what the charge will cover, and tells them to make their closing arguments. After closing arguments, and before either side has given the judge any written requests for instructions, the judge instructs the jury in the words that have been printed in the Case Files. (Most federal judges actually would ask for your written requested instructions well before this point in the trial and would probably tell you in a final pretrial conference order when your written requests should be filed. Frequently, the time would be several days prior to the commencement of trial, with the right to make further requests if they were necessitated by surprise occurrences at the trial.) After giving the instructions, and before the jury retires to deliberate, the judge turns to you, representing the City. Would you have a right to ask for clarifying or additional instructions? Be prepared to tell the judge under the applicable provisions of the Rules what, if anything, you want the judge now to instruct the jury prior to their deliberations.

6. As you continue to consider your views about the civil jury and about the many methods that have developed both to guide and control it, consider an example of what we know about an actual case. Our sources are an article by Steven Brill, the editor-in-chief of American Lawyer (Steven Brill, *Inside the Jury Room at the Washington Post Libel Trial, American Lawyer,* Nov. 1982, at 937), and the Order and Memorandum dated May 2, 1983, of Judge Oliver Gasch of the U.S. District Court, District of Columbia, in *Tavoulareas v. The Washington Post Company, et al.,* C.A. No. 80-3032. The additional defendants included Post editors Ben Bradlee and Bob Woodward. Tavoulareas was the president of Mobil Oil, and his son, Peter, was in the oil tanker business. In 1979, the Post published two articles about the father, a famous self-made man, and his son. The headline of the story, which appeared on the front page, was "Mobil Chief Sets Up Son in Venture." The lead paragraph stated: "Mobil Oil Corp. president William P. Tavoulareas set up his son five years ago as a partner in a London-based shipping management firm that has since done millions of dollars in business operating Mobil-owned ships under exclusive, no-bid contracts." The father, who claimed that he helped his son only when an opportunity arose, was upset that his "unblemished reputation" (Brill's words) had been sullied. He talked with Ben Bradlee four days after the first story, seeking a retraction, and only got a brief subsequent story adding a little information.

Tavoulareas said he tried to get the Post to admit their mistakes for a year, "[b]ut they're so damn arrogant. I kept telling them I'd sue." The lawsuit alleged libel. The plaintiffs were represented by John Walsh, a trial lawyer at the well-known Wall Street firm of Cadwallader, Wickersham & Taft (Taft was President William Howard Taft's brother and Wickersham was appointed to the initial Advisory Committee that drafted the Federal Rules of Civil Procedure). The Post and its staff were represented by the legendary Washington, D.C., firm of Williams & Connolly (the Williams, of course, was Edward Bennett Williams). Irving Younger, who at the time was probably the country's most famous lecturer on evidence and jury strategy (although he "insists he always prefers a judge to a jury") was chosen to be lead counsel for the Post. Prior to Younger's involvement, Williams & Connolly insisted on a jury trial.

The trial lasted nineteen days. The judge instructed the jury: "It is not the defendants' burden to prove that the articles are true. The burden is upon the plaintiffs to prove to you that are they are substantially false. . . . It is not enough for William Tavoulareas to prove the defendants did not conduct a thorough investigation of the facts or that they were negligent in the way they wrote or edited the articles. To recover, William Tavoulareas must prove the defendants had a high degree of awareness that the articles were false or probably false and that they were recklessly disregarded, whether the articles were false or not. If you find the defendants believed the sources of information in the story to be reliable and believed the story to be accurate when published, you must find the defendants have not acted with actual malice as to William Tavoulareas." Brill reports that the jury foreman, who was going to attend law school the next fall, and the five other jurors, under his insistent lead, "operated as if these instructions had not been given." The jury foreman insisted that it was the obligation of the Post to prove in the article itself that the headline that the father had "set up his son" was accurate. In fact, Irving Younger had pitched his defense, which Brill thought was a mistake, on the ground that the article was accurate. Younger's experience had taught him that stressing burden of proof was not a good way to argue or win a law suit when one's client is accused of wrongdoing; instead, you should argue and prove that your client is in the right.

One of the jurors told the judge that a written copy of the instructions would be helpful, but the judge, with the agreement of counsel, did not allow that out of fear that "the instructions might be read piecemeal instead of taken as a whole." Brill reports: "four jurors would later volunteer to me that, as one put it, 'we never understood the instructions and never pretended to.'" Although the first vote of the jury was 4-2 in favor of the Post on all counts, the young jury foreman kept "yelling," according to one juror, "where's the set-up?" By the third day of deliberations, the last of the six jurors gave in and compromised on a $250,000 verdict for compensatory damages for the father, William Tavoulareas, against the Post, an investigative reporter, and a freelance reporter. After a brief trial for the jury to consider punitive damages, at which the Post conceded its healthy financial condition and William Tavoulareas testified to a legal bill of about $1.8 million, the jury awarded the father an additional $1.8 million in punitive damages.

In later discussing the case and what prompted their decision, "[s]everal jurors . . . mentioned the judge's vacation plans and the humiliation of a hung jury." The final juror to relent, several recalled, told the others "that the pressure was too much for her, that she felt sick, and that this case was why, in her view, that there should be 12 jurors as there had been when she's served on jury panels in the past." When asked what would have happened if the jury had just been asked to decide "whether the Post had been recklessly or deliberately inaccurate or unfair," a juror answered; "Oh, in that case, there's no way the plaintiff would have won. We all, even . . . [the foreman], I think, conceded they hadn't done anything careless or on purpose."

Both sides appealed, the plaintiffs' counsel arguing that if the Post was liable to the father, then the son should have also won, and the defendants' counsel continuing to insist that there was no evidence to support the verdict, and seeking a judgment n.o.v. or a reduction of damages. Months later, in a nine-page single space memorandum opinion, the bulk of which meticulously reviewed the evidence in the light most favorable to plaintiff, the judge concluded: "Under the standards enunciated by the Supreme Court, . . . the jury verdict in this case will withstand the motions for judgment n.o.v. only if there is sufficient evidence in the record from which a jury could reasonably find, by clear and convincing proof,* that the defendants published the November 30 article with actual malice. The article in question falls far short of being a model of fair, unbiased, investigative journalism. There is no evidence in the record, however, to show that it contained knowing lies or statements made in reckless disregard of the truth. Reviewed under the stringent test set forth by the Supreme Court in *New York Times Co. v. Sullivan,* the verdict in plaintiff's favor must be set aside." Consequently, the judge granted the defendants' motions for judgment n.o.v.

So, that's the story. Does this change your mind about jury cases? What lessons about civil litigation and jury trials do you draw from it?

7. We have now considered bifurcation, different types of jury verdicts, and jury instructions. The remaining "jury control" doctrine relates to what are called *remittitur* and *additur*. To understand these concepts, you will have to recall what you learned about motions for a new trial based on the contention, in whole or in part, that the monetary amount of the jury verdict was too large or too small "as a matter of law." Given the time and expense to society and the parties resulting from the grant of a new trial, some courts devised the practice of conditioning the grant of a new trial (when damages were excessive) on the plaintiff's refusal to consent to a reduction of damages to a specific amount (called *nisi remittitur damna*). Put another way, the judge is either explicitly or implicitly saying to plaintiff's counsel: "I agree with the defendant that the damages are excessive, and will grant defendant's motion for a new trial, unless your client agrees to reduce the verdict by X amount of dollars."

There are additional, longer-standing precedents for the remittitur, which reduces damages, than for the additur, which increases them. In the additur situation, the judge is either explicitly or implicitly saying to the defendant's counsel: "The plaintiff, although winning the case, has moved for a new trial on the grounds that the damages given in the verdict are inadequate. I agree with the plaintiff, and intend to grant the plaintiff's motion for a new trial unless your client agrees to increase the damages by X dollars. It is your client's choice."

Before considering what you think of these devices, you should be aware of both constitutional and practical considerations. In *Dimick v. Schiedt,* 293 U.S. 474 (1935), the Supreme Court considered the constitutionality of additur and, in a 5-4 decision, found it unconstitutional for federal courts to use the device. The Court distinguished remittitur and

---

* This is not the burden in the ordinary civil case; in the typical case, the plaintiff does not have to adduce "clear and convincing proof," but must merely convince the jury on the evidence (including all reasonable inferences) that it is more likely than not that all elements of the prima facie case are true.

implied, in dicta, that it would permit that device to stand. The points of distinction, according to the majority, were some evidence of the practice of remittitur in England prior to 1791 and that in the case of remittitur "what remains is included in the verdict along with the unlawful excess—in that sense it has been found by the jury—and the remittitur has the effect of merely lopping off the excrescence." The additur, according to the majority, is a "bald addition of something which in no sense can be said to be included in the verdict." *Id.* at 486. The Supreme Court has since given mixed signals about whether it would continue to hold additur unconstitutional. In *Tull v. United States*, 481 U.S. 412, 533 n.16 (1996), the Court implied that *Dimick* was an anomaly and hinted that the Court may "rethink" the additur question "on a later day." But more recently, in *Feltner v. Columbia Pictures Television, Inc.*, 118 S. Ct. 1279 (1998), the Supreme Court found a jury trial right in assessing damages under the federal copyright statute and suggested that *Tull* was "at least in tension with" prior Supreme Court precedent, including *Dimick*, 118 S. Ct. at 188 n.9. Additur, and more frequently remittitur, have been permitted by the highest court of some states. State courts have been more willing to permit additur in cases where the amount to be added is a liquidated amount, such as a fixed financial amount in a contract, or readily calculable interest.

Assuming that a court is permitted to grant the motion for a new trial unless the nonmoving party agrees to lesser or greater damages, the question remains how a court should set the amount to be remitted or added. Consider these three possibilities in remittitur. The judge will grant defendant's motion for a new trial unless the plaintiff agrees to (1) remit the least amount possible that will bring the verdict into the range of what the judge believes is a permissible verdict; (2) remit the amount that will make the verdict what the judge believes a reasonable jury should have awarded; (3) remit the greatest amount possible that will bring the verdict to the smallest award that the judge believes to be rational, given the evidence.

If the plaintiff refuses to remit (or the defendant refuses to add) and the judge, therefore, decides to grant the motion for a new trial, the judge may also consider whether to grant a total new trial, or only a new trial on damages. To grant a new trial only on damages, of course, raises many of the same issues as bifurcation.

Some evidence suggests that plaintiffs in the United States often collect considerably less than the total amounts of their verdicts and the accrued interest. The widespread use of remittitur is one reason; another is settlement pending new trials or appeals, or during the period that plaintiffs try to collect on their judgments. Perhaps most important, the financial straits of defendants (such as bankruptcy or a lack of funds or property to pay the award) may result in plaintiffs' taking a good deal less than the damages award plus interest.

Although there are few empirical studies on the postverdict adjustment of jury awards, one such study demonstrated that, at least in larger cases, plaintiffs ultimately recover substantially less than the jury award:

> Ivy Broder reviewed a sample of 198 jury awards of $1 million or more that occurred between 1984 and 1985. Plaintiffs received the original jury award in just slightly more than a quarter of the cases. On average, the final aggregate disbursement to plaintiffs was 57% lower than the original verdict. The amount of the reduction varied by case type. Medical malpractice awards, for example, were reduced by 27% on average. However, the average statistic obscures the fact that larger awards were reduced more than smaller awards. Broder's report did not indicate whether the reduction was made by the trial judge or an appeal court or whether it resulted from post-verdict settlements or inability to collect from the defendant.

Neil Vidmar, Felicia Gross, & Mary Rose, *Jury Awards for Medical Malpractice and Post-Verdict Adjustments of Those Awards,* 48 DePaul L. Rev. 265, 279-280 (1998) (summarizing Ivy E. Broder, *Characteristics of Million Dollar Awards: Jury Verdicts and Final Disbursements,* 11 Just. Sys. J. 349, 350 (1986)).

8. What is the specific constitutional problem raised by remittitur or additur? Scrutinize the language of the Seventh Amendment to the United States Constitution. Does the majority's constitutional distinction in *Dimick* make sense to you? Why might a state constitutional decision on additur come out differently from the *Dimick* case? When a defendant moves for a new trial based on excessive damages and the plaintiff remits the amount suggested by the judge so that the new trial motion is denied, should the defendant still be able to appeal the case? Can the defendant's appeal, if allowed at all, include the excessiveness of damages even after the remittitur? Can it include the excessiveness of damages before the remittitur? When a remittitur has been made, what risks does the defendant's counsel run if he or she decides to appeal the verdict?

In addition to checking the Seventh Amendment, please apply your common sense to all of these questions. There is no need for you to do additional research on them at this time, but when you determine where you are going to practice, you will want to acquaint yourself with both the law and the custom.

Consider the options provided in the immediately preceding question on the test that the judge should use in determining the amount of remittitur. What are the pros and cons of each test? Which would you choose? In granting a motion for new trial based on excessive or inadequate damages, should the new trial be on all issues, or on damages only? What are the pros and cons of each? In this regard, would you treat some types of cases differently from others?

9. Review the methods of jury control we have considered: rules of evidence, summary judgment, directed verdict, judgment n.o.v., instructions, new-trial motions because the verdict is against the weight of the

evidence, new-trial motions based on excessive or inadequate damages, specialized types of verdicts or interrogatories for the jury, bifurcation and trifurcation, and remittitur and additur. Which, if any, offend your sense of how juries should work? Which methods seem most sensible and fair to you?

Practice Exercise No. 22: Motions to Challenge a Jury Verdict

John Dinkins, a successful 32-year-old black male, has just won a malpractice claim against Forsyth Laboratories in state court in the State of Crabtree. The jury came in with a general verdict for Mr. Dinkins for $50,000. Forsyth Laboratories misread a laboratory test that would have diagnosed stomach cancer in its early stages. As a result of the lab's error, Mr. Dinkins' cancer was not detected until it had spread to other organs. Had the test been read accurately by the lab, Mr. Dinkins would have had a 90-95 percent survival rate after prompt removal of the cancer. Because of the delayed diagnosis, Mr. Dinkins had to endure two major operations, and is currently undergoing chemotherapy. His likelihood of survival has decreased to 50-60%.

In the past 18 months in the State of Crabtree, four similar cases have been successfully tried by plaintiffs similarly situated as to age (pre- and postincident), earning capacity, estimated life expectancy prior to the cancer, and survival rate after the misdiagnosis. These four jury verdicts averaged exactly $200,000. All plaintiffs in these four cases were white males.

The plaintiff believes that the low jury verdict was due to racial prejudice and stereotyping by jurors, as well as social devaluation of black males generally. During the trial, the defendants introduced medical evidence that black males have a higher rate of heart disease—both hereditarily and as a result of their dietary and lifestyle choices—than males of other races. The defendants also introduced evidence that Mr. Dinkins, although financially stable, chose to live in the inner city and to drive a fast, fancy sports car.

Question: If you represented Dinkins, what motions would you bring to challenge this verdict? What arguments would you make? Anticipate Forsyth's justifications and strategies.

G. CLOSING ARGUMENTS

One of the most exciting moments in a trial lawyer's life is standing up to give a closing argument. Some lawyers start thinking about their closing arguments early in their analysis and preparation of a case, as a means of focusing their case preparation on what aspects of the case will eventually provide their most persuasive advocacy. Before moving on to other aspects of procedure, we want you to read about some of that sense of exhilaration.

■ LLOYD PAUL STRYKER,
THE ART OF ADVOCACY
(1954)

. . . The summation is the high point in the art of advocacy; it is the combination and the culmination of all of its many elements. It is the climax of the case. It is the opportunity to rescue a cause until that time perhaps seemingly lost. It calls for every skill the advocate possesses. It calls for more than skill—it is a summons to his courage, a testing ground of his character, a trial of his logic and reasoning powers, his memory, his patience and his tact, his ability to express himself in convincing words; in short, it is an assay of every power of persuasion he possesses. Small wonder, then, that there have been few great summations. . . .

An advocate is one who has been called to the aid of a fellow citizen in deep trouble. You are that advocate, and your one, sole and single aim is to aid that fellow citizen with all your heart and soul and mind.

The jury is watching you with an even greater scrutiny than that with which they looked at you while you were making, now so long ago, your opening address. They remember what you promised them; they have a good recollection of the evidence that followed and they are challenging you to persuade them that you have proved all that you promised them you would prove.

But if they have been studying you, your scrutiny of them has been no less intense. You will remember how they looked when certain evidence was introduced, how they reacted to your cross-examinations. Some one or more of them may have asked questions of a witness on the stand, and you will be thinking now, as you thought then, of the significance of those questions and the way in which the questioner received the answers. If you have succeeded thus far in the trial in establishing some credit with the jury, if your firmness, your good manners, and your complete integrity have won you some measure of approval in the jury box, you will strain now to avoid everything that may forfeit that good will and you will do all within your power to strengthen it. . . .

For each new case the lawyer has a special problem. He alone has seen and heard the witnesses. He, not some master of the past, has divined the feeling of his judge and jury; he alone has felt the atmosphere of his own courtroom and is, therefore, in a better position to decide upon his course of action than all the silent mentors of the printed page.

Imagination is of incalculable aid. An illustration of how it can be used was once given by a great Chicago lawyer, Weymouth Kirkland. He had been called upon to defend a group of insurance companies which were resisting claims based on the alleged death of an engineer named Peck. The plaintiff contended that Peck had fallen overboard from a steamer while crossing Lake Michigan. The defendants, on the other hand, were seeking to establish that Peck had never fallen overboard, that he had left his coat in his stateroom as a ruse, and that when the boat docked in the early morning, he had quietly slipped down the gangplank.

Much evidence was adduced by the plaintiff for the purpose of establishing that if Peck had in fact fallen overboard, the current and the prevailing winds would have carried his body to a particular spot. One of the plaintiff's witnesses was a cook on another steamer whose ship, three days after Peck's disappearance, sailed past the exact spot where other witnesses had said the currents would have carried Peck's body. On his direct examination, the cook said that exactly at that spot he happened to glance out from his locker, saw the body, and recognized it as that of his old friend, Peck.

It was a nice opportunity for cross-examination, and Mr. Kirkland used it in this way:

Q. How long had you known Peck?
A. Fifteen years.
Q. You knew him well?
A. Yes, sir.
Q. How did you happen to see his body?
A. I looked out of the porthole.
Q. You recognized it beyond doubt as the body of Peck?
A. Yes, sir.
Q. Did you make any outcry when you saw the body?
A. No, sir.
Q. Did you ask the captain to stop the ship?
A. No, sir.
Q. What were you doing when you happened to look out of the window and saw the body?
A. I was peeling potatoes.
Q. And when the body of your old friend, Peck, floated by, you just kept on peeling potatoes?
A. Yes, sir.

It was a bit of cross-examination well done. And how was it used in the summing up? Did Mr. Kirkland tell the jury that the cook's testimony was palpably untrue? Did he denounce the absurdity of the answers? He handled it far more adroitly. As he stood before the jury for his final appeal, he produced a potato from one pocket and a knife from another. Thus equipped, he rested one foot on a chair and proceeded to peel the potato, saying: "What ho? What have we here? Who is this floating past? As I live and breathe, if it isn't my old friend Peck! I shall tell the captain about this in the morning. In the meantime, I must go right on peeling my potatoes."

By innuendo he had destroyed all the cook's testimony. A little wit had accomplished far more than the finest rhetoric or the fiercest denunciation of this perjurer.

If I were asked to name the prerequisites of an advocate, I would mention imagination among the first. One seeking to persuade a court or jury which does not possess that quality would be a man impervious to all the overtones and subtle possibilities presented by the facts. Imagination for the trial lawyer is as essential as for the novelist, the artist, or the poet. Poetry and literature and painting are the products of a mental synthesis of ideas fused from many elements; and so it is that by the formation and expression of mental images that your true advocate brings before the jury [the] essence of his contention. In a single flood he dramatizes the real point and makes his hearers see a picture which their untrained senses had not yet dismissed.

Whatever means you employ, you must lift your jury from mere logic to the springs of action that transcend cold reasoning, to the feelings and the emotions that govern, inspire, and produce the verdict. Never for an instant forget that it is a favorable verdict you are seeking.

The most impregnable of syllogisms will not secure it for you. Nothing will do it but the hearts and wills of twelve men whom you must capture. You must find a way to reach those hearts. How better can you do this than by such a systematic arrangement and presentation of the facts that each bit of evidence fits into the pattern of your theory and every circumstance advances your contention. But persuasion is far more than that— persuasion is effected only when you make those who hear you want to follow you, only when you have, as it were, so proselytized your listeners as to turn them into zealots for your cause.

If you had the Stradivarius, you would not possess a more glorious instrument than the hearts and souls of twelve men. And if you had all the skill of Paganini, Ysaye, or Zimbalist, if you had all of Mischa Elman's magic, you would not have too much with which to make your jurors' heartstrings vibrate. There ranged before you they court the inspired touch of a master's hand.

And yet all your artistry will fail if your listeners who hear and feel your art suspect that it is nothing else. Plain men like to think themselves above emotion, impervious to rhetoric and susceptible only to cold reason. Knowing this, it will be yours somehow to disguise your highest flights so that Pegasus seems only a rather well-built and serviceable draft horse.

You must not be only a musician but an actor. You must have studied your client so perceptively that you can understudy him. You must be him. You must not merely play Hamlet, you must be Hamlet himself. More than a musician or an actor, you must be a soldier and a leader. You must be a general and a humble platoon leader who knows how to gain compliance with the most potent of all military orders: "Follow me!" You must make your jury follow you even as they follow your eyes that search them through and through. The true advocate is even more than that; he is a conqueror whose will has brought about subjection and surrender. Is advocacy an art? Is there anywhere a greater one?. . .

Practice Exercise No. 23: Analyzing Closing Arguments in *City of Cleveland*

Edited portions of the three closing arguments in the firefighters case are in the Case Files. The case was a bit unusual in that initially the §1983 cause of action was to be decided by a jury, and the Title VII cause of action was to be tried solely to the judge. The judge permitted the evidence on both counts to come in at the same time and to be heard both by him and the jury. By the end of the case, however, the §1983 cause of action had been eliminated at the directed verdict stage. Consequently, the portions of the final arguments you are about to read were presented to the judge, without a jury, and were solely on the count under Title VII.

Mr. Calipari represented the United States government as plaintiff against the defendants in a case that had been consolidated with the class action against the defendants. Ms. Jennifer represented the plaintiffs in the class action. Mr. Solimine represented the City of Cleveland and the other defendants in both cases.

Consider these questions as you read the final arguments:

(1) How does the speaker perceive his or her audience? What types of arguments does the speaker think will be most persuasive?

(2) What are the relative importance of facts, law, emotions, and morality to the arguments?

(3) In what ways do the speakers' own personalities and views of the litigation process inform their closing arguments?

(4) Can you outline each argument, and is it an outline that makes sense to you, given the purpose or purposes of the closing argument?

(5) Does the speaker have a major theory of the case or a major focus for his or her argument? If so, what is it?

(6) In what ways, if any, would the arguments have differed if they were to a jury?

(7) What arguments do you think were most persuasive? Would they have influenced or persuaded you if you were the judge or a member of a jury?

(8) What would you have done differently?

Practice Exercise No. 24: Preparing and Delivering Closing Arguments in *City of Cleveland*

With this exercise, we hope to provide you with an opportunity (1) to prepare and perhaps present a closing argument in a case that you know in great detail; (2) to help you experience how the formal litigation process (elements, causes of action, burdens of proof) and the passion, morality, and common sense of a real life story come together in creative advocacy; and (3) to help you see an important aspect of the near-end of a process so that you can better understand the relationships among several parts of the process (complaint, discovery, motions, trial).

Accordingly, prepare a closing argument to a jury for the plaintiffs or the City of Cleveland on the §1983 cause of action in the *City of Cleveland* case. Prepare a typed outline of your closing argument (not more than three pages double-spaced) and hand it in at the end of class. Along with your name, please put at the top of the page the side you represent. The choices of client and whether to have a jury are up to you. Do not concern yourself with the class action aspects of the case. Assume that the directed verdict motion on §1983 was denied and that the City of Cleveland is the only remaining defendant. The case will go to the jury only on liability issues (including causation), not on damages. The judge will instruct the jury after both closing arguments with the same instructions you have in your Case Files, except there will only be a general verdict. Assume that the City's counsel will argue first and the plaintiffs' lawyer second. Assume that the jury will be given only general verdict slips. You should be able to make a credible argument that lasts no more than fifteen minutes.

You may argue using any evidence that appears anywhere in the *City of Cleveland* Case Files, including even (for this purpose only) allegations in the complaint, the initial plaintiffs' memorandum, and the closing arguments. Most importantly, you may use any of the evidence noted in the Judge's Trial Notebook (in the Case Files). Feel free to consult anyone. You may use the library, but you need not. Regardless of what help you get, your written outline should be your own. And, of course, your oral argument, if you are called upon, should be your own.

Note: Tips on Making a Closing Argument   **P**

Most lawyers making a closing argument have a very good idea of what they are going to say; they have an outline, but they do not read the argument. They want to make eye contact with the judge or jury, and, if they are not arguing first, they want to adjust their argument to what the other lawyers have already argued.

Closing arguments to a jury usually state in general form the major instructions that the judge will give (if she hasn't already given them). The lawyer wants the jury to consider the law that they have to apply as they listen to the closing argument. Closing arguments usually rely heavily on the evidence that has come in during the trial, and they suggest how that evidence and natural inferences drawn therefrom support the conclusion. A good closing is not simply a summary of the testimony of the witnesses and other evidence; instead, a good argument uses select pieces to advance an argument. Often, closing arguments will address the motivation of important parties and witnesses, focusing on the credibility of certain so-called evidence. Closing arguments try to tell a story—to give a picture in words—that draws the jury to the desired conclusion and leaves a mark that jurors will remember throughout their deliberations.

Closing arguments may not include references to evidence that is not in the record. Also, as in most legal arguments, it is important not to ignore your opponents' strongest points. Rather, you must address them and undermine them—whether through evidence, logic, legal doctrine, morality, or otherwise. Explain to the jury why the picture painted by the opponent is inaccurate or at least incomplete.

If there are important exhibits, remember that the jury will usually have them in the jury room during their deliberations. Some lawyers like to weave the exhibits into their closing argument, so that the jury will be reminded of their argument as they review the exhibits.

It is unethical for a lawyer to say who or what they believe during a closing argument. Instead, you will use phrases like "The evidence suggests . . ." or "The evidence permits only one sound conclusion. . . ." Be sure to tell the fact finder exactly what you want them to do. For example, it is not patronizing and, in fact, is helpful to be as direct as "If you agree with me, ladies and gentlemen of the jury, you should put an 'x' on the line on the jury slip that says 'for the defendant.'" When damages are involved in a matter, you will need to check with local law and custom to ascertain to what extent you may discuss particular sums of money. In many, if not most, jurisdictions you are not allowed in closing argument to ask the jury to "be in the plaintiff's shoes," nor are you allowed to suggest that they consider the value of having one day without the plaintiff's injury and multiplying that by life expectancy.

Most important, realize that there is no single right—or even best— way to make a closing. The effectiveness of the closing arguments depends on your personality, the type of case, the evidence, your witnesses, the jury, the judge, the ambience of the courtroom, and your ability to process each of these influences. Rhetoric—the art of persuasion—is an ancient and admirable enterprise. Enjoy.

H. APPEALS

The value of a favorable trial verdict is materially diminished if it cannot survive appellate review. Winners can quickly become losers, and losers have a second chance to convince the court that a verdict in their favor is the just result or that a new trial is necessary.

The appellate process differs from the trial proceedings in the lower courts in both its procedure and its purpose. The attorneys do not try their case as if the first trial had never happened, but rather present alleged errors of the trial judge for the appellate court to review. The appellate court serves the purpose of supervising the trial judges' decisions and establishing uniformity of the law within its jurisdiction. During the proceedings below, the trial judge may not have the time to consider the issues with the care and reflection afforded to appellate judges. Furthermore, the perspective of the appellate court offers a check on the potential arbitrariness of the trial judge and may instill confidence in the trial process by reaffirming the judges' decisions.

Unlike a trial court, an appellate court looks somewhat beyond the rights of the parties in the specific case before them. The appellate courts are the voice of authority on the law in their jurisdiction and thus attempt to create a uniform body of law for predicting the outcome of future cases. Procedures for achieving these goals may vary, but the Federal Rules of Appellate Procedure establish mechanisms for the federal courts, and substantially similar rules have been adopted in many state courts.

The Judiciary Act of 1789 established three levels of courts in the federal system: the Supreme Court, circuit courts, and district courts. There are currently thirteen courts of appeals—eleven for numbered circuits, one for the District of Columbia, and the Court of Appeals for the Federal Circuit, established in 1982. The United States Courts of Appeals may hear the decisions of the federal district courts of the states and territories in their regions. For practical purposes, the right to appeal is statutory, not constitutional.

The appellate courts will hear only alleged errors that are revealed in the trial record, and ordinarily no new factual findings will be taken into consideration. The trial record must also reveal that the aggrieved party made a timely objection to the alleged error. The alleged error must have materially affected the outcome of the case and must be necessary to the decree in order to be reviewable. If the party does not raise an error that is found in the trial record the appellate court will usually consider it waived.

Federal courts and most state courts require finality in the trial court as a basis for appellate jurisdiction. This requirement, known as the final judgment rule, ensures that the proceedings below are completed before the review process begins. The timing of an appeal usually requires notice within thirty days after the final judgment is rendered.

The main principle behind this final judgment rule is the conservation of judicial resources. Finality requires that the trial below end on the merits and "leave nothing for the court to do but execute the judgment." *Catlin v. United States*, 324 U.S. 229, 233 (1945). If finality is not present, the appeal may be unnecessary. The pending proceedings may settle, or the issue may have become moot as a result of the trial. Also, denying immediate review prevents the use of expensive delaying tactics and harassment of opposing parties.

Not all requests for immediate appeal are denied. Immediate review can be important in providing guidance to the trial court and in preventing hardship. Exceptions to the final judgment rule include the collateral order doctrine, interlocutory appeals, and writs of mandamus and prohibition.

The collateral order doctrine is a judicial exception to the final judgment rule and exempts only a small number of cases—those in which there is an order that is an offshoot of the principle litigation, and where the appeal does not require delving into the merits of the case: "[T]he order must conclusively determine the disputed question, resolve an important issue completely separate from the merits of the action, and be effectively unreviewable on appeal from a final judgment." *Coopers & Lybrand v. Livesay*, 437 U.S. 463, 468 (1978).

An interlocutory decision is made while the case is pending in the trial court, but prior to the final determination of the merits. Under 28 U.S.C.S. §1292, an interlocutory appeal may be taken from interlocutory orders with respect to injunctions, receiverships, and the rights and liabilities of parties to admiralty cases. Also, district court judges can, under limited circumstances, state in an interlocutory order that they think an immediate appeal would "materially advance the ultimate termination of the litigation," and the court of appeals, upon application, has discretion to permit such on appeal.

Writs of mandamus and prohibition seek an order from the appellate court to order a requirement or a prohibition of a certain action by a public official. The public official may be a judge of a lower court, making the procedure similar to interlocutory orders. In *Kerr v. United States District Court*, 426 U.S. 394 (1976), the United States Supreme Court stated, "the remedy of mandamus is a drastic one" and "only exceptional circumstances amounting to judicial 'usurpation of power' will justify the invocation of this extraordinary remedy." *Kerr* also set forth various conditions for which the court would issue a writ, including if the party seeking the writ has no other adequate means to attain the desired relief, and if the party is able to establish that the need for the issuance is "clear and indisputable."

In the courts of appeals, ordinarily a panel of three judges reaches its decision by a majority vote. (On occasion, all of the judges of a court of appeals will hear an appeal.) Even though the panel may decide that the trial court erred in its decision, not all errors at trial are grounds for reversal. The likelihood of reversal depends on the standard of review. In reviewing the district court's finding of fact, the appellate court normally will defer to the authority of the trial judge, who has greater familiarity with the entire case and has observed the demeanor evidence at trial. Under Rule 52(a) of the Federal Rules of Appellate Procedure, the appellate court will set aside findings of fact only if they are "clearly erroneous." In *United States v. U.S. Gypsum Co.*, 333 U.S. 364, 395 (1948), the Court defined the clearly erroneous standard as "when the reviewing court on the entire evidence is left with definite and firm conviction that a mistake has been committed." The trial judge must have misunderstood the law or made a finding without adequate evidentiary support. However, if the case below was a jury trial, the appellate court gives even greater deference to the findings of fact.

Fed. R. App. P. 52(a) does not require a "clearly erroneous" standard for reviewing conclusions of law. The absence of a standard for conclusions of law in the Federal Rules of Appellate Procedure has left the appellate courts with complete authority to freely consider conclusions of law. However, the appellate court will reverse only if it thinks the trial court, more likely than not, erred in its decision. The standard to be applied in cases of mixed fact and law is generally the same standard as that applied to questions of pure law, although the courts have determined which standard to use in certain cases, like contract cases. Where a trial court judge makes a conclusion of law based on the four corners of the document, the appellate court will review the appeal *de novo*. But where the trial court considers extrinsic evidence to make a conclusion, the conclusion rests on findings of fact, and therefore, may be reviewable by the "clearly erroneous" standard.

Finally, when a trial judge makes a discretionary ruling, the standard for review is "abuse of discretion." Since the trial judge is in the best position to make discretionary rulings, the ruling will be overturned only if the appellate court is convinced that the judge was clearly wrong.

After a court of appeals renders its decision, an aggrieved party may seek an appeal at the next level of review. Seeking review from a United States Court of Appeals to the Supreme Court of the United States is almost always done through the discretionary writ of certiorari. Whether the Supreme Court grants the writ depends on such criteria as conflicts among circuits, the general importance of the legal questions involved, and the public importance of the case.

If the case originated in a state court, the party ordinarily has the right of appeal to the state's intermediate appellate court. As in the federal court system, most states require a petition to the state's highest court, which is granted only by the discretion of that court. Under 28 U.S.C. §1257, if a question of federal law exists, and a final judgment or decree has been "rendered by the highest court of a State in which a decision could be had . . ." then the decision "may be reviewed by the [United States] Supreme Court by writ of certiorari. . . ."

Only a small percentage of the cases in which review is sought by the Supreme Court of the United States are granted certiorari and disposed of by a written opinion. In fact, the number of Supreme Court written opinions has been declining. For example, in 1980, 4,174 cases were docketed and 159 were disposed of by written opinion. In 1994, 6,996 cases were docketed, resulting in disposition by just 95 written opinions. Richard H. Fallon, Jr., Daniel J. Meltzer, & David L. Shapiro, *The Federal Courts and The Federal System* 57 (1996).

I. REVIEW

This question is designed to help you determine how much you have learned in the course to date, to help you review and learn some more, and to practice tackling typical law school exam questions.

You will benefit most from the quiz if you follow the directions: Put aside at least two hours to take this quiz; if you finish early, you should assume that you did not use sufficient precision and detail in your answer. Use only your rule book. Try the exam on your own before discussing it with your study group.

Memorandum

To: Summer Judicial Intern
From: Judge Moran, State Trial Court Judge
Date: November 10, 2000

In March, 2000 Wayne Earnest and Cleveland Grover (hereafter, "Earnest" and "Grover," respectively) filed one complaint in my trial court and requested a jury. The statute of limitations for all cases in this jurisdiction is two years. Our state has adopted the Federal Rules of Civil Procedure in all relevant respects.* Our state does not have a contribution statute.

The complaint alleges: the plaintiffs' names and the names of Jill Joke and Sally Sales, as defendants (hereafter, "Joke" and "Sales," respectively); that on Halloween, October 31, 1998, at 9:15 A.M., Earnest entered The Joke Shop, owned and managed by Joke; at 3:30 P.M. Grover did the same; at about the time each opened the door, a ghost suddenly appeared, and then there was the sound of a loud explosion; as a result, each plaintiff was greatly scared; Earnest required seven weeks of medical care for his resulting fright, and Grover, as a result, did and still does require and re-

---

* In this state, however, the complaint does not have to allege subject matter jurisdiction because the trial courts are courts of general jurisdiction and can hear almost all types of cases.

ceive medical care for his resulting fright; as a result each has incurred large medical expenses, missed several months of work, has severe anxiety and headaches, and has difficulty sleeping; wherefore each demands $200,000 in damages. The complaint is signed by a lawyer.

Joke filed a timely answer, in which she (1) admitted ownership and general management of The Joke Shop, denied all other allegations, and alleged that on October 31, 1998 she was not working in The Joke Shop; nor was it supposed to be open; nor was Sales an employee of hers at the time; (2) raised a 12(b)(6) defense; and (3) counterclaimed against Grover for failing to pay for $2,500 of goods purchased from The Joke Shop between January 1 and October 31, 1998, under terms that the price of each purchase was due at the time of purchase. Joke also filed an impleader claim against Sales stating that "Sales had been fired on October 15, 1998, and had no right being in The Joke Shop on October 31, 1998; that she, Joke, had intended and ordered that the Shop be closed that day; and that if she, Joke, is held liable, it would be as a result of Sales' negligence and trespass, and that Sales should therefore indemnify her." Joke also filed an impleader claim against Carl Cap alleging that if "on October 31, 1998 Carl Cap caused an explosion, I had nothing to do with it, since I was not there and knew nothing about it; that Grover alleges said explosion scared him; if it did, and if I am held liable, then Cap must indemnify me."

After discovery, Joke filed an affidavit that restates under oath everything alleged in her answer, counterclaim, and two impleaders. Joke also submitted a portion of deposition taken of Grover's doctor, which says "Grover was anxious and had all the same symptoms before October 31, 1998 as he had after. I do not believe that the October 31st incident, if it happened at all, caused him any harm." Joke also filed interrogatory answers of Sales in which she states, among other things, that "I was working in the Joke Shop with permission on October 31, 1998, but by noon I had discontinued all pranks. Carl Cap, whom both Joke and I had forbidden to come in the store, played a loud recording of an explosion outside the store window, which may have surprised Earnest. I only saw Cap after it happened." Grover filed an affidavit that states "Although I was anxious before the October 31, 1998, negligence of Joke and Sales, I felt much worse afterwards and probably would have gone back to work sooner and required less medical help, had the ghost and loud explosion noise not frightened me."

Although there was extensive discovery in which every party sought all relevant information, I have provided you (in this memo) all relevant portions of pleadings, affidavits, and discovery that you need to help me decide the motions before me.

I have to rule on:

1. Joke's 12(b)(6);
2. A motion for summary judgment by Joke against Grover;

3. A motion by Joke to dismiss against Grover for misjoinder, or, in the alternative, to sever the two plaintiffs' cases;
4. Motions by Sales and Cap to dismiss each respective impleader as improper;
5. A motion by Grover to dismiss Joke's counterclaim against him as improper;
6. A motion filed two weeks ago by Grover to amend his complaint by adding: "In addition, when I came back the next day to complain to Joke, Joke intentionally punched me in the nose, broke it, and caused me to incur headaches, medical expense, and lose additional work."

How should I rule on each of the above motions? (*Notice the date of this memorandum and assume that you are responding on this date.*) Please give me your analysis and reasons. Rule on all of the motions, even if one or more rulings might render others moot. There are, of course, additional pleadings and motions in the Earnest and Sales portions of the case, but I do not have to decide those yet.

6

Questioning and Taming the Current System

Critics of the American federal and state civil justice systems cite costs and delays as serious, chronic problems. The special problems of delay and cost associated with pretrial discovery constitute only part of the problem produced by explosive numbers of court filings, lawyer-driven pleadings, and conventional judicial passivity. For those who are litigants and those who cannot afford to be, the quality of justice is reduced when it is delayed and expensive. A separate line of criticism points to the assumptions and effects of adversariness. Adversarial process is supposed to promote truth-telling, fairness, and the enforcement of rights. Critics allege that instead, as actually operated, the adversarial system promotes nondisclosure, manipulation, and winner-take-all solutions, rather than promoting constructive problem solving.

Others focus on the capacity—or incapacity—of courts to deal with lawsuits crafted under liberal pleading rules that permit multiparty, multiclaim suits involving complex social and economic problems. Some emphasize the need for sharp limits on adjudication, while others defend the creative responses of judges to the contemporary shape of litigation, including litigation involving public institutions and public values.

This chapter examines the premises and criticisms of the adversary system, its relationship to lawyers' roles, the debates over the capacity of courts to address complex litigation, the controversy over whether there indeed is a crisis of litigation in the United States, and descriptions and evaluations of alternatives developed both within the context of litigation and beyond the courts. Given the fact that most cases filed in the United States and state courts never reach trial, the options of settlement, negotiation, arbitration, and mediation are crucial to every piece of litigation.

A. THINKING ABOUT THE ADVERSARY SYSTEM

A crucial assumption in notions of due process is adversariness. Whether used to express a search for the truth through competing presentations or instead to underscore a democratic distrust of centralized authority, adversariness underlies formal litigation and influences dispute processing more generally in the United States. How well do the assumed benefits of adversariness stand up under scrutiny, and what are the possible benefits and drawbacks to alternatives, such as mediation and arbitration? The vast numbers of both civil and criminal cases filed in state and federal court end in settlement; how should this be evaluated, promoted, or deterred?

1. Evaluating the Adversary System

In a comprehensive study of lawyers and justice, the philosopher David Luban considers how much of the conventional U.S. lawyer's role has been justified on the basis of the presumed benefits of the adversary system. As you read his critique of the system, consider which steps in his argument you find persuasive, and which less so; also consider the consequences of his argument for notions of due process.

■ DAVID LUBAN, LAWYERS AND JUSTICE: AN ETHICAL STUDY
Princeton Univ. Press 67-103 (1988)

WHY HAVE AN ADVERSARY SYSTEM?

Prior to the Norman invasion, Anglo-Saxon legal procedure left adjudication up to God through trial by ordeal and trial by "compurgation." In the latter, a litigant rested his case on his own credibility, attested to by oaths sworn by so-called "compurgators." Only if the compurgators could complete their oaths without stumbling or making mistakes were the oaths valid, and the divine hand was expected to twist the compurgators tongues if the litigant was lying. Needless to say, it was not long before professional compurgators arose who could negotiate the most complex oaths without making a mistake, and some accounts have it that the Anglo-American legal profession originated in those compurgators-for-hire.

The Anglo-Saxon adversary system thus originated in superstition, and dogmatic belief in the system's intrinsic superiority as a truth finder amounts to little more than superstition perpetuated. The question we must address is whether the modern adversary system can be defended by hard-headed arguments, or whether adversary trial still requires God as its copilot.

The numerous writers who have defended the adversary system have offered a bewildering variety of arguments on its behalf, but all of them fall into two broad categories: arguments that the adversary system is the best way of achieving various goals (consequentialist arguments), and arguments that it is intrinsically good (non-consequentialist arguments). To begin we shall look at three versions of the former: one, that the adversary system is the best way of ferreting out truth; second, that it is the best way of defending litigants' legal rights; and third, that by establishing checks and balances it is the best way of safeguarding against excesses.

Then we shall turn to three nonconsequentialist arguments. According to the first, the lawyer-client relationship established by the adversary system is itself intrinsically valuable. According to the second, the adversary system is required to honor human dignity by granting every litigant a voice in the legal process. And according to the third, the adversary system is so tightly woven into the very fabric of society that it would be unjust or imprudent to tinker with it.

My aim is to show that none of these arguments is sound, but that the adversary system is nonetheless justified. I conclude the chapter by offering what I shall immodestly claim is the only legitimate reason for maintaining the adversary system: the unexciting pragmatic argument that it is no worse than the plausible alternatives.

The point of all this will emerge in the following chapters, where I shall argue that the kind of justification offered for the adversary system matters crucially in deciding whether the system is capable of underwriting institutional excuses for lawyers. If the usual arguments on its behalf—the six consequentialist and non-consequentialist arguments we shall now examine—could be sustained, the answer might well be "yes"; but given the real reason for maintaining the adversary system, the answer turns out to be a surprising "no."

CONSEQUENTIALIST JUSTIFICATIONS OF THE ADVERSARY SYSTEM

Truth

The question of whether the adversary system is, all in all, the best way of uncovering the facts of a case at bar sounds like an empirical question. I happen to think that it is an empirical question, moreover, which has scarcely been investigated and that is most likely impossible to answer. This is because we do not, after a trial is over, find the parties coming forth to make a clean breast of the conflict and enlighten the world as to what really happened. A trial is not a quiz show with the right answer waiting in a sealed envelope. We can't learn directly whether the facts are really as the trier determined them because we don't ever find out the facts. . . .

It is not surprising to discover that the arguments purporting to show the advantages of the adversary system as a fact-finder have mostly been nonempirical, a mix of a priori theories of inquiry and armchair psychology.

Here is one such argument: it bases itself on the idea very similar to Sir Karl Popper's theory of scientific rationality, that the way to get at the truth is a wholehearted dialectic of assertion and refutation. . . .

This theory is open to a number of objections. First of all, the analogy to Popperian scientific methodology is not a good one. Perhaps science proceeds by advancing conjectures and then trying to refute them; but it does not proceed by advancing conjectures that the scientist knows to be false and then using procedural rules to exclude probative evidence. Yet that is what discrediting the truthful witness or "hiding the ball" through the attorney-client privilege amounts to.

The two adversary attorneys, moreover, are each under an obligation to present the facts in the manner most consistent with their clients' posi-tion—to prevent the introduction of unfavorable evidence, to undermine the credibility of opposing witnesses, to set unfavorable facts in a context in which their importance is minimized, to attempt to provoke inferences in their client's favor. The assumption is that two such accounts will cancel out, leaving the truth of the matter. But there is no earthly reason to think this will happen—the facts may simply pile up in confusion.

This is particularly likely in those frequent cases when the facts in question concern someone's character or state of mind. Out comes the parade of psychiatrists, what Hannah Arendt once called "the comedy of the soul-experts." Needless to say, they have been prepared by the lawyers, sometimes without knowing it. . . .

The other side, of course, can cross-examine such a witness to get the truth out. The late Irving Younger, who was perhaps the most popular lecturer on trial tactics in the country, told how. Among his famous "Ten Commandments of Cross-Examination" are these:

(1) Never ask anything but a leading question.
(2) Never ask a question to which you don't already know the answer.
(3) Never permit the witness to explain his or her answers.
(4) Don't bring out your conclusions in the cross-examination. Save them for closing arguments when the witness is in no position to refute them.

Of course, the opposition may be prepared for this; they may have seen Younger's three-hour videotape on how to examine expert witnesses.

They may know, therefore, that the cross-examiner is saving her conclusions for the closing argument. Not to worry! Younger knew how to stop an attorney from distorting the truth in closing arguments. "If the opposing lawyer is holding the jury spellbound . . . the spell must be broken at all cost. [Younger] suggests the attorney leap to his or her feet and make furious and spurious objections. They will be overruled, but they might at least break the opposing counsel's concentration."

My guess is that this is not quite what Sir Karl Popper had in mind when he wrote, "The Western rationalist tradition . . . is the tradition of critical discussion—of examining and testing propositions or theories by attempting to refute them."

All this does not mean that the adversary system may not in fact get at the truth in many hard cases. (Trial lawyers' war stories present mixed results.) I suppose that it is as good a system as its rivals. But to repeat the point I began with, nobody knows how good that is.

LEGAL RIGHTS

It is sometimes said, however, that the point of the adversary system is not that it is the best way of getting at the truth, but rather the best way of defending individuals' legal rights. This is clearly a version of the theory of zealous advocacy pertinent to criminal cases. Freedman points out that if the sole purpose of a trial were to get at the truth we would not have our Fourth, Fifth, and Sixth Amendment rights; the fact that improperly obtained evidence cannot be used against us and that we cannot be required to testify against ourselves indicates that our society considers other values more central than truth. And, according to the theory we shall now consider, these other values have to do with legal rights.

The argument is that the best way to guarantee that an individual's legal rights are protected, in civil no less than criminal matters, is to provide her with a zealous adversary advocate who will further her interests.

This argument, we should note, is slightly different from Freedman's, according to which counsel by a zealous advocate is not merely the best way of defending one's legal rights, but is itself one of those rights. That, of course, would make the adversary system necessary for the defense of legal rights, but only in the trivial sense that taking away her counsel infringes a person's right to counsel and you can't defend a right by infringing it. Freedman suggests that adversary advocacy is a constitutional value, but this is not obvious. The Constitution makes no explicit mention of the adversary system. . . . It is not clear that the Court would find common law or statutory tinkering with the adversary format a denial of due process, and it is not clear that a constitutional amendment would be required to change to a nonadversarial system. . . .

The argument we are considering is rather that the right to counsel aside, adversary advocacy is the best defense of our other legal rights. The no-holds-barred zealous advocate tries to get everything the law can give (if that is the client's wish), and thereby does a better job of defending the client's legal rights than a less committed lawyer would do.

Put this way, however, it is clear that the argument contains a confusion. My legal rights are everything I am in fact legally entitled to, not everything the law can be made to give. For obviously a good lawyer may be able to get me things to which I am not entitled, but this, to call a spade a spade, is an example of infringing my opponent's legal rights, not defending mine. . . .

To this it might be replied that looking at it this way leaves the opponent's lawyer out of the picture. Of course, the reply continues, no one is claiming that a zealous adversary advocate is attempting to defend legal rights: she is attempting to win. The claim is only that the clash of two such adversaries will in fact defend legal rights most effectively. . . .

It is obvious that litigators pride themselves on their won-lost records. The National Law Journal described "the world's most successful criminal lawyer—229 murder acquittals without a loss!", and goes on to mention the Inner Circle, a lawyer's club whose membership requirement is winning a seven-figure verdict. You never know, of course, maybe each of these cases really had legal right on its side. And when a coin comes up heads 229 times in a row it may be fair—but there is another explanation. Lawyers themselves do not see the point of what they do as defending their clients' legal rights, but as using the law to get their clients what they want. . . .

Let me be clear about what the objection is. It is not that the flaw in the adversary system as a defender of legal rights is overkill on the part of morally imperfect victory-hungry lawyers. The objection is that under the adversary system, an exemplary lawyer is required to indulge in overkill to obtain as legal rights benefits that in fact may not be legal rights. . . .

ETHICAL DIVISION OF LABOR

This argument is no longer that the excesses of zealous advocacy are excused by appealing to the promotion of truth or to the defense of legal rights. Rather, it is that they are excused by what Thomas Nagel calls an "ethical division of labor." . . . The idea is that behavior that looks wrong from the point of view of common morality is justified by the fact that other social roles exist whose purpose is to counteract the excesses resulting from the questionable role behavior. Zealous adversary advocacy is justified by the fact that the other side is also furnished with a zealous advocate; the impartial arbiter provides a further check. . . .

The problem is this. The checks-and-balances notion is desirable because if other parts of the system exist to rectify one's excesses, one will be able to devote undivided attention to the job at hand and do it better. It is analogous to wearing protective clothing in a sport such as fencing: knowing that one's opponent is protected, one is justified in going all out in the match. But in the adversary system, the situation is different, since the attorney is actively trying to get around the checks and balances: here the analogy is to a fencer who uses a special foil that can cut through the opponent's protective clothing. To put the point another way, the adversary advocate attempts to evade the system of checks and balances, not to rely on it to save people from her. You cannot argue that the adversary system works because it is self-checking, since it is self-checking only if it works. . . .

NONCONSEQUENTIALIST JUSTIFICATIONS
OF THE ADVERSARY SYSTEM

It may be thought, however, that assessing the adversary system in consequentialist terms of how it will get some job done misses the point. Some social institutions, such as participatory democracy, are justifiable despite the fact that—maybe even because—they are inefficient. The moral standing of such institutions has a noninstrumental basis.

I wish to consider three nonconsequentialist justifications of the adversary system. The first, and perhaps the boldest, is an attempt to justify the adversary system in the widest sense, in or out of litigation: it is the argument that the traditional lawyer-client relation is an intrinsic moral good. The second is an argument that the adversary system is required by proper respect for human dignity. And the third is a cluster of related arguments: that adversary adjudication is a valued and valuable tradition, that it enjoys the consent of the governed, and that it is thus an integral part of our social fabric.

Adversary advocacy as intrinsically good

When we seek out the services of a professional we seek more than a mere quid pro quo. Perhaps this is because the quo may be of vital importance to us; perhaps it is because a lot of quid may be required to hire those services. In any event, we have the sense of entrusting a large chunk of our life to this person, and the fact that she takes on so intimate a burden and handles it in a trustworthy and skillful manner when the stakes are high seems commendable in itself. Nor does the fact that the professional makes a living by providing this service seem to mitigate the praiseworthiness of it. The business aspect moves along a different moral dimension: it explains how the relationship came about, not what it involves. Finally, our being able to bare our weaknesses and mistakes to the professional and receive assistance without condemnation enhances our sense that beneficence or moral graciousness is at work here. Our lawyer, mirabile dictu, forgives us our transgressions.

Feelings such as these are quite real; the question is whether they are more than feelings. If they are, that may show that Schwartz's two principles and thus the adversary system and the behavior it countenances are themselves positive moral goods.

Such arguments are, in fact, frequently made: they are based on the "service ethic," the idea that providing service is intrinsically good. No finer statement of this ideal exists than Mellinkoff's. He sees the paradigm client as the "man-in-trouble": . . .

> The lawyer, as lawyer, is no sweet kind loving moralizer. He assumes he is needed, and that no one comes to see him to pass the time of day. He is a prober, an analyzer, a scrapper, a man with a strange devotion to his client. Beautifully strange, or so it seems to the man-in-trouble; ugly strange to the untroubled onlooker.

Charles Fried thinks of the lawyer as a "special-purpose friend" whose activity—enhancing the client's autonomy and individuality—is an intrinsic moral good. This is true even when the lawyer's "friendship" consists in assisting the profiteering slumlord to evict an indigent tenant, or enabling Pakel to run the statute of limitations to avoid an honest debt to Zabella.

I mention Mellinkoff's and Fried's arguments together because, it seems to me, they express similar ideas, while the unsavory conclusion of the latter exposes the limitations of the former. Both arguments are attempts to show that a lawyer serving a client constitutes an intrinsic moral good. Mellinkoff's depiction of this service, however, really shows something much weaker, that a lawyer serving a man-in-trouble is (or even more cautiously, can be) engaged in an intrinsic moral good. If the client is a company laying off workers a few at a time to blackmail the FTC into permitting a merger we are confronted with no man-in-trouble and the intuitions to which Mellinkoff's argument appeals disappear. . . . The trouble with Mellinkoff's argument is that he makes all clients look more pitiable than they often are.

Fried, on the other hand, is willing to bite the bullet and argue that it is morally good to represent the man-in-no-trouble-in-particular, the man-who-troubles-others. Fried's idea is that the abstract connection between a remote person (even a person-in-trouble) and the agent exercises too slight a claim on the agent to override the agent's inclination to promote the interests of concrete others such as friends, family, or clients. This argument justifies lavishing special care on our friends, even at the expense of "abstract others," and since lavishing care is morally praiseworthy, once we swallow the notion that a lawyer is a special-purpose friend, we are home free and can guarantee the intrinsic moral worth of the lawyer-client relationship. . . .

The friendship analogy undercuts rather than establishes the principle of nonaccountability. We are not—except for the Gordon Liddys of the world—willing to do grossly immoral things to help our friends, nor should we be. Lord Brougham's apology may be many things, but it is not a credo of human friendship in any form. Fried realizes the danger, for he confesses that not only would I not lie or steal for . . . my friends, I probably also would not pursue socially noxious schemes, foreclose the mortgages of widows or orphans, or assist in the avoidance of just punishment. So we must be careful lest the whole argument unravel on us at this point.

The method for saving the argument, however, is disappointing. Fried distinguishes between personal wrongs committed by a lawyer, such as abusing a witness, and institutional wrongs occasioned by the lawyer, such as foreclosing on widows. The latter are precisely those done by the lawyer in her proper role of advancing the client's legal autonomy and—a preestablished harmony?—they are precisely the ones that are morally okay. That is because the lawyer isn't really doing them, the system is.

This last distinction has not been very popular since the Second World War, and Fried takes pains to restrict it to "generally just and decent" systems, not Nazi Germany. With this qualification, he can more comfortably assert: "We should absolve the lawyer of personal moral responsibility for the result he accomplishes because the wrong is wholly institutional." . . .

The human dignity argument

The philosopher Alan Donagan has interpreted the kernel of Fried's (and Freedman's) justification of adversary advocacy so as to provide a different nonconsequentialist defense of the adversary system. In Donagan's view, the core notion underlying the adversary system is the human dignity of the client. A society respects our human dignity by provisionally treating the positions we maintain in legal disputes (civil or criminal) as good faith positions, even when they are not. . . .

In short: the concept of human dignity underwrites an adversary system only to the extent of requiring that the parties be able to present their own good faith positions in court, assisted by attorneys. That is something, to be sure, but it is not a lot. It is as a matter of fact no more than inquisitorial systems such as those of France and Germany offer. The argument surely does not justify anything as robust as the Anglo-American version of adversary procedure; and, since it justifies neither of the standard conception's two principles, it actually undercuts the wide sense of the adversary system discussed earlier in this chapter.

The social fabric argument

The remaining arguments are distinct but closely related. They are two variants of the following idea, which may be called the "social fabric argument": regardless of whether the adversary system is efficacious, it is an integral part of our culture, and that fact by itself justifies it. The first variation is based on democratic theory: it claims that the adversary system is justified because it enjoys the consent of the governed. The second variation is based on conservative theory: it claims that the adversary system is justified because it is a deeply rooted part of our tradition.

According to the social fabric argument, the moral reason for staying with our institutions is precisely that they are ours. We live under them, adapt our lives and practices to them, assess our neighbors' behavior in their light, employ them as a standard against which to measure other ways of life. Traditional institutions bind us—morally and legitimately bind us—because we assimilate ourselves to our tradition (variation two). In the language of political theory, we consent to them (variation one). They express who we are and what we stand for. . . .

An immediate problem with the argument, however, is that we do not explicitly consent to the adversary system. Nobody asked us, and I don't suppose anyone intends to, whether or not we accept the adversary system as a mode of adjudication. . . .

Thus the most we get from tacit consent arguments, such as Walzer's appeal to our "common life," is a demonstration that we are not obligated to dismantle the adversary system. To get anything stronger we must appeal to a different concept in democratic theory than consent: we must show that people want the adversary system. In Rousseau's language, we must show that having an adversary system is our "general will."

Does the adversary system pass such a test? The answer, I think, is clearly no. Few of our institutions are trusted less than adversary adjudication, precisely because it seems to license lawyers to trample on the truth, and legal rights, and morality. . . .

[T]he argument from tradition ignores the fact that there is no constant tradition: common law constantly modifies the adversary system. Indeed, adversary advocacy is a recent invention within that changing tradition. In Great Britain, felony defense lawyers were not permitted to address the courts until 1836; in America, indigent criminal defendants were not guaranteed free counsel until *Gideon* was decided in 1963. Indigent civil litigants are still not guaranteed free counsel, even in quasi-criminal matters, such as a state's attempt to take a child from its parent. It is hard to see the adversary system as "a clause in the great primaeval contract."

In the second place, the adversary system is an ancillary institution compared with those with which Burke was concerned. . . .

THE REAL REASON FOR THE ADVERSARY SYSTEM

So far the course of argument has been purely negative, a persecution and assassination of the adversary system. By this time you are entitled to ask what I propose putting in its place. The answer is: nothing, for I think the adversary system is justified.

I do not, let me quickly say, have an argumentative novelty to produce. It would be strange indeed for a social institution to be justified on the basis of virtues other than the tried and true ones, virtues that no one had noticed in it before. My justification is a modest one, carrying no ideological freight: I shall call it the "pragmatic justification" or "pragmatic argument," to suggest its affinity with the relaxed, problem-oriented, and historicist notion of justification associated with American pragmatism. The justification is this: first, the adversary system, despite its imperfections, irrationalities, loop-holes, and perversities seems to do as good a job as any at finding truth and protecting legal rights. None of its existing rivals, in particular the inquisitorial system and the socialist system, are demonstrably better and some, such as trial by ordeal, are demonstrably worse. Indeed, even if one of the other systems were slightly better, the human costs—in terms of effort, confusion, anxiety, disorientation, inadvertent miscarriages of justice due to improper understanding, re-training, resentment, loss of tradition, you name it—would outweigh reasons for replacing the existing system.

Second, some adjudicatory system is necessary.

Third, it's the way we have always done things.

These propositions constitute a pragmatic argument: if a social institution does a reasonable enough job of its sort that the costs of replacing it outweigh the benefits, and if we need that sort of job done, we should stay with what we have. . . .

AN EXAMPLE: THE WEST GERMAN PROCEDURAL SYSTEM*

The reader may at this point feel that my "pragmatic justification" amounts to sending her away hungry. An argument that is logically weak but practically strong seems more like resignation than justification.

The problem, of course, is that the abstract assertion that the adversary system "does a reasonable enough job of its sort that the costs of replacing it outweigh the benefits" inevitably arouses the suspicion that it is simply a whitewash designed to justify the status quo. To make the argument more convincing, I propose to make it more concrete. Let us compare the American adversary system with one so-called "inquisitorial" system, that of the German Federal Republic.

The label "inquisitorial" is quite misleading, of course. It evokes images of the auto-da-fe and the Iron Maiden, the Pit and the Pendulum. In fact, the term refers simply to the much greater role played by the court in a trial. . . .

Few exclusionary rules exist in German procedure. In particular, rules such as the exclusion of hearsay evidence, which exist in common law countries because of the fear that lay jurors would be unable to evaluate it, are unheard of. In Germany the lay "jurors" deliberate together with the professional judges, and it is assumed that the latter will be able to explain the value of evidence to the lay participants.

---

*[Editor's Note: For more on the German civil justice process, see Oscar Chase, *Legal Processes and National Culture*, 5 Cardozo J. Intl. & Comp. L. 1 (1997); John H. Langbein, *Cultural Chauvinism in Comparative Law*, 5 Cardozo J. Intl. & Comp. L. 41 (1997); and John H. Langbein, *The German Advantage in Civil Procedure*, 52 U. Chi. L. Rev. 823 (1985).]

After the judge has questioned witnesses, the lawyers and the defendant may ask further questions. Except in political trials, however, it is rare for them to exercise this option, and almost unheard of that a lawyer would ask more than one or two questions. . . .

In civil cases, there is no jury. A judge or panel of judges engages in a series of conferences with the parties and their lawyers. The object of these conferences is to clarify the issues of the case. To this end the lawyers submit written pleadings—shockingly informal ones by American standards—which are continually revised and updated as the case develops. . . .

As in a criminal trial, the court decides issues of law on its own, on the principle "the court knows the law" (*jura novit curia*). It is facilitated in deciding the law, of course, because in civil law countries such as Germany, law is statutory rather than precedential (though precedent is coming to play an increasingly important role in German law), which simplifies legal research considerably. . . .

Of course, a procedural system such as the German one requires that lawyers will not engage in large-sale obfuscations after the fashion of their American brothers and sisters, since the courts hardly have the resources or time to discover them. This is one function of the official code of legal ethics. Its basic principle defines the lawyer's status as an independent organ of the administration of justice (*unabhängiges Organ der Rechtspflege*); and the commentaries make clear that this means independence from the client as well as from the state. . . .

Three other arrangements bear mention because they contribute to the German lawyer's independence as an organ of justice administration. The first is an ethical rule entitled "Questioning and Advising Witnesses." One of the key features of litigation in America is the fact that each litigant chooses its own witnesses after independently investigating the case. The witnesses are often intensively rehearsed, or coached, to prepare them for the trial. . . .

The German rule, by contrast, forbids the lawyer to influence witnesses and thus strongly discourages contact with witnesses. . . .

Secondly, we may contrast German and American legal education. Quite simply, German students learn law from the standpoint of the judge, while Americans learn it from the standpoint of the advocate. . . .

Finally, the German fee structure may help to preserve the lawyer's independence by lessening the financial incentives to excessive zeal. Fees are set by the Federal Lawyers' Fees Act (BRAGO) as a function of the amount at issue (*Gegenstandswert*), and the lawyer receives the same fee whether the case is won or lost. . . .

How well does the German system work? According to John Merryman, an eminent comparativist:

> For those who are concerned about the relative justice of the two systems, a statement made by an eminent scholar after long and careful

study is instructive: he said that if he were innocent he would prefer to be tried by a civil law court, but that if he were guilty he would prefer to be tried by a common law court. This is, in effect, a judgment that criminal proceedings in the civil law world are more likely to distinguish accurately between the guilty and the innocent.

And, notwithstanding the Joint Conference Report's a priori psychological arguments to the contrary, most observers believe that German judges are highly skilled and effective examiners of witnesses. Additional advantages of the German procedure are easy to see: German proceedings are much less formal and cumbersome; the direct participation of the parties injects a human element (one thinks of the title character's mother in the film Morgan: "Your father always said that crime puts the human element in the law"); courtroom theatrics and such American legal pastimes as discovery abuse and interminable motion-practice do not exist; legal fees are considerably lower. Many American authorities note with pleasure the virtual absence of plea-bargaining due to the nonexistence of the guilty plea. (A prosecutor can plea-bargain only by reducing the charge to a misdemeanor.)

Nevertheless, I believe that most Americans would find the German procedures quite uninviting. This is the nub of the pragmatic argument: despite its numerous attractions, the German procedure requires other changes in the legal system and the nexus of values enveloping it that would make the trade-off unacceptable. (You can't change just one part of the system.) . . .

One way of looking at this problem is that the German system requires a great deal more trust in the integrity and impartiality of its judges than Americans are likely to find plausible or even tolerable, particularly in a criminal trial. And once we have noticed this, it becomes a *Leitmotiv* of the German system, reflected in numerous practices and institutions.

In civil matters, for example, there is no prosecutor and thus no dossier. For that reason it is an essential, not an accidental feature of the system, that the trial be broken up into discrete sessions or conferences with significant intervals of time in between them: because the judge must understand the case, she must have the opportunity to study it, prepare for it in ways analogous to the preparation of American trial lawyers, and digest what she has learned. But once the trial is subdivided, it becomes unworkable to impanel a jury—after all, you can't force people to absent themselves from their jobs and commitments again and again. Thus, the absence of the jury is also an essential feature of German civil procedure, just as the perhaps-too-cozy relationship between judges and prosecutors is an essential feature of German criminal procedure. . . .

I have noted that the German fee system is an important part of restraining lawyers from adversarial monkeyshines, which is in turn essential if the judge-driven trial is not to collapse into a shambles. We saw as well that the abolition of contingent fees requires a comprehensive system of state-provided legal aid. But a system of total legal aid carries its own additional imperative: it must weed out nuisance suits or groundless suits to avoid a litigation explosion. The courts therefore decide whether legal aid is to be granted in a lawsuit—and that means that more trust and power is vested in the judiciary.

Additional trust in governmental agency is of course required because of BRAGO: whatever the merits of a state-imposed schedule of lawyers fees—these merits are obvious—such an arrangement would require a readjustment of mentality in America on the part of clients as well as lawyers. (And notice that a rigid, nondiscretionary schedule of fees based upon *Gegenstandswert* is two-edged: it holds down maximum fees, but raises minimum fees. Some German lawyers complained to me that their foreign clients were outraged when a valuable but very simple case, requiring little work from the lawyers, was billed at a high rate.)

The fact that in Germany the judges, not the parties, choose expert witnesses is similarly two-edged. It does prevent one of the most unseemly and disgraceful spectacles in American adjudication, the combat of extravagantly compensated, carefully coached, uncompromisingly partisan experts. But since the German judge usually appoints only one expert and relies on her testimony, any biases in the judge's selection process or the expert's views will be disastrous for the luckless party. Thus the system requires a great deal of trust in the integrity of both judges and experts. . . .

Moreover, a judge-driven system requires a very large judiciary; 28 percent of all German jurists are judges—seventeen thousand judges in a country of sixty-one million—as compared with 4 percent in the United States (about eighteen thousand judges for a country of two hundred forty million). This abundance of judges adds both to the relative anonymity of the judiciary and to the risk that it will be governed by bureaucratic imperatives and thereby converted to an even more insulated elite.

One must also consider whether judge-driven procedure is possible in a common law regime. The common law is extremely complex, and it takes a great deal of time to research legal issues thoroughly. In our adversary system, this time is invested mostly by the two attorneys, out of court and at their clients' expense. In an inquisitorial system, however, the research burden would be passed on to the court and the expense to the state. We observed that this is not outrageously burdensome in Germany because of the relative ease of legal research. That, in turn, is a function of two factors: the preponderance of statutory law over precedent and the existence of authoritative commentary. Americans, however, are hardly likely to abandon the common law, nor are they likely to invest great trust in the professoriat, which dwelleth near Olympus in Germany but in America is regarded with a mixture of suspicion and amused condescension. . . .

Finally, let us recall that a key to inquisitorial procedure is that the court decides what evidence to take. The court, however, has limited time and resources, and so in complex cases many stones will of necessity be left unturned. This does not mean, of course, that the inquisitorial court is less likely to find out the facts of the matter: the "total war" litigation tactics employed by large American law firms representing rich clients (and that is mostly what we are talking about when we speak of complex litigation) often call to mind giant squids squirting the ink of obfuscation in each other's direction—these tactics consist of delay, endless discovery, vexatious motions, and the complementary shenanigans needed to parry such thrusts. Nevertheless, our ideology of "getting one's day in court"—or perhaps one's half-year—means being able to present the case that one's lawyers want, more or less as they want to present it. We would have to think that our judges were awfully good to let them stage-manage that day in court. Even Judge Wapner does not get that kind of deference.

Let me summarize. Hegel thought of the civil service or bureaucracy as a "universal class" that would realize common interests against particularistic ones; he also (mis)quoted Goethe, saying "the masses are respectable hands at fighting, but miserable hands at judging." Some such antipopulist views, if I am right, undergird the German inquisitorial system. My guess is that, despite the many attractive features of the system, Americans would find the imperatives of inquisitorial procedure unacceptable. These imperatives center around the need to repose a great trust in a large, self-consciously lebensfremd officialdom and auxiliary governmental agencies.

One never knows, of course—perhaps the transition could be accomplished without much dislocation. But I am inclined to doubt it. Even if it could—say, by introducing inquisitorial elements into adversary procedures very gradually—the fact remains that by so doing we would be sacrificing some important elements of popular control over the legal system.

And, if I am right about this, we see why a pragmatic justification of the adversary system makes sense. Let me emphasize that I am not arguing that the changes required to switch to inquisitorial procedure are bad— the point is simply that they are trade-offs rather than clear-cut improvements. The argument should work equally well to explain to Germans why they should not rush to abandon a more efficient, competent, and professional inquisitorial system in favor of expensive and theatrical adversarial procedure. The adversary and inquisitorial systems have more-or-less complementary pluses and minuses; why, then, look for greener grass on the other side of the fence?

2. What Are the Strengths and Limitations of Courts?

Some kinds of disputes may not lend themselves to the adversarial process. Professors Lon Fuller and Abram Chayes explore the debate over the capacity of courts to address complex social and economic problems.

As you read, keep in mind lawsuits over segregated schools, violent prisons, and failing economic entities, such as railroads, as well as your own views about the debate. Consider Lon Fuller's discussion of the limits of adjudication; what kinds of legal disputes do you think fit his notion of a "polycentric task"? Should they be sent out of courts to some other settings for dispute resolution, or is there a way that the adversarial process can be modified to meet them?

■ LON FULLER, THE FORMS AND LIMITS OF ADJUDICATION
92 Harv. L. Rev. 353 (1978)

Attention is now directed to the question, What kinds of tasks are inherently unsuited to adjudication? The test here will be that used throughout. If a given task is assigned to adjudicative treatment, will it be possible to preserve the meaning of the affected party's participation through proofs and arguments?

[For purposes of addressing the question of limits, this] section introduces a concept—that of the "polycentric task"—which has been derived from Michael Polanyi's book *The Logic of Liberty* [(1951)]. In approaching that concept it will be well to begin with a few examples.

Some months ago a wealthy lady by the name of Timken died in New York leaving a valuable, but somewhat miscellaneous, collection of paintings to the Metropolitan Museum and the National Gallery "in equal shares," her will indicating no particular apportionment. When the will was probated the judge remarked something to the effect that the parties seemed to be confronted with a real problem. The attorney for one of the museums spoke up and said, "We are good friends. We will work it out somehow or other." What makes this problem of effecting an equal division of the paintings a polycentric task? It lies in the fact that the disposition of any single painting has implications for the proper disposition of every other painting. If it gets the Renoir, the Gallery may be less eager for the Cézanne but all the more eager for the Bellows, etc. If the proper apportionment were set for argument, there would be no clear issue to which either side could direct its proofs and contentions. Any judge assigned to hear such an argument would be tempted to assume the role of mediator or to adopt the classical solution: Let the older brother (here the Metropolitan) divide the estate into what he regards as equal shares, let the younger brother (the National Gallery) take his pick.

As a second illustration suppose in a socialist regime it were decided to have all wages and prices set by courts which would proceed after the usual forms of adjudication. It is, I assume, obvious that here is a task that could not successfully be undertaken by the adjudicative method. . . .

We may visualize this kind of situation by thinking of a spider web. A pull on one strand will distribute tensions after a complicated pattern throughout the web as a whole. Doubling the original pull will, in all likelihood, not simply double each of the resulting tensions but will create a different complicated pattern of tensions. This would certainly occur, for example, if the doubled pull caused one or more of the weaker strands to snap. This is a "polycentric" situation because it is "many centered"—each crossing of strands is a distinct center for distributing tensions. . . .

It should be carefully noted that a multiplicity of affected persons is not an invariable characteristic of polycentric problems. This is sufficiently illustrated in the case of Mrs. Timken's will. That case also illustrated the fact that rapid changes with time are not an invariable characteristic of such problems. On the other hand, in practice polycentric problems of possible concern to adjudication will normally involve many affected parties and a somewhat fluid state of affairs. Indeed, the last characteristic follows from the simple fact that the more interacting centers there are, the more the likelihood that one of them will be affected by a change in circumstances, and, if the situation is polycentric, this change will communicate itself after a complex pattern to other centers. . . .

Now, if it is important to see clearly what a polycentric problem is, it is equally important to realize that the distinction involved is often a matter of degree. There are polycentric elements in almost all problems submitted to adjudication. A decision may act as a precedent, often an awkward one, in some situation not foreseen by the arbiter. Again, suppose a court in a suit between one litigant and a railway holds that it is an act of negligence for the railway not to construct an underpass at a particular crossing. There may be nothing to distinguish this crossing from other crossings on the line. As a matter of statistical probability it may be clear that constructing underpasses along the whole line would cost more lives (through accidents in blasting, for example) than would be lost if the only safety measure were the familiar "Stop, Look & Listen" sign. If so, then what seems to be a decision simply declaring the rights and duties of two parties is in fact an inept solution for a polycentric problem, some elements of which cannot be brought before the court in a simple suit by one injured party against a defendant railway. In lesser measure, concealed polycentric elements are probably present in almost all problems resolved by adjudication. It is not, then, a question of distinguishing black from white. It is a question of knowing when the polycentric elements have become so significant and predominant that the proper limits of adjudication have been reached. . . .

The first question to be addressed is this: When an attempt is made to deal by adjudicative forms with a problem that is essentially polycentric, what happens? As I see it, three things can happen, sometimes all at once. *First,* the adjudicative solution may fail. Unexpected repercussions make the decision unworkable; it is ignored or modified, sometimes repeatedly. *Second,* the purported arbiter ignores judicial proprieties—he "tries out" various solutions in posthearing conferences, consults parties not represented at the hearings, guesses at facts not proved and not properly matters for anything like judicial notice. *Third,* instead of accommodating his procedures to the nature of the problem he confronts, he may reformulate the problem so as to make it amenable to solution through adjudicative procedures.

Only the last of these needs illustration. Suppose it is agreed that an employer's control over promotions shall be subject to review through arbitration. Now obviously an arbiter cannot decide whether when Jones was made a Machinist Class A there was someone else more deserving in the plant, or whether, in view of Jones' age, it would have been better to put him in another job with comparable pay. This is the kind of allocative problem for which adjudication is utterly unsuited. There are, however, two ways of obtaining a workable control over promotions through arbitration. One of these is through the posting of jobs; when a job is vacant, interested parties may apply for promotion into it. At the hearing, only those who have made application are entitled to be considered, and of course only the posted job is in issue. Here the problem is simplified in advance to the point where it can be arbitrated, though not without difficulty, particularly in the form of endless arguments as to whether there was in fact a vacancy that ought to have been posted, and whether a claimant filed his application on time and in the proper form, etc. The other way of accommodating the problem to arbitration is for the arbiter to determine not who should be promoted but who *has* been promoted. That is, the contract contains certain "job descriptions" with the appropriate rate for each; the claimant asserts that he is in fact doing the work of a Machinist A, though he is still assigned the pay and title of a Machinist B. The controversy has two parties—the company and the claimant as represented by the union— and a single factual issue, is the claimant in fact doing the work of a Machinist A?

In practice the procedure of applying for appointment to posted jobs will normally be prescribed in the contract itself, so that the terms of the agreement keep the arbitrator's function with respect to promotions within manageable limits. The other method of making feasible a control of promotions through arbitration will normally result from the arbitrator's own perception of the limitations of his role. The contract may simply contain a schedule of job rates and job classifications and a general clause stating that "discharges, promotions, and layoffs shall be subject to the grievance procedure." If the arbitrator were to construe such a contract to give him general supervision over promotions, he would embark himself upon managerial tasks wholly unsuited to solution by any arbitrative procedure. An instinct toward preserving the integrity of his role will move him, therefore, to construe the contract in the manner already indicated, so that he avoids any responsibility with respect to the assignment of duties and merely decides whether the duties actually assigned make appropriate the classification assigned by the company to the complaining employee. . . .

In closing this discussion of polycentricity, it will be well to caution against two possible misunderstandings. The suggestion that polycentric problems are often solved by a kind of "managerial intuition" should not be taken to imply that it is an invariable characteristic of polycentric problems that they resist rational solution. There are rational principles for building bridges of structural steel. But there is no rational principle which states, for example, that the angle between girder A and girder B must always be 45 degrees. This depends on the bridge as a whole. One cannot construct a bridge by conducting successive separate arguments concerning the proper angle for every pair of intersecting girders. One must deal with the whole structure.

Finally, the fact that an adjudicative decision affects and enters into a polycentric relationship does not of itself mean that the adjudicative tribunal is moving out of its proper sphere. On the contrary, there is no better illustration of a polycentric relationship than an economic market, and yet the laying down of rules that will make a market function properly is one for which adjudication is generally well suited. The working out of our common law of contracts case by case has proceeded through adjudication, yet the basic principle underlying the rates thus developed is that they should promote the free exchange of goods in a polycentric market. The court gets into difficulty, not when it lays down rules about contracting, but when it attempts to write contracts. . . .

■ ABRAM CHAYES, THE ROLE OF THE JUDGE IN PUBLIC LAW LITIGATION
89 Harv. L. Rev. 1281 (1976)

. . . We are witnessing the emergence of a new model of civil litigation and, I believe, our traditional conception of adjudication and the assumptions upon which it is based provide an increasingly unhelpful, indeed misleading framework for assessing either the workability or the legitimacy of the roles of judge and court within this model.

In our received tradition, the lawsuit is a vehicle for settling disputes between private parties about private rights. The defining feature of this conception of civil adjudication are:

> (1) The lawsuit is bipolar. Litigation is organized as a contest between two individuals or at least two unitary interests, diametrically opposed, to be decided on a winner-take-all basis.

(2) Litigation is *retrospective*. The controversy is about an identified set of completed events: whether they occurred, and if so with what consequences for the legal relations of the parties.

(3) *Right and remedy are interdependent*. The scope of the relief is derived more or less logically from the substantive violation under the general theory that the plaintiff will get compensation measured by the harm caused by the defendant's breach of duty—in contract by giving plaintiff the money he would have had absent the breach; in tort by paying the value of the damage caused.

(4) The lawsuit is a *self-contained* episode. The impact of the judgment is confined to the parties. If plaintiff prevails there is a simple compensatory transfer, usually of money, but occasionally the return of a thing or the performance of a definite act. If defendant prevails, a loss lies where it has fallen. In either case, entry of judgment ends the court's involvement.

(5) The process is *party-initiated* and *party-controlled*. The case is organized and the issues defined by exchanges between the parties. Responsibility for fact development is theirs. The trial judge is a neutral arbiter of their interactions who decides questions of law only if they are put in issue by an appropriate move of a party. . . .

Whatever its historical validity, the traditional model is clearly invalid as a description of much current civil litigation in the federal district courts. Perhaps the dominating characteristic of modern federal litigation is that lawsuits do not arise out of disputes between private parties about private rights. Instead, the object of litigation is the vindication of constitutional or statutory policies. The shift in the legal basis of the lawsuit explains many, but not all, facets of what is going on "in fact" in federal trial courts. For this reason, although the label is not wholly satisfactory, I shall call the emerging model "public law litigation."

The characteristic features of the public law model are very different from those of the traditional model. The party structure is sprawling and amorphous, subject to change over the course of the litigation. The traditional adversary relationship is suffused and intermixed with negotiating and mediating processes at every point. The judge is the dominant figure in organizing and guiding the case, and he draws for support not only on the parties and their counsel, but on a wide range of outsiders—masters, experts, and oversight personnel. Most important, the trial judge has increasingly become the creator and manager of complex forms of ongoing relief, which have widespread effects on persons not before the court and require the judge's continuing involvement in administration and implementation. School desegregation, employment discrimination, and prisoners' or inmates' rights cases come readily to mind as avatars of this new form of litigation. But it would be mistaken to suppose that it is confined to these areas. Antitrust, securities fraud and other aspects of the conduct of corporate business, bankruptcy and reorganizations, union governance, consumer fraud, housing discrimination, electoral reapportionment, environmental management—cases in all these fields display in varying degrees the features of public law litigation. . . .

II. THE PUBLIC LAW LITIGATION MODEL

Sometime after 1875, the private law theory of civil adjudication became increasingly precarious in the face of a growing body of legislation designed explicitly to modify and regulate basic social and economic arrangements. At the same time, the scientific and deductive character of judicial lawmaking came under attack, as the political consequences of judicial review of that legislation became urgent.

These developments are well known and have become an accepted part of our political and intellectual history. I want to address in somewhat greater detail the correlative changes that have occurred in the procedural structure of the lawsuit. Most discussion of these procedural developments, while recognizing that change has been far-reaching, proceeds on the assumption that the new devices are no more than piecemeal "reforms" aimed at improving the functional characteristics or the efficacy of litigation conducted essentially in the traditional mode. I suggest, however, that these developments are interrelated as members of a recognizable, if changing, system and that taken together they display a new model of judicial action and the judicial role, both of which depart sharply from received conceptions.

A. THE DEMISE OF BIPOLAR STRUCTURE

Joinder of parties, which was strictly limited at common law, was very liberalized under the codes to conform with the approach of equity calling for joinder of all parties having an "interest" in the controversy. The codes, however, did not at first produce much freedom of joinder. Instead, the courts defined the concept of "interest" narrowly to exclude those without an independent legal right to the remedy to be given in the main dispute. . . .

. . . Today, the Supreme Court is struggling manfully, but with questionable success, to establish a formula for delimiting who may sue that stops short of "anybody who might be significantly affected by the situation he seeks to litigate."

"Anybody"—even "almost anybody" can be a lot of people, particularly where the matters in issue are not relatively individualized private transactions or encounters. Thus, the stage is set for the class action. . . . Whatever the resolution of the current controversies surrounding class actions, I think it unlikely that the class action will ever be taught to behave in accordance with the precepts of the traditional model of adjudication. The class suit is a reflection of our growing awareness that a host of important public and private interactions—perhaps the most important in defining the conditions and opportunities of life for most people—are conducted on a routine or bureaucratized basis and can no longer be visualized as bilateral transactions between private individuals. From another angle, the class action responds to the proliferation of more or less well-organized groups in our society and the tendency to perceive interests as group interests, at least in very important aspects. . . .

B. THE TRIUMPH OF EQUITY

One of the most striking procedural developments of this century is the increasing importance of equitable relief. It is perhaps too soon to reverse the traditional maxim to read that money damages will be awarded only when no suitable form of specific relief can be devised. But surely, the old sense of equitable remedies as "extraordinary" has faded.

I am not concerned here with specific performance—the compelled transfer of a piece of land or a unique thing. This remedy is structurally little different from traditional money-damages. It is a one-time, one-way transfer requiring for its enforcement no continuing involvement of the court. Injunctive relief, however, is different in kind, even when it takes the form of a simple negative order. Such an order is a presently operative prohibition, enforceable by contempt, and it is a much greater constraint on activity than the risk of future liability implicit in the damage remedy. Moreover, the injunction is continuing. Over time, the parties may resort to the court for enforcement or modification of the original order in light of changing circumstances. Finally, by issuing the injunction, the court takes public responsibility for any consequences of its decree that may adversely affect strangers to the action.

Beyond these differences, the prospective character of the relief introduces large elements of contingency and prediction into the proceedings. Instead of a dispute retrospectively oriented toward the consequences of a closed set of events, the court has a controversy about future probabilities. Equitable doctrine, naturally enough, given the intrusiveness of the injunction and the contingent nature of the harm, calls for a balancing of the interests of the parties. And if the immediate parties' interests were to be weighed and evaluated, it was not too difficult to proceed to a consideration of other interests that might be affected by the order. . . .

C. THE CHANGING CHARACTER OF FACTFINDING

The traditional model of adjudication was primarily concerned with assessing the consequences for the parties of specific past instances of conduct. This retrospective orientation is often inapposite in public law litigation, where the lawsuit generally seeks to enjoin future or threatened action, or to modify a course of conduct presently in train or a condition presently existing. In the former situation the question whether threatened action will materialize, in what circumstances, and with what consequences can, in the nature of things, be answered only by an educated guess. In the latter case, the inquiry is only secondarily concerned with how the condition came about, and even less with the subjective attitudes of the actors, since positive regulatory goals are ordinarily defined without reference to such matters. Indeed, in dealing with the actions of large political or corporate aggregates, notions of will, intention, or fault increasingly become only metaphors.

In the remedial phases of public law litigation, factfinding is even more clearly prospective. . . . [T]he contours of relief are not derived logically from the substantive wrong adjudged, as in the traditional model. The elaboration of a decree is largely a discretionary process within which the trial judge is called upon to assess and appraise the consequences of alternative programs that might correct the substantive fault. In both the liability and remedial phases, the relevant inquiry is largely the same: How can the policies of a public law best be served in a concrete case?

In public law litigation, then, factfinding is principally concerned with "legislative" rather than "adjudicative" fact. And "fact evaluation" is perhaps a more accurate term than "factfinding." The whole process begins to look like the traditional description of legislation: Attention is drawn to a "mischief," existing or threatened, and the activity of the parties and court is directed to the development of on-going measures designed to cure that mischief. Indeed, if, as is often the case, the decree sets up an affirmative regime governing the activities in controversy for the indefinite future and having binding force for persons within its ambit, then it is not very much of a stretch to see it as, pro tanto, a legislative act. . . .

The courts, it seems, continue to rely primarily on the litigants to produce and develop factual materials, but a number of factors make it impossible to leave the organization of the trial exclusively in their hands. With the diffusion of the party structure, fact issues are no longer sharply drawn in a confrontation between two adversaries, one asserting the affirmative and the other the negative. The litigation is often extraordinarily complex and extended in time, with a continuous and intricate interplay between factual and legal elements. It is hardly feasible and, absent a jury, unnecessary to set aside a contiguous block of time for a "trial stage" at which all significant factual issues will be presented. The scope of the fact investigation and the sheer volume of factual material that can be exhumed by the discovery process pose enormous problems of organization and assimilation. All these factors thrust the trial judge into an active role in shaping, organizing and facilitating the litigation. We may not yet have reached the investigative judge of the continental systems, but we have left the passive arbiter of the traditional model a long way behind.

D. THE DECREE

The centerpiece of the emerging public law model is the decree. It differs in almost every relevant characteristic from relief in the traditional model of adjudication, not the least in that it is the centerpiece. The decree seeks to adjust future behavior, not to compensate for past wrong. It is deliberately fashioned rather than logically deduced from the nature of the legal harm suffered. It provides for a complex, on-going regime of performance rather than a simple, one-shot, one-way transfer. Finally, it prolongs and deepens, rather than terminates, the court's involvement with the dispute. . . .

I suggested above that a judicial decree establishing an ongoing regime of conduct is pro tanto a legislative act. But in actively shaping and monitoring the decree, mediating between the parties, developing his own sources of expertise and information, the trial judge has passed beyond even the role of legislator and has become a policy planner and manager.

E. A MORPHOLOGY OF PUBLIC LAW LITIGATION

The public law litigation model portrayed in this paper reverses many of the crucial characteristics and assumptions of the traditional concept of adjudication:

(1) The scope of the lawsuit is not exogenously given but is shaped primarily by the court and parties.

(2) The party structure is not rigidly bilateral but sprawling and amorphous.

(3) The fact inquiry is not historical and adjudicative but predictive and legislative.

(4) Relief is not conceived as compensation for past wrong in a form logically derived from the substantive liability and confined in its impact to the immediate parties; instead, it is forward looking, fashioned ad hoc on flexible and broadly remedial lines, often having important consequences for many persons including absentees.

(5) The remedy is not imposed but negotiated.

(6) The decree does not terminate judicial involvement in the affair: its administration requires the continuing participation of the court.

(7) The judge is not passive, his function limited to analysis and statement of governing rules; he is active, with responsibility not only for credible fact evaluation but for organizing and shaping the litigation to ensure a just and viable outcome.

(8) The subject matter of the lawsuit is not a dispute between private individuals about private rights, but a grievance about the operation of public policy.

In fact, one might say that, from the perspective of the traditional model, the proceeding is recognizable as a lawsuit only because it takes place in a courtroom before an official called a judge. But that is surely too sensational in tone. All of the procedural mechanisms outlined above were historically familiar in equity practice. It is not surprising that they should be adopted and strengthened as the importance of equity has grown in modern times. . . .

IV. SOME THOUGHTS ON LEGITIMACY

. . . As the traditional model has been displaced in recent years, . . . questions of judicial legitimacy and accountability have reasserted themselves. . . .

In my view, judicial action only achieves such legitimacy by responding to, indeed by stirring, the deep and durable demand for justice in our society. I confess some difficulty in seeing how this is to be accomplished by erecting the barriers of the traditional conception to turn aside, for example, attacks on exclusionary zoning and police violence, two of the ugliest remaining manifestations of official racism in American life. In practice, if not in words, the American legal tradition has always acknowledged the importance of substantive results for the legitimacy and accountability of judicial action. . . .

Comments and Questions

1. What are the sources for the criteria and judgments used by Fuller and Chayes in the debate over the function and capacities of courts? Fuller relies on a notion of rationality at the core of the judicial process. Is this notion intrinsic to due process? Is it intrinsic to the ideal of a court or to the reality of courts as operated in the contemporary United States? Chayes relies on examples of courts engaged in innovative practices. Do such examples give hope for the capacity of all courts, or do they merely illuminate the abilities of extraordinary judges? Where, if at all, do commitments to democratic participation and accountability to the broad public fit in his scheme?

2. In the debate over the role of courts in addressing complex or "polycentric" disputes (in Fuller's terms), what concerns emerge about judicial legitimacy and the efficacy of the courts' actions?

3. Do the public law courts described by Chayes abandon the premises of adversarial justice? How important are those premises to the tasks of fact finding, judgment, and enforcement? Can those tasks be accomplished as well, and as legitimately, through party collaboration and negotiation?

4. If collaboration and negotiation are central to managing complex disputes, should alternative institutions be involved? Techniques of alternative dispute resolution—including mediation and arbitration—could

be deployed to process individual claims gathered in large-scale class actions, as well as to develop the terms of such claims-management procedures. *See, e.g.,* Mark Z. Edell et al., *Resolutions of Mass Tort Litigation: A Practitioner's Guide to Existing Methods and Emerging Trends,* C949 A.L.I.-A.B.A. Court of Study: Products Liability 37 (1994) (available in WEST-LAW, ALI-ABA Database); Kenneth R. Feinberg, *Response to Deborah Hensler, A Glass Half Full, A Glass Half Empty: The Use of Alternative Dispute Resolution in Mass Personal Injury Litigation,* 73 Tex. L. Rev. 1647 (1995). Courts can also create claims-processing methods for mass cases. *See* Linda S. Mullenix, *Resolving Aggregate Mass Tort Litigation: The New Private Law Dispute Resolution Paradigm,* 33 Val. U. L. Rev. 413 (1999); *see also* Chapter 6, Section C, *infra.*

B. IS THERE A LITIGATION CRISIS?   Ⓟ Ⓒ

Related to debates about court involvement in complex disputes, and to arguments over the adversary system, is the controversy over the litigation crisis in the United States. Is there too much litigation for the courts to handle, or for the good of society? Or is the perception of "too much litigation" itself a response to particular substantive legal developments, such as pro-plaintiff tort law? These issues ultimately are normative ones, but they arise from such basic controversies as how to describe the facts. (Indeed, more disputes, in law and in life, probably concern disagreements about the facts than about the norms that should govern.)

Here are some factual materials, and claims about those facts, relevant to assessing whether there is a litigation crisis. The perception that there is such a crisis has helped generate a variety of alternatives to court-based dispute processing, as well as innovations within courts to manage large caseloads, which are the subject of the next sections of this chapter.

1. Responding to mounting public and professional concern with congestion, delay, and cost in federal court litigation, Congress directed the Chief Justice of the United States Supreme Court to conduct a fifteen-month study of the problems of the federal courts. On April 2, 1990, the Report of the Federal Courts Study Committee presented the analysis and recommendations of this study. The Report pointed out that between 1958 and 1988, the number of cases filed in federal courts tripled, and the number of appellate filings increased ten-fold. In response, Congress more than doubled the number of district court and appellate judgeships and added other court personnel, such as magistrates, law clerks, circuit executives, and staff attorneys. "As a result, the percentage of federal court employees who are judges has fallen from 10 percent in 1958 to 3 percent" in 1990. Despite this Congressional expansion of the court system, the pattern of increased filing exceeded the number of additional judges appointed to the federal bench. The Committee on Long Range Planning

for the Judicial Conference of the United States, Long Range Plan for the Federal Courts 15 (1995)(hereinafter cited as Long Range Plan). Thus, "civil filings increased from 207 per judgeship in 1955 to 448 per judgeship in 1990." Kim Dayton, *The Myth of Alternative Dispute Resolution in Federal Courts*, 76 Iowa L. Rev. 889, 889-890 (1991). Estimates are that the caseload of the federal court system will increase by more than one million new cases by the year 2020, with a projected need for more than 4,000 federal judges. Long Range Plan, App. A, Table 1, at 161.

2. The caseload surge since the 1960s is attributed to some expansive Supreme Court interpretations of individual rights under the Constitution, habeas corpus, and statutes. *See* Judge Richard A. Posner, *The Federal Courts* 80-81 (1985). Yet others emphasize that a considerable portion of the growth is somewhat attributable to increasing criminal prosecutions. Judge Roger J. Miner, *The Federal Courts: Challenge and Reform*, 46 Cath. U.L. Rev. 1189, 1190 (1997). More basically, flexible pleading rules, growth in the legal profession, political agendas of both liberals and conservatives, and a cultural shift toward expecting "total justice" rather than accepting misfortune contribute to the rising court filings. *See* Lawrence Friedman, *Total Justice* (1985).

3. The increased number of federal filings contributes to a lengthening time between filing and trial. A 1987 survey shows that the average time between filing and trial for a typical civil damages suit was 15 months in federal court and 18 months in a state forum. The average time for disposition without trial (by settlement or dismissal) was 10 months in federal court and 12 months in state court. Taylor, *Judges Identify Causes of Delay in Civil Litigation*, 14 Litigation News 3 (Dec. 1988)(summarizing Louis Harris and Associates Inc. Survey, Judicial Attitudes Toward Issues in Civil Procedure (1987)). Of course, averages can be misleading. Here, the averages hide what percentage of the cases were more than three years old, as well as differences among different types of cases and among different districts and states.

4. In the face of mounting caseloads, federal appellate judges increasingly cut back on oral argument, "although such argument ensures essential communication between lawyers and judges, promotes judicial accountability, and provides at least some assurance to the parties that their arguments have been heard and considered by real live judges." Judge Stephen Reinhardt, *Commentary: Developing the Mission: Another View*, 27 Conn. L. Rev. 877, 879 (1995). Federal appellate judges also increasingly issue unpublished opinions, with the risk of undermining the credibility of the judicial process, and rely heavily on staff members including law clerks, court counsel, and magistrates. *Id.* at 879-880. *See also* Robert G. Vaugh, *Normative Controversies Underlying Contemporary Debates About Civil Justice Reform: A Way of Talking About Bureaucracy and the Future of the Federal Courts*, 76 Denv. U. L. Rev. 217 (1998).

5. About 90 percent of the nation's judicial business is handled by state, not federal courts. The Institute for Civil Justice, a division of the

RAND research center, does many studies of civil litigation in both state and federal courts. RAND studies have found that the estimated 1982 government expenditure for processing torts cases in the 50 states' courts of general jurisdiction and the U.S. district court was $320 million. Less than 10 percent of those cases went on to a jury trial, but jury cases accounted for about half of the government expenditures in the states studied. James S. Akakalik and Abby E. Robyn, *Costs of the Civil Justice System: Court Expenditures for Processing Tort Cases* (R-2888-ICJ). Some 87.5 million cases filed in 1966 were processed through 16,236 state trial courts in 1966. National Center for State Courts, *Examining the Work of State Courts* (1996). In 1998, according to the Administrative Office of the U.S. Courts and the National Center for State Courts, there were 2,030 federal judges and 29,808 state judges.

6. The vast proportion of all cases filed settle or otherwise end long before trial. *See, e.g.,* David Trubek et al., *The Costs of Ordinary Litigation,* 31 U.C.L.A. L. Rev. 73, 89 (1983)(in large sample of state and federal cases, fewer than 8 percent went to trial).

7. Probably only a small percentage of cases account for a large percentage of complaints about large numbers of parties, legal complexity, excessive fees, and discovery abuse. *See* Wayne Brazil, *Civil Discovery: Lawyers' Views of Its Effectiveness, Its Principal Problems and Abuses,* 4 A.B.F. Research J. 789 (1980).

8. Numerous observers argue that claims of a litigation explosion and inefficient dispute processing by courts are exaggerated or are unsupported by data. For example, Marc Galanter of the University of Wisconsin Law School used known data to argue that only a small portion of troubles and injuries become disputes, and only a small portion of disputes become lawsuits. The vast majority of lawsuits, in turn, are abandoned, settled, or resolved without full-blown adjudication. While litigation rates have risen recently, the present levels have precedents in the nineteenth century. Suggestive, though not conclusive, comparisons with data from other jurisdictions show that per capita rates of litigation in the United States, though higher than in many industrialized countries, fall in the same general range as those of England, Australia, and Ontario (Canada). Media coverage, changes in governmental activity, and other cultural shifts enlarge the symbolic presence of litigation in the lives of Americans, even when direct personal experience of full-blown adjudication has become relatively less frequent. Claims of pathological litigiousness reflect particular political agendas and the inadequacies of empirical research about law. *See* Marc Galanter, *Reading the Landscape of Disputes: What We Know and Don't Know (and Think We Know) About Our Allegedly Contentious and Litigious Society,* 31 U.C.L.A. L. Rev. 4, 5 (1983). A thorough, recent study of the U.S. tort system reached similar conclusions about exaggerated claims of litigiousness. Although the author outlines in great detail the limitations of existing knowledge, he concludes:

At nearly every stage, the tort litigation system operates to diminish the likelihood that injurers will have to compensate victims. Only a small fraction of the costs created by actionable injuries will ever be paid by the injurers. Although the tort system plays only a tiny part in the compensation of victims of accidental injury, and does so at relatively high transaction costs, it may be more efficient and effective as a deterrent. At the same time that it provides such infrequent and partial compensation, it succeeds in generating huge overestimates of its potency in the minds of potential defendants.

Michael Saks, *Do We Really Know Anything About the Behavior of the Tort Litigation System — and Why Not?*, 140 U. Pa. L. Rev. 1147, 1287-1288 (1992).

9. A renewed push for reform has further challenged the growing outcry about a litigation crisis. Indeed, a recent study by the National Center for State Courts and the Conference of State Court Administrators in Williamsburg, Virginia, rejects the notion of a litigation crisis. The survey found that tort filings, in the 16 states surveyed, have actually declined from 330,124 in 1986 to 303,606 in 1993. Similarly, tort filings in a broader survey of 27 states dropped 6 percent between 1991 and 1993. Less populous states such as Hawaii, Indiana, and Nevada saw filings rise significantly during that period, but more populous states, such as California and New Jersey, experienced decreases of 23 percent and 13 percent, respectively. Reformers point to windfalls for plaintiffs in products liability and malpractice suits, but the Center's study of the dockets of ten states found that product suits comprised only 4 percent, and malpractice suits only 7 percent of all filings in 1993. Only 51 percent of tort plaintiffs prevailed at trial; far fewer prevailed in products liability and medical malpractice actions. Among prevailing plaintiffs, the average products liability award was $260,000, and the average medical malpractice award only $200,000. Plaintiffs won punitive damages in only 6 percent of all cases, and most commonly where there was a finding of an intentional tort such as defamation or fraud. The median punitive damage award found was $50,000. *See* John E. Morris, *Tort Crisis? What Crisis?*, American Lawyer 18 (June 1995) (summarizing the survey).

C. ALTERNATIVE DISPUTE RESOLUTION

One dominant response both to critiques of the adversary system and to the burdening workload of the courts is the development of alternative dispute processes. Alternative Dispute Resolution (ADR) processes seek to solve human problems with greater use of negotiation, compromise, and party participation than the formal, adversarial trial process and with greater guidance and support than informal, unaided settlement. ADR often is championed as a way to circumvent the cost and delay of litigation, although it is also criticized for exposing parties to the results of unequal bargaining power, secrecy, and compromise of rights that a court could enforce.

Chief alternatives include the following:

Mediation: A neutral actor facilitates an agreement between the disputants. Some mediators work on improving communications; some make proposals to the parties and try to break dead-locks; some press for agreement by the parties by using moral pressure or estimates of what would happen if the dispute ends up before a judge. Ideally, the participants engage voluntarily in the process; sometimes, though, mediation is mandated before parties may have access to a judge.

Summary jury trial: Invented by Judge Thomas Lambros, this is a court-initiated and supervised settlement process, designed to be voluntary, nonbinding, and confidential, that gives each party a chance to present their factual case before a jury. The jury then presents its reaction to the conflicting evidence, to give the settlement process a more objective sense of the weaknesses in each party's case. *See* Thomas D. Lambros, *The Summary Jury Trial: An Effective Aid to Settlement*, 77 Judicature 6 (1993). Variations of this process offer early neutral evaluation by allowing the parties to present their factual case before a retired judge, a practicing lawyer, or an expert in valuing claims, and to proceed to settlement negotiations in light of the comments and views of that independent third party.

Rent-a-judge: Authorized by law in California, this process starts when the parties choose a referee and request the trial judge to issue an order of reference or appointment to authorize that referee to hear the case. That order may call for following, changing, or abandoning formal rules of procedure and evidence. The parties usually split the costs and agree upon where the trial will take place. The referee issues a report containing findings of fact and conclusions of law; the decision must be guided by existing substantive law and is both binding and appealable. In some jurisdictions, parties may have an option to elect trial before a retired judge or a magistrate judge who is a judicial officer.

Arbitration: A neutral and skilled actor, agreed upon by the opposing parties, makes a judgment based on the presentation of the parties, and the parties agree to abide by that judgment and forego appeal. The procedures can be quite informal or can mirror procedures used in a courtroom. The arbitration process can be free-standing or annexed to a court system.

These processes may take place entirely outside the court system, in private (or even public) dispute resolution centers, mediation programs, and the like. Or these alternative processes may be annexed to courts or even administered by courts. In some scenarios, judges themselves can become problem solvers who use mediation or other techniques to resolve disputes. Here, judges are not simply managing court dockets but are transforming the work of courts altogether. Advocates and critics of these developments present a range of views, represented in the following readings.

■ JETHRO K. LIEBERMAN AND JAMES F. HENRY, LESSONS FROM THE ALTERNATIVE DISPUTE RESOLUTION MOVEMENT
53 U. Chi. L. Rev. 424 (1986)

. . . THE THEORY BEHIND ADR

OPENING THE LINES OF COMMUNICATION

What often prevents disputes from being resolved is a failure to communicate stemming from a lack of trust between the parties. ADR is premised on the hypothesis that if the parties could overcome this distrust, they could voluntarily reach a settlement as just as the result a court would impose.

The adversary process—the engine of the adjudicatory system—operates on a theory of fundamental distrust: Never put faith in the adversary. Litigation thus becomes formal, tricky, divisive, time-consuming, and distorting. These characteristics are reflected in the common image of discovery in large-scale commercial cases that takes years to conduct, in the careful coaching and preparation of witnesses, and in the skillful impeachment of sound witnesses during cross-examination. In contrast, the creation of trust is central to the design of many ADR processes.

Consider the example of the mini-trial. The mini-trial is not in fact a trial at all, but a highly-structured settlement process. Because it is a flexible device that can be tailored to the precise needs of the parties, no single procedural model of the mini-trial has yet prevailed. But in general, the known mini-trials share many of the following characteristics.

1. The parties negotiate a set of procedural ground rules (a protocol) that will govern the nonbinding mini-trial.
2. The time for preparation is relatively short—between six weeks and three months—and the amount of discovery is relatively limited.
3. The hearing itself is sharply abbreviated—usually no more than two days.
4. The hearing is often conducted by a third-party neutral, typically called the "neutral advisor."
5. The case is presented to representatives of the parties with authority to settle; there is no judge or jury.
6. The lawyers present their "best" case; they do not have time to delve into side issues.

7. Immediately after the hearing, the party representatives meet privately to negotiate a settlement.

8. If they cannot reach a settlement, the neutral advisor may render an advisory opinion on how he thinks a judge would rule if the case were to go to court.

9. The proceedings are confidential: the parties generally commit themselves to refrain from disclosing details of the proceedings to any outsider.

Several observations are in order about the trust-building capacity of the mini-trial. First, the very process of negotiating the protocol tends to foster trust. Second, by concentrating on their best possible case, the lawyers usually feel constrained to discuss the central issues. Third, the kind of lawyerly hairsplitting, namecalling, and pettifogging that might delight courtroom regulars would leave the business executives to whom mini-trials are presented singularly unamused. Finally, the presence at the hearing of a neutral advisor, to whom both parties have consented, enhances the prospect that they will credit any advisory opinion that he renders.

Mediation leads to the building of trust in a somewhat different way. Mediation permits a neutral to learn intimate facts from both sides that they would never have shared with each other in the course of trial preparation. By building on the parties' trust in the mediator, the process thus allows the parties to explore workable options. With the knowledge that he gains, the mediator can learn how far apart the parties are and devise ways of bridging the gap.

One lesson that ADR teaches, then, is that processes designed to restore and build trust can overcome the suspicion and mutual hostility fostered by the adversary system and can lead the parties to settle their differences. When the substantive outcome is compared to the likely result in court—and the costs of continued litigation are weighed in the balance—both parties generally benefit from ADR.

THE SUPERIORITY OF RESULTS

A working hypothesis of ADR is that the results of ADR are often superior to court judgments—and even more clearly superior to conventional settlements. Although the hypothesis is difficult to test, it is supported by several considerations.

First, adjudication is characterized by a "winner-take-all" outcome. This cannot be wholly true, for jury damage awards can work compromises, and the parties can shape consent decrees through bargaining. Nevertheless, in many cases, the fundamental issue of liability can be resolved only by holding for the plaintiff or the defendant. ADR, by contrast, is not bound by the zero-sum game of adjudication. While we have defined ADR as concerned with "legal disputes," participants in ADR are free to go beyond the legal definition of the scope of their dispute. They can reach for creative solutions to the problem that gave rise to the dispute, and those solutions may be far more novel than any remedy a court has the power to provide. In a mini-trial held by Texaco and Borden, for example, the parties resolved a breach-of-contract claim and antitrust counterclaim totaling in the hundreds of millions of dollars by renegotiating the entire contract for the supply of natural gas. Both parties claimed a net gain. No court could have ordered the parties to renegotiate; at best a judge or jury could only have compromised on the amount of damages it awarded the winner.

Second, in classes of cases involving complex institutions, negotiations conducted by executives are likely to yield results superior to those conducted by the lawyers. The executives are far more familiar than their lawyers with the nuances of their business and can respond more quickly and creatively to proposals raised by their counterparts. We do not mean to diminish the role or responsibilities of lawyers in the negotiations; their legal knowledge will often be crucial to successful settlements and good lawyer-negotiators may be more skillful than poorly trained executive-negotiators. Nevertheless, the business executive may be presumed to be less distracted by the shadow the law casts over the dispute; the executive will look at the complete business picture, unconstrained by the narrow parameters imposed by legal doctrine.

Third, direct involvement by the client can obviate or minimize difficulties arising from the self-interest of lawyers. This point may be particularly instructive for judges. By requiring clients to attend pretrial conferences, judges can be sure that the clients know and approve of the propositions their lawyers will assert in court on their behalf.

Fourth, ADR techniques and processes can be far more systematic than the horsetrading of conventional settlement negotiations. Settlement negotiations are often perceived as consisting of sharp tactics and bluff. "Unprincipled" negotiations occur in large part because the parties lack a means of communicating with each other. ADR processes permit realistic assessments of whether offers and counteroffers are in good faith.

Fifth, properly designed ADR processes make it more likely that settlement decisions will be based on the merits of disputes. As Richard A. Posner has suggested, various factors may contribute to more or less settlement. Delay in the judicial system tends to "increase the likelihood of settlement by reducing the stake in the case," in part because delay diminishes the present value of the ultimate award. Other factors include rules governing prejudgment interest and the availability of pretrial discovery. This analysis could lead the courts to advocate policies that would increase delay (or other costs of litigation) in order to prompt settlement. The resulting settlements would not necessarily be just, however, because they would not have taken account of power disparities. The party with the more meritorious claim might not prevail because he is too poor to amass the requisite evidence through the discovery process. Society may have the power to foster higher settlement rates by manipulating the factors that induce people to stay out of court, but many proponents of ADR would not view such policies as consonant with the ADR philosophy. A dispute should not merely be settled; it should be settled justly.

. . . Finally, a sixth reason to think that ADR leads to "better" outcomes is that the use of private neutrals permits the parties to submit their dispute to one with greater expertise in their particular subject than does the luck of the draw in the courtroom. Many complex disputes involve data and concepts that lie beyond the knowledge of generalist judges (and of all juries). The ADR neutral can be selected for a particular expertise, thus saving the parties the cost of educating the fact-finder (and the risk of failing to do so).* Moreover, if the parties have personally participated in selecting the neutral, they may be psychologically disposed to accept is statement of the case, whether it is a binding decision (as in arbitration) or an advisory opinion (as in a mini-trial). . . .

■ OWEN M. FISS, AGAINST SETTLEMENT
93 Yale L.J. 1073 (1984)

. . . The movement promises to reduce the amount of litigation initiated, and accordingly the bulk of its proposals are devoted to negotiation and mediation prior to suit. But the interest in the so-called "gentler arts" has not been so confined. It extends to ongoing litigation as well, and the advocates of ADR have sought new ways to facilitate and perhaps even pressure parties into settling pending cases. . . . Rule 16 of the Federal Rules of Civil Procedure was [recently] amended to strengthen the hand of the trial judge in brokering settlements: The "facilitation of settlement" became an explicit purpose of pretrial conferences and participants were officially invited, if that is the proper word, to consider "the possibility of settlement or the use of extrajudicial procedure to resolve the dispute." [In 1983, the] Advisory Committee on Civil Rules proposed to amend Rule 68 to sharpen the incentives for settlement: Under this amendment, a party who rejects a settlement offer and then receives a judgment less favorable than that offer would have to pay the attorney's fees of the other party. . . .

The advocates of ADR are led to support such measures and to exalt the idea of settlement more generally because they view adjudication as a process to resolve disputes. They act as though courts arose to resolve

---

* *Eds. Note:* For several decades, and with increasing intensity, various states have experimented with specialized courts for specific types of cases, such as commercial litigation. *See, e.g.*, Rocehelle C. Dreyfuss, *Forums of the Future: The Role of Specialized Courts in Resolving Business Disputes*, 61 Brook. L. Rev. 1 (1995); Robert L. Haig, *Can New York's New Commercial Division Resolve Business Disputes as Well as Anyone?* 13 Touro L. Rev. 191 (1996).

quarrels between neighbors who had reached an impasse and turned to a stranger for help. Courts are seen as an institutionalization of the stranger and adjudication is viewed as the process by which the stranger exercises power. The very fact that the neighbors have turned to someone else to resolve their dispute signifies a breakdown in their social relations; the advocates of ADR acknowledge this, but nonetheless hope that the neighbors will be able to reach agreement before the stranger renders judgment. Settlement is that agreement. It is a truce more than a true reconciliation, but it seems preferable to judgment because it rests on the consent of both parties and avoids the cost of a lengthy trial.

THE IMBALANCE OF POWER

By viewing the lawsuit as a quarrel between two neighbors, the dispute-resolution story that underlies ADR implicitly asks us to assume a rough equality between the contending parties. It treats settlement as the antici-pation of the outcome of trial and assumes that the terms of settlement are simply a product of the parties' predictions of that outcome. In truth, however, settlement is also a function of the resources available to each party to finance the litigation, and those resources are frequently distrib-uted unequally. Many lawsuits do not involve a property dispute between two neighbors, or between AT&T and the government (to update the story), but rather concern a struggle between a member of a racial minor-ity and a municipal police department over alleged brutality, or a claim by a worker against a large corporation over work-related injuries. In these cases, the distribution of financial resources, or the ability of one party to pass along its costs, will invariably infect the bargaining process, and the settlement will be at odds with a conception of justice that seeks to make the wealth of the parties irrelevant.

The disparities in resources between the parties can influence the set-tlement in three ways. First, the poorer party may be less able to amass and analyze the information needed to predict the outcome of the litigation, and thus be disadvantaged in the bargaining process. Second, he may need the damages he seeks immediately and thus be induced to settle as a way of accelerating payment, even though he realizes he would get less now than he might if he awaited judgment. All plaintiffs want their damages immediately, but an indigent plaintiff may be exploited by a rich defendant because his need is so great that the defendant can force him to accept a sum that is less than the ordinary present value of the judg-ment. Third, the poorer party might be forced to settle because he does not have the resources to finance the litigation, to cover either his own projected expenses, such as his lawyer's time, or the expenses his oppo-nent can impose through the manipulation of procedural mechanisms such as discovery. It might seem that settlement benefits the plaintiff by allowing him to avoid the costs of litigation, but this is not so. The defendant can anticipate the plaintiff's costs if the case were to be tried fully and decrease his offer by that amount. The indigent plaintiff is a victim of the costs of litigation even if he settles. . . .

Of course, imbalances of power can distort judgment as well: Resources influence the quality of presentation, which in turn has an important bearing on who wins and the terms of victory. We count, however, on the guiding presence of the judge, who can employ a number of measures to lessen the impact of distributional inequalities. He can, for example, supplement the parties' presentations by asking questions, calling his own witnesses, and inviting other persons and institutions to participate as amici. These measures are likely to make only a small contribution toward moderating the influence of distributional inequalities, but should not be ignored for that reason. Not even these small steps are possible with settlement. There is, moreover, a critical difference between a process like settlement, which is based on bargaining and accepts inequalities of wealth as an integral and legitimate component of the process, and a process like judgment, which knowingly struggles against those inequalities. Judgment aspires to an autonomy from distributional inequalities, and it gathers much of its appeal from this aspiration.

THE ABSENCE OF AUTHORITATIVE CONSENT

The argument for settlement presupposes that the contestants are individuals. These individuals speak for themselves and should he bound by the rules they generate. In many situations, however, individuals are ensnared in contractual relationships that impair their autonomy. Lawyers or insurance companies might, for example, agree to settlements that are in their interests but are not in the best interests of their clients, and to which their client would not agree if the choice were still theirs. But a deeper and more intractable problem arises from the fact that many parties are not individuals but rather organizations or groups. We do not know who is entitled to speak for these entities and to give the consent upon which so much of the appeal of settlement depends.

These problems become even more pronounced when we turn from organizations and consider the fact that much contemporary litigation involves even more nebulous social entities, namely, groups. Some of these groups, such as ethnic or racial minorities, inmates of prisons, or residents of institutions for mentally retarded people, may have an identity or existence that transcends the lawsuit, but they do not have any formal organizational structure and therefore lack any procedures for generating authoritative consent. The absence of such a procedure is even more pronounced in cases involving a group, such as the purchasers of Cuisinarts between 1972 and 1982, which is constructed solely in order to create funds large enough to make it financially attractive for lawyers to handle the case. . . .

Going to judgment does not altogether eliminate the risk of unauthorized action, any more than it eliminates the distortions arising from disparities in resources. The case presented by the representative of a group or an organization admittedly will influence the outcome of the suit, and that outcome will bind those who might also be bound by a settlement. On the other hand, judgment does not ask as much from the so-called representatives. There is a conceptual and normative distance between what the representatives do and say and what the court eventually decides, because the judge tests those statements and actions against independent procedural and substantive standards. The authority of judgment arises from the law, not from the statements or actions of the putative representatives, and thus we allow judgment to bind persons not directly involved in the litigation even when we are reluctant to have settlement do so.

The procedures that have been devised for policing the settlement process when groups or organizations are involved have not eliminated the difficulties of generating authoritative consent. Some of these procedures provide a substantive standard for the approval of the settlement and do not even consider the issue of consent. A case in point is the Tunney Act. The Act establishes procedures for giving outsiders notice of a proposed settlement in a government antitrust suit and requires the judge to decide whether a settlement proposed by the Department of Justice is in "the public interest." This statute implicitly acknowledges the difficulty of determining who is entitled to speak for the United States in some authoritative fashion and yet provides the judge with virtually no guidance in making this determination or in deciding whether to approve the settlement. The public-interest standard in fact seems to invite the consideration of such nonjudicial factors as popular sentiment and the efficient allocation of prosecutorial resources.

Other policing mechanisms, such as Rule 23, which governs class actions, make no effort to articulate a substantive standard for approving settlements, but instead entrust the whole matter to the judge. In such cases, the judge's approval theoretically should turn on whether the group consents, but determining whether such consent exists is often impossible, since true consent consists of nothing less than the expressed unanimity of all the members of a group, which might number in the hundreds of thousands and be scattered across the United States. The judge's approval instead turns on how close or far the proposed settlement is from what he imagines would be the judgment obtained after suit. The basis for approving a settlement, contrary to what the dispute-resolution story suggests, is therefore not consent but rather the settlement's approximation to judgment. This might appear to remove my objection to settlement, except that the judgment being used as a measure of the settlement is very odd indeed: It has never in fact been entered, but only imagined. It has been constructed without benefit of a full trial, and at a time when the judge can no longer count on the thorough presentation promised by the adversary system. The contending parties have struck a bargain, and have every interest in defending the settlement and in convincing the judge that it is in accord with the law.

THE LACK OF A FOUNDATION FOR CONTINUING JUDICIAL INVOLVEMENT

The dispute-resolution story trivializes the remedial dimensions of lawsuits and mistakenly assumes judgment to be the end of the process. It supposes that the judge's duty is to declare which neighbor is right and which wrong, and that this declaration will end the judge's involvement (save in that most exceptional situation where it is also necessary for him to issue a writ directing the sheriff to execute the declaration). Under these assumptions, settlement appears as an almost perfect substitute for judgment, for it too can declare the parties' rights. Often, however, judgment is not the end of a lawsuit but only the beginning. The involvement of the court may continue almost indefinitely. In these cases, settlement cannot provide an adequate basis for that necessary continuing involvement, and thus is no substitute for judgment.

The parties may sometimes be locked in combat with one another and view the lawsuit as only one phase in a long continuing struggle. The entry of judgment will then not end the struggle, but rather change its terms and the balance of power. One of the parties will invariably return to the court and again ask for its assistance, not so much because conditions have changed, but because the conditions that preceded the lawsuit have unfortunately not changed. This often occurs in domestic-relations cases, where the divorce decree represents only the opening salvo in an endless series of skirmishes over custody and support.

The structural reform cases that play such a prominent role on the federal docket provide another occasion for continuing judicial involvement. In these cases, courts seek to safeguard public values by restructuring large-scale bureaucratic organizations. The task is enormous, and our knowledge of how to restructure on-going bureaucratic organizations is limited. As a consequence, courts must oversee and manage the remedial process for a long time—maybe forever. This, I fear, is true of most school desegregation cases, some of which have been pending for twenty or thirty years. It is also true of antitrust cases that seek divesture or reorganization of an industry. . . .

The allure of settlement in large part derives from the fact that it avoids the need for a trial. Settlement must thus occur before the trial is complete and the judge has entered findings of fact and conclusions of law. As a consequence, the judge confronted with a request for modification of a consent decree must retrospectively reconstruct the situation as it existed at the time the decree was entered, and decide whether conditions today have sufficiently changed to warrant a modification in that decree. . . . Such an inquiry . . . is likely to dissipate whatever savings in judicial resources the initial settlement may have produced.

Settlement also impedes vigorous enforcement, which sometimes requires the use of contempt power. As a formal matter, contempt is available to punish violations of a consent decree. But courts hesitate to use that power to enforce decrees that rest solely on consent, especially when enforcement is aimed at high public officials. . . . Courts do not see a mere bargain between the parties as a sufficient foundation for the exercise of their coercive powers. . . .

JUSTICE RATHER THAN PEACE

The dispute-resolution story makes settlement appear as a perfect substitute for judgment, as we just saw, by trivializing the remedial dimensions of a lawsuit, and also by reducing the social function of the suit to one of resolving private disputes: In that story, settlement appears to achieve exactly the same purpose as judgment—peace between the parties—but at considerably less expense to society. The two quarreling neighbors turn to a court in order to resolve their dispute, and society makes courts available because it wants to aid in the achievement of their private ends or to secure the peace.

In my view, however, the purpose of adjudication should be understood in broader terms. Adjudication uses public resources, and employs not strangers chosen by the parties but public officials chosen by a process in which the public participates. These officials, like members of the legislative and executive branches, possess a power that has been defined and conferred by public law, not by private agreement. Their job is not to maximize the ends of private parties, nor simply to secure the peace, but to explicate and give force to the values embodied in authoritative texts such as the Constitution and statutes: to interpret those values and to bring reality into accord with them. This duty is not discharged when the parties settle. . . .

■ HARRY T. EDWARDS,[*]
ALTERNATIVE DISPUTE RESOLUTION:
PANACEA OR ANATHEMA?
99 Harv. L. Rev. 668 (1986)

. . . In strictly private disputes, ADR mechanisms such as arbitration often are superior to adjudication. Disputes can be resolved by neutrals with substantive expertise, preferably chosen by the parties, and the substance of disputes can be examined without issue-obscuring procedural rules. Tens of thousands of cases are resolved this way each year by labor and commercial arbitration, and even more private disputes undoubtedly could be better resolved through ADR than by adjudication.

---

[*] *Eds. Note:* Harry T. Edwards is Chief Judge, United States Court of Appeals for the District of Columbia Circuit.

However, if ADR is extended to resolve difficult issues of constitutional or public law—making use of nonlegal values to resolve important social issues or allowing those the law seeks to regulate to delimit public rights and duties—there is real reason for concern. An oft-forgotten virtue of adjudication is that it ensures the proper resolution and application of public values. In our rush to embrace alternatives to litigation, we must be careful not to endanger what law has accomplished or to destroy this important function of formal adjudication. . . .

The concern here is that ADR will replace the rule of law with nonlegal values. J. Anthony Lucas' masterful study of Boston during the busing crisis highlights the critical point that often our nation's most basic values— such as equal justice under the law—conflict with local nonlegal mores. This was true in Boston during the school desegregation battle, and it was true in the South during the civil rights battles of the sixties. This conflict, however, between national public values reflected in rules of law and nonlegal values that might be embraced in alternative dispute resolution exists in even more mundane public issues.

For example, many environmental disputes are now settled by negotiation and mediation instead of adjudication. Indeed, as my colleague Judge Wald recently observed, there is little hope that Superfund legislation can solve our nation's toxic waste problem unless the vast bulk of toxic waste disputes are resolved through negotiation, rather than litigation. Yet, as necessary as environmental negotiation may be, it is still troubling. When Congress or a government agency has enacted strict environmental protection standards, negotiations that compromise these strict standards with weaker standards result in the application of values that are simply inconsistent with the rule of law. Furthermore, environmental mediation and negotiation present the danger that environmental standards will be set by private groups without the democratic checks of governmental institutions. . . .

We must also be concerned lest ADR become a tool for diminishing the judicial development of legal rights for the disadvantaged. Professor Tony Amsterdam has aptly observed that ADR may result in the reduction of possibilities for legal redress of wrongs suffered by the poor and underprivileged, "in the name of increased access to justice and judicial efficiency." Inexpensive, expeditious, and informal adjudication is not always synonymous with fair and just adjudication. The decision-makers may not understand the values at stake and parties to disputes do not always possess equal power and resources. Sometimes because of this inequality and sometimes because of deficiencies in informal processes lacking procedural protections, the use of alternative mechanisms will produce nothing more than inexpensive and ill-informed decisions. And these decisions may merely legitimate decisions made by the existing power structure within society. Additionally, by diverting particular types of cases away from adjudication, we may stifle the development of law in certain disfavored areas of law. Imagine, for example, the impoverished nature of civil rights law that would have resulted had all race discrimination cases in the sixties and seventies been mediated rather than adjudicated. The wholesale diversion of cases involving the legal rights of the poor may result in the definition of these rights by the powerful in our society rather than by the application of fundamental societal values reflected in the rule of law. . . .

Once a body of law is well developed, arbitration and other ADR mechanisms can be structured in such a way that public rights and duties would not be defined and delimited by private groups. The recent experience of labor arbitrators in the federal sector, who are required to police compliance with laws, rules, and regulations, suggests that the interpretation and application of law may not lie outside the competence of arbitrators. So long as we restrict arbitrators to the application of clearly defined rules of law, and strictly confine the articulation of public law to our courts, ADR can be an effective means of reducing mushrooming caseloads. Employment discrimination cases offer a promising example. Many employment discrimination cases are highly fact-bound and can be resolved by applying established principles of law. Others, however, present novel questions that should be resolved by a court. If the more routine cases could be certified to an effective alternative dispute resolution system that would have the authority to make some final determinations, the courts could devote greater attention to novel legal questions, and the overall efficiency of an anti-discrimination law might be enhanced.

In other areas, we could capitalize on the substantive expertise and standards developed by well-established ADR mechanisms. For example, the experience and standards developed through decades of labor arbitration and mediation could prove particularly useful in settling disputes between nonunionized employees and their employers in cases of "unjust dismissal." . . .

Finally, there are some disputes in which community values—coupled with the rule of law—may be a rich source of justice. Mediation of disputes between parents and schools about special education programs for handicapped children has been very successful. A majority of disputes have been settled by mediation, and parents are generally positive about both the outcome and the process. At issue in these mediations is the appropriate education for a child, a matter best resolved by parents and educators—not courts. Similarly, many landlord-tenant disputes can ultimately be resolved only by negotiation. Most tenant "rights" are merely procedural rather than substantive. Yet tenants desire *substantive* improvement in housing conditions or assurances that they will not be evicted. Mediation of landlord-tenant disputes, therefore, can be very successful—often more successful than adjudication—because both parties have much to gain by agreement.

In both of these examples, however, the option of ultimate resort to adjudication is essential. It is only because handicapped children have a statutory right to education that parent-school mediation is successful.

It is only because tenants have procedural rights that landlords will bargain at all.

ADR can thus play a vital role in constructing a judicial system that is both more manageable and more responsive to the needs of our citizens. It is essential—as the foregoing examples illustrate—that this role of ADR be strictly limited to prevent the resolution of important constitutional and public law issues by ADR mechanisms that are independent of our courts. Fortunately, few ADR programs have attempted to remove public law issues from the courts. Although this may merely reflect the relative youth of the ADR movement, it may also manifest an awareness of the danger of public law resolution in nonjudicial fora. . . .

■ LISA BERNSTEIN, UNDERSTANDING THE LIMITS OF COURT-CONNECTED ADR: A CRITIQUE OF FEDERAL COURT-ANNEXED ARBITRATION PROGRAMS
141 U. Pa. L. Rev. 2169 (1993)

. . . A primary goal of CAA [court-annexed arbitration] programs is to reduce the private and social cost of disputing. However, a review of the empirical literature on federal CAA programs (which do not have post-arbitration fee and cost-shifting disincentives to requesting a trial) suggests that there is no conclusive evidence that CAA programs reduce either the private or social cost of disputing.

One measure of social cost is the per-case processing cost. A recent study of the North Carolina CAA program found that "the average cost to the court of each closed . . . [arbitration track] case was $1209 and the average cost to the court of each closed control group case was $1240," but cautioned that "[t]he difference in cost was not statistically significant." One district discontinued its program "due to disproportionately high administrative costs . . . 14% of the district's administrative resources were devoted to handling arbitration cases, which represented only 7.2% of its civil caseload."

Even if CAA programs had no effect on the per-case processing cost, they might produce aggregate social cost savings if they reduced the trial rate. There is no conclusive evidence, however, that the programs have reduced the trial rate, and because so few of the cases subject to the programs would have gone to trial in a trial-only jurisdiction, it would take many years of data to reliably detect changes in the trial rate.

There is some evidence that the programs may slightly reduce the private costs of disputing, but the reductions reported are small, the studies are inconclusive, and the results may be marred by serious response bias. Furthermore, studies that found some reduction in the private cost of disputing to the plaintiff did not observe any changes in the contingent fee percentages charged by plaintiff's lawyers. This suggests that in the tort context CAA programs may benefit plaintiff's lawyers, but not plaintiffs themselves. . . .

Another goal of CAA programs is to reduce delay. A Federal Judicial Center study of the time from filing to disposition concluded that "speedier dispositions are not an automatic benefit of arbitration programs," and a RAND study found no statistically significant difference in disposition times. Nevertheless, even if the programs did succeed in reducing average case processing times, as long as the arbitration award is non-binding, the party with the superior ability to bear the costs of delay can still threaten to request a trial. . . .

One of the most important features of private ADR is the secrecy of both the proceedings and the outcome. Advertisements for private ADR providers tend to emphasize secrecy.

Secrecy can affect both the likelihood of settlement and the settlement value of a claim. In situations where a party is frequently involved in litigation and has an interest in having a reputation as a hard bargainer, secrecy may remove the benefit of being perceived as a hard bargainer in a particular case and make him more likely to settle. Conversely, a party who would have settled to avoid revelation of proprietary information in the absence of an ADR agreement may refuse to settle when such an agreement exists, secure in the knowledge that the proceedings will remain secret.

An additional benefit of secrecy is that it enables the litigants to minimize the damage to their reputation. Although this might not be important in the context of smaller claims to the extent that the existence of a dispute may affect a party's access to capital during the pendency of the dispute, it is an important advantage of private ADR.

Federal court-connected ADR programs cannot offer parties the same degree of secrecy as private ADR programs. Even in court-connected ADR proceedings where the hearing is closed to the public so that the information revealed in the proceeding is kept private, the existence of the dispute and the allegations in the pleadings are a matter of public record. In addition, although the Sixth Circuit has held that summary jury trials may be closed to the public, the constitutionality of closing other types of federal court-connected ADR proceedings to the public has not yet been considered by any federal court.

According to ADR professionals, informality is an important reason that parties opt for private ADR. Informal processes are said to be better than formal adversary proceedings at preserving ongoing business relationships. However, it is precisely in the relational contract setting, where the parties have dealt with each other on a repeat basis over a long period of time and know the types of disputes that are most likely to arise, that the barriers to contracting for private ADR are the lowest, the benefits from doing so are largest, and the parties can most easily select a trier of fact who they feel will justly and amicably resolve any dispute that may arise. In such a situation, failure to include an ADR provision in a contract is likely to reflect a deliberate choice made by the parties and to signal their preference for traditional adjudication should a dispute arise that cannot be amicably resolved.

The ability of court-connected ADR proceedings to fully capture the benefits of informality that are available when the parties opt to use relatively informal private ADR processes is limited. First, the success of most informal dispute resolution processes is due, in large part, to the fact that parties consent to their use. An informal process is unlikely to lead to a consensual settlement when one party does not wish to participate. Second, the history of agency adjudication suggests that court-connected ADR programs and proceedings are likely to become increasingly formal and complex. . . .

The ability of courts and private ADR tribunals to enforce their judgments may differ substantially. Private (extralegal) dispute resolution tribunals are often preferred because they have the ability to impose legal sanctions, such as money damages and specific performance, as well as extralegal sanctions. These extralegal sanctions put additional pressures on the parties to comply with the arbitrated judgments, pressures that are unavailable to courts. For instance, in a well-organized industry, a trade association tribunal may be able to quickly translate an unpaid judgment into damage to reputation. Some trade associations and commodities exchanges require members to sign an agreement to submit disputes to the organization's dispute resolution tribunal and to promptly comply with their judgments. By threatening to expel a member or to publicize his failure to comply with a judgment rendered against him, these associations can make a credible threat to put a noncomplying disputant out of business. In the diamond industry, where all disputes among members of the world's diamond exchanges are decided by exchange-run mediation and arbitration tribunals, the existence and outcome of disputes are kept secret as long as the decisions of the dispute resolution tribunal are complied with, but a party who fails to promptly pay a judgment rendered against him will have his picture hung in every diamond exchange in the world along with a prominent notice describing his wrongdoing and the fact that he failed to pay a judgment. At the Chicago Mercantile Exchange, where the mere existence of a dispute can threaten the public's perception of the integrity of the market, both the existence of a dispute and the judgment of the Exchange's dispute resolution tribunal are posted outside the trading floor even when the guilty party promptly pays the judgment rendered against him. Although exchange rules limit the maximum fine that can be imposed, the reputational effect of making the dispute and judgment public greatly increases the significance of the sanction.

A court-appointed arbitrator, in contrast, cannot take advantage of these types of extralegal enforcement mechanisms; he cannot bring any unique pressures to bear on the parties to induce them to accept his decision, and the fact that he has rendered a decision may have no more effect on the parties' reputations than the mere filing of a claim.

In sum, the private benefits available from the inclusion of private ADR provisions go far beyond the ex post reduction in delay and dispute resolution costs. When the parties are able to agree on acceptable neutral, narrowly tailored ADR provisions may reduce the costs of entering into a contract and can be used to reduce the actual damage suffered by the promisee in the event of breach and thereby increase the value of a contractual promise. In addition, such clauses can broaden the range of credible contractual commitments available to the parties and, in certain contexts, can be used to secure enforcement advantages and the full benefit of reputation bonds. While some of these gains can be captured through the use of private ex post ADR agreements, they cannot, for the most part, be captured by requiring parties to participate in a non-binding CAA hearing conducted by a volunteer member of the local bar. Thus, evidence of the popularity and success of private, consensual, binding ADR should not be used to justify mandatory non-binding court-annexed arbitration programs, and should be used with caution in analyzing the desirability of other types of court-connected ADR programs. . . .

■ GEORGE W. COOMBE, JR., THE RESOLUTION OF TRANSNATIONAL COMMERCIAL DISPUTES: A PERSPECTIVE FROM NORTH AMERICA
5 Ann. Surv. Intl. & Comp. Law 13 (1999)

The resolution of international ("transnational") commercial disputes requires careful appraisal of the underlying business transactions from which a given dispute arises. Particular attention must be paid to several attendant problems—political, economic, jurisprudential, and cultural—that are seldom encountered in the resolution of domestic commercial disputes. Business executives, if properly counseled, will consider at some length the implications of those problems before negotiating a transnational agreement. Indeed, it is not enough to understand the implications of these problems in legal and pragmatic terms; the negotiating process itself should reflect that understanding. Accordingly, an important component of such an agreement should be a dispute resolution clause that reflects the parties' explicit intention to anticipate future disputes and resolve them in a manner conducive to preserving the business relationship.

Over the years, the resolution of transnational disputes has been addressed exclusively by a small number of so-called "international law firms" which are well versed in the intricacies of international litigation and arbitration. Until recently, litigation and arbitration represented the only resolution techniques. The last decade however has witnessed an expansion of the available techniques, which manifests growing business confidence in the practice of resolving disputes through the use of voluntary, non-binding processes such as negotiation, mediation, conciliation, and the minitrial. . . .

The North American Free Trade Agreement (NAFTA) provides for direct arbitration between a foreign investor and a member state. NAFTA provides that an investor may submit a dispute to international arbitration pursuant to the rules of either the International Centre for the Settlement of Investment Disputes (ICSID), or of the United Nations Commission on International Trade Law (UNCITRAL). Further, NAFTA expressly promotes international commercial arbitration: "Each party shall, to the maximum extent possible, encourage and facilitate the use of arbitration and other means of alternative dispute resolution for the settlement of international commercial disputes between private parties in the free trade area."

NAFTA has encouraged the development of new arbitration and mediation centers to address private transborder disputes. The Commercial Arbitration and Mediation Centre for the Americas (CAMCA) was created to facilitate the resolution of private transborder disputes within the North American free trade area. CAMCA was formed by the efforts of its constituent members: the American Arbitration Association (AAA), the British Columbia Commercial Arbitration Center, the Mexico City National Chamber of Commerce, and the Quebec National and International Commercial Arbitration Centre. CAMCA is jointly administered by each of these leading dispute resolution centers in the three NAFTA countries. CAMCA provides arbitration and mediation services under a uniform set of rules published in the three languages of the NAFTA countries. Furthermore, CAMCA has established a multi-national roster of arbitrators and mediators, and has created a neutral mechanism to fix the situs of arbitration or mediation in the absence of party agreement. . . .

Despite recent economic problems in the region, more foreign investment has been committed more rapidly to Asia and the Pacific during the past ten years than in any decade in world history. As a result of those capital flows, two billion people—two and a half times as many as those living in the industrialized west—are bringing themselves into modernity in the space of a single generation.

Due to the commercial importance of Asia to the United States and Canada, it is not surprising that Asian traditions influence U.S. and Canadian thinking. One such tradition—conciliation of commercial disputes—is already firmly established throughout North America as a useful augmentation to arbitration. Business executives and their counsel have come to appreciate, through direct negotiating experience with their Asian counterparts, that Asian values emphasizing preservation of the business relationship and maintenance of party credibility and trust are the very heart of responsible commercial dispute resolution.

Stimulated by a growing recognition of the counter-productive features of formal adjudicatory procedures for resolving disputes, such as litigation and arbitration, many members of the legal profession in the U.S. and in Canada have begun to search for better ways to resolve legal disputes. The objectives which have motivated the search for alternative procedures mirror the list of problems identified as inherent in the conventional adjudicatory procedures: the desire for party participation; the need to resolve the dispute without terminating the underlying business relationship or destroying the confidence upon which it is based; the need to focus the parties' attention on the main issues in the dispute and to minimize the diversions of time and energy to procedural and other ancillary issues; and the encouragement of free dialogue.

In light of the foregoing considerations, and to take advantage of the non-binding negotiations procedures favored throughout Asia, those procedures can be structured within the framework of arbitral procedures. Indeed, the arbitral framework affords the parties great flexibility which will permit them to define the scope and mechanics of the proceeding so as to accomplish the main objectives of the alternative procedures and still lead to a final adjudication in the event that a negotiated settlement is not reached.

Thus, it is possible to design arbitration agreements under which the demand for arbitration would automatically trigger preliminary non-binding procedures, prior to the appointment of arbitrators. If properly structured, such provisions not only insulate such procedures from judicial interference, but also enable the party invoking the alternative procedure to obtain the assistance of a court to compel a recalcitrant opponent to pursue the alternative procedure as an integral part of the arbitration. At present, use of the arbitral framework offers the most promising approach for the application of alternative non-binding, negotiation procedures to transnational business disputes. As a result, we shall continue to look to the values and traditions of Asia and its growing influence upon transnational business and upon the decent resolution of transnational business disputes. . . .

■ RICHARD DELGADO, ET AL., FAIRNESS AND FORMALITY: MINIMIZING THE RISK OF PREJUDICE IN ALTERNATIVE DISPUTE RESOLUTION
1985 Wis. L. Rev. 1359

ADR offers a number of clear-cut benefits. It can shape a decree flexibly so as to protect a continuing relationship between the parties. It is low-cost, speedy, and for some at least, nonintimidating. Yet there is little benefit for a minority disputant in a quick, painless hearing that renders an adverse decision tainted by prejudice.

Part III showed that the risk of prejudice is greatest when a member of an in-group confronts a member of an out-group; when that confrontation is direct, rather than through intermediaries; when there are few rules to constrain conduct; when the setting is closed and does not make clear that "public" values are to preponderate; and when the controversy concerns an intimate, personal matter rather than some impersonal question. Our review also indicated that many minority participants will press their claims most vigorously when they believe that what they do and say will make a difference, that the structure will respond, and that the outcome is predictable and related to effort and merit.

It follows that ADR is most apt to incorporate prejudice when a person of low status and power confronts a person or institution of high status and power. In such situations, the party of high status is more likely than in other situations to attempt to call up prejudiced responses; at the same time, the individual of low status is less likely to press his or her claim energetically. The dangers increase when the mediator or other third party is a member of the superior group or class. Examples of ADR settings that may contain these characteristics are prison and other institutional review boards, consumer complaint panels, and certain types of cases referred to an ombudsman. In these situations, minorities and members of other outgroups should opt for formal in-court adjudication, and the justice system ought to avoid pressuring them to accept an alternate procedure. ADR should be reserved for cases in which parties of comparable power and status confront each other.

ADR also poses heightened risks of prejudice when the issue to be adjudicated touches a sensitive or intimate area of life, for example, housing or culture-based conduct. Thus, many landlord-tenant, interneighbor, and intrafamilial disputes are poor candidates for ADR. When the parties are of unequal status and the question litigated concerns a sensitive, intimate area, the risks of an outcome colored by prejudice are especially great. If, for reasons of economy or efficiency ADR must be resorted to in these situations, the likelihood of bias can be reduced by providing rules that clearly specify the scope of the proceedings and forbid irrelevant or intrusive inquiries, by requiring open proceedings, and by providing some form of higher review. The third-party facilitator or decisionmaker should be a professional and be acceptable to both parties. Any party desiring one should be provided with an advocate, ideally an attorney, experienced with representation before the forum in question. To avoid atomization and lost opportunities to aggregate claims and inject public values into dispute resolution, ADR mechanisms should not be used in cases that have a broad societal dimension, but forward them to court for appropriate treatment.

Would measures like these destroy the very advantages of economy, simplicity, speed, and flexibility that make ADR attractive? Would such measures render ADR proceedings as expensive, time-consuming, formalistic, and inflexible as trials? These measures do increase the costs, but, on balance, those costs seem worth incurring. The ideal of equality before the law is too insistent a value to be compromised in the name of more mundane advantages. Continued growth of ADR consistent with goals of basic fairness will require two essential adjustments: (1) It will be necessary to identify those areas and types of ADR in which the dangers of prejudice are greatest and to direct those grievances to formal court adjudication; (2) In those areas in which the risk of prejudice exists, but is not so great as to require an absolute ban, checks and formalities must be built into ADR to ameliorate these risks as much as possible. . . .

■ FRANK E. A. SANDER, VARIETIES OF DISPUTE PROCESSING
The Pound Conference: Perspectives on Justice in the Future 65, 83-84
(American Bar Association)

. . . What I am thus advocating is a flexible and diverse panoply of dispute resolution processes, with particular types of cases being assigned to differing processes (or combinations of processes), according to some of the criteria mentioned. Conceivably such allocation might be accomplished for a particular class of cases at the outset by the legislature; that in effect is what was done by the Massachusetts legislature for malpractice cases. Alternatively one might envision by the year 2000 not simply a court house but a Dispute Resolution Center, where the grievant would be channeled through a screening clerk who would then direct him to the process (or sequence of processes) most appropriate to his type of case. The room directory in the lobby of such a Center might look as follows:

Screening Clerk	Room 1
Mediation	Room 2
Arbitration	Room 3
Fact Finding	Room 4
Malpractice Screening Panel	Room 5
Superior Court	Room 6
Ombudsman	Room 7

. . . [One concern is] the need to retain the courts as the ultimate agency capable of effectively protecting the rights of the disadvantaged. This is a legitimate concern which I believe to be consistent with the goals I have advocated. I am not maintaining that cases asserting novel constitutional claims ought to be diverted to mediation or arbitration. On the contrary, the goal is to reserve the courts for those activities for which they are best suited and to avoid swamping and paralyzing them with cases that do not require their unique capabilities.

■ CARRIE MENKEL-MEADOW, PURSUING SETTLEMENT IN AN ADVERSARY CULTURE: A TALE OF INNOVATION CO-OPTED OR "THE LAW OF ADR"
19 Fla. St. U.L. Rev. 1 (1991)

In what has become a commonly recognized division in the literature and advocacy about ADR, we see two basically different justifications for processes that resolve cases short of trial—what I call quantitative-efficiency claims versus qualitative-justice claims. These different conceptions of the purposes of ADR represent vastly different ideologies and perspectives on how disputes should be resolved in our society. Although efficiency has become the more prominent concern, I believe the "quality of justice" proponents actually came first in very recent history. In the 1960s, as part of several other social movements advocating more democratic participation in our various social institutions, a variety of groups urged that dispute resolution should more fully involve the participants in disputes. This would allow individuals to make their own decisions about what should happen to them. Thus, a model of community empowerment, party participation, and access to justice was championed by those concerned with substantive justice and democratic process. This "movement" resulted in the funding and support of "neighborhood justice centers" and a variety of more indigenous community dispute resolution centers—many of these justified on the grounds of increased participation and access to justice.

Others, like myself, have argued that outcomes derived from our adversarial judicial system or the negotiation that occurs in its shadows are inadequate for solving many human problems. Our legal system produces binary win-lose results in adjudication. It also produces unreflective compromise—"split the difference" results in negotiated settlements that may not satisfy the underlying needs or interests of the parties. Human problems become stylized and simplified because they must take a particular legal form for the stating of a claim. Furthermore, the "limited remedial imagination" of courts in providing outcomes restricts what possible solutions the parties could develop. Some of us have argued that alternative forms of dispute resolution, or new conceptualizations of old processes, could lead to outcomes that were efficient in the Pareto-optimal sense of making both parties better off without worsening the position of the other. In addition, the processes themselves would be better because they would provide a greater opportunity for party participation and recognition of party goals. Thus, the "quality" school includes both elements of process and substantive justice claims. Some of the arguments here have been supported by the jurisprudential and anthropological work of those studying the different structures that human beings have developed in response to different disputing functions. . . .

The crucial point here is that different constituencies have pursued settlement or ADR for vastly different reason—cheaper and faster is not necessarily the same thing as better. Those different reasons have led to very different institutionalized forms of ADR. Confusion about the purposes behind a particular form of innovation had led to important policy decisions and legal rulings which have given expression to different values underlying particular forms of ADR.

Partly because of the institutionalization of ADR, some of its earliest proponents, including anthropologist Laura Nader, now oppose ADR because it does not foster communitarian and self-determination goals. Instead, it is used to restrict access to courts for some groups, just at the time when these less powerful groups have achieved some legal rights. Indeed, some critics have argued that ADR actually hurts those who are less powerful in our society—like women or racial and ethnic minorities—by leaving them unprotected by formal rules and procedures in situations where informality permits the expression of power and domination that is unmediated by legal restraints. In other criticisms, proceduralists have argued that various forms of ADR compromise our legal system by privatizing law making, shifting judicial roles, compromising important legal and political rights and principles, and failing to grant parties the benefits of hundreds of years of procedural protections afforded by our civil and criminal justice rules. . . .

As ADR proceeds in its various forms through the courts, advocates have raised issues about violations of the right to jury trial, due process, equal protection, and separation of powers. Most of these claims have failed, and it is clear that with certain protections like nonbinding results, rights to *de novo* hearings, and limited penalties, ADR can constitutionally be conducted in the courts. Thus, in the constitutional arena the key issue is how the particular ADR programs are structured. Nonbinding settlement devices have virtually all been sustained against constitutional challenges. Binding procedures, or those that tax too greatly the choice of process (such as cost or feeshifting penalties), are likely to be more problematic. Constitutional challenges are not likely to eliminate or abolish ADR in the courts, though they may have some role in shaping the particular forms that are used.

More interesting to consider and watch are the myriad of legal claims that will now be developed by adversarial advocates forced to seek peace and settlement. As the use of ADR in the courts increases, cases are beginning to filter up to the appellate courts challenging such things as discovery rights, failure to fully participate, or the use of ADR as a "second chance" on the merits. Other challenges involve rights of confrontation and cross-examination, adequate notice, judicial interference or bias, and lack of neutrality on the part of third party neutrals. Courts will soon have to grapple with the manipulative uses of ADR—scheduling a summary jury trial or arbitration just to hear the other side's case for preparation of rebuttal or simply to inject a little delay into the case.

As advocates have grabbed hold of ADR, they have transformed it into another arena of battle. The interesting question is what are the implications of this "capture" of ADR by the courts and its advocates? . . .

The use of settlement activity in the courts should be understood as the clash of two cultures. To the extent that settlement activity seeks to promote consensual agreement through the analysis of the point of view of the other side, it requires some different skills and a very different mind-set from what litigators usually employ. Thus, the issue is whether judges and lawyers in the courts can learn to reorient their cultures and behaviors when trying to settle cases or whether those seeking settlement continue to do so from an adversarial perspective. To the extent that we cannot identify different behaviors in each sphere, we may see the corruption of both processes. If one of the purposes of the legal system is to specify legal entitlements from which settlements may be measured, or from which the parties may depart if they so choose, then having adjudicators engage in too much mediative conduct may compromise the ability of judges to engage in both fact-finding and rulemaking. If courts fail to provide sufficient baselines in their judgments, we will have difficulties determining if particular settlements are wise or truly consensual. There is danger in the possibility that good settlement practice will be marred by overzealous advocacy or by overzealous desire to close cases that may require either full adjudication or a public hearing. . . .

1. To what extent will courts lose their legitimacy as courts if too many other forms of case-processing are performed within their walls? If the "other" processes are not considered legitimate within public institutions, they will be legally challenged and transformed so that they will no longer be "alternatives," but only watered-down versions of court adjudication. These watered-down versions may be violative of the legal rights and rules our courts are intended to safeguard. Are theorists, practitioners, and citizens capable of changing our views of what courts should do?

2. Should some case types be excluded from alternative treatment?

3. What are the purposes for using particular forms of alternative dispute resolution? Caseload management and docket reduction may suggest entirely different processes than a search for a better quality solution which might be quite costly and time-consuming. If the goals and purposes of particular ADR institutions are clarified now, future problems based on overly abstract goals may be avoided.

4. What forms of ADR should be institutionalized? Not all ADR devices are the same. There is a tendency in the literature and in the rhetoric to homogenize widely different approaches to dispute resolution. A more thorough and careful consideration of each of the devices might lead to different conclusions about the utility and legitimacy of these devices.

Mandatory settlement conferences, for example, may become quite acceptable if the judicial officer attending the conference will not also be ruling on the evidence at trial. Similarly, we might feel differently about summary trials if they were as accessible to the public as any other activity conducted in open court and if jurors were told about what they were doing. These distinctions implicate all of the legal policy issues in drafting the rules of procedure. How much regulation of each process should there be? How clear should the rules be before parties can elect different processes or before they can be "ordered" to attend? How should Rules 16, 39, 68, and 83 of the Federal Rules of Civil Procedure be read or amended to reflect the changes in settlement policy? What values should these rules serve? By what standards should practices under these rules be evaluated?

5. What are the politics of ADR? Does ADR serve the interests of particular groups? This is not an easy question to answer. Many have argued that "minor" disputes have been siphoned out of the public legal system, while "major" disputes have continued to receive the benefits of the traditional court system. Large corporations are also removing their cases from the court system. Through their increased use of private ADR, the economics of dispute resolution are more subtle. Some may be "forced" out while others choose to opt out. What will this mean for payment and subsidies of dispute resolution? Will "free market" forces decide the fate of ADR? Who will control decision-making about ADR— judges, lawyers, clients, or legislators? If those with the largest stake in the system exit, who will supply the impetus and resources for court and rule reform? At the level of institutional decision-making, are these issues for individual judges, for the Congress, or for the United States Supreme Court to decide?

6. What are the cultural forces producing these legal changes at these particular times? Has the larger culture around us changed since particular legal innovations were adopted? If attempts to incorporate party participation in disputing were made in the "participatory" 1960s and 1970s, then does the 1980s era of privatization of public services dictate other considerations in the use of ADR? How has the rhetoric of quality justice been transformed into a rhetoric of quantity and case processing?

7. How are different forms of ADR actually functioning? This is the evaluation question. We need to know more about how these processes actually work in terms of processes used and outcome achieved, as well as the more common measures of party satisfaction.

Comments and Questions

1. To what extent do mediation, arbitration, summary jury trials, and other alternative dispute processes help to realize the enforcement of law,

the right to be heard, client autonomy and control, client participation, peacemaking, and efficiency? In which respects are they likely to do better—and worse—than conventional adjudication?

2. How do the alternatives meet public or community needs?

3. Would becoming a mediator help you resolve some of your concerns about becoming a lawyer? Since there seems to be a relatively small market for mediators (compared to the demand for lawyers), as a lawyer you might wish to consider how the skills of a mediator can be used in the daily practice of law.

4. To what extent does and should your own personality influence what you will advise your clients about ADR options?

5. The Civil Justice Reform Act of 1990, which was a portion of the Judicial Improvements Act of 1990, combined authority for judicial case management with a mandate to include alternative dispute mechanisms within federal courts. Citing problems with discovery, motions practice, and general costs and barriers to prompt results in the courts, the Act called for each district court to develop a plan to reduce civil justice expense and delay while also calling for further study and evaluation of the experiments launched under the Act.

Practice Exercise No. 25: Alternative Dispute Resolution Under Local Rule

Here is a local rule for the United States District Court for the District of Massachusetts on Alternative Dispute Resolution, and a letter that one judge in the district requires lawyers to mail to their clients. These apparently were responses to requirements under the Civil Justice Reform Act of 1990. Assume that an identical local rule is in effect for the *City of Cleveland* case. Your clients have received a form letter identical to the one that follows, and you have told them that you will discuss the letter with them. (If your last name begins with letter A through J, you represent the City; and if your last name begins with letter K through Z, you represent the plaintiffs.) In class, you will engage in a strategy session discussing what you should recommend to your client about ADR and the letter's options in their case. Your instructor is an older lawyer in your office. Most people use the terms "mediation" and "conciliation" interchangeably. This technique employs a third party to help the litigants reach a resolution of the dispute on their own agreed-upon terms. In arbitration, a third party (or group of people) hear evidence, usually at a formal hearing, and give a formal decision, in much the same way a judge would. The litigants can agree, or a previous contract can compel, that the arbitration decision be binding, enforceable, and have a claim-preclusion effect. Many, if not most, arbitrators would say that they are applying the applicable law to the facts that they believe to be true after hearing and weighing the evidence.

The descriptions of mini-trial, summary jury trial, and early neutral evaluation that are in the Local Rule and judge's letter are rather straightforward.

District of Massachusetts Local Rule 16.4
Alternative Dispute Resolution

(1) The judicial officer shall encourage the resolution of disputes by settlement or other alternative dispute resolution programs.

(2) *Settlement.* At every conference conducted under these rules, the judicial officer shall inquire as to the utility of the parties' conducting settlement negotiations, explore means of facilitating those negotiations, and offer whatever assistance may be appropriate in the circumstances. Assistance may include a reference of the case to another judicial officer for settlement purposes. Whenever a settlement conference is held, a representative of each party who has settlement authority shall attend or be available by telephone.

(3) *Other Alternative Dispute Resolution Programs.*

(A) Discretion of Judicial Officer. The judicial officer, following an exploration of the matter with all counsel, may refer appropriate cases to alternative dispute resolution programs that have been designated for use in the district court or that the judicial officer may make available. The dispute resolution programs described in subdivisions (2) through (4) are illustrative, not exclusive.

(B) Mini-trial.

(i) The judicial officer may convene a mini-trial upon the agreement of all parties, either by written motion or their oral motion in open court entered upon the record.

(ii) Each party, with or without the assistance of counsel, shall present his or her position before:

(a) selected representatives for each party, or

(b) an impartial third party, or

(c) both selected representatives for each party and an impartial third party.

(iii) An impartial third party may issue an advisory opinion regarding the merits of the case.

(iv) Unless the parties agree otherwise, the advisory opinion of the impartial third party is not binding.

(v) The impartial third party's advisory opinion is not appealable.

(vi) Neither the advisory opinion of an impartial third party nor the presentations of the parties shall be admissible as evidence in any subsequent proceeding, unless otherwise admissible under the rules of evidence. Also, the occurrence of the mini-trial shall not be admissible.

(D) Summary jury trial.

(i) The judicial officer may convene a summary jury trial:

(a) with the agreement of all parties, either by written motion or their oral motion in court entered upon the record, or

(b) upon the judicial officer's determination that a summary jury trial would be appropriate, even in the absence of the agreement of all the parties.

(ii) There shall be six (6) jurors on the panel, unless the parties agree otherwise.

(iii) The panel may issue an advisory opinion regarding:

(a) the respective liability of the parties, or

(b) the damages of the parties, or

(c) both the respective liability and the damages of the parties. Unless the parties agree otherwise, the advisory opinion is not binding and it shall not be appealable.

(iv) Neither the panel's advisory opinion nor its verdict, nor the presentations of the parties shall be admissible as evidence in any subsequent proceeding, unless otherwise admissible under the rules of evidence. Also, the occurrence of the summary jury trial shall not be admissible.

(E) Mediation.

(i) The judicial officer may grant mediation upon the agreement of all parties.

(ii) The mediator selected may be an individual, group of individuals or institution. The mediator shall be compensated as agreed by the parties.

(iii) The mediator shall meet, either jointly or separately, with each party and counsel for each party and shall take any steps that may appear appropriate in order to assist the parties to resolve the impasse or controversy.

(iv) If mediation does not result in a resolution of the dispute, the parties shall promptly report the termination of mediation to the judicial officer.

(v) If an agreement is reached between the parties on any issues, the mediator shall make appropriate note of that agreement and shall refer the parties to the judicial officer for entry of a court order.

(vi) Any communication related to the subject matter of the dispute made during the mediation by any participant, mediator, or any other person present at the mediation shall be a confidential communication to the full extent contemplated by Fed. R. Evid. 408. No admission, representation, statement, or other confidential communication made in setting up or conducting the proceedings not otherwise discoverable or obtainable shall be admissible as evidence or subject to discovery.

UNITED STATES DISTRICT COURT
DISTRICT OF MASSACHUSETTS
BOSTON, 02109

William G. Young
District Judge

Date: _____

Dear Litigant:

Your case has been assigned to this session of the United States District Court for all pretrial proceedings and trial. I assure you that our goal is to give your case a fair, impartial, and just trial as soon as possible. To that end, I have today met with the attorneys and placed your case on the running trial list in this session as of _____.

As you may appreciate, full-scale trials are expensive, and the time spent awaiting trial is frequently lengthy. Therefore, I want you to be aware of various other programs we offer that may possibly resolve your case to your satisfaction with less expense and delay. Each of these programs is voluntary, and all parties to the lawsuit must agree before implementing any such program in your case. I list these programs in the order that they most resemble a trial in this Court.

1. *Trial before a Magistrate Judge*: You may agree to try your case, with or without a jury, before a United States Magistrate Judge. A Magistrate Judge is a judicial officer appointed by the judges of this Court for this purpose. The trial takes place in this courthouse and, if a jury has been claimed, before a federal jury. The advantage of this program is its speed—cases can usually be reached for trial before a Magistrate Judge within a few months. Moreover, the parties can usually agree with the Magistrate Judge upon a specific day to begin the trial. There is no charge for this service.

2. *Trial before a retired Superior Court Justice*: You may agree to try your case to a federal jury before a distinguished retired justice of the Massachusetts Superior Court. The Superior Court is "the great trial court of the Commonwealth," and its justices are experts on jury trials and issues of Massachusetts law. The advantages are the same as for trials before Magistrate Judges—a speedy hearing and definite trial date. The cost of this program to you will be $250 per trial day plus sharing the per trial day cost of a court reporter. The trial will take place in this courthouse before a federal jury.

3. *Arbitration*: You may agree to resolve your case by submitting it to a skilled neutral arbitrator or group of arbitrators. You will have a chance to participate in the choice of arbitrators. Advantages of this program are that prompt arbitration hearings may be scheduled and the arbitrators may be technically skilled in the issues raised in this lawsuit. You and the

other parties will share the costs of the arbitrators and the administration of the arbitration program.

4. *Summary jury trial*: You may agree to a summary jury trial. This is an advisory one-day proceeding before a federal jury. Each party will have the chance to make a brief presentation of its position, and, properly charged as to the law, the jury will render a nonbinding advisory verdict. I will meet with the attorneys that same day to discuss whether a settlement of the case is possible and proper. It may be helpful to you and the other parties to obtain the views of the summary jury in order to better evaluate your position. There is no cost for this program.

5. *Mediation*: You may agree to voluntary mediation. If you agree, I will appoint a skilled, neutral, and experienced mediator promptly to explore with all parties and their attorneys whether a settlement of this case may be reached that will satisfy your basic concerns. Unlike the previous options, mediation never imposes a result on the parties. Rather, it seeks to reach agreement. Prompt mediation may minimize your overall litigation costs.

6. *Early neutral evaluation*: You may agree to have your case evaluated by a neutral attorney skilled in the issues raised in this case. This may assist you in evaluating your position and may aid you in deciding whether to settle, press on to trial, or avail yourself of one or more of these other options.

Your attorney is familiar with each of these options and can advise you in detail concerning what advantages they may offer you. If the parties can agree, you may pursue variations on these options with the support of this Court.

Should you wish further information on any of these points or should all parties agree to pursue any one or a variant of any of them, your attorney should feel free to consult with Courtroom Deputy Clerk Kate Myrick, Esq., or Docket Clerk Elizabeth Smith.

D. CREATIVE JUDICIAL ALTERNATIVES: MANAGERIAL JUDGING AND COURT-SPONSORED DISPUTE RESOLUTION

Echoing concerns first expressed by Dean Roscoe Pound in 1909, Simon Rifkind observed in 1979 that "there is a growing—and justified— apprehension that (1) Quantitatively, the courts are carrying too heavy a burden—and probably a burden beyond the capability of mitigation by merely increasing the number of judges; and (2) Qualitatively, the courts are being asked to solve problems for which they are not institutionally equipped, or not as well equipped as are other available agencies." Simon H. Rifkind, *Are We Asking Too Much of Our Courts?* in *The Pound Conference: Perspectives on Justice in the Future* (West 1979).

To deal with complex court cases and heavy dockets, many judges have experimented with managerial techniques such as using their role as judge to promote settlement, directing cases to mediation or other alternative dispute resolution methods, and employing court-appointed assistants to create claims-processing mechanisms. One prominent lawyer, who has served as a court-appointed master establishing claims-processing mechanisms in several contexts, explains, "This is not really Alternative Dispute Resolution. What I do is not really ADR. It is CJM—creative judicial management of a very serious problem that inundates the courts." Kenneth R. Feinberg, *Response to Deborah Hensler, A Glass Half Full, a Glass Half Empty: The Use of Alternative Dispute Resolution in Mass Personal Injury Litigation*, 73 Tex. L. Rev. 1647, (1995).

Consider the arguments offered in two relatively early articles on case management, one by an enthusiast (Judge William W. Schwarzer), and one by a critic (Professor Judith Resnik, who coined the term "managerial judging" in a longer influential article entitled *Managerial Judges*, 97 Harv. L. Rev. 374 (1982)). How would their arguments apply to judicial supervision of mechanisms to collect massive numbers of individual claims for purposes of mass settlement? The third section, by Professor Martha Minow, describes and largely defends Judge Jack Weinstein's supervision of a settlement of mass tort claims in the Agent Orange litigation.

The section then offers excerpts from a recent judicial opinion issued as part of a managerial approach to a body of numerous claims, and a related practice exercise. You will want to reread Fed. R. Civ. P. 16 as you proceed through this section.

■ WILLIAM W. SCHWARZER,
MANAGING CIVIL LITIGATION:
THE TRIAL JUDGE'S ROLE
61 Judicature 400 (1978)

My concern here is less with the judge's role at trial than before trial. Most civil cases are terminated before trial: in the federal system, less than 10 percent of the cases filed go to trial. Most judicial and private effort is expended on litigation that never reaches trial, through discovery, motions and other formal and informal interlocutory proceedings. It is a frequent complaint that costs incurred even before trial make litigation uneconomical. In addition, what is done in proceedings before trial tends to determine the scope and dimensions of the trial itself. The role of the judge in the pretrial stage of litigation is therefore of sufficient importance to warrant consideration.

Because of the great impact of pretrial activity and proceedings on the magnitude of the burden imposed by litigation on the courts and parties, and because there is room for improvement in the disposition of litigation, whether or not it is eventually tried, I urge that judges intervene in civil litigation and take an appropriately active part in its management from the beginning. If that role is discharged in a fair, informed and sensitive manner, it should aid greatly in achieving these objectives:

1. Define the issues to be litigated and limit pretrial activity to relevant matters;
2. Control pretrial discovery and other activity to avoid unnecessary expense and burden;
3. Arrive at a settlement of the controversy as early as possible or attempt to discover methods for resolving it as expeditiously and economically as possible; and
4. Insure that any trial will be well prepared and limited strictly to matters that cannot be otherwise disposed of.

JUDICIAL MANAGEMENT POWER

No reform of the judicial system is needed to enable the trial judge to perform these kinds of litigation management functions on his own motion, as many judges already do. In the federal system, the Federal Rules of Civil Procedure, particularly Rule 16, give the judge sufficient authority and discretion to intervene sua sponte in pretrial proceedings. Moreover, the U.S. Supreme Court has recognized "the power inherent in every court to control the disposition of the causes on its docket with economy of time and effort for itself, for counsel and for litigants.

Neither the court's inherent management power nor its power under Rule 16 is unlimited. Parties cannot be compelled to litigate the case according to the court's discretion. They can, however, be compelled to comply with pretrial procedures reasonably necessary to implement Rule 1 of the Federal Rules of Civil Procedure to assure the "just, speedy and inexpensive determination of every action." While the courts appear not to be wholly in agreement on where to draw the line, judges clearly have the power to require that cases be fully and adequately prepared before they go to trial and that pretrial activity be conducted economically and efficiently.

Although adequate power exists for judicial intervention, the concept of judicial intervention runs counter to accepted notions. The first of these . . . is the traditional conception of the judge's role in the adversary process: that the judge is supposed to be passive and let lawyers litigate without interference except when one side or the other calls upon him. As Justice David W. Peck has put it, lawyers and judges "are apt to think of themselves as representing opposite poles and exercising divergent functions. The lawyer partisan, the judge reflective."

Judge Frankel, in his recent Cardozo lecture, "The Search for Truth — An Umpireal View," argued that

> Our system does not allow much room for effective or just intervention by
> the trial judge in the adversary fight about the facts. The judge views the
> case from a peak of Olympian ignorance. His intrusion will in too many
> cases result from partial or skewed insights. . . .

Marvin Frankel, *The Search for Truth—An Umpireal View*, 123 U. Pa. L. Rev.
1031, 1042 (1975). Later in the lecture, he stressed that

> the ignorance and unpreparedness of the judge are intended axioms of the
> system. . . . The judge is not to have investigated or explored the evidence
> before trial . . . without an investigative file, the American trial judge is a
> blind and blundering intruder, acting in spasms as sudden flashes of seem-
> ing light may lead or mislead him at odd times.

Id. Though each of these observers was discussing the judge's role at trial,
rather than before trial, they reflect an attitude to which pretrial intervention would be foreign. It somehow equates ignorance with impartiality,
and it fails to take into account the extent to which even the passive judge
must in the normal course intervene in the fight about the facts and make
rulings regardless of any ignorance or lack of preparation. In every interlocutory dispute about discovery, amendments, joinder, class action determination and pretrial relief, the judge must make decisions which (1) are
made without the benefit of a full and complete record, and (2) have a
direct impact on the fight about facts by aiding one party and hampering
the other. Similarly, rulings at the trial on the admissibility of evidence and
the scope of examination must be based on the judge's current appraisal
of the facts of the case and his judgment concerning the course the trial
should follow.

THE NEED FOR INTERVENTION

The judge is, of course, not to become a third party in a general
search for the truth. But ignorance and lack of preparation do not
insulate him from having direct control over how counsel conduct the litigation, whether he acts sua sponte or only when called upon by the
parties. His rulings through the litigation, even procedural ones, implicate
the merits and affect the outcome, yet must be made on the strength of
whatever knowledge of the case the judge is able to acquire along the way.
In any case, therefore, the cause of justice would seem to be better served
by an informed and prepared judge capable of making sound rulings than
by Judge Frankel's model of "the ignorant and unprepared judge [who]
is, ideally, the properly bland figurehead in the adversary scheme of
things." . . .

The reform of pretrial discovery under the Federal Rules of Civil Procedure, it is true, was intended to minimize judicial intervention. But, that
philosophy, though still widely held, is giving way to a growing recognition

that it imposes unacceptable costs. For complex litigation, for example, courts have adopted procedures under the Manual for Complex Litigation premised on active judicial management of the litigation from the outset. The time has come to consider a similar approach for civil litigation generally.

The present crisis might well be relieved by revised or new rules of procedure in such areas as discovery and class actions. But the utility of rules is directly proportional to the wisdom and firmness with which they are administered. Because each case is unique in its facts, personalities and needs, general rules do not obviate the need for individualized judicial management.

No Threat to Fairness

It may be argued that intervention sua sponte jeopardizes the judge's appearance of impartiality. Inasmuch as action resulting from intervention may be interpreted as favoring one party at the expense of the other, the fact that the action was taken on the initiative of the judge, not in response to one party's application, may give rise to suspicions of bias. The argument lacks force, however, where the judge acts in a reasoned and fair manner after having heard the parties and having considered their views.

Moreover, justice is not better served by the passive judge who by inaction permits litigation to blunder along its costly way toward exhaustion of the litigants, when it might have long been settled or at least controlled to everyone's benefit. One may fairly ask whether the parties left to themselves can always be depended on to prosecute litigation diligently, economically and in good faith; to avoid wars of attrition and harassment, obstruction and delay; and to exclude extraneous personal considerations from the conduct of the litigation. . . .

Judges must appear, as well as be, fair in their conduct, but they ought not to be hobbled by the fear that entirely proper actions might arouse suspicion. . . .

The Efficiency Issue

Finally, judicial intervention is met by contradictory arguments from opposing camps. First, some criticize preoccupation with efficiency, placing quantity above quality in dispensing justice. Implying judges are becoming subservient to computers and productivity statistics, they argue "slow justice is always preferable to speedy injustice."

That argument, however, does not undercut the case for judicial management of litigation when the purpose is to achieve the optimum allocation of resources, judicial and private. If by judicial intervention, discovery burdens are lightened, the interests of justice are served for litigants directly involved and for others whose cases are pending.

Then there are those who argue that judicial intervention is an inefficient use of the judge's limited time, and that judges should "minimize . . . [their] investment of time through the early stages of a case." Statistics have been offered to prove that pretrial conferences resulted in a net loss of judicial time, but many judges disagree. An hour or less spent reviewing the case file and meeting with lawyers may often produce substantial time savings by, for example, obviating future discovery disputes and motions, disclosing areas of factual or legal agreement, eliminating issues from trial, bringing about an earlier settlement, or reducing the time required for trial.

As we will discuss later, the controversy is likely to assume more modest dimensions and more manageable shape after the judge, with his knowledge and experience, has discussed the case with the parties and directs them to talk to each other. And as cases are brought to a more rapid conclusion than under the traditional "laissez-faire" system, the quality of justice improves because judges will have more time to devote to the cases remaining on their docket. It seems, therefore, that the busier the judge and the heavier his case load, the more urgent the need for intervention early in civil cases, especially when calendars are burdened with criminal cases entitled to priority. . . .

The time has come to discard the stereotype of "the ignorant and unprepared judge [as] the properly bland figurehead in the adversary scheme of things," the fear that the interests of justice will be compromised by judicial intervention, and the assumption that judges are too busy to use their time wisely. It is time to clear the way for active judicial participation in the management of civil litigation.

THE PROCESS OF INTERVENTION

The purpose of judicial intervention is to promote the "just, speedy, and inexpensive determination to every action." It contemplates that the judge, having familiarized himself with the file and the controlling law and discussed the case informally with counsel, will then supply the appropriate degree of guidance based on his judgment and experience.

Probably the most effective setting is an informal conference in chambers with both counsel and, where appropriate, the clients. The formality of the courtroom, with its trappings of adversary confrontation, hardly promotes the reasoned dialogue, flexibility and accommodation to which the judge's intervention should lead.

Discovery disputes, for example, generally are more readily and constructively resolved by in-chambers discussion moderated by the judge than by formal motion. Similarly, a determination of whether or not a particular issue is in dispute and requires trial may be better made in chambers. Settlement conferences certainly belong in chambers, not in the courtroom. And settlement negotiations are often the next logical step after informal discussion has revealed that the differences between the parties are not as great as conventional litigation posturing had indicated.

As early in the litigation as possible, the judge should urge counsel to define the factual and legal issues, to develop an appropriate discovery program, and to lay out a schedule for motions, pretrial and trial. Working with the judge on these matters, counsel are likely to be more reasonable than if left to themselves. The mere expectation of intervention—the knowledge that the judge is watching or at least available to intervene—is likely to moderate the litigation tactics of the parties, minimizing the need for actual intervention.

Defining and specifying issues at an early conference between court and counsel is of great importance. Rule 8 of the Federal Rules of Civil Procedure requires that the complaint contain "a short and plain statement of the claim showing that the pleader is entitled to relief." Pleadings rarely meet that test. A conference will help disclose just what claim plaintiff asserts to obtain relief and what is in issue. This will narrow the scope of the controversy and focus discovery on essentials. It may reveal areas of agreement and issues that can be disposed of by motion in advance of trial; the judge may call for the filing of motions which appear to him to have possible merit and which a party may have overlooked. It may also indicate that motions contemplated by a party would be futile, thus saving time and expense for everyone.

THE STATUS CONFERENCE

The use of the compulsory status conference to control discovery is one of the principal elements of judicial intervention. It is a way to lay down discovery guidelines, based on discussion of the issues, and is tailored to the needs of the particular case. Such guidelines reduce subsequent discovery disputes and piecemeal motions to compel or for protective orders, and tend to nip in the bud any notion by a party to wage an attrition campaign using discovery as a weapon.

This procedure also enables the judge to suggest to the parties the use of appropriate discovery techniques, thereby avoiding the frustrations and disputes which often arise when parties use the wrong techniques, such as trying to obtain answers to argumentative interrogatories or to compel production of nonexistent documents. Finally, it is an opportunity to arrange for informal exchange of needed information, eliminating some of the expense and delay of formal discovery. Prompt informal exchange of critical items of information may often lead to an early settlement before much litigation expense has been incurred.

Conferences should be held from time to time during the litigation, depending upon the degree of management a particular case requires. . . .

Settlement should be an item on the agenda for each conference. If intervention accomplishes nothing else, it should at least compel communication between opposing counsel and remove the psychological and tactical roadblocks that frequently stand in the way of meaningful negotiations. Inasmuch as over 90 percent of the cases are eventually settled, it benefits everyone if the case settles sooner rather than later. The practice of settling on the courthouse steps results in unnecessary expense in preparing for trial and to cluttered dockets which burden the court and all litigants. . . .

THE JUDGE'S APPROACH

By participating in a settlement conference, the judge must not, and need not, create doubts in the minds of parties about their ability to obtain a fair trial. He may well determine that a settlement conference should be held before another judge who will not try the case or, if he himself has participated in discussions, that another judge should try the case. But a judge need not jeopardize the appearance of impartiality if he simply suggests to the parties how an objective observer might react to some of the evidence and contentions of the parties.

Judicial intervention to promote the settlement of cases should be an exercise in tact and understanding, not coercion. The judge who can listen with a third ear may well receive subliminal messages pointing the way to settlement. And having won the confidence and respect of the parties, a sympathetic and knowledgeable judge will be in a better position to discuss the strengths and weaknesses of the case with each side, perhaps separately, to persuade them of the benefits of settlement and to suggest means to narrow differences. Once the conference procedure has become known to the bar, moreover, counsel, aware of what is expected, will tend to begin negotiations on their own sooner and more seriously.

The passive judge who, conforming to the traditional role model, passes up the opportunity to serve as a catalyst for settlement, will probably try many cases that could have been settled and, in doing so, will render no particular benefit to the administration of justice.

If the case must go to trial, judicial intervention can help assure that it has been thoroughly prepared. Merely holding a pretrial conference, however, accomplishes little. The benefits of pretrial are directly proportional to the amount of effort invested by court and counsel.

At the pretrial conference, the judge, having prepared himself by review of the file, should require each side to specify the disputed legal and factual issues, to identify the proposed witnesses in the order they will appear, to summarize each witness's testimony, and to identify and exchange each proposed exhibit and state its foundation. This process will produce many, sometimes surprising benefits:

1. It will expose the unprepared lawyer and prevent the wasteful charades that pass for trials when lawyers are unprepared;

2. It will enable the judge to spot undisputed issues (which can be disposed of by stipulation) and redundant or unnecessary evidence;
3. It will disclose evidence problems which can be resolved in advance, rather than in time-consuming and disruptive side-bar conferences at trial;
4. It will permit resolution of foundation and authenticity issues concerning exhibits, further saving trial time; and
5. It may indicate the possibility of deciding some issues on motion.

Intervention at this point means that no case goes to trial until the shape and content of the trial have been thoroughly discussed by court and counsel. Experience has shown that the trial time saved as a result of thorough pretrial far exceeds the time required for pretrial. Pretrial should, however, be tailored to the needs of the particular case to spare the parties the expense and burden of complying with boilerplate pretrial orders that impose requirements disproportionate to the case.

Finally, the education the judge receives in the process will enable him to try the case in more informed and effective fashion, perhaps even reducing risk of reversible error.

A WORTHWHILE TASK

Trial judge intervention to manage civil litigation offers the most direct and immediate relief for the litigation crisis, a crisis not confined to large and complex litigation. The party seeking to prosecute a $2000 claim may have proportionately the same problem as one faced with a large class claim. Judicial intervention will help ensure that controversies will be litigated in a manner appropriate to what is truly at issue, and as justly, speedily and inexpensively as possible. . . .

■ JUDITH RESNIK, MANAGERIAL JUDGES AND COURT DELAY: THE UNPROVEN ASSUMPTIONS
23 Judge's Journal 8 (1994)

In growing numbers, federal judges are adopting an increasingly managerial stance. Judges not only adjudicate the merits of issues presented to them by litigants but also meet with parties in chambers to encourage settlement of disputes and to supervise case preparation. As managers, judges learn about cases much earlier than they have in the past, and they negotiate with parties about the course, timing, and scope of pretrial activities.

When acting as pretrial managers, judges typically initiate contact with the parties to a lawsuit. In federal courts, under the new amendments to

Rule 16 of the Federal Rules of Civil Procedure, within 120 days of the filing of a complaint, judges are obliged to issue scheduling orders, detailing the timing for pretrial motions, amendment of pleadings, and discovery. Nearly all cases receive pretrial attention under Rule 16, and some judges have already adopted the supervisory stance contemplated by the recent amendments.

Managerial meetings are usually informal and contrast sharply with the highly stylized structure of the courtroom. Pretrial conferences often occur in chambers; the participants may sit around tables, and the judge may wear business dress. The informal judge-litigant contact provides judges with information beyond that traditionally within their ken. Conference topics are wide-ranging, the judges' concerns broad. The supposedly rigid structure of evidentiary rules, designed to insulate decision-makers from extraneous or impermissible information, is not relevant to case management. Managerial judges are not silent auditors of retrospective events told by witnesses; judges instead become part of the tales.

Pretrial supervision is also relatively private. . . . Many judges conduct pretrials in chambers; generally, neither court reporters nor the public attend. Finally, the decisions reached at pretrial conferences are rarely reviewable until after (and if) a final judgment on the merits is rendered.

Federal judges' new managerial role has emerged for several reasons. The creation in 1938 of pretrial discovery rights generated some disputes that parties brought to court; trial judges undertook the task of resolving discovery disputes and, in the process, became mediators and negotiators. Once involved in pretrial discovery, many judges became convinced that their presence at other points in lawsuits' development would be beneficial; supervision of discovery became a conduit for judicial control over all phases of litigation and thus infused lawsuits with the continual presence of the judge-overseer.

In part because of their new oversight role, and in part because of increasing caseloads, many judges became concerned about the volume of their work. To reduce the pressure, judges turned to efficiency experts, who suggested judicial management as an important technique of calendar control. Under the experts' guidance, judges have increasingly experimented with schemes for speeding the resolution of cases and for persuading litigants whenever possible to settle rather than try cases. During the past decade, enthusiasm for the managerial movement has become widespread. What began as an experiment has become obligatory in virtually all cases in federal courts and is increasingly common in state courts as well.

In the rush to conquer the mountain of work, few have considered whether reliance upon trial judges for informal dispute resolution and for case management is a positive step, and whether judicial management can accomplish the many goals set for it. Little empirical evidence exists to support the claim that judicial management works—either to settle cases or to provide cheaper, quicker, or fairer dispositions.

Proponents of judicial management have also failed to consider the systemic effects of the shift in the judicial role. Management is a new form of judicial activism, a behavior that usually attracts substantial criticism. Judicial management may be teaching judges to value their statistics, such as the number of case dispositions, more than they value the quality of those dispositions. Further, because managerial judging is less visible than traditional adjudication and is usually unreviewable until after final judgments have been rendered, managerial judging gives trial courts more authority and at the same time provides litigants with fewer procedural safeguards to protect them from abuse of that authority. In sum, judicial management merits our close attention and our study before we embrace it as the slogan for the courts of the 1980s.

QUESTIONABLE BENEFITS

Managerial judging's proponents believe that their system of management improves the use of judicial resources. They argue that, with judges in charge of the litigation system, court resources are better allocated, case dispositions speeded and delay reduced while the quality of judicial decision-making is unimpaired. No one can oppose efforts to curtail exploitation of the judicial system and make dispute resolution quick and inexpensive. I do, however, question the extent to which managerial judging contributes to these worthy aims and whether it is wise to rely upon judges to achieve these goals.

Proponents of managerial judging typically assume that management enhances efficiency in three respects. They claim that case management decreases delay, produces more dispositions, and reduces litigation costs. But close examination of the currently available information reveals little support for a firm conclusion that judicial management is responsible for efficiency gains in federal district courts.

Delay Reduction. The first step is assessing the question of delay reduction to decide whether there is a "problem" of delay in federal trial courts. This assessment is not simple to make. In appellate courts, we have shared perception in the amount of time it "should" take to prepare a brief, or the amount of time it "should" take to decide an appeal. In contrast, when we turn to trial courts, it is more difficult to determine the amount of time that "should" be spent to prepare a case for trial. The scope of issues and the number of actors vary greatly among cases as well as throughout the evolution of a single case. Case complexity at the trial level can reasonably require postponement of deadlines not merely by days or weeks (as in the appellate courts) but by months or years. As of yet, we do not have a substantive theory about the proper interval at which cases should proceed through the trial courts.

Moreover, in 1980, the median time for a case to move from filing to disposition in federal district court was only eight months. For cases that were tried, the interval was 20 months. I cannot with confidence assert that such data reveals "delay" in the federal courts. Illustrative of the difficulty in deciding that question is a change in nomenclature. Many researchers who have studied "delay" now address the question of "pace." Such researchers are unable to agree on how to explain why some courts process cases more quickly than others.

But if we were to assume that the pace of some civil litigation had been unduly delayed, we would still encounter problems in assessing the claim that judicial management speeds case processing. Even when we find that some courts with managerial judges have faster disposition rates than some other courts without managerial judges, we have great difficulty identifying the causes for the differences. Cases are filed, withdrawn, settled, or dismissed for a variety of reasons, including changes in legislation, new appellate decisions, shifts in business practices, and fluctuations in the availability of attorneys. Although it is theoretically possible to control for such variables, researchers are hampered by the absence of firsthand, unfiltered information about why cases conclude when they do. . . . Management advocates rely instead on anecdote and intuition to support their claims.

Increasing the Number of Dispositions. In addition to not knowing what impact judicial management has on delay, we also do not know what impact judicial management has on settlement rates. While proponents often claim increased settlement rates as a result of judicial management, most researchers have concluded that intensive judicial settlement efforts do not lead to more dispositions than would have otherwise occurred.

The claim of "the more dispositions the better" raises difficult valuation tasks; decision making must be assessed qualitatively as well as quantitatively. On any given day, are four judges, who speak with parties to 16 lawsuits and report that 12 of those cases ended without trial, more "productive" than four judges who preside at four trials? Is it relevant to an assessment of "productivity" that three of those four trials are settled after ten days of testimony. Or that, in the one case tried to conclusion, the judge writes a 40-page opinion on a novel point of law that is subsequently affirmed by the Supreme Court and thereafter affects thousands of litigants? Measuring judicial accomplishments is complex. Scales designed to measure achievement in other institutions cannot simply be imported into the courtroom.

Reducing Costs. Management advocates assume that judicial supervision not only saves time and produces more dispositions but also limits the ability of litigants to impose unfair financial pressure on their opponents and limits the ability of attorneys to justify excessive billing. Proponents therefore conclude that managerial judges reduce courts' and litigants' costs. But no data exist to support this conclusion. And, if we rely instead on intuition, it is not obvious that judicial supervision averts costly adversarial decisions or attorney misconduct. First, some lawyers use every occasion for contact with judges to argue their clients' cases. Thus, supervision itself can present further opportunities for vigorous adversarial encounters and for more billable hours. Second, the line between attorney misconduct and aggressive but ethical representation is often difficult to discern. Third, even with judicial oversight, lawyers may be able to hide their misconduct; procedural innovations may simply force attorneys to develop new techniques of obfuscation and avoidance.

Moreover, judicial management itself imposes costs. Judges' time is one of the most expensive resources in the courthouse. Rather than concentrate all of their energies on deciding motions, charging juries, and drafting opinions, managerial judges must meet with parties, develop litigation plans, and compel obedience to their new management rules. Managerial judges have more data sheets to complete, more conferences to attend, and ever more elaborate local procedural rules to draft and debate. Even when some of these tasks are delegated to staff, administrative structures must be put into place and then supervised. Although litigants and judges can contain some costs by relying on conference calls, and written exchanges, they still must spend substantial amounts of time and money. Further, because many cases settle without judicial intervention, management may require judges to supervise lawsuits that would not have consumed any judicial resources.

We are not yet able to reach any firm conclusions on whether and how management reduces costs. Until we have data on the number of judge-hours that management consumes and on its costs to the parties, we cannot calculate the net costs of managerial judging and thereby learn whether we have conserved resources. And, if we include in our equation the additional costs discussed below—of the possible increase in erroneous decisions and the loss of public participation—our calculation becomes even more complex.

In sum, I am skeptical of claims that judicial management increases court productivity at reduced costs. Data are not available to support most of these conclusions, and intuition does not compel them. Moreover, managerial proponents have rarely addressed or included in their assessments the effects of judicial management on the nature of adjudication.

Possible Risks

Transforming the judge from adjudicator to manager substantially expands the opportunities for judges to use—or to abuse—their powers. When deciding how much time to allow parties to prepare their cases, when running settlement conferences, when insisting, as some judges do, on ex parte meetings with each side, the trial judge sits unsupervised, virtually beyond review. Judges can create rules for the pretrial phase of lawsuits that parties have no way of challenging; with the individual calendar system in the federal courts, parties must be careful not to offend the one judge who is assigned a case at filing and presides over it until its disposition.

In addition to enhancing the power of judges, management tends to undermine traditional constraints on the use of that power. Judges, when creating management rules, need not submit their ideas to the discipline of written justification or to outside scrutiny. Many decisions are made privately; some are off the record; virtually all are beyond appellate review.

Furthermore, no explicit norms or standards guide judges in their decisions about what to demand of litigants. What does "good," "skilled," or "judicious" management entail? Other than their own intuitions, judges have little to inform them. Few institutional constraints inhibit judges during the informal pretrial phase. During pretrial management, judges are restrained only by personal beliefs about the proper role of judge-managers. . . .

The Threat to Impartiality. A major technique of management is to rely on the private, informal meetings between judges and lawyers to discuss discovery schedules and to explore settlement proposals—meetings beyond the constraints of the formal courtroom setting. But substantial risks inhere in the informality. The extensive information that judges receive during pretrial conferences is not filtered by the rules of evidence. Some of the information is received ex parte, a process that deprives the opposing party of the opportunity to contest the validity of the information received. Moreover, judges are often in close contact with attorneys during the course of management. Such interactions may become occasions for the development of intense feelings about the case or the parties— feelings of admiration, kinship, or antipathy. Management may be a fertile field for the growth of personal bias.

Moreover, judges with supervisory obligations may gain stakes in the case they manage. Their prestige may ride on "efficient" management, as calculated by the speed and number of dispositions. Competition and peer pressure may tempt judges to rush litigants because of reasons unrelated to the merits of the disputes. Reported opinions, as well as attorneys' anecdotes, substantiate the fact that some judges have elevated efficiency and management goals over considerations of fairness.

Unreviewable power, casual contact, and interest in outcome (or in aggregate outcomes) have not traditionally been associated with the "due process" decision-making model. These features do not evoke images of reasoned adjudication, images that form the very basis of both our faith in the judicial process and our enormous grant of power to judges. . . .

Case processing is no longer viewed as a means to an end; instead, it appears to have become the desired goal. Quantity has become all important; quality is occasionally mentioned and then ignored. . . .

CONCLUSION

I argue for reflection before we plunge headlong into judicial management. I do not mean to suggest that adjudication must be frozen into earlier forms or that more efficient decision making is an unworthy aim. Rather, as we reorient the judicial system to accommodate contemporary demands, I believe that we should preserve the core of adjudication.

To help judges remain impartial, we should design rules to limit the flow of untested information to them. To ensure that judges have the patience for deliberation, we should refrain from giving them too many distracting new responsibilities. To hold judges accountable for the quality—not merely the quantity—of their actions, we should require them to act in public and to state reasons for their decisions. In sum we should not simply embrace the new management ethic; we must think carefully about what role judges should take and then craft rules to enable judges to act accordingly.

The following excerpts from *In re Food Lion, Inc.* provide an example of an opinion revealing both the complexity of managerial challenges presented by contemporary litigation and the powers afforded to district court judges to ensure litigant compliance with judicial efforts to manage cases.

■ IN RE FOOD LION, INC.
151 F.3d 1029 (Unpubl.) (4th Cir. June 4, 1998)

PER CURIAM:
In this case we consider appeals from the district court's grant of partial summary judgment in favor of an employer and dismissal of the consolidated Fair Labor Standards Act overtime pay claims of numerous of the employer's salaried and hourly wage employees. For the reasons stated herein, we affirm the district court.

I

Beginning in 1991, several small groups of employees and former employees of Food Lion, Inc. ("Food Lion"), filed civil actions in Federal courts in a number of southern States in which Food Lion owns and operates grocery stores. In each of these actions, the plaintiffs asserted claims for unpaid overtime and penalties under the Fair Labor Standards Act ("FLSA"), 29 U. S. C. §201 et seq. Hourly employees alleged that they were forced to work "off the clock" in order to finish the tasks for which they were responsible under Food Lion's company-wide scheduling system, and several assistant managers claimed that they were not exempt from FLSA's overtime provisions because the tasks they performed did not qualify as "managerial."

On June 13, 1992, the Judicial Panel on Multidistrict Litigation ("JPML" or "Panel") issued an order transferring two of these actions, one from the District of South Carolina (Scott) and the other from the Western District of North Carolina (Ledford), to the Eastern District of North Carolina for "coordinated or consolidated pretrial proceedings" with another action then pending there (McLawhon); all of the cases assigned to Judge Fox. The Panel thereafter transferred six tag-along cases over the next five months. Judge Fox eventually had eleven separate actions before him.

In October 1992, court-approved notices were sent to some 60,000 current and former Food Lion employees who had worked in stores in North Carolina, South Carolina, Florida, Georgia, Virginia, or Tennessee after October 16, 1989. Almost one thousand of these employees (including the named plaintiffs in the eleven separate actions) opted into the litigation by returning "consent forms," and each employee returning a consent form was assigned a "court number." A master file was created in a consolidated case denominated In re: Food Lion, Inc., Fair Labor Standards Act "Effective Scheduling" Litigation, and each "opt-in" plaintiff was assigned to one of the individual cases.

In a series of pretrial orders, Judge Fox dismissed the claims of about half of the plaintiffs on summary judgment. On March 22, 1994, a "suggestion of remand" was filed by the district court and forwarded to the Panel. On June 2, 1994, the Panel remanded eight of the actions to their respective transferor courts.

After remand, one of the two cases remaining in the Eastern District of North Carolina was completed, and an appeal was taken by a number of the plaintiffs whose claims had been dismissed by summary judgment during the consolidated pretrial proceedings (the Royster appeal). At about the same time, some of the plaintiffs who had met a similar fate in Judge Fox's court, but who were part of cases from one of the two other districts in North Carolina, asked for and received Fed. R. Civ. P. 54(b) certifications for immediate appeal from the respective transferor district courts. These two appeals were consolidated with the Royster appeal, and we heard oral argument on October 30, 1995. . . .

. . . [To give dismissed plaintiffs the chance to appeal,] we first heard in abeyance the then-pending appeals from the three North Carolina districts. Second, we directed the Panel to retransfer from the District of South Carolina, the Northern District of Florida, and the Eastern District of Tennessee to the Eastern District of North Carolina those claims that were dismissed by Judge Fox prior to the June 20, 1994 remand by the Panel. Finally, we ordered the district court for the Eastern District of North Carolina, after retransfer, to enter final judgment as to all such claims, pursuant to Fed. R. Civ. P. 54(b) and to allow any appeals taken pursuant to such certifications to be heard in this court. *Id.* at 533.

After our remand and the entry of final judgments by the Eastern District of North Carolina in March 1997, seventy-one plaintiffs from two cases originally filed in the District of South Carolina and eight plaintiffs from the case originally filed in the Northern District of Florida took appeals which were consolidated with the earlier Royster appellants by Order of this court on April 22, 1997. . . .

III. CASE MANAGEMENT DISMISSALS

The hourly employees of Food Lion appeal certain of the district court's case management decisions resulting in dismissals of their claims. In a class action, review of a district court's dismissals for case management reasons is for abuse of discretion. . . . With respect to multi-district litigation, as here, we have instructed, "a district court needs to have broad discretion in coordinating and administering multi-district litigation." *In re Showa Denko K. K. L. Tryptophan Products Liability Litig. II*, 953 F.2d 162, 165 (4th Cir. 1992).

A. LATE CONCERNS

The district court established a January 4, 1993 cutoff date for persons wishing to opt in to the "Effective Scheduling" litigation. Three would-be plaintiffs, Royster, Murchinson, and Mattox, missed the cutoff by several days and were dismissed. Appellants Gore, Losco, O'Neal, and Seidl also failed to file consents by the appointed deadline.

Appellants' sole argument on appeal on this point is nothing more than that the FLSA is remedial and should be stretched to allow in as many such claims as possible. The prerogative of the district court to manage its docket with timetables and deadlines, however, prevents even remedial statutes from stretching to the breaking point. It cannot be gainsaid that the district court was clear about its cut-off deadline. On October 20, 1992, the district court, when it authorized the opt in notice, set a cut-off deadline for persons wishing to opt in on December 31, 1992 (later extended to January 4, 1993). The court stated that late opt-in forms, absent a showing of "exceptional circumstances," would not be considered by the court and such persons sending tardy forms would not be in the class. As the court simply stated, "whoever gets in by the 31st of December is in. Whoever's not in is not in. That's the end of it." Transcript of October 16, 1992 conference at 37.

Several appellants (Losco, O'Neal, and Seidl) later filed affidavits attempting to establish "exceptional circumstances" as an excuse for their untimely opt-in forms. Losco claimed that he mailed his consent form on the appointed date; O'Neal stated that his father was terminally ill when he received the opt-in form and that he mailed the consent after his father died; and Seidl asserted that, after a period of time spent out of town, he completed and mailed the form upon his return. As far as Losco's having mailed his consent only on—not before—the deadline, we have stated in another context that the "litigant who decides to rely on the vagaries of the mail must suffer the consequences." *Thompson v. E. I. DuPont de Nemours & Co.*, 76 F.3d 530, 534 (4th Cir. 1996). With respect to the court's decision declining to find exceptional circumstances accounted for the other tardy consents, we cannot say that court abused its discretion. *See, e.g., Hoffman-LaRouche, Inc. v. Sperling*, 493 U.S. 165, 172 (1989) (holding that a district court is empowered to establish "cut off dates to expedite disposition of the action"). To the extent to which appellants additionally assert that the district court abused its discretion when it dismissed, with prejudice, the claims of the tardy consent filers, sanctions in such a circumstance properly may include dismissal. *See Rabb v. Amatex Corp.*, 769 F. 2d 996, 1000 (4th Cir. 1985).

B. IMPERFECT QUESTIONNAIRES

In May 1993, the district court sent out questionnaires, approved by plaintiffs and defendant, that it required each of the almost one thousand pre-notice and post-notice plaintiffs to complete, notarize, and mail to plaintiffs' counsel by June 11, 1993. Plaintiffs' counsel was then required to pass the questionnaire on to Food Lion's attorneys by June 25, 1993. The court had approved use of the questionnaires in order to streamline discovery of post-notice plaintiffs, provide basic information about each plaintiff's claim, and, thereby, to spur possible settlement negotiations. The court's order alerted the plaintiffs that failure to comply with the above deadlines could result in the dismissal, with prejudice, of the plaintiff's claim.

Many would-be plaintiffs missed the return deadline or sent in incomplete forms (*e.g.*, forms which lacked proper notarization) or the wrong forms (*e.g.*, in April 1993, plaintiffs' counsel had their clients fill out questionnaires for counsel's own use and many plaintiffs wrongly mailed these forms). The district court gave each plaintiff who failed to return a questionnaire or completed the wrong questionnaire an opportunity to show cause by August 2, 1993 why his form was untimely or incomplete. Those plaintiffs who did show cause were not dismissed. The district court found, however, that many claimants did not proffer viable explanations, if any at all was proffered, and entered dismissal orders against them.

Three appellants, Harvey, Bryant, and Clark, failed to submit notarized questionnaires to plaintiffs' counsel by June 11, 1993, and failed to complete and forward the questionnaires to Food Lion before the June 25, 1993 deadline. As well, Bryant and Clark failed to submit timely, properly sworn and notarized explanations in response to the court's show cause order as to why they were late in the first instance. While the three appellants' personal circumstances at the time may explain the tardiness of their questionnaires and may entitle them to some degree of sympathy,[15] because we review the district court's rulings on this point for abuse of discretion, we do not find that the appellants are entitled to legal relief. Given that this consolidated action had almost one thousand claims in the beginning of proceedings, this court will afford the district court significant latitude in its handling of pretrial matters and in its case management directives. The court acted within its discretion when it dismissed the claims of the non-complying appellants. *Rabb, supra,* 769 F.2d at 1000 (holding that failure to comply with a discovery order warrants dismissal).

[The appeals court affirmed the district court's dismissal of the claims of those hourly employees who failed to comply with certain case management deadlines.]

■ MARTHA MINOW, JUDGE FOR THE SITUATION: JUDGE JACK WEINSTEIN, CREATOR OF TEMPORARY ADMINISTRATIVE AGENCIES
97 Colum. L. Rev. 2010, 2020-2026 (1997)

. . . Functionally, court-supervised settlements that establish systems for processing individual claims create temporary administrative agencies without proceeding through the legislative or executive branches. Even without the establishment of such claims facilities, judicial supervision of complex suits resembles administrative agency activity, especially in the use of masters and magistrates authorized to conduct fact-finding hearings, to manage parts of disputes, and to gather expert knowledge. Such solutions provide redress without destroying private defendants and construct flexible procedures and norms intended—by the judge and by the parties' lawyers—to suit particular circumstances. Sometimes, the court-created process is actually integrated into another prepackaged administrative procedure through the bankruptcy framework. At other times, the administrative dimensions of the court-supervised process are illustrated by the reactions of other players; other branches of government, government institutions such as schools, and private actors often send lobbyists to influence the court process, just as administrative agencies have inspired the development of vital advocacy organizations such as the AIDS Action

---

[15]Harvey asserted that he was traveling at the time he received the court questionnaire. He stated that although the questionnaire arrived at his house in South Carolina and was forwarded to him by his wife in a timely manner, he never received it. Nevertheless, even after he did receive the questionnaire, he delayed three weeks before submitting it. Clark stated that he traveled because of his job and was out of town for seven days at the time the questionnaire arrived. Bryant asserted that he had moved around the time the questionnaire was sent and that his mail was not forwarded to him.

Committee and the Natural Resources Defense Council. Judging for the situation, then, involves contextualized efforts to construct procedures tailored for a particular circumstance; judging for the situation involves generating temporary administrative structures responsive to the claims at hand.

. . . Creation of claims processing facilities, use of public hearings, and consultation with community members and experts amount to the establishment of uniquely temporary and contextually specific administrative processes. These devices are framed around the parties to a litigation. The court, and the adjunct actors employed by the court, perform the work of processing claims under simplified procedures and management, seeking to fulfill party expectations swiftly. Exemplifying the range of administrative agencies in this country, some of the court-sponsored processes may be technically competent and efficient while others may be immersed in partisan debates. Typically, the claims-processing activity set up under court approval accomplishes the same shift from fault-based norms to compensation for harms that administrative agencies have adopted in contexts such as black lung disease and workers' compensation for injuries on the job.

Yet, while it is fair to point to the similarities between these judicially created claims procedures and legislatively created administrative agencies, the differences between the two are also striking. Two important differences divide court-created administration systems from established administrative agencies: (1) the fact of court creation rather than legislative or executive authorization, and (2) their temporary, collapsible structure as compared to the more enduring, and at times entrenched, bureaucratic nature of traditional administrative agencies. The first invites intense scrutiny and potentially fatal objection on Article III and separation-of-powers grounds; the second may offer an intriguing challenge to other forms of administration. Both are, in my view, valuable contributions to American law and politics.

1. *Separation of Powers.* —If a federal court, rather than the legislative or executive branches, creates an administrative agency, it is fair to inquire into the potential breach of separation-of-powers requirements and bounded authority for the judiciary. Has the court strayed into the domain of the executive to enforce the law or taken over the task of the legislature to devise prospective rules and establish government agencies? Have appointed judges stepped into the fray reserved for elected officials? Are the judges making political judgments that require accommodation, bargaining, and the accountability of the electoral sanction for democratic legitimacy and efficacy? Answers to these questions are bound to reflect the political preferences of the observer as much as considered theories of democratic governmental structures. Yet, seeing the inevitable infusion of politics into the question restates the problem. A judge who engages in the process of creating administrative responses to social problems is also

inevitably immersed in political views, but lacks the tethering or camouflage of the traditional adjudicatory procedure.

Judge Weinstein himself has not been shy in detailing his own support for compensatory, rather than fault-based, approaches to mass torts, and a cost-sharing approach toward defendants' liability. Similarly, Judge Weinstein has tried to reframe debates over the alleged litigation crisis and difficulties of access to the courts by labeling the issues as the challenge of responding to "the mass of cases working their way through the system." This is the language and conception of administration; it also reflects a choice in favor of redistribution and spreading the costs of injuries across broad communities, rather than other potential responses to harms in the world. For those who think these kinds of questions require the tangling and wrangling of legislative debate, such court actions amount to unchecked fiat, beyond the scope of legal authority and in violation of democratic principles.

Three modest defenses can be offered on behalf of Judge Weinstein and other judges who use judicial resources to respond to such social problems despite inaction by the elected branches: the vacuum created by their inaction leaves judges with properly filed, concrete claims, requiring some sort of response. Kenneth R. Feinberg, sometimes a special master in mass tort cases and always an expert in them, has concluded that no sweeping congressional reform is forthcoming on either the procedural or substantive sides of the field, "[s]o in effect the courts must do what they can with the tools at their disposal." These cases warrant utilization of untraditional means, like special masters, community input, and aggressive case management, because they encompass unanticipated problems with wide-ranging social and political ramifications. As Judge Weinstein insightfully notes, "[a] rigid and unresponsive judiciary, blind to the needs of various communities and of society at large, is far more likely to cause an erosion of public confidence in legal institutions than a judiciary perceived as overly interested in resolving the problems before it."

Judicial action actually may trigger action by the other branches, and thereby promote the vision of overlapping and checking branches of government that lies behind the separation of powers. Judge Weinstein's *Agent Orange* settlement had this effect; Congress responded with a bill to aid veterans affected by exposure to dioxin, and the Veterans' Administration eventually interpreted its mandate to include responding to the needs of these veterans. Unlocking the logjam in the electoral branches may be a rule uniquely assigned to the courts, and thus a basis for justifying judicial action that otherwise seems to interfere with legislative and executive prerogatives. Energetic judging thus may stimulate action by other branches that have been frozen and unresponsive.

Second, judicial action may be defended here as continuous, rather than discontinuous, with other forms of adjudication. There is not an obvious or steady line distinguishing the judicial role involved in selecting strict liability as the standard in a particular tort case from the judicial role involved in supervision of a settlement achieving a similar result. Of course, this line of defense may simply expose even more judicial action to critique as invasive of the ambit of legislative or executive authority. Moreover, if the costs of the administrative process include assessments to the government, and not just to private parties, obtaining public revenues and justifying their use calls for resort to the elected branches. Yet, all judicial action requires appropriations and expenditures of public funds, ranging from the salaries of judges and clerks to outlays for paper and computer disks. Enforcement of the simplest damages award requires the use of personnel to process forms and, at times, to execute liens on property. There is no sharp line separating the tasks of adjudication and the tasks of implementing the law. A separation-of-powers objection starts a debate about appropriate judicial behavior; it does not clinch the debate, nor provide an absolute bar to a temporary administrative apparatus.

Third, exposure and defense of the boundaries between the branches are necessary for reasoned debate: The initiative of someone like Judge Weinstein can generate public debate and analysis to sharpen understandings of separation of powers, a crucial element of our governmental structure. Jack Weinstein's approach to judging renders immediate what otherwise can remain a remote debate about the proper relationship between law and justice. Weinstein's approach reminds lawyers, judges, and theorists that legal rules—ranging from the most technical procedures to the basic constitutional structure—were devised by human beings as means for governing with justice. In Judge Weinstein's court, it is no defense to argue "that's never been done before"; legitimacy and legality are to be measured as much by results as by concordance with precedent. Accordingly, if governing with justice requires bending the rules and altering precedents, then the rules and the precedents need to be bent and altered. Of course, this is only one of many vigorously competing views about the proper relation between justice and law. As a result, Judge Weinstein's landmark cases afford rich, real examples to test the typically abstract debates over this and other competing views of law. In this way, his decisions benefit even those who find his approach to law to be an appalling disregard of its constraints.

2. *Temporary Administration.*—An administrative agency established by the legislature or the executive may have an endpoint or sunset provision terminating its existence, but this is not the common practice. Instead, such administrative agencies, once established, tend to endure and require massive efforts to trim them, much less to close them down. The administrative processes established by courts, in contrast, have very specific time limitations, even if they endure for several years. A claims facility lasts only as long as the fund exists and claims remain to be processed; judicial supervision through masters and magistrates may extend longer than some would like, but it does come to an end when assigned tasks are fulfilled,

when the parties complete their assigned duties or successfully move to modify their obligations, or when the judge involved concludes that no more can be done. These are not perfectly calibrated measures for termination, but they do yield endpoints to judicially sponsored administrative action.

. . . Inventing flexible, responsive administrative practices may be the only alternative to big, blunt bureaucracies on the one hand, and private market mechanisms on the other.

Practice Exercise No. 26: Review of Settlement and Consideration of Judicial Case Management

You are an appellate judge who will be asked to vote, with reasons, on whether to accept or reject a challenge to a federal judge's approval of a settlement for more than 600 consolidated actions, involving more than 2.4 million Vietnam Veterans, their families, and children. The plaintiffs alleged that exposure to Agent Orange, a herbicide used by the U.S. Army to defoliate vegetation in Vietnam, caused various diseases and traumas to those directly and indirectly exposed. They sued chemical manufacturers. Proving such causation would be very difficult, given the state of science at that time, yet the plaintiffs, if they ever reached a jury trial, would present compelling stories to a jury. Judge Jack Weinstein of the Federal Eastern District of New York ultimately presided over settlement negotiations after appointing attorney Kenneth Feinberg to fashion a distribution scheme.

Consider for your appellate review these basic terms of the settlement:

(1) Defendants would pay $180 million plus interest running from a specified date; all co-defendants would release each other and their subsidiary and parent companies from mutual liability;

(2) The settlement fund itself would provide money in advance to pay for class notice and administration expenses associated with settlement;

(3) All parties would reserve the right to sue the United States;

(4) The defendants would reserve the right to reject the settlement if a "substantial" number of class members opted out of the settlement;

(5) The distribution plan from the settlement fund would address the needs of individuals born after the adoption of the settlement, even though they would retain the right to bring new suits;

(6) The settlement terms would be subject to an open "fairness" hearing after all interested parties had notice, giving them an opportunity to express their views about it;

(7) The court-appointed master would develop guidelines, with the judge's help, for distributing the money from the settlement fund

to individual plaintiffs and/or to pay for class-wide benefits, such as lobbying and research.

Judge Weinstein included a 150-page review of all the claims in the case, which did not defend the settlement but instead indicated the ambiguities and difficulties on both sides and the benefits of a settlement, given the uncertainties of continued litigation. He also cited the benefits of a classwide solution to permit some recovery, even in the face of proof problems for the plaintiffs. Under Fed. R. Civ. P. 23 (3), the federal judge has to approve a settlement of claims brought as a class action in order to protect the interests of the unnamed class members. The rule states: "23(e) Dismissal or Compromise. A class action shall not be dismissed or compromised without the approval of the court, and notice of the proposed dismissal or compromise shall be given to all members of the class in such manner as the court directs." The standard for appellate review of a decision under 23(e) is abuse of discretion. Did the judge abuse his discretion in approving this settlement?

Approach this question in light of the readings from this chapter. If they were sitting as judges, how would Fuller and Chayes respond? Lieberman and Henry? Fiss and Edwards? Bernstein and Coombe? Delgado? Sander? Menkel-Meadow? Schwarzer and Resnik? One way to proceed with this exercise would be to meet with other students in small groups to articulate the positions and questions that any or several of the authors would develop in response to the settlement.

As a final exercise, consider this from your own point of view as a law student, as a prospective lawyer and as a citizen: Judge Weinstein was committed to generating a settlement in the case from the moment it reached his courtroom, even though early settlement discussions had failed. He pressed for settlement by appointing an aggressive master to push for one, by rejecting requests to bifurcate the trial or to delay it for more time for discovery, by issuing "tentative" rulings on the substantive law that made both sides worried about losing on the merits, and by directing all counsel to appear in chambers on the Saturday morning four days before trial was scheduled to begin for an around-the-clock negotiation settlement. Ultimately, the $180 million figure came from the judge himself. Does this kind of conduct comport with desirable court-annexed dispute resolution, or does it demonstrate grave problems with that approach?

For a fascinating account of Judge Weinstein's activism and his unconventionally imaginative efforts to force the Agent Orange parties to settle, read Peter H. Schuck, *Agent Orange on Trial* (Belknap 1986).

7

The Choice of an Appropriate Court: Personal Jurisdiction, Notice, and Venue

A. INTRODUCTION

In addition to the issues we have already explored about the plausibility of a claim and the availability of a meaningful remedy, a lawyer contemplating filing a lawsuit must also consider several issues concerning the choice of an appropriate court to hear the case. In order to enter a valid and enforceable judgment, a court must have adjudicatory power consisting of (1) personal jurisdiction over the defendant (or in some cases the defendant's property) and (2) subject matter jurisdiction over the case. Further, the court must be a proper venue for the litigation, and adequate notice must be provided to the defendant of the pendency of the action. The absence of any of these four procedural requisites is grounds for dismissal of the lawsuit, and a judgment entered without proper personal jurisdiction, subject matter jurisdiction, or notice may be successfully challenged either on appeal or in a collateral (separate) proceeding (such as an action to enforce the judgment).

Personal jurisdiction (sometimes referred to as "territorial jurisdiction") is a reflection of the geographic limitations on the judicial power of the sovereign states within our federal system. Assume, for example, that Nancy Carpenter moved to Florida following her husband's tragic death and decided to bring suit against Randall Dee in the courts of that state. Intuitively, it seems unfair to require Dee to defend a lawsuit in a distant state when all the events giving rise to the suit occurred in Massachusetts. We may also question the authority of a Florida court to adjudicate a matter when that state has no connection to the lawsuit other than the fortuitous (and recently adopted) residence of the plaintiff. Both concerns—fairness and power—play a role in the doctrine of personal jurisdiction. Over time (and what could be called a long and winding road), the United States Supreme Court has developed an elaborate constitutional calculus for determining when a court has power to reach a defendant who is beyond its borders and to enter an enforceable judgment against him or her.

While the concept of personal jurisdiction allocates judicial power *among* the states based on power over the defendant, subject matter jurisdiction allocates power *within* states as between the federal and state court systems based on the type of case. Federal courts have limited subject matter jurisdiction; constitutional and statutory provisions restrict their adjudicatory authority to certain types of cases, namely disputes between citizens of different states ("diversity of citizenship" cases), and disputes arising under federal law ("federal question" cases). State courts have general subject matter jurisdiction (they can hear and decide most categories of cases); statutory provisions typically delineate which cases should be filed in which court (such as superior court, housing court, probate court, land court, and so forth).

Even though personal jurisdiction and subject matter jurisdiction are entirely separate and distinct forms of judicial power, students sometimes confuse the two because both have a geographic component. Personal jurisdiction exists over a defendant who is resident within or otherwise connected to the state in which the lawsuit is filed. Subject matter jurisdiction over diversity cases is also obviously dependent on a connection to a state—the citizenship of the parties. Students must look beyond the shared interest in geography to avoid confusing these two quite separate concepts of jurisdiction.

Once the principles of personal and subject matter jurisdiction identify those courts that have power over both the defendant and the case, the concept of *venue* further restricts the location of the lawsuit. Within the federal system, venue determines the appropriate judicial districts in which the case may be filed. The federal trial courts in New York State, for example, are divided into four distinct districts: eastern, western, northern, and southern. Statutory provisions in the Judicial Code assign cases to particular districts based primarily on the residence of the parties or the occurrence of the activities upon which the claim is based. State venue statutes assign cases to particular counties based on similar criteria.

The final prerequisite to the ability of a court to enter a valid judgment is the provision of adequate *notice* to the defendant. Notice and an opportunity to defend the lawsuit reflect the most basic notions of due process of law.

B. JURISDICTION OVER THE PERSON OR PROPERTY OF THE DEFENDANT

Perhaps the most well-known evolution of American case law (certainly to first-year law students!) has occurred in the area of personal jurisdiction. Since the decision in *Pennoyer v. Neff* in 1877, the courts have struggled with the task of defining the requirements that must be met before a court may lawfully summon a nonresident defendant before it and enter an enforceable judgment. The complexity of the problem comes from the very nature of our federal system of government. Each state within the whole retains its own sovereignty, a significant part of which is the power to adjudicate disputes. Yet a judgment entered by a court in State A must under our Constitution be given "full faith and credit" in all other states*—that is to say, State B must (if asked by the plaintiff) recognize and enforce the judgment against the defendant and any assets of the defendant found within State B. Because a judgment may have consequences beyond the borders of the state that renders it and may affect citizens of other states, the adjudication of disputes unavoidably implicates the conflicting authorities of the separate sovereigns.

Although it has always been clear that a state has adjudicatory power over persons and things within its borders, the question remains when that state may reach beyond those borders to entertain a case against a nonresident. *Pennoyer v. Neff*'s traditional concept of jurisdiction, requiring the physical presence of the defendant or his property within the adjudicating state, proved too confining in the years following 1877—a time of tremendous expansion of the national interstate economy. *Pennoyer* inhibited the ability of states to provide a judicial forum for their residents who had claims against nonresidents and who wanted to file suit in their home court. Its demise was thus inevitable.

The breakdown of *Pennoyer* began subtly, with resort to legal fictions (like "constructive presence"), but in 1945 resulted in an entirely new framework for the analysis of personal jurisdiction—*International Shoe Co. v. Washington*'s concept of "minimum contacts." Informed by notions of fair play as much as state power, the modern framework of jurisdiction has proven (like most things "modern") complex and, at times, downright elusive. Indeed, a word of warning about this chapter and the two that follow: we are entering an area of high-density legal doctrine. Be prepared for a change of focus, from procedural rules to appellate case law.

But we get ahead of ourselves.

---

*As we shall see, a judgment is entitled to such universal recognition only if it was entered by a court that had proper adjudicatory power over both the defendant and the case, and that provided adequate notice to the defendant.

C. THE TRADITIONAL CONCEPTION OF PERSONAL JURISDICTION

A Glossary of Terms. Before turning to *Pennoyer* (which generations of law students have insisted is not written in the English language), it is helpful to define certain terms key to the traditional view of personal jurisdiction. *In personam* jurisdiction is the power of a court to enter a binding judgment against the defendant (the judgment may, if necessary, be satisfied by liquidating the defendant's assets). An *in personam* judgment is said to follow the defendant around, meaning that it must be given "full faith and credit" and thus enforced by any state in which the defendant or the defendant's assets are found.

In rem jurisdiction is the power of a court to act with regard to property (usually real estate) within its borders. An *in rem* judgment affects the interests of persons in the property (and may indeed extinguish those interests), but unlike the *in personam* judgment, does not create an obligation on the defendant's part to pay money to the plaintiff. An action to determine title to property is an example of *in rem* jurisdiction.

Quasi in rem jurisdiction is a hybrid of the other two forms of adjudicatory power. It is based on the presence of the defendant's property (either real or personal) within the forum state, but it permits the court to enter a judgment for an amount of money up to the value of the property, to be satisfied from the sale of the property. Unlike the so-called *true* in rem action described above, the claim for relief in a *quasi in rem* action is unrelated to the property that provides the basis for jurisdiction.

A fourth type of jurisdiction permits a court to decide cases concerning the *status* of the litigants, such as the validity of a marriage or the custody of children. A court may, for example, exercise jurisdiction to entertain a divorce action based on the residence of the plaintiff spouse and may order a termination of the marriage relationship, even though the other spouse is beyond the usual reach of adjudicatory power. Entry of a judgment for support payments, however, requires the court to have *in personam* power over the defendant spouse.

■ PENNOYER v. NEFF
95 U.S. 714 (1877)

Justice FIELD delivered the opinion of the Court:

This is an action to recover the possession of a tract of land, of the alleged value of $15,000, situated in the State of Oregon. The plaintiff asserts title to the premises by a patent of the United States issued to him in 1866, under the act of Congress of Sept. 27, 1850, usually known as the Donation Law of Oregon. The defendant claims to have acquired the premises under a sheriff's deed, made upon a sale of the property on execution issued upon a judgment recovered against the plaintiff in one of the circuit courts of the State. The case turns upon the validity of this judgment.

It appears from the record that the judgment was rendered in February, 1866, in favor of J. H. Mitchell, for less than $300, including costs, in an action brought by him upon a demand for services as an attorney; that, at the time the action was commenced and the judgment rendered, the defendant therein, the plaintiff here, was a non-resident of the State that he was not personally served with process, and did not appear therein; and that the judgment was entered upon his default in not answering the complaint, upon a constructive service of summons by publication.

The Code of Oregon provides for such service when an action is brought against a non-resident and absent defendant, who has property within the State. It also provides, where the action is for the recovery of money or damages, for the attachment of the property of the non-resident. And it also declares that no natural person is subject to the jurisdiction of a court of the State, "unless he appear in the court, or be found within the State, or be a resident thereof, or have property therein; and, in the last case, only to the extent of such property at the time the jurisdiction attached." Construing this latter provision to mean, that, in an action for money or damages where a defendant does not appear in the court, and is not found within the State, and is not a resident thereof, but has property therein, the jurisdiction of the court extends only over such property, the declaration expresses a principle of general, if not universal, law. The authority of every tribunal is necessarily restricted by the territorial limits of the State in which it is established. Any attempt to exercise authority beyond those limits would be deemed in every other forum, as has been said by this court, an illegitimate assumption of power, and be resisted as mere abuse. In the case against the plaintiff, the property here in controversy sold under the judgment rendered was not attached, nor in any way brought under the jurisdiction of the court. Its first connection with the case was caused by a levy of the execution. It was not, therefore, disposed of pursuant to any adjudication, but only in enforcement of a personal judgment, having no relation to the property, rendered against a non-resident without service of process upon him in the action, or his appearance therein. The court below did not consider that an attachment of the property was essential to its jurisdiction or to the validity of the sale, but held that the judgment was invalid from defects in the affidavit upon which the order of publication was obtained, and in the affidavit by which the publication was proved.

There is some difference of opinion among the members of this court as to the rulings upon these alleged defects. . . .

If, therefore, we were confined to the rulings of the court below upon the defects in the affidavits mentioned, we should be unable to uphold its decision. But it was also contended in that court, and is insisted upon here, that the judgment in the State court against the plaintiff was void for want of personal service of process on him, or of his appearance in the action in which it was rendered and that the premises in controversy could not be subjected to the payment of the demand of a resident creditor except by a proceeding in rem; that is, by a direct proceeding against the property for that purpose. If these positions are sound, the ruling of the Circuit Court as to the invalidity of that judgment must be sustained, notwithstanding our dissent from the reasons upon which it was made. And that they are sound would seem to follow from two well-established principles of public law respecting the jurisdiction of an independent State over persons and property. The several States of the Union are not, it is true, in every respect independent, many of the rights and powers which originally belonged to them being now vested in the government created by the Constitution. But, except as restrained and limited by that instrument, they possess and exercise the authority of independent States, and the principles of public law to which we have referred are applicable to them. One of these principles is, that every State possesses exclusive jurisdiction and sovereignty over persons and property within its territory. . . . The other principle of public law referred to follows from the one mentioned; that is, that no State can exercise direct jurisdiction and authority over persons or property without its territory. The several States are of equal dignity and authority, and the independence of one implies the exclusion of power from all others. And so it is laid down by jurists, as an elementary principle, that the laws of one State have no operation outside of its territory, except so far as is allowed by comity; and that no tribunal established by it can extend its process beyond that territory so as to subject either persons or property to its decisions. "Any exertion of authority of this sort beyond this limit," says Story, "is a mere nullity, and incapable of binding such persons or property in any other tribunals."

But as contracts made in one State may be enforceable only in another State, and property may be held by non-residents, the exercise of the jurisdiction which every State is admitted to possess over persons and property within its own territory will often affect persons and property without it. To any influence exerted in this way by a State affecting persons resident or property situated elsewhere, no objection can be justly taken; while any direct exertion of authority upon them, in an attempt to give ex-territorial operation to its laws, or to enforce an ex-territorial jurisdiction by its tribunals, would be deemed an encroachment upon the independence of the State in which the persons are domiciled or the property is situated, and be resisted as usurpation. . . .

So the State, through its tribunals, may subject property situated within its limits owned by non-residents to the payment of the demand of its own citizens against them; and the exercise of this jurisdiction in no respect infringes upon the sovereignty of the State where the owners are domiciled. Every State owes protection to its own citizens; and, when non-residents deal with them, it is a legitimate and just exercise of authority to hold and appropriate any property owned by such non-residents to satisfy the claims of its citizens. It is in virtue of the State's jurisdiction over the property of the non-resident situated within its limits that its tribunals can inquire into that non-resident's obligations to its own citizens, and the inquiry can then be carried only to the extent necessary to control the disposition of the property. If the non-resident have no property in the State, there is nothing upon which the tribunals can adjudicate. . . .

Jurisdiction is acquired in one of two modes: first, as against the person of the defendant by the service of process; or, secondly, by a procedure against the property of the defendant within the jurisdiction of the court. In the latter case, the defendant is not personally bound by the judgment beyond the property in question. And it is immaterial whether the proceeding against the property be by an attachment or bill in chancery. It must be substantially a proceeding in rem. . . .

If, without personal service, judgments in personam, obtained ex parte against non-residents and absent parties, upon mere publication of process, which, in the great majority of cases, would never be seen by the parties interested, could be upheld and enforced, they would be the constant instruments of fraud and oppression. Judgments for all sorts of claims upon contracts and for torts, real or pretended, would be thus obtained, under which property would be seized, when the evidence of the transactions upon which they were founded, if they ever had any existence, had perished.

Substituted service by publication, or in any other authorized form, may be sufficient to inform parties of the object of proceedings taken where property is once brought under the control of the court by seizure or some equivalent act. The law assumes that property is always in the possession of its owner, in person or by agent; and it proceeds upon the theory that its seizure will inform him, not only that it is taken into the custody of the court, but that he must look to any proceedings authorized by law upon such seizure for its condemnation and sale. Such service may also be sufficient in cases where the object of the action is to reach and dispose of property in the State, or of some interest therein, by enforcing a contract or a lien respecting the same, or to partition it among different owners, or, when the public is a party, to condemn and appropriate it for a public purpose. In other words, such service may answer in all actions which are substantially proceedings in rem. But where the entire object of the action is to determine the personal rights and obligations of the defendants, that is, where the suit is merely in personam, constructive service in this form upon a non-resident is ineffectual for any purpose. Process from the tribunals of one State cannot run into another State, and summon parties there domiciled to leave its territory and respond to proceedings against them. Publication of process or notice within the State where the tribunal sits cannot create any greater obligation upon the non-resident to appear. Process sent to him out of the State, and process published within it, are equally unavailing in proceedings to establish his personal liability.

The want of authority of the tribunals of a State to adjudicate upon the obligations of non-residents, where they have no property within its limits, is not denied by the court below: but the position is assumed, that, where they have property within the State, it is immaterial whether the property is in the first instance brought under the control of the court by attachment or some other equivalent act, and afterwards applied by its judgment to the satisfaction of demands against its owner; or such demands be first established in a personal action, and the property of the non-resident be afterwards seized and sold on execution. But the answer to this position has already been given in the statement, that the jurisdiction of the court to inquire into and determine his obligations at all is only incidental to its jurisdiction over the property. Its jurisdiction in that respect cannot be made to depend upon facts to be ascertained after it has tried the cause and rendered the judgment. If the judgment be previously void, it will not become valid by the subsequent discovery of property of the defendant, or by his subsequent acquisition of it. The judgment, if void when rendered, will always remain void: it cannot occupy the doubtful position of being valid if property be found, and void if there be none. Even if the position assumed were confined to cases where the non-resident defendant possessed property in the State at the commencement of the action, it would still make the validity of the proceedings and judgment depend upon the question whether, before the levy of the execution, the defendant had or had not disposed of the property. If before the levy the property should be sold, then, according to this position, the judgment would not be binding. This doctrine would introduce a new element of uncertainty in judicial proceedings. The contrary is the law: the validity of every judgment depends upon the jurisdiction of the court before it is rendered, not upon what may occur subsequently. . . .

The force and effect of judgments rendered against non-residents without personal service of process upon them, or their voluntary appearance, have been the subject of frequent consideration in the courts of the United States and of the several States, as attempts have been made to enforce such judgments in States other than those in which they were rendered, under the provision of the Constitution requiring that "full faith and credit shall be given in each State to the public acts, records, and judicial proceedings of every other State"; and the act of Congress providing for the mode of authenticating such acts, records, and proceedings, and declaring that, when thus authenticated, "they shall have such faith and credit given to them in every court within the United States as they have by law or usage in the courts of the State from which they are or shall or taken." In the earlier cases, it was supposed that the act gave to all judgments the same effect in other States which they had by law in the

State where rendered. But this view was afterwards qualified so as to make the act applicable only when the court rendering the judgment had jurisdiction of the parties and of the subject-matter, and not to preclude an inquiry into the jurisdiction of the court in which the judgment was rendered, or the right of the State itself to exercise authority over the person or the subject-matter. . . .

[T]he courts of the United States are not required to give effect to judgments of this character when any right is claimed under them. Whilst they are not foreign tribunals in their relations to the State courts, they are tribunals of a different sovereignty, exercising a distinct and independent jurisdiction, and are bound to give to the judgments of the State courts only the same faith and credit which the courts of another State are bound to give to them.

Since the adoption of the Fourteenth Amendment to the Federal Constitution, the validity of such judgments may be directly questioned, and their enforcement in the State resisted, on the ground that proceedings in a court of justice to determine the personal rights and obligations of parties over whom that court has no jurisdiction do not constitute due process of law. Whatever difficulty may be experienced in giving to those terms a definition which will embrace every permissible exertion of power affecting private rights, and exclude such as is forbidden, there can be no doubt of their meaning when applied to judicial proceedings. They then mean a course of legal proceedings according to those rules and principles which have been established in our systems of jurisprudence for the protection and enforcement of private rights. To give such proceedings any validity, there must be a tribunal competent by its constitution — that is, by the law of its creation — to pass upon the subject-matter of the suit; and, if that involves merely a determination of the personal liability of the defendant, he must be brought within its jurisdiction by service of process within the State, or his voluntary appearance.

Except in cases affecting the personal status of the plaintiff, and cases in which that mode of service may be considered to have been assented to in advance, as hereinafter mentioned, the substituted service of process by publication, allowed by the law of Oregon and by similar laws in other States, where actions are brought against non-residents, is effectual only where, in connection with process against the person for commencing the action, property in the State is brought under the control of the court, and subjected to its disposition by process adapted to that purpose, or where the judgment is sought as a means of reaching such property or affecting some interest therein; in other words, where the action is in the nature of a proceeding in rem. As stated by Cooley in his *Treatise on Constitutional Limitations*, 405, for any other purpose than to subject the property of a non-resident to valid claims against him in the State, "due process of law would require appearance or personal service before the defendant could be personally bound by any judgment rendered."

It is true that, in a strict sense, a proceeding in rem is one taken directly against property, and has for its object the disposition of the property, without reference to the title of individual claimants; but, in a larger and more general sense, the terms are applied to actions between parties, where the direct object is to reach and dispose of property owned by them, or of some interest therein. Such are cases commenced by attachment against the property of debtors, or instituted to partition real estate, foreclose a mortgage, or enforce a lien. So far as they affect property in the State, they are substantially proceedings in rem in the broader sense which we have mentioned. . . .

It follows from the views expressed that the personal judgment recovered in the State court of Oregon against the plaintiff herein, then a non-resident of the State, was without any validity, and did not authorize a sale of the property in controversy.

To prevent any misapplication of the views expressed in this opinion, it is proper to observe that we do not mean to assert, by anything we have said, that a State may not authorize proceedings to determine the status of one of its citizens towards a non-resident, which would be binding within the State, though made without service of process or personal notice to the non-resident. The jurisdiction which every State possesses to determine the civil status and capacities of all its inhabitants involves authority to prescribe the conditions on which proceedings affecting them may be commenced and carried on within its territory. The State, for example, has absolute right to prescribe the conditions upon which the marriage relation between its own citizens shall be created, and the causes for which it may be dissolved. One of the parties guilty of acts for which, by the law of the State, a dissolution may be granted, may have removed to a State where no dissolution is permitted. The complaining party would, therefore, fail if a divorce were sought in the State of the defendant; and if application could not be made to the tribunals of the complainant's domicile in such case, and proceedings be there instituted without personal service of process or personal notice to the offending party, the injured citizen would be without redress.

Neither do we mean to assert that a State may not require a non-resident entering into a partnership or association within its limits, or making contracts enforceable there, to appoint an agent or representative in the State to receive service of process and notice in legal proceedings instituted with respect to such partnership, association, or contracts, or to designate a place where such service may be made and notice given, and provide, upon their failure, to make such appointment or to designate such place that service may be made upon a public officer designated for that purpose, or in some other prescribed way, and that judgments rendered upon such service may not be binding upon the non-residents both within and without the State. . . . Nor do we doubt that a State, on creating corporations or other institutions for pecuniary or charitable purposes, may provide a mode in which their conduct may be investigated, their obligations enforced, or their charters revoked, which shall require other than personal service upon their officers or members. Parties becoming members of such corporations or institutions would hold their interest subject to the conditions prescribed by law.

In the present case, there is no feature of this kind, and, consequently, no consideration of what would be the effect of such legislation in enforcing the contract of a non-resident can arise. The question here respects only the validity of a money judgment rendered in one State, in an action upon a simple contract against the resident of another, without service of process upon him, or his appearance therein.

Judgment affirmed.

[The dissenting opinion of Justice HUNT is omitted.]

Comments and Questions

1. For the fascinating story behind *Pennoyer* and its cast of characters, *see* Wendy Collins Perdue, *Sin, Scandal, and Substantive Due Process: Personal Jurisdiction and Pennoyer Reconsidered*, 62 Wash. L. Rev. 479 (1987).

2. Trace the legal proceedings leading to the Supreme Court decision in *Pennoyer v. Neff*. What was the claim asserted in the prior case of *Mitchell v. Neff*? In which court was it filed, and what was the basis for that court's assertion of jurisdiction over the defendant? Was the jurisdiction *in personam* or *in rem*? Answer the same questions regarding the trial court proceedings in *Neff v. Pennoyer*.

3. Reconstruct the line of the arguments presented by the parties before the Supreme Court in *Pennoyer v. Neff*.

4. What were the bases for the exercise of jurisdiction provided in the Code of Oregon? How did the Supreme Court decision in *Pennoyer* modify these requirements?

5. Why should the Due Process Clause of the Fourteenth Amendment set the outer limits of the permissible reach of state court power? What values are protected by the clause in this context? Why are geographic boundaries so important to the Supreme Court's conception of personal jurisdiction? Regarding Justice Field's invocation of the Due Process Clause, Professor Perdue writes:

> Field's final and most startling step was to introduce the due process clause of the fourteenth amendment into his jurisdictional analysis. This step was unnecessary and surprising for several reasons. First, that clause had not been raised or argued by either party or by the court below. Second, Field had already concluded that the federal courts were not required to (and hence would not) enforce the prior Oregon judgment. Third, the due process discussion was dictum for the additional reason that the fourteenth amendment did not exist at the relevant time. Finally, the specific due

process "holding" of the case—that a judgment rendered without personal jurisdiction is unenforceable even in the rendering forum—has been viewed by at least some courts and commentators as itself quite novel.

Perdue, *supra*, 62 Wash. L. Rev. at 499-500.

6. How do the Due Process and Full Faith and Credit Clauses work together on the question of adjudicatory power?

7. What part does notice play in the Court's decision in *Pennoyer*? Was Neff notified of the pendency of *Mitchell v. Neff*? If not, why was the absence of notice not itself a constitutional (due process) defect in the prior proceedings?

8. What does *Pennoyer v. Neff* hold? Compare this holding to the approach of the lower court, which reached the same result—invalidating the sheriff's deed conveying the land to Pennoyer.

9. If you were representing Mitchell in a replay of *Mitchell v. Neff* after the Supreme Court's decision, what procedural options would you follow to ensure proper adjudicatory power over Neff?

10. *When and How to Raise the Issue of Personal Jurisdiction.* How did Neff go about procedurally challenging the exercise of jurisdiction over him by the court in *Mitchell v. Neff*? Why is this approach called a "*collateral attack*"? A more typical collateral attack occurs where a defendant who is aware of the lawsuit nonetheless deliberately fails to show up in court, suffering a default judgment with the intention of challenging jurisdiction when the plaintiff then sues on the judgment in the defendant's home state (look at *McGee v. International Life Insurance Co.*, below). The primary risk of this approach is that the only basis left for opposing the judgment once it becomes final in the original lawsuit is the jurisdictional challenge—the defendant cannot defend "on the merits" in the subsequent enforcement suit. Thus, a collateral attack strategy places all the defendant's eggs in the jurisdictional basket. If the court rejects the challenge, the judgment will be enforced. Under what circumstances might such a risky strategy make sense?

Assuming that Neff had been aware of Mitchell's action against him at the time it was still pending, what other options would have been available to challenge the court's power? Look for an example at Fed. R. Civ. P. 12(b)(2). Could Neff have appeared in the action and successfully argued (in a "*direct attack*") that the court had no adjudicatory power over him? But isn't "appearance" in court one of the *Pennoyer* bases for exercising power over the defendant? How does the device of "*special appearance*" alleviate the defendant's dilemma? (Note the procedural responses of the defendants in the following cases.)

If Neff had appeared in the action, filed an answer denying the facts alleged, and later raised the defense of lack of personal jurisdiction, what result? Look for an example at Fed. R. Civ. P. 12(g) and 12(h)(1). What policy underlies this *waiver* rule, which makes personal jurisdiction a "fragile" defense (that is, one easily lost)?

11. Consider the procedural options concerning personal jurisdiction open to Ultimate Auto's lawyer in the *Carpenter v. Dee* litigation. Assuming Ultimate is a New Hampshire corporation conducting all of its business there, its "nonresidency" in the forum state of Massachusetts triggers the possibility of a challenge to jurisdiction. Counsel could initiate a direct attack on jurisdiction in the Massachusetts Superior Court action by filing a Rule 12(b)(2) motion to dismiss (Massachusetts has adopted the Federal Rules of Civil Procedure in substantial form in its own courts). If the court grants the motion, the case is over (although plaintiff may appeal). If the motion is denied, Ultimate can defend the case on the merits, while preserving the jurisdictional objection for appeal. Counsel must, of course, raise the jurisdictional objection in a timely fashion (*see* the preceding note) or it is lost forever.

Alternatively, Ultimate could simply fail to appear in the Massachusetts action and suffer a default judgment. The plaintiff must then sue in a separate action to enforce the judgment, most likely in Ultimate's home state of New Hampshire. Since Ultimate had not raised or waived its jurisdictional challenge in the first case, it could collaterally attack the default judgment in this second case as being invalid for want of personal jurisdiction. If this challenge fails—that is, the New Hampshire court concludes that the Massachusetts Superior Court did have proper adjudicatory power over Ultimate and this ruling is upheld on appeal—then Ultimate will have lost its right to defend the case on the merits. Therein lies the risk of the collateral attack strategy. Where the stakes are not high, or there is no legitimate defense on the merits, the strategy may make sense. It also may provide the defendant with a home court advantage—more sympathetic judges, juries, or court personnel in a contest with a nonresident.

12. *Why do litigants and their lawyers care about personal jurisdiction?* By the end of this chapter we will have read more than a dozen cases in which parties, through their lawyers, vigorously fight over the issue of personal jurisdiction. Like all such procedural disputes in court, these are not primarily abstract or philosophical conflicts, but rather are firmly rooted in competing strategic and practical concerns.

The plaintiff chooses the forum in which the lawsuit is filed. Plaintiffs usually choose their home state, for reasons of convenience and familiarity as well as in the hope that they will somehow benefit from a home court advantage. This is particularly likely where the defendant is from a distant state, as increased inconvenience may translate into a favorable (to plaintiff) settlement of the case. Choice-of-law issues, such as the availability of punitive damages or the appropriate statute of limitations, may also favor one forum over another, and of course some venues are considered pro-plaintiff or pro-defendant.

The defendant will of course attempt to undo any advantage that the plaintiff gains by choice of forum, and the issue will be joined on the motion to dismiss for lack of personal jurisdiction over the defendant.

13. As you read the post-*Pennoyer* cases that follow, consider Professor Perdue's observation: "[Justice] Field's approach to personal jurisdiction continues to dominate modern personal jurisdiction doctrine. His opinion in *Pennoyer* not only laid the foundation for treating personal jurisdiction as a substantive liberty interest, but also established that geographic boundaries are central in the protection of that interest." 62 Wash. L. Rev. at 480.

14. Would the strict *Pennoyer* rules permit the exercise of jurisdiction over the defendants in *Hess v. Pawloski* and *Harris v. Balk*, the next two cases? Can you identify those portions of the opinion that permit some room for future expansion?

■ HESS v. PAWLOSKI
274 U.S. 352 (1927)

Justice BUTLER delivered the opinion of the Court:

This action was brought by defendant in error to recover damages for personal injuries. The declaration alleged that plaintiff in error negligently and wantonly drove a motor vehicle on a public highway in Massachusetts, and that by reason thereof the vehicle struck and injured defendant in error. Plaintiff in error is a resident of Pennsylvania. No personal service was made on him, and no property belonging to him was attached. The service of process was made in compliance with chapter 90, General Laws of Massachusetts, as amended by Stat. 1923, c. 431, §2, the material parts of which follow:

> The acceptance by a nonresident of the rights and privileges conferred by section three or four, as evidence by his operating a motor vehicle thereunder, or the operation by a nonresident of a motor vehicle on a public way in the commonwealth other than under said sections, shall be deemed equivalent to an appointment by such nonresident of the registrar or his successor in office, to be his true and lawful attorney upon whom may be served all lawful processes in any action or proceeding against him, growing out of any accident or collision in which said nonresident may be involved while operating a motor vehicle on such a way, and said acceptance or operation shall be a signification of his agreement that any such process against him which is so served shall be of the same legal force and validity as if served on him personally. Service of such process shall be made by leaving a copy of the process with a fee of two dollars in the hands of the registrar, or in his office, and such service shall be sufficient service upon the said nonresident: Provided, that notice of such service and a copy of the process are forthwith sent by registered mail by the plaintiff to the defendant, and the defendant's return receipt and the plaintiff's affidavit of compliance herewith are appended to the writ and entered with the declaration. The court in which the action is pending may order such continuances as may be necessary to afford the defendant reasonable opportunity to defend the action.

Plaintiff in error appeared specially for the purpose of contesting jurisdiction, and filed an answer in abatement and moved to dismiss on the ground that the service of process, if sustained, would deprive him of his property without due process of law, in violation of the Fourteenth Amendment. The court overruled the answer in abatement and denied the motion. The Supreme Judicial Court held the statute to be a valid exercise of the police power, and affirmed the order. . . .

The question is whether the Massachusetts enactment contravenes the due process clause of the Fourteenth Amendment.

The process of a court of one state cannot run into another and summon a party there domiciled to respond to proceedings against him. Notice sent outside the state to a nonresident is unavailing to give jurisdiction in an action against him personally for money recovery. *Pennoyer v. Neff*, 95 U.S. 741. There must be actual service within the state of notice upon him or upon someone authorized to accept service for him. A personal judgment rendered against a nonresident, who has neither been served with process nor appeared in the suit, is without validity. The mere transaction of business in a state by nonresident natural persons does not imply consent to be bound by the process of its courts. The power of a state to exclude foreign corporations, although not absolute, but qualified, is the ground on which such an implication is supported as to them. But a state may not withhold from nonresident individuals the right of doing business therein. The privileges and immunities clause of the Constitution (Section 2, Art. 4), safeguards to the citizens of one state the right "to pass through, or to reside in any other state for purposes of trade, agriculture, professional pursuits, or otherwise." And it prohibits state legislation discriminating against citizens of other states. Motor vehicles are dangerous machines, and, even when skillfully and carefully operated, their use is attended by serious dangers to persons and property. In the public interest the state may make and enforce regulations reasonably calculated to promote care on the part of all, residents and nonresidents alike, who use its highways. The measure in question operates to require a nonresident to answer for his conduct in the state where arise causes of action alleged against him, as well as to provide for a claimant a convenient method by which he may sue to enforce his rights. Under the statute the implied consent is limited to proceedings growing out of accidents or collisions on a highway in which the nonresident may be involved. It is required that he shall actually receive and receipt for notice of the service and a copy of the process. And it contemplates such continuances as may be found necessary to give reasonable time and opportunity for defense. It makes no hostile discrimination against nonresidents, but tends to put them on the same footing as residents. Literal and precise equality in respect of this matter is not attainable; it is not required. The state's power to regulate the use of its highways extends to their use by nonresidents as well as by residents. And, in advance of the operation of a motor vehicle on its highway by a nonresident, the state may require him to appoint one of its officials as his agent on whom process may be served in proceedings growing out of such use. And, in advance of the operation of a motor vehicle on its highway by a nonresident, the state may require him to appoint one of its officials as his agent on whom process may be served in proceedings growing out of such use. *Kane v. New Jersey*, 242 U.S. 160. That case recognized power of the state to exclude a nonresident until the formal appointment is made. And, having the power so to exclude, the state may declare that the use of the highway by the nonresident is the equivalent of the appointment of the registrar as agent on whom process may be served. The difference between the formal and implied appointment is not substantial, so far as concerns the application of the due process clause of the Fourteenth Amendment.

Judgment affirmed.

Comments and Questions

1. What is the basis for the exercise of jurisdiction over the nonresident motorist in *Hess*? Is this consistent with the *Pennoyer* rules? What portion of the *Pennoyer* decision arguably permits this?

2. Why would the United States Supreme Court resort to so questionable a fiction as "implied consent to suit"? What is the relevance of the fact that "motor vehicles are dangerous machines" to the issue of personal jurisdiction?

3. Note that both the Massachusetts statute and the Supreme Court decision upholding it treat the issue of notice as being separate and apart from the issue of adjudicatory power. Within the original *Pennoyer* scheme, notice and jurisdiction were virtually inseparable because the basis for establishing *in personam* jurisdiction, namely service of process within the state, simultaneously provided notice of the lawsuit to the defendant. With the change in focus from service *on the defendant* to activities conducted *by the defendant* within the state (a move finally accomplished in *International Shoe, infra*), power over the defendant and notice to the defendant began to travel divergent paths.

■ HARRIS v. BALK
198 U.S. 215 (1905)

The facts are as follows: The plaintiff in error, Harris, was a resident of North Carolina at the time of the commencement of this action, in 1896, and prior to that time was indebted to the defendant in error, Balk, also a resident of North Carolina, in the sum of $180, for money borrowed from Balk by Harris during the year 1896, which Harris verbally promised to repay, but there was no written evidence of the obligation. During the year above mentioned one Jacob Epstein, a resident of Baltimore, in the state of Maryland, asserted that Balk was indebted to him in the sum of over $300. In August, 1896, Harris visited Baltimore for the purpose of purchasing merchandise, and while he was in that city temporarily on August 6, 1896, Epstein caused to be issued out of a proper court in Baltimore a foreign or nonresident writ of attachment against Balk, attaching the debt due Balk from Harris, which writ the sheriff at Baltimore laid in the hands of Harris, with a summons to appear in the court at a day named. With that attachment, a writ of summons and a short declaration against Balk (as provided by the Maryland statute) were also delivered to the sheriff, and by him set up at the courthouse door, as required by the law of Maryland. Before the return day of the attachment writ Harris left Baltimore, and returned to his home in North Carolina. He did not contest the garnishee process, which was issued to garnish the debt which Harris owed Balk. After his return Harris made an affidavit on August 11, 1896, that he owed Balk $180, and stated that the amount had been attached by Epstein, of Baltimore, and by his counsel in the Maryland proceeding Harris consented therein to an order of condemnation against him as such garnishee for $180, the amount of his debt to Balk. Judgment was thereafter entered against the garnishee, and in favor of the plaintiff, Epstein, for $180. After the entry of the garnishee judgment, condemning the $180 in the hands of the garnishee, Harris paid the amount of the judgment to one Warren, an attorney of Epstein, residing in North Carolina. On August 11, 1896, Balk commenced an action against Harris before a justice of the peace in North Carolina, to recover the $180 which he averred Harris owed him. The plaintiff in error, by way of answer to the suit, pleaded in bar the recovery of the Maryland judgment and his payment thereof, and contended that it was conclusive against the defendant in error in this action, because that judgment was a valid judgment in Maryland, and was therefore entitled to full faith and credit in the courts of North Carolina. This contention was not allowed by the trial court, and judgment was accordingly entered against Harris for the amount of his indebtedness to Balk, and that judgment was affirmed by the supreme court of North Carolina. The ground of such judgment was that the Maryland court obtained no jurisdiction to attach or garnish the debt due from Harris to Balk, because Harris was but temporarily in the state, and the situs of the debt was in North Carolina.

Justice PECKHAM, after making the foregoing statement, delivered the opinion of the Court:

The state court of North Carolina has refused to give any effect in this action to the Maryland judgment; and the Federal question is whether it did not thereby refuse the full faith and credit to such judgment which is required by the Federal Constitution. If the Maryland court had jurisdiction to award it, the judgment is valid and entitled to the same full faith and credit in North Carolina that it has in Maryland as a valid domestic judgment.

The defendant in error contends that the Maryland court obtained no jurisdiction to award the judgment of condemnation, because the garnishee, although at the time in the state of Maryland, and personally served with process therein, was a nonresident of that state, only casually or temporarily within its boundaries; that the situs of the debt due from Harris, the garnishee, to the defendant in error herein, was in North Carolina, and did not accompany Harris to Maryland; that, consequently, Harris, though within the state of Maryland, had not possession of any property of Balk, and the Maryland state court therefore obtained no jurisdiction over any property of Balk in the attachment proceedings, and the consent of Harris to the entry of the judgment was immaterial. The plaintiff in error, on the contrary, insists that, though the garnishee were but temporarily in Maryland, yet the laws of that state provide for an attachment of this nature if the debtor, the garnishee, is found in the state, and the court obtains jurisdiction over him by the service of process therein; that the judgment, condemning the debt from Harris to Balk, was a valid judgment, provided Balk could himself have sued Harris for the debt in Maryland. This, it is asserted, he could have done, and the judgment was therefore entitled to full faith and credit in the courts of North Carolina. . . .

We regard the contention of the plaintiff in error as the correct one. . . .

There can be no doubt that Balk, as a citizen of the state of North Carolina, had the right to sue Harris in Maryland to recover the debt which Harris owed him. Being a citizen of North Carolina, he was entitled to all the privileges and immunities of citizens of the several states, one of which is the right to institute actions in the courts of another state. The law of Maryland provides for the attachment of credits in a case like this. . . .

It thus appears that Balk could have sued Harris in Maryland to recover his debt, notwithstanding the temporary character of Harris' stay there; it also appears that the municipal law of Maryland permits the debtor of the principal debtor to be garnished, and therefore if the court of the state where the garnishee is found obtains jurisdiction over him, through the service of process upon him within the state, then the judgment entered is a valid judgment. . . .

It seems to us, therefore, that the judgment against Harris in Maryland, condemning the $180 which he owed to Balk, was a valid judgment, because the court had jurisdiction over the garnishee by personal service of process within the state of Maryland. . . .

The judgment of the Supreme Court of North Carolina must be reversed, and the cause remanded for further proceedings not inconsistent with the opinion of this court.

Reversed.

Justice HARLAN and Justice DAY dissented.

Comments and Questions

1. What is the basis for the exercise of jurisdiction by the Maryland court over the defendant Balk? Is this consistent with the *Pennoyer* rules? What portion of the *Pennoyer* decision arguably permits this exercise of judicial power? What type of jurisdiction is this?

2. Why would the United States Supreme Court uphold a procedure as dubious as basing jurisdiction on attachment of a debt by seizing the debtor?

3. What was the procedural posture of Balk's challenge to the jurisdiction of the Maryland court? Is this more like the posture of *Pennoyer* or of *Hess*?

4. What role does notice play in the Court's analysis in *Harris v. Balk*?

D. THE MODERN CONCEPTION OF PERSONAL JURISDICTION

Under pressure from an ever-expanding interstate economy, the rigid *Pennoyer* framework was stretched and pulled to accommodate the aggressive reach of states that were seeking to provide a local forum for citizens litigating claims against nonresident persons and corporations. In 1945, the Supreme Court finally discarded the old structure, and with it such fictions as the implied consent of *Hess v. Pawloski,* in favor of a revised theory of personal jurisdiction. The result was the following landmark case.

■ INTERNATIONAL SHOE CO. v. STATE OF WASHINGTON, OFFICE OF UNEMPLOYMENT COMPENSATION AND PLACEMENT
326 U.S. 310 (1945)

Chief Justice STONE delivered the opinion of the Court:

The questions for decision are (1) whether, within the limitations of the due process clause of the Fourteenth Amendment, appellant, a Delaware corporation, has by its activities in the State of Washington rendered itself amenable to proceedings in the courts of that state to recover unpaid contributions to the state unemployment compensation fund exacted by state statutes, Washington Unemployment Compensation Act, Washington Revised Statutes, §9998—103a through §9998—123a, 1941 Supp., and (2) whether the state can exact those contributions consistently with the due process clause of the Fourteenth Amendment.

The statutes in question set up a comprehensive scheme of unemployment compensation, the costs of which are defrayed by contributions required to be made by employers to a state unemployment compensation fund. The contributions are a specified percentage of the wages payable annually by each employer for his employees' services in the state. The assessment and collection of the contributions and the fund are administered by respondents. Section 14(c) of the Act, Wash. Rev. Stat. 1941 Supp., §9998—114c, authorizes respondent Commissioner to issue an order and notice of assessment of delinquent contributions upon prescribed personal service of the notice upon the employer if found within the state, or, if not so found, by mailing the notice to the employer by registered mail at his last known address. That section also authorizes the Commissioner to collect the assessment by distraint if it is not paid within ten days after service of the notice. By §§14(e) and 6(b) the order of assessment may be administratively reviewed by an appeal tribunal within the office of unemployment upon petition of the employer, and this determination is by §6(i) made subject to judicial review on questions of law by the state Superior Court, with further right of appeal in the state Supreme Court as in other civil cases.

In this case notice of assessment for the years in question was personally served upon a sales solicitor employed by appellant in the State of Washington, and a copy of the notice was mailed by registered mail to appellant at its address in St. Louis, Missouri. Appellant appeared specially before the office of unemployment and moved to set aside the order and notice of assessment on the ground that the service upon appellant's salesman was not proper service upon appellant; that appellant was not a corporation of the State of Washington and was not doing business within the state; that it had no agent within the state upon whom service could be made; and that appellant is not an employer and does not furnish employment within the meaning of the statute.

The motion was heard on evidence and a stipulation of facts by the appeal tribunal which denied the motion and ruled that respondent Commissioner was entitled to recover the unpaid contributions. That action was affirmed by the Commissioner; both the Superior Court and the Supreme Court affirmed. 154 P.2d 801. Appellant in each of these courts assailed the statute as applied, as a violation of the due process clause of the Fourteenth Amendment, and as imposing a constitutionally prohibited burden on interstate commerce. The cause comes here on appeal, appellant assigning as error that the challenged statutes as applied infringe the due process clause of the Fourteenth Amendment and the commerce clause.

The facts as found by the appeal tribunal and accepted by the state Superior Court and Supreme Court, are not in dispute. Appellant is a Delaware corporation, having its principal place of business in St. Louis, Missouri, and is engaged in the manufacture and sale of shoes and other footwear. It maintains places of business in several states, other than Washington, at which its manufacturing is carried on and from which its merchandise is distributed interstate through several sales units or branches located outside the State of Washington.

Appellant has no office in Washington and makes no contracts either for sale or purchase of merchandise there. It maintains no stock of merchandise in that state and makes there no deliveries of goods in intrastate commerce. During the years from 1937 to 1940, now in question, appellant employed eleven to thirteen salesmen under direct supervision and control of sales managers located in St. Louis. These salesmen resided in Washington; their principal activities were confined to that state; and they were compensated by commissions based upon the amount of their sales. The commissions for each year totaled more than $31,000. Appellant supplies its salesmen with a line of samples, each consisting of one shoe of a pair, which they display to prospective purchasers. On occasion they rent permanent sample rooms, for exhibiting samples, in business buildings, or rent rooms in hotels or business buildings temporarily for that purpose. The cost of such rentals is reimbursed by appellant.

The authority of the salesmen is limited to exhibiting their samples and soliciting orders from prospective buyers, at prices and on terms fixed by appellant. The salesmen transmit the orders to appellant's office in St. Louis for acceptance or rejection, and when accepted the merchandise for filling the orders is shipped f.o.b. from points outside Washington to the purchasers within the state. All the merchandise shipped into Washington is invoiced at the place of shipment from which collections are made. No salesman has authority to enter into contracts or to make collections.

The Supreme Court of Washington was of opinion that the regular, and systematic solicitation of orders in the state by appellant's salesmen, resulting in a continuous flow of appellant's product into the state, was sufficient to constitute doing business in the state so as to make appellant amenable to suit in its courts. But it was also of opinion that there were sufficient additional activities shown to bring the case within the rule frequently stated, that solicitation within a state by the agents of a foreign corporation plus some additional activities there are sufficient to render the corporation amenable to suit brought in the courts of the state to enforce an obligation arising out of its activities there. The court found such additional activities in the salesmen's display of samples sometimes in permanent display rooms, and the salesmen's residence within the state, continued over a period of years, all resulting in a substantial volume of merchandise regularly shipped by appellant to purchasers within the state. The court also held that the statute as applied did not invade the constitutional power of Congress to regulate interstate commerce and did not impose a prohibited burden on such commerce.

Appellant's argument, renewed here, that the statute imposes an unconstitutional burden on interstate commerce need not detain us. . . . It is no longer debatable that Congress, in the exercise of the commerce power, may authorize the states, in specified ways, to regulate interstate commerce or impose burdens upon it.

Appellant also insists that its activities within the state were not sufficient to manifest its "presence" there and that in its absence the state courts were without jurisdiction, that consequently it was a denial of due process for the state to subject appellant to suit. It refers to those cases in which it was said that the mere solicitation of orders for the purchase of goods within a state, to be accepted without the state and filled by shipment of the purchased goods interstate, does not render the corporation seller amenable to suit within the state. And appellant further argues that since it was not present within the state, it is a denial of due process to subject it to taxation or other money exaction. It thus denies the power of the state to lay the tax or to subject appellant to a suit for its collection.

Historically the jurisdiction of courts to render judgment in personam is grounded on their de facto power over the defendant's person. Hence his presence within the territorial jurisdiction of court was prerequisite to its rendition of a judgment personally binding him. *Pennoyer v. Neff,* 95 U.S. 714, 733. But now that the capias ad respondendum has given way to personal service of summons or other form of notice, due process requires only that in order to subject a defendant to a judgment in personam, if he be not present within the territory of the forum, he have certain minimum contacts with it such that the maintenance of the suit does not offend "traditional notions of fair play and substantial justice." *Milliken v. Meyer,* 311 U.S. 457, 463.

Since the corporate personality is a fiction, although a fiction intended to be acted upon as though it were a fact, it is clear that unlike an individual its "presence" without, as well as within, the state of its origin can be manifested only by activities carried on in its behalf by those who are authorized to act for it. To say that the corporation is so far "present" there as to satisfy due process requirements, for purposes of taxation or the maintenance of suits against it in the courts of the state, is to beg the question to be decided. For the terms "present" or "presence" are used merely to symbolize those activities of the corporation's agent within the state which courts will deem to be sufficient to satisfy the demands of due process. Those demands may be met by such contacts of the corporation with the state of the forum as make it reasonable, in the context of our federal system of government, to require the corporation to defend the particular suit which is brought there. An "estimate of the inconveniences" which would result to the corporation from a trial away from its "home" or principal place of business is relevant in this connection.

"Presence" in the state in this sense has never been doubted when the activities of the corporation there have not only been continuous and systematic, but also give rise to the liabilities sued on, even though no consent to be sued or authorization to an agent to accept service of process has been given. Conversely it has been generally recognized that the casual presence of the corporate agent or even his conduct of single or isolated items of activities in a state in the corporation's behalf are not enough to subject it to suit on causes of action unconnected with the activities there. To require the corporation in such circumstances to defend the suit away from its home or other jurisdiction where it carries on more substantial activities has been thought to lay too great and unreasonable a burden on the corporation to comport with due process.

While it has been held in cases on which appellant relies that continuous activity of some sorts within a state is not enough to support the demand that the corporation be amenable to suits unrelated to that activity, there have been instances in which the continuous corporate operations within a state were thought so substantial and of such a nature as to justify suit against it on causes of action arising from dealings entirely distinct from those activities.

Finally, although the commission of some single or occasional acts of the corporate agent in a state sufficient to impose an obligation or liability on the corporation has not been thought to confer upon the state authority to enforce it, other such acts, because of their nature and quality and the circumstances of their commission, may be deemed sufficient to render the corporation liable to suit. True, some of the decisions holding the corporation amenable to suit have been supported by resort to the legal fiction that it has given its consent to service and suit, consent being implied from its presence in the state through the acts of its authorized agents. But more realistically it may be said that those authorized acts were of such a nature as to justify the fiction.

It is evident that the criteria by which we mark the boundary line between those activities which justify the subjection of a corporation to suit, and those which do not, cannot be simply mechanical or quantitative. The test is not merely, as has sometimes been suggested, whether the activity, which the corporation has seen fit to procure through its agents in another state, is a little more or a little less. Whether due process is satisfied must depend rather upon the quality and nature of the activity in relation to the fair and orderly administration of the laws which it was the purpose of the due process clause to insure. That clause does not contemplate that a state may make binding a judgment in personam against an individual or corporate defendant with which the state has no contacts, ties, or relations. *Cf. Pennoyer v. Neff, supra.*

But to the extent that a corporation exercises the privilege of conducting activities within a state, it enjoys the benefits and protection of the laws of that state. The exercise of that privilege may give rise to obligations; and, so far as those obligations arise out of or are connected with the activities within the state, a procedure which requires the corporation to respond to a suit brought to enforce them can, in most instances, hardly be said to be undue.

Applying these standards, the activities carried on in behalf of appellant in the State of Washington were neither irregular nor casual. They were systematic and continuous throughout the years in question. They resulted in a large volume of interstate business, in the course of which appellant received the benefits and protection of the laws of the state, including the right to resort to the courts for the enforcement of its rights. The obligation which is here sued upon arose out of those very activities. It is evident that these operations establish sufficient contacts or ties with the state of the forum to make it reasonable and just according to our traditional conception of fair play and substantial justice to permit the state to enforce the obligations which appellant has incurred there. Hence we cannot say that the maintenance of the present suit in the State of Washington involves an unreasonable or undue procedure.

We are likewise unable to conclude that the service of the process within the state upon an agent whose activities establish appellant's "presence" there was not sufficient notice of the suit, or that the suit was so unrelated to those activities as to make the agent an inappropriate vehicle for communicating the notice. It is enough that appellant has established such contacts with the state that the particular form of substituted service adopted there gives reasonable assurance that the notice will be actual. Nor can we say that the mailing of the notice of suit to appellant by registered mail at its home office was not reasonably calculated to apprise appellant of the suit. . . .

Appellant having rendered itself amenable to suit upon obligations arising out of the activities of its salesmen in Washington, the state may maintain the present suit in personam to collect the tax laid upon the exercise of the privilege of employing appellant's salesmen within the state. . . .

Affirmed.

Justice JACKSON took no part in the consideration of the case.

Justice BLACK delivered the following opinion.

. . . I believe that the Federal Constitution leaves to each State, without any "ifs" or "buts," a power to tax and to open the doors of its courts for its citizens to sue corporations whose agents do business in those States. Believing that the Constitution gave the States that power, I think it a judicial deprivation to condition its exercise upon this Court's notion of "fair play," however appealing that term may be. Nor can I stretch the meaning of due process so far as to authorize this Court to deprive a State of the right to afford judicial protection to its citizens on the ground that it would be more "convenient" for the corporation to be sued somewhere else.

There is a strong emotional appeal in the words "fair play," "justice," and "reasonableness." But they were not chosen by those who wrote the original Constitution or the Fourteenth Amendment as a measuring rod for this Court to use in invalidating State or Federal laws passed by elected legislative representatives. No one, not even those who most feared a democratic government, ever formally proposed that courts should be given power to invalidate legislation under any such elastic standards. . . . For application of this natural law concept, whether under the terms "reasonableness," "justice," or "fair play," makes judges the supreme arbiters of the country's laws and practices. This result, I believe, alters the form of government our Constitution provides. I cannot agree.

Comments and Questions

1. Consider how the International Shoe Co. structured its business practices in the years before the Supreme Court's decision. No offices or inventory were maintained outside Missouri. Sales representatives had no authority to enter into contracts in the states in which they worked—they merely solicited orders and transmitted them back to headquarters in St. Louis. Product was sent F.O.B. St. Louis, which meant in effect that customers took possession at the point of shipment, thus avoiding the appearance of deliveries beyond the borders of Missouri. The only items belonging to International Shoe Co. that could be found outside Missouri were the single shoe samples that the sales reps displayed to potential purchasers.

Given the state of doctrine regarding the exercise of jurisdiction prior to the *International Shoe* decision, can you see why the Company's business was structured this way? What went wrong with this strategy to avoid suits in other states?

2. Reconstruct the line of the arguments presented by the parties before the Supreme Court in *International Shoe.*

3. What is the basis set forth by the Court for the exercise of jurisdiction over the defendant corporation? How would you articulate the new doctrine of personal jurisdiction? What (if anything) is left of the *Pennoyer* rules? What has happened to the concept of "presence"?

4. Under Chief Justice Stone's formulation, what is the link between the nonresident defendant's level of activity in the forum state and the relation of the plaintiff's claim to that activity? Consider the following diagram:

Level of Activity	Single Act	Mid-Range	Continuous, Substantial, Systematic
Relation to Claim	Only Related Claims	Only Related Claims	All Claims, Related or Not

What policy considerations would draw the Court to focus on these two variables?

5. In which category on the diagram did Chief Justice Stone place the defendant in *International Shoe*? Was it necessary to decide whether the defendant fell in the Mid-Range or the Continuous, Substantial, and Systematic category? Why or why not?

6. In which category on the diagram would you place *Hess v. Pawloski*? Can you find a place on the diagram for *Pennoyer* and *Harris v. Balk*? Or do those exercises of jurisdiction fall outside Chief Justice Stone's categories because they were not *in personam*? We will return to this question in *Shaffer v. Heitner, infra.*

7. If the claim asserted against the company arose from a collision between an International Shoe truck and a citizen of Washington that occurred in California, would the state court in Washington have jurisdiction?

8. Can you articulate the benefit / burden rationale that underlies Chief Justice Stone's theory of personal jurisdiction? Subsequent decisions will return to this rationale much more explicitly.

9. Employing between eleven and thirteen sales representatives in Washington state who generate total commissions of $31,000 per year was deemed sufficient minimum contacts for suit against the employer on the State's unemployment compensation fund claim. Would six sales reps have sufficed? Three? What about *no* sales reps, but instead a catalogue operation run out of state?

Note the Court's admonition that the minimum contacts analysis "cannot be simply mechanical or quantitative." Whether due process standards are met "must depend rather upon the quality and nature of the activity in relation to the fair and orderly administration of the laws which it was the purpose of the due process clause to insure."

10. One court has admonished regarding *International Shoe*:

> This rule of law has been truncated in the minds and jargon of lawyers to "minimum contact"; however, minimum contact does not mean "minimum" or "slight" contact. Minimum contact requires that a foreign defendant have at least enough contact with [the forum] to satisfy minimum standards of due process.

Leonard v. USA Petroleum Corp., 829 F. Supp. 882 (S.D. Tex. 1993).

11. What does Justice Black think of terms like "fair play" and "reasonableness" as the measuring rods for analysis of adjudicatory power? What standard would he substitute?

12. One writer has observed:

> The idea of black letter law seduces us. We crave coherence and certainty in the law as we do in many areas of our lives. We know better, of course. We know that legal doctrine is often indeterminate—that in a particular case, perfectly convincing arguments supporting one conclusion can often be countered by perfectly convincing arguments supporting the opposite conclusion.

Yet we continue to search for rules, principles, tests, approaches—anything that will impose order on doctrine. Nowhere is the inherent frustration of this quest more vividly illustrated than in the debates concerning the due process limitations on the assertion of personal jurisdiction by state courts.

Richard K. Greenstein, *The Nature of Legal Argument: The Personal Jurisdiction Paradigm*, 38 Hastings. L.J. 855 (1987).

E. NOTE ON LONG-ARM STATUTES

International Shoe established a constitutional basis for the exercise of personal jurisdiction that focused on the nonresident's* activities or contacts within the forum state. Constitutional power is not, however, self-executing. A court must first be authorized by appropriate legislation to assert jurisdiction (look back at the Code of Oregon in *Pennoyer* and §14(c) of the Washington Statutes in *International Shoe*). Only then is the minimum-contacts analysis used to determine whether the particular assertion is permissible within the limits of due process.

In the years following the Court's decision in *International Shoe*, many states enacted "long-arm statutes," which authorized their courts to exercise jurisdiction over nonresidents who engaged in certain enumerated acts within the state. Typical among them is the New York statute which reads as follows:

> NY CPLR §302. Personal jurisdiction by acts of non-domiciliaries
>
> (a) Acts which are the basis of jurisdiction. As to a cause of action arising from any of the acts enumerated in this section, a court may exercise personal jurisdiction over any non-domiciliary, or his executor or administrator, who in person or through an agent:
>
> 1. transacts any business within the state or contracts anywhere to supply goods or services in the state; or
>
> 2. commits a tortious act within the state, except as to a cause of action for defamation of character arising from the act; or
>
> 3. commits a tortious act without the state causing injury to person or property within the state, except as to a cause of action for defamation of character arising from the act, if he
>
>> (i) regularly does or solicits business, or engages in any other persistent course of conduct, or derives substantial revenue from goods used or consumed or services rendered, in the state, or
>>
>> (ii) expects or should reasonably expect the act to have consequences in the state and derives substantial revenue from interstate or international commerce; or
>
> 4. owns, uses or possesses any real property situated within the state.

---

*Although *International Shoe* involved a corporate defendant, we will see that the minimum contacts analysis was soon applied to individual defendants as well.

Note that the jurisdiction authorized by the long-arm statute is limited to claims arising out of the enumerated act. (Look back at Chief Justice Stone's constitutional analysis in *International Shoe* to see why this is so.) In *Crocker v. Hilton International Barbados, Ltd.*, 976 F.2d 797 (1st Cir. 1992), for example, where the plaintiff alleged that her rape resulted from negligent security at the Barbados hotel, the court affirmed dismissal of the complaint for lack of personal jurisdiction in Massachusetts. The plaintiff premised jurisdiction on the facts that she had booked the room through a travel agency in the state and that the parent company, Hilton International, had advertised the Barbados hotel in Massachusetts. It is not enough, the court observed, that a defendant transacts business in the state within the meaning of the long-arm statute; the "crucial question to be answered" is whether plaintiff's claim "*arose out of*" this activity, and the court held here that it did not. For a discussion of the concept of "relatedness" between the claim and defendant's activities, *see* Lea Brilmayer, *Related Contacts and Personal Jurisdiction*, 101 Harv. L. Rev. 1444 (1988); Mary Twitchell, *A Rejoinder to Professor Brilmayer*, 101 Harv. L. Rev 1465 (1988).

Regarding notice of the lawsuit, long-arm statutes usually provide for some form of substituted service (that is, other than personal in-hand service), such as service by mail.

Determining whether a court may assert jurisdiction over a nonresident pursuant to a long-arm statute requires a two-step inquiry: (1) Does the statute apply to the particular case? (2) If so, does it reach beyond the constitutional constraints of *International Shoe*'s minimum-contacts analysis? The first question is one of statutory construction; the second involves the substantial body of case law that has developed since 1945, to be explored below.

Some states have instead adopted an open-ended statutory approach: "A court of this state may exercise jurisdiction on any basis not inconsistent with the Constitution of this state or of the United States." Cal. Code Civ. Proc. §410.10.* This effectively collapses the usual two-step inquiry (statutory authority and constitutionality of application) into one.

---

*The Rhode Island statute similarly provides:

Every foreign corporation, every individual not a resident of this state or his executor or administrator, and every partnership or association, composed of any person or persons, not such residents, that shall have the necessary minimum contacts with the state of Rhode Island, shall be subject to the jurisdiction of the state of Rhode Island, and the courts of this state shall hold such foreign corporations and such nonresident individuals or their executors or administrators, and such partnerships or associations amenable to suit in Rhode Island in every case not contrary to the provisions of the constitution or laws of the United States. R.I. St. 9-5-33.

F. NOTE ON SPECIFIC AS COMPARED TO GENERAL JURISDICTION

Long-arm statutes do not supplant the traditional grounds for *in personam* jurisdiction, namely domicile, incorporation in the forum state, service of process on the defendant in the state, appearance in court, and consent. Rather, they supplement those bases by implementing the authority recognized in *International Shoe* to reach nonresidents who, falling outside the traditional categories, engage in specific activities in the state that give rise to the plaintiff's claim. The *specific jurisdiction* authorized by long-arm statutes is distinct from *general jurisdiction*, which is power over *all* claims, whether related to defendant's activities within the forum state or not. General jurisdiction derives from the traditional bases of jurisdiction noted above, as well as from the conduct of such systematic, continuous and substantial business that (in the words of *International Shoe*) it would not be unfair to bind the defendant, even though the claim asserted does not arise from anything defendant did in the forum.

An example of the latter basis for adjudicatory power is *Perkins v. Benguet Consolidated Mining Co.*, 342 U.S. 437 (1952), where the Court held that an Ohio state court could properly exercise jurisdiction over a Philippine corporation on a stockholder's claim, even though it did not arise from or relate to anything the defendant did in Ohio. The mining company had halted operations and temporarily relocated its president in Ohio for the duration of the Japanese military occupation of the Philippine Islands. At his office in Ohio, the president maintained the company files, carried on correspondence, drew salary checks, maintained a bank account, and held director's meetings — in short, he carried on "a continuous and systematic supervision of the necessarily limited wartime activities of the company." It would not, therefore, violate due process for Ohio to assert jurisdiction over the company on the plaintiff's "unrelated" claim for dividends. We will have more to say about general jurisdiction later in this chapter.

Representing the opposite end of the activity spectrum is *McGee v. International Life Insurance Co.*, 355 U.S. 220 (1957). There, the defendant had no office or agent in the forum state of California and, indeed, had not (as far as the record indicated) ever solicited or done any insurance business there except for the one policy that was sued upon by the beneficiary McGee. The California court exercised specific jurisdiction based on a statute subjecting nonresident corporations to suit on insurance contracts entered into with residents of the state. The plaintiff recovered a default judgment, which she sought to collect in Texas, the defendant's home state. The Texas courts refused to enforce the judgment, however, holding that it was not entitled to full faith and credit because the California court lacked jurisdiction over International Life Ins. Co. The Supreme Court reversed in a decision authored by Justice Black, who noted a "clearly discernible trend" toward expanding the scope of jurisdiction over nonresident corporations and individuals. Black attributed this to

> the fundamental transformation of our national economy over the years. Today many commercial transactions touch two or more States and may involve parties separated by the full continent. With this increasing nationalization of commerce has come a great increase in the amount of business conducted by mail across state lines. At the same time modern transportation and communication have made it much less burdensome for a party sued to defend himself in a State where he engages in economic activity.

Id. at 222-23.

Reflecting the high-water mark of specific jurisdiction, the *McGee* Court concluded that the Due Process Clause did not preclude the California court from entering a judgment binding on the Texas insurance company.

> It is sufficient for purposes of due process that the suit was based on a contract that had substantial connection with that state. The contract was delivered in California, the premiums were mailed from there, and the insured was a resident of that state when he died. It cannot be denied that California has a manifest interest in providing effective means of redress for its residents when their insurers refuse to pay claims. These residents would be at a severe disadvantage if they were forced to follow the insurance company to a distant state in order to hold it legally accountable. When claims were small or moderate, individual claimants frequently could not afford the cost of bringing an action in a foreign forum—thus in effect making the company judgment-proof. Often the crucial witnesses—as here on the company's defense of suicide—will be found in the insured's locality. Of course, there may be inconvenience to the insurer if it is held amenable to suit in California, where it had this contract, but certainly nothing that amounts to a denial of due process. There is no contention that respondent did not have adequate notice or sufficient time to prepare its defenses and appear.

355 U.S. at 222-24.

Can you find a foreshadowing of this approach to personal jurisdiction in Justice Black's dissent in *International Shoe?* Is the issue of personal jurisdiction purely technical and procedural? What social policy considerations entered into Justice Black's elaboration of due process doctrine? Does *McGee* suggest that personal jurisdiction may exist when small- or moderate-income plaintiffs are suing a large corporate defendant, but not in the reverse situation?

As you read the remaining cases, consider Justice Black's observation of a "clearly discernible trend" toward expanding specific jurisdiction. As in other fields, prediction of legal trends can be quite risky.

G. NOTE ON PERSONAL JURISDICTION IN FEDERAL COURT

A common source of confusion for civil procedure students is the issue of personal jurisdiction in federal court. Given the focus on *state* sovereignty and *state* boundaries in *Pennoyer* and *International Shoe*, together with the fact that the Fourteenth Amendment Due Process Clause limits only *state* power,* one might assume that a *federal* trial court would not be limited by state geography in its personal jurisdiction reach. This assumption would, however, be in error. Although it is true that there are no *constitutional* constraints on a federal court's exercise of jurisdiction over a defendant found anywhere within the national boundaries, Congress and the Supreme Court have chosen not to give the federal courts the full extent of their potential jurisdictional power.

The vehicle controlling personal jurisdiction in federal court is Fed. R. Civ. P. 4, which on its face seems only to deal with service of process. But look at 4(k)(1)(A), which effectively incorporates the territorial limits of the courts of the state in which the federal district is located, that is, the state long-arm statute (as constrained by the minimum-contacts test). The jurisdictional reach of a federal district court in Ohio is, in other words, determined by and equivalent to the reach of the state trial courts there. (If the federal courts offered plaintiffs a longer reach than state courts, consider the incentives for forum shopping that would be created.)

There are some notable exceptions to the equation of federal and state personal jurisdiction. Look at Fed. R. Civ. P. 4(k)(1)(B) (the so-called 100-mile bulge rule) and (C) (providing for nationwide service in federal interpleader actions in order to facilitate a single litigation among competing claimants to a property or fund). More dramatically, 4(k)(2) (added by amendment in 1993) extends federal power to its outermost constitutional limits in federal claims cases. Can you think of a situation where that rule would apply to "establish personal jurisdiction over the person of any defendant who is not subject to the jurisdiction of the courts of general jurisdiction of any state?" *See* the Advisory Committee Notes to the 1993 Amendments.

H. MINIMUM-CONTACTS ANALYSIS IN OPERATION

The *International Shoe* formulation of the "minimum contacts" test (like most legal doctrine in its initial stages) left many unanswered

---

* The Fifth Amendment contains a due process clause limiting federal power, but the appropriate territorial borders would be national.

questions and considerable room for analytical development by courts in the face of live cases.

One of the early and most important elaborations came in *Hanson v. Denkla,* 357 U.S. 235 (1958). While residing in Pennsylvania, Dora Donner established a trust with the Wilmington Trust Co. of Delaware as trustee. She retained the right to receive the income from the trust until her death and to designate the beneficiaries who would ultimately get the substantial assets. Donner later moved to Florida, where she designated the children of one of her three daughters to receive $400,000 from the trust upon her death. She died a resident of Florida. The two daughters whose children were not provided for filed suit in Florida challenging the disposition of the trust. The court exercised jurisdiction over the Delaware trustee, an indispensable party to the action, and invalidated the trust on the technical grounds that Donner had retained too much control over it during her life. When the Florida decree was sought to be enforced against the trustee in Delaware, however, the courts of that state ruled that it was not entitled to full faith and credit because the Florida court had neither *in personam* jurisdiction over the Delaware trustee, nor *in rem* jurisdiction over the assets of the trust, which were located in Delaware. The United States Supreme Court agreed:

> [The parties seeking to enforce the Florida decree] urge that the circumstances of this case amount to sufficient affiliation with the State of Florida to empower its courts to exercise personal jurisdiction over this nonresident defendant. Principal reliance is placed upon *McGee v. International Life Ins. Co.* In *McGee* the Court noted the trend of expanding personal jurisdiction over nonresidents. As technological progress has increased the flow of commerce between States, the need for jurisdiction over nonresidents has undergone a similar increase. At the same time, progress in communications and transportation has made the defense of a suit in a foreign tribunal less burdensome. In response to these changes, the requirements for personal jurisdiction over nonresidents have evolved from the rigid rule of *Pennoyer v. Neff* to the flexible standard of *International Shoe Co. v. State of Washington.* But it is a mistake to assume that this trend heralds the eventual demise of all restrictions on the personal jurisdiction of state courts. Those restrictions are more than a guarantee of immunity from inconvenient or distant litigation. They are a consequence of territorial limitations on the power of the respective States. However minimal the burden of defending in a foreign tribunal, a defendant may not be called upon to do so unless he has had the "minimal contacts" with that State that are a prerequisite to its exercise of power over him.
>
> We fail to find such contacts in the circumstances of this case. The defendant trust company has no office in Florida, and transacts no business there. None of the trust assets has ever been held or administered in Florida, and the record discloses no solicitation of business in that State either in person or by mail.
>
> The cause of action in this case is not one that arises out of an act done or transaction consummated in the forum State. In that respect, it differs

from *McGee v. International Life Ins. Co.* In *McGee*, the nonresident defendant solicited a reinsurance agreement with a resident of California. The offer was accepted in that State, and the insurance premiums were mailed from there until the insured's death. Noting the interest California has in providing effective redress for its residents when nonresident insurers refuse to pay claims on insurance they have solicited in that State, the Court upheld jurisdiction because the suit was based on a contract which had substantial connection with that State. In contrast, this action involves the validity of an agreement that was entered without any connection with the forum State. The agreement was executed in Delaware by a trust company incorporated in that State and a settlor domiciled in Pennsylvania. The first relationship Florida had to the agreement was years later when the settlor became domiciled there, and the trustee remitted the trust income to her in that State. From Florida Mrs. Donner carried on several bits of trust administration that may be compared to the mailing of premiums in *McGee*. But the record discloses no instance in which the trustee performed any acts in Florida that bear the same relationship to the agreement as the solicitation in *McGee*. Consequently, this suit cannot be said to be one to enforce an obligation that arose from a privilege the defendant exercised in Florida.

357 U.S. at 250-52.

The Court went on to emphasize that the "unilateral activity of those who claim some relationship with a nonresident defendant cannot satisfy the requirement of contact with the forum State. The application of that rule will vary with the quality and nature of the defendant's activity, but it is essential in each case that there be some act by which the defendant purposefully avails itself of the privilege of conducting activities within the forum State, thus invoking the benefits and protections of its laws." 357 U.S. at 253. This "purposeful availment" gloss on the minimum-contacts analysis will prove to be a crucial constraint in many cases, such as *World-Wide Volkswagen Corp. v. Woodson*, which follows below. *See also Leonard v. USA Petroleum Corp.*, 829 F. Supp. 882 (S.D. Tex. 1993) ("It is USA Petroleum's own acts, not the acts of [plaintiff, a Texas resident who claimed he was owed a commission on an oral contract because while he was in Texas he located and produced a buyer for defendant's service stations in Puerto Rico], that establish the jurisdictional minimum contact with a state. To be subject to jurisdiction in Texas, USA Petroleum must itself have acted to establish meaningful contact with the state. . . . [A]ll of the acts [plaintiff] describes were done on his own initiative.")

Are you persuaded by the *Hanson* Court's attempt to distinguish *McGee*? Was the Wilmington Trust Co. really less connected to Florida than International Life Insurance Co. was to California? If not, what could explain the dramatic difference in result between the two cases—decided within a year of each other? Perhaps part of the explanation lies in the implications of enforcing the Florida judgment. The Court noted that the two daughters who successfully challenged the disposition of the trust to their sister's children were "already [themselves] the recipients of over $500,000 each [from their mother's will]." 357 U.S. at 240.

What happened to the trend, observed by Justice Black, toward liberalizing the restrictions on personal jurisdiction? What trend does the next case reflect?

■ WORLD-WIDE VOLKSWAGEN CORP. v. WOODSON
444 U.S. 286 (1980)

Justice WHITE delivered the opinion of the Court:

The issue before us is whether, consistently with the Due Process Clause of the Fourteenth Amendment, an Oklahoma court may exercise in personam jurisdiction over a nonresident automobile retailer and its wholesale distributor in a products-liability action, when the defendants' only connection with Oklahoma is the fact that an automobile sold in New York to New York residents became involved in an accident in Oklahoma.

I

Respondents Harry and Kay Robinson purchased a new Audi automobile from petitioner Seaway Volkswagen, Inc. (Seaway), in Massena, N.Y., in 1976. The following year the Robinson family, who resided in New York, left that State for a new home in Arizona. As they passed through the State of Oklahoma, another car struck their Audi in the rear, causing a fire which severely burned Kay Robinson and her two children.[1]

The Robinsons subsequently brought a products-liability action in the District Court for Creek County, Okla., claiming that their injuries resulted from defective design and placement of the Audi's gas tank and fuel system. They joined as defendants the automobile's manufacturer, Audi NSU Auto Union Aktiengesellschaft (Audi); its importer Volkswagen of America, Inc. (Volkswagen); its regional distributor, petitioner World-Wide Volkswagen Corp. (World-Wide); and its retail dealer, petitioner Seaway. Seaway and World-Wide entered special appearances,[3] claiming that Oklahoma's exercise of jurisdiction over them would offend the limitations on the State's jurisdiction imposed by the Due Process Clause of the Fourteenth Amendment.

The facts presented to the District Court showed that World-Wide is incorporated and has its business office in New York. It distributes

---

1. The driver of the other automobile does not figure in the present litigation.

3. Volkswagen also entered a special appearance in the District Court, but unlike World-Wide and Seaway did not seek review in the Supreme Court of Oklahoma and is not a petitioner here. Both Volkswagen and Audi remain as defendants in the litigation pending before the District Court in Oklahoma.

vehicles, parts, and accessories, under contract with Volkswagen, to retail dealers in New York, New Jersey, and Connecticut. Seaway, one of these retail dealers, is incorporated and has its place of business in New York. Insofar as the record reveals, Seaway and World-Wide are fully independent corporations whose relations with each other and with Volkswagen and Audi are contractual only. Respondents adduced no evidence that either World-Wide or Seaway does any business in Oklahoma, ships or sells any products to or in that State, has an agent to receive process there, or purchases advertisements in any media calculated to reach Oklahoma. In fact, as respondents' counsel conceded at oral argument, there was no showing that any automobile sold by World-Wide or Seaway has ever entered Oklahoma with the single exception of the vehicle involved in the present case.

Despite the apparent paucity of contacts between petitioners and Oklahoma, the District Court rejected their constitutional claim and reaffirmed that ruling in denying petitioners' motion for reconsideration. Petitioners then sought a writ of prohibition in the Supreme Court of Oklahoma to restrain the District Judge, respondent Charles S. Woodson, from exercising in personam jurisdiction over them. They renewed their contention that, because they had no "minimal contacts," with the State of Oklahoma, the actions of the District Judge were in violation of their rights under the Due Process Clause.

The Supreme Court of Oklahoma denied the writ, holding that personal jurisdiction over petitioners was authorized by Oklahoma's "long-arm" statute Okla. Stat., Tit. 12, §1701.03(a)(4) (1971).[7] Although the court noted that the proper approach was to test jurisdiction against both statutory and constitutional standards, its analysis did not distinguish these questions, probably because §1701.03(a)(4) has been interpreted as conferring jurisdiction to the limits permitted by the United States Constitution. The court's rationale was contained in the following paragraph:

> In the case before us, the product being sold and distributed by the petitioners is by its very design and purpose so mobile that petitioners can foresee its possible use in Oklahoma. This is especially true of the distributor, who has the exclusive right to distribute such automobile in New York, New Jersey and Connecticut. The evidence presented below demonstrated that goods sold and distributed by the petitioners were used in the State of

---

7. This subsection provides: "A court may exercise personal jurisdiction over a person, who acts directly or by an agent, as to a cause of action or claim for relief arising from the person's . . . causing tortious injury in this state by an act or omission outside this state if he regularly does or solicits business or engages in any other persistent course of conduct, or derives substantial revenue from goods used or consumed or services rendered, in this state . . ." The State Supreme Court rejected jurisdiction based on §1701.03(a)(3), which authorizes jurisdiction over any person "causing tortious injury in this state by an act or omission in this state." Something in addition to the infliction of tortious injury was required.

Oklahoma, and under the facts we believe it reasonable to infer, given the retail value of the automobile, that the petitioners derive substantial income from automobiles which from time to time are used in the State of Oklahoma. This being the case, we hold that under the facts presented, the trial court was justified in concluding that the petitioners derive substantial revenue from goods used or consumed in this State.

We granted certiorari to consider an important constitutional question with respect to state-court jurisdiction and to resolve a conflict between the Supreme Court of Oklahoma and the highest courts of at least four other States. We reverse.

II

The Due Process Clause of the Fourteenth Amendment limits the power of a state court to render a valid personal judgment against a nonresident defendant. A judgment rendered in violation of due process is void in the rendering State and is not entitled to full faith and credit elsewhere. *Pennoyer v. Neff,* 95 U.S. 714, 732-733 (1878). Due process requires that the defendant be given adequate notice of the suit, *Mullane v. Central Hanover Trust Co.,* 339 U.S. 306, 313-314 (1950), and be subject to the personal jurisdiction of the court, *International Shoe Co. v. Washington,* 326 U.S. 310 (1945). In the present case, it is not contended that notice was inadequate; the only question is whether these particular petitioners were subject to the jurisdiction of the Oklahoma courts.

As has long been settled, and as we reaffirm today, a state court may exercise personal jurisdiction over a nonresident defendant only so long as there exist "minimum contacts" between the defendant and the forum State. *International Shoe Co. v. Washington, supra,* at 316. The concept of minimum contacts, in turn, can be seen to perform two related, but distinguishable, functions. It protects the defendant against the burdens of litigating in a distant or inconvenient forum. And it acts to ensure that the States through their courts, do not reach out beyond the limits imposed on them by their status as coequal sovereigns in a federal system.

The protection against inconvenient litigation is typically described in terms of "reasonableness" or "fairness." We have said that the defendant's contacts with the forum State must be such that maintenance of the suit "does not offend 'traditional notions of fair play and substantial justice.'" *International Shoe Co. v. Washington, supra,* at 316, *quoting Milliken v. Meyer,* 311 U.S. 457, 463 (1940). The relationship between the defendant and the forum must be such that it is "reasonable . . . to require the corporation to defend the particular suit which is brought there." 326 U.S. at 317. Implicit in this emphasis on reasonableness is the understanding that the burden on the defendant, while always a primary concern, will in an appropriate case be considered in light of other relevant factors, including the forum State's interest in adjudicating the dispute, *see McGee v. International Life Ins. Co.*, 355 U.S. 220, 223 (1957); the plaintiff's interest in obtaining convenient and effective relief, *see Kulko v. California Superior Court* [436 U.S. 84, 92 (1978)], at least when that interest is not adequately protected by the plaintiff's power to choose the forum, *cf. Shaffer v. Heitner*, 433 U.S. 186, 211, n.37 (1977); the interstate judicial system's interest in obtaining the most efficient resolution of controversies; and the shared interest of the several States in furthering fundamental substantive social policies, *see Kulko v. California Superior Court, supra*, 436 U.S. at 93, 98.

The limits imposed on state jurisdiction by the Due Process Clause, in its role as a guarantor against inconvenient litigation, have been substantially relaxed over the years. As we noted in *McGee v. International Life Ins. Co.* [355 U.S. 220, 222-23 (1957)], this trend is largely attributable to a fundamental transformation in the American economy: "Today many commercial transactions touch two or more States and may involve parties separated by the full continent. With this increasing nationalization of commerce has come a great increase in the amount of business conducted by mail across state lines. At the same time modern transportation and communication have made it much less burdensome for a party sued to defend himself in a State where he engages in economic activity." The historical developments noted in *McGee*, of course, have only accelerated in the generation since that case was decided.

Nevertheless, we have never accepted the proposition that state lines are irrelevant for jurisdictional purposes, nor could we, and remain faithful to the principles of interstate federalism embodied in the Constitution. The economic interdependence of the States was foreseen and desired by the Framers. In the Commerce Clause, they provided that the Nation was to be a common market, a "free trade unit" in which the States are debarred from acting as separable economic entities. But the Framers also intended that the States retain many essential attributes of sovereignty, including, in particular, the sovereign power to try causes in their courts. The sovereignty of each State, in turn, implied a limitation on the sovereignty of all of its sister States—a limitation express or implicit in both the original scheme of the Constitution and the Fourteenth Amendment.

Hence, even while abandoning the shibboleth that "[t]he authority of every tribunal is necessarily restricted by the territorial limits of the State in which it is established," *Pennoyer v. Neff, supra*, 95 U.S. at 720, we emphasized that the reasonableness of asserting jurisdiction over the defendant must be assessed "in the context of our federal system of government," *International Shoe Co. v. Washington*, 326 U.S. at 317, and stressed that the Due Process Clause ensures not only fairness, but also the "orderly administration of the laws," *id.*, at 319. As we noted in *Hanson v. Denckla*, 357 U.S. 235, 250-251 (1958): "As technological progress has increased the flow of commerce between the States, the need for jurisdiction over nonresidents has undergone a similar increase. At the same time, progress in communications and transportation has made the defense of a suit in a foreign tribunal less burdensome. In response to these changes, the requirements for personal jurisdiction over nonresidents have evolved from the rigid rule of *Pennoyer v. Neff*, 95 U.S. 714, to the flexible standard of *International Shoe Co. v. Washington*, 326 U.S. 310. But it is a mistake to assume that this trend heralds the eventual demise of all restrictions on the personal jurisdiction of state courts. Those restrictions are more than a guarantee of immunity from inconvenient or distant litigation. They are a consequence of territorial limitations on the power of the respective States."

Thus, the Due Process Clause "does not contemplate that a state may make binding a judgment in personam against an individual or corporate defendant with which the state has no contacts, ties, or relations." *International Shoe Co. v. Washington*, 326 U.S. at 319. Even if the defendant would suffer minimal or no inconvenience from being forced to litigate before the tribunals of another State; even if the forum State has a strong interest in applying its law to the controversy; even if the forum State is the most convenient location for litigation, the Due Process Clause, acting as an instrument of interstate federalism, may sometimes act to divest the State of its power to render a valid judgment. *Hanson v. Denckla, supra*, 357 U.S. at 251, 254.

III

Applying these principles to the case at hand, we find in the record before us a total absence of those affiliating circumstances that are a necessary predicate to any exercise of state-court jurisdiction. Petitioners carry on no activity whatsoever in Oklahoma. They close no sales and perform no services there. They avail themselves of none of the privileges and benefits of Oklahoma law. They solicit no business there either through salespersons or through advertising reasonably calculated to reach the State. Nor does the record show that they regularly sell cars at wholesale or retail to Oklahoma customers or residents or that they indirectly, through others, serve or seek to serve the Oklahoma market. In short, respondents seek to base jurisdiction on one, isolated occurrence and whatever inferences can be drawn therefrom: the fortuitous circumstance that a single Audi automobile, sold in New York to New York residents, happened to suffer an accident while passing through Oklahoma.

It is argued, however, that because an automobile is mobile by its very design and purpose it was "foreseeable" that the Robinsons' Audi would cause injury in Oklahoma. Yet "foreseeability" alone has never been a sufficient benchmark for personal jurisdiction under the Due Process Clause. In *Hanson v. Denckla, supra*, it was no doubt foreseeable that the settlor of a Delaware trust would subsequently move to Florida and seek to exercise a power of appointment there; yet we held that Florida courts could not constitutionally exercise jurisdiction over a Delaware trustee that had no other contacts with the forum State. In *Kulko v. California Superior Court,* 436 U.S. 84 (1978), it was surely "foreseeable" that a divorced wife would move to California from New York, the domicile of the marriage, and that a minor daughter would live with the mother. Yet we held that California could not exercise jurisdiction in a child-support action over the former husband who had remained in New York.

If foreseeability were the criterion, a local California tire retailer could be forced to defend in Pennsylvania when a blowout occurs there, *see Erlanger Mills, Inc. v. Cohoes Fibre Mills, Inc.,* 239 F.2d 502, 507 (4th Cir. 1956); a Wisconsin seller of a defective automobile jack could be haled before a distant court for damage caused in New Jersey, *Reilly v. Phil Tolkan Pontiac, Inc.,* 372 F. Supp. 1205 (N.J. 1974); or a Florida soft-drink concessionaire could be summoned to Alaska to account for injuries happening there, *see Uppgren v. Executive Aviation Services, Inc.,* 304 F. Supp. 165, 170-171 (Minn. 1969). Every seller of chattels would in effect appoint the chattel his agent for service of process. His amenability to suit would travel with the chattel. We recently abandoned the outworn rule of *Harris v. Balk,* 198 U.S. 215 (1905), that the interest of a creditor in a debt could be extinguished or otherwise affected by any State having transitory jurisdiction over the debtor. *Shaffer v. Heitner,* 433 U.S. 186 (1977). Having interred [*sic*] the mechanical rule that a creditor's amenability to a quasi in rem action travels with his debtor, we are unwilling to endorse an analogous principle in the present case.

This is not to say, of course, that foreseeability is wholly irrelevant. But the foreseeability that is critical to due process analysis is not the mere likelihood that a product will find its way into the forum State. Rather, it is that the defendant's conduct and connection with the forum State are such that he should reasonably anticipate being haled into court there. *See Kulko v. California Superior Court, supra,* 436 U.S. at 97-98; *Shaffer v. Heitner,* 433 U.S. at 216, and *see id.* at 217-219 (Stevens, J., concurring in judgment). The Due Process Clause, by ensuring the "orderly administration of the laws," *International Shoe Co. v. Washington,* 326 U.S. at 319, gives a degree of predictability to the legal system that allows potential defendants to structure their primary conduct with some minimum assurance as to where that conduct will and will not render them liable to suit.

When a corporation "purposefully avails itself of the privilege of conducting activities within the forum State," *Hanson v. Denckla,* 357 U.S. at 253, it has clear notice that it is subject to suit there, and can act to alleviate the risk of burdensome litigation by procuring insurance, passing the expected costs on to customers, or, if the risks are too great, severing its connection with the State. Hence if the sale of a product of a manufacturer or distributor such as Audi or Volkswagen is not simply an isolated occurrence, but arises from the efforts of the manufacturer or distributor to serve directly or indirectly, the market for its product in other States, it is not unreasonable to subject it to suit in one of those States if its allegedly defective merchandise has there been the source of injury to its owner or to others. The forum State does not exceed its powers under the Due Process Clause if it asserts personal jurisdiction over a corporation that delivers its products into the stream of commerce with the expectation that they will be purchased by consumers in the forum State. *Cf. Gray v. American Radiator & Standard Sanitary Corp.*, 22 Ill. 2d 432 (1961).

But there is no such or similar basis for Oklahoma jurisdiction over World-Wide or Seaway in this case. Seaway's sales are made in Massena, N.Y. World-Wide's market, although substantially larger, is limited to dealers in New York, New Jersey, and Connecticut. There is no evidence of record that any automobiles distributed by World-Wide are sold to retail customers outside this tristate area. It is foreseeable that the purchasers of automobiles sold by World-Wide and Seaway may take them to Oklahoma. But the mere "unilateral activity of those who claim some relationship with a nonresident defendant cannot satisfy the requirement of contact with the forum State." *Hanson v. Denckla, supra*, at 253.

In a variant on the previous argument, it is contended that jurisdiction can be supported by the fact that petitioners earn substantial revenue from goods used in Oklahoma. The Oklahoma Supreme Court so found, 585 P.2d at 354-355, drawing the inference that because one automobile sold by petitioners had been used in Oklahoma, others might have been used there also. While this inference seems less than compelling on the facts of the instant case, we need not question the court's factual findings in order to reject its reasoning.

This argument seems to make the point that the purchase of automobiles in New York, from which the petitioners earn substantial revenue, would not occur but for the fact that the automobiles are capable of use in distant States like Oklahoma. Respondents observe that the very purpose of an automobile is to travel, and that travel of automobiles sold by petitioners is facilitated by an extensive chain of Volkswagen service centers throughout the country, including some in Oklahoma. However, financial benefits accruing to the defendant from a collateral relation to the forum State will not support jurisdiction if they do not stem from a constitutionally cognizable contact with that State. *See Kulko v. California Superior Court*, 436 U.S. at 94-95. In our view, whatever marginal revenues petitioners may receive by virtue of the fact that their products are capable of use in Oklahoma is far too attenuated a contact to justify that State's exercise of in personam jurisdiction over them.

Because we find that petitioners have no "contacts, ties, or relations" with the State of Oklahoma, *International Shoe Co. v. Washington, supra*, 326 U.S. at 319, the judgment of the Supreme Court of Oklahoma is Reversed.

Justice BRENNAN, dissenting:

. . . In [this case], I would find that the forum State has an interest in permitting the litigation to go forward, the litigation is connected to the forum, the defendant is linked to the forum, and the burden of defending is not unreasonable. Accordingly, I would hold that it is neither unfair nor unreasonable to require these defendants to defend in the forum State. . . .

The interest of the forum State and its connection to the litigation is strong. The automobile accident underlying the litigation occurred in Oklahoma. The plaintiffs were hospitalized in Oklahoma when they brought suit. Essential witnesses and evidence were in Oklahoma. *See Shaffer v. Heitner*, 433 U.S. at 208. The State has a legitimate interest in enforcing its laws designed to keep its highway system safe, and the trial can proceed at least as efficiently in Oklahoma as anywhere else.

The petitioners are not unconnected with the forum. Although both sell automobiles within limited sales territories, each sold the automobile which in fact was driven to Oklahoma where it was involved in an accident. It may be true, as the Court suggests, that each sincerely intended to limit its commercial impact to the limited territory, and that each intended to accept the benefits and protection of the laws only of those States within the territory. But obviously these were unrealistic hopes that cannot be treated as an automatic constitutional shield.

An automobile simply is not a stationary item or one designed to be used in one place. An automobile is intended to be moved around. Someone in the business of selling large numbers of automobiles can hardly plead ignorance of their mobility or pretend that the automobiles stay put after they are sold. It is not merely that a dealer in automobiles foresees that they will move. 444 U.S. at 295. The dealer actually intends that the purchasers will use the automobiles to travel to distant States where the dealer does not directly "do business." The sale of an automobile does purposefully inject the vehicle into the stream of interstate commerce so that it can travel to distant States. *See Kulko*, 436 U.S. at 94; *Hanson v. Denckla*, 357 U.S. 235, 253 (1958).

. . . The Court accepts that a State may exercise jurisdiction over a distributor which "serves" that State "indirectly" by "deliver[ing] its products into the stream of commerce with the expectation that they will be purchased by consumers in the forum State." 444 U.S. at 297-298. It is difficult to see why the Constitution should distinguish between a case involving goods which reach a distant State through a chain of distribution and a case involving goods which reach the same State because a consumer, using them as the dealer knew the customer would, took them there. In each case the seller purposefully injects the goods into the stream of commerce and those goods predictably are used in the forum State.

Furthermore, an automobile seller derives substantial benefits from States other than its own. A large part of the value of automobiles is the extensive, nationwide network of highways. Significant portions of that network have been constructed by and are maintained by the individual States, including Oklahoma. The States, through their highway programs, contribute in a very direct and important way to the value of petitioners' businesses. Additionally, a network of other related dealerships with their service departments operates throughout the country under the protection of the laws of the various States, including Oklahoma, and enhances the value of petitioners' businesses by facilitating their customers' traveling.

Thus, the Court errs in its conclusion, 444 U.S. at 299, that "petitioners have no 'contacts, ties, or relations'" with Oklahoma. There obviously are contacts, and, given Oklahoma's connection to the litigation, the contacts are sufficiently significant to make it fair and reasonable for the petitioners to submit to Oklahoma's jurisdiction. . . .

The plaintiffs in [this] case brought suit in a forum with which they had significant contacts and which had significant contacts with the litigation. I am not convinced that the defendants would suffer any "heavy and disproportionate burden" in defending the suits. Accordingly, I would hold that the Constitution should not shield the defendants from appearing and defending in the plaintiffs' chosen fora.

Justice MARSHALL, with whom Justice BLACKMUN joins, dissenting:

For over 30 years the standard by which to measure the constitutionally permissible reach of state-court jurisdiction has been well established: "[D]ue process requires only that in order to subject a defendant to a judgment in personam, if he be not present within the territory of the forum, he have certain minimum contacts with it such that the maintenance of the suit does not offend 'traditional notions of fair play and substantial justice.'" *International Shoe Co. v. Washington,* 326 U.S. 310, 316 (1945), *quoting Milliken v. Meyer,* 311 U.S. 457, 463 (1940). The corollary, that the Due Process Clause forbids the assertion of jurisdiction over a defendant "with which the state has no contacts, ties, or relations," 326 U.S. at 319, is equally clear. The concepts of fairness and substantial justice as applied to an evaluation of "the quality and nature of the [defendant's] activity," *ibid.,* are not readily susceptible of further definition, however, and it is not surprising that the constitutional standard is easier to state than to apply.

This is a difficult case, and reasonable minds may differ as to whether respondents have alleged a sufficient "relationship among the defendant[s], the forum, and the litigation," *Shaffer v. Heitner,* 433 U.S. 186 (1977), to satisfy the requirements of *International Shoe.* I am concerned, however, that the majority has reached its result by taking an unnecessarily narrow view of petitioners' forum-related conduct. The majority asserts that "respondents seek to base jurisdiction on one, isolated occurrence and whatever inferences can be drawn therefrom: the fortuitous circumstance that a single Audi automobile, sold in New York to New York residents, happened to suffer an accident while passing through Oklahoma."

Ante, at 566. If that were the case, I would readily agree that the minimum contacts necessary to sustain jurisdiction are not present. But the basis for the assertion of jurisdiction is not the happenstance that an individual over whom petitioner had no control made a unilateral decision to take a chattel with him to a distant State. Rather, jurisdiction is premised on the deliberate and purposeful actions of the defendants themselves in choosing to become part of a nationwide, indeed a global, network for marketing and servicing automobiles.

Petitioners are sellers of a product whose utility derives from its mobility. The unique importance of the automobile in today's society, which is discussed in Mr. Justice Blackmun's dissenting opinion, needs no further elaboration. Petitioners know that their customers buy cars not only to make short trips, but also to travel long distances. In fact, the nationwide service network with which they are affiliated was designed to facilitate and encourage such travel. Seaway would be unlikely to sell many cars if authorized service were available only in Massena, N.Y. Moreover, local dealers normally derive a substantial portion of their revenues from their service operations and thereby obtain a further economic benefit from the opportunity to service cars which were sold in other States. It is apparent that petitioners have not attempted to minimize the chance that their activities will have effects in other States; on the contrary, they have chosen to do business in a way that increases that chance, because it is to their economic advantage to do so.

To be sure, petitioners could not know in advance that this particular automobile would be driven to Oklahoma. They must have anticipated, however, that a substantial portion of the cars they sold would travel out of New York. Seaway, a local dealer in the second most populous State, and World-Wide, one of only seven regional Audi distributors in the entire country, would scarcely have been surprised to learn that a car sold by them had been driven in Oklahoma on Interstate 44, a heavily traveled transcontinental highway. In the case of the distributor, in particular, the probability that some of the cars it sells will be driven in every one of the contiguous States must amount to a virtual certainty. This knowledge should alert a reasonable businessman to the likelihood that a defect in the product might manifest itself in the forum State—not because of some unpredictable, aberrant, unilateral action by a single buyer, but in the normal course of the operation of the vehicles for their intended purpose.

It is misleading for the majority to characterize the argument in favor of jurisdiction as one of "'foreseeability' alone." As economic entities petitioners reach out from New York, knowingly causing effects in other States and receiving economic advantage both from the ability to cause such effects themselves and from the activities of dealers and distributors in other States. While they did not receive revenue from making direct sales in Oklahoma, they intentionally became part of an interstate economic network, which included dealerships in Oklahoma, for pecuniary gain. In light of this purposeful conduct I do not believe it can be said that petitioners "had no reason to expect to be haled before a[n] Oklahoma court." *Shaffer v. Heitner, supra,* 433 U.S. at 216, and *Kulko v. California Superior Court,* 436 U.S. 84, 97-98 (1978).

The majority apparently acknowledges that if a product is purchased in the forum State by a consumer, that State may assert jurisdiction over everyone in the chain of distribution. With this I agree. But I cannot agree that jurisdiction is necessarily lacking if the product enters the State not through the channels of distribution but in the course of its intended use by the consumer. We have recognized the role played by the automobile in the expansion of our notions of personal jurisdiction. *See Shaffer v. Heitner, supra,* 433 U.S. at 204; *Hess v. Pawloski,* 274 U.S. 352 (1927). Unlike most other chattels, which may find their way into States far from where they were purchased because their owner takes them there, the intended use of the automobile is precisely as a means of traveling from one place to another. In such a case, it is highly artificial to restrict the concept of the "stream of commerce" to the chain of distribution from the manufacturer to the ultimate consumer.

I sympathize with the majority's concern that the persons ought to be able to structure their conduct so as not to be subject to suit in distant forums. But that may not always be possible. Some activities by their very nature may foreclose the option of conducting them in such a way as to avoid subjecting oneself to jurisdiction in multiple forums. This is by no means to say that all sellers of automobiles should be subject to suit everywhere; but a distributor of automobiles to a multistate market and a local automobile dealer who makes himself part of a nationwide network of dealerships can fairly expect that the cars they sell may cause injury in distant States and that they may be called on to defend a resulting lawsuit there. . . .

Of course, the Constitution forbids the exercise of jurisdiction if the defendant had no judicially cognizable contacts with the forum. But as the majority acknowledges, if such contacts are present the jurisdictional inquiry requires a balancing of various interests and policies. *Rush v. Savchuk,* 444 U.S. at 332. I believe such contacts are to be found here and that, considering all of the interests and policies at stake, requiring petitioners to defend this action in Oklahoma is not beyond the bounds of the Constitution. Accordingly, I dissent.

Justice BLACKMUN, dissenting:

I confess that I am somewhat puzzled why the plaintiffs in this litigation are so insistent that the regional distributor and the retail dealer, the petitioners here, who handled the ill-fated Audi automobile involved in this litigation, be named defendants. It would appear that the manufacturer and the importer, whose subjectability to Oklahoma jurisdiction is not challenged before this Court, ought not to be judgment-proof. It may, of course, ultimately amount to a contest between insurance companies that, once begun, is not easily brought to a termination. Having made this much of an observation, I pursue it no further.

For me, a critical factor in the disposition of the litigation is the nature of the instrumentality under consideration. It has been said that we are a nation on wheels. What we are concerned with here is the automobile and its peripatetic character. One need only examine our national network of interstate highways, or make an appearance on one of them, or observe the variety of license plates present not only on those highways but in any metropolitan area, to realize that any automobile is likely to wander far from its place of licensure or from its place of distribution and retail sale. Miles per gallon on the highway (as well as in the city) and mileage per tankful are familiar allegations in manufacturers' advertisements today. To expect that any new automobile will remain in the vicinity of its retail sale—like the 1914 electric driven car by the proverbial "little old lady"—is to blink at reality. The automobile is intended for distance as well as for transportation within a limited area.

It therefore seems to me not unreasonable—and certainly not unconstitutional and beyond the reach of the principles laid down in *International Shoe Co. v. Washington*, 326 U.S. 310 (1945), and its progeny—to uphold Oklahoma jurisdiction over this New York distributor and this New York dealer when the accident happened in Oklahoma. I see nothing more unfair for them than for the manufacturer and the importer. All are in the business of providing vehicles that spread out over the highways of our several States. It is not too much to anticipate at the time of distribution and at the time of retail sale that this Audi would be in Oklahoma. . . .

Comments and Questions

1. By the time *World-Wide Volkswagen* was decided, it was well settled that the commission of a tort *within* a state established jurisdiction over a nonresident tortfeasor for a claim arising from the conduct. Had the Robinsons collided on the Oklahoma highway with a car driven by a Texas citizen, for example, that person could have been sued in Oklahoma on a claim arising from the accident. The actual lawsuit filed by the Robinsons fell in a murkier area—the plaintiffs were complaining about something that happened *outside* the state (the design and manufacture of the Audi) that merely had (or so they alleged) *effects* within the state. In an influential case cited by the Court in *World-Wide Volkswagen*, the Illinois Supreme Court had held an out-of-state component manufacturer amenable to suit in that state on just such an effects theory. *See Gray v. American Radiator & Standard Sanitary Corp.*, 22 Ill. 2d 432 (1961). Defendant Titan Valve manufactured its allegedly defective safety valve in Ohio, then sold it to American

Radiator, which incorporated the valve into a water heater at its plant in Pennsylvania. The heater was then sold to plaintiff Phyllis Gray in Illinois, where it exploded.

Whether this more tenuous connection between a defendant and the forum state creates personal jurisdiction has sharply divided the Supreme Court, as both *World-Wide Volkswagen* and *Asahi Metal Industry Co. v. Superior Court, infra*, illustrate.

2. Can you articulate the Court's definition of "foreseeability" in the context of the minimum-contacts test? Consider Justice White's explanation: "[T]he foreseeability that is critical to due process analysis is not the mere likelihood that a product will find its way into the forum State. Rather, it is that the defendant's conduct and connection with the forum State are such that he should reasonably anticipate being haled into court there." Does this mean that foreseeability of suit becomes equated with the existence of minimum contacts, and thus washes out as an independent criterion of due process? Put another way, isn't the Court saying that a defendant can reasonably foresee a suit only where it has minimum contacts? Do you sense some circular motion here? Justice Brennan, in an omitted section of his dissent, argues that the Court's analysis "begs the question." He explains: "A defendant cannot know if his actions will subject him to jurisdiction in another State until we have declared what the law of jurisdiction is." 444 U.S. 286, 311 n.18.

How do the dissenting justices define foreseeability in their analysis? What is the significance to the dissenters of the mobility of the defendants' product in *World-Wide Volkswagen*?

3. On the issue of foreseeability of suit in the forum state, would it have made a difference to the majority if the Robinsons had actually told their salesperson at the World-Wide dealership that they would be taking their Audi through Oklahoma on the way to Arizona? What might the dissenters have done with this information? Should amenability to suit turn on the (fortuitous) substance of such a conversation?

4. What role should geographical proximity play? What if the Robinsons' accident had occurred in Rhode Island, within a two-hour drive of the dealership? Shouldn't World-Wide have reasonably anticipated one of its cars ending up in Rhode Island? Justice Brennan reads the majority as "exclud[ing] jurisdiction in a contiguous State such as Pennsylvania as surely as in more distant States such as Oklahoma." 444 U.S. at 306 n.10.

5. The majority in *World-Wide Volkswagen* concedes that a "forum State does not exceed its powers under the Due Process Clause if it asserts personal jurisdiction over a corporation that delivers its products into the stream of commerce with the expectation that they will be purchased by consumers in the forum State." The disagreement on the Court seems to focus on the nature and extent of the "expectation," which gets us back to the "foreseeability" issue. The Court will elaborate on the "stream of commerce" concept in *Asahi Metal Industry Co. v. Superior Court, infra*.

6. The opinion of the Court clearly resists an interpretation of due process that would subject a local retailer or distributor to suit in distant locations where their products happen to end up. Why does this raise the specter of *Harris v. Balk*, whose "outworn rule" the Court had recently abandoned?

7. Are you as "puzzled" as Justice Blackmun about why the Robinsons were so intent on keeping World-Wide and Seaway in the lawsuit, when the "big fish," Audi and VW, no longer contested jurisdiction (probably because they were conducting a sufficient level of activities to be subject to general jurisdiction) and could certainly pay any judgment rendered? *In World-Wide Volkswagon v. Woodson—The Rest of the Story*, 72 Neb. L. Rev. 1122 (1993), Professor Adams reveals that the plaintiffs' counsel, believing a state court jury would be more generous to his clients than a federal jury, sought to prevent removal of the case from state to federal court. (We will explore removal procedure later.) In order to avoid removal, it was necessary to maintain non-diverse parties on each side of the case; and since the Robinsons were still citizens of New York, maintaining World-Wide and Seaway (also New York entities) as defendants would block removal. Following the Supreme Court decision holding that these defendants were not amenable to suit in Oklahoma, the case was in fact removed and tried in federal district court. The jury rendered a verdict for the defendants.

8. In what ways does Justice Brennan's dissent in *World-Wide Volkswagen* reflect the same philosophy of personal jurisdiction expressed by Justice Black in *International Shoe* and *McGee*? In an omitted section, Justice Brennan observes that "a courtroom just across the state line from a defendant may often be far more convenient for the defendant than a courtroom in a distant corner of his own State." 444 U.S. 286, 301 n.1. How would you compare the majority's philosophy of state court power?

9. If, as Justice White asserts for the Court, "the Due Process Clause, acting as an instrument of interstate federalism, may sometimes act to divest the State of its power to render a valid judgment" even if the defendant would suffer "minimal or no inconvenience," how can it be that the defendant can waive the personal jurisdiction objection (either deliberately or inadvertently, *see* Fed. R. Civ. P. 12(h)(1))? Note that the defense of lack of subject matter jurisdiction *cannot* be waived by the parties and may even be raised by the court on its own initiative. *See* Fed. R. Civ. P. 12(h)(3) and Advisory Committee Note.

10. Only two years after *World-Wide Volkswagen Corporation v. Woodson* (with its emphasis on state sovereignty), the Court wrote the following:

> The personal jurisdiction requirement recognizes and protects an individual liberty interest. It represents a restriction on judicial power *not as a matter of sovereignty*, but as a matter of individual liberty. . . . It is true that we have stated that the requirement of personal jurisdiction, as applied to state

courts, reflects an element of federalism and the character of state sovereignty vis-à-vis other States. For example, in *World-Wide Volkswagen Corp. v. Woodson*, 444 U.S. 286, 291-292 (1980), we stated: "[A] state court may exercise personal jurisdiction over a nonresident defendant only so long as there exist 'minimum contacts' between the defendant and the forum State. The concept of minimum contacts, in turn, can be seen to perform two related, but distinguishable, functions. It protects the defendant against the burdens of litigating in a distant or inconvenient forum. And it acts to ensure that the States, through their courts, do not reach out beyond the limits imposed on them by their status as coequal sovereigns in a federal system." . . . The restriction on state sovereign power described in *World-Wide Volkswagen Corp.*, however, must be seen as ultimately a function of the individual liberty interest preserved by the Due Process Clause. That Clause is the only source of the personal jurisdiction requirement and the Clause itself makes no mention of federalism concerns. Furthermore, if the federalism concept operated as an independent restriction on the sovereign power of the court, it would not be possible to waive the personal jurisdiction requirement: Individual actions cannot change the powers of sovereignty, although the individual can subject himself to powers from which he may otherwise be protected.

Because the requirement of personal jurisdiction represents first of all an individual right, it can, like other such rights, be waived.

Insurance Corp. of Ireland, Ltd. v. Compagnie des Bauxites de Guinée, 456 U.S. 694 (1982). Has the federalism / state sovereignty dimension of personal jurisdiction been left by the wayside so soon after its triumph in *World-Wide Volkswagen*?

11. *World-Wide Volkswagen* appears to reject categorically the argument that merely causing an effect or injury in a state is a sufficient basis for the exercise of personal jurisdiction over the actor. How then can we explain the result in the next case?

■ CALDER v. JONES
465 U.S. 783 (1994)

Justice REHNQUIST delivered the opinion of the Court:

Respondent Shirley Jones brought suit in California Superior Court claiming that she had been libeled in an article written and edited by petitioners in Florida. The article was published in a national magazine with a large circulation in California. Petitioners were served with process by mail in Florida and caused special appearances to be entered on their behalf, moving to quash the service of process for lack of personal jurisdiction. The superior court granted the motion on the ground that First Amendment concerns weighed against an assertion of jurisdiction otherwise proper under the Due Process Clause. The California Court of Appeal reversed, rejecting the suggestion that First Amendment considerations enter into the jurisdictional analysis. We now affirm.

Respondent lives and works in California. She and her husband brought this suit against the National Enquirer, Inc., its local distributing company, and petitioners for libel, invasion of privacy, and intentional infliction of emotional harm. The Enquirer is a Florida corporation with its principal place of business in Florida. It publishes a national weekly newspaper with a total circulation of over 5 million. About 600,000 of those copies, almost twice the level of the next highest State, are sold in California. Respondent's and her husband's claims were based on an article that appeared in the Enquirer's October 9, 1979 issue. Both the Enquirer and the distributing company answered the complaint and made no objection to the jurisdiction of the California court.

Petitioner South is a reporter employed by the Enquirer. He is a resident of Florida, though he frequently travels to California on business. South wrote the first draft of the challenged article, and his byline appeared on it. He did most of his research in Florida, relying on phone calls to sources in California for the information contained in the article. [4] Shortly before publication, South called respondent's home and read to her husband a draft of the article so as to elicit his comments upon it. Aside from his frequent trips and phone calls, South has no other relevant contacts with California.

Petitioner Calder is also a Florida resident. He has been to California only twice—once, on a pleasure trip, prior to the publication of the article and once after to testify in an unrelated trial. Calder is president and editor of the Enquirer. He "oversee[s] just about every function of the Enquirer." J.A., at 24. He reviewed and approved the initial evaluation of the subject of the article and edited it in its final form. He also declined to print a retraction requested by respondent. Calder has no other relevant contacts with California. . . .

The Due Process Clause of the Fourteenth Amendment to the United States Constitution permits personal jurisdiction over a defendant in any State with which the defendant has "certain minimum contacts . . . such that the maintenance of the suit does not offend 'traditional notions of fair play and substantial justice.'" In judging minimum contacts, a court properly focuses on "the relationship among the defendant, the forum, and the litigation." The plaintiff's lack of "contacts" will not defeat otherwise proper jurisdiction, but they may be so manifold as to permit jurisdiction when it would not exist in their absence. Here, the plaintiff is the focus of the activities of the defendants out of which the suit arises.

The allegedly libelous story concerned the California activities of a California resident. It impugned the professionalism of an entertainer

---

4. The superior court found that South made at least one trip to California in connection with the article. South hotly disputes this finding, claiming that an uncontroverted affidavit shows that he never visited California to research the article. Since we do not rely for our holding on the alleged visit, see n.6, *supra*, we find it unnecessary to consider the contention.

whose television career was centered in California. [The article alleged that respondent drank so heavily as to prevent her from fulfilling her professional obligations.] The article was drawn from California sources, and the brunt of the harm, in terms both of respondent's emotional distress and the injury to her professional reputation, was suffered in California. In sum, California is the focal point both of the story and of the harm suffered. Jurisdiction over petitioners is therefore proper in California based on the "effects" of their Florida conduct in California. *World-Wide Volkswagen Corp. v. Woodson*, 444 U.S. 286, 297-298 (1980).

Petitioners argue that they are not responsible for the circulation of the article in California. A reporter and an editor, they claim, have no direct economic stake in their employer's sales in a distant State. Nor are ordinary employees able to control their employer's marketing activity. The mere fact that they can "foresee" that the article will be circulated and have an effect in California is not sufficient for an assertion of jurisdiction. *World-Wide Volkswagen Corp. v. Woodson*, 444 U.S. at 295. They do not "in effect appoint the [article their] agent for service of process." *World-Wide Volkswagen Corp. v. Woodson*, 444 U.S. at 296. Petitioners liken themselves to a welder employed in Florida who works on a boiler which subsequently explodes in California. Cases which hold that jurisdiction will be proper over the manufacturer, *Buckeye Boiler Co. v. Superior Court*, 71 Cal. 2d 893 (1969); *Gray v. American Radiator & Standard Sanitary Corp.*, 22 Ill. 2d 432 (1961), should not be applied to the welder who has no control over and derives no direct benefit from his employer's sales in that distant State.

Petitioners' analogy does not wash. Whatever the status of their hypothetical welder, petitioners are not charged with mere untargeted negligence. Rather, their intentional, and allegedly tortious, actions were expressly aimed at California. Petitioner South wrote and petitioner Calder edited an article that they knew would have a potentially devastating impact upon respondent. And they knew that the brunt of that injury would be felt by respondent in the State in which she lives and works and in which the National Enquirer has its largest circulation. Under the circumstances, petitioners must "reasonably anticipate being haled into court there" to answer for the truth of the statements made in their article. *World-Wide Volkswagen Corp. v. Woodson*, 444 U.S. at 297. An individual injured in California need not go to Florida to seek redress from persons who, though remaining in Florida, knowingly cause the injury in California.

Petitioners are correct that their contacts with California are not to be judged according to their employer's activities there. On the other hand, their status as employees does not somehow insulate them from jurisdiction. Each defendant's contacts with the forum State must be assessed individually. In this case, petitioners are primary participants in an alleged wrongdoing intentionally directed at a California resident, and jurisdiction over them is proper on that basis. . . .

We hold that jurisdiction over petitioners in California is proper because of their intentional conduct in Florida calculated to cause injury to respondent in California. The judgment of the California Court of Appeal is affirmed.

Comments and Questions

1. Why did defendant National Enquirer file an answer without raising an objection to personal jurisdiction (as Calder and South did)? (Hint: There are many inquiring minds in the Golden State.)

2. Note the Court's effort to distinguish *World-Wide Volkswagen*:

[The *Calder* defendants] are not charged with mere untargeted negligence, but rather their intentional, and allegedly tortious, actions were expressly aimed at California. They wrote and edited an article that they knew would have a potentially devastating impact upon respondent, and they knew that the brunt of that injury would be felt by respondent in the State in which she lives and works and in which the magazine has its largest circulation. Under these circumstances, [defendants] must "reasonably anticipate being haled into court there" to answer for the truth of the statements made in the article.

465 U.S. at 789-90. Are you persuaded by these distinctions?

3. In *Keeton v. Hustler Magazine, Inc.*, 465 U.S. 770 (1984), decided the same day as *Calder*, the Court held that the sale in New Hampshire of thousands of copies of the magazine each month constituted sufficient purposeful contacts to justify jurisdiction over the Ohio corporate defendant in a libel action brought by a New York resident. This permitted plaintiff, whose previous lawsuit against Hustler had been dismissed in the Ohio courts because that state's statute of limitations had run, to take advantage of New Hampshire's longer statute of limitations and thus pursue her action seeking damages for nationwide circulation of the magazine.

Even though the New York Daily News sends only 13 daily editions and 18 Sunday editions to subscribers in California, the Ninth Circuit Court of Appeals held that there was jurisdiction in that state over the newspaper and its columnist in a libel action brought by a California resident. *See Gordy v. Daily News, L.P.*, 95 F.3d 829 (9th Cir. 1996). Although so few papers were distributed in California, the Court found determinative that the plaintiff lived in the state and that the column "was of a nature that would clearly have a severe impact on Gordy as an individual. It is reasonable to expect the bulk of the harm from defamation of an individual to be felt in his domicile." 95 F.3d at 833.

4. Do *Calder* and *Keeton* limit *World-Wide Volkswagen*'s rejection of jurisdiction premised on causing injury within the forum (that is, the "effects test") to *non*-intentional torts, or is the Court instead creating a special

rule for defamation actions? The Ninth Circuit Court of Appeals has read *Calder* as establishing that "personal jurisdiction can be predicated on (1) intentional actions (2) expressly aimed at the forum state (3) causing harm, the brunt of which is suffered—and which the defendant knows is likely to be suffered—in the forum state." *Core-Vent Corp. v. Nobel Industries,* 11 F.3d 1482 (9th Cir. 1993). Does the next case, *Asahi Metal Industry Co., Ltd. v. Superior Court,* help us put these cases in perspective?

5. *Calder* allowed suit against the Enquirer's editor and the reporter who wrote the story on the theory that each knew that the major impact of the story could be felt in California, and that that constituted a purposeful connection to the forum. Could that theory justify exercising jurisdiction over *the source* of a story as well?

In *Hugel v. McNell,* 886 F.2d 1 (1st Cir. 1989), *cert. denied* 494 U.S. 1079 (1990), the First Circuit answered in the affirmative. As sources of information leading to the publication of an article in the Washington Post that forced plaintiff Hugel to resign his post as Deputy Director of Operations of the Central Intelligence Agency, the McNells argued that a default judgment against them in the federal district court in New Hampshire was void for lack of personal jurisdiction. The front page story, entitled "CIA Spymaster Accused of Improper Stock Practices," was disseminated throughout the country via national news services and TV and radio networks. After this media blitz, Hugel resigned his CIA position and over a year later filed a defamation action.

The First Circuit Court of Appeals held that there was *in personam* jurisdiction over the nonresident defendants: "The McNells knew that release of the allegedly false information would have a devastating impact on Hugel, and it can be fairly inferred that they intended the brunt of the injury to be felt in New Hampshire where Hugel had an established reputation as a businessman and public servant. . . . The McNells could reasonably expect to be haled into a New Hampshire court to answer for their conduct, and thus the assertion of in personam jurisdiction over the McNells satisfies the dictates of due process."

But compare *National Association of Real Estate Appraisers, Inc. v. Schaeffer,* 1989 WL 267762 (C.D. Cal. 1989). There, a Rhode Island defendant was sued for slander and libel after applying for and obtaining appraisal certification from the plaintiff association for its pet cat Tobias, and then publicizing the incident as an example of the lax standards for certification in the industry. While in Rhode Island, Schaeffer received a telephone call from a reporter with the Orange County Register; he responded to the questions and at the reporter's request sent a photo of Tobias. The California newspaper published the story, which was then widely disseminated nationwide. The district court granted the defendant's motion to dismiss for lack of personal jurisdiction, concluding that Shaeffer's response to an unsolicited phone call from the forum state was insufficient to constitute purposeful minimum contacts. The court distinguished *Calder* on the grounds that the plaintiff National Association of Real Estate Appraisers, Inc. was an Arizona corporation with its principal place of business in that state; unlike *Calder*, therefore, where the defendants knew that Shirley Jones would bear the brunt of her injury in her home state of California, the plaintiff here was not a resident of California and it could not be said that the defendant's conduct outside the forum was calculated to cause injury in the state.

Jurisdiction was similarly found lacking in *Madara v. Hall*, 916 F.2d 1510 (11th Cir. 1990), a libel action arising from a telephone interview that the defendant gave while in New York to a magazine reporter in California. The action was filed in Florida, which had a generous statute of limitations and where a small number of copies of the magazine in which the story appeared were sold. (The defendant had also performed occasional concerts in Florida, and his records were sold there, but these activities were unrelated to the allegedly libelous interview and thus provided no basis for jurisdiction.) The court of appeals concluded that the defendant had not established purposeful minimum contacts with Florida:

> Simply giving an interview to a reporter is not enough to cause Hall to anticipate being haled into court in Florida. Hall was not the magazine's publisher and did not control its circulation and distribution; thus, he is in a qualitatively different position than the defendant [magazine] in *Keeton*. . . .
> By giving the interview, Hall did not appoint copies of the magazine as his agent for service of process wherever a third party, the publisher, might choose to send these magazines.

Id. at 1519.

■ ASAHI METAL INDUSTRY CO., LTD. v. SUPERIOR COURT OF CALIFORNIA, SOLANO COUNTY
480 U.S. 102 (1987)

Justice O'CONNOR announced the judgment of the Court and delivered the unanimous opinion of the Court with respect to Part I, the opinion of the Court with respect to Part II-B, in which the CHIEF JUSTICE, Justice BRENNAN, Justice WHITE, Justice MARSHALL, Justice BLACKMUN, Justice POWELL, and Justice STEVENS join, and an opinion with respect to Parts II-A and III, in which the CHIEF JUSTICE, Justice POWELL, and Justice SCALIA join:

This case presents the question whether the mere awareness on the part of a foreign defendant that the components it manufactured, sold, and delivered outside the United States would reach the forum State in the stream of commerce constitutes "minimum contacts" between the defendant and the forum State such that the exercise of jurisdiction "does not offend 'traditional notions of fair play and substantial justice.'" *International Shoe Co. v. Washington*, 326 U.S. 310, 316 (1945), *quoting Milliken v. Meyer*, 311 U.S. 457, 463 (1940).

I

On September 23, 1978, on Interstate Highway 80 in Solano County, California, Gary Zurcher lost control of his Honda motorcycle and collided with a tractor. Zurcher was severely injured, and his passenger and wife, Ruth Ann Moreno, was killed. In September 1979, Zurcher filed a product liability action in the Superior Court of the State of California in and for the County of Solano. Zurcher alleged that the 1978 accident was caused by a sudden loss of air and an explosion in the rear tire of the motorcycle, and alleged that the motorcycle tire, tube, and sealant were defective. Zurcher's complaint named, inter alia, Cheng Shin Rubber Industrial Co., Ltd. (Cheng Shin), the Taiwanese manufacturer of the tube. Cheng Shin in turn filed a cross-complaint seeking indemnification from its codefendants and from petitioner, Asahi Metal Industry Co., Ltd. (Asahi), the manufacturer of the tube's valve assembly. Zurcher's claims against Cheng Shin and the other defendants were eventually settled and dismissed, leaving only Cheng Shin's indemnity action against Asahi.

California's long-arm statute authorizes the exercise of jurisdiction "on any basis not inconsistent with the Constitution of this state or of the United States." Cal. Civ. Proc. Code Ann. §410.10 (West 1973). Asahi moved to quash Cheng Shin's service of summons, arguing the State could not exert jurisdiction over it consistent with the Due Process Clause of the Fourteenth Amendment.

In relation to the motion, the following information was submitted by Asahi and Cheng Shin. Asahi is a Japanese corporation. It manufactures tire valve assemblies in Japan and sells the assemblies to Cheng Shin, and to several other tire manufacturers, for use as components in finished tire tubes. Asahi's sales to Cheng Shin took place in Taiwan. The shipments from Asahi to Cheng Shin were sent from Japan to Taiwan. Cheng Shin bought and incorporated into its tire tubes 150,000 Asahi valve assemblies in 1978; 500,000 in 1979; 500,000 in 1980; 100,000 in 1981; and 100,000 in 1982. Sales to Cheng Shin accounted for 1.24 percent of Asahi's income in 1981 and 0.44 percent in 1982. Cheng Shin alleged that approximately 20 percent of its sales in the United States are in California. Cheng Shin purchases valve assemblies from other suppliers as well, and sells finished tubes throughout the world.

In 1983 an attorney for Cheng Shin conducted an informal examination of the valve stems of the tire tubes sold in one cycle store in Solano County. The attorney declared that of the approximately 115 tire tubes in the store, 97 were purportedly manufactured in Japan or Taiwan, and of those 97, 21 valve stems were marked with the circled letter "A", apparently Asahi's trademark. Of the 21 Asahi valve stems, 12 were incorporated into Cheng Shin tire tubes. The store contained 41 other Cheng Shin tubes that incorporated the valve assemblies of other manufacturers.

Declaration of Kenneth B. Shepard in Opposition to Motion to Quash Subpoena, App. to Brief for Respondent 5-6. An affidavit of a manager of Cheng Shin whose duties included the purchasing of component parts stated: "'In discussions with Asahi regarding the purchase of valve stem assemblies the fact that my Company sells tubes throughout the world and specifically the United States has been discussed. I am informed and believe that Asahi was fully aware that valve stem assemblies sold to my Company and to others would end up throughout the United States and in California.'" 39 Cal. 3d 35, 48, n.4 (1985). An affidavit of the president of Asahi, on the other hand, declared that Asahi "'has never contemplated that its limited sales of tire valves to Cheng Shin in Taiwan would subject it to lawsuits in California.'" *Ibid.* The record does not include any contract between Cheng Shin and Asahi. Tr. of Oral Arg. 24.

Primarily on the basis of the above information, the Superior Court denied the motion to quash summons, stating: "Asahi obviously does business on an international scale. It is not unreasonable that they defend claims of defect in their product on an international scale." Order Denying Motion to Quash Summons, *Zurcher v. Dunlop Tire & Rubber Co.*, No. 76180 (Super. Ct., Solano County, Cal., Apr. 20, 1983).

The Court of Appeal of the State of California issued a peremptory writ of mandate commanding the Superior Court to quash service of summons. The court concluded that "it would be unreasonable to require Asahi to respond in California solely on the basis of ultimately realized foreseeability that the product into which its component was embodied would be sold all over the world including California." App. to Pet. for Cert. B5-B6.

The Supreme Court of the State of California reversed and discharged the writ issued by the Court of Appeal. 39 Cal. 3d 35 (1985). The court observed: "Asahi has no offices, property or agents in California. It solicits no business in California and has made no direct sales [in California]." *Id.*, at 48. Moreover, "Asahi did not design or control the system of distribution that carried its valve assemblies into California." *Id.* at 49. Nevertheless, the court found the exercise of jurisdiction over Asahi to be consistent with the Due Process Clause. It concluded that Asahi knew that some of the valve assemblies sold to Cheng Shin would be incorporated into tire tubes sold in California, and that Asahi benefited indirectly from the sale in California of products incorporating its components. The court considered Asahi's intentional act of placing its components into the stream of commerce—that is, by delivering the components to Cheng Shin in Taiwan—coupled with Asahi's awareness that some of the components would eventually find their way into California, sufficient to form the basis for state court jurisdiction under the Due Process Clause.

We granted certiorari, and now reverse.

II

A

The Due Process Clause of the Fourteenth Amendment limits the power of a state court to exert personal jurisdiction over a nonresident defendant. "[T]he constitutional touchstone" of the determination whether an exercise of personal jurisdiction comports with due process "remains whether the defendant purposefully established 'minimum contacts' in the forum State." *Burger King Corp. v. Rudzewicz,* 471 U.S. 462, 474 (1985), *quoting International Shoe Co. v. Washington,* 326 U.S. at 316. Most recently we have reaffirmed the oft-quoted reasoning of *Hanson v. Denckla,* 357 U.S. 235, 253 (1958), that minimum contacts must have a basis in "some act by which the defendant purposefully avails itself of the privilege of conducting activities within the forum State, thus invoking the benefits and protections of its laws." *Burger King,* 471 U.S. at 475. "Jurisdiction is proper . . . where the contacts proximately result from actions by the defendant himself that create a 'substantial connection' with the forum State." *Ibid., quoting McGee v. International Life Insurance Co.,* 355 U.S. 220, 223 (1957).

Applying the principle that minimum contacts must be based on an act of the defendant, the Court in *World-Wide Volkswagen Corp. v. Woodson,* 444 U.S. 286 (1980), rejected the assertion that a consumer's unilateral act of bringing the defendant's product into the forum State was a sufficient constitutional basis for personal jurisdiction over the defendant. It had been argued in *World-Wide Volkswagen* that because an automobile retailer and its wholesale distributor sold a product mobile by design and purpose, they could foresee being haled into court in the distant States into which their customers might drive. The Court rejected this concept of foreseeability as an insufficient basis for jurisdiction under the Due Process Clause. *Id.,* at 295-296. The Court disclaimed, however, the idea that "foreseeability is wholly irrelevant" to personal jurisdiction, concluding that "[t]he forum State does not exceed its powers under the Due Process Clause if it asserts personal jurisdiction over a corporation that delivers its products into the stream of commerce with the expectation that they will be purchased by consumers in the forum State." *Id.,* at 297-298 (citation omitted). The Court reasoned: "When a corporation 'purposefully avails itself of the privilege of conducting activities within the forum State,' *Hanson v. Denckla,* 357 U.S. [235,] 253 [(1958)], it has clear notice that it is subject to suit there, and can act to alleviate the risk of burdensome litigation by procuring insurance, passing the expected costs on to customers, or, if the risks are too great, severing its connection with the State. Hence if the sale of a product of a manufacturer or distributor . . . is not simply an isolated occurrence, but arises from the efforts of the manufacturer or distributor to serve, directly or indirectly, the market for its product in other States, it is not unreasonable to subject it to suit in one of those States if its allegedly defective merchandise has there been the source of injury to its owners or to others." *Id.* at 297.

In *World-Wide Volkswagen* itself, the state court sought to base jurisdiction not on any act of the defendant, but on the foreseeable unilateral actions of the consumer. Since *World-Wide Volkswagen,* lower courts have been confronted with cases in which the defendant acted by placing a product in the stream of commerce, and the stream eventually swept defendant's product into the forum State, but the defendant did nothing else to purposefully avail itself of the market in the forum State. Some courts have understood the Due Process Clause, as interpreted in *World-Wide Volkswagen,* to allow an exercise of personal jurisdiction to be based on no more than the defendant's act of placing the product in the stream of commerce. Other courts have understood the Due Process Clause and the above-quoted language in *World-Wide Volkswagen* to require the action of the defendant to be more purposefully directed at the forum State than the mere act of placing a product in the stream of commerce.

The reasoning of the Supreme Court of California in the present case illustrates the former interpretation of *World-Wide Volkswagen.* The Supreme Court of California held that, because the stream of commerce eventually brought some valves Asahi sold Cheng Shin into California, Asahi's awareness that its valves would be sold in California was sufficient to permit California to exercise jurisdiction over Asahi consistent with the requirements of the Due Process Clause. The Supreme Court of California's position was consistent with those courts that have held that mere foreseeability or awareness was a constitutionally sufficient basis for personal jurisdiction if the defendant's product made its way into the forum State while still in the stream of commerce. *See Bean Dredging Corp. v. Dredge Technology Corp.,* 744 F.2d 1081 (5th Cir. 1984); *Hedrick v. Daiko Shoji Co.,* 715 F.2d 1355 (9th Cir. 1983).

Other courts, however, have understood the Due Process Clause to require something more than that the defendant was aware of its product's entry into the forum State through the stream of commerce in order for the State to exert jurisdiction over the defendant. In the present case, for example, the State Court of Appeal did not read the Due Process Clause, as interpreted by *World-Wide Volkswagen,* to allow "mere foreseeability that the product will enter the forum state [to] be enough by itself to establish jurisdiction over the distributor and retailer." . . .

We now find this latter position to be consonant with the requirements of due process. The "substantial connection," *Burger King,* 471 U.S. at 475; *McGee,* 355 U.S. at 223, between the defendant and the forum State necessary for a finding of minimum contacts must come about by an action of the defendant purposefully directed toward the forum State. *Burger King, supra,* 471 U.S. at 476; *Keeton v. Hustler Magazine, Inc.,* 465 U.S. 770, 774 (1984). The placement of a product into the stream of commerce, without more, is not an act of the defendant purposefully directed toward the forum State. Additional conduct of the defendant may indicate an intent or purpose to serve the market in the forum State, for example, designing the product for the market in the forum State, advertising in the forum State, establishing channels for providing regular advice to customers in the forum State, or marketing the product through a distributor who has agreed to serve as the sales agent in the forum State. But a defendant's awareness that the stream of commerce may or will sweep the product into the forum State does not convert the mere act of placing the product into the stream into an act purposefully directed toward the forum State.

Assuming, *arguendo*, that respondents have established Asahi's awareness that some of the valves sold to Cheng Shin would be incorporated into tire tubes sold in California, respondents have not demonstrated any action by Asahi to purposefully avail itself of the California market. Asahi does not do business in California. It has no office, agents, employees, or property in California. It does not advertise or otherwise solicit business in California. It did not create, control, or employ the distribution system that brought its valves to California. There is no evidence that Asahi designed its product in anticipation of sales in California. On the basis of these facts, the exertion of personal jurisdiction over Asahi by the Superior Court of California* exceeds the limits of due process.

B

The strictures of the Due Process Clause forbid a state court to exercise personal jurisdiction over Asahi under circumstances that would offend "'traditional notions of fair play and substantial justice.'" *International Shoe Co. v. Washington*, 326 U.S. at 316; *quoting Milliken v. Meyer*, 311 U.S. at 463.

We have previously explained that the determination of the reasonableness of the exercise of jurisdiction in each case will depend on an evaluation of several factors. A court must consider the burden on the defendant, the interests of the forum State, and the plaintiff's interest in obtaining relief. It must also weigh in its determination "the interstate judicial system's interest in obtaining the most efficient resolution of controversies; and the shared interest of the several States in furthering fundamental substantive social policies." *World-Wide Volkswagen*, 444 U.S. at 292.

A consideration of these factors in the present case clearly reveals the unreasonableness of the assertion of jurisdiction over Asahi, even apart from the question of the placement of goods in the stream of commerce.

Certainly the burden on the defendant in this case is severe. Asahi has been commanded by the Supreme Court of California not only to traverse the distance between Asahi's headquarters in Japan and the Superior

---

*We have no occasion here to determine whether Congress could, consistent with the Due Process Clause of the Fifth Amendment, authorize federal court personal jurisdiction over alien defendants based on the aggregate of national contacts, rather than on the contacts between the defendant and the State in which the federal court sits.

Court of California in and for the County of Solano, but also to submit its dispute with Cheng Shin to a foreign nation's judicial system. The unique burdens placed upon one who must defend oneself in a foreign legal system should have significant weight in assessing the reasonableness of stretching the long arm of personal jurisdiction over national borders.

When minimum contacts have been established, often the interests of the plaintiff and the forum in the exercise of jurisdiction will justify even the serious burdens placed on the alien defendant. In the present case, however, the interests of the plaintiff and the forum in California's assertion of jurisdiction over Asahi are slight. All that remains is a claim for indemnification asserted by Cheng Shin, a Taiwanese corporation, against Asahi. The transaction on which the indemnification claim is based took place in Taiwan; Asahi's components were shipped from Japan to Taiwan. Cheng Shin has not demonstrated that it is more convenient for it to litigate its indemnification claim against Asahi in California rather than in Taiwan or Japan.

Because the plaintiff is not a California resident, California's legitimate interests in the dispute have considerably diminished. The Supreme Court of California argued that the State had an interest in "protecting its consumers by ensuring that foreign manufacturers comply with the state's safety standards." The State Supreme Court's definition of California's interest, however, was overly broad. The dispute between Cheng Shin and Asahi is primarily about indemnification rather than safety standards. Moreover, it is not at all clear at this point that California law should govern the question whether a Japanese corporation should indemnify a Taiwanese corporation on the basis of a sale made in Taiwan and a shipment of goods from Japan to Taiwan. The possibility of being haled into a California court as a result of an accident involving Asahi's components undoubtedly creates an additional deterrent to the manufacture of unsafe components; however, similar pressures will be placed on Asahi by the purchasers of its components as long as those who use Asahi components in their final products, and sell those products in California, are subject to the application of California tort law.

World-Wide Volkswagen also admonished courts to take into consideration the interests of the "several States," in addition to the forum State, in the efficient judicial resolution of the dispute and the advancement of substantive policies. In the present case, this advice calls for a court to consider the procedural and substantive policies of other nations whose interests are affected by the assertion of jurisdiction by the California court. The procedural and substantive interests of other nations in a state court's assertion of jurisdiction over an alien defendant will differ from case to case. In every case, however, those interests, as well as the Federal interest in Government's foreign relations policies, will be best served by a careful inquiry into the reasonableness of the assertion of jurisdiction in the particular case, and an unwillingness to find the serious burdens on an alien defendant outweighed by minimal interests on the part of the plaintiff or the forum State. "Great care and reserve should be exercised when extending our notions of personal jurisdiction into the international field." *United States v. First National City Bank*, 379 U.S. 378, 404 (1965) (Harlan, J., dissenting). *See* Born, Reflections on Judicial Jurisdiction in International Cases, to be published in 17 Ga. J. Int'l & Comp. L. 1 (1987).

Considering the international context, the heavy burden on the alien defendant, and the slight interests of the plaintiff and the forum State, the exercise of personal jurisdiction by a California court over Asahi in this instance would be unreasonable and unfair.

III

Because the facts of this case do not establish minimum contacts such that the exercise of personal jurisdiction is consistent with fair play and substantial justice, the judgment of the Supreme Court of California is reversed, and the case is remanded for further proceedings not inconsistent with this opinion.

It is so ordered.

Justice BRENNAN, with whom Justice WHITE, Justice MARSHALL, and Justice BLACKMUN join, concurring in part and concurring in the judgment.

I do not agree with the interpretation in Part II-A of the stream-of-commerce theory, nor with the conclusion that Asahi did not "purposely avail itself of the California market." *Ante*, at 1034. I do agree, however, with the Court's conclusion in Part II-B that the exercise of personal jurisdiction over Asahi in this case would not comport with "fair play and substantial justice," *International Shoe Co. v. Washington*, 326 U.S. 310, 320 (1945). This is one of those rare cases in which "minimum requirements inherent in the concept of 'fair play and substantial justice' . . . defeat the reasonableness of jurisdiction even [though] the defendant has purposefully engaged in forum activities." *Burger King Corp. v. Rudzewicz*, 471 U.S. 462, 477-478 (1985). I therefore join Parts I and II-B of the Court's opinion, and write separately to explain my disagreement with Part II-A.

Part II-A states that "a defendant's awareness that the stream of commerce may or will sweep the product into the forum State does not convert the mere act of placing the product into the stream into an act purposefully directed toward the forum State." *Ante*, at 1033. Under this view, a plaintiff would be required to show "[a]dditional conduct" directed toward the forum before finding the exercise of jurisdiction over the defendant to be consistent with the Due Process Clause. *Ibid.* I see no need for such a showing, however. The stream of commerce refers not to unpredictable currents or eddies, but to the regular and anticipated flow of products from manufacture to distribution to retail sale. As long as a participant in this process is aware that the final product is being marketed in the forum State, the possibility of a lawsuit there cannot come as a surprise. Nor will the litigation present a burden for which there is no corresponding benefit. A defendant who has placed goods in the stream of commerce benefits economically from the retail sale of the final product in the forum State, and indirectly benefits from the State's laws that regulate and facilitate commercial activity. These benefits accrue regardless of whether that participant directly conducts business in the forum State, or engages in additional conduct directed toward that State. Accordingly, most courts and commentators have found that jurisdiction premised on the placement of a product into the stream of commerce is consistent with the Due Process Clause, and have not required a showing of additional conduct.

The endorsement in Part II-A of what appears to be the minority view among Federal Courts of Appeals represents a marked retreat from the analysis in *World-Wide Volkswagen v. Woodson*, 444 U.S. 286 (1980). In that case, "respondents [sought] to base jurisdiction on one, isolated occurrence and whatever inferences can be drawn therefrom: the fortuitous circumstance that a single Audi automobile, sold in New York to New York residents, happened to suffer an accident while passing through Oklahoma." *Id.* at 295. The Court held that the possibility of an accident in Oklahoma, while to some extent foreseeable in light of the inherent mobility of the automobile, was not enough to establish minimum contacts between the forum State and the retailer or distributor. *Id.* at 295-296. The Court then carefully explained:

> [T]his is not to say, of course, that foreseeability is wholly irrelevant. But the foreseeability that is critical to due process analysis is not the mere likelihood that a product will find its way into the forum State. Rather, it is that the defendant's conduct and connection with the forum State are such that he should reasonably anticipate being haled into Court there.

Id. at 297. The Court reasoned that when a corporation may reasonably anticipate litigation in a particular forum, it cannot claim that such litigation is unjust or unfair, because it "can act to alleviate the risk of burdensome litigation by procuring insurance, passing the expected costs on to consumers, or, if the risks are too great, severing its connection with the State." *Ibid.* . . .

In this case, the facts found by the California Supreme Court support its finding of minimum contacts. The court found that "[a]lthough Asahi did not design or control the system of distribution that carried its valve assemblies into California, Asahi was aware of the distribution system's operation, and it knew that it would benefit economically from the sale in California of products incorporating its components."[4] Accordingly, I cannot join the determination in Part II-A that Asahi's regular and extensive

---

4. Moreover, the Court found that "at least 18 percent of the tubes sold in a particular California motorcycle supply shop contained Asahi valve assemblies," and that Asahi had an ongoing business relationship with Cheng Shin involving average annual sales of hundreds of thousands of valve assemblies.

sales of component parts to a manufacturer it knew was making regular sales of the final product in California is insufficient to establish minimum contacts with California.

Justice STEVENS, with whom Justice WHITE and Justice BLACKMUN join, concurring in part and concurring in the judgment.

The judgment of the Supreme Court of California should be reversed for the reasons stated in Part II-B of the Court's opinion. While I join Parts I and II-B, I do not join Part II-A for two reasons. First, it is not necessary to the Court's decision. An examination of minimum contacts is not always necessary to determine whether a state court's assertion of personal jurisdiction is constitutional. *See Burger King Corp. v. Rudzewicz*, 471 U.S. 462, 476-478 (1985). Part II-B establishes, after considering the factors set forth in *World-Wide Volkswagen Corp. v. Woodson*, 444 U.S. 286, 292 (1980), that California's exercise of jurisdiction over Asahi in this case would be "unreasonable and unfair." This finding alone requires reversal; this case fits within the rule that "minimum requirements inherent in the concept of 'fair play and substantial justice' may defeat the reasonableness of jurisdiction even if the defendant has purposefully engaged in forum activities." *Burger King*, 471 U.S. at 477- 478 (*quoting International Shoe Co. v. Washington*, 326 U.S. 310, 320 (1945)). Accordingly, I see no reason in this case for the plurality to articulate "purposeful direction" or any other test as the nexus between an act of a defendant and the forum State that is necessary to establish minimum contacts.

Second, even assuming that the test ought to be formulated here, Part II-A misapplies it to the facts of this case. The plurality seems to assume that an unwavering line can be drawn between "mere awareness" that a component will find its way into the forum State and "purposeful availment" of the forum's market. *Ante,* at 1033. Over the course of its dealings with Cheng Shin, Asahi has arguably engaged in a higher quantum of conduct than "[t]he placement of a product into the stream of commerce, without more. . . ." Whether or not this conduct rises to the level of purposeful availment requires a constitutional determination that is affected by the volume, the value, and the hazardous character of the components. In most circumstances I would be inclined to conclude that a regular course of dealing that results in deliveries of over 100,000 units annually over a period of several years would constitute "purposeful availment" even though the item delivered to the forum State was a standard product marketed throughout the world.

Comments and Questions

1. List the facts pertinent to the jurisdictional issue in *Asahi*, as well as the gaps in what is known about Asahi's connections to California.

2. What issue is raised by the conflicting affidavits submitted by Cheng Shin and Asahi? How does the Court treat the issue of foreseeability of suit in the forum state? What does *Asahi* add to our understanding of the interplay between foreseeability, purposeful availment, and minimum contacts?

3. What does *Asahi* actually hold? Answering this question obviously requires a close reading of the opinion of the Court, authored by Justice O'Connor, as well as of the separate opinions of Justice Brennan (and three colleagues) and Justice Stevens. Sketch out the areas of agreement and disagreement between the O'Connor group, the Brennan group, and Justice Stevens. Although all agree on the end result—that jurisdiction cannot be exercised over Asahi—they travel distinct paths to that point.

If you are frustrated by this lack of unanimity, you are not alone. The Fifth Circuit Court of Appeals expressed it this way:

> Because the [Supreme] Court's splintered view of minimum contacts in *Asahi* provides no clear guidance on this issue, we continue to gauge [the nonresident defendant]'s contacts with Texas by the stream of commerce standard as described in *World-Wide Volkswagen* and embraced in this circuit.

Ruston Gas Turbines, Inc. v. Donaldson Company, Inc., 9 F.3d 415, 420 (5th Cir. 1993) (citation omitted). What is "the stream of commerce standard as described in *World-Wide Volkswagen*"?

4. As you recall, the Court said in *World-Wide Volkswagen* that a "forum State does not exceed its powers under the Due Process Clause if it asserts personal jurisdiction over a corporation that delivers its products into the stream of commerce with the expectation that they will be purchased by consumers in the forum State." What is the status of "stream of commerce" theory after *Asahi*? Where does Justice O'Connor's notion of "additional conduct" fit in?

5. Does *Asahi* permit a manufacturer to insulate itself from suit in a state merely by using an intermediary distributor, even when it is aware that its products are being sold and used in the state?

6. What role do the "fair play" factors play in the decision? For example, what is the significance of the facts that (1) defendant Asahi is a foreign corporation; (2) the claim against Asahi was a third-party claim for indemnification asserted by another foreign corporation (plaintiff Zurcher having settled out); (3) the sale of valve assemblies occurred in Taiwan and the items were shipped from Japan? What result if the valve manufacturer had been an Ohio corporation whose valves are shipped to Pennsylvania for assembly, and then the tire explodes in California?

7. What is the relation between the "fair play" factors and the "minimum contacts" test after *Asahi*?

8. The issues raised by *Asahi* divided the business community as well as the Court. The American Chamber of Commerce in the United Kingdom submitted an amicus brief in support of Asahi, arguing that "a rule of U.S. law that a foreign component part manufacturer is subject to the personal jurisdiction of any U.S. court in the territory in which it may be aware its foreign customer's products might come to rest, would substantially increase the costs and uncertainties of international trade for British manufacturers," and could lead to retaliatory measures adversely affecting free trade. The California Manufacturers Association (CMA) countered in its amicus brief in support of the exercise of jurisdiction by California, arguing that the lower court decision "has protected the California consumer from duplicative and costly litigation which would otherwise be made necessary but for the granting of jurisdiction; and the manufacturer doing business in California, subjected to the sword of myriad state laws, rules and regulations, should be entitled to seek a shield of protection from those same laws when faced with defending an action in court commenced as a result of the use of a faulty foreign or alien component." The CMA further asserted that a "reversal of the California court's holding may jeopardize the lives, safety and health of California consumers, businesses and manufacturers, by providing another barrier which increases the difficulty an individual or company presently confronts when seeking a legitimate and lawful solution to the assignment of responsibility."

Practice Exercise No. 27: Applying a Long-Arm Statute in *Carpenter*

Prepare for an information and strategy session among you, other associates, and the partner who represents Nancy Carpenter in *Carpenter v. Dee*, in which the defendants are now Randall and Peter Dee, Ultimate Auto, Inc. and the City of Lowell. There are a few changes in the facts, however, as you will learn from the following memo.

Memorandum

To: Associate
From: Carol Coblentz
Re: *Carpenter v. Dee*

As you know, this case is pending in Massachusetts Superior Court, and we have been permitted to amend and join Ultimate Auto, Inc. as a party defendant. I have just learned some new facts, however. Ultimate Auto is incorporated in New Hampshire, and its principal and only place of business is in Nashua, New Hampshire. The other facts we already know about Ultimate Auto and its relationship to Randall Dee are the same.

Ultimate Auto placed in its answer a motion to dismiss under 12(b)(2). I expect there to be a briefing and hearing scheduled on this motion, so I'd like you to get started on this right away.

I sent a separate set of interrogatories to Ultimate Auto on personal jurisdiction matters and gained some additional information. (I may also have time for a deposition.) Ultimate Auto's officers all live in Nashua, NH, except for the Vice President, William Q. Manconi, who lives in Lawrence, MA. Manconi commutes to work, but sometimes does paper work for the company in his study at home. Ultimate advertises only in New Hampshire newspapers and on two Nashua radio stations. It most frequently uses advertising copy, both for newsprint and radio, that states "Buy Ultimate, the ultimate in tires. Our tires will take you softly and safely on the streets of Nashua through the White and Green Mountains, to the Berkshires and the Alleghenies, in cities as tough as Boston, New York, and Chicago, prairies as beautiful as North Dakota, and farms as rolling as Nebraska. Our expertise and prices will not be beat throughout New England. We are the ultimate in tires." One of Ultimate Auto's employees also maintains a personal web site that mentions his employer and satirizes the Company's advertising credo.

Ultimate Auto keeps no records of what percentage of its sales are to people who reside outside of Nashua or outside of New Hampshire. Its manager and sales people do know that "lots of people come from Northern Massachusetts to buy from us. We are particularly well-known by hunters, sportsmen, and car buffs." Four years ago, Ultimate set up a booth at the Auto Show in Boston.

I know that when I drive in Lawrence, Massachusetts, I can pick up only one of the two radio stations that Ultimate Auto advertises on. And a Nashua newspaper in which Ultimate Auto advertises is for sale at one of the Lawrence newsstands.

I have grown out of touch with recent case law on personal jurisdiction, but have read something about the minimum contacts test. I would like the associates to be prepared to explain the facts and holding(s) of *World-Wide Volkswagen, Calder* and *Asahi* to me, and their relevance, if any, to this matter. Specifically with regard to *Asahi*, I am having trouble figuring out the whole "placing in the stream of commerce" and "targeting to a specific market" question, as well as the relative place of the fair play test. Is the new test applicable in every case? After establishing these cases at the start of the session, I hope we can concentrate on what further factual information I should try to get in this case, how we will obtain it, and how we should think about structuring our argument. Indeed, please be ready to say how the memorandum of law should be organized.

I think you will need the Massachusetts Long Arm statute, which I have attached. For purposes of this meeting, do not worry about any case law specifically interpreting the Massachusetts statute; that research will be conducted later.

Massachusetts General Laws
Jurisdiction of Courts Over Persons in Other States and Countries

M.G.L. c. 223A §3. Transactions or conduct for personal jurisdiction

A court may exercise personal jurisdiction over a person, who acts directly or by an agent, as to a cause of action in law or equity arising from the person's

(a) transacting any business in this commonwealth; (booth) ?prob. doesn't suffice

(b) contracting to supply services or things in this commonwealth;

(c) causing tortious injury by an act or omission in this commonwealth;

(d) causing tortious injury in this commonwealth by an act or omission outside this commonwealth if he regularly does or solicits business, or engages in any other persistent course of conduct, or derives substantial revenue from goods used or consumed or services rendered, in this commonwealth;

accident in commonwealth

(e) having an interest in, using or possessing real property in this commonwealth;

(f) contracting to insure any person, property or risk located within this commonwealth at the time of contracting;

(g) maintaining a domicile in this commonwealth while a party to a personal or marital relationship out of which arises a claim for divorce, alimony, property settlement, parentage of a child, child support or child custody; or the commission of any act giving rise to such a claim; or

(h) having been subject to the exercise of personal jurisdiction of a court of the commonwealth which has resulted in an order of alimony, custody, child support or property settlement, notwithstanding the subsequent departure of one of the original parties from the commonwealth, if the action involves modification of such order or orders and the moving party resides in the commonwealth, or if the action involves enforcement of such order notwithstanding the domicile of the moving party.

———————————

How, if at all, should the personal jurisdiction calculus change when we move from the tort context (encounters between strangers) to the commercial context, where the parties have chosen to deal with one another by negotiating and executing a contractual arrangement (which, all too often, goes sour)? Consider the next case.

■BURGER KING CORP.
v. RUDZEWICZ
471 U.S. 462 (1985)

Justice BRENNAN delivered the opinion of the Court:

The State of Florida's long-arm statute extends jurisdiction to "[a]ny person, whether or not a citizen or resident of this state," who, *inter alia,* "[b]reach[es] a contract in this state by failing to perform acts required by the contract to be performed in this state," so long as the cause of action arises from the alleged contractual breach. Fla. Stat. §48.193(1)(g) (Supp. 1984). The United States District Court for the Southern District of Florida, sitting in diversity, relied on this provision in exercising personal jurisdiction over a Michigan resident who allegedly had breached a franchise agreement with a Florida corporation by failing to make required payments in Florida. The question presented is whether this exercise of long-arm jurisdiction offended "traditional conception[s] of fair play and substantial justice" embodied in the Due Process Clause of the Fourteenth Amendment. *International Shoe Co. v. Washington,* 326 U.S. 310, 320 (1945).

I

A

Burger King Corporation is a Florida corporation whose principal offices are in Miami. It is one of the world's largest restaurant organizations, with over 3,000 outlets in the 50 States, the Commonwealth of Puerto Rico, and 8 foreign nations. Burger King conducts approximately 80% of its business through a franchise operation that the company styles the "Burger King System"—"a comprehensive restaurant format and operating system for the sale of uniform and quality food products." Burger King licenses its franchisees to use its trademarks and service marks for a period of 20 years and leases standardized restaurant facilities to them for the same term. In addition, franchisees acquire a variety of proprietary information concerning the "standards, specifications, procedures and methods for operating a Burger King Restaurant." They also receive market research and advertising assistance; ongoing training in restaurant management;[2] and accounting, cost-control, and inventory-control guidance. By permitting franchisees to tap into Burger King's established national reputation and to benefit from proven procedures for dispensing standardized fare, this system enables them to go into the restaurant business with significantly lowered barriers to entry.

In exchange for these benefits, franchisees pay Burger King an initial $40,000 franchise fee and commit themselves to payment of monthly

---

2. Mandatory training seminars are conducted at Burger King University in Miami and at Whopper College Regional Training Centers around the country.

royalties, advertising and sales promotion fees, and rent computed in part from monthly gross sales. Franchisees also agree to submit to the national organization's exacting regulation of virtually every conceivable aspect of their operations. Burger King imposes these standards and undertakes its rigid regulation out of conviction that "[u]niformity of service, appearance, and quality of product is essential to the preservation of the Burger King image and the benefits accruing therefrom to both Franchisee and Franchisor."

Burger King oversees its franchise system through a two-tiered administrative structure. The governing contracts provide that the franchise relationship is established in Miami and governed by Florida law, and call for payment of all required fees and forwarding of all relevant notices to the Miami headquarters. The Miami headquarters sets policy and works directly with its franchisees in attempting to resolve major problems. See nn. 7, 9, *infra.* Day-to-day monitoring of franchisees, however, is conducted through a network of 10 district offices which in turn report to the Miami headquarters.

The instant litigation grows out of Burger King's termination of one of its franchisees, and is aptly described by the franchisee as "a divorce proceeding among commercial partners." The appellee John Rudzewicz, a Michigan citizen and resident, is the senior partner in a Detroit accounting firm. In 1978, he was approached by Brian MacShara, the son of a business acquaintance, who suggested that they jointly apply to Burger King for a franchise in the Detroit area. MacShara proposed to serve as the manager of the restaurant if Rudzewicz would put up the investment capital; in exchange, the two would evenly share the profits. Believing that MacShara's idea offered attractive investment and tax-deferral opportunities, Rudzewicz agreed to the venture.

Rudzewicz and MacShara jointly applied for a franchise to Burger King's Birmingham, Michigan, district office in the autumn of 1978. Their application was forwarded to Burger King's Miami headquarters, which entered into a preliminary agreement with them in February 1979. During the ensuing four months it was agreed that Rudzewicz and MacShara would assume operation of an existing facility in Drayton Plains, Michigan. MacShara attended the prescribed management courses in Miami during this period, and the franchisees purchased $165,000 worth of restaurant equipment from Burger King's Davmor Industries division in Miami. Even before the final agreements were signed, however, the parties began to disagree over site-development fees, building design, computation of monthly rent, and whether the franchisees would be able to assign their liabilities to a corporation they had formed. During these disputes Rudzewicz and MacShara negotiated both with the Birmingham district office and with the Miami headquarters.[7] With some misgivings,

---

7. Although Rudzewicz and MacShara dealt with the Birmingham district office on a regular basis, they communicated directly with the Miami headquarters in forming the contracts; moreover, they learned that the district office had "very little" decisionmaking authority and accordingly turned directly to headquarters in seeking to resolve their disputes.

Rudzewicz and MacShara finally obtained limited concessions from the Miami headquarters, signed the final agreements, and commenced operations in June 1979. By signing the final agreements, Rudzewicz obligated himself personally to payments exceeding $1 million over the 20-year franchise relationship.

The Drayton Plains facility apparently enjoyed steady business during the summer of 1979, but patronage declined after a recession began later that year. Rudzewicz and MacShara soon fell far behind in their monthly payments to Miami. Headquarters sent notices of default, and an extended period of negotiations began among the franchisees, the Birmingham district office, and the Miami headquarters. After several Burger King officials in Miami had engaged in prolonged but ultimately unsuccessful negotiations with the franchisees by mail and by telephone,[9] headquarters terminated the franchise and ordered Rudzewicz and MacShara to vacate the premises. They refused and continued to occupy and operate the facility as a Burger King restaurant.

B

Burger King commenced the instant action in the United States District Court for the Southern District of Florida in May 1981, invoking that court's diversity jurisdiction pursuant to 28 U.S.C. §1332(a) and its original jurisdiction over federal trademark disputes pursuant to §1338(a).[10] Burger King alleged that Rudzewicz and MacShara had breached their franchise obligations "within [the jurisdiction of] this district court" by failing to make the required payments "at plaintiff's place of business in Miami, Dade County, Florida," and also charged that they were tortiously infringing its trademarks and service marks through their continued, unauthorized operation as a Burger King restaurant. Burger King sought damages, injunctive relief, and costs and attorney's fees. Rudzewicz and MacShara entered special appearances and argued, inter alia, that because they were Michigan residents and because Burger King's claim did not "arise" within the Southern District of Florida, the District Court lacked personal jurisdiction over them. The District Court denied their motions after a hearing, holding that, pursuant to Florida's long-arm statute, "a non-resident Burger King franchisee is subject to the personal jurisdiction of this Court in actions arising out of its franchise agreements." Rudzewicz and MacShara then filed an answer and a counterclaim seeking damages for alleged violations by Burger King

---

9. Miami's policy was to "deal directly" with franchisees when they began to encounter financial difficulties, and to involve district office personnel only when necessary. 5 id., at 95. In the instant case, for example, the Miami office handled all credit problems, ordered cost-cutting measures, negotiated for a partial refinancing of the franchisees' debts, communicated directly with the franchisees in attempting to resolve the dispute, and was responsible for all termination matters.

10. Rudzewicz and MacShara were served in Michigan with summonses and copies of the complaint pursuant to Federal Rule of Civil Procedure 4.

of Michigan's Franchise Investment Law, Mich. Comp. Laws §445.1501 *et seq.* (1979).

After a 3-day bench trial, the court again concluded that it had "jurisdiction over the subject matter and the parties to this cause." Finding that Rudzewicz and MacShara had breached their franchise agreements with Burger King and had infringed Burger King's trademarks and service marks, the court entered judgment against them, jointly and severally, for $228,875 in contract damages. The court also ordered them "to immediately close Burger King Restaurant Number 775 from continued operation or to immediately give the keys and possession of said restaurant to Burger King Corporation," found that they had failed to prove any of the required elements of their counterclaim, and awarded costs and attorney's fees to Burger King.

Rudzewicz appealed to the Court of Appeals for the Eleventh Circuit.[11] A divided panel of that Circuit reversed the judgment, concluding that the District Court could not properly exercise personal jurisdiction over Rudzewicz pursuant to Fla. Stat. §48.193(1)(g) (Supp. 1984) because "the circumstances of the Drayton Plains franchise and the negotiations which led to it left Rudzewicz bereft of reasonable notice and financially unprepared for the prospect of franchise litigation in Florida." *Burger King Corp. v. MacShara*, 724 F.2d 1505, 1513 (1984). Accordingly, the panel majority concluded that "[j]urisdiction under these circumstances would offend the fundamental fairness which is the touchstone of due process." *Ibid.*

Burger King appealed the Eleventh Circuit's judgment to this Court pursuant to 28 U.S.C. §1254(2), and we postponed probable jurisdiction. Because it is unclear whether the Eleventh Circuit actually held that Fla. Stat. §48.193(1)(g) (Supp. 1984) itself is unconstitutional as applied to the circumstances of this case, we conclude that jurisdiction by appeal does not properly lie and therefore dismiss the appeal. Treating the jurisdictional statement as a petition for a writ of certiorari, *see* 28 U.S.C. §2103, we grant the petition and now reverse.

II

A

The Due Process Clause protects an individual's liberty interest in not being subject to the binding judgments of a forum with which he has

11. MacShara did not appeal his judgment. In addition, Rudzewicz entered into a compromise with Burger King and waived his right to appeal the District Court's finding of trademark infringement and its entry of injunctive relief. Accordingly, we need not address the extent to which the tortious act provisions of Florida's long-arm statute, *see* Fla. Stat. §48.193(1)(b) (Supp. 1984), may constitutionally extend to out-of-state trademark infringement. *Cf. Calder v. Jones*, 465 U.S. 783, 788-789 (1984) (tortious out-of-state conduct); *Keeton v. Hustler Magazine, Inc.*, 465 U.S. 770, 776 (1984) (same).

established no meaningful "contacts, ties, or relations." *International Shoe Co. v. Washington*, 326 U.S. at 319.[13] By requiring that individuals have "fair warning that a particular activity may subject [them] to the jurisdiction of a foreign sovereign," *Shaffer v. Heitner*, 433 U.S. 186, 218 (1977) (Stevens, J., concurring in judgment), the Due Process Clause "gives a degree of predictability to the legal system that allows potential defendants to structure their primary conduct with some minimum assurance as to where that conduct will and will not render them liable to suit," *World-Wide Volkswagen Corp. v. Woodson*, 444 U.S. 286, 297 (1980).

Where a forum seeks to assert specific jurisdiction over an out- of-state defendant who has not consented to suit there,[14] this "fair warning" requirement is satisfied if the defendant has "purposefully directed" his activities at residents of the forum, *Keeton v. Hustler Magazine, Inc.*, 465 U.S. 770, 774 (1984), and the litigation results from alleged injuries that "arise out of or relate to" those activities, *Helicopteros Nacionales de Colombia, S.A. v. Hall*, 466 U.S. 408, 414 (1984).[15] Thus "[t]he forum State does not exceed its powers under the Due Process Clause if it asserts personal jurisdiction over a corporation that delivers its products into the stream of commerce with the expectation that they will be purchased by consumers in the forum State" and those products subsequently injure forum consumers. *World-Wide Volkswagen Corp. v. Woodson, supra*, 444 U.S. at 297-298. Similarly, a publisher who distributes magazines in a distant State may fairly be held accountable in that forum for damages resulting there from an allegedly defamatory story. *Keeton v. Hustler Magazine, Inc., supra; see also Calder v. Jones*, 465 U.S. 783 (1984) (suit against author and editor). And with respect to interstate contractual obligations, we have emphasized that parties who "reach out beyond one state and create continuing relationships and obligations with citizens of another state" are subject to regulation and sanctions in the other State for the consequences of their activities.

13. Although this protection operates to restrict state power, it "must be seen as ultimately a function of the individual liberty interest preserved by the Due Process Clause" rather than as a function "of federalism concerns." *Insurance Corp. of Ireland v. Compagnie des Bauxites de Guinée*, 456 U.S. 694 (1982).

14. We have noted that, because the personal jurisdiction requirement is a waivable right, there are a "variety of legal arrangements" by which a litigant may give "express or implied consent to the personal jurisdiction of the court." *Insurance Corp. of Ireland v. Compagnie des Bauxites de Guinée, supra*, at 703. For example, particularly in the commercial context, parties frequently stipulate in advance to submit their controversies for resolution within a particular jurisdiction. *See National Equipment Rental, Ltd. v. Szukhent*, 375 U.S. 311 (1964). Where such forum-selection provisions have been obtained through "freely negotiated" agreements and are not "unreasonable and unjust," *The Bremen v. Zapata Off-Shore Co.*, 407 U.S. 1, 15 (1972), their enforcement does not offend due process.

15. "Specific" jurisdiction contrasts with "general" jurisdiction, pursuant to which "a State exercises personal jurisdiction over a defendant in a suit not arising out of or related to the defendant's contacts with the forum." *Helicopteros Nacionales de Colombia, S.A. v. Hall*, 466 U.S. at 414, n.9; *see also Perkins v. Benguet Consolidated Mining Co.*, 342 U.S. 437 (1952).

We have noted several reasons why a forum legitimately may exercise personal jurisdiction over a nonresident who "purposefully directs" his activities toward forum residents. A State generally has a "manifest interest" in providing its residents with a convenient forum for redressing injuries inflicted by out-of-state actors. Moreover, where individuals "purposefully derive benefit" from their interstate activities, *Kulko v. California Superior Court,* 436 U.S. 84, 96 (1978), it may well be unfair to allow them to escape having to account in other States for consequences that arise proximately from such activities; the Due Process Clause may not readily be wielded as a territorial shield to avoid interstate obligations that have been voluntarily assumed. And because "modern transportation and communications have made it much less burdensome for a party sued to defend himself in a State where he engages in economic activity," it usually will not be unfair to subject him to the burdens of litigating in another forum for disputes relating to such activity. *McGee v. International Life Insurance Co., supra,* 355 U.S. at 223.

Notwithstanding these considerations, the constitutional touchstone remains whether the defendant purposefully established "minimum contacts" in the forum State. *International Shoe Co. v. Washington, supra,* 326 U.S. at 316. Although it has been argued that foreseeability of causing injury in another State should be sufficient to establish such contacts there when policy considerations so require, the Court has consistently held that this kind of foreseeability is not a "sufficient benchmark" for exercising personal jurisdiction. *World-Wide Volkswagen Corp. v. Woodson,* 444 U.S. at 295. Instead, "the foreseeability that is critical to due process analysis . . . is that the defendant's conduct and connection with the forum State are such that he should reasonably anticipate being haled into court there." *Id.,* at 297. In defining when it is that a potential defendant should "reasonably anticipate" out-of-state litigation, the Court frequently has drawn from the reasoning of *Hanson v. Denckla,* 357 U.S. 235, 253 (1958):

> The unilateral activity of those who claim some relationship with a nonresident defendant cannot satisfy the requirement of contact with the forum State. The application of that rule will vary with the quality and nature of the defendant's activity, but it is essential in each case that there be some act by which the defendant purposefully avails itself of the privilege of conducting activities within the forum State, thus invoking the benefits and protections of its laws.

This "purposeful availment" requirement ensures that a defendant will not be haled into a jurisdiction solely as a result of "random," "fortuitous," or "attenuated" contacts, *Keeton v. Hustler Magazine, Inc.,* 465 U.S. at 774; *World-Wide Volkswagen Corp. v. Woodson, supra,* 444 U.S. at 299, or of the "unilateral activity of another party or a third person," *Helicopteros Nacionales de Colombia, S.A. v. Hall, supra,* 466 U.S. at 417.[17] Jurisdiction is proper, however, where the contacts proximately result from actions by the defendant himself that create a "substantial connection" with the forum State. *McGee v. International Life Insurance Co., supra,* 355 U.S. at 223; *see also Kulko v. California Superior Court, supra,* 436 U.S. at 94, n.7.[18] Thus where the defendant "deliberately" has engaged in significant activities within a State, *Keeton v. Hustler Magazine, Inc., supra,* 465 U.S. at 781, or has created "continuing obligations" between himself and residents of the forum, *Travelers Health Assn. v. Virginia,* 339 U.S. at 648, he manifestly has availed himself of the privilege of conducting business there, and because his activities are shielded by "the benefits and protections" of the forum's laws it is presumptively not unreasonable to require him to submit to the burdens of litigation in that forum as well.

Jurisdiction in these circumstances may not be avoided merely because the defendant did not physically enter the forum State. Although territorial presence frequently will enhance a potential defendant's affiliation with a State and reinforce the reasonable foreseeability of suit there, it is an inescapable fact of modern commercial life that a substantial amount of business is transacted solely by mail and wire communications across state lines, thus obviating the need for physical presence within a State in which business is conducted. So long as a commercial actor's efforts are "purposefully directed" toward residents of another State, we have consistently rejected the notion that an absence of physical contacts can defeat personal jurisdiction there. *Keeton v. Hustler Magazine, Inc., supra,* 465 U.S. at 774-775; *see also Calder v. Jones,* 465 U.S. at 778-790; *McGee v. International Life Insurance Co.,* 355 U.S. at 222-223.

Once it has been decided that a defendant purposefully established minimum contacts within the forum State, these contacts may be consid-

---

17. Applying this principle, the Court has held that the Due Process Clause forbids the exercise of personal jurisdiction over an out-of-state automobile distributor whose only tie to the forum resulted from a customer's decision to drive there, *World-Wide Volkswagen Corp. v. Woodson, supra;* over a divorced husband sued for child-support payments whose only affiliation with the forum was created by his former spouse's decision to settle there, *Kulko v. California Superior Court,* 436 U.S. 84 (1978); and over a trustee whose only connection with the forum resulted from the settlor's decision to exercise her power of appointment there, *Hanson v. Denckla,* 357 U.S. 235 (1958). In such instances, the defendant has had no "clear notice that it is subject to suit" in the forum and thus no opportunity to "alleviate the risk of burdensome litigation" there. *World-Wide Volkswagen Corp. v. Woodson, supra,* 444 U.S. at 297.

18. So long as it creates a "substantial connection" with the forum, even a single act can support jurisdiction. *McGee v. International Life Insurance Co.,* 355 U.S. at 223. The Court has noted, however, that "some single or occasional acts" related to the forum may not be sufficient to establish jurisdiction if "their nature and quality and the circumstances of their commission" create only an "attenuated" affiliation with the forum. *International Shoe Co. v. Washington,* 326 U.S. 310, 318 (1945); *World-Wide Volkswagen Corp. v. Woodson,* 444 U.S. at 299. This distinction derives from the belief that, with respect to this category of "isolated" acts, *id.* at 297, the reasonable foreseeability of litigation in the forum is substantially diminished.

ered in light of other factors to determine whether the assertion of personal jurisdiction would comport with "fair play and substantial justice." *International Shoe Co. v. Washington,* 326 U.S. at 320. Thus courts in "appropriate case[s]" may evaluate "the burden on the defendant," "the forum State's interest in adjudicating the dispute," "the plaintiff's interest in obtaining convenient and effective relief," "the interstate judicial system's interest in obtaining the most efficient resolution of controversies," and the "shared interest of the several States in furthering fundamental substantive social policies." *World-Wide Volkswagen Corp. v. Woodson, supra,* 444 U.S. at 292. These considerations sometimes serve to establish the reasonableness of jurisdiction upon a lesser showing of minimum contacts than would otherwise be required. *See, e.g., Keeton v. Hustler Magazine, Inc., supra,* 465 U.S. at 780; *Calder v. Jones, supra,* 465 U.S. at 788-789; *McGee v. International Life Insurance Co., supra,* 355 U.S. at 223-224. On the other hand, where a defendant who purposefully has directed his activities at forum residents seeks to defeat jurisdiction, he must present a compelling case that the presence of some other considerations would render jurisdiction unreasonable. Most such considerations usually may be accommodated through means short of finding jurisdiction unconstitutional. For example, the potential clash of the forum's law with the "fundamental substantive social policies" of another State may be accommodated through application of the forum's choice-of-law rules. Similarly, a defendant claiming substantial inconvenience may seek a change of venue. Nevertheless, minimum requirements inherent in the concept of "fair play and substantial justice" may defeat the reasonableness of jurisdiction even if the defendant has purposefully engaged in forum activities. *World-Wide Volkswagen Corp. v. Woodson, supra,* 444 U.S. at 292; *see also Restatement (Second) of Conflict of Laws* §§36-37 (1971). As we previously have noted, jurisdictional rules may not be employed in such a way as to make litigation "so gravely difficult and inconvenient" that a party unfairly is at a "severe disadvantage" in comparison to his opponent. *The Bremen v. Zapata Off-Shore Co.,* 407 U.S. 1, 18 (1972) (re forum-selection provisions); *McGee v. International Life Insurance Co., supra,* 355 U.S. at 223-224.

B

(1)

Applying these principles to the case at hand, we believe there is substantial record evidence supporting the District Court's conclusion that the assertion of personal jurisdiction over Rudzewicz in Florida for the alleged breach of his franchise agreement did not offend due process. At the outset, we note a continued division among lower courts respecting whether and to what extent a contract can constitute a "contact" for purposes of due process analysis. If the question is whether an individual's contract with an out-of-state party alone can automatically establish sufficient minimum contacts in the other party's home forum, we believe the answer clearly is that it cannot. The Court long ago rejected the notion that personal jurisdiction might turn on "mechanical" tests, *International Shoe Co. v. Washington, supra,* 326 U.S. at 319, or on "conceptualistic . . . theories of the place of contracting or of performance." Instead, we have emphasized the need for a "highly realistic" approach that recognizes that a "contract" is "ordinarily but an intermediate step serving to tie up prior business negotiations with future consequences which themselves are the real object of the business transaction." It is these factors—prior negotiations and contemplated future consequences, along with the terms of the contract and the parties' actual course of dealing—that must be evaluated in determining whether the defendant purposefully established minimum contacts within the forum.

In this case, no physical ties to Florida can be attributed to Rudzewicz other than MacShara's brief training course in Miami. Rudzewicz did not maintain offices in Florida and, for all that appears from the record, has never even visited there. Yet this franchise dispute grew directly out of "a contract which had a substantial connection with that State." *McGee v. International Life Insurance Co.,* 355 U.S. at 223 (emphasis added). Eschewing the option of operating an independent local enterprise, Rudzewicz deliberately "reach[ed] out beyond" Michigan and negotiated with a Florida corporation for the purchase of a long-term franchise and the manifold benefits that would derive from affiliation with a nationwide organization. Upon approval, he entered into a carefully structured 20-year relationship that envisioned continuing and wide-reaching contacts with Burger King in Florida. In light of Rudzewicz' voluntary acceptance of the long-term and exacting regulation of his business from Burger King's Miami headquarters, the "quality and nature" of his relationship to the company in Florida can in no sense be viewed as "random," "fortuitous," or "attenuated." *Hanson v. Denckla,* 357 U.S. at 253; *Keeton v. Hustler Magazine, Inc.,* 465 U.S. at 774; *World-Wide Volkswagen Corp. v. Woodson,* 444 U.S. at 299. Rudzewicz' refusal to make the contractually required payments in Miami, and his continued use of Burger King's trademarks and confidential business information after his termination, caused foreseeable injuries to the corporation in Florida. For these reasons it was, at the very least, presumptively reasonable for Rudzewicz to be called to account there for such injuries.

The Court of Appeals concluded, however, that in light of the supervision emanating from Burger King's district office in Birmingham, Rudzewicz reasonably believed that "the Michigan office was for all intents and purposes the embodiment of Burger King" and that he therefore had no "reason to anticipate a Burger King suit outside of Michigan." This reasoning overlooks substantial record evidence indicating that Rudzewicz most certainly knew that he was affiliating himself with an enterprise based primarily in Florida. The contract documents themselves emphasize that Burger King's operations are conducted and supervised from the Miami headquarters, that all relevant notices and payments must be sent there, and that the agreements were made in and enforced from Miami. Moreover, the parties' actual course of dealing repeatedly confirmed that decisionmaking authority was vested in the Miami headquarters and that the district office served largely as an intermediate link between the head-quarters and the franchisees. When problems arose over building design, site-development fees, rent computation, and the defaulted payments, Rudzewicz and MacShara learned that the Michigan office was powerless to resolve their disputes and could only channel their communications to Miami. Throughout these disputes, the Miami headquarters and the Michigan franchisees carried on a continuous course of direct communi-cations by mail and by telephone, and it was the Miami headquarters that made the key negotiating decisions out of which the instant litigation arose.

Moreover, we believe the Court of Appeals gave insufficient weight to provisions in the various franchise documents providing that all disputes would be governed by Florida law. The franchise agreement, for example, stated: "This Agreement shall become valid when executed and accepted by BKC at Miami, Florida; it shall be deemed made and entered into in the State of Florida and shall be governed and construed under and in accordance with the laws of the State of Florida. The choice of law designation does not require that all suits concerning this Agreement be filed in Florida." The Court of Appeals reasoned that choice-of-law provisions are irrelevant to the question of personal jurisdiction, relying on *Hanson v. Denckla* for the proposition that "the center of gravity for choice-of-law purposes does not necessarily confer the sovereign preroga-tive to assert jurisdiction." This reasoning misperceives the import of the quoted proposition. The Court in *Hanson* and subsequent cases has emphasized that choice-of-law analysis—which focuses on all elements of a transaction, and not simply on the defendant's conduct—is distinct from minimum-contacts jurisdictional analysis—which focuses at the threshold solely on the defendant's purposeful connection to the forum. Nothing in our cases, however, suggests that a choice-of-law provision should be ignored in considering whether a defendant has "purposefully invoked the benefits and protections of a State's laws" for jurisdictional purposes. Although such a provision standing alone would be insufficient to confer jurisdiction, we believe that, when combined with the 20-year interdependent relationship Rudzewicz established with Burger King's Miami headquarters, it reinforced his deliberate affiliation with the forum State and the reasonable foreseeability of possible litigation there. As Judge Johnson argued in his dissent below, Rudzewicz "purposefully availed himself of the benefits and protections of Florida's laws" by entering into contracts expressly providing that those laws would govern franchise disputes.[24]

(2)

Nor has Rudzewicz pointed to other factors that can be said persuasively to outweigh the considerations discussed above and to establish the unconstitutionality of Florida's assertion of jurisdiction. We cannot conclude that Florida had no "legitimate interest in holding [Rudzewicz] answerable on a claim related to" the contacts he had established in that State. *Keeton v. Hustler Magazine, Inc.*, 465 U.S. at 776; *See also McGee v. International Life Insurance Co.*, 355 U.S. at 223 (noting that State frequently will have a "manifest interest in providing effective means of redress for its residents").[25] Moreover, although Rudzewicz has argued at some length that Michigan's Franchise Investment Law, Mich. Comp. Laws §445.1501 *et seq.* (1979), governs many aspects of this franchise relationship, he has not demonstrated how Michigan's acknowledged interest might possibly render jurisdiction in Florida unconstitutional.[26] Finally, the Court of Appeals' assertion that the Florida litigation "severely impaired [Rudzewicz'] ability to call Michigan witnesses who might be essential to his defense and counterclaim," is wholly without support in the record. And even to the extent that it is inconvenient for a party who has minimum contacts with a forum to litigate there, such considerations most frequently can be accommodated through a change of venue. Although the Court has suggested that inconvenience may at some point become so

---

24. In addition, the franchise agreement's disclaimer that the "choice of law designation does not require that all suits concerning this Agreement be filed in Florida," App. 72 (emphasis added), reasonably should have suggested to Rudzewicz that by negative implication such suits could be filed there. The lease also provided for binding arbitration in Miami of certain condemnation disputes, *id.*, at 113, and Rudzewicz conceded the validity of this provision at oral argument, Tr. of Oral Arg. 37. Although it does not govern the instant dispute, this provision also should have made it apparent to the franchisees that they were dealing directly with the Miami headquarters and that the Birmingham district office was not "for all intents and purposes the embodiment of Burger King."

25. Complaining that "when Burger King is the plaintiff, you won't 'have it your way' because it sues all franchisees in Miami," Brief for Appellee 19, Rudzewicz contends that Florida's interest in providing a convenient forum is negligible given the company's size and ability to conduct litigation anywhere in the country. We disagree. Absent compelling considerations, *cf. McGee v. International Life Insurance Co.*, 355 U.S. at 223, a defendant who has purposefully derived commercial benefit from his affiliations in a forum may not defeat jurisdiction there simply because of his adversary's greater net wealth.

26. Rudzewicz has failed to show how the District Court's exercise of jurisdiction in this case might have been at all inconsistent with Michigan's interests. To the contrary, the court found that Burger King had fully complied with Michigan law, and there is nothing in Michigan's franchise Act suggesting that Michigan would attempt to assert exclusive jurisdiction to resolve franchise disputes affecting its residents. In any event, minimum-contacts analysis presupposes that two or more States may be interested in the outcome of a dispute, and the process of resolving potentially conflicting "fundamental substantive social policies," *World-Wide Volkswagen Corp. v. Woodson*, 444 U.S. at 292, can usually be accommodated through choice-of-law rules rather than through outright preclusion of jurisdiction in one forum. *See* n.19, *supra*.

substantial as to achieve constitutional magnitude, *McGee v. International Life Insurance Co., supra,* 355 U.S. at 223, this is not such a case.

The Court of Appeals also concluded, however, that the parties' dealings involved "a characteristic disparity of bargaining power" and "elements of surprise," and that Rudzewicz "lacked fair notice" of the potential for litigation in Florida because the contractual provisions suggesting to the contrary were merely "boilerplate declarations in a lengthy printed contract." Rudzewicz presented many of these arguments to the District Court, contending that Burger King was guilty of misrepresentation, fraud, and duress; that it gave insufficient notice in its dealings with him; and that the contract was one of adhesion. After a 3-day bench trial, the District Court found that Burger King had made no misrepresentations, that Rudzewicz and MacShara "were and are experienced and sophisticated businessmen," and that "at no time" did they "ac[t] under economic duress or disadvantage imposed by" Burger King. Federal Rule of Civil Procedure 52(a) requires that "[f]indings of fact shall not be set aside unless clearly erroneous," and neither Rudzewicz nor the Court of Appeals has pointed to record evidence that would support a "definite and firm conviction" that the District Court's findings are mistaken. To the contrary, Rudzewicz was represented by counsel throughout these complex transactions and, as Judge Johnson observed in dissent below, was himself an experienced accountant "who for five months conducted negotiations with Burger King over the terms of the franchise and lease agreements, and who obligated himself personally to contracts requiring over time payments that exceeded $1 million." Rudzewicz was able to secure a modest reduction in rent and other concessions from Miami headquarters; moreover, to the extent that Burger King's terms were inflexible, Rudzewicz presumably decided that the advantages of affiliating with a national organization provided sufficient commercial benefits to offset the detriments.[28]

III

Notwithstanding these considerations, the Court of Appeals apparently believed that it was necessary to reject jurisdiction in this case as a prophylactic measure, reasoning that an affirmance of the District Court's judgment would result in the exercise of jurisdiction over "out-of-

---

28. We do not mean to suggest that the jurisdictional outcome will always be the same in franchise cases. Some franchises may be primarily intrastate in character or involve different decisionmaking structures, such that a franchisee should not reasonably anticipate out-of-state litigation. Moreover, commentators have argued that franchise relationships may sometimes involve unfair business practices in their inception and operation. *See* H. Brown, *Franchising Realities and Remedies* 4-5 (2d ed. 1978). For these reasons, we reject Burger King's suggestion for "a general rule, or at least a presumption, that participation in an interstate franchise relationship" represents consent to the jurisdiction of the franchisor's principal place of business. Brief for Appellant 46.

state consumers to collect payments due on modest personal purchases" and would "sow the seeds of default judgments against franchisees owing smaller debts." 724 F.2d at 1511. We share the Court of Appeals' broader concerns and therefore reject any talismanic jurisdictional formulas; "the facts of each case must [always] be weighed" in determining whether personal jurisdiction would comport with "fair play and substantial justice." *Kulko v. California Superior Court*, 436 U.S. at 92.[29] The "quality and nature" of an interstate transaction may sometimes be so "random," "fortuitous," or "attenuated"[30] that it cannot fairly be said that the potential defendant "should reasonably anticipate being haled into court" in another jurisdiction. *World-Wide Volkswagen Corp. v. Woodson*, 444 U.S. at 297. We also have emphasized that jurisdiction may not be grounded on a contract whose terms have been obtained through "fraud, undue influence, or overweening bargaining power" and whose application would render litigation "so gravely difficult and inconvenient that [a party] will for all practical purposes be deprived of his day in court." *The Bremen v. Zapata Off-Shore Co.*, 407 U.S. at 12, 18. *Cf. Fuentes v. Shevin*, 407 U.S. 67, 94-96 (1972); *National Equipment Rental, Ltd. v. Szukhent*, 375 U.S. 311, 329 (1964) (Black, J., dissenting) (jurisdictional rules may not be employed against small consumers so as to "crippl[e] their defense"). Just as the Due Process Clause allows flexibility in ensuring that commercial actors are not effectively "judgment proof" for the consequences of obligations they voluntarily assume in other States, *McGee v. International Life Insurance Co.*, 355 U.S. at 223, so too does it prevent rules that would unfairly enable them to obtain default judgments against unwitting customers. *Cf. United States v. Rumely*, 345 U.S. 41, 44 (1953) (courts must not be "blind" to what " [a]ll others can see and understand").

For the reasons set forth above, however, these dangers are not present in the instant case. Because Rudzewicz established a substantial and continuing relationship with Burger King's Miami headquarters, received fair notice from the contract documents and the course of dealing that he might be subject to suit in Florida, and has failed to demonstrate how jurisdiction in that forum would otherwise be fundamentally unfair, we conclude that the District Court's exercise of jurisdiction pursuant to Fla. Stat. §48.193(1)(g) (Supp. 1984) did not offend due process. The judgment of the Court of Appeals is accordingly reversed, and the case is remanded for further proceedings consistent with this opinion.

It is so ordered.

29. This approach does, of course, preclude clear-cut jurisdictional rules. But any inquiry into "fair play and substantial justice" necessarily requires determinations "in which few answers will be written 'in black and white. The greys are dominant and even among them the shades are innumerable.'" *Kulko v. California Superior Court*, 436 U.S. at 92.

30. *Hanson v. Denckla*, 357 U.S. at 253; *Keeton v. Hustler Magazine, Inc.*, 465 U.S. at 774; *World-Wide Volkswagen Corp. v. Woodson*, 444 U.S. at 299.

Justice POWELL took no part in the consideration or decision of this case.

Justice STEVENS, with whom Justice WHITE joins, dissenting.

In my opinion there is a significant element of unfairness in requiring a franchisee to defend a case of this kind in the forum chosen by the franchisor. It is undisputed that appellee maintained no place of business in Florida, that he had no employees in that State, and that he was not licensed to do business there. Appellee did not prepare his French fries, shakes, and hamburgers in Michigan, and then deliver them into the stream of commerce "with the expectation that they [would] be purchased by consumers in" Florida. *Ante,* at 2182. To the contrary, appellee did business only in Michigan, his business, property, and payroll taxes were payable in that State, and he sold all of his products there.

Throughout the business relationship, appellee's principal contacts with appellant were with its Michigan office. Notwithstanding its disclaimer, the Court seems ultimately to rely on nothing more than standard boilerplate language contained in various documents to establish that appellee "'purposefully availed himself of the benefits and protections of Florida's laws.'" Such superficial analysis creates a potential for unfairness not only in negotiations between franchisors and their franchisees but, more significantly, in the resolution of the disputes that inevitably arise from time to time in such relationships. . . .

Comments and Questions

1. The franchise agreement that Rudzewicz entered into with Burger King provided that the "agreement shall become valid when executed and accepted by BKC at Miami, Florida; it shall be deemed made and entered into in the State of Florida and shall be governed and construed under and in accordance with the laws of the State of Florida. The choice-of-law designation does not require that all suits concerning this Agreement be filed in Florida." Why isn't that clause sufficient in itself to establish jurisdiction over Rudzewicz by consent? *See* the Court's footnotes 14 and 24. We will discuss "forum selection" clauses later.

2. Were Rudzewicz's connections to Florida more "purposeful" than World-Wide's to Oklahoma? Were his hamburgers more mobile than *World-Wide Volkswagen*'s Audi? How does the Court distinguish *World-Wide Volkswagen*?

3. Suppose Rudzewicz had been a management consultant retained by Burger King to evaluate its operations in Michigan. His consulting contract was sent from the Miami headquarters to his office in Michigan; he signed and returned it by mail. The contract called for the project to be com-

pleted within three months. Dissatisfied with his work product, Burger King Corporation filed a breach of contract action in Florida. Is there jurisdiction over the defendant? How might the Court distinguish that case?

4. Suppose Rudzewicz clipped a mail order form from a magazine and sent it to the Sunshine Fitness Company in Miami, and the company shipped its Row-Your-Pounds-Away Exerciser to him in Michigan. If Rudzewicz fails to pay the bill, can Sunshine sue him in Florida? How does this contract differ from the one Rudzewicz signed with Burger King?

5. Suppose Rudzewicz is injured on the Exerciser and decides to file a product liability action against Sunshine. Is there jurisdiction in Michigan? How is this case different from *Sunshine v. Rudzewicz* in note 4?

6. What does *Burger King* teach us about the relation between the "fair play" factors and the "minimum contacts" test?

7. Although Burger King won the case, the Court refused to hold that participation in an interstate franchise relationship would constitute consent to jurisdiction in the franchiser's principal place of business. *See* the Court's footnote 28. Was counsel for Burger King wise in basing its proposed rule on a consent theory? Look back at the evolution of law from *Hess v. Pawloski* to *International Shoe*. Why do you think the Court is so adamant about not adopting any general rules in the area of personal jurisdiction? (Don't discount masochism as one possible explanation.)

Practice Exercise No. 28: Ruling on a Rule 12(b)(2) Motion to Dismiss

To: Law Clerk
From: U.S. District Judge, District of Massachusetts
Re: Recommendation on 12(b)(2) Motion in
    Shaw v. Northern Law School

Norris Shaw, a Massachusetts citizen, has filed a diversity action against Northern Law School of Vermont ("NLS") and one of its faculty, Albert Gloss. In a two-count complaint, Shaw seeks damages against the school for breach of contract and against Gloss for intentional infliction of emotional distress.

Shaw alleges that after reading an article about Northern Law School in the Boston Sunday Globe's Education Section, and intrigued by the prospect of learning the law amidst the beauty of the Green Mountains (and in close proximity to Ben & Jerry's Ice Cream), he wrote the school and expressed interest. NLS responded by mailing its catalogue and application form to Shaw's home in Massachusetts. He filled out the application, mailed it to back NLS, and in the spring received by mail an acceptance letter from the school. Shaw sent in his $1500 deposit and enrolled as a law student in the fall of 1996.

In his second year at NLS, Shaw took a course entitled "Extremely Complex Litigation" from Professor Gloss (a lifelong Vermonter). Although he thought he had mastered the materials, Shaw received a failing grade; as a result, he was dismissed from the school. (His GPA was sufficiently unimpressive that the F put him under the required minimum.) After attempting unsuccessfully to have the grade changed through the school's appeals procedure, Shaw returned to Massachusetts and filed the instant lawsuit.

The plaintiff alleges that he regularly disagreed with Professor Gloss in class and that Gloss failed him in retaliation. He asserts that the professor acted with the intent to inflict emotional damage, which he did, and further alleges that the school's refusal to reverse the grade constitutes a breach of its contract with Shaw.

Defendants NLS and Gloss have both moved to dismiss the complaint under Fed. R. Civ. Pro. 12(b)(2). The school has filed an affidavit asserting that its only place of business is in Vermont, that it has never maintained any office, mailing address, or telephone listing in Massachusetts, and that it has never done business or advertised there. The affidavit does concede that NLS occasionally sends recruiters to Massachusetts to inform pre-law advisors and undergraduates about the school. Gloss has filed an affidavit asserting that he has never set foot in Massachusetts and has no connection whatever with the state.

I need a memorandum from you recommending how I should rule on these two motions. You will recall that the Massachusetts Long-Arm statute is reprinted in Practice Exercise No. 27.

I. JURISDICTION BASED ON THE PRESENCE OF DEFENDANT'S PROPERTY

Would it make any difference on the issue of adjudicatory power over Professor Gloss in the preceding Practice Exercise if he owned a vacation home on Martha's Vineyard in Massachusetts? If Gloss had graded Shaw's work while at the home, arguably there might be specific jurisdiction over Shaw's claim. But assuming no such connection, ownership of the home raises two other possible bases of jurisdiction that go back to the original *Pennoyer* formulation. First, Shaw could try to have the professor served with process at the home—service within the forum state constitutes physical "presence" under the *Pennoyer* scheme. We will explore the current status of this basis for court power in the next section.

Second, Shaw could cause the home to be attached and assert *quasi in rem* jurisdiction—under the *Pennoyer* scheme, presence of his property creates jurisdiction over Gloss on the unrelated tort claim, permitting the entry of a judgment up to the value of the property. (You will recall that this was the basis for entering judgment against Neff in *Pennoyer* and Balk in *Harris*.) The Court's 1977 decision in the next case radically altered this category of adjudicatory power.

■ SHAFFER v. HEITNER
433 U.S. 186 (1977)

Justice MARSHALL delivered the opinion of the Court:

The controversy in this case concerns the constitutionality of a Delaware statute that allows a court of that State to take jurisdiction of a lawsuit by sequestering any property of the defendant that happens to be located in Delaware. Appellants contend that the sequestration statute as applied in this case violates the Due Process Clause of the Fourteenth Amendment both because it permits the state courts to exercise jurisdiction despite the absence of sufficient contacts among the defendants, the litigation, and the State of Delaware and because it authorizes the deprivation of defendants' property without providing adequate procedural safeguards. We find it necessary to consider only the first of these contentions.

I

Appellee Heitner, a nonresident of Delaware, is the owner of one share of stock in the Greyhound Corp., a business incorporated under the laws of Delaware with its principal place of business in Phoenix, Ariz. On May 22, 1974, he filed a shareholder's derivative suit in the Court of Chancery for New Castle County, Del., in which he named as defendants Greyhound, its wholly owned subsidiary Greyhound Lines, Inc.,[1] and 28 present or former officers or directors of one or both of the corporations. In essence, Heitner alleged that the individual defendants had violated their duties to Greyhound by causing it and its subsidiary to engage in actions that resulted in the corporation's being held liable for substantial damages in a private antitrust suit[2] and a large fine in a criminal contempt action.[3] The activities which led to these penalties took place in Oregon.

Simultaneously with his complaint, Heitner filed a motion for an order of sequestration of the Delaware property of the individual defendants

---

1. Greyhound Lines, Inc., is incorporated in California and has its principal place of business in Phoenix, Ariz.

2. A judgment of $13,146,090 plus attorneys' fees was entered against Greyhound in *Mt. Hood Stages, Inc. v. Greyhound Corp.*, 1972-3 Trade Cas. P 74,824, *aff'd*, 555 F.2d 687 (9th Cir. 1977).

3. *See United States v. Greyhound Corp.*, 363 F. Supp. 525 (N.D. Ill. 1973) and 370 F. Supp. 881 (N.D. Ill.), *aff'd*, 508 F.2d 529 (7th Cir. 1974). Greyhound was fined $100,000 and Greyhound Lines $500,000.

pursuant to Del. Code Ann., Tit. 10, §366 (1975).[4] This motion was accompanied by a supporting affidavit of counsel which stated that the individual defendants were nonresidents of Delaware. The affidavit identified the property to be sequestered as

> common stock, 3% Second Cumulative Preferred Stock and stock unit credits of the Defendant Greyhound Corporation, a Delaware corporation, as well as all options and all warrants to purchase said stock issued to said individual Defendants and all contractural [sic] obligations, all rights, debts or credits due or accrued to or for the benefit of any of the said Defendants under any type of written agreement, contract or other legal instrument of any kind whatever between any of the individual Defendants and said corporation.

The requested sequestration order was signed the day the motion was filed. Pursuant to that order, the sequestrator "seized" approximately 82,000 shares of Greyhound common stock belonging to 19 of the defendants,[7] and options belonging to another 2 defendants. These seizures

4. Section 366 provides:

(a) If it appears in any complaint filed in the Court of Chancery that the defendant or any one or more of the defendants is a nonresident of the State, the Court may make an order directing such nonresident defendant or defendants to appear by a day certain to be designated. Such order shall be served on such nonresident defendant or defendants by mail or otherwise, if practicable, and shall be published in such manner as the Court directs, not less than once a week for 3 consecutive weeks. The Court may compel the appearance of the defendant by the seizure of all or any part of his property, which property may be sold under the order of the Court to pay the demand of the plaintiff, if the defendant does not appear, or otherwise defaults. Any defendant whose property shall have been so seized and who shall have entered a general appearance in the cause may, upon notice to the plaintiff, petition the Court for an order releasing such property or any part thereof from the seizure. The Court shall release such property unless the plaintiff shall satisfy the Court that because of other circumstances there is a reasonable possibility that such release may render it substantially less likely that plaintiff will obtain satisfaction of any judgment secured. If such petition shall not be granted, or if no such petition shall be filed, such property shall remain subject to seizure and may be sold to satisfy any judgment entered in the case. The Court may at any time release such property or any part thereof upon the giving of sufficient security.

(b) The Court may make all necessary rules respecting the form of process, the manner of issuance and return thereof, the release of such property from seizure and for the sale of the property so seized, and may require the plaintiff to give approved security to abide any order of the Court respecting the property.

(c) Any transfer or assignment of the property so seized after the seizure thereof shall be void and after the sale of the property is made and confirmed, the purchaser shall be entitled to and have all the right, title and interest of the defendant in and to the property so seized and sold and such sale and confirmation shall transfer to the purchaser all the right, title and interest of the defendant in and to the property as fully as if the defendant had transferred the same to the purchaser in accordance with law.

7. The closing price of Greyhound stock on the day the sequestration order was issued was $14 3/8. New York Times, May 23, 1974, p. 62. Thus, the value of the sequestered stock was approximately $1.2 million.

were accomplished by placing "stop transfer" orders or their equivalents on the books of the Greyhound Corp. So far as the record shows, none of the certificates representing the seized property was physically present in Delaware. The stock was considered to be in Delaware, and so subject to seizure, by virtue of Del. Code Ann., Tit. 8, §169 (1975), which makes Delaware the situs of ownership of all stock in Delaware corporations.[9]

All 28 defendants were notified of the initiation of the suit by certified mail directed to their last known addresses and by publication in a New Castle County newspaper. The 21 defendants whose property was seized (hereafter referred to as appellants) responded by entering a special appearance for the purpose of moving to quash service of process and to vacate the sequestration order. They contended that the ex parte sequestration procedure did not accord them due process of law and that the property seized was not capable of attachment in Delaware. In addition, appellants asserted that under the rule of *International Shoe Co. v. Washington*, 326 U.S. 310 (1945), they did not have sufficient contacts with Delaware to sustain the jurisdiction of that State's courts.

The Court of Chancery rejected these arguments in a letter opinion which emphasized the purpose of the Delaware sequestration procedure:

> The primary purpose of "sequestration" as authorized by 10 Del. C. §366 is not to secure possession of property pending a trial between resident debtors and creditors on the issue of who has the right to retain it. On the contrary, as here employed, "sequestration" is a process used to compel the personal appearance of a nonresident defendant to answer and defend a suit brought against him in a court of equity. It is accomplished by the appointment of a sequestrator by this Court to seize and hold property of the nonresident located in this State subject to further Court order. If the defendant enters a general appearance, the sequestered property is routinely released, unless the plaintiff makes special application to continue its seizure, in which event the plaintiff has the burden of proof and persuasion.

This limitation on the purpose and length of time for which sequestered property is held, the court concluded, rendered inapplicable the due process requirements enunciated in *Sniadach v. Family Finance Corp.*, 395 U.S. 337 (1969); *Fuentes v. Shevin*, 407 U.S. 67 (1972); and *Mitchell v. W. T. Grant Co.*, 416 U.S. 600 (1974). The court also found no state-law or federal constitutional barrier to the sequestrator's reliance on Del. Code Ann., Tit. 8, §169 (1975). Finally, the court held that the statutory Delaware situs of the stock provided a sufficient basis for the exercise of quasi in rem jurisdiction by a Delaware court.

9. Section 169 provides: "For all purposes of title, action, attachment, garnishment and jurisdiction of all courts held in this State, but not for the purpose of taxation, the situs of the ownership of the capital stock of all corporations existing under the laws of this State, whether organized under this chapter or otherwise, shall be regarded as in this State."

On appeal, the Delaware Supreme Court affirmed the judgment of the Court of Chancery. Most of the Supreme Court's opinion was devoted to rejecting appellants' contention that the sequestration procedure is inconsistent with the due process analysis developed in the *Sniadach* line of cases. The court based its rejection of that argument in part on its agreement with the Court of Chancery that the purpose of the sequestration procedure is to compel the appearance of the defendant, a purpose not involved in the *Sniadach* cases. The court also relied on what it considered the ancient origins of the sequestration procedure and approval of that procedure in the opinions of this Court, Delaware's interest in asserting jurisdiction to adjudicate claims of mismanagement of a Delaware corporation, and the safeguards for defendants that it found in the Delaware statute.

Appellants' claim that the Delaware courts did not have jurisdiction to adjudicate this action received much more cursory treatment. The court's analysis of the jurisdictional issue is contained in two paragraphs: "There are significant constitutional questions at issue here but we say at once that we do not deem the rule of *International Shoe* to be one of them. . . . The reason of course, is that jurisdiction under §366 remains . . . *quasi in rem* founded on the presence of capital stock here, not on prior contact by defendants with this forum. Under 8 Del. C. §169 the "'situs of the ownership of the capital stock of all corporations existing under the laws of this State . . . [is] in this State,' and that provides the initial basis for jurisdiction. Delaware may constitutionally establish situs of such shares here, . . . it has done so and the presence thereof provides the foundation for §366 in this case. . . ."

We reverse.

II

The Delaware courts rejected appellants' jurisdictional challenge by noting that this suit was brought as a quasi in rem proceeding. Since quasi in rem jurisdiction is traditionally based on attachment or seizure of property present in the jurisdiction, not on contacts between the defendant and the State, the courts considered appellants' claimed lack of contacts with Delaware to be unimportant. This categorical analysis assumes the continued soundness of the conceptual structure founded on the century-old case of *Pennoyer v. Neff*, 95 U.S. 714 (1878). . . .

[U]nder *Pennoyer* state authority to adjudicate was based on the jurisdiction's power over either persons or property. This fundamental concept is embodied in the very vocabulary which we use to describe judgments. If a court's jurisdiction is based on its authority over the defendant's person, the action and judgment are denominated "in personam" and can impose a personal obligation on the defendant in favor of the plaintiff. If jurisdiction is based on the court's power over property within its territory, the action is called "in rem" or "quasi in rem." The effect of a judgment in such a case is limited to the property that supports jurisdiction and does not impose a personal liability on the property owner, since he is not before the court. In *Pennoyer's* terms, the owner is affected only "indirectly" by an in rem judgment adverse to his interest in the property subject to the court's disposition.

By concluding that "[t]he authority of every tribunal is necessarily restricted by the territorial limits of the State in which it is established," *Pennoyer* sharply limited the availability of in personam jurisdiction over defendants not resident in the forum State. If a nonresident defendant could not be found in a State, he could not be sued there. On the other hand, since the State in which property was located was considered to have exclusive sovereignty over that property, in rem actions could proceed regardless of the owner's location.

The *Pennoyer* rules generally favored nonresident defendants by making them harder to sue. This advantage was reduced, however, by the ability of a resident plaintiff to satisfy a claim against a nonresident defendant by bringing into court any property of the defendant located in the plaintiff's State. . . .

[In *International Shoe*] the relationship among the defendant, the forum, and the litigation, rather than the mutually exclusive sovereignty of the States on which the rules of *Pennoyer* rest, became the central concern of the inquiry into personal jurisdiction. The immediate effect of this departure from *Pennoyer's* conceptual apparatus was to increase the ability of the state courts to obtain personal jurisdiction over nonresident defendants.

No equally dramatic change has occurred in the law governing jurisdiction in rem. There have, however, been intimations that the collapse of the *in personam* wing of *Pennoyer* has not left that decision unweakened as a foundation for in rem jurisdiction. Well-reasoned lower court opinions have questioned the proposition that the presence of property in a State gives that State jurisdiction to adjudicate rights to the property regardless of the relationship of the underlying dispute and the property owner to the forum. The overwhelming majority of commentators have also rejected *Pennoyer's* premise that a proceeding "against" property is not a proceeding against the owners of that property. Accordingly, they urge that the "traditional notions of fair play and substantial justice" that govern a State's power to adjudicate in personam should also govern its power to adjudicate personal rights to property located in the State.

Although this Court has not addressed this argument directly, we have held that property cannot be subjected to a court's judgment unless reasonable and appropriate efforts have been made to give the property owners actual notice of the action. This conclusion recognizes, contrary to *Pennoyer,* that an adverse judgment in rem directly affects the property owner by divesting him of his rights in the property before the court. Moreover, in *Mullane* we hold that Fourteenth Amendment rights cannot depend on the classification of an action as in rem or in personam, since that is "a classification for which the standards are so elusive and confused generally and which, being primarily for state courts to define, may and do vary from state to state."

It is clear, therefore, that the law of state-court jurisdiction no longer stands securely on the foundation established in *Pennoyer*. We think that the time is ripe to consider whether the standard of fairness and substantial justice set forth in *International Shoe* should be held to govern actions in rem as well as in personam.

[handwritten margin note: Int'l Shoe should apply to all]

III

The case for applying to jurisdiction in rem the same test of "fair play and substantial justice" as governs assertions of jurisdiction in personam is simple and straightforward. It is premised on recognition that "[t]he phrase, 'judicial jurisdiction over a thing,' is a customary elliptical way of referring to jurisdiction over the interests of persons in a thing." *Restatement (Second) of Conflict of Laws* §56, Introductory Note (1971) (hereafter Restatement). This recognition leads to the conclusion that in order to justify an exercise of jurisdiction in rem, the basis for jurisdiction must be sufficient to justify exercising "jurisdiction over the interests of persons in a thing." [23] The standard for determining whether an exercise of jurisdiction over the interests of persons is consistent with the Due Process Clause is the minimum-contacts standard elucidated in *International Shoe*.

This argument, of course, does not ignore the fact that the presence of property in a State may bear on the existence of jurisdiction by providing contacts among the forum State, the defendant, and the litigation. For example, when claims to the property itself are the source of the underlying controversy between the plaintiff and the defendant, it would be unusual for the State where the property is located not to have jurisdiction. In such cases, the defendant's claim to property located in the State would normally indicate that he expected to benefit from the State's protection of his interest. The State's strong interests in assuring the marketability of property within its borders and in providing a procedure for peaceful resolution of disputes about the possession of that property would also support jurisdiction, as would the likelihood that important records and witnesses will be found in the State. The presence of property may also favor jurisdiction in cases such as suits for injury suffered on the land of an absentee owner, where the defendant's

23. It is true that the potential liability of a defendant in an in rem action is limited by the value of the property, but that limitation does not affect the argument. The fairness of subjecting a defendant to state-court jurisdiction does not depend on the size of the claim being litigated.

ownership of the property is conceded but the cause of action is otherwise related to rights and duties growing out of that ownership.[29]

It appears, therefore, that jurisdiction over many types of actions which now are or might be brought in rem would not be affected by a holding that any assertion of state-court jurisdiction must satisfy the *International Shoe* standard. For the type of quasi in rem action typified by *Harris v. Balk* and the present case, however, accepting the proposed analysis would result in significant change. These are cases where the property which now serves as the basis for state-court jurisdiction is completely unrelated to the plaintiff's cause of action. Thus, although the presence of the defendant's property in a State might suggest the existence of other ties among the defendant, the State, and the litigation, the presence of the property alone would not support the State's jurisdiction. If those other ties did not exist, cases over which the State is now thought to have jurisdiction could not be brought in that forum.

Since acceptance of the *International Shoe* test would most affect this class of cases, we examine the arguments against adopting that standard as they relate to this category of litigation. Before doing so, however, we note that this type of case also presents the clearest illustration of the argument in favor of assessing assertions of jurisdiction by a single standard. For in cases such as *Harris* and this one, the only role played by the property is to provide the basis for bringing the defendant into court. Indeed, the express purpose of the Delaware sequestration procedure is to compel the defendant to enter a personal appearance.[33] In such cases, if a direct assertion of personal jurisdiction over the defendant would violate the Constitution, it would seem that an indirect assertion of that jurisdiction should be equally impermissible.

The primary rationale for treating the presence of property as a sufficient basis for jurisdiction to adjudicate claims over which the State would not have jurisdiction if *International Shoe* applied is that a wrongdoer "should not be able to avoid payment of his obligations by the expedient of removing his assets to a place where he is not subject to an in personam suit." *Restatement* §66, Comment a. *Accord,* Developments 955. This justification, however, does not explain why jurisdiction should be recognized without regard to whether the property is present in the State because of an effort to avoid the owner's obligations. Nor does it support jurisdiction to adjudicate the underlying claim. At most, it suggests that a State in which property is located should have jurisdiction to attach that property, by use of proper procedures,[34] as security for a judgment being sought in

---

29. If such an action were brought under the in rem jurisdiction rather than under a long-arm statute, it would be a quasi in rem action. . . .

33. This purpose is emphasized by Delaware's refusal to allow any defense on the merits unless the defendant enters a general appearance, thus submitting to full in personam liability.

34. *See North Georgia Finishing, Inc. v. Di-Chem, Inc.* 419 U.S. 601 (1975); *Mitchell v. W. T. Grant Co.,* 416 U.S. 600 (1974); *Fuentes v. Shevin,* 407 U.S. 67 (1972); *Sniadach v. Family Finance Corp.,* 395 U.S. 337 (1969).

a forum where the litigation can be maintained consistently with *International Shoe*. Moreover, we know of nothing to justify the assumption that a debtor can avoid paying his obligations by removing his property to a State in which his creditor cannot obtain personal jurisdiction over him. The Full Faith and Credit Clause, after all, makes the valid in personam judgment of one State enforceable in all other States.[36]

It might also be suggested that allowing in rem jurisdiction avoids the uncertainty inherent in the *International Shoe* standard and assures a plaintiff of a forum.[37] We believe, however, that the fairness standard of *International Shoe* can be easily applied in the vast majority of cases. Moreover, when the existence of jurisdiction in a particular forum under *International Shoe* is unclear, the cost of simplifying the litigation by avoiding the jurisdictional question may be the sacrifice of "fair play and substantial justice." That cost is too high.

We are left, then, to consider the significance of the long history of jurisdiction based solely on the presence of property in a State. Although the theory that territorial power is both essential to and sufficient for jurisdiction has been undermined, we have never held that the presence of property in a State does not automatically confer jurisdiction over the owner's interest in that property. This history must be considered as supporting the proposition that jurisdiction based solely on the presence of property satisfies the demands of due process, *cf. Ownbey v. Morgan*, 256 U.S. 94 (1921), but it is not decisive. "[T]raditional notions of fair play and substantial justice" can be as readily offended by the perpetuation of ancient forms that are no longer justified as by the adoption of new procedures that are inconsistent with the basic values of our constitutional heritage. The fiction that an assertion of jurisdiction over property is anything but an assertion of jurisdiction over the owner of the property supports an ancient form without substantial modern justification. Its continued acceptance would serve only to allow state-court jurisdiction that is fundamentally unfair to the defendant.

We therefore conclude that all assertions of state-court jurisdiction must be evaluated according to the standards set forth in *International Shoe* and its progeny.[39]

---

36. Once it has been determined by a court of competent jurisdiction that the defendant is a debtor of the plaintiff, there would seem to be no unfairness in allowing an action to realize on that debt in a State where the defendant has property, whether or not that State would have jurisdiction to determine the existence of the debt as an original matter.

37. This case does not raise, and we therefore do not consider, the question whether the presence of a defendant's property in a State is a sufficient basis for jurisdiction when no other forum is available to the plaintiff.

39. It would not be fruitful for us to re-examine the facts of cases decided on the rationales of *Pennoyer* and *Harris* to determine whether jurisdiction might have been sustained under the standard we adopt today. To the extent that prior decisions are inconsistent with this standard, they are overruled.

IV

The Delaware courts based their assertion of jurisdiction in this case solely on the statutory presence of appellants' property in Delaware. Yet that property is not the subject matter of this litigation, nor is the underlying cause of action related to the property. Appellants' holdings in Greyhound do not, therefore, provide contacts with Delaware sufficient to support the jurisdiction of that State's courts over appellants. If it exists, that jurisdiction must have some other foundation.

Appellee Heitner did not allege and does not now claim that appellants have ever set foot in Delaware. Nor does he identify any act related to his cause of action as having taken place in Delaware. Nevertheless, he contends that appellants' positions as directors and officers of a corporation chartered in Delaware provide sufficient "contacts, ties, or relations," *International Shoe Co. v. Washington*, 326 U.S. at 319, with that State to give its courts jurisdiction over appellants in this stockholder's derivative action. This argument is based primarily on what Heitner asserts to be the strong interest of Delaware in supervising the management of a Delaware corporation. That interest is said to derive from the role of Delaware law in establishing the corporation and defining the obligations owed to it by its officers and directors. In order to protect this interest, appellee concludes, Delaware's courts must have jurisdiction over corporate fiduciaries such as appellants.

This argument is undercut by the failure of the Delaware Legislature to assert the state interest appellee finds so compelling. Delaware law bases jurisdiction, not on appellants' status as corporate fiduciaries, but rather on the presence of their property in the State. Although the sequestration procedure used here may be most frequently used in derivative suits against officers and directors, the authorizing statute evinces no specific concern with such actions. Sequestration can be used in any suit against a nonresident, and reaches corporate fiduciaries only if they happen to own interests in a Delaware corporation, or other property in the State. But as Heitner's failure to secure jurisdiction over seven of the defendants named in his complaint demonstrates, there is no necessary relationship between holding a position as a corporate fiduciary and owning stock or other interests in the corporation. If Delaware perceived its interest in securing jurisdiction over corporate fiduciaries to be as great as Heitner suggests, we would expect it to have enacted a statute more clearly designed to protect that interest.

Moreover, even if Heitner's assessment of the importance of Delaware's interest is accepted, his argument fails to demonstrate that Delaware is a fair forum for this litigation. The interest appellee has identified may support the application of Delaware law to resolve any controversy over appellants' actions in their capacities as officers and directors. But we have rejected the argument that if a State's law can properly be applied to a dispute, its courts necessarily have jurisdiction over the parties to that dispute.

"[The State] does not acquire . . . jurisdiction by being the 'center of gravity' of the controversy, or the most convenient location for litigation. The issue is personal jurisdiction, not choice of law. It is resolved in this case by considering the acts of the (appellants)." *Hanson v. Denckla,* 357 U.S. 235, 254 (1958).

Appellee suggests that by accepting positions as officers or directors of a Delaware corporation, appellants performed the acts required by *Hanson v. Denckla.* He notes that Delaware law provides substantial benefits to corporate officers and directors, and that these benefits were at least in part the incentive for appellants to assume their positions. It is, he says, "only fair and just" to require appellants, in return for these benefits, to respond in the State of Delaware when they are accused of misusing their power.

But like Heitner's first argument, this line of reasoning establishes only that it is appropriate for Delaware law to govern the obligations of appellants to Greyhound and its stockholders. It does not demonstrate that appellants have "purposefully avail[ed themselves] of the privilege of conducting activities within the forum State," *Hanson v. Denckla, supra,* at 253, in a way that would justify bringing them before a Delaware tribunal. Appellants have simply had nothing to do with the State of Delaware. Moreover, appellants had no reason to expect to be haled before a Delaware court. Delaware, unlike some States, has not enacted a statute that treats acceptance of a directorship as consent to jurisdiction in the State. And "(i)t strains reason . . . to suggest that anyone buying securities in a corporation formed in Delaware 'impliedly consents' to subject himself to Delaware's . . . jurisdiction on any cause of action." Appellants, who were not required to acquire interests in Greyhound in order to hold their positions, did not by acquiring those interests surrender their right to be brought to judgment only in States with which they had had "minimum contacts."

Delaware's assertion of jurisdiction over appellants in this case is inconsistent with that constitutional limitation on state power. The judgment of the Delaware Supreme Court must, therefore, be reversed. It is so ordered.

Justice REHNQUIST took no part in the consideration or decision of this case.

Justice POWELL, concurring.

I agree that the principles of *International Shoe Co. v. Washington,* 326 U.S. 310 (1945), should be extended to govern assertions of in rem as well as in personam jurisdiction in a state court. I also agree that neither the statutory presence of appellants' stock in Delaware nor their positions as directors and officers of a Delaware corporation can provide sufficient contacts to support the Delaware courts' assertion of jurisdiction in this case.

I would explicitly reserve judgment, however, on whether the ownership of some forms of property whose situs is indisputably and permanently located within a State may, without more, provide the contacts necessary to subject a defendant to jurisdiction within the State to the extent of the value of the property. In the case of real property, in particular, preservation of the common-law concept of quasi in rem jurisdiction arguably would avoid the uncertainty of the general *International Shoe* standard without significant cost to "'traditional notions of fair play and substantial justice.'"

Subject to the foregoing reservation, I join the opinion of the Court.

Justice STEVENS, concurring in the judgment:

The Due Process Clause affords protection against "judgments without notice." *International Shoe Co. v. Washington*, 326 U.S. 310, 324 (opinion of Black, J.). Throughout our history the acceptable exercise of in rem and quasi in rem jurisdiction has included a procedure giving reasonable assurance that actual notice of the particular claim will be conveyed to the defendant. Thus, publication, notice by registered mail, or extraterritorial personal service has been an essential ingredient of any procedure that serves as a substitute for personal service within the jurisdiction.

The requirement of fair notice also, I believe, includes fair warning that a particular activity may subject a person to the jurisdiction of a foreign sovereign. If I visit another State, or acquire real estate or open a bank account in it, I knowingly assume some risk that the State will exercise its power over my property or my person while there. My contact with the State, though minimal, gives rise to predictable risks.

Perhaps the same consequences should flow from the purchase of stock of a corporation organized under the laws of a foreign nation, because to some limited extent one's property and affairs then become subject to the laws of the nation of domicile of the corporation. As a matter of international law, that suggestion might be acceptable because a foreign investment is sufficiently unusual to make it appropriate to require the investor to study the ramifications of his decision. But a purchase of securities in the domestic market is an entirely different matter.

One who purchases shares of stock on the open market can hardly be expected to know that he has thereby become subject to suit in a forum remote from his residence and unrelated to the transaction. As a practical matter, the Delaware sequestration statute creates an unacceptable risk of judgment without notice. Unlike the 49 other States, Delaware treats the place of incorporation as the situs of the stock, even though both the owner and the custodian of the shares are elsewhere. Moreover, Delaware denies the defendant the opportunity to defend the merits of the suit unless he subjects himself to the unlimited jurisdiction of the court. Thus, it coerces a defendant either to submit to personal jurisdiction in a forum which could not otherwise obtain such jurisdiction or to lose the securities which have been attached. If its procedure were upheld, Delaware would, in effect, impose a duty of inquiry on every purchaser of securities in the national market. For unless the purchaser ascertains both the State of incorporation of the company whose shares he is buying, and also the idiosyncrasies of its law, he may be assuming an unknown risk of litigation. I therefore agree with the Court that on the record before us no adequate basis for jurisdiction exists and that the Delaware statute is unconstitutional on its face.

How the Court's opinion may be applied in other contexts is not entirely clear to me. I agree with Mr. Justice Powell that it should not be read to invalidate quasi in rem jurisdiction where real estate is involved. I would also not read it as invalidating other long-accepted methods of acquiring jurisdiction over persons with adequate notice of both the particular controversy and the fact that their local activities might subject them to suit. My uncertainty as to the reach of the opinion, and my fear that it purports to decide a great deal more than is necessary to dispose of this case, persuade me merely to concur in the judgment.

Justice BRENNAN, concurring in part and dissenting in part:

I join Parts I-III of the Court's opinion. I fully agree that the minimum-contacts analysis developed in *International Shoe Co. v. Washington*, 326 U.S. 310 (1945), represents a far more sensible construct for the exercise of state-court jurisdiction than the patchwork of legal and factual fictions that has been generated from the decision in *Pennoyer v. Neff*, 95 U.S. 714 (1878). It is precisely because the inquiry into minimum contacts is now of such overriding importance, however, that I must respectfully dissent from Part IV of the Court's opinion.

I

The primary teaching of Parts I-III of today's decision is that a State, in seeking to assert jurisdiction over a person located outside its borders, may only do so on the basis of minimum contacts among the parties, the contested transaction, and the forum State. The Delaware Supreme Court could not have made plainer, however, that its sequestration statute, Del. Code Ann., Tit. 10, §366 (1975), does not operate on this basis, but instead is strictly an embodiment of quasi in rem jurisdiction, a jurisdictional predicate no longer constitutionally viable: "[J]urisdiction under §366 remains . . . *quasi in rem* founded on the presence of capital stock here, not on prior contact by defendants with this forum." *Greyhound Corp. v. Heitner*, 361 A.2d 225, 229 (1976). This state-court ruling obviously comports with the understanding of the parties, for the issue of the existence of minimum contacts was never pleaded by appellee, made the subject of discovery, or ruled upon by the Delaware courts. These facts notwithstanding, the Court in Part IV reaches the minimum-contacts question and finds such contacts lacking as applied to appellants. Succinctly stated, once having properly and persuasively decided that the quasi in rem statute that Delaware admits to having enacted is invalid, the Court then proceeds to find that a minimum-contacts law that Delaware expressly denies having enacted also could not be constitutionally applied in this case.

In my view, a purer example of an advisory opinion is not to be found . . . .

My concern with the inappropriateness of the Court's action is highlighted by two other considerations. First, an inquiry into minimum contacts inevitably is highly dependent on creating a proper factual foundation detailing the contacts between the forum State and the controversy in question. Because neither the plaintiff-appellee nor the state courts viewed such an inquiry as germane in this instance, the Court today is unable to draw upon a proper factual record in reaching its conclusion; moreover, its disposition denies appellee the normal opportunity to seek discovery on the contacts issue. Second, it must be remembered that the Court's ruling is a constitutional one and necessarily will affect the reach of the jurisdictional laws of all 50 States. Ordinarily this would counsel restraint in constitutional pronouncements. Certainly it should have cautioned the Court against reaching out to decide a question that, as here, has yet to emerge from the state courts ripened for review on the federal issue.

II

Nonetheless, because the Court rules on the minimum-contacts question, I feel impelled to express my view. While evidence derived through discovery might satisfy me that minimum contacts are lacking in a given case, I am convinced that as a general rule a state forum has jurisdiction to adjudicate a shareholder derivative action centering on the conduct and policies of the directors and officers of a corporation chartered by that State. Unlike the Court, I therefore would not foreclose Delaware from asserting jurisdiction over appellants were it persuaded to do so on the basis of minimum contacts.

It is well settled that a derivative lawsuit as presented here does not inure primarily to the benefit of the named plaintiff. Rather, the primary beneficiaries are the corporation and its owners, the shareholders. "The cause of action which such a plaintiff brings before the court is not his own but the corporation's. . . . Such a plaintiff often may represent an important public and stockholder interest in bringing faithless managers to book."

Viewed in this light, the chartering State has an unusually powerful interest in insuring the availability of a convenient forum for litigating claims involving a possible multiplicity of defendant fiduciaries and for vindicating the State's substantive policies regarding the management of its domestic corporations. I believe that our cases fairly establish that the State's valid substantive interests are important considerations in assessing whether it constitutionally may claim jurisdiction over a given cause of action.

In this instance, Delaware can point to at least three interrelated public policies that are furthered by its assertion of jurisdiction. First, the State has a substantial interest in providing restitution for its local corporations that allegedly have been victimized by fiduciary misconduct, even if the managerial decisions occurred outside the State. The importance of this general state interest in assuring restitution for its own residents previously found expression in cases that went outside the then-prevailing due process framework to authorize state-court jurisdiction over nonresident motorists who injure others within the State. *Hess v. Pawloski*, 274 U.S. 352 (1927). More recently, it has led States to seek and to acquire jurisdiction over nonresident tortfeasors whose purely out-of-state activities produce domestic consequences. *E.g., Gray v. American Radiator & Standard Sanitary Corp.*, 22 Ill. 2d 432 (1961). Second, state courts have legitimately read their jurisdiction expansively when a cause of action centers in an area in which the forum State possesses a manifest regulatory interest. *E.g., McGee v. International Life Ins. Co.*, 355 U.S. 220 (1957) (insurance regulation). Finally, a State like Delaware has a recognized interest in affording a convenient forum for supervising and overseeing the affairs of an entity that is purely the creation of that State's law. For example, even following our decision in *International Shoe*, New York courts were permitted to exercise complete judicial authority over nonresident beneficiaries of a trust created under state law, even though, unlike appellants here, the beneficiaries personally entered into no association whatsoever with New York. *Mullane v. Central Hanover Bank & Trust Co.*, 339 U.S. 306, 313 (1950). I, of course, am not suggesting that Delaware's varied interests would justify its acceptance of jurisdiction over any transaction touching upon the affairs of its domestic corporations. But a derivative action which raises allegations of abuses of the basic management of an institution whose existence is created by the State and whose powers and duties are defined by state law fundamentally implicates the public policies of that forum . . .

I, therefore, would approach the minimum-contacts analysis differently than does the Court. Crucial to me is the fact that appellants voluntarily associated themselves with the State of Delaware, "invoking the benefits and protections of its laws," by entering into a long-term and fragile relationship with one of its domestic corporations. They thereby elected to assume powers and to undertake responsibilities wholly derived from that State's rules and regulations, and to become eligible for those benefits that Delaware law makes available to its corporations' officials. While it is possible that countervailing issues of judicial efficiency and the like might clearly favor a different forum, they do not appear on the meager record before us and, of course, we are concerned solely with "minimum" contacts, not the "best" contacts. I thus do not believe that it is unfair to insist that appellants make themselves available to suit in a competent forum that Delaware might create for vindication of its important public policies directly pertaining to appellants' fiduciary associations with the State.

Comments and Questions

1. What does *Shaffer* hold? How would you state the broadest version of the holding? The narrowest?

2. Does Professor Gloss's vacation home in the earlier Practice Exercise provide a basis for exercising jurisdiction over him after this decision? What, if any, *in rem* and *quasi in rem* cases remain alive and well after *Shaffer*?

3. What are the points of disagreement with the Court's opinion set forth by Justices Powell and Stevens in their separate opinions? How, for example, would they treat Gloss's vacation home as a basis for court power over him? What are the implications of these disagreements for subsequent cases?

4. What is the basis for Justice Brennan's accusation that the Court was rendering an "advisory opinion"? Even if true, what's wrong with the Court's offering "advice"?

5. Spell out Justice Brennan's argument that, measured against the *International Shoe* due process standard, the Delaware courts did have proper constitutional power over the defendants. Does this anticipate the importance that the "fairness factors" would come to play a decade later in *Asahi* and *Burger King*?

6. If Delaware had had a long-arm statute similar to California's ("A court of this state may exercise jurisdiction on any basis not inconsistent with the Constitution of this state or of the United States." Cal. Code Civ. Proc. §410.10), would the case have come out differently? Was the Court's problem with Delaware's exercise of jurisdiction over Shaffer et al. prompted by constitutional concerns or by the particular statutory basis for the exercise?

In response to *Shaffer*, Delaware enacted Del. St. Ti. 10 §3114:

Every nonresident of this State who after September 1, 1977, accepts election or appointment as a director, trustee or member of the governing body of a corporation organized under the laws of this State or who after June 30,

1978, serves in such capacity and every resident of this State who so accepts election or appointment or serves in such capacity and thereafter removes residence from this State shall, by such acceptance or by such service, be deemed thereby to have consented to the appointment of the registered agent of such corporation (or, if there is none, the Secretary of State) as an agent upon whom service of process may be made in all civil actions or proceedings brought in this State, by or on behalf of, or against such corporation, in which such director, trustee or member is a necessary or proper party, or in any action or proceeding against such director, trustee or member for violation of a duty in such capacity, whether or not the person continues to serve as such director, trustee or member at the time suit is commenced. Such acceptance or service as such director, trustee or member shall be a signification of the consent of such director, trustee or member that any process when so served shall be of the same legal force and validity as if served upon such director, trustee or member within this State and such appointment of the registered agent (or, if there is none, the Secretary of State) shall be irrevocable.

The Delaware Supreme Court upheld the statute in *Armstrong v. Pomerance*, 423 A.2d 174 (1980), ruling that the state has a substantial interest in overseeing the conduct of those owing fiduciary duties to shareholders of Delaware corporations. The court reasoned that such interest far outweighs any burden to defendants (who have voluntarily associated themselves with such corporations by accepting directorships) in being required to submit to the jurisdiction of the courts. Would the United States Supreme Court agree?

7. Note the Court's distinction between a state's power to attach property located within its borders as security for a judgment entered in another state or to enforce such judgment, and jurisdiction to adjudicate the underlying claim. *See* the Court's footnote 36 and accompanying text. Is this distinction more meaningful than the one between in personam and in rem jurisdiction, which *Shaffer* purports to inter?

8. A 1993 amendment to the Federal Rules of Civil Procedure limits the use of attachment jurisdiction to situations where there is "a showing that personal jurisdiction over a defendant cannot, in the district where the action is brought, be obtained with reasonable efforts by service of summons in any manner authorized by this rule." Fed. R. Civ. P. 4(n)(2). Does this change make sense? Why or why not?

9. Justice Marshall's opinion for the Court holds that "*all* assertions of state-court jurisdiction must be evaluated according to the standards set forth in *International Shoe* and its progeny." 433 U.S. at 212 (emphasis added). Does the next case persuade you of the danger of such broad categorical judicial pronouncements?

J. JURISDICTION BASED SOLELY ON PERSONAL SERVICE WITHIN THE FORUM STATE

■ BURNHAM v. SUPERIOR COURT OF CALIFORNIA
495 U.S. 604 (1990)

Justice SCALIA announced the judgment of the Court and delivered an opinion in which the CHIEF JUSTICE and Justice KENNEDY join, and in which Justice WHITE joins with respect to Parts I, II-A, II-B, and II-C.

The question presented is whether the Due Process Clause of the fourteenth Amendment denies California courts jurisdiction over a non-resident, who was personally served with process while temporarily in that State, in a suit unrelated to his activities in the State.

I

Petitioner Dennis Burnham married Francie Burnham in 1976 in West Virginia. In 1977 the couple moved to New Jersey, where their two children were born. In July 1987 the Burnhams decided to separate. They agreed that Mrs. Burnham, who intended to move to California, would take custody of the children. Shortly before Mrs. Burnham departed for California that same month, she and petitioner agreed that she would file for divorce on grounds of "irreconcilable differences."

In October 1987, petitioner filed for divorce in New Jersey state court on grounds of "desertion." Petitioner did not, however, obtain an issuance of summons against his wife and did not attempt to serve her with process. Mrs. Burnham, after unsuccessfully demanding that petitioner adhere to their prior agreement to submit to an "irreconcilable differences" divorce, brought suit for divorce in California state court in early January 1988.

In late January, petitioner visited southern California on business, after which he went north to visit his children in the San Francisco Bay area, where his wife resided. He took the older child to San Francisco for the weekend. Upon returning the child to Mrs. Burnham's home on January 24, 1988, petitioner was served with a California court summons and a copy of Mrs. Burnham's divorce petition. He then returned to New Jersey.

Later that year, petitioner made a special appearance in the California Superior Court, moving to quash the service of process on the ground that the court lacked personal jurisdiction over him because his only contacts with California were a few short visits to the State for the purposes of conducting business and visiting his children. The Superior Court denied the motion, and the California Court of Appeal denied mandamus relief, rejecting petitioner's contention that the Due Process Clause prohibited California courts from asserting jurisdiction over him because he lacked

"minimum contacts" with the State. The court held it to be "a valid jurisdictional predicate for in personam jurisdiction" that the "defendant
[was] present in the forum state and personally served with process." We
granted certiorari.

II

A

The proposition that the judgment of a court lacking jurisdiction is
void traces back to the English Year Books, and was made settled law by
Lord Coke in *Case of the Marshalsea*, 10 Coke Rep. 68b, 77a, 77 Eng. Rep.
1027, 1041 (K.B. 1612). Traditionally that proposition was embodied in
the phrase coram non judice, "before a person not a judge"—meaning, in
effect, that the proceeding in question was not a judicial proceeding because lawful judicial authority was not present, and could therefore not
yield a judgment. American courts invalidated, or denied recognition to,
judgments that violated this common-law principle long before the Fourteenth Amendment was adopted. In *Pennoyer v. Neff*, 95 U.S. 714 (1878),
we announced that the judgment of a court lacking personal jurisdiction
violated the Due Process Clause of the Fourteenth Amendment as well.

To determine whether the assertion of personal jurisdiction is consistent with due process, we have long relied on the principles traditionally
followed by American courts in marking out the territorial limits of each
State's authority. That criterion was first announced in *Pennoyer v. Neff*,
supra, in which we stated that due process "mean[s] a course of legal proceedings according to those rules and principles which have been established in our systems of jurisprudence for the protection and enforcement
of private rights," including the "well-established principles of public law
respecting the jurisdiction of an independent State over persons and
property." In what has become the classic expression of the criterion, we
said in *International Shoe Co. v. Washington*, 326 U.S. 310 (1945), that a state
court's assertion of personal jurisdiction satisfies the Due Process Clause if
it does not violate "'traditional notions of fair play and substantial
justice.'" Since *International Shoe*, we have only been called upon to decide
whether these "traditional notions" permit States to exercise jurisdiction
over absent defendants in a manner that deviates from the rules of jurisdiction applied in the 19th century. We have held such deviations permissible, but only with respect to suits arising out of the absent defendant's
contacts with the State.[1] *See, e.g., Helicopteros Nacionales de Colombia v. Hall*,

---

1. We have said that "[e]ven when the cause of action does not arise out of or relate to
the foreign corporation's activities in the forum State, due process is not offended by a
State's subjecting the corporation to its in personam jurisdiction when there are sufficient
contacts between the State and the foreign corporation." *Helicopteros Nacionales de Colombia v.
Hall*, 466 U.S. at 414. Our only holding supporting that statement, however, involved
"regular service of summons upon [the corporation's] president while he was in [the forum

466 U.S. 408, 414 (1984). The question we must decide today is whether due process requires a similar connection between the litigation and the defendant's contacts with the State in cases where the defendant is physically present in the State at the time process is served upon him.

B

Among the most firmly established principles of personal jurisdiction in American tradition is that the courts of a State have jurisdiction over nonresidents who are physically present in the State. The view developed early that each State had the power to hale before its courts any individual who could be found within its borders, and that once having acquired jurisdiction over such a person by properly serving him with process, the State could retain jurisdiction to enter judgment against him, no matter how fleeting his visit. That view had antecedents in English common-law practice, which sometimes allowed "transitory" actions, arising out of events outside the country, to be maintained against seemingly nonresident defendants who were present in England. Justice Story believed the principle, which he traced to Roman origins, to be firmly grounded in English tradition: "[B]y the common law[,] personal actions, being transitory, may be brought in any place, where the party defendant may be found," for "every nation may . . . rightfully exercise jurisdiction over all persons within its domains."

Recent scholarship has suggested that English tradition was not as clear as Story thought, *see* Hazard, A General Theory of State-Court Jurisdiction, 1965 S. Ct. Rev. 241, 253-260; Ehrenzweig, The Transient Rule of Personal Jurisdiction: The "Power" Myth and Forum Conveniens, 65 Yale L.J. 289 (1956). Accurate or not, however, judging by the evidence of contemporaneous or near-contemporaneous decisions, one must conclude that Story's understanding was shared by American courts at the crucial time for present purposes: 1868, when the Fourteenth Amendment was adopted. . . .

Decisions in the courts of many States in the 19th and early 20th centuries held that personal service upon a physically present defendant sufficed to confer jurisdiction, without regard to whether the defendant was only briefly in the State or whether the cause of action was related to his activities there. . . . Most States, moreover, had statutes or common-law rules that exempted from service of process individuals who were brought into the forum by force or fraud, or who were there as a party or witness in

---

State] acting in that capacity." *See Perkins v. Benguet Consolidated Mining Co.*, 342 U.S. 437, 440 (1952). It may be that whatever special rule exists permitting "continuous and systematic" contacts to support jurisdiction with respect to matters unrelated to activity in the forum applies only to corporations, which have never fitted comfortably in a jurisdictional regime based primarily upon "*de facto* power over the defendant's person." *International Shoe Co. v. Washington*, 326 U.S. 310, 316 (1945). We express no views on these matters—and, for simplicity's sake, omit reference to this aspect of "contacts"-based jurisdiction in our discussion.

unrelated judicial proceedings. These exceptions obviously rested upon the premise that service of process conferred jurisdiction. Particularly striking is the fact that, as far as we have been able to determine, not one American case from the period (or, for that matter, not one American case until 1978) held, or even suggested, that in-state personal service on an individual was insufficient to confer personal jurisdiction.

This American jurisdictional practice is, moreover, not merely old; it is continuing. . . . We do not know of a single state or federal statute, or a single judicial decision resting upon state law, that has abandoned in-state service as a basis of jurisdiction. Many recent cases reaffirm it.

C

Despite this formidable body of precedent, petitioner contends, in reliance on our decisions applying the *International Shoe* standard, that in the absence of "continuous and systematic" contacts with the forum, a nonresident defendant can be subjected to judgment only as to matters that arise out of or relate to his contacts with the forum. This argument rests on a thorough misunderstanding of our cases.

The view of most courts in the 19th century was that a court simply could not exercise in personam jurisdiction over a nonresident who had not been personally served with process in the forum. *Pennoyer v. Neff,* while renowned for its statement of the principle that the Fourteenth Amendment prohibits such an exercise of jurisdiction, in fact set that forth only as dictum and decided the case (which involved a judgment rendered more than two years before the Fourteenth Amendment's ratification) under "well-established principles of public law." Those principles, embodied in the Due Process Clause, required (we said) that when proceedings "involv[e] merely a determination of the personal liability of the defendant, he must be brought within [the court's] jurisdiction by service of process within the State, or his voluntary appearance." We invoked that rule in a series of subsequent cases, as either a matter of due process or a "fundamental principl[e] of jurisprudence."

Later years, however, saw the weakening of the *Pennoyer* rule. In the late 19th and early 20th centuries, changes in the technology of transportation and communication, and the tremendous growth of interstate business activity, led to an "inevitable relaxation of the strict limits on state jurisdiction" over nonresident individuals and corporations. *Hanson v. Denckla,* 357 U.S. 235, 260 (1958) (Black, J., dissenting). States required, for example, that nonresident corporations appoint an in-state agent upon whom process could be served as a condition of transacting business within their borders, and provided in-state "substituted service" for nonresident motorists who caused injury in the State and left before personal service could be accomplished. We initially upheld these laws under the Due Process Clause on grounds that they complied with *Pennoyer's* rigid requirement of either "consent," *see, e.g., Hess v. Pawloski, supra,* or "presence." As many observed, however, the consent and presence were purely fictional. Our opinion in *International Shoe* cast those fictions aside and made explicit the underlying basis of these decisions: Due process does not necessarily require the States to adhere to the unbending territorial limits on jurisdiction set forth in *Pennoyer*. The validity of assertion of jurisdiction over a nonconsenting defendant who is not present in the forum depends upon whether "the quality and nature of [his] activity" in relation to the forum renders such jurisdiction consistent with "'traditional notions of fair play and substantial justice.'" Subsequent cases have derived from the *International Shoe* standard the general rule that a State may dispense with in-forum personal service on nonresident defendants in suits arising out of their activities in the State. As *International Shoe* suggests, the defendant's litigation-related "minimum contacts" may take the place of physical presence as the basis for jurisdiction: "Historically the jurisdiction of courts to render judgment in personam is grounded on their de facto power over the defendant's person. Hence his presence within the territorial jurisdiction of a court was prerequisite to its rendition of a judgment personally binding on him. *Pennoyer v. Neff,* 95 U.S. 714, 733. But now that the *capias ad respondendum* has given way to personal service of summons or other form of notice, due process requires only that in order to subject a defendant to a judgment in personam, if he be not present within the territory of the forum, he have certain minimum contacts with it such that the maintenance of the suit does not offend 'traditional notions of fair play and substantial justice.'"

Nothing in *International Shoe* or the cases that have followed it, however, offers support for the very different proposition petitioner seeks to establish today: that a defendant's presence in the forum is not only unnecessary to validate novel, nontraditional assertions of jurisdiction, but is itself no longer sufficient to establish jurisdiction. That proposition is unfaithful to both elementary logic and the foundations of our due process jurisprudence. The distinction between what is needed to support novel procedures and what is needed to sustain traditional ones is fundamental, as we observed over a century ago:

> [A] process of law, which is not otherwise forbidden, must be taken to be due process of law, if it can show the sanction of settled usage both in England and in this country; but it by no means follows that nothing else can be due process of law. . . . [That which], in substance, has been immemorially the actual law of the land . . . therefor[e] is due process of law. But to hold that such a characteristic is essential to due process of law, would be to deny every quality of the law but its age, and to render it incapable of progress or improvement. It would be to stamp upon our jurisprudence the unchangeableness attributed to the laws of the Medes and Persians.

The short of the matter is that jurisdiction based on physical presence alone constitutes due process because it is one of the continuing traditions of our legal system that define the due process standard of "traditional notions of fair play and substantial justice." That standard was developed by analogy to "physical presence," and it would be perverse to say it could now be turned against that touchstone of jurisdiction.

D

Petitioner's strongest argument, though we ultimately reject it, relies upon our decision in *Shaffer v. Heitner*, 433 U.S. 186 (1977). In that case, a Delaware court hearing a shareholder's derivative suit against a corporation's directors secured jurisdiction quasi in rem by sequestering the out-of-state defendants' stock in the company, the situs of which was Delaware under Delaware law. Reasoning that Delaware's sequestration procedure was simply a mechanism to compel the absent defendants to appear in a suit to determine their personal rights and obligations, we concluded that the normal rules we had developed under *International Shoe* for jurisdiction over suits against absent defendants should apply—*viz.*, Delaware could not hear the suit because the defendants' sole contact with the State (ownership of property there) was unrelated to the lawsuit.

It goes too far to say, as petitioner contends, that *Shaffer* compels the conclusion that a State lacks jurisdiction over an individual unless the litigation arises out of his activities in the State. *Shaffer*, like *International Shoe*, involved jurisdiction over an absent defendant, and it stands for nothing more than the proposition that when the "minimum contact" that is a substitute for physical presence consists of property ownership it must, like other minimum contacts, be related to the litigation. Petitioner wrenches out of its context our statement in *Shaffer* that "all assertions of state-court jurisdiction must be evaluated according to the standards set forth in *International Shoe* and its progeny." When read together with the two sentences that preceded it, the meaning of this statement becomes clear:

> The fiction that an assertion of jurisdiction over property is anything but an assertion of jurisdiction over the owner of the property supports an ancient form without substantial modern justification. Its continued acceptance would serve only to allow state-court jurisdiction that is fundamentally unfair to the defendant.
>
> We therefore conclude that all assertions of state-court jurisdiction must be evaluated according to the standards set forth in *International Shoe* and its progeny.

Ibid. Shaffer was saying, in other words, not that all bases for the assertion of in personam jurisdiction (including, presumably, in-state service) must be treated alike and subjected to the "minimum contacts" analysis of *International Shoe*; but rather that quasi in rem jurisdiction, that fictional "ancient form," and in personam jurisdiction, are really one and the same and must be treated alike—leading to the conclusion that quasi in rem jurisdiction, i.e., that form of in personam jurisdiction based upon a "property ownership" contact and by definition unaccompanied by personal, in-state service, must satisfy the litigation-relatedness requirement of *International Shoe*. The logic of *Shaffer*'s holding—which places all suits against absent nonresidents on the same constitutional footing, regardless of whether a separate Latin label is attached to one particular basis of contact—does not compel the conclusion that physically present defendants must be treated identically to absent ones. As we have demonstrated at length, our tradition has treated the two classes of defendants quite differently, and it is unreasonable to read *Shaffer* as casually obliterating that distinction. *International Shoe* confined its "minimum contacts" requirement to situations in which the defendant "be not present within the territory of the forum," and nothing in *Shaffer* expands that requirement beyond that.

It is fair to say, however, that while our holding today does not contradict *Shaffer*, our basic approach to the due process question is different. We have conducted no independent inquiry into the desirability or fairness of the prevailing in-state service rule, leaving that judgment to the legislatures that are free to amend it; for our purposes, its validation is its pedigree, as the phrase "traditional notions of fair play and substantial justice" makes clear. *Shaffer* did conduct such an independent inquiry, asserting that "'traditional notions of fair play and substantial justice' can be as readily offended by the perpetuation of ancient forms that are no longer justified as by the adoption of new procedures that are inconsistent with the basic values of our constitutional heritage." Perhaps that assertion can be sustained when the "perpetuation of ancient forms" is engaged in by only a very small minority of the States. Where, however, as in the present case, a jurisdictional principle is both firmly approved by tradition and still favored, it is impossible to imagine what standard we could appeal to for the judgment that it is "no longer justified." While in no way receding from or casting doubt upon the holding of *Shaffer* or any other case, we reaffirm today our time-honored approach. For new procedures, hitherto unknown, the Due Process Clause requires analysis to determine whether "traditional notions of fair play and substantial justice" have been offended. But a doctrine of personal jurisdiction that dates back to the adoption of the Fourteenth Amendment and is still generally observed unquestionably meets that standard.

III

A few words in response to Justice Brennan's opinion concurring in the judgment: It insists that we apply "contemporary notions of due process" to determine the constitutionality of California's assertion of jurisdiction. But our analysis today comports with that prescription, at least if we give it the only sense allowed by our precedents. The "contemporary notions of due process" applicable to personal jurisdiction are the enduring "traditional notions of fair play and substantial justice" established as the test by *International Shoe.* By its very language, that test is satisfied if a state court adheres to jurisdictional rules that are generally applied and have always been applied in the United States.

But the concurrence's proposed standard of "contemporary notions of due process" requires more: It measures state-court jurisdiction not only against traditional doctrines in this country, including current state-court practice, but also against each Justice's subjective assessment of what is fair and just. Authority for that seductive standard is not to be found in any of our personal jurisdiction cases. It is, indeed, an outright break with the test of "traditional notions of fair play and substantial justice," which would have to be reformulated "our notions of fair play and substantial justice."

The subjectivity, and hence inadequacy, of this approach becomes apparent when the concurrence tries to explain why the assertion of jurisdiction in the present case meets its standard of continuing-American-tradition-plus-innate-fairness. Justice Brennan lists the "benefits" Mr. Burnham derived from the State of California—the fact that, during the few days he was there, "[h]is health and safety [were] guaranteed by the State's police, fire, and emergency medical services; he [was] free to travel on the State's roads and waterways; he likely enjoy[ed] the fruits of the State's economy." Three days' worth of these benefits strike us as powerfully inadequate to establish, as an abstract matter, that it is "fair" for California to decree the ownership of all Mr. Burnham's worldly goods acquired during the 10 years of his marriage, and the custody over his children. We daresay a contractual exchange swapping those benefits for that power would not survive the "unconscionability" provision of the Uniform Commercial Code. Even less persuasive are the other "fairness" factors alluded to by Justice Brennan. It would create "an asymmetry," we are told, if Burnham were permitted (as he is) to appear in California courts as a plaintiff, but were not compelled to appear in California courts as defendant; and travel being as easy as it is nowadays, and modern procedural devices being so convenient, it is no great hardship to appear in California courts. The problem with these assertions is that they justify the exercise of jurisdiction over everyone, whether or not he ever comes to California. The only "fairness" elements setting Mr. Burnham apart from the rest of the world are the three days' "benefits" referred to above—and even those do not set him apart from many other people who have enjoyed three days in the Golden State (savoring the fruits of its economy, the availability of its roads and police services) but who were fortunate enough not to be served with process while they were there and thus are not (simply by reason of that savoring) subject to the general jurisdiction of California's courts. In other words, even if one agreed with Justice Brennan's conception of an equitable bargain, the "benefits" we have been discussing would explain why it is "fair" to assert general jurisdiction over Burnham-returned-to-New-Jersey-after-service only at the expense of proving that it is also "fair" to assert general jurisdiction over Burnham-returned-to-New-Jersey-without-service—which we know does not conform with "contemporary notions of due process."

There is, we must acknowledge, one factor mentioned by Justice Brennan that both relates distinctively to the assertion of jurisdiction on the basis of personal in-state service and is fully persuasive—namely, the fact that a defendant voluntarily present in a particular State has a "reasonable expectatio[n]" that he is subject to suit there. By formulating it as a "reasonable expectation" Justice Brennan makes that seem like a "fairness" factor; but in reality, of course, it is just tradition masquerading as "fairness." The only reason for charging Mr. Burnham with the reasonable expectation of being subject to suit is that the States of the Union assert adjudicatory jurisdiction over the person, and have always asserted adjudicatory jurisdiction over the person, by serving him with process during his temporary physical presence in their territory. That continuing tradition, which anyone entering California should have known about, renders it "fair" for Mr. Burnham, who voluntarily entered California, to be sued there for divorce—at least "fair" in the limited sense that he has no one but himself to blame. Justice Brennan's long journey is a circular one, leaving him, at the end of the day, in complete reliance upon the very factor he sought to avoid: The existence of a continuing tradition is not enough, fairness also must be considered; fairness exists here because there is a continuing tradition.

While Justice Brennan's concurrence is unwilling to confess that the Justices of this Court can possibly be bound by a continuing American tradition that a particular procedure is fair, neither is it willing to embrace the logical consequences of that refusal—or even to be clear about what consequences (logical or otherwise) it does embrace. Justice Brennan says that "[f]or these reasons [*i.e.*, because of the reasonableness factors enumerated above], as a rule the exercise of personal jurisdiction over a defendant based on his voluntary presence in the forum will satisfy the requirements of due process." The use of the word "rule" conveys the reassuring feeling that he is establishing a principle of law one can rely upon—but of course he is not. Since Justice Brennan's only criterion of constitutionality is "fairness," the phrase "as a rule" represents nothing more than his estimation that, usually, all the elements of "fairness" he discusses in the present case will exist. But what if they do not? Suppose, for example, that a defendant in Mr. Burnham's situation enjoys not three days' worth of California's "benefits," but 15 minutes' worth. Or suppose we remove one of those "benefits"—"enjoy[ment of] the fruits of the State's economy"—by positing that Mr. Burnham had not come to California on business, but only to visit his children. Or suppose that Mr. Burnham were demonstrably so impecunious as to be unable to take advantage of the modern means of transportation and communication that Justice Brennan finds so relevant. Or suppose, finally, that the California courts lacked the "variety of procedural devices" that Justice Brennan says can reduce the burden upon out-of-state litigants. One may also make additional suppositions, relating not to the absence of the factors that Justice Brennan discusses, but to the presence of additional factors bearing upon the ultimate criterion of "fairness." What if, for example, Mr. Burnham were visiting a sick child? Or a dying child? *Cf. Kulko v. Superior Court of California, City and County of San Francisco*, 436 U.S. 84, 93 (1978) (finding the exercise of long-arm jurisdiction over an absent parent unreasonable because it would "discourage parents from entering into reasonable visitation agreements"). Since, so far as one can tell, Justice Brennan's approval of applying the in-state service rule in the present case rests on the presence of all the factors he lists, and on the absence of any others, every different case will present a different litigable issue. Thus, despite the fact that he manages to work the word "rule" into his formulation, Justice Brennan's approach does not establish a rule of law at all, but only a "totality of the circumstances" test, guaranteeing what traditional territorial rules of jurisdiction were designed precisely to avoid: uncertainty and litigation over the preliminary issue of the forum's competence. It may be that those evils, necessarily accompanying a freestanding "reasonableness" inquiry, must be accepted at the margins, when we evaluate nontraditional forms of jurisdiction newly adopted by the States, *see, e.g.*, *Asahi Metal Industry Co. v. Superior Court of California, Solano County*, 480 U.S. 102, 115 (1987). But that is no reason for injecting them into the core of our American practice, exposing to such a "reasonableness" inquiry the ground of jurisdiction that has hitherto been considered the very baseline of reasonableness, physical presence.

The difference between us and Justice Brennan has nothing to do with whether "further progress [is] to be made" in the "evolution of our legal system." It has to do with whether changes are to be adopted as progressive by the American people or decreed as progressive by the Justices of this Court. Nothing we say today prevents individual States from limiting or entirely abandoning the in-state-service basis of jurisdiction. And nothing prevents an overwhelming majority of them from doing so, with the consequence that the "traditional notions of fairness" that this Court applies may change. But the States have overwhelmingly declined to adopt such limitation or abandonment, evidently not considering it to be progress.[5] The question is whether, armed with no authority other than

5. I find quite unacceptable as a basis for this Court's decisions Justice Brennan's view that "the raison d'être of various constitutional doctrines designed to protect out-of-staters, such as the Art. IV Privileges and Immunities Clause and the Commerce Clause," entitles this Court to brand as "unfair," and hence unconstitutional, the refusal of all 50 States "to limit or abandon bases of jurisdiction that have become obsolete," *ibid.* "Due process" (which is the constitutional text at issue here) does not mean that process which shifting majorities of this

individual Justices' perceptions of fairness that conflict with both past and current practice, this Court can compel the States to make such a change on the ground that "due process" requires it. We hold that it cannot. . . .

Because the Due Process Clause does not prohibit the California courts from exercising jurisdiction over petitioner based on the fact of in-state service of process, the judgment is

Affirmed.

[handwritten margin note: doesn't argue Part D]

Justice WHITE, concurring in part and concurring in the judgment:

I join Parts I, II-A, II-B, and II-C of Justice Scalia's opinion and concur in the judgment of affirmance. The rule allowing jurisdiction to be obtained over a nonresident by personal service in the forum State, without more, has been and is so widely accepted throughout this country that I could not possibly strike it down, either on its face or as applied in this case, on the ground that it denies due process of law guaranteed by the Fourteenth Amendment. Although the Court has the authority under the Amendment to examine even traditionally accepted procedures and declare them invalid, *e.g., Shaffer v. Heitner,* 433 U.S. 186 (1977), there has been no showing here or elsewhere that as a general proposition the rule is so arbitrary and lacking in common sense in so many instances that it should be held violative of due process in every case. Furthermore, until such a showing is made, which would be difficult indeed, claims in individual cases that the rule would operate unfairly as applied to the particular nonresident involved need not be entertained. At least this would be the case where presence in the forum State is intentional, which would almost always be the fact. Otherwise, there would be endless, fact-specific litigation in the trial and appellate courts, including this one. Here, personal service in California, without more, is enough, and I agree that the judgment should be affirmed.

[handwritten margin note: think history doesn't should be the only factor, need to also look @ fairness]

Justice BRENNAN, with whom Justice MARSHALL, Justice BLACKMUN, and Justice O'CONNOR join, concurring in the judgment.

I agree with Justice Scalia that the Due Process Clause of the Fourteenth Amendment generally permits a state court to exercise jurisdiction over a defendant if he is served with process while voluntarily present in the forum State.[1] I do not perceive the need, however, to decide that a jurisdictional rule that "'has been immemorially the actual law of the

---

Court feel to be "due"; but that process which American society—self-interested American society, which expresses its judgments in the laws of self-interested States—has traditionally considered "due." The notion that the Constitution, through some penumbra emanating from the Privileges and Immunities Clause and the Commerce Clause, establishes this Court as a Platonic check upon the society's greedy adherence to its traditions can only be described as imperious.

1. I use the term "transient jurisdiction" to refer to jurisdiction premised solely on the fact that a person is served with process while physically present in the forum State.

land,'" automatically comports with due process simply by virtue of its "pedigree." Although I agree that history is an important factor in establishing whether a jurisdictional rule satisfies due process requirements, I cannot agree that it is the only factor such that all traditional rules of jurisdiction are, ipso facto, forever constitutional. Unlike Justice Scalia, I would undertake an "independent inquiry into the . . . fairness of the prevailing in-state service rule." I therefore concur only in the judgment.

I

I believe that the approach adopted by Justice Scalia's opinion today—reliance solely on historical pedigree—is foreclosed by our decisions in *International Shoe Co. v. Washington*, 326 U.S. 310 (1945), and *Shaffer v. Heitner*, 433 U.S. 186 (1977). In *International Shoe*, we held that a state court's assertion of personal jurisdiction does not violate the Due Process Clause if it is consistent with "'traditional notions of fair play and substantial justice.'" 326 U.S. at 316.[2] In *Shaffer*, we stated that "all assertions of state-court jurisdiction must be evaluated according to the standards set forth in *International Shoe* and its progeny." 433 U.S. at 212 (emphasis added). The critical insight of *Shaffer* is that all rules of jurisdiction, even ancient ones, must satisfy contemporary notions of due process. No longer were we content to limit our jurisdictional analysis to pronouncements that "[t]he foundation of jurisdiction is physical power," and that "every State possesses exclusive jurisdiction and sovereignty over persons and property within its territory." *Pennoyer v. Neff*, 95 U.S. 714, 722 (1878). While acknowledging that "history must be considered as supporting the proposition that jurisdiction based solely on the presence of property satisfie[d] the demands of due process," we found that this factor could not be "decisive." 433 U.S. at 211-212. We recognized that "'[t]raditional notions of fair play and substantial justice' can be as readily offended by the perpetuation of ancient forms that are no longer justified as by the adoption of new procedures that are inconsistent with the basic values of our constitutional heritage." I agree with this approach and continue to believe that "the minimum-contacts analysis developed in *International Shoe* . . . represents a far more sensible construct for the exercise of state-court jurisdiction than the patchwork of legal and factual fictions that has been generated from the decision in *Pennoyer v. Neff*." *Id.*, at 219 (Brennan, J., concurring in part and dissenting in part) (citation omitted).

2. Our reference in *International Shoe* to "'traditional notions of fair play and substantial justice,'" meant simply that those concepts are indeed traditional ones, not that, as Justice Scalia's opinion suggests, *see ante*, their specific content was to be determined by tradition alone. We recognized that contemporary societal norms must play a role in our analysis. *See, e.g.*, 326 U.S. at 317 (considerations of "reasonable[ness], in the context of our federal system of government").

While our holding in *Shaffer* may have been limited to quasi in rem jurisdiction, our mode of analysis was not. Indeed, that we were willing in *Shaffer* to examine anew the appropriateness of the quasi in rem rule—until that time dutifully accepted by American courts for at least a century—demonstrates that we did not believe that the "pedigree" of a jurisdictional practice was dispositive in deciding whether it was consistent with due process. We later characterized *Shaffer* as "abandon[ing] the outworn rule of *Harris v. Balk*, 198 U.S. 215 (1905), that the interest of a creditor in a debt could be extinguished or otherwise affected by any State having transitory jurisdiction over the debtor." *World-Wide Volkswagen Corp. v. Woodson*, 444 U.S. 286, 296 (1980); *see also Rush v. Savchuk*, 444 U.S. 320, 325-326 (1980). If we could discard an "ancient form without substantial modern justification" in *Shaffer*, we can do so again. Lower courts, commentators, and the American Law Institute all have interpreted *International Shoe* and *Shaffer* to mean that every assertion of state-court jurisdiction, even one pursuant to a "traditional" rule such as transient jurisdiction, must comport with contemporary notions of due process. Notwithstanding the nimble gymnastics of Justice Scalia's opinion today, it is not faithful to our decision in *Shaffer*.

II

Tradition, though alone not dispositive, is of course relevant to the question whether the rule of transient jurisdiction is consistent with due process.[7] Tradition is salient not in the sense that practices of the past are automatically reasonable today; indeed, under such a standard, the legitimacy of transient jurisdiction would be called into question because the rule's historical "pedigree" is a matter of intense debate. The rule was a stranger to the common law and was rather weakly implanted in American jurisprudence "at the crucial time for present purposes: 1868, when the Fourteenth Amendment was adopted." For much of the 19th century, American courts did not uniformly recognize the concept of transient jurisdiction, and it appears that the transient rule did not receive wide currency until well after our decision in *Pennoyer v. Neff*, 95 U.S. 714 (1878).

---

7. I do not propose that the "contemporary notions of due process" to be applied are no more than "each Justice's subjective assessment of what is fair and just." Rather, the inquiry is guided by our decisions beginning with *International Shoe Co. v. Washington*, 326 U.S. 310 (1945), and the specific factors that we have developed to ascertain whether a jurisdictional rule comports with "traditional notions of fair play and substantial justice." *See, e.g., Asahi Metal Industry Co. v. Superior Court of California, Solano County*, 480 U.S. 102, 113 (1987) (noting "several factors," including "the burden on the defendant, the interests of the forum State, and the plaintiff's interest in obtaining relief"). This analysis may not be "mechanical or quantitative," *International Shoe*, but neither is it "freestanding" or dependent on personal whim. Our experience with this approach demonstrates that it is well within our competence to employ.

Rather, I find the historical background relevant because, however murky the jurisprudential origins of transient jurisdiction, the fact that American courts have announced the rule for perhaps a century (first in dicta, more recently in holdings) provides a defendant voluntarily present in a particular State today "clear notice that [he] is subject to suit" in the forum. *World-Wide Volkswagen Corp. v. Woodson*, 444 U.S. at 297. Regardless of whether Justice Story's account of the rule's genesis is mythical, our common understanding now, fortified by a century of judicial practice, is that jurisdiction is often a function of geography. The transient rule is consistent with reasonable expectations and is entitled to a strong presumption that it comports with due process. "If I visit another State, . . . I knowingly assume some risk that the State will exercise its power over my property or my person while there. My contact with the State, though minimal, gives rise to predictable risks." . . .

By visiting the forum State, a transient defendant actually "avail[s]" himself of significant benefits provided by the State. His health and safety are guaranteed by the State's police, fire, and emergency medical services; he is free to travel on the State's roads and waterways; he likely enjoys the fruits of the State's economy as well. Moreover, the Privileges and Immunities Clause of Article IV prevents a state government from discriminating against a transient defendant by denying him the protections of its law or the right of access to its courts. Subject only to the doctrine of *forum non conveniens*, an out-of-state plaintiff may use state courts in all circumstances in which those courts would be available to state citizens. Without transient jurisdiction, an asymmetry would arise: A transient would have the full benefit of the power of the forum State's courts as a plaintiff while retaining immunity from their authority as a defendant.

The potential burdens on a transient defendant are slight. "'[M]odern transportation and communications have made it much less burdensome for a party sued to defend himself'" in a State outside his place of residence. That the defendant has already journeyed at least once before to the forum—as evidenced by the fact that he was served with process there—is an indication that suit in the forum likely would not be prohibitively inconvenient. Finally, any burdens that do arise can be ameliorated by a variety of procedural devices.[13] For these reasons, as a rule

---

13. For example, in the federal system, a transient defendant can avoid protracted litigation of a spurious suit through a motion to dismiss for failure to state a claim or though a motion for summary judgment. Fed. Rules Civ. Proc. 12(b)(6) and 56. He can use relatively inexpensive methods of discovery, such as oral deposition by telephone (Rule 30(b)(7)), deposition upon written questions (Rule 31), interrogatories (Rule 33), and requests for admission (Rule 36), while enjoying protection from harassment (Rule 26(c)), and possibly obtaining costs and attorney's fees for some of the work involved (Rules 37(a)(4), (b)-(d)). Moreover, a change of venue may be possible. 28 U.S.C. §1404. In state court, many of the same procedural protections are available, as is the doctrine of *forum non conveniens*, under which the suit may be dismissed. *See generally* Abrams, Power, Convenience, and the Elimination of Personal Jurisdiction in the Federal Courts, 58 Ind. L.J. 1, 23-25 (1982).

the exercise of personal jurisdiction over a defendant based on his voluntary presence in the forum will satisfy the requirements of due process.[14]

In this case, it is undisputed that petitioner was served with process while voluntarily and knowingly in the State of California. I therefore concur in the judgment.

Justice STEVENS, concurring in the judgment:

As I explained in my separate writing, I did not join the Court's opinion in *Shaffer v. Heitner*, 433 U.S. 186 (1977) because I was concerned by its unnecessarily broad reach. The same concern prevents me from joining either Justice Scalia's or Justice Brennan's opinion in this case. For me, it is sufficient to note that the historical evidence and consensus identified by Justice Scalia, the considerations of fairness identified by Justice Brennan, and the common sense displayed by Justice White, all combine to demonstrate that this is, indeed, a very easy case. Accordingly, I agree that the judgment should be affirmed.

Comments and Questions

1. Keep in mind that the controversy in *Burnham* concerns whether personal service within the forum is *itself* sufficient to establish jurisdiction over a nonresident. In such situations, service of process serves the dual purpose of creating adjudicatory power and providing notice of the litigation.

2. Justice Marshall's opinion in *Shaffer*, which undid *quasi in rem* jurisdiction despite its "long history," observed that due process "can be as readily offended by the perpetuation of ancient forms that are no longer

14. Justice Scalia's opinion maintains that, viewing transient jurisdiction as a contractual bargain, the rule is "unconscionabl[e]" according to contemporary conceptions of fairness. But the opinion simultaneously insists that because of its historical "pedigree," the rule is "the very baseline of reasonableness." Thus is revealed Justice Scalia's belief that tradition alone is completely dispositive and that no showing of unfairness can ever serve to invalidate a traditional jurisdictional practice. I disagree both with this belief and with Justice Scalia's assessment of the fairness of the transient jurisdiction bargain. I note, moreover, that the dual conclusions of Justice Scalia's opinion create a singularly unattractive result. Justice Scalia suggests that when and if a jurisdictional rule becomes substantively unfair or even "unconscionable," this Court is powerless to alter it. Instead, he is willing to rely on individual States to limit or abandon bases of jurisdiction that have become obsolete. This reliance is misplaced, for States have little incentive to limit rules such as transient jurisdiction that make it easier for their own citizens to sue out-of-state defendants. That States are more likely to expand their jurisdiction is illustrated by the adoption by many States of long-arm statutes extending the reach of personal jurisdiction to the limits established by the Federal Constitution. Out-of-staters do not vote in state elections or have a voice in state government. We should not assume, therefore, that States will be motivated by "notions of fairness" to curb jurisdictional rules like the one at issue here. The reasoning of Justice Scalia's opinion today is strikingly oblivious to the raison d'être of various constitutional doctrines designed to protect out-of-staters, such as the Art. IV Privileges and Immunities Clause and the Commerce Clause.

justified as by the adoption of new procedures." Contrast Justice Scalia's virtual equation of tradition and due process (while upholding transient jurisdiction) in *Burnham*. What arguments favor each position? How should one weigh predictability and certainty against flexibility and adaptability in the law? Note Justice White's condemnation of an approach to in-state service that would require "endless, fact-specific litigation." Does that accurately describe the operation of the "minimum contacts/fundamental fairness" approach?

3. As in *Asahi*, the Justices agree on the end result in *Burnham*, but not on the path leading to it. What does *Burnham* actually hold? In the previous Practice Exercise, would service on Professor Gloss in Massachusetts establish valid jurisdiction over him? Would we need to know more about his relationship to the state (that is, what benefits he enjoyed)?

4. In the oft-cited case of *Grace v. MacArthur*, 170 F. Supp. 442 (E.D. Ark. 1959), the defendant, a citizen of Tennessee, contested the exercise of jurisdiction over him which was based on an affidavit of the U.S. Marshall attesting that he personally served the defendant on Braniff Airlines Flight No. 337, a nonstop flight from Memphis, Tennessee, to Dallas, Texas, at a time when "said airplane was in the Eastern District of Arkansas and directly above Pine Bluff, Arkansas, in said District." Without addressing the *International Shoe* issue, the court upheld jurisdiction based on the transient service. Do you see why some have dubbed this "tag" jurisdiction? Would a court reach the same result after *Burnham*?

5. *Xuncax v. Gramajo*, 886 F. Supp. 162 (D. Mass 1995) was an action by nine expatriate citizens of Guatemala against the former defense minister of that country seeking damages under the Torture Victim Protection Act, 28 U.S.C. §1350 (note), for injuries suffered by themselves and members of their families at the hands of the military. Gramajo was served with process while attending his commencement at Harvard's Kennedy School of Government. A default judgment for $47 million was entered after Gramajo returned to Guatemala and declined to appear in the action.

In an earlier action, the Second Circuit Court of Appeals had held that the federal courts have jurisdiction in such cases whenever the alleged torturer is found and served within the United States. In *Filartiga v. Pena-Irala*, 630 F.2d 876 (1980), the defendant was served with a summons and complaint while being held at the Brooklyn Navy Yard pending deportation back to Paraguay, where as Inspector General of the Police he allegedly had had the plaintiffs' son kidnapped and tortured to death in retaliation for his father's political activities. *See also Kadic v. Karadzic*, 70 F.3d 232 (2d Cir. 1995), in which the defendant Bosnian leader was held subject to personal jurisdiction in an action brought by victims of alleged atrocities, based on service of process in Manhattan, where he was attending the United Nations. As the court describes it, Karadzic was approached by process servers in the lobby of his hotel, but after they identified themselves and attempted to hand him the complaint from a distance of two feet his security guards seized it and knocked the papers to the floor. 70 F.3d, at 246. The court rejected Karadzic's argument that he was immune from service because he was in the city on United Nations business.

Subject matter jurisdiction (discussed in the next chapter) was held to exist in these cases based upon the Alien Tort Statute, part of the First Judiciary Act of 1789 and codified at 28 U.S.C. §1350, which provides the district courts with jurisdiction over civil actions brought by aliens alleging torts committed in violation of the "law of nations or a treaty of the United States."

6. Does in-state service work on corporate defendants? In *Wenche Siemer v. Learjet Acquisition Corp.*, 966 F.2d 179 (5th Cir. 1992), the court held that service in Texas on the designated corporate agent of Learjet did not satisfy the requirements of due process so as to permit suit in Texas. The air crash out of which the lawsuit arose occurred in Egypt, on a flight en route from Greece to Saudi Arabia; the decedents and the plaintiff-survivors were all residents of Greece or other European countries; the plane had been based in Greece and operated by a Greek company; the plane was not designed, manufactured, or serviced in Texas; nor had it ever been owned by a Texas resident. The court rejected the plaintiffs' assertion that jurisdiction could be based solely on in-state service on the corporate agent, finding their reliance on *Burnham* "puzzling": "*Burnham* did not involve a corporation and did not decide any jurisdictional issue pertaining to corporations." 966 F.2d, at 182. In so ruling, the court quoted Justice Scalia's observation in his *Burnham* footnote 1 that corporations "have never fitted comfortably in a jurisdictional regime based primarily upon de facto power over the defendant's person." Judicial power over corporations must thus be based, the Fifth Circuit held, on either one of the two constitutionally permissible bases—specific-act jurisdiction over claims related to in-state activities, or such continuous and systematic conduct in the forum so as to justify general jurisdiction over an unrelated claim.

7. What are the limitations on the rule equating physical presence with adjudicatory power? What if a defendant is tricked into coming into the state or is there to testify as a witness in another matter? There is a generally recognized immunity from service of process for nonresidents while they are within the forum state to attend a trial as a witness, party, or attorney, and for defendants who are in the forum by way of trickery, force, or fraud. *See* Fleming James, Jr., Geoffrey Hazard, & John Leubsdorf, *Civil Procedure* 79, 83 (4th ed. 1992). In *Voice Systems Marketing Co. v. Appropriate Technology Corp.*, 153 F.R.D. 117 (E.D. Mich. 1994), the court granted the defendants' motion to dismiss for insufficiency of service after finding that plaintiff induced the defendant's president to travel from California to Michigan ostensibly to correct problems with security products sold to the plaintiff, but actually to serve him with process in a breach of contract action.

K. GENERAL JURISDICTION

Although the main focus of the Supreme Court's considerable output on the personal jurisdiction issue has concerned specific jurisdiction, Chief Justice Stone described another form of adjudicatory power in *International Shoe*, namely, general jurisdiction: this applies when the activities of a corporate defendant in the forum are so continuous and substantial as to justify suits on claims unrelated to those activities. This is the effective counterpart to the general jurisdiction that a state has over each of its residents—that is, a resident may be sued there on any claim, even one arising from something that occurred in another state, based on domicile or residence in the state. *See generally* Jack H. Friedenthal, Mary Kay Kane, & Arthur R. Miller, *Civil Procedure* §3.6 (3d ed. 1999).*

General jurisdiction is held to exist over a corporate defendant whose headquarters or principal place of business is in the forum state, as was the case (at least for the duration of World War II) in *Perkins v. Benguet Consolidated Mining Co.*, 342 U.S. 437 (1952), discussed above. Short of that level of activity, may general jurisdiction be exercised? What does the following case teach us?

■ HELICOPTEROS NACIONALES DE COLOMBIA v. HALL
466 U.S. 408 (1984)

Justice BLACKMUN delivered the opinion of the Court:
We granted certiorari in this case to decide whether the Supreme Court of Texas correctly ruled that the contacts of a foreign corporation with the State of Texas were sufficient to allow a Texas state court to assert jurisdiction over the corporation in a cause of action not arising out of or related to the corporation's activities within the State.

I

Petitioner Helicopteros Nacionales de Colombia, S.A. (Helicol), is a Colombian corporation with its principal place of business in the city of Bogota in that country. It is engaged in the business of providing helicopter transportation for oil and construction companies in South America. On January 26, 1976, a helicopter owned by Helicol crashed in Peru. Four United States citizens were among those who lost their lives in the accident. Respondents are the survivors and representatives of the four decedents.

---

*Thus a state may enter a personal judgment against a domiciliary who is absent from the state and thus not amenable to service of process. This assures that there will always be one forum in which defendant may be sued.

At the time of the crash, respondents' decedents were employed by Consorcio, a Peruvian consortium, and were working on a pipeline in Peru. Consorcio is the alter ego of a joint venture named Williams-Sedco-Horn (WSH). The venture had its headquarters in Houston, Tex. Consorcio had been formed to enable the venturers to enter into a contract with Petro Peru, the Peruvian state-owned oil company. Consorcio was to construct a pipeline for Petro Peru running from the interior of Peru westward to the Pacific Ocean. Peruvian law forbade construction of the pipeline by any non-Peruvian entity.

Consorcio/WSH needed helicopters to move personnel, materials, and equipment into and out of the construction area. In 1974, upon request of Consorcio/WSH, the chief executive officer of Helicol, Francisco Restrepo, flew to the United States and conferred in Houston with representatives of the three joint venturers. At that meeting, there was a discussion of prices, availability, working conditions, fuel, supplies, and housing. Restrepo represented that Helicol could have the first helicopter on the job in 15 days. The Consorcio/WSH representatives decided to accept the contract proposed by Restrepo. Helicol began performing before the agreement was formally signed in Peru on November 11, 1974.[3] The contract was written in Spanish on official government stationery and provided that the residence of all the parties would be Lima, Peru. It further stated that controversies arising out of the contract would be submitted to the jurisdiction of Peruvian courts. In addition, it provided that Consorcio/WSH would make payments to Helicol's account with the Bank of America in New York City.

Aside from the negotiation session in Houston between Restrepo and the representatives of Consorcio/WSH, Helicol had other contacts with Texas. During the years 1970-1977, it purchased helicopters (approximately 80% of its fleet), spare parts, and accessories for more than $4 million from Bell Helicopter Company in Fort Worth. In that period, Helicol sent prospective pilots to Fort Worth for training and to ferry the aircraft to South America. It also sent management and maintenance personnel to visit Bell Helicopter in Fort Worth during the same period in order to receive "plant familiarization" and for technical consultation. Helicol received into its New York City and Panama City, Fla., bank accounts over $5 million in payments from Consorcio/WSH drawn upon First City National Bank of Houston.

Beyond the foregoing, there have been no other business contacts between Helicol and the State of Texas. Helicol never has been authorized to do business in Texas and never has had an agent for the service of process within the State. It never has performed helicopter operations in Texas or sold any product that reached Texas, never solicited business in

---

3. Respondents acknowledge that the contract was executed in Peru and not in the United States.

Texas, never signed any contract in Texas, never had any employee based there, and never recruited an employee in Texas. In addition, Helicol never has owned real or personal property in Texas and never has maintained an office or establishment there. Helicol has maintained no records in Texas and has no shareholders in that State. None of the respondents or their decedents were domiciled in Texas,[5] but all of the decedents were hired in Houston by Consorcio/WSH to work on the Petro Peru pipeline project.

Respondents instituted wrongful-death actions in the District Court of Harris County, Tex., against Consorcio/WSH, Bell Helicopter Company, and Helicol. Helicol filed special appearances and moved to dismiss the actions for lack of in personam jurisdiction over it. The motion was denied. After a consolidated jury trial, judgment was entered against Helicol on a jury verdict of $1,141,200 in favor of respondents.

The Texas Court of Civil Appeals, Houston, First District, reversed the judgment of the District Court, holding that in personam jurisdiction over Helicol was lacking. The Supreme Court of Texas, with three justices dissenting, initially affirmed the judgment of the Court of Civil Appeals. Seven months later, however, on motion for rehearing, the court withdrew its prior opinions and, again with three justices dissenting, reversed the judgment of the intermediate court. In ruling that the Texas courts had in personam jurisdiction, the Texas Supreme Court first held that the State's long-arm statute reaches as far as the Due Process Clause of the Fourteenth Amendment permits.[7] Thus, the only question remaining for the

---

5. Respondents' lack of residential or other contacts with Texas of itself does not defeat otherwise proper jurisdiction. *Keeton v. Hustler Magazine, Inc.*, 465 U.S. 770, 780 (1984); *Calder v. Jones*, 465 U.S. 783 (1984). We mention respondents' lack of contacts merely to show that nothing in the nature of the relationship between respondents and Helicol could possibly enhance Helicol's contacts with Texas. The harm suffered by respondents did not occur in Texas. Nor is it alleged that any negligence on the part of Helicol took place in Texas.

7. The State's long-arm statute is Tex. Rev. Civ. Stat. Ann., Art. 2031b (Vernon 1964 and Supp. 1982-1983). It reads in relevant part:

Sec. 3. Any foreign corporation . . . that engages in business in this State, irrespective of any Statute or law respecting designation or maintenance of resident agents, and does not maintain a place of regular business in this State or a designated agent upon whom service may be made upon causes of action arising out of such business done in this State, the act or acts of engaging in such business within this State shall be deemed equivalent to an appointment by such foreign corporation . . . of the Secretary of State of Texas as agent upon whom service of process may be made in any action, suit or proceedings arising out of such business done in this State, wherein such corporation . . . is a party or is to be made a party.

Sec. 4. For the purpose of this Act, and without including other acts that may constitute doing business, any foreign corporation . . . shall be deemed doing business in this State by entering into contract by mail or otherwise with a resident of Texas to be performed in whole or in part by either party in this State, or the committing of any tort in whole or in part in this State. The act of recruiting Texas residents, directly or through an intermediary located in Texas, for employment inside or outside of Texas shall be deemed doing business in this State.

court to decide was whether it was consistent with the Due Process Clause for Texas courts to assert in personam jurisdiction over Helicol.

II

The Due Process Clause of the Fourteenth Amendment operates to limit the power of a State to assert in personam jurisdiction over a nonresident defendant. *Pennoyer v. Neff*, 95 U.S. 714 (1878). Due process requirements are satisfied when in personam jurisdiction is asserted over a nonresident corporate defendant that has "certain minimum contacts with [the forum] such that the maintenance of the suit does not offend 'traditional notions of fair play and substantial justice.'" *International Shoe Co. v. Washington*, 326 U.S. 310, 316 (1945). When a controversy is related to or "arises out of" a defendant's contacts with the forum, the Court has said that a "relationship among the defendant, the forum, and the litigation" is the essential foundation of in personam jurisdiction. *Shaffer v. Heitner*, 433 U.S. 186 (1977).[8]

Even when the cause of action does not arise out of or relate to the foreign corporation's activities in the forum State,[9] due process is not offended by a State's subjecting the corporation to its in personam jurisdiction when there are sufficient contacts between the State and the foreign corporation. *Perkins v. Benguet Consolidated Mining Co.*, 342 U.S. 437 (1952). In *Perkins*, the Court addressed a situation in which state courts had asserted general jurisdiction over a defendant foreign corporation. During the Japanese occupation of the Philippine Islands, the president and general manager of a Philippine mining corporation maintained an office in Ohio from which he conducted activities on behalf of the company. He kept company files and held directors' meetings in the office, carried on correspondence relating to the business, distributed salary checks drawn on two active Ohio bank accounts, engaged an Ohio bank

---

The last sentence of §4 was added by 1979 Tex. Gen. Laws, ch. 245, §1, and became effective August 27, 1979. The Supreme Court of Texas in its principal opinion relied upon rulings in *U-Anchor Advertising, Inc. v. Burt*, 553 S.W.2d 760 (Tex. 1977); *Hoppenfeld v. Crook*, 498 S.W.2d 52 (Tex. Civ. App. 1973); and *O'Brien v. Lanpar Co.*, 399 S.W.2d 340 (Tex. 1966). It is not within our province, of course, to determine whether the Texas Supreme Court correctly interpreted the State's long-arm statute. We therefore accept that court's holding that the limits of the Texas statute are coextensive with those of the Due Process Clause.

8. It has been said that when a State exercises personal jurisdiction over a defendant in a suit arising out of or related to the defendant's contacts with the forum, the State is exercising "specific jurisdiction" over the defendant. *See* Von Mehren & Trautman, *Jurisdiction to Adjudicate: A Suggested Analysis*, 79 Harv. L. Rev. 1121, 1144-1164 (1966).

9. When a State exercises personal jurisdiction over a defendant in a suit not arising out of or related to the defendant's contacts with the forum, the State has been said to be exercising "general jurisdiction" over the defendant. *See* Brilmayer, *How Contacts Count: Due Process Limitations on State Court Jurisdiction*, 1980 S. Ct. Rev. 77, 80-81; Von Mehren & Trautman, 79 Harv. L. Rev., at 1136-1144; *Calder v. Jones*, 465 U.S. at 786.

to act as transfer agent, and supervised policies dealing with the rehabilitation of the corporation's properties in the Philippines. In short, the foreign corporation, through its president, "ha[d] been carrying on in Ohio a continuous and systematic, but limited, part of its general business," and the exercise of general jurisdiction over the Philippine corporation by an Ohio court was "reasonable and just."

All parties to the present case concede that respondents' claims against Helicol did not "arise out of," and are not related to, Helicol's activities within Texas.[10] We thus must explore the nature of Helicol's contacts with the State of Texas to determine whether they constitute the kind of continuous and systematic general business contacts the Court found to exist in *Perkins*. We hold that they do not.

It is undisputed that Helicol does not have a place of business in Texas and never has been licensed to do business in the State. Basically, Helicol's contacts with Texas consisted of sending its chief executive officer to Houston for a contract-negotiation session; accepting into its New York bank account checks drawn on a Houston bank; purchasing helicopters, equipment, and training services from Bell Helicopter for substantial sums; and sending personnel to Bell's facilities in Fort Worth for training.

The one trip to Houston by Helicol's chief executive officer for the purpose of negotiating the transportation-services contract with Consorcio/WSH cannot be described or regarded as a contact of a "continuous and systematic" nature, as *Perkins* described it, *see also International Shoe Co. v. Washington*, 326 U.S. at 320, and thus cannot support an assertion of in personam jurisdiction over Helicol by a Texas court. Similarly, Helicol's acceptance from Consorcio/WSH of checks drawn on a Texas bank is of negligible significance for purposes of determining whether Helicol had sufficient contacts in Texas. There is no indication that Helicol ever requested that the checks be drawn on a Texas bank or that there was any negotiation between Helicol and Consorcio/WSH with respect to the

10. Because the parties have not argued any relationship between the cause of action and Helicol's contacts with the State of Texas, we, contrary to the dissent's implication, assert no "view" with respect to that issue. The dissent suggests that we have erred in drawing no distinction between controversies that "relate to" a defendant's contacts with a forum and those that "arise out of" such contacts. This criticism is somewhat puzzling, for the dissent goes on to urge that, for purposes of determining the constitutional validity of an assertion of specific jurisdiction, there really should be no distinction between the two. We do not address the validity or consequences of such a distinction because the issue has not been presented in this case. Respondents have made no argument that their cause of action either arose out of or is related to Helicol's contacts with the State of Texas. Absent any briefing on the issue, we decline to reach the questions (1) whether the terms "arising out of" and "related to" describe different connections between a cause of action and a defendant's contacts with a forum, and (2) what sort of tie between a cause of action and a defendant's contacts with a forum is necessary to a determination that either connection exists. Nor do we reach the question whether, if the two types of relationship differ, a forum's exercise of personal jurisdiction in a situation where the cause of action "relates to," but does not "arise out of," the defendant's contacts with the forum should be analyzed as an assertion of specific jurisdiction.

location or identity of the bank on which checks would be drawn. Common sense and everyday experience suggest that, absent unusual circumstances, the bank on which a check is drawn is generally of little consequence to the payee and is a matter left to the discretion of the drawer. Such unilateral activity of another party or a third person is not an appropriate consideration when determining whether a defendant has sufficient contacts with a forum State to justify an assertion of jurisdiction. *See Kulko v. California Superior Court,* 436 U.S. 84, 93 (1978) (arbitrary to subject one parent to suit in any State where other parent chooses to spend time while having custody of child pursuant to separation agreement); *Hanson v. Denckla,* 357 U.S. 235, 253 (1958) ("The unilateral activity of those who claim some relationship with a nonresident defendant cannot satisfy the requirement of contact with the forum State.")

The Texas Supreme Court focused on the purchases and the related training trips in finding contacts sufficient to support an assertion of jurisdiction. We do not agree with that assessment. . . . [P]urchases and related trips, standing alone, are not a sufficient basis for a State's assertion of jurisdiction. . . .

III

We hold that Helicol's contacts with the State of Texas were insufficient to satisfy the requirements of the Due Process Clause of the Fourteenth Amendment.[13] Accordingly, we reverse the judgment of the Supreme Court of Texas. It is so ordered.

Justice BRENNAN, dissenting:

. . . I believe that the undisputed contacts in this case between petitioner Helicol and the State of Texas are sufficiently important, and sufficiently related to the underlying cause of action, to make it fair and reasonable for the State to assert personal jurisdiction over Helicol for the wrongful-death actions filed by the respondents. Given that Helicol has purposefully availed itself of the benefits and obligations of the forum, and given the direct relationship between the underlying cause of action and Helicol's contacts with the forum, maintenance of this suit in the Texas courts "does not offend [the] 'traditional notions of fair play and substantial justice,'" *International Shoe Co. v. Washington,* 326 U.S. 310, 316

13. As an alternative to traditional minimum-contacts analysis, respondents suggest that the Court hold that the State of Texas had personal jurisdiction over Helicol under a doctrine of "jurisdiction by necessity." *See Shaffer v. Heitner,* 433 U.S. 186, 211, n.37 (1977). We conclude, however, that respondents failed to carry their burden of showing that all three defendants could not be sued together in a single forum. It is not clear from the record, for example, whether suit could have been brought against all three defendants in either Colombia or Peru. We decline to consider adoption of a doctrine of jurisdiction by necessity—a potentially far-reaching modification of existing law—in the absence of a more complete record.

(1945), that are the touchstone of jurisdictional analysis under the Due Process Clause. I therefore dissent.

. . . [T]he contacts between petitioner Helicol and the State of Texas . . . are significantly related to the cause of action alleged in the original suit filed by the respondents. Accordingly, in my view, it is both fair and reasonable for the Texas courts to assert specific jurisdiction over Helicol in this case.

By asserting that the present case does not implicate the specific jurisdiction of the Texas courts, the Court necessarily removes its decision from the reality of the actual facts presented for our consideration.[3] More- over, the Court refuses to consider any distinction between contacts that are "related to" the underlying cause of action and contacts that "give rise" to the underlying cause of action. In my view, however, there is a substan- tial difference between these two standards for asserting specific jurisdic- tion. Thus, although I agree that the respondents' cause of action did not formally "arise out of" specific activities initiated by Helicol in the State of Texas, I believe that the wrongful-death claim filed by the respondents is significantly [related] to the undisputed contacts between Helicol and the forum. On that basis, I would conclude that the Due Process Clause allows the Texas courts to assert specific jurisdiction over this particular action.

The wrongful-death actions filed by the respondents were premised on a fatal helicopter crash that occurred in Peru. Helicol was joined as a defendant in the lawsuits because it provided transportation services, in- cluding the particular helicopter and pilot involved in the crash, to the joint venture that employed the decedents. Specifically, the respondent Hall claimed in her original complaint that "Helicol is . . . legally re- sponsible for its own negligence through its pilot employee." Viewed in light of these allegations, the contacts between Helicol and the State of Texas are directly and significantly related to the underlying claim filed by the respondents. The negotiations that took place in Texas led to the contract in which Helicol agreed to provide the precise transportation services that were being used at the time of the crash. Moreover, the

3. Nor do I agree with the Court that the respondents have conceded that their claims are not related to Helicol's activities within the State of Texas. Although parts of their written and oral arguments before the Court proceed on the assumption that no such relationship exists, other portions suggest just the opposite: "If it is the concern of the Solicitor General [appearing for the United States as amicus curiae] that a holding for Respondents here will cause foreign companies to refrain from purchasing in the United States for fear of exposure to general jurisdiction on unrelated causes of action, such concern is not well founded.

"Respondents' cause is not dependent on a ruling that mere purchases in a state, to- gether with incidental training for operating and maintaining the merchandise purchased can constitute the ties, contacts and relations necessary to justify jurisdiction over an unre- lated cause of action. However, regular purchases and training coupled with other contacts, ties and relations may form the basis for jurisdiction." Brief for Respondents 13-14. Thus, while the respondents' position before this Court is admittedly less than clear, I believe it is preferable to address the specific jurisdiction of the Texas courts because Helicol's contacts with Texas are in fact related to the underlying cause of action.

helicopter involved in the crash was purchased by Helicol in Texas, and the pilot whose negligence was alleged to have caused the crash was actually trained in Texas. This is simply not a case, therefore, in which a state court has asserted jurisdiction over a nonresident defendant on the basis of wholly unrelated contacts with the forum. Rather, the contacts between Helicol and the forum are directly related to the negligence that was alleged in the respondent Hall's original complaint.[4] Because Helicol should have expected to be amenable to suit in the Texas courts for claims directly related to these contacts, it is fair and reasonable to allow the assertion of jurisdiction in this case.

Despite this substantial relationship between the contacts and the cause of action, the Court declines to consider whether the courts of Texas may assert specific jurisdiction over this suit. Apparently, this simply reflects a narrow interpretation of the question presented for review. It is nonetheless possible that the Court's opinion may be read to imply that the specific jurisdiction of the Texas courts is inapplicable because the cause of action did not formally "arise out of" the contacts between Helicol and the forum. In my view, however, such a rule would place unjustifiable limits on the bases under which Texas may assert its jurisdictional power.

Limiting the specific jurisdiction of a forum to cases in which the cause of action formally arose out of the defendant's contacts with the State would subject constitutional standards under the Due Process Clause to the vagaries of the substantive law or pleading requirements of each State. For example, the complaint filed against Helicol in this case alleged negligence based on pilot error. Even though the pilot was trained in Texas, the Court assumes that the Texas courts may not assert jurisdiction over the suit because the cause of action "did not 'arise out of,' and [is] not related to," that training. If, however, the applicable substantive law required that negligent training of the pilot was a necessary element of a cause of action for pilot error, or if the respondents had simply added an allegation of negligence in the training provided for the Helicol pilot, then presumably the Court would concede that the specific jurisdiction of the Texas courts was applicable.

Our interpretation of the Due Process Clause has never been so dependent upon the applicable substantive law or the State's formal pleading requirements. At least since *International Shoe Co. v. Washington* the principal focus when determining whether a forum may constitutionally assert jurisdiction over a nonresident defendant has been on fairness and reasonableness to the defendant. To this extent, a court's specific

4. The jury specifically found that "the pilot failed to keep the helicopter under proper control," that "the helicopter was flown into a treetop fog condition, whereby the vision of the pilot was impaired," that "such flying was negligence," and that "such negligence . . . was a proximate cause of the crash." On the basis of these findings, Helicol was ordered to pay over $1 million in damages to the respondents.

jurisdiction should be applicable whenever the cause of action arises out of or relates to the contacts between the defendant and the forum. It is eminently fair and reasonable, in my view, to subject a defendant to suit in a forum with which it has significant contacts directly related to the underlying cause of action. Because Helicol's contacts with the State of Texas meet this standard, I would affirm the judgment of the Supreme Court of Texas.

Comments and Questions

1. What is the test for general jurisdiction? Did Helicol's contacts with Texas even approach the level of activity of the defendant mining company in *Perkins*? Justice Brennan, although dissenting, concedes that "the Court's holding on this issue is neither implausible nor unexpected."

2. In *Nichols v. G. D. Searle & Co.*, 991 F.2d 1195 (4th Cir. 1993), defendant Searle & Company had considerably more contacts with Maryland than Helicol did with Texas, but nonetheless was held beyond the reach of Maryland's general jurisdiction. The plaintiffs, whose product liability action was directed at the defendant's intrauterine device, argued that the defendant's employment of seventeen to twenty-one marketing representatives in Maryland (together with company automobiles, samples, and promotional materials) generating annual sales between $9 and $13 million (approximately 2 percent of its total sales) subjected it to suit there, even though the claims arose elsewhere and the plaintiffs themselves were nonresidents. The Fourth Circuit disagreed, observing: "[B]ecause specific jurisdiction has expanded tremendously, plaintiffs now may generally bring their claims in the forum in which they arose. As a result, obsolescing notions of general jurisdiction, which functioned primarily to ensure that a forum was available for plaintiffs to bring their claims, have been rendered largely unnecessary. Thus broad constructions of general jurisdiction should be generally disfavored." 991 F.2d at 1200 (citations omitted).

Compare *Nichols* with *Kenerson v. Stevenson*, 604 F. Supp. 792 (D. Me. 1985), in which a New Hampshire hospital was held subject to general jurisdiction in a malpractice action in Maine because it had solicited patients in Maine, conferred with doctors there, and referred patients to Maine hospitals. The lawsuit arose out of the plaintiff's treatment at the hospital in New Hampshire, and thus the claim for relief was not related to any of the defendant's contacts with Maine. Nonetheless, the court found continuous and systematic contacts because 7 percent of the hospital's in-patient caseload and between 7 and 13 percent of the out-patient caseload were Maine residents, because the hospital was part of a regional medical system including Maine, and because it regularly received reimbursement from that state for treatment of its residents. While conceding that the hospital was "an essentially local entity," the court concluded that it "cannot reasonably expect, in view of the substantiality of these contacts, not to be haled into court in Maine when claims arise from treatment extended to Maine residents on the basis of such a continuous and systematic business practice." 604 F. Supp. at 795-796 (citations omitted). *See also Hughes v. K-Ross Building Supply Center, Inc.*, 624 F. Supp. 1136 (D. Me. 1986) (court had general jurisdiction over nonresident defendant on claim unrelated to its forum activities where defendant shipped $6 million worth of goods to Maine in past six years, maintains a customer list of over twenty Maine businesses to which it sends a catalogue, and sends a sales representative to the state every six weeks).

Can these cases be reconciled?

3. Should a corporation's contacts with the forum be measured at the time the claim arose, the time the complaint is filed, or any time—including after the complaint is filed? While not resolving this question, U.S. District Judge Stearns observed (in a case in which plaintiff argued general jurisdiction based on contacts occurring two years after the alleged tortious conduct) that "to the extent that foreseeability is a touchstone of due process logic would measure general jurisdiction as of the date the tortious act is committed. Foreseeability in hindsight is after all an oxymoron." *Noonan v. Colour Library Books, Ltd.*, 947 F. Supp. 564, 571 (D. Mass. 1996).

4. What does *Helicopteros Nacionales de Colombia* add to our understanding of *specific* jurisdiction? How would you articulate the disagreement between Justice Brennan and the majority on this point? What is the difference between a claim "arising out of" and "relating to" the defendant's contacts within the forum? Which is the broader standard?

5. Construct the best argument you can that Helicol should be subject to specific jurisdiction in this case. Did the plaintiffs at least suggest such an argument to the Court? *See* Justice Brennan's footnote 3.

6. Some courts have abandoned the strict dichotomy between general and specific jurisdiction. The Maryland Court of Appeals, for example, has noted that in cases where it is not clear whether general or specific jurisdiction is applicable, "the proper approach is to identify the approximate position of the case on the continuum that exists between the two extremes, and apply the corresponding standard, recognizing that the quantum of required contacts increases as the nexus between the contacts and the cause of action decreases." *Camelback Ski Corp. v. Behning*, 539 A.2d 1107, 1111 (1988).

7. *Helicopteros Nacionales de Colombia* was decided in 1984. Does the 1987 decision in *Asahi* suggest another way the Court could reach the same result if *Helicopteros* were before it today? SoC

L. CONSENT

One of the traditional bases for the exercise of adjudicatory power is consent. A defendant can of course voluntarily appear in court and submit to jurisdiction. *Pennoyer* permitted states to require nonresidents conducting certain activities within the state to consent to the appointment of an agent to receive service of process for actions arising out of those activities. In the post-*Pennoyer* years, courts even resorted to the fiction of *implied* consent to justify the exercise of jurisdiction over nonresidents. *See, e.g, Hess v. Pawloski, supra.*

We have also seen that a defendant who fails to assert a defense of lack of personal jurisdiction in a timely fashion waives that objection—in effect a form of involuntary consent. *See* Fed. R. Civ. Proc. 12(h)(1). Similarly, a finding of jurisdiction can flow as a court sanction under the Federal Rules of Civil Procedure from a defendant's failure to comply with discovery orders seeking information related to jurisdiction. *See Insurance Corporation of Ireland, Ltd. v. Compagnie des Bauxites de Guinée*, 456 U.S. 694 (1982).

By operation of a forum-selection clause, consent to jurisdiction can take place before the dispute even arises, as illustrated in the next case.

■ CARNIVAL CRUISE LINES, INC. v. SHUTE
499 U.S. 585 (1991)

Justice BLACKMUN delivered the opinion of the Court:

In this admiralty case we primarily consider whether the United States Court of Appeals for the Ninth Circuit correctly refused to enforce a forum-selection clause contained in tickets issued by petitioner Carnival Cruise Lines, Inc., to respondents Eulala and Russel Shute.

I

The Shutes, through an Arlington, Wash., travel agent, purchased passage for a 7-day cruise on petitioner's ship, the Tropicale. Respondents paid the fare to the agent who forwarded the payment to petitioner's headquarters in Miami, Fla. Petitioner then prepared the tickets and sent them to respondents in the State of Washington. The face of each ticket, at its left-hand lower corner, contained this admonition: "SUBJECT TO CONDITIONS OF CONTRACT ON LAST PAGES IMPORTANT! PLEASE READ CONTRACT—ON LAST PAGES 1, 2, 3" App. 15.

The following appeared on "contract page 1" of each ticket:

TERMS AND CONDITIONS OF PASSAGE CONTRACT TICKET
    . . . 3. (a) The acceptance of this ticket by the person or persons named hereon as passengers shall be deemed to be an acceptance and

agreement by each of them of all of the terms and conditions of this
Passage Contract Ticket.

. . . 8. It is agreed by and between the passenger and the Carrier that
all disputes and matters whatsoever arising under, in connection with or
incident to this Contract shall be litigated, if at all, in and before a Court
located in the State of Florida, U.S.A., to the exclusion of the Courts of any
other state or country.

The last quoted paragraph is the forum-selection clause at issue.

II

Respondents boarded the Tropicale in Los Angeles, Cal. The ship
sailed to Puerto Vallarta, Mexico, and then returned to Los Angeles. While
the ship was in international waters off the Mexican coast, respondent
Eulala Shute was injured when she slipped on a deck mat during a guided
tour of the ship's galley. Respondents filed suit against petitioner in the
United States District Court for the Western District of Washington,
claiming that Mrs. Shute's injuries had been caused by the negligence of
Carnival Cruise Lines and its employees.

Petitioner moved for summary judgment, contending that the forum
clause in respondents' tickets required the Shutes to bring their suit
against petitioner in a court in the State of Florida. Petitioner contended,
alternatively, that the District Court lacked personal jurisdiction over
petitioner because petitioner's contacts with the State of Washington were
insubstantial. The District Court granted the motion, holding that
petitioner's contacts with Washington were constitutionally insufficient to
support the exercise of personal jurisdiction.

The Court of Appeals reversed . . . [concluding] that the forum
clause should not be enforced because it "was not freely bargained for." As
an "independent justification" for refusing to enforce the clause, the
Court of Appeals noted that there was evidence in the record to indicate
that "the Shutes are physically and financially incapable of pursuing this
litigation in Florida" and that the enforcement of the clause would operate to deprive them of their day in court. . . .

In evaluating the reasonableness of the forum clause at issue in this
case, [a]s an initial matter, we do not adopt the Court of Appeals' determination that a nonnegotiated forum-selection clause in a form ticket
contract is never enforceable simply because it is not the subject of
bargaining. Including a reasonable forum clause in a form contract of this
kind well may be permissible for several reasons: First, a cruise line has a
special interest in limiting the fora in which it potentially could be subject
to suit. Because a cruise ship typically carries passengers from many
locales, it is not unlikely that a mishap on a cruise could subject the cruise
line to litigation in several different fora. Additionally, a clause establishing ex ante the forum for dispute resolution has the salutary effect of

dispelling any confusion about where suits arising from the contract must be brought and defended, sparing litigants the time and expense of pretrial motions to determine the correct forum and conserving judicial resources that otherwise would be devoted to deciding those motions. Finally, it stands to reason that passengers who purchase tickets containing a forum clause like that at issue in this case benefit in the form of reduced fares reflecting the savings that the cruise line enjoys by limiting the fora in which it may be sued.

We also do not accept the Court of Appeals' "independent justification" for its conclusion that . . . the clause should not be enforced because "[t]here is evidence in the record to indicate that the Shutes are physically and financially incapable of pursuing this litigation in Florida." . . . In dismissing the case for lack of personal jurisdiction over petitioner, the District Court made no finding regarding the physical and financial impediments to the Shutes' pursuing their case in Florida. . . . In the present case, Florida is not a "remote alien forum," nor—given the fact that Mrs. Shute's accident occurred off the coast of Mexico—is this dispute an essentially local one inherently more suited to resolution in the State of Washington than in Florida. [W]e conclude that they have not satisfied the "heavy burden of proof" required to set aside the clause on grounds of inconvenience.

It bears emphasis that forum-selection clauses contained in form passage contracts are subject to judicial scrutiny for fundamental fairness. In this case, there is no indication that petitioner set Florida as the forum in which disputes were to be resolved as a means of discouraging cruise passengers from pursuing legitimate claims. Any suggestion of such a bad-faith motive is belied by two facts: Petitioner has its principal place of business in Florida, and many of its cruises depart from and return to Florida ports. Similarly, there is no evidence that petitioner obtained respondents' accession to the forum clause by fraud or overreaching. Finally, respondents have conceded that they were given notice of the forum provision and, therefore, presumably retained the option of rejecting the contract with impunity. In the case before us, therefore, we conclude that the Court of Appeals erred in refusing to enforce the forum-selection clause.

The judgment of the Court of Appeals is reversed. It is so ordered.

Justice STEVENS, with whom Justice MARSHALL joins, dissenting:

The Court prefaces its legal analysis with a factual statement that implies that a purchaser of a Carnival Cruise Lines passenger ticket is fully and fairly notified about the existence of the choice of forum clause in the fine print on the back of the ticket. Even if this implication were accurate, I would disagree with the Court's analysis. But, given the Court's preface, I begin my dissent by noting that only the most meticulous passenger is likely to become aware of the forum-selection provision. I have therefore appended to this opinion a facsimile of the relevant text, using the type size that actually appears in the ticket itself. A careful reader will find the forum-selection clause in the 8th of the 25 numbered paragraphs.

Of course, many passengers, like the respondents in this case, will not have an opportunity to read paragraph 8 until they have actually purchased their tickets. By this point, the passengers will already have accepted the condition set forth in paragraph 16(a), which provides that "[t]he Carrier shall not be liable to make any refund to passengers in respect of . . . tickets wholly or partly not used by a passenger." Not knowing whether or not that provision is legally enforceable, I assume that the average passenger would accept the risk of having to file suit in Florida in the event of an injury, rather than canceling—without a refund—a planned vacation at the last minute. The fact that the cruise line can reduce its litigation costs, and therefore its liability insurance premiums, by forcing this choice on its passengers does not, in my opinion, suffice to render the provision reasonable.

Even if passengers received prominent notice of the forum-selection clause before they committed the cost of the cruise, I would remain persuaded that the clause was unenforceable. . . . These clauses are typically the product of disparate bargaining power between the carrier and the passenger, and they undermine the strong public interest in deterring negligent conduct. . . .

Forum-selection clauses in passenger tickets involve the intersection of two strands of traditional contract law that qualify the general rule that courts will enforce the terms of a contract as written. Pursuant to the first strand, courts traditionally have reviewed with heightened scrutiny the terms of contracts of adhesion, form contracts offered on a take-or-leave basis by a party with stronger bargaining power to a party with weaker power. Some commentators have questioned whether contracts of adhesion can justifiably be enforced at all under traditional contract theory because the adhering party generally enters into them without manifesting knowing and voluntary consent to all their terms.

The common law, recognizing that standardized form contracts account for a significant portion of all commercial agreements, has taken a less extreme position and instead subjects terms in contracts of adhesion to scrutiny for reasonableness. . . .

The stipulation in the ticket that Carnival Cruise sold to respondents certainly lessens or weakens their ability to recover for the slip and fall incident that occurred off the west coast of Mexico during the cruise that originated and terminated in Los Angeles, California. It is safe to assume that the witnesses—whether other passengers or members of the crew— can be assembled with less expense and inconvenience at a west coast forum than in a Florida court several thousand miles from the scene of the accident. . . .

Under these circumstances, the general prohibition against stipulations purporting "to lessen, weaken, or avoid" the passenger's right to a trial certainly should be construed to apply to the manifestly unreasonable stipulation in these passengers' tickets. . . .

I respectfully dissent.

Comments and Questions

1. *Carnival Cruise Lines* aptly illustrates the strategic importance of the personal jurisdiction question. The Ninth Circuit Court of Appeals had concluded that "the Shutes are physically and financially incapable of pursuing this litigation in Florida" and that the enforcement of the clause would operate to deprive them of their day in court. In an article highly critical of the Supreme Court's decision, Professor Linda Mullenix writes that "[a]s a practical matter, these [forum selection] clauses cause unwitting plaintiffs to forfeit legitimate legal claims due to the plaintiff's frequent inability to mount a case in a distant, inconvenient forum," and "tips the procedural balance in favor of well-heeled, savvy defendants." She accuses the Court of "tacitly encouraging highly-skilled, high-stakes forum shopping." Linda Mullenix, *Another Easy Case, Some More Bad Law: Carnival Cruise Lines and Contractual Personal Jurisdiction*, 27 Tex. Intl. L.J. 323 (1992).

Congress in effect overruled *Carnival Cruise Lines* by amending an admiralty statute in 1992 to provide that a vessel passenger had a statutory right to bring an action for personal injury in any court of the plaintiff's choice and, further, that the right could not be limited by a forum selection clause in a passenger ticket. For a discussion of the unusual legislative route followed, *see* Michael F. Sturley, *Congressional Action "Overruling" the Supreme Court*, 24 J. Mar. L. & Com. 399 (1993); Note, *Statutory Revision to Carnival Cruise Lines, Inc. v. Shute*, 6 U.S. F. Mar. L.J. 259 (1993).

2. Why would the Court "sell out" consumers in these situations with such apparent indifference? Is *Carnival Cruise Lines* simply a reflection of the Court's pro-business bias? Or might it reflect a desire to preserve a basis for adjudicatory authority free from the extraordinary complexity of the due process analysis?

3. Would the Court have enforced a no-liability clause (disclaiming any liability for injuries suffered during the cruise) inserted into the contract in the same way? Why or why not? If not, doesn't the forum selection clause amount to the same thing for passengers like the Shutes who lack the wherewithal to litigate in the distant forum?

4. Under what circumstances would the majority in *Carnival Cruise Lines* refuse to enforce a forum selection clause?

5. Does it make a difference when the forum selection clause forces a consumer to *defend* in a distant forum? What if Carnival Cruise Lines had sued the Shutes in Florida because the check they used to pay for the cruise was returned unpaid?

6. Have you looked at the back of your long-distance telephone bill lately? The following has appeared on the monthly statement from Sprint Communications: "Pursuant to K.S.A. 60-308(b)(11), as a business customer, you may be subject to jurisdiction in Kansas for any dispute relating to your telephone service with Sprint. This is because you have arranged for or continued to receive phone service managed, operated or monitored in the State of Kansas." Is this a forum-selection clause? Is it enforceable? Explain.

7. We will come back to the issue of the enforceability of forum selection clauses when we discuss *Stewart Organization, Inc. v. Ricoh Corp.*, 487 U.S. 22 (1988) in Chapter 9.

Practice Exercise No. 29: Considering Personal Jurisdiction in the Digital Age

To: Associate
From: Partner
Re: Advice on *CompuServe Inc. v. New Technologies*

Our client New Technologies (NT), a software development company located here in Los Angeles, has just been served with a complaint filed in U.S. District Court in Ohio. The plaintiff, CompuServe Inc., alleges that NT infringed on one of its tradenames and engaged in deceptive trade practices and unfair competition when it recently offered its Easy Navigator on NT's Internet Web site. CompuServe is claiming that the new release is designed to exploit the dramatic success of CompuServe's own "Easy Web Navigator" by deceiving customers into ordering the NT product instead.

It strikes me that jurisdiction over our client in Ohio is questionable. NT's only ties to that state are electronic, Ohio being the headquarters of CompuServe and the base of its operations. NT is a CompuServe subscriber who accesses the system from California through a modem and telephone line and pays fees for the use. In turn, NT is permitted to market its own products to other CompuServe users through its Web site. I've asked the NT people to check their records, and their total sales to users in Ohio over the past two years amounts to less than $1,000 (a meager portion of their total sales; none of the Ohio sales, by the way, involved the Navigator that's the subject of this lawsuit). NT has no office in Ohio, doesn't advertise there except over the Internet, and no NT person has ever set foot in the state.

One thing that worries me a bit is that the basic CompuServe user agreement states that the agreement is "made and performed in Ohio" and governed by that state's law. Subscribers must type "AGREE" on their computer next to these terms and conditions before being allowed into the CompuServe network. But that doesn't look like a forum-selection clause, does it? And even if it is, can it be forced upon NT like this?

Before we invest much time in researching whatever case law there is on cyber-jurisdiction, I'd like your initial thoughts on the potential for a 12(b)(2) motion here. (After all, you're much closer in time to all that *International Shoe* stuff from law school than I am). I await your prompt attention (by way of memo, please).

I've looked up the Ohio long-arm statute. It allows an Ohio court to exercise personal jurisdiction over nonresidents of Ohio on claims arising from, *inter alia,* the nonresident's transacting any business in Ohio. Ohio Rev. Code Ann. §2307.382(A) (Anderson 1995). *See CompuServe, Inc. v. Patterson,* 89 F.3d 1257(6th Cir. 1996).

M. NOTICE

Under the *Pennoyer* scheme, dominated by the concept of "presence," notice of the lawsuit occurred simultaneously with the act that typically gave rise to jurisdiction, namely personal service within the state. As the basis for adjudicatory power became divorced from "presence," however, notifying a defendant had to be accomplished through other means. Remember in *Hess v. Pawloski,* for example, that the nonmotorist statute required that notice be sent by registered mail to the defendant's residence. The following case defines the constitutional parameters of adequate notice.

■ MULLANE v. CENTRAL HANOVER BANK & TRUST CO.
339 U.S. 306 (1950)

Justice JACKSON delivered the opinion of the Court:

This controversy questions the constitutional sufficiency of notice to beneficiaries on judicial settlement of accounts by the trustee of a common trust fund established under the New York Banking Law, Consol. Laws, c. 2. The New York Court of Appeals considered and overruled objections that the statutory notice contravenes requirements of the Fourteenth Amendment and that by allowance of the account beneficiaries were deprived of property without due process of law. The case is here on appeal. . . .

Common trust fund legislation is addressed to a problem appropriate for state action. Mounting overheads have made administration of small trusts undesirable to corporate trustees. In order that donors and testators of moderately sized trusts may not be denied the service of corporate fiduciaries, the District of Columbia and some thirty states other than New York have permitted pooling small trust estates into one fund for investment administration. The income, capital gains, losses and expenses of the collective trust are shared by the constituent trusts in proportion to their contribution. By this plan, diversification of risk and economy of management can be extended to those whose capital standing alone would not obtain such advantage.

Statutory authorization for the establishment of such common trust funds is provided in the New York Banking Law, §100-c, c. 687, L. 1937, as amended by c. 602, L. 1943 and c. 158, L. 1944. Under this Act a trust company may, with approval of the State Banking Board, establish a common fund and, within prescribed limits, invest therein the assets of an unlimited number of estates, trusts or other funds of which it is trustee. Each participating trust shares ratably in the common fund, but exclusive management and control is in the trust company as trustee, and neither a fiduciary nor any beneficiary of a participating trust is deemed to have ownership in any particular asset or investment of this common fund. The trust company must keep fund assets separate from its own, and in its fiduciary capacity may not deal with itself or any affiliate. Provisions are made for accountings twelve to fifteen months after the establishment of a fund and triennially thereafter. The decree in each such judicial settlement of accounts is made binding and conclusive as to any matter set forth in the account upon everyone having any interest in the common fund or in any participating estate, trust or fund.

In January, 1946, Central Hanover Bank and Trust Company established a common trust fund in accordance with these provisions, and in March, 1947, it petitioned the Surrogate's Court for settlement of its first account as common trustee. During the accounting period a total of 113 trusts, approximately half inter vivos and half testamentary, participated in the common trust fund, the gross capital of which was nearly three million dollars. The record does not show the number or residence of the beneficiaries, but they were many and it is clear that some of them were not residents of the State of New York.

The only notice given beneficiaries of this specific application was by publication in a local newspaper in strict compliance with the minimum requirements of N.Y. Banking Law §100-c(12): "After filing such petition (for judicial settlement of its account) the petitioner shall cause to be issued by the court in which the petition is filed and shall publish not less than once in each week for four successive weeks in a newspaper to be designated by the court a notice or citation addressed generally without naming them to all parties interested in such common trust fund and in such estates, trusts or funds mentioned in the petition, all of which may be described in the notice or citation only in the manner set forth in said petition and without setting forth the residence of any such decedent or donor of any such estate, trust or fund." Thus the only notice required, and the only one given, was by newspaper publication setting forth merely the name and address of the trust company, the name and the date of establishment of the common trust fund, and a list of all participating estates, trusts or funds.

At the time the first investment in the common fund was made on behalf of each participating estate, however, the trust company, pursuant to the requirements of §100-c(9), had notified by mail each person of full age and sound mind whose name and address was then known to it and who was "entitled to share in the income therefrom . . . [or] . . . who would be entitled to share in the principal if the event upon which such estate, trust or fund will become distributable should have occurred at the time of sending such notice." Included in the notice was a copy of those provisions of the Act relating to the sending of the notice itself and to the judicial settlement of common trust fund accounts.

Upon the filing of the petition for the settlement of accounts, appellant was, by order of the court pursuant to §100-c(12), appointed special guardian and attorney for all persons known or unknown not otherwise appearing who had or might thereafter have any interest in the income of the common trust fund; and appellee Vaughan was appointed to represent those similarly interested in the principal. There were no other appearances on behalf of anyone interested in either interest or principal.

Appellant appeared specially, objecting that notice and the statutory provisions for notice to beneficiaries were inadequate to afford due process under the Fourteenth Amendment, and therefore that the court was without jurisdiction to render a final and binding decree. Appellant's objections were entertained and overruled, the Surrogate holding that the notice required and given was sufficient. A final decree accepting the accounts has been entered, affirmed by the Appellate Division of the Supreme Court.

The effect of this decree, as held below, is to settle "all questions respecting the management of the common fund." We understand that every right which beneficiaries would otherwise have against the trust company, either as trustee of the common fund or as trustee of any individual trust, for improper management of the common trust fund during the period covered by the accounting is sealed and wholly terminated by the decree.

We are met at the outset with a challenge to the power of the State—the right of its courts to adjudicate at all as against those beneficiaries who reside without the State of New York. It is contended that the proceeding is one in personam in that the decree affects neither title to nor possession of any res, but adjudges only personal rights of the beneficiaries to surcharge their trustee for negligence or breach of trust. Accordingly, it is said, under the strict doctrine of *Pennoyer v. Neff*, 95 U.S. 714, the Surrogate is without jurisdiction as to nonresidents upon whom personal service of process was not made.

Distinctions between actions in rem and those in personam are ancient and originally expressed in procedural terms what seems really to have been a distinction in the substantive law of property under a system quite unlike our own. The legal recognition and rise in economic importance of incorporeal or intangible forms of property have upset the ancient simplicity of property law and the clarity of its distinctions, while new forms of proceedings have confused the old procedural classification. American courts have sometimes classed certain actions as in rem because personal service of process was not required, and at other times have held personal service of process not required because the action was in rem.

Judicial proceedings to settle fiduciary accounts have been sometimes termed in rem, or more indefinitely quasi in rem, or more vaguely still, "in the nature of a proceeding in rem." It is not readily apparent how the courts of New York did or would classify the present proceeding, which has some characteristics and is wanting in some features of proceedings both in rem and in personam. But in any event we think that the requirements of the Fourteenth Amendment to the Federal Constitution do not depend upon a classification for which the standards are so elusive and confused generally and which, being primarily for state courts to define, may and do vary from state to state. Without disparaging the usefulness of distinctions between actions in rem and those in personam in many branches of law, or on other issues, or the reasoning which underlies them, we do not rest the power of the State to resort to constructive service in this proceeding upon how its courts or this Court may regard this historic antithesis. It is sufficient to observe that, whatever the technical definition of its chosen procedure, the interest of each state in providing means to close trusts that exist by the grace of its laws and are administered under the supervision of its courts is so insistent and rooted in custom as to establish beyond doubt the right of its courts to determine the interests of all claimants, resident or nonresident, provided its procedure accords full opportunity to appear and be heard.

Quite different from the question of a state's power to discharge trustees is that of the opportunity it must give beneficiaries to contest. Many controversies have raged about the cryptic and abstract words of the Due Process Clause but there can be no doubt that at a minimum they require that deprivation of life, liberty or property by adjudication be preceded by notice and opportunity for hearing appropriate to the nature of the case.

In two ways this proceeding does or may deprive beneficiaries of property. It may cut off their rights to have the trustee answer for negligent or illegal impairments of their interests. Also, their interests are presumably subject to diminution in the proceeding by allowance of fees and expenses to one who, in their names but without their knowledge, may conduct a fruitless or uncompensatory contest. Certainly the proceeding is one in which they may be deprived of property rights and hence notice and hearing must measure up to the standards of due process.

Personal service of written notice within the jurisdiction is the classic form of notice always adequate in any type of proceeding. But the vital interest of the State in bringing any issues as to its fiduciaries to a final settlement can be served only if interests or claims of individuals who are outside of the State can somehow be determined. A construction of the Due Process Clause which would place impossible or impractical obstacles in the way could not be justified.

Against this interest of the State we must balance the individual interest sought to be protected by the Fourteenth Amendment. This is defined by our holding that "the fundamental requisite of due process of law is the opportunity to be heard." This right to be heard has little reality or worth unless one is informed that the matter is pending and can choose for himself whether to appear or default, acquiesce or contest.

The Court has not committed itself to any formula achieving a balance between these interests in a particular proceeding or determining when constructive notice may be utilized or what test it must meet. Personal service has not in all circumstances been regarded as indispensable to the process due to residents, and it has more often been held unnecessary as to nonresidents. We disturb none of the established rules on these subjects. No decision constitutes a controlling or even a very illuminating precedent for the case before us. But a few general principles stand out in the books.

An elementary and fundamental requirement of due process in any proceeding which is to be accorded finality is notice reasonably calculated, under all the circumstances, to apprise interested parties of the pendency of the action and afford them an opportunity to present their objections. The notice must be of such nature as reasonably to convey the required information, and it must afford a reasonable time for those interested to make their appearance. But if with due regard for the practicalities and peculiarities of the case these conditions are reasonably met the constitutional requirements are satisfied. . . .

But when notice is a person's due, process which is a mere gesture is not due process. The means employed must be such as one desirous of actually informing the absentee might reasonably adopt to accomplish it. The reasonableness and hence the constitutional validity of any chosen method may be defended on the ground that it is in itself reasonably certain to inform those affected, or, where conditions do not reasonably permit such notice, that the form chosen is not substantially less likely to bring home notice than other of the feasible and customary substitutes.

It would be idle to pretend that publication alone, as prescribed here, is a reliable means of acquainting interested parties of the fact that their rights are before the courts. It is not an accident that the greater number of cases reaching this Court on the question of adequacy of notice have been concerned with actions founded on process constructively served through local newspapers. Chance alone brings to the attention of even a local resident an advertisement in small type inserted in the back pages of a newspaper, and if he makes his home outside the area of the newspaper's normal circulation the odds that the information will never reach him are large indeed. The chance of actual notice is further reduced when as here the notice required does not even name those whose attention it is supposed to attract, and does not inform acquaintances who might call it to attention. In weighing its sufficiency on the basis of equivalence with actual notice we are unable to regard this as more than a feint.

Nor is publication here reinforced by steps likely to attract the parties' attention to the proceeding. It is true that publication traditionally has been acceptable as notification supplemental to other action which in itself may reasonably be expected to convey a warning. The ways or [*sic*] an owner with tangible property are such that he usually arranges means to learn of any direct attack upon his possessory or proprietary rights. Hence, [seizure] of a ship, attachment of a chattel or entry upon real estate in the name of law may reasonably be expected to come promptly to the owner's attention. When the state within which the owner has located such property seizes it for some reason, publication or posting affords an additional measure of notification. A state may indulge the assumption that one who has left tangible property in the state either has abandoned it, in which case proceedings against it deprive him of nothing, or that he has left some caretaker under a duty to let him know that it is being jeopardized. . . .

In the case before us there is, of course, no abandonment. On the other hand these beneficiaries do have a resident fiduciary as caretaker of their interest in this property. But it is their caretaker who in the accounting becomes their adversary. Their trustee is released from giving notice of jeopardy, and no one else is expected to do so. Not even the special guardian is required or apparently expected to communicate with his ward and client, and, of course, if such a duty were merely transferred from the trustee to the guardian, economy would not be served and more likely the cost would be increased.

This Court has not hesitated to approve of resort to publication as a customary substitute in another class of cases where it is not reasonably possible or practicable to give more adequate warning. Thus it has been recognized that, in the case of persons missing or unknown, employment of an indirect and even a probably futile means of notification is all that the situation permits and creates no constitutional bar to a final decree foreclosing their rights.

Those beneficiaries represented by appellant whose interests or whereabouts could not with due diligence be ascertained come clearly within this category. As to them the statutory notice is sufficient. However great the odds that publication will never reach the eyes of such unknown parties, it is not in the typical case much more likely to fail than any of the choices open to legislators endeavoring to prescribe the best notice practicable.

Nor do we consider it unreasonable for the State to dispense with more certain notice to those beneficiaries whose interests are either conjectural or future or, although they could be discovered upon investigation, do not in due course of business come to knowledge of the common trustee. Whatever searches might be required in another situation under ordinary standards of diligence, in view of the character of the proceedings and the nature of the interests here involved we think them unnecessary. We recognize the practical difficulties and costs that would be attendant on frequent investigations into the status of great numbers of beneficiaries, many of whose interests in the common fund are so remote as to be ephemeral; and we have no doubt that such impracticable and extended searches are not required in the name of due process. The expense of keeping informed from day to day of substitutions among even current income beneficiaries and presumptive remaindermen, to say nothing of the far greater number of contingent beneficiaries, would impose a severe burden on the plan, and would likely dissipate its advantages. These are practical matters in which we should be reluctant to disturb the judgment of the state authorities.

Accordingly we overrule appellant's constitutional objections to published notice insofar as they are urged on behalf of any beneficiaries whose interests or addresses are unknown to the trustee.

As to known present beneficiaries of known place of residence, however, notice by publication stands on a different footing. Exceptions in the name of necessity do not sweep away the rule that within the limits of practicability notice must be such as is reasonably calculated to reach interested parties. Where the names and post office addresses of those affected by a proceeding are at hand, the reasons disappear for resort to means less likely than the mails to apprise them of its pendency.

The trustee has on its books the names and addresses of the income beneficiaries represented by appellant, and we find no tenable ground for dispensing with a serious effort to inform them personally of the accounting, at least by ordinary mail to the record addresses. Certainly sending them a copy of the statute months and perhaps years in advance does not answer this purpose. The trustee periodically remits their income to them, and we think that they might reasonably expect that with or apart from their remittances word might come to them personally that steps were being taken affecting their interests.

We need not weigh contentions that a requirement of personal service of citation on even the large number of known resident or nonresident beneficiaries would, by reasons of delay if not of expense, seriously interfere with the proper administration of the fund. Of course personal service even without the jurisdiction of the issuing authority serves the end of actual and personal notice, whatever power of compulsion it might lack. However, no such service is required under the circumstances. This type of trust presupposes a large number of small interests. The individual interest does not stand alone but is identical with that of a class. The rights of each in the integrity of the fund and the fidelity of the trustee are shared by many other beneficiaries. Therefore notice reasonably certain to reach most of those interested in objecting is likely to safeguard the interests of all, since any objections sustained would inure to the benefit of all. We think that under such circumstances reasonable risks that notice might not actually reach every beneficiary are justifiable. "Now and then an extraordinary case may turn up, but constitutional law, like other mortal contrivances, has to take some chances, and in the great majority of instances, no doubt, justice will be done."

The statutory notice to known beneficiaries is inadequate, not because in fact it fails to reach everyone, but because under the circumstances it is not reasonably calculated to reach those who could easily be informed by other means at hand. However it may have been in former times, the mails today are recognized as an efficient and inexpensive means of communication. Moreover, the fact that the trust company has been able to give mailed notice to known beneficiaries at the time the common trust fund was established is persuasive that postal notification at the time of accounting would not seriously burden the plan.

In some situations the law requires greater precautions in its proceedings than the business world accepts for its own purposes. In few, if any, will it be satisfied with less. Certainly it is instructive, in determining the reasonableness of the impersonal broadcast notification here used, to ask whether it would satisfy a prudent man of business, counting his pennies but finding it in his interest to convey information to many persons whose names and addresses are in his files. We are not satisfied that it would. Publication may theoretically be available for all the world to see, but it is too much in our day to suppose that each or any individual beneficiary does or could examine all that is published to see if something may be tucked away in it that affects his property interests. We have before indicated in reference to notice by publication that, "Great caution should be used not to let fiction deny the fair play that can be secured only by a pretty close adhesion to fact."

We hold the notice of judicial settlement of accounts required by the New York Banking Law §100-c(12) is incompatible with the requirements of the Fourteenth Amendment as a basis for adjudication depriving known persons whose whereabouts are also known of substantial property rights. Accordingly the judgment is reversed and the cause remanded for further proceedings not inconsistent with this opinion.

Reversed.

Justice DOUGLAS took no part in the consideration or decision of this case.

Justice BURTON, dissenting:

These common trusts are available only when the instruments creating the participating trusts permit participation in the common fund. Whether or not further notice to beneficiaries should supplement the notice and representation here provided is properly within the discretion of the State. The Federal Constitution does not require it here.

Comments and Questions

1. How does *Mullane* rely on *Pennoyer*? On the other hand, how does *Mullane* anticipate *Shaffer v. Heitner*'s repudiation of *Pennoyer*? Can you see why it is viewed as a pivotal case?

2. According to Justice Jackson, what is the basis for jurisdiction over the nonresident beneficiaries? Reread this passage:

> It is sufficient to observe that, whatever the technical definition of its chosen procedure, the interest of each state in providing means to close trusts that exist by the grace of its laws and are administered under the supervision of its courts is so insistent and rooted in custom as to establish beyond doubt the right of its courts to determine the interests of all claimants, resident or nonresident, provided its procedure accords full opportunity to appear and be heard.

339 U.S. at 313. Is this jurisdiction by necessity?

3. Why would the Court set so elastic a constitutional standard as "notice reasonably calculated, under all the circumstances [and with due regard for the practicalities and peculiarities of the case], to apprise interested parties of the pendency of the action and afford them an opportunity to present their objections"? Doesn't such a *test* ensure endless litigation on the adequacy of notice? What is the alternative?

4. Decisions since *Mullane* have set notice by mail as the constitutional minimum for defendants whose addresses can be ascertained by reasonably diligent efforts. *See Walker v. City of Hutchinson*, 352 U.S. 112 (1956) (where landowner's name was known to city, newspaper publication was inadequate notice of condemnation proceedings); *Greene v. Lindsey*, 456 U.S. 444 (1982) (posting notices of eviction proceedings on doors of public housing tenants violated due process where evidence indicated notices were often removed); *Mennonite Board of Missions v. Adams*, 462 U.S. 791 (1983) (notice by publication and posting inadequate to notify mortgagee identified in the public record of pending tax sale).

5. Fed. R. of Civ. P. 4 controls notice in federal actions. The requirements for service on defendants were considerably liberalized by amendments in 1983 and 1993. Work through the "waiver of service" procedures under Rule 4(d). What are the incentives for a defendant to waive service?

Is it accurate to say that Rule 4(d) permits "service by mail"? Read the Advisory Committee's Note to the 1993 Amendment, particularly on subdivision (d).

N. VENUE AND *FORUM NON CONVENIENS*

Beyond the constraints of personal jurisdiction (and, as we will see in the next chapter, subject matter jurisdiction), venue requirements operate as a further limit on the plaintiff's choice of court. State venue rules identify the counties within a state in which an action may be brought,* while federal venue requirements locate a case within particular judicial districts. Venue serves as a geographical funnel to direct cases to locales that have a connection to the parties or the events that gave rise to the litigation. The basic concept is to assign the case to a court that is in proximity either to the parties, or to the witnesses and the evidence.

Read 28 U.S.C. §1391. The federal venue statute sets up somewhat different venue rules depending upon whether the subject matter jurisdiction over the case is based on diversity of citizenship or a federal question (*see* Chapter 8). In both types of case, venue is proper in a judicial district where any defendant resides (if all reside in the same state) or in which a substantial part of the events giving rise to the claim occurred. If neither of these produces an appropriate district (as where, for example, defendants are from different states and the events giving rise to the claim occurred in a foreign country), then a diversity action may be filed in a district where any defendant is subject to personal jurisdiction, §1391(a), and a federal question case in a district where any defendant "may be found" (presumably something less than being subject to personal jurisdiction). §1391(b). A corporate defendant is deemed to reside in any district where it is subject to personal jurisdiction. §1391(c).

Like personal jurisdiction, an objection to venue must be raised in a timely manner or it is waived. *See* Fed. R. Civ. Proc. 12(1). Unlike personal jurisdiction, proper venue is not a constitutional requirement for a valid judgment, and thus cannot be raised by way of collateral attack.

---

*The Massachusetts venue statute applicable in *Carpenter v. Dee*, for example, provides that a "transitory action" shall be brought in the county where any resident party lives or has a usual place of business. Mass. Gen. Laws c. 233 §1. If one party is a corporation, the action may be brought in any county "in which the corporation might sue or be sued." Mass. Gen. Laws c. 233 §8. "Local actions," as contrasted with "transitory actions," are actions involving real estate and must be brought in the county where the real estate is located. If Nancy Carpenter, Randall and Peter Dee, Ultimate Auto, the City of Lowell and McGill's Garage were all situated in different counties in the Commonwealth, where would venue properly lie for an action in which they were all original parties?

If a case is filed in a district in which venue does not properly lie, the court may, as an alternative to dismissal, transfer the case to a district "in which it could have been brought," that is, in which the requirements of personal jurisdiction, subject matter jurisdiction, and venue are all met. *See* 28 U.S.C. §1406. The next case addresses the change of venue provision at §1404 and the common law doctrine of *forum non conveniens*.

■ PIPER AIRCRAFT CO. v. REYNO
454 U.S. 235 (1981)

Justice MARSHALL delivered the opinion of the Court:

These cases arise out of an air crash that took place in Scotland. Respondent, acting as representative of the estates of several Scottish citizens killed in the accident, brought wrongful-death actions against petitioners that were ultimately transferred to the United States District Court for the Middle District of Pennsylvania. Petitioners moved to dismiss on the ground of *forum non conveniens*. After noting that an alternative forum existed in Scotland, the District Court granted their motions. The United States Court of Appeals for the Third Circuit reversed. The Court of Appeals based its decision, at least in part, on the ground that dismissal is automatically barred where the law of the alternative forum is less favorable to the plaintiff than the law of the forum chosen by the plaintiff. Because we conclude that the possibility of an unfavorable change in law should not, by itself, bar dismissal, and because we conclude that the District Court did not otherwise abuse its discretion, we reverse.

I

A

In July 1976, a small commercial aircraft crashed in the Scottish highlands during the course of a charter flight from Blackpool to Perth. The pilot and five passengers were killed instantly. The decedents were all Scottish subjects and residents, as are their heirs and next of kin. There were no eyewitnesses to the accident. At the time of the crash the plane was subject to Scottish air traffic control.

The aircraft, a twin-engine Piper Aztec, was manufactured in Pennsylvania by petitioner Piper Aircraft Co. (Piper). The propellers were manufactured in Ohio by petitioner Hartzell Propeller, Inc. (Hartzell). At the time of the crash the aircraft was registered in Great Britain and was owned and maintained by Air Navigation and Trading Co., Ltd. (Air Navigation). It was operated by McDonald Aviation, Ltd. (McDonald), a Scottish air taxi service. Both Air Navigation and McDonald were organized in the United Kingdom. The wreckage of the plane is now in a hangar in Farnsborough, England.

The British Department of Trade investigated the accident shortly after it occurred. A preliminary report found that the plane crashed after developing a spin, and suggested that mechanical failure in the plane or the propeller was responsible. At Hartzell's request, this report was reviewed by a three-member Review Board, which held a 9-day adversary hearing attended by all interested parties. The Review Board found no evidence of defective equipment and indicated that pilot error may have contributed to the accident. The pilot, who had obtained his commercial pilot's license only three months earlier, was flying over high ground at an altitude considerably lower than the minimum height required by his company's operations manual.

In July 1977, a California probate court appointed respondent Gaynell Reyno administratrix of the estates of the five passengers. Reyno is not related to and does not know any of the decedents or their survivors; she was a legal secretary to the attorney who filed this lawsuit. Several days after her appointment, Reyno commenced separate wrongful-death actions against Piper and Hartzell in the Superior Court of California, claiming negligence and strict liability. Air Navigation, McDonald, and the estate of the pilot are not parties to this litigation. The survivors of the five passengers whose estates are represented by Reyno filed a separate action in the United Kingdom against Air Navigation, McDonald, and the pilot's estate. Reyno candidly admits that the action against Piper and Hartzell was filed in the United States because its laws regarding liability, capacity to sue, and damages are more favorable to her position than are those of Scotland. Scottish law does not recognize strict liability in tort. Moreover, it permits wrongful-death actions only when brought by a decedent's relatives. The relatives may sue only for "loss of support and society."

On petitioners' motion, the suit was removed to the United States District Court for the Central District of California. Piper then moved for transfer to the United States District Court for the Middle District of Pennsylvania, pursuant to 28 U.S.C. § 1404(a).[4] Hartzell moved to dismiss for lack of personal jurisdiction, or in the alternative, to transfer.[5] In December 1977, the District Court quashed service on Hartzell and transferred the case to the Middle District of Pennsylvania. Respondent then properly served process on Hartzell.

B

In May 1978, after the suit had been transferred, both Hartzell and Piper moved to dismiss the action on the ground of *forum non conveniens*.

---

4. Section 1404(a) provides: "For the convenience of parties and witnesses, in the interest of justice, a district court may transfer any civil action to any other district or division where it might have been brought."

5. The District Court concluded that it could not assert personal jurisdiction over Hartzell consistent with due process. However, it decided not to dismiss Hartzell because the corporation would be amenable to process in Pennsylvania.

The District Court granted these motions in October 1979. It relied on the balancing test set forth by this Court in *Gulf Oil Corp. v. Gilbert,* 330 U.S. 501 (1947), and its companion case, *Koster v. Lumbermen's, Mut. Cas. Co.,* 330 U.S. 518 (1947). In those decisions, the Court stated that a plaintiff's choice of forum should rarely be disturbed. However, when an alternative forum has jurisdiction to hear the case, and when trial in the chosen forum would "establish . . . oppressiveness and vexation to a defendant . . . out of all proportion to plaintiff's convenience," or when the "chosen forum [is] inappropriate because of considerations affecting the court's own administrative and legal problems," the court may, in the exercise of its sound discretion, dismiss the case. *Koster, supra,* at 524. To guide trial court discretion, the Court provided a list of "private interest factors" affecting the convenience of the litigants, and a list of "public interest factors" affecting the convenience of the forum. *Gilbert, supra,* 330 U.S. at 508-509.[6]

After describing our decisions in *Gilbert* and *Koster,* the District Court analyzed the facts of these cases. It began by observing that an alternative forum existed in Scotland; Piper and Hartzell had agreed to submit to the jurisdiction of the Scottish courts and to waive any statute of limitations defense that might be available. It then stated that plaintiff's choice of forum was entitled to little weight. The court recognized that a plaintiff's choice ordinarily deserves substantial deference. It noted, however, that Reyno "is a representative of foreign citizens and residents seeking a forum in the United States because of the more liberal rules concerning products liability law," and that "the courts have been less solicitous when the plaintiff is not an American citizen or resident, and particularly when the foreign citizens seek to benefit from the more liberal tort rules provided for the protection of citizens and residents of the United States."

The District Court next examined several factors relating to the private interests of the litigants, and determined that these factors strongly pointed towards Scotland as the appropriate forum. Although evidence concerning the design, manufacture, and testing of the plane and propeller is located in the United States, the connections with Scotland are otherwise "overwhelming." *Id.,* at 732. The real parties in interest are citizens of Scotland, as were all the decedents. Witnesses who could testify regarding the maintenance of the aircraft, the training of the pilot, and

---

6. The factors pertaining to the private interests of the litigants included the "relative ease of access to sources of proof; availability of compulsory process for attendance of unwilling, and the cost of obtaining attendance of willing, witnesses; possibility of view of premises, if view would be appropriate to the action; and all other practical problems that make trial of a case easy, expeditious and inexpensive." The public factors bearing on the question included the administrative difficulties flowing from court congestion; the "local interest in having localized controversies decided at home"; the interest in having the trial of a diversity case in a forum that is at home with the law that must govern the action; the avoidance of unnecessary problems in conflict of laws, or in the application of foreign law; and the unfairness of burdening citizens in an unrelated forum with jury duty.

the investigation of the accident—all essential to the defense—are in Great Britain. Moreover, all witnesses to damages are located in Scotland. Trial would be aided by familiarity with Scottish topography, and by easy access to the wreckage.

The District Court reasoned that because crucial witnesses and evidence were beyond the reach of compulsory process, and because the defendants would not be able to implead potential Scottish third-party defendants, it would be "unfair to make Piper and Hartzell proceed to trial in this forum." The survivors had brought separate actions in Scotland against the pilot, McDonald, and Air Navigation. "[I]t would be fairer to all parties and less costly if the entire case was presented to one jury with available testimony from all relevant witnesses." Although the court recognized that if trial were held in the United States, Piper and Hartzell could file indemnity or contribution actions against the Scottish defendants, it believed that there was a significant risk of inconsistent verdicts.[7]

The District Court concluded that the relevant public interests also pointed strongly towards dismissal. The court determined that Pennsylvania law would apply to Piper and Scottish law to Hartzell if the case were tried in the Middle District of Pennsylvania. As a result, "trial in this forum would be hopelessly complex and confusing for a jury." In addition, the court noted that it was unfamiliar with Scottish law and thus would have to rely upon experts from that country. The court also found that the trial would be enormously costly and time-consuming; that it would be unfair to burden citizens with jury duty when the Middle District of Pennsylvania has little connection with the controversy; and that Scotland has a substantial interest in the outcome of the litigation.

In opposing the motions to dismiss, respondent contended that dismissal would be unfair because Scottish law was less favorable. The District Court explicitly rejected this claim. It reasoned that the possibility that dismissal might lead to an unfavorable change in the law did not deserve significant weight; any deficiency in the foreign law was a "matter to be dealt with in the foreign forum."

C

On appeal, the United States Court of Appeals for the Third Circuit reversed and remanded for trial. The decision to reverse appears to be based on two alternative grounds. First, the Court held that the District Court abused its discretion in conducting the *Gilbert* analysis. Second, the Court held that dismissal is never appropriate where the law of the alternative forum is less favorable to the plaintiff. . . .

---

7. The District Court explained that inconsistent verdicts might result if petitioners were held liable on the basis of strict liability here, and then required to prove negligence in an indemnity action in Scotland. Moreover, even if the same standard of liability applied, there was a danger that different juries would find different facts and produce inconsistent results.

We granted certiorari in these cases to consider the questions they raise concerning the proper application of the doctrine of *forum non conveniens*.

II

The Court of Appeals erred in holding that plaintiffs may defeat a motion to dismiss on the ground of *forum non conveniens* merely by showing that the substantive law that would be applied in the alternative forum is less favorable to the plaintiffs than that of the present forum. The possibility of a change in substantive law should ordinarily not be given conclusive or even substantial weight in the *forum non conveniens* inquiry. . . .

[B]y holding that the central focus of the *forum non conveniens* inquiry is convenience, *Gilbert* implicitly recognized that dismissal may not be barred solely because of the possibility of an unfavorable change in law. Under *Gilbert*, dismissal will ordinarily be appropriate where trial in the plaintiff's chosen forum imposes a heavy burden on the defendant or the court, and where the plaintiff is unable to offer any specific reasons of convenience supporting his choice.[15] If substantial weight were given to the possibility of an unfavorable change in law, however, dismissal might be barred even where trial in the chosen forum was plainly inconvenient.

The Court of Appeals' decision is inconsistent with this Court's earlier *forum non conveniens* decisions in another respect. Those decisions have repeatedly emphasized the need to retain flexibility. In *Gilbert*, the Court refused to identify specific circumstances "which will justify or require either grant or denial of remedy." Similarly, in *Koster*, the Court rejected the contention that where a trial would involve inquiry into the internal affairs of a foreign corporation, dismissal was always appropriate. "That is one, but only one, factor which may show convenience." And in *Williams v. Green Bay & Western R. Co.*, 326 U.S. 549 (1946), we stated that we would not lay down a rigid rule to govern discretion, and that "[e]ach case turns on its facts." If central emphasis were placed on any one factor, the *forum non conveniens* doctrine would lose much of the very flexibility that makes it so valuable.

In fact, if conclusive or substantial weight were given to the possibility of a change in law, the *forum non conveniens* doctrine would become virtually useless. Jurisdiction and venue requirements are often easily satisfied. As a result, many plaintiffs are able to choose from among several forums. Ordinarily, these plaintiffs will select that forum whose choice-of-law rules are most advantageous. Thus, if the possibility of an

---

15. In other words, *Gilbert* held that dismissal may be warranted where a plaintiff chooses a particular forum, not because it is convenient, but solely in order to harass the defendant or take advantage of favorable law. This is precisely the situation in which the Court of Appeals' rule would bar dismissal.

unfavorable change in substantive law is given substantial weight in the *forum non conveniens* inquiry, dismissal would rarely be proper. . . .

The Court of Appeals' approach is not only inconsistent with the purpose of the *forum non conveniens* doctrine, but also poses substantial practical problems. If the possibility of a change in law were given substantial weight, deciding motions to dismiss on the ground of *forum non conveniens* would become quite difficult. Choice-of-law analysis would become extremely important, and the courts would frequently be required to interpret the law of foreign jurisdictions. First, the trial court would have to determine what law would apply if the case were tried in the chosen forum, and what law would apply if the case were tried in the alternative forum. It would then have to compare the rights, remedies, and procedures available under the law that would be applied in each forum. Dismissal would be appropriate only if the court concluded that the law applied by the alternative forum is as favorable to the plaintiff as that of the chosen forum. The doctrine of *forum non conveniens*, however, is designed in part to help courts avoid conducting complex exercises in comparative law. As we stated in *Gilbert*, the public interest factors point towards dismissal where the court would be required to "untangle problems in conflict of laws, and in law foreign to itself."

Upholding the decision of the Court of Appeals would result in other practical problems. At least where the foreign plaintiff named an American manufacturer as defendant, a court could not dismiss the case on grounds of *forum non conveniens* where dismissal might lead to an unfavorable change in law. The American courts, which are already extremely attractive to foreign plaintiffs, would become even more attractive. The flow of litigation into the United States would increase and further congest already crowded courts.

The Court of Appeals based its decision, at least in part, on an analogy between dismissals on grounds of *forum non conveniens* and transfers between federal courts pursuant to §1404(a). In *Van Dusen v. Barrack*, 376 U.S. 612 (1964), this Court ruled that a §1404(a) transfer should not result in a change in the applicable law. Relying on dictum in an earlier Third Circuit opinion interpreting *Van Dusen*, the court below held that that principle is also applicable to a dismissal on *forum non conveniens* grounds. However §1404(a) transfers are different than dismissals on the ground of *forum non conveniens*.

Congress enacted §1404(a) to permit change of venue between federal courts. Although the statute was drafted in accordance with the doctrine of *forum non conveniens*, it was intended to be a revision rather than a codification of the common law. District courts were given more discretion to transfer under §1404(a) than they had to dismiss on grounds of *forum non conveniens*.

The reasoning employed in *Van Dusen v. Barrack* is simply inapplicable to dismissals on grounds of *forum non conveniens*. That case did not discuss the common-law doctrine. Rather, it focused on "the construction and application" of §1404(a). Emphasizing the remedial purpose of the statute, Barrack concluded that Congress could not have intended a transfer to be accompanied by a change in law. The statute was designed as a "federal housekeeping measure," allowing easy change of venue within a unified federal system. The Court feared that if a change in venue were accompanied by a change in law, forum-shopping parties would take unfair advantage of the relaxed standards for transfer. The rule was necessary to ensure the just and efficient operation of the statute.

We do not hold that the possibility of an unfavorable change in law should never be a relevant consideration in a *forum non conveniens* inquiry. Of course, if the remedy provided by the alternative forum is so clearly inadequate or unsatisfactory that it is no remedy at all, the unfavorable change in law may be given substantial weight; the district court may conclude that dismissal would not be in the interests of justice. In these cases, however, the remedies that would be provided by the Scottish courts do not fall within this category. Although the relatives of the decedents may not be able to rely on a strict liability theory, and although their potential damages award may be smaller, there is no danger that they will be deprived of any remedy or treated unfairly.

III

The Court of Appeals also erred in rejecting the District Court's *Gilbert* analysis. The Court of Appeals stated that more weight should have been given to the plaintiff's choice of forum, and criticized the District Court's analysis of the private and public interests. However, the District Court's decision regarding the deference due plaintiff's choice of forum was appropriate. Furthermore, we do not believe that the District Court abused its discretion in weighing the private and public interests.

A

The District Court acknowledged that there is ordinarily a strong presumption in favor of the plaintiff's choice of forum, which may be overcome only when the private and public interest factors clearly point towards trial in the alternative forum. It held, however, that the presumption applies with less force when the plaintiff or real parties in interest are foreign.

The District Court's distinction between resident or citizen plaintiffs and foreign plaintiffs is fully justified. In *Koster*, the Court indicated that a plaintiff's choice of forum is entitled to greater deference when the plaintiff has chosen the home forum. When the home forum has been chosen, it is reasonable to assume that this choice is convenient. When the plaintiff is foreign, however, this assumption is much less reasonable. Because the central purpose of any *forum non conveniens* inquiry is to ensure that the trial is convenient, a foreign plaintiff's choice deserves less deference.

B

The *forum non conveniens* determination is committed to the sound discretion of the trial court. It may be reversed only when there has been a clear abuse of discretion; where the court has considered all relevant public and private interest factors, and where its balancing of these factors is reasonable, its decision deserves substantial deference. . . . In examining the District Court's analysis of the public and private interests, however, the Court of Appeals seems to have lost sight of this rule, and substituted its own judgment for that of the District Court.

(1)

In analyzing the private interest factors, the District Court stated that the connections with Scotland are "overwhelming." This characterization may be somewhat exaggerated. Particularly with respect to the question of relative ease of access to sources of proof, the private interests point in both directions. As respondent emphasizes, records concerning the design, manufacture, and testing of the propeller and plane are located in the United States. She would have greater access to sources of proof relevant to her strict liability and negligence theories if trial were held here. However, the District Court did not act unreasonably in concluding that fewer evidentiary problems would be posed if the trial were held in Scotland. A large proportion of the relevant evidence is located in Great Britain. . . .

The District Court correctly concluded that the problems posed by the inability to implead potential third-party defendants clearly supported holding the trial in Scotland. Joinder of the pilot's estate, Air Navigation, and McDonald is crucial to the presentation of petitioners' defense. If Piper and Hartzell can show that the accident was caused not by a design defect, but rather by the negligence of the pilot, the plane's owners, or the charter company, they will be relieved of all liability. It is true, of course, that if Hartzell and Piper were found liable after a trial in the United States, they could institute an action for indemnity or contribution against these parties in Scotland. It would be far more convenient, however, to resolve all claims in one trial. The Court of Appeals rejected this argument. Forcing petitioners to rely on actions for indemnity or contributions would be "burdensome" but not "unfair." Finding that trial in the plaintiff's chosen forum would be burdensome, however, is sufficient to support dismissal on grounds of *forum non conveniens.*

(2)

The District Court's review of the factors relating to the public interest was also reasonable. On the basis of its choice-of-law analysis, it concluded that if the case were tried in the Middle District of Pennsylvania,

Pennsylvania law would apply to Piper and Scottish law to Hartzell. It stated that a trial involving two sets of laws would be confusing to the jury. It also noted its own lack of familiarity with Scottish law. Consideration of these problems was clearly appropriate under *Gilbert*; in that case we explicitly held that the need to apply foreign law pointed towards dismissal. [Moreover] all other public interest factors favored trial in Scotland.

Scotland has a very strong interest in this litigation. The accident occurred in its airspace. All of the decedents were Scottish. Apart from Piper and Hartzell, all potential plaintiffs and defendants are either Scottish or English. As we stated in *Gilbert,* there is "a local interest in having localized controversies decided at home." Respondent argues that American citizens have an interest in ensuring that American manufacturers are deterred from producing defective products, and that additional deterrence might be obtained if Piper and Hartzell were tried in the United States, where they could be sued on the basis of both negligence and strict liability. However, the incremental deterrence that would be gained if this trial were held in an American court is likely to be insignificant. The American interest in this accident is simply not sufficient to justify the enormous commitment of judicial time and resources that would inevitably be required if the case were to be tried here.

IV

The Court of Appeals erred in holding that the possibility of an unfavorable change in law bars dismissal on the ground of *forum non conveniens*. It also erred in rejecting the District Court's *Gilbert* analysis. The District Court properly decided that the presumption in favor of the respondent's forum choice applied with less than maximum force because the real parties in interest are foreign. It did not act unreasonably in deciding that the private interests pointed towards trial in Scotland. Nor did it act unreasonably in deciding that the public interests favored trial in Scotland. Thus, the judgment of the Court of Appeals is Reversed.

[The opinion of Justice WHITE, concurring in part and dissenting in part, has been omitted. The dissenting opinion of Justice STEVENS, joined by Justice BRENNAN, likewise has been omitted.]

Comments and Questions

1. Be prepared to explain the strategies and procedural moves of defendants Piper and Hartzell. How did the case get from the state court in California (where it was filed) to the federal district court in Pennsylvania?

2. Can you explain the differences between a change of venue under §1404, a transfer under §1406, and a dismissal for *forum non conveniens*? *LAST CHANCE*

3. Given the vitality of transient presence as a valid basis for personal jurisdiction, *forum non conveniens* gives courts one last fail-safe mechanism for avoiding litigation in a forum obviously inconvenient to the defendant and/or far removed from the witnesses and the evidence. In *MacLeod v. MacLeod*, 383 A.2d 39 (1978), for example, the plaintiff, a Virginia resident, sued her former husband for breach of a French divorce decree entered while she was living in France (the couple having married in New York City). The basis for jurisdiction in Maine (and indeed the only connection at all to that state) was service of process upon the former husband (an employee of the CIA who lived abroad and moved frequently) while he was in the state to attend his parents' golden wedding anniversary. The Supreme Judicial Court of Maine affirmed dismissal of the action: "The present action concerns a nonresident plaintiff suing a nonresident defendant upon transitory causes of action which did not arise in the State of Maine. Given those facts, the trial court could rightly consider exercising its discretionary power, notwithstanding the existence of both subject matter and personal jurisdiction, to decline jurisdiction over the action." *Id.* at 41. The court noted, however, that a plaintiff's choice of forum should generally control, and that in any event there can be no dismissal under *forum non conveniens* without an assurance that there is an alternative forum. The order below was thus modified to condition dismissal on the defendant's acceptance of service in Virginia, where the plaintiff was a resident and the defendant still held a driver's license.

4. After a chemical company was sued in New York by victims of the devastating gas plant disaster in Bhopal, India, the Second Circuit Court of Appeals affirmed dismissal for *forum non conveniens*, conditioned upon defendant's agreement to submit to jurisdiction in India and to waive the statute of limitations defense. *See In Re Union Carbide Corporation Gas Plant Disaster*, 809 F.2d 195 (2nd Cir. 1984):

> The vast majority of material witnesses and documentary proof bearing on causation of and liability for the accident is located in India, not the United States, and would be more accessible to an Indian court than to a United States court. The records are almost entirely in Hindi or other Indian languages, understandable to an Indian court without translation. The witnesses for the most part do not speak English but Indian languages understood by an Indian court but not by an American court. These witnesses could be required to appear in an Indian court but not in a court of the United States. Although witnesses in the United States could not be subpoenaed to appear in India, they are comparatively few in number and most are employed by UCC which, as a party, would produce them in India, with lower overall transportation costs than if the parties were to attempt to bring hundreds of Indian witnesses to the United States. Lastly, Judge Keenan

properly concluded that an Indian court would be in a better position to direct and supervise a viewing of the Bhopal plant, which was sealed after the accident. Such a viewing could be of help to a court in determining liability issues.

809 F.2d at 201.

5. Some states have a legislative formulation of *forum non conveniens* written into their long-arm statute. *See, e.g.,* Mass. Gen. Laws c. 223A, §5: "When the court finds that in the interest of substantial justice the action should be heard in another forum, the court may stay or dismiss the action in whole or in part on any conditions that may be just." *See, e.g., Green v. Manhattanville College,* 40 Mass. App. 76, 661 N.E.2d 123 (1996) (dismissing negligence action against New York college alleging that plaintiff was beaten by fellow students while attending college, conditioned on defendant waiving time bar defense in similar case filed in New York).

6. The presence of a forum selection clause is an important (though not conclusive) factor to be weighed when a court rules on a motion for transfer of venue under §§1404 or 1406. *Stewart Organization, Inc. v. Ricoh Corp.,* 487 U.S. 22 (1988). *See, e.g., Detroit Coke Corp. v. NKK Chemical USA, Inc.,* 794 F. Supp. 214 (E.D. Mich. 1992) (granting defendants' motion to transfer venue to Western District of Pennsylvania pursuant to forum selection clause in purchase agreement); *Flake v. Medline Industries, Inc.,* 882 F. Supp. 947 (E.D. Cal. 1995) (age discrimination case transferred to Northern District of Illinois pursuant to clause in employment contract). Does the routine enforcement of these clauses bring us back to the *Pennoyer* days, in that the plaintiff's choice of the forum is trumped?

7. Generally, how would you characterize the evolution of jurisdiction from *Pennoyer* to the present? Are you encouraged, at least in this area, that our judicial system learns from its mistakes and builds on its successes? Why or why not?

8

■

The Choice of an Appropriate Court: Subject Matter Jurisdiction and Removal

A. INTRODUCTION TO SUBJECT MATTER JURISDICTION

As noted in the introduction to the previous chapter, subject matter jurisdiction is one of the three constitutional requirements for a valid and enforceable judgment, the other two being personal jurisdiction and notice. The issue of subject matter jurisdiction, or the authority of the court to hear a particular type of case, focuses our attention on the choice between federal and state court. A plaintiff may file in a federal court if and only if the case falls within the limited parameters of federal subject matter authority—mainly cases between diverse citizens and cases in which the claim arises from federal law. Otherwise, there is no federal court option. As we will see, a defendant can also exercise the option when a case filed in state court falls within federal subject matter jurisdiction—such a case may usually be "removed" to federal court by the defendant. *See* 28 U.S.C. §1441.

We emphasize that the federal and state courts largely share authority— or, as it is often described, have concurrent jurisdiction. In other words, diversity and federal question cases generally may be heard in *either* federal or state court. (In certain cases, such as patent, copyright, and bankruptcy, the federal courts have exclusive jurisdiction.) However, non-diverse, non-federal questions cases can only be heard in state court. As represented in the diagram below, state courts generally can hear cases falling within both the larger and smaller circles, while federal courts are limited to those that fall within the smaller circle.

Concurrent Subject Matter Jurisdiction

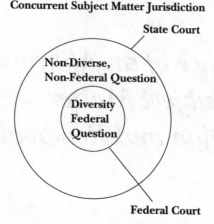

As with personal jurisdiction, the limitations on federal subject matter authority are both constitutional and statutory. Article III, Section 2 sets the constitutional parameters of federal judicial power, extending it (most importantly for our purposes) to cases "arising under this Constitution, the Laws of the United States, and Treaties made," as well as the cases "between citizens of different States." It was left to Congress to establish the lower federal courts and effectuate the grant of judicial power, which it has done in 28 U.S.C. §§1331 and 1332. Note that the former statutory provision empowering the federal courts to hear "all civil actions arising under the Constitution, laws, or treaties of the United States" appears to implement the full extent of constitutional authority over "federal question" cases.* Does the latter provision do the same for "diversity" cases? What about the amount in controversy requirement? Why do you think Congress added this further limitation on federal jurisdiction?

In practice, the choice of federal or state court is usually dictated by strategic and pragmatic concerns. A plaintiff in a civil rights action may prefer a federal to a state judge, the former usually being more experienced in such matters. *See* Burt Neuborne, *The Myth of Parity*, 90 Harv. L. Rev. 1105 (1977). Similarly, wider availability of discovery may attract a plaintiff's counsel in a products liability case to federal rather than state court. Nonetheless, the argument between the lawyers about access to the federal forum will (as usual) concentrate on legal doctrine.

---

*It is interesting to note that Congress did not grant the lower federal courts jurisdiction over federal question cases until 1875. "In the early days of our republic, Congress was content to leave the task of interpreting and applying federal laws in the first instance to the state courts." *See Merrell Dow Pharmaceuticals, Inc. v. Thompson*, 478 U.S. 804, 826 (1986) (Brennan, J., dissenting).

While many commentators have viewed the parallel state and federal court systems as dysfunctional redundancy, Professor Robert Cover discerned distinct advantages for both litigants and the judicial system. *See* Robert Cover, *The Uses of Jurisdictional Redundancy: Interest, Ideology and Innovation,* 22 Wm. & Mary L. Rev. 639 (1981).

B. FEDERAL QUESTION JURISDICTION

■ LOUISVILLE & NASHVILLE RAILROAD COMPANY v. MOTTLEY
211 U.S. 149 (1908)

Statement by Justice MOODY:

The appellees (husband and wife), being residents and citizens of Kentucky, brought this suit in equity in the circuit court of the United States for the western district of Kentucky against the appellant, a railroad company and a citizen of the same state. The object of the suit was to compel the specific performance of the following contract: Louisville, Ky., Oct. 2d, 1871. The Louisville & Nashville Railroad Company, in consideration that E. L. Mottley and wife, Annie E. Mottley, have this day released company from all damages or claims for damages for injuries received by them on the 7th of September, 1871, in consequence of a collision of trains on the railroad of said company at Randolph's Station, Jefferson County, Kentucky, hereby agrees to issue free passes on said railroad and branches now existing or to exist, to said E. L. & Annie E. Mottley for the remainder of the present year, and thereafter to renew said passes annually during the lives of said Mottley and wife or either of them.

The bill alleged that in September, 1871, plaintiffs, while passengers upon the defendant railroad, were injured by the defendant's negligence, and released their respective claims for damages in consideration of the agreement for transportation during their lives, expressed in the contract. It is alleged that the contract was performed by the defendant up to January 1, 1907, when the defendant declined to renew the passes. The bill then alleges that the refusal to comply with the contract was based solely upon that part of the act of Congress of June 29, 1906 which forbids the giving of free passes or free transportation. The bill further alleges: First, that the act of Congress referred to does not prohibit the giving of passes under the circumstances of this case; and, second, that, if the law is to be construed as prohibiting such passes, it is in conflict with the 5th Amendment of the Constitution, because it deprives the plaintiffs of their property without due process of law. The defendant demurred to the bill. The judge of the circuit court overruled the demurrer, entered a decree for the relief prayed for, and the defendant appealed directly to this court.

Justice MOODY, after making the foregoing statement, delivered the opinion of the court:

Two questions of law were raised by the demurrer to the bill, were brought here by appeal, and have been argued before us. They are, first, whether that part of the act of Congress of June 29, 1906 which forbids the giving of free passes or the collection of any different compensation for transportation of passengers than that specified in the tariff filed, makes it unlawful to perform a contract for transportation of persons who, in good faith, before the passage of the act, had accepted such contract in satisfaction of a valid cause of action against the railroad; and, second, whether the statute, if it should be construed to render such a contract unlawful, is in violation of the 5th Amendment of the Constitution of the United States. We do not deem it necessary, however, to consider either of these questions, because, in our opinion, the court below was without jurisdiction of the cause. Neither party has questioned that jurisdiction, but it is the duty of this court to see to it that the jurisdiction of the circuit court, which is defined and limited by statute, is not exceeded. This duty we have frequently performed of our own motion.

There was no diversity of citizenship, and it is not and cannot be suggested that there was any ground of jurisdiction, except that the case was a "suit . . . arising under the Constitution or laws of the United States." It is the settled interpretation of these words, as used in this statute, conferring jurisdiction, that a suit arises under the Constitution and laws of the United States only when the plaintiff's statement of his own cause of action shows that it is based upon those laws or that Constitution. It is not enough that the plaintiff alleges some anticipated defense to his cause of action, and asserts that the defense is invalidated by some provision of the Constitution of the United States. Although such allegations show that very likely, in the course of the litigation, a question under the Constitution would arise, they do not show that the suit, that is, the plaintiff's original cause of action, arises under the Constitution. In *Tennessee v. Union & Planters' Bank*, 152 U.S. 454, the plaintiff, the state of Tennessee, brought suit in the circuit court of the United States to recover from the defendant certain taxes alleged to be due under the laws of the state. The plaintiff alleged that the defendant claimed an immunity from the taxation by virtue of its charter, and that therefore the tax was void, because in violation of the provision of the Constitution of the United States, which forbids any state from passing a law impairing the obligation of contracts. The cause was held to be beyond the jurisdiction of the circuit court, the court saying, by Mr. Justice Gray (p. 464): "A suggestion of one party, that the other will or may set up a claim under the Constitution or laws of the United States, does not make the suit one arising under that Constitution or those laws." Again, in *Boston & M. Consol. Copper & S. Min. Co. v. Montana Ore Purchasing Co.*, 188 U.S. 632, the plaintiff brought suit in the circuit court of the United States for the conversion of copper ore and for an injunction against its continuance. The plaintiff then alleged, for the purpose of showing jurisdiction, in substance, that the defendant would set up in defense certain laws of the United States. The cause was held to be beyond the jurisdiction of the circuit court, the court saying, by Mr. Justice Peckham (pp. 638, 639):

> It would be wholly unnecessary and improper, in order to prove complainant's cause of action, to go into any matters of defense which the defendants might possibly set up, and then attempt to reply to such defense, and thus, if possible, to show that a Federal question might or probably would arise in the course of the trial of the case. To allege such defense and then make an answer to it before the defendant has the opportunity to itself plead or prove its own defense is inconsistent with any known rule of pleading, so far as we are aware, and is improper.
>
> The rule is a reasonable and just one that the complainant in the first instance shall be confined to a statement of its cause of action, leaving to the defendant to set up in his answer what his defense is, and, if anything more than a denial of complainant's cause of action, imposing upon the defendant the burden of proving such defense.
>
> Conforming itself to that rule, the complainant would not, in the assertion or proof of its cause of action, bring up a single Federal question. The presentation of its cause of action would not show that it was one arising under the Constitution or laws of the United States.
>
> The only way in which it might be claimed that a Federal question was presented would be in the complainant's statement of what the defense of defendants would be, and complainant's answer to such defense. Under these circumstances the case is brought within the rule laid down in *Tennessee v. Union & Planters' Bank, supra.* That case has been cited and approved many times since.

The interpretation of the act which we have stated was first announced in *Metcalf v. Watertown,* 128 U.S. 286, and has since been repeated and applied in [cases]. The application of this rule to the case at bar is decisive against the jurisdiction of the circuit court.

It is ordered that the judgment be reversed and the case remitted to the circuit court with instructions to dismiss the suit for want of jurisdiction.

Comments and Questions

1. At the outset of *Mottley,* the Court notes that although neither party questioned subject matter jurisdiction, the lower court had the duty to raise the issue on its own. Would this be true if the issue had been one of personal jurisdiction? Explain. Look back at Fed. R. Civ. P. 12(h), and compare subdivisions (1) and (3). Why the different treatment?

2. Can you articulate the Court's definition of when a lawsuit "arises under" the Constitution or laws of the United States? Why is the *Mottley* case described as establishing a "well-pleaded complaint" rule?

3. Is the *Mottley* result dictated by the language of Art. III, Sec. 2, or the language of 28 U.S.C. §1331? Explain. If neither, why would the Court adopt a more restrictive view of federal question jurisdiction than either the Constitution or statutory provisions appear to require? Put another way, in a case like *Mottley*, where issues of federal law are likely to dominate the proceedings, why deny access to a federal forum simply because the source of the federal law is something other than the plaintiff's "well-pleaded" complaint?

4. Professor Charles Alan Wright has observed:

> Because of [the *Mottley*] rule, it does not suffice for jurisdiction that the answer raises a federal question. If the basis for original federal-question jurisdiction is that the federal courts have a special expertness in applying federal law, and that assertions of federal law will be received more hospitably in a federal court, it would seem that the courts should have jurisdiction where there is some federal issue regardless of which pleading raises it. The rule to the contrary probably stems from the conceptual notion that unless the initial pleading is sufficient to invoke the jurisdiction of the court, the court lacks power to require responsive pleadings or take any other act in the case.

Charles Alan Wright, *Law of Federal Courts* 109 (5th ed. 1994).

5. Despite acknowledging that the well-pleaded complaint rule "may produce awkward results," the Court has concluded that it generally "makes sense as a quick rule of thumb," and continues to apply it. *See Franchise Tax Board v. Construction Laborers Vacation Trust*, 463 U.S. 1, 11 (1983); *Merrell Dow Pharmaceuticals Inc. v. Thompson*, 478 U.S. 804 (1986). The rule also controls in the context of removal jurisdiction (discussed *infra*), since a defendant may remove a case only if it could originally have been brought in federal court. *See Oklahoma Tax Commission v. Graham*, 489 U.S. 838 (1989) (possible existence of tribal sovereign immunity defense did not convert state tax claims into federal questions).

6. How would you redraft §1331 to overturn *Mottley* and expand federal judicial power to its constitutional limits?

7. What would have happened if the litigation roles of the Mottleys and the Railroad had been reversed? Assume that the Railroad had seized the initiative and brought a declaratory judgment action (28 U.S.C. §§2201 and 2202) in federal court, claiming that the Act of Congress of June 29, 1906, invalidated the Mottleys' free pass and further seeking a determination that this was not in conflict with the Due Process Clause of the Fifth Amendment. Wouldn't that complaint arise under the Constitution and laws of the United States? Is the "well-pleaded complaint" rule so easily circumvented?

The courts have been mindful of the danger of permitting a party with a defense arising under federal law to anticipate the coming lawsuit and thus obtain a federal forum. *See, e.g., Franchise Tax Board v. Construction*

Laborers Vacation Trust, 463 U.S. 1 (1983); *Skelly Oil. Co. v. Phillips Petroleum Co.,* 339 U.S. 667 (1950). "To sanction suits for declaratory relief as within the jurisdiction of the District Courts merely because, as in this case, artful pleading anticipates a defense based on federal law would contravene the whole trend of jurisdictional legislation by Congress, disregard the effective functioning of the federal judicial system and distort the limited procedural purpose of the Declaratory Judgment Act." 339 U.S. at 673-674.

8. Counterclaims arising under federal law have not fared any better than defenses under the *Mottley* rule. Federal jurisdiction cannot be created by a defendant's pleading a counter-claim arising under federal law. *See Rath Packing Co. v. Becker,* 530 F.2d 1295, 1303 (9th Cir. 1975), *affirmed on other grounds sub nom. Jones v. Rath Packing Co.,* 430 U.S. 519 (1977).

9. A recurrent problem under §1331 is whether there is jurisdiction over claims that arise from a mixture of federal and state law. In *Merrell Dow Pharmaceuticals Inc. v. Thompson,* 478 U.S. 804 (1986), for example, the plaintiffs sought damages for birth deformities allegedly caused by the drug bendectin. The complaint asserted state law claims of negligence and product liability; it also alleged violations of the Federal Food, Drug and Cosmetic Act, which, although not giving rise to an independent private right of action, nonetheless constituted negligence *per se.* Merrell Dow removed the case from state to federal court, arguing that it was founded in part on a claim arising under federal law. The Supreme Court ultimately ruled that removal was improper because "a complaint alleging a violation of a federal statute as an element of a state cause of action, when Congress has determined that there should be no private, federal cause of action for the violation, does not state a claim 'arising under the Constitution, laws or treaties of the United States.'"

10. Attempting to summarize the scope of federal question jurisdiction, Justice Stevens wrote in *Merrell Dow:*

> There is no single, precise definition of that concept; rather, the phrase "arising under" masks a welter of issues regarding the interrelation of federal and state authority and the proper management of the federal judicial system. This much, however, is clear. The vast majority of cases that come within this grant of jurisdiction are covered by Justice Holmes' statement that a "suit arises under the law that creates the cause of action." Thus, the vast majority of cases brought under the general federal-question jurisdiction of the federal courts are those in which federal law creates the cause of action.

Merrell Dow Pharmaceuticals, Inc. v. Thompson, 478 U.S. 804, 808 (1986).

11. 28 U.S.C. §1343(a)(3) grants jurisdiction over federal civil rights actions alleging the deprivation of rights secured by the Constitution or laws of the United States. Why was this grant of special federal question jurisdiction thought necessary, given that it overlaps with §1331? (Hint: Until 1980, §1331 required that there be $10,000 in controversy.)

C. DIVERSITY JURISDICTION

While it is understandable that the Framers would grant the federal courts authority to hear cases arising under federal law, it is harder to explain the provision of diversity jurisdiction (which, after all, places state law claims in federal court). No doubt, a major impetus was the concern (at a time when persons identified more with their locality rather than with the new national entity) that the state courts might not be level playing fields in cases pitting nonresident litigants against forum residents. This does not, however, explain the availability under Article III and 28 U.S.C. §1332 (originally enacted in 1789) of the federal forum to the resident plaintiff suing a nonresident defendant.* Nor does the fear of local prejudice carry much weight in the modern era.

The questionable basis for the diversity grant may partly explain legislative and judicial efforts to contain it, as well as recent attempts in Congress to abolish it. Congress has always imposed an amount in controversy requirement, originally $500 and currently $75,000. An early Supreme Court opinion, *Strawbridge v. Curtiss*, 7 U.S. (3 Cranch) 267 (1806), imposed another significant limitation by requiring "complete diversity"—that is, every plaintiff must be a citizen of a different state from every defendant. Shared citizenship between any two parties across the "v." defeats jurisdiction. Significantly, *Strawbridge v. Curtiss* has been read as an interpretation of §1332, and not Article III, meaning that Congress is free to modify the complete diversity requirement. *See State Farm Fire & Casualty Co. v. Tashire*, 386 U.S. 523 (1967) (upholding the federal interpleader statute, 28 U.S.C. §1335, which provides a federal forum based on minimal diversity, that is, mere diversity between any two rival claimants without regard to the citizenship of other litigants).

1. Citizenship

The citizenship of a natural person is determined for diversity purposes by the concept of *domicile*. Domicile is defined as the person's "true, fixed, and permanent home and principal establishment, and to which he has the intention of returning whenever he is absent therefrom. . . ." *Mas v. Perry*, 489 F.2d 1396, 1399 (5th Cir. 1974). Thus, current residence itself is not sufficient; there must be an intention to remain indefinitely. Domicile is changed only by (1) taking up residence in another state, with (2) the intention to remain there. A recurrent issue is whether minors retain their parents' domicile when they attend school in a different state. *Compare Dunlap v. Wells*, 741 F.2d 165 (8th Cir. 1984) (eight-year-old

---

*As we shall see below, however, a defendant may remove an action from state to federal court only if "none of the defendants is a citizen of the State in which such action is brought." 28 U.S.C. §1441(b).

retarded boy did not become citizen of Texas, even though his Arkansas parents placed him in a special care home in that state and a local guardian was appointed for him), and *Gordon v. Steele*, 376 F. Supp. 575 (W.D. Pa. 1974) (emancipated college student living in an apartment at school became citizen of Idaho, even though she retained her Pennsylvania driver's license and returned there for vacations).

How does §1332 treat an American citizen domiciled in a foreign country? In a contract dispute arising from the film *Cleopatra*, the motion picture studio sought to recover an alleged $25,000,000 in damages from Richard Burton, a British subject, and Elizabeth Taylor, an American citizen living abroad. *See Twentieth Century-Fox Film Corporation v. Taylor and Burton*, 239 F. Supp. 913 (S.D.N.Y. 1965). On the question of the removability of the action from state to federal court based on diversity of citizenship among the parties, Judge Weinfeld assumed there was no diversity between Taylor and Twentieth Century-Fox, a Delaware corporation, because Taylor was not a citizen of any state, as envisioned by §1332. Burton was treated as diverse from plaintiff, being a "subject of a foreign state." *See* 28 U.S.C. §1332(a)(2).

For diversity purposes, a corporation is a citizen of its state of incorporation and the state where it has its principal place of business. *See* 28 U.S.C. §1332(c). Unlike a natural person, a corporation may thus be a citizen of more than one state if it is incorporated in a state different from the state in which its headquarters is located. For the various tests used to determine a corporation's "principal place of business" (primarily the "nerve center test" and the "place of operations test"), *see Industrial Tectonics, Inc. v. Aero Alloy*, 912 F.2d 1090 (9th Cir. 1990).

Finally, diversity of citizenship must exist at the time the complaint is filed, and jurisdiction is unaffected by subsequent changes in the citizenship of the parties. *Mas v. Perry, supra*, 489 F.2d at 1399.

2. Amount in Controversy

The amount in controversy is determined by the amount claimed by the plaintiff in good faith, and the standard for dismissal of an action for lack of the jurisdictional minimum is high: "It must appear to a legal certainty that the claim is really for less than the jurisdictional amount to justify dismissal." *St. Paul Mercury Indemnity Co. v. Red Cab Co.*, 303 U.S. 283 (1938). *See, e.g., Sellers v. O'Connell*, 701 F.2d 575 (6th Cir. 1983)(complaint dismissed where plaintiff was only entitled to recover $9,875 in pension benefits). Federal jurisdiction is not lost because a judgment is ultimately entered for less than the jurisdictional minimum. *See Mas v. Perry, supra*, 489 F.2d at 1400. Consider the implications of a rule that would require dismissal for lack of jurisdiction whenever a judgment was rendered after trial for less than the statutory minimum.

Federal judges are not, however, without power to otherwise penalize a plaintiff who recovers less than the requisite minimum. Look at §1332(b).

Like the "well-pleaded complaint" rule for federal question jurisdiction, the aim here is to determine jurisdiction early in the litigation. And once jurisdiction "attaches," subsequent events do not deprive the court of power. Do you see how the interests of efficiency and certainty dictate this approach? What would happen to the system if the question of subject matter jurisdiction were contingent on the resolution of the merits of the case?

For purposes of the amount in controversy, a plaintiff may aggregate all of his or her claims (related or not, see Fed. R. Civ. P. 18) brought against a defendant in the complaint. Plaintiffs joining together under Fed. R. Civ. P. 20 or pursuing a class action under Fed. R. Civ. P. 23 may not, however, aggregate their claims against a defendant to reach the jurisdictional minimum. See Snyder v. Harris, 394 U.S. 332 (1969); Zahn v. International Paper Co., 414 U.S. 291 (1973). There is a split of authority in the lower courts as to whether 28 U.S.C. §1367, discussed below, changes the rule against aggregation among plaintiffs. See Richard D. Freer, Toward a Principled Statutory Approach to Supplemental Jurisdiction in Diversity of Citizenship Cases, 74 Ind. L. J. 5, 18–21 (1999).

D. SUPPLEMENTAL JURISDICTION

Although the federal courts possess only limited subject matter jurisdiction, a small margin of supplemental jurisdiction has been recognized to encompass claims that do not fall within the federal question or diversity categories but that are intimately connected to claims already being entertained by the court. As you read the next cases, consider the reasons underlying this "stretch" jurisdiction.

■ UNITED MINE WORKERS OF AMERICA v. GIBBS
383 U.S. 715 (1966)

Justice BRENNAN delivered the opinion of the Court:

Respondent Paul Gibbs was awarded compensatory and punitive damages in this action against petitioner United Mine Workers of America (UMW) for alleged violations of §303 of the Labor Management Relations Act, 1947, 61 Stat. 158, as amended, and of the common law of Tennessee. The case grew out of the rivalry between the United Mine Workers and the Southern Labor Union over representation of workers in the southern Appalachian coal fields. Tennessee Consolidated Coal Company, not a party here, laid off 100 miners of the UMW's Local 5881 when it closed one of its mines in southern Tennessee during the spring of 1960. Late that summer, Grundy Company, a wholly-owned subsidiary of Consolidated, hired respondent as mine superintendent to attempt to open a new mine on Consolidated's property at nearby Gray's Creek through use of members of the Southern Labor Union. As part of the arrangement, Grundy also gave respondent a contract to haul the mine's coal to the nearest railroad loading point.

On August 15 and 16, 1960, armed members of Local 5881 forcibly prevented the opening of the mine, threatening respondent and beating an organizer for the rival union. The members of the local believed Consolidated had promised them the jobs at the new mine; they insisted that if anyone would do the work, they would. At this time, no representative of the UMW, their international union, was present. George Gilbert, the UMW's field representative for the area including Local 5881, was away at Middlesboro, Kentucky, attending an Executive Board meeting when the members of the local discovered Grundy's plan; he did not return to the area until late in the day of August 16. There was uncontradicted testimony that he first learned of the violence while at the meeting, and returned with explicit instructions from his international union superiors to establish a limited picket line, to prevent any further violence, and to see to it that the strike did not spread to neighboring mines. There was no further violence at the mine site; a picket line was maintained there for nine months; and no further attempts were made to open the mine during that period.

Respondent lost his job as superintendent, and never entered into performance of his haulage contract. He testified that he soon began to lose other trucking contracts and mine leases he held in nearby areas. Claiming these effects to be the result of a concerted union plan against him, he sought recovery not against Local 5881 or its members, but only against petitioner, the international union. The suit was brought in the United States District Court for the Eastern District of Tennessee, and jurisdiction was premised on allegations of secondary boycotts under §303. The state law claim, for which jurisdiction was based upon the doctrine of pendent jurisdiction, asserted "an unlawful conspiracy and an unlawful boycott aimed at him and (Grundy) to maliciously, wantonly and willfully interfere with his contract of employment and with his contract of haulage."

. . . The jury's verdict was that the UMW had violated both §303 and state law. Gibbs was awarded $60,000 as damages under the employment contract and $14,500 under the haulage contract; he was also awarded $100,000 punitive damages. On motion, the trial court set aside the award of damages with respect to the haulage contract on the ground that damage was unproved. It also held that union pressure on Grundy to discharge respondent as supervisor would constitute only a primary dispute with Grundy, as respondent's employer, and hence was not cognizable as a claim under §303. Interference with the employment relationship was cognizable as a state claim, however, and a remitted award was sustained on the state law claim. The Court of Appeals for the Sixth Circuit affirmed. We granted *certiorari*. We reverse.

I.

. . . The Court held in *Hurn v. Oursler*, 289 U.S. 238, that state law claims are appropriate for federal court determination if they form a separate but parallel ground for relief also sought in a substantial claim based on federal law. The Court distinguished permissible from non-permissible exercises of federal judicial power over state law claims by contrasting "a case where two distinct grounds in support of a single cause of action are alleged, one only of which presents a federal question, and a case where two separate and distinct causes of action are alleged, one only of which is federal in character. In the former, where the federal question averred is not plainly wanting in substance, the federal court, even though the federal ground be not established, may nevertheless retain and dispose of the case upon the nonfederal ground; in the latter it may not do so upon the nonfederal cause of action." The question is into which category the present action fell.

Hurn was decided in 1933, before the unification of law and equity by the Federal Rules of Civil Procedure. At the time, the meaning of "cause of action" was a subject of serious dispute; the phrase might "mean one thing for one purpose and something different for another." . . .

With the adoption of the Federal Rules of Civil Procedure and the unified form of action, Fed. Rule Civ. Proc. 2, much of the controversy over "cause of action" abated. The phrase remained as the keystone of the *Hurn* test, however, and, as commentators have noted, has been the source of considerable confusion. Under the Rules, the impulse is toward entertaining the broadest possible scope of action consistent with fairness to the parties; joinder of claims, parties and remedies is strongly encouraged.[10] Yet because the *Hurn* question involves issues of jurisdiction as well as convenience, there has been some tendency to limit its application to cases in which the state and federal claims are, as in *Hurn*, "little more than the equivalent of different epithets to characterize the same group of circumstances."

This limited approach is unnecessarily grudging. Pendent jurisdiction, in the sense of judicial power, exists whenever there is a claim "arising under [the] Constitution, the Laws of the United States, and Treaties made, or which shall be made, under their Authority . . ." U.S. Const., Art. III, §2, and the relationship between that claim and the state claim permits the conclusion that the entire action before the court comprises but one constitutional "case."[12] The federal claim must have substance sufficient to

10. *See, e.g.*, Fed. Rules Civ. Proc. 2, 18-20, 42.

12. The question whether joined state and federal claims constitute one "case" for jurisdictional purposes is to be distinguished from the often equally difficult inquiry whether any "case" at all is presented, although the issue whether a claim for relief qualifies as a case "arising under . . . the Laws of the United States" and the issue whether federal and state claims constitute one "case" for pendent jurisdiction purposes may often appear together.

confer subject matter jurisdiction on the court. *Levering & Garrigues Co. v. Morrin*, 289 U.S. 103. The state and federal claims must derive from a common nucleus of operative fact. But if, considered without regard to their federal or state character, a plaintiff's claims are such that he would ordinarily be expected to try them all in one judicial proceeding, then, assuming substantiality of the federal issues, there is power in federal courts to hear the whole.[13]

That power need not be exercised in every case in which it is found to exist. It has consistently been recognized that pendent jurisdiction is a doctrine of discretion, not of plaintiff's right. Its justification lies in considerations of judicial economy, convenience and fairness to litigants; if these are not present a federal court should hesitate to exercise jurisdiction over state claims, even though bound to apply state law to them, *Erie R. Co. v. Tompkins*, 304 U.S. 64. Needless decisions of state law should be avoided both as a matter of comity and to promote justice between the parties, by procuring for them a surer-footed reading of applicable law.[15] Certainly, if the federal claims are dismissed before trial, even though not insubstantial in a jurisdictional sense, the state claims should be dismissed as well. Similarly, if it appears that the state issues substantially predominate, whether in terms of proof, of the scope of the issues raised, or of the comprehensiveness of the remedy sought, the state claims may be dismissed without prejudice and left for resolution to state tribunals. There may, on the other hand, be situations in which the state claim is so closely tied to questions of federal policy that the argument for exercise of pendent jurisdiction is particularly strong. In the present case, for example, the allowable scope of the state claim implicates the federal doctrine of pre-emption; while this interrelationship does not create statutory federal question jurisdiction, *Louisville & N.R. Co. v. Mottley*, 211 U.S. 149, its existence is relevant to the exercise of discretion. Finally, there may be reasons independent of jurisdictional considerations, such as the likelihood of jury confusion in treating divergent legal theories of relief, that would justify separating state and federal claims for trial, Fed. Rule Civ. Proc. 42(b). If so, jurisdiction should ordinarily be refused.

13. *Cf. Armstrong Paint and Varnish Works v. Nu-Enamel Corp.*, 305 U.S. 315, 325. Note, Problems of Parallel State and Federal Remedies, 71 Harv. L. Rev. 513, 514 (1958). While it is commonplace that the Federal Rules of Civil Procedure do not expand the jurisdiction of federal courts, they do embody "the whole tendency of our decisions . . . to require a plaintiff to try his . . . whole case at one time," *Baltimore S.S. Co. v. Phillips, supra*, and to that extent emphasize the basis of pendent jurisdiction.

15. Some have seen this consideration as the principal argument against exercise of pendent jurisdiction. Thus, before *Erie*, it was remarked that "the limitations (on pendent jurisdiction) are in the wise discretion of the courts to be fixed in individual cases by the exercise of that statesmanship which is required of any arbiter of the relations of states to nation in a federal system." In his oft-cited concurrence in *Strachman v. Palmer*, 177 F.2d 427 (C.A.1st Cir. 1949), Judge Magruder counseled that "[f]ederal courts should not be overeager to hold on to the determination of issues that might be more appropriately left to settlement in state court litigation."

The question of power will ordinarily be resolved on the pleadings. But the issue whether pendent jurisdiction has been properly assumed is one which remains open throughout the litigation. Pretrial procedures or even the trial itself may reveal a substantial hegemony of state law claims, or likelihood of jury confusion, which could not have been anticipated at the pleading stage. Although it will of course be appropriate to take account in this circumstance of the already completed course of the litigation, dismissal of the state claim might even then be merited. For example, it may appear that the plaintiff was well aware of the nature of his proofs and the relative importance of his claims; recognition of a federal court's wide latitude to decide ancillary questions of state law does not imply that it must tolerate a litigant's effort to impose upon it what is in effect only a state law case. Once it appears that a state claim constitutes the real body of a case, to which the federal claim is only an appendage, the state claim may fairly be dismissed.

We are not prepared to say that in the present case the District Court exceeded its discretion in proceeding to judgment on the state claim. We may assume for purposes of decision that the District Court was correct in its holding that the claim of pressure on Grundy to terminate the employment contract was outside the purview of §303. Even so, the §303 claims based on secondary pressures on Grundy relative to the haulage contract and on other coal operators generally were substantial. Although §303 limited recovery to compensatory damages based on secondary pressures, and state law allowed both compensatory and punitive damages, and allowed such damages as to both secondary and primary activity, the state and federal claims arose from the same nucleus of operative fact and reflected alternative remedies. Indeed, the verdict sheet sent in to the jury authorized only one award of damages, so that recovery could not be given separately on the federal and state claims.

It is true that the §303 claims ultimately failed and that the only recovery allowed respondent was on the state claim. We cannot confidently say, however, that the federal issues were so remote or played such a minor role at the trial that in effect the state claim only was tried. Although the District Court dismissed as unproved the §303 claims that petitioner's secondary activities included attempts to induce coal operators other than Grundy to cease doing business with respondent, the court submitted the §303 claims relating to Grundy to the jury. The jury returned verdicts against petitioner on those §303 claims, and it was only on petitioner's motion for a directed verdict and a judgment n.o.v. that the verdicts on those claims were set aside. The District Judge considered the claim as to the haulage contract proved as to liability, and held it failed only for lack of proof of damages. Although there was some risk of confusing the jury in joining the state and federal claims—especially since, as will be developed, differing standards of proof of UMW involvement applied— the possibility of confusion could be lessened by employing a special verdict form, as the District Court did. Moreover, the question whether the permissible scope of the state claim was limited by the doctrine of pre-emption afforded a special reason for the exercise of pendent jurisdiction; the federal courts are particularly appropriate bodies for the application of pre-emption principles. We thus conclude that although it may be that the District Court might, in its sound discretion, have dismissed the state claim, the circumstances show no error in refusing to do so.

[The Court went on to reverse the verdict of conspiracy under state law, as Gibbs had not met the necessary burden of proof.]

[The concurring opinion of Justice HARLAN is omitted.]

Comments and Questions

1. Where does the Court find constitutional authority in Article III for "pendent jurisdiction"? Was there statutory authority at the time *Gibbs* was decided? 28 U.S.C. §1367 (discussed below) is of much more recent vintage.

2. What are the pragmatic and judicial efficiency arguments that underlie the Court's approval of pendent jurisdiction? Consider a plaintiff in Gibbs's situation, with an injury that he believes gives rise to claims under both federal and state law. Absent the recognition of pendent jurisdiction (and without diversity of citizenship between the parties), what would his options be in choosing a proper court? If such a plaintiff, desiring a federal forum for his federal claim, is forced (because of lack of jurisdiction) to file the related state claim in state court, haven't we spawned two cases with duplicative facts and evidence and created the risk of inconsistent results?

3. What is the standard for the exercise of pendent jurisdiction under *Gibbs*? If this test is met, must the federal court exercise pendent jurisdiction? If not, under what circumstances may a court decline to assert power over state claims that arise out of the same nucleus of facts as the federal claim?

4. If the justification in *Gibbs* for the expansion of federal adjudicatory power over a state law claim is that the latter is appended to a federal claim being entertained, how can the federal court resolve the state claim even after the federal claim fails (as it did in *Gibbs*)? Does this mean a plaintiff can access pendent jurisdiction merely by asserting some federal claim, no matter how frivolous? What does Justice Brennan say about this?

In *Maguire v. Marquette University*, 814 F.2d 1213 (7th Cir. 1987), the plaintiff brought an action under Title VII of the Civil Rights Act of 1964, alleging she was denied appointment to the Jesuit school's theology department because of her gender. After discovery, she amended her complaint to add a pendent claim asserting breach of Wisconsin's law of academic freedom, alleging she was rejected because of her views favoring abortion. The defendant's motion for summary judgment on the Title VII count was granted on the grounds that the plaintiff's own submissions confirmed the defendant's denial of gender discrimination by showing that the motivating factor behind her rejection was her outspoken opinion, which was inconsistent with Catholic doctrine. The district court then proceeded to decide and dismiss the state law claim. On appeal, the Seventh Circuit held that the district court had erred in reaching the merits of the academic freedom claim. Citing *Gibbs* (383 U.S. at 726), the court ruled that "[w]hen, as here, the federal claim is dismissed before trial, the district court should relinquish jurisdiction of any pendent state law claim unless there is some independent basis of federal jurisdiction." *Maguire*, 814 F.2d at 1218.

5. Just as pendent jurisdiction stretches a federal court's authority over a federal claim to include a state law claim arising from the same facts, "ancillary jurisdiction" enlarges the authority of a federal court entertaining a diversity action, as illustrated by the next case.

■ OWEN EQUIPMENT AND ERECTION COMPANY v. KROGER
437 U.S. 365 (1978)

Justice STEWART delivered the opinion of the Court:

In an action in which federal jurisdiction is based on diversity of citizenship, may the plaintiff assert a claim against a third-party defendant when there is no independent basis for federal jurisdiction over that claim? The Court of Appeals for the Eighth Circuit held in this case that such a claim is within the ancillary jurisdiction of the federal courts. We granted *certiorari* because this decision conflicts with several recent decisions of other Courts of Appeals.

I

On January 18, 1972, James Kroger was electrocuted when the boom of a steel crane next to which he was walking came too close to a high-tension electric power line. The respondent (his widow, who is the administratrix of his estate) filed a wrongful-death action in the United States District Court for the District of Nebraska against the Omaha Public Power District (OPPD). Her complaint alleged that OPPD's negligent construction, maintenance, and operation of the power line had caused Kroger's death. Federal jurisdiction was based on diversity of citizenship, since the respondent was a citizen of Iowa and OPPD was a Nebraska corporation.

OPPD then filed a third-party complaint pursuant to Fed. Rule Civ. Proc. 14(a) against the petitioner, Owen Equipment and Erection Co. (Owen), alleging that the crane was owned and operated by Owen, and that Owen's negligence had been the proximate cause of Kroger's death.[3] OPPD later moved for summary judgment on the respondent's complaint against it. While this motion was pending, the respondent was granted leave to file an amended complaint naming Owen as an additional defendant. Thereafter, the District Court granted OPPD's motion for summary judgment in an unreported opinion. The case thus went to trial between the respondent and the petitioner alone.

The respondent's amended complaint alleged that Owen was "a Nebraska corporation with its principal place of business in Nebraska." Owen's answer admitted that it was "a corporation organized and existing under the laws of the State of Nebraska," and denied every other allegation of the complaint. On the third day of trial, however, it was disclosed that the petitioner's principal place of business was in Iowa, not Nebraska,[5] and that the petitioner and the respondent were thus both citizens of Iowa.[6] The petitioner then moved to dismiss the complaint for lack of jurisdiction. The District Court reserved decision on the motion, and the jury thereafter returned a verdict in favor of the respondent. In an unreported opinion issued after the trial, the District Court denied the petitioner's motion to dismiss the complaint.

The judgment was affirmed on appeal. The Court of Appeals held that under this Court's decision in *Mine Workers v. Gibbs*, 383 U.S. 715, the District Court had jurisdictional power, in its discretion, to adjudicate the respondent's claim against the petitioner because that claim arose from the "core of 'operative facts' giving rise to both [respondent's] claim against OPPD and OPPD's claim against Owen." It further held that the District Court had properly exercised its discretion in proceeding to decide the case even after summary judgment had been granted to OPPD, because the petitioner had concealed its Iowa citizenship from the respondent. Rehearing en banc was denied by an equally divided court.

---

3. Under Rule 14(a), a third-party defendant may not be impleaded merely because he may be liable to the plaintiff. While the third-party complaint in this case alleged merely that Owen's negligence caused Kroger's death, and the basis of Owen's alleged liability to OPPD is nowhere spelled out, OPPD evidently relied upon the state common-law right of contribution among joint tortfeasors. The petitioner has never challenged the propriety of the third-party complaint as such.

5. The problem apparently was one of geography. Although the Missouri River generally marks the boundary between Iowa and Nebraska, Carter Lake, Iowa, where the accident occurred and where Owen had its main office, lies west of the river, adjacent to Omaha, Neb. Apparently the river once avulsed at one of its bends, cutting Carter Lake off from the rest of Iowa.

6. Title 28 U.S.C. §1332(c) provides that "[f]or the purposes of [diversity jurisdiction] . . . , a corporation shall be deemed a citizen of any State by which it has been incorporated and of the State where it has its principal place of business."

II

It is undisputed that there was no independent basis of federal jurisdiction over the respondent's state-law tort action against the petitioner, since both are citizens of Iowa. And although Fed. Rule Civ. Proc. 14(a) permits a plaintiff to assert a claim against a third-party defendant, it does not purport to say whether or not such a claim requires an independent basis of federal jurisdiction. Indeed, it could not determine that question, since it is axiomatic that the Federal Rules of Civil Procedure do not create or withdraw federal jurisdiction. Fed. Rule Civ. Proc. 82.

In affirming the District Court's judgment, the Court of Appeals relied upon the doctrine of ancillary jurisdiction, whose contours it believed were defined by this Court's holding in *Mine Workers v. Gibbs, supra.* The *Gibbs* case differed from this one in that it involved pendent jurisdiction, which concerns the resolution of a plaintiff's federal- and state-law claims against a single defendant in one action. By contrast, in this case there was no claim based upon substantive federal law, but rather state-law tort claims against two different defendants. Nonetheless, the Court of Appeals was correct in perceiving that *Gibbs* and this case are two species of the same generic problem: Under what circumstances may a federal court hear and decide a state-law claim arising between citizens of the same state? But we believe that the Court of Appeals failed to understand the scope of the doctrine of the *Gibbs* case.

The plaintiff in *Gibbs* alleged that the defendant union had violated the common law of Tennessee as well as the federal prohibition of secondary boycotts. This Court held that, although the parties were not of diverse citizenship, the District Court properly entertained the state-law claim as pendent to the federal claim. The crucial holding was stated as follows:

> Pendent jurisdiction, in the sense of judicial power, exists whenever there is a claim "arising under [the] Constitution, the Laws of the United States, and Treaties made, or which shall be made, under their Authority . . . ," U.S. Const., Art. III, §2, and the relationship between that claim and the state claim permits the conclusion that the entire action before the court comprises but one constitutional "case." . . . The state and federal claims must derive from a common nucleus of operative fact. But if, considered without regard to their federal or state character, a plaintiff's claims are such that he would ordinarily be expected to try them all in one judicial proceeding, then, assuming substantiality of the federal issues, there is power in federal courts to hear the whole.

It is apparent that *Gibbs* delineated the constitutional limits of federal judicial power. But even if it be assumed that the District Court in the present case had constitutional power to decide the respondent's lawsuit against the petitioner,[10] it does not follow that the decision of the Court of Appeals was correct. Constitutional power is merely the first hurdle that must be overcome in determining that a federal court has jurisdiction over a particular controversy. For the jurisdiction of the federal courts is limited not only by the provisions of Art. III of the Constitution, but also by Acts of Congress.

That statutory law as well as the Constitution may limit a federal court's jurisdiction over nonfederal claims[11] is well illustrated by two recent decisions of this Court, *Aldinger v. Howard*, 427 U.S. 1 and *Zahn v. International Paper Co.*, 414 U.S. 291. In *Aldinger* the Court held that a Federal District Court lacked jurisdiction over a state-law claim against a county, even if that claim was alleged to be pendent to one against county officials under 42 U.S.C. §1983. In *Zahn* the Court held that in a diversity class action under Fed. Rule Civ. Proc. 23(b)(3), the claim of each member of the plaintiff class must independently satisfy the minimum jurisdictional amount set by 28 U.S.C. §1332(a), and rejected the argument that jurisdiction existed over those claims that involved $10,000 or less as ancillary to those that involved more. In each case, despite the fact that federal and nonfederal claims arose from a "common nucleus of operative fact," the Court held that the statute conferring jurisdiction over the federal claim did not allow the exercise of jurisdiction over the nonfederal claim.[12]

The *Aldinger* and *Zahn* cases thus make clear that a finding that federal and nonfederal claims arise from a "common nucleus of operative fact," the test of *Gibbs*, does not end the inquiry into whether a federal court has power to hear the nonfederal claims along with the federal ones. Beyond this constitutional minimum, there must be an examination of the posture in which the nonfederal claim is asserted and of the specific statute that confers jurisdiction over the federal claim, in order to determine whether "Congress in [that statute] has . . . expressly or by implication negated" the exercise of jurisdiction over the particular nonfederal claim. *Aldinger v. Howard, supra*, 427 U.S. at 18.

10. Federal jurisdiction in *Gibbs* was based upon the existence of a question of federal law. The Court of Appeals in the present case believed that the "common nucleus of operative fact" test also determines the outer boundaries of constitutionally permissible federal jurisdiction when that jurisdiction is based upon diversity of citizenship. We may assume without deciding that the Court of Appeals was correct in this regard.

11. As used in this opinion, the term "nonfederal claim" means one as to which there is no independent basis for federal jurisdiction. Conversely, a "federal claim" means one as to which an independent basis for federal jurisdiction exists.

12. In *Monell v. New York City Dept. of Social Services*, 436 U.S. 658 we have overruled *Monroe v. Pape*, 365 U.S. 167 insofar as it held that political subdivisions are never amenable to suit under 42 U.S.C. §1983—the basis of the holding in *Aldinger* that 28 U.S.C. §1343(3) does not allow pendent jurisdiction of a state-law claim against a county. But *Monell* in no way qualifies the holding of *Aldinger* that the jurisdictional questions presented in a case such as this one are statutory as well as constitutional, a point on which the dissenters in *Aldinger* agreed with the Court.

III

The relevant statute in this case, 28 U.S.C. §1332(a)(1), confers upon federal courts jurisdiction over "civil actions where the matter in controversy exceeds the sum or value of $10,000 . . . and is between . . . citizens of different States." This statute and its predecessors have consistently been held to require complete diversity of citizenship.[13] That is, diversity jurisdiction does not exist unless each defendant is a citizen of a different state from each plaintiff. Over the years Congress has repeatedly reenacted or amended the statute conferring diversity jurisdiction, leaving intact this rule of complete diversity. Whatever may have been the original purposes of diversity-of-citizenship jurisdiction, this subsequent history clearly demonstrates a congressional mandate that diversity jurisdiction is not to be available when any plaintiff is a citizen of the same state as any defendant.

Thus it is clear that the respondent could not originally have brought suit in federal court naming Owen and OPPD as co-defendants, since citizens of Iowa would have been on both sides of the litigation. Yet the identical lawsuit resulted when she amended her complaint. Complete diversity was destroyed just as surely as if she had sued Owen initially. In either situation, in the plain language of the statute, the "matter in controversy" could not be "between . . . citizens of different States."

It is a fundamental precept that federal courts are courts of limited jurisdiction. The limits upon federal jurisdiction, whether imposed by the Constitution or by Congress, must be neither disregarded nor evaded. Yet under the reasoning of the Court of Appeals in this case, a plaintiff could defeat the statutory requirement of complete diversity by the simple expedient of suing only those defendants who were of diverse citizenship and waiting for them to implead nondiverse defendants.[17] If, as the Court of Appeals thought, a "common nucleus of operative fact" were the only requirement for ancillary jurisdiction in a diversity case, there would be no principled reason why the respondent in this case could not have joined her cause of action against Owen in her original complaint as ancillary to her claim against OPPD. Congress' requirement of complete diversity would thus have been evaded completely.

It is true, as the Court of Appeals noted, that the exercise of ancillary jurisdiction over nonfederal claims has often been upheld in situations

---

13. *E.g., Strawbridge v. Curtiss*, 3 Cranch 267. It is settled that complete diversity is not a constitutional requirement. *State Farm Fire & Cas. Co. v. Tashire*, 386 U.S. 523.

17. This is not an unlikely hypothesis, since a defendant in a tort suit such as this one would surely try to limit his liability by impleading any joint tortfeasors for indemnity or contribution. Some commentators have suggested that the possible abuse of third-party practice could be dealt with under 28 U.S.C. §1359, which forbids collusive attempts to create federal jurisdiction. The dissenting opinion today also expresses this view. But there is nothing necessarily collusive about a plaintiff's selectively suing only those tortfeasors of diverse citizenship, or about the named defendants' desire to implead joint tortfeasors. Nonetheless, the requirement of complete diversity would be eviscerated by such a course of events.

involving impleader, cross-claims or counterclaims. But in determining whether jurisdiction over a nonfederal claim exists, the context in which the nonfederal claim is asserted is crucial. And the claim here arises in a setting quite different from the kinds of nonfederal claims that have been viewed in other cases as falling within the ancillary jurisdiction of the federal courts.

First, the nonfederal claim in this case was simply not ancillary to the federal one in the same sense that, for example, the impleader by a defendant of a third-party defendant always is. A third-party complaint depends at least in part upon the resolution of the primary lawsuit. Its relation to the original complaint is thus not mere factual similarity but logical dependence. The respondent's claim against the petitioner, however, was entirely separate from her original claim against OPPD, since the petitioner's liability to her depended not at all upon whether or not OPPD was also liable. Far from being an ancillary and dependent claim, it was a new and independent one.

Second, the nonfederal claim here was asserted by the plaintiff, who voluntarily chose to bring suit upon a state-law claim in a federal court. By contrast, ancillary jurisdiction typically involves claims by a defending party haled into court against his will, or by another person whose rights might be irretrievably lost unless he could assert them in an ongoing action in a federal court. A plaintiff cannot complain if ancillary jurisdiction does not encompass all of his possible claims in a case such as this one, since it is he who has chosen the federal rather than the state forum and must thus accept its limitations. "[T]he efficiency plaintiff seeks so avidly is available without question in the state courts."

It is not unreasonable to assume that, in generally requiring complete diversity, Congress did not intend to confine the jurisdiction of federal courts so inflexibly that they are unable to protect legal rights or effectively to resolve an entire, logically entwined lawsuit. Those practical needs are the basis of the doctrine of ancillary jurisdiction. But neither the convenience of litigants nor considerations of judicial economy can suffice to justify extension of the doctrine of ancillary jurisdiction to a plaintiff's cause of action against a citizen of the same State in a diversity case. Congress has established the basic rule that diversity jurisdiction exists under 28 U.S.C. §1332 only when there is complete diversity of citizenship. "The policy of the statute calls for its strict construction." To allow the requirement of complete diversity to be circumvented as it was in this case would simply flout the congressional command.

Accordingly, the judgment of the Court of Appeals is reversed.

It is so ordered.

Justice WHITE, with whom Mr. Justice BRENNAN joins, dissenting:

The Court today states that "[i]t is not unreasonable to assume that, in generally requiring complete diversity, Congress did not intend to confine the jurisdiction of federal courts so inflexibly that they are unable . . . effectively to resolve an entire, logically entwined lawsuit." In spite of this recognition, the majority goes on to hold that in diversity suits federal courts do not have the jurisdictional power to entertain a claim asserted by a plaintiff against a third-party defendant, no matter how entwined it is with the matter already before the court, unless there is an independent basis for jurisdiction over that claim. Because I find no support for such a requirement in either Art. III of the Constitution or in any statutory law, I dissent from the Court's "unnecessarily grudging" approach.

The plaintiff below, Mrs. Kroger, chose to bring her lawsuit against the Omaha Public Power District (OPPD) in Federal District Court. No one questions the power of the District Court to entertain this claim, for Mrs. Kroger at the time was a citizen of Iowa, OPPD was a citizen of Nebraska, and the amount in controversy was greater than $10,000; jurisdiction therefore existed under 28 U.S.C. §1332(a). As permitted by Fed. Rule Civ. Proc. 14(a), OPPD impleaded petitioner Owen Equipment & Erection Co. (Owen). Although OPPD's claim against Owen did not raise a federal question and although it was alleged that Owen was a citizen of the same State as OPPD, the parties and the court apparently believed that the district Court's ancillary jurisdiction encompassed this claim. Subsequently, Mrs. Kroger asserted a claim against Owen, everyone believing at the time that these two parties were citizens of different States. Because it later came to light that Mrs. Kroger and Owen were in fact both citizens of Iowa, the Court concludes that the District Court lacked jurisdiction over the claim.

In *Mine Workers v. Gibbs*, 383 U.S. 715, we held that once a claim has been stated that is of sufficient substance to confer subject-matter jurisdiction on the federal district court, the court has judicial power to consider a nonfederal claim if it and the federal claim are derived from "a common nucleus of operative fact." Although the specific facts of that case concerned a state claim that was said to be pendent to a federal-question claim, the Court's language and reasoning were broad enough to cover the instant factual situation: "[I]f, considered without regard to their federal or state character, a plaintiff's claims are such that he would ordinarily be expected to try them all in one judicial proceeding, then, assuming substantiality of the federal issues, there is power in federal courts to hear the whole." In the present case, Mrs. Kroger's claim against Owen and her claim against OPPD derived from a common nucleus of fact; this is necessarily so because in order for a plaintiff to assert a claim against a third-party defendant, Fed. Rule Civ. Proc. 14(a) requires that it "aris[e] out of the transaction or occurrence that is the subject matter of the plaintiff's claim against the third-party plaintiff. . . ." Furthermore, the substantiality of the claim Mrs. Kroger asserted against OPPD is unquestioned. Accordingly, as far as Art. III of the Constitution is concerned, the District Court had power to entertain Mrs. Kroger's claim against Owen.

The majority correctly points out, however, that the analysis cannot stop here. As *Aldinger v. Howard*, 427 U.S. 1 (1976), teaches, the jurisdictional power of the federal courts may be limited by Congress, as well as by the Constitution. In *Aldinger*, although the plaintiff's state claim against Spokane County was closely connected with her 42 U.S.C. §1983 claim against the county treasurer, the Court held that the District Court did not have pendent jurisdiction over the state claim, for, under the Court's precedents at that time, it was thought that Congress had specifically determined not to confer on the federal courts jurisdiction over civil rights claims against cities and counties. That being so, the Court refused to allow "the federal courts to fashion a jurisdictional doctrine under the general language of Art. III enabling them to circumvent this exclusion. . . .

In the present case, the only indication of congressional intent that the Court can find is that contained in the diversity jurisdictional statute, 28 U.S.C. §1332(a), which states that "district courts shall have original jurisdiction of all civil actions where the matter in controversy exceeds the sum or value of $10,000 . . . and is between . . . citizens of different States. . . ." Because this statute has been interpreted as requiring complete diversity of citizenship between each plaintiff and each defendant, *Strawbridge v. Curtiss*, 3 Cranch 267 (1806), the Court holds that the District Court did not have ancillary jurisdiction over Mrs. Kroger's claim against Owen. In so holding, the Court unnecessarily expands the scope of the complete-diversity requirement while substantially limiting the doctrine of ancillary jurisdiction.

The complete-diversity requirement, of course, could be viewed as meaning that in a diversity case, a federal district court may adjudicate only those claims that are between parties of different states. Thus, in order for a defendant to implead a third-party defendant, there would have to be diversity of citizenship; the same would also be true for cross-claims between defendants and for a third-party defendant's claim against a plaintiff. Even the majority, however, refuses to read the complete-diversity requirement so broadly; it recognizes with seeming approval the exercise of ancillary jurisdiction over nonfederal claims in situations involving impleader, cross-claims, and counterclaims. Given the Court's willingness to recognize ancillary jurisdiction in these contexts, despite the requirements of §1332(a), I see no justification for the Court's refusal to approve the District Court's exercise of ancillary jurisdiction in the present case.

It is significant that a plaintiff who asserts a claim against a third-party defendant is not seeking to add a new party to the lawsuit. In the present case, for example, Owen had already been brought into the suit by OPPD, and, that having been done, Mrs. Kroger merely sought to assert against Owen a claim arising out of the same transaction that was already before the court. . . .

Because in the instant case Mrs. Kroger merely sought to assert a claim against someone already a party to the suit, considerations of judicial economy, convenience, and fairness to the litigants—the factors relied upon in *Gibbs*—support the recognition of ancillary jurisdiction here. Already before the court was the whole question of the cause of Mr. Kroger's death. Mrs. Kroger initially contended that OPPD was responsible; OPPD in turn contended that Owen's negligence had been the proximate cause of Mr. Kroger's death. In spite of the fact that the question of Owen's negligence was already before the District Court, the majority requires Mrs. Kroger to bring a separate action in state court in order to assert that very claim. Even if the Iowa statute of limitations will still permit such a suit, considerations of judicial economy are certainly not served by requiring such duplicative litigation.[4]

The majority, however, brushes aside such considerations of convenience, judicial economy, and fairness because it concludes that recognizing ancillary jurisdiction over a plaintiff's claim against a third-party defendant would permit the plaintiff to circumvent the complete-diversity requirement and thereby "flout the congressional command." Since the plaintiff in such a case does not bring the third-party defendant into the suit, however, there is no occasion for deliberate circumvention of the diversity requirement, absent collusion with the defendant. In the case of such collusion, of which there is absolutely no indication here, the court can dismiss the action under the authority of 28 U.S.C. §1359.[6] In the absence of such collusion, there is no reason to adopt an absolute rule prohibiting the plaintiff from asserting those claims that he may properly assert against the third-party defendant pursuant to Fed. Rule Civ. Proc. 14(a). The plaintiff in such a situation brings suit against the defendant only with absolutely no assurance that the defendant will decide or be able to implead a particular third-party defendant. Since the plaintiff has no control over the defendant's decision to implead a third party, the fact that he could not have originally sued that party in federal court should be irrelevant. Moreover, the fact that a plaintiff in some cases may be able to foresee the subsequent chain of events leading to the impleader does not seem to me to be a sufficient reason to declare that a district court does not have the power

4. It is true that prior to trial OPPD was dismissed as a party to the suit and that, as we indicated in *Gibbs*, the dismissal prior to trial of the federal claim will generally require the dismissal of the nonfederal claim as well. Given the unusual facts of the present case, however—in particular, the fact that the actual location of Owen's principal place of business was not revealed until the third day of trial—fairness to the parties would lead me to conclude that the District Court did not abuse its discretion in retaining jurisdiction over Mrs. Kroger's claim against Owen. Under the Court's disposition, of course, it would not matter whether or not the federal claim is tried, for in either situation the court would have no jurisdiction over the plaintiff's nonfederal claim against the third-party defendant.

6. Section 1359 states: "A district court shall not have jurisdiction of a civil action in which any party, by assignment or otherwise, has been improperly or collusively made or joined to invoke the jurisdiction of such court."

to exercise ancillary jurisdiction over the plaintiff's claims against the third-party defendant.[7]

Accordingly, the majority's concerns that lead it to conclude that ancillary jurisdiction should not be recognized in the present situation could be met on a case-by-case basis, rather than by the absolute rule it adopts. . . .

I would hold that in a diversity case the District Court has power, both constitutional and statutory, to entertain all claims among the parties arising from the same nucleus of operative fact as the plaintiff's original, jurisdiction-conferring claim against the defendant. Accordingly, I dissent from the Court's disposition of the present case.

Comments and Questions

1. Under the doctrine of ancillary jurisdiction, it has long been recognized that a federal district court could entertain an impleader against a third-party defendant even though addition of that party defeats complete diversity between all plaintiffs and all defendants, or if diversity is lacking between D1 and the new D2. Thus, in a products liability action against a car dealer who allegedly sells a dangerously defective automobile to the injured plaintiff, the dealer may implead the manufacturer under Rule 14, asserting a "claim over" (that is, the manufacturer "is or may be liable" for all or part of plaintiff's claim against the original defendant), even though the third-party defendant shares citizenship with either defendant or with plaintiff. The impleader claim is dependent upon the original claim in the sense that if the latter fails, the former does as well.[*]

The rationale for this jurisdictional stretch is that since the impleader is merely ancillary to the main claim, a side action so to speak, strong policy reasons support permitting it to play out together with the main case: avoidance of multiple litigation fosters judicial efficiency and avoids the risk of inconsistent results. Ancillary jurisdiction is generally applied as well to compulsory counterclaims (Rule 13(a)), cross-claims (Rule 13(g)), and interventions as a matter of right (Rule 24(a)).

2. How does the *Kroger* Court distinguish the assertion of jurisdiction over plaintiff's claim against Owen Equipment from the well-established authority to entertain OPPD's third-party claim against Owen? What is the

---

7. Under the *Gibbs* analysis, recognition of the district court's power to hear a plaintiff's nonfederal claim against a third-party defendant in a diversity suit would not mean that the court would be required to entertain such claims in all cases. The district court would have the discretion to dismiss the nonfederal claim if it concluded that the interests of judicial economy, convenience, and fairness would not be served by the retention of the claim in the federal lawsuit.

*If Carpenter v. Dee were in federal district court on grounds of diversity between Nancy Carpenter and Randall Dee, Dee would be able to implead Ultimate Auto even though Ultimate was a Massachusetts entity sharing citizenship with Nancy Carpenter.

policy rationale for drawing the line here? What do the dissenters have to say about this line? Which view of federal power do you find more compelling from a philosophical perspective? From a pragmatic perspective?

3. Given the Court's logic, would it have made a difference to the result in the case if the original claim against OPPD had *not* been dismissed on summary judgment? Why or why not? Look at the dissent's footnote 4. 🖉⌐

4. *Pendent* jurisdiction permits a federal court to entertain a related[*] nonfederal claim against a party already in court answering to a federal claim. *Ancillary* jurisdiction permits a federal court to entertain a related claim against a party *not* already in the case but impleaded by a defendant on an ancillary claim. The following case treats a hybrid referred to as *pendent party* jurisdiction.

■ FINLEY v. UNITED STATES
490 U.S. 545 (1989)

Justice SCALIA delivered the opinion of the Court:

On the night of November 11, 1983, a twin-engine plane carrying petitioner's husband and two of her children struck electric transmission lines during its approach to a San Diego, California, airfield. No one survived the resulting crash. Petitioner brought a tort action in state court, claiming that San Diego Gas and Electric Company had negligently positioned and inadequately illuminated the transmission lines, and that the city of San Diego's negligent maintenance of the airport's runway lights had rendered them inoperative the night of the crash. When she later discovered that the Federal Aviation Administration (FAA) was in fact the party responsible for the runway lights, petitioner filed the present action against the United States in the United States District Court for the Southern District of California. The complaint based jurisdiction upon the Federal Tort Claims Act (FTCA), 28 U.S.C. §1346(b), alleging negligence in the FAA's operation and maintenance of the runway lights and performance of air traffic control functions. Almost a year later, she moved to amend the federal complaint to include claims against the original state-court defendants, as to which no independent basis for federal jurisdiction existed. The District Court granted petitioner's motion and asserted "pendent" jurisdiction under *Mine Workers v. Gibbs*, 383 U.S. 715 (1966), finding it "clear" that "judicial economy and efficiency" favored trying the actions together, and concluding that they arose "from a common nucleus of operative facts." The District Court certified an interlocutory appeal to the Court of Appeals for the Ninth Circuit under 28 U.S.C. §1292(b). That court summarily reversed . . . , categorically reject[ing] pendent-party jurisdiction under the FTCA. We granted

---

* "Related" in this sense means arising from the same facts.

certiorari to resolve a split among the Circuits on whether the FTCA permits an assertion of pendent jurisdiction over additional parties.

The FTCA provides that "the district courts . . . shall have exclusive jurisdiction of civil actions on claims against the United States" for certain torts of federal employees acting within the scope of their employment. 28 U.S.C. §1346(b). Petitioner seeks to append her claims against the city and the utility to her FTCA action against the United States, even though this would require the District Court to extend its authority to additional parties for whom an independent jurisdictional base—such as diversity of citizenship, 28 U.S.C. §1332(a)(1)—is lacking.

In 1807 Chief Justice Marshall wrote for the Court that "courts which are created by written law, and whose jurisdiction is defined by written law, cannot transcend that jurisdiction." . . . It remains rudimentary law that "[a]s regards all courts of the United States inferior to this tribunal, two things are necessary to create jurisdiction, whether original or appellate. The Constitution must have given to the court the capacity to take it, and an act of Congress must have supplied it. . . . To the extent that such action is not taken, the power lies dormant."

Despite this principle, in a line of cases by now no less well established we have held, without specific examination of jurisdictional statutes, that federal courts have "pendent" claim jurisdiction—that is, jurisdiction over nonfederal claims between parties litigating other matters properly before the court—to the full extent permitted by the Constitution. *Mine Workers v. Gibbs*, which has come to stand for the principle in question, held that "[p]endent jurisdiction, in the sense of judicial power, exists whenever there is a claim 'arising under [the] Constitution, the Laws of the United States, and Treaties made, or which shall be made, under their Authority . . . ,' U.S. Const., Art. III, §2, and the relationship between that claim and the state claim permits the conclusion that the entire action before the court comprises but one constitutional 'case.'" The requisite relationship exists, *Gibbs* said, when the federal and nonfederal claims "derive from a common nucleus of operative fact" and are such that a plaintiff "would ordinarily be expected to try them in one judicial proceeding." Petitioner contends that the same criterion applies here, leading to the result that her state-law claims against San Diego Gas and Electric Company and the city of San Diego may be heard in conjunction with her FTCA action against the United States.

Analytically, petitioner's case is fundamentally different from *Gibbs* in that it brings into question what has become known as pendent-party jurisdiction, that is, jurisdiction over parties not named in any claim that is independently cognizable by the federal court. We may assume, without deciding, that the constitutional criterion for pendent-party jurisdiction is analogous to the constitutional criterion for pendent-claim jurisdiction, and that petitioner's state-law claims pass that test. Our cases show, however, that with respect to the addition of parties, as opposed to the addition of only claims, we will not assume that the full constitutional power has been congressionally authorized, and will not read jurisdictional statutes broadly. In *Zahn v. International Paper Co.*, 414 U.S. 291 (1973), we refused to allow a plaintiff pursuing a diversity action worth less than the jurisdictional minimum of $10,000 to append his claim to the jurisdictionally adequate diversity claims of other members of a plaintiff class—even though all of the claims would together have amounted to a single "case" under *Gibbs*, see *Owen Equipment & Erection Co. v. Kroger*, 437 U.S. 365 (1978). We based this holding upon "the statutes defining the jurisdiction of the District Court," and did not so much as mention *Gibbs*.

Two years later, the nontransferability of *Gibbs* to pendent-party claims was made explicit. In *Aldinger v. Howard*, 427 U.S. 1 (1976), the plaintiff brought federal claims under 42 U.S.C. §1983 against individual defendants, and sought to append to them a related state claim against Spokane County, Washington. (A federal §1983 claim was unavailable against the county because of this Court's decision in *Monroe v. Pape*, 365 U.S. 167 (1961).)[3] We specifically disapproved application of the *Gibbs* mode of analysis, finding a "significant legal difference." "[T]he addition of a completely new party," we said, "would run counter to the well-established principle that federal courts . . . are courts of limited jurisdiction marked out by Congress." "Resolution of a claim of pendent-party jurisdiction . . . calls for careful attention to the relevant statutory language." We held in *Aldinger* that the jurisdictional statute under which suit was brought, 28 U.S.C. §1343, which conferred district court jurisdiction over civil actions of certain types "authorized by law to be commenced," did not mean to include as "authorized by law" a state-law claim against a party that had been statutorily insulated from similar federal suit. The county had been "excluded from liability in §1983, and therefore by reference in the grant of jurisdiction under §1343(3)."

We reaffirmed and further refined our approach to pendent-party jurisdiction in *Owen Equipment & Erection Co. v. Kroger, supra*—a case, like *Zahn*, involving the diversity statute, 28 U.S.C. §1332(a)(1), but focusing on the requirement that the suit be "between . . . citizens of different states," rather than the requirement that it "excee[d] the sum or value of $10,000." We held that the jurisdiction which §1332(a)(1) confers over a "matter in controversy" between a plaintiff and defendant of diverse citizenship cannot be read to confer pendent jurisdiction over a different, nondiverse defendant, even if the claim involving that other defendant meets the *Gibbs* test. "*Gibbs*," we said, "does not end the inquiry into whether a federal court has power to hear the nonfederal claims along with the federal ones. Beyond this constitutional minimum, there must be an examination of the posture in which the nonfederal claim is

---

3. *Monroe v. Pape* was later overruled by *Monell v. New York City Dept. of Social Services*, 436 U.S. 658 (1978).

asserted and of the specific statute that confers jurisdiction over the federal claim."

The most significant element of "posture" or of "context" in the present case (as in *Zahn, Aldinger,* and *Kroger*) is precisely that the added claims involve added parties over whom no independent basis of jurisdiction exists. While in a narrow class of cases a federal court may assert authority over such a claim "ancillary" to jurisdiction otherwise properly vested . . . we have never reached such a result solely on the basis that the *Gibbs* test has been met. And little more basis than that can be relied upon by petitioner here. As in *Kroger,* the relationship between petitioner's added claims and the original complaint is one of "mere factual similarity," which is of no consequence since "neither the convenience of the litigants nor considerations of judicial economy can suffice to justify extension of the doctrine of ancillary jurisdiction." It is true that here, unlike in *Kroger,* the party seeking to bring the added claims had little choice but to be in federal rather than state court, since the FTCA permits the Federal Government to be sued only there. But that alone is not enough. . . .

The second factor invoked by *Kroger,* the text of the jurisdictional statute at issue, likewise fails to establish petitioner's case. The FTCA, §1346(b), confers jurisdiction over "civil actions on claims against the United States." It does not say "civil actions on claims that include requested relief against the United States," nor "civil actions in which there is a claim against the United States"—formulations one might expect if the presence of a claim against the United States constituted merely a minimum jurisdictional requirement, rather than a definition of the permissible scope of FTCA actions. Just as the statutory provision "between . . . citizens of different States" has been held to mean citizens of different states and no one else, so also here we conclude that "against the United States" means against the United States and no one else. "Due regard for the rightful independence of state governments . . . requires that [federal courts] scrupulously confine their own jurisdiction to the precise limits which the statute has defined." The statute here defines jurisdiction in a manner that does not reach defendants other than the United States. . . .

Because the FTCA permits the Government to be sued only in federal court, our holding that parties to related claims cannot necessarily be sued there means that the efficiency and convenience of a consolidated action will sometimes have to be forgone in favor of separate actions in state and federal courts. . . . [T]he present statute permits no other result. . . .

For the foregoing reasons, the judgment of the Court of Appeals is Affirmed.

Justice BLACKMUN, dissenting:

. . . Where, as here, Congress' preference for a federal forum for a certain category of claims makes the federal forum the only possible one in which the constitutional case may be heard as a whole, the sensible result is to permit the exercise of pendent-party jurisdiction. . . . I therefore dissent.

Justice STEVENS, with whom Justice BRENNAN and Justice MARSHALL join, dissenting:

The Court's holding is not faithful to our precedents and casually dismisses the accumulated wisdom of our best judges. As we observed more than 16 years ago, "numerous decisions throughout the courts of appeals since [*Mine Workers v. Gibbs*, 383 U.S. 715 (1966),] have recognized the existence of judicial power to hear pendent claims involving pendent parties where 'the entire action before the court comprises but one constitutional case' as defined in *Gibbs*." I shall first explain why the position taken by the overwhelming consensus of federal judges is correct and then comment on major flaws in the opinion the Court announces today. . . .

Immediately after *Gibbs* was decided, federal judges throughout the Nation recognized that its reasoning applied to cases in which it was necessary to add an additional party on a pendent, nonfederal claim in order to grant complete relief. . . .

I would thus hold that the grant of jurisdiction to hear "civil actions on claims against the United States" authorizes the federal courts to hear state-law claims against a pendent party. [T]he fact that such claims are within the exclusive federal jurisdiction, together with the absence of any evidence of congressional disapproval of the exercise of pendent-party jurisdiction in FTCA cases, provides a fully sufficient justification for applying the holding in *Gibbs* to this case. . . .

The doctrine of pendent jurisdiction rests in part on a recognition that forcing a federal plaintiff to litigate his or her case in both federal and state courts impairs the ability of the federal court to grant full relief, and "imparts a fundamental bias against utilization of the federal forum owing to the deterrent effect imposed by the needless requirement of duplicate litigation if the federal forum is chosen." "The courts, by recognizing pendent jurisdiction, are effectuating Congress' decision to provide the plaintiff with a federal forum for litigating a jurisdictionally sufficient claim." This is especially the case when, by virtue of the grant of exclusive federal jurisdiction, "only in a federal court may all of the claims be tried together." In such circumstances, in which Congress has unequivocally indicated its intent that the federal right be litigated in a federal forum, there is reason to believe that Congress did not intend that the substance of the federal right be diminished by the increased costs in efficiency and convenience of litigation in two forums. No such special federal interest is present when federal jurisdiction is invoked on the basis of the diverse citizenship of the parties and the state-law claims may be litigated in a state forum. *See Owen Equipment & Erection Co. v. Kroger*, 437 U.S., at 376. . . .

I respectfully dissent.

Note on *Finley* and 28 U.S.C. §1367

In response to *Finley,* Congress passed a new "Supplemental Jurisdiction" statute, 28 U.S.C. §1367.

§1367. Supplemental jurisdiction

(a) Except as provided in subsections (b) and (c) or as expressly provided otherwise by Federal statute, in any civil action of which the district courts have original jurisdiction, the district courts shall have supplemental jurisdiction over all other claims that are so related to claims in the action within such original jurisdiction that they form part of the same case or controversy under Article III of the United States Constitution. Such supplemental jurisdiction shall include claims that involve the joinder or intervention of additional parties.

(b) In any civil action of which the district courts have original jurisdiction founded solely on section 1332 of this title, the district courts shall not have supplemental jurisdiction under subsection (a) over claims by plaintiffs against persons made parties under Rule 14, 19, 20, or 24 of the Federal Rules of Civil Procedure, or over claims by persons proposed to be joined as plaintiffs under Rule 19 of such rules, or seeking to intervene as plaintiffs under Rule 24 of such rules, when exercising supplemental jurisdiction over such claims would be inconsistent with the jurisdictional requirements of section 1332.

(c) The district courts may decline to exercise supplemental jurisdiction over a claim under subsection (a) if:

(1) the claim raises a novel or complex issue of State law,

(2) the claim substantially predominates over the claim or claims over which the district court has original jurisdiction,

(3) the district court has dismissed all claims over which it has original jurisdiction, or

(4) in exceptional circumstances, there are other compelling reasons for declining jurisdiction.

(d) The period of limitations for any claim asserted under subsection (a), and for any other claim in the same action that is voluntarily dismissed at the same time as or after the dismissal of the claim under subsection (a), shall be tolled while the claim is pending and for a period of 30 days after it is dismissed unless State law provides for a longer tolling period.

(e) As used in this section, the term "State" includes the District of Columbia, the Commonwealth of Puerto Rico, and any territory or possession of the United States.

The following are excerpts from the legislative history of §1367.

■ HOUSE REPORT NO. 101-734
1990 U.S. Code Congressional and Admin. News 6873

. . . The doctrines of pendent and ancillary jurisdiction, in this section jointly labeled supplemental jurisdiction, refer to the authority of the federal courts to adjudicate, without an independent basis of subject matter jurisdiction, claims that are so related to other claims within the district courts' original jurisdiction that they form part of the same cases or controversy under Article III of the United States Constitution.

Supplemental jurisdiction has enabled federal courts and litigants to take advantage of the federal procedural rules on claim and party joinder to deal economically in single rather than multiple litigation with related matters, usually those arising from the same transaction, occurrence, or series of transactions or occurrences. Moreover, the district court's exercise of supplemental jurisdiction, by making federal court a practical arena for the resolution of an entire controversy, has effectuated Congress' intent in the jurisdictional statutes to provide plaintiffs with a federal forum for litigating claims within original federal jurisdiction.

Recently, however, in *Finley v. United States*, the Supreme Court cast substantial doubt on the authority of the federal courts to hear some claims within supplemental jurisdiction. In *Finley* the Court held that a district court, in a Federal Tort Claims Act suit against the United States, may not exercise supplemental jurisdiction over a related claim by the plaintiff against an additional, nondiverse defendant. The Court's rationale that "with respect to the addition of parties, as opposed to the addition of only claims, we will not assume that the full constitutional power has been congressionally authorized, and will not read jurisdictional statutes broadly," threatens to eliminate other previously accepted forms of supplemental jurisdiction. Already, for example, some lower courts have interpreted *Finley* to prohibit the exercise of supplemental jurisdiction in formerly unquestioned circumstances.

Legislation, therefore, is needed to provide the federal courts with statutory authority to hear supplemental claims. Indeed, the Supreme Court has virtually invited Congress to codify supplemental jurisdiction by commenting in *Finley*, "Whatever we say regarding the scope of jurisdiction . . . can of course be changed by Congress. What is of paramount importance is that Congress be able to legislate against a background of clear interpretive rules, so that it may know the effect of the language it adopts." This section would authorize jurisdiction in a case like *Finley*, as well as essentially restore the pre-*Finley* understandings of the authorization for and limits on other forms of supplemental jurisdiction. In federal-question cases, it broadly authorizes the district courts to exercise supplemental jurisdiction over additional claims, including claims involving the joinder of additional parties. In diversity cases, the district courts may exercise supplemental jurisdiction, except when doing so would be inconsistent with the jurisdictional requirements of the diversity statute. In both cases, the district courts, as under current law, would have discretion to decline supplemental jurisdiction in appropriate circumstances.

[§1367(a)] generally authorizes the district court to exercise jurisdiction over a supplemental claim whenever it forms part of the same constitutional case or controversy as the claim or claims that provide the basis of the district court's original jurisdiction. In providing for supplemental jurisdiction over claims involving the addition of parties, subsection (a) explicitly fills the statutory gap noted in *Finley v. United States*.

[§1367 (b)] prohibits a district court in a case over which it has jurisdiction founded solely on the general diversity provision, 28 U.S.C. §1332, from exercising supplemental jurisdiction in specified circumstances. In diversity-only actions the district courts may not hear plaintiffs' supplemental claims when exercising supplemental jurisdiction would encourage plaintiffs to evade the jurisdictional requirement of 28 U.S.C. §1332 by the simple expedient of naming initially only those defendants whose joinder satisfies §1332's requirements and later adding claims not within original federal jurisdiction against other defendants who have intervened or been joined on a supplemental basis. In accord with case law, the subsection also prohibits the joinder or intervention of persons and plaintiffs if adding them is inconsistent with §1332's requirements. . . .

[§1367(c)] codifies the factors that the Supreme Court has recognized as providing legitimate bases upon which a district court may decline jurisdiction over a supplemental claim, even though it is empowered to hear the claim. Subsection (c)(1)-(3) codifies the factors recognized as relevant under current law. Subsection (c)(4) acknowledges that occasionally there may exist other compelling reasons for a district court to decline supplemental jurisdiction, which the subsection does not foreclose a court from considering in exceptional circumstances. As under current law, subsection (c) requires the district court, in exercising its discretion, to undertake a case-specific analysis. . . .

[§1367(d)] provides a period of tolling of statutes of limitations for any supplemental claim that is dismissed under this section and for any other claims in the same action voluntarily dismissed at the same time or after the supplemental claim is dismissed. The purpose is to prevent the loss of claims to statutes of limitations where state law might fail to toll the running of the period of limitations while a supplemental claim was pending in federal court. It also eliminates a possible disincentive from such a gap in tolling when a plaintiff might wish to seek voluntary dismissal of other claims in order to pursue an entire matter in state court when a federal court dismisses a supplemental claim.

Comments and Questions

1. House Report No. 101-734 notes that "subsection (a) codifies the scope of supplemental jurisdiction first articulated by the Supreme Court

in *United Mine Workers v. Gibbs*, 383 U.S. 715 (1966)" and the "net effect of subsection (b) is to implement the principal rationale of *Owen Equipment & Erection Co. v. Kroger*, 437 U.S. 365 (1978)." Can you identify the language that accomplishes these results? What language overturns *Finley*? How would you improve the drafting of §1367 to achieve its stated purposes more clearly?

2. David D. Siegel, in his Commentary on the 1988 Revision, observes that since pendent and ancillary jurisdiction "have been brought under the single caption of 'supplemental jurisdiction,' there is probably no need to draw a line between them at all." But are there not some lingering differences in treatment between §1367(a) and (b)?

3. The language in §1367 referring to claims so related that "they form part of the same case or controversy under Article III" codifies the *Gibbs* concept of federal and non-federal claims deriving from "a common nucleus of operative fact." Does House Report 101-734 help us understand how broad this concept is? Consider the following example offered by Professor Martin Redish:

> [A]ssume a traffic accident, followed by a fist fight between the drivers. Driver A sues driver B for negligence in causing the accident; driver B counterclaims for battery arising out of the postaccident fight. On a purely linguistic or conceptual level, these two incidents could be characterized as either being part of the same occurrence or not. Courts that define the phrase in terms of evidentiary overlap would probably decline to find these incidents to be part of the same occurrence, because there likely will be little, if any, evidentiary overlap. Yet courts that define the phrase in terms of the broader concept of "logical relationship would quite probably find that the incidents are, in fact, part of the same occurrence."

Martin Redish, *Reassessing the Allocation of Judicial Business Between State and Federal Courts: Federal Jurisdiction and the "Martian Chronicles,"* 78 Va. L. Rev. 1769, 1822-1823 (1992). Given the policy underlying §1367, which approach makes most sense? The issue of defining "same claim" or "same transaction" is of course familiar to us from our look at joinder in Chapter 3 and will be encountered again with regard to the doctrine of finality, in Chapter 10.

Practice Exercise No. 30: Challenging Subject Matter Jurisdiction in *City of Cleveland*

Review the complaint in the *City of Cleveland* case. Assume that the plaintiffs' case survived all pretrial challenges and has gone to trial. At the close of the evidence, the case went to the jury, which is in the midst of deliberating. Counsel for the City has now appeared in court with a motion to dismiss the statutory civil service fraud count of the complaint for lack of subject matter jurisdiction.

The judge agrees to hear the motion immediately and asks to hear first from the moving party. Students with last names beginning with the letters A-M represent the defendant City, all others represent the plaintiffs in opposition.

Practice Exercise No. 31: Challenging Subject Matter Jurisdiction in *Carpenter*

Review the amended complaint and third-party complaints in the *Carpenter* case. Assume, however, that Nancy Carpenter has always resided in New Hampshire and that her action is filed in federal district court in Massachusetts. She sues Dee and Ultimate Auto, both Massachusetts citizens; Ultimate has impleaded McGill's Garage, also a Massachusetts corporation, and its owner, Dale McGill, a citizen of New Hampshire. Nancy does not amend her complaint to sue either the Garage or McGill. The latter two parties have now moved to dismiss for lack of subject matter jurisdiction or, in the alternative, to sever the impleader for purposes of trial under Fed. R. Civ. P. 42(b).

The judge is ready to hear the motion, and asks to hear first from the moving parties. Students with last names beginning with the letters N-Z represent McGill's Garage and Dale McGill; all others represent Ultimate Auto in opposition.

E. REMOVAL

As you recall, the federal and state courts overlap considerably in their jurisdictional authority. (*See* diagram in Section A of this chapter.) Plaintiffs have the initial choice of federal or state court in both federal question and diversity cases (assuming in the latter case the amount in controversy is met). If a plaintiff opts for the state court, however, the defendant in such a case may usually remove the matter to federal court under 28 U.S.C. §1441. (We say "usually" because the defendant's right to remove to federal court is not completely coextensive with the plaintiff's initial right to the federal forum. Read §1441, especially §1441(b), second sentence.) Why would Congress withhold the federal court option from a defendant sued in a diversity of citizenship case in his home state?

As you read the next case, consider the strategy considerations that would lead the plaintiffs to file in state court and the defendants to remove to federal court. What "mistakes" in lawyering can you identify? As a matter of policy, how much "forum shopping" between state and federal court should we allow?

■ BURNETT v. BIRMINGHAM
BOARD OF EDUCATION
861 F. Supp. 1036 (N.D. Ala. 1994)

ACKER, District Judge.

Following defendants' removal of the above-entitled case from the Circuit Court of Jefferson County pursuant to 23 U.S.C. §§1331 and 1343, upon the allegation that a federal question under 42 U.S.C. §1983 is presented, plaintiffs timely filed a motion to remand, invoking 28 U.S.C. §1441(c) and asserting that because state law predominates the entire "matter" should be remanded.

Plaintiffs, Emma Burnett, et al., are employees of defendant, Birmingham Board of Education. Plaintiffs' state court complaint consisted of a petition for writ of mandamus seeking to force defendant Board and its superintendent, defendant Dr. Cleveland Hammonds, to pay plaintiffs in accordance with the scale allegedly called for by their job classification. This was and is clearly a state-law claim. They added a claim under state law for breach of contract. Then, they threw in, as the proverbial "kitchen sink," a count claiming that they were in some undescribed way deprived of the due process guaranteed them by the Constitution of Alabama and by the Constitution of the United States, in the latter instance invoking 42 U.S.C. §1983 as the statutory vehicle for enforcement. The battle lines are drawn around whether or not 28 U.S.C. §1441(c) permits a remand on these procedural facts.

Plaintiffs' motion does not complain of the failure of the notice of removal to contain a copy of the summons served on the Board. The absence of a copy of this "process" was a clear procedural defect under 28 U.S.C. §1446(a) and one which would have been fatal if it had been raised by plaintiffs within the thirty-(30) day period allowed by 22 U.S.C. §1447(c). This defect has, however, been waived.

Plaintiffs understandably rely upon this very court's opinions in *Martin v. Drummond Coal Co., Inc.*, 756 F. Supp. 524 (N.D. Ala. 1991), and *Holland v. World Omni Leasing, Inc.*, 764 F. Supp. 1442 (N.D. Ala. 1991). *Martin* was the very first decision to apply 28 U.S.C. §1441(c) as amended by the Federal Courts Study Committee Implementation Act of 1990, to a federal question removal in which state law was claimed to predominate. *Holland,* which followed on the heals of *Martin,* simply elaborated on *Martin.* Defendants spend their time and energy attempting to explain why their case is different from *Martin* and *Holland.* Defendants have neither asked this court to revisit *Martin* and *Holland* in the light of subsequent cases, nor to find that in this case state law does not predominate. Instead, defendants have simply tried to convince this court that §1441(c) cannot apply, and that this court has no right to exercise the discretion which would be afforded if §1441(c) did apply. Defendants bet entirely on the one distinction between the instant case and *Martin* and *Holland* created by the fact that in both of those cases the only statutory peg for removal was §1331, whereas this removal was based both on §1331 and on §1343(a)(3) and (4). To refresh recollection, §1441(c) provides:

> Whenever a separate and independent claim or cause of action within the jurisdiction conferred by section 1331 of this title is joined with one or more otherwise non-removable claims or causes of action, the entire case may be removed and the district court may determine all issues therein, or, in its discretion, may remand all matters in which State law predominates.

Also, to refresh recollection, §1331 provides: "The district courts shall have original jurisdiction of all civil actions arising under the Constitution, laws, or treaties of the United States." Emphasized by defendants to the exclusion of everything else is the fact that in their notice of removal they not only invoked §1331 but also §1343(a)(3) and (4), which provides:

> The district courts shall have original jurisdiction of any civil action authorized by law to be commenced by any person: . . .
>
> (3) To redress the deprivation, under color of any State's law, statute, ordinance, regulation, custom or usage, of any right, privilege or immunity secured by the Constitution of the United States or by any Act of Congress providing for equal rights of citizens or of all persons within the jurisdiction of the United States.
>
> (4) To recover damages or to secure equitable or other relief under any Act of Congress providing for the protection of civil rights, including the right to vote.

The core of defendants' argument is that §1441(c) is only available if the removal was based solely upon §1331, and therefore that §1441(c) is not available here because this removal was based on another jurisdictional statute, namely, §1343, as well as upon §1331. The court has an answer to defendants' contention. The first, last and best answer is that defendants did, in fact, invoke §1331, and properly so, bringing themselves clearly within the ambit of §1441(c). Using the language of §1441(c), "jurisdiction [was] conferred [on this court] by section 1331." Plaintiffs' invocation of the Fourteenth Amendment and §1983 contained the essential elements for stating a civil cause of action arising under the Constitution and the laws of the United States. This is true even if original jurisdiction was redundantly conferred on this court by §1343(a)(3) and/or (4). Employing the routinely accepted proposition that removal statutes are always to be construed against removal, the language of §1441(c) cannot be interpreted to recognize an exception for all state cases which simply contain a claim invoking 42 U.S.C. §1983 as to which state courts have concurrent jurisdiction. Original federal court access may be available under §1343 (a)(3) and/or (4), when §1983 is relied upon by the plaintiff, but access to a federal court is just as available under §1331, as proven by defendants' reliance upon both. Defendants have not presented any authority standing for the intriguing proposition upon which they here depend. The nearest case on point is *Administaff, Inc. v. Kaster,* 799 F. Supp. 685 (W.D. Tex. 1992), in which the district court was considering a case that had been removed, as was the instant case, both under 28 U.S.C. §§1331 and 1343. Because the *Administaff* court expressed no opinion on the dual reliance on §§1331 and 1343, perhaps because the case was remanded not under §1441(c) but on the general principle "that remand is proper when state law claims predominate in actions involving pendent jurisdiction," there is no real lesson for this court in *Administaff.* Fortunately, this court is not being called upon to rule upon a motion to remand a case removed under §1441(a) but invoking only §1343(a) for the existence of original federal jurisdiction. It would be an interesting dictum to speak to such a hypothetical situation, but this court resists the temptation to express its thoughts on a non-issue. . . .

The clear trend among the few jurisdictions that have considered this question . . . is that the amended remand clause of §1441(c) now allows for a remand of the entire case, federal claim included, where "state law predominates." . . .

After oral argument defendants did finally get around in a letter memo to arguing that §1441(c) "was not intended to have any application to federal question claims to which pendent state law claims have been attached, and which are properly removed under 28 U.S.C. §1441(a) and (b)," or, in other words, that §1441(c) "addresses only the removal of 'completely unrelated' state law claims that are not within the pendent jurisdiction of the court." . . . The instant case is more like a federal claim tacked onto a state claim than vice versa. This court does not find a nucleus of operative fact common to the state and federal claims in the instant case. The state law claims are not pendent to the federal claim but are dominant. . . .

A separate order granting plaintiffs' motion to remand will be entered.

Comments and Questions

1. Removal is yet another civil procedure issue that lies at the inter-section of federal and state power. When a case between diverse parties, or one raising a federal claim, is removed from state to federal court, the federal court clearly has constitutional authority to hear the case, which could have originally been brought there by the plaintiff. A federal claim case that also includes related state law claims may, as we have seen, be entertained by a federal court under its supplemental jurisdiction, and may therefore be heard upon removal from state court. But where is the constitutional authority for the provision of §1441(c) authorizing the federal court to "determine all issues therein," including "otherwise

non-removable claims" [presumably outside the scope of supplemental jurisdiction]? Some commentators have questioned the constitutionality of that provision. *See generally* Joan Steinman, *Supplemental Jurisdiction in §1441 Removed Cases: An Unsurveyed Frontier of Congress' Handiwork*, 35 Ariz. L. Rev. 305 (1993), and Edward Hartnett, *A New Trick from an Old and Abused Dog: §1441(c) Lives and Now Permits the Remand of Federal Question Cases*, 63 Fordham L. Rev. 1099 (1995). On the other side of the coin, why should federal judges be given the authority to remand to state court "all matters in which State law predominates" when a case is properly removed under §1441(a), and thus could have originally been filed in federal court?

2. On a more practical level, if the presence of a nonremovable claim completely defeats removal, then a plaintiff could easily block the defendant's access to the federal forum by simply joining such a claim (under the generally liberal state rules of joinder). Section 1441(c) is designed in part to protect a defendant's access to federal court by at least giving the federal court discretion to "determine all issues therein."

3. Both the amended §1441(c) and the new supplemental jurisdiction provision, §1367, were part of the same statute—the Judicial Improvements Act of 1990. How do you think Congress envisioned the two working together? Note the similarity in language between §1367(c)(2), permitting the federal court to decline supplemental jurisdiction when "the [state law] claim substantially predominates," and §1441(c), permitting remand in that same circumstance.

4. Doesn't §1441(a), in combination with §1367, *already* permit removal of all federal question cases in which supplemental jurisdiction claims are asserted? If so, what does §1441(c) add in that regard?

5. What lessons does *Burnett* teach plaintiff's counsel who want to keep their client's cases in state court?

F. REVIEW

Use the following final exam essay question to review the topics from Chapters 7 and 8.

Question One
(Suggested Time: 1½ hours)

You have been consulted by the Very-Clean Vacuum Company regarding the following matter.

On May 1st of this calendar year, Very-Clean was served with a summons and complaint at its headquarters in St. Louis, Missouri. The complaint reads as follows:

UNITED STATES DISTRICT COURT
FOR THE SOUTHERN DISTRICT OF NEW YORK

Jane Whitecroft and John Whitecroft, Plaintiffs,	Civil Action No._____
v.	COMPLAINT
Very-Clean Vacuum Company, Inc., Defendants.	

1. Plaintiffs are husband and wife and residents of the State of Connecticut. Defendant is incorporated in the State of Delaware and has its principal place of business in Missouri. The matter in controversy exceeds $75,000.

2. On April 15, 1999, plaintiffs purchased a Very-Clean Model 500S Vacuum at the Ace Discount Store in White Plains, New York.

3. Exactly 16 days after purchasing the Very-Clean Model 500S Vacuum, plaintiff John Whitecroft was vacuuming the living room in his house shared with plaintiff Jane Whitecroft. The machine suddenly emitted a large electrical spark and exploded in flames.

4. As a result, plaintiff John Whitecroft was severely burned, suffering permanent and disabling injuries. The plaintiffs' home was destroyed by fire and all their personal belongings lost in the blaze.

5. Plaintiffs allege, upon information and belief, that the fire resulted from the negligence of defendant Very-Clean Vacuum Company, Inc., in the manufacture of the Model 500S and the subsequent reckless failure to warn consumers who had purchased the machines of the danger.

WHEREFORE, plaintiffs pray that judgment be rendered against defendant in the amount of $6,000,000, with interest and costs, and for such other relief as may be appropriate.

/s/
Christine Webber
Attorney for Plaintiffs
1001 3rd Avenue
New York, New York 10022

Very-Clean's corporate counsel informs you that the Company is very nervous about this action, especially given the amount of damages sought. The Company has a great safety record, but he concedes there have been other reported problems with the Model 500S. Very-Clean has received letters from several other purchasers reporting electrical problems with the same model, although none has suffered the type of catastrophic injuries that the Whitecrofts allege. Several of these purchasers have also threatened suit.

Nonetheless, the Company stands behind its product. The people in engineering believe that the accidents with the Model 500S have likely resulted because the consumers have plugged the machines into two-pronged, ungrounded electrical sockets instead of the three-pronged grounded sockets recommended in the instructions.

The Company has always relied upon Second-Guess Testing Labs, located nearby in St. Louis, to assure the quality of its products. Very-Clean has retained them for years to put each of its prospective products through a series of grueling tests prior to placing the product on the market. Second-Guess tested the Model 500S and certified its safety and dependability to Very-Clean. If there is a defect in the product, Second-Guess failed to detect it.

The corporate counsel is quite surprised that the Company's products are being sold in New York, since Very-Clean now distributes only to retailers in the Midwest. (At one time about fifteen years ago, when the Company was just getting started, it did ship products to stores in New York, New Jersey, and Connecticut, but discontinued such sales because they proved unprofitable, given the high transportation costs.) It appears that one of the retail stores Very-Clean supplies in the Midwest went out of business and its inventory was acquired by the Ace Discount national chain, which explains how the Model 500S ended up on sale in an Ace store in White Plains, New York. Very-Clean does advertise regularly in several national magazines that are widely sold and read in New York, but does not ship its products directly anywhere in the eastern United States.

Very-Clean has learned that Jane Whitecroft has been enrolled for the past two years as a doctoral student at Washington University in St. Louis, Missouri. She subleases an apartment near the university, which she lives in while school is in session, but spends the rest of the year with her husband in Connecticut, where she is writing her dissertation.

Finally, corporate counsel informs you that after the accident the Whitecrofts engaged in a vicious publicity campaign against Very-Clean, appearing on talk shows and news programs and characterizing the Company as reckless with the public's safety. This has significantly hurt Very-Clean's reputation and business.

For your information, your associate has advised you that the New York state long-arm statute provides as follows:

§302. A court may exercise personal jurisdiction over a person who acts directly or by an agent as to a cause of action arising from the person's
   (a) transacting any business in the state;
   (b) contracting to supply services or things in the state;
   (c) causing tortious injury by an act or omission in this state;
   (d) causing tortious injury in this state by an act or omission outside this state if he regularly does or solicits business, or engages in any other

persistent course of conduct, or derives substantial revenue from good used or consumed or services rendered, in this state;

(e) having an interest in, using or possessing real property in this state.

1. Prepare a memorandum for the corporate counsel discussing how Very-Clean should respond to this complaint. Consider all possible procedural objections and defenses, including jurisdictional. For each, outline the manner in which it should be raised (such as pleading or motion), the specific Federal Rules of Civil Procedure to be invoked, and the likelihood of prevailing on the objection or defense in court. Include a list of any additional facts you may need to investigate to complete your analysis and explain how the information would be used. (45 minutes)

2. Prepare a memorandum for the corporate counsel discussing the joinder options open to defendant Very-Clean. What additional claims and/or parties should Very-Clean consider? For each, outline the manner in which it should be raised (such as pleading or motion) and the specific provisions of the Federal Rules Civil Procedure invoked. Include a discussion of the jurisdictional problems (if any) of each option. (30 minutes)

3. NOW ASSUME INSTEAD THAT YOU WERE CONSULTED BY JANE AND JOHN WHITECROFT BEFORE THEY FILED SUIT. You also were contacted by several other dissatisfied purchasers of the Model 500S, who want to assert their own claims against the Company. Most of the other dissatisfied purchasers suffered damages to their property as a result of electrical malfunctions; some suffered minor personal injuries. What is the possibility of joining all of these persons in one action? Discuss the joinder options, noting the specific provisions of the Federal Rules of Civil Procedure invoked. Briefly identify any jurisdictional problems that would concern you. (15 minutes).

Permissive Joinder under Rule 20

9

Choice of Federal or State Law — The Erie v. Tompkins Problem

You learned in Chapter 8 that a federal court has subject matter jurisdiction of a civil action if: (1) the action raises a "federal question," 28 U.S.C. §1331; or (2) the court has diversity jurisdiction under 28 U.S.C. §1332. In the former instance, courts apply the *federal* substantive law that is implicated by the federal question. For example, in an action filed under the Civil Rights Act of 1968 (42 U.S.C. §§3601 *et seq.*) alleging discrimination in the rental of housing units, the court will apply the federal statute and the federal decisional law interpreting it.

In diversity cases, however, there is no obvious answer to the question of which law applies in federal court. If for example a personal injury tort action between citizens of different states is being heard in U.S. District Court, will the court apply federal or state negligence law? And, if it is state negligence law that should be applied, should the court apply the laws of the state of residence of Citizen #1? Of Citizen #2? Of the location of the court?

Choice of law issues arise because although a court has jurisdictional power over a case, it does not necessarily also have the authority to apply its own law to resolve the matter. A California state court may have jurisdiction over a tort case based solely on proper service of process on the defendant while present in that state. If neither party is a California resident and the accident occurred elsewhere, would it be fair and just for the California law of negligence to apply? What if the plaintiff "shopped" for the California forum because its negligence law is more favorable to plaintiffs?

837

The choice of law problem has two dimensions. The "vertical" choice of law issue is the choice between federal and state law. The "horizontal" choice of law issue arises when state law is held to apply and the question is *which* state's law? This latter question is taken up in a course on conflict of laws and will not be treated at length here. Our focus will be on the vertical choice of law issues, which implicate fundamental questions about the operation of our parallel court systems and the concept of federalism.

Consider the following case: Harry Tompkins, a resident and citizen of Pennsylvania, was walking along railroad tracks owned by the Erie Railroad in Pennsylvania when he was struck by an open door of a passing freight train and was severely injured. The Erie Railroad was a New York corporation and, thus, Tompkins could have sued in the state courts of either Pennsylvania or New York. The conflict of laws doctrine in both states pointed toward the state in which the accident occurred, and, thus, suit in either state's court would have compelled the application of Pennsylvania law. However, the case law in Pennsylvania would treat Tompkins as a trespasser and therefore hold the Railroad to a lower duty of care (that is, merely to refrain from reckless or wanton conduct). If Tompkins could prove nothing more than that the Railroad had been negligent, he would not recover under Pennsylvania law. The diversity of citizenship between Tompkins and the Railroad, however, gave Tompkins's counsel the option to bring his case in federal court, and the opportunity to argue that Pennsylvania state law did not apply there. This issue was the focus of the following landmark opinion.

■ ERIE RAILROAD CO. v. TOMPKINS
304 U.S. 64 (1938)

Justice BRANDEIS delivered the opinion of the Court:

The question for decision is whether the oft-challenged doctrine of *Swift v. Tyson* shall now be disapproved.

Tompkins, a citizen of Pennsylvania, was injured on a dark night by a passing freight train of the Erie Railroad Company while walking along its right of way at Hughestown in that State. He claimed that the accident occurred through negligence in the operation, or maintenance, of the train; that he was rightfully on the premises as licensee because on a commonly used beaten footpath which ran for a short distance alongside the tracks; and that he was struck by something which looked like a door projecting from one of the moving cars. To enforce that claim he brought an action in the federal court for southern New York, which had jurisdiction because the company is a corporation of that State. It denied liability; and the case was tried by a jury.

The Erie insisted that its duty to Tompkins was no greater than that owed to a trespasser. It contended, among other things, that its duty to

Tompkins, and hence its liability, should be determined in accordance with the Pennsylvania law; that under the law of Pennsylvania, as declared by its highest court, persons who use pathways along the railroad right of way—that is a longitudinal pathway as distinguished from a crossing—are to be deemed trespassers; and that the railroad is not liable for injuries to undiscovered trespassers resulting from its negligence, unless it be wanton or wilful. Tompkins denied that any such rule had been established by the decisions of the Pennsylvania courts; and contended that, since there was no statute of the State on the subject, the railroad's duty and liability is to be determined in federal courts as a matter of general law.

The trial judge refused to rule that the applicable law precluded recovery. The jury brought in a verdict of $30,000; and the judgment entered thereon was affirmed by the Circuit Court of Appeals, which held that it was unnecessary to consider whether the law of Pennsylvania was as contended, because the question was one not of local, but of general, law and that "upon questions of general law the federal courts are free, in the absence of a local statute, to exercise their independent judgment as to what the law is; and it is well settled that the question of the responsibility of a railroad for injuries caused by its servants is one of general law. . . . Where the public has made open and notorious use of a railroad right of way for a long period of time and without objection, the company owes to persons on such permissive pathway a duty of care in the operation of its trains. . . . It is likewise generally recognized law that a jury may find that negligence exists toward a pedestrian using a permissive path on the railroad right of way if he is hit by some object projecting from the side of the train."

The Erie had contended that application of the Pennsylvania rule was required, among other things, by §34 of the Federal Judiciary Act of September 24, 1789, c. 20, 28 U. S. C. §725, which provides:

> The laws of the several States, except where the Constitution, treaties, or statutes of the United States otherwise require or provide, shall be regarded as rules of decision in trials at common law, in the courts of the United States, in cases where they apply.

Because of the importance of the question whether the federal court was free to disregard the alleged rule of the Pennsylvania common law, we granted certiorari.

First. *Swift v. Tyson*, 16 Pet. 1, 18, held that federal courts exercising jurisdiction on the ground of diversity of citizenship need not, in matters of general jurisprudence, apply the unwritten law of the State as declared by its highest court; that they are free to exercise an independent judgment as to what the common law of the State is—or should be; and that, as there stated by Mr. Justice Story:

> the true interpretation of the thirty-fourth section limited its application to state laws strictly local, that is to say, to the positive statutes of the state, and

the construction thereof adopted by the local tribunals, and to rights and titles to things having a permanent locality, such as the rights and titles to real estate, and other matters immovable and intraterritorial in their nature and character. It never has been supposed by us, that the section did apply, or was intended to apply, to questions of a more general nature, not at all dependent upon local statutes or local usages of a fixed and permanent operation, as, for example, to the construction of ordinary contracts or other written instruments, and especially to questions of general commercial law, where the state tribunals are called upon to perform the like functions as ourselves, that is, to ascertain upon general reasoning and legal analogies, what is the true exposition of the contract or instrument, or what is the just rule furnished by the principles of commercial law to govern the case.

The Court in applying the rule of §34 to equity cases, in *Mason v. United States*, 260 U.S. 545, 559, said: "The statute, however, is merely declarative of the rule which would exist in the absence of the statute." The federal courts assumed, in the broad field of "general law," the power to declare rules of decision which Congress was confessedly without power to enact as statutes. Doubt was repeatedly expressed as to the correctness of the construction given §34, and as to the soundness of the rule which it introduced. But it was the more recent research of a competent scholar, who examined the original document, which established that the construction given to it by the Court was erroneous; and that the purpose of the section was merely to make certain that, in all matters except those in which some federal law is controlling, the federal courts exercising jurisdiction in diversity of citizenship cases would apply as their rules of decision the law of the State, unwritten as well as written.[5]

Criticism of the doctrine became widespread after the decision of *Black & White Taxicab Co. v. Brown & Yellow Taxicab Co.*, 276 U.S. 518. There, Brown and Yellow, a Kentucky corporation owned by Kentuckians, and the Louisville and Nashville Railroad, also a Kentucky corporation, wished that the former should have the exclusive privilege of soliciting passenger and baggage transportation at the Bowling Green, Kentucky, railroad station; and that the Black and White, a competing Kentucky corporation, should be prevented from interfering with that privilege. Knowing that such a contract would be void under the common law of Kentucky, it was arranged that the Brown and Yellow reincorporate under the law of Tennessee, and that the contract with the railroad should be executed there. The suit was then brought by the Tennessee corporation in the federal court for western Kentucky to enjoin competition by the Black and White; an injunction issued by the District Court was sustained by the Court of Appeals; and this Court, citing many decisions in which the doctrine of *Swift v. Tyson* had been applied, affirmed the decree.

5. Charles Warren, *New Light on the History of the Federal Judiciary Act of 1789*, 37 Harv. L. Rev. 49, 51-52, 81-88, 108 (1923).

Second. Experience in applying the doctrine of *Swift v. Tyson* had revealed its defects, political and social; and the benefits expected to flow from the rule did not accrue. Persistence of state courts in their own opinions on questions of common law prevented uniformity; and the impossibility of discovering a satisfactory line of demarcation between the province of general law and that of local law developed a new well of uncertainties.

On the other hand, the mischievous results of the doctrine had become apparent. Diversity of citizenship jurisdiction was conferred in order to prevent apprehended discrimination in state courts against those not citizens of the State. *Swift v. Tyson* introduced grave discrimination by non-citizens against citizens. It made rights enjoyed under the unwritten "general law" vary according to whether enforcement was sought in the state or in the federal court; and the privilege of selecting the court in which the right should be determined was conferred upon the non-citizen. Thus, the doctrine rendered impossible equal protection of the law. In attempting to promote uniformity of law throughout the United States, the doctrine had prevented uniformity in the administration of the law of the State.

The discrimination resulting became in practice far-reaching. This resulted in part from the broad province accorded to the so-called "general law" as to which federal courts exercised an independent judgment. In addition to questions of purely commercial law, "general law" was held to include the obligations under contracts entered into and to be performed within the State, the extent to which a carrier operating within a State may stipulate for exemption from liability for his own negligence or that of his employee; the liability for torts committed within the State upon persons resident or property located there, even where the question of liability depended upon the scope of a property right conferred by the State; and the right to exemplary or punitive damages. Furthermore, state decisions construing local deeds, mineral conveyances, and even devises of real estate were disregarded.

In part the discrimination resulted from the wide range of persons held entitled to avail themselves of the federal rule by resort to the diversity of citizenship jurisdiction. Through this jurisdiction individual citizens willing to remove from their own State and become citizens of another might avail themselves of the federal rule. And, without even change of residence, a corporate citizen of the State could avail itself of the federal rule by re-incorporating under the laws of another State, as was done in the Taxicab case.

The injustice and confusion incident to the doctrine of *Swift v. Tyson* have been repeatedly urged as reasons for abolishing or limiting diversity of citizenship jurisdiction. Other legislative relief has been proposed. If only a question of statutory construction were involved, we should not be prepared to abandon a doctrine so widely applied throughout nearly a century. But the unconstitutionality of the course pursued has now been made clear and compels us to do so.

Third. Except in matters governed by the Federal Constitution or by Acts of Congress, the law to be applied in any case is the law of the State. And whether the law of the State shall be declared by its Legislature in a statute or by its highest court in a decision is not a matter of federal concern. There is no federal general common law. Congress has no power to declare substantive rules of common law applicable in a State whether they be local in their nature or "general," be they commercial law or a part of the law of torts. And no clause in the Constitution purports to confer such a power upon the federal courts. As stated by Mr. Justice Field when protesting in *Baltimore & Ohio R. Co. v. Baugh,* 149 U.S. 368, 401, against ignoring the Ohio common law of fellow servant liability:

> I am aware that what has been termed the general law of the country— which is often little less than what the judge advancing the doctrine thinks at the time should be the general law on a particular subject—has been often advanced in judicial opinions of this court to control a conflicting law of a State. I admit that learned judges have fallen into the habit of repeating this doctrine as a convenient mode of brushing aside the law of a State in conflict with their views. And I confess that, moved and governed by the authority of the great names of those judges, I have, myself, in many instances, unhesitatingly and confidently, but I think now erroneously, repeated the same doctrine. But, notwithstanding the great names which may be cited in favor of the doctrine, and notwithstanding the frequency with which the doctrine has been reiterated, there stands, as a perpetual protest against its repetition, the Constitution of the United States, which recognizes and preserves the autonomy and independence of the States—independence in their legislative and independence in their judicial departments. Supervision over either the legislative or the judicial action of the States is in no case permissible except as to matters by the Constitution specifically authorized or delegated to the United States. Any interference with either, except as thus permitted, is an invasion of the authority of the State and, to that extent, a denial of its independence.

The fallacy underlying the rule declared in *Swift v. Tyson* is made clear by Mr. Justice Holmes. The doctrine rests upon the assumption that there is "a transcendental body of law outside of any particular State but obligatory within it unless and until changed by statute," that federal courts have the power to use their judgment as to what the rules of common law are; and that in the federal courts "the parties are entitled to an independent judgment on matters of general law":

> [B]ut law in the sense in which courts speak of it today does not exist without some definite authority behind it. The common law so far as it is enforced in a State, whether called common law or not, is not the common law generally but the law of that State existing by the authority of that State without regard to what it may have been in England or anywhere else. . . . [T]he authority and only authority is the State, and if that be so, the voice

adopted by the State as its own [whether it be of its Legislature or of its Supreme Court] should utter the last word.

Thus the doctrine of *Swift v. Tyson* is, as Mr. Justice Holmes said, "an unconstitutional assumption of powers by courts of the United States which no lapse of time or respectable array of opinion should make us hesitate to correct." In disapproving that doctrine we do not hold unconstitutional §34 of the Federal Judiciary Act of 1789 or any other Act of Congress. We merely declare that in applying the doctrine this Court and the lower courts have invaded rights which in our opinion are reserved by the Constitution to the several States.

Fourth. The defendant contended that by the common law of Pennsylvania as declared by its highest court in *Falchetti v. Pennsylvania R. Co.*, 307 Pa. 203, the only duty owed to the plaintiff was to refrain from wilful or wanton injury. The plaintiff denied that such is the Pennsylvania law. In support of their respective contentions the parties discussed and cited many decisions of the Supreme Court of the State. The Circuit Court of Appeals ruled that the question of liability is one of general law; and on that ground declined to decide the issue of state law. As we hold this was error, the judgment is reversed and the case remanded to it for further proceedings in conformity with our opinion. Reversed.

Justice CARDOZO took no part in the consideration or decision of this case.

Justice REED, concurring:

I concur in the conclusion reached in this case, in the disapproval of the doctrine of *Swift v. Tyson*, and in the reasoning of the majority opinion except in so far as it relies upon the unconstitutionality of the "course pursued" by the federal courts.

The "doctrine of *Swift v. Tyson*," as I understand it, is that the words "the laws," as used in §34, line one, of the Federal Judiciary Act of September 24, 1789, do not include in their meaning "the decisions of the local tribunals." Mr. Justice Story, in deciding that point, said:

> Undoubtedly, the decisions of the local tribunals upon such subjects are entitled to, and will receive, the most deliberate attention and respect of this Court; but they cannot furnish positive rules, or conclusive authority, by which our own judgments are to be bound up and governed.

To decide the case now before us and to "disapprove" the doctrine of *Swift v. Tyson* requires only that we say that the words "the laws" include in their meaning the decisions of the local tribunals. As the majority opinion shows, by its reference to Mr. Warren's researches and the first quotation from Mr. Justice Holmes, that this Court is now of the view that "laws" includes "decisions," it is unnecessary to go further and declare that the "course pursued" was "unconstitutional," instead of merely erroneous.

The "unconstitutional" course referred to in the majority opinion is apparently the ruling in *Swift v. Tyson* that the supposed omission of Congress to legislate as to the effect of decisions leaves federal courts free to interpret general law for themselves. I am not at all sure whether, in the absence of federal statutory direction, federal courts would be compelled to follow state decisions. There was sufficient doubt about the matter in 1789 to induce the first Congress to legislate. No former opinions of this Court have passed upon it. Mr. Justice Holmes evidently saw nothing "unconstitutional" which required the overruling of *Swift v. Tyson*, for he said in the very opinion quoted by the majority, "I should leave *Swift v. Tyson* undisturbed, . . . but I would not allow it to spread the assumed dominion into new fields." *Black & White Taxicab Co. v. Brown & Yellow Taxicab Co.*, 276 U.S. 518, 535. If the opinion commits this Court to the position that the Congress is without power to declare what rules of substantive law shall govern the federal courts, that conclusion also seems questionable. The line between procedural and substantive law is hazy but no one doubts federal power over procedure. The Judiciary Article and the "necessary and proper" clause of Article One may fully authorize legislation, such as this section of the Judiciary Act.

In this Court, *stare decisis*, in statutory construction, is a useful rule, not an inexorable command. It seems preferable to overturn an established construction of an Act of Congress, rather than, in the circumstances of this case, to interpret the Constitution. There is no occasion to discuss further the range or soundness of these few phrases of the opinion. It is sufficient now to call attention to them and express my own non-acquiescence.

[In his dissenting opinion, Justice BUTLER, joined by Justice McREYNOLDS, argued for adherence to the long-standing *Swift v. Tyson* precedent.]

Comments and Questions

1. Justice Brandeis's critique of *Swift v. Tyson*, which had permitted the federal courts to apply "federal general common law" in cases like *Tompkins*, weaves several rhetorical threads. How would you identify and articulate the policy argument made against *Swift*? The statutory argument? The constitutional argument?

2. What are the "mischievous results" of *Swift* referred to by Brandeis? How are these illustrated by the *Black & White Taxicab* case discussed by the Court?

Imagine the following scenario: Tompkins was walking with a friend at the time of the tragic accident, and the friend suffers a similar grievous injury. Both men come to your law office seeking advice on how they should proceed to obtain compensation from the Erie Railroad. If the friend were a resident of New York state, how would you assess his chances of recovery compared to Tompkins's under the regime of *Swift v. Tyson?* How would you explain this anomaly to a layperson? Can you see why Brandeis wrote that *Swift* "rendered impossible equal protection of the law"?

3. How was Justice Story able in *Swift* to construe §34 of the Judiciary Act of 1789 in a manner that permitted the federal courts to ignore state "laws" when they came in the form of case law as opposed to statutory law? Is this consistent with the plain meaning of the language? If not, what motivated the *Swift* Court to stray so far from the ordinary meaning of "laws"?

4. What provision of the Constitution does Brandeis rely upon for the conclusion that *Swift* represented "an unconstitutional assumption of powers by the Courts of the United States?"

5. Why did Justice Reed write a separate opinion? Professor George D. Brown has observed: "*Erie*'s ambiguities are several and obvious. If the decision rests on statutory grounds, the constitutional portion may be unnecessary *dictum.* Even if it is constitutionally based, the Court confused the matter by failing to cite directly any provision of the Constitution and by placing some of the apparent constitutional analysis in the portion of the opinion that rests on other grounds. One can find in the opinion possible invocations of the doctrines of due process, equal protection, separation of powers, and federalism." George D. Brown, *The Ideologies of Forum Shopping—Why Doesn't a Conservative Court Protect Defendants?* 71 U.N.C. L. Rev. 649, 657 (1993).

6. Two distinctions made by Justice Reed in his concurrence play a significant role in the post-*Erie* era. First, he suggests that *Congress* may very well have the authority to declare substantive law that governs in federal diversity cases, even if a federal *judge* does not have this authority. Second, and more important from the perspective of the cases we take up next, Justice Reed distinguishes "substantive" from "procedural" law, observing that the line between the two may be "hazy," but "no one doubts federal power over procedure."

With regard to Justice Reed's comments about "federal power over procedure," it is important to note that the *Erie* decision and the adoption of the Federal Rules of Civil Procedure both occurred in 1938. Prior to the Federal Rules of Civil Procedure, federal district courts were required by the Conformity Act to follow the procedure of the state courts in the states in which they sat, thus depriving them of a uniform national body of procedure and creating what many federal court practitioners considered sheer chaos. In 1934, Congress set the federal rule-making process in motion with the Rules Enabling Act,* which authorized the Supreme Court to "prescribe by general rules, the forms of process, writs, pleadings, and motions, and the practice and procedure of the district courts and courts of

* The current version is at 28 U.S.C. §2072.

appeals in the United States in civil actions. . . ." The Act provided that "[s]uch rules shall not abridge, enlarge, or modify any substantive right. . . ." As Professor Mary Kay Kane has observed: "The year 1938 thus began a new era in the balance of power between state and federal courts—one that was to be controlled by the wavering (sometimes almost evanescent) line between substance and procedure." Mary Kay Kane, *The Golden Wedding Years: Erie Railroad Company v. Tompkins and the Federal Rules,* 63 Notre Dame L. Rev. 671, 673 (1988).

7. The challenging task after *Erie Railroad Co. v. Tompkins* was classifying issues as either procedural or substantive. As you read the following cases, compare your own intuition about what is "procedural" or "substantive" with the Court's reasoning and conclusions.

8. *Note on Horizontal Choice-of-Law.* The horizontal choice-of-law question in *Erie* was whether to apply Pennsylvania or New York state law. Under principles then prevailing, courts generally applied the law of the state in which the accident occurred. *See* William M. Richman & William L. Reynolds, *Understanding Conflict of Laws* 170-172 (2d ed. 1993). In 1971, adoption of the Second Restatement of Conflict of Laws heralded a more flexible approach, weighing a number of factors designed to identify the law of the state with "the most significant relationship" to the issue in question. *Id.* at 195-198. Nevertheless, each state has its own conflicts of law principles.

This leads to another horizontal choice of law question: when a federal court sits in diversity, which state's conflicts of law doctrine should the federal court apply to determine, in turn, which state's substantive law applies? In *Klaxon Co. v. Stentor Electric Mfg. Co.*, 313 U.S. 487 (1941), the Court ruled that federal courts should apply the conflict of laws rules applied by the courts of the state in which they sit. "Otherwise, the accident of diversity of citizenship would constantly disturb equal administration of justice in coordinate state and federal courts sitting side by side." 313 U.S. at 496. Thus, in the *Klaxon Co.* breach of contract action brought in federal district court in Delaware, the court was bound to apply the law of whatever state the Delaware courts would look to in such an action.

■ GUARANTY TRUST CO. v. YORK
326 U.S. 99 (1945)

Justice FRANKFURTER delivered the opinion of the Court:
. . . [Guaranty Trust Co., acting as trustee, agreed to a buy-out plan in which noteholders of the Van Sweringen Corporation received only 50% of the face value of their notes.] The suit, instituted as a class action on behalf of nonaccepting noteholders and brought in a federal court solely because of diversity of citizenship, is based on an alleged breach of trust by Guaranty in that it failed to protect the interests of the noteholders in assenting to the exchange offer and failed to disclose its self-interest

when sponsoring the offer. Petitioner moved for summary judgment, which was granted [on grounds the action was time-barred]. On appeal, the Circuit Court of Appeals, one Judge dissenting, . . . held that in a suit brought on the equity side of a federal district court that court is not required to apply the State statute of limitations that would govern like suits in the courts of a State where the federal court is sitting even though the exclusive basis of federal jurisdiction is diversity of citizenship. The importance of the question for the disposition of litigation in the federal courts led us to bring the case here. . . . Our only concern is with the holding that the federal courts in a suit like this are not bound by local law.

We put to one side the considerations relevant in disposing of questions that arise when a federal court is adjudicating a claim based on a federal law. Our problem only touches transactions for which rights and obligations are created by one of the States, and for the assertion of which, in case of diversity of the citizenship of the parties, Congress has made a federal court another available forum.

Our starting point must be the policy of federal jurisdiction which *Erie R. Co. v. Tompkins*, 304 U.S. 64, embodies. In overruling *Swift v. Tyson*, *Erie R. Co. v. Tompkins* did not merely overrule a venerable case. It overruled a particular way of looking at law which dominated the judicial process long after its inadequacies had been laid bare. Law was conceived as a "brooding omnipresence" of Reason, of which decisions were merely evidence and not themselves the controlling formulations. Accordingly, federal courts deemed themselves free to ascertain what Reason, and therefore Law, required wholly independent of authoritatively declared State law, even in cases where a legal right as the basis for relief was created by State authority and could not be created by federal authority and the case got into a federal court merely because it was "between Citizens of different States" under Art. III, §2 of the Constitution of the United States.

This impulse to freedom from the rules that controlled State courts regarding State-created rights was so strongly rooted in the prevailing views concerning the nature of law, that the federal courts almost imperceptibly were led to mutilating construction even of the explicit command given to them by Congress to apply State law in cases purporting to enforce the law of a State. *See* §34 of the Judiciary Act of 1789. The matter was fairly summarized by the statement that "During the period when *Swift v. Tyson* (1842-1938) ruled the decisions of the federal courts, its theory of their freedom in matters of general law from the authority of state courts pervaded opinions of this Court involving even state statutes or local law." . . . Since it was conceived that there was "a transcendental body of law outside of any particular State but obligatory within it unless and until changed by statute," State court decisions were not "the law" but merely someone's opinion—to be sure an opinion to be respected—concerning the content of this all-pervading law. Not unnaturally, the federal courts assumed power to find for themselves the content of such a body of law.

The notion was stimulated by the attractive vision of a uniform body of federal law. To such sentiments for uniformity of decision and freedom from diversity in State law the federal courts gave currency, particularly in cases where equitable remedies were sought, because equitable doctrines are so often cast in terms of universal applicability when close analysis of the source of legal enforceability is not demanded. . . .

And so this case reduces itself to the narrow question whether, when no recovery could be had in a State court because the action is barred by the statute of limitations, a federal court in equity can take cognizance of the suit because there is diversity of citizenship between the parties. Is the outlawry, according to State law, of a claim created by the States a matter of "substantive rights" to be respected by a federal court of equity when that court's jurisdiction is dependent on the fact that there is a State-created right, or is such statute of "a mere remedial character," which a federal court may disregard?

Matters of "substance" and matters of "procedure" are much talked about in the books as though they defined a great divide cutting across the whole domain of law. But, of course, "substance" and "procedure" are the same keywords to very different problems. Neither "substance" nor "procedure" represents the same invariants. Each implies different variables depending upon the particular problem for which it is used. And the different problems are only distantly related at best, for the terms are in common use in connection with situations turning on such different considerations as those that are relevant to questions pertaining to ex post facto legislation, the impairment of the obligations of contract, the enforcement of federal rights in the State courts and the multitudinous phases of the conflict of laws.

Here we are dealing with a right to recover derived not from the United States but from one of the States. When, because the plaintiff happens to be a non-resident, such a right is enforceable in a federal as well as in a State court, the forms and mode of enforcing the right may at times, naturally enough, vary because the two judicial systems are not identic. But since a federal court adjudicating a State-created right solely because of the diversity of citizenship of the parties is for that purpose, in effect, only another court of the State, it cannot afford recovery if the right to recover is made unavailable by the State nor can it substantially affect the enforcement of the right as given by the State.

And so the question is not whether a statute of limitations is deemed a matter of "procedure" in some sense. The question is whether such a statute concerns merely the manner and the means by which a right to recover, as recognized by the State, is enforced, or whether such statutory limitation is a matter of substance in the aspect that alone is relevant to our problem, namely, does it significantly affect the result of a litigation for a federal court to disregard a law of a State that would be controlling in an action upon the same claim by the same parties in a State court?

It is therefore immaterial whether statutes of limitation are character-ized either as "substantive" or "procedural" in State court opinions in any use of those terms unrelated to the specific issue before us. *Erie R. Co. v. Tompkins* was not an endeavor to formulate scientific legal terminology. It expressed a policy that touches vitally the proper distribution of judicial power between State and federal courts. In essence, the intent of that decision was to insure that, in all cases where a federal court is exercising jurisdiction solely because of the diversity of citizenship of the parties, the outcome of the litigation in the federal court should be substantially the same, so far as legal rules determine the outcome of a litigation, as it would be if tried in a State court. The nub of the policy that underlies *Erie R. Co. v. Tompkins* is that for the same transaction the accident of a suit by a non-resident litigant in a federal court instead of in a State court a block away should not lead to a substantially different result. And so, putting to one side abstractions regarding "substance" and "procedure," we have held that in diversity cases the federal courts must follow the law of the State as to burden of proof, *Cities Service Co. v. Dunlap*, 308 U.S. 208, as to conflict of laws, *Klaxon Co. v. Stentor Co.*, 313 U.S. 487, as to contribu-tory negligence, *Palmer v. Hoffman*, 318 U.S. 109, 117. *And see Sampson v. Channell*, 110 F.2d 754. *Erie R. Co. v. Tompkins* has been applied with an eye alert to essentials in avoiding disregard of State law in diversity cases in the federal courts. A policy so important to our federalism must be kept free from entanglements with analytical or terminological niceties.

Plainly enough, a statute that would completely bar recovery in a suit if brought in a State court bears on a State-created right vitally and not merely formally or negligibly. As to consequences that so intimately affect recovery or non-recovery a federal court in a diversity case should follow State law . . . [I]f a plea of the statute of limitations would bar recovery in a State court, a federal court ought not to afford recovery.

. . . To make an exception to *Erie R. Co. v. Tompkins* on the equity side of a federal court is to reject the considerations of policy which, after long travail, led to that decision. Judge Augustus N. Hand thus summa-rized below the fatal objection to such inroad upon *Erie R. Co. v. Tompkins*:

> In my opinion it would be a mischievous practice to disregard state statutes of limitation whenever federal courts think that the result of adopting them may be inequitable. Such procedure would promote the choice of United States rather than of state courts in order to gain the advantage of different laws. The main foundation for the criticism of *Swift v. Tyson* was that a liti-gant in cases where federal jurisdiction is based only on diverse citizenship may obtain a more favorable decision by suing in the United States courts.

143 F.2d 503, 529, 531.

Diversity jurisdiction is founded on assurance to nonresident litigants of courts free from susceptibility to potential local bias. The Framers of the Constitution, according to Marshall, entertained "apprehensions" lest distant suitors be subjected to local bias in State courts, or, at least, viewed with "indulgence the possible fears and apprehensions" of such suitors. *Bank of the United States v. Deveaux*, 5 Cranch 61, 87. And so Congress afforded out-of-State litigants another tribunal, not another body of law. The operation of a double system of conflicting laws in the same State is plainly hostile to the reign of law. Certainly, the fortuitous circumstance of residence out of a State of one of the parties to a litigation ought not to give rise to a discrimination against others equally concerned but locally resident. The source of substantive rights enforced by a federal court under diversity jurisdiction, it cannot be said too often, is the law of the States. Whenever that law is authoritatively declared by a State, whether its voice be the legislature or its highest court, such law ought to govern in litigation founded on that law, whether the forum of application is a State or a federal court and whether the remedies be sought at law or may be had in equity. . . .

The judgment is reversed and the case is remanded for proceedings not inconsistent with this opinion.

So ordered.

[The dissenting opinion of Justice RUTLEDGE is omitted]

Comments and Questions

1. How would you synthesize the cases of *Erie* and *York*—put another way, after *York*, what is the standard for determining whether state or federal law applies to a particular issue in a diversity case? How does a statute of limitations issue become "substantive" for purposes of choice of law? How does "substantive" become "outcome determinative"?

2. *York* reads the intent of *Erie* "to insure that, in all cases where a federal court is exercising jurisdiction solely because of the diversity of citizenship of the parties, the outcome of the litigation in the federal court should be substantially the same, so far as legal rules determine the outcome of a litigation, as it would be if tried in a State court." Taken literally, doesn't that mean that the newly adopted Fed. R. Civ. P. are in reality a dead letter, and that state rules of procedure would continue to control in federal diversity cases? Isn't it clear after *York* that the two aforementioned events of 1938, the *Erie* decision and the adoption of the Fed. R. Civ. P., are now on a collision course?

3. What would impel the Court to a position that seems so demeaning to the federal courts (established, of course, by authority of Article III of the Constitution)—a position that Judge Charles E. Clark (principal draftsperson of the Fed. R. Civ. P.) remarked reduced federal judges to "ventriloquists' dummies" mouthing state law? *See* Daniel J. Meador, *Transformation of the American Judiciary*, 46 Ala. L Rev 763, 765 (1995).

Clearly the Court was troubled by the "operation of a double system of conflicting laws in the same State," which it found "plainly hostile to the reign of law." Tompkins should not be allowed to shop for a more favorable law of tort recovery than his fictional friend from New York, also injured by the freight car but not of diverse citizenship from Erie Railroad. The outcome test devised in *York* certainly solves that problem, but the puzzle after *York* was whether the cure was more injurious to the operation of the judicial system than the disease. One federal practice after another fell in the wake of the outcome test juggernut. *See Ragan v. Merchants Transfer & Warehouse Co.*, 337 U.S. 530 (1949) (federal practice under Fed. R. Civ. P. 3 of deeming a case commenced for purposes of statute of limitations upon filing complaint was displaced by state statute providing for tolling only upon service of process on defendant); *Cohen v. Beneficial Industrial Loan Corp.*, 337 U.S. 541 (1949) (state law requiring plaintiffs in shareholder derivative actions to post security to indemnify defendant for costs including attorneys fees in event defendant prevails required dismissal of federal diversity action even though Fed. R. Civ. P. 23 required no such security); *Bernhardt v. Polygraphic Co. of America*, 350 U.S. 198 (1956) (federal court could not enforce an arbitration agreement contained in an employment contract sued upon in diversity action in face of state law rendering arbitration agreements revocable).

4. It was left to the ingenuity of two great Supreme Court Justices to reassert the independence of the federal courts in the *Byrd* and *Hanna* cases that follow.

■ BYRD v. BLUE RIDGE RURAL ELECTRIC COOPERATIVE, INC.
356 U.S. 525 (1958)

Justice BRENNAN delivered the opinion of the Court:

This case was brought in the District Court for the Western District of South Carolina. Jurisdiction was based on diversity of citizenship. 28 U.S.C. §1332. The petitioner, a resident of North Carolina, sued respondent, a South Carolina corporation, for damages for injuries allegedly caused by the respondent's negligence. He had judgment on a jury verdict. The Court of Appeals for the Fourth Circuit reversed and directed the entry of judgment for the respondent. We granted certiorari, and subsequently ordered reargument.

The respondent is in the business of selling electric power to subscribers in rural sections of South Carolina. The petitioner was employed as a lineman in the construction crew of a construction contractor. The contractor, R. H. Bouligny, Inc., held a contract with the respondent in the amount of $334,300 for the building of some 24 miles of new power lines, the reconversion to higher capacities of about 88 miles of existing lines, and the construction of 2 new substations and a breaker station. The petitioner was injured while connecting power lines to one of the new substations.

One of respondent's affirmative defenses was that, under the South Carolina Workmen's Compensation Act, the petitioner — because the work contracted to be done by his employer was work of the kind also done by the respondent's own construction and maintenance crews — had the status of a statutory employee of the respondent and was therefore barred from suing the respondent at law because obliged to accept statutory compensation benefits as the exclusive remedy for his injuries. Two questions concerning this defense are before us: (1) whether the Court of Appeals erred in directing judgment for respondent without a remand to give petitioner an opportunity to introduce further evidence; and (2) whether petitioner, state practice notwithstanding, is entitled to a jury determination of the factual issues raised by this defense.

[After deciding that a remand was necessary on the issue of whether Byrd was an "employee" within the meaning of the workers' compensation statute, the Court addressed the second question.]

A question is also presented as to whether on remand the factual issue is to be decided by the judge or by the jury. The respondent argues on the basis of the decision of the Supreme Court of South Carolina in *Adams v. Davison-Paxon Co.*, 230 S.C. 532, that the issue of immunity should be decided by the judge and not by the jury. That was a negligence action brought in the state trial court against a store owner by an employee of an independent contractor who operated the store's millinery department. The trial judge denied the store owner's motion for a directed verdict made upon the ground that §72-111 barred the plaintiff's action. The jury returned a verdict for the plaintiff. The South Carolina Supreme Court reversed, holding that it was for the judge and not the jury to decide on the evidence whether the owner was a statutory employer, and that the store owner had sustained his defense. The court rested its holding on decisions involving judicial review of the Industrial Commission and said:

> Thus the trial court should have in this case resolved the conflicts in the evidence and determined the fact of whether . . . [the independent contractor] was performing a part of the "trade, business or occupation" of the department store-appellant and, therefore, whether . . . [the employee's] remedy is exclusively under the Workmen's Compensation Law.

The respondent argues that this state-court decision governs the present diversity case and "divests the jury of its normal function" to decide the disputed fact question of the respondent's immunity under §72-111. This is to contend that the federal court is bound under *Erie R. Co. v. Tompkins*, 304 U.S. 64, to follow the state court's holding to secure uniform enforcement of the immunity created by the State.

First. It was decided in *Erie R. Co. v. Tompkins* that the federal courts in diversity cases must respect the definition of state-created rights and obligations by the state courts. We must, therefore, first examine the rule in *Adams v. Davison-Paxon Co.* to determine whether it is bound up with these rights and obligations in such a way that its application in the federal court is required. The Workmen's Compensation Act is administered in South Carolina by its Industrial Commission. The South Carolina courts hold that, on judicial review of actions of the Commission under §72-111, the question whether the claim of an injured workman is within the Commission's jurisdiction is a matter of law for decision by the court, which makes its own findings of fact relating to that jurisdiction. The South Carolina Supreme Court states no reasons in *Adams v. Davison-Paxon Co.* why, although the jury decides all other factual issues raised by the cause of action and defenses, the jury is displaced as to the factual issue raised by the affirmative defense under §72-111. The decisions cited to support the holding are . . . concerned solely with defining the scope and method of judicial review of the Industrial Commission. A State may, of course, distribute the functions of its judicial machinery as it sees fit. The decisions relied upon, however, furnish no reason for selecting the judge rather than the jury to decide this single affirmative defense in the negligence action. They simply reflect a policy that administrative determination of "jurisdictional facts" should not be final but subject to judicial review. The conclusion is inescapable that the *Adams* holding is grounded in the practical consideration that the question had theretofore come before the South Carolina courts from the Industrial Commission and the courts had become accustomed to deciding the factual issue of immunity without the aid of juries. We find nothing to suggest that this rule was announced as an integral part of the special relationship created by the statute. Thus the requirement appears to be merely a form and mode of enforcing the immunity, *Guaranty Trust Co. v. York*, 326 U.S. 99, 108, and not a rule intended to be bound up with the definition of the rights and obligations of the parties. The situation is therefore not analogous to that in *Dice v. Akron, C. & Y. R. Co.*, 342 U.S. 359, where this Court held that the right to trial by jury is so substantial a part of the cause of action created by the Federal Employers' Liability Act that the Ohio courts could not apply, in an action under that statute, the Ohio rule that the question of fraudulent release was for determination by a judge rather than by a jury.

Second. But cases following *Erie* have evinced a broader policy to the effect that the federal courts should conform as near as may be—in the absence of other considerations—to state rules even of form and mode where the state rules may bear substantially on the question whether the litigation would come out one way in the federal court and another way in the state court if the federal court failed to apply a particular local rule. *E.g., Guaranty Trust Co. v. York, supra; Bernhardt v. Polygraphic Co.*, 350 U.S. 198. Concededly the nature of the tribunal which tries issues may be important in the enforcement of the parcel of rights making up a cause of action or defense, and bear significantly upon achievement of uniform enforcement of the right. It may well be that in the instant personal-injury case the outcome would be substantially affected by whether the issue of immunity is decided by a judge or a jury. Therefore, were "outcome" the only consideration, a strong case might appear for saying that the federal court should follow the state practice.

But there are affirmative countervailing considerations at work here. The federal system is an independent system for administering justice to litigants who properly invoke its jurisdiction. An essential characteristic of that system is the manner in which, in civil common-law actions, it distributes trial functions between judge and jury and, under the influence—if not the command[10]—of the Seventh Amendment, assigns the decisions of disputed questions of fact to the jury. The policy of uniform enforcement of state-created rights and obligations, see, e.g., *Guaranty Trust Co. v. York*, *supra*, cannot in every case exact compliance with a state rule[12]—not bound up with rights and obligations—which disrupts the federal system of allocating functions between judge and jury. *Herron v. Southern Pacific Co.*, 283 U.S. 91. Thus the inquiry here is whether the federal policy favoring jury decisions of disputed fact questions should yield to the state rule in the interest of furthering the objective that the litigation should not come out one way in the federal court and another way in the state court.

We think that in the circumstances of this case the federal court should not follow the state rule. It cannot be gainsaid that there is a strong federal policy against allowing state rules to disrupt the judge-jury relationship in the federal courts. In *Herron v. Southern Pacific Co.*, *supra*, the trial judge in a personal-injury negligence action brought in the District Court for Arizona on diversity grounds directed a verdict for the defendant when it appeared as a matter of law that the plaintiff was guilty of contributory negligence. The federal judge refused to be bound by a provision of the Arizona Constitution which made the jury the sole arbiter of the question of contributory negligence. This Court sustained the action of the trial judge, holding that "state laws cannot alter the essential character or function of a federal court" because that function "is not in any sense a local matter, and state statutes which would interfere with the appropriate performance of that function are not binding upon the federal court under either the Conformity Act or the 'rules of decision' Act." Perhaps even more clearly in light of the influence of the Seventh Amendmet the function assigned to the jury "is an essential factor in the process

---

10. Our conclusion makes unnecessary the consideration of—and we intimate no view upon—the constitutional question whether the right of jury trial protected in federal courts by the Seventh Amendment embraces the factual issue of statutory immunity when asserted, as here, as an affirmative defense in a common law negligence action.

12. This Court held in *Sibbach v. Wilson & Co.*, 312 U.S. 1, that Federal Rule of Civil Procedure 35 should prevail over a contrary state rule.

for which the Federal Constitution provides." Concededly the *Herron* case was decided *before Erie R. Co. v. Tompkins*, but even when *Swift v. Tyson*, 16 Pet. 1, was governing law and allowed federal courts sitting in diversity cases to disregard state decisional law, it was never thought that state statutes or constitutions were similarly to be disregarded. Yet *Herron* held that state statutes and constitutional provisions could not disrupt or alter the essential character or function of a federal court.

Third. We have discussed the problem upon the assumption that the outcome of the litigation may be substantially affected by whether the issue of immunity is decided by a judge or a jury. But clearly there is not present here the certainty that a different result would follow, *cf. Guaranty Trust Co. v. York, supra,* or even the strong possibility that this would be the case, *cf. Bernhardt v. Polygraphic Co., supra.* There are factors present here which might reduce that possibility. The trial judge in the federal system has powers denied the judges of many States to comment on the weight of evidence and credibility of witnesses, and discretion to grant a new trial if the verdict appears to him to be against the weight of the evidence. We do not think the likelihood of a different result is so strong as to require the federal practice of jury determination of disputed factual issues to yield to the state rule in the interest of uniformity of outcome.[15]

The Court of Appeals did not consider other grounds of appeal raised by the respondent because the ground taken disposed of the case. We accordingly remand the case to the Court of Appeals for the decision of the other questions, with instructions that, if not made unnecessary by the decision of such questions, the Court of Appeals shall remand the case to the District Court for a new trial of such issues as the Court of Appeals may direct.

Reversed and remanded.

[The concurring and dissenting opinions of Justices WHITTAKER, FRANKFURTER, and HARLAN are omitted. The persistence of the *York* outcome analysis among some on the Court is reflected in the following excerpt from Justice Whittaker:

It thus seems to be settled under the South Carolina Workmen's Compensation Law, and the decisions of the highest court of that State construing it, that the question whether exclusive jurisdiction, in cases like this, is vested in its Industrial Commission or in its courts of general jurisdiction is one for

15. *Stoner v. New York Life Ins. Co.*, 311 U.S. 464, is not contrary. It was there held that the federal court should follow the state rule defining the evidence sufficient to raise a jury question whether the state-created right was established. But the state rule did not have the effect of nullifying the function of the federal judge to control a jury submission as did the Arizona constitutional provision which was denied effect in *Herron*. The South Carolina rule here involved affects the jury function as the Arizona provision affected the function of the judge: The rule entirely displaces the jury without regard to the sufficiency of the evidence to support a jury finding of immunity.

decision by the court, not by a jury. The Federal District Court, in this diversity case, is bound to follow the substantive South Carolina law that would be applied if the trial were to be held in a South Carolina court, in which State the Federal District Court sits. *Erie R. Co. v. Tompkins,* 304 U.S. 64. A Federal District Court sitting in South Carolina may not legally reach a substantially different result than would have been reached upon a trial of the same case "in a State court a block away." *Guaranty Trust Co. v. York,* 326 U.S. 99, 109.]

Comments and Questions

1. Why doesn't the Seventh Amendment provide a simple answer to the jury trial issue in *Byrd*? Look at the Court's footnote 10.

2. To what degree does the *Byrd* decision "rescue" federal practice and procedure? What are the limitations of Justice Brennan's rescue effort?

3. How would you articulate the analysis adopted by the Court to determine whether federal or state practice will control? What interests are to be balanced? What has happened to the outcome test of *York*?

4. How would you compare the extent to which the outcome of the litigation may be affected by the choice of law issue in *Byrd* with the extent of outcome-determination in *York*? How does Justice Brennan use that distinction?

5. What are the strategic implications of the choice between having a judge or a jury decide whether Byrd was an "employee" of the Cooperative? Can you understand why the parties thought the issue was worth taking all the way to the United States Supreme Court?

The second phase of the federal practice "rescue" follows.

■ HANNA v. PLUMER
380 U.S. 460 (1965)

Chief Justice WARREN delivered the opinion of the Court:

The question to be decided is whether, in a civil action where the jurisdiction of the United States district court is based upon diversity of citizenship between the parties, service of process shall be made in the manner prescribed by state law or that set forth in Rule 4(d)(1) of the Federal Rules of Civil Procedure.

On February 6, 1963, petitioner, a citizen of Ohio, filed her complaint in the District Court for the District of Massachusetts, claiming damages in excess of $10,000 for personal injuries resulting from an automobile accident in South Carolina, allegedly caused by the negligence of one Louise Plumer Osgood, a Massachusetts citizen deceased at the time of the filing of the complaint. Respondent, Mrs. Osgood's executor and also a Massachusetts citizen, was named as defendant. On February 8, service was made by leaving copies of the summons and the complaint with respondent's wife at his residence, concededly in compliance with Rule 4(d)(1),* which provides:

> The summons and complaint shall be served together. The plaintiff shall furnish the person making service with such copies as are necessary. Service shall be made as follows:
>
> (1) Upon an individual other than an infant or an incompetent person, by delivering a copy of the summons and of the complaint to him personally or by leaving copies thereof at his dwelling house or usual place of abode with some person of suitable age and discretion then residing therein. . . .

Respondent filed his answer on February 26, alleging, inter alia, that the action could not be maintained because it had been brought "contrary to and in violation of the provisions of Massachusetts General Laws (Ter. Ed.) Chapter 197, Section 9." That section provides:

> Except as provided in this chapter, an executor or administrator shall not be held to answer to an action by a creditor of the deceased which is not commenced within one year from the time of his giving bond for the performance of his trust, or to such an action which is commenced within said year unless before the expiration thereof the writ in such action has been served by delivery in hand upon such executor or administrator or service thereof accepted by him or a notice stating the name of the estate, the name and address of the creditor, the amount of the claim and the court in which the action has been brought has been filed in the proper registry of probate. . . .

Mass. Gen. Laws Ann., c. 197, §9 (1958). On October 17, 1963, the District Court granted respondent's motion for summary judgment, citing *Ragan v. Merchants Transfer Co.*, 337 U.S. 530, and *Guaranty Trust Co. v. York*, 326 U.S. 99, in support of its conclusion that the adequacy of the service was to be measured by §9, with which, the court held, petitioner had not complied. On appeal, petitioner admitted noncompliance with §9, but argued that Rule 4(d)(1) defines the method by which service of process is to be effected in diversity actions. The Court of Appeals for the First Circuit, finding that "relatively recent amendments [to §9] evince a clear legislative purpose to require personal notification within the year," [1]concluded

---

Eds. Note: The rule discussed by the court now appears at Fed. R. Civ. P. 4(e)(2).

1. Section 9 is in part a statue of limitations, providing that an executor need not "answer to an action . . . which is not commenced within one year from the time of his giving bond. . . ." This part of the statute, the purpose of which is to speed the settlement of estates, *Spaulding v. McConnell,* 307 Mass. 144, 146 (1940); *Doyle v. Moylan,* 141 F. Supp. 95 (D. Mass. 1956), is not involved in this case, since the action clearly was timely commenced. (Respondent filed bond on March 1, 1962; the complaint was filed February 6, 1963; and the service—the propriety of which is in dispute—was made on February 8, 1963.) 331 F.2d at

that the conflict of state and federal rules was over "a substantive rather than a procedural matter," and unanimously affirmed. 331 F.2d 157. Because of the threat to the goal of uniformity of federal procedure posed by the decision below, we granted certiorari.

We conclude that the adoption of Rule 4(d)(1), designed to control service of process in diversity actions,[3] neither exceeded the congressional mandate embodied in the Rules Enabling Act nor transgressed constitutional bounds, and that the Rule is therefore the standard against which the District Court should have measured the adequacy of the service. Accordingly, we reverse the decision of the Court of Appeals.

The Rules Enabling Act, 28 U.S.C. §2072 (1958 ed.), provides, in pertinent part:

> The Supreme Court shall have the power to prescribe, by general rules, the forms of process, writs, pleadings, and motions, and the practice and procedure of the district courts of the United States in civil actions.
>
> Such rules shall not abridge, enlarge or modify any substantive right and shall preserve the right of trial by jury. . . .

Under the cases construing the scope of the Enabling Act, Rule 4(d)(1) clearly passes muster. Prescribing the manner in which a defendant is to be notified that a suit has been instituted against him, it relates to the "practice and procedure of the district courts." "The test must be whether a rule really regulates procedure,—the judicial process for enforcing rights and duties recognized by substantive law and for justly administering remedy and redress for disregard or infraction of them." *Sibbach v. Wilson & Co.*, 312 U.S. 1, 14.

In *Mississippi Pub. Corp. v. Murphree*, 326 U.S. 438, this Court upheld Rule 4(f), which permits service of a summons anywhere within the State (and not merely the district) in which a district court sits:

> We think that Rule 4(f) is in harmony with the Enabling Act. . . . Undoubtedly most alterations of the rules of practice and procedure may and

---

159. *Cf. Guaranty Trust Co. v. York, supra; Ragan v. Merchants Transfer Co., supra.* Section 9 also provides for the manner of service. Generally, service of process must be made by "delivery in hand," although there are two alternatives: acceptance of service by the executor, or filing of a notice of claim, the components of which are set out in the statute, in the appropriate probate court. The purpose of this part of the statute, which is involved here, is, as the court below noted, to insure that executors will receive actual notice of claims. *Parker v. Rich*, 297 Mass. 111, 113-114 (1937). Actual notice is of course also the goal of Rule 4(d)(1); however, the Federal Rule reflects a determination that this goal can be achieved by a method less cumbersome than that prescribed in §9. In this case the goal seems to have been achieved; although the affidavit filed by respondent in the District Court asserts that he had not been served in hand nor had he accepted service, it does not allege lack of actual notice.

3. "These rules govern the procedure in the United States district courts in all suits of a civil nature whether cognizable as cases at law or in equity, with the exceptions stated in Rule 81. . . ." Fed. R. Civ. P. 1. This case does not come within any of the exceptions noted in Rule 81.

often do affect the rights of litigants. Congress' prohibition of any alteration of substantive rights of litigants was obviously not addressed to such incidental effects as necessarily attend the adoption of the prescribed new rules of procedure upon the rights of litigants who, agreeably to rules of practice and procedure, have been brought before a court authorized to determine their rights. *Sibbach v. Wilson & Co.*, 312 U.S. 1, 11-14. The fact that the application of Rule 4(f) will operate to subject petitioner's rights to adjudication by the district court for northern Mississippi will undoubtedly affect those rights. But it does not operate to abridge, enlarge or modify the rules of decision by which that court will adjudicate its rights.

Id., at 445-446.

Thus were there no conflicting state procedure, Rule 4 (d)(1) would clearly control. However, respondent, focusing on the contrary Massachusetts rule, calls to the Court's attention another line of cases, a line which— like the Federal Rules—had its birth in 1938. *Erie R. Co. v. Tompkins*, 304 U.S. 64, overruling *Swift v. Tyson*, 16 Pet. 1, held that federal courts sitting in diversity cases, when deciding questions of "substantive" law, are bound by state court decisions as well as state statutes. The broad command of *Erie* was therefore identical to that of the Enabling Act: federal courts are to apply state substantive law and federal procedural law. However, as subsequent cases sharpened the distinction between substance and procedure, the line of cases following *Erie* diverged markedly from the line construing the Enabling Act. *Guaranty Trust Co. v. York*, 326 U.S. 99, made it clear that *Erie*-type problems were not to be solved by reference to any traditional or common-sense substance-procedure distinction:

And so the question is not whether a statute of limitations is deemed a matter of "procedure" in some sense. The question is . . . does it significantly affect the result of a litigation for a federal court to disregard a law of a State that would be controlling in an action upon the same claim by the same parties in a State court?

326 U.S. at 109. Respondent, by placing primary reliance on *York* and *Ragan*, suggests that the *Erie* doctrine acts as a check on the Federal Rules of Civil Procedure, that despite the clear command of Rule 4 (d)(1), *Erie* and its progeny demand the application of the Massachusetts rule. Reduced to essentials, the argument is: (1) *Erie*, as refined in *York*, demands that federal courts apply state law whenever application of federal law in its stead will alter the outcome of the case. (2) In this case, a determination that the Massachusetts service requirements obtain will result in immediate victory for respondent. If, on the other hand, it should be held that Rule 4 (d)(1) is applicable, the litigation will continue, with possible victory for petitioner. (3) Therefore, *Erie* demands application of the Massachusetts rule. The syllogism possesses an appealing simplicity, but is for several reasons invalid.

In the first place, it is doubtful that, even if there were no Federal Rule making it clear that in-hand service is not required in diversity actions, the *Erie* rule would have obligated the District Court to follow the Massachusetts procedure. "Outcome-determination" analysis was never intended to serve as a talisman. *Byrd v. Blue Ridge Cooperative*, 356 U.S. 525, 537. Indeed, the message of *York* itself is that choices between state and federal law are to be made not by application of any automatic, "litmus paper" criterion, but rather by reference to the policies underlying the *Erie* rule. *Guaranty Trust Co. v. York, supra*, at 108-112.

The *Erie* rule is rooted in part in a realization that it would be unfair for the character or result of a litigation materially to differ because the suit had been brought in a federal court. "Diversity of citizenship jurisdiction was conferred in order to prevent apprehended discrimination in state courts against those not citizens of the State. *Swift v. Tyson* introduced grave discrimination by non-citizens against citizens. It made rights enjoyed under the unwritten 'general law' vary according to whether enforcement was sought in the state or in the federal court; and the privilege of selecting the court in which the right should be determined was conferred upon the non-citizen. Thus, the doctrine rendered impossible equal protection of the law." *Erie R. Co. v. Tompkins*, supra, at 74-75.

The decision was also in part a reaction to the practice of "forum-shopping" which had grown up in response to the rule of *Swift v. Tyson*. 304 U.S. at 73-74. That the *York* test was an attempt to effectuate these policies is demonstrated by the fact that the opinion framed the inquiry in terms of "substantial" variations between state and federal litigation. 326 U.S. at 109. Not only are nonsubstantial, or trivial, variations not likely to raise the sort of equal protection problems which troubled the Court in *Erie* they are also unlikely to influence the choice of a forum. The "outcome-determination" test therefore cannot be read without reference to the twin aims of the *Erie* rule: discouragement of forum-shopping and avoidance of inequitable administration of the laws.[9]

The difference between the conclusion that the Massachusetts rule is applicable, and the conclusion that it is not, is of course at this point

9. The Court of Appeals seemed to frame the inquiry in terms of how "important" §9 is to the State. In support of its suggestion that §9 serves some interest the State regards as vital to its citizens, the court noted that something like §9 has been on the books in Massachusetts a long time, that §9 has been amended a number of times, and that §9 [was] designed to make sure that executors receive actual notice. *See* note 1, *supra.* The apparent lack of relation among these three observations is not surprising, because it is not clear to what sort of question the Court of Appeals was addressing itself. One cannot meaningfully ask how important something is without first asking "important for what purpose?" *Erie* and its progeny make clear that when a federal court sitting in a diversity case is faced with a question of whether or not to apply state law, the importance of a state rule is indeed relevant, but only in the context of asking whether application of the rule would make so important a difference to the character or result of the litigation that failure to enforce it would unfairly discriminate against citizens of the forum State, or whether application of the rule would have so important an effect upon the fortunes of one or both of the litigants that failure to enforce it would be likely to cause a plaintiff to choose the federal court.

"outcome-determinative" in the sense that if we hold the state rule to apply, respondent prevails, whereas if we hold that Rule 4(d)(1) governs, the litigation will continue. But in this sense every procedural variation is "outcome-determinative." For example, having brought suit in a federal court, a plaintiff cannot then insist on the right to file subsequent pleadings in accord with the time limits applicable in the state courts, even though enforcement of the federal timetable will, if he continues to insist that he must meet only the state time limit, result in determination of the controversy against him. So it is here. Though choice of the federal or state rule will at this point have a marked effect upon the outcome of the litigation, the difference between the two rules would be of scant, if any, relevance to the choice of a forum. Petitioner, in choosing her forum, was not presented with a situation where application of the state rule would wholly bar recovery; rather, adherence to the state rule would have resulted only in altering the way in which process was served.[11] Moreover, it is difficult to argue that permitting service of defendant's wife to take the place of in-hand service of defendant himself alters the mode of enforcement of state-created rights in a fashion sufficiently "substantial" to raise the sort of equal protection problems to which the *Erie* opinion alluded.

There is, however, a more fundamental flaw in respondent's syllogism: the incorrect assumption that the rule of *Erie R. Co. v. Tompkins* constitutes the appropriate test of the validity and therefore the applicability of a Federal Rule of Civil Procedure. The *Erie* rule has never been invoked to void a Federal Rule. It is true that there have been cases where this Court has held applicable a state rule in the face of an argument that the situation was governed by one of the Federal Rules. But the holding of each such case was not that *Erie* commanded displacement of a Federal Rule by an inconsistent state rule, but rather that the scope of the Federal Rule was not as broad as the losing party urged, and therefore, there being no Federal Rule which covered the point in dispute, *Erie* commanded the enforcement of state law. . . . (Here, of course, the clash is unavoidable; Rule 4(d)(1) says—implicitly, but with unmistakable clarity—that in-hand service is not required in federal courts.) At the same time, in cases adjudicating the validity of Federal Rules, we have not applied the *York* rule or other refinements of *Erie*, but have to this day continued to decide questions concerning the scope of the Enabling Act and the constitutionality of specific Federal Rules in light of the distinction set forth in *Sibbach*. E.g., *Schlagenhauf v. Holder*, 379 U.S. 104.

Nor has the development of two separate lines of cases been inadvertent. The line between "substance" and "procedure" shifts as the legal

---

11. We cannot seriously entertain the thought that one suing an estate would be led to choose the federal court because of a belief that adherence to Rule 4(d)(1) is less likely to give the executor actual notice than §9, and therefore, more likely to produce a default judgment. Rule 4(d)(1) is well designed to give actual notice, as it did in this case. *See* note 1, *supra*.

context changes. "Each implies different variables depending upon the particular problem for which it is used." *Guaranty Trust Co. v. York, supra,* at 108; Cook, The Logical and Legal Bases of the Conflict of Laws, pp. 154-183 (1942). It is true that both the Enabling Act and the *Erie* rule say, roughly, that federal courts are to apply state "substantive" law and federal "procedural" law, but from that it need not follow that the tests are identical. For they were designed to control very different sorts of decisions. When a situation is covered by one of the Federal Rules, the question facing the court is a far cry from the typical, relatively unguided *Erie* choice: the court has been instructed to apply the Federal Rule, and can refuse to do so only if the Advisory Committee, this Court, and Congress erred in their prima facie judgment that the Rule in question transgresses neither the terms of the Enabling Act nor constitutional restrictions.

We are reminded by the *Erie* opinion that neither Congress nor the federal courts can, under the guise of formulating rules of decision for federal courts, fashion rules which are not supported by a grant of federal authority contained in Article I or some other section of the Constitution; in such areas state law must govern because there can be no other law. But the opinion in *Erie,* which involved no Federal Rule and dealt with a question which was "substantive" in every traditional sense (whether the railroad owed a duty of care to Tompkins as a trespasser or a licensee), surely neither said nor implied that measures like Rule 4(d)(1) are unconstitutional. For the constitutional provision for a federal court system (augmented by the Necessary and Proper Clause) carries with it congressional power to make rules governing the practice and pleading in those courts, which in turn includes a power to regulate matters which, though falling within the uncertain area between substance and procedure, are rationally capable of classification as either. Neither *York* nor the cases following it ever suggested that the rule there laid down for coping with situations where no Federal Rule applies is coextensive with the limitation on Congress to which *Erie* had adverted. Although this Court has never before been confronted with a case where the applicable Federal Rule is in direct collision with the law of the relevant State, courts of appeals faced with such clashes have rightly discerned the implications of our decisions.

> One of the shaping purposes of the Federal Rules is to bring about uniformity in the federal courts by getting away from local rules. This is especially true of matters which relate to the administration of legal proceedings, an area in which federal courts have traditionally exerted strong inherent power, completely aside from the powers Congress expressly conferred in the Rules. The purpose of the *Erie* doctrine, even as extended in *York* and *Ragan,* was never to bottle up federal courts with "outcome-determinative" and "integral-relations" stoppers—when there are "affirmative countervailing [federal] considerations" and when there is a Congressional mandate (the Rules) supported by constitutional authority.

Lumbermen's Mutual Casualty Co. v. Wright, 322 F.2d 759, 764 (5th Cir. 1963). *Erie* and its offspring cast no doubt on the long-recognized power of Congress to prescribe housekeeping rules for federal courts even though some of those rules will inevitably differ from comparable state rules. "When, because the plaintiff happens to be a non-resident, such a right is enforceable in a federal as well as in a State court, the forms and mode of enforcing the right may at times, naturally enough, vary because the two judicial systems are not identic." *Guaranty Trust Co. v. York, supra,* at 108; *Cohen v. Beneficial Loan Corp.,* 337 U.S. 541, 555. Thus, though a court, in measuring a Federal Rule against the standards contained in the Enabling Act and the Constitution, need not wholly blind itself to the degree to which the Rule makes the character and result of the federal litigation stray from the course it would follow in state courts, *Sibbach v. Wilson & Co., supra,* at 13-14, it cannot be forgotten that the *Erie* rule, and the guidelines suggested in York, were created to serve another purpose altogether. To hold that a Federal Rule of Civil Procedure must cease to function whenever it alters the mode of enforcing state-created rights would be to disembowel either the Constitution's grant of power over federal procedure or Congress' attempt to exercise that power in the Enabling Act. Rule 4 (d) (1) is valid and controls the instant case. Reversed.

Justice HARLAN, concurring:

It is unquestionably true that up to now *Erie* and the cases following it have not succeeded in articulating a workable doctrine governing choice of law in diversity actions. I respect the Court's effort to clarify the situation in today's opinion. However, in doing so I think it has misconceived the constitutional premises of *Erie* and has failed to deal adequately with those past decisions upon which the courts below relied.

Erie was something more than an opinion which worried about "forum-shopping and avoidance of inequitable administration of the laws," although to be sure these were important elements of the decision. I have always regarded that decision as one of the modern cornerstones of our federalism, expressing policies that profoundly touch the allocation of judicial power between the state and federal systems. *Erie* recognized that there should not be two conflicting systems of law controlling the primary activity of citizens, for such alternative governing authority must necessarily give rise to a debilitating uncertainty in the planning of everyday affairs.[1] And it recognized that the scheme of our Constitution envisions an allocation of law-making functions between state and federal legislative processes which is undercut if the federal judiciary can make substantive law affecting state affairs beyond the bounds of congressional legislative powers in

---

1. Since the rules involed in the present case are parallel rather than conflicting, this rationale does not come into play here.

this regard. Thus, in diversity cases *Erie* commands that it be the state law governing primary private activity which prevails.

The shorthand formulations which have appeared in some past decisions are prone to carry untoward results that frequently arise from oversimplification. The Court is quite right in stating that the "outcome-determinative" test of *Guaranty Trust Co. v. York*, 326 U.S. 99, if taken literally, proves too much, for any rule, no matter how clearly "procedural," can affect the outcome of litigation if it is not obeyed. In turning from the "outcome" test of *York* back to the unadorned forum-shopping rationale of *Erie,* however, the Court falls prey to like oversimplification, for a simple forum-shopping rule also proves too much; litigants often choose a federal forum merely to obtain what they consider the advantages of the Federal Rules of Civil Procedure or to try their cases before a supposedly more favorable judge. To my mind the proper line of approach in determining whether to apply a state or a federal rule, whether "substantive" or "procedural," is to stay close to basic principles by inquiring if the choice of rule would substantially affect those primary decisions respecting human conduct which our constitutional system leaves to state regulation. If so, *Erie* and the Constitution require that the state rule prevail, even in the face of a conflicting federal rule.

The Court weakens, if indeed it does not submerge, this basic principle by finding, in effect, a grant of substantive legislative power in the constitutional provision for a federal court system (*compare Swift v. Tyson*, 16 Pet. 1), and through it, setting up the Federal Rules as a body of law inviolate. "The constitutional provision for a federal court system . . . carries with it congressional power . . . to regulate matters which, though falling within the uncertain area between substance and procedure, are rationally capable of classification as either." So long as a reasonable man could characterize any duly adopted federal rule as "procedural," the Court, unless I misapprehend what is said, would have it apply no matter how seriously it frustrated a State's substantive regulation of the primary conduct and affairs of its citizens. Since the members of the Advisory Committee, the Judicial Conference, and this Court who formulated the Federal Rules are presumably reasonable men, it follows that the integrity of the Federal Rules is absolute. Whereas the unadulterated outcome and forum-shopping tests may err too far toward honoring state rules, I submit that the Court's "arguably procedural, ergo constitutional" test moves too fast and far in the other direction.

The courts below relied upon this Court's decisions in *Ragan v. Merchants Transfer Co.*, 337 U.S. 530, and *Cohen v. Beneficial Loan Corp.*, 337 U.S. 541. Those cases deserve more attention than this Court has given them, particularly *Ragan* which, if still good law, would in my opinion call for affirmance of the result reached by the Court of Appeals. Further, a discussion of these two cases will serve to illuminate the "diversity" thesis I am advocating.

In *Ragan* a Kansas statute of limitations provided that an action was deemed commenced when service was made on the defendant. Despite Federal Rule 3 which provides that an action commences with the filing of the complaint, the Court held that for purposes of the Kansas statute of limitations a diversity tort action commenced only when service was made upon the defendant. The effect of this holding was that although the plaintiff had filed his federal complaint within the state period of limitations, his action was barred because the federal marshal did not serve a summons on the defendant until after the limitations period had run. I think that the decision was wrong. At most, application of the Federal Rule would have meant that potential Kansas tort defendants would have to defer for a few days the satisfaction of knowing that they had not been sued within the limitations period. The choice of the Federal Rule would have had no effect on the primary stages of private activity from which torts arise, and only the most minimal effect on behavior following the commission of the tort. In such circumstances the interest of the federal system in proceeding under its own rules should have prevailed.

Cohen v. Beneficial Loan Corp. held that a federal diversity court must apply a state statute requiring a small stockholder in a stockholder derivative suit to post a bond securing payment of defense costs as a condition to prosecuting an action. Such a statute is not "outcome determinative"; the plaintiff can win with or without it. The Court now rationalizes the case on the ground that the statute might affect the plaintiff's choice of forum, but as has been pointed out, a simple forum-shopping test proves too much. The proper view of *Cohen* is, in my opinion, that the statute was meant to inhibit small stockholders from instituting "strike suits," and thus it was designed and could be expected to have a substantial impact on private primary activity. Anyone who was at the trial bar during the period when *Cohen* arose can appreciate the strong state policy reflected in the statute. I think it wholly legitimate to view Federal Rule 23 as not purporting to deal with the problem. But even had the Federal Rules purported to do so, and in so doing provided a substantially less effective deterrent to strike suits, I think the state rule should still have prevailed. That is where I believe the Court's view differs from mine; for the Court attributes such overriding force to the Federal Rules that it is hard to think of a case where a conflicting state rule would be allowed to operate, even though the state rule reflected policy considerations which, under *Erie*, would lie within the realm of state legislative authority.

It remains to apply what has been said to the present case. The Massachusetts rule provides that an executor need not answer suits unless in-hand service was made upon him or notice of the action was filed in the proper registry of probate within one year of his giving bond. The evident intent of this statute is to permit an executor to distribute the estate which he is administering without fear that further liabilities may be outstanding for which he could be held personally liable. If the Federal District Court in Massachusetts applies Rule 4(d)(1) of the Federal Rules of Civil Procedure instead of the Massachusetts service rule, what effect would that have on the speed and assurance with which estates are distributed? As I see it, the effect would not be substantial. It would mean simply that an executor would have to check at his own house or the federal courthouse as well as the registry of probate before he could distribute the estate with impunity. As this does not seem enough to give rise to any real impingement on the vitality of the state policy which the Massachusetts rule is intended to serve, I concur in the judgment of the Court.

Comments and Questions

1. Does Chief Justice Warren foreshadow early on how this decision will come out when he ends the second paragraph as follows: "Because of the threat to the goal of uniformity of federal procedure posed by the decision below, we granted certiorari."

2. How would you compare the extent to which the outcome of the litigation may be affected by the choice of law issue in *Hanna* with the extent of outcome-determination in *Erie, York* and *Byrd*? What about the relative risks of the plaintiff's forum shopping in each of these cases? How does Chief Justice Warren use these comparisons to justify his decision in *Hanna?*

3. What is the test after *Hanna* for determining whether in a diversity case to apply a Federal Rule of Civil Procedure that is in conflict with a state practice?

4. From the point of view of political science, can you see why the Supreme Court would grant more authority to a practice contained in the Federal Rules of Civil Procedure, which has the imprimatur of the elaborate Rules Enabling Act process behind it, than to a practice that merely represents the decision of lower court federal judges?

5. Is Justice Harlan correct in arguing that under the Court's test "the integrity of the Federal Rules is absolute" and "it is hard to think of a case where a conflicting state rule would be allowed to operate, even though the state rule reflected policy considerations which, under *Erie*, would lie within the realm of state legislative authority"? Consider Justice Harlan's prediction when you read *Walker v. ARMCO Steel Corp.*, the case that follows.

6. What alternative test would Justice Harlan impose for the choice of law issue? Is his "primary activity" standard workable, or is it too fuzzy?

7. Does the Supreme Court have a conflict of interest when it rules on the validity of a Federal Rule of Civil Procedure, which it itself adopted under the Rules Enabling Act? Justices Black and Douglas, in dissenting from the adoption of proposed amendments to the Federal Rules of Civil Procedure in 1963, suggested that the responsibility for drafting should be shifted: "Transfer of the function to the Judicial Conference would relieve us of the embarrassment of having to sit in judgment on the constitutional-

ity of rules which we have approved and which in given circumstances might have to be declared invalid." 374 U.S. 865, 869-870 (1963). Justice White joined this view in 1993, adding: "I did my share of litigating when in practice and once served on the Advisory Committee for the Civil Rules, but the trial practice is a dynamic profession, and the longer one is away from it the less likely it is that he or she should presume to second-guess the careful work of the active professionals manning the rulemaking committees, work that the Judicial Conference has approved." 146 F.R.D. 501, 504 (1993).

8. Professor Stephen Burbank has exhaustively researched the history of the Rules Enabling Act of 1934 and concluded that its prevailing interpretation as reflected in *Hanna,* namely, that the second sentence prescribing that the rules adopted "shall neither abridge, enlarge nor modify the substantive rights of any litigant" was intended to preserve state law is wrong. Instead, the clause was "intended to allocate power between the Supreme Court as rulemaker and Congress and thus to circumscribe the delegation of legislative power." . . . "[T]he protection of state law was deemed a probable effect, rather than the primary purpose of the [procedure/substance] allocation scheme established by the Act." Stephen Burbank, *The Rules Enabling Act of 1934,* 130 U. Pa. L. Rev. 1015 (1982). If Burbank is right that the Act addresses the separation of powers *within* the federal government and not the relation *between* the federal government and the states, what are the implications for the analysis adopted by *Hanna?*

■ WALKER v. ARMCO STEEL CORP.
446 U.S. 740 (1980)

Justice MARSHALL delivered the opinion of the Court:

This case presents the issue whether in a diversity action the federal court should follow state law or, alternatively, Rule 3 of the Federal Rules of Civil Procedure in determining when an action is commenced for the purpose of tolling the state statute of limitations.

I

According to the allegations of the complaint, petitioner, a carpenter, was injured on August 22, 1975, in Oklahoma City, Okla., while pounding a Sheffield nail into a cement wall. Respondent was the manufacturer of the nail. Petitioner claimed that the nail contained a defect which caused its head to shatter and strike him in the right eye, resulting in permanent injuries. The defect was allegedly caused by respondent's negligence in manufacture and design.

Petitioner is a resident of Oklahoma, and respondent is a foreign corporation having its principal place of business in a State other than

Oklahoma. Since there was diversity of citizenship, petitioner brought suit in the United States District Court for the Western District of Oklahoma. The complaint was filed on August 19, 1977. Although summons was issued that same day, service of process was not made on respondent's authorized service agent until December 1, 1977.[2] On January 5, 1978, respondent filed a motion to dismiss the complaint on the ground that the action was barred by the applicable Oklahoma statute of limitations. Although the complaint had been filed within the 2-year statute of limitations, Okla. Stat., Tit. 12, §95 (1971), state law does not deem the action "commenced" for purposes of the statute of limitations until service of the summons on the defendant, Okla. Stat., Tit. 12, §97 (1971). If the complaint is filed within the limitations period, however, the action is deemed to have commenced from that date of filing if the plaintiff serves the defendant within 60 days, even though that service may occur outside the limitations period. In this case, service was not effectuated until long after this 60-day period had expired. Petitioner in his reply brief to the motion to dismiss admitted that his case would be foreclosed in state court, but he argued that Rule 3 of the Federal Rules of Civil Procedure governs the manner in which an action is commenced in federal court for all purposes, including the tolling of the state statute of limitations.

The District Court dismissed the complaint as barred by the Oklahoma statute of limitations. The court concluded that Okla. Stat., Tit. 12, §97 (1971) was "an integral part of the Oklahoma statute of limitations," and therefore under *Ragan v. Merchants Transfer & Warehouse Co.*, 337 U.S. 530 (1949), state law applied. The court rejected the argument that *Ragan* had been implicitly overruled in *Hanna v. Plumer*, 380 U.S. 460 (1965).

The United States Court of Appeals for the Tenth Circuit affirmed. 592 F.2d 1133 (1979). That court concluded that Okla. Stat., Tit. 12, §97 (1971), was in "direct conflict" with Rule 3. 592 F.2d, at 1135. However, the Oklahoma statute was "indistinguishable" from the statute involved in *Ragan*, and the court felt itself "constrained" to follow *Ragan*. 592 F.2d, at 1136.

We granted certiorari, because of a conflict among the Courts of Appeals. We now affirm.

II

The question whether state or federal law should apply on various issues arising in an action based on state law which has been brought in

---

2. The record does not indicate why this delay occurred. The face of the process record shows that the United States Marshal acknowledged receipt of the summons on December 1, 1977, and that service was effectuated that same day. At oral argument counsel for petitioner stated that the summons was found "in an unmarked folder in the filing cabinet" in counsel's office some 90 days after the complaint had been filed. Counsel conceded that the summons was not delivered to the Marshal until December 1. It is unclear why the summons was placed in the filing cabinet.

federal court under diversity of citizenship jurisdiction has troubled this Court for many years. In the landmark decision of *Erie R. Co. v. Tompkins*, 304 U.S. 64 (1938), we overturned the rule expressed in *Swift v. Tyson*, 16 Pet. 1 (1842), that federal courts exercising diversity jurisdiction need not, in matters of "general jurisprudence," apply the nonstatutory law of the State. The Court noted that "[diversity] of citizenship jurisdiction was conferred in order to prevent apprehended discrimination in state courts against those not citizens of the State." The doctrine of *Swift v. Tyson* had led to the undesirable results of discrimination in favor of noncitizens, prevention of uniformity in the administration of state law, and forum shopping. In response, we established the rule that "[except] in matters governed by the Federal Constitution or by Acts of Congress, the law to be applied in any [diversity] case is the law of the State."

In *Guaranty Trust Co. v. York*, 326 U.S. 99 (1945), we addressed ourselves to "the narrow question whether, when no recovery could be had in a State court because the action is barred by the statute of limitations, a federal court in equity can take cognizance of the suit because there is diversity of citizenship between the parties." The Court held that the *Erie* doctrine applied to suits in equity as well as to actions at law. In construing *Erie* we noted that "[in] essence, the intent of that decision was to insure that, in all cases where a federal court is exercising jurisdiction solely because of the diversity of citizenship of the parties, the outcome of the litigation in the federal court should be substantially the same, so far as legal rules determine the outcome of a litigation, as it would be if tried in a State court." We concluded that the state statute of limitations should be applied. "Plainly enough, a statute that would completely bar recovery in a [§1983] suit if brought in a State court bears on a State-created right vitally and not merely formally or negligibly. As to consequences that so intimately affect recovery or non-recovery a federal court in a diversity case should follow State law."

The decision in *York* led logically to our holding in *Ragan v. Merchants Transfer & Warehouse Co., supra*. In *Ragan*, the plaintiff had filed his complaint in federal court on September 4, 1945, pursuant to Rule 3 of the Federal Rules of Civil Procedure. The accident from which the claim arose had occurred on October 1, 1943. Service was made on the defendant on December 28, 1945. The applicable statute of limitations supplied by Kansas law was two years. Kansas had an additional statute which provided: "An action shall be deemed commenced within the meaning of [the statute of limitations], as to each defendant, at the date of the summons which is served on him. . . . An attempt to commence an action shall be deemed equivalent to the commencement thereof within the meaning of this article when the party faithfully, properly and diligently endeavors to procure a service; but such attempt must be followed by the first publication or service of the summons within sixty days." Kan. Gen. Stat. §60-308 (1935). The defendant moved for summary judgment on the ground that the Kansas statute of limitations barred the action since service had not been made within either the 2-year period or the 60-day period. It was conceded that had the case been brought in Kansas state court it would have been barred. Nonetheless, the District Court held that the statute had been tolled by the filing of the complaint. The Court of Appeals reversed because "the requirement of service of summons within the statutory period was an integral part of that state's statute of limitations." *Ragan*, 337 U.S. at 532.

We affirmed, relying on *Erie* and *York*. "We cannot give [the cause of action] longer life in the federal court than it would have had in the state court without adding something to the cause of action. We may not do that consistently with *Erie R. Co. v. Tompkins*." 337 U.S. at 533-534. We rejected the argument that Rule 3 of the Federal Rules of Civil Procedure governed the manner in which an action was commenced in federal court for purposes of tolling the state statute of limitations. Instead, we held that the service of summons statute controlled because it was an integral part of the state statute of limitations, and under *York* that statute of limitations was part of the state-law cause of action.

Ragan was not our last pronouncement in this difficult area, however. In 1965 we decided *Hanna v. Plumer*, 380 U.S. 460, holding that in a civil action where federal jurisdiction was based upon diversity of citizenship, Rule 4(d)(1) of the Federal Rules of Civil Procedure, rather than state law, governed the manner in which process was served. Massachusetts law required in-hand service on an executor or administrator of an estate, whereas Rule 4 permits service by leaving copies of the summons and complaint at the defendant's home with some person "of suitable age and discretion." The Court noted that in the absence of a conflicting state procedure, the Federal Rule would plainly control. We stated that the "outcome-determination" test of *Erie* and *York* had to be read with reference to the "twin aims" of *Erie*: "discouragement of forum-shopping and avoidance of inequitable administration of the laws." We determined that the choice between the state in-hand service rule and the Federal Rule "would be of scant, if any, relevance to the choice of a forum," for the plaintiff "was not presented with a situation where application of the state rule would wholly bar recovery; rather, adherence to the state rule would have resulted only in altering the way in which process was served." *Id.* at 469 (footnote omitted). This factor served to distinguish that case from *York* and *Ragan*.

The Court in *Hanna*, however, pointed out "a more fundamental flaw" in the defendant's argument in that case. The Court concluded that the *Erie* doctrine was simply not the appropriate test of the validity and applicability of one of the Federal Rules of Civil Procedure:

> The *Erie* rule has never been invoked to void a Federal Rule. It is true that there have been cases where this Court had held applicable a state rule in the face of an argument that the situation was governed by one of the

Federal Rules. But the holding of each such case was not that *Erie* commanded displacement of a Federal Rule by an inconsistent state rule, but rather that the scope of the Federal Rule was not as broad as the losing party urged, and therefore, there being no Federal Rule which covered the point in dispute, *Erie* commanded the enforcement of state law.

380 U.S. at 470. The Court cited *Ragan* as one of the examples of this proposition, 380 U.S. at 470, n.12. The Court explained that where the Federal Rule was clearly applicable, as in *Hanna*, the test was whether the Rule was within the scope of the Rules Enabling Act, 28 U.S.C. §2072, and if so, within a constitutional grant of power such as the Necessary and Proper Clause of Art. I. 380 U.S. at 470-472.

III

The present case is indistinguishable from *Ragan*. The statutes in both cases require service of process to toll the statute of limitations, and in fact the predecessor to the Oklahoma statute in this case was derived from the predecessor to the Kansas statute in *Ragan*. Here, as in *Ragan*, the complaint was filed in federal court under diversity jurisdiction within the 2-year statute of limitations, but service of process did not occur until after the 2-year period and the 60-day service period had run. In both cases the suit would concededly have been barred in the applicable state court, and in both instances the state service statute was held to be an integral part of the statute of limitations by the lower court more familiar than we with state law. Accordingly, as the Court of Appeals held below, the instant action is barred by the statute of limitations unless *Ragan* is no longer good law.

Petitioner argues that the analysis and holding of *Ragan* did not survive our decision in *Hanna*. Petitioner's position is that Okla. Stat., Tit. 12, §97 (1971), is in direct conflict with the Federal Rule. Under *Hanna*, petitioner contends, the appropriate question is whether Rule 3 is within the scope of the Rules Enabling Act and, if so, within the constitutional power of Congress. In petitioner's view, the Federal Rule is to be applied unless it violates one of those two restrictions. This argument ignores both the force of *stare decisis* and the specific limitations that we carefully placed on the *Hanna* analysis.

We note at the outset that the doctrine of *stare decisis* weighs heavily against petitioner in this case. Petitioner seeks to have us overrule our decision in *Ragan*. *Stare decisis* does not mandate that earlier decisions be enshrined forever, of course, but it does counsel that we use caution in rejecting established law. In this case, the reasons petitioner asserts for overruling *Ragan* are the same factors which we concluded in *Hanna* did not undermine the validity of *Ragan*. A litigant who in effect asks us to reconsider not one but two prior decisions bears a heavy burden of supporting such a change in our jurisprudence. Petitioner here has not met that burden. This Court in *Hanna* distinguished *Ragan* rather than overruled it, and for good reason. Application of the *Hanna* analysis is premised on a "direct collision" between the Federal Rule and the state law. In *Hanna* itself the "clash" between Rule 4(d)(1) and the state in-hand service requirement was "unavoidable." The first question must therefore be whether the scope of the Federal Rule in fact is sufficiently broad to control the issue before the Court. It is only if that question is answered affirmatively that the *Hanna* analysis applies.[9]

As has already been noted, we recognized in *Hanna* that the present case is an instance where "the scope of the Federal Rule [is] not as broad as the losing party [urges], and therefore, there being no Federal Rule which [covers] the point in dispute, *Erie* [commands] the enforcement of state law." Rule 3 simply states that "[a] civil action is commenced by filing a complaint with the court." There is no indication that the Rule was intended to toll a state statute of limitations, much less that it purported to displace state tolling rules for purposes of state statutes of limitations. In our view, in diversity actions Rule 3 governs the date from which various timing requirements of the Federal Rules begin to run, but does not affect state statutes of limitations.

In contrast to Rule 3, the Oklahoma statute is a statement of a substantive decision by that State that actual service on, and accordingly actual notice by, the defendant is an integral part of the several policies served by the statute of limitations. The statute of limitations establishes a deadline after which the defendant may legitimately have peace of mind; it also recognizes that after a certain period of time it is unfair to require the defendant to attempt to piece together his defense to an old claim. A requirement of actual service promotes both of those functions of the statute. It is these policy aspects which make the service requirement an "integral" part of the statute of limitations both in this case and in *Ragan*. As such, the service rule must be considered part and parcel of the statute of limitations. Rule 3 does not replace such policy determinations found in state law. Rule 3 and Okla. Stat., Tit. 12, §97 (1971), can exist side by side, therefore, each controlling its own intended sphere of coverage without conflict.

Since there is no direct conflict between the Federal Rule and the state law, the *Hanna* analysis does not apply. Instead, the policies behind *Erie* and *Ragan* control the issue whether, in the absence of a federal rule directly on point, state service requirements which are an integral part of the state statute of limitations should control in an action based on state

---

9. This is not to suggest that the Federal Rules of Civil Procedure are to be narrowly construed in order to avoid a "direct collision" with state law. The Federal Rules should be given their plain meaning. If a direct collision with state law arises from that plain meaning, then the analysis developed in *Hanna v. Plumer* applies.

law which is filed in federal court under diversity jurisdiction. The reasons for the application of such a state service requirement in a diversity action in the absence of a conflicting federal rule are well explained in *Erie* and *Ragan,* and need not be repeated here. It is sufficient to note that although in this case failure to apply the state service law might not create any problem of forum shopping,[15] the result would be an "inequitable administration" of the law. *Hanna v. Plumer,* 380 U.S., at 468. There is simply no reason why, in the absence of a controlling federal rule, an action based on state law which concededly would be barred in the state courts by the state statute of limitations should proceed through litigation to judgment in federal court solely because of the fortuity that there is diversity of citizenship between the litigants. The policies underlying diversity jurisdiction do not support such a distinction between state and federal plaintiffs, and *Erie* and its progeny do not permit it.

The judgment of the Court of Appeals is Affirmed.

Comments and Questions

1. What does *Walker* do to the goal of uniformity of federal procedure articulated by Chief Justice Warren in *Hanna?* What's left of the *Byrd/Hanna* rescue operation?

2. Synthesize the line of cases from *Erie* through *Walker.* How would you articulate the different tests (and their rationales) for federal/state choice of law in diversity cases where (1) state law conflicts directly with a Fed. R. Civ. P.; (2) state law is not in direct conflict with any Fed. R. Civ. P. (what *Hanna* refers to as the "relatively unguided *Erie* choice"); (3) state law conflicts with a federal practice that reflects (as in *Byrd*) an "essential characteristic" of federal litigation? What's left of the *Erie v. Tompkins* decision? Given the same facts, would *Erie* come out the same way today?

3. In *Stewart Organization, Inc. v. Ricoh Corp.,* 487 U.S. 22 (1988), the Court extended the *Hanna* Fed. R. Civ. P. analysis to cases of conflicts between federal *statutory* provisions and state practice. Defendant in the diversity action in Alabama federal district court filed a motion under 28 U.S.C. §1404(a) to transfer the action to the Southern District of New York, seeking to invoke a forum selection clause contained in the dealership contract sued upon which required the case to be filed in New York City. The district court denied the motion based upon Alabama state law, which refused to recognize such clauses. The Eleventh Circuit Court of

---

15. There is no indication that when petitioner filed his suit in federal court he had any reason to believe that he would be unable to comply with the service requirements of Oklahoma law or that he chose to sue in federal court in an attempt to avoid those service requirements.

Appeals reversed, holding that venue is a matter of federal procedure and that under federal law principles the forum selection clause was enforceable. *See* Chapter 7.

The United States Supreme Court agreed, holding that because §1404(a) was a validly enacted federal statute (that is, it addressed a matter of practice and procedure) that directly conflicted with state law (it places discretion in the district judge to weigh all factors of convenience and fairness, including the existence of a forum selection clause), it must control the issue, and there was no need to evaluate the outcome-determinative effect of the choice (as there is in "unguided" *Erie* cases).

Justice Scalia dissented, viewing the conflict here as similar to that in *Walker* where the federal rule was not broad enough to cover the issue in dispute. In the absence of a direct conflict between federal and state practice, Scalia fell back upon the outcome test and concluded that application of §1404 to displace the Alabama rule against enforcement of forum selection clauses would encourage forum shopping and produce the inequitable administration of the laws, the twin evils *Erie* was designed to avoid. Scalia's observation that "[t]he decision of an important legal issue should not turn on the accident of diversity of citizenship" brings us back full circle to *Erie* and *York*. How do you think Justice Scalia would define "important"?

Practice Exercise No. 32: Analyzing Vertical Choice of Law Issues in *Carpenter*

Assume, as we did in the previous Practice Exercise, that there is diversity of citizenship between the parties in the *Carpenter* case, thus making available both a federal and a state forum for the action. In weighing the advantages and disadvantages of each, we discover that the Massachusetts legislature has recently adopted a "tort reform" statute providing among other things that a plaintiff seeking punitive damages against a defendant in the state courts must: (1) plead with particularity the facts and circumstances upon which the claim for punitive damages in based, and may not make said allegations upon information and belief; and (2) pay the costs and reasonable attorneys' fees of the defendant if the claim for punitive damages is ultimately unsuccessful. The legislative history recites findings that claims for punitive damages are often made without merit, tend to substantially enlarge the time necessary to try the case, and have turned the litigation system into a lottery in which some plaintiffs win huge windfalls and some defendants are driven into bankruptcy.

One of our associates has suggested that if we filed in federal district court in Massachusetts, we would not be subject to the state tort reform statute. Prepare for a brainstorming session on this strategy for choice of forum. What guidance does the following case provide?

■ GASPERINI v. CENTER FOR HUMANITIES, INC.
518 U.S. 415 (1996)

Justice GINSBURG delivered the opinion of the Court:

Under the law of New York, appellate courts are empowered to review the size of jury verdicts and to order new trials when the jury's award "deviates materially from what would be reasonable compensation." N.Y. Civ. Prac. Law and Rules (CPLR) §5501(c) (McKinney 1995). Under the Seventh Amendment, which governs proceedings in federal court, but not in state court, "the right of trial by jury shall be preserved, and no fact tried by a jury, shall be otherwise re-examined in any Court of the United States, than according to the rules of the common law." U.S. Const., Amdt. 7. The compatibility of these provisions, in an action based on New York law but tried in federal court by reason of the parties' diverse citizenship, is the issue we confront in this case. We hold that New York's law controlling compensation awards for excessiveness or inadequacy can be given effect, without detriment to the Seventh Amendment, if the review standard set out in CPLR §5501(c) is applied by the federal trial court judge, with appellate control of the trial court's ruling limited to review for "abuse of discretion."

I

Petitioner William Gasperini, a journalist for CBS News and the Christian Science Monitor, began reporting on events in Central America in 1984. He earned his living primarily in radio and print media and only occasionally sold his photographic work. During the course of his seven-year stint in Central America, Gasperini took over 5,000 slide transparencies, depicting active war zones, political leaders, and scenes from daily life. In 1990, Gasperini agreed to supply his original color transparencies to The Center for Humanities, Inc. (Center) for use in an educational videotape, Conflict in Central America. Gasperini selected 300 of his slides for the Center; its videotape included 110 of them. The Center agreed to return the original transparencies, but upon the completion of the project, it could not find them.

Gasperini commenced suit in the United States District Court for the Southern District of New York, invoking the court's diversity jurisdiction pursuant to 28 U.S.C. §1332.[1] He alleged several state-law claims for relief, including breach of contract, conversion, and negligence. The Center conceded liability for the lost transparencies and the issue of damages was tried before a jury.

---

1. Plaintiff Gasperini, petitioner here, is a citizen of California; defendant Center, respondent here, is incorporated, and has its principal place of business, in New York.

At trial, Gasperini's expert witness testified that the "industry standard" within the photographic publishing community valued a lost transparency at $1,500. This industry standard, the expert explained, represented the average license fee a commercial photograph could earn over the full course of the photographer's copyright, *i.e.*, in Gasperini's case, his life-time plus 50 years. Gasperini estimated that his earnings from photography totaled just over $10,000 for the period from 1984 through 1993. He also testified that he intended to produce a book containing his best photographs from Central America.

After a three-day trial, the jury awarded Gasperini $450,000 in compensatory damages. This sum, the jury foreperson announced, "is [$]1500 each, for 300 slides." Moving for a new trial under Federal Rule of Civil Procedure 59, the Center attacked the verdict on various grounds, including excessiveness. Without comment, the District Court denied the motion.

The Court of Appeals for the Second Circuit vacated the judgment entered on the jury's verdict. Mindful that New York law governed the controversy, the Court of Appeals endeavored to apply CPLR §5501(c), which instructs that, when a jury returns an itemized verdict, as the jury did in this case, the New York Appellate Division "shall determine that an award is excessive or inadequate if it deviates materially from what would be reasonable compensation." . . . Surveying Appellate Division decisions that reviewed damage awards for lost transparencies, the Second Circuit concluded that testimony on industry standard alone was insufficient to justify a verdict; prime among other factors warranting consideration were the uniqueness of the slides' subject matter and the photographer's earning level.

Guided by Appellate Division rulings, the Second Circuit held that the $450,000 verdict "materially deviates from what is reasonable compensation." 66 F.3d at 431. Some of Gasperini's transparencies, the Second Circuit recognized, were unique, notably those capturing combat situations in which Gasperini was the only photographer present. But others "depicted either generic scenes or events at which other professional photojournalists were present." *Id.* at 431. No more than 50 slides merited a $1,500 award, the court concluded, after "giving Gasperini every benefit of the doubt." *Ibid.* Absent evidence showing significant earnings from photographic endeavors or concrete plans to publish a book, the court further determined, any damage award above $100 each for the remaining slides would be excessive. Remittiturs "present difficult problems for appellate courts," the Second Circuit acknowledged, for court of appeals judges review the evidence from "a cold paper record." *Ibid.* Nevertheless, the Second Circuit set aside the $450,000 verdict and ordered a new trial, unless Gasperini agreed to an award of $100,000.

This case presents an important question regarding the standard a federal court uses to measure the alleged excessiveness of a jury's verdict in an action for damages based on state law. We therefore granted certiorari.

II

Before 1986, state and federal courts in New York generally invoked the same judge-made formulation in responding to excessiveness attacks on jury verdicts: courts would not disturb an award unless the amount was so exorbitant that it "shocked the conscience of the court." *See Consorti*, 72 F.3d at 1012-1013 (collecting cases). As described by the Second Circuit:

> The standard for determining excessiveness and the appropriateness of re-mittitur in New York is somewhat ambiguous. Prior to 1986, New York law employed the same standard as the federal courts, *see Matthews v. CTI Container Transport Int'l Inc.*, 871 F.2d 270, 278 (2d Cir. 1989), which authorized remittitur only if the jury's verdict was so excessive that it "shocked the conscience of the court."

Id. at 1012. *See also* D. Siegel, Practice Commentaries C5501:10, *reprinted in* 7B McKinney's Consolidated Laws of New York Ann., p. 25 (1995) ("conventional standard for altering the verdict was that its sum was so great or so small that it 'shocked the conscience' of the court").

In both state and federal courts, trial judges made the excessiveness assessment in the first instance, and appellate judges ordinarily deferred to the trial court's judgment. *See, e.g., McAllister v. Adam Packing Corp.*, 66 App. Div. 2d 975, 976 (3d Dept. 1978) ("The trial court's determination as to the adequacy of the jury verdict will only be disturbed by an appellate court where it can be said that the trial court's exercise of discretion was not reasonably grounded."); *Martell v. Boardwalk Enterprises, Inc.*, 748 F.2d 740, 750 (2d Cir. 1984) ("The trial court's refusal to set aside or reduce a jury award will be overturned only for abuse of discretion.").

In 1986, as part of a series of tort reform measures,[3] New York codified a standard for judicial review of the size of jury awards. Placed in CPLR §5501(c), the prescription reads:

> In reviewing a money judgment . . . in which it is contended that the award is excessive or inadequate and that a new trial should have been granted unless a stipulation is entered to a different award, the appellate division shall determine that an award is excessive or inadequate if it deviates materially from what would be reasonable compensation. . . .

III

In cases like Gasperini's, in which New York law governs the claims for relief, does New York law also supply the test for federal-court review of the size of the verdict? The Center answers yes. The "deviates materially"

---

3. The legislature sought, particularly, to curtail medical and dental malpractice, and to contain "already high malpractice premiums." Legislative Findings and Declaration, Ch. 266, 1986 N.Y. Laws 470 (McKinney).

standard, it argues, is a substantive standard that must be applied by federal appellate courts in diversity cases. The Second Circuit agreed. *See* 66 F.3d, at 430; *see also Consorti,* 72 F.3d, at 1011 ("[CPLR §5501(c)] is the substantive rule provided by New York law."). Gasperini, emphasizing that §5501(c) trains on the New York Appellate Division, characterizes the provision as procedural, an allocation of decisionmaking authority regarding damages, not a hard cap on the amount recoverable. Correctly comprehended, Gasperini urges, §5501(c)'s direction to the Appellate Division cannot be given effect by federal appellate courts without violating the Seventh Amendment's Reexamination Clause.

As the parties' arguments suggest, CPLR §5501(c), appraised under *Erie R. Co. v. Tompkins,* 304 U.S. 64 (1938), and decisions in *Erie*'s path, is both "substantive" and "procedural": "substantive" in that §5501(c)'s "deviates materially" standard controls how much a plaintiff can be awarded; "procedural" in that §5501(c) assigns decisionmaking authority to New York's Appellate Division. Parallel application of §5501(c) at the federal appellate level would be out of sync with the federal system's division of trial and appellate court functions, an allocation weighted by the Seventh Amendment. The dispositive question, therefore, is whether federal courts can give effect to the substantive thrust of §5501(c) without untoward alteration of the federal scheme for the trial and decision of civil cases.

A

Federal diversity jurisdiction provides an alternative forum for the adjudication of state-created rights, but it does not carry with it generation of rules of substantive law. As *Erie* read the Rules of Decision Act: "Except in matters governed by the Federal Constitution or by Acts of Congress, the law to be applied in any case is the law of the State." 304 U.S. at 78. Under the *Erie* doctrine, federal courts sitting in diversity apply state substantive law and federal procedural law.

Classification of a law as "substantive" or "procedural" for *Erie* purposes is sometimes a challenging endeavor.[7] *Guaranty Trust Co. v. York,* 326 U.S. 99 (1945), an early interpretation of *Erie,* propounded an "outcome-determination" test: "Does it significantly affect the result of a litigation

---

7. Concerning matters covered by the Federal Rules of Civil Procedure, the characterization question is usually unproblematic: It is settled that if the Rule in point is consonant with the Rules Enabling Act, 28 U.S.C. §2072, and the Constitution, the Federal Rule applies regardless of contrary state law. *See Hanna v. Plumer,* 380 U.S. 460 (1965); *Burlington Northern R. Co. v. Woods,* 480 U.S. 1, 4-5(1987). Federal courts have interpreted the Federal Rules, however, with sensitivity to important state interests and regulatory policies. *See, e.g., Walker v. Armco Steel Corp.,* 446 U.S. 740, 750-752 (1980)(reaffirming decision in *Ragan v. Merchants Transfer & Warehouse Co.,* 337 U.S. 530 (1949), that state law rather than Rule 3 determines when a diversity action commences for the purposes of tolling the state statue of limitations; Rule 3 makes no reference to the tolling of state limitations, the Court observed, and accordingly found no "direct conflict"); *S. A. Healy Co. v. Milwaukee Metropolitan Sewerage Dist.,* 60 F.3d 305, 310-312 (7th Cir. 1995) state provision for offers of settlement by plaintiffs is compatible with Federal Rule 68, which is limited to offers by defendants).

for a federal court to disregard a law of a State that would be controlling in an action upon the same claim by the same parties in a State court?" 326 U.S. at 109. Ordering application of a state statute of limitations to an equity proceeding in federal court, the Court said in *Guaranty Trust*: "Where a federal court is exercising jurisdiction solely because of the diversity of citizenship of the parties, the outcome of the litigation in the federal court should be substantially the same, so far as legal rules determine the outcome of a litigation, as it would be if tried in a State court." *Ibid.; see also Ragan v. Merchants Transfer & Warehouse Co.*, 337 U.S. 530, 533 (1949) (when local law that creates the cause of action qualifies it, "federal court must follow suit," for "a different measure of the cause of action in one court than in the other [would transgress] the principle of *Erie*"). A later pathmarking case, qualifying *Guaranty Trust*, explained that the "outcome-determination" test must not be applied mechanically to sweep in all manner of variations; instead, its application must be guided by "the twin aims of the *Erie* rule: discouragement of forumshopping and avoidance of inequitable administration of the laws." *Hanna v. Plumer*, 380 U.S. 460, 468.

Informed by these decisions, we address the question whether New York's "deviates materially" standard, codified in CPLR §5501(c), is outcome affective in this sense: Would "application of the [standard] . . . have so important an effect upon the fortunes of one or both of the litigants that failure to [apply] it would [unfairly discriminate against citizens of the forum State, or] be likely to cause a plaintiff to choose the federal court"? *Id.*, at 468, n.9.

We start from a point the parties do not debate. Gasperini acknowledges that a statutory cap on damages would supply substantive law for *Erie* purposes. *See* Reply Brief for Petitioner 2 ("The state as a matter of its substantive law may, among other things, eliminate the availability of damages for a particular claim entirely, limit the factors a jury may consider in determining damages, or place an absolute cap on the amount of damages available, and such substantive law would be applicable in a federal court sitting in diversity."); *see also* Tr. of Oral Arg. 4-5, 25; *Consorti*, 72 F.3d, at 1011. Although CPLR §5501(c) is less readily classified, it was designed to provide an analogous control.

New York's Legislature codified in §5501(c) a new standard, one that requires closer court review than the commonlaw "shock the conscience" test. More rigorous comparative evaluations attend application of §5501(c)'s "deviates materially" standard. To foster predictability, the legislature required the reviewing court, when overturning a verdict under §5501(c), to state its reasons, including the factors it considered relevant. *See* CPLR §5522(b). We think it a fair conclusion that CPLR §5501(c) differs from a statutory cap principally "in that the maximum amount recoverable is not set forth by statute, but rather is determined by case law." Brief for City of New York as Amicus Curiae 11. In sum, §5501(c) contains a procedural instruction, but the State's objective is manifestly substantive. *Cf. S. A. Healy Co. v. Milwaukee Metropolitan Sewerage Dist.*, 60 F.3d 305, 310 (7th Cir. 1995). It thus appears that if federal courts ignore the change in the New York standard and persist in applying the "shock the conscience" test to damage awards on claims governed by New York law, "'substantial' variations between state and federal [money judgments]" may be expected. *See Hanna*, 380 U.S. at 467-468. We therefore agree with the Second Circuit that New York's check on excessive damages implicates what we have called *Erie*'s "twin aims." Just as the *Erie* principle precludes a federal court from giving a state-created claim "longer life . . . than [the claim] would have had in the state court," *Ragan*, 337 U.S. at 533-534, so *Erie* precludes a recovery in federal court significantly larger than the recovery that would have been tolerated in state court. . . .

[A discussion of the Seventh Amendment re-examination clause is omitted.]

c

. . . In *Byrd*, the Court faced a one-or-the-other choice: trial by judge as in state court, or trial by jury according to the federal practice. In the case before us, a choice of that order is not required, for the principal state and federal interests can be accommodated. The Second Circuit correctly recognized that when New York substantive law governs a claim for relief, New York law and decisions guide the allowable damages. *See* 66 F.3d, at 430; *see also Consorti*, 72 F.3d, at 1011. But that court did not take into account the characteristic of the federal-court system that caused us to reaffirm: "The proper role of the trial and appellate courts in the federal system in reviewing the size of jury verdicts is . . . a matter of federal law." *Donovan v. Penn Shipping Co.*, 429 U.S. 648, 649 (1977) (*per curiam*); *see also Browning-Ferris*, 492 U.S. at 279 ("The role of the district court is to determine whether the jury's verdict is within the confines set by state law. . . . The court of appeals should then review the district court's determination under an abuse-of-discretion standard.").

New York's dominant interest can be respected, without disrupting the federal system, once it is recognized that the federal district court is capable of performing the checking function, *i.e.*, that court can apply the State's "deviates materially" standard in line with New York case law evolving under CPLR §5501(c).[22] We recall, in this regard, that the "deviates

---

22. Justice Scalia finds in Federal Rule of Civil Procedure 59 a "federal standard" for new trial motions in "'direct collision'" with, and "'leaving no room for the operation of,'" a state law like CPLR §5501(c). The relevant prescription, Rule 59(a), has remained unchanged since the adoption of the Federal Rules by this Court in 1937. 302 U.S. 783. Rule 59(a) is as encompassing as it is uncontroversial. It is indeed "Hornbook" law that a most usual ground for a Rule 59 motion is that "the damages are excessive." *See* C. Wright, *Law of Federal Courts* 676-677 (5th ed. 1994). Whether damages are excessive for the claim-in-suit must be governed by some law. And there is no candidate for that governance other than the law that gives rise to the claim for relief—here, the law of New York. *See* 28 U.S.C. §2072(a) and (b)("Supreme Court shall have the power to prescribe general rules of . . . procedure";

materially" standard serves as the guide to be applied in trial as well as appellate courts in New York. *See supra*, at 425.

Within the federal system, practical reasons combine with Seventh Amendment constraints to lodge in the district court, not the court of appeals, primary responsibility for application of §5501(c)'s "deviates materially" check. Trial judges have the "unique opportunity to consider the evidence in the living courtroom context," *Taylor v. Washington Terminal Co.*, 409 F.2d 145, 148 (D.C. Cir. 1969), while appellate judges see only the "cold paper record," 66 F.3d at 431.

District court applications of the "deviates materially" standard would be subject to appellate review under the standard the Circuits now employ when inadequacy or excessiveness is asserted on appeal: abuse of discretion. *See* 11 Wright & Miller, Federal Practice and Procedure §2820, at 212-214, and n.24 (collecting cases); *see* 6A *Moore's Federal Practice* ¶59.08[6], at 59-177 to 59-185 (same). In light of *Erie*'s doctrine, the federal appeals court must be guided by the damage-control standard state law supplies, but as the Second Circuit itself has said: "If we reverse, it must be because of an abuse of discretion. . . . The very nature of the problem counsels restraint. . . . We must give the benefit of every doubt to the judgment of the trial judge." *Dagnello*, 289 F.2d, at 806.

IV

It does not appear that the District Court checked the jury's verdict against the relevant New York decisions demanding more than "industry standard" testimony to support an award of the size the jury returned in this case. As the Court of Appeals recognized, *see* 66 F.3d, at 429, the uniqueness of the photographs and the plaintiff's earnings as photographer—past and reasonably projected—are factors relevant to appraisal of the award. *See, e.g., Blackman v. Michael Friedman Publishing Group, Inc.*, 201 App. Div. 2d 328 (1st Dept. 1994); *Nierenberg v. Wursteria, Inc.*, 189 App. Div. 2d 571, 571-572 (1st Dept. 1993). Accordingly, we vacate the judgment of the Court of Appeals and instruct that court to remand the case to the District Court so that the trial judge, revisiting his ruling on the new trial motion, may test the jury's verdict against CPLR §5501(c)'s "deviates materially" standard.

[The dissenting opinions of Justice STEVENS and Justice SCALIA, respectively, the latter of which was joined by Chief Justice REHNQUIST and Justice THOMAS, are omitted.]

"[s]uch rules shall not abridge, enlarge or modify any substantive right"); *Browning-Ferris*, 492 U.S. at 279 ("standard of excessiveness" is a "matte[r] of state, and not federal, common law"); *see also* R. Fallon, D. Meltzer, & D. Shapiro, *Hart and Wechsler's The Federal Courts and the Federal System* 729-730 (4th ed. 1996) (observing that Court "has continued since *Hanna v. Plumer*, 380 U.S. 460 (1965) to interpret the federal rules to avoid conflict with important state regulatory policies," *citing Walker v. Armco Steel Corp.*, 446 U.S. 740 (1980)).

10

Finality and Preclusion

A. INTRODUCTION TO FINALITY

Suppose that Joe and Sally are involved in an automobile accident. Sally then files a lawsuit against Joe, alleging that his negligence caused the accident and seeking compensation for the broken left headlight on her car. She litigates that case to conclusion, and a final judgment is entered (whether in her favor or against her). Sally then files a second lawsuit arising from the same accident, again alleging that Joe's negligence caused the accident and this time seeking recovery for the broken *right* headlight on her car. Could any dispute resolution system permit such relitigation?

In the American system, the doctrine of *res judicata*, also called *claim preclusion*, prevents Sally from litigating subsequent suits arising from the same accident that has already been the subject of litigation between the same parties. In addition to the obvious inefficiency and waste of resources, relitigation would be unfair to the harassed defendant, and would permit a plaintiff to spin the roulette wheel as many times as necessary to find a jury that would grant relief.

What if Sally files her claim against Joe for damages arising from the automobile accident, but does not include a claim that she has against him for an unpaid loan unrelated to the accident? Must she assert both of these claims in the same lawsuit, or can she choose to litigate those claims separately? We would certainly like Sally to have the option of joining the two claims (and, of course, she does have this option under Fed. R. Civ. P. 18); but we need not *compel* her to do so in order to protect the system or the defendant from harassing lawsuits that rehash the same matters. The two cases contemplated here involve different incidents and transactions, and the evidence presented at the trials would not be redundant. Because the accident claim and the loan claim are not the "same claim," separate litigation is allowed.

It is clear then that the actual operation of the doctrine of *res judicata* or claim preclusion will depend on the breadth of our definition of "claim"—the broader the definition, the more joinder we are going to mandate. And you can imagine several factual circumstances that would explore the margins of that definition. For example, what if Sally's unpaid loan to Joe had helped Joe purchase the car that was involved in the accident? And what if Joe and Sally were in their respective automobiles arguing with each other about the unpaid loan at an intersection, and that argument occasioned the accident?

It should also be noted that this finality doctrine operates in two time frames of critical importance to lawyers. First, in planning the case, a plaintiff's lawyer must be certain to include in the complaint all matters that might be considered part of the *same claim* against that defendant, or risk being precluded from raising the matter in the future. Second, once final judgment of a case has been entered, subsequent litigation between the same parties may require a determination of whether Case 2 is precluded because it represents a "splitting" into two lawsuits of matters that should have been raised in Case 1 because they constitute the same claim. As we will see, claim preclusion operates regardless of whether the plaintiff won or lost Case 1; either way, Case 2 is barred if it is deemed to derive from the same claim.

Now suppose that A and B have executed a contract that requires B to clear timber from A's land every June for ten years. B performs on the contract for two years, but then is sued by A for failure to clear the land in year three. B defends by challenging the validity of the contract, and the case is tried, resulting in a jury verdict and judgment for the plaintiff. Subsequently, A sues B for failure to clear the land in year seven. Assuming that this represents a different claim from the first case because it arises out of a different breach of the multiyear contractual arrangement, and thus the second case is not precluded by claim preclusion, we will see that another doctrine, *issue preclusion* or *collateral estoppel*, will come into play. Once an issue has been adjudicated between adverse parties, that issue cannot be relitigated in another lawsuit between the same parties. While claim preclusion prevents Case 2 from proceeding at all, issue preclusion operates to foreclose only the issue that has previously been litigated and resolved.

The highly influential American Law Institute *Restatement (Second) of Judgments* summarizes the finality doctrines as follows:

■ AMERICAN LAW INSTITUTE, RESTATEMENT (SECOND) OF JUDGMENTS

§17. Effects of Former Adjudication — General Rules

A valid and final personal judgment is conclusive between the parties, except on appeal or other direct review, to the following extent:

(1) If the judgment is in favor of the plaintiff, the claim is extinguished and merged in the judgment and a new claim may arise on the judgment;

(2) If the judgment is in favor of the defendant, the claim is extinguished and the judgment bars a subsequent action on that claim;

(3) A judgment in favor of either the plaintiff or the defendant is conclusive, in a subsequent action between them on the same or a different claim, with respect to any issue actually litigated and determined if its determination was essential to that judgment.

COMMENT

a. Merger (Subsection (1)). When a valid and final personal judgment is rendered in favor of the plaintiff, the claim is generally merged in the judgment. This means that the claim, whether it was valid or not, is extinguished, and the judgment with new rights of enforcement thereof is substituted for the claim.

b. Bar (Subsection (2)). When a valid and final personal judgment is rendered in favor of the defendant, the judgment is generally a bar to a subsequent action on the claim. It is sometimes said that there is an "estoppel by judgment," but that term is not used in the Restatement of this subject. If the original claim was valid, it is extinguished by the judgment; if it was not valid, the effect of the judgment is conclusively to establish its invalidity.

c. Issue preclusion (Subsection (3)). A valid and final personal judgment, whether in favor of the plaintiff or of the defendant, has a further effect — that of issue preclusion. In a subsequent action between the parties, the judgment generally is conclusive as to the issues raised in the subsequent action if those issues were actually litigated and determined in the prior action and if their determination was essential to the judgment. When the subsequent action is on a different claim, this effect of the judgment is sometimes designated a collateral estoppel.

d. Erroneous judgment. The general rules stated in this Section are applicable to a valid and final judgment, even if it is erroneous and subject to reversal. If the judgment is erroneous, the unsuccessful party's remedy is to have it set aside or reversed in the original proceedings. Such a remedy may be sought by a motion for a new trial or other relief in the court that rendered the judgment, or by an appeal or other proceedings for review of the judgment in an appellate court.

The black letter law and the policies underlying the finality doctrines are easy to understand. "*Res judicata* and collateral estoppel relieve parties of the cost and vexation of multiple law suits, conserve judicial resources, and, by preventing inconsistent decisions, encourage reliance on adjudication." *Allen v. McCurry*, 449 U.S. 90, 94 (1980). The challenge, as usual, is applying the doctrine to the variety of fact situations that arise in litigation in a way that produces fair and just outcomes.

The finality doctrines of claim and issue preclusion must not be confused with the principle of *stare decisis*, by which courts generally follow past precedent in resolving questions of law. *Stare decisis* "is a basic self-governing principle within the Judicial Branch" which is designed to ensure that the law will not change erratically, and which "permits society to presume that bedrock principles are founded in the law rather than in the proclivities of individuals." *Patterson v. McLean Credit Union*, 491 U.S. 164, 172 (1989). While precedents are not sacrosanct, the burden is certainly on the party advocating abandonment of established precedent. In our *Sally v. Joe* lawsuit, for example, decisional law in that jurisdiction that establishes contributory negligence as a complete bar to recovery would control unless Sally's lawyers were successful in arguing for a departure from precedent.

B. CLAIM PRECLUSION (*RES JUDICATA*) — "SPEAK NOW OR FOREVER HOLD YOUR PEACE"

Fed. R. Civ. P. 8(c) requires *res judicata* to be pled as an affirmative defense (can you explain why?). And in order for *res judicata* to bar a plaintiff's claim, three elements must be shown:

(1) a prior suit that proceeded to a final valid judgment on the merits;
(2) the present suit arises out of the same claim as the prior suit; and
(3) the parties in both suits are the same, or in privity.

1. What Constitutes the "Same Claim"?

The defining unit for the operation of claim preclusion is the meaning of a "claim." The following sections of the *Restatement (Second) of Judgments* explain the rationale of the modern transactional definition.

■ AMERICAN LAW INSTITUTE, RESTATEMENT (SECOND) OF JUDGMENTS

§24. DIMENSIONS OF "CLAIM" FOR PURPOSES OF MERGER OR BAR — GENERAL RULE CONCERNING "SPLITTING"

(1) When a valid and final judgment rendered in an action extinguishes the plaintiff's claim pursuant to the rules of merger or bar, the claim extinguished includes all rights of the plaintiff to remedies against the defendant with respect to all or any part of the transaction, or series of connected transactions, out of which the action arose.

(2) What factual grouping constitutes a "transaction," and what groupings constitute a "series," are to be determined pragmatically, giving weight to such considerations as whether the facts are related in time, space, origin, or motivation, whether they form a convenient trial unit, and whether their treatment as a unit conforms to the parties' expectations or business understanding or usage.

COMMENT

a. Rationale of a transactional view of claim. In defining claim to embrace all the remedial rights of the plaintiff against the defendant growing out of the relevant transaction (or series of connected transactions), this Section responds to modern procedural ideas which have found expression in the Federal Rules of Civil Procedure and other procedural systems.

"Claim," in the context of *res judicata*, has never been broader than the transaction to which it related. But in the days when civil procedure still bore the imprint of the forms of action and the division between law and equity, the courts were prone to associate claim with a single theory of recovery, so that, with respect to one transaction, a plaintiff might have as many claims as there were theories of the substantive law upon which he could seek relief against the defendant. Thus, defeated in an action based on one theory, the plaintiff might be able to maintain another action based on a different theory, even though both actions were grounded upon the defendant's identical act or connected acts forming a single life-situation. In those earlier days there was also some adherence to a view that associated claim with the assertion of a single primary right as accorded by the substantive law, so that, if it appeared that the defendant had invaded a number of primary rights conceived to be held by the plaintiff, the plaintiff had the same number of claims, even though they all sprang from a unitary occurrence. There was difficulty in knowing which rights were primary and what was their extent, but a primary right and the corresponding claim might turn out to be narrow. Thus it was held by some courts that a judgment for or against the plaintiff in an action for personal injuries did not preclude an action by him for property damage occasioned by the same negligent conduct on the part of the defendant—this deriving from the idea that the right to be free of bodily injury was distinct from the property right. Still another view of claim looked to sameness of evidence; a second action was precluded where the evidence to support it was the same as that needed to support the first. Sometimes this was made the sole test of identity of claim; sometimes it figured as a positive but not as a negative test; that is, in certain situations a second action might be precluded although the evidence material to it varied from that in the first action. Even so, claim was not coterminous with the transaction itself.

The present trend is to see claim in factual terms and to make it coterminous with the transaction regardless of the number of substantive theories, or variant forms of relief flowing from those theories, that may be available to the plaintiff; regardless of the number of primary rights that may have been invaded; and regardless of the variations in the evidence needed to support the theories or rights. The transaction is the basis of the litigative unit or entity which may not be split.

. . . A modern procedural system . . . permits the presentation in the action of all material relevant to the transaction without artificial confinement to any single substantive theory or kind of relief and without regard to historical forms of action or distinctions between law and equity. . . . The law of *res judicata* now reflects the expectation that parties who are given the capacity to present their "entire controversies" shall in fact do so.

b. Transaction: application of a pragmatic standard. The expression "transaction, or series of connected transactions," is not capable of a mathematically precise definition; it invokes a pragmatic standard to be applied with attention to the facts of the cases. And underlying the standard is the need to strike a delicate balance between, on the one hand, the interests of the defendant and of the courts in bringing litigation to a close and, on the other, the interest of the plaintiff in the vindication of a just claim.

It should be emphasized that the concept of a transaction is here used in the broad sense it has come to acquire in the interpretation of statutes and rules governing pleading and other aspects of civil procedure. Thus the overtones of voluntary interchange often associated with the term in normal speech do not obtain.

In general, the expression connotes a natural grouping or common nucleus of operative facts. Among the factors relevant to a determination whether the facts are so woven together as to constitute a single claim are their relatedness in time, space, origin, or motivation, and whether, taken together, they form a convenient unit for trial purposes. Though no single factor is determinative, the relevance of trial convenience makes it appropriate to ask how far the witnesses or proofs in the second action would tend to overlap the witnesses or proofs relevant to the first. If there is a substantial overlap, the second action should ordinarily be held precluded. But the opposite does not hold true; even when there is not a substantial overlap, the second action may be precluded if it stems from the same transaction or series.

c. Transaction may be single despite different harms, substantive theories, measures or kinds of relief. A single transaction ordinarily gives rise to but one claim by one person against another. When a person by one act takes a number of chattels belonging to another, the transaction is single, and judgment for the value of some of the goods exhausts the claim and precludes the injured party from maintaining one action for the remainder. In the more complicated case where one act causes a number of harms to, or invades a number of different interests of the same person, there is still but one transaction; a judgment based on the act usually prevents the person from maintaining another action for any of the harms not sued for in the first action. . . .

That a number of different legal theories casting liability on an actor may apply to a given episode does not create multiple transactions and hence multiple claims. This remains true although the several legal theories depend on different shadings of the facts, or would emphasize different elements of the facts, or would call for different measures of liability or different kinds of relief.

Consider the application of the definition of "claim" in the next case.

■ CAR CARRIERS, INC., v. FORD MOTOR COMPANY
789 F.2d 589 (7th Cir. 1989)

RIPPLE, Circuit Judge.

In this case, we are asked to decide whether the present litigation is barred by an earlier lawsuit under the doctrine of *res judicata.* For the reasons which follow, we hold that the present suit is barred by the earlier judgment and, accordingly, affirm the judgment of the district court.

In 1982, Car Carriers, Inc. (Car Carriers) and six related entities brought an action against Ford Motor Company (Ford) and Nu-Car Carriers, Inc. (Nu-Car). Count I of the six count complaint (1982 Complaint) accused Ford and Nu-Car of conspiring in violation of the Act, 15 U.S.C. §1. The remaining five counts asserted pendent state law claims.

The district court dismissed the entire action. The court found the antitrust claim lacking because the plaintiffs failed "to suffer the type of harm the antitrust laws were designed to recompense." Further, since the court found that this defect was "noncurable," the antitrust claim was dismissed with prejudice. Having dismissed the complaint's only federal claim, the district court declined to exercise pendent jurisdiction over the remaining state law claims and dismissed them without prejudice. On appeal, a panel of this court affirmed the district court's decision in all respects.

Undaunted by their first unfruitful journey through the federal courts, Car Carriers and its related entities filed the present action on October 25, 1983 (1983 Complaint). The 1983 Complaint consisted of twenty-four counts: Counts I-VI alleged violations of the Racketeer Influenced and Corrupt Organizations Act (RICO), 18 U.S.C. §1961 *et seq.*; Count XXIV alleged a violation of the Interstate Commerce Act, 49 U.S.C. §§11902-11904; the remaining seventeen counts alleged violations of Illinois law.

The district court again dismissed the entire action. The court held that the federal claims arose from the same "basic fact situation" as that alleged in support of the 1982 Complaint's antitrust claim and, therefore, were barred by the doctrine of *res judicata*. For reasons which are not relevant here, this dismissal was without prejudice. The state law claims were again dismissed without prejudice as not pendent to any valid federal claim. After unsuccessful attempts to clarify or amend the district court's judgment, this appeal followed.

I

Before addressing Car Carriers' substantive claims, it will be helpful to set out the occurrences which sparked the 1982 Complaint—the initial litigation in this matter. As set forth in that complaint, from 1968 until 1981, Car Carriers transported new Ford vehicles from Ford's plants and railheads in the Chicago area. As a transport company, Car Carriers was regulated by both the Illinois and Interstate Commerce Commissions; accordingly, Car Carriers' rates were subject to approval by both agencies. The complaint alleged that Ford had the power to control these rates either by formally opposing any rate increase sought before the agencies or by simply terminating the carrier.

According to Car Carriers, as early as 1975, Ford and its alleged co-conspirators entered into contracts and continuing combinations which were designed to restrain trade in the business of providing haul-away motor transportation for new Ford automobiles. As explained in this court's earlier opinion, Car Carriers accused Ford of employing the following method to implement its goal:

First, the carrier selected for elimination (the so-called "target carrier") would be required to make substantial investments in new tractor-trailer equipment, real estate, and new terminal facilities. In return, Ford would promise additional transportation traffic and "complete agreement with increased tariff rates necessary to pay for these acquisitions." After the "target" carriers had made these investments, however, Ford would then prevent them from obtaining the rate increases necessary for profitable operations.

Second, Ford, with support of other carriers, "interfered with and prevented [the] target haulaway carriers and their affiliates from selling their businesses and assets as going business concerns or prevented [the] target haulaway carriers from consolidation or merger with other carriers." Finally, Ford would apparently terminate its relationship with the target carrier at this point, thereby allowing the favored carriers to "acquire the businesses and assets of [the target carriers] at distress prices or for less than fair market value as going business concerns."

Car Carriers further averred that its demise generally followed the pattern just described: In 1975, Ford directed . . . Car Carriers to sell . . . [its] assets and business to a second Ford carrier. After Car Carriers had entered into negotiations for a sale with the E & L Transport Co, . . . however, Ford "unreasonably interfered with and prevented" the consummation of the agreement by inducing the corporate parent of E & L to repudiate an executed letter of intent. In 1977 and 1978, Ford induced Car Carriers to purchase over $6,000,000 worth of new tractor-trailer equipment with the promise that Car Carriers "would be able to recover the cost of such equipment with additional transport business and higher tariff rates." However, during the entire period of 1975 to 1981, Ford caused Car Carriers's operations in Chicago to be unprofitable through its "refusal to allow adequate published tariff rates or other compensation" for Car Carriers and by "refusing to allow adequate temporary rate adjustments."

In 1979, Ford prevented Car Carriers from acquiring the outstanding stock of Automobile Transport, Inc. ("ATI"), which was at that time Ford's carrier in Wayne, Michigan and other areas. This action by Ford "prevented a carrier consolidation which would have generated valuable backhaul business and resulted in significant operating efficiencies and cost reduction benefits" to ATI, Car Carriers, and Ford. Later that year, Ford terminated ATI and awarded the substantial portion of ATI's business to Nu-Car and E & L on the basis of "sham and knowingly predatory bids."

In 1981, Ford solicited bid proposals for Chicago haulaway services from Car Carriers and other Ford transporters. In October of that year, Ford terminated Car Carriers and awarded the haulaway contract for the Chicago area to Nu-Car on the basis of the latter's "sham and knowingly predatory bid." To minimize the losses from the termination, Car Carriers attempted to sell its facilities and other assets to Nu-Car. However, the effort was frustrated when Ford and Nu-Car insisted on "walkaway and other onerous provisions . . . as well as unacceptable covenants and releases" of Car Carriers's claims against Ford, Nu-Car, and Associated Transport, Inc.; Nu-Car eventually constructed its own terminal facility near the Ford plant on land provided by Ford.

In this litigation, the appellants present [two] issues for our review. First, they ask that we reject the district court's fact-oriented test for *res judicata* in favor of an analysis which would differentiate causes of action based on the rights, duties, and injuries allegedly redressed by each claim. Second, assuming we adopt the district court's approach, the appellants ask that we relieve them of their *res judicata* burden because some of their claims were based on facts which—while admittedly in existence prior to the 1982 Complaint—were unknown to them until after judgment on that complaint.

II

The district court found that the federal claims alleged in the 1983 Complaint arose out of the same factual context as described in the 1982 Complaint. Thus, the court dismissed these claims as barred by the doctrine of *res judicata*. The appellants do not disagree with the district court's finding that both complaints arose out of a common core of operative fact; rather, they attempt to overturn the district court's decision by persuading us to adopt an alternate formulation for determining the application of *res judicata*. Under this alternate test, *res judicata* would not bar a second lawsuit when "an analysis of the rights, duties, and injuries involved in the second lawsuit reveals that they are materially different from those in issue in the first." Appellants' Br. at 28. For the reasons which will be explained in the following section, we decline to adopt the appellants' suggested formulation.

Res judicata is designed to ensure the finality of judicial decisions. It is not "a mere matter of practice or procedure inherited from a more technical time than ours. It is a rule of fundamental and substantial justice, 'of public policy and of private peace,' which should be cordially regarded and enforced by the courts. . . ." *Hart Steel Co. v. Railroad Supply Co.*, 244 U.S. 294, 299 (1917). It "encourages reliance on judicial decisions, bars vexatious litigation, and frees the courts to resolve other disputes." As we recently stated in *Alexander v. Chicago Park District*, 773 F.2d 850 (7th Cir. 1985), "'its enforcement is essential to the maintenance of social order; for, the aid of judicial tribunals would not be invoked for the vindication of rights of person and property, if . . . conclusiveness did not attend the judgments of such tribunals.'" *Id.* at 853.

A

"Under *res judicata*, 'a final judgment on the merits bars further claims by parties or their privies based on the same cause of action.'" In determining the scope of a "cause of action," this circuit has utilized the "same transaction" test. *Alexander*, 773 F.2d at 854. Under this test, a "cause of action" consists of "'a single core of operative facts' which give rise to a remedy." *Alexander*, 773 F.2d at 854. This "same transaction" test is decidedly fact-oriented. Once a transaction has caused injury, all claims arising from that transaction must be brought in one suit or be lost. Thus, "a mere change in the legal theory does not create a new cause of action."

Alexander, 773 F.2d at 854. Therefore, prior litigation acts as a bar not only to those issues which were raised and decided in the earlier litigation but also to those issues which could have been raised in that litigation. *Federated Department Stores, Inc. v. Moitie*, 452 U.S. 394, 398 (1981).

As the commentators have noted, this approach is consistent with the general litigation scheme established by the Federal Rules of Civil Procedure. Litigants have great latitude in joining claims and amending pleadings. *See* Fed. R. Civ. P. 15, 18. Thus, to further the purpose of the rules, it is appropriate that *res judicata* be defined with sufficient breadth to encourage parties to present all their related claims at one time. Further, we note that the Federal Rules define compulsory counterclaims as those claims which have arisen out of the same transaction or occurrence that prompted the plaintiffs' action. *See* Fed. R. Civ. P. 13(a). By compelling defendants to bring their claims in the same action, the rule encourages the simultaneous and final resolution of all claims which arise from a common factual background. Thus, if the Federal Rules impose this obligation on defendants, we believe that it is appropriate to interpret the doctrine of *res judicata* in such a way as to further that same goal by imposing a similar obligation on plaintiffs.

The appellants argue that, while the "same transaction" test may be the primary test for defining a "cause of action," it is not the universal test. The appellants argue that a more appropriate test in this case would be one which scrutinized the theories of relief (RICO, Interstate Commerce Act, Sherman Act) in search of differences between the rights, duties and injuries addressed by each.

We do not disagree that [the cases relied upon] contain language suggesting that *res judicata* analysis can involve a comparison of the rights, duties and injuries that have been alleged. We believe, however, that this language must be read cautiously lest it undermine the fundamental policies of *res judicata*: "that there be an end of litigation; that those who have contested an issue shall be bound by the result of the contest, and that matters once tried shall be considered forever settled as between the parties." *Baldwin v. Iowa State Traveling Men's Association*, 283 U.S. 522 (1931). It is no accident that the "same transaction" test has become "the present trend among courts nationwide." *Hagee v. City of Evanston*, 729 F.2d 510, 513 n.5 (7th Cir. 1984). It preserves—far more firmly than the alternate formulation—the fundamental policy concerns of the doctrine. In our view, these policy concerns counsel against using in this case the "right-duty" approach which the appellants have suggested. Indeed, even in *Harper Plastics*, a case upon which the appellants heavily rely, the court explicitly warned that an unsuccessful party ought not be able to "frustrate the doctrine of *res judicata* by cloaking the same cause of action in the language of a theory of recovery untried in the previous litigation." 657 F.2d at 945. Therefore, the "right-duty" approach should not be used as a substitute for the "same transaction" test absent compelling circumstances and a clear showing that such a substitution will not undermine the policies of *res judicata*. Appellants have made absolutely no such showing in this case.

B

We turn now to an application of the "transactional" test to the facts of this case. We must determine whether Car Carriers' RICO and Interstate Commerce Act claims could have been brought in the earlier litigation; in other words, we must decide whether these claims are part of the same cause of action which spawned the earlier Sherman Act claim. [The three threshold requirements of *res judicata* are (1) an identity of the parties or their privies, (2) an identity of the causes of action, and (3) a final judgment on the merits.]

In this appeal, neither party has contested the "final judgment" element. Further, neither party has questioned the identity of the parties in the two actions. While N & W was a new party defendant in the second action, *see* supra note 3, it did not join in the *res judicata* motion; and even though the named plaintiffs were not identical in both actions, the additional plaintiffs in the second action did "not deny their obvious privity with the plaintiffs in the 1982 Action." 583 F. Supp. at 223. Therefore, the only open question concerns the identity of the causes of action involved in both suits.

In concluding that both the 1982 and the 1983 Complaints alleged the same cause of action, the district court first relied on an analysis derived from the doctrine of pendent jurisdiction. As enunciated in *United Mine Workers v. Gibbs*, 383 U.S. 715 (1966), a federal court may exercise pendent jurisdiction over a state law claim if both the state and federal claims derive from a common nucleus of operative fact. In this case, the alleged pendent claims were virtually identical to the state law claims alleged in the 1982 Complaint. Thus, according to the district court's reasoning, the appellants had admitted that the Sherman Act, RICO, and Interstate Commerce Act claims derived from a common nucleus of operative fact. Therefore, the district court concluded that *res judicata* was appropriate because the 1983 Complaint's RICO and Interstate Commerce Act claims arose out of the same set of facts as did the 1982 Complaint's Sherman Act claim.

There is a good deal of merit to the trial court's position. However, we are reluctant to rely on that ground alone. Mere allegations that state claims are pendent to a federal action do not create pendent jurisdiction. When dismissing both the 1982 Complaint's federal claims and the 1983 Complaint's federal claims, the district court also dismissed the state claims without determining whether they had properly been brought as pendent claims. Therefore, since the district court's decision did not disclose whether pendent jurisdiction would have been proper had the federal claims survived, we must find a more solid basis for our decision.

As an alternate ground for its decision, the district court also specifically found that the RICO and Sherman Act counts arose out of the same underlying facts. The court stated: "Like the present RICO claims, the earlier antitrust claims alleged Ford induced Car Carriers to make investments it could not recoup. Like the earlier antitrust claims, the current RICO claims allege Car Carriers was terminated due to a sham and predatory bid, and Ford and Nu-Car refused to buy Car Carriers' assets upon its termination." We agree; the RICO and Sherman Act claims arose out of a single core of operative facts and, thus, were parts of the same cause of action.

The district court did not specifically mention the Interstate Commerce Act claim—Count XXIV of the 1983 Complaint. Yet, a brief review of that count makes clear that it too was part of the same cause of action. Paragraph 504, the first paragraph of that count, states in relevant part:

> Count XXIV seeks damages from Ford and Nu-Car as a result of their individual and joint violations of 49 U.S.C. §§11902, 11903(a) and (b) and 11904(a)(3) and (b) wherein they both solicited, gave, granted, accepted, received, and offered rebates, concessions and discrimination by various direct and indirect means in a continuing course of conduct from July 1981 until about June 1983, which conduct was designed to replace Car Carriers at Chicago, to install Nu-Car as Ford's driveaway and haulaway carrier, and to secure Nu-Car improvement of Ford owned real estate in Chicago by Nu-Car at no cost to Ford. These Ford/Nu-Car violations grew out of Ford's request for bids to replace CCI in Chicago, Nu-Car's response to that request and Ford's subsequent actions in installing Nu-Car in Chicago and elsewhere with incremental traffic effective October 1981.

This allegation parallels the facts underlying the 1982 Complaint. Accordingly, the district court did not err by dismissing this count. [While we are aware that the actions alleged in Count XXIV extend beyond the time period alleged in the 1982 Complaint, we believe that this discrepancy is unimportant. In this case, it is sufficient that there is some chronological overlap and that the two complaints arise out of the same common nucleus of operative fact. To the extent that Count XXIV addresses events occurring after the first judgment, we note that the 1983 Complaint was dismissed without prejudice specifically to allow such a claim to be brought later.]

In sum, we hold that the district court properly applied the "same transaction test" to dismiss all of Car Carriers' federal claims.

III

As a second ground for appeal, Car Carriers asks that we lift the *res judicata* bar for some of its claims because Car Carriers did not discover the facts supporting those claims until after the 1982 Complaint had been dismissed. In essence, Car Carriers claims that since *res judicata* will not bar actions based on facts occurring after the initial judgment, *see Lawlor v. National Screen Service Corp.*, 349 U.S. 322 (1955) — presumably because those facts were unknown to the plaintiffs when they initiated their first action — *res judicata* should likewise not bar claims based on prejudgment facts which were unknown to the plaintiffs when they filed. We find this contention to be absolutely without merit.

As we concluded in Part II, *supra*, all of the appellants' claims were part of the same cause of action; they all arose from a single core of operative fact. Since all claims arose from the same factual context and since the appellants had sufficient knowledge to sue on one claim, they also had sufficient knowledge to sue on the rest of their claims. When a litigant files a lawsuit, the courts have a right to presume that he has done his legal and factual homework. It would undermine the basic policies protected by the doctrine of *res judicata* to permit the appellants to once again avail themselves of judicial time and energy while another litigant, who has yet to be heard even once, waits in line behind them. . . .

IV

In disposing of the 1983 Complaint, the district court properly analyzed the *res judicata* effect of its earlier decision. We note, in addition, that since Counts I and II were properly dismissed as barred by *res judicata*, all actions against the appellee Norfolk & Western Railway Company were properly dismissed inasmuch as they were derivative. Therefore, the decision of the district court is Affirmed.

Comments and Questions

1. The *Car Carriers* plaintiff-appellants argue, first, that *res judicata* doctrine should not be controlled by a transactional analysis of what constitutes the "same claim," but rather by a narrower definition based on rights, duties, and injuries. Some jurisdictions following this latter approach have concluded that separate claims for property damage and personal injury may arise out of the same accident, since the right to recover for property damage is distinct from the right to be compensated for personal injuries. *See Restatement (Second) of Judgments* §24, Comment c and Illustration 1. Why do you suppose these jurisdictions are increasingly in the minority?

2. Plaintiff-appellants' second argument is that *res judicata* should not

apply because some of the facts upon which they rely in the second case were not known to them until after the judgment in the first case. The court dismissed this contention as "absolutely without merit." Could finality doctrine accommodate a "newly discovered facts" exception?

3. What is the relationship between Fed. R. Civ. P. 13(a) and claim preclusion? If there were no compulsory counterclaim rule, would general *res judicata* principles still achieve the same result?

4. In *Heacock v. Heacock.*, 402 Mass. 21 (1988), Carla Heacock filed a tort action in Superior Court against her former husband Gregg, alleging that while they were still married he had assaulted her violently, causing traumatic epilepsy, and seeking damages for her personal injuries. Gregg filed a motion to dismiss, asserting that the tort action was precluded by the prior divorce action and judgment in the Probate Court. The divorce on the ground of irretrievable breakdown had been granted following a hearing in which Carla presented evidence as to, among other things, the assault and her injuries.

The trial court judge dismissed Carla's tort action "on the basis of issue preclusion, collateral estoppel, *res judicata*, or any one of those three, whichever happens to be the best one." 402 Mass. at 23. Can you help the judge out? Compare your analysis with that of the Supreme Judicial Court on Carla's appeal:

> 1. Claim preclusion. The doctrine of claim preclusion makes a valid, final judgment conclusive on the parties and their privies, and bars further litigation of all matters that were or should have been adjudicated in the action. This is so even though the claimant is prepared in a second action to present different evidence or legal theories to support his claim, or seeks different remedies. The doctrine is a ramification of the policy considerations that underlie the rule against splitting a cause of action, and is "based on the idea that the party to be precluded has had the incentive and opportunity to litigate the matter fully in the first lawsuit." As such, it applies only where both actions were based on the same claim.
>
> A tort action is not based on the same underlying claim as an action for divorce. The purpose of a tort action is to redress a legal wrong in damages; that of a divorce action is to sever the marital relationship between the parties, and, where appropriate, to fix the parties' respective rights and obligations with regard to alimony and support, and to divide the marital estate. Although a judge in awarding alimony and dividing marital property must consider, among other things, the conduct of the parties during the marriage, the purposes for which these awards are made do not include compensating a party in damages for injuries suffered. The purpose of an award of alimony is to provide economic support to a dependent spouse; that of the division of marital property is to recognize and equitably recompense the parties' respective contributions to the marital partnership. The plaintiff could not have recovered damages for the tort in the divorce action, as the Probate Court does not have jurisdiction to hear tort actions

and award damages.* The policy considerations commonly advanced to justify the doctrine of claim preclusion are not implicated in the circumstances of this case. Maintenance of the tort claim will not subject the defendant and the courts to the type of piecemeal litigation that the doctrine of claim preclusion seeks to prevent. As such, nothing in the doctrine or in the policy considerations underlying it warrants its application in the circumstances of this case.

2. Issue preclusion. To defend successfully on the ground of issue preclusion, the defendant must establish that the issue of fact sought to be foreclosed actually was litigated and determined in a prior action between the parties or their privies, and that the determination was essential to the decision in the prior action. Because a judge in awarding alimony and dividing marital property must consider a number of factors, and the judge who presided over the Heacocks' divorce action did not make any findings of fact to support his judgment, we cannot say that the judge necessarily resolved any issue relating to the defendant's assault of the plaintiff. Accordingly, the doctrine of issue preclusion does not apply.

Id., 402 Mass. at 23-25.

2. What Constitutes a Final Valid Judgment on the Merits?

Next consider the *Restatement*'s explanations of the concepts "judgment on the merits" and "final judgment." *See also* Fed. R. Civ. P. 41(b).

■ AMERICAN LAW INSTITUTE, RESTATEMENT (SECOND) OF JUDGMENTS

§20. JUDGMENT FOR DEFENDANT—EXCEPTIONS TO THE GENERAL RULE OF BAR

(1) A personal judgment for the defendant, although valid and final, does not bar another action by the plaintiff on the same claim:

(a) When the judgment is one of dismissal for lack of jurisdiction, for improper venue, or for nonjoinder or misjoinder of parties; or

---

* *Editor's Note:* For obvious reasons, claim preclusion does not apply where the "plaintiff was unable to rely on a certain theory of the case or to seek a certain remedy or form of relief in the first action because of the limitations on the subject matter jurisdiction of the courts or restrictions on their authority to entertain multiple theories or demands for multiple remedies or forms of relief in a single action, and the plaintiff desires in the second action to rely on that theory or to seek that remedy or form of relief. *See Restatement (Second) of Judgments* §26(1)(c).

(b) When the plaintiff agrees to or elects a nonsuit (or voluntary dismissal) without prejudice or the court directs that the plaintiff be nonsuited (or that the action be otherwise dismissed) without prejudice; or

(c) When by statute or rule of court the judgment does not operate as a bar to another action on the same claim, or does not so operate unless the court specifies, and no such specification is made. . . .

ILLUSTRATION

1. A brings an action against B for personal injuries, and the action is dismissed for improper venue on the ground that the judicial district in which suit was brought was not the district of defendant's residence as required by law. Although A is not barred from maintaining an action on the claim in another district, the rules of issue preclusion are applicable to the determination that venue was improper in the initial action.

2. A brings an action against B for personal injuries in a federal court, basing jurisdiction on diversity of citizenship. The action is dismissed on the ground that the alleged diversity does not in fact exist. A is not barred from bringing another action on the same claim in a court of competent jurisdiction.

3. The Parties Are the Same or Are in Privity

■ GONZALEZ v. BANCO CENTRAL CORP.
27 F.3d 751 (1st Cir. 1994)

SELYA, Circuit Judge.

This appeal raises tantalizing questions concerning the application of the doctrine of *res judicata* to nonparties. Because we conclude that appellants cannot lawfully be precluded from bringing their action in the circumstances at bar, we reverse the district court's order of dismissal and remand for further proceedings.

I. BACKGROUND

In the 1970s, a consortium of real estate developers sold subdivided lots of undeveloped land to approximately 3,000 purchasers, most of whom resided in Puerto Rico. Contrary to the promoters' glowing representations, the real estate proved to be Florida swampland, unsuitable for development.

In 1982, a gaggle of duped purchasers (whom we shall call "the Rodriguez plaintiffs") commenced a civil action in the United States District Court for the District of Puerto Rico. They sued the sellers, the banks that financed the project, and several related individuals. The Rodriguez plaintiffs alleged violations of the Interstate Land Sales Full Disclosure Act ("ILSFDA"), 15 U.S.C. §1703, the Securities Exchange Act of 1934, 15 U.S.C. §78j, Rule 10b-5 thereunder, 17 C.F.R. §240.10b-5, and the Racketeering Influenced and Corrupt Organizations Act ("RICO"), 18 U.S.C. §§1961-1964. Some of the plaintiffs then assisted in the formation of the Sunrise Litigation Group. The group's members paid fees that helped defray the costs of the litigation and exchanged information that sometimes proved to be of use in pursuing the litigation.

After several years of discovery and numerous amendments to the pleadings, the Rodriguez plaintiffs, 152 strong, sought to convert their suit to a class action. In April of 1987, the district court refused either to certify a class or to permit additional plaintiffs to intervene. Almost immediately thereafter, several prospective plaintiffs who had tried in vain to join the Rodriguez litigation initiated the instant action. The new coalition of claimants (whom we shall call "the Gonzalez plaintiffs") were represented by the same lawyers who represented the Rodriguez plaintiffs. They sued the same defendants and their complaint mimicked a proposed amended complaint on file (but never allowed) in the Rodriguez litigation. . . .

Despite strong evidence of skullduggery, the Rodriguez plaintiffs frittered away much of their case through a series of pretrial blunders. The Rodriguez plaintiffs ultimately lost what remained of their case after a seven-week jury trial when Judge Fuste directed verdicts for the defendants on the only surviving claims and this court upheld his ruling on appeal, *see Rodriguez v. Banco Central Corp.*, 990 F.2d 7, 14 (1st Cir. 1993).

Following the interment of the Rodriguez litigation, renewed attention focused on the Gonzalez litigation (which was pending before Judge Laffitte). By then, the Gonzalez plaintiffs were pressing certain claims that replicated those pressed and lost by the Rodriguez plaintiffs, e.g., claims under the ILSFDA, Rule 10b-5, and RICO (premised on securities fraud), and certain additional claims that had been neglected or abandoned by the Rodriguez plaintiffs, e.g., RICO claims premised on mail fraud, state-law claims for fraud, and claims for breach of contract.

After silhouetting the Gonzalez plaintiffs' suit against the backdrop of the completed Rodriguez litigation, Judge Laffitte, by way of an unpublished memorandum opinion, dismissed the action in its entirety on grounds of *res judicata*. The Gonzalez plaintiffs appeal.

II. ANALYSIS

Although appellants were not parties to the earlier litigation, the court below applied *res judicata* in bar of their claims under a theory of privity. The applicability vel non of the doctrine of *res judicata* presents a question of law over which we exercise plenary appellate review. . . .

The accepted formulation of *res judicata* for federal court use teaches that "a final judgment on the merits of an action precludes the parties or their privies from relitigating issues that were or could have been raised in that action." *Allen v. McCurry*, 449 U.S. 90, 94 (1980). Accordingly, the elements of *res judicata* are (1) a final judgment on the merits in an earlier suit, (2) sufficient identicality between the causes of action asserted in the earlier and later suits, and (3) sufficient identicality between the parties in the two suits.

In the present situation, the first element in this tripartite test provokes no controversy; appellants concede that the earlier (Rodriguez) suit resulted in final judgment on the merits. Thus, we concentrate our energies on the remaining two prongs of the test.

IDENTICALITY OF CAUSES OF ACTION

To determine whether sufficient subject matter identity exists between an earlier and a later suit, federal courts employ a transactional approach. This approach recognizes that a valid and final judgment in an action will extinguish subsequent claims "with respect to all or any part of the transaction, or series of connected transactions, out of which the action arose."

To understand the transactional approach, it is necessary to appreciate that a single transaction or series of transactions can—and often does—give rise to a multiplicity of claims. Phrased another way, "[a] single cause of action can manifest itself in an outpouring of different claims, based variously on federal statutes, state statutes, and the common law." The necessary identity will be found to exist if both sets of claims—those asserted in the earlier action and those asserted in the subsequent action—derive from a common nucleus of operative facts. *See id.* This principle pertains no matter how diverse or prolific the claims themselves may be. *See* J. Moore, 1B *Federal Practice* ¶ 0.410[1] at 350 (2d ed. 1993) (explaining that "the 'cause of action' or 'claim' . . . is bounded by the injury for which relief is demanded, and not by the legal theory"). It follows that the omission of a particular statement of claim from the original suit is of no great consequence; if the transaction is the same and the other components of the test are satisfied, principles of *res judicata* will bar all claims that either were or could have been asserted in the initial action. The key is to define the underlying injury.

This definitional process is not a purely mechanical exercise. "What factual grouping constitutes a 'transaction', and what groupings constitute a 'series,' are [matters that should] be determined pragmatically," taking into consideration a wide variety of relevant factors, including but not limited to such things as "whether the facts are related in time, space, origin, or motivation, whether they form a convenient trial unit, and whether their treatment as a unit conforms to the parties' expectations. . . ."

Given these criteria, we believe that there is sufficient identicality here between the earlier and later actions to satisfy the requisite standard. Without exception, appellants' claims stem from the same series of transactions as the claims asserted in the initial litigation. Although the individual sales contracts are different, all of them arise out of a single course of conduct undertaken by a band of allied defendants. By like token, while each purchaser acquired a different lot at a different price, all the lots are part of the same development and all were sold by means of the same ballyhoo. At the very least, the two sets of claims are closely related in time, origin, and geography.

Moreover, if merged, the two sets of claims would form a well-integrated unit. The same kinds of land sale contracts that the Rodriguez plaintiffs attacked under ILSFDA and sought to characterize as "securities" for purposes of their RICO claim underlie appellants' current claims. To be sure, appellants have negotiated the procedural minefield more nimbly than their predecessors, and have, therefore, assembled a more varied assortment of legal theories; but their claims—including both those that replicate the Rodriguez plaintiffs' claims and those that do not—implicate the same series of interconnected transactions that gave rise to the causes of action litigated in the earlier lawsuit. In short, both sets of claims, though dressed in different legal garb, grow out of a common nucleus of operative facts. No more is exigible.

IDENTICALITY OF PARTIES

Concluding, as we do, that the district court's analysis passes muster on the first two components of the tripartite test, we turn to the third essential ingredient needed to invoke the doctrine of *res judicata*: the presence of a sufficient identity between the parties to the earlier and later actions. Short of situations in which precisely the same parties appear in both suits, this element is almost always difficult to gauge.

1. Nonparty Preclusion. We step back to gain a sense of perspective. We are aware that a Supreme Court dictum can be read to suggest that *res judicata* is inoperative as a matter of law insofar as nonparties are concerned. *See Montana v. United States*, 440 U.S. 147, 154 (1979) ("Preclusion of . . . nonparties falls under the rubric of collateral estoppel rather than *res judicata* because the latter doctrine presupposes identity between causes of action. And the cause of action which a nonparty has vicariously asserted differs by definition from that which he subsequently seeks to litigate in his own right.") (dictum). We believe it is highly improbable, however, that the Montana Court, whose primary interest lay in molding the contours of the related doctrine of collateral estoppel, meant categorically to banish privity—a time-honored concept that collapses distinctions between form and substance in respect to party status—from use in conjunction with principles of *res judicata*.

This conclusion is firmly supported not only by respectable precedent but also by practical considerations. Notwithstanding the Montana dictum, several courts, including this court, continue to apply *res judicata* to nonparties when the circumstances warrant. *See, e.g., Aunyx*, 978 F.2d at 7-8 (applying *res judicata* to preclude the alter ego of a corporation from relitigating); *In re Air Crash at Dallas/Fort Worth Airport*, 861 F.2d 814,

816-18 (5th Cir. 1988) (applying *res judicata* to bar decedent's daughter from relitigating); *see also Restatement (Second) of Judgments* §§40, 41 (endorsing application of claim preclusion to nonparties in specified circumstances). In the same vein, courts continue routinely to formulate *res judicata* as a doctrine that bars parties "or their privies" from relitigating claims.

There are also strong practical considerations that counsel against blind adherence to the Montana dictum. The doctrine of *res judicata* serves many desirable ends, among them finality and efficiency. Logic suggests that the doctrine can achieve its goals only if its preclusive effects occasionally can reach persons who, technically, were not parties to the original action. The pitfalls of a more mechanical rule are obvious; making party status a sine qua non for the operation of *res judicata* opens the door to countless varieties of manipulation, including claim-splitting, suits by proxy, and forum-shopping.

Finally, reading Montana's dictum as categorically eliminating *res judicata* whenever there are technically distinct parties is at loggerheads with the hoary concept of privity—a concept long since integrated into the legal lexicon and routinely applied in analogous situations. We are loath to assume that the Court intended to wrest this concept from the jurisprudence of *res judicata* by a casual observation, bereft of any meaningful discussion or explanation. As a rule, appellate courts do not operate in so Delphic a fashion.

We find this combination of precedent, policy, and practicalities to be irresistible. Consequently, we hold that, under federal law, *res judicata* can sometimes operate to bar the maintenance of an action by persons who, technically, were not parties to the initial action (to which preclusive effect is attributed). Nonetheless, we appreciate that this is a murky corner of the law and caution the district courts to tread gingerly in applying *res judicata* to nonparties.[4]

PRIVITY

The most familiar mechanism for extending *res judicata* to nonparties without savaging important constitutional rights is the concept of privity—a concept that furnishes a serviceable framework for an exception to the rule that *res judicata* only bars relitigation of claims by persons who were parties to the original litigation. Although privity can be elusive, this case does not require us to build four walls around it. Here, the *res judicata* defense is based not on some exotic doctrinal refinement but on commonly accepted principles of how privity operates to bring about

---

4. The perils of nonparty preclusion are real. Prominent among them is the prospect that an overly expansive arrangement of the concept, or too free use of it, may endanger constitutional rights. *See Meza v. General Battery Corp.*, 908 F.2d 1262, 1266 (5th Cir. 1990) (approving concept but noting the due process concerns implicit in the ideal that, in general, every party is entitled to her own "day in court").

nonparty preclusion. The theory underlying defendants' iteration of the defense is that privity exists (and, therefore, nonparty preclusion potentially obtains) if a nonparty either substantially controlled a party's involvement in the initial litigation or, conversely, permitted a party to the initial litigation to function as his de facto representative.[5] We accept defendants' theoretical premise, but, after close perscrutation of the record as a whole, we conclude that neither stripe of privity exists here.

SUBSTANTIAL CONTROL

The doctrine of *res judicata* rests upon the bedrock principle that, for claim preclusion to apply, a litigant first must have had a full and fair opportunity to litigate his claim. If a nonparty either participated vicariously in the original litigation by exercising control over a named party or had the opportunity to exert such control, then the nonparty effectively enjoyed his day in court, and it is appropriate to impute to him the legal attributes of party status for purposes of claim preclusion.

Substantial control means what the phrase implies; it connotes the availability of a significant degree of effective control in the prosecution or defense of the case—what one might term, in the vernacular, the power—whether exercised or not—to call the shots. *Restatement (Second) of Judgments* §39, comment c, at 384 (stating that control, for purposes of issue preclusion, refers to the right to exercise "effective choice as to the legal theories and proofs to be advanced," as well as "control over the opportunity to obtain review").

As the proverb suggests, a picture is sometimes worth a thousand words. Along these lines, we suspect that the concept of substantial control can be illustrated better by examples than by linguistic constructs. For instance, substantial control has been found in the case of a liability insurer that assumes the insured's defense, *see, e.g., Iacaponi v. New Amsterdam Cas. Co.*, 379 F.2d 311, 312 (3d Cir. 1967), *cert. denied*, 389 U.S. 1054 (1968), an indemnitor who participates in defending an action brought against the indemnitee, *see, e.g., Bros, Inc. v. W. E. Grace Mfg. Co.*, 261 F.2d 428, 430-31 (5th Cir. 1958), and the owner of a close corporation who assumes control of litigation brought against the firm, *see, e.g., Kreager v. General Elec. Co.*, 497 F.2d 468, 471-72 (2d Cir.), *cert. denied*, 419 U.S. 1041 (1974). Conversely, courts have refused to find substantial control merely because a nonparty retained the attorney who represented a party to the earlier action, *see Freeman v. Lester Coggins Trucking, Inc.*, 771 F.2d 860, 864 (5th Cir. 1985); *Ramey v. Rockefeller*, 348 F. Supp. 780, 785 (E.D.N.Y. 1972), or because the nonparty assisted in financing the earlier action, *see Rumford Chem.*, 215 U.S. at 159-60; *General Foods Corp. v. Massachusetts Dep't of Pub. Health*, 648 F.2d 784, 787-88 (1st Cir. 1981), or

---

5. The sobriquet "virtual representation" frequently is used to describe this type of de facto representation. It fits equally well under the label "representation by proxy."

because the nonparty testified as a witness in the earlier action, *see Benson & Ford, Inc. v. Wanda Petroleum Co.*, 833 F.2d 1172, 1174-75 (5th Cir. 1987); *Ponderosa Devel. Corp. v. Bjordahl*, 787 F.2d 533, 536-37 (10th Cir. 1986), or because the nonparty procured witnesses or evidence, *see Carl Zeiss Stiftung v. V.E.B. Carl Zeiss, Jena*, 293 F. Supp. 892, 921 (S.D.N.Y. 1968), *modified*, 433 F.2d 686 (2d Cir. 1970), *cert. denied*, 403 U.S. 905 (1971), or because the nonparty furnished his attorney's assistance, *see Cofax Corp. v. Minn. Mining & Mfg. Co.*, 79 F. Supp. 842, 844 (S.D.N.Y. 1947).

In the last analysis, there is no bright-line test for gauging substantial control. The inquiry must be case-specific, and fact patterns are almost endlessly variable. The critical judgment cannot be based on isolated facts. Consequently, an inquiring court must consider the totality of the circumstances to determine whether they justify a reasonable inference of a nonparty's potential or actual involvement as a decisionmaker in the earlier litigation. The nonparty's participation may be overt or covert, and the evidence of it may be direct or circumstantial—so long as the evidence as a whole shows that the nonparty possessed effective control over a party's conduct of the earlier litigation as measured from a practical, as opposed to a purely theoretical, standpoint. The burden of persuasion ultimately rests with him who asserts that control (or the right to exercise it) existed to such a degree as would warrant invoking nonparty preclusion.

Applying this standard, there is no principled way in which it can be said that the *Gonzalez* plaintiffs substantially controlled the *Rodriguez* plaintiffs in regard to the original litigation. The only facts to which the district court alluded in ruling that nonparty preclusion loomed involve the similarity of the complaints at one point in time, the parties' common legal representation, and the planned use of some discovered materials in both litigations. In our view, these facts do not begin to show that the *Gonzalez* plaintiffs exercised any meaningful degree of control over the course of the *Rodriguez* litigation. Nor did they have either the right or the opportunity to demand such control.

Moreover, the record contains much additional evidence indicating the absence of substantial control. No useful purpose would be served by marshalling this evidence. We do, however, remark the most telling datum: that the *Rodriguez* plaintiffs sought to amend their complaint to add those who later became the *Gonzalez* plaintiffs a full half-decade after the start of the litigation—a datum strongly suggesting that appellants had no involvement in the initial five years of litigation. This lack of participation at the early stages of the *Rodriguez* litigation is particularly probative on the issue of substantial control, for it was during this period that many pivotal strategic decisions were made, resulting in the virtual forfeiture of some especially promising causes of action (including the mail fraud and state-law claims). Obviously, appellant had no chance to share in this decisionmaking.

The defendants also attempt to sustain the application of *res judicata* by employing principles of virtual representation to demonstrate that privity exists. The attempt stalls. Following defendants' itinerary would require us to imbue the theory of virtual representation with a much greater cruising range than either the law or the facts permit.

Although rooted in the eighteenth century law of estates, virtual representation has only recently emerged as a vehicle for general nonparty preclusion. *See* Robert G. Bone, *Rethinking the "Day in Court" Ideal and Nonparty Preclusion*, 67 N.Y.U. L. Rev. 193, 206-219 (1992). Its recent jurisprudential history has been characterized by breadth of initial articulation followed by abrupt retrenchment in actual application. These pererrations, and the competing centrifugal and centripetal forces that account for them, are most easily explained by reference to the due process analyses that must guide any effort to place the theory into practice.

The courts that first rode the warhorse of virtual representation into battle on the *res judicata* front invested their steed with near-magical properties. They suggested that mere identity of interests between party and nonparty warranted application of the theory and, hence, authorized nonparty preclusion. *See, e.g., Aerojet-General Corp. v. Askew*, 511 F.2d 710, 719 (5th Cir.) (holding that, under federal law, "a person may be bound by a judgment even though not a party if one of the parties to the suit is so closely aligned with his interests as to be his virtual representative"), *cert. denied*, 423 U.S. 908 (1975). Despite such sweeping generalities, courts soon came to realize that, though virtual representation was not the old gray mare, neither should it be confused with Pegasus; finding virtual representation based solely on identity of interests, and then deploying the theory to justify nonparty preclusion in a broad spectrum of cases, would threaten the core principles underpinning the due process equation. *See Martin v. Wilks*, 490 U.S. 755, 761-62 (1989). For this reason, contemporary caselaw has placed the theory of virtual representation on a short tether, significantly restricting its range. *See Benson & Ford*, 833 F.2d at 1175 (observing that the theory of virtual representation must be kept within strict confines); *Pollard v. Cockrell*, 578 F.2d 1002, 1008-09 (5th Cir. 1978) (explicitly limiting *Aerojet* holding).

The upshot is that, today, while identity of interests remains a necessary condition for triggering virtual representation, it is not alone a sufficient condition. More is required to bring the theory to bear. *See General Foods*, 648 F.2d at 789 (holding that "identity of interests" between a party and a nonparty "does not bind [the nonparty] to the judgment"); *Griffin v. Burns*, 570 F.2d 1065, 1071 (1st Cir. 1978) (explaining that "mere similarity of interests and a quantum of representation" is insufficient to trigger virtual representation); *Petit v. City of Chicago*, 766 F. Supp. 607, 612 (N.D. Ill. 1991) (holding that "identity of interests alone . . . is not sufficient to yield a finding of privity"); *see also Benson & Ford*, 833 F.2d at 1174-76 (declining to find nonparty preclusion anent an antitrust claim growing out of the same facts where the nonparty plaintiff testified at the earlier trial and had the same attorney).

To say that a litigant advocating virtual representation, and seeking thereby to preclude a nonparty's suit, must show more than an identity of interests is to state the nature of the problem, not to solve it. Many of the ensuing questions—questions like "how much more?" and "what comprises 'more'?"—seem to have no categorical answers. Not surprisingly, then, the cases in which courts have dealt with the doctrine, taken as an array, are resistant to doctrinal rationalization in the form of a single elegant limiting principle of the "one size fits all" variety. There is no black-letter rule. *See Colby v. J. C. Penney Co.*, 811 F.2d 1119, 1125 (7th Cir. 1987) (commenting that "no uniform pattern has emerged from the cases"); *Ethnic Employees of Library of Congress v. Boorstin*, 751 F.2d 1405, 1411 n.8 (D.C. Cir. 1985) (noting that the virtual representation doctrine has a "highly uncertain scope"); *see also* Bone, *supra*, 67 N.Y.U. L. Rev. at 220 (acknowledging absence of clear organizing framework). In the end, virtual representation is best understood as an equitable theory rather than as a crisp rule with sharp corners and clear factual predicates, such that a party's status as a virtual representative of a nonparty must be determined on a case-by-case basis, *see Bonilla Romero*, 836 F.2d at 43.

Although the need for individualized analysis persists, a common thread binds these variegated cases together: virtual representation has a pronounced equitable dimension. Thus, notwithstanding identity of interests, virtual representation will not serve to bar a nonparty's claim unless the nonparty has had actual or constructive notice of the earlier litigation,[10] and the balance of the relevant equities tips in favor of preclusion. For example, courts have applied the doctrine in situations in which a nonparty has given actual or implied consent to be bound by the results in a prior action, *see e.g., Boyd v. Jamaica Plain Co-op Bank*, 386 N.E.2d 775, 778-81 (Mass. App. Ct. 1979); *see also Benson & Ford*, 833 F.2d at 1176 (finding "tacit agreement[s]" to be bound characteristic of cases applying virtual representation), or in which there has been "an express or implied legal relationship in which parties to the first suit are accountable to nonparties who file a subsequent suit raising identical issues," *Pollard*, 578 F.2d at 1008; *see also In re Medomak Canning Co.*, 922 F.2d 895, 900-01 (1st Cir. 1990) (holding that creditors were represented by the trustee in bankruptcy, who had a fiduciary relationship to them), or in which certain

---

10. Notice is a very important factor. With the possible exception of *Aerojet*, 511 F.2d 710 (a case that has since been narrowed by the Fifth Circuit), counsel have cited us to no case in which a court has precluded a nonparty, based on a theory of virtual representation, where the nonparty had not received timely notice (actual or constructive) of the initial litigation.

types of familial relationships link parties and nonparties, *see, e.g., Eubanks v. FDIC*, 977 F.2d 166, 170 (5th Cir. 1992) (holding wife bound by outcome of bankrupt husband's prior action); *Stone v. Williams*, 970 F.2d 1043, 1058-61 (2d Cir. 1992) (binding decedent's son to a prior ruling concerning legacies), *cert. denied*, 124 L. Ed. 2d 243, or in which courts have detected tactical maneuvering designed unfairly to exploit technical nonparty status in order to obtain multiple bites of the litigatory apple, *see, e.g., Petit,* 766 F. Supp. at 611-13; *Crane v. Comm'r of Dep't of Agric.*, 602 F. Supp. 280, 286-88 (D. Me. 1985); Bone, *supra,* at 222. Implicit in all these scenarios is the existence of actual or constructive notice.

We have considered, and rejected, another possible common characteristic. Some courts have suggested that adequacy of representation is also a condition precedent to nonparty preclusion grounded upon virtual representation. *See, e.g., Clark v. Amoco Prods. Co.*, 794 F.2d 967, 973-74 (5th Cir. 1986) (suggesting that virtual representation "closely resembles the common law theory of concurrent privity . . . which in turn is really only [an] adequate representation of interests analysis"); *Delta Air Lines, Inc. v. McCoy Restaurants, Inc.*, 708 F.2d 582, 587 (11th Cir. 1983) (finding no virtual representation because nonparty was not "adequately represented"). Properly viewed, however, adequacy of representation is not itself a separate and inflexible requirement for engaging principles of virtual representation,[12] although it is one of the factors that an inquiring court should weigh in attempting to balance the equities.

Based on these benchmarks, the Gonzalez plaintiffs cannot plausibly be said to have been virtually represented by the Rodriguez plaintiffs notwithstanding the identity of interests between the two groups. Here, the equities counsel very strongly against deploying the theory of virtual representation. In the first place, there has been no showing that the Gonzalez plaintiffs had timely notice of the first suit. In the second place, the parties' independence—the inescapable fact that the Rodriguez plaintiffs were not legally responsible for, or in any other way accountable to, the Gonzalez plaintiffs—weighs heavily against a finding of virtual representation. In the third place, the lack of a special type of close relationship between the two groups of plaintiffs (who are, for the most part, unrelated lambs purportedly fleeced by the same cadre of unscrupulous sheepherders) also weighs against a finding of virtual representation. Fourth, the fact that the Gonzalez plaintiffs never consented, either explicitly or constructively, to be bound by the verdict in the earlier action

---

12. A contrary view would fly in the teeth of the general rule that, in civil litigation, the sins of the lawyer routinely are visited upon the client. *See, e.g., Link v. Wabash R.R.*, 370 U.S. 626, 633-36, 8 L. Ed. 2d 734, 82 S. Ct. 1386 (1961); *Thibeault v. Square D Co.*, 960 F.2d 239, 242 (1st Cir. 1992). We do not understand why a nonparty who comes within the doctrinal framework for virtual representation—a framework in which party and nonparty share identical interests, and that provides for notice and a weighing of equitable considerations—should be treated differently from a party in this regard.

is significant, especially since they actually initiated the later action while the earlier action was still pending. And, finally, far from engaging in tactical maneuvering aimed at gaining unfair advantage, appellants sought to join the Rodriguez action—and were thwarted in the effort because the defendants objected and the district court, siding with the defendants, barred appellants' path.

Of course, given the discretionary character of virtual representation, we would not conclude that a case falls outside the theory's purview solely because it does not fit snugly into some preconceived niche or mirror some established fact pattern. But, here, the sequence of events itself confirms the inappropriateness of bringing virtual representation to the fore in this case. The district court, after refusing to certify a class, prohibited appellants from joining the original suit, yet thereafter precluded them from prosecuting their own action. This whipsawing placed appellants in an untenable position. Short of a class action, with all the concomitant safeguards that class certification portends, *see, e.g.*, Fed. R. Civ. P. 23, we do not think that the Due Process Clause comfortably can accommodate such a paradigm. In any event, on the facts of this case the prospect of depriving these plaintiffs of their day in court offends our collective sense of justice and fair play. Consequently, we hold that the theory of virtual representation cannot be galvanized to preclude appellants from maintaining their suit.

III. CONCLUSION

We need go no further. Because the appellants were neither parties to the initial action nor in privity with the plaintiffs therein, the district court erred in dismissing their suit under principles of *res judicata*. Reversed and remanded for further proceedings. Costs to appellants.

Comments and Questions

We have encountered the question of when a nonparty may be bound by a judgment before. Look back at our very first case—*United States v. Hall*. Is Judge Selya's analysis in *Gonzalez* consistent with Judge Wisdom's in *Hall*? What is Judge Selya's definition of privity? Would it apply to Mr. Hall? We will return to this question in the last chapter, because it is at the core of the issues surrounding class actions. *See* Chapter 11.

4. *Review Problems*

1. Assume that the plaintiffs in *City of Cleveland* lost their case. The City subsequently changes the selection procedures that it has used when

evaluating applicants for firefighter, including the development of a new physical agility test. The new test, like the old, measures only anaerobic capacity and not stamina. Can the same group of plaintiffs sue the City alleging that the new test unlawfully discriminates against women, or will they be barred by claim preclusion? SAME Ⓟ | SAME TRANSACTION

2. Suppose three of the female firefighters who unsuccessfully sued the City in *City of Cleveland* were African American. After *Barbara Zoll v. City of Cleveland*, can these women bring a subsequent suit against the City alleging that the firefighter test is discriminatory against African Americans?

3. Now let's turn to the facts of *Carpenter v. Dee*. Assume that, prior to filing suit, Nancy Carpenter's lawyer learned that Ms. Carpenter had already sued Randall Dee in Small Claims Court, alleging that he was responsible for the death of her husband, and after a trial (at which the parties appeared pro se) was awarded $2,000 (the maximum amount that can be awarded in that court). What are the implications for the proposed lawsuit in Massachusetts Superior Court (a court of general jurisdiction)?

4. Assume that Nancy Carpenter files an action in Superior Court against the City of Lowell based on the failure of its police officers, who had stopped Randall Dee while he was operating his Jeep, to advise Dee that the vehicle was illegally modified or otherwise to take action to prevent its operation in a dangerous condition. The action is dismissed by the trial court on defendant's 12(b)(6) motion, the court relying on an old case decided by the Supreme Judicial Court holding that municipalities are not liable for the negligence of their employees. No appeal is filed, and a final judgment is entered for the City. One week later, the Supreme Judicial Court, in an unrelated case, repudiated the prior precedent and announced a new rule making municipalities liable for the negligent acts of their agents and employees. May Nancy Carpenter take advantage of this development and file another suit against the City? Why or why not? Doesn't justice require that Carpenter get another bite of the apple since the judgment against her rests on a now-discarded legal principle? Remember these concerns when you read *Federated Department Stores v. Motie, infra.*

C. ISSUE PRECLUSION (COLLATERAL ESTOPPEL)

■ DAVID P. HOULT v. JENNIFER HOULT
157 F.3d (1st Cir. 1998)

BOUDIN, Circuit Judge.

In July 1988, when she was 27 years old, Jennifer Hoult brought suit in the district court against her father, David Hoult, alleging assault and battery, intentional infliction of emotional distress, and breach of fiduciary duty. To support these claims, she alleged that her father had sexually abused, raped and threatened her from the time that she was about four years old until she was about sixteen years old.

The statute of limitations presented an obvious obstacle. Jennifer Hoult sought to overcome it by showing that the alleged abuse caused her to repress her memory of the events until she began to recapture those memories during therapy sessions in October 1985. *See* M.G.L. 260 §4C. The claim of repressed memory was supported at trial by testimony from a psychiatrist, Dr. Renee Brandt, who appeared as an expert witness on repression caused by traumatic abuse.

In June 1993, the district court conducted an eight day jury trial in which Jennifer Hoult testified at length, giving detailed descriptions of extensive alleged abuse by her father; in addition to other forms of abuse, she testified to five specific episodes of rape. Supporting testimony was provided by her former therapist and by Dr. Brandt. In defense, David Hoult testified on his own behalf, flatly denying the allegations, but presented no other witnesses.

On July 1, 1993, the jury returned a verdict in favor of Jennifer Hoult and ordered damages in the amount of $500,000. This verdict was preceded by a separate finding by the jury accepting the statute of limitations defense; in effect the jury found that Jennifer Hoult had repressed memory of the abuse until it was rediscovered within the limitations period. David Hoult appealed both from the judgment against him and the denial of a motion for a new trial, but both appeals were ultimately dismissed for lack of prosecution.

Later, Jennifer Hoult wrote letters to several professional associations in which she repeated the charge that her father had raped her. David Hoult then brought the present action in the district court against Jennifer Hoult, claiming that her charge of rape against him was defamatory. Jennifer Hoult moved to dismiss on the ground that the jury verdict in her earlier assault action had determined that David Hoult had raped her and that David Hoult was barred by collateral estoppel from relitigating this finding.

Initially, the district court denied the motion to dismiss, saying that the evidence adduced at the trial could have led the jury to impose liability because David Hoult had sexually abused Jennifer Hoult "in ways that did not amount to rape" or could even have done so on the basis of Jennifer Hoult's testimony that David Hoult had "threatened her with murder, chased her around the house with a knife, and fondled her in a sexual manner, among other incidents of violence and assault."

By motion for reconsideration, Jennifer Hoult argued that the jury's finding of repression, in rejecting the statute of limitations defense, was necessarily based on Dr. Brandt's expert opinion that the repression required "repeated acts" of sexual abuse; and the only repeated acts of sexual abuse (Jennifer Hoult argued) were her descriptions of five separate incidents of rape. Accepting this argument, the district court allowed Jennifer Hoult's motion to dismiss the action, and David Hoult now appeals.

The governing legal doctrine of collateral estoppel, which we briefly summarize, is largely undisputed; the problem is one of applying the doctrine to this case. . . . Subject to certain exceptions, the general rule on "issue preclusion" is as follows: When an issue of fact or law is actually litigated and determined by a valid and final judgment, and the determination is essential to the judgment, the determination is conclusive in a subsequent action between the parties, whether on the same or a different claim. Restatement (Second) Judgments §27 (1982). Neither side disputes that this formulation sets forth the governing law.

David Hoult . . . says—as did the district judge in his original order refusing to dismiss—that there is no proof that the jury ever determined that David Hoult had committed the alleged rapes. The burden is upon Jennifer Hoult, as the party invoking collateral estoppel, to establish that the jury did so determine in the original action. *See Commercial Associates v. Tilcon Gammino, Inc.*, 998 F.2d 1092, 1098 (1st Cir. 1993).

Admittedly, the jury made no explicit finding that rapes occurred. Nevertheless, "[a]n issue may be 'actually' decided [for collateral estoppel purposes] even if it is not explicitly decided, for it may have constituted, logically or practically, a necessary component of the decision reached." *Dennis v. Rhode Island Hospital Trust National Bank*, 744 F.2d 893, 899 (1st Cir. 1984). The court in the second case may examine the full record in the earlier one to decide "whether a rational jury could have grounded its verdict upon an issue other than that which the [moving party] seeks to foreclose from consideration." *Ashe v. Swenson*, 397 U.S. 436 (1970).

Whether the jury did find, or must have found, rape in the earlier trial is perhaps question of fact. But where (as here) the question is answered by looking only at the paper record of the earlier trial, appeals courts tend to review the district court ruling de novo. The more difficult threshold issue is how clear it must be that the jury found the fact in question. The maxim of Lord Coke which is sometimes quoted by courts is that "an estoppel must 'be certain to every intent.'" *Russell v. Place*, 94 U.S. (4 Otto) 606, 610, 24 L. Ed. 214 (1876).

This is more demanding than the "more likely than not" standard commonly applied in civil matters, but sensibly so. Telling a party that it cannot prove or contest a fact of importance in the case at hand is a severe measure. Courts have been willing to take that step only where it is certain that the issue has already been decided in a prior case (normally one involving the same parties). . . . Confronted with a general verdict in the earlier case, courts commonly ask whether a finding was "necessary" to the judgment, and answer the question by looking primarily to the instructions and the result. But a finding is "necessary" if it was central to the route that led the factfinder to the judgment reached, even if the result "could have been achieved by a different, shorter and more efficient route." *Commercial Associates v. Tilcon Gammino, Inc.*, 998 F.2d 1092, 1097 (1st Cir. 1993). And in deciding whether the jury did make and rest centrally upon a finding not expressly made, it is proper to consider—as *Dennis* said—not only what was "logically" but also what was "practically" a "necessary component of the decision reached." *Dennis*, 744 F.2d at 899.

Here, the rape charges were the centerpiece of Jennifer Hoult's case. In the opening statement, her counsel said that Jennifer Hoult would have to live with her "memories of the rape, torture, and sexual abuse" by her father and that her father had had "intercourse" with her. Defense counsel answered that Jennifer Hoult could not have been "raped by her father some 3,000 times," as she had once claimed, and he promised evidence to show the unlikelihood that numerous rapes could have occurred without detection by other family members.

Jennifer Hoult then testified specifically to five incidents of rape and said that there were other like rapes whose details she could not recollect. On cross-examination by defense counsel, she said:

> I know based on the specific memories that I have of him attacking me and based on my perceptions, and memories of my life as a whole that he assaulted me regularly, and that rape, even the narrower definition [simple sexual intercourse] was a regular part of the way that he assaulted me.

In closing argument, defense counsel—who argued first—said at the outset:

> Specifically, Jennifer alleges that her father sexually abused her. More specifically, Jennifer claims that her father raped her, and I will call your attention now, as I did in my opening statement, that Jennifer describes rape as forcible vaginal intercourse.

In response, Jennifer Hoult's counsel said: "And this is not about hugging and kissing. She is claiming he assaulted her. He raped her. It's not inappropriate hugging and kissing."

A further consideration, stressed by the district court, is Dr. Brandt's testimony and the jury's finding on the statute of limitations. Dr. Brandt testified that repeated sexual abuse can cause repression of memory of the abuse and that Jennifer Hoult's symptoms "correlated" with such a syndrome. In finding that the statute of limitations had run, the only plausible explanation is that the jury accepted Jennifer Hoult's testimony as to the rapes, which were the salient and specific acts of repeated abuse to which she testified.

Theoretically, the jury could have concluded that Jennifer Hoult had made up or imagined the rapes, and it could then have found repressed memory and awarded the $500,000 judgment because of improper sexual fondlings and threats or acts of violence. But this is a wholly unrealistic assessment of a trial in which the rapes were the central and pivotal issue, the fondlings were the preface to the rapes, and the violence was connected to the rapes (either as part of the rapes or to encourage silence). In our view the jury necessarily decided that rapes had occurred.

The present law suit seeks, in the guise of a defamation action, to retry the central issue in the prior assault case between the same litigants. That issue—ultimately a credibility contest between the two opposing parties—was resolved by the jury at the first trial. Whether the jury was right or wrong, its decision about what happened is not now open to relitigation.

Affirmed.

Comments and Questions

1. *Hoult* illustrates the difficulty that may arise in applying issue preclusion where the previous judgment is (as it usually is) a general verdict. How did Judge Boudin go about reconstructing what the jury had decided in reaching the prior verdict?

2. Read Fed. R. Civ. P. 49, authorizing the discretionary use of special verdicts as well as interrogatories accompanying a general verdict. What are the advantages and disadvantages of these alternatives to the general verdict? See Mark S. Brodin, *Accuracy, Efficiency, and Accountability in the Litigation Process—The Case for the Fact Verdict*, 59 U. Cinn. L. Rev. 15 (1990).

3. Was David Hoult denied "due process of law" by operation of issue preclusion?

■ PARKLANE HOSIERY CO., INC. v. SHORE
439 U.S. 322 (1979)

Justice STEWART delivered the opinion of the Court:

This case presents the question whether a party who has had issues of fact adjudicated adversely to it in an equitable action may be collaterally estopped from relitigating the same issues before a jury in a subsequent legal action brought against it by a new party.

The respondent brought this stockholder's class action against the petitioners in a Federal District Court. The complaint alleged that the petitioners, Parklane Hosiery Co., Inc. (Parklane), and 13 of its officers, directors, and stockholders, had issued a materially false and misleading proxy statement in connection with a merger. The proxy statement, according to the complaint, had violated §§14(a), 10(b), and 20(a) of the Securities Exchange Act of 1934, 48 Stat. 895, 891, 899, as amended, 15 U.S.C. §§78n(a), 78j(b), and 78t(a), as well as various rules and regulations promulgated by the Securities and Exchange Commission (SEC). The complaint sought damages, rescission of the merger, and recovery of costs.

Before this action came to trial, the SEC filed suit against the same defendants in the Federal District Court, alleging that the proxy statement that had been issued by Parklane was materially false and misleading in essentially the same respects as those that had been alleged in the respondent's complaint. Injunctive relief was requested. After a 4-day trial, the District Court found that the proxy statement was materially false and misleading in the respects alleged, and entered a declaratory judgment to that effect. The Court of Appeals for the Second Circuit affirmed this judgment. The respondent in the present case then moved for partial summary judgment against the petitioners, asserting that the petitioners were collaterally estopped from relitigating the issues that had been resolved against them in the action brought by the SEC.[2] The District Court denied the motion on the ground that such an application of collateral estoppel would deny the petitioners their Seventh Amendment right to a jury trial. The Court of Appeals for the Second Circuit reversed, holding that a party who has had issues of fact determined against him after a full and fair opportunity to litigate in a nonjury trial is collaterally estopped from obtaining a subsequent jury trial of these same issues of fact. The appellate court concluded that "the Seventh Amendment preserves the right to jury trial only with respect to issues of fact, [and] once those issues have been fully and fairly adjudicated in a prior proceeding, nothing remains for trial, either with or without a jury." Because of an intercircuit conflict, we granted certiorari.

I

The threshold question to be considered is whether, quite apart from the right to a jury trial under the Seventh Amendment, the petitioners can

---

2. A private plaintiff in an action under the proxy rules is not entitled to relief simply by demonstrating that the proxy solicitation was materially false and misleading. The plaintiff must also show that he was injured and prove damages. *Mills v. Electric Auto-Lite Co.*, 396 U.S. 375, 386-390. Since the SEC action was limited to a determination of whether the proxy statement contained materially false and misleading information, the respondent conceded that he would still have to prove these other elements of his prima facie case in the private action. The petitioners' right to a jury trial on those remaining issues is not contested.

be precluded from relitigating facts resolved adversely to them in a prior equitable proceeding with another party under the general law of collateral estoppel. Specifically, we must determine whether a litigant who was not a party to a prior judgment may nevertheless use that judgment "offensively" to prevent a defendant from relitigating issues resolved in the earlier proceeding.[4]

A

Collateral estoppel, like the related doctrine of *res judicata*,[5] has the dual purpose of protecting litigants from the burden of relitigating an identical issue with the same party or his privy and of promoting judicial economy by preventing needless litigation. *Blonder-Tongue Laboratories, Inc. v. University of Illinois Foundation,* 402 U.S. 313, 328-329. Until relatively recently, however, the scope of collateral estoppel was limited by the doctrine of mutuality of parties. Under this mutuality doctrine, neither party could use a prior judgment as an estoppel against the other unless both parties were bound by the judgment. Based on the premise that it is somehow unfair to allow a party to use a prior judgment when he himself would not be so bound,[7] the mutuality requirement provided a party who had litigated and lost in a previous action an opportunity to relitigate identical issues with new parties.

By failing to recognize the obvious difference in position between a party who has never litigated an issue and one who has fully litigated and lost, the mutuality requirement was criticized almost from its inception. Recognizing the validity of this criticism, the Court in *Blonder-Tongue Laboratories, Inc. v. University of Illinois Foundation, supra,* abandoned the mutuality requirement, at least in cases where a patentee seeks to relitigate the validity of a patent after a federal court in a previous lawsuit has already declared it invalid. The "broader question" before the Court, however, was "whether it is any longer tenable to afford a litigant more than one full and fair opportunity for judicial resolution of the same

---

4. In this context, offensive use of collateral estoppel occurs when the plaintiff seeks to foreclose the defendant from litigating an issue the defendant has previously litigated unsuccessfully in an action with another party. Defensive use occurs when a defendant seeks to prevent a plaintiff from asserting a claim the plaintiff has previously litigated and lost against another defendant.

5. Under the doctrine of *res judicata,* a judgment on the merits in a prior suit bars a second suit involving the same parties or their privies based on the same cause of action. Under the doctrine of collateral estoppel, on the other hand, the second action is upon a different cause of action and the judgment in the prior suit precludes relitigation of issues actually litigated and necessary to the outcome of the first action.

7. It is a violation of due process for a judgment to be binding on a litigant who was not a party or a privy and therefore has never had an opportunity to be heard. *Blonder-Tongue Laboratories, Inc. v. University of Illinois Foundation,* 402 U.S. 313, 329; *Hansberry v. Lee,* 311 U.S. 32, 40.

issue." 402 U.S., at 328. The Court strongly suggested a negative answer to that question:

> In any lawsuit where a defendant, because of the mutuality principle, is forced to present a complete defense on the merits to a claim which the plaintiff has fully litigated and lost in a prior action, there is an arguable misallocation of resources. To the extent the defendant in the second suit may not win by asserting, without contradiction, that the plaintiff had fully and fairly, but unsuccessfully, litigated the same claim in the prior suit, the defendant's time and money are diverted from alternative uses—productive or otherwise—to relitigation of a decided issue. And, still assuming that the issue was resolved correctly in the first suit, there is reason to be concerned about the plaintiff's allocation of resources. Permitting repeated litigation of the same issue as long as the supply of unrelated defendants holds out reflects either the aura of the gaming table or "a lack of discipline and of disinterestedness on the part of the lower courts, hardly a worthy or wise basis for fashioning rules of procedure." *Kerotest Mfg. Co. v. C-O-Two Co.*, 342 U.S. 180, 185 (1952). Although neither judges, the parties, nor the adversary system performs perfectly in all cases, the requirement of determining whether the party against whom an estoppel is asserted had a full and fair opportunity to litigate is a most significant safeguard. *Id.*, at 329. n.10.

B

The *Blonder-Tongue* case involved defensive use of collateral estoppel—a plaintiff was estopped from asserting a claim that the plaintiff had previously litigated and lost against another defendant. The present case, by contrast, involves offensive use of collateral estoppel—a plaintiff is seeking to estop a defendant from relitigating the issues which the defendant previously litigated and lost against another plaintiff. In both the offensive and defensive use situations, the party against whom estoppel is asserted has litigated and lost in an earlier action. Nevertheless, several reasons have been advanced why the two situations should be treated differently.

First, offensive use of collateral estoppel does not promote judicial economy in the same manner as defensive use does. Defensive use of collateral estoppel precludes a plaintiff from relitigating identical issues by merely "switching adversaries." *Bernhard v. Bank of America Nat. Trust & Savings Assn.*, 19 Cal. 2d at 813 n.12. Thus defensive collateral estoppel gives a plaintiff a strong incentive to join all potential defendants in the first action if possible. Offensive use of collateral estoppel, on the other hand, creates precisely the opposite incentive. Since a plaintiff will be able to rely on a previous judgment against a defendant but will not be bound by that judgment if the defendant wins, the plaintiff has every incentive to adopt a "wait and see" attitude, in the hope that the first action by another plaintiff will result in a favorable judgment. Thus offensive use of collateral estoppel will likely increase rather than decrease the total amount of litigation, since potential plaintiffs will have everything to gain and nothing to lose by not intervening in the first action.

A second argument against offensive use of collateral estoppel is that it may be unfair to a defendant. If a defendant in the first action is sued for small or nominal damages, he may have little incentive to defend vigorously, particularly if future suits are not foreseeable. Allowing offensive collateral estoppel may also be unfair to a defendant if the judgment relied upon as a basis for the estoppel is itself inconsistent with one or more previous judgments in favor of the defendant.[14] Still another situation where it might be unfair to apply offensive estoppel is where the second action affords the defendant procedural opportunities unavailable in the first action that could readily cause a different result.[15]

C

We have concluded that the preferable approach for dealing with these problems in the federal courts is not to preclude the use of offensive collateral estoppel, but to grant trial courts broad discretion to determine when it should be applied. The general rule should be that in cases where a plaintiff could easily have joined in the earlier action or where, either for the reasons discussed above or for other reasons, the application of offensive estoppel would be unfair to a defendant, a trial judge should not allow the use of offensive collateral estoppel.

In the present case, however, none of the circumstances that might justify reluctance to allow the offensive use of collateral estoppel is present. The application of offensive collateral estoppel will not here reward a private plaintiff who could have joined in the previous action, since the respondent probably could not have joined in the injunctive action brought by the SEC even had he so desired. Similarly, there is no unfairness to the petitioners in applying offensive collateral estoppel in this case. First, in light of the serious allegations made in the SEC's complaint against the petitioners, as well as the foreseeability of subsequent private suits that

14. In Professor Currie's familiar example, a railroad collision injures 50 passengers all of whom bring separate actions against the railroad. After the railroad wins the first 25 suits, a plaintiff wins in suit 26. Professor Currie argues that offfensive use of collateral estoppel should not be applied so as to allow plaintifffs 27 through 50 automatically to recover. Currie, *Mutuality of Estoppel: Limits of the Bernhard Doctrine*, 9 Stan. L. Rev. 281, 304 (1957).

15. If, for example, the defendant in the first action was forced to defend in an inconvenient forum and therefore was unable to engage in full scale discovery or call witnesses, application of offensive collateral estoppel may be unwarranted. Indeed, differences in available procedures may sometimes justify not allowing a prior judgment to have estoppel effect in a subsequent action even between the same parties, or where defensive estoppel is asserted against a plaintiff who has litigated and lost. The problem of unfairness is particularly acute in cases of offensive estoppel, however, because the defendant against whom estoppel is asserted typically will not have chosen the forum in the first action.

typically follow a successful Government judgment, the petitioners had every incentive to litigate the SEC lawsuit fully and vigorously.[18] Second, the judgment in the SEC action was not inconsistent with any previous decision. Finally, there will in the respondent's action be no procedural opportunities available to the petitioners that were unavailable in the first action of a kind that might be likely to cause a different result.[19]

We conclude, therefore, that none of the considerations that would justify a refusal to allow the use of offensive collateral estoppel is present in this case. Since the petitioners received a "full and fair" opportunity to litigate their claims in the SEC action, the contemporary law of collateral estoppel leads inescapably to the conclusion that the petitioners are collaterally estopped from relitigating the question of whether the proxy statement was materially false and misleading.

II

The question that remains is whether, notwithstanding the law of collateral estoppel, the use of offensive collateral estoppel in this case would violate the petitioners' Seventh Amendment right to a jury trial.[20]

A

"[The] thrust of the [Seventh] Amendment was to preserve the right to jury trial as it existed in 1791." *Curtis v. Loether*, 415 U.S. 189, 193. At common law, a litigant was not entitled to have a jury determine issues that had been previously adjudicated by a chancellor in equity.

Recognition that an equitable determination could have collateral-estoppel effect in a subsequent legal action was the major premise of this Court's decision in *Beacon Theatres, Inc. v. Westover*, 359 U.S. 500. . . .

B

Despite the strong support to be found both in history and in the recent decisional law of this Court for the proposition that an equitable determination can have collateral-estoppel effect in a subsequent legal action, the petitioners argue that application of collateral estoppel in this case would nevertheless violate their Seventh Amendment right to a jury

18. After a 4-day trial in which the petitioners had every opportunity to present evidence and call witnesses, the District Court held for the SEC. The petitioners then appealed to the Court of Appeals for the Second Circuit, which affirmed the judgment against them. Moreover, the petitioners were already aware of the action brought by the respondent, since it had commenced before the filing of the SEC action.

19. It is true, of course, that the petitioners in the present action would be entitled to a jury trial of the issues bearing on whether the proxy statement was materially false and misleading had the SEC action never been brought—a matter to be discussed in Part II of this opinion. But the presence or absence of a jury as factfinder is basically neutral, quite unlike, for example, the necessity of defending the first lawsuit in an inconvenient forum.

20. The Seventh Amendment provides: "In Suits at common law, where the value in controversy shall exceed twenty dollars, the right to jury trial shall be preserved. . . ."

trial. The petitioners contend that since the scope of the Amendment must be determined by reference to the common law as it existed in 1791, and since the common law permitted collateral estoppel only where there was mutuality of parties, collateral estoppel cannot constitutionally be applied when such mutuality is absent.

The petitioners have advanced no persuasive reason, however, why the meaning of the Seventh Amendment should depend on whether or not mutuality of parties is present. A litigant who has lost because of adverse factual findings in an equity action is equally deprived of a jury trial whether he is estopped from relitigating the factual issues against the same party or a new party. In either case, the party against whom estoppel is asserted has litigated questions of fact, and has had the facts determined against him in an earlier proceeding. In either case there is no further factfinding function for the jury to perform, since the common factual issues have been resolved in the previous action.

The Seventh Amendment has never been interpreted in the rigid manner advocated by the petitioners. On the contrary, many procedural devices developed since 1791 that have diminished the civil jury's historic domain have been found not to be inconsistent with the Seventh Amendment. *See Galloway v. United States*, 319 U.S. 372, 388-393 (directed verdict does not violate the Seventh Amendment); *Gasoline Products Co. v. Champlin Refining Co.*, 283 U.S. 494, 497-498 (retrial limited to question of damages does not violate the Seventh Amendment even though there was no practice at common law for setting aside a verdict in part); *Fidelity & Deposit Co. v. United States*, 187 U.S. 315, 319-321 (summary judgment does not violate the Seventh Amendment).

The *Galloway* case is particularly instructive. There the party against whom a directed verdict had been entered argued that the procedure was unconstitutional under the Seventh Amendment. In rejecting this claim, the Court said:

> The Amendment did not bind the federal courts to the exact procedural incidents or details of jury trial according to the common law in 1791, any more than it tied them to the common-law system of pleading or the specific rules of evidence then prevailing. Nor were "the rules of the common law" then prevalent, including those relating to the procedure by which the judge regulated the jury's role on questions of fact, crystallized in a fixed and immutable system. . . .
>
> The more logical conclusion, we think, and the one which both history and the previous decisions here support, is that the Amendment was designed to preserve the basic institution of jury trial in only its most fundamental elements, not the great mass of procedural forms and details, varying even then so widely among common-law jurisdictions." 319 U.S., at 390, 392 (footnote omitted).

The law of collateral estoppel, like the law in other procedural areas defining the scope of the jury's function, has evolved since 1791. Under the rationale of the *Galloway* case, these developments are not repugnant to the Seventh Amendment simply for the reason that they did not exist in 1791. Thus if, as we have held, the law of collateral estoppel forecloses the petitioners from relitigating the factual issues determined against them in the SEC action, nothing in the Seventh Amendment dictates a different result, even though because of lack of mutuality there would have been no collateral estoppel in 1791.

The judgment of the Court of Appeals is Affirmed.

Justice REHNQUIST, dissenting:

It is admittedly difficult to be outraged about the treatment accorded by the federal judiciary to petitioners' demand for a jury trial in this lawsuit. Outrage is an emotion all but impossible to generate with respect to a corporate defendant in a securities fraud action, and this case is no exception. But the nagging sense of unfairness as to the way petitioners have been treated, engendered by the imprimatur placed by the Court of Appeals on respondent's "heads I win, tails you lose" theory of this litigation, is not dispelled by this Court's antiseptic analysis of the issues in the case. It may be that if this Nation were to adopt a new Constitution today, the Seventh Amendment guaranteeing the right of jury trial in civil cases in federal courts would not be included among its provisions. But any present sentiment to that effect cannot obscure or dilute our obligation to enforce the Seventh Amendment, which was included in the Bill of Rights in 1791 and which has not since been repealed in the only manner provided by the Constitution for repeal of its provisions.

The right of trial by jury in civil cases at common law is fundamental to our history and jurisprudence. Today, however, the Court reduces this valued right, which Blackstone praised as "the glory of the English law," to a mere "neutral" factor and in the name of procedural reform denies the right of jury trial to defendants in a vast number of cases in which defendants, heretofore, have enjoyed jury trials. Over 35 years ago, Mr. Justice Black lamented the "gradual process of judicial erosion which in one-hundred-fifty years has slowly worn away a major portion of the essential guarantee of the Seventh Amendment." *Galloway v. United States,* 319 U.S. 372, 397 (1943) (dissenting opinion). Regrettably, the erosive process continues apace with today's decision.[1]

The Seventh Amendment provides:

> In Suits at common law, where the value in controversy shall exceed twenty dollars, the right of trial by jury shall be preserved, and no fact tried by a jury, shall be otherwise reexamined in any Court of the United States, than according to the rules of the common law. . . .

---

1. Because I believe that the use of offensive collateral estoppel in this particular case was improper, it is not necessary for me to decide whether I would approve its use in circumstances where the defendant's right to a jury trial was not impaired.

It is perhaps easy to forget, now more than 200 years removed from the events, that the right of trial by jury was held in such esteem by the colonists that its deprivation at the hands of the English was one of the important grievances leading to the break with England. The extensive use of vice-admiralty courts by colonial administrators to eliminate the colonists' right of jury trial was listed among the specific offensive English acts denounced in the Declaration of Independence. And after war had broken out, all of the 13 newly formed States restored the institution of civil jury trial to its prior prominence; 10 expressly guaranteed the right in their state constitutions and the 3 others recognized it by statute or by common practice. Indeed, "[the] right to trial by jury was probably the only one universally secured by the first American state constitutions. . . ." L. Levy, *Legacy of Suppression: Freedom of Speech and Press in Early American History* 281 (1960). . . .

The founders of our Nation considered the right of trial by jury in civil cases an important bulwark against tyranny and corruption, a safeguard too precious to be left to the whim of the sovereign, or, it might be added, to that of the judiciary. Those who passionately advocated the right to a civil jury trial did not do so because they considered the jury a familiar procedural device that should be continued; the concerns for the institution of jury trial that led to the passages of the Declaration of Independence and to the Seventh Amendment were not animated by a belief that use of juries would lead to more efficient judicial administration. Trial by a jury of laymen rather than by the sovereign's judges was important to the founders because juries represent the layman's common sense, the "passional elements in our nature," and thus keep the administration of law in accord with the wishes and feelings of the community. O. Holmes, *Collected Legal Papers* 237 (1920). Those who favored juries believed that a jury would reach a result that a judge either could not or would not reach. It is with these values that underlie the Seventh Amendment in mind that the Court should, but obviously does not, approach the decision of this case. . . .

Judged by the foregoing principles, I think it is clear that petitioners were denied their Seventh Amendment right to a jury trial in this case. Neither respondent nor the Court doubts that at common law as it existed in 1791, petitioners would have been entitled in the private action to have a jury determine whether the proxy statement was false and misleading in the respects alleged. The reason is that at common law in 1791, collateral estoppel was permitted only where the parties in the first action were identical to, or in privity with, the parties to the subsequent action. It was not until 1971 that the doctrine of mutuality was abrogated by this Court in certain limited circumstances. *Blonder-Tongue Laboratories, Inc. v. University of Illinois Foundation*, 402 U.S. 313. But developments in the judge-made doctrine of collateral estoppel, however salutary, cannot, consistent with the Seventh Amendment, contract in any material fashion the right to a jury trial that a defendant would have enjoyed in 1791. In the instant case, resort to the doctrine of collateral estoppel does more than merely contract the right to a jury trial: It eliminates the right entirely and therefore contravenes the Seventh Amendment.

Even accepting, *arguendo*, the majority's position that there is no violation of the Seventh Amendment here, I nonetheless would not sanction the use of collateral estoppel in this case. The Court today holds:

> The general rule should be that in cases where a plaintiff could easily have joined in the earlier action or where, either for the reasons discussed above or for other reasons, the application of offensive estoppel would be unfair to a defendant, a trial judge should not allow the use of offensive collateral estoppel.

Ante, at 331. In my view, it is "unfair" to apply offensive collateral estoppel where the party who is sought to be estopped has not had an opportunity to have the facts of his case determined by a jury. Since in this case petitioners were not entitled to a jury trial in the Securities and Exchange Commission (SEC) lawsuit, I would not estop them from relitigating the issues determined in the SEC suit before a jury in the private action. I believe that several factors militate in favor of this result.

First, the use of offensive collateral estoppel in this case runs counter to the strong federal policy favoring jury trials, even if it does not, as the majority holds, violate the Seventh Amendment. . . .

Second, I believe that the opportunity for a jury trial in the second action could easily lead to a different result from that obtained in the first action before the court and therefore that it is unfair to estop petitioners from relitigating the issues before a jury. This is the position adopted in the *Restatement (Second) of Judgments*, which disapproves of the application of offensive collateral estoppel where the defendant has an opportunity for a jury trial in the second lawsuit that was not available in the first action. The Court accepts the proposition that it is unfair to apply offensive collateral estoppel "where the second action affords the defendant procedural opportunities unavailable in the first action that could readily cause a different result." Differences in discovery opportunities between the two actions are cited as examples of situations where it would be unfair to permit offensive collateral estoppel. But in the Court's view, the fact that petitioners would have been entitled to a jury trial in the present action is not such a "procedural [opportunity]" because "the presence or absence of a jury as factfinder is basically neutral, quite unlike, for example, the necessity of defending the first lawsuit in an inconvenient forum."

As is evident from the prior brief discussion of the development of the civil jury trial guarantee in this country, those who drafted the Declaration of Independence and debated so passionately the proposed Constitution during the ratification period, would indeed be astounded to learn that the presence or absence of a jury is merely "neutral," whereas the availability of discovery, a device unmentioned in the Constitution, may be controlling. It is precisely because the Framers believed that they might receive a different result at the hands of a jury of their peers than at the mercy of the sovereign's judges, that the Seventh Amendment was adopted. And I suspect that anyone who litigates cases before juries in the 1970's would be equally amazed to hear of the supposed lack of distinction between trial by court and trial by jury. The Court can cite no authority in support of this curious proposition. The merits of civil juries have been long debated, but I suspect that juries have never been accused of being merely "neutral" factors.

Contrary to the majority's supposition, juries can make a difference, and our cases have, before today at least, recognized this obvious fact. Thus, in *Colgrove v. Battin*, 413 U.S., at 157, we stated that "the purpose of the jury trial in . . . civil cases [is] to assure a fair and equitable resolution of factual issues, *Gasoline Products Co. v. Champlin Co.*, 283 U.S. 494, 498 (1931). . . ." And in *Byrd v. Blue Ridge Rural Electrical Cooperative, supra*, at 537, the Court conceded that "the nature of the tribunal which tries issues may be important in the enforcement of the parcel of rights making up a cause of action or defense. . . . It may well be that in the instant personal-injury case the outcome would be substantially affected by whether the issue of immunity is decided by a judge or a jury." *See Curtis v. Loether*, 415 U.S., at 198; *cf. Duncan v. Louisiana*, 391 U.S. 145, 156 (1968). Jurors bring to a case their common sense and community values; their "very inexperience is an asset because it secures a fresh perception of each trial, avoiding the stereotypes said to infect the judicial eye." H. Kalven & H. Zeisel, *The American Jury* 8 (1966).

The ultimate irony of today's decision is that its potential for significantly conserving the resources of either the litigants or the judiciary is doubtful at best. That being the case, I see absolutely no reason to frustrate so cavalierly the important federal policy favoring jury decisions of disputed fact questions. The instant case is an apt example of the minimal savings that will be accomplished by the Court's decision. As the Court admits, even if petitioners are collaterally estopped from relitigating whether the proxy was materially false and misleading, they are still entitled to have a jury determine whether respondent was injured by the alleged misstatements and the amount of damages, if any, sustained by respondent. Thus, a jury must be impaneled in this case in any event. The time saved by not trying the issue of whether the proxy was materially false and misleading before the jury is likely to be insubstantial. It is just as probable that today's decision will have the result of coercing defendants to agree to consent orders or settlements in agency enforcement actions in order to preserve their right to jury trial in the private actions. In that event, the Court, for no compelling reason, will have simply added a powerful club to the administrative agencies' arsenals that even Congress was unwilling to provide them.

Comments and Questions

1. How does the mutuality doctrine (effectively abrogated by *Parklane*) differ from the due process safeguard preventing estoppel against a party who has not had a full and fair opportunity to litigate the issue in the previous case? What are the implications of this difference for Justice Stewart and the Court, insofar as offensive use of collateral estoppel is concerned?

2. How does the operation of defensive collateral estoppel differ from that of offensive collateral estoppel? What are the implications of this difference for Justice Stewart and the Court, insofar as the constraints they place on offensive collateral estoppel?

3. How would Professor Currie's "familiar example," *see* the Court's footnote 14, be resolved under the *Parklane* analysis?

4. Given Justice Rehnquist's eloquent invocation of the Seventh Amendment, has the Court not elevated the doctrine of finality above the constitutional right to trial by jury? What could possibly justify this result?

D. THE COUNTERWEIGHTS TO FINALITY

Are there any circumstances in which countervailing policy concerns would outweigh the doctrine of finality? What if the decision in the prior case is based on what is now recognized to be an erroneous reading of the law? Does the interest in arriving at the correct result trump the interest in putting disputes to rest once and for all? The next case illustrates the priority placed on finality.

■ FEDERATED DEPARTMENT STORES, INC. v. MOITIE
452 U.S. 394 (1981)

Reversal

Justice REHNQUIST delivered the opinion of the Court:

The only question presented in this case is whether the Court of Appeals for the Ninth Circuit validly created an exception to the doctrine of *res judicata*. The court held that *res judicata* does not bar relitigation of an unappealed adverse judgment where, as here, other plaintiffs in similar actions against common defendants successfully appeal the judgments against them. We disagree with the view taken by the Court of Appeals for the Ninth Circuit and reverse.

I

In 1976 the United States brought an antitrust action against petitioners, owners of various department stores, alleging that they had violated §1 of the Sherman Act, 15 U.S.C. §1, by agreeing to fix the retail price of women's clothing sold in northern California. Seven parallel civil actions were subsequently filed by private plaintiffs seeking treble damages on behalf of proposed classes of retail purchasers, including that of respondent Moitie in state court (*Moitie I*) and respondent Brown (*Brown I*) in the United States District Court for the Northern District of California. Each of these complaints tracked almost verbatim the allegations of the Government's complaint, though the *Moitie I* complaint referred solely to state law. All of the actions originally filed in the District Court were assigned to a single federal judge, and the *Moitie I* case was removed there on the basis of diversity of citizenship and federal-question jurisdiction. The District Court dismissed all of the actions "in their entirety" on the ground that plaintiffs had not alleged an "injury" to their "business or property" within the meaning of §4 of the Clayton Act, 15 U.S.C. §15.

Plaintiffs in five of the suits appealed that judgment to the Court of Appeals for the Ninth Circuit. The single counsel representing Moitie and Brown, however, chose not to appeal and instead refiled the two actions in state court, *Moitie II* and *Brown II*. Although the complaints purported to raise only state-law claims, they made allegations similar to those made in the prior complaints, including that of the Government. Petitioners removed these new actions to the District Court for the Northern District of California and moved to have them dismissed on the ground of *res judicata*. In a decision rendered July 8, 1977, the District Court first denied respondents' motion to remand. It held that the complaints, though artfully couched in terms of state law, were "in many respects identical" with the prior complaints, and were thus properly removed to federal court because they raised "essentially federal law" claims. The court then concluded that because *Moitie II* and *Brown II* involved the "same parties, the same alleged offenses, and the same time periods" as *Moitie I* and *Brown I*, the doctrine of *res judicata* required that they be dismissed. This time, Moitie and Brown appealed.

Pending that appeal, this Court on June 11, 1979, decided *Reiter v. Sonotone Corp.*, 442 U.S. 330, holding that retail purchasers can suffer an "injury" to their "business or property" as those terms are used in §4 of the Clayton Act. On June 25, 1979, the Court of Appeals for the Ninth Circuit reversed and remanded the five cases which had been decided with *Moitie I* and *Brown I*, the cases that had been appealed, for further proceedings in light of *Reiter*. When *Moitie II* and *Brown II* finally came before the Court of Appeals for the Ninth Circuit, the court reversed the decision of the District Court dismissing the cases.[2] Though the court recognized that a "strict application of the doctrine of *res judicata* would preclude our review of the instant decision," it refused to apply the doctrine to the facts of this case. It observed that the other five litigants . . . had successfully appealed the decision against them. It then asserted that "non-appealing parties may benefit from a reversal when their position is closely interwoven with that of appealing parties," and concluded that "[because] the instant dismissal rested on a case that has been effectively overruled," the doctrine of *res judicata* must give way to "public policy" and "simple justice." We granted certiorari to consider the validity of the Court of Appeals' novel exception to the doctrine of *res judicata*.

II

There is little to be added to the doctrine of *res judicata* as developed in the case law of this Court. A final judgment on the merits of an action precludes the parties or their privies from relitigating issues that were or could have been raised in that action. Nor are the *res judicata* consequences of a final, unappealed judgment on the merits altered by the fact that the judgment may have been wrong or rested on a legal principle subsequently overruled in another case. As this Court explained in *Baltimore S.S. Co. v. Phillips*, 274 U.S. 316, 325 (1927), an "erroneous conclusion" reached by the court in the first suit does not deprive the defendants in the second action "of their right to rely upon the plea of *res judicata*. . . . A judgment merely voidable because based upon an erroneous view of the law is not open to collateral attack, but can be corrected only by a direct review and not by bringing another action upon the same cause [of action]." We have observed that "[the] indulgence of a contrary view would result in creating elements of uncertainty and confusion and in undermining the conclusive character of judgments, consequences which it was the very purpose of the doctrine of *res judicata* to avert." *Reed v. Allen*, 286 U.S. 191, 201 (1932). In this case, the Court of Appeals conceded that the "strict application of the doctrine of *res judicata*" required that *Brown II*

---

2. The Court of Appeals also affirmed the District Court's conclusion that *Brown II* was properly removed to federal court, reasoning that the claims presented were "federal in nature." We agree that at least some of the claims had a sufficient federal character to support removal. As one treatise puts it, courts "will not permit plaintiff to use artful pleading to close off defendant's right to a federal forum . . . [and] occasionally the removal court will seek to determine whether the real nature of the claim is federal, regardless of plaintiff's characterization." 14 C. Wright, A. Miller, & E. Cooper, *Federal Practice and Procedure* §3722, pp. 564-566 (1976) (citing cases) (footnote omitted). The District Court applied that settled principle to the facts of this case. After "an extensive review and analysis of the origins and substance of" the two Brown complaints, it found, and the Court of Appeals expressly agreed, that respondents had attempted to avoid removal jurisdiction by "[artfully]" casting their "essentially federal law claims" as state-law claims. We will not question here that factual finding.

be dismissed. By that, the court presumably meant that the "technical elements" of *res judicata* had been satisfied, namely, that the decision in *Brown I* was a final judgment on the merits and involved the same claims and the same parties as *Brown II*.[3] The court, however, declined to dismiss *Brown II* because, in its view, it would be unfair to bar respondents from relitigating a claim so "closely interwoven" with that of the successfully appealing parties. We believe that such an unprecedented departure from accepted principles of *res judicata* is unwarranted. Indeed, the decision below is all but foreclosed by our prior case law.

. . . Indeed, this case presents even more compelling reasons to apply the doctrine of *res judicata* than did [prior cases]. Respondents here seek to be the windfall beneficiaries of an appellate reversal procured by other independent parties, who have no interest in respondents' case, not a reversal in interrelated cases procured . . . by the same affected party. Moreover, . . . it is apparent that respondents here made a calculated choice to forgo their appeals. *See also Ackermann v. United States*, 340 U.S. 193, 198 (1950) (holding that petitioners were not entitled to relief under Federal Rule of Civil Procedure 60(b) when they made a "free, calculated, deliberate [choice]" not to appeal). The Court of Appeals also rested its opinion in part on what it viewed as "simple justice." But we do not see the grave injustice which would be done by the application of accepted principles of *res judicata*. "Simple justice" is achieved when a complex body of law developed over a period of years is evenhandedly applied. The doctrine of *res judicata* serves vital public interests beyond any individual judge's ad hoc determination of the equities in a particular case. There is simply "no principle of law or equity which sanctions the rejection by a federal court of the salutary principle of *res judicata*." The Court of Appeals' reliance on "public policy" is similarly misplaced. This Court has long recognized that "[public] policy dictates that there be an end of litigation; that those who have contested an issue shall be bound by the result of the contest, and that matters once tried shall be considered forever settled as between the parties." We have stressed that "[the] doctrine of *res judicata* is not a mere matter of practice or procedure inherited from a more technical time than ours. It is a rule of fundamental and substantial justice, 'of public policy and of private peace,' which should be cordially regarded and enforced by the courts. . . ." The language used by this Court half a century ago is even more compelling in view of today's crowded dockets:

The predicament in which respondent finds himself is of his own making. . . .
[We] cannot be expected, for his sole relief, to upset the general and well-

3. The dismissal for failure to state a claim under Federal Rule of Civil Procedure 12(b)(6) is a "judgment on the merits." *See Angel v. Bullington*, 330 U.S. 183, 190 (1947); *Bell v. Hood*, 327 U.S. 678 (1946).

established doctrine of res judicata, conceived in the light of the maxim that the interest of the state requires that there be an end to litigation—a maxim which comports with common sense as well as public policy. And the mischief which would follow the establishment of precedent for so disregarding this salutary doctrine against prolonging strife would be greater than the benefit which would result from relieving some case of individual hardship.

Reed v. Allen, 286 U.S., at 198-199. Respondents make no serious effort to defend the decision of the Court of Appeals. They do not ask that the decision below be affirmed. Instead, they conclude that the "the writ of certiorari should be dismissed as improvidently granted." In the alternative, they argue that "the district court's dismissal on grounds of *res judicata* should be reversed, and the district court directed to grant respondent's motion to remand to the California state court." In their view, *Brown I* cannot be considered *res judicata* as to their state-law claims, since *Brown I* raised only federal-law claims and *Brown II* raised additional state-law claims not decided in *Brown I,* such as unfair competition, fraud, and restitution.

It is unnecessary for this Court to reach that issue. It is enough for our decision here that *Brown I* is *res judicata* as to respondents' federal-law claims. Accordingly, the judgment of the Court of Appeals is reversed, and the cause is remanded for proceedings consistent with this opinion. It is so ordered.

Justice BLACKMUN, with whom Justice MARSHALL joins, concurring in the judgment.

While I agree with the result reached in this case, I write separately to state my views on two points.

First, I, for one, would not close the door upon the possibility that there are cases in which the doctrine of *res judicata* must give way to what the Court of Appeals referred to as "overriding concerns of public policy and simple justice." . . . [R]espondents were not "caught in a mesh of procedural complexities." Instead, they made a deliberate tactical decision not to appeal. Nor would public policy be served by making an exception to the doctrine in this case; to the contrary, there is a special need for strict application of *res judicata* in complex multiple party actions of this sort so as to discourage "break-away" litigation. Finally, this is not a case "where the rights of appealing and non-appealing parties are so interwoven or dependent on each other as to require a reversal of the whole judgment when a part thereof is reversed."

Second, and in contrast, I would flatly hold that *Brown I* is *res judicata* as to respondents' state-law claims. Like the District Court, the Court of Appeals found that those state-law claims were simply disguised federal claims; since respondents have not cross-petitioned from that judgment, their argument that this case should be remanded to state court should be itself barred by *res judicata.* More important, even if the state and federal claims are distinct, respondents' failure to allege the state claims in *Brown I* manifestly bars their allegation in *Brown II*. The dismissal of *Brown I* is *res judicata* not only as to all claims respondents actually raised, but also as to all claims that could have been raised. Since there is no reason to believe that it was clear at the outset of this litigation that the District Court would have declined to exercise pendent jurisdiction over state claims, respondents were obligated to plead those claims if they wished to preserve them. Because they did not do so, I would hold the claims barred.

Justice BRENNAN, dissenting.

In its eagerness to correct the decision of the Court of Appeals for the Ninth Circuit, the Court today disregards statutory restrictions on federal-court jurisdiction, and, in the process, confuses rather than clarifies long-established principles of *res judicata*. I therefore respectfully dissent.

I

Respondent Floyd R. Brown filed this class action (*Brown II*) against petitioners in California state court. The complaint stated four state-law causes of action: (1) fraud and deceit, (2) unfair business practices, (3) civil conspiracy, and (4) restitution. Plaintiffs' Complaint, paras. 11-14. It alleged "not less than $600" damages per class member, and in addition sought "appropriate multiple damages," exemplary and punitive damages, interest from date of injury, attorney's fees and costs, and other relief. All four of the causes of action rested wholly on California statutory or common law; none rested in any fashion on federal law.

Nonetheless, petitioners removed the suit to the United States District Court for the Northern District of California, where respondent Brown filed a motion to remand on the ground that his action raised no federal question within the meaning of 28 U.S.C. §1441 (b). Respondent's motion was denied by the District Court, which stated that "[from] start to finish, plaintiffs have essentially alleged violations by defendants of federal antitrust laws." The court reasoned that "[artful] pleading" by plaintiffs cannot "convert their essentially federal law claims into state law claims," and held that respondent's complaint was properly removed "because [it] concerned federal questions which could have been originally brought in Federal District Court without satisfying any minimum amount in controversy." The court then dismissed the action, holding that, under the doctrine of *res judicata*, *Brown II* was barred by the adverse decision in an earlier suit in federal court (*Brown I*) involving "the same parties, the same alleged offenses, and the same time periods." *Ibid.*

The Court of Appeals affirmed the District Court's decision not to remand, stating that "[the] court below correctly held that the claims presented were federal in nature." However, the Court of Appeals reversed the District Court's order of dismissal, and remanded for trial.

II

The provision authorizing removal of actions from state to federal courts on the basis of a federal question[2] is found in 28 U.S.C. §1441 (b):

Any civil action of which the district courts have original jurisdiction founded on a claim or right arising under the Constitution, treaties or laws of the United States shall be removable without regard to the citizenship or residence of the parties.

Removability depends solely upon the nature of the plaintiff's complaint: an action may be removed to federal court only if a "right or immunity created by the Constitution or laws of the United States [constitutes] an element, and an essential one, of the plaintiff's cause of action." An action arising under state law may not be removed solely because a federal right or immunity is raised as a defense. *Tennessee v. Union & Planters' Bank*, 152 U.S. 454 (1894).

An important corollary is that "the party who brings a suit is master to decide what law he will rely upon and therefore does determine whether he will bring a 'suit arising under' the . . . [laws] of the United States" by the allegations in his complaint. Where the plaintiff's claim might be brought under either federal or state law, the plaintiff is normally free to ignore the federal question and rest his claim solely on the state ground. If he does so, the defendant has no general right of removal.

This corollary is well grounded in principles of federalism. So long as States retain authority to legislate in subject areas in which Congress has legislated without pre-empting the field, and so long as state courts remain the preferred forum for interpretation and enforcement of state law, plaintiffs must be permitted to proceed in state court under state law. It would do violence to state autonomy were defendants able to remove state claims to federal court merely because the plaintiff could have asserted a federal claim based on the same set of facts underlying his state claim. . . .

This lawsuit concerns the area of antitrust in which federal laws have not displaced state law. Thus, respondent Brown had the option of proceeding under state or federal law, or both. So far as is apparent from the complaint, which was carefully limited to four California state-law

---

2. As the District Court acknowledged, *Brown II* could not be removed on the basis of diversity of citizenship, because the amount in controversy did not exceed $10,000. The court correctly noted, however, that the action could have been removed without regard to the amount in controversy, if it could have been brought as an original action in federal court without meeting any minimum amount in controversy. Actions under the Clayton Act, 15 U.S.C. §15, may be brought in federal court without regard to amount in controversy. *See also* 28 U.S.C. §1331 (1976 ed., Supp. IV), and note following §1331 (repeal of minimum amount in controversy for federal-question cases pending as of date of enactment).

causes of action, this case arises wholly without reference to federal law. Under settled principles of federal jurisdiction, therefore, respondent's lawsuit should not have been removed to federal court.

The Court today nonetheless sustains removal of this action on the ground that "at least some of the claims had a sufficient federal character to support removal." I do not understand what the Court means by this. Which of the claims are federal in character? Why are the claims federal in character? In my view, they are all predicated solely on California law. Certainly, none of them purports to state a claim under the federal antitrust laws, and the mere fact that plaintiffs might have chosen to proceed under the Clayton Act surely does not suffice to transmute their state claims into federal claims.

The Court relies on what it calls a "factual finding" by the District Court, with which the Court of Appeals agreed, that "respondents had attempted to avoid removal jurisdiction by '[artfully]' casting their 'essentially federal law claims' as state-law claims." *Ibid.* But this amounts to no more than a pejorative characterization of respondents' decision to proceed under state rather than federal law. "Artful" or not, respondents' complaints were not based on any claim of a federal right or immunity, and were not, therefore, removable. . . .

Even assuming that this Court and the lower federal courts have jurisdiction to decide this case, however, I dissent from the Court's disposition of the *res judicata* issue. Having reached out to assume jurisdiction, the Court inexplicably recoils from deciding the case. The Court finds it "unnecessary" to reach the question of the *res judicata* effect of *Brown I* on respondents' "state-law claims." "It is enough for our decision here," the Court says, "that *Brown I* is *res judicata* as to respondents' federal-law claims." *Ibid.* But respondents raised only state-law claims; respondents did not raise any federal-law claims. Thus, if the Court fails to decide the disposition of respondents' state-law claims, it decides nothing. And in doing so, the Court introduces the possibility—heretofore foreclosed by our decisions—that unarticulated theories of recovery may survive an unconditional dismissal of the lawsuit.

Like Justice Blackmun, I would hold that the dismissal of *Brown I* is *res judicata* not only as to every matter that was actually litigated, but also as to every ground or theory of recovery that might also have been presented. An unqualified dismissal on the merits of a substantial federal antitrust claim precludes relitigation of the same claim on a state-law theory. The Court's failure to acknowledge this basic principle can only create doubts and confusion where none were before, and may encourage litigants to split their causes of action, state from federal, in the hope that they might win a second day in court.

I therefore respectfully dissent, and would vacate the judgment of the Court of Appeals with instructions to remand to the District Court with instructions to remand to state court.

Comments and Questions

1. Note the Court's equation of finality and justice:

"Simple justice" is achieved when a complex body of law developed over a period of years is evenhandedly applied. The doctrine of *res judicata* serves vital public interests beyond any individual judge's ad hoc determination of the equities in a particular case. There is simply "no principle of law or equity which sanctions the rejection by a federal court of the salutary principle of *res judicata*." The Court of Appeals' reliance on "public policy" is similarly misplaced. This Court has long recognized that "[public] policy dictates that there be an end of litigation; that those who have contested an issue shall be bound by the result of the contest, and that matters once tried shall be considered forever settled as between the parties." We have stressed that "[the] doctrine of *res judicata* is not a mere matter of practice or procedure inherited from a more technical time than ours. It is a rule of fundamental and substantial justice, 'of public policy and of private peace,' which should be cordially regarded and enforced by the courts. . . ."

When you read *Martin v. Wilks*, the last case reprinted in this book, consider whether the Court there (again through Justice Rehnquist) accords the interest in finality the same absolute deference as in *Moitie*. Can the two cases be reconciled?

2. Can you reconcile the *Moitie* Court's suggestion that *Brown I* was *res judicata* only to the *federal law* claims with the well established concept that claim preclusion operates as to all transactionally related claims that were raised *and that could have been raised*? Do Justices Blackmun, Marshall, and Brennan stay closer to this principle in their analysis?

3. What is the relationship between the preclusion issue and the question of removability in *Moitie*? Is there not another contradiction between the Court's conclusion that *Brown II* was properly removed, because of the federal nature of its claims, and its suggestion that *Brown II*'s state-law claims may not be precluded by *Brown I*?

4. In *United States v. Mendoza*, 464 U.S. 154 (1984), Justice Rehnquist carved out an exception to the use of issue preclusion against the Government as litigant. Like Moitie and Brown, the Government left unappealed a decision against it, here a ruling by a United States District Court that the due process rights of Filipino veterans of World War II had been violated when their citizenship naturalization process was suspended. Mendoza brought a suit raising the same issue, and the Ninth Circuit held that the Government was estopped from relitigating it. The Supreme Court disagreed:

A rule allowing nonmutual collateral estoppel against the Government in such cases would substantially thwart the development of important questions of law by freezing the first final decision rendered on a particular legal issue. Allowing only one final adjudication would deprive this Court of the benefit it receives from permitting several courts of appeals to explore a difficult question before this Court grants certiorari.

Clearly, then, some policy concerns can outweigh the usually strict application of preclusion doctrine.

5. As the next case demonstrates, the rules of preclusion operate across all kinds of lines—state and federal courts; civil and criminal cases. Issues resolved between A and B in state court are routinely precluded from being relitigated between A and B in federal court, and vice versa; issues resolved against the defendant in a criminal case will usually preclude relitigation by that party in a civil case (however, there is no *vice versa* here because the "preponderance of the evidence" burden of proof in civil litigation is considerably lower than the "beyond a reasonable doubt" standard in the criminal case).

6. What policy concerns are invoked by the dissent in the next case to outweigh the usually strict application of preclusion doctrine in the context of a federal civil rights action following on the heels of a state criminal prosecution? How does the Court answer these concerns?

■ ALLEN v. MCCURRY
449 U.S. 90 (1980)

Justice STEWART delivered the opinion of the Court:

. . . In April 1977, several undercover police officers, following an informant's tip that McCurry was dealing in heroin, went to his house in St. Louis, Mo., to attempt a purchase. Two officers, petitioners Allen and Jacobsmeyer, knocked on the front door, while the other officers hid nearby. When McCurry opened the door, the two officers asked to buy some heroin "caps." McCurry went back into the house and returned soon thereafter, firing a pistol at and seriously wounding Allen and Jacobsmeyer. After a gun battle with the other officers and their reinforcements, McCurry retreated into the house; he emerged again when the police demanded that he surrender. Several officers then entered the house without a warrant, purportedly to search for other persons inside. One of the officers seized drugs and other contraband that lay in plain view, as well as additional contraband he found in dresser drawers and in auto tires on the porch.

McCurry was charged with possession of heroin and assault with intent to kill. At the pretrial suppression hearing, the trial judge excluded the evidence seized from the dresser drawers and tires, but denied suppression of the evidence found in plain view. McCurry was convicted of both the heroin and assault offenses.

McCurry subsequently filed the present §1983* action for $1 million in damages against petitioners Allen and Jacobsmeyer, other unnamed individual police officers, and the city of St. Louis and its police department. The complaint alleged a conspiracy to violate McCurry's Fourth Amendment rights, an unconstitutional search and seizure of his house, and an assault on him by unknown police officers after he had been arrested and handcuffed. The petitioners moved for summary judgment. The District Court apparently understood the gist of the complaint to be the allegedly unconstitutional search and seizure and granted summary judgment, holding that collateral estoppel prevented McCurry from relitigating the search-and-seizure question already decided against him in the state courts.

The Court of Appeals reversed the judgment and remanded the case for trial. The appellate court said it was not holding that collateral estoppel was generally inapplicable in a §1983 suit raising issues determined against the federal plaintiff in a state criminal trial. But noting that [caselaw] barred McCurry from federal habeas corpus relief, and invoking "the special role of the federal courts in protecting civil rights," the court concluded that the §1983 suit was McCurry's only route to a federal forum for his constitutional claim and directed the trial court to allow him to proceed to trial unencumbered by collateral estoppel.

II

The federal courts have traditionally adhered to the related doctrines of *res judicata* and collateral estoppel. Under *res judicata*, a final judgment on the merits of an action precludes the parties or their privies from relitigating issues that were or could have been raised in that action. Under collateral estoppel, once a court has decided an issue of fact or law necessary to its judgment, that decision may preclude relitigation of the issue in a suit on a different cause of action involving a party to the first case. As this Court and other courts have often recognized, *res judicata* and collateral estoppel relieve parties of the cost and vexation of multiple lawsuits, conserve judicial resources, and, by preventing inconsistent decisions, encourage reliance on adjudication.

In recent years, this Court has reaffirmed the benefits of collateral estoppel in particular, finding the policies underlying it to apply in contexts not formerly recognized at common law. Thus, the Court has elimi-

---

* ["Every person who, under color of any statute, ordinance, regulation, custom, or usage, of any State or Territory, subjects, or causes to be subjected, any citizen of the United States or other person within the jurisdiction thereof to the deprivation of any rights, privileges, or immunities secured by the Constitution and laws, shall be liable to the party injured in an action at law, suit in equity, or other proper proceeding for redress." 42 U.S.C. §1983.]

nated the requirement of mutuality in applying collateral estoppel to bar relitigation of issues decided earlier in federal-court suits, and has allowed a litigant who was not a party to a federal case to use collateral estoppel "offensively" in a new federal suit against the party who lost on the decided issue in the first case, *Parklane Hosiery Co. v. Shore*, 439 U.S. 322. But one general limitation the Court has repeatedly recognized is that the concept of collateral estoppel cannot apply when the party against whom the earlier decision is asserted did not have a "full and fair opportunity" to litigate that issue in the earlier case.

The federal courts generally have also consistently accorded preclusive effect to issues decided by state courts. Thus, *res judicata* and collateral estoppel not only reduce unnecessary litigation and foster reliance on adjudication, but also promote the comity between state and federal courts that has been recognized as a bulwark of the federal system. Indeed, though the federal courts may look to the common law or to the policies supporting *res judicata* and collateral estoppel in assessing the preclusive effect of decisions of other federal courts, Congress has specifically required all federal courts to give preclusive effect to state-court judgments whenever the courts of the State from which the judgments emerged would do so:

> [Judicial] proceedings [of any court of any State] shall have the same full faith and credit in every court within the United States and its Territories and Possessions as they have by law or usage in the courts of such State. . . .

28 U.S.C. §1738. It is against this background that we examine the relationship of §1983 and collateral estoppel, and the decision of the Court of Appeals in this case.

III

This Court has never directly decided whether the rules of *res judicata* and collateral estoppel are generally applicable to §1983 actions. But in *Preiser v. Rodriguez*, 411 U.S. 475, 497, the Court noted with implicit approval the view of other federal courts that *res judicata* principles fully apply to civil rights suits brought under that statute. And the virtually unanimous view of the Courts of Appeals since *Preiser* has been that §1983 presents no categorical bar to the application of *res judicata* and collateral estoppel concepts. These federal appellate court decisions have spoken with little explanation or citation in assuming the compatibility of §1983 and rules of preclusion, but the statute and its legislative history clearly support the courts' decisions. . . .

Moreover, the legislative history of §1983 does not in any clear way suggest that Congress intended to repeal or restrict the traditional doctrines of preclusion. The main goal of the Act was to override the corrupting influence of the Ku Klux Klan and its sympathizers on the governments and law enforcement agencies of the Southern States, *see Monroe v. Pape*, 365 U.S. 167, 174, and of course the debates show that one strong motive behind its enactment was grave congressional concern that the state courts had been deficient in protecting federal rights, *Mitchum v. Foster*, 407 U.S. 225, 241-242; *Monroe v. Pape*, *supra*, at 180 n.13. But in the context of the legislative history as a whole, this congressional concern lends only the most equivocal support to any argument that, in cases where the state courts have recognized the constitutional claims asserted and provided fair procedures for determining them, Congress intended to override §1738 or the common-law rules of collateral estoppel and *res judicata*. Since repeals by implication are disfavored, *Radzanower v. Touche Ross & Co.*, 426 U.S. 148, 154, much clearer support than this would be required to hold that §1738 and the traditional rules of preclusion are not applicable to §1983 suits.

As the Court has understood the history of the legislation, Congress realized that in enacting §1983 it was altering the balance of judicial power between the state and federal courts. *See Mitchum v. Foster*, *supra*, at 241. But in doing so, Congress was adding to the jurisdiction of the federal courts, not subtracting from that of the state courts. The debates contain several references to the concurrent jurisdiction of the state courts over federal questions, and numerous suggestions that the state courts would retain their established jurisdiction so that they could, when the then current political passions abated, demonstrate a new sensitivity to federal rights. . . .

To the extent that it did intend to change the balance of power over federal questions between the state and federal courts, the 42d Congress was acting in a way thoroughly consistent with the doctrines of preclusion. In reviewing the legislative history of §1983 in *Monroe v. Pape*, *supra*, the Court inferred that Congress had intended a federal remedy in three circumstances: where state substantive law was facially unconstitutional, where state procedural law was inadequate to allow full litigation of a constitutional claim, and where state procedural law, though adequate in theory, was inadequate in practice. In short, the federal courts could step in where the state courts were unable or unwilling to protect federal rights. *Id.* at 176. This understanding of §1983 might well support an exception to *res judicata* and collateral estoppel where state law did not provide fair procedures for the litigation of constitutional claims, or where a state court failed to even acknowledge the existence of the constitutional principle on which a litigant based his claim. Such an exception, however, would be essentially the same as the important general limit on rules of preclusion that already exists: Collateral estoppel does not apply where the party against whom an earlier court decision is asserted did not have a full and fair opportunity to litigate the claim or issue decided by the first court. But the Court's view of §1983 in *Monroe* lends no strength to any argument that Congress intended to allow relitigation of federal issues decided after a full and fair hearing in a state court simply because the state court's decision may have been erroneous. . . .

The only . . . conceivable basis for finding a universal right to litigate a federal claim in a federal district court is hardly a legal basis at all, but rather a general distrust of the capacity of the state courts to render correct decisions on constitutional issues. . . .

The Court of Appeals erred in holding . . . the doctrine of collateral estoppel inapplicable to his §1983 suit. Accordingly, the judgment is reversed, and the case is remanded to the Court of Appeals for proceedings consistent with this opinion.

It is so ordered.

Justice BLACKMUN, with whom Justice BRENNAN and Justice MARSHALL join, dissenting.

The legal principles with which the Court is concerned in this civil case obviously far transcend the ugly facts of respondent's criminal convictions in the courts of Missouri for heroin possession and assault.

The Court today holds that notions of collateral estoppel apply with full force to this suit brought under 42 U.S.C. §1983. In my view, the Court, in so ruling, ignores the clear import of the legislative history of that statute and disregards the important federal policies that underlie its enforcement. It also shows itself insensitive both to the significant differences between the §1983 remedy and the exclusionary rule, and to the pressures upon a criminal defendant that make a free choice of forum illusory. I do not doubt that principles of preclusion are to be given such effect as is appropriate in a §1983 action. In many cases, the denial of *res judicata* or collateral estoppel effect would serve no purpose and would harm relations between federal and state tribunals. Nonetheless, the Court's analysis in this particular case is unacceptable to me. It works injustice on this §1983 plaintiff, and it makes more difficult the consistent protection of constitutional rights, a consideration that was at the core of the enacters' intent. Accordingly, I dissent. . . .

In this case, the police officers seek to prevent a criminal defendant from relitigating the constitutionality of their conduct in searching his house, after the state trial court had found that conduct in part violative of the defendant's Fourth Amendment rights and in part justified by the circumstances. I doubt that the police officers, now defendants in this §1983 action, can be considered to have been in privity with the State in its role as prosecutor. Therefore, only "issue preclusion" is at stake. The following factors persuade me to conclude that this respondent should not be precluded from asserting his claim in federal court. First, at the time §1983 was passed, a nonparty's ability, as a practical matter, to invoke collateral estoppel was nonexistent. One could not preclude an opponent from relitigating an issue in a new cause of action, though that issue had been determined conclusively in a prior proceeding, unless there was "mutuality." Additionally, the definitions of "cause of action" and "issue" were narrow. As a result, and obviously, no preclusive effect could arise out of a criminal proceeding that would affect subsequent civil litigation. Thus, the 42d Congress could not have anticipated or approved that a criminal defendant, tried and convicted in state court, would be precluded from raising against police officers a constitutional claim arising out of his arrest.

Also, the process of deciding in a state criminal trial whether to exclude or admit evidence is not at all the equivalent of a §1983 proceeding. The remedy sought in the latter is utterly different. In bringing the civil suit the criminal defendant does not seek to challenge his conviction collaterally. At most, he wins damages. In contrast, the exclusion of evidence may prevent a criminal conviction. A trial court, faced with the decision whether to exclude relevant evidence, confronts institutional pressures that may cause it to give a different shape to the Fourth Amendment right from what would result in civil litigation of a damages claim. Also, the issue whether to exclude evidence is subsidiary to the purpose of a criminal trial, which is to determine the guilt or innocence of the defendant, and a trial court, at least subconsciously, must weigh the potential damage to the truth-seeking process caused by excluding relevant evidence.

A state criminal defendant cannot be held to have chosen "voluntarily" to litigate his Fourth Amendment claim in the state court. The risk of conviction puts pressure upon him to raise all possible defenses. He also faces uncertainty about the wisdom of forgoing litigation on any issue, for there is the possibility that he will be held to have waived his right to appeal on that issue. The "deliberate bypass" of state procedures, which the imposition of collateral estoppel under these circumstances encourages, surely is not a preferred goal. To hold that a criminal defendant who raises a Fourth Amendment claim at his criminal trial "freely and without reservation submits his federal claims for decision by the state courts," is to deny reality. The criminal defendant is an involuntary litigant in the state tribunal, and against him all the forces of the State are arrayed. To force him to a choice between forgoing either a potential defense or a federal forum for hearing his constitutional civil claim is fundamentally unfair.

I would affirm the judgment of the Court of Appeals.

Comments and Questions

1. Four years after *Allen v. McCurry* the Court revisited the question of whether preclusion doctrine should be suspended in order to provide a federal forum for civil rights claims. Dr. Ethel D. Migra brought a state court breach of contract action against the Board of Education when it reneged on its earlier renewal of her contract as supervisor of elementary

education. She prevailed and was awarded reinstatement and compensatory damages. She subsequently filed a §1983 action in federal court alleging that her nonrenewal was in retaliation against her for her role as an advocate of desegregation in the school district, thereby depriving her of rights protected by the First, Fifth, and Fourteenth Amendments to the Constitution. The District Court granted summary judgment for the defendants and dismissed the complaint on the basis of *res judicata.* In *Migra v. Warren City School District Board of Education,* 465 U.S. 75 (1984), the Supreme Court affirmed, writing:

> The Court in *Allen* left open the possibility . . . that the preclusive effect of a state-court judgment might be different as to a federal issue that a §1983 litigant could have raised but did not raise in the earlier state-court proceeding. That is the central issue to be resolved in the present case. Petitioner did not litigate her §1983 claim in state court, and she asserts that the state-court judgment should not preclude her suit in federal court simply because her federal claim could have been litigated in the state-court proceeding. Thus, petitioner urges this Court to interpret the interplay of §1738 and §1983 in such a way as to accord state-court judgments preclusive effect in §1983 suits only as to issues actually litigated in state court.
>
> It is difficult to see how the policy concerns underlying §1983 would justify a distinction between the issue preclusive and claim preclusive effects of state-court judgments. The argument that state-court judgments should have less preclusive effect in §1983 suits than in other federal suits is based on Congress' expressed concern over the adequacy of state courts as protectors of federal rights. *Allen* recognized that the enactment of §1983 was motivated partially out of such concern, but *Allen* nevertheless held that §1983 did not open the way to relitigation of an issue that had been determined in a state criminal proceeding. Any distrust of state courts that would justify a limitation on the preclusive effect of state judgments in §1983 suits would presumably apply equally to issues that actually were decided in a state court as well as to those that could have been. If §1983 created an exception to the general preclusive effect accorded to state-court judgments, such an exception would seem to require similar treatment of both issue preclusion and claim preclusion. Having rejected in *Allen* the view that state-court judgments have no issue preclusive effect in §1983 suits, we must reject the view that §1983 prevents the judgment in petitioner's state-court proceeding from creating a claim preclusion bar in this case.
>
> Petitioner suggests that to give state-court judgments full issue preclusive effect but not claim preclusive effect would enable litigants to bring their state claims in state court and their federal claims in federal court, thereby taking advantage of the relative expertise of both forums. Although such a division may seem attractive from a plaintiff's perspective, it is not the system established by §1738. That statute embodies the view that it is more important to give full faith and credit to state-court judgments than to ensure separate forums for federal and state claims. This reflects a variety of concerns, including notions of comity, the need to prevent vexatious litigation, and a desire to conserve judicial resources. In the present litigation, petitioner does

not claim that the state court would not have adjudicated her federal claims had she presented them in her original suit in state court. Alternatively, petitioner could have obtained a federal forum for her federal claim by litigating it first in a federal court. Section 1983, however, does not override state preclusion law and guarantee petitioner a right to proceed to judgment in state court on her state claims and then turn to federal court for adjudication of her federal claims. We hold, therefore, that petitioner's state-court judgment in this litigation has the same claim preclusive effect in federal court that the judgment would have in the Ohio state courts.

465 U.S. at 83-85.

2. What are the lessons of *Allen* and *Migra* for lawyers who represent litigants in similar circumstances? This is a good review of the pitfalls generally to be avoided with regard to the doctrines of finality.

Practice Exercise No. 33:
Applying Preclusion Principles

On March 8, 1998, Malcolm-Jinwala Warner (a citizen of Maine) was severely injured in a head on collision with a Ford Wrangler Jeep driven by Carmen Padros. The accident took place on the corner of Centre Street and Spring Park Avenue in Jamaica Plain, Massachusetts. The accident occurred when Warner was waiting at a stop sign on Spring Park Avenue. Padros was driving on Centre Street and attempting to make a left on Spring Park Avenue when all of a sudden Padros lost control of the Jeep and it rolled over on top of Warner's car. Warner's wife, who was following in her own car, saw the entire accident.

Through an investigation by Warner's attorney, Warner learned that Padros was stopped by the Boston police an hour before the accident and was found to have a blood alcohol level of 0.10. Even though Padros was legally intoxicated, the police let her go when she promised to drive directly home. In addition, his attorney found that four months prior to the accident, Padros had modified her Jeep with a suspension lift kit and oversize tires purchased from Ultimate Auto in Lowell. The body of the Jeep was further lifted by metal rods.

In a prosecution arising out of the accident, Padros has been tried for the criminal offense of illegally raising the height of her Jeep and found guilty. She received a suspended sentence and one year of probation.

Warner has now brought suit in federal court against Padros, the police officers who had stopped her prior to the accident, the Boston Police Department, the City of Boston, and Ultimate Auto, alleging negligence and gross negligence.

Assume that four days after Warner files his complaint, a federal court jury in the Jeep case of *Carpenter v. Dee* finds in favor of the plaintiff and against the Lowell Police Department and Ultimate Auto on all counts. Assume this verdict is a general verdict on each count, and is now pending appeal in the First Circuit Court of Appeals.

Warner's attorney, with whom you are working, believes that all defendants may be collaterally estopped in ways that will significantly help Warner's case. A hearing is scheduled on Warner's motion for partial summary judgment motion, collaterally estopping the defendants from contesting key facts and issues.

1. What issues would you ask the judge to collaterally estop the defendants from challenging? How should the judge rule on each?

2. Assume Warner knew about the first Jeep case and was invited to join the case as a co-plaintiff but refused. Would this change your answer to question # 1?

3. Assume the jury in the *Carpenter* case also came in (in addition to the general verdict) with an answer to an interrogatory (Fed. R. Civ. P. 50(b)), which declared that Ultimate Auto's actions were willful, wanton or reckless. How does this affect your issue preclusion arguments?

4. In your research you discover a previous civil case where the Boston Police Department and the City were found grossly negligent after two police officers stopped a driver, measured his blood alcohol level of 0.10, issued a citation, and then let him continue to drive. The driver then struck a plaintiff who brought suit. Would this previous case collaterally estop any of the parties in the *Warner* case? Could you use the case in any other way?

5. Warner alleges that as a result of the accident with Padros his left leg was broken in three places. Padros's attorney finds that a worker's compensation board found that Warner's left leg was broken on March 1, 1998, as result of a work-related injury. Will the board's finding collaterally estop Warner from claiming that his leg was broken as a result of the car accident? Can Padros get any mileage from the worker's compensation case?

6. If Warner prevails against Padros, can Warner's wife now successfully sue for infliction of emotional distress or will *res judicata* bar her claim?

E. REVIEW

Memorandum

To: Judicial Law Clerks
From: Trial Judge
Re: *Collector v. Gallery*

In *Charles Collector ("Collector") v. Cape Gallery, Inc. ("Gallery")*, commenced June 10, 1998, both sides (subsequent to discovery) have moved for total or partial summary judgment, relying on preclusion law. Our state Supreme Court has, in other cases, affirmed the application of nonmutual collateral estoppel, when deemed appropriate. Please tell me how to rule and why. Please don't write more than two double spaced typed pages (or its equivalent). I need careful but concise analysis.

Collector's complaint alleges in relevant part: (1) on March 4, 1997, he purchased a painting ("Truro Fog") from Gallery for $7200, which Sally Sales, while working for Gallery, and with authority, guaranteed him in writing was painted by Karl Knaths ("Knaths") in 1958; (2) on May 4, 1998, Collector first realized the painting was a forgery; (3) if it were an original Knaths, the painting would be worth $30,000, but instead it is valueless; (4) Gallery owes Collector $30,000 as a result of breach of written guarantee. Gallery's answer admits all allegations in "1"; states, as to "2" that it is without sufficient knowledge to answer when Collector realized anything and denies the allegation of forgery; and denies all allegations in "3" and "4". Gallery alleged the affirmative defense of *res judicata*. Both parties demand a jury trial.

To support its summary judgment motion Collector points to the pleadings and has filed three affidavits. One affidavit, signed by Collector, states that each allegation of his complaint is true, he is an experienced appraiser of oil paintings, he has had much experience buying and selling paintings by Knaths, if the Knaths was not a forgery it would be worth $30,000, but if the painting he bought is not a Knaths it is worthless. A second affidavit, signed by Carla Expert, says that she has been a professor of Modern Art at the Museum School for 22 years; she has compared "Wellfleet Sunset" and "Provincetown Pier" (both 1958 paintings allegedly by Knaths, which are in the Museum School Collection) with "Truro Fog" and there is no way that the painter of "Truro Fog" was the same painter who painted "Wellfleet Sunset" and "Provincetown Pier": the colors, brush strokes, types of paint, and sense of abstraction are too different. The third affidavit is signed by the appropriate clerk of court and states that the attached docket, pleadings, complete transcript, and opinion are accurate copies. These documents show that in the case of *The Museum School v. Gallery*, commenced January 3, 1995, in the Superior Court (with no jury), an action to rescind for reason of mutual mistake or fraud a contract to buy "Wellfleet Sunset" and "Provincetown Pier" on the grounds the paintings were not by Knaths, the judge found in favor of Gallery and wrote in her opinion that "I find in this hotly contested case that was tried for six days in September, 1995, with many witnesses on both sides, that both paintings were painted in 1958 by Karl Knaths. Gallery's experts were persuasive as to the authenticity of the two Knaths." Final judgment was entered for Gallery on October 22, 1995, and no appeal was taken.

Gallery filed an affidavit of the appropriate clerk in the Superior Court case of Collector against Gallery, commenced on August 1, 1998, with copies of the docket, pleadings, defendant's interrogatories, motions and court order. The complaint stated that from January 1, 1997, through July 31, 1998, Collector had purchased three paintings on three different occasions from Gallery (all modern paintings but only one by Knaths, "Moon Over Eastham," allegedly a 1956 painting), each with a separate written guarantee of authenticity, signed by different Gallery employees, and that Collector sought to rescind the purchases for fraud or mutual mistake, on the ground that none of the three were by their purported painters. Gallery admitted the sales and guarantees, denied the fraud and mistake, and alleged that each painting was authentic. The papers showed that, despite a court order, Collector had repeatedly refused to answer interrogatories or show up for depositions, and that the judge ordered the case dismissed with prejudice pursuant to the state counterpart of Fed. R. Civ. P. 37(b)(2)(C). Gallery also filed an interrogatory answer by Collector in the case presently before me, stating that Collector was paying Carla Expert $100 per hour for all work performed on this case, and an affidavit by Gallery's lawyer that she intended to cross-examine both Collector and Expert at the trial to show their bias, among other things.

11

Complexity: It All Comes Together

We think that you will find this an interesting and rewarding end to your introductory course in Civil Procedure. The issues presented in this chapter are interesting because they survey the contours of some of the most advanced and controversial concepts in contemporary discourse on civil procedure and its reform. Completion of this chapter should be rewarding because these complex and controversial issues are simply applications, interactions, and integrations of the policies, rules, and ideas we explored in previous chapters. In other words, we hope that upon completion of this chapter, you will appreciate that civil procedure is an integrated whole, in which various policies, rules, and ideas continually interact.

This chapter focuses primarily on Fed. R. Civ. P. 19, 22, 23, and 24. In Part A, we introduce the concepts of necessary and indispensable parties under Rule 19 and intervention under Rule 24. In Part B, we briefly introduce Rule 22 and the doctrine of interpleader. In Part C, we explore the role of Rule 23 class actions in contemporary civil procedure. And in Part D we wrap up this introduction to complex litigation with a landmark case and practice exercise that weave the concepts in this chapter into the tapestry that is the policies, rules, and ideas we have explored throughout this text.

A. NECESSARY AND INDISPENSABLE PARTIES: THE ATTEMPT TO SET BOUNDARIES ON LAWSUITS

One way to think about law is as a discipline that attempts to establish order. As you first saw in Chapter 3, the law determines which events—from among myriad social interchanges that each of us encounters each day—give rise to legal relief; elements and causes of action are legal concepts that facilitate order. In several chapters, we have seen the drafters of the Federal Rules use the words "transaction" and "occurrence" to define the outer boundary of facts underlying a legal story.

In this chapter we explore another dimension of this effort to set boundaries on lawsuits: which characters are essential to the lawsuit? This chapter thus supplements what we already learned in Chapter 3 about the permissive aspects of the joinder of parties. You will recall that the standard for permissive joinder under Fed. R. Civ. P. 20 includes both a transactional commonality and a common question of law or fact. The question who *must* be joined is more difficult.

Consider the following examples:

(1) A thinks that B has illegally claimed ownership in and has taken possession of A's land. A sues B and wants the court to award A possession and title to the land. However, formal title to the land in fact belongs to C, who has asserted title as trustee for the benefit of B. Should A be required to include C in the lawsuit?

(2) A and B have the same formal name, Roy Adams. Both A and B claim to be the beneficiary of a life insurance policy issued by insurance carrier L on the life of C, who has died. A sues L. L fears that if the court tells it to pay the policy amount to A, another suit could be filed by B, and L may again be ordered to pay the policy amount (this time, to B). Should A be required to include B in the lawsuit against L? Should A be required to include all persons named Roy Adams in the lawsuit? Is L able to force A and B into the same lawsuit?

(3) A says that R, a restaurant chain, was obligated under a contract (with A) to give A an exclusive franchise to operate the only R restaurant in a small town in Missouri. At some point after A and R executed their contract, B opened an R franchise in the same town, claiming that it has an exclusive franchise. A sues R to enforce the exclusive franchise agreement. Should A be required to include B as a party in this lawsuit?

Consider your answers to these questions. What principles did you apply? What weight did you give to efficiency concerns? Were you "fair" to named parties? Were you "fair" to those who could or should be named parties?

Our discussion of "necessary and indispensable parties" begins with *Bank of California v. Superior Court.* Although this is a 1940 opinion that was not governed by the Federal Rules of Civil Procedure, it provides a rich exploration of the underlying principles and useful historical context. As you read the case, consider these questions, and be prepared to discuss them in class: What are Bertha Smedley, the niece, and her attorney trying to achieve? Why couldn't they achieve it all in probate court in California? In what ways would it have been better if all of the legatees could be joined in one action? Why couldn't they be joined? What alternatives were available to the court?

■ **BANK OF CALIFORNIA NAT. ASSN. v. SUPERIOR COURT IN AND FOR CITY AND COUNTY OF SAN FRANCISCO**
16 Cal. 2d 516 (1940)

GIBSON, Chief Justice.

This is a petition for a writ of prohibition, to restrain the respondent superior court from proceeding with the trial of an action without bringing in certain parties alleged to be "necessary and indispensable."

Sara M. Boyd, the widow of Colin M. Boyd, died testate in June, 1937, leaving an estate valued at about $225,000. On July 8, 1937, in the superior court in San Francisco, her will was admitted to probate, and petitioner, Bank of California, was appointed executor. The will left individual legacies and bequests amounting to $60,000 to a large number of legatees, including charitable institutions and individuals, some residing in other states and in foreign countries. Petitioner, St. Luke's Hospital, was named residuary legatee and devisee, and thereby received the bulk of the estate.

On October 14, 1937, Bertha M. Smedley, a niece and legatee, brought an action to enforce the provisions of an alleged contract by which decedent agreed to leave her entire estate to the plaintiff. The complaint named as parties defendant the executor and all of the beneficiaries under the will, and prayed for a decree adjudging that plaintiff is, by virtue of the agreement, the owner of the entire estate of the decedent after payment of debts and expenses. It was further prayed that plaintiff's title to the property be quieted; that defendants be ordered to execute deeds to her, and that upon the failure of any defendant to do so the clerk should execute such an instrument.

Summons was served only upon petitioners, the executor and the residuary legatee. No other defendants were served, and none appeared. Petitioners filed separate answers. The action came to trial on November 15, 1939. Immediately upon its opening, petitioners made a motion under section 389 of the Code of Civil Procedure for an order to bring in the other defendants, and to have summons issued and served upon them. The motion was made on the ground that all of the other defendants were "necessary and indispensable parties" to the action, and that the court could not proceed without them. The motion was denied by respondent court. Petitioners then applied for a writ of prohibition to restrain the trial until these other parties should be brought in.

In support of their application, petitioners point out that the complaint challenges the right of every legatee and devisee to share in the estate, and prays for an award of the entire property to plaintiff. It is contended that a trial and judgment without the absent defendants would adversely affect the rights of such parties, would result in a multiplicity of suits, and would subject the petitioning executor to inconvenience, expense and the burden of future litigation.

To test the theory of petitioners, it will be necessary to examine briefly the origin and nature of the rules on required or compulsory joinder of parties. We may eliminate, at the outset, the field of permissive joinder of "proper parties," for there is no doubt that the absent defendants are interested in the issues and subject of the action, and could properly be joined. For the same reason, these legatees, if they had not been named as defendants, could no doubt have intervened in the action. These propositions are conceded by all parties, and the precise issue is thus made clear, whether the absent defendants are not only proper parties but "indispensable parties" in the sense that service upon them or their appearance is essential to the jurisdiction of the court to proceed in the action. Prohibition, of course, cannot issue unless the procedural defect of parties is jurisdictional.

At common law, joinder of plaintiffs was compulsory where the parties, under the substantive law, were possessed of joint rights. Joint promisees under a contract, partners, and joint tenants were familiar examples. Equity courts developed another theory of compulsory joinder, to carry out the policy of avoiding piecemeal litigation and multiplicity of suits. Those persons necessary to a complete settlement of the controversy were usually required to be joined, in order that the entire matter might be concluded by a single suit. Obviously, this theory of joinder covered many situations where the substantive rights were not joint, and accordingly joinder would not have been required in an action at law. *See* Charles Clark, *Code Pleading*, pp. 241, 242, 245. Generally speaking, the modern rule under the codes carries out the established equity doctrine. Thus, section 389 of the Code of Civil Procedure states: "The court may determine any controversy between parties before it, when it can be done without prejudice to the rights of others, or by saving their rights; but when a complete determination of the controversy cannot be had without the presence of other parties, the court must then order them to be brought in. . . ." Such statutes have been interpreted as declaratory of the equity rule and practice. *See* Charles Clark, *Code Pleading*, p. 250.

But the equity doctrine as developed by the courts is loose and ambiguous in its expression and uncertain in its application. Sometimes it is stated as a mandatory rule, and at other times as a matter of discretion, designed to reach an equitable result if it is practicable to do so. And despite various attempts at reconciliation of conflicting expressions, a great deal of confusion still remains in the cases. *See* Notes, 48 Harv. L. Rev. 995; 23 Cal. L. Rev. 320, 321. Bearing in mind the fundamental purpose of the doctrine, we should, in dealing with "necessary" and "indispensable" parties, be careful to avoid converting a discretionary power or a rule of fairness in procedure into an arbitrary and burdensome requirement which may thwart rather than accomplish justice. These two terms have frequently been coupled together as if they have the same meaning; but there appears to be a sound distinction, both in theory and practice, between parties deemed "indispensable" and those considered merely "necessary." As Professor Clark has remarked: "It has been objected that the terms "necessary" and "indispensable" convey the same idea. . . . But a distinction has been drawn. While necessary parties are so interested in the controversy that they should normally be made parties in order to enable the court to do complete justice, yet if their interests are separable from the rest and particularly where their presence in the suit cannot be obtained, they are not indispensable parties. The latter are those without whom the court cannot proceed." Charles Clark, *Code Pleading*, p. 245, note 21.

First, then, what parties are indispensable? There may be some persons whose interests, rights, or duties will inevitably be affected by any decree which can be rendered in the action. Typical are the situations where a number of persons have undetermined interests in the same property, or in a particular trust fund, and one of them seeks, in an action, to recover the whole, to fix his share, or to recover a portion claimed by him. The other persons with similar interests are indispensable parties. The reason is that a judgment in favor of one claimant for part of the property or fund would necessarily determine the amount or extent which remains available to the others. Hence, any judgment in the action would inevitably affect their rights. Thus, in an action by one creditor against assignees for the benefit of creditors, seeking an accounting and payment of his share of the assets, the other creditors were held indispensable (*McPherson v. Parker*, 30 Cal. 455, 89 Am. Dec. 129); and in an action by plaintiff to enforce a trust, where he claimed the property in his own right, to the exclusion of another actual beneficiary, failure to join the latter was held fatal to the judgment. *O'Connor v. Irvine*, 74 Cal. 435, 16 P. 236. Where, also, the plaintiff seeks some other type of affirmative relief which, if granted, would injure or affect the interests of a third person not joined that third person is an indispensable party. Thus, in an action by a lessor against a sublessee to forfeit a parent lease because of acts of the sublessee, the sublessors (original lessees) were indispensable parties, since a decree of forfeiture would deprive them of their lease. *Hartman Ranch Co. v. Associated Oil Co.*, 10 Cal. 2d 232, 262. And in a suit to cancel illegal registration of voters, all voters whose registration was challenged were indispensable parties. *Ash v. Superior Court*, 33 Cal. App. 800. Many other cases, illustrating the reasons for compulsory joinder, may be found.

All of these persons are, of course, "necessary" parties, but the decisions show that they come within a special classification of necessary parties, to which the term "indispensable" seems appropriate. An attempt to adjudicate their rights without joinder is futile. Many cases go so far as to say that the court would have no jurisdiction to proceed without them, and that its purported judgment would be void and subject to collateral attack. The objection is so fundamental, it need not be raised by the parties themselves; the court may, of its own motion, dismiss the proceedings, or refuse to proceed, until these indispensable parties are brought in. It follows that if the court does attempt to proceed, it is acting beyond its jurisdiction and may be restrained by prohibition.

The other classification includes persons who are interested in the sense that they might possibly be affected by the decision, or whose interests in the subject matter or transaction are such that it cannot be finally and completely settled without them; but nevertheless their interests are so separable that a decree may be rendered between the parties before the court without affecting those others. These latter may perhaps be "necessary" parties to a complete settlement of the entire controversy or transaction, but are not "indispensable" to any valid judgment in the particular case. They should normally be joined, and the court, following the equity rule, will usually require them to be joined, in order to carry out the policy of complete determination and avoidance of multiplicity of suits. But, since the rule itself is one of equity, it is limited and qualified by considerations of fairness, convenience, and practicability. Where, for example, it is impossible to find these other persons or impracticable to bring them in, the action may proceed as to those parties who are present. . . .

[T]he present action may be examined to determine whether the absent defendants are indispensable or only necessary parties. The nature of such an action has been frequently discussed by the courts. The probate court cannot, of course, take cognizance of the contract, and an equity court cannot compel the making of a will. Hence, there is no specific performance of the contract in the strict sense. But equity gives relief which is the equivalent of a specific performance. Though the estate may be probated and the property distributed accordingly, the court will, in an action by the promisee, impose a constructive trust upon any particular property in the hands of the individual distributee. This relief is sometimes called "quasi-specific performance," since it accomplishes the substantial result of enforcement of the contract.

The action in these cases is against the distributee personally, and not against the estate; and it is independent of the will and the probate proceeding. Each distributee is individually held as a constructive trustee solely of the property which came to him, and none is interested in the granting or denial of similar relief as to any other. Where there are a number of legatees and devisees, they would all appear to be "necessary" parties in the sense that the main issue, the validity of the testamentary disposition of the property of decedent, affects their property interests, and the entire matter, the disposition of all of the decedent's property, cannot be finally settled without a binding adjudication for or against every legatee or devisee. Hence, the court will usually order them served and brought in unless there is some good reason for not doing so. But the absent defendants in such a case are not indispensable parties. Unlike the situations discussed above, in which any judgment would necessarily affect the rights of the absent persons, the case here is one where plaintiff may litigate her claim against the appearing defendants alone and obtain a decree which binds them alone. The absent defendants, not being before the court, will not be bound by the judgment, whether favorable or unfavorable, and their property interests will not be affected. . . .

If, in this kind of action, the court has jurisdiction to try the case, and may render a valid judgment where the plaintiff sues or maintains the suit against less than all of the distributees, it must be clear that they are not indispensable parties. So, in the present case, the absent defendants are not indispensable parties, and the court has jurisdiction to proceed without them, to determine the rights of the parties actually before it.

Much stress is laid by petitioners upon the fact that plaintiff prays for judgment against all the defendants, and has not dismissed as to the absent parties. It is also pointed out that the prayer seeks a decree quieting title to the property. Petitioners argue that the court cannot have jurisdiction over the action in the form in which plaintiff seeks to maintain it, without bringing in the absent parties. The answer to this contention is that the court cannot lose jurisdiction of a proceeding merely because the prayer of the complaint seeks relief beyond that to which the plaintiff is entitled. The court may try the matters within its jurisdiction and render a valid judgment. It is not bound to follow plaintiff's theory and certainly it will not be presumed that it will follow an erroneous theory and act beyond its jurisdiction. . . .

Comments and Questions

1. What is the difference between a "necessary party" and an "indispensable party" according to the Supreme Court of California? Give examples of each. In *Carpenter v. Dee*, if two passengers were killed, would both of them be necessary or indispensable parties who must be joined as plaintiffs? Why or why not? Would Randall Dee and Ultimate Auto have to be joined as defendants? Was Twyla Burrell and/or Peter Dee necessary or indispensable, or neither, given the way the initial complaint in the Jeep case was conceived and constructed?

2. In *Bank of California*, why didn't plaintiff just serve all of the legatees, since it would be to her advantage to have an adjudication against them all?

3. Why are those legatees who were not served held by the court to be "necessary" but not "indispensable"?

4. What does the California Supreme Court mean by "intervention," and why is intervention relevant to the case?

5. What is the relationship among the concepts underlying "necessary and indispensable parties," preclusion law, personal jurisdiction, and due process? This is worth thinking about at some length, because you should now be able to see the integrated nature of these doctrines.

6. Now look at Fed. R. Civ. P. 19 and 24, particularly 24(a). What language do they have in common? What situations is each trying to cover? Note that Fed. R. Civ. P. 19(a) lists those who should be made parties, if feasible, or in other words, if they are subject to personal jurisdiction in the courts in question, if the court can assert subject matter jurisdiction over them (for instance, do they destroy diversity of citizenship?), or if they do not legitimately object to venue. If it is feasible to join a 19(a) person, then that person must be joined. If it is not feasible, the rule requires you to apply Fed. R. Civ. P. 19(b) in order to see whether the court should proceed in the absence of the 19(a) person or whether the case should be dismissed. Reconsider the *Bank of California* case. How would it have come out procedurally under the current Federal Rules?

The fact situation in the next case is complicated, but a complete understanding is worthwhile because the opinion explains how federal courts approach Rule 19 problems. Here is a quick summary of the facts to help you get started: The litigation arose out of a fatal traffic accident involving a car that was driven by Donald Cionci and a truck that was driven by Thomas Smith. Both of the drivers were fatally injured in the accident, along with one of Cionci's (two) passengers, John Lynch. Cionci's other passenger, John Harris, was injured but survived the accident. The owner of the car, Edward Dutcher, was not present during the accident, but had allegedly given Cionci the keys and permission to drive his car. Provident Tradesmens Bank was the administrator of Lynch's estate. The Lumbermens Mutual Casualty Company held the liability insurance policy on Dutcher's car. Patterson is the representative of Cionci's estate.

■ PROVIDENT TRADESMENS BANK & TRUST CO. v. PATTERSON
390 U.S. 102 (1968)

Justice HARLAN delivered the opinion of the Court:

This controversy, involving in its present posture the dismissal of a declaratory judgment action for nonjoinder of an "indispensable" party, began nearly 10 years ago with a traffic accident. An automobile owned by

Edward Dutcher, who was not present when the accident occurred, was being driven by Donald Cionci, to whom Dutcher had given the keys. John Lynch and John Harris were passengers. The automobile crossed the median strip of the highway and collided with a truck being driven by Thomas Smith. Cionci, Lynch, and Smith were killed and Harris was severely injured.

Three tort actions were brought. Provident Tradesmens Bank, the administrator of the estate of passenger Lynch and petitioner here, sued the estate of the driver, Cionci, in a diversity action. Smith's administratrix, and Harris in person, each brought a state-court action against the estate of Cionci, Dutcher, the owner, and the estate of Lynch. These Smith and Harris actions, for unknown reasons, have never gone to trial and are still pending. The Lynch action against Cionci's estate was settled for $50,000, which the estate of Cionci, being penniless, has never paid.

Dutcher, the owner of the automobile and a defendant in the as yet untried tort actions, had an automobile liability insurance policy with Lumbermens Mutual Casualty Company, a respondent here. That policy had an upper limit of $100,000 for all claims arising out of a single accident. This fund was potentially subject to two different sorts of claims by the tort plaintiffs. First, Dutcher himself might be held vicariously liable as Cionci's "principal"; the likelihood of such a judgment against Dutcher is a matter of considerable doubt and dispute. Second, the policy by its terms covered the direct liability of any person driving Dutcher's car with Dutcher's "permission."

The insurance company had declined, after notice, to defend in the tort action brought by Lynch's estate against the estate of Cionci, believing that Cionci had not had permission and hence was not covered by the policy. The facts allegedly were that Dutcher had entrusted his car to Cionci, but that Cionci had made a detour from the errand for which Dutcher allowed his car to be taken. The estate of Lynch, armed with its $50,000 liquidated claim against the estate of Cionci, brought the present diversity action for a declaration that Cionci's use of the car had been "with permission" of Dutcher. The only named defendants were the company and the estate of Cionci. The other two tort plaintiffs were joined as plaintiffs. Dutcher, a resident of the State of Pennsylvania as were all the plaintiffs, was not joined either as plaintiff or defendant. The failure to join him was not adverted to at the trial level.

The major question of law contested at trial was a state-law question. The District Court had ruled that, as a matter of the applicable (Pennsylvania) law, the driver of an automobile is presumed to have the permission of the owner. Hence, unless contrary evidence could be introduced, the tort plaintiffs, now declaratory judgment plaintiffs, would be entitled to a directed verdict against the insurance company. The only possible contrary evidence was testimony by Dutcher as to restrictions he had imposed on Cionci's use of the automobile. The two estate plaintiffs claimed, however, that under the Pennsylvania "Dead Man Rule" Dutcher was incompetent to testify on this matter as against them. The District Court upheld this claim. It ruled that under Pennsylvania law Dutcher was incompetent to testify against an estate if he had an "adverse" interest to that of the estate. It found such adversity in Dutcher's potential need to call upon the insurance fund to pay judgments against himself, and his consequent interest in not having part or all of the fund used to pay judgments against Cionci. The District Court, therefore, directed verdicts in favor of the two estates. Dutcher was, however, allowed to testify as against the live plaintiff, Harris. The jury, nonetheless, found that Cionci had had permission, and hence awarded a verdict to Harris also.

Lumbermens appealed the judgment to the Court of Appeals for the Third Circuit, raising various state-law questions. The Court of Appeals did not reach any of these issues. Instead, after reargument *en banc*, it decided, 5-2, to reverse on two alternative grounds neither of which had been raised in the District Court or by the appellant.

The first of these grounds was that Dutcher was an indispensable party. The court held that the "adverse interests" that had rendered Dutcher incompetent to testify under the Pennsylvania Dead Man Rule also required him to be made a party. The court did not consider whether the fact that a verdict had already been rendered, without objection to the nonjoinder of Dutcher, affected the matter. Nor did it follow the provision of Rule 19 of the Federal Rules of Civil Procedure that findings of "indispensability" must be based on stated pragmatic considerations. It held, to the contrary, that the right of a person who "may be affected" by the judgment to be joined is a "substantive" right, unaffected by the federal rules; that a trial court "may not proceed" in the absence of such a person; and that since Dutcher could not be joined as a defendant without destroying diversity jurisdiction the action had to be dismissed.

Since this ruling presented a serious challenge to the scope of the newly amended Rule 19, we granted certiorari. Concluding that the inflexible approach adopted by the Court of Appeals in this case exemplifies the kind of reasoning that the rule was designed to avoid, we reverse.

I

We may assume, at the outset, that Dutcher falls within the category of persons who, under [Rule 19(a)], should be "joined if feasible." The action was for an adjudication of the validity of certain claims against a fund. Dutcher, faced with the possibility of judgments against him, had an interest in having the fund preserved to cover that potential liability. Hence there existed, when this case went to trial, at least the possibility that a judgment might impede Dutcher's ability to protect his interest, or lead to later relitigation by him.

The optimum solution, an adjudication of the permission question that would be binding on all interested persons, was not "feasible," however, for Dutcher could not be made a defendant without destroying diversity. Hence the problem was the one to which Rule 19(b) appears to address itself: in the absence of a person who "should be joined if feasible," should the court dismiss the action or proceed without him? Since this problem emerged for the first time in the Court of Appeals, there were also two subsidiary questions. First, what was the effect, if any, of the failure of the defendants to raise the matter in the District Court? Second, what was the importance, if any, of the fact that a judgment, binding on the parties although not binding on Dutcher, had already been reached after extensive litigation? The three questions prove, on examination, to be interwoven.

We conclude, upon consideration of the record and applying the "equity and good conscience" test of Rule 19(b), that the Court of Appeals erred in not allowing the judgment to stand.

Rule 19(b) suggests four "interests" that must be examined in each case to determine whether, in equity and good conscience, the court should proceed without a party whose absence from the litigation is compelled. Each of these interests must, in this case, be viewed entirely from an appellate perspective since the matter of joinder was not considered in the trial court. First, the plaintiff has an interest in having a forum. Before the trial, the strength of this interest obviously depends upon whether a satisfactory alternative forum exists. On appeal, if the plaintiff has won, he has a strong additional interest in preserving his judgment. Second, the defendant may properly wish to avoid multiple litigation, or inconsistent relief, or sole responsibility for a liability he shares with another. After trial, however, if the defendant has failed to assert this interest, it is quite proper to consider it foreclosed.

Third, there is the interest of the outsider whom it would have been desirable to join. Of course, since the outsider is not before the court, he cannot be bound by the judgment rendered. This means, however, only that a judgment is not *res judicata* as to, or legally enforceable against, a nonparty. It obviously does not mean either (a) that a court may never issue a judgment that, in practice, affects a nonparty or (b) that (to the contrary) a court may always proceed without considering the potential effect on nonparties simply because they are not "bound" in the technical sense. Instead, as Rule 19(a) expresses it, the court must consider the extent to which the judgment may "as a practical matter impair or impede his ability to protect" his interest in the subject matter. When a case has reached the appeal stage the matter is more complex. The judgment appealed from may not in fact affect the interest of any outsider even though there existed, before trial, a possibility that a judgment affecting his interest would be rendered. When necessary, however, a court of appeals should, on its own initiative, take steps to protect the absent party, who of course had no opportunity to plead and prove his interest below.

Fourth, there remains the interest of the courts and the public in complete, consistent, and efficient settlement of controversies. We read the Rule's third criterion, whether the judgment issued in the absence of the nonjoined person will be "adequate," to refer to this public stake in settling disputes by wholes, whenever possible, for clearly the plaintiff, who himself chose both the forum and the parties defendant, will not be heard to complain about the sufficiency of the relief obtainable against them. After trial, considerations of efficiency of course include the fact that the time and expense of a trial have already been spent.

Rule 19(b) also directs a district court to consider the possibility of shaping relief to accommodate these four interests. Commentators had argued that greater attention should be paid to this potential solution to a joinder stymie, and the Rule now makes it explicit that a court should consider modification of a judgment as an alternative to dismissal. Needless to say, a court of appeals may also properly require suitable modification as a condition of affirmance.

Had the Court of Appeals applied Rule 19's criteria to the facts of the present case, it could hardly have reached the conclusion it did. We begin with the plaintiff's viewpoint. It is difficult to decide at this stage whether they would have had an "adequate" remedy had the action been dismissed before trial for nonjoinder: we cannot here determine whether the plaintiffs could have brought the same action, against the same parties plus Dutcher, in a state court. After trial, however, the "adequacy" of this hypothetical alternative, from the plaintiffs' point of view, was obviously greatly diminished. Their interest in preserving a fully litigated judgment should be overborne only by rather greater opposing considerations than would be required at an earlier stage when the plaintiffs' only concern was for a federal rather than a state forum.

Opposing considerations in this case are hard to find. The defendants had no stake, either asserted or real, in the joinder of Dutcher. They showed no interest in joinder until the Court of Appeals took the matter into its own hands. This properly forecloses any interest of theirs, but for purposes of clarity we note that the insurance company, whose liability was limited to $100,000, had or will have full opportunity to litigate each claim on that fund against the claimant involved. Its only concern with the absence of Dutcher was and is to obtain a windfall escape from its defeat at trial.

The interest of the outsider, Dutcher, is more difficult to reckon. The Court of Appeals, concluding that it should not follow Rule 19's command to determine whether, as a practical matter, the judgment impaired the nonparty's ability to protect his rights, simply quoted the District Court's reasoning on the Dead Man issue as proof that Dutcher had a "right" to be joined:

> The subject matter of this suit is the coverage of Lumbermens' policy issued to Dutcher. Depending upon the outcome of this trial, Dutcher may have the policy all to himself or he may have to share its coverage with the Cionci Estate, thereby extending the availability of the proceeds of the policy to

satisfy verdicts and judgments in favor of the two Estate plaintiffs. Sharing the coverage of a policy of insurance with finite limits with another, and thereby making that policy available to claimants against that other person is immediately worth less than having the coverage of such policy available to Dutcher alone. By the outcome in the instant case, to the extent that the two Estate plaintiffs will have the proceeds of the policy available to them in their claims against Cionci's estate, Dutcher will lose a measure of protection. Conversely, to the extent that the proceeds of this policy are not available to the two Estate plaintiffs Dutcher will gain. . . . It is sufficient for the purpose of determining adversity (of interest) that it appears clearly that the measure of Dutcher's protection under this policy of insurance is dependent upon the outcome of this suit. That being so, Dutcher's interest in these proceedings is adverse to the interest of the two Estate plaintiffs, the parties who represent, on this record, the interests of the deceased persons in the matter in controversy.

There is a logical error in the Court of Appeals' appropriation of this reasoning for its own quite different purposes: Dutcher had an "adverse" interest (sufficient to invoke the Dead Man Rule) because he would have been benefited by a ruling in favor of the insurance company; the question before the Court of Appeals, however, was whether Dutcher was harmed by the judgment against the insurance company.

The two questions are not the same. If the three plaintiffs had lost to the insurance company on the permission issue, that loss would have ended the matter favorably to Dutcher. If, as has happened, the three plaintiffs obtain a judgment against the insurance company on the permission issue, Dutcher may still claim that as a nonparty he is not estopped by that judgment from relitigating the issue. At that point it might be argued that Dutcher should be bound by the previous decision because, although technically a nonparty, he had purposely bypassed an adequate opportunity to intervene. We do not now decide whether such an argument would be correct under the circumstances of this case. If, however, Dutcher is properly foreclosed by his failure to intervene in the present litigation, then the joinder issue considered in the Court of Appeals vanishes, for any rights of Dutcher's have been lost by his own inaction.

If Dutcher is not foreclosed by his failure to intervene below, then he is not "bound" by the judgment in favor of the insurance company and, in theory, he has not been harmed. There remains, however, the practical question whether Dutcher is likely to have any need and if so will have any opportunity, to relitigate. The only possible threat to him is that if the fund is used to pay judgments against Cionci the money may in fact have disappeared before Dutcher has an opportunity to assert his interest. Upon examination, we find this supposed threat neither large nor unavoidable.

The state-court actions against Dutcher had lain dormant for years at the pleading stage by the time the Court of Appeals acted. Petitioner asserts here that under the applicable Pennsylvania vicarious liability law there is virtually no chance of recovery against Dutcher. We do not accept this assertion as fact, but the matter could have been explored below. Furthermore, even in the event of tort judgments against Dutcher, it is unlikely that he will be prejudiced by the outcome here. The potential claimants against Dutcher himself are identical with the potential claimants against Cionci's estate. Should the claimants seek to collect from Dutcher personally, he may be able to raise the permission issue defensively, making it irrelevant that the actual monies paid from the fund may have disappeared: Dutcher can assert that Cionci did not have his permission and that therefore the payments made on Cionci's behalf out of Dutcher's insurance policy should properly be credited against Dutcher's own liability. Of course, when Dutcher raises this defense he may lose, either on the merits of the permission issue or on the ground that the issue is foreclosed by Dutcher's failure to intervene in the present case, but Dutcher will not have been prejudiced by the failure of the District Court here to order him joined.

If the Court of Appeals was unconvinced that the threat to Dutcher was trivial, it could nevertheless have avoided all difficulties by proper phrasing of the decree. The District Court, for unspecified reasons, had refused to order immediate payment on the Cionci judgment. Payment could have been withheld pending the suits against Dutcher and relitigation (if that became necessary) by him. In this Court, furthermore, counsel for petitioners represented orally that they, the tort plaintiffs, would accept a limitation of all claims to the amount of the insurance policy. Obviously such a compromise could have been reached below had the Court of Appeals been willing to abandon its rigid approach and seek ways to preserve what was, as to the parties, subject to the appellants' other contentions, a perfectly valid judgment.

The suggestion of potential relitigation of the question of "permission" raises the fourth "interest" at stake in joinder cases—efficiency. It might have been preferable, at the trial level, if there were a forum available in which both the company and Dutcher could have been made defendants, to dismiss the action and force the plaintiffs to go elsewhere. Even this preference would have been highly problematical, however, for the actual threat of relitigation by Dutcher depended on there being judgments against him and on the amount of the fund, which was not revealed to the District Court. By the time the case reached the Court of Appeals, however, the problematical preference on efficiency grounds had entirely disappeared: there was no reason then to throw away a valid judgment just because it did not theoretically settle the whole controversy.

II

Application of Rule 19(b)'s "equity and good conscience" test for determining whether to proceed or dismiss would doubtless have led to a contrary result below. The Court of Appeals' reasons for disregarding the rule remain to be examined. The majority of the court concluded that the rule was inapplicable because "substantive" rights are involved, and substantive rights are not affected by the Federal Rules. Although the court did not articulate exactly what the substantive rights are, or what law determines them, we take it to have been making the following argument: (1) there is a category of persons called "indispensable parties"; (2) that category is defined by substantive law and the definition cannot be modified by rule; (3) the right of a person falling within that category to participate in the lawsuit in question is also a substantive matter, and is absolute.

With this we may contrast the position that is reflected in Rule 19. Whether a person is "indispensable," that is, whether a particular lawsuit must be dismissed in the absence of that person, can only be determined in the context of particular litigation. There is a large category, whose limits are not presently in question, of persons who, in the Rule's terminology, should be "joined if feasible," and who, in the older terminology, were called either necessary or indispensable parties. Assuming the existence of a person who should be joined if feasible, the only further question arises when joinder is not possible and the court must decide whether to dismiss or to proceed without him. To use the familiar but confusing terminology, the decision to proceed is a decision that the absent person is merely "necessary" while the decision to dismiss is a decision that he is "indispensable." The decision whether to dismiss (*i.e.*, the decision whether the person missing is "indispensable") must be based on factors varying with the different cases, some such factors being substantive, some procedural, some compelling by themselves, and some subject to balancing against opposing interests. Rule 19 does not prevent the assertion of compelling substantive interests; it merely commands the courts to examine each controversy to make certain that the interests really exist. To say that a court "must" dismiss in the absence of an indispensable party and that it "cannot proceed" without him puts the matter the wrong way around: a court does not know whether a particular person is "indispensable" until it had examined the situation to determine whether it can proceed without him. . . .

III

We think it clear that the judgment below cannot stand. The judgment is vacated and the case is remanded to the Court of Appeals for consideration of those issues raised on appeal that have not been considered, and, should the Court of Appeals affirm the District Court as to those issues, for appropriate disposition preserving the judgment of the District Court and protecting the interests of nonjoined persons.

It is so ordered. Judgment vacated and case remanded to Court of Appeals.

Comments and Questions

1. At this point you should be able to (1) identify all of the named and potential parties in *Provident Tradesmens Bank*; (2) understand the underlying fact pattern of that case, including the three tort actions and the declaratory judgment case that reached the Supreme Court; and (3) explain what happened in the district court and in the court of appeals.

2. Many states have what are called "Dead Man" or "Dead Person" Rules or Statutes. They often differ in their exact wording and application, but most have the same purpose. In situations in which an estate of a deceased is in effect the party (particularly the defendant), there is a fear that witnesses who stand to gain from the litigation have too great a motivation and opportunity to fabricate, since the deceased cannot testify and refute them. Consequently, some states prohibit testimony by interested witnesses about the transaction or occurrence to which the deceased would have testified if alive. Historically, courts have used such purple prose as "since death has sealed the lips of the deceased, the Dead Man Statute assures that so too will the lips of a living opponent be sealed." Why should a federal court look to a state evidence statute? As you know, the Federal Rules of Evidence—like the Federal Rules of Civil Procedure—normally apply in federal court.

3. Exactly how does the Supreme Court say Rule 19 should operate in a case such as this? Some lawyers now feel they have to do the Fed. R. Civ. P. 19(b) analysis two somewhat different ways. Why?

4. What should happen next in *Provident Tradesmens*?

5. Notice how Rule 19 can be used as an attempt by defendants to achieve a dismissal. Give some examples of circumstances in which the Rule 19 defense will lead to a dismissal. Will such a dismissal have a *res judicata* effect? What might be the impact of statutes of limitations?

6. Why does Fed. R. Civ. P. 12(h)(2) add "a defense of failure to join a party indispensable under Rule 19" to those which can be made as late as "at the trial on the merits"?

7. Each of the subsections of Fed. R. Civ. P. 19(a) raises interpretative problems that may not be immediately apparent from the language. First, note the language in Fed. R. Civ. P. 19(a)(1) about "complete relief." Consider, for example, in *Carpenter*, whether the City, the Garage, and Ultimate Auto would be Rule 19(a) parties if Carpenter had sued only Randall Dee. Indeed, Dee may be virtually judgment-proof, and thus Carpenter may not be able to obtain "complete relief" were she unable to collect. Nevertheless, the answer is that these potential defendants are *not* Rule 19(a) parties, because she would be able to get whatever relief against Dee the law permits (notwithstanding her inability to collect on a judgment).

Next, consider Fed. R. Civ. P. 19(a)(2)(ii) and the meaning of "inconsistent obligations." Assume that Carpenter sued (only) Randall Dee and, in that trial, a jury found for the plaintiff and awarded damages of $100,000. Assume, then, that Carpenter brought a second action against (only) Ultimate Auto and, in that second trial, a jury found for the plaintiff and awarded damages of $500,000. (And assume further Ultimate Auto could not use nonmutual defensive collateral estoppel against Carpenter on the amount of her harm.) But would this constitute "inconsistent obligations" within the meaning of Fed. R. Civ. P. 19(a)? Again the answer is *no*, even though the *verdicts* certainly are inconsistent.* An inconsistent *obligation* occurs if one court orders a party to do one thing (for instance, deed Blackacre to *A*) and another court orders the same party to perform an inconsistent act (for instance, deed Blackacre to *B*).

Additional ambiguous language in Rule 19 appears in Fed. R. Civ. P. 19(a)(2)(i). As you study this subpart, realize that

- Courts often recognize only legally protected "interest[s]," not merely financial interests;
- Courts often interpret "relating to the subject of the action" to mean that the absent party must have a direct stake in the litigation;
- Courts may view very differently what set of facts constitute practical impairment (for example, courts disagree whether an adverse *stare decisis* effect is enough of a potential harm).

Preclusion law introduces still more complication. One might expect the Due Process Clause to solve the problem, as no absentee can be bound unless it is named as a party in the litigation. The exception, of course, is for an absentee that is in privity with a named party; but, in that instance, the absent party will, in effect, have had its day in court by virtue of its privity with the named party. However, consider the facts of *Lopez v. Martin Luther King, Jr., Hospital*, 97 F.R.D. 24 (C.D. Cal. 1983). There the parents of a child sued the hospital and various doctors, alleging medical malpractice in the course of childbirth, for recovery of damages suffered by them (*not* the child). (Under California law, the parents had a cause of action separate from the child's.) The child was not named as a plaintiff, because it would have destroyed the diversity jurisdiction of the federal court. (The Lopez parents were Mexican nationals; the child was a citizen of California.) The district court held that the child *might* be later precluded because a California court could find privity. Applying Fed. R. Civ. P. 19(b), then, the court dismissed the case because it could have been brought in a state court with both the parents and the child as plaintiffs. The court's characterization of the flexibility of Fed. R. Civ. P. 19(a) is instructive:

---

* Inconsistent *verdicts* are not uncommon. Frequently, when nonjoined plaintiffs sue a defendant on the same theory (*e.g.*, asbestos, tobacco, handguns, mass disaster), some plaintiffs win and others lose — even if the relevant facts are virtually identical.

. . . Rule 19 matters should be governed by practical considerations. Indeed, the Rule was amended in 1966 in an attempt to forestall what was developing as a rigid, formalistic approach to compulsory joinder under the old version of the Rule. . . . What constitutes an "interest relating to the subject of the action" has not been clearly defined, although it has been suggested that the interest requirement be broadly construed in order to require joinder of all conditionally necessary parties. . . . The Court recognizes that the alleged interest must be something more than a financial interest or an interest of convenience. However, the Rule does not require a "legal" interest; it merely requires "an interest relating to the subject of the action." Whether this interest exists must be determined from a practical perspective, not through the adoption of strict legal definitions and technicalities. . . .

Lopez, supra, 97 F.R.D. at 28.

8. As in *Lopez*, a defendant can use a Rule 19 motion to have a case dismissed in situations where a Rule 19(a) party, if joined, would defeat diversity jurisdiction. Although in such situations the absent party typically would be a defendant, a judge has discretion to realign the parties in a manner that considers with which one the absent party has common and adverse interests. Such realignment of the parties labels and interests may occur also under Fed. R. Civ. P. 24 (Intervention) or, for that matter, in any instance where diversity jurisdiction is implicated. *See* Jack H. Friedenthal, Mary Kay Kane, & Arthur R. Miller, *Civil Procedure* 28-29, 349 (3rd ed. 1999).

9. For a critical look at English and American antecedents to "necessary and indispensable party" doctrine, *see* Geoffrey C. Hazard, Jr., *Indispensable Party: The Historical Origin of a Procedural Phantom*, 61 Colum. L. Rev. 1254 (1961). For additional information and citations on the various interpretations of the subparts of Fed. R. Civ. P. 19(a), *see* James Wm. Moore, 4 *Federal Practice* ¶¶19.03[3][a]-[f] (Daniel R. Coquillette et al., eds., 3rd ed. 1999).

10. Some courts have developed what has been called a *public rights* or *public interest exception* to Rule 19, basing the exception on *National Licorice Co. v. NLRB*, 309 U.S. 350 (1940):

In some cases, the courts have not insisted on Rule 19 joinder of those whose interests will "be impaired or impeded" by a litigation if their position is already advanced by another party . . . , if mandatory joinder would be unwieldy or impossible, and if there was a strong public interest that the case proceed. In an environmental suit brought by the Sierra Club, for example, the District Court for the Eastern District of California held that although miners' property rights would be affected, the miners were not necessary parties: "where what is at stake are essentially issues of public concern and the nature of the case would require joinder of a large number of persons, Rule 19's joinder requirements need not be satisfied." [*Sierra Club v. Watt*, 608 F. Supp. 305, 321–324 (E.D. Cal. 1985).] Also citing Federal Rule 1, the district court reasoned that "[s]urely justice cannot be done if public interest litigation is precluded by virtue of the requirements of joinder."

Phyllis Tropper Baumann, Judith Olans Brown, and Stephen N. Subrin, *Substance in the Shadow of Procedure: The Integration of Substantive and Procedural Law in Title VII Cases*, 33 B.C. L. Rev. 211, 281-82 (1992) (footnotes omitted). The context of the quote is criticism of the holding and reasoning of *Martin v. Wilks*, 490 U.S. 755 (1989), which is the last case in this book.

11. The *Provident Tradesmens* decision highlights a connection between Fed. R. Civ. P. 19 and 24. That relationship will be discussed again in *Martin v. Wilks, infra.* In that case, the Supreme Court makes clear that Fed. R. Civ. P. 24 does not compel an absent party to intervene. You surely have noticed that the intervention as-a-matter-of-right language in Fed. R. Civ. P. 24(a) tracks the language of Fed. R. Civ. P. 19(a). Does it make sense to you that these two rules would have similar language? Consider that the rules are not identical—either in language or in usage. Further, while Rule 19 typically is used by a defendant to force the plaintiff to add a party, Rule 24 is used by an absentee party to become a party. Also, Fed. R. Civ. P. 24(a) contains the additional clause, "unless the applicant's interest is adequately represented by existing parties." Moreover, since there is a more lenient test for intervention under Fed. R. Civ. P. 24(b) (permissive intervention), a judge may permit an absentee to intervene without having to apply the more stringent requirements of Fed. R. Civ. P. 24(a)(1). Some judges have been extremely lenient in permitting a wide range of intervening parties, yet have severely curtailed independent participation. *See, e.g., United States v. Reserve Mining Co.*, 56 F.R.D. 408 (1972).

12. Remember that the drafters of the supplemental jurisdiction statute chose not to permit plaintiffs to expand diversity jurisdiction. Indeed, the limits on supplemental jurisdiction in diversity cases specifically address claims by plaintiffs under Fed. R. Civ. P. 19 and 24, as well as "claims by persons proposed to be joined as plaintiffs under Rule 19 . . . or seeking to intervene as plaintiffs under Rule 24 . . . when exercising supplemental jurisdiction over such claims would be inconsistent with the supplemental jurisdiction requirements of Section 1332." 28 U.S.C. §1367(b).

B. INTERPLEADER

Rule 22 offers a method of joining parties in cases where a stakeholder faces claims "such that [it] is or may be exposed to double or multiple liability." Fed. R. Civ. P. 22. For example, a life insurance company may be uncertain whom to pay among persons alleging they are beneficiaries entitled to the same proceeds of a deceased's policy. The life insurance company can *interplead* all of those alleging rights to the proceeds. The company seeks a determination of whom to pay so that it doesn't have to pay more then the policy amount. Consequently, the insurance company, which ordinarily would be the defendant in a case in which a beneficiary makes a claim, becomes the plaintiff in an interpleader.

Two types of interpleader are available in federal court. In the first, statutory provisions require only $500 in controversy, permit nationwide service of process, and establish venue wherever one or more of the claimants reside. 28 U.S.C. §§1335, 1397, and 2361. "Nonstatutory interpleader is available under Rule 22, but the jurisdictional and procedural requirements there are the same as in an ordinary civil action." Charles Wright, *Law of Federal Courts*, §74 (5th ed. 1994).

Interpleader is also available to a stakeholder who is sued by one of the claimants, allowing it to interplead the other claimants by way of a third-party claim, cross-claim, or counterclaim. A trial court deciding an interpleader action considers, first, whether there is real potential for exposure to multiple liability for a single "claim," and only in that instance, second, the merits of the interpleader action.

Comments and Questions

1. Why does Fed. R. Civ. P. 22(1) have language similar to Fed. R. Civ. P. 19(a)(2)(ii)? Are both provisions necessary? Explain.

2. Make sure that you can explain the difference between and among intervention, interpleader, impleader, and indispensable party.

3. Under what circumstances would a stakeholder use Rule 22 rather than §1335 to interplead claimants? The answer lies in the language of the statute.

C. CLASS ACTIONS

At the beginning of this chapter, we discussed endeavors to bound lawsuits. In this section, we consider situations where plaintiffs want to expand the lawsuit beyond named plaintiffs or beyond named defendants. In a class action, named parties represent unnamed people that are members of the class. Accordingly, a host of conceptual and practical problems and questions might spring to mind:

- What about the Due Process Clause?
- How do the jurisidictional requirements—subject matter jurisdiction, personal jurisdiction, venue, and service of process—operate in a class action?
- How does a class either conduct or respond to discovery?
- What happens when hundreds or even millions of people have their rights adjudicated in a single proceeding?

Of course, whether the legal system should even permit class actions is another question that you should consider as you read this section.

Before we introduce you to the class action device, we offer a few preliminary cautions—and words of reassurance. Most law schools have courses in advanced civil procedure, complex litigation, or mass torts, which delve into class actions in depth. This chapter is merely an introduction. At the same time, however, you already know quite a bit about class actions. For example, although we have not yet focused on this aspect of the case, the *City of Cleveland* case was filed as a class action. And, as you learned in Chapter 10 that a nonparty could be bound by privity, a class is bound by the named representatives in a class action. Nor are representative suits particularly unusual; trustees sue to protect and bind the interests of beneficiaries; corporations file and defend suits that bind shareholders. And finally, you are familiar with the procedural and practical obstacles that one encounters when joining multiple parties together in one lawsuit. (Briefly review *Mullane v. Central Hanover Bank and Trust Co.*) You explored a basic tension between efficiency and the potential for prejudice (or confusion) when you learned about joinder of parties (Fed. R. Civ. P. 20) and consolidation of trials (Fed. R. Civ. P. 42).

Throughout this course, you have been invited to examine the role of the attorney as both an advocate and as a professional simply trying to earn a living by charging fees. The fees issue surfaces in the class action context as many wonder whether an attorney who stands to gain huge fees from a class action is putting his personal interests before those of the class—especially in the typical situation where members of a class action receive relatively small financial sums.

Opponents of the expanded use of class actions argue that class actions deprive class members of rights to client autonomy and control. Yet these opponents must address how individuals who suffer harms but cannot sue can otherwise vindicate their rights. Indeed, given the declining availability of resources (government or otherwise) to enforce certain safety, environmental, consumer protection, or other standards, what alternative to the private class action will otherwise deter certain wrongdoing? And, although an individual class member has little autonomy or control over the direction of a lawsuit, query just how much autonomy or control an ordinary client possesses in an ordinary lawsuit.

There is much literature on the pros and cons of the class action. Professor John C. Coffee, Jr., of Columbia Law School has written several articles on the economic incentives of lawyers who bring class actions. *See, e.g.,* John C. Coffee, Jr., *The Regulation of Entrepreneurial Litigation: Balancing Fairness and Efficiency in the Large Class Action,* 54 U.Chi.L. Rev. 877(1987); and John C. Coffee, Jr., *Understanding the Plaintiff's Attorney: The Implications of Economic Theory for Private Enforcement of Law Through Class and Derivative Actions,* 86 Colum. L. Rev. 669 (1986). A fascinating defense of the individual lawsuit is Roger H. Trangsrud, *Mass Trials in Mass*

Tort Cases: A Dissent, 1989 U. Ill. L. Rev. 69 (portions of which are reprinted in Chapter 5, *supra*). An empirical counterview, demonstrating the minimal control that the ordinary client possesses in the ordinary lawsuit, is set forth in Deborah R. Hensler, *Resolving Mass Toxic Torts: Myths and Realities*, 1989 U. Ill. L. Rev. 89. The best history of the origins of the modern class action is Stephen C. Yeazell, *From Medieval Group Litigation to the Modern Class Action* (1987). For an extensive bibliography of publications dealing with the use of class actions in litigation, *see* David L. Shapiro, *Class Actions: The Class as Party and Client*, 73 Notre Dame L. Rev. 913, 914-916 n.2 (1998).

In this section, we introduce you to the conceptual and constitutional basis for the class action with the seminal case, *Hansberry v. Lee*. (Note that this case was commenced in state court and, thus, was not governed by the Federal Rules.) We begin with some history behind this case that's in the nature of a contextual orientation essay.

1. *Hansberry v. Lee*

■ ALLEN R. KAMP, THE HISTORY BEHIND *HANSBERRY v. LEE*
20 U.C. Davis L. Rev. 481 (1987)

INTRODUCTION

This Article, investigating *Hansberry v. Lee*'s factual background, grew out of a student's comment after a civil procedure class. In teaching class actions, *Hansberry* is a classic, usually the first case in the class action section of civil procedure textbooks. My class session went according to plan. I initially explained racially restrictive covenants and their validity until *Shelley v. Kraemer* in 1948, and then began a Socratic examination of *Hansberry*. The case sought to enforce a racially restrictive covenant and the covenant's validity turned on the result of a prior case. The question then becomes whether Hansberry is bound by the prior case, *Burke v. Kleiman*, which was a class action. The Court held he was not bound because the class was composed of members with conflicting goals:

> It is quite another to hold that all those who are free alternatively either to assert rights or to challenge them are of a single class, so that any group, merely because it is of the class so constituted, may be deemed adequately to represent any others of the class in litigating their interests in either alternative.

Then the students realized that (a) it is constitutional to have a class action that binds the class members to the class judgment; (b) whether the prior class action binds the class members may be decided collaterally in a subsequent lawsuit; and (c) without "adequate representation" the class members are not bound. I discussed Rule 23's requirements of "adequate representation" and "typicality." Afterward, I upset the students' complacency by asking how much consistency between class members' views is required: what if some members in a prison suit are masochists and like cruel and unusual punishment? What if, in a school desegregation suit, some students do not want to be bussed? I discussed questions of opt-out rights and social policy concerning the advisability of representative lawsuits in general and class actions in particular, and then wrapped up.

This analysis of *Hansberry* was upset by one of my students, Mr. C. O. Travis, who, while working as a garbageman, was attending John Marshall Law School at night. "Professor, did you know that Hansberry in *Hansberry v. Lee* was Lorraine Hansberry's father and that *A Raisin in the Sun* was based on her family's experience?" Lorraine Hansberry had attended Mr. Travis' high school in Chicago. I did not know, and at first did not believe it. Some investigation, however, revealed that Mr. Travis was right. What was the history of the Hansberry family? The answer involves black, Chicago, and legal history, leads to a re-examination of the *Hansberry* case, and provides insights into the judicial process.

THE BACKGROUND OF THE *HANSBERRY* CASE

The conflict in *Hansberry*, caused by the Hansberrys' move into an all-white neighborhood, derived from Chicago's increasing black population. Between 1900 and 1934, the city's black population grew from 30,000 to 236,000. During this time, however, blacks were continuously more segregated. In 1910, 25% of blacks lived in areas of under 5% black population. None lived in areas of over 90% concentration. By 1934, less than 5% lived in areas of under 5% concentration, while 65% lived in areas that were 90% or more black. Geographically, blacks were concentrated in two narrow corridors stretching westward and southward from downtown Chicago.

This segregation was accomplished in two ways: violence and the racially restrictive covenant. After the violence of the 1910's and 1920's subsided, racially restrictive covenants were developed. "Around these black zones, an organized endeavor was put in place to subject the property to racially restrictive covenants. Although prior to the '20's, several individual owners and developers had placed race restrictions on their deeds, covenants covering entire neighborhoods were uncommon in Chicago." Such covenants were legal—in 1926, the Supreme Court dismissed for want of jurisdiction a case upholding a racially restrictive covenant in *Corrigan v. Buckley*.

After the *Corrigan* decision, the Chicago Real Estate Board started a program to cover neighborhoods with the covenants. They prepared a model covenant. (The *Hansberry* covenant was based on this model.)

Then the Board sent out speakers and organizers across the city to get the covenants adopted. Organizing a neighborhood to adopt a covenant was a massive task. Legal descriptions and signatures had to be obtained, and then the covenants had to be filed with the Recorder of Deeds. Notary publics were hired to notarize and then record signatures. Subsequently, if any black persons moved into the area, they were reported, a suit filed against their occupancy, and an injunction obtained. By the late 1920's, black neighborhoods were hemmed in on all sides by the racial covenants. Up to 85 percent of Chicago was covered by such covenants.

The racially restrictive covenants legally prevented occupancy by blacks. They bound the signer and subsequent purchasers, showing up as an "objection" in any title search. Courts would routinely enforce the covenants, ordering vacation of the premises on pain of contempt. . . .

The covenant was useful only if most of the owners had signed it. Thus, a covenant's effectiveness required that a certain percentage of owners participate. Thus, the issue in dispute in *Hansberry*—actual percentage of the signatures in the affected area—was a key requirement:

> This agreement and the restrictions herein contained shall be of no force or effect unless this agreement or a substantially similar agreement, shall be signed by the owners above enumerated of ninety-five per cent of the frontage above described, or their heirs or assigns, and recorded in the office of the Recorder of Deeds of Cook County, Illinois, on or before December 31, 1928.

The covenant challenged by the Hansberrys covered a subdivision known as "South Park" or "Washington Park." This area was a three by four block rectangle bounded on the north by Washington Park, on the east by Cottage Grove, on the south by 63rd Street, and on the west by South Park Avenue. A race track, torn down in 1908, formerly occupied the land. This area was populated by whites, but surrounded on the west and south by black areas.

In 1940, only three black families lived in the area. West of the subdivision, the population went from 10% to 100% nonwhite. To the south, 90 to 100% of the population was nonwhite.

To the east, however, were the white areas of Hyde Park and Woodlawn, where the nonwhite population was only .1 to 9.9%. The South Park subdivision, therefore, was seen as a barrier between the black community and Woodlawn.

In 1928, a group of white businessmen, the Woodlawn Property Owners Association, organized a covenant to cover the South Park neighborhood. The covenant had the support of outside real estate organizations, institutions, banks, and mortgage companies. Contradictory evidence exists about the participation of the University of Chicago, located in Hyde Park. A 1937 article stated that the university was trying to establish a "buffer state," and had contributed funds to the Woodlawn Property Owners Association. The University did not deny this. Robert Hutchins, then president of the university, stated: "However unsatisfactory they [the covenants] may be they are the only means at present available by which the members of the associations [neighborhood associations] can stabilize the conditions under which they desire to live."

The effective system of segregation created by the racially restrictive covenants began to break down in the 1930's. Two phenomena contributed to this breakdown: the growth of Chicago's black population and the Depression. Together they produced an increased black demand for housing and a depressed market for white housing. Hansberry was able to buy his house because he was the only person who wanted it.

Chicago's black population grew in the first third of the twentieth century. In 1900, it was 30,000; in 1934, 236,000. At the same time, the process of continually increasing segregation restricted blacks to the ghetto. In 1910, 24% of the total black population lived in areas in which 95% of the people were white. In 1934, only 3% of the black population lived in such areas. In 1910, the highest concentration of blacks to the general population was between 60-69%; in 1934, 87% of blacks lived in areas that were over 70% black; 69% lived in areas that were 99% black. In 1937, it was estimated that there were 50,000 more black people than units available. Blacks had to pay 20 to 50% more than whites for comparable housing.

Contemporaneously, the Depression reduced the market for white housing. In the Washington Park subdivision, the population decreased by 13.8 percent between 1930 and 1934. In the 1930's, "there was no market among white people for property in the subdivision." The prior owner of the Hansberry home, Burke, had left the house vacant at the time he moved from the subdivision. Thus, most of those who wanted to rent or buy in white areas were blacks:

> The Supreme Court eventually ruled in favor of the blacks, but even before that ruling [*Hansberry*], other white property owners opened their buildings to blacks and extracted high rentals for accommodations which were unable to attract white tenants. Rather than suffer financial losses, they elected to violate existing covenants and fill their vacant units with blacks.

One of these owners was Burke, who was an officer in the Woodlawn Property Owners Association and whose wife, Olive Ida Burke, had successfully sued, in *Burke v. Kleiman*, to enforce the covenant. Burke afterwards "resigned his position and withdrew from the association with ill feelings, and stated several times that he would put negroes in every block of that property." In order to sell to the Hansberrys, Burke set up a dummy transaction in which Jan D. Crook bought the property to convey to the Hansberrys. In the suit to enforce the covenant against the Hansberrys, it was alleged that through fraudulent concealment on the part of the defendants James T. Burke and Harry A. Price, from the Bank [First National Bank of Englewood], of the fact that Hansberry was a negro and that the property was being purchased for him, a deed was produced from the bank to Jay D. Crook who, in fact, purchased for Hansberry.

Thus, Mr. Burke was one of the defendants in *Hansberry*, attacking the decree obtained in a prior suit by his wife, Olive.

The defendant, Carl A. Hansberry, was an active man who had had varied careers, including deputy United States Marshal, businessman, and unsuccessful Republican candidate for Congress. He distributed pamphlets on black civil rights under the name of "The Hansberry Foundation." His daughter Lorraine described him:

My father was typical of a generation of Negroes who believed that the "American way" could successfully be made to work to democratize the United States. Thus, twenty-five years ago, he spent a small personal fortune, his considerable talents, and many years of his life fighting, in association with NAACP attorneys, Chicago's "restrictive covenants" in one of this nation's ugliest ghettoes.

That fight also required that our family occupy the disputed property in a hellishly hostile "white neighborhood" in which literally howling mobs surrounded our house. . . . One of these missiles almost took the life of the then eight-year old signer of this letter. My memories of this "correct" way of fighting white supremacy in America include being spat at, cursed and pummeled in the daily trek to and from school. And I also remember my desperate and courageous mother, patrolling our household all night with a loaded German luger, doggedly guarding her four children, while my father fought the respectable part of the battle in the Washington court.

The fact that my father and the NAACP "won" a Supreme Court decision, in a now famous case which bears his name in the law books, is—ironically—the sort of "progress" our satisfied friends allude to when they presume to deride the more radical means of struggle. The cost, in emotional turmoil, time and money, which contributed to my father's early death as a permanently embittered exile in a foreign country when he saw that after such sacrificial efforts the Negroes of Chicago were as ghetto-locked as ever, does not seem to figure in their calculations.

The sale generated the lawsuit to enforce the covenant and evict the Hansberrys, *Lee v. Hansberry*. The complaint alleged a conspiracy on the part of the defendants to destroy the agreement by selling or leasing property in the restricted area to Negroes. Plaintiffs were successful below, the court restraining Burke "from leasing or selling any real estate within the restricted area to negroes, or to white persons for the purpose of selling or leasing to negroes, restraining . . . the Supreme Liberty Life Insurance company from making any further loans on real estate in the restricted area to negroes or for occupancy by negroes; declaring the conveyance to

Hansberry and wife void and ordering them to remove from the premises, and holding the restrictive agreement valid and in full force and effect."

The main arguments considered by the Illinois Supreme Court concerned the covenant's interpretation and validity under its own terms. No constitutional objection was considered.

The evidentiary basis of the rulings against the defendants below were not challenged except as to one Israel Katz. The court found that his statement that "he would sell his property to anybody, including negroes," was sufficient evidence to enjoin him from doing so.

The appellants argued that enjoining the mortgage company from making loans in the restricted area to Negroes or for Negro occupancy was improper, because mortgages were exempted from the restrictive agreement. The Illinois Supreme Court ruled that the language merely provided that violating the restrictive agreement was an insufficient reason to invalidate a mortgage. "It does not give mortgagees a license to conspire to destroy the agreement, as the evidence shows this insurance company was doing."

The main argument in the case revolved around the question whether the requisite number of owners had signed the agreement. The agreement was to be "of no force or effect" unless signed by owners of 95 percent of the area's frontage. The plaintiffs in *Lee* argued that this question was *res judicata*, determined by the prior case of *Burke*. The trial court in *Hansberry* found that actually only 54 percent had signed the agreement, but that the question was *res judicata*.

The complainant's contention was "that unless an injunction is granted, said neighborhood will become mixed, both white and colored with its attendant evils." In *Burke*, the defense was that conditions had so changed in the area that enforcing the decree would be inequitable. Certain facts were stipulated, including that more than the required 95 percent of frontage owners had signed the covenants. The court in *Burke* found that the neighborhood had not changed materially and affirmed the decree, summarily rejecting the constitutional argument.

The Illinois Supreme Court, in *Lee v. Hansberry*, found that *Burke* "was a class or representative suit." Thus, "other members of the class are bound by the results in the case unless it is reversed or set aside on direct proceedings." That the finding was stipulated did not render the decree any less binding. The court found no evidence of fraud or collusion in procuring the stipulation. Thus the questions of execution and validity were *res judicata*, and *res judicata* extends to all matters that might have been raised. The covenant's validity could not be relitigated and the decree evicting the Hansberrys was affirmed.

Hansberry petitioned for *certiorari* to the Supreme Court. His lawyers hoped to have racially restrictive covenants declared unconstitutional. Their main arguments, however, went to the propriety of the class action—only their last argument went to the purported constitutional violation. . . .

■ HANSBERRY v. LEE
311 U.S. 32 (1940)

Justice STONE delivered the opinion of the Court:

The question is whether the Supreme Court of Illinois, by its adjudication that petitioners in this case are bound by a judgment rendered in an earlier litigation to which they were not parties, has deprived them of the due process of law guaranteed by the Fourteenth Amendment.

Respondents brought this suit in the Circuit Court of Cook County, Illinois, to enjoin the breach by petitioners of an agreement restricting the use of land within a described area of the City of Chicago, which was alleged to have been entered into by some five hundred of the land owners. The agreement stipulated that for a specified period no part of the land should be "sold, leased to or permitted to be occupied by any person of the colored race," and provided that it should not be effective unless signed by the "owners of 95 per centum of the frontage" within the described area. The bill of complaint set up that the owners of 95 per cent of the frontage had signed; that respondents are owners of land within the restricted area who have either signed the agreement or acquired their land from others who did sign and that petitioners Hansberry, who are Negroes, have, with the alleged aid of the other petitioners and with knowledge of the agreement, acquired and are occupying land in the restricted area formerly belonging to an owner who had signed the agreement.

To the defense that the agreement had never become effective because owners of 95 per cent of the frontage had not signed it, respondents pleaded that that issue was *res judicata* by the decree in an earlier suit. *Burke v. Kleiman*, 277 Ill. App. 519. To this petitioners pleaded, by way of rejoinder, that they were not parties to that suit or bound by its decree, and that denial of their right to litigate, in the present suit, the issue of performance of the condition precedent to the validity of the agreement would be a denial of due process of law guaranteed by the Fourteenth Amendment. It does not appear, nor is it contended that any of petitioners is the successor in interest to or in privity with any of the parties in the earlier suit.

The circuit court, after a trial on the merits, found that owners of only about 54 per cent of the frontage had signed the agreement, and that the only support of the judgment in the *Burke* case was a false and fraudulent stipulation of the parties that 95 per cent had signed. But it ruled that the issue of performance of the condition precedent to the validity of the agreement was *res judicata* as alleged and entered a decree for respondents. The Supreme Court of Illinois affirmed. We granted certiorari to resolve the constitutional question. . . .

It is a principle of general application in Anglo-American jurisprudence that one is not bound by a judgment in personam in a litigation in which he is not designated as a party or to which he has not been made a party by service of process. *Pennoyer v. Neff*, 95 U.S. 714; 1 *Freeman on Judgments*, 5th Ed., §407. A judgment rendered in such circumstances is not entitled to the full faith and credit which the Constitution and statute of the United States, R.S. §905, 28 U.S.C. §687, 28 U.S.C.A. §687, prescribe, *Pennoyer v. Neff, supra; Lafayette Ins. Co. v. French*, 18 How. 404, 15 L. Ed. 451; *Hall v. Lanning*, 91 U.S. 160; *Baker v. Baker, E. & Co.*, 242 U.S. 394, and judicial action enforcing it against the person or property of the absent party is not that due process which the Fifth and Fourteenth Amendments require. *Postal Telegraph-Cable Co. v. Neport*, 247 U.S. 464; *Old Wayne Mut.L. Ass'n v. McDonough*, 204 U.S. 8.

To these general rules there is a recognized exception that, to an extent not precisely defined by judicial opinion, the judgment in a "class" or "representative" suit, to which some members of the class are parties, may bind members of the class or those represented who were not made parties to it.

The class suit was an invention of equity to enable it to proceed to a decree in suits where the number of those interested in the subject of the litigation is so great that their joinder as parties in conformity to the usual rules of procedure is impracticable. Courts are not infrequently called upon to proceed with causes in which the number of those interested in the litigation is so great as to make difficult or impossible the joinder of all because some are not within the jurisdiction or because their whereabouts is unknown or where if all were made parties to the suit its continued abatement by the death of some would prevent or unduly delay a decree. In such cases where the interests of those not joined are of the same class as the interests of those who are, and where it is considered that the latter fairly represent the former in the prosecution of the litigation of the issues in which all have a common interest, the court will proceed to a decree.

It is evident that the considerations which may induce a court thus to proceed, despite a technical defect of parties, may differ from those which must be taken into account in determining whether the absent parties are bound by the decree or, if it is adjudged that they are, in ascertaining whether such an adjudication satisfies the requirements of due process and of full faith and credit. Nevertheless there is scope within the framework of the Constitution for holding in appropriate cases that a judgment rendered in a class suit is *res judicata* as to members of the class who are not formal parties to the suit. Here, as elsewhere, the Fourteenth Amendment does not compel state courts or legislatures to adopt any particular rule for establishing the conclusiveness of judgments in class suits; nor does it compel the adoption of the particular rules thought by this court to be appropriate for the federal courts. With a proper regard for divergent local institutions and interests, *cf. Jackson County v. United States*, 308 U.S. 343, 351, this Court is justified in saying that there has been a failure of due process only in those cases where it cannot be said that the procedure adopted, fairly insures the protection of the interests of absent parties who are to be bound by it. *Chicago, B. & Q.R. Co. v. Chicago,* 166 U.S. 226, 235.

It is familiar doctrine of the federal courts that members of a class not present as parties to the litigation may be bound by the judgment where they are in fact adequately represented by parties who are present, or where they actually participate in the conduct of the litigation in which members of the class are present as parties, *Plumb v. Goodnow* (*Plumb v. Crane*), 123 U.S. 560; *Confectioners' Machinery Co. v. Racine Engine & Mach. Co.,* 7 Cir., 163 F. 914; *Id.,* 7 Cir., 170 F. 1021; *Bryant El. Co. v. Marshall, C.C.,* 169 F. 426, or where the interest of the members of the class, some of whom are present as parties, is joint, or where for any other reason the relationship between the parties present and those who are absent is such as legally to entitle the former to stand in judgment for the latter. *Smith v. Swormstedt, supra; cf. Christopher v. Brusselback, supra,* 302 U.S. at pages 503, 504, and cases cited.

In all such cases, so far as it can be said that the members of the class who are present are, by generally recognized rules of law, entitled to stand in judgment for those who are not, we may assume for present purposes that such procedure affords a protection to the parties who are represented though absent, which would satisfy the requirements of due process and full faith and credit. Nor do we find it necessary for the decision of this case to say that, when the only circumstance defining the class is that the determination of the rights of its members turns upon a single issue of fact or law, a state could not constitutionally adopt a procedure whereby some of the members of the class could stand in judgment for all, provided that the procedure were so devised and applied as to insure that those present are of the same class as those absent and that the litigation is so conducted as to insure the full and fair consideration of the common issue. We decide only that the procedure and the course of litigation sustained here by the plea of *res judicata* do not satisfy these requirements.

The restrictive agreement did not purport to create a joint obligation or liability. If valid and effective its promises were the several obligations of the signers and those claiming under them. The promises ran severally to very other signer. It is plain that in such circumstances all those alleged be bound by the agreement would not constitute a single class in any ration brought to enforce it. Those who sought to secure its benefits by rcing it could not be said to be in the same class with or represent whose interest was in resisting performance, for the agreement by its imposes obligations and confers rights on the owner of each plot of ho signs it. If those who thus seek to secure the benefits of the nt were rightly regarded by the state Supreme Court as constitut- ss, it is evident that those signers or their successors who are in challenging the validity of the agreement and resisting its e are not of the same class in the sense that their interests are identical so that any group who had elected to enforce rights conferred by the agreement could be said to be acting in the interest of any others who were free to deny its obligation.

Because of the dual and potentially conflicting interests of those who are putative parties to the agreement in compelling or resisting its performance, it is impossible to say, solely because they are parties to it, that any two of them are of the same class. Nor without more, and with the due regard for the protection of the rights of absent parties which due process exacts, can some be permitted to stand in judgment for all.

It is one thing to say that some members of a class may represent other members in a litigation where the sole and common interest of the class in the litigation is either to assert a common right or to challenge an asserted obligation. *Smith v. Swormstedt, supra; Supreme Tribe of Ben-Hur v. Cauble, supra; Groves v. Farmers State Bank,* 368 Ill. 35, 12 N.E.2d 618. It is quite another to hold that all those who are free alternatively either to assert rights or to challenge them are of a single class, so that any group merely because it is of the class so constituted, may be deemed adequately to represent any others of the class in litigating their interests in either alternative. Such a selection of representatives for purposes of litigation, whose substantial interests are not necessarily or even probably the same as those whom they are deemed to represent, does not afford that protection to absent parties which due process requires. The doctrine of representation of absent parties in a class suit has not hitherto been thought to go so far. Apart from the opportunities it would afford for the fraudulent and collusive sacrifice of the rights of absent parties, we think that the representation in this case no more satisfies the requirements of due process than a trial by a judicial officer who is in such situation that he may have an interest in the outcome of the litigation in conflict with that of the litigants.

The plaintiffs in the *Burke* case sought to compel performance of the agreement in behalf of themselves and all others similarly situated. They did not designate the defendants in the suit as a class or seek any injunction or other relief against others than the named defendants, and the decree which was entered did not purport to bind others. In seeking to enforce the agreement the plaintiffs in that suit were not representing the petitioners here whose substantial interest is in resisting performance. The defendants in the first suit were not treated by the pleadings or decree as representing others or as foreclosing by their defense the rights of others, and even though nominal defendants, it does not appear that their interest in defeating the contract outweighed their interest in establishing its validity. For a court in this situation to ascribe to either the plaintiffs or defendants the performance of such functions on behalf of petitioners here, is to attribute to them a power that it cannot be said that they had assumed to exercise, and a responsibility which, in view of their dual interests it does not appear that they could rightly discharge.

Comments and Questions

1. Describe the basic lawsuits at issue in *Hansberry*. Who sued whom? Who wanted to bind whom and on what theory? What precisely was the procedural (constitutional) question, and how was it resolved?

2. Why does it ever make sense for a suit to bind people other than the named parties? How representative must the interests of the class representative be vis-à-vis the rest of the class? As Professor Kamp queried, "What if, in a school desegregation suit, some students do not want to be bussed?" At what point in a class action lawsuit may the class no longer challenge the representativeness of the named plaintiffs?

3. The *Hansberry* opinion cites two well-known prior cases. In *Smith v. Swormstedt*, 57 U.S. (16 How.) 288 (1853), six plaintiffs, who represented 1500 traveling preachers of the Methodist Episcopal Church South, sued three defendants, as representatives of 3800 traveling preachers of the Methodist Episcopal Church North. The Methodist Episcopal Church had split over the slavery issue, and the plaintiffs wanted to divide the church property. The Court permitted the case to proceed in a manner that would bind both the plaintiffs' and defendants' classes. In *Supreme Tribe of Ben-Hur v. Cauble*, 255 U.S. 356 (1921), a prior federal suit had been brought by certain Class A certificate holders of a fraternal benefit association that purported to represent more than 70,000 other holders. The named petitioners sought to overturn a reclassification of their certificates, but the defendant won. Thereafter, a second group of Class A certificate holders sued on the same issue, and the Court held that they were bound by the prior decree. Why were these cases particularly suitable for class action treatment of a kind that would bind all members of the class? What Federal Rule or Rules that you have already had might apply to these situations? Do you think that all members of the classes in *Swormstedt* and *Ben-Hur* should be entitled to notification of the pendency of the suit and be granted an opportunity to opt out (that is, to announce that they did not want to participate in the suit and would not be bound by its results)?

4. As you read the following orientation to the doctrine of Fed. R. Civ. P. 23, consider how *Hansberry*, *Swormstedt*, and *Supreme Tribe of Ben-Hur* would have been decided under the current Federal Rule.

2. The Federal Rule*

The prerequisites for a federal class action are set forth in Fed. R. Civ. P. 23 (a) and (b). Subsection (a) contains four requirements—*all* of which must be satisfied to maintain any federal class action. The four

---

*There are many aspects of the class action that we do *not* explore in this chapter. These topics include defendant class actions, which have their own unique problems, and securities class actions, which are largely statutory. We also do not address class actions under state procedure.

prerequisites are numerosity, commonality, typicality, and representativeness. Subsection (b) also contains four requirements, but each of these constitutes a different type of class action, and thus, only *one* must be satisfied in order to maintain a class action under Rule 23.

a. The Prerequisites

In this subsubsection we outline each of the four prerequisites* set forth in Rule 23(a):

- Numerosity,
- Commonality,
- Typicality,
- Representativeness.

First, Fed. R. Civ. P. 23(a)(1) requires that "the class is so numerous that joinder of all members is impracticable." However, there is no set number of members to satisfy this requirement of numerosity; indeed, groups of as many as 350 have been held too small for a class action, yet groups of 25 or more have been held sufficient. *See* Charles Wright, *Law of Federal Courts* §72 (5th ed. 1994).

Second, Fed. R. Civ. P. 23(a)(2) requires "questions of law or fact common to the class." This requirement of commonality demands an analysis similar to what you learned to do under Fed. R. Civ. P. 20 (permissive joinder) and under Fed. R. Civ. P. 42(a) (consolidation).

Third, Fed. R. Civ. P. 23(a)(3) requires that "the claims and defenses of the representatives parties are typical of the claims and defenses of the class." This typicality requirement originates with the Due Process Clause, which, in turn, requires that the interests of a party be adequately represented and protected in order for that party to be bound by the decision of a court.

Fourth, and finally, Fed. R. Civ. P. 23(a)(4) requires that the representatives named in the class action "fairly and adequately protect the interests of the class." This requirement, usually labeled representativeness, requires the judge to consider whether the named representatives and their counsel have the sufficient expertise, capacity, and interests at stake to represent the class. And it is the responsibility of the class counsel to persuade the trial judge that the named class representatives are truly representative of the class.

To be sure, the four requirements set forth in Fed. R. Civ. P. 23(a) overlap. Trial judges are usually afforded broad discretion on the question whether these initial requirements have been met.

---

*One might instead suggest that there are five prerequisites: the four identified here plus identification of the class. Rule 23(a) identifies the four and presumes the fifth.

b. The Typology

Class actions that satisfy Fed. R. Civ. P. 23(a) must also meet the requirements of one of the four kinds of class actions described in Fed. R. Civ. P. 23(b):

- 23(b)(1)(A) Incompatible Standards Class Actions
- 23(b)(1)(B) Limited Funds Class Actions
- 23(b)(2) Injunctive/Declaratory Relief Class Actions
- 23(b)(3) Predominance/Superiority Class Actions

First, the incompatible standards class action is permitted only in instances where the putative class counsel can persuade the trial judge that "the prosecution of separate actions by or against individual members of the class would create a risk of inconsistent or varying adjudications with respect to individual members of the class which would establish incompatible standards of conduct for the party opposing the class." Fed. R. Civ. P. 23(b)(1)(A). Put another way, this type of class action is appropriate if and only if, absent a class action, the defendant(s) could be subject to incompatible mandates as to its *future* conduct:

> The class is designed to protect against the non-class party's being placed in a stalemated or conflicted position and is applicable only to actions in which there is not only a risk of inconsistent adjudications but also where the non-class party could be sued for *different and incompatible affirmative relief.*

Employers Insurance of Wausau v. FDIC, 112 F.R.D. 52, 54 (E.D. Tenn. 1986). This concept should be familiar to you, as it resembles the test under Fed. R. Civ. P. 19(a)(2)(ii) for necessary parties.

Second, the limited funds class action is permitted only in instances where there is a risk that "adjudications with respect to individual members of the class . . . would as a practical matter be dispositive of the interests of the other members not parties to the adjudications or substantially impair or impede their ability to protect their interests." Fed. R. Civ. P. 23(b)(1)(B). The putative class counsel thus must persuade the district court judge that the defendants' available assets would be insufficient to pay all claims, and that the limited funds class action is the best mechanism to promote equal treatment of all litigants. A significant aspect of such a class is its mandatory character, as there is no opt-out provision.

Third, a class action is permitted under Fed. R. Civ. P. 23(b)(2) when "the party opposing the class has acted or refused to act on grounds generally applicable to the class, thereby making appropriate final injunctive relief or corresponding declaratory relief with respect to the case as a whole." As the 1966 Advisory Committee Notes to this Rule state, and as our experience with this rule confirms, this type of class action is particularly appropriate in civil rights cases "where a party is charged with discriminating unlawfully against a class, usually one whose members are incapable of specific enumeration."

> The provisions of Rule 23(b)(2) are designed to cover cases in which the primary concern is the grant of injunctive or declaratory relief. In such cases, there is no requirement that notice be given to all of the class members, and there is no opportunity for putative class members to "opt out."

Consider other types of illegal activity that would justify injunctive or declaratory relief that would inure to the benefit of the entire class.

The fourth and final type of class action is the most controversial. Class actions under Fed. R. Civ. P. 23(b)(3) require a finding "that the questions of law or fact common to the members of the class predominate over any questions affecting only individual members, and that a class action is superior to other available methods for the fair and efficient adjudication of the controversy." Under this type of class action, all class members "who can be identified through reasonable effort" must be given individual notice of the class action as well as the opportunity to opt out of the class action lawsuit. *See* Fed. R. Civ. P. 23(c)(2). The cost of notifying a putative class of plaintiffs can be prohibitively expensive. *See Eisen v. Carlisle & Jacquelin*, 417 U.S. 156 (1974) (notice by publication plus notification to a portion of the class held inadequate, and the cost of sending notice could not be shifted to the defendant); *Oppenheimer Fund v. Sanders*, 437 U.S. 340 (1978) (burden of identifying class members could not be shifted to defendant as part of discovery, when information was not otherwise relevant). Moreover, the threat or reality of numerous opt-outs can make a settlement of the class action much harder to obtain.

There also are special requirements for a 23(b)(3) class action. In particular, the putative class counsel must persuade the court that common questions of law or fact predominate over individual questions and also that a class action is superior to other available, fair, and efficient methods of adjudication. The rule then identifies four matters that are "pertinent" to these requirements: (1) the particular interests of class members to control their own lawsuits; (2) the (prior) commencement of other relevant lawsuits; (3) the desirability of concentrating the litigation into a single forum; and (4) the manageability of the class. These considerations often accent a concern for what frequently is referred to as the *splintering* problem, *i.e.*, the issues for each putative class member are unique, requiring individualized evidence, thus diminishing or eliminating the advantages of a class action.

The 23(b)(3) class action is often a vehicle for the vindication of consumer rights. An individual who wishes to challenge the manufacturer of defective siding or wishes to challenge the credit card issuer with unfair credit card policies may not have the realistic option to file an individual case against a large company (or, in certain instances, against an entire industry). However, it may be in this very same category of cases that the circumstances of some or many members are particularly unique. Indeed, the Advisory Committee Notes to the 1966 amendments to Rule 23 suggest that the 23(b)(3) class action would not ordinarily be appropriate for fraud or mass accident cases, because of the splintering on issues of liablity, causation, damages, and defenses. Notwithstanding the warning, numerous fraud, mass accident, and even mass tort cases have been certified as this type of class action.

c. Certification and Implications

Fed. R. Civ. P. 23(c) states that "[a]s soon as practicable after the commencement of an action brought as a class action, the court shall determine by order whether it is to be so maintained." This is what lawyers and judges mean when they talk about *certifying* a class action. In order to determine whether the case should be certified as a class action, the court requires the party or parties seeking a class action to define who the members of the class will be. Fed. R. Civ. P. 23(c)(4). The class must be defined so that the judge can determine whether the basic four requirements for a class action have been met and whether the class can be certified as one of the four types, which, in turn, helps determine who is entitled to notice and/or the opportunity to opt out.

The class action puts an interesting twist into most every procedural and practice question that appears in the first ten chapters of this book. We can emphasize only a few points here, and necessarily must leave the rest for another course.

Subject Matter Jurisdiction. In class action diversity cases, only the named plaintiffs and defendants require complete diversity. *Supreme Tribe of Ben-Hur v. Cauble,* 255 U.S. 356 (1921). Oddly, however, it is an open question whether every class member must meet the statutory amount in controversy. *cf. Zahn v. International Paper Co.,* 414 U.S. 291 (1971) with 28 U.S.C. §1367(b) (Rule 23 class members are conspicuously absent from the list of persons who cannot be added as parties by the plaintiff in a manner that escapes the prohibitions of Section 1332 diversity jurisdiction).

Personal Jurisdiction. The Supreme Court held in *Phillips Petroleum Company v. Shutts,* 472 U.S. 797 (1985) that the Due Process Clause did not require the court to have personal jurisdiction over the absent plaintiff class members in that case, because they had received notice and were afforded the opportunity to opt out.

Conflict of Law. The application of different substantive laws to members of a class has proven to be a serious hurdle to the certification of national class actions. In *Shutts,* the Court cautioned that there are due process limitations on judges' inclinations to "nationalize" substantive law in order to avoid the application of varying state laws.

Statutes of Limitations. Generally speaking, the statute of limitations is tolled at the commencement of the class action suit for all of the putative members of the class. If the class is not certified, the tolling ends, and the statutory period resumes where it left off. *Crown Cork & Seal Co. v. Parker*, 462 U.S. 345 (1983). The fact that states have different statutes of limitation, however, is yet another impediment to national class actions.

Before you read a few class action cases that apply various portions of the rule, you should also be made aware of some practical implications of pursuing a class action. Of course, there are tremendous advantages and opportunities when representing a class. First, the defendant(s) cannot moot your case by simply giving the named representative or representatives the relief that they want. A class action is also a way to provide legal representation and relief to hundreds or thousands of individuals who cannot afford lawyers or may not even be aware of their legal rights. A class action may be a good way to rally support and publicity for a cause, and it may be the only way to attract good lawyers to engage in expensive and time-consuming litigation. The mere threat of bringing a class action may leverage a better settlement for your client.

At the same time, however, filing a class action is not without risk. First, you must be prepared to shift your loyalty from your individual client(s) to the entire class. And in a class action, the named representatives usually are entitled only to the same relief as all other class members. The time, expense, and commitment of pursuing a class action can be enormous, dwarfing other demands on your time. You may also prepare to be challenged as the lead counsel, and may end up in a subsidiary role or even excluded. Further, if a case is certified as a class action, you should expect the district judge to play a much more active role in case management than she otherwise might. *See* Fed. R. Civ. P. 23(d). You should also expect to cede the ability to settle the case as you see fit, as the settlement or dismissal of a class action usually involves a hearing and always requires notification to class members and court approval. Fed. R. Civ. P. 23(e).

In sum, the decision whether to pursue a class action is a crucial one— for your client, for you, your law partners, and for "the cause."

■ GENERAL TELEPHONE CO. v. FALCON
457 U.S. 147 (1982)

Justice STEVENS delivered the opinion of the Court:

The question presented is whether respondent Falcon, who complained that petitioner did not promote him because he is a Mexican-American, was properly permitted to maintain a class action on behalf of Mexican-American applicants for employment whom petitioner did not hire.

I

In 1969 petitioner initiated a special recruitment and training program for minorities. Through that program, respondent Falcon was hired in

July 1969 as a groundman, and within a year he was twice promoted, first to lineman and then to lineman-in-charge. He subsequently refused a promotion to installer-repairman. In October 1972 he applied for the job of field inspector; his application was denied even though the promotion was granted several white employees with less seniority.

Falcon thereupon filed a charge with the Equal Employment Opportunity Commission stating his belief that he had been passed over for promotion because of his national origin and that petitioner's promotion policy operated against Mexican-Americans as a class. *Falcon v. General Telephone Co. of Southwest*, 626 F.2d 369, 372, n.2 (C.A.5 1980). In due course he received a right-to-sue letter from the Commission and, in April 1975, he commenced this action under Title VII of the Civil Rights Act of 1964, 78 Stat. 253, as amended, 42 U.S.C. §2000e *et seq.* (1976 ed. and Supp. IV), in the United States District Court for the Northern District of Texas. His complaint alleged that petitioner maintained "a policy, practice, custom, or usage of: (a) discriminating against [Mexican-Americans] because of national origin and with respect to compensation, terms, conditions, and privileges of employment, and (b) . . . subjecting [Mexican-Americans] to continuous employment discrimination." Respondent claimed that as a result of this policy whites with less qualification and experience and lower evaluation scores than respondent had been promoted more rapidly. The complaint contained no factual allegations concerning petitioner's hiring practices.

Respondent brought the action "on his own behalf and on behalf of other persons similarly situated, pursuant to Rule 23(b)(2) of the Federal Rules of Civil Procedure." The class identified in the complaint was "composed of Mexican-American persons who are employed, or who might be employed, by GENERAL TELEPHONE COMPANY at its place of business located in Irving, Texas, who have been and who continue to be or might be adversely affected by the practices complained of herein."

After responding to petitioner's written interrogatories, respondent filed a memorandum in favor of certification of "the class of all hourly Mexican-American employees who have been employed, are employed, or may in the future be employed and all those Mexican-Americans who have applied or would have applied for employment had the Defendant not practiced racial discrimination in its employment practices." App. 46-47. His position was supported by the ruling of the United States Court of Appeals for the Fifth Circuit in *Johnson v. Georgia Highway Express, Inc.*, 417 F.2d 1122 (1969), that any victim of racial discrimination in employment may maintain an "across the board" attack on all unequal employment practices alleged to have been committed by the employer pursuant to a policy of racial discrimination. Without conducting an evidentiary hearing, the District Court certified a class including Mexican-American employees and Mexican-American applicants for employment who had not been hired.

Following trial of the liability issues, the District Court entered separate findings of fact and conclusions of law with respect first to respondent and then to the class. The District Court found that petitioner had not discriminated against respondent in hiring, but that it did discriminate against him in its promotion practices. App. to Pet. for Cert. 35a, 37a. The court reached converse conclusions about the class, finding no discrimination in promotion practices, but concluding that petitioner had discriminated against Mexican-Americans at its Irving facility in its hiring practices. *Id.*, at 39a-40a.

After various post-trial proceedings, the District Court ordered petitioner to furnish respondent with a list of all Mexican-Americans who had applied for employment at the Irving facility during the period between January 1, 1973, and October 18, 1976. Respondent was then ordered to give notice to those persons advising them that they might be entitled to some form of recovery. Evidence was taken concerning the applicants who responded to the notice, and backpay was ultimately awarded to 13 persons, in addition to respondent Falcon. The total recovery by respondent and the entire class amounted to $67,925.49, plus costs and interest.

Both parties appealed. The Court of Appeals rejected respondent's contention that the class should have encompassed all of petitioner's operations in Texas, New Mexico, Oklahoma, and Arkansas. On the other hand, the court also rejected petitioner's argument that the class had been defined too broadly. For, under the Fifth Circuit's across-the-board rule, it is permissible for "an employee complaining of one employment practice to represent another complaining of another practice, if the plaintiff and the members of the class suffer from essentially the same injury. In this case, all of the claims are based on discrimination because of national origin." 626 F.2d, at 375. The court relied on *Payne v. Travenol Laboratories, Inc.*, 565 F.2d 895 (1978), *cert. denied*, 439 U.S. 835, in which the Fifth Circuit stated:

> Plaintiffs' action is an "across the board" attack on unequal employment practices alleged to have been committed by Travenol pursuant to a policy of racial discrimination. As parties who have allegedly been aggrieved by some of those discriminatory practices, plaintiffs have demonstrated a sufficient nexus to enable them to represent other class members suffering from different practices motivated by the same policies.

565 F.2d, at 900, *quoted in* 626 F.2d, at 375.

On the merits, the Court of Appeals upheld respondent's claim of disparate treatment in promotion, but held that the District Court's findings relating to disparate impact in hiring were insufficient to support recovery on behalf of the class. After this Court decided *Texas Dept. of Community Affairs v. Burdine*, 450 U.S. 248, we vacated the judgment of the Court of Appeals and directed further consideration in the light of that opinion.

General Telephone Co. of Southwest v. Falcon, 450 U.S. 1036. The Fifth Circuit thereupon vacated the portion of its opinion addressing respondent's promotion claim but reinstated the portions of its opinion approving the District Court's class certification. 647 F.2d 633 (1981). With the merits of both respondent's promotion claim and the class hiring claims remaining open for reconsideration in the District Court on remand, we granted certiorari to decide whether the class action was properly maintained on behalf of both employees who were denied promotion and applicants who were denied employment.

II

The class-action device was designed as "an exception to the usual rule that litigation is conducted by and on behalf of the individual named parties only." *Califano v. Yamasaki,* 442 U.S. 682, 700-701. Class relief is "peculiarly appropriate" when the "issues involved are common to the class as a whole" and when they "turn on questions of law applicable in the same manner to each member of the class." *Id.,* at 701. For in such cases, "the class-action device saves the resources of both the courts and the parties by permitting an issue potentially affecting every [class member] to be litigated in an economical fashion under Rule 23." *Ibid.*

Title VII of the Civil Rights Act of 1964, as amended, authorizes the Equal Employment Opportunity Commission to sue in its own name to secure relief for individuals aggrieved by discriminatory practices forbidden by the Act. *See* 42 U.S.C. §2000e-5(f)(1). In exercising this enforcement power, the Commission may seek relief for groups of employees or applicants for employment without complying with the strictures of Rule 23. *General Telephone Co. of Northwest v. EEOC,* 446 U.S. 318. Title VII, however, contains no special authorization for class suits maintained by private parties. An individual litigant seeking to maintain a class action under Title VII must meet "the prerequisites of numerosity, commonality, typicality, and adequacy of representation" specified in Rule 23(a). *Id.,* at 330. These requirements effectively "limit the class claims to those fairly encompassed by the named plaintiff's claims." *Ibid.*

We have repeatedly held that "a class representative must be part of the class and 'possess the same interest and suffer the same injury' as the class members." *East Texas Motor Freight System, Inc. v. Rodriguez,* 431 U.S. 395, 403 (*quoting Schlesinger v. Reservists Committee to Stop the War,* 418 U.S. 208, 216.) In *East Texas Motor Freight,* a Title VII action brought by three Mexican-American city drivers, the Fifth Circuit certified a class consisting of the trucking company's black and Mexican-American city drivers allegedly denied on racial or ethnic grounds transfers to more desirable line-driver jobs. We held that the Court of Appeals had "plainly erred in declaring a class action." 431 U.S., at 403. Because at the time the class was certified it was clear that the named plaintiffs were not qualified for line-driver positions, "they could have suffered no injury as a result of the allegedly discriminatory practices, and they were, therefore, simply not eligible to represent a class of persons who did allegedly suffer injury." *Id.*, at 403-404.

Our holding in *East Texas Motor Freight* was limited; we noted that "a different case would be presented if the District Court had certified a class and only later had it appeared that the named plaintiffs were not class members or were otherwise inappropriate class representatives." *Id.*, at 406, n.12. We also recognized the theory behind the Fifth Circuit's across-the-board rule, noting our awareness "that suits alleging racial or ethnic discrimination are often by their very nature class suits, involving classwide wrongs," and that "[c]ommon questions of law or fact are typically present." *Id.*, at 405. In the same breath, however, we reiterated that "careful attention to the requirements of Fed. Rule Civ. Proc. 23 remains nonetheless indispensable" and that the "mere fact that a complaint alleges racial or ethnic discrimination does not in itself ensure that the party who has brought the lawsuit will be an adequate representative of those who may have been the real victims of that discrimination." *Id.*, at 405-406.

We cannot disagree with the proposition underlying the across-the-board rule—that racial discrimination is by definition class discrimination. But the allegation that such discrimination has occurred neither determines whether a class action may be maintained in accordance with Rule 23 nor defines the class that may be certified. Conceptually, there is a wide gap between (a) an individual's claim that he has been denied a promotion on discriminatory grounds, and his otherwise unsupported allegation that the company has a policy of discrimination, and (b) the existence of a class of persons who have suffered the same injury as that individual, such that the individual's claim and the class claims will share common questions of law or fact and that the individual's claim will be typical of the class claims. For respondent to bridge that gap, he must prove much more than the validity of his own claim. Even though evidence that he was passed over for promotion when several less deserving whites were advanced may support the conclusion that respondent was denied the promotion because of his national origin, such evidence would not necessarily justify the additional inferences (1) that this discriminatory treatment is typical of petitioner's promotion practices, (2) that petitioner's promotion practices are motivated by a policy of ethnic discrimination that pervades petitioner's Irving division, or (3) that this policy of ethnic discrimination is reflected in petitioner's other employment practices, such as hiring, in the same way it is manifested in the promotion practices. These additional inferences demonstrate the tenuous character of any presumption that the class claims are "fairly encompassed" within respondent's claim.

Respondent's complaint provided an insufficient basis for concluding that the adjudication of his claim of discrimination in promotion would require the decision of any common question concerning the failure of petitioner to hire more Mexican-Americans. Without any specific presentation identifying the questions of law or fact that were common to the claims of respondent and of the members of the class he sought to represent, it was error for the District Court to presume that respondent's claim was typical of other claims against petitioner by Mexican-American employees and applicants. If one allegation of specific discriminatory treatment were sufficient to support an across-the-board attack, every Title VII case would be a potential companywide class action. We find nothing in the statute to indicate that Congress intended to authorize such a wholesale expansion of class-action litigation.

The trial of this class action followed a predictable course. Instead of raising common questions of law or fact, respondent's evidentiary approaches to the individual and class claims were entirely different. He attempted to sustain his individual claim by proving intentional discrimination. He tried to prove the class claims through statistical evidence of disparate impact. Ironically, the District Court rejected the class claim of promotion discrimination, which conceptually might have borne a closer typicality and commonality relationship with respondent's individual claim, but sustained the class claim of hiring discrimination. As the District Court's bifurcated findings on liability demonstrate, the individual and class claims might as well have been tried separately. It is clear that the maintenance of respondent's action as a class action did not advance "the efficiency and economy of litigation which is a principal purpose of the procedure." *American Pipe & Construction Co. v. Utah*, 414 U.S. 538, 553.

We do not, of course, judge the propriety of a class certification by hindsight. The District Court's error in this case, and the error inherent in the across-the-board rule, is the failure to evaluate carefully the legitimacy of the named plaintiff's plea that he is a proper class representative under Rule 23(a). As we noted in *Coopers & Lybrand v. Livesay*, 437 U.S. 463, "the class determination generally involves considerations that are 'enmeshed in the factual and legal issues comprising the plaintiff's cause of action.'" *Id.*, at 469 (*quoting Mercantile Nat. Bank v. Langdeau*, 371 U.S. 555, 558). Sometimes the issues are plain enough from the pleadings to determine whether the interests of the absent parties are fairly encompassed within the named plaintiff's claim, and sometimes it may be necessary for the court to probe behind the pleadings before coming to rest on the certification question. Even after a certification order is entered, the judge remains free to modify it in the light of subsequent developments in the litigation. For such an order, particularly during the period before any notice is sent to members of the class, "is inherently tentative." 437 U.S., at 469, n.11. This flexibility enhances the usefulness of the class-action device; actual, not presumed, conformance with Rule 23(a) remains, however, indispensable.

III

The need to carefully apply the requirements of Rule 23(a) to Title VII class actions was noticed by a member of the Fifth Circuit panel that announced the across-the-board rule. In a specially concurring opinion in *Johnson v. Georgia Highway Express, Inc.*, 417 F.2d, at 1125-1127, Judge Godbold emphasized the need for "more precise pleadings," *id.*, at 1125, for "without reasonable specificity the court cannot define the class, cannot determine whether the representation is adequate, and the employer does not know how to defend," *id.*, at 1126. He termed as "most significant" the potential unfairness to the class members bound by the judgment if the framing of the class is overbroad. *Ibid.* And he pointed out the error of the "tacit assumption" underlying the across-the-board rule that "all will be well for surely the plaintiff will win and manna will fall on all members of the class." *Id.*, at 1127. With the same concerns in mind, we reiterate today that a Title VII class action, like any other class action, may only be certified if the trial court is satisfied, after a rigorous analysis, that the prerequisites of Rule 23(a) have been satisfied.

The judgment of the Court of Appeals affirming the certification order is reversed, and the case is remanded for further proceedings consistent with this opinion.

Chief Justice BURGER, concurring in part and dissenting in part:

I agree with the Court's decision insofar as it states the general principles which apply in determining whether a class should be certified in this case under Rule 23. However, in my view it is not necessary to remand for further proceedings since it is entirely clear on this record that no class should have been certified in this case. I would simply reverse the Court of Appeals and remand with instructions to dismiss the class claim. . . .

. . . [W]hile a judge's decision to certify a class is not normally to be evaluated by hindsight, since the judge cannot know what the evidence will show, there is no reason for us at this stage of these lengthy judicial proceedings not to proceed in light of the evidence actually presented. The Court properly concludes that the Court of Appeals and the District Court failed to consider the requirements of Rule 23. In determining whether to reverse and remand or to simply reverse, we can and should look at the evidence. The record shows that there is no support for the class claim. Respondent's own statistics show that 7.7% of those hired by petitioner between 1972 and 1976 were Mexican-American while the relevant labor force was 5.2% Mexican-American. *Falcon v. General Telephone Company of Southwest*, 626 F.2d 369, 372, 381, n.16 (1980). Petitioner's unchallenged evidence shows that it hired Mexican-Americans in numbers greater than their percentage of the labor force even though Mexican-Americans applied for jobs with petitioner in numbers smaller than their percentage of the labor force. *Id.*, at 373, n.4. This negates any claim of Falcon as a class representative.

Like so many Title VII cases, this case has already gone on for years, draining judicial resources as well as resources of the litigants. Rather than promoting judicial economy, the "across-the-board" class action has promoted multiplication of claims and endless litigation. Since it is clear that the class claim brought on behalf of unsuccessful applicants for jobs with petitioner cannot succeed, I would simply reverse and remand with instructions to dismiss the class claim.

Comments and Questions

1. According to the Court, what provision(s) of Fed. R. Civ. P. 23 did the plaintiff fail to satisfy? What should Falcon have done? Is the Court's decision consistent with notice-pleading and the timing for consideration of burdens of proof? Do you agree with the Court's distinction between the practices of hiring and promotion? Can you reach an alternative conclusion, based upon your understanding of Title VII and the underlying purposes of Fed. R. Civ. P. 23? Explain. Review the Advisory Committee's Notes that explained the 1966 amendment to Rule 23(b)(2).

2. The Practice Exercise that follows these Comments and Questions involves class certification in the *City of Cleveland* case. As you prepare for the exercise, consider the sequence of the arguments for and against class certification. Generally speaking, lawyers focus first on their definition of the class and the efficacy of that definition. In *City of Cleveland*, it was highly controverted whether the class could include not only those who took the examination, but also past, deterred, and future applicants. The ability to identify the members of the class individually at an early stage of the litigation is most critical in a 23(b)(3) class action where individualized notice is a prerequisite. Lawyers typically then address "numerosity," "commonality," "typicality," and "representativeness" issues in Fed. R. Civ. P. 23(a). "Commonality" and "typicality" frequently involve similar arguments. Lawyers opposing class certification will usually focus on the indeterminacy of the definition of those who are members of the class and on all of the reasons that a case, if certified, would splinter into individualized questions for each named plaintiff and for each class member. Plaintiffs normally point to cases that say that if the only splintering will be in respect to damages, then the case should still be certified and there can later be individualized hearings after liability has been established. Finally, the lawyers will turn their attention to the types of class action under 23(b) and any other questions presented by the remainder of the Rule, such as the notice provisions in 23(c) and relevant specific orders under 23(d).

3. *Appealability of Class Certification Decisions.* Plaintiffs have no right to appeal the denial of class certification, and defendants have no right to appeal the grant of class certification. However, under Fed. R. Civ. P.

23(f), the court of appeals may, in the exercise of its discretion, permit such an appeal, if timely filed. (Consider also 28 U.S.C. §§1291, 1292(a)(1) and 1292(b) as possible avenues for appeal; understand how your argument for review would need to be framed in order to fit each of these sections. How likely is it that one of these standards could be met?) Consider the situation where class certification is denied, but the denial effectively terminates the litigation because the individual stake of the representative plaintiffs is too small to justify individual prosecution. This is referred to as the "death knell" concept and has been argued as a justification for interlocutory appellate review of the denial of class certifications. The Supreme Court unequivocally rejected this justification in *Coopers & Lybrand v. Livesay*, 437 U.S. 463 (1978).

4. The courts have had to face the problem of cases that have both 23(b)(2) and 23(b)(3) characteristics. Frequently, class action plaintiffs seek both injunctive or declaratory relief for the class as a whole, and individual damages for each class member. It is critical which category the court selects, because of the usual mandatory nature of a 23(b) case, as opposed to the notice and opt-out provisions applicable to 23(c) cases. Some courts have certified hybrid (b)(2) class actions with an injunctive or declaratory relief first stage, without the right to opt-out, and a second mandatory relief stage under 23(b)(3), in which class members have opt-out rights. *See, e.g., Simon v. World Omni Leasing*, 146 F.R.D. 197 (S.D. Ala 1992).

5. *Derivative actions under Fed. R. Civ. P. 23.1 and 23.2.* The Federal Rules provide for two other types of "joinder" cases, which we are not exploring in this course. (1) Rule 23.1 covers "derivative actions by shareholders." These are law suits in which shareholders of a corporation contend that management of the same corporation will not seek redress on behalf of the corporation. In effect, the minority shareholders are normally attacking the activity or inactivity of management. In most derivative actions, the stockholder sues in behalf of other similarly situated minority stockholders, so that stockholders derivative suits are akin to class actions. (2) Rule 23.2 covers the similar situation of "actions relating to unincorporated associations."

Practice Exercise No. 34: Motion for Class Certification in *City of Cleveland*

Prepare for a session before a federal district judge to hear the motion to certify a plaintiff class in the *City of Cleveland.* Students with last names beginning with the letters A-D will be clerks to the judge; E-O should prepare arguments (for the City) in opposition to the motion; and P-Z should prepare arguments (for the class) in support of the motion.

Assume that the class that the plaintiffs seek to certify is as defined in paragraph 5 of the Complaint in the Case Files. Assume for purposes of this exercise that the plaintiffs' firm has the requisite skill, experience, and financial resources to handle this class action.

d. Settlement

You undoubtedly have read in newspapers and magazines about class actions in asbestos, tobacco, Dalkon shield, diet pills, and other similar cases. The burden of thousands, sometimes hundreds of thousands, of such cases on the courts has caused them to assume the role of case manager, settlement-instigator, and settlement-approver. (One of the best descriptions of this role is Peter Schuck's *Agent Orange on Trial: Mass Toxic Disasters in the Courts* (1986), describing in detail the intensive management of the case and its settlement by U.S. District Judge Jack B. Weinstein. Judge Weinstein's activity in this case is discussed in Chapter 6.) To give you some insight into the tensions between efficiency and fairness that run through this field, you will next read *Amchem Products, Inc. v. Windsor,* one of the recent cases in which the Court invalidated a class action settlement that had been approved by a district judge.

As you read this opinion, consider whether toxic torts cases move civil procedure and/or civil litigation into a qualitatively and quantitatively different place. Examine the roles of client, lawyer, named representative, class member, and judge in this case. How do the values and concepts we have studied in this course—adversariness, efficiency, client autonomy, the ethical obligations of attorneys to clients, judicial neutrality, the right to be heard, the significance of a trial—shed light on the problems that mass tort cases present to the court system and to society?

■ AMCHEM PRODUCTS, INC. v. WINDSOR
521 U.S. 591 (1999)

Justice GINSBURG delivered the opinion of the Court:

This case concerns the legitimacy under Rule 23 of the Federal Rules of Civil Procedure of a class-action certification sought to achieve global settlement of current and future asbestos-related claims. The class proposed for certification potentially encompasses hundreds of thousands, perhaps millions, of individuals tied together by this commonality: each was, or some day may be, adversely affected by past exposure to asbestos products manufactured by one or more of 20 companies. Those companies, defendants in the lower courts, are petitioners here.

The United States District Court for the Eastern District of Pennsylvania certified the class for settlement only, finding that the proposed settlement was fair and that representation and notice had been adequate. That court enjoined class members from separately pursuing asbestos-related personal-injury suits in any court, federal or state, pending the issuance of a final order. The Court of Appeals for the Third Circuit vacated the District Court's orders, holding that the class certification failed to satisfy Rule 23's requirements in several critical respects. We affirm the Court of Appeals' judgment.

I

A

The settlement-class certification we confront evolved in response to an asbestos-litigation crisis. A United States Judicial Conference Ad Hoc Committee on Asbestos Litigation, appointed by The Chief Justice in September 1990, described facets of the problem in a 1991 report:

> [This] is a tale of danger known in the 1930s, exposure inflicted upon millions of Americans in the 1940s and 1950s, injuries that began to take their toll in the 1960s, and a flood of lawsuits beginning in the 1970s. On the basis of past and current filing data, and because of a latency period that may last as long as 40 years for some asbestos related diseases, a continuing stream of claims can be expected. The final toll of asbestos related injuries is unknown. Predictions have been made of 200,000 asbestos disease deaths before the year 2000 and as many as 265,000 by the year 2015.
>
> The most objectionable aspects of asbestos litigation can be briefly summarized: dockets in both federal and state courts continue to grow; long delays are routine; trials are too long; the same issues are litigated over and over; transaction costs exceed the victims' recovery by nearly two to one; exhaustion of assets threatens and distorts the process; and future claimants may lose altogether.

Report of The Judicial Conference Ad Hoc Committee on Asbestos Litigation 2-3 (Mar. 1991).

Real reform, the report concluded, required federal legislation creating a national asbestos dispute-resolution scheme. . . . As recommended by the Ad Hoc Committee, the Judicial Conference of the United States urged Congress to act. To this date, no congressional response has emerged.

In the face of legislative inaction, the federal courts—lacking authority to replace state tort systems with a national toxic tort compensation regime—endeavored to work with the procedural tools available to improve management of federal asbestos litigation. Eight federal judges, experienced in the superintendence of asbestos cases, urged the Judicial Panel on Multidistrict Litigation (MDL Panel), to consolidate in a single district all asbestos complaints then pending in federal courts. Accepting the recommendation, the MDL Panel transferred all asbestos cases then filed, but not yet on trial in federal courts to a single district, the United States District Court for the Eastern District of Pennsylvania; pursuant to the transfer order, the collected cases were consolidated for pretrial proceedings before Judge Weiner. The order aggregated pending cases only;

no authority resides in the MDL Panel to license for consolidated proceedings claims not yet filed.

B

After the consolidation, attorneys for plaintiffs and defendants formed separate steering committees and began settlement negotiations. Ronald L. Motley and Gene Locks—later appointed, along with Motley's law partner Joseph F. Rice, to represent the plaintiff class in this action—co-chaired the Plaintiffs' Steering Committee. Counsel for the Center for Claims Resolution (CCR), the consortium of 20 former asbestos manufacturers now before us as petitioners, participated in the Defendants' Steering Committee. Although the MDL order collected, transferred, and consolidated only cases already commenced in federal courts, settlement negotiations included efforts to find a "means of resolving . . . future cases." . . .

In November 1991, the Defendants' Steering Committee made an offer designed to settle all pending and future asbestos cases by providing a fund for distribution by plaintiffs' counsel among asbestos-exposed individuals. The Plaintiffs' Steering Committee rejected this offer, and negotiations fell apart. CCR, however, continued to pursue "a workable administrative system for the handling of future claims."

To that end, CCR counsel approached the lawyers who had headed the Plaintiffs' Steering Committee in the unsuccessful negotiations, and a new round of negotiations began; that round yielded the mass settlement agreement now in controversy. At the time, the former heads of the Plaintiffs' Steering Committee represented thousands of plaintiffs with then-pending asbestos-related claims—claimants the parties to this suit call "inventory" plaintiffs. CCR indicated in these discussions that it would resist settlement of inventory cases absent "some kind of protection for the future." . . .

Settlement talks thus concentrated on devising an administrative scheme for disposition of asbestos claims not yet in litigation. In these negotiations, counsel for masses of inventory plaintiffs endeavored to represent the interests of the anticipated future claimants, although those lawyers then had no attorney-client relationship with such claimants.

Once negotiations seemed likely to produce an agreement purporting to bind potential plaintiffs, CCR agreed to settle, through separate agreements, the claims of plaintiffs who had already filed asbestos-related lawsuits. In one such agreement, CCR defendants promised to pay more than $200 million to gain release of the claims of numerous inventory plaintiffs. After settling the inventory claims, CCR, together with the plaintiffs' lawyers CCR had approached, launched this case, exclusively involving persons outside the MDL Panel's province—plaintiffs without already pending lawsuits.[3]

3. It is basic to comprehension of this proceeding to notice that no transferred case is included in the settlement at issue, and no case covered by the settlement existed as a civil action at the time of the MDL Panel transfer.

c

The class action thus instituted was not intended to be litigated. Rather, within the space of a single day, January 15, 1993, the settling parties—CCR defendants and the representatives of the plaintiff class described below—presented to the District Court a complaint, an answer, a proposed settlement agreement, and a joint motion for conditional class certification.[4]

The complaint identified nine lead plaintiffs, designating them and members of their families as representatives of a class comprising all persons who had not filed an asbestos-related lawsuit against a CCR defendant as of the date the class action commenced, but who (1) had been exposed—occupationally or through the occupational exposure of a spouse or household member—to asbestos or products containing asbestos attributable to a CCR defendant, or (2) whose spouse or family member had been so exposed.[5] Untold numbers of individuals may fall within this description. All named plaintiffs alleged that they or a member of their family had been exposed to asbestos-containing products of CCR defendants. More than half of the named plaintiffs alleged that they or their family members had already suffered various physical injuries as a result of the exposure. The others alleged that they had not yet manifested any asbestos-related condition. The complaint delineated no subclasses; all named plaintiffs were designated as representatives of the class as a whole.

The complaint invoked the District Court's diversity jurisdiction and asserted various state-law claims for relief, including (1) negligent failure to warn, (2) strict liability, (3) breach of express and implied warranty, (4) negligent infliction of emotional distress, (5) enhanced risk of disease, (6) med-

---

4. Also on the same day, the CCR defendants filed a third-party action against their insurers, seeking a declaratory judgment holding the insurers liable for the costs of the settlement. The insurance litigation, upon which implementation of the settlement is conditioned, is still pending in the District Court.

5. The complaint defines the class as follows:

(a) All persons (or their legal representatives) who have been exposed in the United States or its territories (or while working aboard U.S. military, merchant, or passenger ships), either occupationally or through the occupational exposure of a spouse or household member, to asbestos or to asbestos-containing products for which one or more of the Defendants may bear legal liability and who, as of January 15, 1993, reside in the United States or its territories, and who have not, as of January 15, 1993, filed a lawsuit for asbestos-related personal injury, or damage, or death in any state or federal court against the Defendant(s) (or against entities for whose actions or omissions the Defendant(s) bear legal liability).

(b) All spouses, parents, children, and other relatives (or their legal representatives) of the class members described in paragraph (a) above who have not, as of January 15, 1993, filed a lawsuit for the asbestos-related personal injury, or damage, or death of a class member described in paragraph (a) above in any state or federal court against the Defendant(s) (or against entities for whose actions or omissions the Defendant(s) bear legal liability).

1 App. 13-14.

ical monitoring, and (7) civil conspiracy. Each plaintiff requested unspecified damages in excess of $100,000. CCR defendants' answer denied the
principal allegations of the complaint and asserted 11 affirmative defenses.

A stipulation of settlement accompanied the pleadings; it proposed to
settle, and to preclude nearly all class members from litigating against
CCR companies, all claims not filed before January 15, 1993, involving
compensation for present and future asbestos-related personal injury
or death. An exhaustive document exceeding 100 pages, the stipulation
presents in detail an administrative mechanism and a schedule of payments to compensate class members who meet defined asbestos-exposure
and medical requirements. The stipulation describes four categories of
compensable disease: mesothelioma; lung cancer; certain "other cancers"
(colon-rectal, laryngeal, esophageal, and stomach cancer); and "non-
malignant conditions" (asbestosis and bilateral pleural thickening). Persons with "exceptional" medical claims—claims that do not fall within the
four described diagnostic categories—may in some instances qualify for
compensation, but the settlement caps the number of "exceptional" claims
CCR must cover.

For each qualifying disease category, the stipulation specifies the range
of damages CCR will pay to qualifying claimants. Payments under the
settlement are not adjustable for inflation. Mesothelioma claimants—the
most highly compensated category—are scheduled to receive between
$20,000 and $200,000. The stipulation provides that CCR is to propose
the level of compensation within the prescribed ranges; it also establishes
procedures to resolve disputes over medical diagnoses and levels of
compensation.

Compensation above the fixed ranges may be obtained for "extraordinary" claims. But the settlement places both numerical caps and dollar
limits on such claims.[6] The settlement also imposes "case flow maxi-
mums," which cap the number of claims payable for each disease in a
given year.

Class members are to receive no compensation for certain kinds of
claims, even if otherwise applicable state law recognizes such claims.
Claims that garner no compensation under the settlement include claims
by family members of asbestos-exposed individuals for loss of consortium,
and claims by so-called "exposure-only" plaintiffs for increased risk of
cancer, fear of future asbestos-related injury, and medical monitoring.
"Pleural" claims, which might be asserted by persons with asbestos-related
plaques on their lungs but no accompanying physical impairment, are also
excluded. Although not entitled to present compensation, exposure-only

6. Only three percent of the qualified mesothelioma, lung cancer, and "other cancer"
claims, and only one percent of the total number of qualified "non-malignant condition"
claims can be designated "extraordinary." Average expenditures are specified for claims
found "extraordinary"; mesothelioma victims with compensable extraordinary claims, for example, receive, on average, $300,000.

claimants and pleural claimants may qualify for benefits when and if they develop a compensable disease and meet the relevant exposure and medical criteria. Defendants forgo defenses to liability, including statute of limitations pleas.

Class members, in the main, are bound by the settlement in perpetuity, while CCR defendants may choose to withdraw from the settlement after ten years. A small number of class members — only a few per year — may reject the settlement and pursue their claims in court. Those permitted to exercise this option, however, may not assert any punitive damages claim or any claim for increased risk of cancer. Aspects of the administration of the settlement are to be monitored by the AFL-CIO and class counsel. Class counsel are to receive attorneys' fees in an amount to be approved by the District Court.

D

On January 29, 1993, as requested by the settling parties, the District Court conditionally certified, under Federal Rule of Civil Procedure 23(b)(3), an encompassing opt-out class. The certified class included persons occupationally exposed to defendants' asbestos products, and members of their families, who had not filed suit as of January 15. Judge Weiner appointed Locks, Motley, and Rice as class counsel, noting that "[t]he Court may in the future appoint additional counsel if it is deemed necessary and advisable." . . . At no stage of the proceedings, however, were additional counsel in fact appointed. Nor was the class ever divided into subclasses. In a separate order, Judge Weiner assigned to Judge Reed, also of the Eastern District of Pennsylvania, "the task of conducting fairness proceedings and of determining whether the proposed settlement is fair to the class." . . . Various class members raised objections to the settlement stipulation, and Judge Weiner granted the objectors full rights to participate in the subsequent proceedings. . . .

In preliminary rulings, Judge Reed held that the District Court had subject-matter jurisdiction, and he approved the settling parties' elaborate plan for giving notice to the class. The court-approved notice informed recipients that they could exclude themselves from the class, if they so chose, within a three-month opt-out period.

Objectors raised numerous challenges to the settlement. They urged that the settlement unfairly disadvantaged those without currently compensable conditions in that it failed to adjust for inflation or to account for changes, over time, in medical understanding. They maintained that compensation levels were intolerably low in comparison to awards available in tort litigation or payments received by the inventory plaintiffs. And they objected to the absence of any compensation for certain claims, for example, medical monitoring, compensable under the tort law of several States. Rejecting these and all other objections, Judge Reed concluded that the settlement terms were fair and had been negotiated without collusion. He also found that adequate notice had been given to class members, and that final class certification under Rule 23(b)(3) was appropriate.

As to the specific prerequisites to certification, the District Court observed that the class satisfied Rule 23(a)(1)'s numerosity requirement, a matter no one debates. The Rule 23(a)(2) and (b)(3) requirements of commonality and preponderance were also satisfied, the District Court held, in that

> [t]he members of the class have all been exposed to asbestos products supplied by the defendants and all share an interest in receiving prompt and fair compensation for their claims, while minimizing the risks and transaction costs inherent in the asbestos litigation process as it occurs presently in the tort system. Whether the proposed settlement satisfies this interest and is otherwise a fair, reasonable and adequate compromise of the claims of the class is a predominant issue for purposes of Rule 23(b)(3).

Id., at 316. The District Court held next that the claims of the class representatives were "typical" of the class as a whole, a requirement of Rule 23(a)(3), and that, as Rule 23(b)(3) demands, the class settlement was "superior" to other methods of adjudication.

Strenuous objections had been asserted regarding the adequacy of representation, a Rule 23(a)(4) requirement. Objectors maintained that class counsel and class representatives had disqualifying conflicts of interests. In particular, objectors urged, claimants whose injuries had become manifest and claimants without manifest injuries should not have common counsel and should not be aggregated in a single class. Furthermore, objectors argued, lawyers representing inventory plaintiffs should not represent the newly-formed class.

Satisfied that class counsel had ably negotiated the settlement in the best interests of all concerned, and that the named parties served as adequate representatives, the District Court rejected these objections. Subclasses were unnecessary, the District Court held, bearing in mind the added cost and confusion they would entail and the ability of class members to exclude themselves from the class during the three-month opt-out period. Reasoning that the representative plaintiffs "have a strong interest that recovery for all of the medical categories be maximized because they may have claims in any, or several categories," the District Court found "no antagonism of interest between class members with various medical conditions, or between persons with and without currently manifest asbestos impairment." Declaring class certification appropriate and the settlement fair, the District Court preliminarily enjoined all class members from commencing any asbestos-related suit against the CCR defendants in any state or federal court.

The objectors appealed. The United States Court of Appeals for the Third Circuit vacated the certification, holding that the requirements of Rule 23 had not been satisfied. . . .

II

Objectors assert in this Court, as they did in the District Court and Court of Appeals, an array of jurisdictional barriers. Most fundamentally, they maintain that the settlement proceeding instituted by class counsel and CCR is not a justiciable case or controversy within the confines of Article III of the Federal Constitution. In the main, they say, the proceeding is a nonadversarial endeavor to impose on countless individuals without currently ripe claims an administrative compensation regime binding on those individuals if and when they manifest injuries.

Furthermore, objectors urge that exposure-only claimants lack standing to sue: Either they have not yet sustained any cognizable injury or, to the extent the complaint states claims and demands relief for emotional distress, enhanced risk of disease, and medical monitoring, the settlement provides no redress. Objectors also argue that exposure-only claimants did not meet the then-current amount-in-controversy requirement (in excess of $50,000) specified for federal-court jurisdiction based upon diversity of citizenship. See 28 U.S.C. §1332(a).

As earlier recounted, the Third Circuit declined to reach these issues because they "would not exist but for the [class action] certification." We agree that "[t]he class certification issues are dispositive"; because their resolution here is logically antecedent to the existence of any Article III issues, it is appropriate to reach them first, cf. Arizonans for Official English v. Arizona, 520 U.S. 43, —,117 S. Ct. 1055, 1068 (1997) (declining to resolve definitively question whether petitioners had standing because mootness issue was dispositive of the case). We therefore follow the path taken by the Court of Appeals, mindful that Rule 23's requirements must be interpreted in keeping with Article III constraints, and with the Rules Enabling Act, which instructs that rules of procedure "shall not abridge, enlarge or modify any substantive right," 28 U.S.C. §2072(b). See also Fed. Rule Civ. Proc. 82 ("rules shall not be construed to extend . . . the [subject matter] jurisdiction of the United States district courts").

III

[We have omitted the description of Fed. R. Civ. P. 23(a) and the first three types of 23(b) class actions.]

In the 1966 class-action amendments, Rule 23(b)(3), the category at issue here, was "the most adventuresome" innovation. See Kaplan, A Prefatory Note, 10 B.C. Ind. & Com. L. Rev. 497, 497 (1969) (hereinafter Kaplan, Prefatory Note). Rule 23(b)(3) added to the complex-litigation arsenal class actions for damages designed to secure judgments binding all class members save those who affirmatively elected to be excluded. . . .

While the text of Rule 23(b)(3) does not exclude from certification cases in which individual damages run high, the Advisory Committee had dominantly in mind vindication of "the rights of groups of people who individually would be without effective strength to bring their opponents into court at all." Kaplan, Prefatory Note 497. As concisely recalled in a recent Seventh Circuit opinion:

> The policy at the very core of the class action mechanism is to overcome the problem that small recoveries do not provide the incentive for any individual to bring a solo action prosecuting his or her rights. A class action solves this problem by aggregating the relatively paltry potential recoveries into something worth someone's (usually an attorney's) labor.

In the decades since the 1966 revision of Rule 23, class action practice has become ever more "adventuresome" as a means of coping with claims too numerous to secure their "just, speedy, and inexpensive determination" one by one. *See* Fed. Rule Civ. Proc. 1. The development reflects concerns about the efficient use of court resources and the conservation of funds to compensate claimants who do not line up early in a litigation queue.

Among current applications of Rule 23(b)(3), the "settlement only" class has become a stock device. . . . Although all Federal Circuits recognize the utility of Rule 23(b)(3) settlement classes, courts have divided on the extent to which a proffered settlement affects court surveillance under Rule 23's certification criteria.

In *GM Trucks*, 55 F.3d, at 799-800, and in the instant case, 83 F.3d, at 624-626, the Third Circuit held that a class cannot be certified for settlement when certification for trial would be unwarranted. Other courts have held that settlement obviates or reduces the need to measure a proposed class against the enumerated Rule 23 requirements. . . .

A proposed amendment to Rule 23 would expressly authorize settlement class certification, in conjunction with a motion by the settling parties for Rule 23(b)(3) certification, "even though the requirements of subdivision (b)(3) might not be met for purposes of trial." Proposed Amendment to Fed. Rule Civ. Proc. 23(b), 117 S. Ct. No. 1 CXIX, CLIV to CLV (Aug. 1996) (Request for Comment). In response to the publication of this proposal, voluminous public comments—many of them opposed to, or skeptical of, the amendment—were received by the Judicial Conference Standing Committee on Rules of Practice and Procedure. The Committee has not yet acted on the matter. We consider the certification at issue under the rule as it is currently framed.

IV

We granted review to decide the role settlement may play, under existing Rule 23, in determining the propriety of class certification. . . .

Confronted with a request for settlement-only class certification, a district court need not inquire whether the case, if tried, would present intractable management problems, *see* Fed. Rule Civ. Proc. 23(b)(3)(D), for the proposal is that there be no trial. But other specifications of the rule—those designed to protect absentees by blocking unwarranted or overbroad class definitions—demand undiluted, even heightened, attention in the settlement context. Such attention is of vital importance, for a court asked to certify a settlement class will lack the opportunity, present when a case is litigated, to adjust the class, informed by the proceedings as they unfold. *See* Fed. Rule Civ. Proc. 23(c), (d).[16]

And, of overriding importance, courts must be mindful that the rule as now composed sets the requirements they are bound to enforce. Federal Rules take effect after an extensive deliberative process involving many reviewers: a Rules Advisory Committee, public commenters, the Judicial Conference, this Court, the Congress. *See* 28 U.S.C. §§2073, 2074. The text of a rule thus proposed and reviewed limits judicial inventiveness. Courts are not free to amend a rule outside the process Congress ordered, a process properly tuned to the instruction that rules of procedure "shall not abridge . . . any substantive right." §2072(b).

Rule 23(e), on settlement of class actions, reads in its entirety: "A class action shall not be dismissed or compromised without the approval of the court, and notice of the proposed dismissal or compromise shall be given to all members of the class in such manner as the court directs." This prescription was designed to function as an additional requirement, not a superseding direction, for the "class action" to which Rule 23(e) refers is one qualified for certification under Rule 23(a) and (b). *Cf. Eisen*, 417 U.S., at 176-177 (adequate representation does not eliminate additional requirement to provide notice). Subdivisions (a) and (b) focus court attention on whether a proposed class has sufficient unity so that absent members can fairly be bound by decisions of class representatives. That dominant concern persists when settlement, rather than trial, is proposed.

The safeguards provided by the Rule 23(a) and (b) class-qualifying criteria, we emphasize, are not impractical impediments—checks shorn of utility—in the settlement class context. First, the standards set for the protection of absent class members serve to inhibit appraisals of the chancellor's foot kind—class certifications dependent upon the court's gestalt judgment or overarching impression of the settlement's fairness.

Second, if a fairness inquiry under Rule 23(e) controlled certification, eclipsing Rule 23(a) and (b), and permitting class designation despite the impossibility of litigation, both class counsel and court would be disarmed. Class counsel confined to settlement negotiations could not use the threat of litigation to press for a better offer, *see* Coffee, *Class Wars: The Dilemma of the Mass Tort Class Action*, 95 Colum. L. Rev. 1343, 1379-1380 (1995), and the court would face a bargain proffered for its approval without benefit of adversarial investigation, *see, e.g., Kamilewicz v. Bank of Boston Corp.*, 100 F.3d 1348, 1352 (C.A.7 1996) (Easterbrook, J., dissenting from denial of

---

16. Portions of the opinion dissenting in part appear to assume that settlement counts only one way—in favor of certification. To the extent that is the dissent's meaning, we disagree. Settlement, though a relevant factor, does not inevitably signal that class action certification should be granted more readily than it would be were the case to be litigated. For reasons the Third Circuit aired, proposed settlement classes sometimes warrant more, not less caution on the question of certification.

rehearing en banc) (parties "may even put one over on the court, in a staged performance"), *cert. denied*, 520 U.S. — , 117 S. Ct. 1569 (1997).

Federal courts, in any case, lack authority to substitute for Rule 23's certification criteria a standard never adopted—that if a settlement is "fair," then certification is proper. Applying to this case criteria the rule-makers set, we conclude that the Third Circuit's appraisal is essentially correct. Although that court should have acknowledged that settlement is a factor in the calculus, a remand is not warranted on that account. The Court of Appeals' opinion amply demonstrates why—with or without a settlement on the table—the sprawling class the District Court certified does not satisfy Rule 23's requirements.[17]

A

We address first the requirement of Rule 23(b)(3) that "[common] questions of law or fact . . . predominate over any questions affecting only individual members." The District Court concluded that predominance was satisfied based on two factors: class members' shared experience of asbestos exposure and their common "interest in receiving prompt and fair compensation for their claims, while minimizing the risks and transaction costs inherent in the asbestos litigation process as it occurs presently in the tort system." The settling parties also contend that the settlement's fairness is a common question, predominating over disparate legal issues that might be pivotal in litigation but become irrelevant under the settlement.

The predominance requirement stated in Rule 23(b)(3), we hold, is not met by the factors on which the District Court relied. The benefits asbestos-exposed persons might gain from the establishment of a grand-scale compensation scheme is a matter fit for legislative consideration, *see supra* at 2237-2238, but it is not pertinent to the predominance inquiry. That inquiry trains on the legal or factual questions that qualify each class member's case as a genuine controversy, questions that preexist any settlement.

The Rule 23(b)(3) predominance inquiry tests whether proposed classes are sufficiently cohesive to warrant adjudication by representation. *See* 7A Wright, Miller, & Kane 518-519.[19] The inquiry appropriate under Rule 23(e), on the other hand, protects unnamed class members "from unjust or unfair settlements affecting their rights when the representatives become fainthearted before the action is adjudicated or are able to secure satisfaction of their individual claims by a compromise." *See* 7B Wright, Miller, & Kane §1797, at 340-341. But it is not the mission of Rule 23(e) to assure the class cohesion that legitimizes representative action in the first

---

17. We do not inspect and set aside for insufficient evidence district court findings of fact. Rather, we focus on the requirements of Rule 23, and endeavor to explain why those requirements cannot be met for a class so enormously diverse and problematic as the one the District Court certified.

19. This case, we note, involves no "limited fund" capable of supporting class treatment under Rule 23(b)(1)(B), which does not have a predominance requirement.

place. If a common interest in a fair compromise could satisfy the predominance requirement of Rule 23(b)(3), that vital prescription would be stripped of any meaning in the settlement context. . . .

No settlement class called to our attention is as sprawling as this one. *Cf. In re Asbestos Litigation*, 90 F.3d at 976, n.8 ("We would likely agree with the Third Circuit that a class action requesting individual damages for members of a global class of asbestos claimants would not satisfy [Rule 23] requirements due to the huge number of individuals and their varying medical expenses, smoking histories, and family situations."). Predominance is a test readily met in certain cases alleging consumer or securities fraud or violations of the antitrust laws. Even mass tort cases arising from a common cause or disaster may, depending upon the circumstances, satisfy the predominance requirement. The Advisory Committee for the 1966 revision of Rule 23, it is true, noted that "mass accident" cases are likely to present "significant questions, not only of damages but of liability and defenses of liability, . . . affecting the individuals in different ways." And the Committee advised that such cases are "ordinarily not appropriate" for class treatment. But the text of the rule does not categorically exclude mass tort cases from class certification, and district courts, since the late 1970s, have been certifying such cases in increasing number. The Committee's warning, however, continues to call for caution when individual stakes are high and disparities among class members great. As the Third Circuit's opinion makes plain, the certification in this case does not follow the counsel of caution. That certification cannot be upheld, for it rests on a conception of Rule 23(b)(3)'s predominance requirement irreconcilable with the rule's design.

B

Nor can the class approved by the District Court satisfy Rule 23(a)(4)'s requirement that the named parties "will fairly and adequately protect the interests of the class." The adequacy inquiry under Rule 23(a)(4) serves to uncover conflicts of interest between named parties and the class they seek to represent. *See General Telephone Co. of Southwest v. Falcon*, 457 U.S. 147, 157-158, n.13. "[A] class representative must be part of the class and 'possess the same interest and suffer the same injury' as the class members." *East Tex. Motor Freight System, Inc. v. Rodriguez*, 431 U.S. 395, 403 (*quoting Schlesinger v. Reservists Comm. to Stop the War*, 418 U.S. 208, 216 (1974)).[20]

20. The adequacy-of-representation requirement "tend[s] to merge" with the commonality and typicality criteria of Rule 23(a), which "serve as guideposts for determining whether . . . maintenance of a class action is economical and whether the named plaintiff's claim and the class claims are so interrelated that the interests of the class members will be fairly and adequately protected in their absence." *General Telephone Co. of Southwest v. Falcon*, 457 U.S. 147, 157, n.13 (1982). The adequacy heading also factors in competency and conflicts of class counsel. *See id.*, at 157-158, n.13. Like the Third Circuit, we decline to address adequacy-of-counsel issues discretely in light of our conclusions that common questions of law or fact do not predominate and that the named plaintiffs cannot adequately represent the interests of this enormous class.

As the Third Circuit pointed out, named parties with diverse medical conditions sought to act on behalf of a single giant class rather than on behalf of discrete subclasses. In significant respects, the interests of those within the single class are not aligned. Most saliently, for the currently injured, the critical goal is generous immediate payments. That goal tugs against the interest of exposure-only plaintiffs in ensuring an ample, inflation-protected fund for the future.

The disparity between the currently injured and exposure-only categories of plaintiffs, and the diversity within each category are not made insignificant by the District Court's finding that petitioners' assets suffice to pay claims under the settlement. Although this is not a "limited fund" case certified under Rule 23(b)(1)(B), the terms of the settlement reflect essential allocation decisions designed to confine compensation and to limit defendants' liability. For example, as earlier described, *see supra* at 2240-2241, the settlement includes no adjustment for inflation; only a few claimants per year can opt out at the back end; and loss-of-consortium claims are extinguished with no compensation.

The settling parties, in sum, achieved a global compromise with no structural assurance of fair and adequate representation for the diverse groups and individuals affected. Although the named parties alleged a range of complaints, each served generally as representative for the whole, not for a separate constituency. . . .

The Third Circuit found no assurance here—either in the terms of the settlement or in the structure of the negotiations—that the named plaintiffs operated under a proper understanding of their representational responsibilities. That assessment, we conclude, is on the mark.

c

Impediments to the provision of adequate notice, the Third Circuit emphasized, rendered highly problematic any endeavor to tie to a settlement class persons with no perceptible asbestos-related disease at the time of the settlement. Many persons in the exposure-only category, the Court of Appeals stressed, may not even know of their exposure, or realize the extent of the harm they may incur. Even if they fully appreciate the significance of class notice, those without current afflictions may not have the information or foresight needed to decide, intelligently, whether to stay in or opt out.

Family members of asbestos-exposed individuals may themselves fall prey to disease or may ultimately have ripe claims for loss of consortium. Yet large numbers of people in this category—future spouses and children of asbestos victims—could not be alerted to their class membership. And current spouses and children of the occupationally exposed may know nothing of that exposure.

Because we have concluded that the class in this case cannot satisfy the requirements of common issue predominance and adequacy of representation, we need not rule, definitively, on the notice given here. In accord with the Third Circuit, however, we recognize the gravity of the question whether class action notice sufficient under the Constitution and Rule 23 could ever be given to legions so unselfconscious and amorphous.

V

The argument is sensibly made that a nationwide administrative claims processing regime would provide the most secure, fair, and efficient means of compensating victims of asbestos exposure. Congress, however, has not adopted such a solution. And Rule 23, which must be interpreted with fidelity to the Rules Enabling Act and applied with the interests of absent class members in close view, cannot carry the large load CCR, class counsel, and the District Court heaped upon it. . . .

For the reasons stated, the judgment of the Court of Appeals for the Third Circuit is Affirmed.

Justice O'CONNOR took no part in the consideration or decision of this case.

Justice BREYER, with whom Justice STEVENS joins, concurring in part and dissenting in part:

Although I agree with the Court's basic holding that "settlement is relevant to a class certification," I find several problems in its approach that lead me to a different conclusion. First, I believe that the need for settlement in this mass tort case, with hundreds of thousands of lawsuits, is greater than the Court's opinion suggests. Second, I would give more weight than would the majority to settlement-related issues for purposes of determining whether common issues predominate. Third, I am uncertain about the Court's determination of adequacy of representation, and do not believe it appropriate for this Court to second-guess the District Court on the matter without first having the Court of Appeals consider it. Fourth, I am uncertain about the tenor of an opinion that seems to suggest the settlement is unfair. And fifth, in the absence of further review by the Court of Appeals, I cannot accept the majority's suggestions that "notice" is inadequate.

These difficulties flow from the majority's review of what are highly fact-based, complex, and difficult matters, matters that are inappropriate for initial review before this Court. The law gives broad leeway to district courts in making class certification decisions, and their judgments are to be reviewed by the Court of Appeals only for abuse of discretion. See *Califano v. Yamasaki*, 442 U.S. 682, 703 (1979). Indeed, the District Court's certification decision rests upon more than 300 findings of fact reached after five weeks of comprehensive hearings. Accordingly, I do not believe that we should in effect set aside the findings of the District Court. That court is far more familiar with the issues and litigants than is a court of appeals or are we, and therefore has "broad power and discretion . . . with respect to matters involving the certification" of class actions.

I do not believe that we can rely upon the Court of Appeals' review of the District Court record, for that review, and its ultimate conclusions, are infected by a legal error. *E.g., Georgine v. Amchem Products, Inc.*, 83 F.3d 610, 626 (C.A.3 1996) (holding that "considered as a litigation class," the class cannot meet Rule 23's requirements). There is no evidence that the Court of Appeals at any point considered the settlement as something that would help the class meet Rule 23. I find, moreover, the fact-related issues presented here sufficiently close to warrant further detailed appellate court review under the correct legal standard. And I shall briefly explain why this is so.

I

First, I believe the majority understates the importance of settlement in this case. Between 13 and 21 million workers have been exposed to asbestos in the workplace—over the past 40 or 50 years—but the most severe instances of such exposure probably occurred three or four decades ago. This exposure has led to several hundred thousand lawsuits, about 15% of which involved claims for cancer and about 30% for asbestosis. About half of the suits have involved claims for pleural thickening and plaques—the harmfulness of which is apparently controversial. (One expert below testified that they "don't transform into cancer" and are not "predictor[s] of future disease," App. 781.) Some of those who suffer from the most serious injuries, however, have received little or no compensation. . . . These lawsuits have taken up more than 6% of all federal civil filings in one recent year, and are subject to a delay that is twice that of other civil suits. Judicial Conference Report 7, 10-11.

Delays, high costs, and a random pattern of noncompensation led the Judicial Conference Ad Hoc Committee on Asbestos Litigation to transfer all federal asbestos personal-injury cases to the Eastern District of Pennsylvania in an effort to bring about a fair and comprehensive settlement. It is worth considering a few of the Committee's comments. . . .

Although the transfer of the federal asbestos cases did not produce a general settlement, it was intertwined with and led to a lengthy year-long negotiation between the co-chairs of the Plaintiff's Multi-District Litigation Steering Committee (elected by the Plaintiff's Committee Members and approved by the District Court) and the 20 asbestos defendants who are before us here. These "protracted and vigorous" negotiations led to the present partial settlement, which will pay an estimated $1.3 billion and compensate perhaps 100,000 class members in the first 10 years. "The negotiations included a substantial exchange of information" between class counsel and the 20 defendant companies, including "confidential data" showing the defendants' historical settlement averages, numbers of claims filed and settled, and insurance resources. "Virtually no provision" of the settlement "was not the subject of significant negotiation," and the settlement terms "changed substantially" during the negotiations. *Ibid.* In the end, the negotiations produced a settlement that, the District Court determined based on its detailed review of the process, was "the result of arms-length adversarial negotiations by extraordinarily competent and experienced attorneys."

The District Court, when approving the settlement, concluded that it improved the plaintiffs' chances of compensation and reduced total legal fees and other transaction costs by a significant amount. Under the previous system, according to the court, "[t]he sickest of victims often go uncompensated for years while valuable funds go to others who remain unimpaired by their mild asbestos disease." The court believed the settlement would create a compensation system that would make more money available for plaintiffs who later develop serious illnesses.

I mention this matter because it suggests that the settlement before us is unusual in terms of its importance, both to many potential plaintiffs and to defendants, and with respect to the time, effort, and expenditure that it reflects. All of which leads me to be reluctant to set aside the District Court's findings without more assurance than I have that they are wrong. I cannot obtain that assurance through comprehensive review of the record because that is properly the job of the Court of Appeals and that court, understandably, but as we now hold, mistakenly, believed that settlement was not a relevant (and, as I would say, important) consideration.

Second, the majority, in reviewing the District Court's determination that common "issues of fact and law predominate," says that the predominance "inquiry trains on the legal or factual questions that qualify each class member's case as a genuine controversy, questions that preexist any settlement." I find it difficult to interpret this sentence in a way that could lead me to the majority's conclusion. If the majority means that these pre-settlement questions are what matters, then how does it reconcile its statement with its basic conclusion that "settlement is relevant" to class certification, or with the numerous lower court authority that says that settlement is not only relevant, but important?

Nor do I understand how one could decide whether common questions "predominate" in the abstract—without looking at what is likely to be at issue in the proceedings that will ensue, namely, the settlement. Every group of human beings, after all, has some features in common, and some that differ. How can a court make a contextual judgment of the sort that Rule 23 requires without looking to what proceedings will follow? Such guideposts help it decide whether, in light of common concerns and differences, certification will achieve Rule 23's basic objective— "economies of time, effort, and expense." . . .

Of course, as the majority points out, there are also important differences among class members. Different plaintiffs were exposed to different products for different times; each has a distinct medical history and a different history of smoking; and many cases arise under the laws of different States. The relevant question, however, is how much these differences matter in respect to the legal proceedings that lie ahead. Many, if not all, toxic tort class actions involve plaintiffs with such differences. And the differences in state law are of diminished importance in respect to a proposed settlement in which the defendants have waived all defenses and agreed to compensate all those who were injured.

These differences might warrant subclasses, though subclasses can have problems of their own. "There can be a cost in creating more distinct subgroups, each with its own representation. . . . [T]he more subclasses created, the more severe conflicts bubble to the surface and inhibit settlement. . . . The resources of defendants and, ultimately, the community must not be exhausted by protracted litigation." Jack Weinstein, *Individual Justice in Mass Tort Litigation,* at 66. Or these differences may be too serious to permit an effort at group settlement. This kind of determination, as I have said, is one that the law commits to the discretion of the district court—reviewable for abuse of discretion by a court of appeals. I believe that we are far too distant from the litigation itself to reweigh the fact-specific Rule 23 determinations and to find them erroneous without the benefit of the Court of Appeals first having restudied the matter with today's legal standard in mind.

Third, the majority concludes that the "representative parties" will not "fairly and adequately protect the interests of the class." Rule 23(a)(4). It finds a serious conflict between plaintiffs who are now injured and those who may be injured in the future because "for the currently injured, the critical goal is generous immediate payments," a goal that "tugs against the interest of exposure-only plaintiffs in ensuring an ample, inflation-protected fund for the future."

I agree that there is a serious problem, but it is a problem that often exists in toxic tort cases. . . . And it is a problem that potentially exists whenever a single defendant injures several plaintiffs, for a settling plaintiff leaves fewer assets available for the others. With class actions, at least, plaintiffs have the consolation that a district court, thoroughly familiar with the facts, is charged with the responsibility of ensuring that the interests of no class members are sacrificed. . . .

[C]ertain details of the settlement that are not discussed in the majority opinion suggest that the settlement may be of greater benefit to future plaintiffs than the majority suggests. The District Court concluded that future plaintiffs receive a "significant value" from the settlement due to variety of its items that benefit future plaintiffs, such as: (1) tolling the statute of limitations so that class members "will no longer be forced to file premature lawsuits or risk their claims being time-barred"; (2) waiver of defenses to liability; (3) payment of claims, if and when members become sick, pursuant to the settlement's compensation standards, which avoids "the uncertainties, long delays and high transaction costs [including attorney's fees] of the tort system"; (4) "some assurance that there will be funds available if and when they get sick," based on the finding that each defendant "has shown an ability to fund the payment of all qualifying claims" under the settlement; and (5) the right to additional compensation if cancer develops (many settlements for plaintiffs with noncancerous conditions bar such additional claims). 157 F.R.D. at 292. For these reasons, and others, the District Court found that the distinction between present and future plaintiffs was "illusory." 157 F.R.D. at 317-318.

I do not know whether or not the benefits are more or less valuable than an inflation adjustment. But I can certainly recognize an argument that they are. (To choose one more brief illustration, the majority chastises the settlement for extinguishing loss-of-consortium claims, but does not note that, as the District Court found, the "defendants' historical [settlement] averages, upon which the compensation values are based, include payments for loss of consortium claims, and, accordingly, the Compensation Schedule is not unfair for this ascribed reason.") The difficulties inherent in both knowing and understanding the vast number of relevant individual fact-based determinations here counsel heavily in favor of deference to district court decisionmaking in Rule 23 decisions. Or, at the least, making certain that appellate court review has taken place with the correct standard in mind.

Fourth, I am more agnostic than is the majority about the basic fairness of the settlement. The District Court's conclusions rested upon complicated factual findings that are not easily cast aside. . . . I do not intend to pass judgment upon the settlement's fairness, but I do believe that these matters would have to be explored in far greater depth before I could reach a conclusion about fairness. And that task, as I have said, is one for the Court of Appeals.

Finally, I believe it is up to the District Court, rather than this Court, to review the legal sufficiency of notice to members of the class. The District Court found that the plan to provide notice was implemented at a cost of millions of dollars and included hundreds of thousands of individual notices, a wide-ranging television and print campaign, and significant additional efforts by 35 international and national unions to notify their members. Every notice emphasized that an individual did not currently have to be sick to be a class member. And in the end, the District Court was "confident" that Rule 23 and due process requirements were satisfied because, as a result of this "extensive and expensive notice procedure," "over six million" individuals "received actual notice materials," and "millions more" were reached by the media campaign. Although the majority, in principle, is reviewing a Court of Appeals' conclusion, it seems to me that its opinion might call into question the fact-related determinations of the District Court. To the extent that it does so, I disagree, for such findings cannot be so quickly disregarded. And I do not think that our precedents permit this Court to do so.

II

The issues in this case are complicated and difficult. The District Court might have been correct. Or not. Subclasses might be appropriate. Or not. I cannot tell. And I do not believe that this Court should be in the business of trying to make these fact-based determinations. That is a job suited to the district courts in the first instance, and the courts of appeal on review. But there is no reason in this case to believe that the Court of Appeals conducted its prior review with an understanding that the settlement could have constituted a reasonably strong factor in favor of class certification. For this reason, I would provide the courts below with an opportunity to analyze the factual questions involved in certification by vacating the judgment, and remanding the case for further proceedings.

Comments and Questions

1. What does *Amchem* hold? If the court of appeals was wrong, why did the majority affirm? Precisely what mistake(s) did the district court make when it certified the class and allowed the settlement? And why was the settlement that adverse parties reached, when dealing at arm's-length, nevertheless overturned?

2. Describe the attitudes that inhere in the rhetoric of the majority and dissenting opinions. Now describe the reasoning processes.

3. Another recent opinion of the Court addressing settlement class actions is *Ortiz v. Fibreboard Corporation*, 527 U.S. 815 (1999). In *Ortiz*, there was a mandatory limited funds class action against an asbestos manufacturer and two insurance companies that had been mired for decades in litigation. The district court had approved and the Fifth Circuit affirmed a $1.535 billion global settlement of 45,000 pending and all future claims. However, Justice Souter, writing for the majority, held that a limited funds class action established for the purpose of extinguishing unliquidated tort claims was not what the Advisory Committee had envisioned when drafting Fed. R. Civ. P. 23(b)(1)(B). Even were such a class ever contemplated by the Advisory Committee, Justice Souter wrote, this class was also defective because (1) there was insufficient inquiry by the lower courts into whether there was a sufficient inadequacy of funds (noting that "Fibreboard was allowed to retain virtually its entire net worth"); (2) the class definition excluded plaintiffs with certain causes of action; and (3) the class representatives recovered disproportionately more than the class members. Chief Justice Rehnquist wrote a concurring opinion, joined by Justices Scalia and Kennedy, reiterating again that the asbestos situation

"cries out for a legislative solution." And Justice Breyer, again, as in *Am-chem*, wrote a dissenting opinion joined by Justice Stevens that criticized the majority for their lack of sensitivity to the need for judicial flexibility and creativity in the face of the flood of asbestos cases; "when 'calls for national legislation' go unanswered . . . , judges can and should search aggressively for ways, within the framework of existing law, to avoid delay and expense so great as to bring about a massive denial of justice."

4. There has developed a new genre of literature capturing the details and drama of complex litigation. We already have mentioned Peter Schuck's superb book, *Agent Orange on Trial: Mass Toxic Disasters in the Courts* (1986). Another excellent book that is the likely progenitor of this genre is Gerald Stern's *The Buffalo Creek Disaster* (1977). The story of the Dalkon Shield litigation is told in several paperback books: Ronald J. Bacigal, *The Limits of Litigation: The Dalkon Shield Controversy* (1990); Richard B. Solbol, *Bending the Law: The Story of the Dalkon Shield Bankruptcy* (1991); and Karen M. Hicks, *Surviving the Dalkon Shield IUD: Women v. the Pharmaceutical Industry* (1994). Another fascinating book is Sheldon D. Englemayaer & Robert Wagman, *Lord's Justice: One Judge's Battle to Expose the Deadly Dalkon Shield I.U.D.* (1985). The story of asbestos litigation is told in Paul Brodeur's *Outrageous Misconduct: The Asbestos Industry on Trial* (1985). Another very good book co-authored by Deborah H. Henseler, William L. F. Felstiner, Molly Selvin, & Patricia A. Abener is entitled *Asbestos in the Courts: The Challenge of Mass Toxic Torts* (1985). The bendectin litigation is chronicled in Michael Green's *Bendectin and Birth Defects: The Challenge of Mass Toxic Substances Litigation* (1995). And perhaps the most well-known of this genre, though not involving a class action suit, is Jonathan Harr's *A Civil Action* (1995).

5. As you near the end of this civil procedure course, consider whether our procedural system needs to be retooled in order to accommodate the demands of cases that affect thousands and hundreds of thousands of citizens. Would your adjustments be practical? Conceptual? Targeted only at the elephantine cases? Explain.

6. Judge Robert M. Parker of the U.S. Court of Appeals was the trial judge (sitting by designation) who initially certified the settlement class action in *Ortiz*. Judge Parker is a former U.S. District Judge and is well-known and respected for his judicial creativity. In his efforts to resolve the thousands of asbestos cases that were assigned to him, he used phased trials to adjudicate various defenses and 30 illustrative plaintiffs to try issues of liability. Thwarted in these efforts by the Fifth Circuit, *see In re Fibreboard Corp.*, 893 F.2d 706 (5th Cir. 1990), upon remand, Judge Parker again used certain sample jury verdicts and extrapolation techniques to determine the amount of (settlement) recovery by certain members in the class. Again, he was reversed by the Fifth Circuit, which held that such trial by statistics violated the Seventh Amendment. *Cimino v. Raymark Industries, Inc.*, 151 F.3d 297 (5th Cir. 1998). Is trial by statistics unfair? Or

are statistically based awards in fact more accurate and fair, since "[e]very verdict is itself merely a sample from the large population of potential awards"? *See* Michael J. Saks & Peter David Blanck, *Justice Improved: The Unrecognized Benefits of Sampling and Aggregation in the Trial of Mass Torts*, 44 Stan. L. Rev. 815, 833-835 (1992); *cf.* Kenneth S. Bordens & Irwin A. Horowitz, *The Limits of Sampling and Consolidation in Mass Tort Trials: Justice Improved or Justice Altered?*, 22 Law & Psychol. Rev. 43 (1998).

7. Perhaps there are better ways of conceptualizing the class action. Professor David Shapiro has suggested that it may make more sense to view class actions "as not involving the claimants as a number of individuals, or even as an 'aggregation' of individuals, but rather as an entity in itself for the critical purposes of determining the nature of the lawsuit, the role of the lawyer and the judge, and the significance of the disposition," his own deep belief in "virtues of autonomy and individual choice" notwithstanding:

> Assuming that public prosecutors are not to constitute the sole means of enforcement in [a small claims price-fixing conspiracy case alleging violation of federal antitrust laws], the small claim class action strikes me as one that serves the purpose not of compensating those harmed in any significant sense, or of providing them a sense of personal vindication, but rather, and perhaps entirely, the purpose of allowing a private attorney general to contribute to social welfare by bringing an action whose effect is to internalize to the wrongdoer the cost of the wrong. The purpose of the action, in other words, is solely to deter the kind of wrong that causes a small injury to a large number (just as the availability to an individual of a private civil action to recover for a substantial injury can serve to deter the wrongful conduct of those who would cause an equivalent social harm, but in the form of a large injury to only one victim). Although some actions of this kind may not be justifiable except as a means of contributing to the income of lawyers, surely others are fully warranted, and the question whether the action should be allowed to go forward is quite different from the question of the nature of the action once it is certified on behalf of a plaintiff class.

David L. Shapiro, *Class Actions: The Class as Party and Client*, 73 Notre Dame L. Rev. 913, 924 (1998). Shapiro argues that mass tort cases would also be better viewed in terms of the entity model from the perspective of the major objectives of the tort system, as well as the desirability for members of the affected class. He is influenced, among other reasons, by the expense and delay in the traditional individual autonomy model, and by "uncertain outcomes, and professional representatives who make decisions for their clients at least as often as they follow their clients' instructions." *Id.* at 934. Professor Shapiro concludes that "the choice is not so much between two workable models as between a model that offers some hope of a reasonably prompt and fair disposition and one that does not." *Id.*

8. Dean Edward Sherman has suggested that American civil litigation has moved in the direction of the European inquisitorial form of litigation; as evidence, he identifies the growing reliance on the admission of written testimony, summarized testimony, and pre-packaged videotaped depositions. Edward F. Sherman, *The Evolution of American Civil Trial Process Towards Greater Congruence with Continental Trial Practice*, 7 Tul. J. Intl. & Comp. L. 125 (1999). Similarly, Professor Howard Erichson has noted that the use of court-appointed experts and settlement class actions has drawn our system close to the inquisitorial model: "So far, neither the judiciary nor the legislature has proved itself very effective, on the whole, at handling mass torts. But we can be cheered by glimpses of what may be formative moments in an evolution toward more effective inquisitorial judging in mass tort litigation." Howard M. Erichson, *Mass Tort Litigation and Inquisitorial Justice*, 87 Geo. L.J. 1983, 2024 (1999). As a counterpoint, Professor Richard Marcus has expressed skepticism about moving away from the trial model and away from live narrative with its capacity to evoke empathy. Richard L. Marcus, *Completing Equity's Conquest? Reflections on the Future of Trial Under the Federal Rules of Civil Procedure*, 50 U. Pitt. L. Rev. 725 (1989).

D. THE MYSTERIES OF *MARTIN v. WILKS*

You have now reached the point where you should be able to grapple with a case that integrates almost all of the rules introduced in this chapter. Moreover, the case will force you to reconsider many of the underlying purposes of a procedural system, due process, and discrimination law. After you read *Martin v. Wilks*, study the applicable section of the Civil Rights Act of 1991 (which is printed after the case) and prepare for the final practice exercise.

■ MARTIN v. WILKS
490 U.S. 755 (1989)

Chief Justice REHNQUIST delivered the opinion of the Court:

A group of white firefighters sued the city of Birmingham, Alabama (City), and the Jefferson County Personnel Board (Board) alleging that they were being denied promotions in favor of less qualified black firefighters.* They claimed that the City and the Board were making promotion decisions on the basis of race in reliance on certain consent decrees,

---

* Eds Note: For more information about the history of race relations in Birmingham, *see* Chapter 2, Section E.

and that these decisions constituted impermissible racial discrimination in violation of the Constitution and federal statute. The District Court held that the white firefighters were precluded from challenging employment decisions taken pursuant to the decrees, even though these firefighters had not been parties to the proceedings in which the decrees were entered. We think this holding contravenes the general rule that a person cannot be deprived of his legal rights in a proceeding to which he is not a party.

The litigation in which the consent decrees were entered began in 1974, when the Ensley Branch of the National Association for the Advancement of Colored People and seven black individuals filed separate class-action complaints against the City and the Board. They alleged that both had engaged in racially discriminatory hiring and promotion practices in various public service jobs in violation of Title VII of the Civil Rights Act of 1964, 42 U.S.C. §2000e *et seq.*, and other federal law. After a bench trial on some issues, but before judgment, the parties entered into two consent decrees, one between the black individuals and the City and the other between them and the Board. These proposed decrees set forth an extensive remedial scheme, including long-term and interim annual goals for the hiring of blacks as firefighters. The decrees also provided for goals for promotion of blacks within the fire department.

The District Court entered an order provisionally approving the decrees and directing publication of notice of the upcoming fairness hearings. Notice of the hearings, with a reference to the general nature of the decrees, was published in two local newspapers. At that hearing, the Birmingham Firefighters Association (BFA) appeared and filed objections as *amicus curiae*. After the hearing, but before final approval of the decrees, the BFA and two of its members also moved to intervene on the ground that the decrees would adversely affect their rights. The District Court denied the motions as untimely and approved the decrees. *United States v. Jefferson County*, 28 F.E.P. Cases 1834 (N.D. Ala. 1981). Seven white firefighters, all members of the BFA, then filed a complaint against the City and the Board seeking injunctive relief against enforcement of the decrees. The seven argued that the decrees would operate to illegally discriminate against them; the District Court denied relief.

Both the denial of intervention and the denial of injunctive relief were affirmed on appeal. *United States v. Jefferson County*, 720 F.2d 1511 (CA11 1983). The District Court had not abused its discretion in refusing to let the BFA intervene, thought the Eleventh Circuit, in part because the firefighters could "institut[e] an independent Title VII suit, asserting specific violations of their rights." *Id.*, at 1518. And, for the same reason, petitioners had not adequately shown the potential for irreparable harm from the operation of the decrees necessary to obtain injunctive relief. *Id.*, at 1520.

A new group of white firefighters, the Wilks respondents, then brought suit against the City and the Board in District Court. They too alleged that, because of their race, they were being denied promotions in favor of less qualified blacks in violation of federal law. The Board and the City admitted to making race conscious employment decisions, but argued that the decisions were unassailable because they were made pursuant to the consent decrees. A group of black individuals, the Martin petitioners, were allowed to intervene in their individual capacities to defend the decrees.

The defendants moved to dismiss the reverse discrimination cases as impermissible collateral attacks on the consent decrees. The District Court denied the motions, ruling that the decrees would provide a defense to claims of discrimination for employment decisions "mandated" by the decrees, leaving the principal issue for trial whether the challenged promotions were indeed required by the decrees. After trial the District Court granted the motion to dismiss. The court concluded that "if in fact the City was required to [make promotions of blacks] by the consent decree, then they would not be guilty of [illegal] racial discrimination" and that the defendants had "establish[ed] that the promotions of the black individuals . . . were in fact required by the terms of the consent decree."

On appeal, the Eleventh Circuit reversed. It held that, "[b]ecause . . . [the Wilks respondents] were neither parties nor privies to the consent decrees, . . . their independent claims of unlawful discrimination are not precluded." . . .

We granted certiorari, and now affirm the Eleventh Circuit's judgment. All agree that "[i]t is a principle of general application in Anglo-American jurisprudence that one is not bound by a judgment in personam in a litigation in which he is not designated as a party or to which he has not been made a party by service of process." *Hansberry v. Lee*, 311 U.S. 32, 40 (1940). *See, e.g., Parklane Hosiery Co. v. Shore*, 439 U.S. 322, 327, n.7. *See, e.g., Blonder-Tongue Laboratories, Inc. v. University Foundation*, 402 U.S. 313, 328-329 (1971); *Zenith Radio Corp. v. Hazeltine Research, Inc.*, 395 U.S. 100, 110 (1969). This rule is part of our "deep-rooted historic tradition that everyone should have his own day in court." 18 C. Wright, A. Miller, & E. Cooper, Federal Practice and Procedure §4449, p. 417 (1981)(18 Wright). A judgment or decree among parties to a lawsuit resolves issues as among them, but it does not conclude the rights of strangers to those proceedings. [In a footnote, Justice Rehnquist added: "We have recognized an exception to the general rule when, in certain limited circumstances, a person, although not a party, has his interests adequately represented by someone with the same interests who is a party. *See Hansberry v. Lee*, 311 U.S. 32, 41-42 (1940) ('class' or 'representative' suits); Fed. Rule Civ. Proc. 23 (same); *Montana v. United States*, 440 U.S. 147, 154-155 (1979) (control of litigation on behalf of one of the parties in the litigation). Additionally, where a special remedial scheme exists expressly foreclosing successive litigation by nonlitigants, as for example in bankruptcy or probate, legal proceedings may terminate preexisting rights if the scheme is otherwise consistent with due process. *See NLRB v. Bildisco & Bildisco,* 465 U.S. 513, 529-530, n.10 (1984)('proof of claim must be presented to the Bankruptcy Court . . . or be lost'); *Tulsa Professional Collection Services, Inc. v. Pope,* 485 U.S. 478 (1988) (nonclaim statute terminating unsubmitted claims against the estate). Neither of these exceptions, however, applies in this case."]

Petitioners argue that, because respondents failed to timely intervene in the initial proceedings, their current challenge to actions taken under the consent decree constitutes an impermissible "collateral attack." They argue that respondents were aware that the underlying suit might affect them, and if they chose to pass up an opportunity to intervene, they should not be permitted to later litigate the issues in a new action. The position has sufficient appeal to have commanded the approval of the great majority of the Federal Courts of Appeals, but we agree with the contrary view expressed by the Court of Appeals for the Eleventh Circuit in this case.

We begin with the words of Justice Brandeis in *Chase National Bank v. Norwalk,* 291 U.S. 431 (1934): "The law does not impose upon any person absolutely entitled to a hearing the burden of voluntary intervention in a suit to which he is a stranger. . . . Unless duly summoned to appear in a legal proceeding, a person not a privy may rest assured that a judgment recovered therein will not affect his legal rights." *Id.,* at 441. While these words were written before the adoption of the Federal Rules of Civil Procedure, we think the Rules incorporate the same principle; a party seeking a judgment binding on another cannot obligate that person to intervene; he must be joined. *See Hazeltine, supra,* 395 U.S., at 110 (judgment against Hazeltine vacated because it was not named as a party or served, even though as the parent corporation of one of the parties it clearly knew of the claim against it and had made a special appearance to contest jurisdiction). Against the background of permissive intervention set forth in *Chase National Bank,* the drafters cast Rule 24, governing intervention, in permissive terms. *See* Fed. Rule Civ. Proc. 24(a) (intervention as of right) ("Upon timely application anyone shall be permitted to intervene"); Fed. Rule Civ. Proc. 24(b)(permissive intervention) ("Upon timely application anyone may be permitted to intervene"). They determined that the concern for finality and completeness of judgments would be "better [served] by mandatory joinder procedures." 18 Wright §4452, p. 453. Accordingly, Rule 19(a) provides for mandatory joinder in circumstances where a judgment rendered in the absence of a person may "leave . . . persons already parties subject to a substantial risk of incurring . . . inconsistent obligations . . ." Rule 19(b) sets forth the factors to be considered by a court in deciding whether to allow an action to proceed in the absence of an interested party.

Joinder as a party, rather than knowledge of a lawsuit and an opportunity to intervene, is the method by which potential parties are subjected to the jurisdiction of the court and bound by a judgment or decree. The parties to a lawsuit presumably know better than anyone else the nature and scope of relief sought in the action, and at whose expense such relief might be granted. It makes sense, therefore, to place on them a burden of bringing in additional parties where such a step is indicated, rather than placing on potential additional parties a duty to intervene when they acquire knowledge of the lawsuit. The linchpin of the "impermissible collateral attack" doctrine—the attribution of preclusive effect to a failure to intervene—is therefore quite inconsistent with Rule 19 and Rule 24.

Petitioners argue that . . . *Provident Tradesmens Bank & Trust Co. v. Patterson*, 390 U.S. 102 (1968) suggest[s] an opposite result. . . . In that case we discussed Rule 19 shortly after parts of it had been substantially revised, but we expressly left open the question whether preclusive effect might be attributed to a failure to intervene. 390 U.S., at 114-115.

Petitioners contend that a different result should be reached because the need to join affected parties will be burdensome and ultimately discouraging to civil rights litigation. Potential adverse claimants may be numerous and difficult to identify; if they are not joined, the possibility for inconsistent judgments exists. Judicial resources will be needlessly consumed in relitigation of the same question.

Even if we were wholly persuaded by these arguments as a matter of policy, acceptance of them would require a rewriting rather than an interpretation of the relevant Rules. But we are not persuaded that their acceptance would lead to a more satisfactory method of handling cases like this one. It must be remembered that the alternatives are a duty to intervene based on knowledge, on the one hand, and some form of joinder, as the Rules presently provide, on the other. No one can seriously contend that an employer might successfully defend against a Title VII claim by one group of employees on the ground that its actions were required by an earlier decree entered in a suit brought against it by another, if the later group did not have adequate notice or knowledge of the earlier suit.

The difficulties petitioners foresee in identifying those who could be adversely affected by a decree granting broad remedial relief are undoubtedly present, but they arise from the nature of the relief sought and not because of any choice between mandatory intervention and joinder. Rule 19's provisions for joining interested parties are designed to accommodate the sort of complexities that may arise from a decree affecting numerous people in various ways. We doubt that a mandatory intervention rule would be any less awkward. As mentioned, plaintiffs who seek the aid of the courts to alter existing employment policies, or the employer who might be subject to conflicting decrees, are best able to bear the burden of designating those who would be adversely affected if plaintiffs prevail; these parties will generally have a better understanding of the scope of likely relief than employees who are not named but might be affected. Petitioners' alternative does not eliminate the need for, or difficulty of, identifying persons who, because of their interests, should be included in a lawsuit. It merely shifts that responsibility to less able shoulders.

Nor do we think that the system of joinder called for by the Rules is likely to produce more relitigation of issues than the converse rule. The breadth of a lawsuit and concomitant relief may be at least partially shaped in advance through Rule 19 to avoid needless clashes with future litigation. And even under a regime of mandatory intervention, parties who did not have adequate knowledge of the suit would relitigate issues. Additional questions about the adequacy and timeliness of knowledge would inevitably crop up. We think that the system of joinder presently contemplated by the rules best serves the many interests involved in the run of litigated cases, including cases like the present one.

Petitioners also urge that the congressional policy favoring voluntary settlement of employment discrimination claims, referred to in cases such as *Carson v. American Brands, Inc.*, 450 U.S. 79 (1981), also supports the "impermissible collateral attack" doctrine. But once again it is essential to note just what is meant by "voluntary settlement." A voluntary settlement in the form of a consent decree between one group of employees and their employer cannot possibly "settle," voluntarily or otherwise, the conflicting claims of another group of employees who do not join in the agreement. This is true even if the second group of employees is a party to the litigation: "[P]arties who choose to resolve litigation through settlement may not dispose of the claims of a third party . . . without that party's agreement. A court's approval of a consent decree between some of the parties therefore cannot dispose of the valid claims of nonconsenting intervenors." *Firefighters v. Cleveland,* 478 U.S. 501, 529 (1986).

Insofar as the argument is bottomed on the idea that it may be easier to settle claims among a disparate group of affected persons if they are all before the court, joinder bids fair to accomplish that result as well as a regime of mandatory intervention.

For the foregoing reasons we affirm the decision of the Court of Appeals for the Eleventh Circuit. That court remanded the case for trial of the reverse discrimination claims. *Birmingham Reverse Discrimination,* 833 F.2d, at 1500-1502. Petitioners point to language in the District Court's findings of fact and conclusions of law which suggests that respondents will not prevail on the merits. We agree with the view of the Court of Appeals, however, that the proceedings in the District Court may have been affected by the mistaken view that respondents' claims on the merits were barred to the extent they were inconsistent with the consent decree. Affirmed.

Justice STEVENS with whom Justice BRENNAN, Justice MARSHALL, and Justice BLACKMUN join, dissenting:

As a matter of law there is a vast difference between persons who are actual parties to litigation and persons who merely have the kind of interest that may as a practical matter be impaired by the outcome of a case.

Persons in the first category have a right to participate in a trial and to appeal from an adverse judgment; depending on whether they win or lose, their legal rights may be enhanced or impaired. Persons in the latter category have a right to intervene in the action in a timely fashion, or they may be joined as parties against their will. But if they remain on the sidelines, they may be harmed as a practical matter even though their legal rights are unaffected. One of the disadvantages of sideline-sitting is that the bystander has no right to appeal from a judgment no matter how harmful it may be.

In these cases the Court quite rightly concludes that the white firefighters who brought the second series of Title VII cases could not be deprived of their legal rights in the first series of cases because they had neither intervened nor been joined as parties. *See Firefighters v. Cleveland*, 478 U.S. 501, 529-530 (1986); *Parklane Hosiery Co. v. Shore*, 439 U.S. 322, 327, n.7 (1979). The consent decrees obviously could not deprive them of any contractual rights, such as seniority, *cf. W. R. Grace & Co. v. Rubber Workers*, 461 U.S. 757 (1983), or accrued vacation pay, *cf. Massachusetts v. Morash*, 490 U.S. 107 (1989), or of any other legal rights, such as the right to have their employer comply with federal statutes like Title VII, *cf. Firefighters v. Cleveland, supra*, 478 U.S., at 529. There is no reason, however, why the consent decrees might not produce changes in conditions at the white firefighters' place of employment that, as a practical matter, may have a serious effect on their opportunities for employment or promotion even though they are not bound by the decrees in any legal sense. The fact that one of the effects of a decree is to curtail the job opportunities of nonparties does not mean that the nonparties have been deprived of legal rights or that they have standing to appeal from that decree without becoming parties.

Persons who have no right to appeal from a final judgment—either because the time to appeal has elapsed or because they never became parties to the case—may nevertheless collaterally attack a judgment on certain narrow grounds. If the court had no jurisdiction over the subject matter, or if the judgment is the product of corruption, duress, fraud, collusion, or mistake, under limited circumstances it may be set aside in an appropriate collateral proceeding. *See Restatement (Second) of Judgments* §§69-72 (1982); *Griffith v. Bank of New York*, 147 F.2d 899, 901 (CA2) (Clark, J.), *cert. denied*, 325 U.S. 874 (1945). This rule not only applies to parties to the original action, but also allows interested third parties collaterally to attack judgments. In both civil and criminal cases, however, the grounds that may be invoked to support a collateral attack are much more limited than those that may be asserted as error on direct appeal. Thus, a person who can foresee that a lawsuit is likely to have a practical impact on his interests may pay a heavy price if he elects to sit on the sidelines instead of intervening and taking the risk that his legal rights will be impaired.

In these cases there is no dispute about the fact that respondents are not parties to the consent decrees. It follows as a matter of course that they are not bound by those decrees. Those judgments could not, and did not, deprive them of any legal rights. The judgments did, however, have a practical impact on respondents' opportunities for advancement in their profession. For that reason, respondents had standing to challenge the validity of the decrees, but the grounds that they may advance in support of a collateral challenge are much more limited than would be allowed if they were parties prosecuting a direct appeal.

The District Court's rulings in this case have been described incorrectly by both the Court of Appeals and this Court. The Court of Appeals repeatedly stated that the District Court had "in effect" held that the white firefighters were "bound" by a decree to which they were not parties. And this Court's opinion seems to assume that the District Court had interpreted its consent decrees in the earlier litigation as holding "that the white firefighters were precluded from challenging employment decisions taken pursuant to the decrees." It is important, therefore, to make clear exactly what the District Court did hold and why its judgment should be affirmed.

I

The litigation in which the consent decrees were entered was a genuine adversary proceeding. In 1974 and 1975, two groups of private parties and the United States brought three separate Title VII actions against the city of Birmingham (City), the Personnel Board of Jefferson County (Board), and various officials, alleging discrimination in hiring and promotion in several areas of employment, including the fire department. After a full trial in 1976, the District Court found that the defendants had violated Title VII and that a test used to screen job applicants was biased. App. 553. After a second trial in 1979 that focused on promotion practices—but before the District Court had rendered a decision—the parties negotiated two consent decrees, one with the City defendants and the other with the Board. App. to Pet. for Cert. 122a (City decree), 202a (Board decree). The United States is a party to both decrees. The District Court provisionally approved the proposed decrees and directed that the parties provide notice "to all interested persons informing them of the general provisions of the Consent Decrees . . . and of their right to file objections." App. 695. Approximately two months later, the District Court conducted a fairness hearing, at which a group of black employees objected to the decrees as inadequate and a group of white firefighters—represented in part by the Birmingham Firefighters Association (BFA)—opposed any race-conscious relief. *Id.*, at 727. The District Court overruled both sets of objections and entered the decrees in August 1981.

In its decision approving the consent decrees, the District Court first noted "that there is no contention or suggestion that the settlements are fraudulent or collusive." *Id.*, at 238a. The court then explained why it was satisfied that the affirmative-action goals and quotas set forth in the decrees were "well within the limits upheld as permissible" in *Steelworkers v. Weber*, 443 U.S. 193 (1979), and other cases. It pointed out that the decrees "do not preclude the hiring or promotion of whites and males even for a temporary period of time," and that the City's commitment to promote blacks and whites to the position of fire lieutenant at the same rate was temporary and was subject both to the availability of qualified candidates and "to the caveat that the decree is not to be interpreted as requiring the hiring or promotion of a person who is not qualified or of a person who is demonstrably less qualified according to a job-related selection procedure." It further found that the record provided "more than ample reason" to conclude that the City would eventually be held liable for discrimination against blacks at high-level positions in the fire and police departments. Based on its understanding of the wrong committed, the court concluded that the remedy embodied in the consent decrees was "reasonably commensurate with the nature and extent of the indicated discrimination." *Cf. Milliken v. Bradley*, 418 U.S. 717, 744 (1974). The District Court then rejected other specific objections, pointing out that the decrees would not impinge on any contractual rights of the unions or their members. Finally, after noting that it had fully considered the white firefighters' objections to the settlement, it denied their motion to intervene as untimely.

Several months after the entry of the consent decrees, the Board certified to the City that five black firefighters, as well as eight whites, were qualified to fill six vacancies in the position of lieutenant. A group of white firefighters then filed suit against the City and Board challenging their policy of "certifying candidates and making promotions on the basis of race under the assumed protection of consent settlements." The complaint alleged, in the alternative, that the consent decrees were illegal and void, or that the defendants were not properly implementing them. The plaintiffs filed motions for a temporary restraining order and a preliminary injunction. After an evidentiary hearing, the District Court found that the plaintiffs' collateral attack on the consent decrees was "without merit" and that four of the black officers were qualified for promotion in accordance with the terms of the decrees. Accordingly, it denied the motions, and, for the first time in its history, the City had a black lieutenant in its fire department.

The plaintiffs' appeal from that order was consolidated with the appeal that had been previously taken from the order denying the motion to intervene filed in the earlier litigation. The Court of Appeals affirmed both orders. *See United States v. Jefferson County*, 720 F.2d 1511 (CA11 1983). While that appeal was pending, in September 1983, the Wilks respondents filed a separate action against petitioners. The Wilks complaint alleged that petitioners were violating Title VII, but it did not contain any challenge to the validity of the consent decrees. After various preliminary proceedings, the District Court consolidated these cases, along with four other reverse discrimination actions brought against petitioners, under the caption *In re: Birmingham Reverse Discrimination Litigation.* In addition, over the course of the litigation, the court allowed further parties to intervene.

On February 18, 1985, the District Court ruled on the City's motion for partial summary judgment and issued an opinion that, among other things, explained its understanding of the relevance of the consent decrees to the issues raised in the reverse discrimination litigation. After summarizing the proceedings that led up to the entry of the consent decrees, the District Court expressly "recognized that the consent decrees might not bar all claims of 'reverse discrimination' since [the plaintiffs] had not been parties to the prior suits." The court then took a position with respect to the relevance of the consent decrees that differed from that advocated by any of the parties. The plaintiffs contended that the consent decrees, even if valid, did not constitute a defense to their action, *cf. W. R. Grace & Co. v. Rubber Workers,* 461 U.S. 757 (1983), and, in the alternative, that the decrees did not authorize the promotion of black applicants ahead of higher scoring white applicants and thus did not justify race-conscious promotions. The City, on the other hand, contended that the promotions were immunized from challenge if they were either required or permitted by the terms of the decrees. *Id.,* at 282. The District Court took the intermediate position that promotions required by—and made because of—the decrees were justified. However, it denied the City's summary judgment motion because it raised factual issues requiring a trial.

In December 1985, the court conducted a 5-day trial limited to issues concerning promotions in the City's fire and engineering departments. At that trial, respondents challenged the validity of the consent decrees; to meet that challenge, petitioners introduced the records of the 1976 trial, the 1979 trial, and the fairness hearing conducted in 1981. Respondents also tried to prove that they were demonstrably better qualified than the black firefighters who had been promoted ahead of them. At the conclusion of the trial, the District Court entered a partial final judgment dismissing portions of the plaintiffs' complaints. The judge explained his ruling in an oral opinion dictated from the bench, supplemented by the adoption, with some changes, of detailed findings and conclusions drafted by the prevailing parties.

In his oral statement, the judge adhered to the legal position he had expressed in his February ruling. He stated: "The conclusions there expressed either explicitly or implicitly were that under appropriate circumstances, a valid consent decree appropriately limited can be the basis for a defense against a charge of discrimination, even in the situation in which it is clear that the defendant to the litigation did act in a racially conscious manner. In that February order, it was my view as expressed then, that if the City of Birmingham made promotions of blacks to positions as fire lieutenant, fire captain and civil engineer, because the City believed it was required to do so by the consent decree, and if in fact the City was required to do so by the Consent Decree, then they would not be guilty of racial discrimination, either under Title 7, Section 1981, 1983 or the 14th Amendment. That remains my conclusion given the state of the law as I understand it." He then found as a matter of fact that petitioners had not promoted any black officers who were not qualified or who were demonstrably less qualified than the whites who were not promoted. He thus rejected respondents' contention that the City could not claim that it simply acted as required by terms of the consent decree:

> In this case, under the evidence as presented here, I find that even if the burden of proof be placed on the defendants, they have carried that proof and that burden of establishing that the promotions of the black individuals in this case were in fact required by the terms of the consent decree.

The written conclusions of law that he adopted are less clear than his oral opinion. He began by unequivocally stating: "The City Decree is lawful." He explained that "under all the relevant case law of the Eleventh Circuit and the Supreme Court, it is a proper remedial device, designed to overcome the effects of prior, illegal discrimination by the City of Birmingham." In that same conclusion, however, he did state that "plaintiffs cannot collaterally attack the Decree's validity." Yet, when read in context—and particularly in light of the court's finding that the decree was lawful under Eleventh Circuit and Supreme Court precedent—it is readily apparent that, at the extreme, this was intended as an alternative holding. More likely, it was an overstatement of the rule that collateral review is narrower in scope than appellate review. In any event, and regardless of one's reading of this lone sentence, it is absolutely clear that the court did not hold that respondents were bound by the decree. Nowhere in the District Court's lengthy findings of fact and conclusions of law is there a single word suggesting that respondents were bound by the consent decree or that the court intended to treat them as though they had been actual parties to that litigation and not merely as persons whose interests, as a practical matter, had been affected. Indeed, respondents, the Court of Appeals, and the majority opinion all fail to draw attention to any point in this case's long history at which the judge may have given the impression that any nonparty was legally bound by the consent decree.

II

Regardless of whether the white firefighters were parties to the decrees granting relief to their black co-workers, it would be quite wrong to assume that they could never collaterally attack such a decree. If a litigant has standing, he or she can always collaterally attack a judgment for certain narrowly defined defects. On the other hand, a district court is not required to retry a case—or to sit in review of another court's judgment—every time an interested nonparty asserts that some error that might have been raised on direct appeal was committed. Such a broad allowance of collateral review would destroy the integrity of litigated judgments, would lead to an abundance of vexatious litigation, and would subvert the interest in comity between courts. Here, respondents have offered no circumstance that might justify reopening the District Court's settled judgment.

The implementation of a consent decree affecting the interests of a multitude of nonparties, and the reliance on that decree as a defense to a charge of discrimination in hiring and promotion decisions, raise a legitimate concern of collusion. No such allegation, however, has been raised. Moreover, there is compelling evidence that the decrees were not collusive. In its decision approving the consent decrees over the objection of the BFA and individual white firefighters, the District Court observed that there had been "no contention or suggestion" that the decrees were fraudulent or collusive. The record of the fairness hearing was made part of the record of this litigation, and this finding was not contradicted. More significantly, the consent decrees were not negotiated until after the 1976 trial and the court's finding that the City had discriminated against black candidates for jobs as police officers and firefighters, and until after the 1979 trial, at which substantial evidence was presented suggesting that the City also discriminated against black candidates for promotion in the fire department. Like the record of the 1981 fairness hearing, the records of both of these prior proceedings were made part of the record in this case. Given this history, the lack of any indication of collusion, and the District Court's finding that "there is more than ample reason for . . . the City of Birmingham to be concerned that [it] would be in time held liable for discrimination against blacks at higher level positions in the police and fire departments," it is evident that the decree was a product of genuine arm's-length negotiations.

Nor can it be maintained that the consent judgment is subject to reopening and further litigation because the relief it afforded was so out of line with settled legal doctrine that it "was transparently invalid or had only a frivolous pretense to validity." *Walker v. Birmingham*, 388 U.S. 307, 315 (1967)(suggesting that a contemner might be allowed to challenge contempt citation on ground that underlying court order was "transparently invalid"). To the contrary, the type of race-conscious relief ordered in the consent decrees is entirely consistent with this Court's approach to affirmative action. Given a sufficient predicate of racial discrimination, neither the Equal Protection Clause of the Fourteenth Amendment nor Title VII of the Civil Rights Act of 1964 erects a bar to affirmative action plans that benefit non-victims and have some adverse effect on nonwrongdoers. As Justice O'Connor observed in *Wygant v. Jackson Bd. of Education*, 476 U.S. 267 (1986): "This remedial purpose need not be accompanied by contemporaneous findings of actual discrimination to be accepted as legitimate as long as the public actor has a firm basis for believing that remedial action is required." *Id.*, at 286 (opinion concurring in part and concurring in judgment). Such a belief was clearly justified in these cases. After conducting the 1976 trial and finding against the City and after listening to the five days of testimony in the 1979 trial, the judge was well qualified to conclude that there was a sound basis for believing that the City would likely have been found to have violated Title VII if the action had proceeded to a litigated judgment.

Hence, there is no basis for collaterally attacking the judgment as collusive, fraudulent, or transparently invalid. Moreover, respondents do not claim—nor has there been any showing of—mistake, duress, or lack of jurisdiction. Instead, respondents are left to argue that somewhat different relief would have been more appropriate than the relief that was actually granted. Although this sort of issue may provide the basis for a direct appeal, it cannot, and should not, serve to open the door to relitigation of a settled judgment.

III

The facts that respondents are not bound by the decree and that they have no basis for a collateral attack, moreover, do not compel the conclusion that the District Court should have treated the decree as nonexistent for purposes of respondents' discrimination suit. That the decree may not directly interfere with any of respondents' legal rights does not mean that it may not affect the factual setting in a way that negates respondents' claim. The fact that a criminal suspect is not a party to the issuance of a search warrant does not imply that the presence of a facially valid warrant may not be taken as evidence that the police acted in good faith. Similarly, the fact that an employer is acting under court compulsion may be evidence that the employer is acting in good faith and without discriminatory intent. Indeed, the threat of a contempt citation provides as good a reason to act as most, if not all, other business justifications.

After reviewing the evidence, the District Court found that the City had in fact acted under compulsion of the consent decree. Based on this finding, the court concluded that the City carried its burden of coming forward with a legitimate business reason for its promotion policy, and, accordingly, held that the promotion decisions were "not taken with the requisite discriminatory intent" necessary to make out a claim of disparate treatment under Title VII or the Equal Protection Clause. For this reason, and not because it thought that respondents were legally bound by the consent decree, the court entered an order in favor of the City and defendant-intervenors.

Of course, in some contexts a plaintiff might be able to demonstrate that reference to a consent decree is pretextual. *See Texas Dept. of Community Affairs v. Burdine*, 450 U.S. 248 (1981). For example, a plaintiff might be able to show that the consent decree was collusive and that the defendants simply obtained the court's rubber stamp on a private agreement that was in no way related to the eradication of pervasive racial discrimination. The plaintiff, alternatively, might be able to show that the defendants were not bound to obey the consent decree because the court that entered it was without jurisdiction. *See United States v. Mine Workers*, 330 U.S. 258, 291-294 (1947). Similarly, although more tenuous, a plaintiff might argue that the parties to the consent judgment were not bound because the order was "transparently invalid" and thus unenforceable. If the defendants were as a result not bound to implement the affirmative-action program, then the plaintiff might be able to show that the racial preference was not a product of the court order.

In a case such as this, however, in which there has been no showing that the decree was collusive, fraudulent, transparently invalid, or entered without jurisdiction, it would be "unconscionable" to conclude that obedience to an order remedying a Title VII violation could subject a defendant to additional liability. Rather, all of the reasons that support the Court's view that a police officer should not generally be held liable when he carries out the commands in a facially valid warrant apply with added force to city officials, or indeed to private employers, who obey the commands contained in a decree entered by a federal court. In fact, Equal Employment Opportunity Commission regulations concur in this assessment. They assert: "The Commission interprets Title VII to mean that actions taken pursuant to the direction of a Court Order cannot give rise to liability under Title VII." 29 C.F.R. §1608.8 (1989). Assuming that the District Court's findings of fact were not clearly erroneous—which of course is a matter that is not before us—it seems perfectly clear that its judgment should have been affirmed. Any other conclusion would subject large employers who seek to comply with the law by remedying past discrimination to a never-ending stream of litigation and potential liability. It is unfathomable that either Title VII or the Equal Protection Clause demands such a counter-productive result.

IV

The predecessor to this litigation was brought to change a pattern of hiring and promotion practices that had discriminated against black citizens in Birmingham for decades. The white respondents in this case are not responsible for that history of discrimination, but they are nevertheless beneficiaries of the discriminatory practices that the litigation was designed to correct. Any remedy that seeks to create employment conditions that would have obtained if there had been no violations of law will necessarily have an adverse impact on whites, who must now share their job and promotion opportunities with blacks. Just as white employees in the past were innocent beneficiaries of illegal discriminatory practices, so is it inevitable that some of the same white employees will be innocent victims who must share some of the burdens resulting from the redress of the past wrongs.

There is nothing unusual about the fact that litigation between adverse parties may, as a practical matter, seriously impair the interests of third persons who elect to sit on the sidelines. Indeed, in complex litigation this Court has squarely held that a sideline-sitter may be bound as firmly as an actual party if he had adequate notice and a fair opportunity to intervene and if the judicial interest in finality is sufficiently strong.

There is no need, however, to go that far in order to agree with the District Court's eminently sensible view that compliance with the terms of a valid decree remedying violations of Title VII cannot itself violate that statute or the Equal Protection Clause. The city of Birmingham, in entering into and complying with this decree, has made a substantial step toward the eradication of the long history of pervasive racial discrimination that has plagued its fire department. The District Court, after conducting a trial and carefully considering respondents' arguments, concluded that this effort is lawful and should go forward. Because respondents have thus already had their day in court and have failed to carry their burden, I would vacate the judgment of the Court of Appeals and remand for further proceedings consistent with this opinion.

■ CIVIL RIGHTS ACT OF 1991
Pub. L. No. 102-166, §402(a), 105 Stat. 1071, 1099,
reprinted at 42 U.S.C. §2000e-2(n)(1)(Supp. V. 1993)

§108. [A]n employment practice that implements and is within the scope of a litigated or consent judgment or order that resolves a claim of employment discrimination under the Constitution or Federal civil rights laws may not be challenged . . . in a claim under the Constitution or Federal civil rights laws:

(i) by a person who, prior to the entry of the judgment or order . . . had—

(1) actual notice of the proposed judgment or order sufficient to apprise such person that such judgment or order might adversely affect the interests and legal rights of such person and that an opportunity was available to present objections to such judgment or order by a future date certain; and

(2) a reasonable opportunity to present objections to such judgment or order;

or

(ii) by a person whose interests were adequately represented by another person who had previously challenged the judgment or order on the same legal grounds and with a similar factual situation, unless there has been an intervening change in law or fact.

Practice Exercise No. 35: The Supreme Court
Addressess the Constitutionality of Preclusion
Under the Civil Rights Act

Assume that the year is 2005 and that there are a number of new Justices on the Supreme Court of the United States. Moreover, the provisions of the Civil Rights Act of 1991 dealing with *Martin v. Wilks,* which are printed immediately after that case, are still in effect. Assume further that the *City of Cleveland* case, with essentially the same facts and same parties which you have studied throughout this course, was commenced in January 2001 in federal court and resulted, after a full trial before a judge without a jury, in a verdict and judgment for the plaintiffs under Title VII and an injunction ordering the City of Cleveland to use a non-gender-biased written and physical examination in the future which results in qualified women being hired for the Cleveland fire department and granting them as of the hiring date (if they have previously taken the discriminatory tests, and now passed the new tests) seniority, pay, and the positions that they would have had if they had previously passed the test and been hired at that time. The judgment entered and decree ordered as a result of that suit were appealed to the Court of Appeals and affirmed. This decree has adversely affected some current male members of the fire department, who have, in effect, placed lower on the seniority scale and who have been prejudiced already, they argue, by a reduced opportunity to become officers in the department. Fifteen women have already been hired since the new nondiscriminatory tests have been administered, and three of these are already captains. Moreover, the women who were now hired at larger salaries left a diminished salary pool from which current male members could receive raises.

The current male members of the Cleveland Fire Department, claiming that they were prejudiced by the initial suit, brought a class action against the women on the Department and the City of Cleveland to void the judgment and the injunction on the grounds that they were indispensable parties to the initial suit brought in behalf of the women. The named white male class representatives admitted in depositions that within six months of the commencement of the 2001 suit they had read about it in the newspapers, but they also said that they did not realize the impact that "victory for the women" would have on them. They allege that the district court in the 2001 class action knew about them and their concerns at least by January 2003, three months before the trial commenced in that case, which is when they moved to intervene for the first time; their motion to intervene was denied, and that decision was affirmed by the appeals court, after hearing their argument. They further argued that they cannot be bound and harmed by a suit to which they were not a party. The district court granted summary judgment to the women on the force and to the City of Cleveland, on the grounds that the initial verdict and judgment were valid, the male firefighters were not necessary and indispensable parties, the *Martin v. Wilks* amendment found in the Civil Rights Act is dispositive, and that the trial judge in the initial suit acted within his appropriate discretion in denying the late attempt to intervene. The court of appeals affirmed on all points. The Supreme Court has granted cert.

The plaintiffs in the current class action suit, the male firefighters, argue that *Martin v. Wilks* governs, that the initial decree is invalid on Rule 19 and due process grounds, that they had a right to intervene and the denial to grant their motion was improper, and that the *Martin v. Wilks* amendment found in Civil Rights Act of 1991 is unconstitutional on due process grounds for it purports to bind them without formal notice, service, and the right to be heard. The women firefighters and the City of Cleveland argue that this suit is in a procedurally incorrect posture, that *Martin v. Wilks* doesn't apply to their initial case or to this one because it is distinguishable, that the current court should decide the *Martin v. Wilks* issue differently for it was wrongly decided in 1989 (regardless of the Civil Rights Act of 1991), that the Civil Rights Act of 1991 does apply and is constitutional, and that the plaintiffs in the current suit lost any rights they might otherwise have had because of their tardy attempt to intervene in the first suit (the district court judge did not abuse her discretion in denying the motion to intervene and that preclusion law prevents their now appealing a motion denied in the prior law suit).

The women firefighters and the City of Cleveland have hired the same lawyer. Students with last names beginning with the letters A-M will argue for the appellees; all others will argue for the male appellants. Each student should be prepared to give a complete oral argument before the Supreme Court, unless you chose the option which follows. You will be picked at random. Appellants' counsel will be called upon first.

Option: You may wish to prepare your arguments as a team (of three or less). Make sure you team with students representing the same party (or parties). If any member of your team is selected, all should come forward to argue; divide the alloted time as you see fit.

Case Files

Case Files
Carpenter v. Dee
Contents

Initial Memorandum

To: Associates

From: Carol Coblentz (senior partner)

Re: Nancy Carpenter—potential client of Needham, Shaker &
        Coblentz

At 7:00 p.m. on August 29, 1998, twenty-five-year-old Charlie Carpenter was riding as a passenger with his friend Randall Dee in Dee's Jeep CJ-7. They were on their way to pick up their swimming trunks so they could return to a friend's barbecue and pool party. On the corner of Palmer and Franklin streets in Lowell, MA, Dee lost control of the Jeep and it rolled over. Dee suffered only minor injuries, but Charlie Carpenter was pinned under the vehicle and killed.

Charlie Carpenter was survived by his wife Nancy who was pregnant and later delivered a premature but healthy son on January 10th, 1999. She named the boy Charlie Jr. At the time of the accident Mr. Carpenter was employed as a custodian at Forsythe University, where he received benefits, which applied to his wife and would have covered his child as well. Charlie Sr. was killed just prior to qualifying for University-funded life insurance benefits. Prior to his custodian job, Charlie worked as an auto mechanic for a variety of local auto body shops.

Months prior to the incident Randall Dee had modified the Jeep with a suspension lift kit and oversize tires. These modifications affected the Jeep's handling characteristics and were a significant factor in the roll over of the Jeep. Dee had been stopped by Lowell police on several occasions prior to the accident for various suspected motor vehicle offenses. However, we believe that the police never advised him that the Jeep was illegally modified and that the authorities took no other action to prevent the Jeep from being driven in its dangerously modified condition.

On July 27, 1999, Randall Dee was convicted in criminal court on four counts in relation to the incident on August 29, 1998: (1) negligent homicide; (2) failing to slow at an intersection; (3) speeding; and (4) altering the height of a motor vehicle. He received a one-year suspended sentence for the homicide count and was required to serve two years probation and 200 hours of community service. Fines for the other charges amounted to $100.

The Jeep that Dee was driving was owned by his ex-girlfriend, Twyla Burrell. Ms. Burrell maintained a minimum liability insurance policy on the Jeep in the amount of $10,000. Ms. Burrell had lived with Dee for more than a year, and when she moved out, she left the Jeep with Dee, ostensibly because he had done so much work on it.

We'll need to investigate further to discover the extent of the modifications made to the Jeep, but Ms. Carpenter knows that they included a suspension lift and hugely oversized tires. I'm not entirely clear about the next bit, but Ms. Carpenter insists that the body of the Jeep was lifted even further off the frame by using hockey pucks that were bolted to the frame at various points around the vehicle. A Massachusetts statute prohibits raising the height of a vehicle more than two inches off of the frame, and Ms. Carpenter says she's certain that the jeep was lifted at least a foot. Although she believes that the roll over was caused by the modifications—and from what I hear in the news about hiked up vehicles, this sounds plausible—none of these modifications broke or were damaged as a part of the accident.

We know that Dee has been stopped by uniformed Lowell police officers previously and that on one prior occasion he was found guilty of the offense of driving while intoxicated (for which his license was suspended for 30 days). Further, we know that at some time prior to that conviction (but still subsequent to the modifications of the Jeep) Dee was stopped by a uniformed Lowell police officer for driving without a side view mirror and instructed not to drive the Jeep until he got a mirror. Dee was stopped on at least one other occasion by Lowell police for driving an unregistered, uninsured vehicle—at which time it was taken from him and towed away; Dee later proved that there was insurance on the Jeep and was fined only for driving it unregistered.

From what we can tell, Randall Dee is not a wealthy man. He is unmarried and lives in his family home with his brother, Peter. Ms. Carpenter believes they bought the house from the estate of their deceased father. Ms. Carpenter says that she thought the brothers both owned the house, but a mutual friend told her recently that Peter says he owns the house alone. To date, we don't know where Randall Dee bought the parts he used to modify the Jeep, nor do we know if he received any warnings from anyone about creating a dangerous propensity to tip over by raising the Jeep off of the frame. We also don't know if he knew the Jeep was too high under the Mass. Code, nor do we know yet where he had his car inspected for its annual inspection sticker required under Massachusetts law.

Please be prepared to discuss with me who the parties might be in a lawsuit, and what the causes of action might be. Should we take the case?

Note—I advised Ms. Carpenter that if we take the case we would pursue it on a contingent fee basis.

[Eds. Note: The names of the parties have been changed to protect their privacy. The dates of certain events (including the enactment and effective dates of certain Massachusetts regulations) have been modified for pedagogical reasons. With other minor exceptions, the pleadings, motions, and discovery in the Case Files are identical to those filed in the actual case.]

■ M.G.L. c. 229 §2 (WRONGFUL DEATH)

A person who

(1) by his negligence causes the death of a person, or

(2) by willful, wanton or reckless act causes the death of a person under such circumstances that the deceased could have recovered damages for personal injuries if his death had not resulted, or

(3) operates a common carrier of passengers and by his negligence causes the death of a passenger, or

(4) operates a common carrier of passengers and by his willful, wanton or reckless act causes the death of a passenger under such circumstances that the deceased could have recovered damages for personal injuries if his death had not resulted, or

(5) is responsible for a breach of warranty arising under Article 2 of chapter one hundred and six which results in injury to a person that causes death,

shall be liable in damages in the amount of:

(1) the fair monetary value of the decedent to the persons entitled to receive the damages recovered, as provided in section one, including but not limited to compensation for the loss of the reasonably expected net income, services, protection, care, assistance, society, companionship, comfort, guidance, counsel, and advice of the decedent to the persons entitled to the damages recovered;

(2) the reasonable funeral and burial expenses of the decedent;

(3) punitive damages in an amount of not less than five thousand dollars in such case as the decedent's death was caused by the malicious, willful, wanton or reckless conduct of the defendant or by the gross negligence of the defendant;

except that:

(1) the liability of an employer to a person in his employment shall not be governed by this section,

(2) a person operating a railroad shall not be liable for negligence in causing the death of a person while walking or being upon such railroad contrary to law or to the reasonable rules and regulations of the carrier and

(3) a person operating a street railway or electric railroad shall not be liable for negligence for causing the death of a person while walking or being upon that part of the street railway or electric railroad not within the limits of a highway.

A person shall be liable for the negligence or the willful, wanton or reckless act of his agents or servants while engaged in his business to the same extent and subject to the same limits as he would be liable under this section for his own act. Damages under this section shall be recovered in an action of tort by the executor or administrator of the deceased. An action to recover damages under this section shall be commenced within three years from the date of death or within such time thereafter as is provided by section four, four B, nine or ten or chapter two hundred and sixty.*

[The survivorship provisions of M.G.L. c. 229 §1 are as follows:

(1) If the deceased shall have been survived by a wife or husband and no children or issue surviving, then to the use of such surviving spouse.

(2) If the deceased shall have been survived by a wife or husband and by one child or by the issue of one deceased child, then one half to the use of such surviving spouse and one half to the use of such child or his issue by right of representation.

(3) If the deceased shall have been survived by a wife or husband and by more than one child surviving either in person or by issue, then one third to the use of such surviving spouse and two thirds to the use of such surviving children or their issue by right of representation.

(4) If there is no surviving wife or husband, then to the use of the next of kin.]

■ M.G.L. c. 229 §6 (CONSCIOUS SUFFERING)

In any civil action brought under [the Wrongful Death section reprinted above], damages may be recovered for conscious suffering resulting from the same injury, but any sum so recovered shall be held and disposed of by the executors or administrators as assets of the estate of the deceased.

■ M.G.L. c. 109A §§1-10 (FRAUDULENT CONVEYANCE) *

§1 Definitions. In this chapter "Assets" of a debtor means property not exempt from liability for his debts. To the extent that any property is liable for any debts of the debtor, such property shall be included in his assets.

"Conveyance" includes every payment of money, assignment, release, transfer, lease, mortgage or pledge of tangible or intangible property, and also the creation of any lien or encumbrance.

"Creditor" is a person having any claim, whether matured or unmatured, liquidated or unliquidated, absolute, fixed or contingent.

"Debt" includes any legal liability, whether matured or unmatured, liquidated or unliquidated, absolute, fixed or contingent.

Eds. Note: This was the law at the time the actual lawsuit was brought. Massachusetts has since adopted the Uniform Fraudulent Transfer Act, which has similar provisions. *See* M.G.L. c. 109A, effective Oct. 6, 1996.

§2 Insolvency of persons. A person is insolvent within the meaning of this chapter when the present fair salable value of his assets is less than the amount that will be required to pay his probable liability on his existing debts as they become absolute and matured. . . .

§3 Fair consideration. Fair consideration is given for property or obligation—

(a) When in exchange for such property or obligation, as a fair equivalent therefor, and in good faith, property is conveyed or an antecedent debt is satisfied, or

(b) When such property or obligation is received in good faith to secure a present advance or antecedent debt in amount not disproportionately small as compared with the value of the property or obligation obtained. . . .

§4 Conveyances by insolvent. Every conveyance made and every obligation incurred by a person who is or will be thereby rendered insolvent is fraudulent as to creditors without regard to his actual intent if the conveyance is made or the obligation is incurred without a fair consideration. . . .

§6 Conveyances by person about to incur debts beyond ability to pay. Every conveyance made and every obligation incurred without fair consideration when the person making the conveyance or entering into the obligation intends or believes that he will incur debts beyond his ability to pay as they mature is fraudulent as to both present and future creditors.

§7 Conveyances made with intent to defraud. Every conveyance made and every obligation incurred with actual intent, as distinguished from intent presumed in law, to hinder, delay or defraud either present or future creditors, is fraudulent as to both present and future creditors. . . .

§9 Rights of creditors; matured claims.

(1) Where a conveyance or obligation is fraudulent as to a creditor, such creditor, when his claim has matured, may, as against any person except a purchaser for fair consideration without knowledge of the fraud at the time of the purchase, or one who has derived title immediately or immediately from such a purchaser—

(a) Have the conveyance set aside or obligation annulled to the extent necessary to satisfy his claim, or

(b) Disregard the conveyance and attach or levy execution upon the property conveyed.

(2) A purchaser who without actual fraudulent intent has given less than a fair consideration for the conveyance or obligation may retain the property or obligation as security for repayment.

§10 Rights of creditors; immature claims. Where a conveyance made or obligation incurred is fraudulent as to a creditor whose claim has not matured, he may proceed in the supreme judicial or superior court against any person against whom he could have proceeded had his claim matured, and the court may—

    (a) Restrain the defendant from disposing of his property,

    (b) Appoint a receiver to take charge of the property,

    (c) Set aside the conveyance or annul the obligation, or

    (d) Make any order which the circumstances of the case may require.

COMMONWEALTH OF MASSACHUSETTS

MIDDLESEX, SS   SUPERIOR COURT DEPARTMENT
                                       OF THE TRIAL COURT
                                       CIVIL ACTION NO. 99-6144

NANCY CARPENTER, As
Administratrix of the Estate
of Charles Carpenter,
    Plaintiff   COMPLAINT

       vs.   PLAINTIFF CLAIMS
                                       TRIAL BY JURY
RANDALL DEE and PETER DEE,
    Defendants.

PARTIES

1. The plaintiff Nancy Carpenter is a resident of Lowell, Middlesex County, Massachusetts. She brings this action in her capacity as the administratrix of the estate of Charles Carpenter, her late husband, of Lowell, Middlesex County, Massachusetts. She was duly appointed as administratrix by the Middlesex Probate Court, docket number 98P3875A.

2. The defendant Randall Dee is a resident of Lowell, Middlesex County, Massachusetts.

3. The defendant Peter Dee is a resident of Lowell, Middlesex County, Massachusetts.

FACTS

4. On or about August 29, 1998, the plaintiff's intestate, Charles Carpenter, was riding as a passenger in a 1986 Jeep CJ-7 (hereinafter "the Jeep").

5. The Jeep was owned by one Twyla Burrell, and operated by the defendant Randall Dee.

6. At or near the intersection of Palmer and Franklin Streets in Lowell, the operator lost control of the Jeep, and it rolled over, pinning Charles Carpenter beneath it.

7. The loss of control and resulting accident was caused by the negligent and/or grossly negligent and/or wanton and willful, and reckless conduct of the defendant Randall Dee as operator of the Jeep including, but not limited to, the following acts and omissions:

(a) excessive speed;

(b) failing to stop at an intersection; and

(c) illegal and dangerous alteration of the chassis, causing unsafe handling characteristics.

COUNT I—WRONGFUL DEATH

8. The plaintiff repeats and incorporates herein the allegations of paragraphs 1 through 7.

9. As a result of the negligent and/or grossly negligent and/or wanton, willful and reckless conduct of the defendant Randall Dee, the plaintiff's intestate was killed on August 29, 1998.

COUNT II—CONSCIOUS SUFFERING

10. The plaintiff repeats and incorporates herein the allegations of paragraphs 1 through 7.

11. As a result of the conduct of the defendant Randall Dee, as described above, the plaintiff's intestate sustained serious personal injuries, from which he suffered consciously, prior to his death on August 29, 1998.

COUNT III—FRAUDULENT CONVEYANCE

12. The plaintiff repeats and incorporates herein the allegations of paragraphs 1 through 7.

13. At the time of the accident on August 29, 1998, the defendant Randall Dee and the defendant Peter Dee owned as joint tenants a certain parcel of land at 91 Birch Hill Road, Lowell, Massachusetts, containing approximately 11,604 square feet.

14. The defendants Randall Dee and Peter Dee had purchased said property from the estate of their deceased father Rick Dee, for the amount of $80,000 on or about February 13, 1998.

15. On or about October 8, 1998, the defendant Randall Dee conveyed all his right, title and interest in the above property to Peter Dee for "nominal consideration."

16. On information and belief, the transfer of such interest was fraudulent as to creditors, including, but not limited to, the plaintiff, within the meaning of M.G.L. c. 109A, in that:

(a) The conveyance was made without fair consideration, and Randall Dee was thereby rendered insolvent, within the meaning of M.G.L. c. 109A, §4; and/or

(b) The conveyance was made without fair consideration at a time when the defendant Randall Dee believed that he would incur debts beyond his ability to pay, within the meaning of M.G.L. c. 109A, §6; and/or

(c) The transfer was made with an actual intent to hinder, delay, or defraud creditors, including but not limited to the plaintiff, within the meaning of M.G.L. c. 109A, §7.

WHEREFORE, the plaintiff prays for the following relief:

1. Judgment on Count I against the defendant Randall Dee

(a) To compensate the survivors of the plaintiff's intestate for the fair monetary value of the deceased for reasonably expected net income lost, services, protection, care, assistance, society, companionship, comfort, guidance, counsel and advice of the deceased;

(b) Reasonable funeral and burial expenses;

(c) Punitive damages in an amount of at least $5,000.00, pursuant to M.G.L. c. 229, §2.

2. Judgment on Count II against the defendant Randall Dee to compensate the estate of Charles Carpenter for his pain and conscious suffering.

3. That the Court issue a temporary restraining order enjoining the defendant, Randall Dee, until further order of this court, from conveying, encumbering, or in any other manner transferring any interest, legal or equitable, in any of his assets, including but not limited to real estate, bank accounts, certificates of deposit, securities, valuables, and any other asset not immune from execution, except in the ordinary course of business.

4. That the Court issue a preliminary injunction enjoining the defendant Randall Dee, until the disposition of this action on the merits, from conveying, encumbering, or in any other manner transferring any interest, legal or equitable, in any of his assets, including but not limited to real estate, bank accounts, certificates of deposit, securities, valuables, and any other asset not immune from execution, except in the ordinary course of business.

5. That the Court issue a temporary restraining order enjoining the defendant Peter Dee, until further order of this court, from conveying, encumbering, or in any other manner transferring any interest, legal or equitable, in the real estate at 91 Birch Hill Road, Lowell, MA.

6. That the Court issue a preliminary injunction, enjoining the defendant Peter Dee, until the disposition of this action on the merits, from conveying, encumbering, or in any other manner transferring any interest, legal or equitable, in the real estate at 91 Birch Hill Road, Lowell, MA.

7. That the Court, under Count III, declare null and void the conveyance of the interest of Randall Dee in the property at 91 Birch Hill Road, Lowell, and/or allow satisfaction of any judgment in this action Randall Dee to be satisfied against the interest he held in said property prior to the fraudulent conveyance.

8. That the Court issue a temporary restraining order enjoining the defendants, until further order of the Court, from selling, or transferring in any way the Jeep CJ-7 vehicle involved or in any way modifying it, or changing its present condition.

9. That the Court issue a preliminary injunction enjoining the defendants, until the disposition of this action on the merits, from selling, or transferring in any way the Jeep CJ-7 vehicle involved or in any way modifying it, or changing its present condition.

By her attorneys,

By:___/s/ Carol Coblentz____
Carol Coblentz (BBO#304321)
Needham, Shaker and Coblentz
44 Park Place
Boston, MA 02100
(617) 555-5555

Dated: /d/

(*Eds. Note*: Notice that at the beginning of this complaint, the plaintiff's lawyer gives a civil action number, "No. 99-6144." The "99" represents the year 1999. The entire number is a docket number that is given to the case upon the filing of the complaint. Docket numbers often also include a letter or initials that indicates to which judge or session the case has been assigned.)

COMMONWEALTH OF MASSACHUSETTS

MIDDLESEX, SS

SUPERIOR COURT DEPARTMENT
OF THE TRIAL COURT
CIVIL ACTION NO. 99-6144

NANCY CARPENTER, As
Administratrix of the Estate
of Charles Carpenter,
  Plaintiff

vs.

MOTION TO DISMISS

RANDALL DEE and PETER DEE,
  Defendants.

The defendant Randall Dee moves to dismiss Counts I, II, and III (Wrongful Death, Conscious Suffering, and Fraudulent Conveyance) of the Complaint against said defendant pursuant to Mass. R. Civ. P. 12(b)(6) for failure to state claims upon which relief can be granted.

In support thereof Randall Dee says that the Complaint alleges three causes of action against said defendant. It is further alleged that on August 29, 1998, the Plaintiff's intestate was injured and killed while a passenger in a Jeep CJ-7 that rolled over because said Jeep was being driven at an excessive speed while failing to stop at an intersection and with illegal and dangerous alteration of the chassis. The specific allegation against the defendants include the following:

(a) On Count I, the defendant's conduct was negligent and/or grossly negligent and/or wanton, willful and reckless;

(b) On Count II, the defendant's conduct resulted in serious personal injuries to the plaintiff's intestate which resulted in conscious suffering; and

(c) On Count III, the defendant fraudulently conveyed a certain parcel of land that was purchased for the amount of $80,000; and that defendant Randall Dee conveyed all his right, title, and interest in said property to Peter Dee for nominal consideration and that transfer of such interest was fraudulent.

All three counts should be dismissed for the two reasons hereunder set forth:

(1) Randall Dee was not the owner of said Jeep CJ-7.

(2) The complaint does not allege that Randall Dee owed a duty to Charles Carpenter.

Count III should also be dismissed for failure to plead the circumstances with particularity.

RANDALL DEE, by his attorney,

By:___/s/ Robert Orthwein____
Robert Orthwein (BBO#304389)
Chaudhuri, Brown, Orthwein & Guinto
11 Boardwalk
Boston, MA 02100
(617) 555-1111

Dated: /d/

COMMONWEALTH OF MASSACHUSETTS

MIDDLESEX, SS

SUPERIOR COURT DEPARTMENT
OF THE TRIAL COURT
CIVIL ACTION NO. 99-6144

NANCY CARPENTER, As
Administratrix of the Estate
of Charles Carpenter,
  Plaintiff

vs.

MOTION FOR A MORE
DEFINITE STATEMENT

RANDALL DEE and PETER DEE,
  Defendants.

The defendant Randall Dee moves the Court to issue an order for a more definite statement pursuant to Mass. R. Civ. P. 12(e).

The complaint is so vague and ambiguous that defendant should not reasonably be required to prepare a responsive pleading. Plaintiff should be ordered to furnish a more definite statement of the nature of her claim as set forth in her complaint in the following respects:

1. With respect to the allegations contained in Paragraph 7, page 1 of the complaint, plaintiff should be required to state the facts supporting her conclusion that on August 29, 1998, Randall Dee lost control of the 1986 Jeep CJ-7 because of his negligent and/or grossly negligent and/or wanton and willful, conduct by stating the circumstances surrounding the accident: weather conditions, speed of vehicle, proximity to other vehicles, condition and experience of defendant-driver.

2. With respect to the prayer for relief, plaintiff has failed to provide the amount which she is claiming for the loss of the value of the decedent's net income, services, protection, care, assistance, society, companionship, comfort, guidance, counsel and advice of the deceased.

RANDALL DEE, by his attorney,

By:___/s/ Robert Orthwein____
Robert Orthwein (BBO#304389)
Chaudhuri, Brown, Orthwein & Guinto
11 Boardwalk
Boston, MA 02100
(617) 555-1111

Dated: /d/

COMMONWEALTH OF MASSACHUSETTS

MIDDLESEX, SS

SUPERIOR COURT DEPARTMENT
OF THE TRIAL COURT
CIVIL ACTION NO. 99-6144

NANCY CARPENTER, As
Administratrix of the Estate
of Charles Carpenter,
    Plaintiff

vs.

RANDALL DEE and PETER DEE,
    Defendants.

ANSWER OF RANDALL DEE
(AS TO COUNTS I AND II ONLY)

DEFENDANT RANDALL DEE
CLAIMS JURY BY TRIAL

PARTIES

1. The Defendant, Randall Dee, admits the allegations contained in Paragraph One of Plaintiff's Complaint.

2. The Defendant, Randall Dee, admits the allegations contained in Paragraph Two of Plaintiff's Complaint.

3. The Defendant, Randall Dee, admits the allegations contained in Paragraph Three of Plaintiff's Complaint.

FACTS

4. The Defendant, Randall Dee, admits the allegations contained in Paragraph Four of Plaintiff's Complaint.

5. The Defendant, Randall Dee, admits the allegations contained in Paragraph Five of Plaintiff's Complaint.

6. The Defendant, Randall Dee, denies each and every allegation contained in Paragraph Six of Plaintiff's Complaint.

7. The Defendant, Randall Dee, denies each and every allegation contained in Paragraph Seven of Plaintiff's Complaint.

COUNT I—WRONGFUL DEATH

8. The Defendant, Randall Dee, repeats and realleges his answers contained in Paragraphs One through Seven, as if fully stated herein.

9. The Defendant, Randall Dee, denies each and every allegation contained in Paragraph Nine of Plaintiff's Complaint.

COUNT II—CONSCIOUS SUFFERING

10. The Defendant, Randall Dee, repeats and realleges his answers contained in Paragraphs One through Seven, as if fully stated herein.

11. The Defendant, Randall Dee, denies each and every allegation contained in Paragraph Eleven of Plaintiff's Complaint.

FIRST DEFENSE

And further answering, the Defendant says that the Plaintiff's intestate's own negligence caused or contributed to the accident and damages alleged, and therefore the Plaintiff cannot recover.

SECOND DEFENSE

And further answering, the Defendant says that the Plaintiff's intestate was more than 50 percent negligent in causing or contributing to the accident and damages alleged, and therefore the Plaintiff either cannot recover or any verdict or finding in his favor must be reduced by the percentage of negligence attributed to the said Plaintiff's intestate.

THIRD DEFENSE

And further answering, the Defendant says that the Plaintiff's intestate assumed the risk of the accident and damages alleged, and therefore the Plaintiff cannot recover.

FOURTH DEFENSE

And further answering, the Defendant says that the Plaintiff's intestate was in violation of the law at the time and place of the alleged accident, which violation of the law caused or contributed to the happening of said accident, and therefore the Plaintiff cannot recover.

FIFTH DEFENSE

And further answering, the Defendant says that the Plaintiff's intestate's alleged injuries and subsequent death, were caused by persons other than the Defendant, his agents, servants, or employees, and plaintiff's intestate's alleged injuries, if any, were caused by persons for whose conduct the defendant is not responsible, and therefore, the Plaintiff cannot recover.

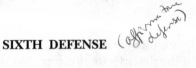

SIXTH DEFENSE (*aff. defense*)

And further answering, the Defendant says that the Plaintiff's intestate's alleged injuries, and subsequent death, do not come within one of the exceptions to the Massachusetts No-Fault Insurance Law, being Massachusetts General Laws, Chapter 231, Section 6D, and therefore the Plaintiff is barred from bringing this action and cannot recover. *(affirmative)*

SEVENTH DEFENSE (*aff. defense*)

And further answering, the Defendant says that the alleged cause of action referred to in the Plaintiff's complaint falls within the purview of Massachusetts General Laws, Chapter 90, Section 34(m), and therefore this action is brought in violation of the law and the Plaintiff cannot recover.

WHEREFORE, the Defendant, Randall Dee, demands judgment against the Plaintiff and further demands that said action be dismissed.

AND, FURTHER, the Defendant, Randall Dee, claims a trial by jury on all the issues.

RANDALL DEE, by his attorney,

By:___/s/ Robert Orthwein____
Robert Orthwein (BBO#304389)
Chaudhuri, Brown, Orthwein & Guinto
11 Boardwalk
Boston, MA 02100
(617) 555-1111

Dated: /d/

[*Eds. Note*: Randall Dee did not answer the allegations in Count III of the complaint. One possible explanation for this is that the parties may have reached an agreement on what to do about the alleged fraudulent conveyance pending a trial on the merits. It also is conceivable that the Randall Dee intended later to answer Count III, but the parties then simply forgot. To be sure, unusual things happen during litigation.

We also wish to emphasize that Randall Dee's third defense, assumption of the risk, is not a defense under Massachusetts comparative negligence law. The sixth and seventh affirmative defenses are completely

baseless. The statutory provisions cited relate to Massachusetts no-fault insurance, and the defenses do not apply in this case. We reprint the Answer
in full, however, because we want you to see what was filed. It also is instructive to learn what happens when one blindly follows forms.]

COMMONWEALTH OF MASSACHUSETTS

MIDDLESEX, SS

SUPERIOR COURT DEPARTMENT
OF THE TRIAL COURT
CIVIL ACTION NO. 99-6144

NANCY CARPENTER, As
Administratrix of the Estate
of Charles Carpenter,
  Plaintiff

vs.

MOTION TO AMEND

RANDALL DEE and PETER DEE,
  Defendants.

Now comes the plaintiff and moves for leave to file an Amended Complaint, a copy of which is attached hereto.

By her attorneys,

By:___/s/ Carol Coblentz___
Carol Coblentz (BBO#304321)
Needham, Shaker and Coblentz
44 Park Place
Boston, MA 02100
(617) 555-5555

Dated: /d/

COMMONWEALTH OF MASSACHUSETTS

MIDDLESEX, SS   SUPERIOR COURT DEPARTMENT
                                OF THE TRIAL COURT
                                CIVIL ACTION NO. 99-6144

NANCY CARPENTER, As
Administratrix of the Estate
of Charles Carpenter,
     Plaintiff   AMENDED COMPLAINT

     vs.
                                PLAINTIFF CLAIMS
RANDALL DEE; PETER DEE;   TRIAL BY JURY
ULTIMATE AUTO, INC.; and
CITY OF LOWELL,
     Defendants.

PARTIES

1. The plaintiff Nancy Carpenter is a resident of Lowell, Middlesex County, Massachusetts. She brings this action in her capacity as the administratrix of the estate of Charles Carpenter, her late husband, of Lowell, Middlesex County, Massachusetts. She was duly appointed as administratrix by the Middlesex Probate Court, docket number 98P3875A.

2. The defendant Randall Dee is a resident of Lowell, Middlesex County, Massachusetts.

3. The defendant Peter Dee is a resident of Lowell, Middlesex County, Massachusetts.

4. Ultimate Auto, Inc. is a Massachusetts corporation, with a usual place of business in Lowell, Middlesex County, Massachusetts.

5. The City of Lowell ("the City"), is a body politic and corporate, with executive offices at 100 Main Street, Lowell, Middlesex County, Massachusetts.

FACTS

6. On or about August 29, 1998, the plaintiff's intestate, Charles Carpenter, was riding as a passenger in a 1986 Jeep CJ-7 (hereinafter "the Jeep").

7. The Jeep was owned by one Twyla Burrell, and operated by the defendant Randall Dee.

8. At or near the intersection of Palmer and Franklin Streets in Lowell, the operator lost control of the Jeep, and it rolled over pinning Charles Carpenter beneath it.

9. The loss of control and resulting accident was caused by the negligent and/or grossly negligent and/or wanton, willful, and reckless conduct of the defendant Randall Dee as operator of the Jeep including, but not limited to, the following acts and omissions:

(a) Excessive speed;
(b) Failing to stop at an intersection; and
(c) Illegal and dangerous alteration of the chassis, causing unsafe handling characteristics.

10. The defendant Randall Dee modified the Jeep, by means of a suspension lift kit and oversize tires. He purchased both items at a retail store owned and operated by the defendant Ultimate Auto.

11. The raised suspension and oversized tires markedly affected the handling characteristics (including, but not limited to, propensity to roll over) of the Jeep, and such modifications were a substantial contributing cause to the accident on August 29, 1998.

12. On several occasions prior to August 29, 1998, police officers of the City of Lowell, acting within the scope of their employment, stopped the defendant Randall Dee while operating the Jeep, in connection with suspected motor vehicle offenses. On no occasion, did any of the officers advise the defendant Dee that the vehicle was illegally modified, or take any other action to prevent the vehicle from being operated in its dangerous condition. The failure of the police to act was a substantial contributing cause to the accident on August 29, 1998.

COUNT I (Wrongful Death, Randall Dee)

13. The plaintiff repeats and incorporates herein the allegations of paragraphs 1-9.

14. As a result of the negligent and/or grossly negligent and/or wanton, willful and reckless conduct of the defendant Randall Dee, the plaintiff's intestate was killed on August 29, 1998.

COUNT II (Conscious Suffering, Randall Dee)

15. The plaintiff repeats and incorporates herein the allegations of paragraphs 1-9.

16. As a result of the conduct of the defendant Randall Dee, as described above, the plaintiff's intestate sustained serious personal injuries, from which he suffered consciously, prior to his death on August 29, 1987.

COUNT III (Fraudulent Conveyance)

17. The plaintiff repeats and incorporates herein the allegations of paragraphs 1-9.

18. At the time of the accident on August 29, 1998, the defendant Randall Dee and the defendant Peter Dee owned as joint tenants a certain parcel of land at 91 Birch Hill Road, Lowell, Massachusetts, containing approximately 11,604 square feet.

19. The defendants Randall Dee and Peter Dee had purchased said property from the estate of their deceased father Richard Dee, for the amount of $80,000.00 on or about February 13, 1998.

20. On or about October 8, 1998, the defendant Randall Dee conveyed all his right, title and interest in the above property to Peter Dee for "nominal consideration."

21. On information and belief, the transfer of such interest was fraudulent as to the creditors, including, but not limited to, the plaintiff, within the meaning of G.L. c. 109A, in that:

(a) The conveyance was made without fair consideration and Randall Dee was thereby rendered insolvent, within the meaning of G.L. c. 109A, §4; and/or

(b) The conveyance was made without fair consideration at a time when the defendant Randall Dee believed that he would incur debts beyond his ability to pay, within the meaning of G.L. c 109A, §6; and/or

(c) The transfer was made with an actual intent to hinder, delay or defraud creditors, including but not limited to the plaintiff, within the meaning of G.L. c. 109A, §7.

COUNT IV (Wrongful Death, Ultimate Auto)

22. The plaintiff repeats and incorporates herein the allegations of paragraphs 1-11.

23. The defendant Ultimate Auto as a retailer of automotive parts, owed a duty to Randall Dee (and to the public generally) to provide appropriate technical advice with regard to the sale of products that could be used to modify vehicles.

24. In breach of that duty, the defendant Ultimate Auto was guilty of negligent and/or grossly negligent and/or wanton, willful and reckless conduct, including, but not limited to, the following acts and omissions:

(a) Selling a suspension lift kit and oversized tires which, individually and in combination, altered the height of the Jeep, affecting its handling characteristics (including, but not limited to, its propensity to roll over) and rendered it unsafe;

(b) Failing to give any kind of warning or instruction to Randall Dee, with respect to the effect of such parts on the handling characteristics of the Jeep;

(c) Selling automotive parts which constituted per se a violation of G.L. c. 90, §7P, with regard to modification of vehicle height;

(d) Failing to advise Randall Dee that the installation of the parts constituted a violation of G.L. c. 90, §7P.

25. As a result of the above acts and omissions, the defendant Randall Dee installed the suspension lift kit and oversized tires, and the acts and omissions of Ultimate Auto were a substantial contributing cause to the loss of control and resulting accident on August 29, 1998.

26. As a result of the negligent and/or grossly negligent and/or wanton, willful and reckless conduct of the defendant, Ultimate Auto, the plaintiff's intestate was killed on August 29, 1998.

COUNT V (Conscious Suffering, Ultimate Auto)

27. The plaintiff repeats and incorporates herein the allegations of paragraph 1-11 and 23-26.

28. As a result of the conduct of the defendant Ultimate Auto, as described above, the plaintiff's intestate sustained serious personal injuries, from which he suffered consciously, prior to his death on August 29, 1998.

COUNT VI (Wrongful Death, Warranties, Ultimate Auto)

29. The plaintiff repeats and incorporates herein the allegations of paragraphs 1-11 and 23-26.

30. The defendant Ultimate Auto was a merchant with respect to sale of the suspension lift kit and oversized tires. The defendant Ultimate Auto

breached implied warranties of merchantability and fitness for a particular purpose, by selling to the defendant Randall Dee, a suspension lift kit and oversized tires which, individually and in combination, rendered the Jeep unreasonably dangerous and/or by selling the suspension lift kit and oversized tires, without adequate warning or instruction with regard to their dangerous propensity.

31. As a result of the said breaches of warranty, the defendant Randall Dee installed the suspension lift kit and oversized tires. The breaches of the defendant Ultimate Auto were a substantial contributing cause to the loss of control and resulting accident on August 29, 1998. As a result of the defendant's breaches of warranty, the plaintiff's intestate was killed on August 29, 1998.

COUNT VII (Conscious Suffering, Warranties, Ultimate Auto)

32. Plaintiff repeats and incorporates herein the allegations of paragraphs 1-11, 23-26 and 29-31.

33. As a result of the breaches of warranty of the defendant Ultimate Auto, as described above, the plaintiff's intestate sustained serious personal injuries, from which he suffered consciously, prior to his death on August 29, 1998.

COUNT VIII (Wrongful Death, City of Lowell)

34. Plaintiff repeats and incorporates herein the allegations of paragraphs 1-12.

35. On or about February 19, 1999, the year after the accident, the plaintiff, through her attorney and pursuant to G.L. c. 258, §4, gave written notice of its claim to the City. No substantive response to that notice has been forthcoming.

36. The modification of the Jeep represented an imminent danger to all persons that might be affected by it, in particular, its occupants, and a clear violation of G.L. c. 90, §7P. As such, it created a special duty of care to those who might be affected by it, including the plaintiff's intestate.

37. Despite the obvious danger of immediate and foreseeable injury presented by the Jeep, police officers of the City of Lowell failed to take any effective action to reduce or eliminate the danger.

38. As a result, the Jeep was being operated in a condition of imminent danger on August 29, 1998, and the negligence of the City, through

its police officers, was a substantial contributing cause to the loss of control and resulting accident on that date.

39. As a result of the negligence of the City, its agents and employees, the plaintiff's intestate was killed on August 29, 1998.

COUNT IX (City of Lowell, Conscious Suffering)

40. The plaintiff repeats and incorporates herein the allegations of paragraphs 1-12 and 34-39.

41. As a result of the conduct of the defendant City as described above, the plaintiff's intestate sustained serious personal injuries, from which he suffered consciously, prior to his death on August 29, 1998.

WHEREFORE the plaintiff prays for the following relief:

1. Judgment on Counts I, IV, VI and VIII against the defendants Randall Dee, Ultimate Auto and City of Lowell.

   (a) To compensate the survivors of the plaintiff's intestate for the fair monetary value of the deceased for reasonably expected net income lost, services, protection, care, assistance, society, companionship, comfort, guidance, counsel and advice of the deceased.

   (b) Reasonable funeral and burial expenses.

   (c) Punitive damages in an amount of at least $5,000.00, pursuant to G.L. c. 229, §2.

2. Judgment on Counts II, V, VII and IX against the defendants Randall Dee, Ultimate Auto and City of Lowell to compensate the estate of Charles Carpenter for his pain and conscious suffering.

3. That the Court issue a temporary restraining order enjoining the defendant, Randall Dee, until further order of this court, from conveying, encumbering, or in any other manner transferring any interest, legal or equitable, in any of his assets, including but not limited to real estate, bank accounts, certificates of deposit, securities, valuables, and any other asset not immune from execution, except in the ordinary course of business.

4. That the Court issue a preliminary injunction enjoining the defendant Randall Dee, until the disposition of this action on the merits, from conveying, encumbering or in any other manner transferring any interest, legal or equitable, in any of his assets, including but not limited to real

estate, bank accounts, certificates of deposit, securities, valuables, and any other asset not immune from execution, except in the ordinary course of business.

5. That the Court issue a Temporary Restraining Order enjoining the defendant Peter Dee, until further order of this court, from conveying, encumbering, or in any other manner transferring any interest, legal or equitable, in the real estate at 91 Birch Hill Road, Lowell, Massachusetts.

6. That the Court issue a preliminary injunction enjoining the defendant, Peter Dee, until the disposition of this action on the merits, from conveying, encumbering, or in any other manner transferring any interest, legal or equitable, in the real estate at 91 Birch Hill Road, Lowell, Massachusetts.

7. That the Court, under Count III, declare null and void the conveyance of the interest of Randall Dee in the property at 91 Birch Hill Road, Lowell and/or allow satisfaction of any judgment in this action against Randall Dee to be satisfied against the interest he held in said property prior to the fraudulent conveyance.

8. That the Court issue a temporary restraining order enjoining the defendants, until further Order of the Court, from selling, or transferring in any way the Jeep CJ-7 vehicle involved or in any way modifying it, or changing its present condition.

9. That the Court issue a preliminary injunction enjoining the defendants, until the disposition of this action on the merits, from selling, or transferring in any way the Jeep CJ-7 vehicle involved or in any way modifying it, or changing its present condition.

10. PLAINTIFF CLAIMS TRIAL BY JURY.

By her attorneys,

By:___/s/ Carol Coblentz____
Carol Coblentz (BBO#304321)
Needham, Shaker and Coblentz
44 Park Place
Boston, MA 02100
(617) 555-5555

Dated: /d/

■ UNIFORM COMMERCIAL CODE §2-314. IMPLIED WARRANTY: MERCHANTABILITY; USAGE OF TRADE

(1) Unless excluded or modified . . . , a warranty that the goods shall be merchantable is implied in a contract for their sale if the seller is a merchant with respect to goods of that kind. . . .

(2) Goods to be merchantable must be at least such as

(a) pass without objection in the trade under the contract description; and

(b) in the case of fungible goods, are of fair average quality within the description; and

(c) are fit for the ordinary purposes for which such goods are used; and

(d) run, within the variations permitted by the agreement, of even kind, quality and quantity within each unit and among all units involved; and

(e) are adequately contained, packaged, and labeled as the agreement may require; and

(f) conform to the promises or affirmations of fact made on the container or label if any.

(3) Unless excluded or modified . . . other implied warranties may arise from course of dealing or usage of trade.

COMMENT

1. The seller's obligation applies to present sales as well as to contracts. . . .

2. The question when the warranty is imposed turns basically on the meaning of the terms of the agreement as recognized in the trade. . . .

3. In an action based on breach of warranty, it is of course necessary to show not only the existence of the warranty but the fact that the - warranty was broken and that the breach of the warranty was the proximate cause of the loss sustained. In such an action an affirmative showing by the seller that the loss resulted from some action or event following his own delivery of the goods can operate as a defense. Equally, evidence indicating that the seller exercised care in the manufacture, processing or selection of the goods is relevant to the issue of whether the warranty was in fact broken. Action by the buyer following an examination of the goods which ought to have indicated the defect complained of can be shown as matter bearing on whether the breach itself was the cause of the injury.

■ UNIFORM COMMERCIAL CODE §2-315. IMPLIED WARRANTY: FITNESS FOR PARTICULAR PURPOSE

Where the seller at the time of contracting has reason to know any particular purpose for which the goods are required and that the buyer is relying on the seller's skill or judgment to select or furnish suitable goods, there is unless excluded or modified under the next section an implied warranty that the goods shall be fit for such purpose.

COMMENT

1. Whether or not this warranty arises in any individual case is basically a question of fact to be determined by the circumstances of the contracting. Under this section the buyer need not bring home to the seller actual knowledge of the particular purpose for which the goods are intended or of his reliance on the seller's skill and judgment, if the circumstances are such that the seller has reason to realize the purpose, intended or that the reliance exists. . . .

2. A "particular purpose" differs from the ordinary purpose for which the goods are used in that it envisages a specific use by the buyer which is peculiar to the nature of his business whereas the ordinary purposes for which goods are used are those envisaged in the concept of merchantability and go to uses which are customarily made of the goods in question. For example, shoes are generally used for the purpose of walking upon ordinary ground, but a seller may know that a particular pair was selected to be used for climbing mountains.

A contract may of course include both a warranty of merchantability and one of fitness for a particular purpose. . . .

■ M.G.L. c. 90 §7P. HEIGHT OF MOTOR VEHICLES; ALTERATION RESTRICTED.

No person shall alter, modify or change the height of a motor vehicle with an original manufacturer's gross vehicle weight rating of up to and including ten thousand pounds, by elevating or lowering the chassis or body by more than two inches above or below the original manufacturer's specified height by use of so-called "shackle lift kits" for leaf springs or by use of lift kits for coil springs, tires, or any other means or device.

The registrar shall establish such rules and regulations for such changes in the height of motor vehicles beyond said two inches. No motor vehicle that has been so altered, modified or changed beyond the provisions of this section or the rules and regulations established by the registrar shall be operated on any way.

■ M.G.L. c. 231B §85. COMPARATIVE NEGLIGENCE; LIMITED EFFECT OF CONTRIBUTORY NEGLIGENCE AS DEFENSE.

Contributory negligence shall not bar recovery in any action by any person or legal representative to recover damages for negligence resulting in death or in injury to person or property, if such negligence was not greater than the total amount of negligence attributable to the person or persons against whom recovery is sought, but any damages allowed shall be diminished in proportion to the amount of negligence attributable to the person for whose injury, damage or death recovery is made. In determining by what amount the plaintiff's damages shall be diminished in such a case, the negligence of each plaintiff shall be compared to the total negligence of all persons against whom recovery is sought. The combined total of the plaintiff's negligence taken together with all of the negligence of all defendants shall equal one hundred per cent.

The violation of a criminal statute, ordinance or regulation by a plaintiff which contributed to said injury, death or damage, shall be considered as evidence of negligence of that plaintiff, but the violation of said statute, ordinance or regulation shall not as a matter of law and for that reason alone, serve to bar a plaintiff from recovery.

The defense of assumption of risk is hereby abolished in all actions hereunder.

The burden of alleging and proving negligence which serves to diminish a plaintiff's damages or bar recovery under this section shall be upon the person who seeks to establish such negligence, and the plaintiff shall be presumed to have been in the exercise of due care.

■ M.G.L. c. 231B §§1-4. CONTRIBUTION AMONG JOINT TORTFEASORS.

§1. (a) Except as otherwise provided in this chapter, where two or more persons become jointly liable in tort for the same injury to person or property, there shall be a right of contribution among them even though judgment has not been recovered against all or any of them.

(b) The right of contribution shall exist only in favor of a joint tortfeasor, hereinafter called tortfeasor, who has paid more than his pro rata share of the common liability, and his total recovery shall be limited to the amount paid by him in excess of his pro rata share. No tortfeasor shall be compelled to make contribution beyond his own pro rata share of the entire liability.

(c) A tortfeasor who enters into a settlement with a claimant shall not be entitled to recover contribution from another tortfeasor in respect to any amount paid in a settlement which is in excess of what was reasonable.

(d) A liability insurer, who by payment has discharged in full or in part the liability of a tortfeasor and has thereby discharged in full its obligation as insurer, shall be subrogated to the tortfeasor's right of contribution to the extent of the amount it has paid in excess of the tortfeasor's pro rata share of the common liability. This provision shall not limit or impair any right of subrogation arising from any other relationship.

(e) This chapter shall not impair any right of indemnity under existing law. Where one tortfeasor is entitled to indemnity from another, the right of the indemnity obligee shall be for indemnity and not contribution, and the indemnity obligor shall not be entitled to contribution from the obligee for any portion of his indemnity obligation.

§2. In determining the pro rata shares of tortfeasors in the entire liability (a) their relative degrees of fault shall not be considered; (b) if equity requires, the collective liability of some as a group shall constitute a single share; and (c) principles of equity applicable to contribution generally shall apply.

§3. (a) Whether or not judgment has been entered in an action against two or more tortfeasors for the same injury, contribution may be enforced by separate action.

(b) Where a judgment has been entered in an action against two or more tortfeasors for the same injury, contribution may be enforced in that action by judgment in favor of one against other judgment defendants by motion upon notice to all parties to the action.

(c) If there is a judgment for the injury against the tortfeasor seeking contribution, any separate action by him to enforce contribution must be commenced within one year after the judgment has become final by lapse of time for appeal or after appellate review.

(d) If there is no judgment for the injury against the tortfeasor seeking contribution, his right of contribution shall be barred unless he has either (1) discharged by payment, the common liability within the statute of limitations period applicable to claimant's right of action against him and has commenced his action for contribution within one year after payment, or (2) agreed, while action is pending against him, to discharge the common liability and has, within one year after the agreement, paid the liability and commenced his action for contribution.

(e) The recovery of a judgment for an injury against one tortfeasor shall not, of itself, discharge the other tortfeasors from liability for the injury unless the judgment is satisfied. The satisfaction of the judgment shall not impair any right of contribution.

(f) The judgment of the court in determining the liability of the several defendants to the claimant for an injury shall be binding as among such defendants in determining their right to contribution.

§4. When a release or covenant not to sue or not to enforce judgment is given in good faith to one or two or more persons liable in tort for the same injury:

(a) It shall not discharge any of the other tortfeasors from liability for the injury unless its terms so provide; but it shall reduce the claim against the others to the extent of any amount stipulated by the release or the covenant, or in the amount of the consideration paid for it, whichever is the greater; and

(b) It shall discharge the tortfeasor to whom it is given from all liability for contribution to any other tortfeasor.

■ WALTER VANBUSKIRK,* "LIFTING" A TRUCK

Driving around on the streets, it is not uncommon to see trucks that are higher off the ground and have larger tires than normal trucks. The process truck owners go through to achieve this effect is called "lifting" the truck. There are three basic ways to life a truck: body lifts, suspension lifts, and larger tires. Each of these types of lifts have different uses and have different effects on the center of gravity of the truck.

BODY LIFTS

All trucks and some cars have frames as the main structural member. The frame is the base which most everything else bolts onto. The body of the truck bolts onto the frame at numerous locations (apparently twelve locations on Randall Dee's Jeep). Normally, there is a small rubber spacer approximately one inch in thickness, called a body mount, between the frame and the body at each of these locations. A body lift uses larger spacers between the body and the frame to raise the body up off the frame. This has the effect of raising the fenders up higher which allows the use of larger tires.

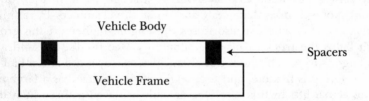

In the case, Randall Dee used hockey pucks as the spacers between the body and the frame. Although this may sound absurd, it is actually very common. However, most people will use spacers made of steel or some specially designed composite material when putting in more than two inches of lift. This approach is preferred, because the rubber hockey pucks are too compressible. Dee used 4 hockey pucks at each body mount location to achieve approximately 4″ of lift.

SUSPENSION LIFTS

Between the truck's axle and frame is the suspension. The suspension is made up of four main components: the shackle, the leaf spring, the

*Walter VanBuskirk is a 1999 graduate of Boston College Law School.

shock absorber, and the U-bolt (Note that the following graphic does not have shock absorbers or U-Bolts). The shackle attaches the leaf spring to the frame. The leaf spring is a series of "arched" strips of metal welded together, which flex to allow the vehicle to move somewhat independently of the tires. If left alone, after you hit a bump the leaf spring would continue to bounce. The shock absorber stops the leaf spring from bouncing. Finally, the U-bolt attaches the leaf spring to the axle.

To raise the suspension in a truck there are numerous options: longer shackles, larger leaf springs, or a spacer between the axle and the leaf spring (you would never use hockey pucks here). Randall Dee used larger leaf springs.

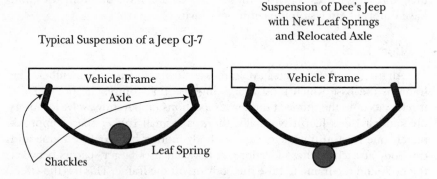

Typical Suspension of a Jeep CJ-7

Suspension of Dee's Jeep
with New Leaf Springs
and Relocated Axle

Suspension lifts are more desirable than body lifts. This type of lift actually raises the frame and everything attached to it further off the ground. Not only does that create additional tire clearance (by raising the fenders over the axle), it also raises the engine higher off the ground, which helps the truck in off-road situations. Dee used a two and a half inch larger spring. This does not always give exactly a two and a half inch lift; the spring is flexible, and the weight of the vehicle has a large effect on the actual lift. In this case Dee actually achieved a three inch lift. It should also be noted that Jeeps are strange in that they are one of the only trucks that have the axle mounted on top of the leaf spring. Most other trucks mount the axle under the leaf spring which allows the use of a spacer between the axle and leaf spring to lift the truck. Randall Dee remounted the axle under the leaf springs. This is a common step performed when lifting a Jeep.

LARGER TIRES

Basically the major use of body lifts and suspension lifts is to allow the use of bigger tires. Bigger tires give the truck more total clearance (they can drive through deeper mud and over bigger rocks). Average tires are around 28″ in diameter. The tires Randall Dee put on his Jeep were 40″ in diameter. This is a twelve inch increase in diameter, which leads to six inches of additional height over his previous tires.

DEE'S JEEP

In the case of Dee's Jeep, he put in four inches of body lift, a three inch suspension lift replacing the leaf springs, three more inches of suspension lift by remounting the axle, and larger tires adding six inches. In total Dee's Jeep is minimum of sixteen inches higher than a regular Jeep.

Randall Dee's CJ-7

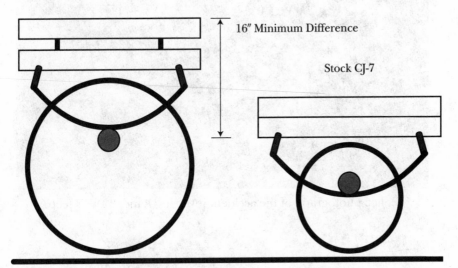

16″ Minimum Difference

Stock CJ-7

■ PHOTOGRAPHS

Police photograph of the accident involving Randall Dee's Jeep.

Police photograph of the accident involving Randall Dee's Jeep.

Close-up of the raised suspension of Randall Dee's Jeep.

COMMONWEALTH OF MASSACHUSETTS

MIDDLESEX, SS

SUPERIOR COURT DEPARTMENT
OF THE TRIAL COURT
CIVIL ACTION NO. 99-6144

NANCY CARPENTER, As
Administratrix of the Estate
of Charles Carpenter,
    Plaintiff

vs.

RANDALL DEE; PETER DEE;
CITY OF LOWELL,
    Defendants.

ULTIMATE AUTO, INC.,
Defendant and Third-Party
    Plaintiff

vs.

DALE MCGILL and
McGILL'S GARAGE, INC.,
    Third-Party Defendants.

MOTION OF DEFENDANT
ULTIMATE AUTO, INC.
TO FILE A THIRD PARTY
COMPLAINT

The defendant, Ultimate Auto, Inc., moves that the Court allow it to file the attached third-party complaint for contribution against Dale McGill and McGill's Garage, Inc.

In support thereof, the defendant Ultimate Auto, Inc. states that discovery has shown that the vehicle, which was allegedly in a defective condition at the time of the accident, had been issued an inspection sticker by the third-party defendants and that the issuance of said inspection sticker was in violation of applicable Massachusetts regulations. Accordingly, the third-party defendants would be liable as joint tortfeasors for the claims made by the plaintiff.

By its Attorneys,

___/s/ Bertram Cohen____
Bertram Cohen (BBO#641311)
Roth, McKnight & Zimmerman
111 Milk Street
Boston, MA 02100
(617) 555-0000

Dated: /d/

COMMONWEALTH OF MASSACHUSETTS

MIDDLESEX, SS

SUPERIOR COURT DEPARTMENT
OF THE TRIAL COURT
CIVIL ACTION NO. 99-6144

NANCY CARPENTER, As
Administratrix of the Estate
of Charles Carpenter,
  Plaintiff

  vs.

RANDALL DEE; PETER DEE;
CITY OF LOWELL,
  Defendants.

ULTIMATE AUTO, INC.,
  Defendant and Third-Party
  Plaintiff

  vs.

DALE MCGILL and
McGILL'S GARAGE, INC.,
  Third-Party Defendants.

THIRD PARTY COMPLAINT
OF ULTIMATE AUTO, INC.

COUNT I

1. The third-party defendant, Dale McGill, is an individual residing in Watertown, Massachusetts, and at all times material was the owner and manager of a service station doing business as McGill's Garage, Inc., in Watertown, Massachusetts.

2. The defendant/third-party plaintiff, Ultimate Auto, Inc., has been named as a party defendant in an action sounding in tort against it and in which it is alleged that the negligence of the defendant/third-party plaintiff entitled the plaintiff to recover for damages allegedly sustained as a result of a motor vehicle accident on August 29, 1998.

3. If the plaintiff did sustain injuries and damages as alleged, such injuries and damages occurred as a direct and proximate result of the negligence and carelessness of the third-party defendant, Dale McGill in approving an inspection sticker on the vehicle involved in the accident alleged in the plaintiff's complaint.

4. The third-party defendant is jointly liable for the injuries and damages allegedly sustained by the plaintiff pursuant to G.L. c. 231B, §§1-3.

WHEREFORE, the defendant/third-party plaintiff, says that if it is found liable to the plaintiff, the third-party defendant, Dale McGill, is liable to the defendant/third-party plaintiff as a joint tortfeasor.

COUNT II

5. The third-party defendant, McGill's Garage, Inc., is a Massachusetts corporation with a usual place of business in Watertown, Massachusetts, and at all times material was in the business of conducting motor vehicle inspections.

6. The defendant/third-party plaintiff, Ultimate Auto, Inc., has been named as a party defendant in an action sounding in tort against it and in which it is alleged that the negligence of the defendant/third-party plaintiff entitled the plaintiff to recover for damages allegedly sustained as a result of a motor vehicle accident on August 29, 1998.

7. If the plaintiff did sustain injuries and damages as alleged, such injuries and damages occurred as a direct and proximate result of the negligence and carelessness of employees or agents of the third-party defendant, McGill's Garage, Inc., in approving or issuing an inspection sticker on the vehicle involved in the accident alleged in the plaintiff's complaint.

8. The third-party defendant is jointly liable for the injuries and damages allegedly sustained by the plaintiff pursuant to G.L. c. 231B, §§1-3.

WHEREFORE, the defendant/third-party plaintiff, says that if it is found liable to the plaintiff, the third-party defendant, McGill's Garage, Inc., is liable to the defendant/third-party plaintiff as a joint tortfeasor.

By its Attorneys,

___/s/ Bertram Cohen____
Bertram Cohen (BBO#641311)
Roth, McKnight & Zimmerman
111 Milk Street
Boston, MA 02100
(617) 555-0000

Dated: /d/

COMMONWEALTH OF MASSACHUSETTS

MIDDLESEX, SS

SUPERIOR COURT DEPARTMENT
OF THE TRIAL COURT
CIVIL ACTION NO. 99-6144

NANCY CARPENTER, As
Administratrix of the Estate
of Charles Carpenter,
   Plaintiff

     vs.

RANDALL DEE; PETER DEE;
CITY OF LOWELL,
   Defendants.

ULTIMATE AUTO, INC.,
Defendant and Third-Party
   Plaintiff

     vs.

DALE MCGILL and
McGILL'S GARAGE, INC.,
   Third-Party Defendants.

ANSWER AND CROSS-CLAIMS
OF ULTIMATE AUTO, INC.

TRIAL BY JURY

FIRST DEFENSE

The Defendant, Ultimate Auto, Inc., ("Ultimate Auto") addresses the separately numbered paragraphs of the Complaint as follows:

1. The Defendant is without knowledge or information sufficient to form a belief as to the truth of the allegations contained in Paragraph 1.

2. The Defendant is without knowledge or information sufficient to form a belief as to the truth of the allegations contained in Paragraph 2.

3. The Defendant is without knowledge or information sufficient to form a belief as to the truth of the allegations contained in Paragraph 3.

4. The Defendant admits the allegations contained in Paragraph 4.

5. The Defendant admits the allegations contained in Paragraph 5.

6. The Defendant is without knowledge or information sufficient to form a belief as to the truth of the allegations contained in Paragraph 6.

7. The Defendant is without knowledge or information sufficient to form a belief as to the truth of the allegations contained in Paragraph 7.

8. The Defendant is without knowledge or information sufficient to form a belief as to the truth of the allegations contained in Paragraph 8.

9. The Defendant denies the allegations contained in Paragraph 9.

10. The Defendant denies the allegations contained in Paragraph 10.

11. The Defendant denies the allegations contained in Paragraph 11.

12. The Defendant is without knowledge or information sufficient to form a belief as to the truth of the allegations contained in Paragraph 12.

13-21. The Defendant makes no answer to the allegations of these Paragraphs because they do not purport to make a claim against it.

22. The Defendant repeats and realleges its answers to Paragraphs 1-11.

23. The Defendant denies the allegations contained in Paragraph 23.

24. The Defendant denies the allegations contained in Paragraph 24.

25. The Defendant denies the allegations contained in Paragraph 25.

26. The Defendant denies the allegations contained in Paragraph 26.

27. The Defendant repeats and realleges its answers to Paragraphs 1-11 and 23-26.

28. The Defendant denies the allegations contained in Paragraph 28.

29. The Defendant repeats and realleges its answers to Paragraphs 1-11 and 23-26.

30. The Defendant denies the allegations contained in Paragraph 30.

31. The Defendant denies the allegations contained in Paragraph 31.

32. The Defendant repeats and realleges its answers to Paragraphs 1-11, 23-26, and 29-31.

33. The Defendant denies the allegations contained in Paragraph 33.

34-41. The Defendant makes no answer to the allegations of these Paragraphs because they do not purport to make a claim against it.

SECOND DEFENSE

This action is barred by operation of the applicable statute of limitations.

THIRD DEFENSE

If the Plaintiff is entitled to recover against the Defendant, any such recovery must be reduced in accordance with the comparative negligence statute as enacted in the Commonwealth, since the Plaintiff's own negligence was the proximate cause of the injury sustained.

FOURTH DEFENSE

Any loss sustained by the Plaintiff resulted from his own negligence, which was greater in degree than any negligence of the Defendant and therefore the Plaintiff is barred from recovery in this action.

FIFTH DEFENSE

The Defendant is exempt from liability to the extent provided by the Massachusetts "no fault" statutes, G.L. c. 90, section 34m, and G.L. c. 231 section 6d.

SIXTH DEFENSE

The Plaintiff has failed to give notice of breach of warranty, and the Defendant has thereby been prejudiced.

CROSS-CLAIM AGAINST RANDALL DEE, PETER DEE AND THE CITY OF LOWELL

1. If the Plaintiff's decedent was injured as alleged by the Plaintiff, he was injured as a result of the negligence of the Defendants, Randall Dee, Peter Dee, and/or the City of Lowell.

2. The Defendants, Randall Dee, Peter Dee, and the City of Lowell, are liable to the Defendant, Ultimate Auto, Inc. for contribution pursuant to G.L. c. 231B.

WHEREFORE, the Defendant Ultimate Auto, Inc., demands judgment for contribution against the Defendants, Randall Dee and Peter Dee.

THE DEFENDANT, ULTIMATE AUTO, INC., DEMANDS TRIAL BY JURY ON ALL CLAIMS.

By its Attorneys,

___/s/ Bertram Cohen____
Bertram Cohen (BBO#641311)
Roth, McKnight & Zimmerman
111 Milk Street
Boston, MA 02100
(617) 555-0000

Dated: /d/

COMMONWEALTH OF MASSACHUSETTS

MIDDLESEX, SS

SUPERIOR COURT DEPARTMENT
OF THE TRIAL COURT
CIVIL ACTION NO. 99-6144

NANCY CARPENTER, As
Administratrix of the Estate
of Charles Carpenter,
    Plaintiff

PLAINTIFF'S REQUEST FOR
PRODUCTION OF DOCUMENTS
BY ULTIMATE AUTO, INC.

    vs.

RANDALL DEE; PETER DEE;
ULTIMATE AUTO, INC.; and
CITY OF LOWELL,
    Defendants.

The plaintiff, Nancy Carpenter, hereby requests of defendant, Ultimate Auto, Inc., that the plaintiff be permitted to inspect and copy the originals and copies of the following designated documents, writings, photographs, or tangible things. Production, inspection and copying shall take place at the office of defendant's counsel, within thirty days of the receipt of this notice or at such other place and time as may be agreed upon by counsel for the parties.

If, in response to any of the following requests, production of a document is denied on the basis of attorney-client privilege or trial-preparation/work-product materials, kindly indicate sufficient information concerning said document and the claimed privilege to enable the court to assess the applicability of said privilege, including the nature of the document withheld, the identity of its author, the current custodian of the document, the date the document was prepared, and the exact privilege being asserted.

DEFINITIONS

A. "The accident" refers to the alleged accident described in plaintiff's complaint as occurring on or about August 29, 1998.

B. "The motor vehicle" means the Jeep CJ-7 alleged to have caused the plaintiff's injuries and described in the plaintiff's complaint.

C. "Ultimate Auto, Inc." means the defendant Ultimate Auto, Inc., its officers, agents, and employees.

D. The term "documents" as used herein includes writings of any sort, drawings, graphs, charts, photographs, and other data compilations.

REQUESTS

1. All promotional and descriptive material in your possession relating in any way to oversize tires.

2. All promotional and descriptive material in your possession relating in any way to suspension lift kits.

3. All documents in your possession which comment upon, or relate in any way to, Massachusetts General Laws c. 90, §7P.

4. A copy of all warnings and instructions which accompany suspension lift kits and/or oversize tires.

5. All warranties pertaining to the above products.

6. All complaints, letters, notices, claims or suit papers which constitute, reflect or relate to any claims as described in plaintiff's Interrogatory No. 11.*

7. All studies, reports, literature, research or documents of any other kind and description, relating in any way to the alteration in vehicle handling or driving characteristics (including, but not limited to change in its propensity to roll over) as result of alteration of vehicle height.

8. Copies of all industry and trade standards which reflect, or relate in any way to, the design, construction or configuration of automobile parts which have the purpose or effect of altering vehicle height.

9. Copies of all insurance policies (primary or excess) affording coverage to the defendant for this loss.

10. Copies of all statements secured at any time from plaintiff, or from any member of the plaintiff's family, and whether such statements be recorded or written, signed or unsigned.

11. All written warnings or instructions, which you have ever furnished to any customer, relating in any way to alteration of the

Eds. Note: Plaintiff's Interrogatory No. 11 can be found reprinted in Ultimate Auto's Answers to Interrogatories in these case files.

handling or driving characteristics of the vehicle (including, but not limited to, its propensity to roll over) as a result of modification of vehicle height.

By her Attorneys,

By:___/s/ Carol Coblentz____
Carol Coblentz (BBO#304321)
Needham, Shaker and Coblentz
44 Park Place
Boston, MA 02100
(617) 555-5555

Dated: /d/

COMMONWEALTH OF MASSACHUSETTS

MIDDLESEX, SS

SUPERIOR COURT DEPARTMENT
OF THE TRIAL COURT
CIVIL ACTION NO. 99-6144

NANCY CARPENTER, As
Administratrix of the Estate
of Charles Carpenter,
   Plaintiff

vs.

RANDALL DEE; PETER DEE;
ULTIMATE AUTO, INC.; and
CITY OF LOWELL,
   Defendants.

RESPONSE OF DEFENDANT
ULTIMATE AUTO, INC. TO
PLAINTIFF'S REQUEST FOR
PRODUCTION OF DOCUMENTS

1. Catalogue and specification sheet to be produced.

2. Manufacturer's brochure to be produced.

3. Registry of Motor Vehicle regulation to be produced.

4. The defendant has no such documents in his possession, custody or control other than the documents produced in response to requests no. 1 and 2.

5. The defendant has no such documents in his possession, custody or control.

6. The defendant has no such documents in his possession, custody or control.

7. The defendant has no such documents in his possession, custody or control.

8. The defendant, by its attorney, objects to this request on the grounds that it is vague and does not specify with particularity the documents sought.

9. Insurance policy to be produced.

10. The defendant has no such documents in his possession, custody or control.

11. The defendant has no such documents in his possession, custody or control.

By its Attorneys,

___/s/ Bertram Cohen___
Bertram Cohen (BBO#641311)
Roth, McKnight & Zimmerman
111 Milk Street
Boston, MA 02100
(617) 555-0000

Dated: /d/

COMMONWEALTH OF MASSACHUSETTS

MIDDLESEX, SS

SUPERIOR COURT DEPARTMENT
OF THE TRIAL COURT
CIVIL ACTION NO. 99-6144

NANCY CARPENTER, As
Administratrix of the Estate
of Charles Carpenter,
    Plaintiff

ANSWERS OF DEFENDANT
ULTIMATE AUTO, INC. TO
PLAINTIFF'S INTERROGATORIES

    vs.

RANDALL DEE; PETER DEE;
ULTIMATE AUTO, INC.; and
CITY OF LOWELL,
    Defendants.

1. Please identify yourself by stating your full name, residential address, business address, employer, occupation and job title.*

Adam Jenkins, 11 Weeping Willow Road, Lexington, MA, President of Ultimate Auto, Inc.

2. Before proceeding further, please consult with all necessary persons, and review all necessary documents, to answer the remaining interrogatories. Have you done so?

Yes.

3. If you are a member of any trade associations, related in any way in whole or in part to the design, manufacture, sale, or use of automotive parts, which have the purpose or effect of modifying the height of vehicles, please identify all such organizations including: (a) name; (b) address; (c) inclusive dates of your membership; and (d) the name of any publications which you regularly receive from such organizations.

Specialty Equipment Manufacturers Associations.

4. Were you, or anyone employed by your company, aware of the existence of Massachusetts General Laws c. 90 section 7P. Unless the answer is

---

* *Eds. Note*: The Local Rules of many courts require that answers to interrogatories also contain the questions being answered. This makes it easier for judges and lawyers to comprehend and use the answers.

in the unqualified negative, kindly state the name, residential address and position with your company of all persons who were so aware.

Yes. Cecil Sylvester.

5. If you expect to call any person as an expert witness at the trial of this case, kindly state (a) the name and address of each person whom you expect to call as an expert witness at trial; (b) the subject matter on which each person whom you expect to call as an expert witness at trial is expected to testify, and his qualifications as an expert in that area; (c) the substance of the facts and opinions to which each expert is expected to testify and a summary of the grounds for each such opinion; and (d) the formal education (including the college and post-graduate education) of each such expert, each job or position such person has held in his area of expertise and the dates of such employment, membership in professional societies of each such expert, and identify all publications of each such subject in his field of expertise.

Unknown at the present time.

6. With respect to any primary, or excess liability insurance applicable to the plaintiff's claim, please state the insurer, effective dates of the policy, and applicable coverage limits.

$500,000/$500,000 single limit bodily injury coverage, The Travelers Insurance Company, effective on the date of the loss alleged in the plaintiff's complaint.

7. Please identify all automotive parts ever purchased by the defendant, Randall Dee, at your company, including the exact description of such parts, date or purchase and purchase price.

It is unknown what, if any, any automotive parts were ever purchased by Randall Dee from Ultimate Auto. This question is presently being investigated by my attorney in connection with discovery in this action.

8. If you provided Randall Dee with any oral or written warning or instruction, relating in any way to change in the driving characteristics of modified vehicles (including, but not limited to, an increased propensity to rollover) please state (a) the exact content of such warning; (b) the date; and (c) the person or persons who gave such warning or instruction.

It is unknown what, if any, automotive parts were ever purchased by Randall Dee from Ultimate Auto. This question is presently being investigated by my attorney in this action.

9. Are you, or is anyone in your company, aware that Monster Tire's 38 inch "Monster Mudder" tires (hereinafter "the Monster Tires") if mounted on a 1986 Jeep CJ7 (with necessary modifications to allow the mounting of such tires) could alter the driving and handling characteristics of the vehicle. Unless the answer is in the unqualified negative, kindly state (a) when you first became aware of this; (b) the name, address and company position of all persons with such awareness; and (c) in as much detail as possible, please describe what characteristics you were aware could be affected.

The defendant, by his attorney, objects to this interrogatory on the grounds that it is not clear what modifications are included in the term "necessary." Without waiving this objection the defendant states that both at, and after, the date of the accident, alleged in the plaintiff's complaint Adam Jenkins was aware that any modification to the center of gravity of a vehicle by the addition of tires could, depending on the vehicle, and other variables, affect the handling of the vehicle.

10. Are you, or is anyone in your company, aware that Rodeo Suspension kit lifts if mounted on a 1986 Jeep CJ7 could alter the driving and handling characteristics of the vehicle. Unless the answer is in the unqualified negative, kindly state (a) when you first became aware of this; (b) the name, address and company position of all persons with such awareness; and (c) in as much detail as possible, please describe what characteristics you were aware could be affected.

No.

11. If you have ever received any claim or lawsuit, relating in any way to a vehicle rolling over, after the installation of any parts (including, but not limited to suspension lift kits and tires) purchased at your company, please state as to each such claim or lawsuit (a) the name of the person or persons involved in such claim or lawsuit; (b) name of plaintiff's attorney, if any; (c) date of receipt of the claim or lawsuit; (d) date of the incident; (e) the current status of such claim or lawsuit; and (f) the court, caption and docket number of each such claim which resulted in litigation.

Not applicable.

12. Please identify the officers, directors, agent, servant or employee of the defendant with the most knowledge as to each of the following topics, including such individuals' full name, residential address, business address and position; (a) training of your company's sales personnel; (b) warnings or instructions issued to customers with regard to changes in

handling or driving characteristics as a result of altering the height of a vehicle; and (c) the status of any claims or lawsuits described in Interrogatory No. 11 above.

Cecil Sylvester.

Signed under the pains and penalties of perjury
ULTIMATE AUTO, INC.

By: ___/s/ Adam Jenkins____
Adam Jenkins

COMMONWEALTH OF MASSACHUSETTS

MIDDLESEX, SS   SUPERIOR COURT DEPARTMENT
                                  OF THE TRIAL COURT
                                  CIVIL ACTION NO. 99-6144

NANCY CARPENTER, As
Administratrix of the Estate
of Charles Carpenter,
   Plaintiff   TRANSCRIPT OF DEPOSITION
                                  OF DEFENDANT RANDALL DEE

   vs.

RANDALL DEE; PETER DEE;
ULTIMATE AUTO, INC.; and
CITY OF LOWELL,
   Defendants.

Deposition of Randall Dee, taken on behalf of the Plaintiff, pursuant to Notice under the applicable Rules of the Massachusetts Rules of Civil Procedure, before Rochelle D. Baron, a Shorthand Reporter and Notary Public in and for the Commonwealth of Massachusetts, at the Offices of Needham, Shaker & Coblentz on Thursday, xxxxx, xx,* commencing at 10:30 a.m.

APPEARANCES
   ROSEMARY NEEDHAM, ESQ. and CAROL COBLENTZ, ESQ., For
      Plaintiff.
   GWENDOLYN FRANCIS, ESQ., For Defendant Randall Dee.
   BERTRAM COHEN, ESQ., For Defendant Ultimate Auto, Inc.
   CAITLIN TALBOT, ESQ., For Defendant City of Lowell.
. . .

---

* *Eds. Note*: In the actual case, this deposition was taken six months after the complaint was filed and prior to the adding of Ultimate Auto, Inc. and the City of Lowell as defendants.

MS. COBLENTZ: Let me propose the following stipulations. The witness will read and sign the deposition. We will waive the notarization, sealing and filing; reserve all objections, except as to form, and reserve all motions to strike, except as to form.

RANDALL DEE, a witness called by the plaintiff, having been first duly sworn, was examined and testified as follows:

DIRECT EXAMINATION BY *MS. COBLENTZ:* Mr. Dee, my name is Carol Coblentz. I represent the plaintiff in this action. I'm going to be asking you a series of questions. It is not my intent to trick you in any way. If you, therefore, don't understand a question or it's unclear to you, please let me know, and I'll rephrase it or repeat it. And if you don't ask me to do that, I will assume you understand it.

If you hear an objection from your attorney, you go ahead and answer unless I instruct you not to answer. And if you want a break at any time, just let me know about that as well. Would you state your name, please?

A: Randall Dee

Q: Where do you live, sir?

A: 91 Birch Hill Road, Lowell.

Q: And how long have you lived at that house?

A: Twenty-five years.

Q: And that's the house that you grew up in that your parents owned?

A: Yes.

Q: What's your Social Security number?

A: I'm not—I don't know it by heart.

Q: Do you have a driver's license with you today?

A: Yes.

Q: Is this your driver's license?

A: Yes.

Q: And is your Social Security number your driver's license as well?

A: Yes.

Q: Mr. Dee, are your parents both deceased?

A: Yes.

Q: And what were their names?

A: Dorothy Dee and Richard Dee.

Q: And do you know approximately when they purchased the house that you live in now, approximately?

A: Twenty-five years ago—about 25 years ago.

[We have omitted three pages of deposition regarding the transfer of the Dee house to Randall and his three siblings.]

Q: Mr. Dee, tell me when you first got your driver's license, approximately.

A: Five years ago.

Q: And what's your current age?

A: Twenty-five.

Q: So it was several years after you were first entitled to apply that you got it.

A: Yes. I think it was about—it might have been two years after or—I'm not sure. I forget. I think I might have been 19.

Q: Did you take driver's education in school?

A: No.

Q: Did you graduate from high school?

A: Yes.

Q: Lowell?

A: Lowell Vocational High School.

Q: And what course did you take there?

A: Auto body.

Q: And you are presently employed?

A: Yes.

Q: By whom?

A: Raytheon of Waltham.

Q: And what do you do, sir?

A: I am a plater, metal finisher.

Q: And how long have you been at Raytheon?

A: Four years.

Q: And your present rate of pay is what?

A: What do you mean?

Q: Are you paid on an hourly basis?

A: Yes.

Q: What do you make an hour?

A: I think it's around $12 or something.

Q: And you work a 40-hour week?

A: Yes.

Q: Do you get overtime as well?

A: Very little but I do.

Q: And that's time and a half?

A: Yes.

Q: Did you take driving instruction from anyone?

A: No.

Q: Just kind of learned O.J.T., as they say?

A: Yes.

Q: Have you ever held a job in which driving was a part of your duties?

A: No.

Q: What was the first car that you owned?

A: I never owned a car. I had never actually owned a car.

Q: The Jeep that you were driving at the time of this accident was registered to whom?

A: Twyla Burrell.

Q: And Burrell was an old girlfriend of yours?

A: Yes.

Q: And did you, in fact, live with her at some time?

A: Yes.

Q: Was her legal address 91 Birch Hill Road?

A: For a while before the accident.

Q: Now, when did you and she stop living together, approximately?

A: I'm not—

Q: It was before the accident?

A: Yes.

Q: A year or so before, something like that?

A: Yes.

Q: When was that vehicle purchased by Twyla Burrell?

A: Would have to be around '95 or '94, I'd say.

Q: And it was a 1986 Jeep CJ-7?

A: Yes.

Q: Where was it purchased from?

A: Some car auction, I think, in Concord maybe.

[We have omitted the portion of the deposition regarding Randall's acquisition of the Jeep from Twyla Burrell.]

Q: Can you help me at all in terms of the specific date when the Jeep was purchased?

A: I'm not too sure. It had to be '95 maybe. I could find out, but I'm not too sure.

Q: Now, were any modifications made to the Jeep?

A: Yes.

Q: I want to talk about those in as much detail as we can and to talk about each of them separately. First of all, let me start with tires. When the Jeep was purchased, what kind of tires did it have, if you know?

A: It had stock tires.

Q: And do you know the size of those tires?

A: Fifteen inch.

Q: Would that be stock for a Jeep CJ-7?

A: Yes.

Q: At some point, much larger tires were put on, is that right?

A: Yes.

Q: Were the stock tires that were on it in good condition?

A: No. They were worn out.

Q: So they needed to be replaced anyway.

A: Yes.

Q: Did you immediately replace them with larger tires?

A: I had to lift the Jeep before I could put the bigger tires on.

Q: And when you say "lift the Jeep," you mean raise the suspension?

A: Yes.

Q: And we'll get to that. When and where did you purchase the larger tires?

A: I purchased them at Ultimate Auto, Inc.

Q: And these tires are called Monster Tires, is that right?

A: Yes.

Q: Is that a brand name, or do you know what the brand was?

A: That may be the brand. Though it might be technically something else.

Q: And what size tires were these?

A: They were 40 inch, 15's but 40 inch.

Q: In other words, the inner radius—

A: The rim was 15-inch rim.

Q: Fifteen-inch rim which is the same as the stock rim?

A: Yes.

Q: But the diameter of the tire is much larger.

A: Yes.

Q: And is 40 inch the diameter of the tire?

A: Yes.

Q: So it's over three feet. And the suspension needs to be raised to accommodate that.

A: Yes.

Q: Had you previously raised the suspension before you purchased the tires?

A: Yes.

Q: And tell me what you did to do that.

A: Well, I bought a lift kit, a suspension—a suspension lift kit from the same place, Ultimate Auto and then I—and that raised it, I think, three inches—

Q: The lift kit alone raised it three inches.

A: —and stiffened up the suspension. And then I raised the body from the frame four inches with spaces underneath the body of the Jeep to the frame and that gave—

Q: So that was a total of seven inches—

A: Yes.

Q: —which gave you enough clearance to fit the tires.

A: Fit the tires.

Q: And now, having raised it seven inches, could the car then work? I mean I understand it would have looked silly. Would it have worked on stock tires?

A: Yes.

Q: And if it had stock tires, say, at the roof line, it still would have been even inches higher.

A: Yes.

Q: And with the Monster Tires, how much additional height was added?

A: It probably raised a foot?

Q: So that overall, it had been lifted as much as one foot seven inches, am I right?

A: Approximately.

Q: What I want to do, Mr. Dee, is go into this in detail, and you have to bear with me because I'm not an auto mechanic. And I want to understand it as much as I can.

MS. FRANCIS: Can I just interject. I don't think there's anything to show that there's actual figures or that this is on his own estimate. I understand you've given us your best judgment about the height, and I understand you haven't measured them to the fraction of an inch.

A: Yes.

Q: Did you purchase the lift kit at the same time as you purchased tires to raise the body?

Was that all done at the same time?

A: What do you mean?

Q: Okay. The lift kit contained some specific materials that are used to raise the suspension.

A: Are we talking about now the suspension or the body?

Q: The suspension.

A: They're just springs that are arced greater than a stock spring, and that's what gives you the lift.

Q: And you also purchased a kind of rubber disc as a spacer.

A: Not for the suspension; that's for the body.

Q: Did you do the work yourself?

A: Yes.

Q: Did anyone help you?

A: Charlie did a little bit, but it was mostly me.

Q: Charlie Carpenter?

A: Yes.

Q: Where did you do the work?

A: I did it in my backyard, my driveway.

Q: Did you need a lift to do any of this work?

A: Just a floor jack.

Q: And how long did it take you to do that work?

A: A couple of months, two months.

Q: Let's start by having you describe for me what parts you purchased from Ultimate Auto.

A: Okay. I purchased the Monster Tires, right —

Q: Four of them?

A: Four of them, yes—and—

Q: What was the cost of those? [Discussion off the record.]

Q: Is it your best memory that the tires were $300 each?

A: No. The tires were 200 each and the rims were $50 each for a rim. So four—four rims was $200 and the tires were 200 each.

Q: So that's a thousand.

A: Yes, plus the tax or whatever. It came to roughly—I guess I got the receipt—1200. Gee, and if I had gone to New Hampshire, I would have saved the tax.

Q: So it was about 1200 just for the tires and rims?

A: Yes.

Q: And with tax, excise tax and so forth.

A: Yes.

Q: Am I correct that you purchased those after you had already done the work to lift the car?

A: Yes.

Q: So the first thing you purchased was what?

A: The leaf spring, the suspension lift at Ultimate Auto.

MS. COBLENTZ: I have a pretty good idea what a leaf spring looks like but let's go off the record a minute.

[Discussion off the record.]

Q: We're to do this by drawing of words as opposed to pictures.

A: Yes.

Q: The first thing that you did was you replaced the stock leaf spring with a more arced spring.

A: Yes.

Q: And the upper part of the spring connects to the frame of the Jeep and the lower part connects to the axle.

A: Right.

Q: So that by increasing the arc, it has the effect of raising the frame relative to the axle, is that correct?

A: Yes.

Q: And the stiffer and more arced spring raises the frame relative to the axle by how much, approximately?

A: I think it was a three inch. Two and a half inch it says on the—two and a half inch suspension lift they sell it.

Q: So there is a box that calls it a two and a half inch lift.

A: Yes, Rodeo is the name.

Q: Rodeo?

A: Yes.

Q: Do you, by any chance, have any of the boxes or any of the instructions for that equipment?

A: Probably not.

Q: But it was called Rodeo?

A: Yes.

Q: And this was purchased at Ultimate Auto?

A: Yes.

Q: Now, did you purchase the body lift materials at the same time?

A: No.

Q: Did you buy four springs?

A: Yes.

Q: And what was the cost, approximately?

A: I think it cost 350 or 300 and change.

Q: So about 80 or $85 per spring, correct?

A: About that.

Q: Was that the first thing you

purchased to do the modification?

Q: Yes.

Q: And then at a subsequent time, you purchased the kit to lift the body relative to the frame.

A: Yes.

Q: And what is that called?

A: It's called a body lift.

Q: And is the term "hockey puck" sometimes used to describe that?

A: Well, what happened is I called Crazy Larry's, a place where they sell body lifts. I called the place to purchase it, and they—I don't know who the guy was, but he said, "Everybody's using hockey pucks. It's the hardest rubber in the world." He was buying hockey pucks and using them as body lifts so that's what I did. I went out and I bought a bunch of hockey pucks.

Q: An actual hockey puck in a sporting goods store?

A: Yes.

Q: Do you know where you bought them?

A: City Sports in Waltham.

Q: So you literally used hockey pucks.

A: Yes.

Q: Did you get this advice over the phone?

A: Yes.

Q: From Crazy Larry's?

A: Yes.

Q: Who gave you the advice about the body lifts?

A: I don't remember who it was because I was calling around

a bunch of places looking for a body lift.

Q: Did Ultimate Auto sell body lifts?

A: Yes everybody did.

Q: Do you have any way of remembering who you talked to there?

A: No, no. I called so many locations. I forget who told me. I'm not too sure who said, but he said everybody's using hockey pucks so—

Q: Do you know what that body lift kit looks like?

A: Yes.

Q: Does it, in fact, consist of a rubber—

A: They are Spacers; they're round; some are made out of aluminum; some are made out of steel. And they're just round pieces of metal with a hole through the middle. You just put—you just lift the body a little from the frame and fill it in and put body bolts back in.

Q: So it's just a cylinder really.

A: That's all.

Q: Okay. And does Ultimate Auto specialize in conversion of vehicles?

A: I don't know if—they don't do it themselves. They sell the parts, but they don't actually do any of the work.

Q: And they sell racing tires and so forth.

A: They sell everything.

Q: So it's a specialty store—

A: Yes.

Q: —for people who want to modify cars either in terms of racing them or speeding them up or things of that sort.

A: Or four-wheeling.

Q: Or four-wheeling. Now, when you bought the hockey pucks, what did you do, you drill out a hole in them?

A: Yes.

Q: And you pile—

A: Four on—

Q: —four on top of each other.

A: Yes.

Q: So let's say a hockey puck's about an inch and a half thick.

A: No, an inch thick.

Q: So that raised it four inches.

A: Yes.

Q: When you purchased the hockey pucks, did you, by any chance, tell City Sports what you were going to use them for?

A: No. I told them I owned a hockey team.

Q: So you bought 16 pucks.

A: I bought about 50 of them.

Q: Fifty of them?

A: Sure.

Q: Because they wear out?

A: No. You got—

Q: I thought you said four on each wheel.

A: No. We're talking about the body now. From the frame, you got—you got about 12 mount—12 spots where the body bolts to the frame so you got to put four, four, four and four.

Q: So at every point where the body bolts to the frame you put four hockey pucks as a spacer.

A: Yes.

Q: Is that something you had heard about before, the use—

A: Everybody was doing it.

Q: —the use of hockey pucks?

A: Everybody was doing it. They were cheaper, for one thing. And you are better off having rubber in between to absorb the shock rather than metal, metal to metal.

Everybody was using the hockey pucks.

MS. COBLENTZ: Off the record.

[Discussion off the record.]

Q: And then after you did that, you then went back and purchased the Monster Tires.

A: Yes.

Q: Do you remember the names of the persons you dealt with at Ultimate Auto.

A: No. They changed. He never gets the same salesmen. They come and go at that place. I wouldn't remember.

Q: Is the place still in existence?

A: Yes.

Q: Are Monster Tire tires designed specifically for Jeeps?

A: No.

MS. FRANCIS: I don't know if he'd know that information anyways.

Q: If you know. Are they made for four-wheel-drive vehicles?

A: They're made for anything, any type of vehicle.

Q: Are they designed for off-road use?

A: Yes.

Q: They're pretty knobby?

A: Yes.

Q: But they will also operate on the road?

A: Yes.

Q: And I am correct that with a tire of that size that you would be unable to accommodate it without doing both the suspension lift and the body lift?

A: Yes.

Q: Had you ever had prior experience modifying vehicles?

A: No.

Q: Did you teach yourself to do this?

A: Yes.

Q: Did you use any printed materials to learn how to do it?

A: No. I looked in books, but like Off Road magazine or something. It was a fad. Everybody was lifting.

Q: Did you subscribe to any of those magazines?

A: No.

Q: You just purchased them someplace?

A: Yes.

Q: Do you know the name of any specific ones that you used?

A: Magazine?

Q: Yes.

A: Off Road, I think it's called.

Q: Did you use an article in Off Road as a kind of "how to" or a manual to help you do this?

A: No.

Q: Had you gotten any instruction in this during your high school vocational training?

A: No.

Q: I take it that from a mechanical point of view it wasn't terribly complicated.

A: No.

Q: Now, did you ever learn in high school or from any source that Jeeps were known to have a roll-over problem?

A: Yes.

Q: And where did you first learn that?

A: I think I seen it on the TV, 20/20.

Q: On 20/20 or Sixty Minutes?

A: Something like that there was an article.

Q: Was that before this accident, if you know?

A: I think it was after. I'm not sure.

Q: Did you know at the time when you made the modifications that raising the height of a vehicle can affect its handling characteristics?

A: Yes.

Q: And did you know that raising the height of a vehicle can, among other things, affect its propensity to roll over?

A: I didn't know. I figured it would make it better because the tires were heavier. You got heavy tires at the bottom. Now you got more weight at the bottom of the vehicle now than the top so I figured it would roll less.

Q: You actually thought it would roll less because of the weight of the tires—

A: Yes.

Q: —even though the overall height was raised as much as it was?

A: Yes.

Q: When you purchased the Monster Tires at Ultimate Auto did the salesman give you any instructions concerning their use?

A: No.

Q: Did he tell you about anything to watch out for?

A: No.

Q: Did he ask you what vehicle you were putting them on?

A: No.

Q: Just sold them to you?

A: That's all.

Q: You paid the money and they went out.

A: You got it, right, yes.

Q: Same question with respect to the suspension raiser, suspension lift kit, did you get any warnings or instructions when you purchased that?

A: No, no.

Q: And were there any questions about what use you were going to put these parts to?

A: What do you mean, any questions?

Q: Did he give you any instructions?

A: Oh, the same man?

Q: Yes, the same man.

A: No, they just hand them to you and you give them the money.

Q: Were there any warnings or instructions in the suspension lift kits concerning their use?

A: Not that I know of. I didn't see any.

Q: I may have asked you and I forgot the answer, the manufacturer of the Monster Tires?

A: I think that's their name.

Q: Do they make other kinds of tires? It's not a name that's familiar to me.

A: I'm not too sure. It's not a familiar name. I'm not sure if that's all they make.

Q: Are these tires still on the car?

A: Yes.

Q: And the car is where?

A: It's in my driveway.

Q: And you know that you're not allowed to modify it.

A: I don't even think—it's rotting there.

Q: Did you do maintenance work on the jeep yourself?

A: Yes.

Q: Did you ever have maintenance work on it performed anywhere else?

A: No.

Q: Did you do all the work on it yourself?

A: Yes.

Q: Do you remember any of the maintenance you did on it?

A: Changed the oil, spark plugs.

Q: Did you do any engine work on it at all?

A: No. It's basically stock. I put a header on it, but other than that, it was all stock.

Q: So, to the best of your judgment, that car never saw the inside of an auto mechanic's door after you got it.

A: No.

Q: Do you remember where the vehicle was inspected?

A: Yes.

Q: Where was that?

A: McGill's.

Q: If I suggest to you December of 1997, does that sound about right as the last inspection?

A: I can't recall.

Q: But you know that it was inspected prior to the accident.

A: Yes.

Q: Now, by December 1997, had the modifications all been done?

A: That means before it's been inspected, you mean?

Q: Yes.

A: Oh, yes.

Q: So if, in fact, it was inspected in December of 1997, the inspector was looking at a very modified vehicle, correct—

A: Yes.

Q: —and with all of the modifications we've talked about.

A: Yes.

Q: I'd just like to talk about your driving history. You indicated that you started driving, you thought, about age 19, approximately.

A: I think it was 19.

Q: Prior to this accident, were you charged with any motor vehicle violations, excluding parking.

A: Yes.

Q: And I'd like to talk about them in order, starting with the earliest that you can recall.

A: Let me think. I think the only one was drunk driving.

Q: And do you recall when that was?

MS. FRANCIS: Approximate time.

A: I forget.

MS. FRANCIS: Do you want to go off the record to refresh your recollection?

[Discussion off the record.]

Q: I have some information suggesting that in April of 1998 you were charged with driving under the influence. Does that sound correct?

A: Yes.

Q: Do you know any of the officers involved?

A: Yes.

Q: And who were they? I'm talking about that stop now.

A: With the drunk driving?

Q: Drunk driving, right.

MS. FRANCIS: Do you want to go off the record to refresh your recollection?

A: Ricky Murdoch, the officer was Ricky Murdoch.

Q: M-U-R-D-O-C-H?

A: That's close enough.

Q: Do you know any other of the officers involved with that?

A: No.

Q: Were you driving the Jeep at that time?

A: Yes.

Q: And it had, of course, been modified?

A: Yes.

Q: Did the officers at that time make any comments to you about the Jeep?

A: No.

Q: What was the outcome of that charge?

A: What did they do to me?

Q: Yes.

A: I was found guilty of DWI and I lost my license—loss of license for 30 days, and I had to go to school, drunk driving school, for so many hours. I'm not sure how many hours.

Q: Now, when your license is pulled, do you physically give up your license?

A: Yes.

Q: You hand it, what, to the clerk or something in court?

A: Yes.

Q: And then you get it back later?

A: In 30 days from the date you give it to them, they'll give it back to you providing you go to that—

Q: Now, as I understand it, at the time of this accident, you didn't have your license in your possession, is that correct?

A: Yes.

Q: Am I correct?

A: Yes.

Q: But you did, in fact, have a license at that time.

A: Yes.

Q: It had been returned?

A: Oh, are we talking about—

Q: At the time of this accident that we're here for.

A: I didn't have it on me, but I did have a license.

Q: You mentioned another incident. There was something about there not being a side mirror.

A: Well, I was never cited for that.

Q: But were you pulled over for it?

A: Yes.

Q: Do you know the name of the officer who did that?

A: No.

Q: But it was a uniformed Lowell police officer?

A: Yes.

Q: And when was that, first of all?

A: It was prior to the accident. I'm not too sure.

Q: Was it prior to the drunk driving charge?

A: Yes.

Q: Was it in 1997?

A: Yes.

Q: So it was—and so at that time, the vehicle had been modified again.

A: Yes.

Q: And could you tell me what the officer said?

A: He told me to—he told me—he said, "Take the vehicle home and don't take it back out on the road till you get a mirror on it, a rear view mirror." So I took it home and I put a mirror on it.

Q: You're talking about a side mirror—

A: Yes.

Q: —not the inner rear view mirror.

A: No.

Q: The driver's side mirror.

A: Yes.

Q: And you did that?

A: Yes.

Q: And did that officer make any comment on the height of the vehicle or anything related to its height?

A: No.

Q: And again, that was in 1997?

A: Yes.

Q: Now, were there any other motor vehicle violations that you have had up to this accident?

A: Yes.

Q: And what was that?

A: I was pulled over for being unregistered, uninsured in that Jeep. What happened is it was insured, but the little sticker that goes on your plate there—you know how they send you a card, renewal— registration renewal, well, either I never got the card or something so I didn't notice that little sticker had expired. So I was pulled over in that Jeep. They towed the vehicle, and they cited me for unregistered, uninsured.

Q: And when was that?

A: That was prior to the accident. It could have been in '87 or '86.

Q: You mean '97.

A: I'm sorry, '97.

Q: But it was after the vehicle had been modified.

A: Yes.

Q: Am I correct that you did the modification fairly shortly after you got the Jeep?

A: Yes.

Q: So let me recap. On at least three occasions prior to the accident this vehicle, in its modified form, came under the scrutiny of the Lowell Police Department.

A: Yes.

Q: And on none of those occasions did the police officers comment to you at all about its height, am I correct?

A: Yes.

Q: Was there any court appearance involved with that unregistered, uninsured charge?

A: Yes.

Q: What was the outcome of that?

A: I proved that it was insured. I brought in proof that it was insured so he dismissed that charge, but he did fine me for being unregistered, and that's it.

Q: So, in fact, for whatever reason, you couldn't show that the car was registered.

A: It had expired.

Q: It had expired.

A: But it was insured.

Q: Okay. Were you fined?

A: Yes.

Q: So presumably there are court records relating to that.

A: Yes.

Q: Who was your insurance agent?

A: I don't remember.

Q: Is the Jeep insured now?

A: No.

Q: Is it in a driveable condition?

A: No.

Q: Because?

A: The windshield broke, it's missing the hood and fender.

Q: So it hasn't been driven since the day of the accident.

A: No.

Q: How did it get from the accident site back to you house?

A: Towed.

Q: Do you know who towed it?

A: McGill's.

Q: Do you know how it was towed?

A: Just a normal—

Q: Was it dollied?

A: No. It was just towed, lift the front end.

Q: Towed on the rear wheels?

A: Yes.

Q: I'd like to turn to the happening of the accident itself. The date of the accident, sir, was what, do you recall?

A: August, 1998.

MS. COBLENTZ: Off the record a second.

[Discussion off the record.]

Q: What day of the week was that, do you know?

A: Saturday.

Q: And what did you do that morning?

A: What did I do?

Q: Yes.

A: I got up—

Q: Do you remember anything special about the day?

A: No, just regular day.

Q: Did you have plans for the day?

A: Well, it was my brother's birthday.

Q: Peter's?

A: Yes. They invited a few friends over to his girlfriend's house. It was a hot day. She has a pool in the backyard, which is about a hundred—a hundred feet away from the accident where she lives.

Q: And her name is what?

A: Keisha Ramsay.

Q: How do you spell that?

A: K-E-I-S-H-A, R-A-M-S-A-Y.

MS. COBLENTZ: Off the record.
[Discussion off the record.]

Q: Does she still live there?

A: Yes.

Q: Do you know the address?

A: No.

Q: Does your brother still go out with her?

A: Yes.

Q: Who was present at the party?

A: There was myself, my wife, my brother, his girlfriend Keisha, her mother—was that—her brother-in-law with his two children.

Q: What's his name?

A: Stony; that's his last name, Stony. I'm not sure of his first name.

Q: And she has been here with us today.

A: Yes.

Q: When were you married?

A: [No response.]

Q: Nobody ever remembers that. Don't feel bad.

A: That's a toughie.

Q: Were you married at the time of this accident?

A: No.

Q: I should never have asked.

A: I'm in trouble now.

Q: It's just the pressure of the occasion. When did you arrive at the party?

A: I'd say around 4:30 or 5.

Q: And was Charlie invited to the party?

A: Yes.

Q: Did you invite him?

A: No, my brother did.

Q: Was Charlie more your friend or your brother's friend?

A: He was both.

Q: And you had known him for a long time?

A: Oh, yes. We were like brothers.

Q: Did Charlie arrive separately from you?

A: Yes.

Q: How did he get to the party?

A: His car.

Q: And what kind of car did he have?

A: I think he had a green Mustang.

Q: How long were you at the party?

A: About an hour before he came.

Q: You were there an hour before Charlie came?

A: About that.

Q: So Charlie would have come around 5:30 or so.

A: Yes.

Q: Was this party for a dinner?

A: It was a cookout, barbecue, whatever.

Q: And did you, in fact, have dinner?

A: Yes.

Q: Was there any alcohol served at this party?

A: There was beer.

Q: Did you have beer?

A: No.

Q: You had none?

A: No.

Q: How do you remember that?

A: I just was—just didn't drink. I wasn't drinking that day, I remember.

Q: How much did you drink then? Did you have an occasional beer?

A: That's all; on the weekends, maybe a Saturday.

Q: Have you ever had any kind of drinking problem?

A: No.

Q: Did Charlie have anything to drink?

A: I don't know.

Q: What time did you leave the party?

A: Let's see. I'd say around 6:30 - 7 or—we were just leaving to get our bathing suits to go swimming, me and Charlie.

Q: Were you going to go back to each of your houses to get suits?

A: Yes.

Q: And where were you on your way first, to your house or his?

A: Probably his; his was—let me think—yes, his house would be closer.

[Discussion off the record.]

Q: And the accident happened at the corner of Palmer and Franklin, is that right?

A: Yes.

Q: I'd like you to draw, just if you could, a little map showing the path from the party to where the accident happened.

A: Okay.

[Witness drawing.]

MS. FRANCIS: May I just inquire, are you intending to use this for future reference, this sketch, or is it just for questions?

MS. COBLENTZ: Well, I'll mark it.

MS. FRANCIS: Of course, it's completely out of scale.

MS. COBLENTZ: I want to get the relationship of one street to the other.

THE WITNESS: I'm not too sure of the spelling or whatever, but I think that's how it was, basically.

MS. COBLENTZ: Let me mark this sketch as the next exhibit.

[A sketch drawn by the witness was marked as Exhibit No. 4 for identification.]

Q: Exhibit 4 is your sketch indicating the house where—

A: Yes.

Q: And the accident happened in the course of the left turn onto Franklin Street; is that correct?

A: Yes.

Q: Now, before we get into that, in previous occasions when you had driven the vehicle, had there been anytime when you felt it leaning or starting to roll over?

A: No.

Q: Had you driven it off the road at all?

A: Very little, a few times.

Q: Where did you drive it off road?

A: Prospect Hill.

Q: Prospect Hill in Waltham?

A: Yes.

Q: Did you drive up the hill there or just kind of around those grounds there?

A: Around the grounds.

Q: Had you ever driven it off road under conditions where you had any real need for the extra clearance that all the modifications had given you?

A: Yes.

Q: And are there, for example, rocks and boulders there that you need to clear?

A: There's rocks and boulders and muddy, and I took it up there in the snow. And you need the clearance or you'd get hung up in the snow. You know what I mean, you'd actually be stuck in the snow if you weren't that high.

Q: But the primary use that you made of the vehicle was on the road?

A: Yes.

Q: Now, is Palmer and Franklin a regulated intersection? Is there a stop sign or traffic light there?

A: No traffic light; I think there's a stop sign. I'm not sure, but not—I didn't have a stop sign. I think there is the stop sign.

Q: On Franklin?

A: On Franklin.

Q: Can you give me your best estimate of your speed as you were going down Palmer Street before you got to the corner?

A: I'd say it couldn't be no more than 20 because that Jeep with the big tire, I didn't change the gear ratio so it didn't have no power. It took a long time to pick up speed so I say—the distance from about a hundred yards—

Q: Do you remember what gear you were in?

A: First gear, because it was a slight climb, like I said. When I put on the big tires, it took all the power away from it.

Q: You were in first gear all that time?

A: Yes, because it's real short. I don't think I got out of first gear.

Q: Were you in first gear as you made the corner?

A: Yes.

Q: When the Jeep rolled, you were in first gear?

A: I'm pretty sure.

Q: Do you remember turning the corner excessively sharply?

MS. FRANCIS: I object.

Q: Let me rephrase it. Did you turn the corner more sharply than you usually turn a corner?

A: No.

Q: Tell me exactly what happened, as you remember it.

A: I was going down Palmer street and then that intersection or that turn, it's real sharp—no. I wouldn't say sharp. It's a real dangerous turn or something. It dips and then—it dips toward—it's—I don't know. It's a bad—everybody cuts it. No one ever takes the turn. Everybody crosses the yellow line.

Q: In other words, you cut the corner a little bit onto Franklin.

A: You have to. That's the kind of—

Q: Is it, for instance, a 90-degree turn?

MS. FRANCIS: I don't think he'd have any knowledge of that.

Q: If you know.

A: I don't know.

Q: You know what I mean when I say that? Is it more than like a square corner? Are you kind of doubling back when you—

A: I don't think so.

Q: Is there something about the pitch on Franklin Road that creates any difficulty?

A: I would say there is, but—

Q: Have you ever heard about any other accidents at that corner?

A: I seen—the bushes that I hit, a couple of—maybe a month ago, the same bushes, the exact same spot, the bushes were dug up again.

Q: Okay. I'd like you to draw another diagram for me showing the same intersection in larger scale, and I'll draw the streets.

[Ms. Coblentz draws a diagram.]

Q: This is Palmer and this is Franklin. The Jeep is coming from here and making this turn [indicating], correct?

A: Okay.

Q: Right?

A: Yes.

Q: First of all, describe it in words and then we'll figure out what we want on the sketch. You indicated that you had to cut the corner crossing the yellow line as you did so.

A: Yes, very—yes.

Q: And what was the first sensation you had of any problem?

A: I didn't. It just—I don't remember.

Q: Do you remember applying the brakes?

A: Yes, I think so. It happened— you know, I'd say so fast but just—I don't remember. I tried to, you know, block it out. I just can't recall.

Q: As you think back on it, do you have a memory of the vehicle rolling?

A: Barely.

Q: And I take it rolled—if you were looking at the vehicle from behind, it rolled clockwise? In other words, it rolled toward the right?

A: It rolled toward the passenger side.

Q: Right. And do you have any sense about when it started to roll in relation to where you were, on Palmer or Franklin?

A: No.

Q: It was shortly after you had started the turn though, is that right?

A: Oh, yes.

Q: Were you pretty much onto Franklin when it began to roll?

A: I was probably right in the middle of the turn maybe.

Q: What I'd like you to draw for me, as best you can, and try to get the Jeep somewhat in scale, at least relative to the intersection itself, the position of the Jeep at the moment when it first seemed to begin to turn. And the way we draw cars in the law business is like this with a "V" on the front end like that.

A: And what do you want me to do?

Q: I want you to draw the position of the Jeep when it first started to roll.

MS. FRANCIS: Is that what he felt?

Q: When you felt that it first started to roll, as best you can. But I just want to get some sense of where it was in relation to the intersection.

A: I'm coming down here [indicating].

Q: Down here turning onto Franklin like that?

A: And there was a house here. There was bushes here, shrubs.

Q: Why don't you draw the shrubs.

A: How do you—

Q: Just kind of a wavy line to indicate the shrubs.
[Witness complies.]

Q: Those are the shrubs on that corner?

A: I'd say right about—maybe right there.

Q: And can you draw for me the final position that the Jeep was in when it came to rest?

MS. FRANCIS: Can we mark that position with some kind of letter or something?

MS. COBLENTZ: Yes.

Q: Why don't you put "1" inside that. And then draw the position of the Jeep when it came to rest.

MS. FRANCIS: The location, you mean?

MS. COBLENTZ: Yes, the position.

MS. FRANCIS: Because position means situation.
[Witness complies.]

A: Something like that.

Q: So it came to rest partly on the road in these bushes.

A: Yes.

MS. FRANCIS: Can we mark that position with a "2"?

MS. COBLENTZ: Yes.

Q: Can you put a "2" on there?
[Witness complies.]

Q: And at that point, the vehicle was completely flipped over.

A: Yes.

Q: And Charlie was pinned under the roll bar?

A: Yes.

Q: Did it have the roll bar when you got it?

A: Yes.

Q: Were you thrown out of the vehicle?

A: No.

Q: Were you belted in?

A: No.

Q: You were inside the vehicle?

A: Yes. I had the steering wheel, you know, to hold me in. So when it rolled, I slid out of it, like fell out toward the passenger side.

Q: And what did you do when you got out? First of all, you were conscious.

A: Yes.

Q: Were you hurt at all?

A: Yes.

Q: How had you gotten hurt?

A: I think I banged up my knee.

Q: But you weren't seriously hurt at all?

A: No.

Q: Were there people around?

A: Yes.

Q: What's the first thing you did?

A: I checked—I looked to see where Charlie was.

Q: And you saw him pinned under the roll bar.

A: Yes.

Q: What did you do next?

A: I flipped out. I tried to push the Jeep. I just didn't know what to do.

Q: Did you get some people to help you?

A: Some—somebody came over. I just—I don't remember. I know—

Q: Do you remember at some point the vehicle being pushed onto its side?

A: I don't—I'm not sure. It must have been.

Q: Do you remember it being on its side when the police arrived?

A: Yes, I think so.

Q: Do you remember having any conversation with the police that night?

A: No.

Q: What do you mean, after the accident?

A: Yes. They put me in the traffic safety van and—

MS. FRANCIS: Do you remember talking to the police was the question.

A: Yes.

MS. FRANCIS: Was that the question, just talking to the police?

MS. COBLENTZ: Yes.

Q: Well, let me ask this. At some point, you knew you were being charged with some crime.

A: Correct, yes.

Q: Were you informed of it that night?

A: No.

Q: Were you taken to the hospital?

A: Yes.

Q: Was that Lowell's Community Hospital?

A: Yes.

Q: Were you treated and released?

A: What happened is I was waiting—I was waiting to be treated and then I heard that Charlie died. I just flipped out. I refused treatment, and I just walked out of the hospital and went home.

Q: You walked home?

A: Yes.

Q: How far is that?

A: About a mile.

Q: Was the car in the two-wheel drive or four-wheel drive position?

A: Two.

Q: Did you ever use four-wheel drive on the road?

A: Only in the winter in the snow.

Q: Did you tell the police that you had some steering difficulty?

A: I thought there was, but—I'm not sure. I said something about that.

Q: Is it your belief today that there was any steering difficulty?

A: I'm still not sure. I haven't touched the Jeep. I don't know.

Q: Am I correct that at the moment when the vehicle began to roll over, up to that time, you had not been aware of any steering problem?

A: No.

Q: It began to negotiate the curve and accepted steering input as you made it, right?

A: Repeat that.

Q: Yes. You turned the wheel and the vehicle responded to your turning the wheel.

A: Yes, as far as I—yes.

Q: And you're not aware of any breaking problem, is that right?

A: No.

Q: Do you remember the names of the officers you spoke to that night?

A: [No response.]

A: The officers?

Q: Yes.

A: No. I have it at home.

Q: Had you ever seen either of them before?

A: No.

Q: Were you or Charlie yelling anything just prior to the accident?

A: No.

Q: Did you ever hear any information of a witness that said you were?

A: Yes.

Q: How did you hear that?

A: He said it at the probable cause hearing.

Q: And your testimony is that you were not yelling?

A: No.

Q: Were there any repairs made to the Jeep after the accident?

A: No.

Q: At what time was it towed back to your house, do you know?

A: I think it was two days after. It was towed to McGill's Garage, and it was stored back there, I think, for a couple of days, And then it was towed to my house.

Q: I just want to go through the charges and what happened. You were charged with a number of different offenses as a result of this, weren't you—

A: Right.

Q: —of which the most serious, of course, was motor vehicle homicide. You were found guilty of that.

A: I think so, yes.

MS. FRANCIS: Do you recall?

Q: And do you remember what your penalty was for that?

A: Two years suspended sentence.

Q: So that the two years has now elapsed.

A: No. I think it's—I got until May, I think.

Q: And the driving to endanger was dismissed and merged into the count for motor vehicle homicide.

A: Yes.

Q: And you were found not guilty of operating after license had been revoked.

A: Yes.

Q: And you were found guilty for failing to slow at the intersection.

A: Yes.

Q: And you were found guilty of speeding, right?

A: Yes.

Q: And you were found guilty of altering the height of a motor vehicle.

A: Yes.

Q: At the time, sir, when you deeded your interest in your house to your brother, did you have any other substantial property?

A: No.

Q: So it's fair to say that the house was really your sole significant asset.

A: That's it.

Q: And what was your motor vehicle liability insurance at the time of this accident?

A: What option, you mean?

Q: Yes.

A: I think it was option 3.

Q: Do you remember how much liability coverage you had?

A: I think it was 10/20, something like that.

MS. COBLENTZ: Off the record. [Discussion off the record.]

Q: So you knew that you had the minimum amount of liability insurance, correct?

A: Yes.

Q: And you knew at the time, did you not, that one who negligently causes the death of another can be responsible civilly as well as criminally for that?

MS. FRANCIS: I object to that. I don't think he even has the answer to that.

MS. COBLENTZ: I think it relates.

MS. FRANCIS: He knew at which time?

MS. COBLENTZ: At the time he conveyed the house. That's what this goes to.

MS. FRANCIS: That he knew— what was the question again?

Q: At the time when you conveyed the house, you knew that someone who is negli-

gent and causes the death of another person can be responsible to the estate of that person civilly or criminally.

A: I didn't know that.

Q: You didn't know that?

A: No.

Q: You had no concerns whatever about possibly losing an asset?

A: No. I just needed money. I didn't have nowhere to turn. I don't have any credit at all. I needed money before he'd represent me.

Q: Does Raytheon have a credit union?

A: Yes.

Q: Had you gone to the credit union?

A: No.

Q: Did you ever ask?

A: No. I didn't think they'd lend you that much money.

Q: But you didn't inquire.

A: No.

MS. COBLENTZ: I'm done.

MS. FRANCIS: I have a couple of questions.

CROSS EXAMINATION BY MS. FRANCIS

Q: Was there any damage to the Jeep that you described to us?

A: Right now? From the accident, you mean?

Q: From the accident.

A: The windshield broke and the nose—the nose is crushed, like the hood and the two fenders and that's—

Q: Was it driveable after the accident?

A: I don't think so.

Q: Was there any damage to this

new suspension that you installed?

A: No, not that I know of.

Q: In other words, those hockey pucks were still in place?

A: Yes.

Q: Did you have to put separate bolts that you purchased to go through the center of those hockey pucks?

A: Did I, yes.

Q: Longer ones —

A: Yes.

Q: —than were there? Were they still intact after the accident?

A: Yes, yes.

Q: And the springs that you installed, were they still intact?

A: Yes. The whole undercarriage is intact.

Q: Was there any damage to any of the parts that you installed?

A: No, nothing; It didn't roll that hard.

MS. FRANCIS: I have no further questions.

REDIRECT EXAMINATION BY MS. COBLENTZ

Q: Where did you purchase the bolts?

A: A hardware store.

Q: But you didn't get them at a specialty auto store.

A: No.

MS. COBLENTZ: That's all I have.

MS. FRANCIS: We're all set.

[Whereupon, the deposition was concluded at 12:08 p.m.]

COMMONWEALTH OF MASSACHUSETTS

MIDDLESEX, SS

SUPERIOR COURT DEPARTMENT
OF THE TRIAL COURT
CIVIL ACTION NO. 99-6144

NANCY CARPENTER, As
Administratrix of the Estate
of Charles Carpenter,
  Plaintiff

    vs.

RANDALL DEE; PETER DEE;
CITY OF LOWELL,
  Defendants.

ULTIMATE AUTO, INC.,
  Defendant and Third-Party
  Plaintiff

    vs.

DALE MCGILL and
McGILL'S GARAGE, INC.,
  Third-Party Defendants.

THIRD-PARTY DEFENDANT
DALE MCGILL'S AND MCGILL'S
GARAGE INC.'S MOTION FOR
SUMMARY JUDGMENT

Now come the third-party defendants, Dale McGill and McGill's Garage, Inc., by and through counsel and move this court pursuant to Rule 56 for Summary Judgment in their behalf on the basis that there is no genuine issue of material fact as to whether the third-party defendants owed a duty to Plaintiff's decedent, rather, this is a question of law to be decided by this court, as more fully set forth in the third-party defendants' memorandum filed in support of this motion.

Third-party defendants request oral argument of this motion.

Attorney for third-party defendants,

___/s/ Lisa Scottoline____
Lisa Scottoline (BBO#393689)
Scottoline & Turow
One Federal Street
Boston, MA 02100
617/555-7777

Dated: /d/

COMMONWEALTH OF MASSACHUSETTS

MIDDLESEX, SS   SUPERIOR COURT DEPARTMENT
                                       OF THE TRIAL COURT
                                       CIVIL ACTION NO. 99-6144

NANCY CARPENTER, As
Administratrix of the Estate
of Charles Carpenter,
  Plaintiff

                                       MEMORANDUM IN SUPPORT OF
    vs.   THIRD-PARTY DEFENDANT
                                       DALE MCGILL'S AND MCGILL'S
RANDALL DEE; PETER DEE;   GARAGE INC.'S MOTION FOR
CITY OF LOWELL,   SUMMARY JUDGMENT
  Defendants.

ULTIMATE AUTO, INC.,
Defendant and Third-Party
  Plaintiff

    vs.

DALE MCGILL and
McGILL'S GARAGE, INC.,
  Third-Party Defendants.

Now come the third-party defendants, Dale McGill and McGill's Garage, Inc., and in support of their Motion for Summary Judgment, pursuant to Rule 56 state as follows:

I. INTRODUCTION

This instant action arises out of a one vehicle auto incident where a 1986 Jeep CJ-7 (hereinafter referred to as "the Jeep"), operated by defendant, Randall Dee, "rolled-over" allegedly causing the death of plaintiff's decedent, Charles Carpenter, on August 29, 1998. Sometime prior to August 29, 1998, Randall Dee allegedly modified the suspension on the Jeep by installing oversize tires and a suspension kit manufactured and sold by the defendant, Ultimate Auto, Inc. It is alleged by the plaintiff that Ultimate Auto was negligent when it sold the tires and suspension kit which allegedly altered the height of the Jeep and affected its handling characteristics rendering it unsafe. The plaintiff sets forth various specific allegations of negligence in support of its alleged cause of action. (Plaintiff's Complaint Count IV, ¶¶22-25.)

Ultimate Auto later added McGill's Garage, Inc., and Dale McGill as third-party defendants demanding contribution and alleging that Dale McGill, as agent or employee, of McGill's Garage, Inc. was negligent in approving an inspection sticker on said vehicle prior to the date of the accident. At the time alleged McGill's Garage, Inc. was a duly licensed inspection station for the Commonwealth of Massachusetts and engaged, among other things, in inspecting vehicles and either passing or rejecting said vehicles in accordance with the Code of Massachusetts Regulations, 540 CMR, §4.00 through 4.08 then in effect.

It is alleged that a safety inspection sticker was issued by McGill's Garage, Inc., to the Dee vehicle in December of 1997, several months prior to the incident in question and after Dee had altered the Jeep with the tires and suspension kit purchased from Ultimate Auto.

ARGUMENTS AND POINTS OF LAW

Neither Dale McGill (hereinafter called "McGill") nor McGill's Garage, Inc., (hereinafter called "McGill's Garage") are liable to Ultimate Auto as joint tort-feasor for contributions to any loss proven by the plaintiff against Ultimate Auto for the reason that at the time of the alleged incident no duty was owing by either Dale McGill or McGill's Garage to the plaintiff, plaintiff's decedent or anyone else.

Without a duty owing by McGill and/or McGill's Garage to plaintiff or plaintiff's decedent, neither McGill nor McGill's Garage are liable to plaintiff or plaintiff's decedent in tort. Because neither McGill, nor McGill's Garage are liable in tort to plaintiff or plaintiff's decedent, neither is a joint tort-feasor against whom contribution can be had by Ultimate Auto.

General Laws, Chapter 231B, Section 1(a), inserted by St. 1962, Chapter 730, Section 1, provides in pertinent parts: "[W]here two or more persons become jointly liable in tort for the same injury to person or property, there shall be a right of contribution among them." The language of this statute requires that the potential contributor be directly liable to the plaintiff. Without liability in tort, there is no right to contribution.

It therefore follows that, only if McGill's Garage and Dale McGill are directly liable to the plaintiff's decedent, can the defendant/third-party plaintiff state a claim for contribution from McGill's Garage and Dale McGill.

At the time of the alleged issuance of the inspection sticker, December 1997, McGill's Garage, and its employee McGill were required to inspect vehicles in accordance with 540 CMR, Section 4.00 through 4.08 effective March 31, 1995.*

Said regulations did not require McGill's Garage, nor McGill, as employee acting within the scope of his employment when issuing the inspection sticker, to inspect and/or reject any vehicle for alleged violations of any height or suspension alteration requirement.

Although M.G.L., Chapter 90, Section 7P may have prohibited any person from modifying or changing the height of a motor vehicle, with some exceptions, as alleged by the plaintiff, neither McGill nor McGill's Garage altered the Jeep and, therefore, they were not governed by that statute in the issuance of the December 1997 inspection sticker.

As 540 CMR, Section 4.00 through Section 4.08 effective March 31, 1995 did not require inspection for altered height, neither McGill nor McGill's Garage had a duty to do so. In fact, pursuant to 540 CMR Section 4.00 through Section 4.08, neither McGill nor McGill's Garage had any right to inspect and/or reject the subject jeep as the regulations set forth those specific areas only which were governed by the inspection procedure and did not authorize any inspection station to act beyond the specific directions of the regulations.

540 CMR Section 4.00 effective March 31, 1995 was not amended until May 27, 1999 [the year after the accident], after the death of Charlie Carpenter and after the issuance of the sticker in question, the inspection guidelines were changed to include inspection and/or rejection of certain altered height vehicles. 540 CMR Section 4.04 (13)(a).

CONCLUSION

There is only a question of law before this Court; that is, whether an inspection station, in December of 1998 had a duty to, through its agents and/or employees, reject a 1986 Jeep CJ-7 vehicle which had been modified with a suspension kit and tires to alter the height of the vehicle. Dispositive questions of law are properly heard on Motion for Summary Judgment. Clearly, the answer is no. 540 CMR Section 4.00 effective March 31, 1995 through May 27, 1999, set forth the standards for vehicle inspection and was silent as to altered height vehicles. Therefore, neither Dale McGill nor McGill's Garage through any other agent and/or employee had a duty owing to plaintiff or plaintiff's decedent relative to the Dee vehicle.

Having no duty owing to the plaintiff or plaintiff's decedent, neither McGill nor McGill's Garage can be held as a joint tort-feasor with Ultimate

---

* *Note to students*: For this exercise we have changed the effective dates of these regulations in order to make this simulation conform with the sequence of events as they occurred in the actual case.

Auto and others regarding the loss claimed by plaintiff in this action. As neither McGill nor McGill's Garage can be held as joint tort-feasor, neither can be liable to Ultimate Auto for contribution as alleged in the Third-Party Complaint.

WHEREFORE, Dale McGill and McGill's Garage, Inc. move this Court for entry of summary judgment in their respective favors and against the third-party plaintiff, Ultimate Auto, Inc.

Attorney for third-party defendants,

___/s/ Lisa Scottoline____
Lisa Scottoline (BBO#393689)
Scottoline & Turow
One Federal Street
Boston, MA 02100
617/555-7777

Dated: /d/

COMMONWEALTH OF MASSACHUSETTS

MIDDLESEX, SS

SUPERIOR COURT DEPARTMENT
OF THE TRIAL COURT
CIVIL ACTION NO. 99-6144

NANCY CARPENTER, As
Administratrix of the Estate
of Charles Carpenter,
  Plaintiff

       vs.

RANDALL DEE; PETER DEE;
CITY OF LOWELL,
  Defendants.

ULTIMATE AUTO, INC.,
  Defendant and Third-Party
  Plaintiff

       vs.

DALE MCGILL and
McGILL'S GARAGE, INC.,
  Third-Party Defendants.

STIPULATION OF
THIRD-PARTY PLAINTIFF,
ULTIMATE AUTO, INC., AND
THIRD-PARTY DEFENDANTS,
DALE MCGILL AND
MCGILL'S GARAGE, INC.

Defendant and Third-Party Plaintiff, Ultimate Auto, Inc., and Third-Party Defendants, Dale McGill and McGill's Garage, Inc., hereby stipulate as follows:

1. At all relevant times, McGill's Garage, Inc. was a duly licensed inspection station for the Commonwealth of Massachusetts, which was engaged in, among other things, passing or rejecting vehicles; and Dale McGill was a certified inspector.

2. A safety inspection sticker was issued by McGill's Garage, Inc. to the Dee vehicle in question in December of 1997, several months prior to the incident in question and after Dee had altered the Jeep with the tires and suspension kit purchased from Ultimate Auto. Randall Dee paid $15.00 for the inspection and sticker.

3. Dale McGill was at all relevant times the President of, and Chief Mechanic and Inspector at, McGill's Garage, Inc. As of December 1997, he had been a gas station owner for fifteen years; he worked in other gas stations as a mechanic and helper for eight years prior to that.

4. The Commonwealth of Massachusetts Periodic Annual Inspection of All Motor Vehicles regulations [reprinted in the Case Files] were in effect at the time of the December 1997 inspection. G.L. c. 90 §7P [also in the Case Files] also was in effect at all relevant times, including at the time of the inspection.

5. At all relevant times, McGill's Garage had large external signs that said: "Full Service Center," "Gas Station," and "Massachusetts Inspection Station."

6. At several times during 1997 Randall Dee bought gas at McGill's Garage, and Dale McGill was often the individual who pumped the gas into the Jeep. On at least one occasion prior to December 1997, Randall Dee got a change of oil and lubrication for the Jeep at McGill's Garage.

7. The following discovery [not reprinted in the Case Files] has occurred:

(a) In a deposition, Randall Dee said that when he went to McGill's Garage for the December 1997 inspection, he said to Dale McGill words to the effect that "I want my Jeep inspected for a safety sticker." He further states in that deposition that "I thought a safety sticker meant my Jeep was safe."

(b) Randall Dee and Dale McGill both say in depositions that Dale McGill inspected the Jeep in question in December 1997 and put the sticker showing that the vehicle had passed inspection on the front windowshield of the Jeep; both further say that neither Randall Dee nor Dale McGill mentioned the modifications to the Jeep to each other in December 1997 or at any other time.

(c) Plaintiff's lawyers have provided an affidavit during the discovery process in this case from an engineer who states that she has had extensive education and experience in vehicle design and safety. The affidavit further says that in the expert's opinion, based on what she has learned through extensive discovery in the case, inspection of the Jeep in question, and a visit to the relevant site, "a substantial cause of the accident in question was the elevated height of the modified Jeep which made the Jeep a good deal less stable than it would be without the modifications."

8. For purposes of the motion pending before the Court, the Massachusetts Rules of Civil Procedure are identical to the Federal Rules of Civil Procedure. Where the state and federal rules are identical, Massachusetts state courts often look to federal precedents. The Massachusetts Supreme

Court has recently cited *Celotex Corp. v. Catsett,* 477 U.S. 317 (1986) with approval.

9. State courts frequently cite to the Restatements of Law as persuasive authority.

Executed by the parties as of this ____ day of _____, ____.

ULTIMATE AUTO, INC.,	DALE MCGILL and
Third-Party Plaintiff	MCGILL'S GARAGE, INC.,
	Third-Party Defendant

By its Attorney,	By its Attorney,

____/s/ Bertram Cohen_____	____/s/ Lisa Scottoline_____
Bertram Cohen (BBO#641311)	Lisa Scottoline (BBO#393689)
Roth, McKnight & Zimmerman	Scottoline & Turow
111 Milk Street	One Federal Street
Boston, MA 02100	Boston, MA 02100
(617) 555-0000	617/555-7777

■ THE COMMONWEALTH OF MASSACHUSETTS, SECRETARY OF STATE, REGULATION FILING AND PUBLICATION*

1. **REGULATION CHAPTER NUMBER AND HEADING:** 540 CMR 4.00 Periodic Annual Staggered Safety and Combined Safety and Emissions Inspection of All Motor Vehicles.

2. **NAME OF AGENCY: Registry of Motor Vehicles**

3. **READABLE LANGUAGE SUMMARY:** States the general purposes and requirements of this regulation as well as the persons, organizations and businesses affected.

The purpose of 540 CMR 4.00 is to provide for a periodic staggered safety and combined safety and emissions inspection of all motor vehicles registered in the Commonwealth of Massachusetts and to establish licensing procedures for inspection stations, fleet inspection stations and safety inspection stations only authorized to participate in the inspection program. 540 CMR 4.00 establishes regulations and procedures for the issuance of various certificates to owner/operators in accordance with inspection procedures. 540 CMR 4.00 shall affect all persons owning, operating, purchasing and selling automobiles in the Commonwealth and shall affect many businesses relating to motor vehicle industry.

540 CMR: REGISTRY OF MOTOR VEHICLES

4.00 PERIODIC ANNUAL STAGGERED SAFETY AND COMBINED SAFETY AND EMISSION INSPECTION OF ALL MOTOR VEHICLES

. . . The purpose of 540 CMR 4.00 is to provide rules and regulations and to establish inspection procedures for a periodic annual staggered safety and combined safety and emissions inspection of all motor vehicles in accordance with the General Laws of the Commonwealth of Massachusetts.

4.01 SCOPE AND APPLICABILITY

540 CMR 4.00 is adopted by the Registrar of Motor Vehicles in accordance with the authority of M.G.L. c. 90 §31 to establish rules and regulations governing the use and operation of motor vehicles and trailers. 540

---

* *Eds. Note*: These were the applicable regulations at the time of the inspection.

CMR 4.00 establishes rules and regulations which provide for a periodic staggered safety and combined safety and emission inspection of all motor vehicles registered in the Commonwealth of Massachusetts under the authority of M.G.L. c. 90 §7A, establishing regulations for issuance of various certificates in accordance with proper inspection of a motor vehicle pursuant to M.G.L. c. 90 §7V(a)(b)(c) and establishes rules and regulations for licensing stations which are approved to perform safety or combined safety and emissions inspections on motor vehicles pursuant to M.G.L. c. 90 §7W.

4.02 SPECIAL DEFINITIONS

In addition to the definitions set forth in M.G.L. c. 90 §1, the following special definitions shall also apply. . . .

Certificate of Inspection shall mean a serially numbered, adhesive sticker, device or symbol, as may be prescribed by the registrar indicating a motor vehicle has met the inspection requirements established by the registrar for issuance of a certificate. The registrar may prescribe the use of one or more categories of certificate of inspection in accordance with M.G.L. c. 90 §1.

Certificate of Rejection shall mean a serially numbered, adhesive sticker, device or symbol, as may be prescribed by the registrar indicating a motor vehicle has failed to meet the safety or combined safety and emissions inspection requirements as established by the registrar in accordance with M.G.L. c. 90 §1. . . .

Certified Inspector shall mean an individual certified by the commissioner as properly trained to perform an emissions inspection as delineated by the manufacturer of the emissions analyzer in accordance with M.G.L. c. 90 §1. . . .

Exempt Vehicles shall mean motor vehicles whose curb weight exceeds eight thousand pounds, motorcycles, diesel powered vehicles, motor vehicles more than fifteen model years old before the date of inspection, motor vehicles not capable of a speed greater than twenty-five miles per hour under any condition of operation or loading on a level surface and any class of vehicles exempted by the commissioner of Department of Environmental Quality Engineering which present prohibitive inspection problems. . . .

Inspection Station shall mean a proprietorship, partnership, or corporation licensed by the registrar to perform safety or combined safety and emissions inspections on motor vehicles. . . .

Safety Inspection Station Only shall mean a proprietorship, partnership or corporation whose principal business is unique to a particular exempt vehicle.

4.03 REQUIREMENTS FOR INITIAL AND SUBSEQUENT STAGGERED ANNUAL INSPECTION

(1) **General Provisions.** Every owner or person in control of a Massachusetts registered motor vehicle shall submit the vehicle for inspection under the following rules:. . . .

(c) **Inspection Upon Registration.** Every owner or person in control of a motor vehicle which is newly registered in the Commonwealth shall submit such motor vehicle for certificate of inspection within seven days of the date on which the motor vehicle is first registered to said owner in the Commonwealth. . . .

(2) **Subsequent Inspection.** Subsequent to initial inspection, every owner or person in control of a Massachusetts registered motor vehicle shall submit the vehicle for inspection annually during the monthly expiration of the previously issued Certificate of Inspection.

(3) **Validity of Certificates of Inspection.** Certificates of Inspection are valid until such time as they expire or ownership of the vehicle transferred.

4.04 PROCEDURES FOR INSPECTION OF ALL MOTOR VEHICLES

(1) **Prior to beginning inspection,** a visual check of the vehicle should be made to determine that ice and snow accumulation, condition of the suspension, etc., will not impede or interfere with the proper aiming of headlamps. Inspectors shall. . . . collect the established inspection fee and remove any inspection sticker from the windshield of the motor vehicle.

(2) **Check registration certificate** for date of expiration. . . .

(3) **Inspect number plate(s)** to see that they are undamaged, securely mounted, clean and clearly visible. No bumper, trailer hitch or other accessory may interfere with a clear view of them. The number plate must be mounted in the proper location on the rear of the vehicle if the vehicle has been issued one plate. Both number plates must be mounted in the proper location on the rear and front of the vehicle, if the vehicle has been issued two plates.

Any decorative number plate or number plate replica not issued by the Registry of Motor Vehicles on which the word Massachusetts appears must be removed from the vehicle.

(4) **Perform Emission Testing Requirements and Procedures.** . . .

(5) **Test Brakes.**

(a) The adjuster may operate the vehicle in the inspection bay and test the parking and service brake. The parking brake on all vehicles will be tested by accelerating the motor to approximately 1200 to 1300 RPMs with the vehicle in gear in both forward and reverse positions against the brake in the applied position. . . .

(b) Brakes shall be adequate to stop the vehicle from a speed of 20 MPH in not more than the following distances:

Service (foot) Brake	Pleasure Vehicles	25 feet
	Trucks and Buses	35 feet
Parking (hand) Brake	All Vehicles	75 feet

(6) **Examine Muffler and Exhaust System.** Accelerate motor to test for prevention of unnecessary noise and emission of any unreasonable amount of smoke. The exhaust system, exhaust manifold(s), exhaust pipe(s), muffler(s) and tailpipe(s), if designed to be so equipped, shall be tight and free of leaks.

(7) **Check Steering and Suspension.**

(a) Check for free steering by turning the steering wheel through a full right and left turn. Reject a vehicle if binding or interference occurs during the procedure. With the front wheels in the straight ahead position (and the engine running on vehicles equipped with power steering) measure lash or lost movement at the steering wheel rim.

(b) Lash or lost movement on passenger cars and station wagons, as measured at the steering wheel rim, should not exceed 2 inches if the vehicle is equipped with manual steering. Lash or lost movement on antique motor vehicles, trucks, vans and buses will be measured in the same manner with the allowable tolerance on trucks, vans and buses to be determined by steering wheel diameter in accordance with the following schedule:

Steering Wheel Diameter	Lash (shall not exceed)
16″	2″
18″	$2\,{}^1\!/_4$″
20″	$2\,{}^1\!/_2$″
22″	$2\,{}^3\!/_4$″

(c) The front end of all vehicles will be raised by jacking or hoisting and visually examined. Vehicles equipped with ball joints will be raised and checked in accordance with the instructions and recommendations of the Automobile Manufacturers Association. Ball joint tolerance shall not exceed those established by the vehicle manufacturer.

(d) Reject a vehicle with excessive wear or play in any part of the steering mechanism or of the vehicle that would affect proper steering. . . .

(8) **Sound Horn.** Sound horn to test for adequate signal. The horn must be securely fastened to the vehicle.

(9) **Examine Windshield and Rear Windows.**

(a) **Clear Windshield.** . . .

(b) **Ornaments.** Ornaments forward of the operator's line of vision through the windshield must be removed. No poster or sticker shall be attached to the windshield in such a manner so as to obstruct the vision of the operator.

(c) **Rear Windows.** Rear windows must allow an unobstructed view to the rear. On convertible type vehicles, the rear window must be inspected and if clouded, the vehicle must be rejected.

(d) **Windshield Cleaner(s).** Test for proper operation. . . .

(10) **Examine Lighting Devices.**

(a) **Tail Lights.** Every motor vehicle, except a two wheeled motorcycle, an antique motor car and a farm tractor, shall be equipped with two red lights (tail lamps) mounted one at each side of the rear of the vehicle so as to show two red lights from behind and equipped with two stop lights (stop lamps) mounted and displayed in a like manner. A single lamp may combine both the above functions. Every motor vehicle shall be equipped with a white light so arranged as to illuminate the rear number plate so that it is plainly visible at sixty feet.

(b) **Directionals.** Front and rear directional signals will be operable on every vehicle originally equipped with such signals. Every motor vehicle registered in the Commonwealth, which was manufactured for the model year 1967 and for subsequent model years, shall be equipped with a device to permit the front and rear directional signals to flash simultaneously.

(c) **Headlamps.** Headlamps shall be aimed in accordance with the Registrar's specifications. Said specifications shall be forwarded to licensees by the Registry of Motor Vehicles.

(11) **Examine Tires.**

(a) No tire mounted on a motor vehicle or trailer shall be deemed to be in safe operating condition unless it meets the visual and tread depth requirements set forth in these regulations.

1. **Tread Depth.** The amount of tread design on the tire. Tread depth includes both the original, retread and recap tread design; and, in respect to special mileage commercial tires, recut and regrooved tread design. Truck and bus tires having a wheel diameter over 16 inches, having sufficient original tread rubber above the breaker strip may be siped and classed as a siped tread design 2/32 of an inch siped depth shall be considered equal to 2/32 of an inch original tread depth, provided that the cords of the tire are not damaged by the process.

2. **Special Mileage Commercial Tire.** A tire manufactured with an extra layer of rubber between the cord body and original tread design, which extra layer is designed for the purpose of recutting or regrooving, and which tire is specifically labeled as a special mileage commercial tire.

3. **Visual Requirements.** No tire shall be deemed to be in safe operating condition if such tire has:

a. **Fabric Break.** A fabric break, or a cut in excess of one inch in any direction as measured on the outside of the tire and deep enough to reach the body cords, or has been repaired temporarily by the use of blowout patches or boots; or

b. **Bulges.** Any bump, bulge or knot related to separation or partial failure of the tire, structure; or

c. Exposed Cord. Any portion of the ply or cord structure exposed; or

d. Worn Tread. A portion of the tread design completely worn, provided such worn portion is of sufficient size to affect substantially the traction and stopping ability of the tire.

4. **Method of Measuring Tread Depth.** Tire tread depth shall be measured by a tread depth gauge which shall be of a type calibrated in thirty-seconds of an inch. Readings shall be taken in a major tread groove of the tire nearest the center at two points of the circumference at least fifteen inches apart. Readings for a tire which has the tread design running across the tire or for a siped tire, where such tread design is permitted, shall be taken at or near the center of the tire at two points of the circumference of at least fifteen inches apart.

5. **Tread Depth Requirements.** No tire shall be deemed to be in safe operating condition if such tire is worn to the point where less than two-thirty-seconds (2/32) of an inch of tread design remains at both points at which gauge readings are obtained.

6. **Tire Intermix.** The vehicle will be rejected if a radial ply tire is used on the same axle with a conventional non radial tire. The vehicle will be rejected if bias or bias belted ply tires are used on the rear axle when non-radial tires are used on the front axle. . . .

(12) **Examine Bumpers, Fenders, External Sheet Metal and Fuel Tank.** Any motor vehicle will be rejected if any of the following conditions are evident:

(a) **Bumpers.** Broken or bent bumpers, fenders, exterior sheet metal or mouldings having sharp edges or abnormal protrusions extending beyond normal vehicle extremities so as to constitute a danger to pedestrians and other motor vehicle traffic. If bumper face plates are removed, bumper brackets must also be removed. The vehicle hood, door and luggage compartment lid and battery or engine compartment doors or lids, if so equipped, must fully and properly close and be capable of being firmly latched.

(b) **Fenders.** Front and rear fenders must be in place. . . .

(c) **Floor Pans.** Floor pans which are rusted through or otherwise would permit passage of exhaust gases into the passenger or trunk area.

(d) **Fuel Tanks.** Fuel tanks which are not securely attached to the vehicle's body or chassis. . . .

4.07 ISSUANCE OF CERTIFICATES OF INSPECTION, REJECTION, AND WAIVER PROCEDURE

(1) **General Provisions.**

(a) A separate and distinct charge, as established by the Registrar and Commissioner, shall be made for each inspection.

(b) All required entries on certificates and periodic inspection reports must be legibly completed in ink, ball point pen or indelible pencil by the inspection station owner/operator or employee performing the inspection.

(2) **Certificate of Inspection.**

(a) Any motor vehicle subject to Safety Inspection Only or Combined Safety and Emissions Inspection, which, after inspection, is found to be in compliance with all safety or safety and emissions inspection requirements will be issued a Certificate of Inspection. . . .

(3) **Certificate of Rejection.**

(a) Any motor vehicle subject to the Combined Safety and Emissions Inspection which is not in compliance with all safety and emissions inspection requirements and any motor vehicle subject to Safety Inspection Only which is not in compliance with all safety inspection requirements, will be issued a Certificate of Rejection.

(b) **Requirements.** When a Certificate of Rejection is issued on a motor vehicle, entries pertaining to the date of inspection and vehicle registration number of the motor vehicle will be completed by the inspection station owner/operator or employee performing the inspection on the Certificate of Inspection, that would normally have been issued to the motor vehicle, and on the periodic inspection report. The certificate will be retained at the inspection station for a period of twenty days for potential issuance to the affected motor vehicle. If issued to the affected motor vehicle, all required entries on said certificate and on the periodic inspection report will be completed. At the expiration of the twenty day period, unissued certificates with partial entries will be held in an open file for return to the Registry of Motor Vehicles.

4.08 LICENSURE OF INSPECTION STATION

(1) **General Provisions: Licensing Requirements.** Effective April 1, 1983, all inspection stations, which shall include Inspection Stations for

Combined Safety and Emissions Testing, Fleet Inspection Stations and Safety Inspection Stations Only shall be licensed by the Registry of Motor Vehicles to carry out the annual staggered Safety or Safety and Emissions Inspection Program. . . .

(g) **Requirements for Personnel Who Administer Inspections.** Inspections must be performed by the licensee or permanent employees of the licensee who are in possession of a Massachusetts Motor Vehicle Operators License. Persons performing inspections must be able to demonstrate their proficiency in inspecting motor vehicles and in operating, calibrating and maintaining items or equipment required for the inspection of motor vehicles, to personnel of the Registry of Motor Vehicles and the Massachusetts Department of Environmental Quality Engineering assigned to program administration and enforcement. Persons performing Emissions inspections must be certified by the Commissioner. A permanent employee is herein defined as a person carried on the payroll records of the applicant, regularly employed on the premises for a minimum of 20 hours a week. . . .

■ RESTATEMENT (SECOND) OF CONTRACTS

§201. Whose Meaning Prevails.

(1) Where the parties have attached the same meaning to a promise or agreement or a term thereof, it is interpreted in accordance with that meaning.

(2) Where the parties have attached different meanings to a promise or agreement or a term thereof, it is interpreted in accordance with the meaning attached by one of them if at the time the agreement was made

(a) that party did not know of any different meaning attached by the other, and the other knew the meaning attached by the first party; or

(b) that party had no reason to know of any different meaning attached by the other, and the other had reason to know the meaning attached by the first party. . . .

§202. Rules in Aid of Interpretation.

(1) Words and other conduct are interpreted in the light of all the circumstances, and if the principal purpose of the parties is ascertainable it is given great weight.

(2) A writing is interpreted as a whole, and all writings that are part of the same transaction are interpreted together.

(3) Unless a different intention is manifested,

(a) where language has a generally prevailing meaning, it is interpreted in accordance with that meaning;

(b) technical terms and words of art are given their technical meaning when used in a transaction within their technical field.

. . . (5) Wherever reasonable, the manifestations of intention of the parties to a promise or agreement are interpreted as consistent with each other and with any relevant course of performance, course of dealing, or usage of trade.

§207. Interpretation Favoring the Public.

In choosing among the reasonable meanings of a promise or agreement or a term thereof, a meaning that serves the public interest is generally preferred.

■ RESTATEMENT (SECOND) OF TORTS

§299A. Undertaking in Profession or Trade.

Unless he represents that he has greater or less skill or knowledge, one who undertakes to render services in the practice of a profession or trade is required to exercise the skill and knowledge normally possessed by members of that profession or trade in good standing in similar communities.

OFFICIAL COMMENTS

a. Skill, as the word is used in this Section, is something more than the mere minimum competence required of any person who does an act, under the rule stated in §299. It is that special form of competence which is not part of the ordinary equipment of the reasonable man, but which is the result of acquired learning, and aptitude developed by special training and experience. All professions, and most trades, are necessarily skilled, and the word is used to refer to the special competence which they require.

b. Profession or trade. This Section is thus a special application of the rule stated in §299. It applies to any person who undertakes to render services to another in the practice of a profession, such as that of physician or surgeon, dentist, pharmacist, oculist, attorney, accountant, or engineer. It applies also to any person who undertakes to render services to others in the practice of a skilled trade, such as that of airplane pilot, precision machinist, electrician, carpenter, blacksmith, or plumber. This Section states the minimum skill and knowledge which the actor undertakes to exercise, and therefore to have. If he has in fact greater skill than that common to the profession or trade, he is required to exercise that skill, as stated in §299, Comment e.

c. Undertaking. In the ordinary case, the undertaking of one who renders services in the practice of a profession or trade is a matter of contract between the parties, and the terms of the undertaking are either stated expressly, or implied as a matter of understanding. The rule here stated does not, however, depend upon the existence of an enforceable contract between the parties. It applies equally where professional services are rendered gratuitously, as in the case of a physician treating a charity patient, or without any definite understanding, as in the case of one who renders services to a patient who is unconscious, in an emergency. The basis of the rule is the undertaking of the defendant, which may arise apart from contract.

This undertaking is not necessarily a matter of the requirements of the particular task undertaken, although that task will of course have its bearing upon what is understood. A highly skilled individual, as for example, a certified public accountant, may undertake to perform services which normally require little skill, as for example to do ordinary book-keeping, and in performing those services he may, or may not, undertake to exercise his unusually high skill. On the other hand a bookkeeper with little or no accounting skill may undertake to do work which would normally call for a certified public accountant, and he may, or may not, undertake in doing it to exercise the skill of such an accountant. It is a matter of the skill which he represents himself to have, or is understood to undertake to have, rather than of the skill which he actually possesses, or which the task requires.

d. *Special representation.* An actor undertaking to render services may represent that he has superior skill or knowledge, beyond that common to his profession or trade. In that event he incurs an obligation to the person to whom he makes such a representation, to have, and to exercise, the skill and knowledge which he represents himself to have. Thus a physician who holds himself out as a specialist in certain types of practice is required to have the skill and knowledge common to other specialists. On the other hand the actor may make it clear that he has less than the minimum of skill common to the profession or trade; and in that case he is required to exercise only the skill which he represents that he has. Thus a layman who attempts to perform a surgical operation in an emergency, in the absence of any surgeon, and who makes it clear that he does not have the skill or knowledge of a surgeon, is not required to exercise such skill or knowledge. The rule stated in this Section applies only where there is no such special representation.

e. *Standard normally required.* In the absence of any such special representation, the standard of skill and knowledge required of the actor who practices a profession or trade is that which is commonly possessed by members of that profession or trade in good standing. It is not that of the most highly skilled, nor is it that of the average member of the profession or trade, since those who have less than median or average skill may still be competent and qualified. Half of the physicians of America do not automatically become negligent in practicing medicine at all, merely because their skill is less than the professional average. On the other hand, the standard is not that of the charlatan, the quack, the unqualified or incompetent individual who has succeeded in entering the profession or trade. It is that common to those who are recognized in the profession or trade itself as qualified, and competent to engage in it.

f. Schools of thought. Where there are different schools of thought in a profession, or different methods are followed by different groups engaged in a trade, the actor is to be judged by the professional standards of the group to which he belongs. The law cannot undertake to decide technical questions of proper practice over which experts reasonably disagree, or to declare that those who do not accept particular controversial doctrines are necessarily negligent in failing to do so. There may be, however, minimum requirements of skill applicable to all persons, of whatever school of thought, who engage in any profession or trade. Thus any person who holds himself out as competent to treat human ailments must have a minimum skill in diagnosis, and a minimum knowledge of possible methods of treatment. Licensing statutes, or those requiring a basic knowledge of science for the practice of a profession, may provide such a minimum standard.

g. Type of community. Allowance must be made also for the type of community in which the actor carries on his practice. A country doctor cannot be expected to have the equipment, facilities, experience, knowledge or opportunity to obtain it, afforded him by a large city. The standard is not, however, that of the particular locality. If there are only three physicians in a small town, and all three are highly incompetent, they cannot be permitted to set a standard of utter inferiority for a fourth who comes to town. The standard is rather that of persons engaged in similar practice in similar localities, considering geographical location, size, and the character of the community in general.

Such allowance for the type of community is most frequently made in professions or trades where there is a considerable degree of variation in the skill and knowledge possessed by those practicing it in different localities. It has commonly been made in the cases of physicians or surgeons, because of the difference in the medical skill commonly found in different parts of the United States, or in different types of communities. In other professions, such as that of the attorney, such variations either do not exist or are not as significant, and allowance for them has seldom been made. A particular profession may be so uniform, in different localities, as to the skill and knowledge of its members, that the court will not feel required to instruct the jury that it must make such allowance.

■ PEDERSON v. TIME, INC.
404 Mass. 14 (1989)

NOLAN, Justice. A judge in the Superior Court ruled that there is no genuine issue of fact whether Edith Pederson's ward, Alice Totten, was insane so as to toll the running of the statute of limitations against her claims. The judge allowed motions for summary judgment in favor of the defendants, Time, Inc. (Time), Life Magazine (Life) reporter David Friend, photographer Michael O'Brien, and the Department of Mental Health. The guardian appealed the judgment to the Appeals Court. We transferred the case to this court on our own motion. We reverse the judgment.

The guardian filed an unverified complaint on April 27, 1984, alleging various claims against the defendants based on an article appearing in the May, 1981, issue of Life. After a partial judgment on the pleadings, the remaining claims against Time, the publisher of Life, the reporter, and the photographer allege intentional violation of the State privacy statute, G.L. c. 214, §1B (1986 ed.), and intentional infliction of emotional distress. The two remaining counts against the Department of Mental Health allege violation of the Fair Information Practices Act, G.L. c. 66A (1986 ed.).

The guardian's allegations stem from an article entitled, *Emptying the Madhouse: The Mentally Ill Have Become Our Cities' Lost Souls.* The article discussed Totten's mental illness and was illustrated by a photograph of Totten tied spread-eagled to a hospital bed. Friend and O'Brien interviewed and photographed Totten on November 1 and 2, 1980, while she was an in-patient at Northampton State Hospital where she had been admitted following a violent episode. Doctors diagnosed her as schizophrenic. The Life article containing Totten's name and photograph was published on April 21, 1981, and that, all parties agree, is the latest date on which Totten's claims could have accrued. [April 21, 1981, is the date copies of the May, 1981, issue of Life went on sale in western Massachusetts.]

Each of Totten's claims has a three-year statute of limitation. Absent tolling of the period of limitations, the guardian could have seasonably commenced the action at any time up to and including April 22, 1984. She, however, did not file her complaint until April 27, 1984, thus raising the issue whether the statute of limitations should be tolled for the six-day period between April 21, 1981, the date the claims ripened, and April 27, 1981, the date three years following which the guardian commenced the action. If Totten were insane from April 22 to April 27, 1981, the statute providing for the tolling of limitations periods, G.L. c. 260, §7, [General Laws c. 260, §7, provided in relevant part that, if a person is "insane . . . when a right to bring an action first accrues, the action may be commenced within the time hereinbefore limited after the disability is removed."] would apply and would make the April 27, 1984, action timely. . . .

"[I]nsanity" under §7 is "any mental condition which precludes the plaintiff's understanding the nature or effects of his acts" and thus prevents him from comprehending his legal rights.

The crucial question in this case is whether the issue of Totten's insanity could be properly decided in a summary judgment action or whether there existed a genuine issue of material fact for a fact finder. Rule 56(c) of the Massachusetts Rules of Civil Procedure, 365 Mass. 824 (1974), provides that a judge shall grant a motion for summary judgment "if the pleadings, depositions, answers to interrogatories, and admissions on file, together with the affidavits, if any, show that there is no genuine issue as to any material fact and that the moving party is entitled to a judgment as a matter of law." The party moving for summary judgment assumes the burden of affirmatively demonstrating that there is no genuine issue of material fact on every relevant issue, even if he would have no burden on an issue if the case were to go to trial. If the moving party establishes the absence of a triable issue, the party opposing the motion must respond and allege specific facts which would establish the existence of a genuine issue of material fact in order to defeat a motion for summary judgment.

Insanity is a mental state and the generally accepted rule is that the "granting of summary judgment in a case where a party's state of mind. . . constitutes an essential element of the cause of action is disfavored." [Citations omitted.]

The guardian raised the issue of Totten's insanity in the pleadings, and that issue is clearly relevant in this case. The defendants argue that this statement in the complaint does not raise the issue of the tolling statute with specific precision, and thus the issue is not "raised by the pleadings." This argument is incorrect. The complaint raises the issue of Totten's mental incapacity and put the defendants on notice of the theory of the plaintiff's case, and that is all that is necessary under Mass. R. Civ. P. 8, 365 Mass. 749 (1974).

Hence, the defendants had the burden of proving that there existed no genuine issue whether Totten was sane or insane at the relevant time. This they did not do. Their evidence as to the period between March and June of 1981 simply establishes that Totten performed certain functions reasonably well. First, the evidence does not specifically address the days at issue: April 21 to April 27, 1981. Second, the defendants' affidavits and documents do not show that during this six-day period Totten did not have a mental condition which precluded her understanding the nature or effect of her acts. Accordingly, the judgments of the Superior Court are reversed and this case is remanded to the Superior Court. Judgments reversed.

and signed statements in the Coalition files, and I believe that we have evidentiary support for those facts.

A. There are presently no women employed by the city as firefighters, although several cities (such as New York, Columbus, and Seattle) do have female firefighters. The city of Cleveland uses a rank-order written and physical abilities test ostensibly to select candidates who possess the highest skills required to perform the job. Candidates are graded on their test performance, and an eligibility list is compiled in which scores are ranked from high to low. Although the test used by the city is supposed to be designed to eliminate discriminatory hiring, such rank order tests (as opposed to tests resulting in a non-ranked list of those who are qualified to serve) have been shown to have a disparate impact on women. The test used by the city can perhaps be challenged on the grounds that the test measures attributes in which men traditionally excel, such as speed and strength, while it ignored those in which women excel, such as stamina and endurance. This exam also tested for attributes not necessarily related to the skills which the job of firefighting requires.

B. The city hired a consultant to design, administer, and score the entry-level firefighter examination in question. No women were hired after those exams were scored and ranked. Several years ago, the same consultant was hired to design an exam for entry-level firefighters and to administer it. Cognizant of the fact that no women had yet scored high enough to be ranked at a level that evenly remotely provided an opportunity to be selected a firefighter, the consultant prepared a new job analysis and designed his test based on the new job analysis.

C. After the test was developed, but prior to the exam, the city embarked on a program to recruit and train female firefighters. As part of its recruitment program, the city provided potential female recruits with a free twelve-week training course. According to the initial interviews held with the women, this course did not include all components of what eventually would be on the exam.

D. On April 30, 1998, the city administered the written portion of the test, and on May 7 through 13, the physical portion of the text. Although there were originally 3,612 applicants, only 2,212 took the written part of the exam (285 of whom were females) and of those only 1,233 were allowed to take the physical part of the exam. Out of that group 29 females scored high enough to be placed on an eligibility list with 1,069 males. The highest ranking woman was 334 on the list, thus precluding any possibility that a female would be selected for one of the 35 available openings.

I have affidavits from three potential plaintiffs. Here are summaries, although Pat Moss has not yet consented to be a named plaintiff.

Barbara Zoll is a 24-year-old white female and a resident of the City of Cleveland. She is a graduate of Kent State University with a Bachelor's Degree in aerospace technology. She took the written exam, and received a score high enough to be permitted to take the physical agility test.

In January of 1998, While watching a local television news show she became aware of the recruitment program. After calling the Fire Department and asking for additional information she was referred to another program targeted towards minorities. She attended classes as part of the minority program for three weeks until discovering, on her own, the program directed to women recruits. She then began attending the women's recruitment classes four nights a week for four hours each. The classes included physical conditioning as well as academic aspects of the exam.

On the day of the civil service exam she arrived at 9:00 a.m. as instructed, with her yellow admission card indicating name, address, and seat number. There was no additional identification required or requested. On the answer sheet handed her at that time the pertinent information (name, address, and other information) was already filled out. Although it was announced that once testing began no one would be allowed to leave the test area, Zoll witnessed other candidates coming and going from the exam area with no apparent control. During the exam, an exam monitor personally told her of several typographical errors, however no general announcements were made to this effect. The plaintiff found the exam tested for areas of knowledge not previously announced in the civil service posting, or covered by the recruitment program classes. Despite two attempts to receive a copy of her graded exam she has not been allowed to do so.

Although Barbara Zoll was an exceptionally good athlete, the special class for women did not prepare her for the physical portion of the test. The barbell exercise caught her off guard, and the men had a distinct advantage in the dummy-pull. Despite the fact that she was in great shape, Barbara Zoll did much worse on the physical portion than she did on the written portion.

Pat Moss is a thirty-three-year old, white female, who has a Bachelor of Arts in Social Studies and a teaching certificate. She has taken three other civil service exams within the last six months in other smaller communities and has placed eighth (8th), seventh (7th) and fifteenth (15th) respectively. She originally heard about the special women's training program over the local television news. She received additional information from a friend who is a current Cleveland firefighter. On average she attended the classes two (2) days a week, beginning about three (3) weeks after they started. Ten days prior to the exam she saw the consultant and the Civil Service Personnel Administrator attend and observe a class. At the next class she attended, certain aspects of the physical conditioning program were made more rigorous, however it was not until the week before the actual physical exam that she and the other program participants were notified that weight training would be part of the exam.

In addition to the official women's training program, Moss also attended a special private training program. This course was run by a former police chief and cost $500.00. Included in that course of study were a number of general areas not covered in the official training program, but which were eventually on the exam. It was intimated by the facilitator of the private classes that he was in contact with the consultant.

Moss also notes that there were no security measures followed during the administering of the exam. She also had a test monitor point out a typographical error regarding the mislabeling of answers. After the exam, she spoke with a male applicant who informed her that he had been notified about three (3) typographical errors. Her test answer sheet had been filled out in advance with her name, address, and other pertinent personal information.

Because Moss scored a forty-five she was allowed to take the physical agility test, scheduled for a Sunday, May 10, at 4:00 p.m.. Upon arriving on the day the exam was scheduled she was notified by a note posted on the door, that the exam was postponed until the 13th due to rain and cold. On the rescheduled test date the identification system was limited to signing an entry log and receiving a card with her name on it. At the conclusion of each event the monitors wrote down her times and would then initial them. After completing all of the test events the cards were returned by placing them on a pile at a desk. Nobody was able to explain to her how the raw scores would be converted into a final rating for the agility test.

A number of the back tanks (I think this refers to self-contained breathing apparatus or air tanks), required to be worn while dragging a hose to the opposite end from where one starts, were inoperative. This resulted in a line-up at that particular event and a resting period for only some of the test participants. On the day she took the agility test the weather was sunny, dry, and cool.

Moss ranked 587 on the eligibility list. After learning her score she wrote letters to the Mayor and the Director of Public Safety questioning a rumor she heard that minority candidates would be scored differently. The Director of Public Safety responded that the procedure for choosing firefighters is designated by the Charter of the City, however selection of minority candidates has been modified by court order. White female candidates are not considered as minorities under the court order.

Jennifer Grimes is twenty-four years old, white, married, and at the time the exam was given, a resident of Parma, Ohio. She attended the official training program for women firefighters about two nights a week, and she also attended the private class for six weeks prior to the written test being administered. She learned of the private classes through a firefighter neighbor. The private classes are distinguishable from the official classes because they covered specific technical instruction concerning fire fighting techniques and other material taught at the Fire Academy. Two weeks prior to the exam the instructor notified the class that he had received certain information about the exam's content and then proceeded to instruct the class on tips to answer certain types of comprehension questions.

The official training sessions she attended did not cover this material, indeed, she recalls the classes as being focused on basic English, basic math and story problems. These classes appeared to come directly from a generic commercial outline.

The private classes did not focus as heavily on physical conditioning as the official class. However, they were scheduled to practice a simulated physical exam for six Saturdays prior to the exam. One week before the actual physical component of the examination she, along with all the other qualifying applicants, received a copy of the physical test program. The events listed included a barbell event, requiring that a thirty-three pound barbell be pressed thirty-five times without bending knees.

While attending the official women's training sessions she overheard an instructor inform several women that they could not get into the private class because it was full. Furthermore, she heard this same instructor characterize the women's training sessions as equal to the other classes. The son of this instructor was enrolled in the private classes to prepare for the firefighters exam.

Upon arriving at the written exam the yellow entry card was being made available to those individuals who had arrived without one. Her test answer sheet had been filled out in advance with her name, address, etc. She had been informed that the applicants would be filling out this information themselves.

During the exam she observed people changing seats from their assigned seats, smoking and talking. Errors on the exam were corrected by individual monitors assigned to areas of the Convention Center where the exam was held.

Grimes scored high enough to be eligible for the physical agility test. At the physical exam on May 9, 1998, she was informed that she was to proceed directly from one event to another without stopping in between; if she was found to be out of sequence with other candidates she would be disqualified. However, she observed other persons stopping to rest or being permitted to complete events even though they were out of sequence. Additionally, she observed lines forming at certain events, thus allowing some people the opportunity to rest.

Legal Analysis

Here is a summary of the legal research I have done so far in this case. I see four potential claims:

1. Section 1983

One potential remedy for a deprivation of civil rights is 42 U.S.C. §1983, which provides:

Every person who, under color of any statute, ordinance, regulation, custom or usage, of any State or Territory or the District of Columbia, subjects, or causes to be subjected, any citizen of the United States or other person within the jurisdiction thereof to the deprivation of any rights, privileges, or immunities secured by the Constitution and laws, shall be liable to the party injured in an action at law, suit in equity, or other proper proceeding for redress. . . .

The plain language of 42 U.S.C. §1983 mandates that a plaintiff must satisfy two essential requisites to state an actionable claim. First, there must be an alleged violation of a right secured by federal constitutional or statutory laws, such as the Fourth Amendment right to be free from unreasonable searches or the Fourteenth Amendment right to the equal protection of the laws. Second, a §1983 plaintiff must show that the alleged deprivation was caused by a person acting under color (or pretense) of state law. (Most rights secured by the Constitution are protected only against infringement by public entities or their officials, not private parties).

There is case law holding that a municipality (like the City of Cleveland) is "a person" (and thus an appropriate defendant) for purposes of §1983. In order to make out a claim against a local governmental body, it must be shown that the deprivation of rights complained of grows out of either the official policy or the custom and practice of the municipality. Actions by subordinate city officials acting on their own are not covered, unless they are acting in an official policy-making role.

The federal right that we will claim implicates §1983 is the right to equal protection for women under the Fourteenth Amendment. The Supreme Court has held that a plaintiff claiming a violation of the Fourteenth Amendment Equal Protection Clause must prove *discriminatory intent* (*i.e.*, that the challenged action was *deliberately* designed to disadvantage a protected group). *Discriminatory effect* alone is not sufficient to make out an Equal Protection violation. *See Washington v. Davis*, 426 U.S. 229 (1976); *Village of Arlington Heights v. Metropolitan Housing Development Corp.*, 429 U.S. 252 (1977). A plaintiff asserting an equal rights violation in a Section 1983 claim must be prepared to meet both production and persuasion burdens as to discriminatory intent. In *Black v. City of Akron, Ohio*, 831 F.2d 131 (6th Cir. 1987), however, the court held that "statistical proof may be used in actions under 42 U.S.C. §1983" and that "allegations of statistical evidence of an adverse impact might be sufficient to survive summary judgment." *Id.* at 133.

Unless the only relief sought is equitable, the parties have the right to claim a jury in §1983 cases. Section 1983 plaintiffs are entitled to compensatory damages, and also to punitive damages where "evil motive or intent" or "reckless or callous indifference to federally protected rights" is proven. *Smith v. Wade*, 461 U.S. 30 (1983). The court has discretion to allow a prevailing plaintiff (but not the United States) to recover "a reasonable attorney's fee as part of costs" in §1983 cases. (42 U.S.C. §1988).

2. Section 1985

Another potential remedy is found in 42 U.S.C. §1985(3):

> If two or more persons in any State or Territory conspire or go in disguise on the highway or on the premises of another, for the purpose of depriving, either directly or indirectly, any person or class of persons of the equal protection of the laws, or of equal privileges and immunities under the laws; or for the purpose of preventing or hindering the constituted authorities of any State or Territory from giving or securing to all persons within such State or Territory the equal protection of the laws; or if two or more persons conspire to prevent by force, intimidation, or threat, any citizen who is lawfully entitled to vote, from giving his support or advocacy in a legal manner, toward or in favor of the election of any lawfully qualified person as an elector for President or Vice President, or as a Member of Congress of the United States; or to injure any citizen in person or property on account of such support or advocacy; in any case of conspiracy set forth in this section, if one or more persons engaged therein do, or cause to be done, any act in furtherance of the object of such conspiracy, whereby another is injured in his person or property, or deprived of having and exercising any right or privilege of a citizen of the United States, the party so injured or deprived may have an action for the recovery of damages occasioned by such injury or deprivation, against any one or more of the conspirators.

A claim asserted under §1985(3) may be based on a purely private conspiracy (with no government involvement) if it was motivated by "some racial, or perhaps otherwise class-based, invidiously discriminatory animus." *Griffin v. Breckenridge*, 403 U.S. 88, 102 (1971). The conspiracy must be aimed at interfering with rights that are protected in 42 U.S.C. §1985 against encroachment, such as "equal protection of the laws, or of equal privileges and immunities under the laws," so this probably will get us back into having to prove discriminatory animus even when the conspiracy involves state actors. "It remains uncertain whether gender-based motivation qualifies as an actionable animus. . . ." under §1985(3). (1 Harold S. Lewis, Jr., *Litigating Civil Rights and Employment Discrimination Cases* §1.5 (1996)) "The Court in [*Great American Fed. S. & L Ass'n v. Novotny*, 442 U.S. 366 (1979)] held that §1985(3) is unavailable to enforce rights created by Title VII, 'expressing the fear that it might be used to bypass the detailed state and local administrative procedures, conciliation mechanisms and judicial remedies that Congress specified in the modern statute." (Lewis, Jr., *id.*) But, as I read *Novotny*, we can use §1985(3) to recover for a conspiracy to violate the equal protection clause; unlike *Novotny*, we have state action in our case.

Section 1985(3) provides a civil remedy, and consequently the elements of what constitute a civil conspiracy are probably relevant to defining "conspiracy" for §1985(3) purposes. These are: "(1) two or more persons; (2) an object to be accomplished; (3) a meeting of the minds on the object or course of action; (4) one or more unlawful, overt acts; and (5) damages as the proximate result." *Nelson v. Fontenot,* 784 F. Supp. 1528 (E.D. Tex. 1992) (action brought by deputy sheriffs against county officials alleging conspiracy to prohibit deputies from organizing a union).

3. Ohio Civil Service Statute

The Ohio statutory provisions relating to "frauds in examination prohibited" (Title I, Ch. 124, §124.58) are as follows:

No person or officer shall willfully or corruptly, by himself or in cooperation with one or more persons, defeat, deceive, or obstruct any person in respect of his right of examination, appointment, or employment according to sections 124.01 to 124.64 of the Revised Code, or to any rules or regulations prescribed pursuant to such sections; or willfully or corruptly, falsely mark, grade, estimate, or report upon the examination or proper standing of any person examined, registered, or certified pursuant to such sections, or aid in so doing; or willfully or corruptly make any false representations concerning the same, or concerning the person examined; or willfully or corruptly furnish to any person any special or secret information for the purpose of either improving or injuring the prospects or chances of any person so examined, registered, or certified; or to be examined, registered, or certified, or personate any other person, or permit or aid in any manner any person to personate him, in connection with any examination, registration, appointment, application, or request to be examined, registered, or appointed; or shall furnish any false information about himself, or any other person, in connection with any examination, registration, appointment, application, or request to be examined, registered, or appointed.

There is very little case law interpreting this portion of the Ohio civil service statutory provisions or the predecessor Ohio statute. The word "fraud" in its title, and the repetition of words such as "willfully or corrupt," "defeat, deceive, or obstruct," "falsely mark," "personate," and "willfully or corruptly furnish to any person any special or secret information" with respect to civil service examinations suggest to me that the purpose of these provisions is to protect the integrity of the civil service examination system by prohibiting cheating of any kind or the intentional distortion of results by dishonest behavior, such as providing people with the exam in advance, or taking the exam in someone else's name, or altering the true results. In *Resek v. Seven Hills,* 9 Ohio App. 3d 224, 227 (1963), the statutory provisions are cited in a case in which the Chief of Police was removed from his office for, among other things, illegally trying to help a friend who had failed the civil service exam for lieutenant. The Chief of Police had tried to influence a member of the Civil Service Commission (whom he had helped get appointed) to award the person who had failed undeserved credits for efficiency and seniority in service. The Chief of Police also tried to stop other people from getting the promotion to lieutenant, thus making room for his friend. Such behavior, in violation of the civil service provisions, was part of the justification for his removal. Under the predecessor statute to Title I, Ch. 124, §124.58, a civil service commissioner who made a false certificate that an applicant had satisfactorily passed an examination, which was untrue, was found guilty of corrupt use of his office. *Kerr v. Hinkle*, 12 OD (NP) 365 (1902).

4. Title VII

Title VII is, of course, another possibility. 42 U.S.C. §§2000e *et seq.* The statute prohibits discrimination in both private and public employment, and provides in pertinent part:

> (a) It shall be an unlawful employment practice for an employer—
> (1) to fail or refuse to hire or to discharge any individual or otherwise to discriminate against any individual with respect to his compensations, terms, conditions, or privileges of employment, because of such individual's race, color, religion, sex, or national origin; or
> (2) to limit, segregate, or classify his employees or applicants for employment in any way which would deprive or tend to deprive any individual of employment opportunities or otherwise adversely affect his status as an employee, because of such individual's race, color, religion, sex, or national origin. . . .
> (h) Notwithstanding any other provision of this subchapter, it shall not be an unlawful employment practice for an employer . . . to give and to act upon the results of any professionally developed ability test provided that such test, its administration or action upon the results is not designed, intended or used to discriminate because of race, color, religion, sex or national origin. . . .

Generally speaking, a violation of Title VII may be established by showing that (1) a covered employer (fifteen or more employees), (2) discriminated, (3) on one of the prohibited bases of discrimination, (4) with respect to an employment practice covered by the Act. Title VII prohibits two forms of discrimination: (I) disparate treatment, the familiar form of intentional conduct motivated by race, color, religion, sex, or national origin; and (II) disparate impact, the use of ostensibly neutral selection practices which have an adverse effect on a protected group and are not justified by a showing that the device predicts successful job performance. An example of the latter is a written examination which excludes disproportionate numbers of minorities and has no substantial relation to the skills and attributes necessary to perform the job in question.

In a *disparate treatment* case the plaintiff generally first must establish a prima facie case of discrimination, the elements of which are:

> 1) membership in a protected group; 2) application and qualification for a job for which the employer was seeking applicants; 3) rejection, despite the

applicant's qualifications; and 4) the employer's continued solicitation of applicants with qualifications equal to the plaintiff's.

Barbara Lindemann & Paul Grossman, I *Employment Discrimination Law* 15 (3rd ed. 1996). Such a showing raises a rebuttable inference that the rejection was discriminatorily motivated. *See McDonnell Douglas Corp. v. Green*, 411 U.S. 792 (1973). The defendant must then articulate (merely a burden of production) a nondiscriminatory explanation for the rejection. "Reasons that employers often articulate to rebut an inference of discrimination include, among others, lesser comparative qualifications, inability to get along with supervisors or fellow employees, misconduct, business exigencies such as the need to eliminate jobs, insubordination, inferior test scores, poor performance, the need to comply with rules set in union contracts, and greater familiarity with the favored employee's work." Lindemann & Grossman, *id.* at 22. After the employer meets its production burden on nondiscriminatory purpose, the plaintiff has the opportunity to demonstrate that the articulated reason is merely a pretext to cover the discriminatory motivation. The plaintiff ordinarily attempts to accomplish this by comparing his/her record and qualifications with that of individuals of the opposite race or gender who were favorably treated by the employer. The ultimate burden of proof remains with the plaintiff to prove (both in the production and persuasion senses) discriminatory intent on the part of the defendant. In *St. Mary's Honor Center v. Hicks*, 509 U.S. 502 (1993), the Supreme Court held that even if the plaintiff meets its burden in proving pretext (*i.e.*, the factfinder is persuaded that the reason or reasons given by the employer are not the real reasons why the defendant-employer rejected the plaintiff), the plaintiff may still lose unless the factfinder is persuaded that it was pretext for discrimination, as opposed to some other reason the employer is trying to hide. This holding in a 5-4 decision has been highly controversial, and courts disagree as to when the plaintiff's initial prima facie case, accompanied by the factfinder's disbelief of the employer's stated reason (i.e., a finding of pretext) is sufficient to permit an inference of discriminatory intent. Mark S. Brodin, *The Demise of Circumstantial Proof in Employment Discrimination Litigation: St. Mary's Honor Center v. Hicks, Pretext, and the "Personality Excuse,"* 18 Berkeley J. Employment & Lab. L. 183 (1997).

The theory of *disparate impact* was adopted by the Supreme Court in *Griggs v. Duke Power Co.*, 401 U.S. 424, 432 (1971), in which the plaintiffs challenged the employer's requirement of a high school diploma and a passing grade on a standardized general intelligence test in order to be employed at the North Carolina power plant. Evidence presented indicated that because of the inferior educational opportunities afforded to black citizens of the state, these selection requirements disproportionately excluded black applicants. Moreover, the requirements were not shown to have any relation to the performance of jobs at the plant. The Supreme

Court held that in order to establish a disparate impact violation of Title VII, "a plaintiff need only show that the facially neutral standards in question select applicants for hire in a significantly discriminatory pattern." The burden of proof then shifts to the employer to prove (with both production and persuasion burdens) that the challenged requirement had "a manifest relationship to the employment in question." If the employer is successful in proving that the requirement was job-related, the plaintiff could still prevail by proving that alternative selection devices would serve the employer's legitimate interests without a similar discriminatory effect.

Physical qualifications for employment which are ostensibly gender-neutral may nonetheless have a discriminatory impact on one sex. In *Dothard v. Rawlinson*, 433 U.S. 321 (1977), for example, the Court struck down height/weight minimums for the position of prison guard because they excluded disproportionate numbers of female applicants, and were not shown to be job-related.

Disparate impact cases involve some tricky burden of proof problems, which were addressed by the Civil Rights Act of 1991 and now are part of Title VII:

> (k)(1)(A) An unlawful employment practice based on disparate impact is established under this title only if—
>> (i) a complaining party demonstrates that a respondent uses a particular employment practice that causes a disparate impact on the basis of race, color, religion, sex, or national origin and the respondent fails to demonstrate that the challenged practice is job related for the position in question and consistent with business necessity . . .
>
> (B)(i) With respect to demonstrating that a particular employment practice causes a disparate impact as described in subparagraph (A)(i), the complaining party shall demonstrate that each particular challenged employment practice causes a disparate impact, except that if the complaining party can demonstrate to the court that the elements of a respondent's decisionmaking process are not capable of separation for analysis, the decisionmaking process may be analyzed as one employment practice.
>> (ii) If the respondent demonstrates that a specific employment practice does not cause the disparate impact, the respondent shall not be required to demonstrate that such practice is required by business necessity. . . .

The Civil Rights Act of 1991 also clarified the burden of proof in so-called mixed-motive disparate treatment cases:

> *Sec. 107. Clarifying Prohibition Against Impermissible Consideration of Race, Color, Religion, Sex, or National Origin in Employment Practices.*
> Except as otherwise provided in this title, an unlawful employment practice is established when the complaining party demonstrates that race,

color, religion, sex, or national origin was a motivating factor for any employment practice, even though other factors also motivated the practice.

On a claim in which an individual proves a violation under section 703(m) and a respondent demonstrates that the respondent would have taken the same action in the absence of the impermissible motivating factor, the court—

(i) may grant declaratory relief, injunctive relief (except as provided in clause (ii)), and attorney's fees and costs demonstrated to be directly attributable only to the pursuit of a claim under section 703(m); and

(ii) shall not award damages or issue an order requiring any admission, reinstatement, hiring, promotion, or payment, described in subparagraph (A). . . .

One other provision of the Civil Rights Act of 1991 may be of interest:

Sec. 106. Prohibition Against Discriminatory Use of Test Scores.

(1) It shall be an unlawful employment practice for a respondent, in connection with the selection or referral of applicants or candidates for employment or promotion, to adjust the scores of, use different cutoff scores for, or otherwise alter the results of, employment related tests on the basis of race, color, religion, sex, or national origin. . . .

The Civil Right Act of 1991 reaffirms the prior case law that even if the factfinder is persuaded that the defendant's stated "job related" employment practice is "consistent with business necessity," the plaintiff can win if it proves (production and persuasion burdens) that there is an alternative employment practice that the defendant refuses to adopt that would meet the employer's business needs without having a similar discriminatory impact. (Sec. 105, (a)(ii) and (C).)

Under Title VII, a plaintiff can recover compensatory and punitive damages by proving intentional discrimination, but cannot do so in a disparate impact case. Reinstatement and backpay are considered equitable remedies that are available in both disparate impact and disparate treatment cases. In a disparate treatment case, compensatory damages (including damages for future pecuniary losses, emotional pain, suffering, inconvenience, mental anguish, loss of enjoyment of life, and other nonpecuniary losses) and punitive damages are limited for each complaining party to $300,000 against employers with more than 500 employees; but, in addition, the complaining party can be awarded equitable relief. In a case in which the plaintiff seeks compensatory damages (which will be a disparate treatment case requiring the plaintiff to prove intentional discrimination), any party may claim a jury. Parties probably do not have the right to demand a jury in disparate treatment cases. Under Title VII, prevailing plaintiffs can be awarded attorney fees.

**IN THE UNITED STATES DISTRICT COURT
FOR THE NORTHERN DISTRICT OF OHIO
EASTERN DIVISION**

BARBARA ZOLL
902 East 61st Street, Apt. #5
Cleveland, Ohio 44103

JENNIFER GRIMES   C.A. No. 98-2371
1992 Brookdale Road
Parma, Ohio 44134

On behalf of themselves and
all others similarly situated

                                                     COMPLAINT
    Plaintiffs   **CLASS ACTION**

        vs.

CITY OF CLEVELAND
City Hall
601 Lakeside Avenue
Cleveland, Ohio 44114

JAMES KOSOLSKY, MAYOR
City of Cleveland
City Hall
601 Lakeside Avenue
Cleveland, Ohio 44114
    Individually and in his official capacity as Mayor

HARRY N. TARPLEY, DIRECTOR
Department of Public Safety
City of Cleveland
City Hall
601 Lakeside Avenue
Cleveland, Ohio 44114
    Individually and in his official capacity as Director of the
    Department of Public Safety

STEVEN SAPERS, PRESIDENT
Civil Service Commission
4210 Cable Avenue
Cleveland, Ohio 44127
    Individually and in his official capacity as a Civil Service
    Commission member and officer

EVAN W. SPANIOG, VICE PRESIDENT
Civil Service Commission
15089 Harland Avenue
Cleveland, Ohio 44119
  Individually and in his official capacity as a Civil Service
  Commission member and officer

ALICE Q. SIMMONS, SECRETARY
Civil Service Commission
Room 119, City Hall, 601 Lakeside Avenue
Cleveland, Ohio 44114
  Individually and in her official capacity as a Civil Service
  Commission member and officer

BETTY SMITH
1400 Henley Avenue
Cleveland, Ohio 44109
  Individually and in her official capacity as a Civil Service
  Commission member

SAMUEL HAWKINS
4823 East 74th Street
Cleveland, Ohio 44104
  Individually and in his official capacity as a Civil Service
  Commission member

KAREN SHELTON
PERSONNEL ADMINISTRATOR
Civil Service Commission
City of Cleveland
Room 119, City Hall
601 Lakeside Avenue
Cleveland, Ohio 44114
  Individually and in her official capacity as
  Personnel Administrator of the Civil Service Commission

THOMAS McGINNIS, FIRE CHIEF
City of Cleveland
1535 Superior Avenue
Cleveland, Ohio 44114
  Individually and in his official capacity as Fire Chief

SHELDON O. MARSHALL
Personnel Testing And Statistical Analysis
1701 Erie Ave.
Cleveland, Ohio 44114
    Acting as an agent and/or representative of the City of Cleveland
in devising and administering its Civil Service Commission test, and
for the Fire Department of the City of Cleveland, Defendants.

PRELIMINARY STATEMENT

1. This is a class action for declaratory and equitable relief and damages brought by the Plaintiffs against the City of Cleveland, Ohio, and several municipal officials and an agent and/or representative of the City of Cleveland on the grounds that the Defendants have engaged in unlawful discrimination against females with respect to the Defendants' policies and practices concerning the recruiting, training, testing, hiring, and employment of firefighters.

The Plaintiffs seek a judgment and decree that the practices complained of are in violation of rights guaranteed by the Constitution of the United States and applicable civil rights statutes.

Plaintiffs also seek to invoke the Court's supplemental jurisdiction with respect to common law claims arising out of the same common nucleus of facts as her federal claims. In connection with this claim, the Plaintiffs seek a judgment or decree that the practices complained of herein are in violation of the laws of the State of Ohio, ordinances, rules and regulations of the City of Cleveland and its Civil Service Commission.

PARTIES

A. Plaintiffs

2. (a) Plaintiff, Barbara Zoll, is a citizen of the United States residing at 902 East 61st Street, Apt. #5, Cleveland, Ohio 44103.

(b) Barbara Zoll is a white female.

(c) On April 30, 1998, Plaintiff took the City of Cleveland Civil Service Commission written test for eligibility for appointment as a Cleveland firefighter.

(d) Barbara Zoll received a score of 48.50 on the written test and took the physical agility test administered from May 7 through May 13, 1998.

(e) Plaintiff is no. 642 on the current eligibility list for appointment as a Cleveland firefighter.

(f) Barbara Zoll attended classes in a specially funded training program for female applicants for the April 30, 1998, firefighters' Civil Service Commission Test.

3. (a) Plaintiff, Jennifer Grimes, is a citizen of the United States residing at 1992 Brookdale Road, Parma, Ohio 44134. In late January or early February 1998, when she applied to take the City of Cleveland Civil Service Commission test for eligibility for appointment as a Cleveland firefighter, Plaintiff was a bona fide resident of 3448 West 94th Street, Cleveland, Ohio 44102.

(b) Jennifer Grimes is a white female.

(c) On April 30, 1998, Plaintiff took the City of Cleveland Civil Service Commission written test for eligibility for appointment as a Cleveland firefighter.

(d) Jennifer Grimes received a score of 39.50 on the written test, plus an additional 5 points because she is a veteran, and was permitted to take the physical agility test administered on May 9, 1998.

(e) Jennifer Grimes received a score of 28.24 on the physical agility test, and was given an additional 10 points because she was a resident of the City of Cleveland.

(f) Jennifer Grimes is Number 952 on the current eligibility list for appointment as a Cleveland firefighter.

(g) Because of her ranking as No. 952 on the current eligibility list, it is unlikely that Plaintiff will be appointed as a Cleveland firefighter.

(h) Jennifer Grimes attended classes in a specially funded training program for female applicants for the firefighters Civil Service Commission Test.

B. Class Action

4. Plaintiffs bring this action on their own behalf and pursuant to Rules 23(a) and (b)(2), F.R.C.P. on behalf of all others similarly situated.

5. The class which Plaintiffs represent includes all females who at any time applied to take the Civil Service Commission Examination for

eligibility for appointment as a Cleveland firefighter offered on April 30, 1998, and also all females who attended the special training class offered by the City of Cleveland from approximately mid-January 1998 to late-April, 1998, for the purpose of training actual and potential female applicants for the April 30, 1998, Civil Service Examination. The class also includes all females who have been or will be deterred from applying for employment, and also all females who will be employed, or who will apply for employment as firefighters with the City of Cleveland at any time in the future.

6. (a) The Defendants have restricted eligibility of applicants for the position of firefighter to persons 18 years of age or more, who are citizens of the United States and who possess a high school diploma, or the equivalent.

(b) The population of the Standard Metropolitan Statistical Area (SMSA) of Cleveland includes 1,384,025 persons 18 years of age or more.

(c) Of these 1,384,025 persons, approximately 53% are female.

(d) Two hundred eighty-five (285) women took the Civil Service Commission written test for eligibility for appointment as a Cleveland firefighter on April 30, 1998. The number of women who will apply for employment in the future, or who have been or will be deterred from applying is unknown.

(e) The class is so numerous that joinder of all members is impracticable.

7. (a) Defendants issue notices of all Civil Service examinations for the position of firefighter.

(b) Defendants require written tests of all firefighter applicants and agility tests of those who pass the written test.

(c) No (0) female has ever been employed by the City of Cleveland as a firefighter in its history; the woman scoring highest on the examination that began April 30, 1998, is No. 334 on the eligibility list.

(d) A special training program for female applicants or potential applicants was held by the Defendant City of Cleveland for the April 30, 1998, Civil Service Commission examination for the position of Cleveland firefighter. While this program was open to anyone who wished to attend, free of charge, it was referred to as being especially for women.

(e) The above facts are common to the class.

8. Questions of law common to the members of the class concern whether the acts herein alleged to have been committed by the Defendants constitute violations of the United States Constitution and the Civil Rights Acts of 1871, and 1964, as amended.

9. (a) Plaintiff Barbara Zoll applied to take, participated in, and passed the Civil Service Commission written test for eligibility for appointment as a Cleveland firefighter offered on April 30, 1998, and scored a 33.2 on the physical portion.

(b) Plaintiff Jennifer Grimes applied to take, and passed the Civil Service Commission written tests for eligibility for appointment as a Cleveland firefighter offered on April 30, 1998. She attained a score of less than 35 (the requisite passing score) on the physical agility test offered from May 7, 1998, through May 13, 1998, although her name is, nevertheless, listed on the eligibility list for appointment as a Cleveland firefighter.

(c) The City of Cleveland plans to appoint approximately thirty-five (35) firefighters immediately from the current firefighter eligibility list.

(d) The highest-ranking woman who passed both the written test and the physical agility test is ranked Number 334 on the eligibility list.

(e) The City of Cleveland will not reach any woman on the current eligibility list for appointment as a Cleveland firefighter unless it takes women from the eligibility list out of their rank order.

(f) All the named Plaintiffs attended some classes of a specially-funded training program for the April 30, 1998, Cleveland Firefighters Civil Service Commission Examination.

(g) Plaintiffs' claims are typical of the class.

10. (a) Plaintiffs have pursued available administrative remedies by filing charges of employment discrimination based on their sex with the Cleveland Regional Office of the Equal Employment Opportunity Commission.

(b) Plaintiffs have retained counsel and are able fairly and adequately to represent and protect the interests of the class.

11. The Defendants' policies regarding hiring and employment have been and will continue to be generally applicable to the class thereby making appropriate final injunctive and declaratory relief with respect to the

class as a whole. A common relief is sought. A class action is the only practical method of fair and efficient adjudication of this controversy.

C. Defendants

12. (a) Defendant City of Cleveland is a municipal corporation organized and established pursuant to laws of the State of Ohio.

(b) Defendant City of Cleveland, through its mayor and council, formulates, adopts, and implements policies, practices, and procedures with regard to hiring and employment by the municipality.

(c) Defendant City of Cleveland is an employer within the meaning of Title 42 U.S.C. §2000e(a) and (b), as amended.

13. Defendant James Kosolsky is Mayor of the City of Cleveland and, as such, is vested with the authority to enforce the City's ordinances, regulations, and policies. He is sued both in his official capacity and individually.

14. Defendant Harry N. Tarpley is the Director of the Department of Public Safety of the City of Cleveland. As an appointee of the mayor, he is vested with authority to oversee and direct the operations and policies of the various safety divisions of the City of Cleveland, including the Fire Department.

15. Steven Sapers is President of the Civil Service Commission of the City of Cleveland. He is vested with the authority to carry out the ordinances, rules, regulations, and policies of the Civil Service Commission. He is sued in his official capacity and individually.

16. Evan W. Spaniog is Vice President of the Civil Service Commission of the City of Cleveland. He is vested with the authority to carry out the ordinances, rules, regulations, and policies of the Civil Service Commission. He is sued in his official capacity and individually.

17. Alice Q. Simmons is the Secretary of the Civil Service Commission of the City of Cleveland. She is vested with the authority to carry out the ordinances, rules, regulations, and policies of the Civil Service Commission. She is being sued in her official capacity and individually.

18. Betty Smith is a member of the Civil Service Commission of the City of Cleveland. She is vested with the authority to carry out the ordinances, rules, regulations, and policies of the Civil Service Commission. She is being sued in her official capacity and individually.

19. Samuel Hawkins is a member of the Civil Service Commission of the City of Cleveland. He is vested with the authority to carry out the ordinances, rules, regulations, and policies of the Civil Service Commission. He is being sued in his official capacity and individually.

20. Karen Shelton is Personnel Administrator of the Civil Service Commission of the City of Cleveland. She is vested with the authority to carry out the ordinances, rules, regulations, and policies of the Civil Service Commission. She is being sued in her official capacity and individually.

21. (a) Defendant Fire Chief Thomas McGinnis is a sworn officer of the Fire Department of the City of Cleveland.

(b) The Fire Chief supervises approximately 1,000 persons who serve as firefighters for the City.

(c) Defendant Fire Chief McGinnis is an agent of an employer within the meaning of Title 42 U.S.C. § 2000e(a) and (b), as amended.

22. (a) Defendant Sheldon O. Marshall is a professor of psychology at Case-Western Reserve University, Cleveland, Ohio, who offers consulting services in the area of devising, administering, evaluating, and scoring civil service examinations on behalf of local, state, and federal governments.

(b) Pursuant to an agreement with the Defendant City of Cleveland, Defendant Marshall prepared, administered, scored, and evaluated the Civil Service Commission written test for eligibility for appointment as a Cleveland firefighter offered on April 30, 1998, and also the physical agility test of the same examination, offered from May 7 through 13, 1998.

(c) Defendant Marshall is an agent and/or representative of an employer within the meaning of Title 42 U.S.C. §2000e(a) and (b) as amended.

STATEMENT OF THE CLAIM

A. COUNT ONE: TITLE VII

23. On or about October 6, 1994, Sheldon O. Marshall submitted a Proposal to provide a job-related entry-level examination for the position of firefighter—City of Cleveland.

24. Pursuant to Ordinance No. 2618-94 enacted December 6, 1994, the Council of the City of Cleveland selected Defendant Marshall to

provide his professional services in preparing, administering, and defending a job-related, entry-level examination for the position of firefighter.

25. (a) On or about March 15, 1995, pursuant to Ordinance No. 2618-94 enacted by the Council of the City of Cleveland on December 6, 1994, the City of Cleveland entered into a formal agreement with Defendant Marshall that he provide the professional services necessary to prepare, administer, and defend a job-related, entry-level examination for the position of firefighter.

(b) In return, the City of Cleveland has paid or will pay Defendant Marshall an amount equal to or in excess of Thirty-Seven Thousand Five Hundred Fifty Dollars ($37,550.00).

26. On or about January 1, 1998, the Civil Service Commission of the City of Cleveland issued an announcement of an open competitive examination for the position of firefighter, the written portion of which would be administered on April 30, 1998. Said announcement stated:

The written test is designed to measure basic reading and math skills, the ability to follow directions, the ability to recall basic factual materials, and a variety of judgment and skills related to firefighter performance. Knowledge of firefighting procedures is not required on the test.

27. (a) During January, 1998, or February, 1998, the exact date unknown, the City of Cleveland commenced a program allegedly intended to prepare women successfully to pass all phases of the 1998 firefighter entry-level tests.

(b) Classes in this program were free of charge and described as a women's training course.

(c) Classes in the women's training program were supervised by Lt. Kevin Kelly, an agent of the Defendant City of Cleveland.

(d) The content of the classes in this program did not provide adequate preparation for the content of the written test administered on April 30, 1998.

(e) The content of the classes in the women's training program did not include all aspects of the physical agility test administered May 7 through 12, 1998.

28. (a) For several months prior to April 30, 1998, the exact dates being unknown, Buddy Casey offered a program of classes to prepare candidates for the firefighter tests.

(b) Enrollees in Buddy Casey's classes were charged a fee of Five Hundred Dollars ($500.00).

(c) Only eight (8) women attended Casey's classes.

(d) The content of Casey's classes closely paralleled the content of the written test offered on April 30, 1998.

29. On or about April 30, 1998, at the Cleveland Convention Center commencing at 9:30 a.m., the Civil Service Commission administered the written portion of the entry-level firefighters test to all candidates.

30. Those persons determined by the City of Cleveland to have passed the written test successfully were notified to take the physical agility test.

31. Physical agility tests were administered to groups of twenty-five (25) candidates at scheduled half hour intervals commencing May 7, 1998 through May 13, 1998.

32. (a) Sometime during the second half of May, 1998, the Civil Service Commission issued an eligibility list of one thousand ninety-eight (1,098) names of persons who had taken both written and physical portions of the City of Cleveland's entry-level firefighter examination during April-May, 1998.

(b) Of the one thousand ninety-eight (1,098) names appearing on the eligibility list, the names of only twenty-nine (29) women appear.

(c) The highest ranking woman on the May, 1998 eligibility list is F. Huilbert, who is ranked No. 334.

(d) Women have been informed by agents, officers, and representatives of the City of Cleveland that no women will be hired as Cleveland firefighters.

33. (a) The Cleveland firefighter entry-level examination has a disparate adverse impact upon female applicants with respect to both the written and the physical agility portions of the examination.

34. (a) The content of the written portion of the entry-level firefighter test April 30, 1998, is not job-related and/or performance predictive.

(b) The content of the written test does not accord with the content of the Civil Service announcement of January 3, 1998.

(c) Nor was the written test administered April 30, 1998, related to the content of the special women's firefighter training program offered by the City of Cleveland in early 1998.

(d) The firefighter written test discriminates against female applicants on the basis of their sex.

(e) Alternative job-related methods of testing were available, which would not have had as adverse a disparate effect upon females and which would not have discriminated against females on the basis of their sex.

35. (a) The administration of the written test was not in accordance with laws, ordinances, regulations, and policies applicable to the Defendants in this action.

(b) Security for the administration of the test was not uniformly applied to all candidates.

36. (a) The method of grading and evaluating the written test scores discriminated against females upon the basis of their sex.

(b) The method of grading, evaluation, and weighting questions within the written test was not selected until after the candidates had completed and turned in their completed tests.

(c) Five (5) extra points for eligible veterans were added immediately to veterans' written scores thereby enabling many men who otherwise would not have passed the written test to attain a passing grade of thirty-five (35).

(d) Methods of correcting errors in the written test were not uniformly applied to all candidates.

(e) Although various female candidates requested the right to review their graded written tests, their requests were denied.

37. (a) The content of the physical agility test administered from May 7 through May 13, 1998, was not job-related and/or performance predictive of the skills required of an entry-level Cleveland firefighter.

(b) The physical agility test was not related to the content of the special women's firefighter training program offered by the City of Cleveland in early 1998.

(c) The physical agility test was of such difficulty that it was predictable that women would be more likely than men to be eliminated by it.

(d) The physical agility test included items with respect to which women are known to be disadvantaged while excluding those with respect to which females generally are advantaged.

38. The administration of the physical agility test from May 7 through May 13, 1998, was neither consistent, uniform, nor fair.

39. (a) The grading of the physical agility test has had a disparate adverse impact upon women and a discriminatory effect upon women based upon their sex.

(b) Times for each physical agility event were evaluated against the times of other participants, rather than for minimum competency.

(c) The methods of evaluating candidates' time scores varied significantly and without adequate reason, on the different days the physical test was administered.

(d) The method of weighting, evaluating, and scoring the physical agility test was not determined until after the candidates had completed their tests.

(e) The method of determining the physical agility test score sufficient for placement on the eligibility list was not in accordance with the stated requirement set forth in the instruction sheet issued to candidates taking the agility test (see Exhibit A attached).

40. The City of Cleveland, through its officers, agents, and representatives has made statements intended to discourage females from seeking employment with the City of Cleveland's Fire Department.

41. The City of Cleveland and the other named Defendants knew, or should have known, that the written and physical agility firefighters' tests would have a disparate adverse impact and discriminatory effect upon females because of their sex.

42. The procedures described above for the selection of entry-level firefighters were intended by the Defendants to eliminate female candidates from consideration for firefighter positions.

43. By all the acts set forth in paragraphs 23 through 42 above, the Defendants have violated Title VII of the Civil Rights Act of 1964, 42 U.S.C. §§2000e, *et seq.*

44. Plaintiffs have fulfilled the conditions precedent to filing a civil action pursuant to Title VII of the Civil Rights Act of 1964. Both Named Plaintiffs have filed timely charges of discrimination with the Equal Employment Opportunity Commission and requested their Notices of Right to Sue.

RELIEF PRAYED

45. WHEREFORE, Plaintiffs respectfully pray that this Honorable Court:

(a) Declare unlawful the policies and practices of the Defendants set forth in paragraphs 23 through 42 above, as depriving Plaintiffs and the members of the class they represent, employment opportunities protected by Title VII of the Civil Rights Act of 1964, 42 U.S.C. §§2000e, *et seq.*;

(b) Enjoin the Defendants, both preliminarily and permanently, from declaring the Plaintiffs and others of their class to be either ineligible or too low ranking on the eligibility list for appointment to entry-level firefighter positions on the basis of unvalidated tests which have a disparate effect upon females solely because of their sex;

(c) Direct that the Defendant City of Cleveland, its Mayor, department directors, civil service commission, and others undertake a program to formulate, promulgate, and implement a uniform and nondiscriminatory procedure and policy with respect to the recruiting, hiring, and training of female firefighters;

(d) Make Plaintiffs and the members of their class whole by appropriate back pay, including pre-judgment and post-judgment interest at prevailing rates on the amount awarded, and front pay;

(e) Grant Plaintiffs and the members of their class the costs of this action and reasonable attorneys' fees pursuant to 42 U.S.C. §1988, including interest at prevailing rates on all sums awarded;

(f) After a prompt hearing of this action according to law, issue an order retaining jurisdiction of this claim until such time as the Court is assured from the activity of the Defendants and their agents that the violations of rights complained of herein have ceased and are no longer threatened and that the effect of past violations has been remedied; and

(g) Grant such other affirmative relief as the Court deems just and appropriate.

B. COUNT TWO: §1983

46-65. As paragraphs 46 through 65, Plaintiffs restate, as if fully stated herein, paragraphs 23 through 42 of this complaint.

66. By all the acts set forth in paragraphs 46 through 65 above, the Defendants have violated the Civil Rights Act of 1871, 42 U.S.C. §1983, and the Due Process and Equal Protection Clause of the Fourteenth Amendment of the United States Constitution.

RELIEF PRAYED

67. WHEREFORE, Plaintiffs respectfully pray that this Honorable Court:

(a) Pursuant to Title 28 U.S.C. §§ 2201 and 2202, declare unlawful the actions, policies, practices, customs, and usages herein challenged, as being violative of the Civil Rights Act of 1871, 42 U.S.C. §1983, and the Fourteenth Amendment to the United States Constitution;

(b) Enjoin, both preliminarily and permanently, all use of veterans' preference points for male firefighters with respect to the scoring of the City of Cleveland's entry-level firefighter test;

(c) Enjoin the Defendants, both preliminarily and permanently, from declaring the Plaintiffs and others of their class to be either ineligible or too low ranking on the eligibility list for appointment to entry-level firefighter positions on the basis of unvalidated tests which have a disparate effect upon females solely because of their sex;

(d) Direct that the Defendant City of Cleveland, its Mayor, department directors, civil service commission, and others undertake a program to formulate, promulgate, and implement a uniform and nondiscriminatory procedure and policy with respect to the recruiting, hiring, and training of female firefighters;

(e) Make Plaintiffs and the members of their class whole by appropriate back pay, including pre-judgment and post-judgment interest at prevailing rates on the amount awarded, and front pay;

(f) Grant Plaintiffs and the members of their class the costs of this action and reasonable attorneys' fees pursuant to 42 U.S.C. §1988, including interest at prevailing rates on all sums awarded;

(g) Award Plaintiffs and the members of the class they represent compensatory and punitive damages;

(h) After a prompt hearing of this action according to law, issue an order retaining jurisdiction of this claim until such time as the Court is assured from the activity of the Defendants and their agents that the violations of rights complained of herein have ceased and are no longer threatened and that the effect of past violations has been remedied; and

(i) Grant such other affirmative relief as the Court deems just and appropriate.

C. COUNT THREE: CONSPIRACY UNDER §1985(3)

68-87. As paragraphs 68 through 87, Plaintiffs restate, as if fully stated herein, paragraphs 23 through 42 of this complaint.

88. (a) Defendants the City of Cleveland, the officers and members of the Civil Service Commission and Fire Chief McGinnis and other unnamed co-conspirators each and with the others determine the employment needs of the City.

(b) Similarly, the Defendants determine the methods used to publicize the fact that hiring of firefighters for the City will take place.

(c) Further, the above-named Defendants, together with Defendant Sheldon Marshall, select the testing procedures, administer the examination, and evaluate the results.

(d) Finally, the above-named Defendants, together with Defendant Sheldon Marshall, are responsible for deciding which applicants will be hired for available entry-level firefighter position.

89. Defendants employed by the City of Cleveland have conspired with Defendant Marshall and with each other to deprive directly or indirectly, candidates for firefighter positions for the City of Cleveland of their rights to equal employment opportunity guaranteed by the Fourteenth Amendment to the United States Constitution and 42 U.S.C. §§1983 and 2000e, *et seq.*

90. Defendants employed by the City of Cleveland, Defendant Marshall, and any unnamed co-conspirators have met and acted in concert to

deprive the Plaintiffs and members of their class equal opportunities for employment with the City of Cleveland, thereby causing irreparable injury to them in violation of rights guaranteed by the Due Process and Equal Protection Clauses of the Fourteenth Amendment to the United States Constitution and 42 U.S.C. §§1983 and 2000e, *et seq.*

91. By these multiple acts, some of which were taken outside the scope of authority and the official capacities of the Defendants, as set forth in paragraphs 75 through 95 above, the Defendants have violated the Civil Rights Act of 1871, 42 U.S.C. §1985(3).

RELIEF PRAYED

92. WHEREFORE, Plaintiffs respectfully pray that this Honorable Court:

(a) Pursuant to Title 28 U.S.C. §§2201 and 2202 declare unlawful the actions taken in concert by the Defendants conspiring to deprive the Plaintiffs and the members of the class they represent of nondiscriminatory training programs, preparation, development, administration, grading, evaluation, and purported validation of both the written firefighters' test offered on April 30, 1998, and the physical agility firefighters' test offered May 7 through May 13, 1998, and declare unlawful, null and void these same actions and the eligibility list(s) resulting from said tests as being violative of 42 U.S.C. §1985(3);

(b) Enjoin, both preliminarily and permanently, all use of veterans' preference points for male firefighters with the scoring of the City of Cleveland's entry-level firefighter test;

(c) Enjoin the Defendants, both preliminarily and permanently, from declaring the Plaintiffs and others of their class to be either ineligible or too low ranking on the eligibility list for appointment to entry-level firefighter positions on the basis of unvalidated tests which have a disparate effect upon females solely because of their sex;

(d) Direct that the Defendant City of Cleveland, its Mayor, department directors, civil service commission, and others undertake a program to formulate, promulgate, and implement a uniform and nondiscriminatory procedure and policy with respect to the recruiting, hiring, and training of female firefighters;

(e) Make Plaintiffs and the members of their class whole by appropriate back pay, including pre-judgment and post-judgment interest at prevailing rates on the amount awarded, and front pay;

(f) Grant Plaintiffs and the members of their class the costs of this action and reasonable attorneys' fees pursuant to 42 U.S.C. §1988, including interest at prevailing rates on all sums awarded;

(g) Award Plaintiffs and the members of the class they represent compensatory and punitive damages;

(h) After a prompt hearing of this action according to law, issue an order retaining jurisdiction of this claim until such time as the Court is assured from the activity of the Defendants and their agents that the violations of rights complained of herein have ceased and are no longer threatened and that the effect of past violations has been remedied; and

(i) Grant such other affirmative relief as the Court deems just and appropriate.

D. COUNT FOUR: OHIO CIVIL SERVICE FRAUD STATUTE

93-112. As paragraphs 93 through 112, Plaintiffs restate, as if fully stated herein, paragraphs 23 through 42 of this complaint.

113. Rule 4.00 of the Civil Service Rules of the City of Cleveland provide procedures for the conduct of civil service competitive examinations.

114. The importance of proper administrative procedures with respect to the conduct of civil service examinations is underscored by O.R.C. §124.58, which prohibits fraud with respect to defeating, deceiving, or obstructing any person in respect of his right of examination, appointment, or employment. This statute also prohibits willful, corrupt, or false grading of examinations and other matters.

115. Defendants made material representations to the Plaintiffs, falsely and fraudulently, that the City of Cleveland was seeking to appoint women firefighters, thereby inducing Plaintiff to apply to take the Firefighter examination.

116. These representations, whether oral or in writing, by the Defendants were known to be false by some or all of the Defendants at the time these representations were made and were made willfully and maliciously with intent to induce Plaintiffs to take the firefighter examination and to deceive and deny Plaintiffs their civil rights.

117. Plaintiffs, relying upon the false representations and the representation of the Defendants that the women's training program would

adequately prepare them for the firefighter examination, enrolled in the women's training program, spent substantial time preparing for the Civil Service Commission firefighting examination, and completed those tests which they were permitted to take in their attempt to qualify for firefighter positions.

118. The Defendants, having induced the Plaintiffs to take tests which discriminated against women based upon their sex, then also administered and evaluated these tests in a discriminatory, willful, and malicious fashion.

119. As a result of these false and fraudulent representations of the Defendants, Plaintiffs were proximately injured and suffered economic loss, loss of career opportunity, humiliation, and emotional distress.

RELIEF PRAYED

120. WHEREFORE, Plaintiffs respectfully pray that this Honorable Court:

(a) Declare unlawful the policies and practices of the Defendants set forth in paragraphs 23 through 42 above;

(b) Enjoin the Defendants, both preliminarily and permanently, from declaring the Plaintiffs and others of their class to be either ineligible or too low ranking on the eligibility list for appointment to entry-level firefighter positions on the basis of unvalidated tests which have a disparate effect upon females solely because of their sex;

(c) Direct that the Defendant City of Cleveland, its Mayor, department directors, civil service commission, and others undertake a program to formulate, promulgate, and implement a uniform and nondiscriminatory procedure and policy with respect to the recruiting, hiring, and training of female firefighters;

(d) Enjoin, both preliminarily and permanently, all additions of veterans' preference points to written test scores;

(e) Award Plaintiffs and the members of the class they represent compensatory damages, also including back pay;

(f) Award Plaintiffs and the members of the class they represent punitive damages, also including costs and attorneys' fees; and

(g) Grant such other affirmative relief as the Court deems just and appropriate.

Respectfully Submitted
By Their Attorney

___/s/ E. Julia Jennifer____
Elisabeth Julia Jennifer
Jennifer, Berton & Abrahams
56 Joan Street
Cleveland, Ohio 44114

Dated: /d/

EXHIBIT A

CLEVELAND ENTRY LEVEL EXAM FOR FIREFIGHTERS
PART II—PHYSICAL STRENGTH, ENDURANCE, AND ABILITY TEST

Place: Cleveland Fire Academy, 3250 Lakeside Avenue
Date: May 7—May 13, 1998

Your scheduled date and time are marked on your 3 x 5 ticket. . . .

(1) If it is impossible for you to appear at the date and time scheduled on your white ticket, stop at the re-scheduling desk as you leave.

(2) Parking near the Academy is limited, allow time to park and reach the Academy by your scheduled time.

(3) Bring your ticket; it is your ticket of admission to the Academy testing area. You will get no other notice concerning the physical test unless you fail to qualify on the written exam. Persons not scheduled for testing during that specific half-hour session will not be admitted to the Academy testing area.

(4) Wear comfortable clothing and sneakers or rubber-soled shoes similar to those you would wear when participating in a demanding athletic event.

(5) Check with your doctor before participating in the physical ability test if you have circulatory, respiratory, or other problems that have

required medical attention, if you have a blood pressure of 150/100 or higher, or if you are taking medication.

(6) Avoid eating, drinking coffee, or smoking for at least two hours before your scheduled testing session. It is also advisable to allow yourself 10 minutes of warm-up and stretching exercises before signing in to begin the test.

The physical abilities exam is designed to measure aerobic fitness, muscular strength and endurance, balance, and speed as these factors relate to frequently encountered tasks involved in firefighting and rescue. Where possible we have tried to simulate firefighter activities which do not require special prior training. Where special training, safety concerns, or physical constraints exist, test elements have been modified to measure the same skills and abilities in a more practical and standardized manner.

In all cases it is the responsibility of the candidate to complete the exercises as rapidly as possible without risking personal injury through carelessness or reckless actions. Falls and/or minor injuries incurred during an event can cost you far more than one or two extra seconds spent exercising caution.

There are three events as described below. In each case you will earn from 0 to the maximum points listed (in fractional steps), based on your performance. There is no absolute pass/fail cut-off on each individual event, but you must score a total of 35 out of 50 points (70 per cent) to pass the agility test.

Event 1—Upper arm and shoulder muscular endurance—(10 pts.) raise bar bell (approx. 33 lbs.) to chin level. On signal raise barbell overhead to full arm extension and then lower to chin level. Repeat rapidly for 60 seconds or until a maximum of 35 lifts are completed. Score will be based on total successful lifts in one minute up to the maximum of 35. Lifts involving the bending of knees and/or use of legs will be discounted. You must proceed immediately to Event 2. If you delay being tested so that you drop out of the testing sequence, you will be disqualified.

Events 2 and 3 will be run with the applicant carrying a standard self-contained breathing apparatus on his/her back (excluding mask and regulator), weighing approximately 40 lbs.

Event 2—Fire scene set-up and building entry—(25 pts.) Grab one end and drag 100 ft. of 4 1/2-in. hose 90 feet; drop and run to other end of hose; pick up and drag 90 ft. back to start area; run to fire apparatus (70 ft.); remove 12 ft. extension ladder (35 lbs.); enter fire tower (45 ft.

away), place ladder against wall of first landing; continue up the inside stairwell to the fourth story above ground level; return to first landing; remove ladder and replace on fire apparatus. Approximately 340 ft. total run plus 40 ft. vertical ascent and descent. Score based on total time required from beginning of hose drag to return of ladder to side of fire apparatus.

Event 3—Simulated interior fire rescue—(15 pts.) Grasp handle of dead weight (100 lbs); pull 20 ft to low headroom drag area (30 in. high, 40 in. wide); crawl and drag weight through low headroom area (36 ft.); drag weight 16 ft. past marker; return to start area through low headroom drag area. Distance approx. 144 ft. Score based on total time.

All distances, weights, and other measures are approximate. Minor procedural, equipment, and/or measurement changes may be invoked at the time of the exam.

Memorandum Re Directed Verdict*

To: Judicial Clerks

From: Judge Paz, United States District Court for the Northern District of Ohio

Re: Defendant City of Cleveland's Directed Verdict (Judgment as a Matter of Law)

Motion in Barbara Zoll, et al. v. City of Cleveland.

As you know, I have been hearing plaintiff's evidence in this case for the past week. I am sure that the city will move for a directed verdict (now a Fed. R. Civ. P. 50 motion for judgment as a matter of law) as soon as the plaintiffs rest, which should be any hour now. I want to decide the motion fairly quickly, once plaintiffs rest, so that counsel, witnesses, and the jury know what to do. So please be prepared to advise me on a moment's notice.

What I will do now is bring you up to date on the case, and at the end of this memo I will give you a photostat of the relevant portions of my trial notebook summarizing the evidence. If more evidence comes in the next few hours that I think is at all relevant to the motion I will tell you later.

You've seen the complaint previously, and you have told me that during your civil procedure course you were exposed to civil rights actions under Sections 1983 and 1985, and Title VII cases. This is a class action brought on behalf of entry-level female firefighters in the City of Cleveland, challenging the rank-order written and physical capabilities selection examination established by the city as perpetuating the exclusion of women from firefighting positions.

The plaintiffs have proceeded under four causes of action. Count One is for alleged violations of Title VII of the Civil Rights Act of 1964, as amended. Count Two alleges a violation of 42 U.S.C. §1983, based upon violations of the Due Process and Equal Protection Clauses of the Fourteenth Amendment of the United States Constitution. Count Three alleges a conspiracy under 42 U.S.C. §1985(3) to deprive the plaintiffs of their rights under the Due Process and Equal Protection Clauses of the Fourteen Amendment of the U.S. Constitution. Count Four alleges

---

* This memorandum and the following trial notebook are based on the actual trial, but have been drafted solely for the purposes of this book. Some testimony has been modified, added, and eliminated for pedagogical purposes.

violations of the Ohio Revised Code §124.58 ("Frauds in examinations prohibited").

The only defendant remaining in the case is the City of Cleveland. The plaintiffs have settled with Sheldon Marshall, the expert who devised the tests in question, and have now dismissed against all other defendants except the city. Nonetheless, to the extent that a city official's or agent's activity is relevant to making the city liable, such activity can be considered. I assume that the city will move for directed verdict on all four counts. Ignore that this is a class action, and treat the named plaintiffs as individuals for purposes of this motion. Also ignore any issues relating to the type or amount of damages, for I have bifurcated liability from questions of damages or types of injunctive relief.

I have already decided that I will deny any motion for directed verdict against the Title VII count, because I am sure that the plaintiffs' statistics with respect to virtually no hiring of females ("disparate impact") shifts the burdens of production and persuasion to the defendants to prove the "business necessity defense." In the words of the Cook & Sobieski treatise, "Under the 1991 Act, an employer may successfully defend a disparate impact resulting from an employment practice by demonstrating 'that the challenged practice is job related for the position in question and consistent with business necessity.'" I am confident that the plaintiffs' statistical evidence has placed that burden on defendants.

I have asked counsel to consider whether i) they are entitled to a trial by jury on only the Title VII count; and ii) whether they would be willing to have me decide the Title VII count alone, without a jury, since it involves so much detailed information about testing. I think the lawyers are leaning in that direction—proceeding without a jury—if only Title VII remains.

I suspect that the defendant's motion for directed verdict on the other three counts will rely on the following potential weaknesses in plaintiffs' case, which I will explain.* As to the Ohio statute (Ohio Rev. Code, Sec. 124.58), take a look at the exact wording of the statute. The term "frauds" in the title, and the repeated use of such words as "willfully or corruptly" and "deceive," "falsely," and "false" suggest to me that defendants will say there is no evidence of misstatements of existing facts with intent to deceive. My clerks with last names beginning with the letters A-G should particularly be prepared to advise me on the directed verdict motion relating to that count. It is critical that you read each clause of the

---

* Students may also find it useful to reread the legal analysis portions of the Initial Memorandum in these *City of Cleveland* Case Files

statute and analyze the evidence as to each clause. Do the plaintiffs have a stronger shot at surviving the directed verdict motion as to any particularly clause? What evidence makes you think so?

It seems to me that the plaintiffs may have trouble with "conspiracy" aspects of the 42 U.S.C. §1985(3) count, but I want you to also consider what else they have to prove substantively in this count. My clerks with last names beginning with the letters H-P should particularly analyze plaintiffs' production burden with respect to that count. The law is clear that all conspirators do not have to be named as co-defendants nor do they have to remain in the case for the jury to consider whether there was a conspiracy within the meaning of §1985(3). In other words, you will have to analyze the activity of the Mayor, Dr. Marshall, fire department officials, etc., to the extent there is evidence about them, even though the only defendant is now the City. A conspiracy is often defined as follows: "a combination, or an agreement between two or more persons, for accomplishing an unlawful end or a lawful end by unlawful means."

I suspect that 42 U.S.C. §1983 may present the closest case with respect to whether or not the plaintiffs can survive a directed verdict motion. My clerks with last names beginning with the letters Q-Z should concentrate on any directed verdict motion directed to that count. On this cause of action, I suspect the plaintiffs may have problems with both intent and causation. In other words, the prima facie case under §1983 requires that the plaintiffs produce evidence that directly and/or circumstantially (through the use of inferences) would permit a reasonable jury to find that a defendant "purposefully and intentionally" discriminated against women and that the defendant's activity caused the harm claimed, which I take it is the failure of women to secure positions as firefighters. With respect to the city, it is not enough that some official unilaterally had an animus against women, or did not like the idea of women becoming firefighters. The city or the fire department must have had a policy to discriminate, which is different from a series of isolated events. The question is whether a reasonable jury on the evidence could find such a policy, bearing in mind that such a policy need not be articulated in writing or orally; it could be inferred, if such an inference is a reasonable one.

Portions of Judge Paz's Trial Notebook

Evidence Admitted in *Barbara Zoll, Jennifer Grimes, et al. v. City of Cleveland* which might be relevant to directed verdict motion.

Plaintiffs' first witness, Mayor James Kosolsky: testifies that he has been mayor of the City of Cleveland for about eight years. Doesn't know exactly when he found out, but "I certainly knew that the fire department was absent of any women firefighters." (Pl. Ex. 1: "Mayor Policy Statement of Affirmative Action and Equal Employment Opportunity.") He made "a commitment to the city to develop and implement result-oriented goals, procedures and programs to reduce the underutilization of minorities and women and to achieve equity throughout the city's workforce." Wanted testing procedures that "would not preclude women from being members of the Cleveland Fire Department, but at the same time would guarantee that the dept. would have qualified individuals." Knows there are now women firefighters in other fire departments in the U.S. "Hammered away at his people that I want this to be the best doggone test there can be. I don't want anybody charging that we are trying to discriminate or preclude anybody from being a member of any of our departments or the city service." Reads from document that says "Fire Division has set a goal to hire seven blacks and two Hispanics as firefighters." Admits that no number of women specifically listed as a goal. Two years later, a document says: goal to hire one woman as typist in fire department. Testifies that reason number set for black and Hispanic firefighters was result of consent decree in another case. Fire department had 1,010 paid members. Three were women, none as uniformed firefighters.

Cross-examination by city attorney (as on direct): Firefighters job is "to protect the health, safety and welfare of the citizens of Cleveland. That's the overriding thing that we are trying to get done. We are in the service business, and want to get the best service that we can possibly provide and have the best people we can to provide the service."

Q: "Mayor, did you ever intentionally discriminate with respect to the female applicants who sought employment in the Division of Fire?"
A: "Absolutely not."

Re-direct of mayor (as on cross): He's not suggesting in any way that the objective of bringing women into the firefighters' workforce is in conflict with the goal of bringing in firefighters for protection of the health and safety and welfare of the citizens of Cleveland.

Plaintiffs read to the jury certain requests for admission that have been admitted by all defendants, as well as certain stipulations agreed to by all parties. My summary of data on the written and physical examinations to become a uniform firefighter in Cleveland, Ohio (these are the examinations being challenged in this lawsuit): There were initially 3,612 applicants. 2,212 took the written part of the test. 1,233 took the physical part. Each portion of the examination was worth a raw score of 50 points, with a maximum achievable score (with the two tests combined) of 100. The raw scores on the written portion were adjusted by capping the scores from the different sections, by awarding five extra points to qualifying veterans, by awarding ten extra points to city residents, and by adding six points to the scores of minority candidates. The veteran and resident point adjustments were made pursuant to provisions in the city charter. The minority adjustment was undertaken as a means of complying with a consent decree entered against the city in a suit by minority candidates alleging bias in hiring. Only those applicants with adjusted score of at least 35 were eligible to take the physical portion of the exam. 285 females took the written portion; 122 passed. 1,927 males took the written portion; 1,206 passed. The maximum attainable score for candidates on the physical portion of the exam was 50. 35 was considered a passing score. Of the 1,125 men taking the physical test, 1,002 passed. Of the 101 women taking the physical test, 15 passed. After taking the physical portion of the examination, 29 females and 1,069 males scored high enough on both portions of the exam to be placed on the eligibility list. The woman with the highest score ranked 334 on the eligibility list, which was too low to be hired. The class of 35 firefighters hired in the two year period as a result of the exam in question contained no women.

Percentage of males passing the written examination was 62.5%. Percentage of females was 42.8%. 89.3% of males received a score of 35 or higher on the physical portion of the exam in question; 14.0 % of the females who took it had 35 or higher on this portion.

The eligibility list is compiled of those whose combined scores on both tests (including the adjustments on the written portion) was 69.5 or higher. The general practice, based on the city's charter, is for the director of public safety to hire in strict top/down rank numerical order from the eligibility list, the only exception being for the hiring of a Black/Hispanic quota pursuant to a court degree, designed to remedy intentional and egregious racial discrimination. After establishment of the eligibility list, further selection components include a medical test, a psychological test, and a background check. These three procedures are conducted only upon the highest ranking candidates who have any realistic chance of being hired.

The rate at which women received a combined written and physical score high enough to be placed upon the eligibility list was dramatically less than the rate at which men received a combined written and physical score high enough to be placed on the eligibility list.

According to the most relevant United States Census, the workforce in the Cleveland Standard Metropolitan Statistical Area is 46% female.

Plaintiffs' next witness was Janet Quigley. Worked for the Employment Litigation Section, Civil Rights Division, U.S. Department of Justice, Washington, D.C. A mathematical statistician. Based on education and experience, I qualified her as an expert in statistical analysis. She is trained to compute standard deviation numbers—"a measure of fluctuation from what actually occurred in an event from what is expected to occur under normal circumstances or due to chance." She computed standard deviations for the physical performance examination in question. 1,233 applicants took it; of those, 108 or 8.3% were female. On the final eligibility list, 29 or 2.6% were female. In normal circumstances or due to chance, we'd expect to have 91 of those females scoring high enough on the examination. The difference is 62, and the number of standard deviations acquired is 6.76. "The probability of this event is 1 in 10 billion, approximately zero." Used the same method to calculate standard deviation for those applicants (1017) who scored 35 or higher on physical examination. 1,002 or 98.5% were male and 15 or 1.5% were female. Using the same methodology as before, we would have expected 84 females to have scored 35 or higher. The probability of what in fact happened was 1 in 10,000 billion, approximately zero (other similar statistics).

Cross-examination by counsel for the city. Witness admits she just looked at numbers. Didn't know the physical or the mental ability of anyone who took the examinations. Admits that five times as many women took the physical exam in the year in question than when the exam was previously given two years before.

Summary of testimony about the test itself, compiled from testimony of several witnesses, including Dr. Marshall: Test was prepared by Dr. Marshall, who has extensive experience in the area of job analysis and examination development for safety forces, including the position of entry-level firefighter. Interviewed hundreds of firefighters and high ranking officers, read firefighting manuals and books, made and analyzed questionnaires to ascertain the frequency and importance of firefighting tasks. Based on women failing to rank high on previous eligibility lists, he was concerned about gender differences, and wanted to minimize adverse impact tests had on females. At same time, wants test to show best people for job.

Based upon extensive research, and comparison of his findings with manuals and lists of tasks used in other cities, Dr. Marshall developed final written and physical components of the examination. The written component was designed to test reading comprehension, the ability to follow directions, mathematical skills, and other forms of cognitive reasoning.

Much of the information tested came from the Ohio Fire Service Training Manual. The physical component consisted of three events:

Event 1: **Overhead Lift**—using a 33 lb. barbell, candidates must lift the barbell overhead repeatedly for one minute or up to a maximum of 35 lifts. Cannot bend knees; must be locked.

Event: 2: **Fire Scene Set Up and Tower Climb**—while wearing a custom-tailored self-contained breathing apparatus, candidates must drag two lengths of standard 2 1/2 inch hose 180 feet (90 feet one way, drop coupling, run to the other end of the hose, pick up and return 90 feet, drop coupling in designated area), run 75 feet to pumper, remove a one-person ladder (approximately 35 lbs.) from the side of the pumper, carry the ladder into the fire tower, place it against the back rail of the first landing and continue up the inside stairwell to the fifth floor where a monitor observes the candidates' arrival. Then, candidates return to the first landing, retrieve the ladder and place it on the pumper.

Event 3: **Dummy Drag**—still wearing their self-contained breathing apparatus, candidates must drag a 100 lb. bag 70 feet (40 of which includes low headroom), turn and, still dragging the bag, return to the starting point.

Dr. Marshall was paid by the city, and worked closely with fire department officers from the city. Worked most with Assistant Chief Adams on this test, and on previous ones. Marshall had worked for city many times previously. He knew that the barbell event was "something most women wouldn't be familiar with at all." When he saw how badly women did on the event, he decided on his own late one evening after the event to add one and three-quarter points for each women on this event. Many firemen told him and he believes that strength and speed are critical to firefighters, particularly in the first few minutes after the uniform firefighters arrive at a fire. His test concentrated on anaerobic abilities, and he knows women do better on aerobic exercises. But aerobic capacity is tested in the physical given to those who names have been taken from the eligibility list. The sequencing of the three events is not related to how it is done in actually fighting fires. Marshall knew before he created the barbell test that introducing above-your-head lifting had eliminated women from the Cleveland Emergency Medical Technician testing. For the barbell test, applicants were not permitted to bend their knees. Firefighters bend their knees ordinarily when carrying ladders and other heavy objects.

Testimony of Alice Simons, Secretary of the Civil Service Division, Cleveland. She gave out applications and advice re: tests and openings in question. May have said under her breath to a woman applicant: "Why don't you stay home and have babies." (Other witness testifies she said this.) Yes, she did ask one female applicant why she wanted to be a firefighter. Did allow two men to apply late, but they were already in the building when it closed at the end of the last permitted day. Told them to come back first thing the next day the building was open, even though it was beyond the date. "After all, they were already in the building." Late-filing woman was different; she hadn't been in building.

Testimony of William M. Adams. Direct: Employed by Division of Fire for twenty-seven years. Now assistant-chief. In charge of fire suppression forces on one shift for the entire City of Cleveland. Cleveland is one of few cities in state with their own fire training academy. Cleveland part of nationwide program to rate all firefighters into groups, according to proficiency. Group One less proficiency than Two, Two less than Three and Four, etc. The National Fire Protection Association (NFPA) sets standards for fire instruction, equipment, and other matters. NFPA and our department agree you can train firefighters to be better throughout their careers. Cleveland has a firefighters' training manual. Worked extensively with Dr. Marshall in months just before the test in question. He suggested to Dr. Marshall that barbell lifts might be one way to test for important physical skills for firefighters. Doesn't remember if talked about locking the knees. May have suggested the running and dragging event. Can't recall. He had taken prior exams where they had to pick up 120 to 150 pound dummies. Often have to carry heavy things in hurry. Sometimes have to do it crawling. "Hand straps" can be used to carry people out. They weren't used in the physical exam.

Witness had talked to Dr. Marshall before Marshall prepared the tests in question, and they had discussed matters taken directly from the Ohio Fire Service Training Manual. He identifies differences between the ARCO training book and the Fire Service Training Manual. Question: "Now, if someone knew that Dr. Marshall was going to use the Fire Service Training Manual, he or she could do a better job in taking the written test, isn't that true? Answer: "I don't know if that would be a true statement or not." He did tell the women at the Fire Service Training Academy that "if they study hard the Arco book, they would do well on the exam." He knew that in the Buddy Casey course, which applicants paid to take, they were told to study from the Fire Service Training Manual.

Jury is read answers to interrogatories showing that women who took the Casey course did significantly better on both portions of the exam than women who only took the free course that was designed specifically to help women prepare for the exams. The free course specifically designed for women was given by Kevin Kelly.

Yes, he did think that women would be chosen from a different list. This was the "scuttlebutt." Question: "But you communicated to the women that they were going to be hired off the list. Women will testify that they heard you say that. Do you recall making those statements?" Answer: "Yes. Again I wasn't speaking as a Cleveland Fire Department official. I was telling them this is my belief." Yes, he has observed women actually performing, fighting live fires. Maybe 15 to 20 times. Probably all types. Probably saw them using pipe poles and saw them dragging hoses. Probably saw them in two story fires and probably saw them take ladders off the hook and ladder. Probably some of them had higher and some lower scores than men. Question: "And would you rate some of the woman firefighters better than other male cadets?" Answer: "Well they are probably better than some and worse than others, yes." Some of the women observed were lower on eligibility lists then men. Admits in former deposition saying: "Some of these women who were firefighters ranked lower than male cadets, but performed better than those male cadets." Now adds: "On certain tasks they did."

Jury shown the announcement given to all applicants about the tests in question. It did not mention barbells. It said: "The physical agility portion will measure endurance, upper and lower body strength, and hand/eye coordination. Candidates will be required to perform a series of events using actual firefighting equipment and such equipment may have to be carried up and down stairs. You will have to perform a simulated rescue with a dummy of adult body weight. You are recommended to increase your physical endurance in order to maximize your performance on the examination." Previous announcements, also shown to the jury, had been more specific about each aspect of the physical test.

Testimony of Kevin Kelly. Direct. In the department for 22 years. Now a Lieutenant. Has heard firefighters, assistant chiefs, and other officers say many times that women don't belong in fire department, that they aren't strong and fast enough; that they "can't come through in a pinch." Heard such stuff from Assistant Chief Adams as recently as one year before the test in question. Can't recall exact words. He knows women firefighters are presently in the cities of Columbus, Ohio; New York, New York; Seattle, Washington; and other major cities. Some fire departments don't choose by rank order on exams. Instead, they put everyone together who has passed the exams, basically a pass/fail test. Some attempt to achieve diversity from that larger pool. Some have random selection from all those who have passed, pure chance.

Was at meeting when Safety Director Harry Tarpley expressed his view that objections to women as firefighters because of their physical capacity "were invalid." Kelly testifies that Tarpley "expressed his belief that it is an operational need for the City's Fire Department to have a personnel force reflective of Cleveland's population, male and female, because the community expects this kind of reflection— it provides awareness, a sensitivity to community problems and enhances the division's ability to function within the community." Safety Director Tarpley did not recommend any new criteria for the employment of firefighters from those applied in prior years except for an effort to recruit minorities and women. Tarpley had said he was satisfied with the qualifications of applicants on the eligibility list prepared three years before the one in question. He didn't suggest that either the written or physical components of the exam be made more difficult.

Kelly, continuing: Sometime after Marshall's tests had been developed, but before they were administered, the city started a program to recruit and train female firefighters. As part of the recruitment program, the city advertised and gave a free twelve-week training program. There was also a minority pre-test training program conducted by the city which was attended by both males and females. Also there was the $500 course given by Buddy Casey, a retired lieutenant from the department. He had been doing this for years. Because of his interest, and previous experience teaching firefighters, Kelly was chosen to design and implement a pre-examination recruitment and training program for women interested in becoming firefighters. "I undertook this program under the direction of Chief McGinnis, Assistant Chief Gainsley and Safety Director Tarpley." I sought and received funding from the Comprehensive Employment and Training Act (CETA) program for the women's training program to pay for textbooks, equipment, and instructors. I was assigned this project as part of my regular duties, and relieved from doing some other things. But I spent hundreds more hours on this than what I got paid for; "I wanted to do it. It made sense to me."

My course met twelve times, four hours each. Two and a half hours were on physical activities, and the rest on cognitive. Written portion was based primarily on the then current edition of the ARCO Civil Service Test training manual. I thought this would work best and didn't know of Dr. Marshall's reliance on the Ohio Fire Service Training Manual. Physical portion of my course based primarily on the content of previous examinations, including training in such activities as dummy lift and carry, dummy drag, hose drag, tower run, fence climb, ladder lift, balance beam walk, and hose coupling. The program didn't include training in the use of barbells, and I didn't recommend to any of the women that she work with barbells prior to the examination. One week before the actual physical examination, the city notified all applicants of the content of the examination, including the barbell event. I obtained a set of barbells and made them available to my students. "In my opinion, with additional training, the women could have become more proficient with barbells." Chief McGinnis—Chief of the Cleveland Fire Department—never came to any of the classes, and "pretty much left me to design my own course."

Testimony of Buddy Casey: Former lieutenant, Cleveland Fire Department. Father was a policeman. Been giving my course for over ten years. In year in question, 485 persons enrolled in my Police and Fire School. My curriculum based on prior examinations and from study guide previously prepared by Dr. Marshall. These materials indicated to me that mechanical reasoning and technical subjects would be covered on the written component of the exam, including material from the Ohio Fire Training Manual. Based on Marshall's earlier tests, my training included a dummy drag, a hose drag (2 1/2 inch hose), and a stair climb carrying a donut roll of hose. I recommended weight lifting to develop biceps and forearms to enable candidates to carry the donut roll up 5 to 6 flights of stairs. Of the top 100 persons on the eligibility list in question, 48 were my students. Of the top 200, 92 or 93 were mine. Of the top 300, 134 took my class. Six of the nine women who took my course were on the eligibility list. "I am charging them a lot of money. I have a real incentive to give the best course possible."

Testimony of Barbara Zoll: Lives in Cleveland. Applied for and took entry level firefighter examination for year in question. Saw announcement by mayor that city looking for more minorities and women in fire department. Reads from announcement: "Contact our minority and women special recruitment office at 10539 St. Clair, weekdays 9:00 to 8:00 and Saturdays 9:00 to 1:00. You must be 18 or older with a high school diploma or GED. For more information call 555-2000." I thought I'd be good at firefighting. I'm pretty athletic, and run 40 to 60 miles a week. Have been doing it for several years. Had run and finished in D.C. marathon, 26.2 miles. Three years before test, I had finished a marathon in four hours. Had run Honolulu, Revco, Montreal (in 323), and Boston marathons. Friend told me of pretest training program for women—free, I liked that. Went to some of them. I also took the Casey paid course. ARCO manual given me at women's class. Casey went over tests he had prepared, concentrated on tools, electricity, currents, math, physics, fulcrums, pulleys, stuff that appeared on the actual exam. Casey took us at the end of each class to lift weights at Cleveland State. Had us put weights in backpack and run up stairs. Moved to Cleveland proper so I'd get ten more points. I was crazy to pass. I thought they'd for sure hire women, from what I heard. First given details about physical portion right after the written exam. Surprised that barbells now appeared. My physical was eleven days later. Afraid to go work on barbells now, because "if you pull something, you're going to be out of the competition." Got 48.5 out of 50 on the written portion. I felt adequately prepared on that part, had even taken books out of library. Barbell was first part of physical. I did about 22 in allotted time. "When I didn't make the required 35 lifts, I just felt like I had blown all my chances. Really depressed about it." But still did other events. Women's training program didn't teach the sequencing of events—the second test—like it was given. Then had to pull a hundred pound dummy under tables. The training programs did not have this particular dummy event. In the test, every time you got too high the tank caught, and you got stuck. Cost time. I watched others do it. Many of the later people took off their shoes, and went under first (ducking). It was definitely something you easily could have been taught to do better, faster. With shoes off, some people's feet slipped. "So the guys took their shoes off and their socks and were doing it in their bare feet. Your feet are moist, you are not going to slip and they go right through there right underneath." No monitors told them not to do this. These techniques were not taught at the women's training program. Some candidates had more time between three physical tests than others.

I took other city and towns' tests, too, and passed. But not hired. Not large enough departments to have openings. I was ecstatic when I found out I passed the Cleveland exam. Later a neighbor told me I got something from Civil Service. I ran home; was number 642 on list. Overwhelmed, started crying.

Cross-examination. Got 33.32 on physical portion. Not get veteran points. Women's times on marathons not as good as men. Flier she read didn't talk of preferential treatment for women. Thought might get hired because they gave special course for women, and she did well compared to other women in the course. Admits she "washed out" when took Parma, Ohio physical test. Slipped on the water. Disqualified on very first test in Parma. And slipped and lost momentum in Cleveland dummy drag too. Shown exhibit of announcement of test. Admits that it lists she should be prepared to carry equipment up and down stairs. And should be prepared to rescue dummies of adult body weight. Did all or part of the preparatory courses. Ran marathons. Worked a little on nautilus machines. Worked on upper body strength. Two out of three tests concentrate on leg muscles. Was told could rip dummy so could have handle. Those who had more time between tests was random, luck of the draw. No sign said men could take off shoes and women couldn't on the dummy-drag. No problem on application process itself.

Re-direct. Announcement said to wear sneakers or rubber-sole shoes "similar to those you would wear when participating in a demanding athletic event." Would have removed shoes if knew it was allowed for the dummy drag event.

Testimony of Jennifer Grimes: Read article in Plain Dealer saying fire department wanted women to apply. Attracted to fact that there would be special training program for women. Was member of Scandinavia Club, and already working on nautilus. Worked on arms and legs. Went to special Kelly free course for women once or twice every week given. ARCO book used exclusively in that class. "I studied it." Went to Community College and took some math. Eager to prepare for exam in question. "My understanding was that the city intended to hire women and that I believed that they had a certain number that they wanted to hire." I got this understanding at the special women's course. First learned of actual physical events after we finished the written portion. Surprised that barbells listed. Not worked on any types of weights in the special program. Had from April 30 (written) to May 9th to prepare for actual events. Physical given me on May 9. (period was May 7 through May 13; I was given 9th) Didn't start barbell training then; not want to strain self.

Never told to study from Fire Training Manual. ARCO book never mentioned classifications and uses of fire extinguishers. When I took exam, I could see I wasn't adequately trained. I did 33 of 35 barbells, and felt very shaky afterwards. I was surprised how my body acted. Nothing in training prepared me for this. On hose and ladder run, we had trained separately in the class, but never in that type of sequence. If it would have been pass/fail and I could have paced myself, I could have passed that portion. The required speed made it difficult. Dummy had a ring at the end of it. It was different than the one we had in training. One in training the weight was distributed in a way it was easier to pull. Never told I could take off shoes to do the dummy drag.

Took exams in four other towns. Brook Park written exam was more just reading comprehension. Was 13 out of 400 in Brook Park, including both physical and written. More balance and agility tests. Also mile or mile and a half run. Many were pass/fail events.

Not aware that one could apply for Cleveland exam after the date given. Got veteran points in Cleveland. Was 952 on eligibility list. Surprised they didn't hire women after the training programs they put us through.

Cross-examination: No trouble getting or completing application. Never discouraged by any Cleveland official. Was given sample questions by the city. City sent her notice of special training program. Nothing in newspaper article said they would hire women regardless of performance on exams. Would have still taken exam even if hadn't got impression women would be on a separate list. Didn't have to pay for women's course. Knew about $500 course by Buddy Casey. Even though women's course met four times a week for twelve weeks, only went once or twice a week. Sometimes left classes early. Had opportunity in class to do dummy drag. Given practice lifting ladders, and running up tower. Maybe missed some things when not there. And had opportunity to drag a hose at the women's class. And it was timed, like in the exam. And given practice carrying objects, like in the exam. Maybe missed other materials besides the ARCO book when she was absent. Instructors encouraged her to believe in self at the women's course. No males in course when she practiced running the tower and doing the dummy drag and dummy carry.

N.B. There was other evidence from other members of the plaintiff class, but it was cumulative, and didn't add anything for directed verdict purposes.

I asked plaintiffs' counsel whether they were going to put in their expert evidence on alleged deficiencies in the tests during their case in chief. They said that as a matter of strategy, and because the United States Government controlled the expert witnesses, their basic attacks on the content, criterion-related, and construct validity of the tests would await the defendants' defending the tests in the second tier of the Title VII case. In other words, the plaintiffs would use their statistics to shift the burden of going forward to the city on the business necessity defense, and the plaintiffs would then attack the business necessity and try to show "pretext" in the third tier. I suggested that the evidence on pretext might be relevant to "intent" and "purpose" in the Section 1983 case, and that such evidence might be critical to meet their production burden as to the non-Title VII counts. They said they thought the statistics and their other evidence would be sufficient at this stage of the case. I assume they didn't want to tip their hand to the city on test-validity evidence, before the city had to defend their tests at the second tier of the Title VII case.

IN THE UNITED STATES DISTRICT COURT*
FOR THE NORTHERN DISTRICT OF OHIO
EASTERN DIVISION

UNITED STATES OF AMERICA, Plaintiff, vs. CITY OF CLEVELAND, et al., Defendants.	C.A. No. 98-4773 Judge Arthur L. Paz MOTION OF THE PLAINTIFF UNITED STATES TO BIFURCATE FOR TRIAL THE ISSUES OF LIABILITY AND INDIVIDUAL RELIEF

Plaintiff United States hereby moves this Court under Rule 42(b) of the Federal Rules of Civil Procedure to bifurcate the trial of this case into two stages: liability stage (Stage I) and an individual relief stage (Stage II).

The Supreme Court in *International Brotherhood of Teamsters v. United States*, 431 U.S. 324 (1977) has specifically approved such a bifurcated trial of cases of this nature. Moreover, division of the trial into a liability stage and an individual relief stage will serve the interests of judicial economy and accelerate the disposition of this case.

The attached memorandum provides points and authorities in support of this motion. Also attached is a proposed order providing for the bifurcation.

Respectfully submitted,

__/s/ Ruggero Calipari___
Ruggero Calipari
Attorney, U.S. Dept. of Justice
Civil Rights Division
Employment Litigation Section
Washington, D.C. 20530
(202) 555-4171

Dated: /d/

---

* This was the case brought by the United States government on the same facts as the Zoll and Grimes case, but the government sued only under Title VII. The cases were consolidated for trial.

IN THE UNITED STATES DISTRICT COURT*
FOR THE NORTHERN DISTRICT OF OHIO
EASTERN DIVISION

UNITED STATES OF AMERICA, Plaintiff, vs. CITY OF CLEVELAND, et al., Defendants.	C.A. No. 98-4773 Judge Arthur L. Paz MEMORANDUM IN SUPPORT OF MOTION OF THE PLAINTIFF UNITED STATES TO BIFURCATE FOR TRIAL THE ISSUES OF LIABILITY AND INDIVIDUAL RELIEF

BACKGROUND

The United States filed this action against the City of Cleveland, the Cleveland Civil Service Commission, the Cleveland Fire Department, and in their official capacities, the Director of the Department of Public Safety, the Fire Chief of the Cleveland Fire Department and the members of the Cleveland Civil Service Commission (hereinafter collectively referred to as "City," "Cleveland" or "City of Cleveland"), alleging, inter alia, that the City of Cleveland was engaged in a pattern or practice of employment discrimination in violation of Title VII of the Civil Rights Act of 1964, as amended, 42 U.S.C. §2000e *et seq.* against women with respect to entry level employment opportunities as sworn firefighters in the Cleveland Fire Department.

The complaint alleges that the City of Cleveland's employment practices violate Title VII by the use of selection devices that unlawfully discriminate against female applicants for the fire department because they have an adverse impact based upon sex and are not predictors of successful job performance.

ARGUMENT

Plaintiff United States has moved this Court for an order bifurcating the trial with regard to the issues concerning Defendants' liability and general injunctive relief (Stage I) and the issues concerning the entitlement of individuals to monetary and other individual make-whole relief (Stage II). Rule 42(b) of the Federal Rules of Civil Procedure provides for such a bifurcated procedure. Rule 42(b) states in relevant part:

---

* This was the case brought by the United States government on the same facts as the Zoll and Grimes case, but the government sued only under Title VII. The cases were consolidated for trial.

(b) **Separate Trials.** The court, in furtherance of convenience or to avoid prejudice, or when separate trials will be conducive to expedition and economy, may order a separate trial of any . . . issues. . . .

In *International Brotherhood of Teamsters v. United States*, 431 U.S. 324 (1977), the Supreme Court recognized the appropriateness of a bifurcated procedure in pattern or practice suits. The Court explained the first stage of a pattern or practice suit as follows:

The plaintiff in a pattern-or-practice action is the government, and its initial burden is to demonstrate that unlawful discrimination has been a regular procedure or policy followed by an employer or group of employers. . . . At the initial, "liability" stage of a pattern-or-practice suit the Government is not required to offer evidence that each person for whom it will ultimately seek relief was a victim of the employer's discriminatory policy. Its burden is to establish a prima facie case that such a policy existed. The burden then shifts to the employer to defeat the prima facie showing of a pattern-or-practice by demonstrating that the Government's proof is either inaccurate or insignificant. 431 U.S. 360.

When the Government seeks individual relief for the victims of the discriminatory practice, a district court must usually conduct additional proceedings after the liability phase of the trial to determine the scope of individual relief. *Id.* at 361. *See also Equal Employment Opportunity Commission v. Monarch Pattern Tool Co.*, 737 F.2d 1444 (6th Cir. 1984).

The United States submits that the two-stage trial procedure recognized in *Teamsters* should be used in this pattern or practice litigation as well. In so doing, the interests of judicial economy would be served. By reserving the determination of the scope and extent of individual relief for Stage II proceedings, the court will expedite the disposition of this case. Part of the relief sought is make-whole relief for potentially numerous individual women who have been harmed by the discriminatory employment practices alleged in the complaint. *See* Section 706(g), 42 U.S.C. 2000e(g); *Albemarle Paper Co. v. Moody*, 422 U.S. 405 (1975).

It is common practice in employment discrimination cases, where, as here, there are a large number of potential individual claimants, for courts to try liability issues separately from those issues involving individual relief. *See, e.g., United States v. Lee Way Motor Freight, Inc.*, 7 FEP Cases 710, 750 (W.D. Okl. 1973), *aff'd in relevant part*, 625 F.2d 918 (10th Cir. 1979); *United States v. U.S. Steel Corp.*, 520 F.2d 1043, 1052-56 (5th Cir. 1975); *Love v. Pullman Co.*, 12 FEP Cases 331 (D. Colo. 1975), *aff'd*, 569 F.2d 1074 (10th Cir. 1976); *Ellison v. Rock Hill Printing & Finishing Co.*, 64 F.R.D. 415 (D.S.C. 1974). The rationale for bifurcation was explained by the district court in *Love v. Pullman Co., supra*, this way:

If we order bifurcation and if plaintiffs fail to establish liability, then lengthy discovery and complex evidentiary problems concerning individual membership in the class and individual damages will be unnecessary. Of course, should liability be proven, then a subsequent proceeding will, absent a settlement, be required to determine the validity and amount of individual claims. But we are not persuaded by defendant's contention that bifurcation will somehow delay final disposition of the case, assuming liability is established. By limiting discovery to issues of liability, the trial of those issues may be accelerated in time. Then if liability is found, the parties may resume discovery on damages. We do not believe that evidence relating to the fact of damage, as an element of liability for class-wide discrimination, and proof of individual claims overlaps to any significant extent.

From the foregoing, we conclude that separation for trial of the liability issues from the damages issues in the instant case would be "conducive to expedition and economy" and that defendant will suffer no prejudice thereby. *Love v. Pullman Co.*, 12 FEP Cases at 332.

The United States is aware that a private class action, the Barbara Zoll action, has been consolidated with the United States' action for trial. It should be pointed out, however, that courts typically bifurcate the proceedings in private class actions into a liability stage and an individual relief stage, just as is done in government pattern or practice actions.

As in other cases of this type, the United States anticipates that the City of Cleveland's discrimination may entitle a substantial number of persons to individual relief. Little or no discovery has been taken by any of the parties concerning individual make-whole relief. Naturally, we recognize our threshold burden to establish defendants' liability. To avoid the possibility of expending unnecessary efforts by the Court and the parties concerning matters of discovery and evidence related to individual damages, the Court should reserve issues on individual relief for a Stage II proceeding.

Respectfully submitted,

___/s/ Ruggero Calipari____
Ruggero Calipari
Attorney, U.S. Dept. of Justice
Civil Rights Division
Employment Litigation Section
Washington, D.C. 20530
(202) 555-4171

Dated: /d/

Transcript of Jury Instructions (on §1983 action)

THE COURT: Ladies and gentlemen of the jury, we now come to the part of the trial where I will tell you the law.

My charge has been broken down into three laws.

First, the law that applies in just about every civil case, and then I will tell you the law in this case, and then I will tell you about your deliberations.

Now, as I said many times to you, you are the triers of the facts, and I tell you what the law is.

And these instructions are for your guidance in arriving at a verdict in this case. They don't intend to reflect any opinion on the part of the Court, and don't single out any one instruction alone but consider them in their entirety.

You are not concerned with the wisdom of any rule of law, and you are not permitted any personal interpretation. It is your duty to take the law that I give you, and you recall when I picked the jury I said that you must follow the jury instructions regardless of what it was.

Now, in this case it is to be considered as between equal parties. Under our system of law the law is no respector of titles or situations like that, so we have a class of women who are applicants for firefighter against the City of Cleveland.

You are supposed to consider them equal in their standing before the Court.

During the course of the trial the lawyers may have made objections to questions. If I have sustained an objection, you never heard the answer, and don't speculate on what the answer was.

If I overruled the objection, you heard the answer. The lawyers have an obligation to object when they believe an improper question has been asked, so don't hold that against the lawyers because they may have objected.

You are the determiners of the credibility of the witnesses and that really means believability. You can believe all, some of the witnesses' testimony or none of the witnesses' testimony.

Now, witnesses may be discredited or impeached by contradictory evidence, and you heard during the course of the trial that sometimes a witness who had previously been deposed was examined about apparently inconsistent statements between the deposition and now, and you consider all of that in determining the credibility of the witness.

Now, evidence is all of the testimony from the witnesses in the case and usually including exhibits.

In this case it is your combined recollection of all the testimony that will be with you in the jury room, and for simplicity you will rely on your collective recollection of what the evidence is, which is the live testimony of witnesses, and that is how we decide this case.

If a lawyer happens to ask a question in an assertive voice, that is not evidence. The evidence is not what the lawyer says. The lawyer may ask the question, and it may appear to be in the form of testimony, but don't consider the lawyer's statements. It is not evidence, and that includes both opening and closing statements. I told you those were only the lawyer's views of the evidence in the case, and I also permitted the lawyers to tell you before each witness testified, to tell you the purpose of the witness being sworn and testifying, and that you should not consider that as evidence, only the lawyer's view to give you a brief summary of what is to come and give you a better understanding of the witness's testimony.

It is the witness's testimony that is evidence and not the lawyer's preliminary statement.

Now, generally speaking, we have two types of evidence called direct and circumstantial. Now, direct evidence is the testimony or recital of facts by witnesses who have actual knowledge of the incident.

The other is circumstantial or indirect evidence. Circumstantial evidence is evidence of facts or circumstances from which the jury may infer other connected facts which immediately and reasonably follow according to common experience.

There is no distinction between the two. All the law requires is that you find the facts in accordance with a preponderance of all the evidence in the case, both direct and circumstantial.

Now, you heard me mention the word "inference," and while you are to consider only the evidence in the case, you are not limited to the mere bald statements of the witnesses. In other words, you are not limited solely to what you see and hear as the witnesses testify.

In other words, you are permitted to draw from the facts which you find have been proved such reasonable inferences as seem justified in the light of your experiences.

In other words, an inference is a reasonable deduction of fact which logically follows from other facts established by the evidence. In other words, inferences are deductions or conclusions which reason and common sense lead the jury to draw from facts which have been established by the evidence in the case.

The existence of an inference does not change or shift the burden of proof from one party to another. The inference must be weighed along with all the evidence to determine if the issue to which it applies has been established by a preponderance of the evidence.

You are permitted to make any logical and immediate inference from the facts which you find have been established, but you can't make an inference on an inference. You can make an inference or inferences only from the facts.

I already told you about credibility.

Now, burden of proof. That means as follows:

In our system of society when people can't resolve their difference, they resort to litigation, and a person who feels aggrieved will file a lawsuit. That person is the plaintiff.

The other person responds. That's the defendant or defendants.

Now, the plaintiff usually files a complaint in making certain allegations. The allegations of the complaint are not evidence. It only puts the other side on notice what the charges are against them. The other side responds in the form of an answer.

Now, the person who asserts a claim in a complaint has what we call the burden of proof and then must prove the facts that they allege by a preponderance of the evidence, and that's known as burden of proof.

While the burden rests upon the party who asserts an affirmative action to claim by a preponderance of the evidence, they have to prove that claim by the preponderance. It doesn't require absolute certainty, only a preponderance of the evidence.

Simply stated, it is evidence that is more probable, more persuasive and of great probative value. It is the quality of the evidence that must be weighed, and quality may or may not be identical with the quantity, that is, with the greater number of witnesses.

In determining whether or not an issue has been proved by a preponderance of the evidence, you should consider all of the evidence bearing upon that issue regardless of who produced it.

If the evidence is equally balanced or if you are unable to determine which side of an issue has the preponderance, then the party who has the burden of proof has not established such issue by a preponderance of the evidence. That's the simple facts of it.

So that is the general law that is applicable in just about every case, and I am now going to tell you a little bit about the particular law in this case.

This case started with a complaint filed by the plaintiffs. The only defendant now is the City of Cleveland for you to consider, and that would be the only person liable, although we still have some individual—what we call state actors, and I will tell you about that shortly.

Your main concern is whether the City of Cleveland intentionally discriminated against these women firefighters, applicants.

Now, the plaintiffs filed a complaint in which they made the allegations, and I told you about the complaint earlier and you heard the lawyers make reference to the complaint. The allegations in the complaint are not evidence as I told you before.

The City has filed an answer in the form of a general denial which places the simple issues before you as to whether or not the City of Cleveland purposely or purposefully and intentionally discriminated against these women applicants for firefighters in the 1998 examination in the design, the preparation and the administration of the test and in making the eligibility list.

Now, in this case, we are dealing with Title 42, Section 1983. That's what we call a civil rights action, and it provides, in substance, that no person shall be denied his or her constitutional rights under color of law, and if somebody violates their constitutional rights under color of law, they are liable.

Now, the constitutional right alleged to have been violated in this case is under the Fourteenth Amendment, the due process clause—I mean, equal protection clause that says that no state shall make or enforce any law which shall abridge the privileges or immunities of citizens in the United States, nor shall any state deprive any person of life, liberty or property without due process of law nor deny any person within its jurisdiction the equal protection of laws, and I will explain that to you very, very shortly.

Now, this amendment provides in substance, that there shall be no infringement of a person of his constitutional right of equal protection. Now, this applies to classes of people, and all members of a particular class are entitled to equal protection and they should be treated equally.

I already defined this class to you, and it is simply the applicants for firefighters who were women in the City of Cleveland in 1998, and that's basically what you will consider. And the principal allegation is that they were discriminated against by the defendants, the City of Cleveland, in this examination.

Obviously, as I told you about the purpose, the plaintiff has the burden of proving each and every element of the case by a preponderance of the evidence, and I will define various terms for you and other words that have common meaning so I won't necessarily go over them with you.

The three elements that must be proven in this type of case is whether the defendant purposely or intentionally committed the acts which were charged against him and whether they were under color of law and whether they were the proximate cause of the plaintiffs not being placed higher on the examination and so forth.

Now, under color of law, I am telling you is a matter of law that all the action here was under color of law, so you don't have to concern yourself with that, but our main concern is whether we have a constitutional violation which was under the equal protection clause.

I reviewed with you the statute and the constitutional violation.

Now, an employment practice is not unconstitutional as a violation of equal protection simply because it has a disproportionately adverse impact upon one group or another. In this case, the mere fact that the firefighter entry level examination resulted in males scoring higher than females does not make that examination unconstitutional.

The plaintiffs must prove purposeful discrimination. That is, the plaintiffs must prove by a preponderance of the evidence there was purposeful discrimination and this examination was designed, prepared and administered and so forth to discriminate against females.

Now, what do we mean by purposeful, knowingly, intentional?

An act is done knowingly if it is done voluntarily and intentionally and not because of mistake, accident, negligence or other innocent reason.

Now, an act is intentional if it is done knowingly and done voluntarily and done deliberately and not because of mistake, accident, negligence or other innocent reason.

In determining whether the defendant acted intentionally, we can't get in the mind of people, and you will have to take a look at that and make that determination from all of the facts and circumstances. The City of Cleveland can only be liable if the city policy was one of discrimination against women firefighters, and that's the only way the City can be liable.

We have some municipal actors here. They are not parties in the case, so we are only talking about the City of Cleveland and liability can only come from a policy of the City that would make the City liable.

Now, a policy in simple terms is the general principles or rules by which a government is guided in it management of public affairs. We can have statutes, ordinances, rules, regulations or just operative practices and procedures.

All of these can be considered policies, and it is different than just isolated events. It must be a policy.

Now, you could have one series of events. It could be a policy, but the City can only be liable if its policy was to discriminate against women intentionally or purposefully.

Now, I want to tell you about some things that you heard about in the case, but before I do that, you have heard the word "discrimination" referred to over and over again.

Now, it means the effect of an established practice which confers particularly privileges on a class arbitrarily selected from a large number of persons. It is unfair treatment or denial of normal privileges to persons because of their sex and applies in this case, a failure to treat all persons equally where no reasonable distinction can be found between those favored and those not favored.

All of you are familiar with the word "discrimination," so it doesn't need any expert advice to tell you what the word "discrimination" means.

Now, equal protection simply means that all persons shall be treated equally under our laws and under our government procedures.

Now, in order to avoid some confusion, there was a lot of testimony and disputed evidence here and terms and words were used and I better tell you about the legal significance of any of them. The fact that I discuss this with you doesn't mean I have an opinion on them, just what the law is.

Reference was made in the testimony here about other cases and about blacks and Hispanics. Now, this is a case of sex discrimination against women applicant firefighters. Now, I let that testimony in because it may or may not have had an impact on the women applicant firefighters. If you find that it had some relevance and effect on the women firefighters in this case under the charge in this case, then you can consider that along with all the other evidence.

If you find it is totally irrelevant and has no relationship to the issues in this case, you will totally disregard it. The fact that the court of law in another court put an order on the City of Cleveland to give some preferences to black or Hispanic firefighters has no effect on this case unless that policy by that court decree was wrongfully administered to such an extent that it discriminated against women, but to that extent, the City complied, they had to. But don't decide this case based on the facts in that case. You are only dealing with the sex discrimination charge.

Now, you heard some questions about quotas. I am telling you as a matter of law a governmental agency is not required to have a numbered quota, so the fact there was no quota for women has no legal significance.

You heard testimony about affirmative action plan. The City isn't even required to have an affirmative action plan, but once they have such a plan, they are required to implement the plan and comply with the stated policies of the plan.

The City of Cleveland, like all governmental agencies and all private agencies, they are required— prohibited from discriminating against women because of discrimination, because this is a marketplace and a job place and that's the job of the City.

So in regard to the test, you heard a lot of testimony about the test and how it was designed and how it was prepared, how it was administered, how it was graded and how the list was made.

Now, it is for you to decide from all the evidence whether, based on everything you heard, the City policy purposefully and intentionally discriminated against women in regard to the test, and that's what the allegation is.

Once again, I want to remind you we have a thing in law called the totality of the circumstances. You are to decide this based on all of the evidence in the case and all of the direct evidence, all of the circumstantial evidence and all of the inferences that come from the facts that you find have been proven.

Now, the purpose of these tests are they are designed, prepared and administered to select from an adult application pool those candidates most likely to be successful in training and to be successful firefighters, and that's what we call job-related. You heard testimony about job-related in regard to these tests.

Now, you also heard a lot of testimony about the City hiring an expert to prepare the tests. Now, the municipal government has the obligation like the defendant here, to get a qualified testmaker and give him instructions in regard to his guidelines as to the qualifications for the job and the duties to be performed on both the mental and physical aspect of the test, and he should understand what he is doing.

And it is his obligation to develop a test or tests for mental and physical skills that will be job-related and be a fair and reasonable test for skills and abilities and a predictor of successful performance in training as well as a firefighter.

Now, you heard testimony about events and sequence of events, and it is for you to determine from all of the evidence whether there was something in the events that were chosen and the selection of the sequence of whether it resulted in a discriminatory—intentionally discriminatory impact or effect on the women.

If the sequence of the physical test events was not reasonably or rationally related to job announcement or the training program or the training materials or manuals and that the sequence was not designed and/or administered in such a manner as would objectively illustrate that the applicant would be a successful trainee and/or a successful firefighter

and that such sequence of events, in addition to being non-job-related, was more difficult for women than for men, all of this can be considered in determining whether there was intentional discrimination. Obviously, you will consider the corollary of that, and as to numerical ranking, you heard some evidence about numerical ranking.

I am telling you as a matter of law the City of Cleveland charter and the Civil Service Commission requires there be a numerical ranking. There must be a numerical ranking, and it is required that the Civil Service Commission, after they do the written test scoring and the physical test scoring and the other components of the test and the other procedures they then prepare a numerical listing. And then for the number of applicants or for the number of jobs to be filled, they give three names to the appointing authority for each one job.

If there were 35 jobs, they would give them 105 names, and the appointing authority then has to appoint from that list. It is a 1-2-3 rule.

Now, you heard testimony about study materials, study manuals, training material. The City was not obligated to give any training manuals or study materials. They could have just had the announcement for the test. The announcement must be related to the testing.

You can't have an announcement for one purpose to give a test for another. The announcement was to give people general notice of what the test would be and must be reasonably or rationally related to the test, and it is for you to determine whether that was done.

The City was not required to give training material, but once they did, there must be a direct relationship between the training material and what's on the test.

Now, they are not required to give copies of the test or give precisely the exact questions for the written, and they are not required to give precisely or tell the sequence of events. They do it in a very general way.

Obviously, the type of thing on the written and the type of thing on the physical must be reasonably or rationally related to the duties of firefighter and give reasonable notice to the applicants of the general areas to be covered, not the precise areas but the general areas.

They must be done in such a way that the average person would understand them. So while the City is not required to give training material, once they give it, certainly it should be reasonably and rationally related to the test and not be designed in such a way as to be misleading or result in discrimination purposefully and intentionally against women.

The written and physical material for the test should have been designed, prepared and administered in a manner that both men and women should have been treated equally. The test should not have been designed, prepared and/or administered in such a manner that favors one group of applicants over another group of applicants.

In other words, the test should not be designed, prepared or administered in such a fashion or manner that it discriminates against one group of applicants. It must be consistent, as I just said, with the general terms of the announcement by the Civil Service Commission, and the test must be consistent with the job announcement.

All of this, and I am not trying to emphasize any one point, all of this may be or must be considered by you in determining whether the City actually intentionally discriminated.

Now, job related, you have heard that term, and the tests or test must relate or bear a relationship to the work or duties normally performed by the average firefighter in daily firefighting activities. It relates to actual job tasks.

In other words, it relates to actual job tasks, and you heard a lot of testimony about barbells. Now, the fact that the applicants in training classes did not work with barbells and did not practice the physical exercise in the same sequence as they did on the test in and of itself does not mean that the City discriminated against the plaintiffs.

However, this evidence can be considered together with all of the other evidence in determining whether any defendant intentionally discriminated against women firefighter applicants in the design, preparation and administration of the firefighting test in 1998.

So if you, the jury, find by a preponderance of the evidence that the 1998 test was designed, prepared or administered in such a manner or in such a way that it discriminated against women applicants, then you find that the women applicants' constitutional rights to equal protection was denied by the defendant.

On the other hand, if you find by a preponderance of the evidence that the plaintiffs proved that any one of the defendants* violated their constitutional right to equal protection under color of law, you shall find for that plaintiff and against that defendant.

On the other hand, if you find that the plaintiffs failed to prove by a preponderance of the evidence any one of the elements discussed above, you shall return a verdict for that defendant and against the plaintiffs.

One other thing, each applicant for the firefighters examination has the obligation and is required to prepare himself or herself for the written and physical agility tests. The City has no obligation to train the applicants, and the City is not the guarantor of the success of any applicant for the firefighters examination.

However, if the City does give its notice, which it did about the test as I told you before and they

do undertake training, then the training should relate to the subject matter generally that will be on the test, and I told you that before.

The City's obligation is to give a fair and reasonable and physical agility test that tests skills and abilities of the applicants and predicts the probability of a successful training followed by the probability that the applicant will be a successful firefighter and it must be job-related.

Now, that generally is the law on the 1983 equal protection case.

Now, in order for the plaintiffs to prevail, he must have another element, and that is there must be a proximate cause. If you find there was a constitutional violation, you must then find there was a proximate cause by a preponderance of the evidence.

In other words, the action of the City was a proximate cause of the firefighters' applicants who were women for not being placed higher on the list or being hired as firefighters, so if you find all three elements, in other words, that the City violated their constitutional rights and its violation was a proximate cause of them not being—women not being hired on the list, then you will render a verdict for the plaintiff against the defendant.

On the other hand, if the plaintiff failed to prove any one of these elements, you will end up returning a verdict for the defendant.

Now, you will retire very shortly to the jury room and begin your deliberations and elect one

---

* [*Eds. Note:* We do not know why the judge talked about "defendants" here, since only the City of Cleveland remained in this case as a defendant.]

of your members as a foreperson to speak for you.

You heard all of the evidence, and you may not remember all of it individually but you will find collectively you will remember all of it.

The admonition I give you not to form or express an opinion about the case is no longer with you. Otherwise you couldn't deliberate.

You can also talk to each other about the case. You will do all your deliberations in the jury room and only with all of you present.

If any of you has to leave to go to the bathroom, you will stop your deliberations.

Now, I have here—I am going to give you one interrogatory, and the question is, "Did you find that the City of Cleveland intentionally or purposely discriminated against women applicants for the position of firefighters in the design, preparation, administration, scoring and the construction of the eligibility list of the 1998 City of Cleveland firefighters examination?" And it will be yes or no and it must be signed by all nine of you. You will do your deliberations, and when all nine of you have reached a verdict, it must be unanimous, I have two verdict forms.

One is in favor of the plaintiff and one is in favor of the City. It only has to be signed by the foreperson, and the first one—there is no significance by the order which I read them—"We, the jury in the above-captioned case, unanimously find by a preponderance of the evidence for the plaintiffs Barbara Zoll et al. and against the defendant City of Cleveland in the 42 U.S.C. §1983 case."

The other one is, "We, the jury in the above-captioned case, unanimously find for the defendant City of Cleveland and against the plaintiffs Barbara Zoll et al. in the 42 U.S.C. §1983 case."

We have concluded that we are going to decide this case. You have heard the evidence, and you heard some discussion about the exhibits as we went along, but for expediting the proceeding, we are not going to give you any exhibits, just the interrogatory and the verdict form. . . .

Remember, you will elect one of your members as foreperson, and your principal charge is based on these instructions to decide if the City of Cleveland by its policies purposely and intentionally discriminated against women firefighters in this whole procedure, the 1998 firefighters examination.

Excerpts from Transcript of Closing Arguments
Made to the Judge in the Title VII Case

MR. CALIPARI: First of all, the only issue in this case of litigation is whether the [test in question] was job-related. . . . Another point I want to make briefly, your Honor, is under *Connecticut versus Teal,* where any aspect of a selection procedure has an adverse impact, the employer must relate [it to the] job.

[This] Court has also asked a question about whether under Title VII [the] United States was required to show intent. We state that the Supreme Court has expressly ruled showing of discriminatory purpose for intent is not required under Section 7 of Title VII.

However, in this case I think it's pretty clear that even though the burden is not there to show intent, there certainly was intent on the part of the City to exclude women from being part of the fire department. First of all, 1998 was the first time the City set out to recruit women for the job of firefighting. 1998 was also the first year the items on the test were not identified prior to the examination or prior to examination . . . with sufficient time so women could train and all the expert physiologists, experts in exercise physiology agreed that there's a vast improvement with training for women.

In fact, as you recall, the testimony of Dr. Marshall and [the] Chief, the City took steps, intentionally took steps to mislead

individuals as to exactly what was going to be on that examination. The City also went and hired somebody who was not an expert in exercise physiology, or an expert in gender differences. In fact as you recall, the job analysis conducted by Dr. Marshall showed the hand/eye coordination, balance and aerobic capacity were critical and important elements of the job of firefighter. To test for these items would have reduced the gender differences between males and females. They were in fact not tested for, although Dr. Marshall does in his linkage of the abilities to the individual items on the examination, his table indicates that those abilities, hand/eye coordination, balance and aerobic capacity, were in fact tested for. But in fact, [our experts] disagreed as did the expert exercise physiologist for the City. . . .

Job analysis conducted by Dr. Marshall concluded in part that firefighters must possess a high level of aerobic capacity and aerobic fitness, muscular strength, muscular endurance, flexibility, coordination, muscular balance and speed. In fact, Dr. Marshall indicated that he intended to have the firefighters exams test for muscular endurance and aerobic capacity because those traits become particularly important in life-threatening situations.

No one's contraindicated that aerobic capacity and aerobic

fitness are critical to the job of firefighting. However, all the experts in exercise physiology do agree these tests were primarily anaerobic in nature and did not test and measure the aerobic energy system. The 1998 examination of three events, barbell event, the fire scene set-up, tire climb and the dummy drag, there's no evidence that this test is validated on the basis of content validity.

Event number one, barbell event, first of all, there's no evidence that the barbell or overhead lift is an activity performed by firefighters in performance of their duty. Dr. Marshall testified he included the barbell lift to measure absolute muscular endurance of shoulder and upper limbs, not specifically to replicate tasks performed by firefighters. This event had the most adverse impact upon women when you consider its use in a rank order selection procedure. . . .

Event two involved sprinting up and down stairs, performing other tasks in a fashion that is not only dangerous but does not replicate the manner in which firefighters perform their duties. As the Chief indicated, firefighting lasts many hours. It's a coordinated and choreographed activity, and if a firefighter is exhausted, he's unable to perform further firefighting duties.

You recall . . . the City's expert [testified] that these types of events in the way they are run results in a build-up of lactic acid and a build-up of lactic acid results in a person becoming

exhausted and, as the Chief testified, once a person is exhausted, he's of no use to save lives or put out fires.

We heard testimony that event number three was designed to replicate rescues in smoke-filled rooms. While even Dr. Marshall testified, firefighters do not and are not trained to run in smoke-filled rooms to perform rescues. The doctor testified that event number three, the dummy drag, measures a nonspecific item or activity. He says it's a measurement of strength and ability to drag or pull. And he's in direct contradiction to what Dr. Marshall testifies to with that event. You recall Dr. Marshall testified a good time for that event would be dragging a dummy 2 feet per second. One must point out to him in trial that the actual time required in order to pass the test was 4 feet per second, then he changed his opinion.

The event was administered in a nonstandard fashion and you recall Dr. Barrett testifying that a test should be standardized. It was nonstandard because individuals in event number three were able to wrap the rope and the ring around the wrists, his or her wrists, to aid in the dragging. Others were not instructed to do so. Similarly, individuals were allowed to remove shoes to gain better traction. Others were not instructed to do so.

The Court heard testimony that the dummy they used, the fact it was nonarticulated, disadvantages persons with other strengths. You recall a doctor testified although someone may not have the grip strength necessary to pull it, he or she could compensate by using the arms or dragging the dummy in a different manner. If it was an articulated dummy, you'd be able to take advantage of that. The manner in which these three test items are designed to perform does not replicate or approximate the critical and coordinant tasks necessary to perform the job of firefighting.

Your Honor, the United States is seeking three things with respect to these proceedings. First, that the Court find these tests and City selection procedures are unlawful under Title VII. Second, that the Court order the City not to discriminate against women in the future. And third, that the Court order the City to develop a valid, fair and job-related examination for the position of eventual firefighter in the future. As a result of this test, zero women were hired in a position of firefighter . . . there would be no women on the fire department today.

Dr. Marshall, the developer of the examination, developed both written and physical portions of the examination. He has absolutely no expertise in the area of exercise physiology. Dr. Marshall developed the examination and his testimony and that evidence which he sets forth in his report is contradicted by the city's own experts in exercise physiology. The examination was a test for aerobic capacity, aerobic fitness, muscular strength, and so

on. No one's been at disagreement with that, but those are the critical and important elements of firefighting. The City, in fact, did not test for those elements. . . .

Finally, your Honor, the United States asks that the Court strike down these examinations as being not job related or valid under Title VII and find the City has not carried its burden to show that these examinations are job related. Thank you.

MS. JENNIFER: Your Honor, I'll try not to be repetitive of arguments that have been made by Mr. Calipari. . . .

The City has cited to [the] sixth circuit case . . . [of] *Grano Department of Development versus City of Columbus.* . . . Reading through this is an exercise in credulity in that the statements that are made presumably are in there in an attempt to make it appear they apply to our case. Grano is a disparate treatment case, not a disparate impact case, and the language of the opinion specifically points out the difference of standard between the disparate treatment and the disparate impact case. Why it's in here, I don't know. There is a paucity of sixth circuit authority in the conclusions of law that the City has submitted.

One of the other cases . . . is *Louisville Black Police Officers Organization versus the City of Louisville.* There's a citation to the Western District of Kentucky for the proposition that the content validity of employment selection device can be demonstrated, even though all the uniform guidelines are not satisfied. And it indicates that it was affirmed by the sixth circuit.

If one checks the sixth circuit opinion involved, all but [sic] the sixth circuit opinion is the award of attorneys' fees to plaintiff's counsel in that case. We, of course, concur in the importance of that particular sixth circuit opinion, but not for the proposition for which it appears to be cited here in the City's conclusions of law.

With respect to the omissions from the conclusions of law, we don't see any references to *Williams v. Vukovich*. We don't see references to any of the cases that —

MR. SOLIMINE: Objection, your Honor. I thought this was closing.

THE COURT: Go ahead.

MS. JENNIFER: That in fact are at issue in this case, *Columbus v. Vukavich,* and I think that in looking at the law that we have here, it's very important to point out that *Williams versus Vukavich* particularly cites with approval the second circuit's decision, in *Guardians*, which is, of course, the Seminole [sic] case, dealing with a need to validate. If you have a case that you're using—test that you're using in rank order, that you must validate for the use with respect to rank order.

Now, in looking at the standards for determining liability in this case, we of course are looking primarily at a disparate impact case. We put forward evidence with respect to some instances of disparate treatment as well, but they are simply illustrative to show examples of the kind of treatment that was going on during the period of time that the issues concerning this test were before us.

In looking at the disparate impact of the exam, I noticed with interest for the first time in the City's conclusions of law number four, the City now admits that the differential selection rate of males versus females in fact does constitute adverse impact, [a] conclusion they weren't willing to stipulate to at any time. Now, given the fact they've omitted that disparate impact, it appears to be an omission with respect to tests as a whole, or I should say the selection process as a whole, not with respect to the individual components of the test. . . .

Now, in looking at the standards that we have of disparate impact case [sic] with respect to our burden of proof, once the disparate impact is established, then it's up to the defendants to in fact carry a burden of proof, not production, as is set forth in the disparate treatment case, but the burden of proof to be able to show the job necessity for using the procedure that they have used.

Now, that's normally shown through use of validation to show the job-relatedness of the test. But one of the things that's been brought up and that I want to reiterate is that in this case they have used a rank order score which includes components in addition to the written and the physical, and it includes veterans points and includes residents points. If we look at the Court's opinion, *Connecticut versus Teal,* not only is it clear that the individual components must be validated under the circumstances, but it is the entire selection process, the entire selection procedure. And I might add that this is a situation, of course, where the bottom line did not show adverse impact in the *Teal* case. But if we look at even the dissenting opinion in this case, it's clear that it is the total selection procedure that must be validated, and here we have basically an admission from the City that they haven't attempted to do so.

But in any event, we have a system here in which the use of the capping system and the use of a variable number of minority points led to an adverse impact on the rank order of the women on the list, particularly adversely affecting women at the top of the list, the only women who stood a chance of being hired. And that particular problem, the differential effect upon the people at the top of the list, is not unique in this case if we look at *Thomas versus City of Evanston.* We see that the Court there is very attentive to the fact that the importance is the ranking. It's not the average scores. That's a meaningless indication in a case of this kind. It's the position on the list that's all important. Now, in addition to using

veteran points, capping and racial points that created a disparate impact, we also had the irregularities in the administration development of the written test. . . .

Finally, in the last section of the test, the judgment section, we had only 14 questions, and three of them Dr. Marshall reluctantly admitted that, perhaps because he developed this himself, he reluctantly admitted that there were alternate answers that were equally logical to the ones he selected and gave people credit for.

And then there was one question in this section in which Dr. Marshall simply said the answer was wrong. . . . Four of the 14 items of this last section, which supposedly tested judgment, was the only section that did test judgment. We assume judgment is very important in the job of firefighter, but close to 30 percent of these items were deficient.

Now, in looking at the physical, . . . there was no measure established, no specific measure established for the amount of physical strength that the job of firefighter required.

If we look at Supreme Court authority on this point, the height and weight requirement that was at issue in *Dothard versus Rawlinson* felt and the Supreme Court there point out, I'm quoting, that the defendants had produced no evidence correlating the height and weight requirement with the requisite amount of strength thought essential to firefighters and some men at the fire academy that you had to make the written more difficult. So instead, what he does is he sets up a system that weights the physical twice as much as the written.

Now, with respect to pretext, I think it's important to point out that what we've got here is an enormous amount of evidence that deals with intentional discrimination. . . .

When we look at all these things, the effect is foreseeable. That's evidence and intent. The fact that *Penick* was a 1983 case isn't relevant. The fact that evidence comes in here at the last stage as the plaintiff's rebuttal of defendant's case is sufficient for our purposes in making our Title VII case. Thank you, your Honor.

MR. SOLIMINE: Good afternoon, your Honor. I want to begin, your Honor, by thanking the Court, first of all, for giving us so much latitude in trying this case and also for the Court's attentiveness to the issues and testimony herein. Given that I only have about 20 minutes, there are a couple of issues that I do want to address that Ms. Jennifer raised. I want to do that very briefly.

First of all, she indicated that there was [*sic*] some problems with the written part of the examination, that, for example, she noted there were people who during the administration of the written examination, about 300 people have both parts of the—that the first part of the test, they had both the exam answer sheet and the booklet. Again, there's been no evidence that this particular

occurrence in any way benefited males or females. . . .

I need not remind this Court we spent nearly four weeks listening to various witnesses testify in this case. We had nearly 30 witnesses, over 2,500 pages of transcript in this case. That's quite a bit, your Honor. But it was essential that we get what the true issues were that were involved. This Court made clear early on there is a very narrow issue involved here and that issue is whether or not the examination in 1998, the entire examination in 1998 and the hiring processes for firefighters discriminated against women. That's the issue that's presented here, your Honor. This is not a case about whether women can do the job of firefighting, this is not a case of race discrimination. We are not called here to address, your Honor, whether or not the inherent order is improper. The controlling issue is whether or not the City's testing and hiring procedures were discriminatory against women.

Now, your Honor, in my summation, I'm going to talk of principally two points: The first one being adverse impact and the second one being the job-relatedness and validity of the 1998 examination. . . .

Your Honor, I'd be hard pressed to stand here now and argue that the selection rate for females as a result of the 1998 examination did not have an adverse impact or did not reflect adverse impact. In fact, your Honor, any City which gave a valid test for firefighting would be faced with the same dilemma. That's been evidenced in Columbus, Buffalo, New York, New York City, and other cities. That's the reality that we have to live with. When the City hired firefighters . . . , all those hired were males, all those hired were talked down, no females were hired. What we have is the inexorable zero the Courts talk about. We'll have to live with that.

Your Honor, that's the only point we're going to concede and that's the only point that the evidence mandates that we concede. The bottom line, your Honor, is that in this particular case, we have submitted nearly four weeks—strike that. We have spent nearly four years before this Court on this case, four weeks actually in the courtroom, trying this case. There have been numerous depositions. In fact, Dr. Marshall himself has been deposed over eight times. There's countless exhibits, reams and reams of paper, trial transcripts, deposition transcripts, and the bottom line, your Honor, in spite of all of that is that the test is valid.

Your Honor, we could have learned this three years ago, four years ago. We didn't have to wait four years to arrive at that. And another reality, your Honor, that it seems to have taken the plaintiffs four years to get to, is the reality that females didn't score high enough to be selected, that is because like anybody else who didn't score high enough to be selected that they lack the abilities required of the job, principally the physical abilities involved in the job of firefighting. Those are tough realities, your Honor, but that's the way it is.

Now, we accept it as our burden to show that the 1998 examination was job related. . . . We've been at this for four years, [and] might as well go ahead and remind the Court what the evidence shows.

During the trial your Honor, we had one witness that this Court remarked had broken the record for testifying. That witness was Dr. Marshall. We saw him again today. He was on the stand for I believe what amounted to about five days' testifying because he was the one who developed the 1998 examination. . . . [H]e developed the examination[ ] not because we couldn't find anyone better, but because he was the best person for the job. And other court's [*sic*] in this district had knowledge of that skill and experience and competency in test developing. . . .

[Dr. Marshall testified that his] first objective was to make sure that the abilities that were measured were those abilities that were required for the job of firefighter. . . . He also testified that the second objective . . . was to make sure that the tests actually used the kinds of tasks that firefighters performed. . . . Dr. Marshall then identified a third objective . . . and that was to make sure that the test picked those people who do well on the job. . . . By the testimony we know of now, your Honor, all three of these forms of validity are interrelated and Dr. Marshall's goal at that point was to as best as possible be [*sic*] all three of these objectives. . . .

Now, there has been some talk, I guess I have to say more than talk, real serious efforts to turn the 1998 examination into two examinations. Your Honor, there was only one examination. And that is what the candidates had to score high enough on in order to make it on the eligibility list, the entire examination, the cognitive and intellectual part and as well the physical part of the examination.

What's principally at issue here, your Honor, is the physical part of that test, the physical events. We've had some testimony about problems with the written, but no evidence to show that there is even a need to focus soley [*sic*] on the written or soley [*sic*] on the physical. But given the fact, your Honor, that that is what the plaintiffs have sought to do, we certainly have to address the challenge to the physical events. . . .

[E]vent number one was [the] overhead lift or barbell lift. Plaintiffs didn't like event number [one]. And they gave a number of reasons why they didn't like event number one and viewed it as being detrimental to women. Well, there are principally three reasons why they don't like event number one. First of all, they say firefighters don't lift barbells in conduct to perform firefighting task[s]. Your Honor, no one ever said they did.

Number two, they complain about the fact candidates were prohibited [*sic*] bending knees while doing this event.

Third, they claim women are not very familiar with barbells, and therefore, Dr. Marshall specifically put in this event to weed out women. Your Honor, the evidence in this case screens [*sic*] to the contrary.

First of all, the evidence is clear and unequivocal there are tasks firefighters have to perform wherein they use their upper body muscles exclusively, and that's what event number one was capping the candidates upper body strength. . . . They do have to lift firefighting equipment overhead, and we had quite a bit of testimony with respect to what it is that firefighters have to do.

We had testimony to the effect that there are times when they use those upper body muscles and cannot use their legs in order to get the job done. We heard testimony from the Chief in terms of the critical and important tasks that firefighters have to perform in the first few minutes of arriving. He talked about having to perform ventilation. That was something that had to be done quickly. And that the objective is get that done in five minutes.

We heard testimony also from the Chief that when firefighters arrive at the scene, they have to get a ladder off the truck. They have to use those upper body muscles to get that ladder off. They have to go up and straddle a roof and begin to chop a hole in order to ventilate, because as I said before, the straddle method, they're using their upper body muscles exclusively.

We had another firefighter testify here, that was Ken Naig. Ken Naig talked about pulling ceilings, using a pipe pole, and he testified the objective was to get plaster and wood and everything removed so you could check to see where the fires is spreading. If that isn't done as quickly as possible, you're going to be in trouble.

Ken Naig testified that in a minute he's been able to do 50 movements up and down on his ceiling using a pipe pole. We had Ken Naig in court and used with his pipe pole, he was able to do 80 pushes up and down in a minute using the pipe pole.

There was another thing upon mentioning Ken Naig at this point, your Honor, is Dave Hall by his testimony made it clear that firefighters do their job as quickly as possible, be it ventilating, be it performing a rescue, be it getting the supply—they work very hard to get the job done as quickly as possible. That fact, your Honor, the sincerity and dedication of Ken Naig as a firefighter was reflected in a newspaper article that was in today's paper regarding a rescue, and although the article didn't mention it, the firefighter attempted to rescue that six year old, who in fact did get her out. It was Ken Naig, your Honor.

Now, we also heard, as I said before, about a lot of equipment the firefighters have to carry. We heard testimony from Larry Helfer about the fact that since he's only 5 feet 4 inches tall that he has to compensate for his height because he knows the job of firefighter requires him to be strong in his upper body. So he lifts weights to keep himself in shape.

Now, we've had women come in who testified and complained about the bar lift, but most of the women who testified were able to do 35 lifts. Your Honor, I'm not sure what the beef is there.

They have complaints about event number three as well and— but before I go to that it was their expert's view that what you really should do if you want to see whether someone can chop or lift or carry a ladder is you ought to have them do that.

Your Honor, common sense tells us that is ridiculous. Can you imagine the carnage at the exam site when you have novices swinging axes and carrying ladders and trying to raise 60-pound fans overhead? It's ridiculous. . . .

Now, event number [two, the] hose drag. Now, they had several complaints, a couple principal complaints about event two. They were timing and intention. They didn't like the fact that the events measured there were timed. Well, your Honor, the reality is that that event needs to be timed. . . . [A] pump in Cleveland has only about two minutes of water, so it's important the fire department get that line laid out and connected to the hydrant as soon as possible. Hook and ladder people engage in rescue, ventilation work, and it's important that ventilation be done simultaneously with efforts to hook up that line so by the time the line is hooked up, the water is ready to go, the building is ventilated, the heat and smoke is coming out. You can't waste your time doing those activities, your honor. . . .

Now, on to event number three. They have principally three complaints about that. First, they don't like the fact this event was timed. Second, they don't like the weight of the dummy. Again, event number three was timed for the same reason event number two was timed. It demonstrates tasks, it has to be done as quickly as possible. We're talking, event number two, about being able to measure, the candidate's ability to drive themselves by pulling their weight a certain required distance. It's a simulated rescue. It's something that has to be done as quickly as possible. . . .

They didn't like the weight of the dummy. . . . They offered in lieu of the dummy use of an articulated dummy, something with arms and legs your Honor.

We saw the description of how the event number three was set up. There was an overhead barrier they had to crawl up. You can have the legs and arms and everything flailing all over the place. What's the sense of having an articulated dummy. The plaintiff's own witness, Buddy Casey, said he tried using an articulated dummy for his course, five or six people go through with that thing, arms are torn off, legs are torn off. Imagine the complaints we'd have from the plaintiffs had we used an articulated dummy and that dummy was not the exact weight and specification for each candidate that went through. Clearly,

their complaints about the weight are ridiculous.

Third is the grip. This is a real surprise. They didn't like the handle. They wanted to be able to have a dummy or weight designed so each candidate could grab it however they please. What they're ignoring here, your Honor, is they're introducing differentiation, they're eliminating the standardization of this event. If you leave it up to a candidate to figure out how they're going to grab the dummy, imagine the variance you're going to get in your examination. . . .

Again, back to time. I forgot to mention we talked about the time issue. We have firefighters [who talked] about the criticality of rescues. Talked about how when a structure is burning and he goes in to perform a rescue, there are two people's lives at steak [sic], his and the life of the victim. He's going to do everything to make sure he gets the victim out and himself out and alive as soon as possible. . . .

The City of Cleveland is not a laboratory, your Honor, they are real people in this town, real people who when their homes are on fire or the lives of their children — maybe that's funny to some people, but the reality is it's a serious situation when someone's home is on fire and the City cannot afford to experiment with a job that involves such serious dangers to the public. The City certainly deserves to have the best qualified for the job and their very lives depend on that. Thank you.

Table of Cases

Table of Statutes and Rules

Index